# FOR REFERENCE

**Do Not Take From This Room**

John Willis and Ben Hodges

# THEATRE WORLD®

Volume 63 / 2006-2007

**APPLAUSE**

THEATRE AND CINEMA BOOKS

An Imprint of Hal Leonard Corporation

New York

**THEATRE WORLD**
Volume 63
Copyright © 2009 by John Willis and Ben Hodges

Published in 2009 by Applause Theatre & Cinema Books
An Imprint of Hal Leonard Corporation
7777 West Bluemound Road
Milwaukee, WI 53213

Trade Book Division Editorial Offices
19 West 21st Street, New York, NY 10010

Printed in the United States of America
Book design by Tony Meisel

ISBN  978-1-55783-728-8
ISSN 1088–4564

www.applausepub.com

# Dedication

To John Kander and Fred Ebb (April 8, 1933–September 11, 2004), one of the most creatively and commercially successful songwriting teams in American theatre history.

Their Broadway theatrical credits as Kander and Ebb include *A Family Affair* (1962), *Flora the Red Menace* (1965), *Cabaret* (1967 Tony Award, 1967 Grammy Award, 1988 Tony nomination, 1998 Tony Award), *The Happy Time* (1967 Tony Award nomination), Zorba (1969 Tony Award nomination), 70, Girls, 70 (1971), *Chicago* (1976 Tony nomination, 1996 Tony Award), *The Act* (1977 Tony nomination), *Woman of the Year* (1981 Tony nomination), *The Rink* (1984 Tony nomination), *Kiss of the Spiderwoman* (1993 Tony Award, 1993 Drama Desk Award), *Steel Pier* (1997 Tony nomination, 1997 Drama Desk nomination), *Fosse* (1999 Tony Award, 1999 Drama Desk Award), *Chita Rivera: The Dancer's Life* (2005), and *Curtains* (2007 Tony nomination, 2007 Drama Desk nomination). Off-Broadway credits include *2 by 5* (1976), *Diamonds* (1984), and *And the World Goes 'Round* (1992 Lucille Lortel Award). Their film credits include *Cabaret* (1972 Academy Award), *Funny Lady* (1975), *Chicago* (2002 Academy Award nomination), and *New York, New York* (1977).

Ben Hodges, New York, NY
May 2009

**PAST EDITOR**          Daniel Blum (1945–1963)
John Willis (1963–2007)

**EDITOR EMERITUS**      John Willis (1963–2007)

**EDITOR IN CHIEF**      Ben Hodges (1998–present)

**ASSOCIATE EDITORS**:      Scott Denny (2005-present)

Allison Graham (2005-present)

**ASSISTANT EDITOR**      Lisa Kuhnen (2006-present)

**STAFF PHOTOGRAPHERS:**    Henry Grossman, Aubrey Rueben, Michael Riordan, Laura Viade, Michael Viade, Jack Williams

Theatre World would like to extend a very special thank you to all the New York and regional press agents, theatre marketing departments, and theatre photographers for their constant and steadfast support of this publication, as well as for the endless resources that they provide to the editorial staff. Our gratitude is eternally extended to Joan Marcus, Carol Rosegg, Paul Kolnik, Richard Termine, Gerry Goodstein, Michael Daniel, Audrey Ross, John Barlow, Carol Fineman, Michael Hartman, Bethany Larson, Ryan Ratelle, Dennis Crowley, Kevin Roebak, Wayne Wolf, Leslie Baden, Matt Stapleton, Michelle Bergmann, Tom D'Ambrosio, Bill Evans, Jim Randolph, Chris Boneau, Jackie Green, Juliana Hannett, Allison Houseworth, Jessica Johnson, Shanna Marcus, Christine Olver, Joe Perrotta, Matt Polk, Matt Ross, Heath Schwartz, Susanne Tighe, Adrian Bryan-Brown, Jim Byck, Aaron Meier, Brett Singer, Bruce Cohen, Peter Cromarty, David Gersten, Ellen Jacobs, Karen Greco, Helene Davis, Irene Gandy, Jim Baldassare, Jonathan Slaff, Scott Klein, DJ Martin, Bret Oberman, Keith Sherman, Glenna Freedman, Kevin McAnarney, Max Eisen, Beck Lee, Dan Fortune, Miller Wright, Marissa Altamura, Philip Carrubba, Jon Dimond, Richard Hillman, Rick Miramontez, Tony Origlio, Barbara Carroll, Philip Rinaldi, Timothy Haskell, Carrie Friedman, Richard Kornberg, Don Summa, Billy Zavelson, Howard Rubenstein, Robert Lasko, Sam Rudy, Bill Coyle, Adrianna Douzous, Jeremy Shaffer, Dan Demello, Shirley Herz, Ron Lasko, Gary Springer, Joe Trentacosta, Stephen Sunderlin, Susan L Schulman, Judy Jacksina, Bridget Klapinski, Darron Molovinsky, Pete Sanders, Arlene Kriv, Sam Neuman, Candi Adams, Michael Borowski, Marc Thibodeau, and Shayne Miller.

Thanks also to Michael Messina, president of Applause Theatre and Cinema Books, and John Cerullo, executive vice president of Hal Leonard Corporation, Beth Allen, Epitacio Arganza; Jason Baruch and Sendroff and Baruch LLP; Seth Barrish, Lee Brock, Eric Paeper, and The Barrow Group Theater Company/The Barrow Group School; Jed Bernstein and the Commercial Theater Institute; Wayne Besen and Truth Wins Out; Nicole Boyd; Helen Guditis and the Broadway Theater Museum; Fred Cantor; Fred Caruso; Ann Cason and *East Tennessee Life;* Pearl Chang; Michael Che; Jason Cicci, Monday Morning Productions, and Summer Stage New York; Richard Cohen; Sue Cosson; Susan Cosson; Mart Crowley; Robert Dean Davis; Carol and Nick Dawson; Bob and Brenda Denny; Jamie deRoy; Carmen Diaz; Diane Dixon; Craig Dudley; Sherry Eaker; Ben Feldman, Amy Luce, and Emily Feldman; David Fritz; Christine and David Grimsby; the estates of the late Charles J. Grant Jr. and Zan Van Antwerp; Brad Hampton; Laura and Tommy Hanson; Richard M. Henderson Sr. and Patricia Lynn Henderson; Al and Sherry Hodges; Charlie and Phyllis Hurt; Leonard Jacobs; Gretchen, Aaron, Eli, and Max Kerr; Jane, Lynn, and Kris Kircher; Tim Deak, Kim Spanjol, and The Learning Theatre Inc.; David Lowry; Joaquin Matias; Barry Monush and Screen World; Howard Sherman and the American Theatre Wing; Jason Bowcutt, Shay Gines, Nick Micozzi, and the staff and respective voting committees of the New York Innovative Theatre Awards; Barbara O'Malley and John Ford; Petie Dodrill, Craig Johnson, Rob Johnson, Dennis Romer, Katie Robbins, Dean Jo Ann VanSant, Ed Vaughan, the late Dr. Charles O. Dodrill and the staff of Otterbein College/Otterbein College Department of Theatre and Dance, P.J. Owen; William Craver and Paradigm; Hugo Uys and the staff of Paris Commune; John Philip; David Plank; Angie and Drew Powell; Kay Radtke; Carolyn, David, Glenna, and Jonas Rapp; Ric Wanetik, David Hagans, Steve Gelston, Yvonne Ghareeb; Kim Jackson, Mollie Levin, and Ricochet LLC; Jetaun Dobbs, Sydney Davalos, Todd Haimes, and Roundabout Theatre Company; Kate Rushing; Bill Schaap; Emmanuel Serrano; Hannah Richman Slosberg and Jason Slosberg; Charlotte St. Martin and the League of American Theatres and Producers; Susan Stoller; Henry Grossman, Lucy Nathanson, Michael Riordan, John Sala, Mark Snyder, Renée Isely Tobin and Bob, Kate, Eric, Laura, Anna, and Foster Tobin; Bob Ost and Theater Resources Unlimited Inc.; Laura Viade, Michael Viade, Rachel Werbel, and the staff of Theatre World and the John Willis Theatre World/Screen World Archive; Peter Filichia, Tom Lynch, Kati Meister, Erin Oestreich, Scott Denny, Barry Keating, Leigh Giroux, and the board of directors of The Theatre World Awards Inc.; Harry Haun, Howard Kissel, Matthew Murray, Frank Scheck, Michael Sommers, Doug Watt, Linda Winer, and the voting committee of The Theatre World Awards Inc.; Elizabeth Williams, Jack Williams, Barbara Dewey, and the staff of the University of Tennessee at Knoxville; Wilson Valentin; Kathie Packer and the estate of the late Frederic B. Vogel; Sarah and Bill Willis; George Wilson; Shane and Bill Wolters.

# Contents

*Scott Cohen and Jama Williamson in Manhattan Theatre Club's production of* Losing Louie. *Opened at the Biltmore Theatre November 26, 2006 (photo by Joan Marcus)*

*Jay Klaitz, Will Chase, and Christian Anderson in* High Fidelity. *Opened at the Imperial Theatre December 7, 2006 (photo by Joan Marcus)*

*Stephanie J. Block, Jeff McCarthy, and Marcus Chait in* The Pirate Queen. *Opened at the Hilton Theatre April 5, 2007 (photo by Joan Marcus)*

*The Cast of Dr. Seuss' How the Grinch Stole Christmas. Opened at the Hilton Theatre November 8, 2006 (photo by Paul Kolnik)*

*Chandler Williams and Alan Cox in Manhattan Theatre Club's production of* Translations. *Opened at the Biltmore Theatre January 25, 2007 (photo by Joan Marcus)*

*Byron Jennings and Laila Robins in the Roundabout Theatre Company's production of* Heartbreak House. *Opened at the American Airlines Theatre October 11, 2006 (photo by Joan Marcus)*

# BROADWAY

Top to bottom:

*Lea Michele and Jonathan Groff in* Spring Awakening
*(photo by Joan Marcus)*

*The Company of* The Coast of Utopia Part 2 - Shipwreck
*(photo by Paul Kolnik)*

*Orfeh and Laura Bell Bundy in* Legally Blonde *(photo by Paul Kolnik)*

*Nicole Parker, Mary Birdsong, Brooks Ashmanskas and Martin Short in* Martin Short: Fame Becomes Me. *Opened at the Bernard B. Jacobs Theatre August 17, 2006 (photo by Paul Kolnik)*

*The Cast of* A Chorus Line. *Opened at the Gerald Schoenfeld Theatre October 5, 2006 (photo by Paul Kolnik)*

*Nathan Lane in* Butley. *Opened at the Booth Theatre October 25, 2006 (photo by Joan Marcus)*

*Sarah Hyland, Christine Ebersole, Kelsey Fowler, Bob Stillman in* Grey Gardens. *Opened at the Walter Kerr Theatre November 2, 2006 (photo by Joan Marcus)*

*The Company of* Les Misérables. *Opened at the Broadhurst Theatre November 9, 2006 (photo by Michael Le Poer Trench)*

Right: *Tom Everett Scott,*
*Julie White, Johnny Galecki*
*in* The Little Dog Laughed.
*Opened at the Cort Theatre*
*November 13, 2006*
*(photo by Carol Rosegg)*

Below: *Ashley Brown,*
*Katherine Leigh Doherty,*
*Alexander Scheitinger,*
*and Gavin Lee in* Mary
Poppins. *Opened at the*
*New Amsterdam Theatre*
*November 16, 2006.*
*(photo by Joan Marcus)*

*Above: Raúl Esparza and the Cast of* Company. *Opened at the Barrymore Theatre November 29, 2006 (photo by Paul Kolnik)*

*Below: Jason Butler Harner, Billy Crudup, Jennifer Ehle, August Gladstone, Beckett Melville, and Patricia Conolly in Lincoln Center Theater's* The Coast of Utopia–Shipwreck, *part two of Tom Stoppard's trilogy. Opened at the Vivian Beaumont TheaterDecember 21, 2006 (photo by Paul Kolnik)*

*Bill Nighy and Julianne Moore in* The Vertical Hour. *Opened at the Music Box Theatre November 30, 2006 (photo by Paul Kolnik)*

Above: *The Cast of* Spring Awakening. *Opened at the Eugene O'Neill Theatre December 10, 2006 (photo by Doug Hamilton)*

Below: *Kristin Chenoweth and Cast in the Roundabout Theatre Company's revival of* The Apple Tree. *Opened at Studio 54 December 14, 2006 (photo by Joan Marcus)*

Boyd Gaines and Hugh Dancy in Journey's End. *Opened at the Belasco Theatre February 22, 2007 (photo by Paul Kolnik)*

*John Mahoney, Annie Parisse, and Alan Tudyk in Roundabout Theatre Company's revival of* Prelude to a Kiss. *Opened at the American Airlines Theatre March 8, 2007 (photo by Joan Marcus)*

Left: *Liev Schreiber in* Talk Radio. *Opened at the Longacre Theatre March 11, 2007 (photo by Joan Marcus)*

Below: *Jill Paice, David Hyde Pierce and the Cast of* Curtains. *Opened at the Al Hirschfeld Theatre March 22, 2007 (photo by Joan Marcus)*

Above: *Vanessa Redgrave as Joan Didion in* The Year of Magical Thinking. *Opened at the Booth Theatre March 29, 2007* (photo by Brigitte Lacombe)

Left: *Eve Best and Kevin Spacey in the Old Vic revival of* A Moon for the Misbegotten. *Opened at the Brooks Atkinson Theatre April 9, 2007* (photo by Simon Annand)

*Christopher Plummer and Brian Dennehy in the revival of* Inherit the Wind. *Opened at the Lyceum Theatre April 12, 2007 (photo by Joan Marcus)*

Above: *Michael Sheen and Frank Langella in* Frost/Nixon. *Opened at the Bernard B. Jacobs Theatre April 22, 2007 (photo by Joan Marcus)*

Below: *Laura Bell Bundy and the Cast of* Legally Blonde. *Opened at the Palace Theatre April 29, 2007 (photo by Paul Kolnik)*

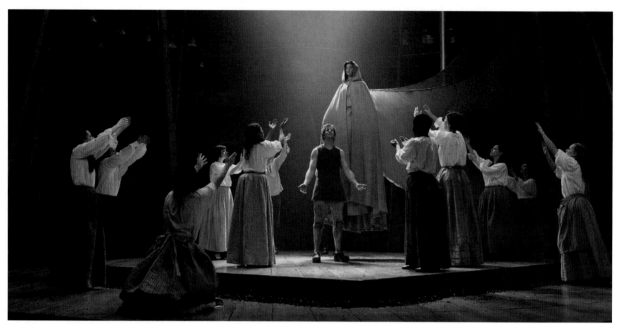

*Ivy Vahanian, Brad Fleischer and the Company of the National Theatre of Great Britain's production of* Coram Boy. *Opened at the Imperial Theatre May 2, 2007 (photo by Joan Marcus)*

*Michael Cerveris and Donna Murphy in Manhattan Theatre Club's production of* LoveMusik. *Opened at the Biltmore Theatre May 3, 2007 (photo by Joan Marcus)*

*Marian Seldes and Angela Lansbury in* Deuce. *Opened at the Music Box Theatre May 6, 2007 (photo by Joan Marcus)*

Above: *Tonya Pinkins and
Harry Lennix in August
Wilson's* Radio Golf, *the final
play of his ten play cycle.
Opened at the Cort Theatre
May 8, 2007
(photo by Carol Rosegg)*

Right: *Audra McDonald and
John Cullum in Roundabout
Theatre Company's revival
of* 110 in the Shade. *Opened
at Studio 54 May 9, 2007
(photo by Joan Marcus)*

# KIKI & HERB: ALIVE ON BROADWAY

Helen Hayes Theatre; First Preview: August 11, 2006 2004; Opening Night: August 15, 2006; Closed September 10, 2006; 5 previews, 27 performances

Created and executed by Justin Bond and Kenny Mellman; Produced by David J. Foster, Jared Geller, Ruth Hendel, Jonathan Reinis, Inc., Billy Zavelson, Jamie Cesa, Anne Strickland Squadron, and Jennifer Manocherian, in association with Gary Allen and Melvin Honowitz; Set, Scott Pask; Costumes, Marc Happel; Lighting, Jeff Croiter; Sound, Brett Jarvis; PSM, Peter Hanson; General Manager, Foster Entertainment (David J. Foster, Executive Director; Jared Geller, Executive Producer; Sally Gibson, General Manager); Production Manager, Aurora Productions (Gene O'Donovan, W. Benjamin Heller II, Bethany Weinstein, Tuesday Curran, Melissa Mazdra); Company Manager, Josh Lowenthal; Wardrobe Coordinator, Jennifer Malloy; Assistant Set, Jeffrey Hinchee; Assistant Lighting, Joel Silver; Assistant to Mr. Croiter, Grant W.S. Yeager; Production: Roger Keller (head property man), Doug Purcell (head carpenter), Joseph Beck (head electrician), Robert Etter (sound technician), Dan Novi (follow spot); Video Production, Sniper Films/Chris Gallagher, Matt Gallagher; Advertising, The Eliran Murphy Group; Marketing and Press, The Karpel Group, Bridget Klapinski, Billy Zavelson

**CAST** Kiki **Justin Bond;** Herb **Kenny Mellman**

A musical cabaret presented without intermission.

**SYNOPSIS** Kiki and Herb make their first appearance on the Great White Way. Kiki is a brash, boozy septuagenarian chanteuse. She's never much cared what other people think, but she's always willing to say what she thinks. On stage with her stalwart accompanist and only living friend Herb, Kiki lets rip with political rants, searing social commentary and confessions about their own highs and lows. As the story goes, a young Kiki & Herb met in the 1930s at the Erie Children's Institutional, where the two would begin an artistic collaboration and close personal relationship that would last a lifetime. Kiki & Herb display their musical prowess with reinventions of songs by great artists old and new such as The Cure, Bob Merrill, the Wu-Tang Clan, Bright Eyes, Dan Fogelberg, The Mountain Goats and many more.

*Kenny Mellman as Herb and Justin Bond as Kiki*
*(photos by Carol Rosegg)*

# MARTIN SHORT: FAME BECOMES ME

Bernard B. Jacobs Theatre; First Preview: July 29, 2006; Opening Night: August 17, 2006; Closed January 7, 2007; 22 previews, 165 performances

Conceived by Martin Short and Scott Wittman with additional material by Alan Zweibel; book by Martin Short and Daniel Goldfarb, music and arrangements by Marc Shaiman, lyrics by Scott Wittman and Marc Shaiman; Produced by Base Entertainment, Harbor Entertainment, Roy Furman, Jeffrey A. Sine, in association with Lisa Lapan and Terry E. Schnuck; Director, Scott Wittman, Choreography, Christopher Gattelli; Sets, Scott Pask; Costumes, Jess Goldstein; Lighting, Chris Lee; Sound, Peter Hylenski; Orchestrations, Larry Blank; Musical Director, Charlie Alterman; Music Coordinator, John Miller; Casting, Telsey + Company; Wigs, Charles LaPointe; PSM, Bess Marie Glorioso; Production Management, Juniper Street Productions; Marketing, TMG - The Marketing Group; Executive Producers, Joanna Hagan, Bernie Brillstein; General Management, Alan Wasser, Allan Williams; Associate Producer, Brown-Pinto Productions; Company Manager, Penelope Daulton; Stage Manager, Ana M. Garcia; ASM, Brent Peterson; Associate Director, Paul Dobie; Assistant Choreographer, Bethany Pettigrew; Associate Design: Orit Jacoby Carroll (set), China Lee (costumes), Jason Jeunnette (lighting), TJ McEvoy (sound); Makeup, Angelina Avallone; Prosthetics, Kevin Haney; Assistant Design: Lauren Alvarez (set), Joel Shier (lighting); Production: David "Pfish" Terry (production carpenter/ZFX operator), Chris Latsch (assistant carpenter/ZFX operator), Ken St. Peter (advance carpenter), Dan D. Coey (production electrician), Brian Dawson (head electrician), Stephen Long (assistant electrician), Rich Tyndall (automated lighting), Robert N. Valli (properties), Jill Johnson (assistant props), Tucker Howard (head sound), Bonnie Runk (assistant sound), Michael Growler (wardrobe supervisor), Susan Corrado (hair/makeup supervisor), Janelle Leone (assistant hair/makeup), Derek Moreno (Mr. Short's dresser); Music Preparation, Paul Holderbaum/Chelsea Music Services; Additional Orchestrations, Peter Myers; Electronic Music Design/Programming, Jim Harp; Dance Captain, Jill Abramovitz; Assistant to Messrs. Shaiman and Wittman, Richard Read; Assistant to John Miller, Charles Butler; Advertising, SpotCo; Press, Barlow • Hartman; Cast recording: Sh-K-Boom/Ghostlight 84420

**CAST** Martin Short; The Comedy All Stars **Brooks Ashmankas, Mary Birdsong, Nicole Parker\*, Capathia Jenkins, Marc Shaiman**

**UNDERSTUDIES** Jill Abramovitz, Charlie Alterman, Aisha de Haas, Edward Staudenmayer

**ORCHESTRA** Charlie Alterman (Conductor/keyboards), Craig Baldwin (Associate Conductor/keyboards); Dave Trigg (trumpet/piccolo trumpet/flugelhorn), Eddie Salkin (tenor sax/alto sax/clarinet/flute), Mike Christianson (trombone/bass trombone), Marc Shaiman (piano), Rich Mercurio (drums), Dick Sarpola (bass/electric bass), Ed Shea (percussion)

**MUSICAL NUMBERS** Another Curtain Goes Up, All I Ask, Three Gorgeous Kids, Babies, The Farmer's Daughter, Sittin' on the Fence, Don't Wanna Be Me, Ba-Ba-Ba-Bu-Duh Broadway!, Hello Boy!, Step Brother de Jesus, Married to Marty, The Triangle Song, Sniff, Sniff, Twelve Step Pappy, Would Ya Like to Star in Our Show?, I Came Just As Soon As I Heard, The Lights Have Dimmed on Broadway, Michael's Song, Heaven, Stop the Show, All I Ask (reprise), Another Curtain Comes Down, Glass Half Full

**2006-2007 AWARDS Theatre World Award**: Mary Birdsong

New York premiere of a comedy musical presented without intermission. Prior to Broadway the show had out-of-town engagements in San Francisco, Toronto, and Chicago.

**SYNOPSIS** Martin Short re-enacts such imagined lifetime high points as his birth in 1976; his abusive father, a legendary Saskatchewan song and dance man; his heartbreaking Golden Globe-nominated performance as a mentally challenged concentration camp survivo,r and even his afterlife in show biz heaven. Along the way, superstars including Sarah Jessica Parker, Liz Taylor, Katharine Hepburn, Jodi Foster, and Renee Zellweger are conjured nightly by the comedy all stars along side Short's unforgettable characters Jiminy Glick, Ed Grimley, and Irving Cohen. Among the many celebrities interviewed by Short's alter ego Jiminy Glick in the celebrity interview portion of the show were Jerry Seinfeld, Steve Martin, Nathan Lane, Rosie O'Donnell, Conan O'Brien, Rosanne Barr, Jimmy Fallon, Regis Philbin, Al Roker, Stephen Colbert, Stanley Tucci, Dennis Miller, Kristin Chenoweth, James Belushi, Tracey Ullman, Martha Stewart, Larry King, and Bette Midler.

*Donna Vivino replaced Nicole Parker from October 3–December 26.

Nicole Parker, Martin Short, and Mary Birdsong

*Martin Short, Nicole Parker, Brooks Ashmanskas, and Mary Birdsong (photos by Paul Kolnik)*

Brooks Ashmanskas, Mary Birdsong, Capathia Jenkins, and Nicole Parker

Mary Birdsong and Martin Short

Capathia Jenkins, Marc Shaiman, Mary Birdsong, and Nicole Parker

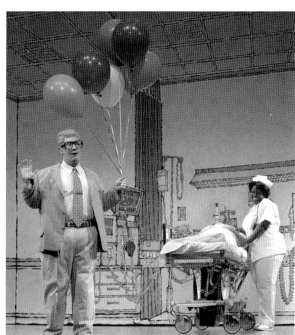

Martin Short and Capathia Jenkins

## JAY JOHNSON: THE TWO AND ONLY

Helen Hayes Theatre; First Preview: September 9, 2006; Opening Night: September 28, 2006; Closed November 26, 2006; 10 previews, 70 performances

Written by Jay Johnson, conceived by Jay Johnson, Murphy Cross, and Paul Kreppel; Produced by Roger Alan Gindi, Stewart F. Lane & Bonnie Comley, Dan Whitten, Herbert Goldsmith Productions, Ken Grossman, Bob & Rhonda Silver, Michael A. Jenkins/Dallas Summer Musicals, and Wetrock Entertainment; Directors, Murphy Cross and Paul Kreppel; Set, Beowulf Boritt; Lighting, Clifton Taylor; Sound, David Gotwald; Original Music, Michael Andreas; Production Management, Robert G. Mahon III, Jeff Wild; PSM, Lori Ann Zepp; Marketing, HHC Marketing (Hugh Hysell); Associate Producer, Jamie deRoy; General Management, Gindi Theatrical Management, Roger Alan Gindi; Company Manager, A. Scott Falk; Associate Set Design, Jo Winarski; Assistant Design, Jessie Moore (set); Nicolas Phillips & Steve O'Shea (lighting); Production: Doug Purcell (head carpenter), Roger Keller (head property man), Joseph Beck (head electrician), Robert Etter (sound); Assistants: Ryan J. Davis (Ms. Cross and Mr. Kreppel), David M. Brenner (Mr. Gindi), Jeanine Holiday & Diana Prince (Mr. Lane), Fiona Landers & Olivia D'Ambrosio (Mr. Whitten), Wand Beth & Jenny Cagle (Mr. Jenkins); Marketing Associates: Amanda Pekoe, Jessica Hinds, Kristen Donnelly; Advertising, Serino Coyne Inc.: Roger Micone, Neal Leibowitz, Christin Seidel, Morgan Schreiber; Press, O+M Co., Tony Origlio, Kip Vanderbilt, Philip Carrubba, Jon Dimond, Yufen Kung, Sarah Talisman, Molly Barnett

Performed by **Jay Johnson**

*Jay Johnson and Darwin (photos by Carol Rosegg)*

**2006-2007 AWARDS** Tony Award: Best Special Theatrical Event

A solo performance play with puppets presented without intermission. Originally produced Off-Broadway at the Atlantic Theater Company, May 13, 2004 (see *Theatre World* Volume 60, page 125).

**SYNOPSIS** In his one-man/several puppet show about the history and art of ventriloquism as refracted through his life and career, Jay Johnson deconstructs and demonstrates his life long obsession with a "cast" that includes Bob, Amigo, Darwin, Long John LaFeat, Nethernore the Bird of Death, Spaulding, Arthur Drew, Jackie and GaGa, and Squeaky. Johnson follows in the footsteps of such performers as Jules Vernon, Fred Russell (and Coster Joe), The Great Lester (and Frank Byron, Jr.), Edgar Bergen (and Charlie McCarthy), and Paul Winchell, who have all helped to define ventriloquism as a bonafide modern art form.

*Jay Johnson and Bob*

# A CHORUS LINE

Gerald Schoenfeld Theatre; First Preview: September 18, 2006; Opening Night: October 5, 2006; 18 previews, 273 performances as of May 31, 2007

Conceived and originally choreographed and directed by Michael Bennett, book by James Kirkwood and Nicholas Dante, music by Marvin Hamlisch, lyrics by Edward Kleban; Originally co-choreographed by Bob Avian; Produced by Vienna Waits; Director, Bob Avian; Choreography restaged by Baayork Lee; Set, Robin Wagner; Costumes, Theoni V. Aldredge; Lighting, Tharon Musser, adapted by Natasha Katz; Sound, Acme Sound Partners; Music Direction and Supervision, Patrick Vaccariello; Orchestrations, Jonathan Tunick, Billy Byers, and Hershy Kay; Vocal Arrangements, Don Pippin; General Management, Alan Wasser Associates; Casting, Jay Binder; Production Manager, Arthur Siccardi; PSM, William Joseph Barnes; Company Manager, Susan Bell; Associate CM, Adam J. Miller; Stage Manager, Laurie Goldfeder; ASM/Assistant Choreographer/Dance Captain, Michael Gorman; Assistant Dance Captain, Lyndy Franklin; Assistant Director, Peter Pileski; Associate Design: Suzy Benzinger (costumes), Yael Lubetzky (lighting); Assistant Design: David Peterson (set), Patrick Wiley (costumes), Aaron Spivey (lighting), Michael Creason (sound); Automated Lights, Matthew Hudson; Music Coordinator, Michael Keller; Production: Curtis Cowley (carpenter), Jimmy Fedigan (electrician), Eric Norris (head electrician), Scott Sanders (sound), Jon Dory (advance sound), Rory Powers (wardrobe supervisor), Heidi Brown (prop coordinator); Music Copying, Emily Grishman/Katherine Edmonds; Synthesizer Programming, Bruce Samuels; Rehearsal Pianist, John O'Neill; Advertising, Serino Coyne Inc.; Marketing, TMG - The Marketing Group; Press, Barlow • Hartman, Wayne Wolfe, Andrew Snyder; Cast recording: Sony BMG Music/Masterworks Broadway 82876-89785-2

**CAST** Bobby **Ken Alan;** Don **Brad Anderson;** Tricia **Michelle Aravena;** Roy **David Baum;** Zach **Michael Berresse;** Tom **Mike Cannon;** Butch **E. Clayton Cornelious;** Diana **Natalie Cortez;** Cassie **Charlotte d'Amboise;** Maggie **Mara Davi;** Val **Jessica Lee Goldyn;** Sheila **Deidre Goodwin;** Larry **Tyler Hanes;** Lois **Nadine Isenegger;** Richie **James T. Lane;** Vicki **Lorin Latarro**[1]**;** Mark **Paul McGill;** Judy **Heather Parcells;** Greg **Michael Paternostro;** Bebe **Alisan Porter;** Mike **Jeffrey Schecter;** Connie **Yuka Takara**[2]**;** Paul **Jason Tam;** Frank **Grant Turner;** Kristine **Chryssie Whitehead;** Al **Tony Yazbeck;** Swings[3] **Joey Dudding, Pamela Fabello, Lyndy Franklin**

**UNDERSTUDIES** Michelle Aravena (Bebe, Connie, Diana, Maggie), David Baum (Al, Bobby, Greg, Mike), Mike Cannon (Al, Mark, Mike, Richie), E. Clayton Cornelious (Don, Larry, Paul, Richie), Joey Dudding (Mark, Paul), Lyndy Franklin (Bebe, Connie, Kristine, Maggie), Jessica Lee Goldyn (Cassie), Tyler Hanes (Bobby, Zach), Nadine Isenegger (Cassie, Val), Pamela Jordan (Judy, Kristine, Sheila, Val), Lorin Latarro (Cassie, Diana, Judy, Sheila), Grant Turner (Don, Greg, Larry, Zach)

**ORCHESTRA** Patrick Vaccariello (Conductor), Jim Laev (Associate Conductor/keyboard 2), Ted Nash (woodwind 1), Lino Gomez (woodwind 2), David Young (woodwind 3), Jacqueline Henderson (woodwind 4), John Chudoba (trumpet 1), Trevor Neumann (trumpet 2), Scott Wenholt (trumpet 3), Michael Seltzer (trombone 1), Ben Herrington (trombone 2), Jack Schatz (bass trombone), Bill Sloat (bass), Greg Anthony (keyboard 1), Maggie Torre (keyboard 3), Dan McMillan (percussion), Brian Brake (drums)

**MUSICAL NUMBERS** I Hope I Get It, I Can Do That, And, At the Ballet, Sing!, Hello Twelve, Hello Thirteen, Hello Love, Nothing, Dance: Ten; Looks: Three, The Music and the Mirror, One, The Tap Combination, What I Did for Love, One: Reprise

*Michael Berresse and Company (photos by Paul Kolnik)*

**SETTING** An Audition. Time: 1975. Place: A Broadway Theatre. Revival of the musical presented without intermission. Originally produced by the Public Theatre in association with Plum Productions on May 21–July 13, 1975, running 101 performances (see *Theatre World* Volume 31, page 132). The show opened on Broadway at the Shubert Theatre October 17, 1975, and ran for 6,137 performances, earning nine Tony Awards, five Drama Desk Awards, the New York Drama Critics Award, Pulitzer Prize for Drama, a special Obie Award, and a Special Theatre World Award (see *Theatre World* Volume 32, page 14).

**SYNOPSIS** Broadway gypsies lay their talents—and hearts—on the line at a unique chorus call audition for a Broadway musical. This musical theatre masterpiece combines dance, song, drama, and human emotion to tell the tale of the American Musical's unsung heroes—the chorus dancers. "This show is dedicated to anyone who has ever danced in a chorus or marched in step…anywhere."—Michael Bennett.

*Succeeded by: 1. Pamela Fabello 2. J. Elaine Marcos, Lisa Ho 3. Additional and/ or replacement: Aaron J. Albano, Dylis Croman, Courtney Laine Mazza, Jessica Lea Patty, Josh Walden

Charlotte d'Amboise, Mara Davi, Brad Anderson, and Tony Yazbeck

Charlotte d'Amboise

James T. Lane and Company

The Finale

# HEARTBREAK HOUSE

American Airlines Theatre; First Preview: September 15, 2006; Opening Night: October 11, 2006; Closed December 17, 2006; 30 previews, 79 performances

*Philip Bosco and Swoosie Kurtz  (photos by Joan Marcus)*

Written by George Bernard Shaw; Produced by the Roundabout Theatre Company (Todd Haimes, Artistic Director; Harold Wolpert, Managing Director; Julia C. Levy, Executive Director); Director, Robin Lefevre; Set, John Lee Beatty; Costumes, Jane Greenwood; Lighting, Peter Kaczorowski; Original Music & Sound, John Gromada; Hair & Wigs, Tom Watson; Dialect Coach, Stephen Gabis; PSM, Leslie C. Lyter; Casting, Jim Carnahan, Mele Nagler; Technical Supervisor, Steve Beers; General Manager, Sydney Beers; Founding Director, Gene Feist; Associate Artistic Director, Scott Ellis; Marketing, David B. Steffen; Finance, Susan Neiman; Development, Jeffory Lawson; Sales, Jim Seggelink; Telesales, Daniel Weiss; Company Manager, Nichole Jennino; Stage Manager, Jonathan Donahue; Associate Director, Todd Lundquist; Assistant Design: Tim Mackabee (set), Jennifer Moeller (costumes), Scott Davis (lighting), Ryan Rumery (sound); Assistant Technical Supervisor, Elisa Kuhar; Production: Glenn Merwede (carpenter), Brian Maiuri (electrician), Andrew Forste (properties), Sean Haines (assistant props), Susan J. Fallon (wardrobe supervisor), Manuela LaPorte (hair & wig supervisor), Dann Wojnar (sound), Melissa Crawford (day wardrobe), Julie Hilimire, Vickie Grecki (dressers), Chris Mattingly (flyman); Advertising, The Eliran Murphy Group; Press, Boneau/Bryan-Brown, Matt Polk, Jessica Johnson, Amy Kass

**CAST** Ellie Dunn **Lily Rabe;** Nurse Guinness **Jenny Sterlin;** Captain Shotover **Philip Bosco;** Ariadne Utterword **Laila Robins;** Hesione Hushabye **Swoosie Kurtz;** Mazzini Dunn **John Christopher Jones;** Hector Hushabye **Byron Jennings;** Boss Mangan **Bill Camp;** Randall Utterword **Gareth Saxe**

**UNDERSTUDIES** Tony Carlin (Hector Hushabye, Boss Mangan, Randall Utterword), Doug Stender (Captain Shotover, Mazzini Dunn), Angela Pierce (Ellie Dunn, Ariadne Utterword), Robin Moseley (Hesione Hushabye, Nurse Guinness)

**SETTING** Sussex; A fine evening at the end of September. Revival of a play presented in two acts.

**SYNOPSIS** *Heartbreak House* follows the unlikely romantic encounters that occur in an estate on the English countryside. Romance springs eternal but never mutual and the most successful relationships have the least to do with love.

*Byron Jennings, Swoosie Kurtz*

*Swoosie Kurtz, Lily Rabe, and Byron Jennings*

# LOSING LOUIE

Biltmore Theatre; First Preview: September 21, 2006; Opening Night: October 12, 2006; Closed November 26, 2006; 24 previews, 53 performances

Written by Simon Mendes DaCosta; Produced by Manhattan Theatre Club (Lynne Meadow, Artistic Director; Barry Grove, Executive Producer) by special arrangement with James L. Nederlander and Michael Codron; Director, Jerry Zaks; Set, John Lee Beatty; Costumes, William Ivey Long; Lighting, Paul Gallo; Sound, Dan Moses Schreier; PSM, Barclay Stiff; Casting, Nancy Piccione & David Caparelliotis; Artistic Operations, Mandy Greenfield; Production Manager, Ryan McMahon; Development, Jill Turner Lloyd; Marketing, Debra A. Waxman; General Manager, Florie Seery; Artistic Development, Paige Evans; Artistic Administration/ Assistant to the Artistic Director, Amy Gilkes Loe; Literary Manager, Emily Shooltz; Musical Development, Clifford Lee Johnson III; Finance, Jeffrey Bledsoe; Associate General Manager, Lindsey Brooks Sag; Subscriber Services, Robert Allenberg; Telesales, George Tetlow; Education, David Shookhoff; Company Manager, Denise Cooper; Stage Manager, David H. Lurie; Dramaturg, Aaron Leichter; Assistant Director, Michael Goldfried; Associate Design: Jennifer Robin Arnold (costumes), John Viesta (lighting); Assistant Design: Yoshinori Tanokura (set), Ryan Rumery (sound); Hair/Makeup Supervisor, Natasha Steinhagen; Lighting Programmer, Marc Polimeni; Dresser, Tim Hanlon; Lighting/Sound Supervisor, Matthew T. Gross; Properties Supervisor, Scott Laule; Costume Supervisor, Erin Hennessy Dean; Advertising, SpotCo; Press, Boneau/Bryan-Brown, Jim Byk, Aaron Meier, Heath Schwartz

**SYNOPSIS** How do our childhood memories affect our lives? How do the mistakes of one generation impact the next? Interwoven events from the past and present blend together as two generations bury and uncover secrets, fifty years apart. Following the death of their father and years of separation, the strain of a family reunion causes moments of social embarrassment for two brothers and their wives. Secrets that refuse to remain buried erupt as they face it out in the bedroom—the place where all the confusion began.

*Matthew Arkin and Mark Linn-Baker*

*Mark Linn-Baker, Matthew Arkin, Patricia Kalember, and Michele Pawk (photos by Joan Marcus)*

**CAST** Bella Holland **Jama Williamson;** Louis Ellis **Scott Cohen;** Tony Ellis **Mark Linn-Baker;** Sheila Ellis **Michele Pawk;** Bobbie Ellis **Rebecca Creskoff;** Elizabeth Ellis **Patricia Kalember;** Reggie Ellis **Matthew Arkin**

**UNDERSTUDIES** John Bolger (Louie, Tony, Reggie), Julie Lauren (Bella, Bobbie), Charlotte Maier (Sheila, Elizabeth)

**SETTING** Time: Early '60s and the present. Place: Pound Ridge, NY. American premiere of a play presented in two acts. Originally presented at Hampstead Theatre, U.K., and the West End's Trafalgar Studio One in March 2005.

*Mark Linn-Baker and Michele Pawk*

# BUTLEY

Booth Theatre; First Preview: October 5, 2006; Opening Night: October 25, 2006; Closed January 14, 2007; 21 previews, 94 performances

Written by Simon Gray; Produced by the Huntington Theatre Company (Nicholas Martin, Artistic Director; Michael Maso, Managing Director), Elizabeth Ireland McCann, Stephanie P. McClelland, Chase Mishkin, Eric Falkenstein, Debra Black, Barbara Manocherian/Larry Hirschhorn, Barbara Freitag, Jeffrey Sine/Frederick Zollo; Executive Producer, Joey Parnes; Director, Nicholas Martin; Set, Alexander Dodge; Costumes, Ann Roth; Lighting, David Weiner; Sound, John Gromada; Wigs & Hair, David Brian Brown; Casting, Jay Binder/Jack Bowdan; Dialect Coach, Stephen Gabis; PSM, Michael McGoff; Marketing, TMG—The Marketing Group; Company Manager, Kim Sellon; Associate Producer, Tommy Demaio; General Management, Joey Parnes; Assistant Producer, S.D. Wagner; Assistant General Manager, John Johnson; Assistant Company Manager, Kit Ingui; ASM, Elizabeth Miller; Assistant to the Director, Michael Matthews; Associate Sound, Christopher Cronin; Assistant Design: Kevin Judge (set), Stephen Boulmetis (lighting), Michelle Matland (costume), David Baker (sound), Carole Morales (wig); Production: Larry Morley (carpenter), Steve Cochrane (electrician), Mike Smanko (props supervisor), Wayne Smith (sound), Ken McDonough (head carpenter), Jeff Turner (head electrician), Jerry Marshall (head props), Dave Olin Rogers (wardrobe supervisor), Diana Sikes (hairdresser), Ken Brown (star dresser), Sandy Binion (dresser); Advertising, SpotCo; Press, Boneau/Bryan-Brown, Jackie Green, Matt Ross

**CAST** Ben Butley **Nathan Lane;** Joseph Keyston **Julian Ovenden;** Miss Heasman **Jessica Stone;** Edna Shaft **Dana Ivey;** Anne Butley **Pamela Gray;** Reg Nuttall **Darren Pettie;** Mr. Gardner **Roderick Hill\*;** Students **Marguerite Stimpson, Chad Hoeppner**

**UNDERSTUDIES** John Leonard Thompson (Ben Butley), Anthony Crane (Reg, Joey), Marguerite Stimpson (Miss Heasman), Gloria Biegler (Edna, Anne Butley), Chad Hoeppner (Joey, Mr. Gardner)

**SETTING** An office in a college of London University, 1971. Revival of a play presented in two acts. Originally produced at the Morosco Theatre October 31, 1972 (see *Theatre World* Volume 29, page 24).

**SYNOPSIS** *Butley* is a dark comedy about a literature professor whose world is crumbling around him. Faced with surprising news from both his wife and his young protégé, Butley fights for his life with his best weapon: his acid wit.

\*Mr. Hill replaced James McMenamin in previews.

*Nathan Lane (photos by Joan Marcus)*

Above: *Pamela Gray and Nathan Lane*

Left: *Nathan Lane, Dana Ivey, and Julian Ovenden*

# THE TIMES THEY ARE A-CHANGIN'

Brooks Atkinson Theatre; First Preview: September 25, 2006; Opening Night: October 26, 2006; Closed November 19, 2006; 35 previews, 28 performances

*Lisa Brescia and Michael Arden (photo by Bruce Glikas)*

Conceived by Twyla Tharp; music and lyrics by Bob Dylan; Produced by James L. Nederlander, Hal Luftig/Warren Trepp, Debra Black, East of Doheny, Rick Steiner/Mayerson Bell Staton Group, Terry Allen Kramer, Patrick Catullo, Jon B. Platt/Roland Sturm; Director & Choreographer, Twyla Tharp; Music Arrangements/Adaptation/Supervisor, Michael Dansicker; Set & Costumes, Santo Loquasto; Lighting, Donald Holder; Sound, Peter Hylenski; Orchestrations, Michael Dansicker & Bob Dylan; Music Director, Henry Aronson; Music Coordinator, Howard Joines; Casting, Jay Binder, Jack Bowdan/Megan Larche; Technical Supervisor, Theatresmith Inc./Smitty; PSM, Arthur Gaffin; Associate Producers, Jesse Huot, Ginger Montel, Rhoda Mayerson; Resident Director, Kim Craven; General Management, The Charlotte Wilcox Company; Company Manager, James Lawson; Associate CM, Alexandra Gushin; Stage Manager, David Sugarman; ASM, Justin Scribner; Dance Captain, Alexander Brady; Associate Design: Wilson Chin (set), Matthew Pachtman (costumes), Jeanne Koenig & Aland Henderson (lighting); Assistant Lighting, Caroline Chao, Ben Krall, Hilary Manners, Carolyn Wong (lighting); Assistant Sound, TJ McEvoy; Assistant to Costume Designer, Sarah Sophia Turner; Makeup, Angelina Avallone; Production: James Maloney (electrician), Gerard Griffin (carpenter), Jeffrey Lunsford (flyman), Brad Robertson (head electrician), Neil Rosenberg (production properties), Eric Castaldo (props), Phillip Lojo (sound engineer), Kathleen Gallagher (wardrobe supervisor), Amber Isaac (assistant wardrobe), Lazaro Arencibia (hair supervisor), Maggie Horkey, Ginene M. Licata, Erin Schindler, Rodney Sovar, Joelyn R. Wikosz (dressers); Advertising, SpotCo; Press, Shaffer-Coyle Public Relations, Jeremy Shaffer, Bill Coyle, Adriana Douzos

**CAST** Coyote **Michael Arden;** Captain Ahrab **Thom Sesma;** Cleo **Lisa Brescia;** Ensemble **Lisa Gajda, Neil Haskell, Jason McDole, Charlie Neshyba-Hodges, Jonathan Nosan, John Selya, Ron Todorowski;** Swings **Alexander Brady, Alaine Kashian, Keith Kühl, Marty Lawson, Joseph Putignano, Cary Tedder**

**STANDBYS** Jason Wooten (Coyote), John Herrera (Captain Ahrab), Katie Klaus (Cleo)

**THE BAND** Henry Aronson (Conductor/keyboards/accordion/percussion), John "J.J." Jackson (guitars/banjo/dobro/harmonica), Dave MacNab (guitars/banjo), Paul Ossola (electric and upright bass), Brian Doherty (drums/percussion)

*Jason McDole and Charlie Neshyba-Hodges (photo by Richard Termine)*

**MUSICAL NUMBERS** The Times They Are A-Changin', Highway 61 Revisited, Don't Think Twice It's All Right, Just Like a Woman, Like a Rolling Stone, Everything is Broken, Desolation Row, Rainy Day Women #12 & 35, Mr. Tambourine Man, Masters of War, Blowin' in the Wind, Please Mrs. Henry, On a Night Like This, Lay Lady Lay, I'll Be Your Baby Tonight, Simple Twist of Fate, Summer Days, Gotta Serve Somebody, Not Dark Yet (Part 1), Knockin' on Heaven's Door, Maggie's Farm, Not Dark Yet (Part 2), I Believe in You, Dignity, Forever Young, Playout: "Country Pie" Medley

**SETTING** Sometime between awake and asleep. A new musical presented without intermission. World premiere presented at the Old Globe Theatre (Jack O'Brien, Artistic Director; Louis G. Spisto, Executive Director), San Diego, California, January 25–March 19, 2006.

**SYNOPSIS** *The Times They Are A-Changin'* is a fable existing in a dreamscape populated by members of a struggling circus: a ringmaster, his son, a runaway, and the clowns. A tale of fathers and sons, of men and women, of leaders and followers, of immobility and change, the musical uses prophecy, parable, metaphor, accusation, and confession—much like the Dylan songs which comprise it—to confront us with images and ideas of who we are and who it is possible to be.

*Thom Sesma*

*Charlie Neshyba-Hodges, Michael Arden, and Ron Todorowski*

*Michael Arden and Cast*

# GREY GARDENS

Walter Kerr Theatre; First Preview: October 3, 2006; Opening Night: November 2, 2006; 240 performances as of May 31, 2007

*Christine Ebersole  (photos by Joan Marcus)*

Book by Doug Wright, music by Scott Frankel, lyrics by Michael Korie; based on the documentary film *Grey Gardens* by David Maysles, Albert Maysles, Ellen Hovde, Muffie Meyer, and Susan Froemke; Produced by East of Doheny, Staunch Entertainment, Randall L. Wreghitt/Mort Swinsky; Michael Alden, Edwin W. Schloss, in association with Playwrights Horizons; Director, Michael Greif; Musical Staging, Jeff Calhoun; Sets, Allen Moyer; Costumes, William Ivey Long; Lighting, Peter Kaczorowski; Sound, Brian Ronan; Projections, Wendall K. Harrington; Hair and Wigs, Paul Huntley; Orchestrations, Bruce Coughlin; Music Director, Lawrence Yurman; Music Coordinator, John Miller; Executive Producer, Beth Williams; General Management, Alan Wasser, Allan Williams; PSM, Judith Schoenfeld; Production Management, Juniper Street Productions; Marketing, TMG—The Marketing Group; Casting, Telsey + Company; Original Casting, Alan Filderman, Alaine Alldaffer, and James Calleri; Company Manager, Mark Shacket; Stage Manager, J. Philip Bassett; ASM, Stephen R. Gruse; Associate Director, Johanna McKeon; Assistant CM, Carrie Sherriff; Associate Choreographer, Jodi Moccia; Dance Captain, Megan Lewis; Dialect Coach, Deborah Hecht; Associate Design: Warren Karp (set), Zachary Borovay (projections), Scott Traugott & Donald Sanders (costumes); Assistant Design: Joel E. Silver & John Viesta III (lighting), David Stollings (sound), Robert Martin (costumes); Production: Anthony Menditto (carpenter), Dan Coey (electrician), Christopher Pantuso (props supervisor), Michael Farfalla (sound), Geoffrey Vaughn (head

carpenter), Mark Hallisey (advance carpenter), Drayton Allison (head electrician), Josh Weitzman (automated lighting), P.J. Stasuk (head sound), Lisa Tucci (wardrobe supervisor), Cindy Demand (hair supervisor), Jill Frese (Ms. Ebersole's dresser), Vangeli Kaselurtis, Timothy Greer, Hilda Garcia Suli (dressers), Vanessa Brown (wrangler); Advertising, Serino Coyne Inc.; Music Copying, Emily Grishman/Katherine Edmonds; Synthesizer Programmer, Randy Cohen; Press, The Publicity Office, Michael Borowski, Marc Thibodeau, Bob Fennell, Candi Adams; Cast recording: PS Classics 642

**CAST** *Prologue (1973):* Edith Bouvier Beale **Mary Louise Wilson;** "Little" Edie Beale **Christine Ebersole;** *Act One (1941):* Edith Bouvier Beale **Christine Ebersole;** Young "Little" Edie Beale **Erin Davie;** George Gould Strong **Bob Stillman;** Brooks, Sr. **Michael Potts;** Jacqueline "Jackie" Bouvier **Sarah Hyland;** Lee Bouvier **Kelsey Fowler;** Joseph Patrick Kennedy Jr. **Matt Cavenaugh;** J.V. "Major" Bouvier **John McMartin;** *Act Two (1973):* Edith Bouvier Beale **Mary Louise Wilson;** "Little" Edie Beale **Christine Ebersole;** Brooks, Jr. **Michael Potts;** Jerry **Matt Cavenaugh;** Norman Vincent Peale **John McMartin**

**STANDBYS** Maureen Moore (for Christine Ebersole), Dale Soules (for Mary Louise Wilson), Abigail Ferenczy (for Sarah Hyland and Kelsey Fowler), Donald Grody (for John McMartin), Michael W. Howell (for Michael Potts), Megan Lewis (for Erin Davie), Asa Somers (for Matt Cavenaugh and Bob Stillman)

*Sarah Hyland, Christine Ebersole, Kelsey Fowler, and Bob Stillman*

**MUSICIANS** Lawrence Yurman (Conductor), Paul Staroba (Associate Conductor/keyboards), Eric DeGioia (violin), Anik Oulianine (cello), Ken Hitchcock and Todd Groves (reeds), Daniel Urness (trumpet/flugelhorn), Patrick Pridemore (French horn), Brian Cassier (acoustic bass), Tim McLafferty (percussion/drums)

**MUSICAL NUMBERS** The Girl Who Has Everything, The Five-Fifteen, Mother Darling, Goin' Places, Marry Well, Hominy Grits, Peas in a Pod, Drift Away, The Five-Fifteen (reprise), Daddy's Girl, The Telegram, Will You?, The Revolutionary Costume for Today, The Cake I Had, Entering Grey Gardens, The House We Live In, Jerry Likes My Corn, Around the World, Will You? (reprise), Choose to Be Happy, Around the World (reprise), Another Winter in a Summer Town, The Girl Who Has Everything (reprise)

**2006-2007 AWARDS** Tony Awards: Best Actress in a Musical (Christine Ebersole), Best Featured Actress in a Musical (Mary Louise Wilson); Best Costumes (William Ivey Long); **Theatre World Award:** Erin Davie

**SETTING** Grey Gardens, East Hampton, Long Island, New York 1941 and 1973; Transfer of the Off–Broadway musical presented in two acts. Originally presented at Playwrights Horizons (Tim Sanford, Artistic Director; Leslie Marcus, Managing Director; William Russo, General Manager) February 10–April 30, 2006 (see *Theatre World* Volume 62, page 165).

**SYNOPSIS** Once among the brightest names in the pre-Camelot social register, the deliciously eccentric aunt and cousin of Jacqueline Kennedy Onassis are now East Hampton's most notorious recluses. Facing an uncertain future, Edith Bouvier Beale and her adult daughter, "Little" Edie, are forced to revisit their storied past and come to terms with it—for better, and for worse.

*Erin Davie and John McMartin*

*Mary Louise Wilson*

*Christine Ebersole*

*Matt Cavenaugh, Mary Louise Wilson, and Christine Ebersole*

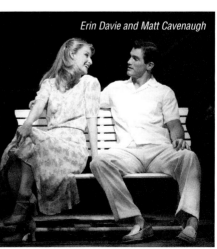

*Erin Davie and Matt Cavenaugh*

# DR. SEUSS' HOW THE GRINCH STOLE CHRISTMAS! THE MUSICAL

Hilton Theatre; First Preview: October 25, 2006; Opening Night: November 8, 2006; Closed January 7, 2007; 22 previews, 107 performances

Book and lyrics by Timothy Mason, music by Mel Marvin, additional music and lyrics by Albert Hague and Dr. Seuss; based on the book *How the Grinch Stole Christmas* by Dr. Seuss; Presented by Target; Produced by Running Subway, EMI Music Publishing, Michael Speyer & Bernie Abrams, with Allen Spivak, Janet Pailet, Spark Productions/Maximum Entertainment/Jonathan Reinis; Created and Supervised by Jack O'Brien; Director, Matt August; Original Choreography, John DeLuca; Choreography Restaged by Bob Richard; Executive Producer, James Sanna; Sets, John Lee Beatty; Lighting, Pat Collins; Costumes, Robert Morgan; Puppets, Michael Curry; Sound, Acme Sound Partners; Wigs/Hair, Thomas Augustine; Makeup, Angelina Avallone; Special Effects, Gregory Meeh; Music Direction/Vocal Arrangements/Incidental Arrangements, Joshua Rosenblum; Orchestrator, Michael Starobin; Dance Music Arrangements, David Krane; Music Coordinator, Seymour Red Press; Casting, Telsey + Company; PSM, Michael Brunner; Technical Supervisor, Don S. Gilmore; Associate Producers, Audrey Geisel, Joshua Rosenblum; General Manager, David Waggett; Marketing, Tomm Miller; Company Manager, Heidi Neven; Advertising, Margeotes Fertitta Powell; ASMs, Daniel S. Rosokoff, Joel Rosen, Dana Williams; Associate CM, Jolie Gabler; Assistant CM, Alyssa Mann; Assistant Director, West Hyler; Assistant Choreographer, Shane Rhoades; Dance Captain, Kurt Kelly; Associate Design: Eric Renschler (set), D.M. Wood (lighting), Nancy Palmatier (costumes), Carmel Vargyas (wigs); Associate Technical Director, Bradley Thompson; Synthesizer Programming, Bruce Samuels; Press, Allison Brod Public Relations

Rusty Ross and Patrick Page

Patrick Page

**CAST** Old Max **John Cullum;** Cindy Lou-Who **Nicole Bocchi** or **Caroline London;** JP Who **Price Waldman;** Mama Who **Kaitlin Hopkins;** Grandpa Seth Who **Michael McCormick;** Grandma Who **Jan Neuberger;** Boo Who **Malcolm Morano** or **Aaron Dwight Conley;** Annie Who **Heather Tepe** or **Caitlin Belcik;** Danny Who **Eamon Foley** or **James Du Chateau;** Betty Who **Brynn Williams** or **Libbie Jacobson;** Citizens of Whoville **Janet Dickinson, André Garner, Josephine Rose Roberts, William Ryall, Pearl Sun, Jeff Skowron;** Little Whos—Red Cast **Antonio D'Amato, Danielle Freid, Jess Leprotto, Katie Micha, Nikki Rose, Corwin Tuggles, Kelley Rock Wiese;** Little Whos –White Cast **Jahaan Amin, Kevin Csolak, Brianna Gentilella, Sky Jarrett, Daniel Manche, Jillian Mueller, Molly J. Ryan;** Young Max **Rusty Ross;** The Grinch **Patrick Page;** Swings **Kurt Kelly, Amy Griffin, Rafael Luis Tillis, Lawson Young;** Standby for Old Max **Martin Van Treuren**

**UNDERSTUDIES** William Ryall (Grinch, Old Max), André Garner (Young Max), Jeff Skowron (JP Who, Grandpa Seth Who), Pearl Sun (Mama Who), Janet Dickinson (Grandma Who), Katie Micha & Molly J. Ryan (Cindy Lou Who), Antonio D'Amato & Daniel Manche (Boo Who), Nikki Rose & Jillian Mueller (Annie Who), Jess Leprotto & Kevin Csolak (Danny Who), Danielle Freid & Jahaan Amin (Betty Who)

*The Company (photos by Paul Kolnik)*

*John Cullum*

**MUSICIANS** Joshua Rosenblum (Conductor); Sue Anschutz (Associate Conductor/keyboards); Mark Mitchell (Assistant Conductor/keyboards); Steven Kenyon, Robert DeBellis, Terrence Cook, John Winder (woodwinds); Christian Jaudes, Philip Granger, Wayne DuMaine (trumpets); Wayne Goodman, Robert Fournier (trombones); Louis Bruno (bass); Gregory Landes (drums); David Roth (percussion)

**MUSICAL NUMBERS** Who Likes Christmas?, I Hate Christmas Eve, Whatchama Who, Welcome Christmas, I Hate Christmas Eve (reprise), Once in a Year, One of a Kind, Now's the Time, You're a Mean One Mr. Grinch, Santa for a Day, You're a Mean One Mr. Grinch (reprise), Who Likes Christmas? (reprise), One of a Kind (reprise), Welcome Christmas (reprise), Finale, Who Likes Christmas?

New York premiere of a musical presented without intermission. Based on the production produced at the Old Globe (Jack O'Brien, Artistic Director; Louis G. Spisto, Executive Director), San Diego, California, and originally commissioned by and produced at The Children's Theatre Company, Minneapolis, Minnesota.

**SYNOPSIS** The mean and scheming Grinch decides to steal Christmas away from the Whos, an endlessly cheerful bunch bursting with holiday spirit. When the Whos still celebrate after the thievery, they melt the miser's heart and the Grinch learns that holidays are about togetherness and love, and not about accumulating material things.

# LES MISÉRABLES

Broadhurst Theatre; First Preview: October 24, 2006; Opening Night: November 9, 2006; 17 previews, 232 performances as of May 31, 2007

*Alexander Gemignani  (photos by Michael Le Poer Trench)*

Book by Alain Boublil and Claude-Michel Schönberg, music by Claude-Michel Schönberg, lyrics by Herbert Kretzmer; based on the novel by Victor Hugo; Original French text by Alain Boublil and Jean-Marc Natel, Additional material by James Fenton; Produced by Cameron Mackintosh; Directed and adapted by John Caird and Trevor Nunn; Design, John Napier; Lighting, David Hershey; Original Sound, Andrew Bruce; Costumes, Adreane Neofitou; Associate Director, Shaun Kerrison; New Orchestrations, Christopher Jahnke; Co-Orchestrator, Stephen Metcalfe; Original Orchestrations, John Cameron; Orchestral Adaptation/Musical Supervision, Stephen Brooker; Music Director, Kevin Stites; Sound, Jon Weston; Executive Producers, Nicholas Allott, Matthew Dalco, Fred Hanson; Casting, Tara Rubin; General Management, Alan Wasser Associates; Technical Production Manager, Jake Bell; PSM, Michael J. Passaro; Stage Managers, Charles Underhill, Jim Athens; Company Manager, Abra Stanley Leonard; Associate CM, Steve Greer; Dance Captain, Matt Clemens; Associate Set Design (U.K.), Sue Jekinson DiAmico, Matt Kinley; Associate Costumes, Elise Napier (U.K.), Rick Kelly (U.S.); Hair, Tom Watson; Music Coordinator, John Miller; Rehearsal Pianists, Paul Raiman, Annbritt duChateau, Andy Grobengieser; Music Copyists, Emily Grishman (U.S.), Dakota Music Service (U.K.); Moving Lights, Alan Boyd, Rob Halliday; Assistant Design: Josh Zangen (set), Mark Simpson (lighting); Associate Sound, Jason Strangfeld; Synthesizer Programming, Stuart Andrews;

Movement Consultant, Kate Flatt; Production: Todd Frank (head carpenter), Robert Fehribach (electrician), Timothy Abel (props), Michael Pitzer (head electrician), Steven Callahan (head props), Patrick Pummill (head sound), Henry Baker (automations), Rick Kelly (wardrobe supervisor), Kevin Phillips (hair/makeup supervisor); Advertising, Serino Coyne Inc.; Press, The Publicity Office, Marc Thibodeau, Bob Fennell, Michael Borowski, Candi Adams, Matthew Fasano

**CAST** Jean Valjean **Alexander Gemignani;** Javert **Norm Lewis**[*1]; Farmer **Doug Kreeger;** Innkeeper **Drew Sarich;** Innkeeper's Wife **Karen Elliott**[*2]; Laborer **J.D. Goldblatt;** The Bishop of Digne **James Chip Leonard;** Constables **Nehal Joshi, Jeff Kready;** Factory Foreman **Robert Hunt**[*3]; Fantine **Daphne Rubin-Vega**[*4]; Factory Girl **Haviland Stillwell;** Factory Workers **Becca Ayers, Daniel Bogart, Justin Bohon**[*5]**, Kate Chapman**[*6]**, Nikki Renée Daniels, Karen Elliott**[*2]**, Marya Grandy**[*7]**, Blake Ginther, JD Goldblatt, Victor Hawks, Nehal Joshi, Jeff Kready, Doug Kreeger, James Chip Leonard, Megan McGinnis, Drew Sarich, Idara Victor;** Sailors **Justin Bohon**[*5]**, Victor Hawks, Nehal Joshi;** Pimp **J.D. Goldblatt;** Madame **Kate Chapman**[*6]; Whores **Becca Ayers, Nikki Renée Daniels, Ali Ewoldt, Celia Keenan-Bolger**[*8]**, Megan McGinnis, Haviland Stilwell, Idara Victor;** Old Woman **Karen Elliott**[*2]; Crone **Marya Grandy**[*7]; Bamatabois **Daniel Bogart;** Fauchelevant **Jeff Kready;** Champmathieu **Robert Hunt**[*3]; Young Cosette **Tess Adams**[*9] or Kylie Liya Goldstein or **Carly Rose Sonenclar;** Thénardier **Gary Beach;** Madame Thénardier **Jenny Galloway**[*10]; Young Eponine **Tess Adams**[*8] or Kylie Liya Goldstein or **Carly Rose Sonenclar;** Old Beggar Woman **Karen Elliott**[*2]; Madeleine **Nikki Renée Daniels;** Gavroche **Brian D'Addario or Jacob Levine**[*11]; Eponine **Celia Keenan-Bolger**[*8]; Cosette **Ali Ewoldt;** Major Domo **Justin Bohon**[*5]; *Thénardier's Gang:* Montparnasse **JD Goldblatt;** Babet **Jeff Kready;** Brujon **Victor Hawks;** Claquesous **James Chip Leonard;** *Students:* Enjolras **Aaron Lazar**[*12]; Marius **Adam Jacobs;** Combeferre **Daniel Bogart;** Feuilly **Blake Ginther;** Courfeyrac **Robert Hunt**[*3]; Joly **Justin Bohon**[*5]; Grantaire **Drew Sarich;** Lesgles **Nehal Joshi;** Jean Prouvaire **Doug Kreeger;** Swings **Matt Clemens, Marissa McGowan, Q. Smith, Stephen Trafton**

**UNDERSTUDIES** For Jean Valjean: Victor Hawks, Jeff Kready; for Javert: Robert Hunt, Drew Sarich; for Thénardier: Victor Hawks, James Chip Leonard; for Madame Thénardier: Karen Elliott, Marya Grandy; for Fantine: Nikki Renée Daniels, Haviland Stillwell; for Cosette: Marissa McGowan, Idara Victor; for Marius: Daniel Bogart, Doug Kreeger; for Eponine: Megan McGinnis, Marissa McGowan; for Enjolras: Nehal Joshi, Drew Sarich

*The Company*

*Celia Keenan-Bolger and Adam Jacobs*

**MUSICIANS** Kevin Stites (Conductor), Paul Raiman (Associate Conductor/keyboards), Annbritt duChateau (Assistant Conductor/keyboards), Bob Bush (flute/piccolo/alto flute/alto recorder), Laura Wallis (oboe/English horn), Jonathan Levine (clarinet/bass clarinet/tenor recorder), Timothy Schadt (trumpet/Flugel), Chris Olness (bass trombone/tuba), Brad Gemeinhardt and Sara Cyrus (French horn), Martin Agee (violin),Debra Shufelt-Dine (viola), Clay C. Ruede (cello), Dave Phillips (bass), Charles Descarfino (mallets/timpani/percussion)

**MUSICAL NUMBERS** Prologue, Soliloquy, At the End of the Day, I Dreamed a Dream, Lovely Ladies, Who Am I, Come to Me, Castle on a Cloud, Master of the House, Thénardier Waltz, Look Down, Stars, Red and Black, Do You Hear the People Sing, In My Life, A Heart Full of Love, One Day More, On My Own, A Little Fall of Rain, Drink With Me to Days Gone By, Bring Him Home, Dog Eats Dog, Soliloquy, Empty Chairs at Empty Tables, Wedding Chorale, Beggars at the Feast, Finale

**SETTING** Paris and surrounding areas, 1815–1832. Revival of a musical presented in two acts. The original American production opened at the Broadway Theatre March 12, 1987 (see *Theatre World* Volume 43, page 32), then transferred to the Imperial Theatre where it played until May 18, 2003, running 6,680 performances. *Les Misérables* is the third longest-running show in Broadway history and on October 8, 2006 passed the twenty-one year old record of *Cats* in London to become the longest-running musical ever on the West End or Broadway with 8,372 performances— a run nearly three years longer than Broadway's record-holder *The Phantom of the Opera*. *Les Misérables* has been seen by over fifty-four million people in thrity-eight countries and twenty-one languages since its first London performance in October 1985.

**SYNOPSIS** The epic musicalization of Hugo's classic novel about paroled convict Jean Valjean who, failing attempts to find work as an honest man with his yellow parole note, tears up his shackles and conceals his identity in order to live his life again; the police inspector Javert, who becomes obsessed with finding Valjean; Fantine, the single mother of Cosette, who is forced to become a prostitute to support her daughter; Marius, a French student who falls in love with Valjean's adopted daughter Cosette; Eponine, the young daughter of the Thénardiers who falls in love with Marius; the Thénardiers, who own an Inn and exploit their customers; and Enjolras and the other students, who are working toward freeing the oppressed lower class of France.

*Succeeded by: 1. Ben Davis 2. Soara-Joye Ross 3. Ben Crawford 4. Lea Salonga 5. Anderson Davis, Kevin David Thomas 6. Lucia Spina 7. Kristine Reese, Marya Grandy 8. Mandy Bruno 9. Kaylie Rubinaccio 10. Ann Harada 11. Zach Rand 12. Max von Essen

*Alexander Gemignani and Norm Lewis*

# THE LITTLE DOG LAUGHED

Cort Theatre; First Preview: October 26, 2006; Opening Night: November 13, 2006; Closed February 18, 2007; 22 previews, 112 performances

Written by Douglas Carter Beane; Produced by Roy Gabay, Susan Dietz, Morris Berchard, Steve Bozeman, Ted Snowdon, Jerry Frankel/Doug Nevin, Jennifer Manocherian/Ina Meibach, and Second Stage Theatre (Carole Rothman, Artistic Director; Ellen Richard, Executive Director); Director, Scott Ellis; Set, Allen Moyer; Costumes, Jeff Marshie; Lighting, Donald Holder; Original Music, Lewis Flinn; Casting, Mele Nagler; PSM, Linda Marvel; Production Management, Robert G. Mahon III, Jeff Wild; General Manager, Roy Gabay Productions; Company Manager, Bruce Kilinger; ASM, Alex Lyu Volckhausen; Assistant Director, Vijay Mathew; Associate Design: Hilary Manners (lighting); Warren Karp (set); Production Properties Coordinator, Susan Barras; Assistants, Kyle LaColla (Mr. Mahshie), Catherine Tate (Mr. Holder), Mark Huang (Mr. Flinn), Stephen Kopel (Ms. Nagler); Angela Sidlow (Ms. Dietz), Ted Seifman (Mr. Snowdon); Associates to Ms. Dietz, Tom Kirdahy, Jayson Raitt, Devlin Elliott; Production: Ed Diaz (carpenter), Scott DeVerna (electrician), Lonnie Gaddy (properties), Kevin Diaz (automation carpenter), John Lofgren (assistant props), Kay Grunder (wardrobe supervisor), Kyle LaColla (dresser); Advertising, SpotCo; For Second Stage: Finance, Janice B. Cwill; Management, Don-Scott Cooper; Development, Sarah Bordy; Marketing, Hector Coris; Associate Artistic Director, Christopher Burney; Ticket Services, Greg Turner; Press, Richard Kornberg & Associates, Tom D'Ambrosio, Don Summa

**CAST** Diane **Julie White;** Mitchell **Tom Everett Scott;** Alex **Johnny Galecki;** Ellen **Ari Graynor**

**UNDERSTUDIES** Brian Henderson (Mitchell/Alex), Dana Slamp (Diane/Ellen)

*Julie White (photos by Carol Rosegg)*

**2006-2007 AWARDS** Tony Award: Best Actress in a Play (Julie White); **Theatre World Award:** Johnny Galecki

**SETTING** New York and Hollywood, the present. Off-Broadway transfer of a play presented in two acts. Originally presented at Second Stage December 13, 2005 (see *Theatre World* Volume 62, page 173).

**SYNOPSIS** In this tell-tale about the last Hollywood taboo—closeted movie stars, an up-and-coming leading man and his brash, tightly-wound Hollywood agent become entangled with a sexy drifter and his naïve girlfriend.

*Ari Graynor and Johnny Galecki*

*Johnny Galecki and Tom Everett Scott*

# MARY POPPINS

New Amsterdam Theatre; First Preview: October 14, 2006; Opening Night: November 16, 2006; 30 previews, 224 performances as of May 31, 2007

Book by Julian Fellowes, original music and lyrics by Richard M. Sherman and Robert B. Sherman; based on the stories of P.L. Travers and the 1964 Walt Disney Film; new songs and additional music and lyrics by George Stiles and Anthony Drewe; Produced and co-created by Cameron Mackintosh; Produced for Disney Theatrical Productions by Thomas Schumacher; Director, Richard Eyre; Co-Director and Choreography, Matthew Bourne; Set and Costumes, Bob Crowley; Lighting, Howard Harrison; Co-choreography, Stephen Mear; Music Supervisor, David Caddick; Music Director, Brad Haak; Orchestrations, William David Brohn; Sound (NY), Steve Canyon Kennedy; Dance/Vocal Arrangements, George Stiles; Associate Choreographer, Geoffrey Garratt; Associate Director, Anthony Lyn; Associate Producer, James Thane; Makeup, Naomi Donne; Casting, Tara Rubin Casting; Technical Director, David Benken; PSM, Tom Capps; Resident Choreographer, Tom Kosis; Company Manager, Dave Ehle; Assistant Company Manager, Laura Eicholz; Production Associate, Jeff Parvin; Associate General Manager, Alan Wasser; Stage Manager, Mark Dobrow; ASMs, Valerie Lau-Kee Lai, Jason Trubitt; Dance Captain, Rommy Sandhu, Dialects/Vocal Coach, Deborah Hecht; Associate Design: Bryan Johnson & Rosalind Coombes (set), Christine Rowland & Mitchell Bloom (costumes), Daniel Walker (lighting), John Shivers (sound); Wigs, Angela Cobbin; Illusions Design, Jim Steinmeyer; Technical Director, David Benken; Scenic Production Supervisor, Patrick Eviston; Assistant Technical Supervisor, Rosemarie Palombo; Foy Flying, Raymond King; Automation, Steve Stackle, David Helk; Properties, Victor Amerling, Tim Abel, Joe Bivone, John Saye; Keyboard Programming, Stuart Andrews; Music Contractor, David Lai; Advertising, Serino Coyne Inc.; Music Copyist, Emily Grishman Music Preparation; Press, Boneau/Bryan-Brown; Original London Cast recording: Disney Theatricals 61391-7

*Ashley Brown, Alexander Scheitinger, Katherine Leigh Doherty, and Gavin Lee (photo by Joan Marcus)*

**CAST** Bert **Gavin Lee;** George Banks **Daniel Jenkins;** Winifred Banks **Rebecca Luker;** Jane Banks **Katherine Doherty**[*1] or **Kathryn Faughnan** or **Delaney Moro**[*2]; Michael Banks **Matthew Gumley** or **Henry Hodges** or **Alexander Scheitinger**[*3]; Katie Nanna **Megan Osterhaus;** Policeman **James Hindman;** Miss Lark **Ann Arvia;** Admiral Boom **Michael McCarty;** Mrs. Brill **Jane Carr;** Robertson Ay **Mark Price;** Mary Poppins **Ashley Brown;** Park Keeper **Nick Corley;** Neleus **Brian Letendre;** Queen Victoria **Ruth Gottschall;** Bank Chairman **Michael McCarty;** Miss Smythe **Ruth Gottschall;** Von Hussler **Sean McCourt;** Northbrook **Matt Loehr;** Bird

*Ashley Brown and Gavin Lee (photo by George Holz)*

Woman **Cass Morgan;** Mrs. Corry **Janelle Anne Robinson;** Fannie **Vasthy E. Mompoint;** Annie **Megan Osterhaus;** Valentine **Tyler Maynard**[*4]; William **Eric B. Anthony;** Mr. Punch **James Hindman;** Glamorous Doll **Catherine Walker;** Miss Andrew **Ruth Gottschall;** Ensemble **Eric B. Anthony, Ann Arvia, Kristin Carbone, Nick Corley, Case Dillard, Ruth Gottschall, James Hindman, Brian Letendre, Matt Loehr, Michelle Lookadoo, Tony Mankser, Tyler Maynard**[*4]**, Michael McCarty, Sean McCourt, Vasthy E. Mompoint, Jesse Nager, Kathleen Nanni, Megan Osterhaus, Dominic Roberts, Janelle Anne Robinson, Shekitra Starke, Catherine Walker, Kevin Samual Yee;** Swings[*5] **Pam Bradley, Brian Collier, Nicholas Dromard, Suzanne Hylenski, Stephanie Kurtzuba, Rommy Sandhu**

**UNDERSTUDIES** Eric B. Anthony (Bert), Ann Arvia (Mrs. Brill), Kristine Carbone (Mary Poppins/Mrs. Banks), Nicholas Dromard (Bert/Von Hussler/Northbrook), James Hindman (George Banks), Matt Loehr (Bert), Tyler Maynard (Robertson Ay), Sean McCourt (George Banks), Megan Osterhaus (Mrs. Banks), Dominic Roberts (Robertson Ay), Catherine Walker (Mary Poppins)

**MUSICIANS**  Brad Haak (Conductor), Kristen Blodgette (Associate Conductor/keyboard); Milton Granger (piano); Peter Donovan (bass), Dave Ratajczak (drums), Daniel Haskins (percussion), Nate Brown (guitar/banjo/E-bow), Russ Rizner & Larry DiBello (horns), Jon Sheppard & Louis Hanzlik (trumpet), Marc Donatelle (trombone/euphonium), Randy Andos (bass trombone/tuba), Paul Garment (clarinet), Alexandra Knoll (oboe/English horn), Brian Miller (flutes), Stephanie Cummins (cello)

**MUSICAL NUMBERS**  Chim Chim Cher-ee, Cherry Tree Lane (Part 1), The Perfect Nanny, Cherry Tree Lane (Part 2), Practically Perfect, Jolly Holiday, Cherry Tree Lane (reprise), Being Mrs. Banks, Jolly Holiday (reprise), A Spoonful of Sugar, Precision and Order, A Man Has Dreams, Feed the Birds, Supercalifragilisticexpialidocious, Temper, Temper, Chim, Chim, Cher-ee (reprise), Cherry Tree Lane (reprise), Brimstone and Treacle (Part 1), Let's Go Fly A Kite, Good For Nothing, Being Mrs Banks (reprise), Brimstone and Treacle (Part 2), Practically Perfect (reprise), Chim Chim Cher-ee (reprise), Step in Time, A Man Has Dreams, A Spoonful of Sugar (reprise), Anything Can Happen, A Spoonful of Sugar (reprise), A Shooting Star

**2006–2007 AWARDS**  Tony Award: Best Scenic Design of a Musical (Bob Crowley); Drama Desk: Outstanding Featured Actor in a Musical (Gavin Lee), Outstanding Set Design of a Musical (Bob Crowley); **Theatre World Award:** Gavin Lee

**SETTING**  In and around the Banks' household somewhere in London at the turn of the last century. American premiere of a new musical presented in two acts. Originally opened in London at the Prince Edward Theatre on December 15, 2004.

**SYNOPSIS**  *Mary Poppins* is the story of the Banks family and how their lives change after the arrival of nanny Mary Poppins at their home at 17 Cherry Tree Lane in London.

*Succeeded by: 1. Nicole Bocchi 2. Devynn Pedell 3. Jacob Levine 4. Mark Ledbetter 5. Additional: Regan Kays, Jeff Metzler

*Rebecca Luker (photo by Andrew Eccles)*

*The Company*

*Rebecca Luker and Daniel Jenkins*

*Ashley Brown and Gavin Lee*
*(photo by George Holz)*

*Gavin Lee and Company (photo by Joan Marcus)*

# THE COAST OF UTOPIA
## Voyage—Shipwreck—Salvage

Vivian Beaumont Theater; October 17, 2006–May 13, 2007

A trilogy of plays by Tom Stoppard; Produced by Lincoln Center Theater (André Bishop, Artistic Director; Bernard Gersten, Executive Producer) in association with Bob Boyett; Director, Jack O'Brien; Sets, Bob Crowley and Scott Pask; Costumes, Catherine Zuber; Lighting, Brian MacDevitt (*Voyage*), Kenneth Posner (*Shipwreck*), Natasha Katz (*Salvage*); Original Music and Sound, Mark Bennett; PSM, Robert Bennett; Casting, Daniel Swee; Development, Hattie K. Jutagir; Marketing, Linda Mason Ross; General Manager, Adam Siegel; Production Manager, Jeff Hamlin; Finance, David S. Brown; Education, Kati Koerner; Music Directors, Mark Bennett, Dan Lipton; Company Manager, Matthew Markoff; Assistant CM, Jessica Perlmeter Cochrane; Associate Director, Benjamin Endsley Klein; Assistant Director, Caitlin Moon; Assistant to the Director, Seth Sklar-Heyn; ASMs, Diane DiVita, Jennifer Rae Moore, Jason Hindelang; Associate Design: Frank McCullough (set), Michael Zecker (costumes), Aaron Spivey (lighting), Leon Rothenberg (sound); Assistant Design: Jeffrey Hinchee, Lauren Alvarez (set), Court Watson (costumes), Kathleen Dobbins (lighting); Assistant Composer, David Ganon; Vocal Music/Instrumental Coach, Dan Lipton; Additional Music Arrangements, Curtis Moore; Projections, William Cusick; Associate Projections, Ryan Holsopple; Hair and Wigs, Tom Watson, Paul Huntley; Props, Scott Laule; Wardrobe Supervisor, Lynn Bowling; Hair Supervisor, Mary Kay Yezerski; Choreographer, Michele Lynch; Production Assistant, Anne Michaelson; Voice/Speech Consultant, Elizabeth Smith; Press, Philip Rinaldi, Barbara Carroll; Original Score Recording: Sh-K-Boom/Ghostlight Records 84422

**2006-2007 AWARDS** Tony Awards: Best Play, Best Featured Actress in a Play (Jennifer Ehle), Best Featured Actor in a Play (Billy Crudup), Best Direction of a Play (Jack O'Brien), Best Scenic Design of a Play (Bob Crowley, Scott Pask), Best Costumes of a Play (Catherine Zuber), Best Lighting Design of a Play (Brian MacDevitt, Kenneth Posner, Natasha Katz); Drama Desk: Outstanding Play, Outstanding Featured Actress in a Play (Martha Plimpton), Outstanding Director of a Play (Jack O'Brien), Outstanding Scenic Design of a Play (Bob Crowley, Scott Pask), Outstanding Costumes of a Play (Catherine Zuber), Outstanding Lighting Design of a Play (Brian MacDevitt, Kenneth Posner, Natasha Katz), Outstanding Music for a Play (Mark Bennett); Outer Critics Circle: Outstanding New Broadway Play, Outstanding Director of a Play (Jack O'Brien), Outstanding Set Design (Bob Crowley, Scott Pask), Outstanding Costumes (Catherine Zuber), Outstanding Lighting Design (Brian MacDevitt, Kenneth Posner, Natasha Katz), Outstanding Featured Actress in a Play (Martha Plimpton)

**SYNOPSIS** *The Coast of Utopia* is the story of six young men, Michael Bakunin, Nicholas Stankevich, Vissarion Belinsky, Ivan Turgenev, Alexander Herzen, and Nicholas Ogarev, who formed the revolutionary backbone to Russia's emergence. Members of the "Generation of the 1840s," the idealistic intellectual young Russian noblemen met as students at the University of Moscow during the difficult, repressive decade in the reign of Tsar Nicholas I. They share deep friendships which lasted throughout their lives as they were buffeted by history and their own triumphs and personal tragedies. Together as friends, they struggled to bring Russia into the modern age. *The Coast of Utopia* was originally produced at London's National Theatre in 2002, directed by Trevor Nunn. The Lincoln Center run included nine Saturday "marathons" in which all three parts were presented in one day.

### Part One—*Voyage*

First Preview: October 17, 2006; Opening Night: November 27, 2006; Closed May 12, 2007; 31 previews, 45 performances

*Billy Crudup and Brian F. O'Byrne (photos by Paul Kolnik)*

**CAST** Alexander Bakunin **Richard Easton**; Varvara, *his wife* **Amy Irving**; Liubov, *a daughter* **Jennifer Ehle**; Varenka, *a daughter* **Martha Plimpton**; Tatiana, *a daughter* **Kellie Overbey**; Miss Chamberlain, *their English governess* **Annie Purcell**; Baron Renne, *betrothed to Liubov* **Bianca Amato**; Semyon, *senior household servant* **Andrew McGinn**; Semyon, *senior household servant,* **David Manis**; Masha, *a maid* **Felicity LaFortune**; Michael Bakunin **Ethan Hawke**; Dyakov, *betrothed to Varenka* **Anthony Cochrane**; Nicholas Stankevich, *a young philosopher* **David Harbour**; Vissarion Belinsky, *a literary critic* **Billy Crudup**; Ivan Turgenev **Jason Butler Harner**; Alexander Herzen **Brian F. O'Byrne**; Nicholas Ogarev, *his friend* **Josh Hamilton**; Nicholas Sazonov, *another friend* **Aaron Krohn**; Nicholas Ketscher, *a young doctor* **Baylen Thomas**; Nicholas Polevoy, *editor of The Messenger* **David Pittu**[*1]; Mrs. Beyer **Patricia Conolly**; Natalie Beyer, *her daughter* **Mia Barron**; Peter Chaadaev, *an essayist* **David Cromwell**; Stepan Shevyrev, *a professor and editor* **Robert Stanton**; Katya, *Belinsky's mistress* **Jennifer Lyon**; Pushkin, *a poet*/Cat **Adam Dannheisser**; Serfs, Servants, Party Guests, Musicians, etc **Larry Bull, Denis Butkus, Michael Carlsen, Amanda Leigh Cobb, Matt Dickson, Scott Parkinson, Erika Rolfsrud, Brian Sgambati, Eric Sheffer Stevens**[*2]**, David Christopher Wells**

*Succeeded by: 1. Eric Sheffer Stevens 2. William Connell

*Jennifer Ehle, Kellie Overbey, Amy Irving, Felicity LaFortune, Richard Easton, David Manis, Ethan Hawke, and Billy Crudup*

**UNDERSTUDIES** Bianca Amato (Katya), Larry Bull (Dyakov, Pushkin/Cat), Amanda Leigh Cobb (Natalie, Tatiana, Alexandra), Anthony Cochrane (Semyon, Nicolas Polevoy, Stephen Shevyrev), Adam Dannheisser (Michael Bakunin), Felicity LaFortune (Miss Chamberlain, Mrs. Beyer, Varvara), Jennifer Lyon (Masha), Andrew McGinn (Nicholas Ogarev), David Manis (Peter Chaadaev, Alexander Bakunin), Scott Parkinson (Vissarion Belinsky, Nicholas Sazonov), Erika Rolfsrud (Liubov, Varenka), Robert Stanton (Baron Renne), Eric Sheffer Stevens (Alexander Herzen), Baylen Thomas (Ivan Turgenev), David Christopher Wells (Nicholas Stankevich, Nicholas Ketscher)

**MUSICIANS** Josh Camp (accordion), Marshall Coid (violin), Kevin Kuhn (balalaika, mandolin), Dan Lipton (piano), Alissa Smith (viola), Bruce Wang (cello)

**SETTING** Act 1: Premukhino, the Bakunin estate 150 miles northwest of Moscow, Summer 1833–Autumn 1841; Act 2: Moscow and St. Petersburg, March 1834–Autumn 1844. American premiere of part one of a trilogy presented in two acts.

*Ethan Hawke, Martha Plimpton, Jennifer Ehle, and Kellie Overbey*

*Kellie Overbey, Jennifer Ehle, and Annie Purcell*

*Ethan Hawke*

## Part Two—*Shipwreck*

First Preview: December 5, 2006; Opening Night: December 21, 2006; Closed May 12, 2007; 12 previews, 45 performances

**CAST** *In Sololovo, Russia:* Alexander Herzen **Brían F. O'Byrne**; Natalie Herzen, *his wife* **Jennifer Ehle**; Sasha Herzen, *their son* **Beckett Melville**; Kolya Herzen, *their younger son* **August Gladstone**; Nurse, *a household serf* **Mia Barron**; Nicholas Ogarev, *a poet* **Josh Hamilton**; Ivan Turgenev, *a writer* **Jason Butler Harner**; Timothy Granovsky, *a historian* **Andrew McGinn**; Nicholas Ketscher, *a doctor* **Baylen Thomas**; Konstatin Aksakov, *a Slavophile* **Scott Parkinson**; Policeman **David Manis**; *In Paris:* Vissarion Belinsky, *a literary critic* **Billy Crudup**; Madame Haag, *Herzen's mother* **Patricia Conolly**; Jean-Marie, *a French servant* **David Cromwell**; George Herwegh, *a German poet* **David Harbour**; Emma Herwegh, *his wife* **Bianca Amato**; Shop Boy **Tolan Aman**; Nicholas Sazonov, *a Russian émigré activist* **Aaron Krohn**; Michael Bakunin **Ethan Hawke**; Marianne on the Barricades **Felicity LaFortune**; Karl Marx **Adam Dannheisser**; Natasha Tuchkov, *Natalie's friend* **Martha Plimpton**; Benoit, *a French servant* **David Pittu**[*1]; Beggar **Scott Parkinson**; Maria Ogarev, *Ogarev's estranged wife* **Amy Irving**; Franz Otto, *a lawyer in Dresden, Saxony* **Robert Stanton**; Leonty Ibayev, *Russian Consul General in Nice* **Richard Easton**; Rocca, *an Italian servant* **David Pittu**[*1]; Rosa, *an Italian maid* **Felicity LaFortune**; Serfs, French Servants, Revolutionaries, Italian Servants **Larry Bull, Denis Butkus, Michael Carlsen, Anthony Cochrane**[*2]**, Amanda Leigh Cobb, Michael D'Addario**[*3]**, Matt Dickson, Jennifer Lyon, Kellie Overbey, Annie Purcell, Erika Rolfsrud, Brian Sgambati, Eric Sheffer Stevens, David Christopher Wells**

*Succeeded by: 1. Anthony Cochrane 2. William Carlsen 3. Maximillian Sherer

**UNDERSTUDIES** Mia Barron (Natasha Tuchkov), Larry Bull (Karl Marx, Jean-Marie), Anthony Cochrane (Benoit, Rocca, Leonty Ibayev), Amanda Leigh Cobb (Rosa, Marianne), Michael D'Addario (Sasha Herzen, Kolya Herzen), Adam Dannheisser (Michael Bakunin), Felicity LaFortune (Madame Haag, Maria Ogarev), Jennifer Lyon (Nurse), David Manis (Franz Otto), Andrew McGinn (Nicholas Ogarev, Nicholas Sazonov), Scott Parkinson (Vissarion Belinsky), Erika Rolfsrud (Natalie Herzen, Emma Herwegh), Eric Sheffer Stevens (Alexander Herzen), Baylen Thomas (Ivan Turgenev, Beggar), David Christopher Wells (Timothy Granovsky, Nicholas Ketscher, George Herwegh)

**MUSICIANS** Dominic Derasse (trumpet), Dan Lipton (piano), Sarah Schram (oboe), Jake Schwartz (guitar), Andrew Sterman (clarinet, flute)

**SETTING** 1846–1852, The Herzens' apartment in Paris, The Herzens' house in Nice (at this time an Italian town), various other locations in and around Moscow, Saxony, Paris, Germany, and a cross-Channel steamer. American premiere of part two of a trilogy presented in two acts.

*Jennifer Ehle and Brian F. O'Byrne (photos by Paul Kolnik)*

*Jason Butler Harner, Billy Crudup, Jennifer Ehle, August Gladstone, Beckett Melville, and Patricia Conolly*

Brian F. O'Byrne, Jason Butler Harner, and David Harbour

Brian F. O'Byrne and Josh Hamilton (photos by Paul Kolnik)

Amy Irving and Jennifer Ehle

Jennifer Ehle, David Harbour, and Martha Plimpton

## Part Three—*Salvage*

First Preview: January 30, 2007; Opening Night: February 15, 2007; Closed May 13, 2007; 13 previews, 34 performances

**CAST** *Herzen's Household:* Alexander Herzen **Brían F. O'Byrne;** Sasha, *his son* **Matt Dickson;** Sasha, *as a child* **Evan Daves;** Tata, *his daughter* **Annie Purcell;** Tata, *as a child* **Kat Peters;** Olga, *his daughter* **Amanda Leigh Cobb;** Olga, *as a child* **Kat Peters;** Olga, *as a young child* **Vivien Kells;** Maria Fomm, *their German nanny* **Felicity LaFortune;** Malwida von Meysenbug, *their German governess and tutor* **Jennifer Ehle;** Mrs. Blainey, *an English nanny* **Patricia Conolly;** Rose, *a parlormaid* **Mia Barron;** English Servants **Tolan Aman, Amanda Leigh Cobb, Matt Dickson, Brian Sgambati;** *The Émigré Circle in London:* Count Stanislaw Worcell, *leading figure of the Polish opposition in exile* **Richard Easton;** Arnold Ruge, *radical German editor and activist of 1848* **David Cromwell;** Gottfried Kinkel, *radical German poet and activist of 1848* **David Manis;** Joanna Kinkel, *his wife, a composer, writer and women's rights activist* **Bianca Amato;** Karl Marx, *author of the Communist Manifesto* **Adam Dannheisser;** Ernest Jones, *radical English Chartist politician, lawyer, and poet* **Robert Stanton;** Emily Jones, *his wife* **Jennifer Lyon;** Giuseppe Mazzini, *Italian nationalist leader in exile* **Brian Sgambati;** Louis Blanc, *French socialist politician, former 1848 Assembly member* **David Pittu**[*1]; Alexandre Ledru-Rollin, *French republican politician, former 1848 Assembly member* **Larry Bull;** Alphonse de Ville, *his aide* **Baylen Thomas;** Lajos Kossuth, *first President of independent Hungary, in exile* **Anthony Cochrane;** Teresa Kossuth, *his wife* **Erika Rolfsrud;** Captain Peks, *his aide* **Denis Butkus;** Zenkowicz, *Chief of Staff to Count Worcell* **David Cromwell;** Tchorzewski, *a Polish bookshop owner* **Michael Carlsen;** Czerniecki, *a Polish printer* **Aaron Krohn;** Polish émigré at the celebration of the new Tsar **Denis Butkus;** Michael Bakunin **Ethan Hawke;** Nicholas Ogarev **Josh Hamilton;** Natasha Tuchkov Ogarev, *his second wife* **Martha Plimpton;** Ivan Turgenev **Jason Butler Harner;** Mary Sutherland, *Ogarev's mistress* **Kellie Overbey;** Henry, *her son* **Tolan Aman;** *Russian visitors—The "New" Generation:* Nicholas Chernyshevsky, *a radical author of "What Is to Be Done?"* **Andrew McGinn;** Doctor at the Seashore (Bazarov) **David Harbour;** Perotkin **David Christopher Wells;** Semlov **Brian Sgambati;** Lt. Korf **Denis Butkus;** Vetoshnikov **David Pittu**[*1]; Sleptsov **Scott Parkinson;** *In Geneva:* Waiter **Brian Sgambati;** Teresina, *Herzen's Italian daughter-in-law, Sasha's wife* **Mia Barron;** Liza, *daughter of Herzen and Natasha Ogarev* **Kat Peters;** Ensemble **Eric Sheffer Stevens**[*2]**, Beckett Melville, Sophie Rudin**

*Succeeded by: 1. Eric Sheffer Stevens 2. William Connell

**UNDERSTUDIES** Bianca Amato (Teresina), Tolan Aman (Sasha as a child), Bianca Amato (Teresina), Mia Barron (Natasha Tuchkov Ogarev, Tata), Larry Bull (Karl Marx), Denis Butkus (Lajos Kossuth, Sasha), Michael Carlsen (Giuseppe Mazzini, Lt. Korf, Sleptsov), Amanda Leigh Cobb (Emily Jones), Anthony Cochrane (Count Stanislaw Worcell, Zenkowicz), Adam Dannheisser (Michael Bakunin), Matt Dickson (Captain Peks, Polish émigré), Aaron Krohn (Doctor at the Seashore, Nicholas Chernyshevsky), Felicity LaFortune (Mrs. Blainey), Jennifer Lyon (Maria Fomm, Rose), Andrew McGinn (Gottfried Kinkel, Nicholas Ogarev), Beckett Melville (Henry), Scott Parkinson (Arnold Ruge), Annie Purcell (Joanna Kinkel), Erika Rolfsrud (Malwida von Meysenbug, Mary Sutherland, Olga), Sophie Rudin (Liza, Olga as a child, Olga as a young child, Tata as a child), Brian Sgambati (Waiter), Eric Sheffer Stevens (Alexander Herzen, Perotkin, Semlov), Baylen Thomas (Alexandre Ledru-Rollin, Ernest Jones, Ivan Turgenev), David Christopher Wells (Alphonse de Ville, Czerniecki, Louis Blanc, Vetoshnikov)

**MUSICIANS** Dan Lipton (piano), Aaron Krohn (guitarist), Dominic Derasse (trumpet), Andrew Sterman (clarinet)

**SETTING** England and, much later, Geneva. Time: 1853–1868; American premiere of part three of a trilogy presented in two acts.

*Josh Hamilton, Kat Peters, Brian F. O'Byrne, Martha Plimpton, and Ethan Hawke (photos by Paul Kolnik)*

*Evan Daves, Brian F. O'Byrne, and Kat Peters*

*The Company*

*Josh Hamilton and Brian F. O'Byrne*

*Josh Hamilton and Martha Plimpton*

# COMPANY

Barrymore Theatre; First Preview: October 30, 2006; Opening Night: November 29, 2006; 217 performances as of May 31, 2007

Music and lyrics by Stephen Sondheim, book by George Furth; Produced by Marc Routh, Richard Frankel, Steven Baruch, Ambassador Theatre Group, Tulchin/Bartner Productions, Darren Bagert, and Cincinnati Playhouse in the Park (Edward Stern, Producing Artistic Director; Buzz Ward, Executive Director); Director and Musical Staging, John Doyle; Musical Supervision and Orchestrations by Mary-Mitchell Campbell; Set, David Gallo; Costumes, Ann Hould-Ward; Lighting, Thomas C. Hase; Sound, Andrew Keister; Hair & Wigs, David Lawrence; Makeup, Angelina Avallone; Casting, Telsey + Company; Associate Director, Adam John Hunter; PSM, Gary Mickelson; Resident Music Supervisor, Lynne Shankel; General Manager, Richard Frankel Productions Inc., Jo Porter; Production Management, Juniper Street Productions Inc.; Company Manager, Sammy Ledbetter; Associate CM, Jason Pelusio; Stage Manager/Dance Captain, Newton Cole; ASM, Claudia Lynch; Production Manager, Hilary Blanken; Production Management Associates, Guy Kwan, Kevin Broomell, Ana Rose Greene, Elana Soderblom; Action Arrangement, Drew Fracher; Associate Design: Mary Hamrick (set), Sidney Shannon (costumes), Paul Miller (lighting); Scenic Model, Frank McCullough; Design Assistants: Josh Zangen (set), Bradley Clements (lighting), Michael Bogden (sound); Production: Fred Gallo (carpenter), Jack Anderson (advance carpenter), Jonathan Lawson (electrician), Tom Lawrey (light board), Michael Wojchik (sound), Joseph P. Harris Jr. (prop master), Dawn Makay (head props), Penny Davis (wardrobe supervisor),Vanessa Anderson (hair and wig supervisor); Advertising, Serino Coyne Inc.; Music Copying, Kaye-Houston Music; Press, Barlow • Hartman, Leslie Baden; Cast recording: Nonesuch 79635

*Elizabeth Stanley, Kelly Jeanne Grant, Angel Desai, and Raúl Esparza (photos by Paul Kolnik)*

**CAST** Robert—*Percussion* **Raúl Esparza;** Joanne—*Orchestra Bells, Percussion* **Barbara Walsh;** Harry—*Trumpet, Trombone* **Keith Buterbaugh;** Peter—*Piano/Keyboards, Double Bass* **Matt Castle;** Paul—*Trumpet, Drums* **Robert Cunningham;** Marta—*Keyboard, Violin, Alto Sax* **Angel Desai;** Kathy—*Flute, Alto Sax* **Kelly Jeanne Grant;** Sarah—*Flute, Alto Sax, Piccolo* **Kristin Huffman;** Susan— *Piano/Keyboards, Orchestra Bells* **Amy Justman;** Amy—*French Horn, Trumpet, Flute* **Heather Laws;** Jenny—*Violin, Guitar, Double Bass* **Leenya Rideout;** David—*Cello, Alto Sax, Tenor Sax* **Fred Rose;** Larry—*Clarinet, Drums* **Bruce Sabath;** April—*Oboe, Tuba, Alto Sax* **Elizabeth Stanley**

**STANDBYS** Fred Rose (Robert), Renée Bang Allen (Sarah, Joanne), Brandon Ellis (David, Paul), David Garry (Harry, Larry, Paul), Jason Ostrowski (Peter), Jessica Wright (Amy, Jenny, Susan), Katrina Yaukey (Marta, Kathy, April)

**MUSICAL NUMBERS** Company, The Little Things You Do Together, Sorry-Grateful, You Could Drive a Person Crazy, Have I Got a Girl for You, Someone is Waiting, Another Hundred People, Getting Married Today, Marry Me a Little, Side by Side by Side, What Would We Do Without You?, Poor Baby, Barcelona, The Ladies Who Lunch, Being Alive

**2006–2007 AWARDS** Tony Award: Best Revival of a Musical; Drama Desk: Outstanding Revival of a Musical, Outstanding Actor in a Musical (Raúl Esparza), Outstanding Orchestrations (Mary-Mitchell Campbell); Outer Critics Circle: Outstanding Revival of a Musical, Outstanding Actor in a Musical (Raúl Esparza)

**SETTING** New York City. Now. Revival of the musical presented in two acts. This production was previously produced at Cincinnati Playhouse in the Park, March 14–April 14, 2006 (see *Theatre World* Volume 62, page 276). Originally produced on Broadway on April 26, 1970, at the Alvin Theatre (see *Theatre World* Volume 26, page 57), and revived by the Roundabout Theatre Company at the Criterion Center on August 30, 1995 (see *Theatre World* Volume 52, page 12). A special Broadway Cares/Equity Fights AIDS concert staging of the show was produced at the Vivian Beaumont Theater on April 11–12, 1993, featuring most of the original cast members (see *Theatre World* Volume 49, page 36).

**SYNOPSIS** A revolutionary, unconventional look at love and commitment in a complex modern world, *Company* is a remarkably honest, clever and sophisticated portrayal of five married couples as seen through the eyes of their mutual friend Robert, a bachelor weighing the pros and cons of wedded life. A comic and touching tale, the show explores not only fear and longing but also the simple joys of being alive. Doyle's production is a bold reinvention of the show (as in his version of the previous season's *Sweeney Todd*) in which the actors sing, dance, and play all of the musical instruments.

*Raúl Esparza*

*The Cast*

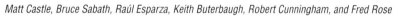

*Matt Castle, Bruce Sabath, Raúl Esparza, Keith Buterbaugh, Robert Cunningham, and Fred Rose*

# THE VERTICAL HOUR

Music Box Theatre; First Preview: November 9, 2006; Opening Night: November 30, 2006; Closed March 11, 2007; 23 previews, 117 performances

Written by David Hare; Produced by Scott Rudin, Robert Fox, Neal Street Productions, Roger Berlind, Debra Black, The Shubert Organization; Director, Sam Mendes; Set, Scott Pask; Costumes, Ann Roth; Lighting, Brian MacDevitt; Sound, Christopher Cronin; Casting, Daniel Swee; U.K. Casting Consultant; Anne McNulty; PSM, James Harker; Associate Director, B.T. McNicholl; Production Management, Aurora Productions (Gene O'Donovan, W. Benjamin Heller II, Bethany Weinstein, Melissa Mazdra, Tuesday Curran); General Management, Stuart Thompson, Caroline Prugh, James Triner; Company Manager, Chris Morey; Stage Manager, Thea Bradshaw Gilles; Hair, Alan D'Angerio; Associate Design: Orit Jacoby Carroll (set), Michelle Matland (costumes), Jennifer Schriever (lighting); Assistant Set, Jeffrey Hinchee; Wardrobe Supervisor, Douglas C. Petitjean; Hair Supervisor, Susan Schectar; Production Assistant, John Bantay; Production: David M. Cohen, Brian G.F. McGarity, Abraham Morrison, Bill Lewis, Laura Beattie, Barry Doss; Assistants: Hannah Bower, Laurent Lambert, Jeffrey Hillock, Ana Pilar Camacho, Susie Graves, Megan Curren; Neal Street Productions Producer, Beth Byrne; Advertising, SpotCo; Press, Barlow • Hartman, Dennis Crowley, Ryan Ratelle

**CAST** Oliver Lucas **Bill Nighy;** Nadia Blye **Julianne Moore;** Dennis Dutton **Dan Bittner;** Philip Lucas **Andrew Scott;** Terri Scholes **Rutina Wesley**

**STANDBYS** Jennifer Roszell (Nadia Blye), Matthew Humphreys (Dennis Dutton, Philip Lucas), Steven Crossley (Oliver Lucas), Crystal Noelle (Terri Scholes)

**2006–2007 AWARDS Theatre World Award:** Bill Nighy

**SETTING** An office at Yale University and a lawn on the Welsh borders, the recent past. World premiere of a new play presented in two acts.

**SYNOPSIS** Nadia Blye is a young American war correspondent turned academic who now teaches Political Studies at Yale. A brief holiday with her boyfriend in the Welsh borders brings her into contact with a kind of Englishman whose culture and beliefs are a surprise and a challenge, both to her and to her relationship. This new play, about the interconnection between our secret motives and our public politics, seeks to illustrate how life has subtly changed for so many people in the West in the new century.

*Julianne Moore*

*Bill Nighy*

*Andrew Scott (photos by Paul Kolnik)*

# HIGH FIDELITY

Imperial Theatre; First Preview: November 20, 2006; Opening Night: December 7, 2006; Closed December 17, 2006; 18 previews, 14 performances

Music by Tom Kitt, Lyrics by Amanda Green, Book by David Lindsay-Abaire, based on the novel *High Fidelity* by Nick Hornsby and the Touchtone Pictures Film; Produced by Jeffrey Seller, Kevin McCollum, Robyn Goodman, Live Nation, Roy Miller, Dan Markley, Ruth Hendel/Danzansky Partners, and Jam Theatricals; Director, Walter Bobbie; Choreographer, Christopher Gattelli; Set, Anna Louizos; Costumes, Theresa Squire; Lighting, Ken Billington; Sound, Acme Sound Partners; Music Director, Adam Ben-David; Orchestrations, Tom Kitt and Alex Lacamoire; Vocal Arrangements, Stephen Oremus; Music Coordinator, Michael Keller; Music Supervision, Alex Lacamoire; Casting, Telsey + Company; Technical Supervisor, Brian Lynch; Marketing, Scott A. Moore; General Manager, John S. Corker; Production Supervisor, Steven Beckler; Company Manager, Brig Berney; Associate Director, Marc Bruni; Associate Producers, Sonny Everett, Mariano Tolentino Jr.; PSM, Steven Beckler; Associate General Manager, R. Erin Craig; Wigs, Charles LaPointe; Stage Manager, Thomas J. Gates; ASM, Timothy R. Semon; Assistant Choreographer, Shanna Van Derwerker; Assistant to the Director, Robert Ross Parker; Associate Design: Donyale Werle, Todd Potter (set), Heather Dunbar (costumes), John Demous (lighting); Design Assistants: Eric Lewis Beauzay, Court Watson (set), Amanda Bujak, Amelia Dombrowski, Chris Rumery, Lisa Zinni (costumes), Anthony Pearson (lighting), Leah Loukas (wigs); Music Copying, Emily Grishman, Katherine Edmonds; Drum Arrangements, Damien Bassman; Moving Light Programmer, David Arch; Carpenter/Associate Technical Supervisor, Christopher Kluth; Properties Coordinator, Kathy Fabian/Propstar; Propmaster, Ronald Groomes; Dance Captain, Paul Castree; Advertising, SpotCo; Press, Sam Rudy Media Relations, Dale R. Heller, Robert Lasko; Cast recording: Sh-K-Boom/Ghostlight Records 84421

*Will Chase, Kirsten Wyatt, Anne Warren, Emily Swallow, Caren Lyn Manuel, and Rachel Stern (photos by Joan Marcus)*

**CAST** Rob **Will Chase;** Hipster/Roadie **Andrew C. Call;** Futon Guy **Justin Brill;** Guy with Mohawk/Neil Young **Matt Caplan;** Dick **Christian Anderson;** Barry **Jay Klaitz;** Laura **Jenn Colella;** Anna/Alison **Kirsten Wyatt;** Penny/Back-up Singer **Anne Warren;** Charlie/Marie LaSalle **Emily Swallow;** Sarah **Caren Lyn Manuel;** Liz/Jackie **Rachel Stern;** T.M.P.M.I.T.W./Bruce **Jon Patrick Walker;** Ian/Middle-Aged Guy **Jeb Brown;** Swings **Paul Castree, George Merrick, Betsy Morgan, Tom Plotkin, J.B. Wing**

**UNDERSTUDIES** Justin Brill (Dick), Andrew C. Call (Barry, T.M.P.M.I.T.W./Bruce), Matt Caplan (Rob, Barry), Paul Castree (Dick), Caren Lyn Manuel (Laura, Liz/Jackie, Charlie/Marie), George Merrick (Ian/Middle-Aged Guy), Betsy Morgan (Laura, Liz/Jackie, Charlie/Marie, Anna/Allison), Tom Plotkin (Ian/Middle-Aged Guy, T.M.P.M.I.T.W./Bruce), Emily Swallow (Laura), Jon Patrick Walker (Rob), Anne Warren (Laura), J.B. Wing (Liz/Jackie, Charlie/Marie, Anna/Allison)

***HIGH FIDELITY* BAND** Adam Ben-David (Conductor/Piano/Harmonica), Matt Gallagher (Associate Conductor/Organ/Keyboard), Kenny Brescia (guitars), Michael Aarons (guitars/sitar/banjo/mandolin), Randy Landau (bass), Damien Bassman (drums/percussion), Dan Willis (reeds), Bud Burridge (trumpet), Antoine Silverman (violin), Peter Sachon (cello), Jim Abbott (synthesizer programmer)

**MUSICAL NUMBERS** The Last Real Record Store, Desert Island Top 5 Break-Ups, It's No Problem, She Goes, Ian's Here, Number Five With A Bullet, Ready To Settle, Nine Percent Chance, I Slept With Someone (Who Slept with Lyle Lovett), I Slept With Someone (Who Handled Kurt Cobain's Intervention), I Slept With Someone (reprise), Exit Sign, Cryin' In The Rain, Conflict Resolution I, Conflict Resolution II, Conflict Resolution III, Goodbye And Goodluck, It's No Problem (reprise), Laura, Laura, Turn The World Off (And Turn You On)

**SETTING** Place: A remote neighborhood in Brooklyn. Time: The recent past. New York premiere of a new musical presented in two acts. *High Fidelity* had out-of-town tryouts at Boston's Colonial Theatre, September 26, 2006.

**SYNOPSIS** The romantic musical comedy follows the adventures of Rob, a record store owner who knows almost everything about pop music, but almost nothing about how to hang onto a girl. Rob's love life, already a broken record of heartache, falls off the charts completely when he gets dumped by Laura... but that just sets him up for one of the top five romantic comebacks ever.

*Will Chase and Jenn Colella*

Above: *Christian Anderson, Will Chase, and Jay Klaitz*

Left: *Jay Klaitz, Will Chase, and Christian Anderson*

# SPRING AWAKENING

Eugene O'Neill Theatre; First Preview: November 17, 2006; Opening Night: December 10, 2006; 28 previews, 204 performances as of May 31, 2007

Book and lyrics by Steven Sater, music by Duncan Sheik, based on the play *The Awakening of Spring* by Frank Wedekind; Produced by Ira Pittelman, Tom Hulce, Jeffrey Richards, Jerry Frankel, The Atlantic Theater Company (Neil Pepe, Artistic Director; Andrew D. Hamingson, Managing Director), Jeffrey Sine, Freddy DeMann, Max Cooper, Mort Swinsky, Cindy and Jay Gutterman, Joe McGinnis, Judith Ann Abrams, ZenDog Productions, CarJac Productions, Aron Bergson Productions, Jennifer Manocherian, Ted Snowdon, Harold Thau, Terry Schnuck, Cold Spring Productions, Amanda Dubois, Elizabeth Eynon Wetherell, Jennifer Maloney, Tamara Tunie, Joe Cilibrasi, StyleFour Productions; Director, Michael Mayer; Choreography, Bill T. Jones; Musical Director, Kimberly Grigsby; Set, Christine Jones; Costumes, Susan Hilferty; Lighting, Kevin Adams; Sound, Brian Ronan; Orchestrations, Duncan Sheik; Vocal Arrangements, AnnMarie Milazzo; Additional Arrangements, Simon Hale; Music Coordinator, Michael Keller; Casting, Jim Carnahan, Carrie Gardner; Fight Director, J. David Brimmer; PSM, Heather Cousens; Associate Producers, Joan Cullman Productions, Patricia Flicker Addiss; Technical Supervision, Neil A. Mazzella; General Management, Abbie M. Strassler; General Management, Iron Mountain Productions; Company Manager, John E. Gendron; Marketing and Promotions, Situation Marketing, Damian Bazadona, Steve Tate; Stage Manager, Rick Steiger; ASM, Bethany Russell, Assistant CM, Bethany Russell; Dance Captain, Lauren Pritchard; Fight Captain, Brian Charles Johnson; National Marketing Consultants, Susan Blond, Simone Smalls, Liza Bychkov; National Press Consultants, Rubenstein Communications, Inc., Amy Jacobs, Andy Shearer, Alice McGillion; Associate Technical Supervision, Sam Ellis; Assistant Director, Beatrice Terry; Assistant Choreographer, Miguel Anaya Jr.; Associate Music Director, Deborah Abramson; Music Copyist, Steven M. Alper; Associate Design: Edward Coco (set), Maiko Matshushima (costumes), Aaron Sporer (lighting), Moving Light Programmer, Bobby Harrell; Conventional Light Programmer, Neil McShane; Assistant Design: David Stollings (sound), Tim McMath, Akiko Kosaka, Amy Rubin, Rob Monaco, Sarah Walsh (sets), Marina Reti (costumes); Production: Donald Robinson (head carpenter), Kevin Maher (fly automations), Thomas Sherman (deck automation), Todd D'Aiuto (electrician), Greg Husinko (head electrician), Kathy Fabian/Propstar (props coordinator), Christopher Beck (props), Francis Elers, Craig Van Tassei (sound), Susan Checklick (wardrobe supervisor), Rufus Mayhem (hair consultant), Nathaniel Hathaway (hair supervisor); Press, Jeffrey Richards Associates, Irene Gandy; Cast recording: Decca Broadway B0008020-02

*The Cast (photo by Doug Hamilton)*

*Phoebe Strole, Remy Zaken, Lea Michele, and Lilli Cooper
(photo by Joan Marcus)*

**CAST** Wendla **Lea Michele;** The Adult Women **Christine Estabrook;** Martha **Lilli Cooper;** Ilse **Lauren Pritchard;** Anna **Phoebe Strole;** Thea **Remy Zaken;** The Adult Men **Stephen Spinella;** Otto **Brian Charles Johnson;** Hanschen **Jonathan B. Wright;** Ernst **Gideon Glick;** Georg **Skylar Astin;** Moritz **John Gallagher Jr.;** Melchior **Jonathan Groff;** Ensemble **Gerard Canonico, Jennifer Damiano, Robert Hager, Krysta Rodriguez;** Swings **Rob Devaney, Frances Mercanti-Anthony**

*John Gallagher Jr. and Stephen Spinella*

Lea Michele and Jonathan Groff

Gideon Glick and Jonathan B. Wright

**UNDERSTUDIES** Robert Hager & Jonathan B. Wright (Melchior); Gerard Canonico & Brian Charles Johnson (Moritz, Georg); Gerard Canonico & Robert Hager (Hanschen, Otto, Ernst, Georg); Rob Devaney (Adult Men); Krysta Rodriguez & Phoebe Strole (Wendla, Ilse); Jennifer Damiano & Krysta Rodriguez (Ana, Martha, Thea); Frances Mercanti-Anthony (Adult Women)

**THE BAND** Kimberly Grigsby (Conductor/keyboards), Thad DeBrock (guitars), George Farmer (bass), Trey Files (Associate Conductor/drums), Benjamin Kalb (cello), Oliver Manchon (violin/guitar), Hiroko Taguchi (violin)

**MUSICAL NUMBERS** Mama Who Bore Me, Mama Who Bore Me (reprise), All That's Known, The Bitch of Living, My Junk, Touch Me, The Word of Your Body, The Dark I Know Well, And Then There Were None, The Mirror-Blue Night, I Believe, The Guilty Ones, Don't Do Sadness, Blue Wind, Left Behind, Totally Fucked, The Word of Your Body (reprise), Whispering, Those You've Known, The Song of Purple Summer

**2006–2007 AWARDS** Tony Awards: Best Musical, Best Book of a Musical (Steven Sater), Best Original Score (Duncan Sheik, Steven Sater), Best Featured Actor in a Musical (John Gallagher, Jr.), Best Choreography (Bill T. Jones), Best Direction of a Musical (Michael Mayer), Best Orchestrations (Duncan Sheik), Best Lighting Design of a Musical (Kevin Adams); Drama Desk: Outstanding Musical, Outstanding Director of a Musical (Michael Mayer), Outstanding Lyrics (Steven Sater), Outstanding Music (Duncan Sheik); Outer Critics Circle: Outstanding New Broadway Musical, Outstanding New Score (Duncan Sheik, Steven Sater), Outstanding Director of a Musical (Michael Mayer); Lortel Awards (from the Off-Broadway production): Outstanding Musical (tie with *In the Heights*), Outstanding Lighting Design (Kevin Adams); **Theatre World Award:** Jonathan Groff

**SETTING** A provincial German town in the 1890s. Transfer of the Off-Broadway musical presented in two acts. Originally produced at the Atlantic Theater Company May 19–August 5, 2006 (see *Theatre World* Volume 62, page 151).

**SYNOPSIS** *Spring Awakening* is the contemporary musical adaptation of one of literature's most controversial plays. The musical centers on a brilliant young student named Melchior, his troubled friend Moritz, and the beautiful young Wendla who is on the verge of womanhood, and boldly depicts a dozen young people and how they make their way through the complicated, confusing, and mysterious time of their sexual awakening. Sheik and Sater's score feature songs that illuminate the urgency of adolescent self-discovery, the burning intensity of teen friendships, and the innate suspicion of the uncomprehending adult world.

Lilli Cooper and Phoebe Strole, Lea Michele (photo by Joan Marcus)

John Gallagher Jr.

Christine Estabrook. Jonathan Groff, and Stephen Spinella

John Gallagher Jr., Jonathan Groff, and Lea Michele

Stephen Spinella

# THE APPLE TREE

Studio 54; First preview: November 29, 2006; Opening Night: December 14, 2006; Closed March 11, 2007; 18 previews, 99 performances

Book, music, and lyrics by Jerry Bock and Sheldon Harnick, additional material by Jerome Coopersmith; based on stories by Mark Twain, Frank. R. Stockton and Jules Feiffer; Produced by the Roundabout Theatre Company (Todd Haimes, Artistic Director; Harold Wolpert, Managing Director; Julia C. Levy, Executive Director); Director, Gary Griffin; Choreography, Andy Blankenbuehler; Music Director/Vocal Arrangements, Rob Fisher; Orchestrations, Jonathan Tunick; Set, John Lee Beatty; Costumes, Jess Goldstein; Lighting, Donald Holder; Sound, Dan Moses Schreier; Hair/Wigs, Charles LaPointe; Music Coordinator, Seymour Red Press; PSM, Peter Hanson; ASM, Jon Krause; Casting, Jim Carnahan; Technical Supervisor, Steve Beers; General Manager, Sydney Beers; Founding Director, Gene Feist; Associate Artistic Director, Scott Ellis; Marketing, David B. Steffen; Development, Jeffory Lawson; Company Manager, Nancy Mulliner; ACM, Katie McKee; Dance Captain, Lorin Latarro; Assistant Director, Todd Lundquist; Assistant Choreographer, Joanne Manning; Assistant Technical Supervisor, Elisa R. Kuhar; Associate Design: Matt Myhrum (set), China Lee (costumes), Mike Jones (lighting); Assistant Design: Yoshinori Tanokura (set), David Withrow (costumes), Catherine Tate (lighting), Phillip Peglow (sound); Makeup, Angelina Avallone; Production: Dan Hoffman (carpenter), Josh Weitzman (electrician), Denise Grillo (properties), Nadine Hetttrel; (wardrobe supervisor), Daryl Terry (hair and wig supervisor), Pitsch Karrer (sound), Paul Ashton (automation), Eric Norris (moving lights); Music Copying, Emily Grishman, Katherine Edmonds; Advertising, The Eliran Murphy Group; Press, Boneau/Bryan-Brown: Adrian Bryan-Brown, Matt Polk, Jessica Johnson, Joe Perrotta

**CAST** Part 1: *The Diary of Adam and Eve* (based on the story by Mark Twain): Adam **Brian d'Arcy James**; Eve **Kristin Chenoweth**; Snake **Marc Kudisch**; Part 2: *The Lady or the Tiger?* (based on the story by Frank R. Stockton): Balladeer **Marc Kudisch**; King Arik **Walter Charles**; Princess Barbára **Kristin Chenoweth**; Prisoner **Mike McGowan**; Tiger **Sean Palmer**; Prisoner's Bride **Sarah Jane Everman**; Nadjira **Lorin Latarro**; Captain Sanjar **Brian d'Arcy James**; Guards **Mike McGowan, Dennis Stowe**; King Arik's Court **Meggie Cansler, Julie Connors, Sarah Jane Everman, Justin Keyes, Lorin Latarro, Mike McGowan, Sean Palmer, Dennis Stowe**; Part 3: *Passionella–A Romance of the 60's* (based on the story by Jules Feiffer): Narrator **Marc Kudisch**; Elle/Passionella **Kristin Chenoweth**; Mr. Fallible/Producer **Walter Charles**; Newsboy **Justin Keyes**; Director **Dennis Stowe**; Film Critic **Julie Connors**; Stage Hand **Mike McGowan**; Flip, The Prince Charming **Brian d'Arcy James**; Flip's Following, Movie Set Crew **Meggie Cansler, Julie Connors, Sarah Jane Everman, Justin Keyes, Lorin Latarro, Mike McGowan, Sean Palmer, Dennis Stowe**; Swings **Jennifer Taylor Farrell, Eric Santagata**

**UNDERSTUDIES** Sarah Jane Everman (Eve, Princess Barbára, Passionella), Mike McGowan (Adam, Sanjar, Flip, King Arik), Sean Palmer (Snake, Balladeer, Narrator)

**ORCHESTRA** Rob Fisher (Conductor), Sam Davis (Associate Conductor/keyboard), Marilyn Reynolds, Sylvia D'Avanzo (violins), David Blinn (viola), Roger Shell (cello), James Ercole, Sean Frank, Mark Thrasher (woodwinds), Dominic Derasse, Charles Porter (trumpets), Clint Sharman (trombone), Roger Wendt (French horn), Susan Jolles (harp), John Beal (bass), Paul Pizzuti (drums/percussion), Bruce Samuels (synthesizer programmer)

**MUSICAL NUMBERS** Part 1: Eden Prelude, Here in Eden, Feelings, Eve, Friends, The Apple Tree (Forbidden Fruit), Beautiful, Beautiful World, It's A Fish, Go to Sleep Whatever You Are, What Makes Him Love Me; Part 2: The Lady or the Tiger Prelude, I'll Tell You a Truth, Make Way, Forbidden Love (In Gaul), The Apple Tree (reprise), I've Got What You Want, Tiger, Tiger, Make Way (reprise), Which Door?, I'll Tell You a Truth (reprise); Part 3: Passionella Mini-Overture,

*Kristin Chenoweth and Marc Kudisch (photos by Joan Marcus)*

*Walter Charles, Brian d'Arcy James, Kristin Chenoweth, and Cast*

Oh to Be a Movie Star, Gorgeous, (Who, Who, Who, Who,) Who is She?, Wealth, You Are Not Real, George L

**SETTING** Part 1: Saturday June 1st, Eden; Part 2: A Long Time Ago, a Semi-Barbaric Kingdom; Part 3: Then, Here. Revival of the musical in three acts, presented with one intermission between parts 1 and 2. This production is based on the City Center *Encores!* production presented May 12–16, 2005 (see *Theatre World* Volume 61, page 177). Originally produced on Broadway at the Shubert Theatre October 18, 1966 (see *Theatre World* Volume 23, page 20).

**SYNOPSIS** *The Apple Tree* is comprised of three one-act musicals about men, women, and a little thing called temptation, based on short stories by three of literature's finest storytellers, Mark Twain, Frank R. Stockton, and Jules Feiffer.

Brian d'Arcy James and
Kristin Chenoweth

Kristin Chenoweth

Kristin Chenoweth
and Cast

# TRANSLATIONS

Biltmore Theatre; First Preview: January 4, 2007; Opening Night: January 25, 2007; Closed March 11, 2007; 24 previews, 53 performances

Written by Brian Friel; Produced by Manhattan Theatre Club (Lynne Meadow, Artistic Director; Barry Grove, Executive Producer), and the McCarter Theatre Center (Emily Mann, Artistic Director; Jeffrey Woodward, Managing Director); Director, Garry Hynes; Set/Costumes, Francis O'Connor; Lighting, Davy Cunningham; Sound, John Leonard; Original Music, Sam Jackson; PSM, Richard Costabile; Casting, Laura Stanczyk, Nancy Piccione/David Caparelliotis; Director of Artistic Operations, Mandy Greenfield; Production Manager, Ryan McMahon; Development, Jill Turner Lloyd; Marketing, Debra A. Waxman; General Manager, Florie Seery; Director of Artistic Development, Paige Evans; McCarter Theatre Center Producing Director, Mara Isaacs; McCarter Theatre Center Director of Production, David York; Artistic Consultant, Daniel Sullivan; Director of Artistic Administration, Amy Gilkes Loe; Literary Manager, Emily Shooltz; Finance, Jeffrey Bledsoe; Associate General Manager, Lindsey Brooks Sag; Education, David Shookhoff; Telesales, George Tetlow; Lighting/Sound Supervisor, Matthew T. Gross; Properties Supervisor, Scott Laule; Costume Supervisor, Erin Hennessy Dean; Company Manager, Seth Shepsle; Stage Manager, Kasey Ostopchuck; Drama League Assistant Director, Gaye-Taylor Upchurch; Dialect Consultant, Charlotte Fleck; Hair/Makeup Supervisor, Taurance Williams; Lighting Programmer, Marc Polimeni; Advertising, SpotCo; Press, Boneau/Bryan-Brown

Chandler Williams, Michael FitzGerald, Morgan Hallett, Geraldine Hughes, Susan Lynch, and Alan Cox

Dermot Crowley and Susan Lynch (photos by Joan Marcus)

**CAST** Manus **David Costabile;** Sarah **Morgan Hallett;** Jimmy Jack **Dermot Crowley;** Maire **Susan Lynch;** Doalty **Michael FitzGerald;** Bridget **Geraldine Hughes;** Hugh **Niall Buggy;** Owen **Alan Cox;** Captain Lancey **Graeme Malcolm;** Lieutenant Yolland **Chandler Williams**

**UNDERSTUDIES** Jeremy Bobb (Manus, Doalty, Owen, Lieutenant Yolland), Diane Landers (Sarah, Maire, Bridget), Kenneth Tigar (Jimmy Jack, Hugh, Captain Lancey)

**SETTING** A hedge school in the townland of Baile Beag/Ballybeg, an Irish-speaking community in County Donegal, late August 1833. Revival of the play presented in three acts with one intermission. Originally produced Off-Broadway at Manhattan Theatre Club, April 7–May 17, 1981 (see *Theatre World* Volume 37, page 128), and on Broadway at the Plymouth Theatre, March 7–April 9, 1995 (see *Theatre World* Volume 51, page 40).

**SYNOPSIS** Clashing cultures and tragedies of miscommunication unfold in Friel's invented Irish county of Ballybeg, a place he has explored in the plays *Dancing at Lughnasa, Aristocrats,* and *Molly Sweeney.* Poignant and moving, *Translations* depicts the power of language to unite and divide people in a time of cultural imperialism.

Niall Buggy

# JOURNEY'S END

Belasco Theatre; First Preview: February 8, 2007; Opening Night: February 22, 2007; 15 previews, 113 performances as of May 31, 2007

Written by R.C. Sherriff; Produced by Boyett Ostar Productions, Stephanie P. McClelland, Bill Rollnick, James D'Orta, Philip Geier; Director, David Grindley; Sets and Costumes, Jonathan Fensom; Lighting, Jason Taylor; Sound, Gregory Clarke; Casting, Jay Binder, Jack Bowdan; PSM, Arthur Gaffin; Technical Supervisor, Larry Morley; Marketing, HHC Marketing; General Management, Alan Wasser, Allan Williams; Company Manager, Penelope Daulton; U.K. Technical Supervisor, The Production Desk Ltd., Paul Hennessy; Stage Manager, David Sugarman; Dialect Coach, Majella Hurley; Fight Director, Thomas Schall; Fight Captain, John Behlmann; Scenic Artist, James Rowse; Scenic Drop Artwork, Alasdair Oliver; Production Props, Eric J. Castaldo; Production: George Dummitt (carpenter), Joe Mortitz (flyman), Susan Goulet (electrician), Neil McShane (Electrician), Heidi Brown (props), Tucker Howard (sound), Brien Brannigan (sound), Kay Grunder (wardrobe supervisor), Jeff McGovney (dresser); U.K. Wardrobe Consultant, Charlotte Bird; US Wardrobe Consultant, Patrick Bevilacqua; U.K. Props Supervisor, Fahmida Bakht; Press, Pete Sanders Group, Glenna Freedman

Richard Poe, Nick Berg Barnes, and Kieran Campion

Stark Sands, John Ahlin, and Boyd Gaines (photos by Paul Kolnik)

**CAST** Captain Hardy/Sergeant Major **John Curless;** Lieutenant Osborne **Boyd Gaines;** Private Mason **Jefferson Mays;** 2nd Lieutenant Raleigh **Stark Sands;** Captain Stanhope **Hugh Dancy;** 2nd Lieutenant Trotter **John Ahlin;** Private Albert Brown **John Behlmann;** 2nd Lieutenant Hibbert **Justin Blanchard;** Colonel **Richard Poe;** German Soldier **Kieran Campion;** Lance Corporal Broughton **Nick Berg Barnes**

**UNDERSTUDIES** John Behlmann (Stanhope, German Soldier, Broughton), Richard Poe (Osborne), John Curless (Mason, Colonel), Kieran Campion (Raleigh, Hibbert, Albert, Broughton), Nick Berg Barnes (Hardy, Sergeant Major, Trotter)

**2006–2007 AWARDS** Tony Award: Best Revival of a Play; Drama Desk: Outstanding Revival of a Play, Outstanding Featured Actor in a Play (Boyd Gaines), Outstanding Sound Design (Gregory Clarke); Outer Critics Circle: Outstanding Revival of a Play, Outstanding Featured Actor in a Play (Boyd Gaines); **Theatre World Award:** Stark Sands

**SETTING** A dugout in the British trenches near St. Quentin, France; Act I: Evening on Monday March 18, 1918; Act II: Tuesday morning and afternoon; Act III: Wednesday afternoon, night, and Thursday, toward dawn. Revival of a play presented in six scenes in three acts with one intermission. This production was based on Mr. Grindley's successful London production which opened at the Comedy Theatre in 2004, toured the U.K., and had runs at three West End Theatres before closing in January 2006. Originally produced on Broadway at Henry Miller's Theatre, March 22, 1929–May, 1930, and revived at the Empire Theatre September 18–30, 1939.

**SYNOPSIS** Based on Sherriff's own experiences in the First World War, *Journey's End* is about a group of British soldiers living together in a cramped trench in France while fighting the last great German offensive in March 1918.

Hugh Dancy and Justin Blanchard

# PRELUDE TO A KISS

American Airlines Theatre; First Preview: February 17, 2007 Opening Night: March 8, 2007; Closed April 29, 2007; 23 previews, 61 performances

Written by Craig Lucas; Produced by the Roundabout Theatre Company (Todd Haimes, Artistic Director; Harold Wolpert, Managing Director; Julia C. Levy, Executive Director); Director, Daniel Sullivan; Set, Santo Loquasto; Costumes, Jane Greenwood; Lighting, Donald Holder; Original Music/Sound, John Gromada; Hair/Wigs, Tom Watson; PSM, Leslie C. Lyter; Casting, Jim Carnahan, Mele Nagler; Technical Supervisor, Steve Beers; General Manager, Sydney Beers; Marketing and Sales Promotion, David B. Steffen; Development, Jeffory Lawson; Founding Director, Gene Feist; Associate Artistic Director, Scott Ellis; Company Manager, Nichole Jennino; Stage Manager, Jonathan Donahue; Assistant Director, Jonathan Solari; Associate Set Design, Jenny B. Sawyers; Assistant Design: Tobin Ost (set), Camille Assaf, Amela Baksic (costumes), Caroline Chao, Rebecca Makus (lighting), Ryan Rumery (sound); Fight Consultant, J. Steven White; Assistant Technical Supervisor, Elisa Kuhar; Properties, Nelson Vaughn; Properties Coordination, Kathy Fabian; Hair/Wig Supervisor, Manuel LaPorte; Production Assistant, Courtney B. James; Production: Glenn Merwede (carpenter/automation), Andrew Forste (props), Chris Mattingly (fly), Hal Fraser (carpenter), Brian Maiuri (electrician), Dann Wojnar (sound), Jill Anania (electrician), Barb Bartel (moving lights), Jeff Rowland (spot), Susan J. Fallon (wardrobe supervisor), Julie Hilmire, Victoria Grecki (dressers), Melanie Mulder (prop assistant); Advertising, Eliran Murphy Group; Press, Boneau/Bryan-Brown: Adrian Bryan-Brown, Matt Polk, Jessica Johnson, Amy Kass

**CAST** Old Man **John Mahoney**; Peter **Alan Tudyk**; Rita **Annie Parisse**; Taylor **Matthew Rauch**; Tom/Jamaican Water **Francois Battiste**; Dr. Boyle **James Rebhorn**; Mrs. Boyle **Robin Bartlett**; Minister **MacIntyre Dixon**; Uncle Fred **John Rothman**; Aunt Dorothy **Marceline Hugot**; Leah **Marceline Hugot**; Ensemble **Brandon J. Dirden, Susan Pellegrino, Karen Walsh**

**UNDERSTUDIES** Brandon J. Dirden (Tom/Jamaican Waiter/Taylor/Minister), MacIntyre Dixon (Old Man/Uncle Fred), Susan Pellegrino (Aunt Dorothy/Leah/Mrs. Boyle), Matthew Rauch (Peter), John Rothman (Dr. Boyle), Karen Walsh (Rita)

**SETTING** Present, New York City. A play presented in two acts; originally produced on Broadway at the Helen Hayes Theatre May 1, 1990, running 440 performances (see *Theatre World* Volume 46, page 36).

**SYNOPSIS** Peter and Rita follow their whirlwind courtship with a storybook wedding. When a mysterious elderly man appears and kisses the bride at the wedding and magically exchanges his soul with hers, the two lovers are sent on a journey that they will never forget. As they struggle to come to terms with their relationship and Rita's nagging doubts, their love is put to the test by unknown forces.

*John Mahoney, Annie Parisse, and Alan Tudyk*

*The Company*

*Alan Tudyk and Annie Parisse (photos by Joan Marcus)*

# TALK RADIO

Longacre Theatre; First Preview: February 15, 2007; Opening Night: March 11, 2007; 29 previews, 93 performances as of May 31, 2007

Written by Eric Bogosian, based on an original idea by Ted Savinar; created for the stage by Eric Bogosian and Ted Savinar; Produced by Jeffrey Richards, Jerry Frankel, Jam Theatricals, Francis Finlay, Ronald Frankel, James Fuld Jr., Steve Green, Judith Hansen, Patty Ann Lacrete, James Riley, Mary Lu Roffe/Mort Swinsky, Sheldon Stein, Terri & Timothy Childs/StyleFour Productions, Irving Welzer/Herb Blodgett; Presented in association with the Atlantic Theater Company; Director, Robert Falls; Set, Mark Wendland; Costumes, Laura Bauer; Lighting, Christopher Akerlind; Sound, Richard Woodbury; Casting, Telsey + Company; PSM, Jane Grey; General Management, Albert Poland; Technical Supervisor, Neil A. Mazzella; Company Manager, Daniel Kuney; Stage Manager, Matthew Farrell; Assistant Director, José Zayas; Associate Design: Bobby Tilley (costumes), Jeremy Lee (sound); Design Assistants: Rachel Nemec (sets), Ben Krall (lighting); Props Coordinator, Kathy Fabian, Carrie Hash; Associate Properties, Carrie Mossman, Melanie Mulder; Prop Furniture, Jason Gandy/Aardvark Interiors; Prop Equipment, Richard Fitzgerald/Sound Associates; Production Assistant, Ben West; Staff Assistants: Roger Mendoza, Mark Barber, Nikole Beckwith, Julie Massey, Michael Altbaum; Associate Technical Supervisor, Sam Ellis; Production: Ed Diaz (carpenter), James Maloney (electrician), Brad Robertson (head electrician), John Lofgren (props), Valerie Spradling (sound), Kristine Bellerud (wardrobe supervisor), Rose Marie C. Cappelluti (Mr. Schreiber's dresser), Sandy Binion (dresser); Dialect Coach, Kate Maré; Advertising, Serino Coyne Inc.; Press, Jeffrey Richards, Irene Gandy

**CAST** Sid Greenberg **Adam Sietz;** Bernie **Cornell Womack;** Spike **Kit Williamson;** Stu Noonan **Michael Laurence;** Linda MacArthur **Stephanie March;** Vince Farber **Marc Thompson;** Barry Champlain **Liev Schreiber;** Dan Woodruff **Peter Hermann;** Jordan Grant **Christy Pusz;** Kent **Sebastian Stan;** Dr. Susan Fleming **Barbara Rosenblat;** Rachael **Christine Pedi;** Caller's Voices **Christine Pedi, Christy Pusz, Barbara Rosenblat, Adam Sietz, Marc Thompson, Cornell Womack**

**STANDBYS/UNDERSTUDIES** Michael Laurence (Barry, Dan), Lee Sellars (Dan, Stu, Spike), Cornell Womack (Stu, Male Callers), Christy Pusz (Linda Mac Arthur, Rachael, Female Callers), Kit Williamson (Kent), Oliver Vaquer (Sid Greenberg, Bernie, Vince Farber, Male Callers), Christine Pedi (Dr. Susan Fleming, Female Callers), Adam Sietz, Marc Thompson (Male Callers)

**SETTING** Spring 1987. Studio B of radio station WTLK in Cleveland, Ohio. Revival of a play presented without intermission. Originally produced Off–Broadway at the Public Theatre May 12, 1987 (see *Theatre World* Volume 43, page 124).

*Liev Schreiber (photos by Joan Marcus)*

**SYNOPSIS** *Talk Radio* follows one night in the career of Barry Champlain, an acid-tongued, late-night talk-show host, whose program is about to be picked up for national syndication. Barry, whose specialty is insulting the pathetic souls who call in the middle of the night to sound off, upsets the sponsors, juggles his love life, and drowns his pain in an alcoholic stupor as he rages his sharp opinions into the airwaves.

Above: *Sebastian Stan and Peter Hermann,*

Left: *Sebastian Stan, Stephanie March, and Liev Schreiber*

# CURTAINS

Al Hirschfeld Theatre; First Preview: February 27, 2007; Opening Night: March 22, 2007; 26 previews, 81 performances as of May 31, 2007

Book by Rupert Holmes, music by John Kander, lyrics by Fred Ebb, original book and concept by Peter Stone, additional lyrics by John Kander and Rupert Holmes; Produced by Roger Berlind, Roger Horchow, Daryl Roth, Jane Bergére, Ted Hartley, Center Theatre Group; Director, Scott Ellis; Choreography, Rob Ashford; Music Director/Vocal Arrangements, David Loud; Orchestrations, William David Brohn; Set, Anna Louizos; Costumes, William Ivey Long; Lighting, Peter Kaczorowski; Sound, Brian Ronan; Hair and Wigs, Paul Huntley; Dance Arrangements, David Chase; Fight Director, Rick Sordelet; Aerial Effects, Paul Rubin; Makeup, Angelina Avallone; Associate Choreographer, JoAnn M. Hunter; Casting, Jim Carnahan; Production Supervisor, Beverly Randolph; Technical Supervisor, Peter Fulbright; Music Coordinator, John Monaco; General Management, 101 Productions Ltd.; Marketing Services, TMG - The Marketing Group; Associate Producers, Barbara and Peter Fodor; Company Manager, Bruce Klinger; Stage Manager, Scott Taylor Rollison; ASM, Kevin Bertolacci, Jerome Vivona; Associate Company Manager, Beverly Edwards; Dance Captain, David Eggers; Assistant Dance Captain, Ashley Amber; Creative Assistant to Mr. Holmes, Teressa Esposito; Assistant Director, Dave Solomon; Assistant to Mr. Ellis, Kathleen Bond; Associate Design, Michael Carnahan (set), Tom Beal (costumes), Hilary Manners (lighting); Assistant to Ms. Louizos, Zhanna Gurvich; Assistant Design, Rachel Attridge (costumes), Cathy Parrott, Brenda Abbandandalo (for Mr. Long), Joel E. Silver (lighting), Lisa Katz (for Mr. Kaczorowski), Josh Weitzman (moving lights programmer), Mike Farfalla (sound); Production: George Wagner (props supervisor), Robert Adams (head props), Michael Gowler (wardrobe supervisor), Larry Boyette (hair supervisor), Erik Hansen (fly automation), Paul Wimmer (carpenter), Rick Styles (deck automation), Richard Mortell (electrician); Keyboard Programmer, Stuart Andrews; Music Copying, Larry H. Abel, Music Preparation International; Advertising, Serino Coyne Inc.; Press, Boneau/Bryan-Brown, Chris Boneau, Jim Byk, Juliana Hannett, Matt Ross; Cast recording: Manhattan Records/EMI Broadway Angel 92212 2

**CAST** Jessica Cranshaw/Connie Subbotin **Patty Goble;** Randy Dexter **Jim Newman;** Niki Harris **Jill Paice;** Bambi Bernét **Megan Sikora;** Bobby Pepper **Noah Racey;** Johnny Harmon **Michael X. Martin;** Georgia Hendricks **Karen Ziemba;** Aaron Fox **Jason Danieley;** Carmen Bernstein **Debra Monk;** Oscar Shapiro **Michael McCormick;** Christopher Belling **Edward Hibbert;** Lieutenant Frank Cioffi **David Hyde Pierce;** Mona Page **Mary Ann Lamb;** Harv Fremont **Matt Farnsworth;** Roberta Wooster **Darcie Roberts;** Sidney Bernstein **Ernie Sabella;** Detective O'Farrell **Kevin Bernard;** Daryl Grady **John Bolton;** Sasha Iljinsky **David Loud;** Marjorie Cook **Paula Leggett Chase;** Arlene Barruca **Nili Bassman;** Roy Stetson **Kevin Bernard;** Brick Hawvermale **Ward Billeisen;** Jan Setler **Jennifer Dunne;** Peg Prentice **Brittany Marcin;** Ronnie Driscoll **Joe Aaron Reid;** Russ Cochran **Christopher Spaulding;** Swings **Ashley Amber, David Eggers, J. Austin Eyer, Allison Spratt, Jerome Vivona**

**UNDERSTUDIES** Ashley Amber (Bambi Bernét), Nili Bassman (Niki Harris), Kevin Bernard (Aaron Fox, Christopher Belling, Lieutenant Frank Cioffi), Ward Billeisen (Bobby Pepper), Paula Leggett Chase (Carmen Bernstein, Georgia Hendricks, Jessica Cranshaw), Jennifer Dunne (Bambi Bernét), David Eggers (Bobby Pepper), Matt Farnsworth (Aaron Fox, Daryl Grady), Patty Goble (Carmen Bernstein), Michael X. Martin (Daryl Grady, Oscar Shapiro, Sidney Bernstein), Jim Newman (Bobby Pepper, Johnny Harmon), Darcie Roberts (Georgia Hendricks, Jessica Cranshaw), Allison Spratt (Niki Harris), Jerome Vivona (Johnny Harmon, Oscar Shapiro, Sidney Bernstein)

**ORCHESTRA** David Loud (Conductor), Sam Davis (Associate Music Director/piano and synthesizer), Steven Kenyon (flute/piccolo/clarinet/alto sax), Al Hunt (oboe, English horn, clarinet, tenor sax), Owen Kotler (clarinet/alto sax/soprano sax), Mark Thrasher (bassoon/bass clarinet/baritone sax/flute/clarinet), R.J. Kelly (French Horn 1), Angela Cordell (French horn 2), Don Downs (trumpet 1),

*Jill Paice, David Hyde Pierce, and Company*

Matthew Peterson (trumpet 2), Charles Gordon (trombone 1/House Contractor), Jennifer Wharton (bass trombone/tuba), Gregory Landes (percussion); Bruce Doctor (drums): Greg Utzig (guitars/banjos); Robert Renino (bass)

**MUSICAL NUMBERS** Wide Open Spaces, What Kind of Man?, Thinking of Him, The Woman's Dead, Show People, Coffee Shop Nights, In the Same Boat 1, I Miss the Music, Thataway!, He Did It, It's a Business, Kansasland, In the Same Boat 2, Thinking of Him (reprise), A Tough Act to Follow, In the Same Boat 3, A Tough Act to Follow (reprise)

**2006–2007 AWARDS** Tony Award: Best Actor in a Musical (David Hyde Pierce); Drama Desk: Outstanding Book of a Musical (Rupert Holmes, Peter Stone), Outstanding Featured Actress in a Musical (Debra Monk); Outer Critics Circle: Outstanding Featured Actress in a Musical (Karen Ziemba)

**SETTING** The Colonial Theatre in Boston, 1959, during the out-of-town tryout of the new musical, *Robbin' Hood!* A new musical presented in two acts. American premiere produced at the Ahmanson Theatre by Center Theatre Group in Los Angeles, August–September, 2006.

**SYNOPSIS** *Curtains* unfolds backstage at Boston's Colonial Theatre in 1959, where a new musical could be a Broadway smash, were it not for the presence of its talent-free leading lady. When the hapless star dies on opening night during her curtain call, Lieutenant Frank Cioffi arrives on the scene to conduct an investigation. But the lure of the theatre proves irresistible and after an unexpected romance blooms for the stage-struck detective, he finds himself just as drawn toward making the show a hit, as he is in solving the murder.

*Debra Monk and Company*

*David Hyde Pierce and Debra Monk (photos by Joan Marcus)*

*Noah Racey and Karen Ziemba*

*Karen Ziemba, Debra Monk, David Hyde Pierce, Michael McCormick, Edward Hibbert and Cast*

# THE YEAR OF MAGICAL THINKING

Booth Theatre; First Preview: March 6, 2007; Opening Night: March 29, 2007; 23 previews, 73 performances as of May 31, 2007

Written by Joan Didion, based on her memoir; Produced by Scott Rudin, Roger Berlind, Debra Black, Daryl Roth, The Shubert Organization (Chairman, Gerald Schoenfeld; President, Philip J. Smith; Executive Vice President, Robert E. Wankel); Executive Producers, Stuart Thompson and John Barlow; Director, David Hare; Set, Bob Crowley; Costumes, Ann Roth; Lighting, Jean Kalman; Sound, Paul Arditti; PSM, Karen Armstrong; Associate Director, B.T. McNicholl; Marketing, Eric Schnall; Production Manager, Aurora Productions; General Manager, Stuart Thompson Productions/James Triner; Company Manager, Cassidy J. Briggs; Casting, Daniel Swee; Hair & Makeup, Naomi Donne; Dialect Coach, Deborah Hecht; Stage Manager, Martha Donaldson; Associate Design: Bryan Johnson, Jeffrey Hinchee (set), Michelle Matland (costumes), Bobby Harrell (lighting), Walter Trarbach & Tony Smolenski IV (sound); Production: Michael Pitzer (electrician), Ronald Fogel (head electrician), Bill Lewis (sound operator), Laura Beattie (wardrobe supervisor), Aleksandra Nesterchuk (hairdresser), Kenneth McDonough (carpenter), Ed White (assistant carpenter), Jimmy Keane (props), Ronnie Burns Sr. (house electrician), Craig Grigg (prop fabrication); Assistant to Ms. Redgrave, Eamonn Burke; Advertising, SpotCo; Press, Boneau/Bryan-Brown, Chris Boneau, Steven Padla, Heath Schwartz

**CAST** Joan Didion **Vanessa Redgrave**

**STANDBY** Maureen Anderman

World premiere of a new solo performance play presented without intermission.

**SYNOPSIS** In the one-woman play, Redgrave plays Didion, reliving a shocking period in the famed author's life. One night, as Didion's daughter Quintana lay in a coma, her husband of forty years, the writer John Gregory Dunne, died suddenly of a massive coronary as the two of them sat down to dinner in their New York apartment. Redgrave, as Didion, recounts the events of that night, Didion's memories of her marriage, the grieving period and the treatment of her daughter, who subsequently passed away as well.

*Vanessa Redgrave*

*Vanessa Redgrave (photos by Brigitte Lacombe)*

*Vanessa Redgrave*

# THE PIRATE QUEEN

Hilton Theatre; First Preview: March 6, 2007; Opening Night: April 5, 2007; 32 previews, 65 performances as of May 31, 2007

Book by Alain Boublil, Claude-Michel Schönberg and Richard Maltby Jr., music by Claude-Michel Schönberg; lyrics by Alain Boublil, Richard Maltby Jr. and John Dempsey; based upon the novel, *Grania—She King of the Irish Seas* by Morgan Llywelyn; Produced by Riverdream, Moya Doherty and John McColgan; Director, Frank Galati; Musical Staging, Graciela Daniele; Orchestrations/Vocal Arrangements/Musical Supervision and Direction, Julian Kelly; Artistic Director, John McColgan; Irish Dance Choreographer, Carol Leavy Joyce; Sets, Eugene Lee; Costumes, Martin Pakledinaz; Lighting, Kenneth Posner; Sound, Jonathan Deans; Hair, Paul Huntley; Special Effects, Gregory Meeh; Aerial Sequence, Paul Rubin; Makeup, Angelina Avallone; Scenic Associate, Edward Pierce; Fight Director, J. Steven White; Associate Director, Tara Young; Associate Choreographer, Rachel Bress; Casting, Tara Rubin; Production Manager, Peter W. Lamb; PSM, C. Randall White; Musical Coordinator, Sam Lutfiyya and Music Services International; Marketing, TMG-The Marketing Group; Associate Producer, Dancap Productions Inc.; Executive Producer (Development), Ronan Smith; Executive Producer, Edgar Dobie; General Manager, Theatre Production Group; Company Manager, Jim Brandeberry; Stage Manager, Kathleen E. Purvis; Assistant Stage Managers, Sandra M. Franck, Charlene Speyerer, Michael Wilhoite; Assistant Company Manager, Elizabeth M. Talmadge; Additional Choreography, Mark Dendy; Associate Musical Director, Brian Connor; Dance Captains, Rachel Bress, Padraic Moyles; Fight Captain/Assistant Fight Director/Dance Captain, Timothy W. Bish; GM Assistant, Tegan Meyer; Associate Design: Philip Rosenberg, Patricia Nichols (lighting), MaryAnn D. Smith (costumes); Assistant Design: Nick Francone, Jen Price (sets), Erin Spivey (lighting), Courtney McClain, Randall E. Klein (costumes), Brian Hsieh (sound), Automated Lighting Programmer, David Arch

*Stephanie J. Block and Company (photos by Joan Marcus)*

(New York), Timothy F. Rogers (Chicago); Art Design Concept, The Apartment Creative Agency; Art Design Development, Zeus Creative (Dublin); Special Effects Assistant, Jeremy Chernick; Electronic Music Programmer, Brett Alan Sommer and Jim Harp; Music Copying/Preparation, Mark Cumberland for Hotstave Ltd. and Anixter Rice Music Service; Irish Music Consultant, David Downes; Production: Don S. Gilmore (carpenter), Jim Kane (head carpenter), Michael S. LoBue (electrician), Jon Mark Davidson (head electrician), Jody Durham (advance electrician), Garth Helm (sound), Simon Matthews (head sound); Joseph P. Harris Jr. (prop master); Michael Bernstein (head props), Robert Guy (wardrobe supervisor), Edward J. Wilson (hair/makeup supervisor); Advertising, SpotCo; Press: Boneau/Bryan-Brown, Matt Polk, Steven Padla, Jessica Johnson, Amy Kass; Cast recording: Sony BMG Masterworks Broadway 7118102

*The Cast performs "The Wedding Ring Dance"*

**CAST** Grace (Grania) O'Malley **Stephanie J. Block;** Tiernan **Hadley Fraser;** Dubhdara **Jeff McCarthy;** Evleen **Áine Uí Cheallaigh;** Queen Elizabeth I **Linda Balgord;** Sir Richard Bingham **William Youmans;** Donal O'Flaherty **Marcus Chait;** Chieftain O'Flaherty **Joseph Mahowald;** Majella **Brooke Elliott;** Eoin **Christopher Grey Misa** or **Steven Barath**; Ensemble **Nick Adams, Richard Todd Adams, Caitlin Allen, Sean Beglan, Jerad Bortz, Troy Edward Bowles, Grady McLeod Bowman, Alexis Ann Carra, Noelle Curran, Bobbie Ann Dunn, Brooke Elliott, Christopher Garbrecht, Eric Hatch, Cristin J. Hubbard, David Koch, Timothy Kochka, Jamie LaVerdiere, Joseph Mahowald, Tokiko Masuda, Padraic Moyles, Brian O'Brien, Kyle James O'Connor, Michael James Scott, Greg Stone, Katie Erin Tomlinson, Daniel Torres, Jennifer Waiser, Briana Yacavone;** Swings **Timothy W. Bish, Rachel Bress, Don Brewer, Kimilee Bryant;** Standby for Grace **Kathy Voytko**

**UNDERSTUDIES** Richard Todd Adams (Donal O'Flaherty, Sir Richard Bingham), Kimilee Bryant (Majella, Queen Elizabeth I), Brooke Elliott (Evleen), Christopher Garbrecht (Dubhdara), Cristin J. Hubbard (Queen Elizabeth I), Jamie LaVerdiere (Tiernan), Joseph Mahowald (Dubhdara, Sir Richard Bingham), Greg Stone (Tiernan), Katie Erin Tomlinson (Grace O'Malley), Daniel Torres (Donal O'Flaherty)

**ORCHESTRA** Julian Kelly (Conductor); Brian Connor (Associate Conductor/ keyboard 1); Joshua Rosenblum (Assistant Conductor/keyboard II); Liz Knowles (fiddle/violin); Kieran O'Hare (Uilleann pipes/whistles); Kenneth Edge (sax/clarinet); Jeff Nelson (horn); Kristen Agresta (harp/Gaelic harp); Steve Roberts (guitars/banjo); Michael Pearce (electric bass); Dave Roth (percussion); Frank Pagano (drums/Bodhran)

**MUSICAL NUMBERS** Prologue, The Pirate Queen, Woman, The Storm, My Grace, Here on This Night, The Waking of the Queen, Rah-Rah, Tip-Top; The Choice Is Mine, The Bride's Song, Boys'll Be Boys, The Wedding, I'll Be There, Boys'll Be Boys (reprise), Trouble at Rockfleet, A Day Beyond Belclare, Go Serve Your Queen, Dubhdara's Farewell, Sail to the Stars; Entr'acte, It's a Boy, Enemy at Port Side, I Dismiss You, If I Said I Loved You, The Role of the Queen, The Christening, Let a Father Stand By His Son, Surrender, She Who Has All, Lament, The Sea of Life, Terra Marique Potens, Woman to Woman, Behind the Screen, Grace's Exit, Finale

**SETTING** Ireland and England, the sixteenth century; New York premiere of a new musical presented in two acts. The show had out-of-town tryouts at Chicago's Cadillac Palace Theatre, October 3–November 26, 2006.

**SYNOPSIS** *The Pirate Queen* combines classic storytelling with a sweeping score and joyous dancing to celebrate the real-life story of legendary Irish chieftain Grace O'Malley: a compelling, inspiring heroine who led an extraordinary life as a pirate, chieftain, lover and mother in 16th-century Ireland. To protect her people and save her one true love, O'Malley must confront the one woman more powerful than her — her fierce rival, Queen Elizabeth I of England.

*Hadley Fraser and Company*

*Linda Balgord*

*Stephanie J. Block, Jeff McCarthy, and Marcus Chait*

# A MOON FOR THE MISBEGOTTEN

Brooks Atkinson Theatre; First Preview: March 24, 2007; Opening Night: April 20, 2007; 13 previews, 59 performances as of May 31, 2007

Written by Eugene O'Neill; Originally produced by the Old Vic Theatre Company (Sally Greene, Chief Executive; Kevin Spacey, Artistic Director); Produced by Elliot Martin, Max Cooper, Ben Sprecher, Nica Burns, Max Weitzenhoffer, The Old Vic, Spring Sirkin, Wendy Federman, Louise Forlenza, Ian Osborne, Thomas Steven Perakos, James L. Nederlander; Director, Howard Davies; Set, Bob Crowley; Costumes, Lynette Mauro; Lighting, Mark Henderson; Sound, Christopher Shutt; Sound System Design, T. Richard Fitzgerald & Carl Casella; Original Music, Dominic Muldowney; U.K. Casting, Maggie Lunn; U.S. Casting, Stuart Howard Associates; Production Manager, Brian Lynch; PSM, Bruce A. Hoover; General Manager, Peter Bogye; Company Manager, Mary Miller; Original London Lighting, Paule Constable; Stage Manager, Bernita Robinson; Production Assistant, Cyrille Blackburn; Assistant Director, Nathan Curry; Associate U.K. Set Design, Paul Atkinson, Alistair Turner; Associate U.S. Set Design, Bryan Johnson; Associate Sound, Colin Pink; Assistant Lighting, Daniel Walker; Production: Carpenter, Thomas A. LaVaia (carpenter), Manuel Becker (electrician), Joseph DePaulo (props), Wallace Flores (sound), Kathleen Gallagher (wardrobe supervisor), Yvonne Jensen (dresser); Advertising, SpotCo; Press, Barlow • Hartman, Dennis Crowley, Ryan Ratelle, Michelle Bergmann

**CAST** Josie Hogan **Eve Best;** Mike Hogan **Eugene O'Hare;** Phil Hogan **Colm Meaney;** Jim Tyrone **Kevin Spacey;** T. Stedman Harder **Billy Carter**

**UNDERSTUDIES** Kati Brazda (Josie), Billy Carter (Phil Hogan), Nick Westrate (Mike, T. Stedman Harder)

**2006–2007 AWARDS** Drama Desk: Outstanding Actress in a Play (Eve Best); **Theatre World Award:** Eve Best

**SETTING** The action takes place in Connecticut, September 1923. Revival of a play presented in two acts. This production was presented by The Old Vic Theatre Company, September 15–December 23, 2006 with this cast. Originally produced on Broadway at the Bijou Theatre May 2, 1957 (see *Theatre World* Volume 13, page 114). The play has had three Broadway revivals prior to this production: The Morosco Theatre, December 29, 1973–November 17, 1974 (see *Theatre World* Volume 30, page 34); The Cort Theatre, May 1–June 9, 1984 (see *Theatre World* Volume 40, page 38); and the Walter Kerr Theatre, March 10–July 2, 2000 (see *Theatre World* Volume 56, page 29).

*Kevin Spacey*

**SYNOPSIS** *A Moon for the Misbegotten* explores the tormented and alcoholic James Tyrone, who finds solace one moonlit night in the healing arms of the shy, virginal Josie Hogan. Possessed by the memory of his dead mother and guilt ridden by his own blasphemous behavior, the doomed Tyrone is the only man Josie will ever really know.

*Eve Best and Colm Meaney (photos by Simon Annand)*

*Colm Meaney and Kevin Spacey*

# INHERIT THE WIND

Lyceum Theatre; First Preview: March 19, 2007; Opening Night: April 12, 2007; 26 previews, 55 performances of May 31, 2007

Written by Jerome Lawrence and Robert E. Lee; Produced by Boyett Ostar Productions, The Shubert Organization, Lawrence Horowitz, Jon Avnet/Ralph Guild, Roy Furman, Debra Black/Daryl Roth, Bill Rollnick/Nancy Ellison Rollnick, Stephanie McClelland; Director, Doug Hughes; Set and Costumes, Santo Loquasto; Lighting, Brian MacDevitt; Original Music and Sound, David Van Tieghem; Hair and Wigs, Paul Huntley; Casting, Jay Binder/Jack Bowdan; PSM, Michael Brunner; Technical Supervisor, Peter Fulbright; Marketing, HHC Marketing; General Management, 101 Productions; Associate Producer, Judith Resnick; Company Manager, Gregg Arst; Stage Manager, Barclay Stiff; Associate Director, Mark Schneider; Music Supervisor, David M. Lutken; Associate Design: Jenny B. Sawyers (set), Matthew Pachtman (costume), Michael O'Connor (lighting), Jill B.C. DuBoff (sound); Design Assistants, Tobin Ost, Kanae Heike (set), Sarah Sophia Turner (costumes); Production: Charley P. Mann (carpenter), Abraham Morrison (props supervisor), Brian G.F. McGarity (electrician), Brien Brannigan (sound supervisor), John Paull III (head props), William Rowland II (head electrician), Marc Polimeni (lighting programmer), Dave Olin Rogers (wardrobe supervisor), Andrea Gonzalez, Kimberly Prentice, Jennifer Barnes, Jennifer Malloy, Paul Riner (dressers), Robin Maginsky Day (hair supervisor), Chris Munnell (assistant); Press, Boneau/Bryan-Brown, Adrian Bryan-Brown, Jackie Green, Danielle Crinnion

*Christopher Plummer and Brian Dennehy*

**CAST** Howard **Conor Donovan**; Melinda **Amanda Sprecher**; Rachel **Maggie Lacey**; Mr. Meeker **Scott Sowers**; Bert Cates **Benjamin Walker**; Mr. Goodfellow **Henry Stram**; Mrs. Krebs **Charlotte Maier**; Reverend Jeremiah Brown **Byron Jennings**; Sillers **Andrew Weems**; Dunlap **Jay Patterson**; Bannister **Bill Buell**; Mrs. Loomis **Anne Bowles**; Mrs. Blair **Pippa Pearthree**; Vendor **Bill Christ**; Elijah **Lanny Flaherty***; Timmy **Matthew Nardozzi**; E.K. Hornbeck **Denis O'Hare**; Monkey Man **Kevin C. Loomis**; Matthew Harrison Brady **Brian Dennehy**; Mrs. Brady **Beth Fowler**; Mayor **Jeff Steitzer**; Judge **Terry Beaver**; Tom Davenport **Jordan Lage**; Photographer **Randall Newsome**; Henry Drummond **Christopher Plummer**; Reuters Reporter/Esterbrook **Erik Steele**; Gospel Quartet **Carson Church, Katie Klaus, Mary Kate Law, David M. Lutken**; Townspeople **Anne Bowles, Steve Brady, Bill Christ, Kit Flanagan, Sherman Howard, Philip LeStrange, Kevin C. Loomis, Charlotte Maier, Matthew Nardozzi, Randall Newsome, Jay Patterson, Pippa Pearthree, Erik Steele, Andrew Weems**

**UNDERSTUDIES** Anne Bowles (Rachel Brown), Steve Brady (Dunlap, Elijah, Sillers), Bill Christ (Mr. Goodfellow, Rev. Jeremiah Brown), Kit Flanagan (Mrs. Blair, Mrs. Brady, Mrs. Krebs), Sherman Howard (Henry Drummond, Monkey Man), Jordan Lage (E. K. Hornbeck), Philip LeStrange (Judge, Mayor, Mr. Bannister), Kevin Loomis (Meeker, Reuter's Man), Matthew Nardozzi (Howard, Melinda), Erik Steele (Bertram Cates, Photographer), Jeff Steitzer (Matthew Harrison Brady)

**SETTING** Place: A small town. Time: Summer. Not too long ago. Revival of a courtroom drama presented in two acts. Originally presented at the National Theatre April 21, 1955–June 22, 1957, running 806 performances (see *Theatre World* Volume 12, page 130). A previous Broadway revival played the Royale Theatre April 3–May 12, 1996 (See *Theatre World* Volume 52, page 46).

**SYNOPSIS** The play is a fictionalized retelling of the famous 1925 "Monkey Trial" in which science teacher John Scopes was tried and convicted for teaching Darwin's theory of evolution, violating a Tennessee law that forbade teaching any theory that conflicted with the Biblical conception of Divine Creation. The role of attorney Matthew Harrison Brady is based on William Jennings Bryan, and the attorney Henry Drummond is based on Clarence Darrow.

*Succeeded by Raynor Scheine

*Christopher Plummer and Brian Dennehy (photos by Joan Marcus)*

# FROST/NIXON

Bernard B. Jacobs Theatre; First Preview: March 31, 2007; Opening Night: April 22, 2007; 23 previews, 45 performances as of May 31, 2007

Written by Peter Morgan; Originally presented by The Donmar Warehouse (Michael Grandage, Artistic Director; Lucy Davies, Executive Producer; James Bierman, General Manager); Produced by Arielle Tepper Madover, Matthew Byam Shaw, Robert Fox, Act Productions, David Binder, Debra Black, Annette Niemtzow/Harlene Freezer, The Weinstein Company; Director, Michael Grandage; Set and Costumes, Christopher Oram; Lighting, Neil Austin; Composer and Sound, Adam Cork; Video, Jon Driscoll; Hair and Wigs, Richard Mawbey; Casting, Daniel Swee (U.S.), Anne McNulty (U.K.); Marketing, Eric Schnall; General Management, 101 Productions Ltd.; PSM, Rick Steiger; Technical Supervisor, Aurora Productions (U.S.), Patrick Molony (U.K.); Company Manager, Alexandra Gushin; Stage Manager, Lisa Buxbaulk; Assistant Director, Seth Sklar-Heyn; Associate Design: Scott Traugott (costumes), Daniel Walker (lighting), Victoria Smerdon (moving light programmer), Chris Cronin (sound); Screen Technician, Colin Barnes; Makeup, Angelina Avallone; Production: Michael Van Praagh (carpenter), Edward Ruggerio (flyman), Jon Lawson, Herbert Messing (electricians), Christopher Kurtz (video), Dave Fulton (props supervisor), Alfred Ricci (house props), John Alban, Daniel Carpio (props), Kelly A. Saxon (wardrobe supervisor), Patrick Bevilacqua, Lyle Jones, Philip Heckman (dressers), Joel Mendenhall (hair supervisor), Timothy Eaker, Brian Maschka, Holly Ferguson (assistants); Advertising, SpotCo; Press, Boneau/Bryan-Brown, Steven Padla, Heath Schwartz

Frank Langella (photos by Joan Marcus)

Michael Sheen and Frank Langella

Remy Auberjonois, Michael Sheen, Armand Schultz, and Stephen Kunken

**CAST** Richard Nixon **Frank Langella;** Jim Reston **Stephen Kunken;** David Frost **Michael Sheen;** Jack Brennan **Corey Johnson;** Evonne Goolagong **Shira Gregory;** John Birt **Remy Auberjonois;** Manolo Sanchez **Triney Sandoval;** Swifty Lazar/Mike Wallace **Stephen Rowe;** Caroline Cushing **Sonya Walger;** Bob Zelnick **Armand Schultz;** Ensemble **Dennis Cockrum, Antony Hagopian, Roxanna Hope**

**UNDERSTUDIES** Bob Ari (Richard Nixon), Remy Auberjonois (David Frost), Dennis Cockrum (Swifty Lazar, Bob Zelnick, Manolo Sanchez), Antony Hagopian (John Birt, Jack Brennan, Manolo Sanchez), Roxanna Hope (Evonne Goolagong, Caroline Cushing), Triney Sandoval (Jim Reston)

**2006–2007 AWARDS** Tony Award: Best Actor in a Play (Frank Langella); Drama Desk: Outstanding Actor in a Play (Frank Langella); Outer Critics Circle: Outstanding Actor in a Play (Frank Langella)

**SETTING** England, Australia, and the U.S., 1977. American premiere of a new play presented without intermission. Originally presented at London's Donmar Warehouse August 15, 2006, and transferred to the Gielgud Theatre, November 16, 2006.

**SYNOPSIS** A dramatization of the events surrounding David Frost's 1977 television interviews with Richard Nixon. *Frost/Nixon* tackles the question: How did David Frost, a famous British talk-show host with a playboy reputation, elicit the apology that the rest of the world was waiting to hear from former President Richard Nixon? The fast-paced new play shows the determination, conviction, and cunning of two men as they square off in one of the most monumental political interviews of all time.

Michael Sheen

# LEGALLY BLONDE

Palace Theatre; First Preview: April 3, 2007; Opening Night: April 29, 2007; 30 previews, 37 performances as of May 31, 2007

Music and lyrics by Laurence O'Keefe and Nell Benjamin, book by Heather Hatch; based upon the novel by Amanda Brown and the MGM motion picture; Produced by Hal Luftig, Fox Theatricals, Dori Berinstein, James L. Nederlander, Independent Presenters Network, Roy Furman, Amanda Lipitz, Broadway Asia, Barbara Whitman, FWPM Group, Ruth Hendel/Cheryl Wiesenfeld, Hal Goldberg/David Binder, James D. Stern/Douglas L. Meyer, Robert Bartner-Michael A. Jenkins/Albert Nocciolino, and Warren Trepp in association with MGM ON STAGE, Darcie Denkert, and Dean Stobler; Produced for Fox Theatricals by Kristin Caskey and Mike Isaacson; Director and Choreographer, Jerry Mitchell; Music Director/Conductor, James Sampliner; Orchestrations, Christopher Jahnke; Arrangements, Laurence O'Keefe & James Sampliner; Music Coordinator, Michael Keller; Sets, David Rockwell; Costumes, Gregg Barnes; Lighting, Ken Posner & Paul Miller; Sound, Acme Sound Partners; Casting, Telsey + Company; Hair, David Brian Brown; Associate Director, Marc Bruni; Associate Choreographer, Denis Jones; Technical Supervisor, Smitty/Theatresmith Inc.; Animal Trainer, William Berloni; PSM, Bonnie L. Becker; General Management, Nina Lannan Associates/Maggie Brohn; Marketing, TMG - The Marketing Group; Associate Producers, PMC Productions, Yasuhiro Kawana, Andrew Asnes/Adam Zotovich; Company Manager, Kimberly Kelley; Associate CM, Nathan Gehan; Assistant Choreographer, Nick Kenkel; Stage Manager, Kimberly Russell; ASM, Scott Rowen; Dance Captains, Rusty Mowery, Michelle Kittrell; Assistant to Mr. Rockwell, Barry Richards; Associate Designer, Richard Jaris; Assistant Design: Todd Ivans, Gaetane Bertol, Brian Drucker, Rob Bissinger, Larry Brown, Corrine Merrill; Set Graphics, Alexi Logothetis, Charles Rush, Jerry Sabatini, Matthew Goodrich; Associate Costumes, Sky Switser; Assistant Costumes, Matthew R. Pachtman; Costume Assistants, Sarah Sophia Turner, Jeriana Hochberg; Assistant Lighting, Jonathan Spencer; Advance Sound, Dan Robillard; Assistant Sound, Jeffrey Yoshi Lee; Automated Lighting Programmer, Timothy F. Rogers; Dialect Coach, Stephen Gabis; Fight Director, Thomas Schall; Makeup, Justen M. Brosnan; Production: Donald J. Oberpriller (carpenter), Dan Coey (head electrician), Robert Biasetti (sound), Robert N. Valli (props), Jessica Scoblick, Dolly Williams (wardrobe supervisors), Carole Morales (hair supervisor); Additional Arrangements, Alex Lacamoire; Music Copyist, Emily Grishman Music Preparation; Synthesizer Programmer, Leland Music Company; Dog Handlers, William Berloni, Rob Cox; Advertising, Serino Coyne Inc.; Press, Barlow • Hartman, Michael Hartman, John Barlow, Carol Fineman, Kevin Robak; Cast recording: Sh-K-Boom/Ghostlight Records 84423

*Laura Bell Bundy (photo by Joan Marcus)*

**CAST** Elle Woods **Laura Bell Bundy;** Warner Huntington III **Richard H. Blake;** Vivienne Kensington **Kate Shindle;** Emmett Forrest **Christian Borle;** Professor Callahan **Michael Rupert;** Paulette **Orfeh;** Serena **Leslie Kritzer;** Margot **Annaleigh Ashford;** Pilar **DeQuina Moore;** Shandi/Brooke Wyndam **Nikki Snelson;** Kate/Chutney **Kate Wetherhead;** Leilani **Becky Gulsvig;** Cece **Michelle Kittrell;** Kristine **April Berry;** Gabby **Beth Curry;** Veronica/Enid **Natalie Joy Johnson;** Judge **Amber Efé;** Mom/Whitney **Gaelen Gilliland;** Grandmaster Chad/Dewey/Kyle **Andy Karl;** Dad/Winthrop **Kevin Pariseau;** Carlos **Matthew Risch;** Padamadan/Nikos **Manuel Herrera;** Aaron/Guard **Noah Weisberg;** Bruiser **Chico;** Rufus **Chloe;** Harvard Students, Marching Band, Cheerleaders, Inmates, Salespeople **April Berry, Paul Canaan, Beth Curry, Amber Efé, Gaelen Gilliland, Jason Gillman, Becky Gulsvig, Manuel Herrera, Natalie Joy Johnson, Andy Karl, Nick Kenkel, Michelle Kittrell, Kevin Pariseau, Matthew Risch, Jason Patrick Sands, Noah Weisberg, Kate Wetherhead;** Swings **Lindsay Nicole Chambers, Tracy Jai Edwards, Rusty Mowery, Rod Harrelson**

*Laura Bell Bundy and Cast (photo by Joan Marcus)*

*Kate Shindle, Richard H. Blake, Laura Bell Bundy, and Michael Rupert (photo by Paul Kolnik)*

**UNDERSTUDIES** Annaleigh Ashford (Elle Woods), Beth Curry (Brooke Wyndam, Shandi), Tracy Jai Edwards (Vivienne Kensington), Amber Efé (Paulette), Gaelen Gilliland (Paulette, Vivienne Kensington), Jason Gillman (Warner Huntington III), Becky Gulsvig (Elle Woods), Andy Karl (Emmett Forrest, Professor Callahan), Michelle Kittrell (Brooke Wyndam, Shandi), Kevin Pariseau (Professor Callahan), Matthew Risch (Warner Huntington III), Noah Weisberg (Emmett Forrest)

**ORCHESTRA** James Sampliner (Conductor/keyboard 1); Jason DeBord (Associate Conductor/keyboard 2); Antoine Silverman (violin/Concert Master); Jonathan Dinklage (viola); Peter Sachon (cello); Dave Trigg; Bud Burridge (trumpets); Keith O'Quinn (trombone); Vincent DellaRocca, Dan Willis, Chad Smith (reeds); Roger Wendt (French horn); Greg Joseph (drums); Mark Vanderpoel (bass); Matt Gallagher (keyboard 3); John Putnam, Kenny Brescia (guitars); Pablo Rieppi (percussion)

**MUSICAL NUMBERS** Omigod You Guys, Serious, Daughter of Delta Nu, What You Want, The Harvard Variations, Blood in the Water, Positive, Ireland, Ireland (reprise), Serious (reprise), Chip on My Shoulder, So Much Better, Whipped Into Shape, Take It Like a Man, Bend and Snap, There! Right There!, Legally Blonde, Legally Blonde Remix, Omigod You Guys (reprise), Find My Way/Finale

**SETTING** In and around the Delta Nu house, Southern California; in and around the Harvard Law campus, Cambridge, Massachusetts. New York premiere of a new musical presented in two acts. The show had an out-of-town tryout in San Francisco at the Golden Gate Theatre, January 23–February 24, 2007.

*Christian Borle and Laura Bell Bundy (photo by Joan Marcus)*

**SYNOPSIS** Sorority star Elle Woods doesn't take "no" for an answer. So when her boyfriend dumps her for someone more "serious," Elle puts down the credit card, hits the books and sets out to go where no Delta Nu has gone before: Harvard Law. Along the way, Elle proves that being true to herself never goes out of style.

*Laura Bell Bundy and Cast (photo by Paul Kolnik)*

*Laura Bell Bundy, Orfeh, and Andy Karl (photo by Paul Kolnik)*

# CORAM BOY

Imperial Theatre; First Preview: April 16, 2007; Opening Night: May 2, 2007; Closed May 27, 2007, 17 previews, 30 performances

Adapted by Helen Edmundson from the novel by Jamila Gavin, music by Adrian Sutton; Originally presented by The National Theatre of Great Britain (Nicholas Hytner, Director; Nick Starr, Executive Director; Sir Hayden Philips, Chairman of the Board); Produced by Boyett Ostar Productions, The Shubert Organization, Roy Furman, Lawrence Horowitz, Stephanie McClelland, Debra Black/Daryl Roth, Eric Falkenstein/Ralph Guild, Elan McAllister/Allan S. Gordon, in association with Jamie deRoy, Jam Theatricals/CPI, Harriet Leve/Ron Nicynski/Laurence Braun, Bill Rollnick/Nancy Ellison Rollnick; Director, Melly Still; Musical Director, Constantine Kitsopoulos; Set/Costumes, Ti Green and Melly Still; Original Lighting, Paule Constable, recreated by Ed McCarthy; Original Sound, Christopher Shutt, recreated by Acme Sound Partners; U.S. Hair and Wigs, David H. Lawrence; U.S. Fight Director, Thomas Schall; Additional Arrangements, Derek Barnes; Music Coordinator, John Miller; Casting, Stanczyk/Cherpakov Casting; Marketing, HHC Marketing; General Management, 101 Productions Ltd.; PSM, Kim Vernace; Technical Supervisors, David Benken and Juniper Street Productions; Company Manager, Thom Clay; Stage Manager, Paul J. Smith; ASM, Matthew Melchiorre; Assistant to the Director, Bruce Perry; Associate Design: Paul Weimer, Ted LeFevre (set), Scott Traugott (costumes), Nick Simmons (U.K. lighting), Nicholas Borsjuk (sound); Dialect Coach, Stephen Gabis; U.K. Dramaturg, Tom Morris; Original Fight Director, Alison De Burgh; Fight Captain, Eric William Morris; Production: Jack Anderson (carpenter), Joe Cangelosi (electrician), Brad Gyorgak (sound supervisor), Steven Wood (properties), Patrick Eviston (advance carpenter), Jason Wilkosz (advance electrician), Nick Simmons (lighting programmer), Karen L. Eifert (wardrobe supervisor), David H. Lawrence (hair supervisor); Synthesizer Programmer, Karl Mansfield; Music Preparation, Anixter Rice Music Services; Press, Boneau/Bryan-Brown, Joe Perotla, Ian Bjorklund

Ivy Vahanian and Cast (photos by Joan Marcus)

**CAST** Act 1—1742: Meshak Gardiner **Brad Fleischer**; Angel **Ivy Vahanian**; Dr. Smith **Quentin Maré**; Young Thomas Ledbury **Charlotte Parry**; Young Alexander Ashbrook **Xanthe Elbrick**; Otis Gardiner **Bill Camp**; Mrs. Lynch **Jan Maxwell**; Miss Price **Angela Linn**; Mr. Claremore **Tom Riis Farrell**; Lady Ashbrook **Christina Rouner**; Isobel Ashbrook **Karron Graves**; Mrs. Milcote **Kathleen McNenny**; Melissa **Ivy Vahanian**; Edward Ashbrook **Laura Heisler**; Alice Ashbrook **Cristin Milioti**; Lord Ashbrook **David Andrew Macdonald**; Adult Alexander Ashbrook **Wayne Wilcox**; Act II—1750: Mrs. Hendry **Jacqueline Antaramian**; Philip Gaddarn **Bill Camp**; Toby **Uzo Aduba**; Aaron **Xanthe Elbrick**; Molly **Jolly Abraham**; Handel **Quentin Maré**; Adult Thomas Ledbury **Dashiell Eaves**

Christina Rouner, David Andrew Macdonald, Ivy Vahanian, Xanthe Elbrick, and Cast

**CHOIR** Philip Anderson, John Arbo, Sean Attebury, Renée Brna, Charlotte Cohn, Sean Cullen, Katie Geissinger, Zachary James, Tinashe Kajese, bj Karpen, Katherine Keys, Evangelia Kingsley, Eric William Morris, Daniel Neer, Nina Negri, Mark Rehnstrom, Martín Solá, Samantha Soule, Alison Weller, Gregory Wright

**UNDERSTUDIES** Renée Brna (Aaron, Edward Ashbrook, Young Alexander Ashbrook, Young Thomas Ledbury), Sean Cullen (Dr. Smith, Handel, Lord Ashbrook, Otis Gardner, Thomas Claymore), Tinashe Kajese (Miss Price, Molly, Toby), Eric William Morris (Adult Alexander Ashbrook, Adult Thomas Ledbury, Meshak Gardiner), Samantha Soule (Alice Ashbrook, Angel, Isobel Ashbrook, Melissa), Alison Weller (Lady Ashbrook, Mrs. Hendry, Mrs. Lynch, Mrs. Milcote)

**MUSICIANS** Constantine Kitsopoulos (Conductor/keyboard), Chip Prince (Associate Conductor/keyboard), Dale Stuckenbruck & Elizabeth Lim-Dutton (violin), Maxine Roach (viola), Deborah Assael (cello), Judith Sugarman (string bass)

**2006–2007 AWARDS Theatre World Award:** Xanthe Elbrick

**SETTING** England, 1742 and 1750. American premiere of a play with music presented in two acts. Prior to its New York debut, *Coram Boy* played two sold-out engagements at the National Theatre, winning the 2006 Time Out Live Best Play Award and receiving rave reviews from the U.K. critics.

**SYNOPSIS** *Coram Boy* tells the tale of two orphans at the Coram Hospital for Deserted Children: Toby, saved from an African slave ship and Aaron, the abandoned son of the heir to a great estate. Featuring an hour's worth of original music and Handel's "Messiah" chorus in the finale, this story of fathers and sons, set in the dark heart of eighteenth-century England, is an epic and thrilling adventurous tale that is also moving and uplifting.

Ivy Vahanian and Xanthe Elbrick

*Charlotte Parry and Xanthe Elbrick*

*Bill Camp and Jan Maxwell*

*Ivy Vahanian, Brad Fleischer, and Cast*

# LOVEMUSIK

Biltmore Theatre; First Preview: April 12, 2007; Opening Night: May 3, 2007; 24 previews, 32 performances as of May 31, 2007

Book by Alfred Uhry, music by Kurt Weill, lyrics by Maxwell Anderson, Bertolt Brecht, Howard Dietz, Roger Fernay, Ira Gershwin, Oscar Hammerstein II, Langston Hughes, Alan Jay Lerner, Maurice Magre, Ogden Nash, Elmer Rice, Kurt Weill; suggested by the letters of Kurt Weill and Lotte Lenya; Produced by Manhattan Theatre Club (Lynne Meadow, Artistic Director; Barry Grove, Executive Producer) in special arrangement with Marty Bell, Aldo Scrofani, Boyett Ostar Productions, Tracy Aron, Roger Berlind/Debra Black, Chase Mishkin, Ted Snowdon; Director, Harold Prince, Musical Staging, Patricia Birch; Sets, Beowulf Boritt; Costumes, Judith Dolan; Lighting, Howell Binkley; Sound, Duncan Robert Edwards; Wigs, Paul Huntley; Makeup, Angelina Avallone; PSM, Joshua Halperin; Casting, Mark Simon; Orchestrations, Jonathan Tunick; Musical Supervisor, Kristen Blodgette; Music Coordinator, Seymour Red Press; Additional Vocal Arrangements, Milton Granger; Director of Artistic Operations, Mandy Greenfield; Production Manager, Ryan McMahon; Development, Jill Turner Lloyd; Marketing, Debra A. Waxman; General Manager, Florie Seery; Director of Artistic Development, Paige Evans; Artistic Consultant, Daniel Sullivan; Director of Artistic Administration/Assistant to the Artistic Director, Amy Gilkes Loe; Finance, Jeffrey Bledsoe; Associate General Manager, Lindsey Brooks Sag; Company Manager, Seth Shepsle; Production Manager, Bridget Markov; Stage Manager, Jason Brouillard; Assistant to Mr. Prince, Daniel Kutner; Assistant Choreographer, Deanna Dys; Dance Captain, Ann Morrison; Rehearsal Pianist, Stan Tucker; Associate Design: Jo Winiarski (set), Ryan O'Gara (lighting); Assistant Design: Camille Connolly, Jessie T. Moore, Jason Lajka (set), Rebecca Lustig (costumes), Brad King (lighting), Nathaniel Hare (sound), Darlene Dannenfelser (hair/wigs); Dialect Consultant, Stephen Gabis; Production: Michelle Sesco (assistant costume supervisor), Patrick Murray (automations); John Fullum/Leomar Susana/Rich Wichrowski (fly); Gerard Fortunato (assistant carpenter), Sue Poulin (assistant props), Hillary Knox (moving lights), J. Day (conventional lights), Timothy Coffey/Matt Maloney (front lights), Suzanne Williams (board operator), Alice Ramos (hair supervisor), Taurance Williams (hair assistant), Jens Muehlhausen (sound engineer); Advertising, SpotCo; Press, Boneau/Bryan-Brown, Jim Byk, Aaron Meier, Heath Schwartz, Christine Olver; Cast recording: Sh-K-Boom/Ghostlight Records 84424

*Rachel Ulanet, David Pittu, Ann Morrison, and Judith Blazer*

*Michael Cerveris and Donna Murphy (photos by Carol Rosegg)*

**CAST** Kurt Weill **Michael Cerveris;** Lotte Lenya **Donna Murphy;** Bertolt Brecht **David Pittu;** George Davis **John Scherer;** Woman on the Stairs/ Brecht Woman **Judith Blazer;** Magistrate/Judge/Auditioner **Herndon Lackey;** Court Secretary/Brecht Woman/Auditioner **Rachel Ulanet;** Brecht Woman/ Photographer **Ann Morrison;** Interviewer/Handyman **Erik Liberman;** Otto/ Allen Lake **Graham Rowat;** Swings **Edwin Cahill, Jessica Wright**

*Michael Cerveris*

**UNDERSTUDIES** Edwin Cahill (Brecht, Weill), Erik Liberman (Brecht), Ann Morrison (Lenya), Graham Rowat (Davis)

**ORCHESTRA** Nicholas Archer (Conductor/piano); Stan Tucker (Associate Conductor); Katherine Livolsi-Landau, Suzy Perelman (violin); David Blinn (viola); Mairi Dorman (cello); James Ercole, John Winder (woodwinds); Christian Jaudes (trumpet); Jeff Cooper (bass); Billy Miller (drums/percussion)

**MUSICAL NUMBERS** Speak Low, Nanna's Lied, Kiddush, Songs of the Rhineland, Klops Lied (Meatball Song), Berlin Im Licht, Wooden Wedding, Tango Ballad, Alabama Song, Girl of the Moment, Moritat, Schickelgruber, Come to Paris, I Don't Love You, Wouldn't You Like to Be on Broadway, Alabama Song (reprise), How Can You Tell an American, Very, Very, Very, It's Never Too Late to Mendelssohn, Surabaya Johnny, Youkali, Buddy on the Night Shift, That's Him, Hosannah Rockefeller, I Don't Love You (reprise), The Illusion Wedding Show, It Never Was You, A Bird of Passage, September Song

**2006–2007 AWARDS** Drama Desk: Outstanding Actress in a Musical (Donna Murphy—tie with Audra McDonald), Outstanding Orchestrations; Outer Critics Circle: Outstanding Actress in a Musical (Donna Murphy)

**SETTING** Europe and America, 1920s–1940s. World premiere of a new musical presented in two acts.

**SYNOPSIS** An epic romance set in Berlin, Paris, Broadway and Hollywood, *LoveMusik* follows the lives of the unlikeliest of lovers—the brilliant, intellectual German composer Kurt Weill and a lusty girl from the streets of Vienna who became his muse and star, Lotte Lenya. The show spans twenty-five years in the lives of this complicated couple.

*Michael Cerveris and David Pittu*

*Donna Murphy*

# DEUCE

Music Box Theatre; First Preview: April 16, 2007; Opening Night: May 6, 2007; 27 previews, 29 performances as of May 31, 2007

Written by Terrence McNally; Produced by Scott Rudin, Stuart Thompson, Maberry Theatricals, The Shubert Organization, Roger Berlind, Debra Black, Bob Boyett, Susan Dietz, Daryl Roth; Director, Michael Blakemore; Set Design, Peter J. Davison; Costumes, Ann Roth; Lighting, Mark Henderson; Video and Projection Design, Sven Ortel; Sound, Paul Charlier; Casting, Telsey + Company; PSM, Steven Beckler; Production Management, Aurora Productions; Company Manager, Brig Berney; General Management, Stuart Thompson Productions, James Triner, Caroline Prugh; Stage Manager, Mary MacLeod; Associate Design: Michelle Matland (costumes), Daniel Walker (lighting), Walter Trarbach, Tony Smolenski IV (sound); Makeup Consultant, Angelina Avallone; Production: Brian G.F. McGarity (electrician), Paul Delcioppo (sound operator), David Cohen (projections operator), Kristin Gardner (wardrobe supervisor), Maeve Fiona Butler (Ms. Lansbury's dresser), Anna Hoffman (hair supervisor); Production Assistant, John Bantay; Dramaturg, Tessa LaNeve; Assistant Director, Kim Weild; Tennis Consultant, Tom Santopietro; Producer Assistants: Diana Short, Jeffrey Hillock, Ana Pilar Camacho, Greg Raby, Diane Murphy, Angela Sidlow; Advertising, SpotCo; Marketing, Leanne Schanzer Promotions; Press, Boneau/Bryan-Brown, Chris Boneau, Jim Byk, Danielle Crinnion

*Angela Lansbury*

**CAST** An Admirer **Michael Mulheren;** Midge Barker **Marian Seldes;** Leona Mullen **Angela Lansbury;** Ryan Becker **Brian Haley;** Kelly Short **Joanna P. Adler**

**STANDBYS** Jennifer Harmon (Midge); Diane Kagan (Leona); Linda Marie Larson (Kelly), Robert Emmet Lunney (Ryan/An Admirer)

**SETTING** U.S. Grand Slam Tennis tournament, now. World premiere of a new play presented without intermission.

**SYNOPSIS** In the winter of their lives, two former doubles tennis legends reunite to watch a championship match, and try to make sense of the partnership that took them to the top of their game.

*Marian Seldes and Angela Lansbury (photos by Joan Marcus)*

*Marian Seldes and Angela Lansbury*

# RADIO GOLF

Cort Theatre; First Preview: April 20, 2007; Opening Night: May 8, 2007; 17 previews, 28 performances as of May 31, 2007

*Tonya Pinkins (photos by Carol Rosegg)*

*John Earl Jelks and Anthony Chisholm*

**CAST** Hammond Wilks **Harry Lennix;** Mame Wilks **Tonya Pinkins;** Roosevelt Hicks **James A. Williams;** Sterling Johnson **John Earl Jelks;** Elder Joseph Barlow **Anthony Chisholm**

**STANDBYS** Rosalyn Coleman (Mame Wilks), Billy Eugene Jones (Hammond Wilks, Roosevelt Hicks), Cedric Young (Elder Joseph Barlow, Sterling Johnson)

**SETTING** The Hill District, Pittsburg, Pennsylvania, 1997. The office of Bedford Hills Redevelopment Inc. in a storefront on Centre Avenue. New York premiere of a new play presented in two acts. Originally produced at Yale Repertory Theatre (James Bundy, Artistic Director; Victoria Nolan, Managing Director) in New Haven, Connecticut, April 2005.

**SYNOPSIS** A fast-paced, dynamic and wonderfully funny work about the world today and the dreams we have for the future, *Radio Golf* is the story of a successful entrepreneur who aspires to become the city's first black mayor. But when the past begins to catch up with him, secrets get revealed that could be his undoing. *Radio Golf* is the final installment in August Wilson's decade-by-decade ten play cycle chronicling the African-American experience in the twentieth century. Wilson passed away October 16, 2005.

Written by August Wilson; Produced by Jujamcyn Theatres (Rocco Landesman, President; Paul Libin, Producing Director; Jack Viertel, Creative Director; Jordan Roth, Vice President), Margo Lion, Jeffrey Richards, Jerry Frankel, Tamara Tunie, Wendell Pierce, Fran Kirmser, The Bunting Management Group, Georgia Frontiere, Open Pictures, Lauren Doll, Steven Greil, The August Wilson Group, Wonder City Inc., Townsend Teague, in association with Jack Viertel and Gordon Davidson; Director, Kenny Leon; Set, David Gallo; Costumes, Susan Hilferty; Lighting, Donald Holder; Original Music/Sound, Dan Moses Schreier; Dramaturg, Todd Kreidler; Casting, Stanczyk/Cherpakov; Production Management, Aurora Productions; PSM, Narda Alcorn; Executive Producer, Nicole Kastrinos; General Manager, 101 Productions Ltd.; Marketing, TMG; Company Manager, Chris Morey; Additional Marketing, Images USA, Walker International Communications Group, Brothers and Sisters Marketing, Situation Marketing; Original Casting, Harriet Bass; Assistant Director, Derrick Sanders; Stage Manager, Marion Friedman; Vocal Coach, Erin Annarella; Associate Design: Charlie Smith (set), Maiko Matsushima (costumes), Hilary Manners (lighting), David Bullard (sound); Production: Ed Diaz (carpenter), Dylan Foley (props supervisor), Scott DeVerna (electrician), Jens McVoy (sound supervisor), Philip Lojo (head sound), Lonnie Gaddy (head props), Eileen Miller (wardrobe supervisor), David Rubie (dresser), Barbara Roman (hair supervisor); Advertising, SpotCo; Press, Barlow • Hartman, John Barlow, Michael Hartman, Dennis Crowley, Michelle Bergmann

*Harry Lennix*

# 110 IN THE SHADE

Studio 54; First Preview: April 13, 2007; Opening Night: May 9, 2007; 27 previews, 27 performances as of May 31, 2007

Book by N. Richard Nash, music by Harvey Schmidt, lyrics by Tom Jones; based on Nash's play *The Rainmaker*; Produced by the Roundabout Theatre Company (Todd Haimes, Artistic Director; Harold Wolpert, Managing Director; Julia C. Levy, Executive Director); Director, Lonny Price; Choreography, Dan Knechtges; Music Direction, Paul Gemignani; Orchestrations, Jonathan Tunick; Set and Costumes, Santo Loquasto; Lighting, Christopher Akerlind; Sound, Dan Moses Schreier; Hair and Wigs, Tom Watson; Dance Music Arrangements, David Krane; Dialect Coach, Stephen Gabis; PSM, Peter Hanson; Fight Director, Rick Sordelet; Casting, Jim Carnahan; Makeup, Angelina Avallone; Technical Supervisor, Steve Beers; General Manager, Sydney Beers; Founding Director, Gene Feist; Associate Artistic Director, Scott Ellis; Marketing and Sales Promotions, David B. Steffen; Development, Jeffory Lawson; Company Manager, Nancy Mulliner; ASM, Dan da Silva; Assistant CM, Dave Solomon; Assistant Director, Matt Cowart; Director's Assistant, Will Nunziata; Dance Captain, Matt Wall; Assistant Choreographer, Caitlin Carter; Assistant Technical Supervisor, Elisa Kuhar; Associate Design: Jenny Sawyers (set), Matthew Pachtman (costumes), Ben Krall (lighting), Phillip Scott Peglow (sound); Synthesizer Programmer, Bruce Samuels; Music Associate, Paul Ford; Music Copying, Emily Grishman Music Preparation; Production Properties, Kathy Fabian; Moving Lights, Victor Seastone; Conventional Light Programmer, Jessica Morton; Rain Equipment, Jauchem & Meeh; Production: Dan Hoffman (carpenter), Josh Weitzman (electrician); John Woodring (assistant electrician), Nadine Hettrell (wardrobe supervisor), Carrie Mossman, Carrie Hash (assistant props), Daryl Terry (hair/wig supervisor), Kat Ventura (stylist); David Gotwald (sound), Paul Ashton (automation), Dorion Fuchs, Dan Schulteis (spots), Steve Jones (flyman), Larry White (deck sound), Al Talbot (deck electrician); Advertising, The Eliran Murphy Group; Press, Boneau/Bryan-Brown, Matt Polk, Jessica Johnson, Amy Kass

*Audra McDonald and John Cullum (photos by Joan Marcus)*

**CAST** File **Christopher Innvar;** H.C. Curry **John Cullum;** Noah Curry **Chris Butler;** Jimmy Curry **Bobby Steggert;** Lizzie Curry **Audra McDonald;** Snookie **Carla Duren;** Starbuck **Steve Kazee;** Little Girl **Valisia Lekae Little;** Clarence **Darius Nichols;** Townspeople: Odetta Clark **Colleen Fitzpatrick;** Vivian Lorraine Taylor **Valisia Lekae Little;** Clarence J. Taylor **Darius Nichols;** Curjith (Curt) McGlaughlin **Devin Richards;** Reverend Clark **Michael Scott;** Cody Bridger **Will Swenson;** Lily Ann Beasley **Elisa Van Duyne;** Katheryn Brawner **Betsy Wolfe**

**UNDERSTUDIES** Colleen Fitzpatrick (Lizzie), Will Swenson (Starbuck), Michael Scott (H.C., File), Devin Richards (Noah), Darius Nichols (Jimmy), Valisia Lekae Little (Snookie)

**ORCHESTRA** Paul Gemignani (Conductor); Mark Mitchell (Associate Conductor/keyboard); Sylvia D'Avanzo, Sean Carney (violins); Joe Gottsman (viola); Roger Shell (cello); Susan Rothoiz (flute/piccolo); Rick Heckman, Eric Weidman, Don McGeen (woodwinds); Dominic Derasse, Mike Ponella (trumpets); Bruce Eidem (trombone); Jennifer Hoult (harp); John Beal (bass); Paul Pizzuti (drums/percussion)

**MUSICAL NUMBERS** Another Hot Day, Lizzie's Coming Home, Love, Don't Turn Away, Poker Polka, Hungry Men, The Rain Song, You're Not Foolin' Me, Raunchy, A Man and a Woman, Old Maid, Evenin' Star, Everything Beautiful, Melisande, Simple Little Things, Little Red Hat, Is It Really Me?, Wonderful Music, The Rain Song (reprise)

**2006–2007 AWARDS** Drama Desk: Outstanding Actress in a Musical (Audra McDonald - tie with Donna Murphy)

**SETTING** July 4, 1936 in the Texas Panhandle. Revival of a musical presented in two acts. Originally produced on Broadway at the Broadhurst Theatre October 24, 1963–August 9, 1964, running 330 performances (see *Theatre World* Volume 20, page 42).

**SYNOPSIS** In the middle of a heat wave in 1930s Texas, when everyone is longing for rain, or a breeze, Lizzie Curry is on the verge of becoming a hopeless old maid. Her wit, intelligence, and skills as a homemaker can't make up for the fact that she can't find true love. Even the town sheriff, for whom she harbors a secret yen, won't take a chance. However, when a charismatic rainmaker named Starbuck enters the town and her family's life, Lizzie's world is turned upside down.

*Audra McDonald and Christopher Innvar*

Left: *Steve Kazee, Audra McDonald*

Below: *Audra McDonald and Company*

# Played Through / Closed this Season

## THE 25th ANNUAL PUTNAM COUNTY SPELLING BEE

Circle in the Square; First Preview: April 15, 2005; Opening Night: May 20, 2005; 21 previews, 867 performances as of May 31, 2007

Music and lyrics by William Finn, book by Rachel Sheinkin, conceived by Rebecca Feldman, and additional material by Jay Reiss; Based on *C-R-E-P-U-S-C-U-L-E*, an original play by The Farm; Produced by David Stone, James L. Nederlander, Barbara Whitman, Patrick Catullo, Barrington Stage Company and Second Stage Theatre (Carole Rothman, Artistic Director; Timothy J. McClimon, Executive Director); Director, James Lapine; Choreography, Dan Knechtges; Set and Lobby Design, Beowulf Boritt; Costumes, Jennifer Caprio; Lighting, Natasha Katz; Sound, Dan Moses Schreier; Orchestrations, Michael Starobin; Music Director, Vadim Feichtner; Vocal Arrangements, Carmel Dean; Music Coordinator, Michael Keller; Casting, Tara Rubin; PSM, Andrea "Spook" Testani; Production Manager, Kai Brothers; General Management, 321 Theatrical Management (Nancy Nagel Gibbs, Nina Essman, Marcia Goldberg); Marketing, The Araca Group; Company Manager, Seth Marquette; Resident Director, Darren Katz; Stage Manager, Kelly Hance; Dance Captain, Derrick Baskin; ASM, Lisa Yuen; Assistant Choreographer, DJ Gray; Hair and Wig Design, Marty Kapulsky; Associate Lighting, Philip Rosenberg; Associate Sound, David Bullard; Associate Production Manager, Jason Block; Music Preparation, Emily Grishman; Advertising, Serino Coyne Inc.; Press, The Publicity Office (2006), Barlow • Hartman (2007); Cast recording: Sh-K-Boom/Ghostlight Records 7915584407-2

**CAST** Mitch Mahoney **Derrick Baskin**[1]; Marcy Park **Deborah S. Craig**[2]; Leaf Coneybear **Jesse Tyler Ferguson**[3]; William Barfee **Josh Gad**[4]; Rona Lisa Peretti **Lisa Howard**[5]; Olive Ostrovsky **Celia Keenan-Bolger**[6]; Chip Tolentino **Jose Llana**[7]; Douglas Panch **Greg Stuhr**[8]; Logainne Schwartzandgrubenierre **Sarah Saltzberg**[9]

*Jennifer Simard and Mo Rocca (photos by Joan Marcus)*

*The Cast*

**UNDERSTUDIES**[10] Todd Buonopane (Douglas, Leaf, William, Chip) Kate Wetherhead (Logainne, Marcy, Olive), Maurice Murphy (Leaf, Chip, Douglas, Mitch), Lisa Yuen (Marcy, Olive, Rona)

**MUSICIANS** Vadim Feichtner (Conductor/piano), Carmel Dean (Associate Conductor/ synthesizer), Rick Heckman (reed), Amy Ralske (cello), Glenn Rhian (drums/percussion)

**MUSICAL NUMBERS** The 25th Annual Putnam County Spelling Bee, The Spelling Bee Rules/My Favorite Moment Of The Bee 1, My Friend, The Dictionary, The First Goodbye, Pandemonium, I'm Not That Smart, The Second Goodbye, Magic Foot, Pandemonium Reprise/My Favorite Moment Of The Bee 2, Prayer Of The Comfort Counselor, My Unfortunate Erection (Chip's Lament), Woe Is Me, I'm Not That Smart (reprise), I Speak Six Languages, The I Love You Song, Woe Is Me (reprise), My Favorite Moment Of The Bee 3/Second, Finale, The Last Goodbye

**SETTING** Now. The Putnam County Junior High School Gymnasium. A new musical presented without intermission. Originally produced Off-Broadway at Second Stage, January 2005, and at the Barrington Stage Company, Sheffield, Massachusetts, July 2004. For original production credits see *Theatre World* Volume 61, page 80.

**SYNOPSIS** Four audience participants and six young people experience the anxiety and pressure of a regional spelling bee. The six kids in the throes of puberty, overseen by grown-ups who barely managed to escape childhood themselves, learn that winning isn't everything and that losing doesn't necessarily make you a loser.

*Succeeded by: 1. James Monroe Iglehart (4/17/07) 2. Greta Lee (4/17/07) 3. Barrett Foa (6/25/06), Stanley Bahorek (4/17/07) 4. Jared Gertner (1/30/07) 5. Jennifer Simard (4/17/07) 6. Jessica-Snow Wilson (9/19/06), Jenni Barber (4/17/07) 7. Aaron J. Albano 8. Mo Rocca (4/17/07) 9. Sara Inbar (4/17/07) 10. Subsequent: Catherine Basile (Marcy, Olive, Rona), Elsa Carmona (Rona), Robin Lee Gallo (Marcy), Brian Gonzales (Leaf, Chip, Douglas, William), Carly Hughes (Marcy, Rona), Kevin Smith Kirkwood (Chip, Mitch), Rory O'Malley (Leaf, Douglas, William), Jacqui Polk (Logainne, Marcy, Olive), Sarah Stiles (Logainne, Marcy, Olive), Law Tarello (Doug, William), Lee Zarrett (Leaf, William)

# AVENUE Q

Golden Theatre; First Preview: July 10, 2003; Opening Night: July 31, 2003; 22 previews, 1,599 performances as of May 31, 2007

Music and lyrics by Robert Lopez and Jeff Marx, book by Jeff Whitty; Produced by Kevin McCollum, Robyn Goodman, Jeffrey Seller, Vineyard Theatre and The New Group; Director, Jason Moore; Choreography, Ken Roberson; Music Supervision/Orchestrations/Arrangements, Stephen Oremus; Puppet Conception and Design, Rick Lyon; Set, Anna Louizos; Costumes, Mirena Rada; Lighting, Howell Binkley; Sound, Acme Sound Partners; Animation, Robert Lopez; Music Director/Incidental Music, Gary Adler; Music Coordinator, Michael Keller; Casting, Cindy Tolan; Technical Supervisor, Brian Lynch; Marketing, TMG—The Marketing Group; General Manager, John Corker; PSM, Robert Witherow; Resident Director, Evan Ensign; Associate Producers, Sonny Everett, Walter Grossman, Morton Swinsky; Company Manager; Mary K. Witte; Dance Captain, Natalie Venetia Belcon/Aymee Garcia; Stage Manager, Christine M. Daly; Assistant Director, Jen Bender; ASM, Aymee Garcia; Associate Set, Todd Potter; Associate Lighting, Timothy F. Rogers; Music Copying, Emily Grishman and Alex Lacamoire; Animation and Video Production, Noodle Soup Production, Jeremy Rosenberg; Sound and Video Design Effects, Brett Jarvis; Advertising, SpotCo; Press, Sam Rudy Media Relations; Cast recording: RCA 82876-55923-2

**CAST** Princeton/Rod **Barrett Foa**[1]; Brian **Evan Harrington;** Kate Monster/Lucy the Slut **Mary Faber**[2]; Nicky/Trekkie Monster/Bad Idea Bear **Rick Lyon**[3]; Christmas Eve **Ann Sanders**[4]; Gary Coleman **Natalie Venetia Belcon**[5]; Mrs. T./Bad Idea Bear/Others **Jennifer Barnhart;** Ensemble[6] **Matt Schreiber, Howie Michael Smith**[6]

**UNDERSTUDIES**[7] Becca Ayers (Kate/Lucy, Mrs. T./Bear), Jennifer Barnhart (Kate Monster/Lucy the Slut), Minglie Chen (Christmas Eve, Mrs. T./Bear), Carmen Ruby Floyd (Gary Coleman, Mrs. T/Bear), Aymee Garcia (Kate/Lucy, Christmas Eve, Mrs. T./Bear), Sala Iwamatsu (Christmas Eve), Howie Michael Smith (Princeton/Rod, Nicky/Trekkie/Bear), Matt Schreiber (Nicky/Trekkie/Bear, Brian)

**ORCHESTRA** Gary Adler (Conductor, keyboard), Mark Hartman/Michael Patrick Walker (Associate Conductor, keyboard), Mary Ann McSweeney (bass), Brian Koonin (guitar), Patience Higgins/Jimmy Cozier (reeds), Michael Croiter (drums)

**MUSICAL NUMBERS** Avenue Q Theme, What Do You Do With a BA in English?/It Sucks to be Me, If You Were Gay, Purpose, Everyone's a Little Bit Racist, The Internet Is for Porn, Mix Tape, I'm Not Wearing Underwear Today, Special, You Can Be as Loud as the Hell You Want (When You're Making Love), Fantasies Come True, My Girlfriend, Who Lives in Canada, There's a Fine, Fine Line, There Is Life Outside Your Apartment, The More You Ruv Someone, Schadenfreude, I Wish I Could Go Back to College, The Money Song, For Now

**SETTING** The present, an outer borough of New York City. A musical presented in two acts. For original production credits see *Theatre World* Volume 60, page 25.

**SYNOPSIS** *Avenue Q* is about real life: finding a job, losing a job, learning about racism, getting an apartment, getting kicked out of your apartment, being different, falling in love, promiscuity, avoiding commitment, and internet porn. Twenty and thirty-something puppets and humans survive life in the big city and search for their purpose in this naughty but timely musical that features "full puppet nudity!"

*Succeeded by: 1. Howie Michael Smith (7/3/06) 2. Kelli Sawyer (10/30/06), Mary Faber (12/20/06) 3. Robert McClure (10/30/06), Christian Anderson (01/07) 4. Sala Iwamatsu, Ann Sanders 5. Haneefah Wood (7/3/06) 6. Jonathan Root; Aymee Garcia, Minglie Chen, Leo Daignault, 7. Additional/Subsequent: Leo Daignault (Bear, Brian, Nicky, Trekkie Monster), Jonathan Root (Ensemble, Princeton/Rod, Nicky/Trekkie/Bear), Jasmin Walker (Gary Coleman)

*Evan Harrington and Ann Sanders (photo by Nick Reuchel)*

*Jennifer Barnhart, Nicky, and Christian Anderson (photo by Carol Rosegg)*

# AWAKE AND SING!

Belasco Theatre; First Preview: March 23, 2006; Opening Night: April 17, 2006; Closed June 25, 2006; 27 previews, 80 performances

Written by Clifford Odets; Produced by Lincoln Center Theater (André Bishop, Artistic Director; Bernard Gersten, Executive Producer); Director, Bartlett Sher; Set, Michael Yeargan; Costumes, Catherine Zuber; Lighting, Christopher Akerlind; Sound, Peter John Still and Marc Salzberg; Stage Manager, Robert Bennett; ASM, Denise Yaney; Casting, Daniel Swee; Development, Hattie Jutagir; Marketing, Linda Mason Ross; General Manager, Adam Siegel; Production Manager, Jeff Hamlin; Company Manager, Matthew Markoff; Assistant Director, Sarna Lapine; Assistant Design: Mikiko Suzuki (set), David Newell and Michael Zecker (costumes), Ben Krall (lighting); Dialect Coach, Ralph Zito; Wigs, Tom Watson, Campbell Young; Makeup, Angelina Avallone; Animal Trainer, William Berloni; Production: Bill Nagle (carpenter), John Weingart (flyman), Mark Dignam (propertyman), Neil McShane (electrician), Valerie Spradling (sound engineer),

*Zoe Wanamaker and Mark Ruffalo*

*Lauren Ambrose and Ben Gazzara (photos by Paul Kolnik)*

Steve Gardner (moving lights), Christopher Schneider (props coordinator), James Wilcox (wardrobe supervisor), Susan Schectar (hair supervisor), Nichole Amburg, Paul Ludick, Rodd Sovar (dressers), Robert Cox (animal handler); Advertising, Serino Coyne Inc.; Technical Supervision, Walter Murphy and Patrick Merryman; Poster Art, James McMullan; Press, Philip Rinaldi, Barbara Carroll

**CAST** Ralph Berger **Pablo Schreiber;** Myron Berger **Jonathan Hadary;** Hennie Berger **Lauren Ambrose;** Jacob **Ben Gazzara;** Bessie Berger **Zoe Wannamaker;** Schlosser **Peter Kybart;** Moe Axelrod **Mark Ruffalo;** Uncle Morty **Ned Eisenberg;** Sam Feinschreiber **Richard Topol**

**UNDERSTUDIES** Tony Campisi (Myron Berger, Uncle Morty), Stan Lachow (Jacob Berger, Schlosser), Annie Purcell (Hennie Berger), Charles Socarides (Ralph Berger), Ed Vassallo (Moe Axelrod, Sam Feinschreiber), Lori Wilner (Bessie Berger)

**SETTING** The mid 1930s. An apartment in the Bronx, New York City. A drama in three acts and four scenes presented with two intermissions. Originally produced at the Belasco Theatre February 19, 1935. This production was the fourth Broadway revival, with the first two revivals running simultaneously in 1939 at Daly's 63rd Street Theatre and the Windsor Theatre, and a third at Circle in the Square on March 8, 1984 (see *Theatre World* Volume 40, page 30).

**SYNOPSIS** Clifford Odets' classic tragicomedy details the struggles of three generations of a Depression-era Jewish family in the Bronx.

*Pablo Schreiber and Ben Gazzara*

# BEAUTY AND THE BEAST

Lunt-Fontanne Theatre; First Preview: Wednesday, March 9, 1994; Opening Night: Monday, April 18, 1994; 46 previews, 5,396 performances as of May 31, 2007

Music by Alan Menken, lyrics by Howard Ashman, Tim Rice, book by Linda Woolverton; based on the Disney animated film directed by Kirk Wise and Gary Trousdale; Produced by Disney Theatrical Productions; Director, Robert Jess Roth; Choreography, Matt West; Sets, Stan Meyer; Costumes, Ann Hould-Ward; Lighting, Natasha Katz; Sound, T. Richard Fitzgerald; Hair, David H. Lawrence; Illusions, Jim Steinmeyer, John Gaughan; Prosthetics, John Dods; Associate Producer/Company Manager, Mark Rozzano; Production Supervisor, Harris Production Services; PSM, John Brigleb; Casting, Binder Casting/Mark Brandon; Fight Director, Rick Sordelet; Dance Arrangements, Glen Kelly; Music Coordinator, John Miller; Orchestrations, Danny Troob; Musical Supervision/ Vocal Arrangements, David Friedman; Musical Director/Incidental Arrangements, Michael Kosarin; Assistant Company Manager, Keith D. Cooper; Stage Managers, M.A. Howard, Michael Biondi, Elizabeth Larson; Dance Captain, Daria Lynn Scatton; Fight Captain, David E. Liddell; Puppet Design Consultant, Michael Curry; Special Effects Consultant, Jauchem & Meeh; Associate Production Supervisor, Tom Bussey; Production Manager, Elisa Cardone; Associate Design: Dennis W. Moyes (set), Gregory Cohen & Dan Walker (lighting), John Petrafesa, Jr. (sound), Tracy Christensen (costumes); Synthesizer Programmer, Dan Tramon, Bruce Samuels; Additional Orchestrations, Michael Starobin, Ned Ginsberg; Music Preparation, Peter R. Miller; Advertising, Serino Coyne Inc.; Press, Boneau/Bryan-Brown; Cast recording: Walt Disney 60861

**CAST** Young Prince **Brian Collier**[*1]; Enchantress **Elizabeth Polito;** Beast **Steve Blanchard;** Belle Sarah Litzsinger[*2]; Bookseller **Glenn Rainey**[*3]; Lefou **Aldrin Gonzalez;** Gaston **Grant Norman**[*4];Three Silly Girls[*5] **Michelle Lookadoo, Elisa Van Duyne, Tia Marie Zorne;** Maurice **Jamie Ross;** Wolves **Ana Maria Andricain, Brian Collier**[*1]**, Christopher DeAngelis**[*6]**, Elizabeth Polito;** Cogsworth **Christopher Duva**[*7]; Lumiere **Jacob Young**[*8]; Babette **Meredith Inglesby**[*9]; Mrs. Potts **Jeanne Lehman;** Chip **Trevor Braun** or **Alexander Scheitinger**[*10]; Madame de la Grande Bouche **Gina Ferrall**[*11]; Salt and Pepper **Garrett Miller, Christopher DeAngelis**[*6];Doormat **Brian Collier**[*1]; Cheesegrater **Rod Roberts**[*12]; Monsieur D'Arque **Glenn Rainey**[*2]; Voice of Prologue Narrator **David Ogden Stiers;** Townspeople/Enchanted Objects[*13] **Ana Maria Andricain, Gina Carlette, Brian Collier, Christopher DeAngelis, Keith Fortner, Alisa Klein, David E. Liddell, Michelle Lookadoo, Stephanie Lynge, Garrett Miller, Bill Nabel, Brian O'Brien, Brynn O'Malley, Elizabeth Polito, Glenn Rainey, Rod Roberts, Daria Lynn Scatton, David Spangenthal, Rob Sutton, Ann Van Cleave, Elisa Van Duyne, Tia Marie Zorne;** Swings **Keith Fortner, Alisa Klein, David E. Liddell, Daria Lynn Scatton**

**UNDERSTUDIES** Ana Maria Andricain (Belle), Alisa Klein (Enchantress, Silly Girls, Wolves, Babette, Madame de la Grande Bouche), Daria Lynn Scatton (Enchantress, Silly Girls, Wolves), Keith Fortner (Young Prince, Bookseller, Lefou, Wolves, Salt/Pepper, Doormat, Cheesegrater), David E. Liddell (Young Prince, Bookseller, Salt/Pepper, Doormat, Cheesegrater), David Spangenthal (Beast, Gaston, Monsieur D'Arque), Rob Sutton (Beast, Gaston), Brynn O'Malley (Belle), Brian Collier/Connor Gallagher (Lefou), Bill Nabel (Maurice, Cogsworth, Lumiere, Monsieur D'Arque), Glenn Rainey/Billy Vitelli (Maurice, Cogsworth), Christopher DeAngelis/Bret Shuford (Lumiere), Michelle Lookadoo/Tracy Generalovich (Babette), Stephanie Lynge (Mrs. Potts, Madame de la Grande Bouche), Ann Van Cleave (Mrs. Potts, Madame de la Grande Bouche)

**ORCHESTRA** Michael Kosarin (Conductor); Kathy Sommer (Associate Conductor/keyboard); Joseph Passaro (Assistant Conductor); Amy Duran (Assistant Conductor); Suzanne Ornstein (Concertmaster); Lorra Aldridge, Evan Johnson, Roy Lewis, Kristina Musser (violins); Caryl Paisner, Joseph Kimura (cellos); Jeffrey Carney (bass); Kathy Fink (flute); Vicki Bodner (oboe); Keriann Kathryn Dibari, Tony Brackett (clarinet/flute); Charles McCracken (bassoon/

contrabassoon); Neil Balm, James de la Garza (trumpets); Jeffrey Lang, Anthony Cecere, Robert Carlisle (French horns); Paul Faulise (bass trombone/tuba); John Redsecker, Joseph Passaro (drums/percussion); Stacey Shames (harp); Madelyn Rubinstein (keyboard)

**MUSICAL NUMBERS** Overture, Prologue (Enchantress), Belle, No Matter What, Me, Home, Gaston, How Long Must This Go On?, Be Our Guest, If I Can't Love Her, Entr'acte/Wolf Chase, Something There, Human Again, Maison des Lunes, Beauty and the Beast, Mob Song, The Battle, Transformation, Finale

A musical presented in two acts. For original production credits see *Theatre World* Volume 50, page 55. World premiere at Houston's Theatre Under the Stars December 2, 1993. The Broadway production originally opened at the Palace Theatre and transferred to the Lunt-Fontanne November 12, 1999. Over one hundred cast alumni gathered at the Lunt-Fontanne on April 18, 2007, for a reunion party to celebrate the show's 13th Anniversary on Broadway. The show was scheduled to close on July 29, 2007.

**SYNOPSIS** A stage adaptation of the animated Walt Disney film about a strong-willed young woman who breaks the spell that turned a handsome prince into a monstrous beast. Trying to save her beloved father from the Beast's clutches, Belle agrees to become his prisoner forever. But once she is inside the Beast's enchanted castle, the members of his court, who have been transformed into household objects like clocks and candlesticks, decide to play matchmakers. As the Beast begins to fall in love with Belle, he becomes progressively less beastly. But the spell can be broken only if the Beast can get her to love him in return.

*Succeeded by: 1. Connor Gallagher 2. Sarah Uriarte Berry (9/19/06), Deborah Lew (12/26/06), Anneliese Van Der Pol (4/3/07) 3. Billy Vitelli 4. Donny Osmond (9/19), Stephen Buntrock (12/26/06) 5. Tracy Generalovich, Jennifer Marcum 6. Bret Shuford, Christopher DeAngelis 7. Jonathan Freeman (11/21/06), Glenn Rainey 8. John Tartaglia (11/21/06), David deVries 9. Ann Mandrella 10. Marlon Sherman 11. Mary Stout 12. Steve Konopelski 13. Steve Konopelski, Deborah Lew, Jennifer Marcum, James Patterson, Jennifer Shrader

*Steve Blanchard (photo by Joan Marcus)*

# BRIDGE AND TUNNEL

Helen Hayes Theatre; First Preview: January 12, 2006; Opening Night: January 26, 2006; Closed August 6, 2006; 16 previews, 213 performances

Written by Sarah Jones; Produced by Eric Falkenstein, Michael Alden, and Boyett Ostar Productions; Director, Tony Taccone; Set, David Korins; Lighting, Howell Binkley; Sound, Christopher Cronin; Music, DJ Rekha, Asa Taccone; Marketing, Nancy Richards and Marcia Pendelton; Assistant Director, Steve Colman; PSM, Laurie Goldfeder; Technical Supervisor, Aurora Productions (Gene O'Donovan, W. Benjamin Heller II, Bethany Weinstein, Hilary Austin); Associate Producers, Tom Wirtshafter, Pat Flicker Addiss, Jayson Jackson/Judith Aidoo, Mark Marmer, Marcia Roberts; General Management, Richards/Climan Inc. (David R. Richards, Tamar Haimes, Laura Cronin); Company Manager, Chris Morey/Jolie Gabler; Associate Set, Rod Lemmond; Assistant Set, Lawrence Hutcheson; Associate Lighting, Sarah Maines; Production: Trevor McGinness (wardrobe supervisor), Joe Lavaia (production carpenter), Joseph Beck (production electrician), Roger Keller (production props), Robert Etter (production sound), Greg Fedigan (spot operator); Vocal Coach, Andrea Haring; Production Assistant, Michelle Dunn; Assistant to the General Manager, Amanda E. Berkowitz; Assistant to Ms. Jones, Caitie Bradley; Advertising, Serino Coyne Inc.; Press, The Pete Sanders Group, Glenna Freedman, Shane Marshall Brown

Performed by **Sarah Jones**

**SETTING** Onstage at a Queens, New York poetry slam, now. A solo performance play presented without intermission. Originally developed at the Berkeley Repertory Theatre and subsequently produced Off-Broadway at the Culture Project (Allan Buchman, Founding Director), February 19, 2004 (see *Theatre World* Volume 60, page 114), and originally developed at Berkeley Repertory Theatre, Berkeley, California.

**SYNOPSIS** Jones transforms into more than a dozen characters of various ethnicities through slight changes in voice and costume. The actress weaves together a community, with each character dealing with assimilation in modern urban America, and delves into portraits of a certain few. Among her melting pot of personae include a Pakistani accountant, an Eastern European Jewish woman, a young Vietnamese male slam poet, a wheelchair-bound Mexican labor organizer, an Australian artist, a Haitian social worker, a Chinese mother and a young Latina. Jones earned a Special Theatre World Award for this performance in 2004.

*Sarah Jones*

*Sarah Jones (photos by Paul Kolnik)*

# CHICAGO

Ambassador Theatre; First Preview: October 23, 1996; Opening Night: November 14, 1996; 25 previews, 4,391 performances as of May 31, 2007

Lyrics by Fred Ebb, music by John Kander, book by Fred Ebb and Bob Fosse; based on the play by Maurine Dallas Watkins; Production based on the 1996 City Center *Encores!* production; Original production directed and choreographed by Bob Fosse; Produced by Barry & Fran Weissler in association with Kardana/Hart Sharp Productions and Live Nation; Director, Walter Bobbie; Choreography, Ann Reinking in the style of Bob Fosse; Supervising Music Director, Rob Fisher; Music Director, Leslie Stifelman; Set, John Lee Beatty; Costumes, William Ivey Long; Lighting, Ken Billington; Sound, Scott Lehrer; Orchestrations, Ralph Burns; Dance Arrangements, Peter Howard; Adaptation, David Thompson; Musical Coordinator, Seymour Red Press; Hair/Wigs, David Brian Brown; Casting, James Calleri/Duncan Stewart (current), Jay Binder (original); Technical Supervisor, Arthur P. Siccardi; Dance Supervisor, Gary Chryst; PSM, David Hyslop; Associate Producer, Alecia Parker; General Manager, B.J. Holt; Company Manager, Hilary Hamilton; Associate CM, Jean Haring; Stage Managers, Terrence J. Witter, Mindy Farbrother; GM Associate, Stephen Spadaro; Assistant Director, Jonathan Bernstein; Assistant Choreographer, Debra McWaters; Dance Captains, Gregory Butler, Mindy Cooper, Bernard Dotson; Associate Lighting, John McKernon; Set Assistants, Eric Renschler, Shelley Barclay; Production: Kevin Woodsworth (wardrobe supervisor), Donald Sanders (costume assistant), Joseph Mooneyham (carpenter), Luciana Fusco (electrician), Michael Guggino (front light operator), John Montgomery (sound engineer), Justen Brosnan (hair supervisor), John Cagney (propman), Jo-Ann Bethell, Kathy Dacey, Paula Davis (dresser); Music Preparation, Chelsea Music Services Inc.; Press, Pete Sanders (1997-2006), Jeremy Shaffer (2007); Cast recording: RCA 68727-2

*John Kander and the girls open the performance with the now classic dialogue penned by his belated lyricist Fred Ebb: "You are about to see a story of murder, greed, corruption, violence, exploitation, adultery, and treachery — all those things we hold near and dear to our hearts." (all photos by Paul Kolnik from the Tenth Anniversary Benefit Performance)*

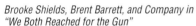

*Brooke Shields, Brent Barrett, and Company in "We Both Reached for the Gun"*

**CAST** Velma Kelly **Brenda Braxton**[*1]; Roxie Hart **Tracy Shane**[*2]; Amos Hart **Ray Bokhour**[*3]; Matron "Mama" Morton **Lillias White**[*4]; Billy Flynn **Obba Babatunde**[*5]; Mary Sunshine **R. Lowe;** Fred Casely **Gregory Butler;** Sergeant Fogarty **Matthew Risch;** Liz **Michelle M. Robinson;** Annie **Angel Reda**[*6]; June **Donna Marie Asbury;** Hunyak **Gabriela Garcia**[*7]; Mona **Bryn Dowling**[*8]; Go-To-Hell-Kitty **Michelle Potterf**[*9]; Harry/The Jury **Shawn Emamjomeh;** Aaron/"Me and My Baby" Specialty Dance **Denis Jones;** Judge/Doctor; **Bernard Dotson**[*10]; Bailiff/Court Clerk **Denny Paschall;** Martin Harrison/"Me and My Baby" Specialty Dance **Eric Jordan Young**

*Chita Rivera and Cast perform "All That Jazz"*

**UNDERSTUDIES** Donna Marie Asbury (Velma, Mama), Bernard Dotson (Billy), Bryn Dowling (Roxie), Gabriela Garcia (Velma), Denis Jones (Amos), Melissa Rae Mahon (Roxie), J. Loeffelholz/N. Adams (Mary Sunshine), David Kent (Fred, Specialty Dance), Denny Paschall (Specialty Dance), Matthew Risch (Fred), Michelle M. Robinson (Mama), Mark Anthony Taylor (Fred, Specialty Dance), Eric Jordan Young (Billy, Amos); For all other roles: Mindy Cooper, David Kent, Gary Kilmer, Sharon Moore, Josh Rhodes, Steven Sofia, Mark Anthony Taylor; Temporary replacements: Julio Agustin (Fred, Sergeant Fogarty), Steven Sofia (Aaron/Specialty Dance), Dan LoBuono (Harry/The Jury)

**ORCHESTRA** Leslie Stifelman (Conductor); Jeffrey Saver, Scott Cady (Associate Conductors/piano/accordion); Seymour Red Press, Jack Stuckey, Richard Centalonza (woodwinds); John Frosk, Darryl Shaw (trumpets); Dave Bargeron, Bruce Bonvissuto (trombones); Jay Berliner (banjo); Ronald Raffio (bass/tuba); Marshall Coid (violin); Ronald Zito (drums/percussion)

**MUSICAL NUMBERS** All That Jazz, Funny Honey, Cell Block Tango, When You're Good to Mama, Tap Dance, All I Care About, A Little Bit of Good, We Both Reached for the Gun, Roxie, I Can't Do It Alone, My Own Best Friend, Entr'acte, I Know a Girl, Me and My Baby, Mister Cellophane, When Velma Takes the Stand, Razzle Dazzle, Class, Nowadays, Hot Honey Rag, Finale.

**SETTING** Chicago, late 1920s. A new production of the 1975 musical presented in two acts. For original production credits see *Theatre World* Volume 53, page 14. Originally produced on Broadway June 3, 1975 at the 46th Street Theatre (now the Richard Rodgers Theatre where this revival first opened), with Gwen Verdon, Chita Rivera, and Jerry Orbach (see *Theatre World* Volume 32, Page 8). This production was first presented at City Center *Encores!* on May 2–4, 1996 (see *Theatre World* Volume 52, page 63). It then transferred to Broadway, opening at the Richard Rodgers Theatre, then transferred to the Shubert Theatre on February 12, 1997, then transferred to the Ambassador Theatre on January 29, 2003.

**SYNOPSIS** Murder, media circus, vaudeville, and celebrity meet in this 1920s tale of two of the windy city's most celebrated felons and their rise to fame amidst a razzle dazzle trial.

**TENTH ANNIVERSARY GALA** On November 14, 2006, *Chicago* celebrated its tenth anniversary with a special gala performance which reunited original stars of the revival as well as seventy other present and past cast members sharing all of the roles. John Kander opened the show with the show's textual introduction, penned by his late collaborator, Fred Ebb. Other highlights included Chita Rivera reprising her role as Velma (from the original Broadway production) for "All That Jazz", the original ensemble members performing an extended version of the Entr'acte, a succession of seven "Billys" singing "Razzle Dazzle," and director Walter Bobbie introducing the production's original Roxie and Velma, Ann Reinking, and Bebe Neuwirth, who performed "Nowadays."

The cast included: Donna Marie Asbury, Obba Babatundé, Brent Barrett, Rob Bartlett, Hinton Battle, Roy Bean, P.J. Benjamin, Ray Bokhour, Jim Bortelmann, Wayne Brady, Brenda Braxton, Greg Butler, Kevin Carolan, Caitlin Carter, Lynda Carter, Kevin Chamberlin, Chuck Cooper, Mindy Cooper, Mamie Duncan-Gibbs, Shawn Emamjomeh, Gabriela Garcia, Joel Grey, Melanie Griffith, Gregory Harrison, Marilu Henner, Ruthie Henshall, Denis Jones, David Kent, Mary Ann Lamb, Sharon Lawrence, Huey Lewis, Marcia Lewis Bryan, Jeff Loeffelholz, Ryan Lowe, Melissa Rae Mahon, Christopher McDonald, Gerry McIntyre, Terra C. MacLeod, Sharon Moore, James Naughton, Bebe Neuwirth, Caroline O'Connor, John O'Hurley, Ron Orbach, Destan Owens, Denny Paschall, Ron Raines, Ann Reinking, Kevin Richardson, Matthew Risch, Chita Rivera, Michelle M. Robinson, Roz Ryan, David Sabella, Ernie Sabella, Brooke Shields, Ashlee Simpson, Mark Anthony Taylor, Rocker Verastique, Jennifer West, Rita Wilson, Bruce Winant, Carol Woods, Tom Wopat, Amra-Faye Wright, Eric Jordan Young, Karen Ziemba, and Leigh Zimmerman.

*Succeeded by: 1. Amra-Faye Wright (11/20/06), Brenda Braxton (12/31/06) 2. Rita Wilson (6/12/06), Michelle DeJean (8/7/06), Bianca Marroquin (8/21/06), Michelle DeJean (10/30/06), Bebe Neuwirth (12/31/06), Bianca Marroquin (4/23/07) 3. Kevin Chamberlin (6/12/06), Rob Bartlett (9/11/06) 4. Roz Ryan (9/11/06), Carol Woods (vacation weeks for Ms. White and Ms. Ryan) 5. Usher Raymond (8/21/06), Christopher McDonald (10/15/06), Huey Lewis (11/20/06), Philip Casnoff (1/15/07), Bernard Dotson (4/23/07), Joey Lawrence (5/4/07) 6. Jennifer West, Solange Sandy 7. Jillana Laufer, Emily Fletcher 8. Robyn Hurder 9. Julie Tolivar, Melissa Rae Mahon 10. Kevin Neal McCready, Bernard Dotson

*Joel Grey, the original "Amos" performs "Mr. Cellophane"*

# THE COLOR PURPLE

Broadway Theatre; First Preview: November 1, 2005; Opening Night: December 1, 2005; 30 previews, 623 performances as of May 31, 2007

Book by Marsha Norman, music and lyrics by Brenda Russell, Allee Willis, Stephen Bray; based on Alice Walker's novel and the Warner Brothers/Amblin Entertainment 1986 film directed by Steven Spielberg; Produced by Oprah Winfrey, Scott Sanders, Roy Furman, Quincy Jones, Creative Battery, Anna Fantaci & Cheryl Lachowicz, Independent Presenters Network, David Lowy, Stephanie P. McClelland, Gary Winnick, Jan Kallish, Nederlander Presentations Inc., Bob & Harvey Weinstein, Andrew Asnes & Adam Zotovich, Todd Johnson; Director, Gary Griffin, Sets, John Lee Beatty, Costumes, Paul Tazewell; Lighting, Brian MacDevitt; Sound, Jon Weston; Choreography, Donald Byrd, Music Supervisor/ Incidental Music, Kevin Stites; Music Director, Linda Twine; Arrangements, Daryl Waters, Joseph Joubert; Music Coordinator, Seymour Red Press; Orchestrations, Jonathan Tunick; Casting, Bernard Telsey; Hair, Charles LaPointe; Production Managers, Arthur Siccardi, Patrick Sullivan; PSM, Kristen Harris; General Management, Amy Jacobs; Marketing, TMG; Company Manager, Kimberly Kelley; Associate Director, Nona Lloyd; Stage Manager, Lisa Dawn Cave; ASM, Neveen Mahmoud; Fight Director, J. Steven White; Fight Captain, James Brown III; Dialects, Deborah Hecht; Makeup, Angelina Avallone; Dance Captain, Stephanie Guiland-Brown; Press, Barlow • Hartman; Cast recording: Angel/EMI 0946 3 42954 2 0

**CAST** Young Nettie/Mister Daughter **Chantylla Johnson;** Young Celie/Mister Daughter/Young Olivia/Henrietta **Zipporah G. Gatling;** Church Soloist **Carol Dennis;** Church Lady/Doris **Kimberly Ann Harris**[*1]; Church Lady/Darlene **Virginia Ann Woodruff**[*2]; Church Lady/Jarenne, Daisy[*3]; **Maia Nkenge Wilson;** Preacher/Prison Guard **Doug Eskew;** Pa/Grady **J.C. Montgomery;** Nettie **Renée Elise Goldsberry**[*4]; Celie **LaChanze**[*5]; Mister **Kingley Leggs**[*6]; Young Harpo, Young Adam **Leon G. Thomas III**[*7]; Harpo **Brandon Victor Dixon**[*8]; Sofia **Felicia P. Fields**[*9]; Squeak **Krisha Marcano;** Shug Avery **Elisabeth Withers-Mendes;** Ol' Mister **Lou Myers**[*10]; Buster/Chief **Nathaniel Stampley**[*11]; Bobby **James Brown III;** Older Olivia **Bahiyah Sayyed Gaines;** Older Adam **Grasan Kingsberry;** Ensemble[*12] **James Brown III, LaTrisa A. Coleman, Carol Dennis, Anika Ellis, Doug Eskew, Bahiyah Sayyed Gaines, Zipporah G. Gatiling, Charles Gray, James Harkness, Francesca Harper, Kimberly Ann Harris**[*1], **Chantylla Johnson, Grasan Kingsberry, JC Montgomery, Lou Myers, Angela Robinson, Nathaniel Stampley**[*11], **Jamal Story, Leon G. Thomas III**[*7], **Mai Nkenge Wilson**[*3], **Virginia Ann Woodruff**[*2]; Swings[*13] **Jeannette I. Bayardelle, Eric L. Christian, Bobby Daye, Stephanie Guiland-Brown, Corinne McFarlane, Daniel J. Watts**

*Fantasia and NaTasha Yvette (photos by Paul Kolnik)*

**ORCHESTRA** Linda Twine (Conductor); Joseph Joubert, (Associate Conductor/ keyboards); Barry Danielian, Brian O'Flaherty, Kamau Adilifu (trumpets); Larry Farrell, Jason Jackson (trombones); Les Scott, Lawrence Feldman, Jay Brandford (woodwinds); Shelton Becton (keyboards); Buddy Williams, Damien Bassman drums/percussion), Steve Bargonetti (guitar/harmonica), Ben Brown (bass), Paul Woodiel, Mineko Yajima (violins), David Creswell (viola), Clay C. Ruede (cello)

**MUSICAL NUMBERS** Huckleberry Pie, Mysterious Ways, Somebody Gonna Love You, Our Prayer, Big Dog, Hell No!, Brown Betty, Shug Avery Comin' to Town, Too Beautiful for Words, Push Da Button, Uh-Oh!, What About Love?, African Homeland, The Color Purple, Mister's Song, Miss Celie's Pants, Any Little Thing, I'm Here, The Color Purple (reprise)

**SETTING** Georgia, 1909–1949. A musical presented in two acts. For original production credits see *Theatre World* Volume 62, page 39. Originally produced in 2004 at Atlanta's Alliance Theatre (Susan Booth, Artistic Director; Thomas Pechar, Managing Director).

**SYNOPSIS** *The Color Purple* is an inspiring story of a woman, who, through love, finds the strength to triumph over adversity and discover her unique voice in the world. Ultimately, it is about hope, a testament to the healing power of love and a celebration of life.

*Succeeded by 1. Charlotte Crossley (03/07) 2. Rosena M. Hill (03/07) 3. Leilani N. Bryant 4. Darlesia Cearcy (1/17/06) 5. Jeannette I. Bayardelle (11/7/06), Kenita R. Miller (2/27/07), Fantasia (4/10/07) 6. Alton Fitzgerald White (11/7/06) 7. Ricky Smith 8. Chaz Lamar Shepherd (03/07) 9. NaTasha Yvette Williams (03/07) 10. Larry Marshall (11/7/06) 11. Gavin Gregory 12. Shelby Braxton-Brooks, Ruby E. Crawford, Kenya Unique Massey, Marla McReynolds, Levensky Smith 13. Kemba Shannon, Deidra H. Brooks, Ashley Reneé Jordan, Jenny Mollet, Teresa Stanley, LaVon Fisher-Wilson, Yolanda Wyns*

*Fantasia and Company*

# DIRTY ROTTEN SCOUNDRELS

Imperial Theatre; First Preview: January 31, 2005; Opening Night: March 3, 2005; Closed September 3, 2006; 36 previews, 627 performances

Book by Jeffrey Lane, music and lyrics by David Yazbek; based on the film written by Dale Launer, Stanley Shapiro and Paul Henning; Produced by Marty Bell, David Brown, Aldo Scrofani, Roy Furman, Dede Harris, Amanda Lipitz, Greg Smith, Ruth Hendel, Chase Mishkin, Barry and Susan Tatelman, Debra Black, Sharon Karmazin, Joyce Schweickert, Bernie Abrams/Michael Speyer, David Belasco[+], Barbara Whitman, Weissberger Theater Group/Jay Harris, Cheryl Wiesenfeld/Jean Cheever, Florenz Ziegfeld[+], Clear Channel Entertainment and Harvey Weinstein; Produced in association with MGM On Stage/Darcie Denkert and Dean Stolber, and the entire Prussian Army[+]; Executive Producers, Marty Bell, Aldo Scrofoni; Director, Jack O'Brien, Choreography, Jerry Mitchell; Music Director/Incidental Music, Ted Sperling; Set, David Rockwell; Costumes, Gregg Barnes; Lighting, Kenneth Posner; Sound, Acme Sound Partners; Casting, Bernard Telsey; Associate Choreographer, Denis Jones; Orchestrations, Harold Wheeler; Vocal Arrangements, Ted Sperling & David Yazbek; Dance Arrangements, Zane Mark; Music Coordinator, Howard Joines; Technical Supervisor, Christopher Smith; PSM, Michael Brunner; Marketing, Margery Singer Company; General Management, The Charlotte Wilcox Company; Company Manager, Matthew Lambert; Stage Manager, Daniel S. Rosokoff; ASM, Dana Williams; Dance Captain, Greg Graham; Makeup, Jorge Vargas; Music Copying, Emily Grishman; Advertising, SpotCo; Press, Barlow • Hartman; Cast recording: Sh-K-Boom/Ghostlight Records, RTADV84406-2

**CAST** Andre Thibault **Gregory Jbara**[*1]; Lawrence Jameson **Jonathan Pryce**[*2]; Lenore/Renee **Rachel deBenedet**; Sophia **Joan Hess**; Muriel Eubanks **Lucie Arnaz**; Conductor **Timothy J. Alex**; Freddy Benson **Norbert Leo Butz**[*3]; Jolene Oakes **Sara Gettelfinger**; Hotel Manager/Sailor #2/Nikos **Tom Galantich**; Christine Colgate **Rachel York**[*4]; Sailor #1 **Will Erat**; Ensemble **Timothy J. Alex, Roxane Barlow, Jacqueline Bayne, Stephen Campanella, Joe Cassidy, Julie Connors, Rachel deBenedet, Laura Marie Duncan, Sally Mae Dunn, Will Erat, Tom Galantich, Jason Gillman, Amy Heggins, Joan Hess, Rachelle Rak, Chuck Saculla, Dennis Stowe, Matt Wall;** Swings **Christine Bokhour, Paula Leggett Chase, Julie Connors, Jeremy Davis, Jenifer Foote, Nina Goldman, Greg Graham, Timothy Smith;** Standby for Lawrence Jameson **Dennis Parlato**

**UNDERSTUDIES** Timothy J. Alex & Joe Cassidy (Andre, Freddy), Paula Leggett Chase (Muriel), Julie Connors (Jolene, Christine), Rachel deBenedet (Muriel), Laura Marie Duncan (Christine, Muriel), Tom Galantich (Lawrence), Jason Gillman (Freddy), Joan Hess (Christine, Muriel), Dennis Parlato (Andre), Michael Paternostro (Andre, Freddy), Rachelle Rak (Jolene)

*Keith Carradine and Brian d'Arcy James*

*Lucie Arnaz (photos by Carol Rosegg)*

**ORCHESTRA** Fred Lassen (Conductor); Jan Rosenberg (Associate Conductor/keyboards); Howard Joines (Assistant Conductor/Musical Coordinator/percussion); Antoine Silverman (Concert Master); Michael Nicholas, Claire Chan (violin), Anja Wood (cello); Andrew Sterman, Dan Willis, Mark Thrasher (woodwinds); Kevin Bryan, Hollis Burridge (trumpet); Mike Boschen (trombone); Theresa MacDonnell (horn); Dan Lipton (keyboards); Erik Della Penna (guitar); Mike DuClos (bass); Dean Sharenow (drums)

**MUSICAL NUMBERS** Overture, Give Them What They Want, What Was a Woman to Do?, Great Big Stuff, Chimp in a Suit, Oklahoma?, All About Ruprecht, What Was a Woman to Do? (reprise), Here I Am, Nothing Is Too Wonderful to Be True, The Miracle (Act I Finale), Entr'acte, Rüffhousin' mit Schüffhausen, Like Zis/Like Zat, The More We Dance, Love Is My Legs, Love Sneaks In, Like Zis/Like Zat (reprise), Son of Great Big Stuff, The Reckoning, Dirty Rotten Number, Finale

**SETTING** The French Riviera, the present. A musical presented in two acts. Originally produced at the Old Globe Theatre, San Diego, California. For original production credits see *Theatre World* Volume 61, page 52.

**SYNOPSIS** Two con men living on the French Riviera unsuccessfully attempt to work together, only to find the town isn't big enough for both of them. They agree on a settlement: the first to extract $50,000 from a young heiress wins and the other has to leave town. A battle of cons ensues, and an unexpected twist leaves the audience laughing and guessing until the end.

[+] Not actual Producers of the show, but listed as a joke in all publicity material.

*Succeeded by: 1. Richard Kind (8/3/06) 2. Keith Carradine (7/21/06) 3. Brian d'Arcy James (7/21/06) 4. Sherie Rene Scott (6/20/06)

# DOUBT

Walter Kerr Theatre; First Preview: March 9, 2005; Opening Night: March 31, 2005; Closed July 2, 2006; 25 previews, 525 performances

Written by John Patrick Shanley; Produced by Carole Shorenstein Hays, Manhattan Theatre Club (Lynne Meadow, Artistic Director; Barry Grove, Executive Producer), Roger Berlind, and Scott Rudin; Director, Doug Hughes; Scenic Design, John Lee Beatty; Costumes, Catherine Zuber; Lighting, Pat Collins; Original Music and Sound, David Van Tieghem; PSM, Charles Means; Casting, Nancy Piccione and David Caparelliotis; Production Manager, Aurora Productions (Gene O'Donovan, W. Benjamin Heller II, Elise Hanley, Bethany Weinstein); Marketing, TMG - The Marketing Group; General Manager, Stuart Thompson Productions/James Triner; Executive Producer, Greg Holland; Company Manager, Bobby Driggers; Stage Manager, Elizabeth Moloney; Dialect Coach, Stephen Gabis; Assistant Company Manager, Laura Penney; Associate Director, Mark Schneider; Associate Set, Eric Renschler; Assistant Set, Yoshinori Tanokura; Associate Lighting, D.M. Wood; Assistant Costumes, T. Michael Hall, Michael Zecker; Assistant Sound, Walter Trarbach; Production: James Gardner (electrician), Rebecca Heroff (props), Paul Delcioppo (sound), Eileen Miller (wardrobe supervisor), Gina Gornick (dresser), Danny Braddish (automation); Advertising, SpotCo; Press, Boneau/Bryan-Brown

**CAST** Sister Aloysius **Eileen Atkins;** Father Flynn **Ron Eldard;** Sister James **Jena Malone;** Mrs. Muller **Adriane Lenox**

**STANDBYS:** Nadia Bowers (Sister James), Lynda Gravátt (Mrs. Muller), Stevie Ray Dallimore (Father Flynn)

**SETTING** St. Nicholas Church School in the Bronx. Autumn 1964. Transfer of the Off-Broadway play presented without intermission. For original production credits see *Theatre World* Volume 61, pages 64 and 185.

**SYNOPSIS** Set against the backdrop of a Bronx Catholic school in 1964, *Doubt* is the story of a strong-minded woman faced with a difficult decision. Should she voice concerns about one of her male colleagues even if she's not entirely certain of the truth?

*Ron Eldard, Jena Malone, and Eileen Atkins (photos by Joan Marcus)*

*Jena Malone,*
*Eileen Atkins*

# THE DROWSY CHAPERONE

Marquis Theatre; First Preview: April 3, 2006; Opening Night: May 1, 2006; 32 previews, 448 performances as of May 31, 2007

Music and lyrics by Lisa Lambert and Greg Morrison, book by Bob Martin and Don McKellar, by special arrangement with Paul Mack; Produced by Kevin McCollum, Roy Miller, Boyett Ostar Productions, Stephanie McClelland, Barbara Freitag, Jill Furman; Director/Choreography, Casey Nicholaw; Sets, David Gallo; Costumes, Gregg Barnes; Lighting, Ken Billington, Brian Monahan; Sound, Acme Sound Partners; Casting, Bernard Telsey; Hair, Josh Marquette; Makeup, Justen M. Brosnan; Orchestrations, Larry Blank; Dance/Incidental Arrangements, Glen Kelly; Music Director/Vocal Arrangements, Phil Reno; Music Coordinator, John Miller; Production Supervisors, Brian Lynch, Chris Kluth; PSM, Karen Moore; Associate Producers; Sonny Everett, Mariano Tolentino Jr.; Marketing, TMG; General Management, Charlotte Wilcox Company; Company Manager, Bruce Kagel; ACM, Robert E. Jones; Stage Manager, Josh Halperin; ASM, Rachel S. McCutchen; Assistant Director, Josh Rhodes; Dance Captain, Angela Pupello; Props, George Wagner; Music Preparation, Hotstave Ltd.; Press, Boneau/Bryan Brown; Cast recording: Sh-K-Boom/Ghostlight Records 7915584411-2

**CAST** Man in Chair **Bob Martin**[*1]; Mrs. Tottendale **Georgia Engel**[*2]; Underling **Edward Hibbert**[*3]; Robert Martin **Troy Britton Johnson**; George **Eddie Korbich**[*4]; Feldzieg **Lenny Wolpe**; Kitty **Jennifer Smith**; Gangster #1 **Jason Kravits**; Gangster #2 **Garth Kravits**; Aldolpho **Danny Burstein**; Janet Van De Graaff **Sutton Foster**[*5]; The Drowsy Chaperone **Beth Leavel**; Trix **Kecia Lewis-Evans**; Ensemble **Linda Griffin, Angela Pupello**[*6]**, Joey Sorge, Patrick Wetzel**; Swings[*7] **Andrea Chamberlain, Jay Douglas, Stacia Fernandez, Kilty Reidy**

*John Glover and Beth Leavel*

**UNDERSTUDIES**[*8]**:** Patrick Wetzel, Jay Douglas (Man in Chair/Feldzieg); Angela Pupello, Andrea Chamberlain (Janet/Kitty); Joey Sorge, Jay Douglas (Robert/Aldolpho) Linda Griffin, Stacia Fernandez (The Drowsy Chaperone/Mrs. Tottendale/Trix); Patrick Wetzel, Kilty Reidy (Underling/George); Joey Sorge, Kilty Reidy (Gangster 1 & 2)

**ORCHESTRA** Phil Reno (Conductor); Lawrence Goldberg (Associate Conductor/keyboards); Matt Perri (keyboards); Edward Joffe, Tom Murray, Tom Christensen, Ron Jannelli (reeds); Dave Stahl, Glenn Drewes, Jeremy Miloszewicz (trumpet); Steve Armour, Jeff Nelson (trombone), Ed Hamilton (guitar); Michael Kuennen (bass); Perry Cavari (drums); Bill Hayes (percussion)

**MUSICAL NUMBERS** Overture, Fancy Dress, Cold Feets, Show Off, As We Stumble Along, I Am Aldolpho, Accident Waiting Happen, Toledo Surprise; Message From a Nightingale, Bride's Lament, Love Is Always Lovely, I Do I Do in the Sky, As We Stumble Along (reprise)

**SETTING** The New York apartment and in the mind of Man in Chair, now. A musical presented without intermission. For original production credits see *Theatre World* Volume 62, page 60.

**SYNOPSIS** To chase his blues, a musical theatre addict drops the needle on his favorite LP—the 1928 musical comedy *The Drowsy Chaperone*. From the crackle of his hi-fi, the musical magically bursts to life, telling the tale of a pampered Broadway starlet who wants to give up show business to get married. Enter her producer who sets out to sabotage the nuptials, the "drowsy" chaperone, the debonair groom, a dizzy chorine, a Latin lover, a couple of gangsters and ruses are played, hi-jinks occur, and the plot spins completely out of control.

*Jo Anne Worley and Peter Bartlett  (photos by Joan Marcus)*

*Succeeded by: 1. Jonathan Crombie (3/20/07), John Glover (4/17/07) 2. Jo Anne Worley (4/17/07) 3. Noble Shropshire (7/3/07), Edward Hibbert (9/12/06), Peter Bartlett (1/16/07) 4. Patrick Wetzel (5/22/07) 5. Janine LaManna (4/17/07) 6. Joanna Young 7. Linda Gabler, Dale Hensley, Kate Loprest, Brian J. Marcum, Bob Walton 8. Linda Gabler (Kitty), Joanna Young (Janet Van De Graaff)

# FAITH HEALER

Booth Theatre; First Preview: April 18, 2006; Opening Night: May 4, 2006; Closed August 13, 2006; 19 previews, 117 performances

Written by Brian Friel; Presented by the Gate Theatre Dublin; Produced by Michael Colgan & Sonia Friedman Productions, The Shubert Organization, Robert Bartner, Roger Berlind, Scott Rudin, and Spring Sirkin; Director, Jonathan Kent; Set and Costumes, Jonathan Fensom; Lighting, Mark Henderson; Sound, Christopher Cronin; Video, Sven Ortel; U.S. Casting, Jim Carnahan; PSM, Jane Grey; Production Management, Aurora Productions; General Management, Stuart Thompson Productions, James Triner; Associate Producer, Lauren Doll; Company Manager, Shawn M. Fertitta; Stage Manager, Sid King; Assistant to the Director, Will MacAdams; Associate Lighting, Kristina Kloss; Production: Brian G.F. McGarity (production electrician), Jim Kane, Donald "Buck" Roberts (production props), Paul Ashton (props assistant), Kenny McDonough (carpenter), Ronnie Burns, Sr. (electrician), Jim Keane (props), Kay Grunder (wardrobe supervisor), Jeff McGovney (dresser), Cynthia Demand (hair/wig supervisor); Advertising, SpotCo; Press, Barlow • Hartman, Dennis Crowley, Ryan Ratelle

**CAST** Frank Hardy **Ralph Fiennes;** Grace Hardy **Cherry Jones;** Teddy **Ian McDiarmid**

**STANDBYS** Patrick Boll (Frank), Jarlath Conroy (Teddy), Robin Moseley (Grace)

A drama presented in four scenes in two acts. Part 1: Freddie, Part 2: Grace, Part 3: Teddy, Part 4: Frank. Originally produced on Broadway at the Longacre Theatre, April 5, 1979 (see *Theatre World* Volume 35, page 39). This production was presented at the Gate Theatre (Dublin, Ireland) from February 6–March 31, 2006, with Mr. Fiennes and Mr. McDiarmid in the cast.

**SYNOPSIS** Told in a series of four monologues, *Faith Healer* looks at mystic experiences and the fine line between artists and con men. A dissolute, charismatic healer, his long-time lover, and his devoted manager travel the back roads of Scotland and Wales peddling miracles. As they wrestle with Frank's genuine but elusive gift for healing, they ask potent questions about who we trust, what we know and why we believe.

Ian McDiarmid (photo by Joan Marcus)

Cherry Jones (photo by Joan Marcus)

*Ralph Fiennes (photo by Anthony Woods)*

# HAIRSPRAY

Neil Simon Theatre; First Preview: July 18, 2002; Opening Night: August 15, 2002; 31 previews, 1,997 performances as of May 31, 2007

Book by Mark O'Donnell and Thomas Meehan, music by Marc Shaiman, lyrics by Marc Shaiman and Scott Wittman; based on the 1988 film written and directed by John Waters; Produced by Margo Lion, Adam Epstein, The Baruch-Viertel-Routh-Frankel Group, James D. Stern/Douglas L. Meyer, Rick Steiner/Frederic H. Mayerson, SEL & GFO, New Line Cinema, in association with Live Nation, Allan S. Gordon, Elan V. McAllister, Dede Harris, Morton Swinsky, John and Bonnie Osher; Director, Jack O'Brien, Choreography, Jerry Mitchell; Sets, David Rockwell; Costumes, William Ivey Long; Lighting, Kenneth Posner; Sound, Steve C. Kennedy; Casting, Telsey + Company; Wigs/Hair, Paul Huntley; PSM, Lois L. Griffing; Associate Director, Matt Lenz; Associate Choreographer, Michele Lynch; Orchestrations, Harold Wheeler; Music Director, Lon Hoyt, Arrangements, Marc Shaiman; Music Coordinator, John Miller; General Management, Richard Frankel, Laura Green; Technical Supervisor, Tech Production Services Inc./Peter Fulbright; Associate Producers, Rhoda Mayerson, the Aspen Group, Daniel C. Staton; Company Managers, Bruce Kagel, Tracy Geltman; Stage Managers, Marisha Ploski, Thomas J. Gates; Makeup, Randy Houston Mercer; Music Copying, Emily Grishman, Katherine Edmonds; Dance Captains, Rusty Mowery, Robbie Roby, Brooke Leigh Engen; Press, Richard Kornberg; Cast recording: Sony SK 87708

**CAST** Tracy Turnblad **Shannon Durig;** Corny Collins **Jonathan Dokuchitz;** Amber Von Tussle **Becky Gulsvig**[*1]; Brad **Michael Cunio;** Tammy **Lindsay Nicole Chambers**[*2]; Fender **Serge Kushnier**[*3]; Brenda **Leslie Goddard;** Sketch **Bryan West;** Shelley **Donna Vivino**[*4]; IQ **Todd Michel Smith**[*5]; Lou Ann **Anne Warren**[*5]; Link Larkin **Andrew Rannells**[*7]; Prudy Pingleton/

Gym Teacher/Matron **Julie Halston**[*8]; Edna Turnblad **Blake Hammond**[*9]; Penny Pingleton **Cassie Levy**[*10]; Velma Von Tussle **Leah Hocking**[*11]; Harriman F. Spritzer/Principal/Mr. Pinky/Guard **Kevin Meaney**[*12]; Wilbur Turnblad **Stephen DeRosa**[*13]; Seaweed J. Stubbs **Tevin Campbell;** Duane **Tyrick Wiltez Jones;** Gilbert **Arbender J. Robinson;** Lorraine **Terita R. Redd;** Thad **Rashad Naylor**[*14]; The Dynamites **Carla Jay Hargrove, Judine Richard Somerville, Candace Marie Woods**[*15]; Little Inez **Chloe Smith**[*16]; Motormouth Maybelle **Darlene Love;** Denizens of Baltimore **Lindsay Nicole Chambers, Michael Cunio, Leslie Goddard, Carla Jay Hargrove, Julie Halston, Tyrick Wiltez Jones, Kevin Meaney, Rashad Naylor, Arbender J. Robinson, Terita R. Redd, Todd Michel Smith; Chloe Smith, Judine Richard Somerville, Donna Vivino, Anne Warren, Bryan West, Candace Marie Woods;** Swings[*17] **Joe Abraham, Cameron Adams, Gretchen Bieber, Michelle Kittrell, Lauren Kling, Abdul Latif, Rusty Mowery, Cjay Hardy Philip, Nicole Powell, Jason Snow, Willis White;** Standby for Tracy: **Katrina Rose Dideriksen**

**ORCHESTRA** Lon Hoyt (Conductor/keyboard), Keith Cotton (Associate conductor/keyboard), Seth Farber (assistant conductor/keyboard), David Spinozza and Peter Calo (guitars), Francisco Centeno (electric bass), Clint de Ganon (drums), Walter "Wally" Usiatynski (percussion), David Mann and Dave Rickenberg (reeds), Danny Cahn (trumpet), Birch Johnson (trombone), Rob Shaw and Carol Pool (violins), Sarah Hewitt Roth (cello)

**MUSICAL NUMBERS** Good Morning Baltimore, The Nicest Kids in Town, Mama I'm a Big Girl Now, I Can Hear the Bells, The Legend of Miss Baltimore Crabs, The Madison, The Nicest Kids in Town (reprise), Welcome to the '60s, Run and Tell That, Big, Blond and Beautiful, The Big Dollhouse, Good Morning Baltimore, Timeless to Me, Without Love, I Know Where I've Been, Hairspray, Cooties, You Can't Stop the Beat

**SETTING** Time: 1962. Place: Baltimore. A musical presented in two acts. For original production credits see *Theatre World* Volume 59, page 25. World premiere at the 5th Avenue Theatre (Seattle, Washington) June 2002.

**SYNOPSIS** *Hairspray* is the story of Tracy Turnblad, who is going to do whatever it takes to dance her way onto TV's most popular show. Can a big girl with big dreams—and even bigger hair—turn the whole town around?

*Succeeded by: 1. Haylie Duff (7/18/06), Tara Macri, Brynn O'Malley (1/19/07) 2. Heather Lindell, Cameron Adams, Hayley Podschun 3. Tyler Hanes, Andrew Rannells, John Jeffrey Martin, Daniel Robinson 4. Lori Eve Marinacci 5. Jesse L. Johnson, Todd Michael Smith 6. Jackie Seiden, Leslie McDonel 7. Aaron Tveit, Ashley Parker Angel 8. Lisa Jolley (10/4/06), Susan Mosher (1/16/07) 9. Paul Vogt (1/30/07) 10. Diana DeGarmo, Alexa Vega (2/13/07) 11. Isabel Keating (6/6/06) 12. Blake Hammond (1/30/07) 13. Jere Burns 14. Tommar Wilson, Dwayne Cooper 15. Iris Burruss 16. Naturi Naughton 17. Ryan Christopher Chotto, Brooke Leigh Engen, Robbie Roby, Lindsay Thomas

*Ashley Parker Angel and Company*

*Jonathan Dokuchitz, Alexa Vega, Kevin Meaney and Susan Mosher (photos by Paul Kolnik)*

# THE HISTORY BOYS

Broadhurst Theatre; First Preview: April 14, 2006; Opening Night: April 23, 2006; Closed October 1, 2006; 10 previews, 185 performances

Written by Alan Bennett; Presented by The National Theatre of Great Britain (Sir Hayden Phillips, Chairman of the Board; Nicholas Hytner, Director; Nick Starr, Executive Director); Produced by Boyett Ostar Productions, Roger Berlind, Debra Black, Eric Falkenstein, Roy Furman, Jam Theatricals, Stephanie P. McClelland, Judith Resnick, Scott Rudin, Jon Avnet/Ralph Guild, Dede Harris/Mort Swinsky; Director, Nicholas Hytner; Set and Costumes, Bob Crowley; Lighting, Mark Henderson; Music, Richard Sisson; Video, Ben Taylor; Sound, Colin Pink; Casting Toby Whale (U.K.), Tara Rubin (U.S.); General Management, 101 Productions, Ltd.; PSM, Michael J. Passaro; Marketing, HHC Marketing; Technical Supervisor, David Benken; Company Manager, Gregg Arst; Stage Manager, Charlie Underhill; U.K. Musical Director, Tom Attwood; Associate Lighting, Daniel Walker; U.K. Associate Production Manager, Andy Ward; Assistant Technical Supervisor, Rosemarie Palombo; Movement Director, Jack Murphy; Moving Lights, Bobby Harrell; Press, Boneau/Bryan-Brown, Jim Byk, Juliana Hannett

**CAST** *The Boys:* Akthar **Sacha Dhawan;** Crowther **Samuel Anderson;** Dakin **Dominic Cooper;** Lockwood **Andrew Knott;** Posner **Samuel Barnett;** Rudge **Russell Tovey;** Scripps **Jamie Parker;** Timms **James Corden;** *The Teachers:* Headmaster **Clive Merrison**[1]; Mrs. Lintott **Frances de la Tour**[2]; Hector **Richard Griffiths**[3]; Irwin **Stephen Campbell Moore;** TV Director **Colin Haigh**[4]; Make-up Lady **Pamela Merrick**[5]; Other Boys[6] **Joseph Attenborough, Tom Attwood, Rudi Dharmalingam**

**UNDERSTUDIES**[7] Joseph Attenborough (Lockwood, Rudge, Timms, TV Director), Tom Attwood (Crowther, Posner, Scripps), Rudi Dharmalingam (Akthar, Crowther, Dakin), Colin Haigh (Headmaster, Hector), Pamela Merrick (Mrs. Lintott)

**SETTING** The mid 1980s at a grammar school (English equivalent of high school) in the north of England. A comedy/drama with music presented in two acts; Originally produced at the Lyttelton Theatre, May 5, 2004, and subsequently a world tour before coming to New York.

**SYNOPSIS** A rambunctious group of smart and funny sixth-form boys are in pursuit of sex, sport, and a place at university as they prepare for their A-level examinations. Led by a headmaster obsessed with results, a history teacher whose methods are untraditional and another whose practices are by the book, the eight students experience the school year that would forever change their lives. Bennett examines rivalry, adolescence, and education with wit and precision.

*Succeeded by: 1. Malcolm Sinclair (7/11-8/20) 2. Maggie Steed (7/11-8/20) 3. Desmond Barrit (7/18–25) 4. Bill Buell 5. Pippa Pearthree 6. LeRoy McClain, Alex Tonetta, Jeffrey Withers 7. Bill Buell (Hector, Headmaster), LeRoy McClain (Dakin, Rudge, Akthar), Pippa Pearthree (Mrs. Lintott), Alex Tonetta (Posner, Scripps, Timms, TV Director), Jeffrey Withers (Irwin, Crowther, Lockwood), Seth Sklar-Heyn (Other Boys, TV Director)

*Jamie Parker, Andrew Knott, Dominic Cooper, and James Corden (photo by Joan Marcus)*

*Russell Tovey, Samuel Anderson, James Corden, Andrew Knott, Dominic Cooper, Samuel Barnett, Jamie Parker, and Sacha Dhawan (photo by Alex Bailey)*

# HOT FEET

Hilton Theatre; First Preview: April 15, 2006; Opening Night: April 30, 2006; Closed July 23, 2006; 12 previews, 97 performances

Conceived by Maurice Hines, book by Heru Ptah, music and lyrics by Maurice White, additional music and lyrics by Philip Bailey, Reginald Burke, Valerie Carter, William B. Champlin, Peter Cor, Eddie Del Barrio, Larry Dunn, David Foster, Garry Glenn, Jay Graydon, James N. Howard, Jonathan G. Lind, Al McKay, Skip Scarbrough, Skylark, Charles Stepney, Beloyd Taylor, Wayne Vaughn, Wanda Vaughn, Verdine White, Cat Gray, Brett Laurence, Bill Meyers, Heru Ptah, and Allee Willis; Produced by Transamerica, Rudy Durand, in association with Laliba Entertainment Inc., Meir A & Eli C LLC, Polymer Global Holdings, and Godley Morris Group LLC; Director and Choreography, Maurice Hines; Set, James Noone; Costumes, Paul Tazewell; Lighting, Clifton Taylor; Sound, Acme Sound Partners; Hair, Qodi Armstrong; Music Director and Conductor, Jeffrey Klitz; Arrangements and Orchestrations, Bill Meyers; Music Coordinator, John Miller; Production Manager, Arthur Siccardi; Casting, Stuart Howard, Amy Schecter, and Paul Hardt; Assistant Director, Ricardo Khan; PSM, Michael E. Harrod; Marketing, HHC Marketing; General Management, Leonard Soloway, Steven M. Levy; Company Manager, Alexandra Gushin; Stage Manager, Dan Shaheen; ASM, Frances W. Falcone; Assistant Choreographer, Danita Salamida, Duane Lee Holland; Assistant Company Manager, Sara Jane Baldwin; Associate Design: Dennis Ballard (costumes), Ed McCarthy (lighting); Automated Lighting, Paul J. Sonnleitner; Music Copyist, Robert Nowak and Associates; Press, Springer Associates, Joe Trentacosta

**CAST** Louie **Allan Hidalgo;** Emma **Samantha Pollino** (evenings)**/Sarah Livingston** (matinees); Kalimba **Vivian Nixon;** Mom **Ann Duquesnay;** Anthony **Michael Balderrama;** Victor **Keith David\*;** Naomi **Wynonna Smith;** Rahim **Daryl Spiers;** Ensemble **Kevin Aubin, Gerrard Carter, Dionne Figgins, Ramón Flowers, Karla Puno Garcia, Nakia Henry, Duane Lee Holland, Iquail S. Johnson, Dominique Kelley, Steve Konopelski, Sumie Maeda, Jon-Paul Mateo, Vasthy Mompoint, Tera-Lee Pollin, Monique Smith, Daryl Spiers, Felicity Stiverson, Hollie E. Wright;** Swings **Jessica Hope Cohen, Dana Marie Ingraham, Terace Jones, Matthew Warner Kiernan, Danita Salamida;** Band Vocalists **Brent Carter, Keith Anthony Fluitt, Theresa Thomason;** Band Vocalist Swings **Marvel J. Allen, John A. James**

**STANDBYS/UNDERSTUDIES** Adrian Bailey (Victor), Sandra Reaves-Phillips (Mom), Caesar Samayoa (Louie), Sarah Livingston (Emma), Dionne Figgins/Hollie E. Wright/Tera-Lee Pollin, (Kalimba), Daryl Spiers/Matthew Warner Kiernan (Anthony), Nakia Henry (Naomi), Jon-Paul Mateo (Rahim)

**ORCHESTRA** Jeffrey Klitz (Conductor/synthesizer); Andy Ezrin (Associate Conductor/synthesizer); Keith Robinson, Bernd Schoenhart (guitar); Artie C. Reynolds, III (electric bass/ bass synthesizer); Brian Dunne (drums); Errol Crusher Bennett (percussion); Dave Keys (synthesizer); Scott Kreitzer (saxophones); Don Downs, David Trigg (trumpets); Keith O'Quinn (trombone)

**MUSICAL NUMBERS** Overture, In the Stone, Rock That/Boogie Wonderland, When I Dance, Dearest Heart, September, Turn It Into Something Good, Ponta de Areia, Thinking of You, Mighty Mighty, Serpentine Fire, Fantasy, Louie's Welcome, Getaway, Dirty, After the Love Has Gone, Can't Hide Love, You Don't Know, Kali, Hot Feet Ballet (Intro, Let Your Feelings Show, System of Survival, Saturday Night, Africano, Star, Faces), Kali (reprise), Mega Mix, September, Shining Star, Gratitude

**SETTING** New York City, now. A dance musical presented in two acts.

**SYNOPSIS** A modern day version of *The Red Shoes* using the music of the pop group Earth Wind and Fire, *Hot Feet* tells the story of Kalimba, a beautiful young dancer, who gets involved in a Faustian bargain when she is persuaded to dance in a pair of enchanted red shoes.

\*Succeeded by Mel Johnson, Jr.

*Anne Duquesnay and Vivian Nixon  (photos by Paul Kolnik)*

*Michael Balderrama and Chuck Cooper*

# JERSEY BOYS

August Wilson Theatre; First Preview: October 4, 2005; Opening Night: November 6, 2005; 38 previews, 655 performances as of May 31, 2007

Book by Marshall Brickman and Rick Elice, music by Bob Gaudio, lyrics by Bob Crewe; Produced by Dodger Theatricals (Michael David, Edward Strong, Rocco Landesman, Des McAnuff), Joseph J. Grano, Pelican Group, Tamara Kinsella and Kevin Kinsella, in association with Latitude Link, Rick Steiner and Osher/Staton/Bell/Mayerson Group; Director, Des McAnuff; Choreography, Sergio Trujillo; Musical Director, Vocal Arrangements/Incidental Music, Ron Melrose; Sets, Klara Zieglerova; Costumes, Jess Goldstein; Lighting, Howell Binkley; Sound, Steve Canyon Kennedy; Projections, Michael Clark; Hair/Wigs, Charles LaPointe; Fight Director, Steve Rankin; PSM, Richard Hester; Orchestrations, Steve Orich; Music Coordinator, John Miller; Technical Supervisor, Peter Fulbright; Casting, Tara Rubin (East), Sharon Bialy, Sherry Thomas (West); Company Manager, Sandra Carlson; Associate Producers, Lauren Mitchell, and Rhoda Mayerson; Executive Producer, Sally Campbell Morse; Promotions, HHC Marketing; Stage Manager, Michelle Bosch; ASM, Michael T. Clarkston; Dialect Coach, Stephen Gabis; Dance Captain/Fight Captain, Peter Gregus; Music Technical Design, Deborah Hurwitz; Associate General Manager, Jennifer F. Vaughan; Marketing, Dodger Marketing; Advertising, Serino Coyne Inc.; Press, Boneau/Bryan-Brown, Susanne Tighe, Heath Schwartz; Cast recording: Rhino R2 73271

**CAST** French Rap Star/Detective #1/Hal Miller/Barry Belson/Police Officer/Davis **Tituss Burgess**[\*1]; Stanley/Hank Majewski/Crewe's PA/Joe Long **Steve Gouveia**[\*2]; Bob Crewe/others **Peter Gregus**; Tommy DeVito **Christian Hoff**; Nick DeVito/Stosh/Billy Dixon/Norman Waxman/Charlie Calello/others **Donnie Kehr**; Joey/Recording Studio Engineer/others **Michael Longoria**; Gyp De Carlo/others **Mark Lotito**; Mary Delgado/Angel/others **Jennifer Naimo**; Church Lady/Miss Frankie Nolan/Bob's Party Girl/Angel/Lorraine/others **Erica Piccininni**; Bob Gaudio **Daniel Reichard**; Frankie's Mother/Nick's Date/Angel/Francine/others **Sara Schmidt**; Nick Massi **J. Robert Spencer**; Frankie Valli **John Lloyd Young**; Thugs **Ken Dow, Joe Payne**; Swings **Heather Ferguson, John Leone, Dominic Nolfi, Matthew Scott**

**UNDERSTUDIES**[\*3] Steve Gouveia[\*2] (Bob Gaudio, Nick Massi), Donnie Kehr (Gyp De Carlo, Tommy DeVito), John Leone (Gyp De Carlo, Nick Massi, Tommy DeVito, Bob Crewe), Michael Longoria (Frankie Valli), Dominic Nolfi (Bob Gaudio, Frankie Valli, Tommy DeVito, Joey), Matthew Scott (Tommy DeVito, Frankie Valli, Bob Gaudio)

*Daniel Reichard, John Lloyd Young, Christian Hoff, J. Robert Spencer (photos by Joan Marcus)*

**MUSICIANS** Ron Melrose (Conductor/keyboards), Deborah Hurwitz (Associate Conductor/keyboards), Stephen "Hoops" Snyder (keyboards), Joe Payne (guitars), Ken Dow (bass), Kevin Dow (drums), Matt Hong and Ben Kono (reeds), David Spier (trumpet)

**MUSICAL NUMBERS** Ces Soirées-La (Oh What a Night), Silhouettes, You're the Apple of My Eye, I Can't Give You Anything But Love, Earth Angel, Sunday Kind of Love, My Mother's Eyes, I Go Ape, (Who Wears) Short Shorts, I'm in the Mood for Love/Moody's Mood for Love, Cry for Me, An Angel Cried, I Still Care, Trance, Sherry, Big Girls Don't Cry, Walk Like a Man, December, 1963 (Oh What a Night), My Boyfriend's Back, My Eyes Adored You, Dawn (Go Away), Walk Like a Man (reprise), Big Man in Town, Beggin', Stay, Let's Hang On (To What We've Got), Opus 17 (Don't You Worry 'Bout Me), Bye Bye Baby, C'mon Marianne, Can't Take My Eyes Off of You, Working My Way Back to You, Fallen Angel, Rag Doll, Who Loves You

**SETTING** New Jersey, New York, and across the U.S., 1950s–now. A new musical presented in two acts. For original production credits see *Theatre World* Volume 62, page 34. World Premiere produced by La Jolla Playhouse, October 5, 2004.

**SYNOPSIS** "How did four blue-collar kids become one of the greatest successes in pop music history? You ask four guys, you get four different answers." *Jersey Boys* is the story of the legendary Four Seasons, blue-collar boys who formed a singing group and reached the heights of rock 'n' roll stardom.

*Succeeded by: 1. Kris Coleman 2. Colin Donnell 3. Additional: Travis Cloer (Frankie Valli, Joey)

*Christian Hoff, J. Robert Spencer, John Lloyd Young, Steve Gouveia, Peter Gregus, and Daniel Reichard*

# THE LIEUTENANT OF INISHMORE

Lyceum Theatre; First Preview: April 18, 2006; Opening Night: May 3, 2006; Closed September 3, 2006; 16 previews, 142 performances

Written by Martin McDonagh; Produced by Randall L. Wreghitt, Dede Harris, Atlantic Theater Company (Neil Pepe, Artistic Director; Andrew D. Hamingson, Managing Director), David Lehrer, Harriet Newman Leve & Ron Nicynski, Zavelson Meyrelles Greiner Group, Mort Swinsky & Redfern Goldman Productions, and Ruth Hendel; Director, Wilson Milam; Set, Scott Pask; Costumes, Theresa Squire; Lighting, Michael Chybowski; Sound, Obadiah Eaves; Music, Matt McKenzie; Arrangements, Andrew Ranken; Casting, Pat McCorkle; Fight Director, J. David Brimmer; Dialect Coach, Stephen Gabis; PSM, James Harker; Stage Manager, Freda Farrell; Production Management, Aurora Productions; General Management, Richards/Climan Inc.; Associate Producer, Braun-McFarlane Productions; Marketing, HHC Marketing; Company Manager, Thom Clay; Assistant to the Director, Nick Leavens; Wigs, Charles LaPointe; Fight Captain, Jeff Binder; Associate Set, Nancy Thun; Assistant Design: Nancy Thun (set), Renee Mariotti (costumes), Dale Knoth (lighting), Ryan Powers (sound); Production: Adam Braunstein (head carpenter), Paul Wimmer (advance carpenter), William Rowland (head electrician), Jenny Montgomery (production sound), Anmaree Rodibaugh (properties supervisor), Leah Nelson (head props), Nancy Schaefer (wardrobe supervisor), Heather Richmond Wright (hair supervisor), Laura Koch & Cathy Prager (props), Edmund Harrison (dresser); Prop Shopper, Peter Sarafin; Casting Associate, Kelly Gillespie; Casting Assistant, Joe Lopick; Production Assistant, Kristen Lake; Advertising, SpotCo; Press, Boneau/Bryan Brown, Susanne Tighe, Heath Schwartz

Brian d'Arcy James, Andrew Connolly, Dashiell Eaves
(photos by Monique Carboni)

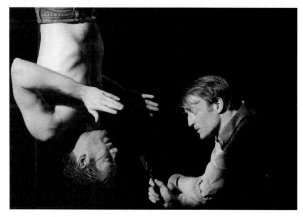

David Wilmot and Alison Pill

**CAST** Davey **Domhnall Gleeson**[1]; Donny **Peter Gerety**; Padraic **David Wilmot**[2]; James **Jeff Binder**[3]; Mairead **Alison Pill**; Christy **Andrew Connolly**; Joey **Dashiell Eaves**; Brendan **Brian d'Arcy James**[4]

**UNDERSTUDIES** John Ahlin (Donny, Christy), Brian Avers (Davey, Padraic, James, Christy, Joey), Cristin Milioti (Mairead), Jordan Bridges (Brendan)

**SETTING** 1993 on the island of Inishmore, County Galway, Ireland. Off-Broadway transfer of a comedy presented in two acts. Originally presented at the Atlantic Theater Company February 27, 2006. The play was originally produced at the Royal Shakespeare Company, Stratford, England, in June 2002.

**SYNOPSIS** Described as Monty Python meets Quentin Tarantino, this wicked black comedy is about a ruthless, violent Irish liberation army enforcer and the one thing he loves more than anything…his black cat. Shocking, gory, yet farcical and hilarious, the play examines the absurdity of political and gun violence in our society.

*Succeeded by: 1. Jerzy Gwiazdowski 2. Christopher Denham 3. Jordan Bridges 4. Andrew Connolly

Left: *Jeff Binder and David Wilmot*

# THE LIGHT IN THE PIAZZA

Vivian Beaumont Theatre; First Preview: March 17, 2005; Opening Night: April 18, 2005; Closed July 2, 2006; 36 previews, 504 performances

Book by Craig Lucas, music and lyrics by Adam Guettel, based on the novel by Elizabeth Spencer; Produced by Lincoln Center Theater (André Bishop, Artistic Director; Bernard Gersten, Executive Producer) by arrangement with Turner Entertainment Co., owner of the original motion picture "Light in the Piazza;" Director, Bartlett Sher; Set, Michael Yeargan; Costumes, Catherine Zuber; Lighting, Christopher Akerlind; Sound, Acme Sound Partners; Orchestrations, Ted Sperling and Adam Guettel; Casting, Janet Foster; Stage Manager, Thom Widmann; Musical Theater Associate Producer, Ira Weitzman; General Manager, Adam Siegel; Production Manager, Jeff Hamlin; Development, Hattie K. Jutagir; Marketing, Linda Mason Ross; Company Manager, Josh Lowenthal; Assistant Company Manager, Jessica Perlmeter Cochrane; Assistant Director, Sarna Lapine; Assistant to Mr. Lucas, Troy Miller; ASM, Claudia Lynch; Dance Captain, Laura Griffith; Associate Sound, Jeffrey Yoshi Lee; Assistant Design: Mikiko Suzuki (set), David Newell, Michael Zecker (costumes), Michael J. Spadaro (lighting); Associate Orchestrations, Bruce Coughlin; Properties, Christopher Schneider; Dialect Coach, Ralph Zito; Hair/Wigs, Jerry Altenburg; Production: Marc Salzberg (soundman), Bruce Rubin (light board), Victor Seastone (moving lights), Lynn Bowling (wardrobe supervisor), Lazaro Arencibia (hair supervisor), Cathy Cline, Virginia Neininger, Liam O'Brien, Jerome Parker, Sarah Rochford, Jane Rottenbach (dressers), Mary Micari, Alice Ramos (hair assistants); Music Copyist, Emily Grishman Music Preparation, Katherine Edmonds; Musical Coordinator, Seymour Red Press; Poster Art, James McMullan; Advertising, Serino Coyne Inc.; Press, Philip Rinaldi; Cast recording: Nonesuch Records, 79829-2

**CAST** Margaret Johnson **Victoria Clark\*;** Clara Johnson, her daughter **Katie Clark;** Fabrizio Naccarelli **Aaron Lazar;** Signor Naccarelli, Fabrizio's father **Chris Sarandon;** Giuseppe Naccarelli, Fabrizio's brother **Michael Berresse;** Franca Naccarelli, Giuseppe's wife **Sarah Uriarte Berry;** Signora Naccarelli, Fabrizio's mother **Patti Cohenour\*;** Roy Johnson. Margaret's husband **Beau Gravitte;** Tour Guide **Felicity LaFortune;** Priest **Joseph Siravo;** Ensemble **David Bonanno, David Burnham, Laura Griffith, Prudence Wright Holmes, Jennifer Hughes, Felicity LaFortune, Michel Moinot, Joseph Siravo;** Swings **Adam Overett, Peter Samuel**

*Kelli O'Hara and Aaron Lazar (photos by Joan Marcus)*

*Victoria Clark (seated) and Katie Clarke*

**UNDERSTUDIES** Glenn Seven Allen (Priest), David Bonanno (Giuseppe Naccarelli), David Burnham (Fabrizio Naccarelli), Patti Cohenour (Margaret Johnson), Laura Griffith (Franca Naccarelli), Jennifer Hughes (Clara Johnson), Felicity LaFortune (Signora Naccarelli), Catherine LaValle (Tour Guide), Joseph Siravo (Roy Johnson, Signor Naccarelli)

**ORCHESTRA** Ted Sperling (Conductor), Dan Riddle (Associate Conductor, piano, celesta), Christian Hebel (Concertmaster), Matthew Lehmann, Sylvia D'Avanzo, James Tsao, Lisa Matricardi, Katherine Livolsi-Stern (violin), Peter Sachon, Ariane Lallemand (celli), Victoria Drake (harp), Richard Heckman (clarinet/English horn/ oboe), Gili Sharett (bassoon), Willard Miller (percussion), Andrew Schwartz (guitar/mandolin)

**MUSICAL NUMBERS** Statues and Stories, The Beauty Is, Il Mondo Era Vuoto, Passeggiata, The Joy You Feel, Dividing Day, Hysteria, Say It Somehow, Aiutami, The Light in the Piazza, Octet, Tirade, Octet (reprise), The Beauty Is (reprise), Let's Walk, Love to Me, Fable

**SETTING** Florence and Rome in the summer of 1953, with occasional side trips to America. A new musical presented in two acts. For original production credits see *Theatre World* Volume 61, page 71. World premiere at the Intiman Theatre Company and The Goodman Theatre; developed with the assistance of The Sundance Theatre Laboratory.

**SYNOPSIS** Margaret and Clara Johnson, A North Carolinian mother and daughter, are traveling through Italy in the summer of 1953, and Clara finds romance with a handsome, high-spirited Florentine, Fabrizio. Margaret's determined efforts to keep the two apart and hide Clara's secret from him and his family are not enough to thwart their true love.

\* Patti Cohenour played Margaret at select Friday evening and Saturday matinee performances. Diane Sutherland played Signora Naccarelli at those performances.

# THE LION KING

Minskoff Theatre; First Preview: October 15, 1997; Opening Night: November 13, 1997; 33 previews, 4,005 performances as of May 31, 2007

Music by Elton John, lyrics by Tim Rice, additional music and lyrics by Lebo M, Mark Mancina, Jay Rifkin, Julie Taymor, Hans Zimmer; book by Roger Allers and Irene Mecchi, adapted from screenplay by Ms. Mecchi, Jonathan Roberts and Linda Woolverton; Produced by Walt Disney Theatrical Productions, Peter Schneider, Thomas Schumacher; Director, Julie Taymor; Choreography, Garth Fagan; Orchestrations, Robert Elhai, David Metzger, Bruce Fowler; Music Director, Karl Jurman; Sets, Richard Hudson; Costumes/Masks/Puppets, Julie Taymor; Lighting, Donald Holder; Masks/Puppets, Michael Curry; Sound, Steve Canyon Kennedy; Hair/Makeup, Michael Ward; Associate Director, John Stefaniuk Production Dance Supervisor, Marey Griffith; Associate Producers, Todd Lacy, Aubrey Lynch II; Technical Director, David Benken; General Manager, Alan Levey; Project Manager, Nina Essman; PSM, Theresa Bailey; Production Supervisor, Doc Zorthian; Senior Production Manager, Anne Quart; Associate Music Producer, Robert Elhai; Stage Managers, Carmen I. Abrazado, Victoria A. Epstein, Antonia Gianino, Ron Vodicka; Company Manager, Thomas Schlenk; Assistant CM, Michael Height; Resident Director, Brian Hill; Resident Dance Supervisor, Ruthlyn Salomons; Executive Music Producer, Chris Montan; Fight Captain, Steven Evan Washington; Vocal Arrangements, Lebo M; Music Coordinator, Michael Keller; Casting, Jay Binder; Press, Boneau/Bryan-Brown; Cast recording: Walt Disney 60802-7

**CAST** Rafiki **Tshidi Manye;** Mufasa **Alton Fitzgerald White;** Sarabi **Jean Michelle Grier;** Zazu **Tony Freeman**[\*1]; Scar **Patrick Page**[\*2]; Young Simba **Justin Martin** or **Jarrell J. Singleton**[\*3]; Young Nala **Ashley Renee Jordan** or **Alex de Castro**[\*4]; Shenzi **Bonita J. Hamilton;** Banzai **Benjamin Sterling Cannon;** Ed **Enrique Segura;** Timon **Danny Rutigliano;** Pumbaa **Tom Alan Robbins**[\*5]; Simba **Josh Tower;** Nala **Kissy Simmons;** Singers[\*6] **Alvin Crawford, Lindiwe Dlamini, Bongi Duma, Andrea Frierson, Jean Michelle Grier, Michael Alexander Henry, Joel Karie, Keswa, Ron Kunene, Sheryl McCallum, S'bu Ngema, Mpume Sikakane, Rema Webb, Kenny Redell Williams, Kyle Wrentz;** Dancers[\*7] **Kristina Michelle Bethel, Kylin Brady, Camille M. Brown, Michelle Aguilar Camaya, Gabriel A. Croom, Vincent Cuny, Alicia Fisher, Gregory A. King, Lisa Lewis, Ray Mercer, Brandon Christopher O'Neal, Ryan Brooke Taylor, Steven Evan Washington;** Swings **Garland Days, Angelica Edwards, Ian Yuri Gardner, Tony James, Dennis Johnston, Cornelius Jones, Jr., Jennifer Harrison Newman, Dawn Noel Pignuola, Sophia N. Stephens, Torya**

**UNDERSTUDIES/SWINGS** John E. Brady (Zazu, Timon, Pumbaa), Kylin Brady (Nala), Camille M. Brown (Sarabi), Alvin Crawford (Mufasa), Garland Days (Banzai), Angelica Edwards (Rafiki, Shenzi), Tony Freeman (Scar), Ian Yuri Gardner (Banzai, Ed), Michael Alexander Henry (Mufasa), Dennis Johnston (Ed, Simba), Cornelius Jones, Jr. (Banzai, Ed, Simba), Joel Karie (Simba), Jack Koenig (Scar, Pumbaa), Sheryl McCallum (Rafiki, Sarabi), Enrique Segura (Zazu, Timon), Mpume Sikakane (Rafiki), Sophia A. Stephens (Shenzi, Nala), Rema Webb (Rafiki, Shenzi, Nala), Kenny Redell Williams (Banzai)

**ORCHESTRA** Karl Jurman (Conductor); Cherie Rosen (Associate Conductor/keyboards), Ted Baker, Paul Ascenzo (synthesizers); David Weiss, Bob Keller (woodwinds); Francisca Mendoza (Concertmaster); Krystof Witek, Avril Brown (violins); Ralph Farris (violin/viola); Eliana Mendoza, Bruce Wang (cellos); Alexander Cook, Katie Dennis, Greg Smith (French horns); Rock Ciccarone (trombone); George Flynn (bass trombone/tuba); Tom Barney (bass); Tommy Igoe (Assistant Conductor/drums); Kevin Kuhn (Guitar); Rolando Morales-Matos (Assistant Conductor/percussion), Valerie Dee Naranjo (percussion/mallets); Junior "Gabu" Wedderburn (percussion)

*The Giraffes from The Lion King (photos by Joan Marcus)*

**MUSICAL NUMBERS** Circle of Life, Morning Report, I Just Can't Wait to Be King, Chow Down, They Live in You, Be Prepared, Hakuna Matata, One by One, Madness of King Scar, Shadowland, Endless Night, Can You Feel the Love Tonight, King of Pride Rock/Finale

A musical presented in two acts. For original production credits see *Theatre World* Volume 54, page 20. Originally opened at the New Amsterdam Theatre and transferred to the Minskoff Theatre June 13, 2006.

**SYNOPSIS** Based on the Disney animated feature film, *The Lion King* tells the story of the epic adventures of a young lion cub named Simba as he struggles to accept the responsibilities of adulthood and his destined role as king.

*Succeeded by: 1. Jeff Binder, Tony Freeman 2. Derek Smith, Patrick Page 3. Christian A. Phenix, Julian Ivey, Shavar McIntosh 4. India, Halley Vargas Sullivan 5. Bob Amaral, Tom Alan Robbins 6. Kyle R. Banks, André Jackson, Meena T. Jahi, Selloane A. Nkhela 7. Christopher Freeman, Dennis Lue, Natalie Ridley, Angelo Rivera, Phillip W. Turner

*Kissy Simmons and Company*

# MAMMA MIA!

Winter Garden Theatre; First Preview: October 5, 2001; Opening Night: October 18, 2001; 14 previews, 2,366 performances as of May 31, 2007

Book by Catherine Johnson, music, lyrics, and orchestrations by Benny Andersson, Björn Ulvaeus, some songs with Stig Anderson; Produced by Judy Craymer, Richard East and Björn Ulvaeus for Littlestar Services Limited, in association with Universal Music Group; Director, Phyllida Lloyd; Choreography, Anthony Van Laast; Set/Costumes, Mark Thompson; Lighting, Howard Harrison; Sound, Andrew Bruce & Bobby Aitken; Musical Supervision, Additional Materials and Orchestrations, Martin Koch; Wigs, Paul Huntley; Musical Coordination, Michael Keller; Resident Director, Martha Banta; Associate Choreographer, Nichola Treherne; Dance Supervisor/Captain, Janet Rothermel; Associate Musical Director, David Holcenberg; Associate Design: Nancy Thun (U.S. set), Jonathan Allen (U.K. set), Lucy Gaiger & Scott Traugott (costumes), Josh Marquette (hair), David Holmes, Ed McCarthy, Andrew Voller (lighting), Brian Beasley, David Patridge (sound); Production Manager, Arthur Siccardi; General Manager, Nina Lannan; Associate General Manager/Company Manager, Rina L. Saltzman; Assistant Company Manager, Liza Garcia; International Executive Producer, Andrew Treagus Associates Limited; PSM, Andrew Fenton; Stage Managers, Sherry Cohen, Charlene Speyerer; Casting, Tara Rubin; Music Coordinator, Michael Keller; Transcription, Anders Neglin; Synthesizer Programmer, Nicholas Gilpin; Press, Boneau/Bryan-Brown; London Cast recording: Polydor 543 115 2

*Samantha Eggers, Carey Anderson, and Veronica J, Kuehn*

**CAST** Sophie Sheridan **Carey Anderson;** Ali **Olivia Oguma**[1]; Lisa **Samantha Eggers;** Tanya **Judy McLane;** Rosie **Olga Merediz**[2]; Donna Sheridan **Leah Hocking**[3]; Sky **Andy Kelso;** Pepper **Ben Gettinger;** Eddie **Raymond J. Lee**[4]; Harry Bright **David Beach**[5]; Bill Austin **Mark L. Montgomery**[6]; Sam Carmicheal **John Dossett**[7]; Father Alexandrios **Brian Scott Johnson;** Ensemble[8] **Meredith Akins, Brent Black, Angela Ara Brown, Isaac Calpito, Christopher Carl, Meghann Dreyfuss, Shakiem Evans, Lori Haley Fox, Bryan Scott Johnson, Erika Mansfield, Corrine Melançon, Steve Morgan, Megan Osterhaus Joi Danielle Price, Sandy Rosenberg, Gerard Salvador, Britt Shubow, Leah Zepel;** Swings **Lanene Charters, Matthew Farver, Ryan Sander, Collette Simmons**

**UNDERSTUDIES** Meredith Akins (Lisa), Brent Black (Bill, Sam, Father Alexandrios), Angela Ara Brown (Ali), Isaac Calpito (Pepper),Christopher Carl (Harry, Bill, Sam, Father Alexandrios), Meghann Dreyfuss (Sophie), Samantha Eggers (Sophie), Shakiem Evans (Eddie), Matthew Farver (Eddie, Father Alexandrios), Lori Haley Fox (Tanya, Donna, Rosie), Bryan Scott Johnson (Harry, Bill, Sam), Corrine Melançon (Tanya, Donna), Steve Morgan (Sky), Joi Danielle Price (Ali), Sandy Rosenberg (Rosie), Gerard Salvador (Pepper), Ryan Sander (Sky, Pepper), Britt Shubow (Sophie, Lisa), Leah Zepel (Ali)

**ORCHESTRA** Wendy Bobbitt Cavett (Conductor/keyboard); Rob Preuss (Associate Conductor/keyboard 3); Steve Marzullo (keyboard 2); Myles Chase (keyboard 4); Doug Quinn, Jeff Campbell (guitars); Paul Adamy (bass); Ray Marchica (drums); David Nyberg (percussion)

**MUSICAL NUMBERS** Chiquitita, Dancing Queen, Does Your Mother Know?, Gimme! Gimmie! Gimmie!, Honey, Honey, I Do, I Do, I Do, I Do, I Have a Dream, Knowing Me Knowing You, Lay All Your Love on Me, Mamma Mia, Money Money Money, One of Us, Our Last Summer, Slipping Through My Fingers, S.O.S., Super Trouper, Take a Chance on Me, Thank You For the Music, The Name of the Game, The Winner Takes All, Under Attack, Voulez-Vous

**SETTING** A wedding weekend. A tiny Greek island. A musical presented in two acts. For original production credits see *Theatre World* Volume 58, page 27.

**SYNOPSIS** Songs of the 1970s group ABBA strung together tell the story of baby boomer wistfulness and a girl's search for her unknown father.

*Succeeded by: 1. Veronica J. Kuehn 2. Gina Ferrall (10/25/06) 3. Carolee Carmello (9/27/06) 4. Michael James Scott, Raymond Lee 5. Michael Mastro (10/25/06) 6. Bryan Scott Johnson, Pearce Bunting (10/25/06) 7. David McDonald 8. Timothy Booth, Jen Burleigh-Bentz, Allyson Carr, Jon-Erik Goldberg, Joelle Graham, Frankie James Grande, Lori Hammel, Monica Kapoor, Courtney Reed, Amina Robinson, Laurie Wells*

*Andy Kelso and Carey Anderson (photos by Joan Marcus)*

# MONTY PYTHON'S SPAMALOT

Shubert Theatre; First Preview: February 14, 2004; Opening Night: March 17, 2005; 34 previews, 910 performances as of May 31, 2007

Book and lyrics by Eric Idle, music by John DuPrez and Eric Idle; based on the screenplay of the motion picture *Monty Python and the Holy Grail* by Eric Idle, John Cleese, Terry Gilliam, Terry Jones, Michael Palin and Graham Chapman; Produced by Boyett Ostar Productions, The Shubert Organization, Arielle Tepper, Stephanie McClelland, Lawrence Horowitz, Élan V. McAllister, Allan S. Gordon, Independent Presenters Network, Roy Furman, GRS Associates, Jam Theatricals, TGA Entertainment Ltd., Clear Channel Entertainment; Associate Producer, Randi Grossman, Tisch/Avnet Financial; Director, Mike Nichols; Choreography, Casey Nicholaw; Sets and Costumes, Tim Hatley; Lighting, Hugh Vanstone; Sound, Acme Sound Partners; Hair/Wigs, David Brian Brown; Special Effects, Gregory Meeh; Projections, Elaine J. McCarthy; Music Director/Vocal Arrangements, Todd Ellison; Orchestrations, Larry Hochman; Music Arrangements, Glen Kelly; Music Coordinator, Michael Keller; Casting, Tara Rubin; Associate Director, Peter Lawrence; PSM, Mahlon Kruse; Associate Choreography, Darlene Wilson; General Management, 101 Productions Ltd. Marketing, HHC Marketing; Company Management, Elie Landau, Steven Lukens; Production Management, Aurora Productions/Gene O'Donovan; Fight Director, David DeBesse; Makeup, Joseph A. Campayno; Stage Management, Jim Woolley, Sheri K. Turner, Chad Lewis; Dance Captain, Pamela Remler, Scott Taylor/Lee Wilkins; Fight Captain, Greg Reuter; Vocal Coach, Kate Wilson; Magic Consultant, Marshall Magoon; Puppetry Consultant, Michael Curry; Music Copying, Emily Grishman; Advertising, Serino Coyne Inc.; Press, Boneau/Bryan-Brown; Cast recording: Decca Broadway B0004265-02

*Michael McGrath and Jonathan Hadary (photos by Joan Marcus)*

**CAST** Historian/Not Dead Fred/French Guard,/Minstrel/Prince Herbert **Christian Borle**[*1]; Mayor/Patsy/Guard 2 **Michael McGrath;** King Arthur **Harry Groener**[*2]; Sir Robin/Guard 1/Brother Maynard **Martin Moran;** Sir Lancelot/The French Taunter/Knight of Ni/Tim the Enchanter **Steve Kazee**[*3]; Sir Dennis Galahad/The Black Knight/Prince Herbert's Father **Christopher Sieber**[*4]; Dennis' Mother/Sir Bedevere/Concorde **Steve Rosen**[*5]; The Lady of the Lake **Lauren Kennedy**[*6]; Sir Not Appearing/Monk **Kevin Covert;** Nun **Brian Shepard;** God **John Cleese;** French Guards **Thomas Cannizzaro, Greg Reuter;** Minstrels **Brad Bradley, Asmeret Ghebremichael**[*7], **Greg Reuter;** Sir Bors **Brad Bradley;** Ensemble **Brad Bradley, Thomas Cannizzaro, Kevin Covert, Jennifer Frankel, Lisa Gajda**[*8], **Asmeret Ghebremichael**[*7], **Kristie Kerwin**[*9], **Abbey O'Brien**[*10], **Ariel Reid**[*11], **Greg Reuter, Brian Shepard, Scott Taylor;** Swings[*12] **Beth Johnson, Pamela Remler, Rick Spaans, Lee A. Wilkins**

**STANDBYS/UNDERSTUDIES** Standbys: Drew McVety[*13], (Arthur, Lancelot, Galahad, Robin, Bedevere), James Ludwig (Robin, Bedevere, Patsy, Historian, Not Dead Fred, Prince Herbert, Lancelot), Rosena M. Hill[*14], (Lady of the Lake); Understudies: Brad Bradley, Thomas Cannizzaro, Jenny Hill, Asmeret Ghebremichael[*7], Greg Reuter, Brian Shepard

**ORCHESTRA** Todd Ellison (Conductor), Ethyl Will (Associate Conductor, keyboard), Ann Labin (Concertmaster), Maura Giannini & Ming Yeh (violins), Richard Brice (viola), Diane Barere (cello), Ken Dybisz and Alden Banta (reeds), John Chudoba (lead trumpet), Anthony Gorruso (trumpet), Mark Patterson (trombone), Zohar Schondorf (French horn), Antony Geralis (keyboard 2), Scott Kuney (guitars), Dave Kuhn (bass), Sean McDaniel (drums), Dave Mancuso (percussion)

**MUSICAL NUMBERS** Fisch Schlapping Song, King Arthur's Song, I Am Not Dead Yet, Come With Me, The Song That Goes Like This, All for One, Knights of

*The Ladies of Spamalot*

the Round Table, The Song That Goes Like This (reprise), Find Your Grail, Run Away, Always Look on the Bright Side of Life, Brave Sir Robin, You Won't Succeed on Broadway, The Diva's Lament, Where Are You?, Here Are You, His Name Is Lancelot, I'm All Alone, The Song That Goes Like This (reprise), The Holy Grail, Find Your Grail Finale—Medley

A new musical presented in two acts. For original production credits see *Theatre World* Volume 61, page 55.

**SYNOPSIS** Telling the legendary tale of King Arthur and the Knights of the Round Table, and their quest for the Holy Grail, *Monty Python's Spamalot* features a chorus line of dancing divas and knights, flatulent Frenchmen, killer rabbits, and one legless knight.

*Succeeded by: 1. Tom Deckman 2. Jonathan Hadary (10/31/06) 3. Chris Hoch (10/3/06), Rick Holmes 4. Lewis Cleale (7/5/06), Christopher Sieber (5/10/07) 5. Jeff Dattilo, Jeffrey Kuhn 6. Marin Mazzie (10/31/06) 7. Emily Hsu 8. Amy Heggins 9. Jenny Hill 10. Vanessa Sonon 11. Brandi Wooten 12. Additional: Lindsay Lopez 13. Anthony Holds, Chris Hoch 14. Napiera Groves

# THE ODD COUPLE

Brooks Atkinson Theatre; First Preview: October 4, 2005; Opening Night: October 27, 2005; Closed June 4, 2006; 28 previews, 249 performances

Written by Neil Simon; Produced by Ira Pittelman, Jeffrey Sine, Ben Sprecher, Max Cooper, Scott E. Nederlander, and Emanuel Azenberg; Director, Joe Mantello; Set, John Lee Beatty; Costumes, Ann Roth; Lighting, Kenneth Posner; Sound, Peter Fitzgerald; Original Music, Marc Shaiman; Casting, Bernard Telsey Casting; Hair, David Brian Brown; Production Supervisor, William Joseph Barnes; PSM, Jill Cordle; Stage Manager, Richard Costabile; Technical Supervisor, Brian Lynch, Neil A. Mazzella; Associate Producers, Roy Furman and Jay Binder; General Manager, Abbie M. Strassler; Company Manager, John E. Gendron; Assistant Director, Lisa Leguillou; Production Supervisor, William Joseph Barnes; Props, Chuck Dague; Makeup, Angelina Avallone; Associate Set, Eric Renschler; Associate Lighting, Philip Rosenberg; Associate Sound, Jill B.C. DuBoff; Production: Manuel Becker (electrician), Wallace Flores (sound), George Wagner (props), Douglas C. Petitjean (wardrobe supervisor), Ken Brown (Mr. Lane's dresser), Mark Trezza (Mr. Broderick's dresser), Maura Clifford, Cesar Porto (dressers), Carmel Vargyas (hair supervisor); Advertising, Serino Coyne Inc./Angelo Desimini; Press, Bill Evans and Associates, Jim Randolph

**CAST** Speed **Rob Bartlett;** Murray **Mike Starr;** Roy **Peter Frechette;** Vinnie **Lee Wilkof;** Oscar Madison **Nathan Lane;** Felix Ungar **Matthew Broderick;** Gwendolyn Pigeon **Olivia d'Abo;** Cecily Pigeon **Jessica Stone**

**UNDERSTUDIES** Rob Bartlett (Oscar), Peter Frechette (Felix), Gene Gabriel (Murray, Oscar, Roy, Speed, Vinnie), Marc Grapey (Felix, Murray, Roy, Speed, Vinnie), Christy Pusz (Cecily, Gwendolyn)

**SETTING** Oscar Madison's Riverside Drive apartment. Summer 1965. A comedy in three acts and four scenes presented with one intermission. Originally produced on Broadway at the Plymouth Theatre and later the Eugene O'Neill Theatre, March 10, 1965, running 966 performances (see *Theatre World* Volume 21, page 84). A revised "female version" of the play was produced at the Broadhurst Theatre, June 11, 1985 (see *Theatre World* Volume 42, page 6).

**SYNOPSIS** In one of Neil Simon's most popular comedies, two divorced men, sportswriter/slob Oscar Madison and fastidious photographer Felix Unger share an apartment with hilarious results.

*Nathan Lane and Matthew Broderick (photos by Carol Rosegg)*

*Nathan Lane, Lee Wilkof, Rob Bartlett, Matthew Broderick, Brad Garrett, and Peter Frechette*

# THE PAJAMA GAME

American Airlines Theatre; First Preview: January 27, 2006; Opening Night: March 2, 2006; Closed June 17, 2006; 41 previews, 129 performances

Book by George Abbott and Richard Bissell, music and lyrics by Richard Adler and Jerry Ross, based on the novel *7½ Cents* by Richard Bissell, book revised by Peter Ackerman; Produced by the Roundabout Theatre Company (Todd Haimes, Artistic Director; Harold Wolpert, Managing Director; Julia C. Levy, Executive Director) with special arrangement with Jeffrey Richards, James Fuld, Jr., and Scott Landis; Director and Choreographer, Kathleen Marshall; Musical Supervisor/Vocal & Dance Arrangements, David Chase; Orchestrations, Dick Lieb & Danny Troob; Set, Derek McLane; Costumes, Martin Pakledinaz; Lighting, Peter Kaczorowski; Sound, Brian Ronan; PSM, David O'Brien; Hair/Wigs, Paul Huntley; Music Coordinator, Seymour Red Press; Casting, Jim Carnahan; Associate Director, Marc Bruni; Associate Choreographer, Musical Director, Rob Berman; Technical Supervisor, Steve Beers; General Manager, Sydney Beers; Founding Director, Gene Feist; Associate Artistic Director, Scott Ellis; Marketing, David B. Steffen; Development, Jeffory Lawson; Company Manager, Denys Baker; ASMs, Stephen R. Gruse, Leslie C. Lyter; Assistant to the Director, Jenny Hogan; Dance Captain, David Eggers; Makeup, Angelina Avallone; Synthesizer Programmer, Andrew Barrett; Associate Design: Shoko Kambara (sets), Karen Spahn (lighting); Advertising, The Eliran Murphy Group; Press, Boneau/Bryan-Brown, Matt Polk, Jessica Johnson, Shanna Marcus; Cast recording: Columbia Records CK 99035

*Kelli O'Hara and the Company (photos by Joan Marcus)*

**CAST** Prez **Peter Benson;** Mae **Joyce Chittick;** Virginia **Bridget Berger;** Charlie **Stephen Berger;** Martha **Kate Chapman;** Brenda **Paula Leggett Chase**; Poopsie **Jennifer Cody;** Lewie **David Eggers;** Cyrus **Michael Halling;** Carmen **Bianca Marroquin;** Jake **Vince Pesce;** Joe **Devin Richards;** Ralph **Jeffrey Schecter;** Shirley **Debra Walton;** Hines **Michael McKean;** Mr. Hasler **Richard Poe;** Gladys **Megan Lawrence;** Mabel **Roz Ryan;** Granzenlicker/Pop **Michael McCormick;** Sid Sorokin **Harry Connick Jr.;** Babe Williams **Kelli O'Hara;** Swings **Michael O'Donnell, Amber Stone**

**UNDERSTUDIES** Bridget Berger (Babe Williams), Stephen Berger (Granzenlicker, Hasler, Pop), Kate Chapman (Mabel), Jennifer Cody (Gladys), Michael Halling (Sid Sorokin), Michael McCormick (Hines), Jeffrey Howard Schecter (Prez), Debra Walton (Mae)

**ORCHESTRA** Rob Berman (Conductor), Chris Fenwick (Associate Conductor/piano), Marilyn Reynolds (violin), Beth Sturdevant (cello), Steven Kenyon, John Winder (reeds), Roger Ingram (trumpet), John Allred, Joe Barati (trombone), Jim Hershman (guitar) Neal Caine (Bass), Paul Pizzuti (drums)

**MUSICAL NUMBERS** Racing With the Clock, A New Town is a Blue Town, I'm Not At All in Love, I'll Never Be Jealous Again, Hey There, Racing With the Clock (reprise), Sleep-Tite, Her Is, Once a Year Day, Her Is (reprise), Small Talk, There Once Was a Man, Hey There (reprise), Steam Heat, The World Around Us, Hey There (reprise), If You Win, You Lose, Think of the Time I Save, Hernando's Hideaway, The Three of Us, 7 1/2 Cents, There Once Was a Man (reprise), The Pajama Game

**SETTING** 1954. The Sleep-Tite Pajama Factory, Cedar Rapids, Iowa. Revival of a musical presented in two acts. Originally produced on Broadway at the St. James Theatre, May 13, 1954 (see *Theatre World* Volume 10, page 100), then transferred to the Schubert Theatre, where it ran for 1063 performances. The show was first revived at the Lunt-Fontanne Theatre on December 9, 1973 for a limited engagement (see *Theatre World* Volume 30, page 26).

**SYNOPSIS** Labor trouble and love go head to head at the Sleep-Tite pajama factory, where worker demands for a seven and a half cent raise are going unheeded. In the midst of a looming strike, an unlikely romance blossoms between Babe Williams, head of the workers' Grievance Committee, and Sid, the new factory superintendent, in this classic musical about love, sex, labor unions, and the workplace.

*Harry Connick Jr. and Kelli O'Hara*

# THE PHANTOM OF THE OPERA

Majestic Theatre; First Preview: January 9, 1988. Opening Night: January 26, 1988; 16 previews, 8,066 performances as of May 31, 2007

Music and book by Andrew Lloyd Webber, lyrics by Charles Hart; additional lyrics and book by Richard Stilgoe; based on the novel by Gaston Leroux; Produced by Cameron Mackintosh and The Really Useful Theatre Company; Director, Harold Prince; Musical Staging/Choreography, Gillian Lynne; Orchestrations, David Cullen, Mr. Lloyd Webber; Design, Maria Björnson; Lighting, Andrew Bridge; Sound, Martin Levan; Original Musical Director and Supervisor, David Caddick; Musical Director, David Lai; Production Supervisor, Peter von Mayrhauser; Casting, Tara Rubin; Original Casting, Johnson-Liff Associates; General Manager, Alan Wasser; Production Dance Supervisor, Denny Berry; Associate Musical Supervisor, Kristen Blodgette; Associate General Manager, Allan Williams; Technical Production Managers, John H. Paull III, Jake Bell; Company Manager, Robert Nolan; Stage Managers, Craig Jacobs, Bethe Ward, Brendan Smith; Assistant Company Manager, Chris D'Angelo; Press, The Publicity Office, Marc Thibodeau, Michael S. Borowski, Jeremy Shaffer; London Cast recording: Polydor 831273

*Howard McGillin (photo by Joan Marcus)*

**CAST** The Phantom of the Opera **Howard McGillin**[*1]; Christine Daae **Rebecca Pitcher;** Christine Daae (alternate). **Jennifer Hope Wills**[*2]; Raoul, Vicomte de Chagny **Michael Shawn Lewis**; Carlotta Giudicelli **Patricia Phillips**[*4]; Monsieur Andre **George Lee Andrews**; Monsieur Firmin **David Cryer;** Madame Giry **Marilyn Caskey;** Ubaldo Piangi **Roland Rusinek**; Meg Giry **Heather McFadden;** Monsieur Reyer/Hairdresser **Peter Lockyer**[*5]; Auctioneer **Carrington Vilmont**[*6]; Jeweler (Il Muto) **Frank Mastrone**; Monsieur Lefevre/Firechief **Kenneth Kantor;** Joseph Buquet **Richard Warren Pugh**[*7]; Don Attilio **Gregory Emanuel Rahming;** Passarino **Carrington Vilmont**[*6]; Slave Master/Solo Dancer (alt.) **Daniel Rychlec**[*8]; Flunky/Stagehand/Solo Dancer **Jack Hayes**[*9]; Page **Kris Koop;** Porter/ Fireman **Jimmy Smagula**[*10]; Spanish Lady **Sally Williams;** Wardrobe Mistress/Confidante Mary Leigh Stahl[*11]; Princess **Susan Owen**[*12]; Madame Firmin **Melody Rubie;** Innkeeper's Wife **Wren Marie Harrington;** Marksman **Stephen Buntrock**[*13]; Ballet Chorus of the Opera Populaire[*14] **Dara Adler, Emily Adonna, Julianne Cavendish, Kara Klein, Gianna Loungway, Mabel Modrono, Carly Blake Sebouhian, Dianna Warren;** Ballet Swing **Harriet Clark;** Swings **Michael Babin, Scott Mikita, James Romick, Janet Saia, Julie Schmidt, Jim Weitzer**

**ORCHESTRA** David Caddick, Kristen Blodgette, David Lai, Tim Stella, Norman Weiss (Conductors); Joyce Hammann (Concert Master), Alvin E. Rogers, Gayle Dixon, Kurt Coble, Jan Mullen, Karen Milne (violins); Stephanie Fricker, Veronica Salas (violas); Ted Ackerman, Karl Bennion (cellos); Melissa Slocum (bass); Henry Fanelli (harp); Sheryl Henze, Ed Matthew, Melanie Feld, Matthew Goodman, Atsuko Sato (woodwinds); Lowell Hershey, Francis Bonny (trumpets); William Whitaker (trombone); Daniel Culpepper, Peter Reit, David Smith (French horn); Eric Cohen, Jan Hagiwara (percussion); Tim Stella, Norman Weiss (keyboards)

**MUSICAL NUMBERS** Think of Me, Angel of Music, Little Lotte/The Mirror, Phantom of the Opera, Music of the Night, I Remember/Stranger Than You Dreamt It, Magical Lasso, Notes/Prima Donna, Poor Fool He Makes Me Laugh, Why Have You Brought Me Here?/Raoul I've Been There, All I Ask of You, Masquerade/ Why So Silent?, Twisted Every Way, Wishing You Were Somehow Here Again, Wandering Child/Bravo Bravo, Point of No Return, Down Once More/Track Down This Murderer, Finale

**SETTING** In and around the Paris Opera House, 1881–1911. A musical presented in two acts with nineteen scenes and a prologue. For original production credits see *Theatre World* Volume 44, page 20. The show became the longest running show in Broadway history on January 9, 2006.

**SYNOPSIS** A disfigured musical genius haunts the catacombs beneath the Paris Opera and exerts strange control over a lovely young soprano.

*Succeeded by: 1. Gary Mauer, Howard McGillin 2. Jennifer Hope Wills 3. Julie Hanson, Susan Owen 4. Anne Runolfsson, Julie Schmidt, Patricia Phillips 5. Geoff Packard 6. Jason Mills 7. Stephen Tewksbury, Michael McCoy, Richard Poole 8. Justin Peck, Corbin Popp, Kyle DesChamps 9. Justin Peck, Corbin Popp, Jack Hayes 10. John Wasiniak 11. Tregoney Shepherd, Julie Schmidt, Katie Banks 12. Sara Jean Ford 13. Michael Babin, Paul A. Schaefer 14. Polly Baird, Jessica Radetsky

# THE PRODUCERS

St. James Theatre; First Preview: March 21, 2001; Opening Night: April 19, 2001; Closed April 22, 2007; 33 previews, 2,502 performances

Book by Mel Brooks and Thomas Meehan, music and lyrics by Mel Brooks; based on the 1967 film written and directed by Mel Brooks; Produced by Rocco Landesman, Live Nation, The Frankel-Baruch-Viertel-Routh Group, Bob and Harvey Weinstein, Rick Steiner, Robert F.X. Sillerman and Mel Brooks, in association with James D. Stern/Douglas L. Meyer and by special arrangement with StudioCanal; Director and Choreography, Susan Stroman; Musical Arrangements/Supervision, Glen Kelly; Set, Robin Wagner; Costumes, William Ivey Long; Lighting, Peter Kaczorowski; Sound, Steve Canyon Kennedy; Casting, Tara Rubin; Original Casting, Johnson-Liff Associates; Associate Director/PSM, Steven Zweigbaum; Associate Choreography, Warren Carlyle; Hair/Wigs, Paul Huntley; Musical Director/Vocal Arrangements, Patrick S. Brady; Orchestrations, Douglas Besterman, Larry Blank; Music Coordinator, John Miller; General Manager, Richard Frankel/Laura Green; Technical Supervisor, Juniper Street Productions; Associate Producers, Frederic H. and Rhoda Mayerson, Jennifer Costello; Company Manager, Kathy Lowe; Associate CM, Jackie Newman; Stage Manager, Ira Mont; ASMs, Casey Aileen Rafter, Alexis Shorter; Assistant Director, Scott Bishop; Assistant Choreographer, Lisa Shriver; Resident Choreographer, Courtney Young; Dance Captain, Justin Greer; Advertising, Serino Coyne Inc.; Press, Barlow • Hartman; Cast recording: Sony SK 89646

**CAST** The Usherettes **Christina Marie Norrup, Ashley Yeater** Max Bialystock **John Treacy Egan**[1]; Leo Bloom **Roger Bart**[2]; Hold-me Touch-me **Madeleine Doherty;** Mr. Marks **Kevin Ligon;** Franz Liebkind **Bill Nolte;**

*Lee Roy Reams*

Carmen Ghia **Brad Musgrove;** Roger De Bris **Gary Beach**[3]; Bryan **Peter Marinos;** Kevin **Kevin Ligon;** Scott **Jim Borstelmann;** Shirley **Pamela Dayton**[4]; Ulla **Angie Schworer;** Lick-me Bite-me **Christina Marie Norrup;** Kiss-me Feel-me **Kathy Fitzgerald;** Jack Lepidus **Peter Marinos;** Donald Dinsmore **Jim Borstelmann;** Jason Green **Kevin Ligon;** Lead Tenor **Eric Gunhus;** Sergeant **Kevin Ligon;** O'Rourke **Will Taylor;** O'Riley **Chris Klink;** O'Houlihan **Robert H. Fowler**[5]; Guard **Jim Borstelmann;** Bailiff **Will Taylor;** Judge **Peter Marinos;** Foreman of the Jury **Kathy Fitzgerald;** Trustee **Kevin Ligon;** Ensemble **Jim Borstelmann, Madeleine Doherty, Kathy Fitzgerald, Robert H. Fowler**[5], **Eric Gunhus, Kimberly Hester, Shauna Hoskin, Kimberly Catherine Jones, Renée Klapmeyer**[6], **Chris Klink, Kevin Ligon, Peter Marinos, Christina Marie Norrup, Will Taylor, Wendy Waring, Ashley Yeater;** Swings **Angie C. Creighton, James Gray, Justin Greer, Stacey Todd Holt, Liz McKendry, Jason Patrick Sands, Courtney Young**

*John Tracey Egan and Hunter Foster (photos by Paul Kolnik)*

**ORCHESTRA** Patrick S. Brady (Conductor); David Gursky (Associate Conductor/keyboards); Vincent DellaRocca, Steven J. Greenfield, Jay Hassler, Alva F. Hunt, Frank Santagata (woodwinds); Nick Marchione, Frank Greene, David Rogers (trumpets); Dan Levine, Tim Sessions, Chris Olness (trombones); Nancy Billman (French horn); Rick Dolan (Concert Master); Ashley D. Horne, Louise Owen, Karen M. Karlsrud, Helen Kim (violins); Laura Bontrager (cello); Anna Reinersman (harp); Robert Renino (bass); Larry Lelli (drums); Benjamin Herman (percussion)

**MUSICAL NUMBERS** Opening Night, The King of Broadway, We Can Do It, I Wanna Be a Producer, In Old Bavaria, Der Guten Tag Hop Clop, Keep It Gay, When You Got It Flaunt It, Along Came Bialy, Act One Finale, That Face, Haben Sie Gehoert das Deutsche Band?, You Never Say "Good Luck" on Opening Night, Springtime for Hitler, Where Did We Go Right?, Betrayed, 'Til Him, Prisoners of Love, Leo and Max, Goodbye!

**SETTING** New York City, 1959. A musical comedy presented in two acts. For original production credits see *Theatre World* Volume 57, page 40.

**SYNOPSIS** A theatrical producer and his accountant hatch a sure-fire scheme to make money: raise more cash than you need for a sure-fire Broadway flop entitled *Springtime for Hitler*. Adapted from the 1968 film written by Mel Brooks, *The Producers* is the most awarded show in Broadway history, and a film version of the musical was made in 2005 featuring many of the original cast members, and directed by Susan Stroman.

*Succeeded by: 1. Tony Danza (12/19/06), John Treacy Egan (3/13/07) 2. Hunter Foster (7/27/06), Roger Bart (12/19/06), Hunter Foster (1/23/07) 3. Lee Roy Reams 4. Kathy Fitzgerald 5. Philip Michael Baskerville, Robert H. Fowler 6. Sarrah Strimel

# RENT

Nederlander Theatre; First Preview: April 16, 1996; Opening Night: April 29, 1996; 16 previews, 4,614 performances as of May 31, 2007

Book, music, and lyrics by Jonathan Larson; Produced by Jeffrey Seller, Kevin McCollum, Allan S. Gordon, and New York Theatre Workshop; Director, Michael Greif; Musical Supervision and Additional Arrangements, Tim Weil; Choreography, Marlies Yearby; Set, Paul Clay; Costumes, Angela Wendt; Lighting, Blake Burba; Sound, Kurt Fischer; Original Concept and Additional Lyrics, Billy Aronson; Arrangements, Steve Skinner; Dramaturg, Lynn M. Thompson; Casting, Telsey + Company; Music Director, David Truskinoff; PSM, John Vivian; General Manager, John Corker; Technical Supervision, Unitech Productions Inc.; Company Manager, Nick Kaledin; Film, Tony Gerber; Stage Manager, Crystal Huntington; ASM, Ryan J. Bell; Assistant Director, Martha Banta; Resident Assistant Director, Evan Ensign; Associate Conductor, John Korba; Company Manager Associates, Andrew Jones, Ginger Montel; Wigs/Hair/Make-up, David Santana; Assistant Costumes, Lisa Zinni; Production: Karen Lloyd, Roberta Chistery (wardrobe supervisors), David Santana (hair/makeup supervisor), Richard J. Beck (electrician), Stephen Clem (console), Tom O'Neill, Holli Shevett (spots), Susan Ash, Greg Freedman (sound board), Emile Lafargue (deck electrician), Joe Ferreri (house carpenter), Joe Ferreri Jr. (assistant house carpenter), Billy Wright (house props), Jan Marasek (prop master), William T. Wright (assistant house props), Elizabeth Floyd, Tamara Kopko (dressers); Dance Captain, Owen Johnston II; Music Preparation, Eva Gianono; Marketing, TMG—The Marketing Group; Advertising, SpotCo; Press, Richard Kornberg, Don Summa, Ian Rand; Cast recording: Dreamworks 50003

**CAST** Roger Davis **Tim Howar;** Mark Cohen **Matt Caplan**[*1]; Tom Collins **Destan Owens**[*2]; Benjamin Coffin III **D'Monroe;** Joanne Jefferson **Kenna J. Ramsey**[*3]; Angel Schunard **Justin Johnson;** Mimi Marquez **Antonique Smith**[*4]; Maureen Johnson **Ava Gaudet**[*5]; Mark's Mom/Alison/Others **Haven Burton;** Christmas Caroler/Mr. Jefferson/Pastor/Others **Marcus Paul James;** Mrs. Jefferson/Woman with Bags/Others **Frenchie Davis**[*6]; Gordon/The Man/Mr. Grey/Others **Luther Creek;** Steve/Man with Squeegee/Waiter/Others **Robin De Jesús**[*7]; Paul/Cop/Others **Shaun Earl;** Alexi Darling/Roger's Mom/Others **Mayumi Ando**[*8]; Swings[*9] **Karmine Allers, Justin Brill, Crystal Monée Hall, Owen Johnston II, Philip Dorian McAdoo, Moeisha McGill, Kyle Post**

**UNDERSTUDIES** Karmine Allers (Maureen, Mimi), Luther Creek & Kyle Post (Mark, Roger), Frenchie Davis, Haven Burton (Maureen), Shaun Earl (Angel), Ava Gaudet (Mimi), Crystal Monée Hall (Joanne), Marcus Paul James (Tom Collins, Benjamin), Owen Johnston II (Mark, Angel), Philip Dorian McAdoo (Tom Collins), Moeisha McGill (Joanne, Mimi), Andy Señor (Angel)

**MUSICAL NUMBERS** Tune Up, Voice Mail (#1–#5), Rent, You Okay Honey?, One Song Glory, Light My Candle, Today 4 U, You'll See, Tango: Maureen, Life Support, Out Tonight, Another Day, Will I?, On the Street, Santa Fe, We're Okay, I'll Cover You, Christmas Bells, Over the Moon, La Vie Boheme/I Should Tell You, Seasons of Love, Happy New Year, Take Me or Leave Me, Without You, Contact, Halloween, Goodbye Love, What You Own, Finale/Your Eyes

**MUSICIANS** David Truskinoff (Conductor/keyboards), Steve Mack (bass), Bobby Baxmeyer (guitar) John Korba (Associate Conductor/guitar), Jeffrey Potter (drums)

**MUSICAL NUMBERS** Tune Up, Voice Mail (#1–#5), Rent, You Okay Honey?, One Song Glory, Light My Candle, Today 4 U, You'll See, Tango: Maureen, Life Support, Out Tonight, Another Day, Will I?, On the Street, Santa Fe, We're Okay, I'll Cover You, Christmas Bells, Over the Moon, La Vie Boheme/I Should Tell You, Seasons of Love, Happy New Year, Take Me or Leave Me, Without You, Contact, Halloween, Goodbye Love, What You Own, Finale/Your Eyes

**SETTING** New York City's East Village, 1990. A musical presented in two acts. For original production credits see *Theatre World* Volume 52, page 58. Originally presented Off-Broadway at the New York Theatre Workshop on February 13, 1996 before it transferred to Broadway. Tragedy occurred when the thirty-five-year-old author, Jonathan Larson, died of an aortic aneurysm after watching the final dress rehearsal of his show on January 24, 1996.

**SYNOPSIS** Based on Puccini's opera La Boheme, the musical centers on a group of impoverished young artists and musicians struggling to survive and create in New York's Alphabet City in the early 1990s, under the shadow of AIDS.

*Succeeded by: 1. Christopher J. Hanke 3. Mark Richard Ford, Troy Horne 3. Nicole Lewis, Tonya Dixon 4. Jaime Lee Kirchner, Antonique Smith, Tamyra Gray 5. Maggie Benjamin, Nicolette Hart 6. Gwen Stewart, Maia Nkenge Wilson 7. Andy Señor, Telly Leung 8. T.V. Carpio, Mayumi Ando 9. Dana Dawson, Todd E. Pettiford

*Christopher Hanke and Tim Hower (photos by Joan Marcus)*

*Tamyra Grey and Tim Hower*

# SHINING CITY

Biltmore Theatre; First Preview: April 20, 2006; Opening Night: May 9, 2006; Closed July 16, 2006; 21 previews, 80 performances

Written by Conor McPherson; Produced by Manhattan Theatre Club (Lynne Meadow, Artistic Director; Barry Grove, Executive Producer) in special arrangement with Scott Rudin, Roger Berlind, and Debra Black; Director, Robert Falls; Set, Santo Loquasto; Costumes, Kaye Voyce; Lighting, Christopher Akerlind; Sound, Obadiah Eaves; Dialect Coach, Deborah Hecht; PSM, Barclay Stiff; Casting, Nancy Piccione/David Caparelliotis; Director of Artistic Operations, Mandy Greenfield; Production Manager, Ryan McMahon; Development, Jill Turner Lloyd; Marketing, Debra A. Waxman; General Manager, Florie Seery; Director of Artistic Development, Paige Evans; Director of Artistic Production, Michael Bush; Associate General Manager, Lindsay T. Brooks; Company Manager, Denise Cooper; Stage Manager, Francesca Russell; Assistant Director, Henry Wishcamper; Associate Set, Jenny B. Sawyers; Technical Director, William Mohney; Advertising, SpotCo; Press, Boneau/Bryan-Brown, Jim Byk, Aaron Meier, Heath Schwartz

**CAST** Ian **Brían F. O'Byrne;** John **Oliver Platt;** Neasa **Martha Plimpton;** Laurence **Peter Scanavino**

**UNDERSTUDIES** Chris Genebach (Ian, Laurence), Fiana Toibin (Neasa)

**SETTING** An office in Dublin, present. Roughly two months separate each scene. American premiere of a drama presented without intermission; Originally produced at the Royal Court Theatre, London, and the Gate Theatre, Dublin, on June 4, 2004.

**SYNOPSIS** *Shining City* is supernatural tale that concerns a widower who visits a first time therapist, claiming to have seen the ghost of his recently deceased wife. The therapist is confronted with his own demons, and the visits between the two become a gripping struggle to survive. A "coup de theatre" thrilling ending leaves them changed for the rest of their lives.

*Oliver Platt and Brian F. O'Byrne (photos by Joan Marcus)*

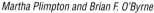

*Martha Plimpton and Brian F. O'Byrne*

# SWEENEY TODD
## The Demon Barber of Fleet Street

Eugene O'Neill Theatre; First Preview: October 3, 2005; Opening Night: November 3, 2005; Closed September 3, 2006; 35 previews, 349 performances

Music and lyrics by Stephen Sondheim, book by Hugh Wheeler, from an adaptation by Christopher Bond; Originally directed on Broadway by Harold Prince; Produced by Tom Viertel, Steven Baruch, Marc Routh, Richard Frankel, Ambassador Theatre Group, Adam Kenwright, Tulchin/Bartner/Bagert; Director/Set/Costumes, John Doyle; Music Supervision/Orchestrations, Sarah Travis; Lighting, Richard G. Jones; Sound, Dan Moses Schreier; Wigs/Hair, Paul Huntley; Resident Music Supervisor, David Loud; Casting, Bernard Telsey Casting; Music Coordinator, John Miller; General Management, Richard Frankel Productions, Jo Porter; PSM, Adam John Hunter; Company Manager, Sammy Ledbetter; Stage Manager, Julia P. Jones/Newton Cole; ASM, David Redman Scott/Aja Kane; Assistant CM, Jason Pelusio; Production Management, Showman Fabricators; Associate Design: Ted LeFevre (set), Paul Miller (lighting), David Bullard (sound); Patrick Chevillot (costumes); Makeup, Angelina Avallone; Advertising, Serino Coyne Inc.; Press, Barlow • Hartman, Rick Miramontez, Leslie Baden; Cast recording: Nonesuch 79946-2

**CAST** Mrs. Lovett—*Tuba, Orchestra Bells, Percussion* **Patti LuPone**[*1]; Sweeney Todd—*Guitar, Orchestra Bells, Percussion* **Michael Cerveris**; Judge Turpin—*Trumpet, Orchestra Bells, Percussion* **Mark Jacoby;** Pirelli—*Accordion, Keyboard, Flute* **Donna Lynne Champlin;** Tobias Ragg—*Violin, Clarinet, Keyboard* **Manoel Felciano;** The Beadle—*Keyboard, Trumpet* **Alexander Gemignani;** Jonas Fogg—*Bass* **John Arbo;** Beggar Woman—*Clarinet* **Diana Dimarzio;** Anthony Hope—*Cello, Keyboard* **Benjamin Magnuson;** Joanna—*Cello, Penny Whistle* **Lauren Molina**

**STANDBYS**[*2] Benjamin Eakeley (Anthony Hope, The Beadle, Tobias Ragg), Merwin Foard (Judge Turpin, Sweeney Todd), Dorothy Stanley (Mrs. Lovett, Pirelli), Elisa Winter (Beggar Woman, Johanna)

**MUSICAL NUMBERS** The Ballad of Sweeney Todd, No Place Like London, The Barber and His Wife, The Worst Pies in London, Poor Thing, My Friends, Green Finch and Linnet Bird, Ah Miss, Johanna, Pirelli's Miracle Elixir, The Contest, Johanna, Wait, Kiss Me, Ladies in Their Sensitivities, Quartet, Pretty Women, Epiphany, A Little Priest, God That's Good!, Johanna, By the Sea, Not While I'm Around, Parlor Songs, City on Fire!, Final Sequence, The Ballad of Sweeney Todd

Revival of a musical presented in two acts. This version was originally presented at the Watermill Theatre, Berkshire, Great Britain. Originally produced on Broadway at the Uris (Gershwin) Theatre, March 1, 1979, running 557 performances (see *Theatre World* Volume 35, page 32). The musical was first revived on Broadway at Circle in the Square, September 14, 1989 (see *Theatre World* Volume 46, page 8).

**SYNOPSIS** Stephen Sondheim's award-winning musical is about a murderous barber, hell bent on revenge, who takes up with his enterprising neighbor in a delicious plot to slice their way through England's upper crust. This unique reinvention of the show utilizes the ten member cast as the musicians.

Succeeded by: 1. Judy Kaye 2. Added: David Hess (Jonas Fogg, Judge Turpin, Sweeney Todd, The Beadle), Stephen McIntyre (Jonas Fogg), Jessica Wright (Beggar Woman, Pirelli)

*Michael Cerveris and Patti LuPone
(photos by Paul Kolnik)*

*The Cast*

# TARZAN

Richard Rodgers Theatre; First Preview: March 24, 2006; Opening Night: May 10, 2006; 35 previews, 443 performances as of May 31, 2007

Music and lyrics by Phil Collins, book by David Henry Hwang; Produced by Disney Theatrical Productions and Thomas Schumacher; based on the 1999 Disney animated feature film (screenplay by Tab Murphy, Bob Tzudiker and Noni White; directed by Kevin Lima & Chris Buck); Based on the story "Tarzan of the Apes" by Edgar Rice Burroughs; Director/Set/Costumes, Bob Crowley; Choreography, Meryl Tankard; Musical Production/Vocal Arrangements, Paul Bogaev; Aerial Design, Pichoón Baldinu; Lighting, Natasha Katz; Sound, John Shivers; Hair, David Brian Brown; Makeup, Naomi Donne; Soundscape, Lon Bender; Special Creatures; Ivo Coveney; Fight Director, Rick Sordelet; Music Director/Dance Arrangements, Jim Abbott; Orchestrations, Doug Besterman; Music Coordinator, Michael Keller; Casting, Bernard Telsey; Production Supervisor, Clifford Schwartz; Technical Supervisor, Tom Shane Bussey; Associate Director, Jeff Lee; Associate Producer, Marshall B. Purdy; Project Manager, Lizbeth Cone; Company Manager, Randy Meyer; Associate Company Manager, Eduardo Castro; Assistant Choreographer, Lenora Stapleton; Assistant Aerial Designer, Angela Phillips; Animated Sequence, Little Airplane Productions; Stage Manager, Frank Lombardi; ASM, Julia P. Jones, Tanya Gillette, Robert Armitage; Dance Captain, Marlyn Ortiz; Fight Captain/Assistant Dance Captain, Stefan Raulston; Music Copyist, Russell Anixter, Donald Rice; Dialogue/Vocal Coach, Deborah Hecht, Advertising, Serino Coyne Inc.; Press, Boneau/Bryan-Brown; Cast recording: Disney Records 61541-7

**CAST** Kerchak **Shuler Hensley**[*1]; Kala **Merle Dandridge;** Young Tarzan **Daniel Manche**[*2] or **Alex Rutherford;** Terk **Chester Gregory II;** Tarzan **Josh Strickland;** Jane Porter **Jenn Gambatese;** Professor Porter **Tim Jerome;** Mr. Clayton **Donnie Keshawarz**[*3]; Snipes/Lead Song of Man Vocals **Horace V. Rogers;** Waterfall Ribbon Dancer **Kara Madrid;** Moth **Andy Pellick;** Ensemble[*4] **Marcus Bellamy, Celina Carvajal, Dwayne Clark, Kearran Giovanni, Michael Hollick, Kara Madrid, Kevin Massey, Anastacia McCleskey, Rika Okamoto, Marlyn Ortiz, John Elliott Oyzon, Andy Pellick, Stefan Raulston, Horace V. Rogers, Sean Samuels, Niki Scalera;** Swings[*5] **Veronica deSoyza, Joshua Kobak, Whitney Osentoski, Angela Phillips, Nick Sanchez, Natalie Silverlieb, JD Aubrey Smith, Rachel Stern;** Standby for Kerchak and Porter **Darrin Baker**[*5]

**UNDERSTUDIES** Joshua Kobak, Kevin Massey (Tarzan); Celina Carvajal, Niki Scalera (Jane); Michael Hollick, Horace V. Rogers (Kerchak); Kearran Giovanni, Natalie Silverlieb (Kala); Dwayne Clark, Nick Sanchez (Terk); Michael Hollick, Joshua Kobak (Clayton); Michael Hollick (Porter); Succeeding: Andrea Dora (Kala), Nicholas Rodriguez (Tarzan), Natalie Silverlieb (Jane)

**ORCHESTRA** Jim Abbott (Conductor/keyboard 1); Ethan Popp (Associate Conductor/keyboard 2); Andrew Barrett (synthesizer programmer); Martyn Axe (keyboard 3); Gary Seligson (drums); Roger Squitero, Javier Diaz (percussion); Hugh Mason (bass); JJ McGeehan (guitar); Leanne LeBlanc (cello); Anders Boström (flutes); Charles Pillow (reeds); Anthony Kadleck (trumpet); Bruce Eidem (trombone); Theresa MacDonnell (French horn)

**MUSICAL NUMBERS** Two Worlds, You'll Be in My Heart, Jungle Funk, Who Better Than Me, No Other Way, I Need to Know, Son of Man, Son of Man (reprise), Sure As Sun Turns to Moon, Waiting for This Moment, Different, Trashin' the Camp, Like No Man I've Ever Seen, Strangers Like Me, Who Better Than Me (reprise), Everything That I Am, You'll Be in My Heart (reprise), Sure As Sun Turns to Moon (reprise), Two Worlds (Finale)

**SETTING** The Coast of Africa, early 1900's. World premiere of a musical presented in two acts.

**SYNOPSIS** Tarzan, a shipwrecked baby who was raised in an African jungle by apes, has his first encounter with humans (including the beautiful Jane) and must choose where he belongs - the "civilized" human world or the "wild" one that nurtured him.

*Succeeded by: 1. Rob Evan 2. Dylan Riley Snyder 3. Michael Hollick, Donnie Keshawarz 3. Veronica deSoyza, Andrea Dora, Gregory Haney, Jonathan Johnson, Nicholas Rodriguez 4. Ven Daniel, Alayna Gallo, Jeslyn Kelly, Allison Thomas Lee 5. Christopher Carl

*Alex Rutherford and Merle Dandridge (photo by Joan Marcus)*

# THREE DAYS OF RAIN

Bernard Jacobs Theatre; First Preview: March 28, 2006; Opening Night: April 19, 2006; Closed June 18, 2006; 26 previews, 70 performances

Written by Richard Greenberg; Produced by Marc Platt, David Stone, and The Shubert Organization; Director, Joe Mantello; Set and Costumes, Santo Loquasto; Lighting, Paul Gallo; Original Music and Sound, David Van Tieghem; Casting, Bernard Telsey Casting; Rain, Jauchem & Meeh; Hair, Lyndell Quiyou; PSM, William Joseph Barnes; Production Management, Aurora Productions (Gene O'Donovan, W. Benjamin Heller II, Bethany Weinstein, Hilary Austin); General Management, Stuart Thompson Productions, Caroline Prugh, James Triner; Stage Manager, Timothy R. Semon; Assistant Director, Michael Silverstone, Associate Design: Jenny Sawyers (set), Paul Miller (lighting), Jill B.C. DuBoff (sound); Assistant Design: Wilson Chin (set), Matthew Pachtman (costumes); Production: Donald "Buck" Roberts (carpenter), Michael LoBue (electrician), Abraham Morrison (props), Christopher Sloan (sound), Kristine Bellerud (wardrobe supervisor), Barry Doss (dresser); GM Assistant, Megan Curran; PA, Maura Farver; Advertising, Serino Coyne Inc.; Press, The Publicity Office, Bob Fennell, Marc Thibodeau, Candi Adams, Michael S. Borowski, Matt Fasano

**CAST** Walker/Ned **Paul Rudd;** Nan/Lina **Julia Roberts;** Pip/Theo **Bradley Cooper**

**UNDERSTUDIES** Michael Dempsey (Walker/Ned, Pip/Theo), Michelle Federer (Nan/Lina)

**SETTING** Act 1: An unoccupied loft space in downtown Manhattan, 1995; Act 2: The same space, 1960. Broadway debut of a play presented in two acts. Originally commissioned and first produced by South Coast Repertory Theatre, and produced Off-Broadway by the Manhattan Theatre Club, October 21, 1997 (see *Theatre World* Volume 54, page 90).

**SYNOPSIS** Brought together for the reading of a will, three young adults—sister, brother, and a long-time friend—unwittingly replay their parents' tangled relationships. The themes of love, friendship, ambition, and betrayal expand exponentially in Act Two, when the same actors play youthful versions of the parents, business partners in love with the same woman.

Paul Rudd and Julia Roberts (photos by Joan Marcus)

Bradley Cooper and Julia Roberts

Paul Rudd and Bradley Cooper

# THE THREEPENNY OPERA

Studio 54; First Preview: March 24, 2006; Opening Night: April 20, 2006; Closed June 25, 2006; 32 previews, 77 performances

Book and lyrics by Bertolt Brecht, music by Kurt Weill, based on Elisabeth Hauptmann's German translation of John Gay's *The Beggar's Opera* with a new translation by Wallace Shawn; Produced by the Roundabout Theatre Company (Todd Haimes, Artistic Director; Harold Wolpert, Managing Director; Julia C. Levy, Executive Director); Director, Scott Elliott; Choreography, Aszure Barton; Music Director, Kevin Stites; Set, Derek McLane; Costumes, Isaac Mizrahi; Lighting, Jason Lyons; Sound, Ken Travis; Hair/Wigs, Paul Huntley; Original Orchestrations, Kurt Weill; Music Coordinator; John Miller; PSM; Peter Hanson; Casting, Jim Carnahan; Technical Supervisor, Steve Beers; General Manager, Sydney Beers; Founding Director, Gene Feist; Associate Artistic Director, Scott Ellis; Marketing, David B. Steffen; Development, Jeffory Lawson; Company Manager, Nichole Larson; Stage Manager, Jon Krause; Assistant Director, Marie Masters; Assistant Choreographer, William Briscoe; Associate Music Director, Paul Raiman; Associate Lighting, Jennifer Schriever; Associate Sound, Tony Smolenski; Makeup, Chantel Miller; Music Copying, Emily Grishman; Advertising, The Eliran Murphy Group; Press, Boneau/Bryan-Brown, Matt Polk, Jessica Johnson, Joe Perrotta

**CAST** Jenny **Cyndi Lauper**; Smith **John Herrera**; Walter/Betty **Maureen Moore**; Jimmy/Dolly **Brooke Sunny Moriber**; Rev. Kimball/Eunice **Terry Burrell**; Robert **Romain Frugé**; Vixen **Deborah Lew**; Matthew **David Cale**; Macheath **Alan Cumming**; Mr. Peachum **Jim Dale**; Beggar/Beatrice **Brian Butterick**; Filch **Carlos Leon**; Mrs. Peachum **Ana Gasteyer**; Polly Peachum **Nellie McKay**; Jacob **Adam Alexi-Malle**; Eddie **Kevin Rennard**; Tiger Brown **Christopher Innvar**; Bruno/Molly **Christopher Kenney**; Harry/Velma **Lucas Steele**; Lucy Brown **Brian Charles Rooney**; Policeman and Beggars: **Maureen Moore, Brooke Sunny Moriber, Terry Burrell, Romain Frugé, Deborah Lew, Brian Butterick, Carlos Leon, Adam Alexi-Malle, Kevin Rennard, Christopher Kenney, Lucas Steel**; Swings **Nehal Joshi, Valisia Lekae Little**

**UNDERSTUDIES** Romain Frugé (Mac), Maureen Moore (Jenny), Brooke Sunny Moriber (Polly), Terry Burrell (Mrs. Peachum), David Cale (Mr. Peachum), Lucas Steele (Lucy) Adam Alexi-Malle (Filch), John Herrera (Tiger)

**ORCHESTRA** Kevin Stites (Conductor), Paul Raiman (Associate Conductor/piano-harmonium-Celeste), Eddie Salkin and Roger Rosenberg (reeds), Tim Schadt and Matt Peterson (trumpets), Mike Christianson (tenor trombone), Charles duChateau (cello/accordion), Greg Utzig (guitar/Hawaiian guitar/banjo/mandolin), Charles Descarfino (percussion/drums), Richard Sarpola (bass)

**MUSICAL NUMBERS** Overture, Song of the Extraordinary Crimes of Mac the Knife, Peachum's Morning Hymn, The 'Rather Than' Song, Wedding Song, Pirate Jenny, The Army Song, Wedding Song (reprise), Love Song, The 'No' Song, Certain Things Make Our Life Impossible, Goodbye, Polly's Song, The Ballad of the Overwhelming Power of Sex, The Ballad of the Pimp, The Ballad of the Happy Life, The Jealously Duet, How Do Humans Live?, The Ballad of the Overwhelming Power of Sex (reprise), The Song of Inadequacy of Human Striving, The Song of Inadequacy of Human Striving (reprise), Lucy's Aria, Cry from the Grave, The Ballad in which Macheath asks Everyone's Forgiveness, Finale

**SETTING** London, 1837. A musical presented in two acts. Originally produced at the Empire Theatre on April 13, 1933. The show was revived previously in 1954 and 1955–1961 at Theater de Lys (Off-Broadway), 1966 at the Billy Rose Theatre, 1976–1977 at the Vivian Beaumont, and in 1989 at the Lunt-Fontanne.

**SYNOPSIS** A notorious bandit marries a girl, much to the chagrin of her father. The peeved patriarch does everything in his power to imprison his son-in-law in this updated version of the political and social satire.

Above: *Alan Cumming and Cyndi Lauper (photos by Joan Marcus)*

Left: *Ana Gasteyer, Nellie McKay, and Jim Dale*

# THE WEDDING SINGER

Al Hirschfeld Theatre; First Preview: March 30, 2006; Opening Night: April 27, 2006; Closed December 31, 2006; 30 previews, 285 performances

Music by Matthew Sklar, book by Chad Beguelin and Tim Herlihy, lyrics by Chad Beguelin, additional music and lyrics by Adam Sandler and Tim Herlihy; based upon the New Line Cinema film written by Tim Herlihy; Produced by Margo Lion, New Line Cinema, The Araca Group, Roy Furman, Douglas L. Meyer/James D. Stern Productions, Rick Steiner/The Staton-Bell-Osher-Mayerson Group, JamTheatricals; Produced in association with Jujamcyn Theatres, Jay Furman, Michael Gill, Dr. Lawrence Horowitz, Marisa Sechrest, Gary Winnick, Élan V. McAllister/Allan S. Gordon/Adam Epstein; Director, John Rando; Choreography, Rob Ashford; Set, Scott Pask; Costumes, Gregory Gale; Lighting, Brian MacDevitt; Sound, Peter Hylenski; Casting, Bernard Telsey; Hair, David Brian Brown; Makeup, Joe Dulude II; Orchestrations, Irwin Fisch; Incidental & Dance Music Arrangements, David Chase; Music Director, James Sampliner; Music Coordinator, John Miller; Executive Producer, Mark Kaufman; Production Manager, Juniper Street Productions; Associate Choreography, JoAnn M. Hunter; PSM, Rolt Smith; Marketing, The Araca Group; General Management, The Charlotte Wilcox Company; Company Manager, Edward Nelson; Associate CM, Beverly Edwards; Stage Manager, Julie Balduff; ASM, Janet Takami; Dance Captains, Angelique Ilo, Michael McGurk; Assistant Director, Jen Bender; Associate Design: Orit Jacoby Carroll (set) Janine Marie McCabe (costumes), Charles Pennebaker (costumes), Josh Marquette (wigs/hair); Press, Richard Kornberg, Don Summa; Cast recording: Sony Classical/BMG 82876-82095-2

Stephen Lynch  (photos by Joan Marcus)

**CAST** Robbie Hart **Stephen Lynch**; Sammy **Matthew Saldívar**[*1]; George **Kevin Cahoon**; Debbie **Ashley Amber**; Harold **Nick Kenkel**[*2]; David/Bad Haircut Guy **David Josefsberg**[*3]; Julia Sullivan **Laura Benanti**[*4]; Holly **Amy Spanger**; Glen Guglia **Richard H. Blake**; Rosie **Rita Gardner**; Linda **Felicia Finley**; Angie/Large Lady/China Clerk/Vegas Airlines Ticket Agent **Adinah Alexander**; Mookie/Ricky **Eric LaJuan Summers**; Crystal **Tracee Beazer**; Donatella **Cara Cooper**[*5]; Shane **Matt Allen**[*6]; Sideburns Lady **Christina Sivrich**; Trekkie **Matthew Stocke**; Bum **Peter Kapetan**; Impersonators **Tracee Beazer, Cara Cooper**[*5]**, Peter Kapetan, J. Elaine Marcos, T. Oliver Reid**[*7]**, Christina Sivrich, Matthew Stocke**; Ensemble **Ashley Amber, Adinah Alexander, Matt Allen**[*6]**, Tracee Beazer, Cara Cooper**[*5]**, Nicolette Hart, David Josefsberg**[*3]**, Peter Kapetan, Spencer Liff, J. Elaine Marcos, T. Oliver Reid**[*7]**, Christina Sivrich, Matthew Stocke, Eric LaJuan Summers**; Swings **Angelique Ilo, Kevin Kern, Joanne Manning, Michael McGurk, Adam Zotovich**; Standby for Julia Sullivan **Tina Madigan**

The Company

**UNDERSTUDIES** Matthew Stocke (Robbie Hart), Cara Cooper (Holly), Matthew Stocke (George, Glen Guglia), David Josefsberg (Sammy), Nicolette Hart (Linda), Christina Sivrich (Rosie)

**ORCHESTRA** James Sampliner/Jim Vukovich (Conductor/keyboards); John Samorian (Associate Conductor/keyboards); Larry Saltzman, Stephen Lynch, John Putnam, Gary Sieger (guitar); Jon Working (keyboards); Irio O'Farrill, Matthew Saldivar (bass); Warren Odze (drums); Clifford Lyones, Jack Bashkow (reeds); Trevor Neumann (trumpet); James Saporito (percussion)

**MUSICAL NUMBERS** It's Your Wedding Day, Right on Time, Awesome, It's Your Wedding Day (reprise), Right on Time (reprise), A Note From Linda, Pop, Somebody Kill Me, Rosie's Note, Casualty of Love, Come Out of the Dumpster, Today You Are a Man, George's Prayer, Not That Kind of Thing, Saturday Night in the City, All About the Green, Right in Front of Your Eyes, Single, If I Told You, Let Me Come Home, If I Told You (reprise), Move That Thang, Grow Old With You, It's Your Wedding Day (Finale)

**SETTING** Ridgefield, New Jersey, 1985. A musical presented in two acts. World premiere presented February 9, 2006, at the 5th Avenue Theatre, Seattle, Washington

**SYNOPSIS** Robbie Hart, New Jersey's favorite wedding singer, is the life of the party until his own fiancée leaves him at the altar. Shot through the heart, Robbie makes every wedding he plays as disastrous as his own. Enter Julia, a winsome waitress who wins his affection, but Julia is about to be married to a Wall Street shark. Unless Robbie can pull off the performance of the decade, the girl of his dreams will be gone forever. *The Wedding Singer* takes us back to a time when hair was big, greed was good, collars were up, and a wedding singer just might be the coolest guy in the room.

*Succeeded by: 1. Constantine Maroulis (9/8/06), Matthew Saldívar (11/7/06) 2. Spencer Liff 3. Andy Karl, David Josefsberg 4. Tina Madigan (8/16/06), Laura Benanti (10/3/06) 5. Joanne Manning, Robyn Hurder 6. David Eggers 7. Jon-Paul Mateo, Dennis Stowe

# WICKED

Gershwin Theatre; First Preview: October 8, 2003; Opening Night: October 30, 2003; 25 previews, 1,496 performances as of May 31, 2007

Book by Winnie Holzman, music and lyrics by Stephen Schwartz; based on the novel by Gregory Maguire; Produced by Marc Platt, Universal Pictures, The Araca Group, Jon B. Platt and David Stone; Director, Joe Mantello; Musical Staging, Wayne Cilento; Music Supervisor, Stephen Oremus; Orchestrations, William David Brohn; Set, Eugene Lee; Costumes, Susan Hilferty; Lighting, Kenneth Posner; Sound, Tony Meola; Projections, Elanie J. McCarthy; Wigs/Hair, Tom Watson; Technical Supervisor, Jake Bell; Arrangements, Alex Lacamoire, Stephen Oremus; Dance Arrangements, James Lynn Abbott; Music Coordinator, Michael Keller; Special Effects, Chic Silber; Production Supervisor, Thom Widmann; Dance Supervisor, Mark Myars; Associate Director, Lisa Leguillou; Casting, Bernard Telsey; PSM, Chris Jamros; General Management, 321 Theatrical Management; Executive Producers, Marcia Goldberg and Nina Essman; Company Management, Susan Sampliner, Robert Brinkerhoff; Stage Management, Jennifer Marik, Christy Ney, Chris Zaccardi; Fight Director, Tom Schall; Flying, Paul Rubin/ZFX Inc.; Dressing/Properties, Kristie Thompson; Makeup, Joe Dulude II; Assistant Choreography, Corrine McFadden-Herrera; Music Preparation, Peter R. Miller; Synthesizer Programming, Andrew Barrett; Advertising, Serino Coyne Inc.; Press, The Publicity Office/Barlow • Hartman; Cast recording: Decca Broadway 0001 682-02

**CAST** Glinda **Kate Reinders**[1]; Witch's Father/Ozian Official **Michael DeVries**; Witch's Mother **Katie Webber**; Midwife **Jan Neuberger**[2]; Elphaba **Eden Espinosa**[3]; Nessarose **Jenna Leigh Green**[4]; Boq **Robb Sapp**[5]; Madame Morrible **Carol Kane**[6]; Doctor Dillamond **Sean McCourt**[7]; Fiyero **Derrick Williams**[8]; The Wonderful Wizard of Oz **David Garrison**; Chistery **Philip Spaeth**[9]; Ensemble[10] **Ioana Alfonso, Sonshine Allen, Kevin Aubin, Jerad Bortz, Ben Cameron, Michael DeVries, Sarah Jane Everman, Lori Ann Ferreri, Adam Fleming, Rhett G. George, Gaelen Gilliland, Kisha Howard, Kenway Hon Wai K. Kua, Brandi Chavonne Massey, Corrine McFadden-Herrera, Barrett Martin, Jan Neuberger, Clifton Oliver, Eddie Pendergraft, Alexander Quiroga, Noah Rivera, Michael Seelbach, Megan Sikora, Philip Spaeth, Heather Spore, Marty Thomas, Katie Webber, Brooke Wendle, Briana Yacavone**; Swings[11] **Stephen Lee Anderson, Clyde Alves, Kristen Leigh Gorski, Anthony Galde, Tiffany Haas, Mark Myars, Carson Reide, Eric Stretch, Terrance Spencer** Standbys **Saycon Sengbloh**[12] (Elphaba), **Katie Adams**[13] (Glinda)

**ORCHESTRA** Robert Billig (Conductor), David Evans (Associate Conductor/piano/synthesizer); Christian Hebel (Concertmaster), Victor Schultz (violin), Kevin Roy (viola), Dan Miller (cello), Konrad Adderly (bass), Greg Skaff & Ric Molina (guitar), John Moses (clarinet/soprano sax), John Campo (bassoon/baritone sax/clarinet), Tuck Lee (oboe), Helen Campo (flute), Jon Owens (lead trumpet), Tom Hoyt (trumpet), Dale Kirkland, Douglas Purviance (trombone), Theo Primis, Chad Yarbrough (French horn), Paul Loesel, David Evans (keyboards), Andy Jones (percussion), Matt Vanderende (drums), Laura Sherman (harp), Ben Cohn (piano/synthesizer)

**MUSICAL NUMBERS** No One Mourns the Wicked, Dear Old Shiz, The Wizard and I, What Is This Feeling?, Something Bad, Dancing Through Life, Popular, I'm Not That Girl, One Short Day, A Sentimental Man, Defying Gravity, No One Mourns the Wicked (reprise), Thank Goodness, The Wicked Witch of the East, Wonderful, I'm Not That Girl (reprise), As Long as You're Mine, No Good Deed, March of the Witch Hunters, For Good, Finale

**SETTING** The Land of Oz. A musical presented in two acts. Premiere presented in San Francisco at the Curran Theatre May 28–June 29, 2003. For original production credits see *Theatre World* Volume 60, page 34.

**SYNOPSIS** *Wicked* explores the early life of the witches of Oz, Glinda, and Elphaba, who meet at Shiz University. Glinda is madly popular and Elphaba is green. After an initial period of mutual loathing, the roommates begin to learn something about each other. Their lives continue to intersect, and eventually their choices and convictions take them on widely different paths.

*Succeeded by: 1. Kendra Kassebaum (1/9/07) 2. Kathy Santen 3. Ana Gasteyer (10/6/06), Julia Murney (1/9/07) 4. Christy Candler 5. Logan Lipton (8/8/06) 6. Jayne Houdyshell (11/14/06) 7. Steven Skybell (8/8/06) 8. Sebastian Arcelus (1/9/07) 9. Manuel I. Herrera, Jonathan Warren 10. Brad Bass, Kathy Deitch, Kristina Fernandez, Lauren Gibbs, Todd Hanebrink, Zach Hensler, Manuel I. Herrera, Reed Kelly, Cassie Levy, Lindsay K. Northen, Brandon Christopher O'Neal, Kathy Santen, Brian Slaman, Charlie Sutton, Shanna VanDerwerker, Jonathan Warren 11. Kristina Fernandez, Afra Hines, Ryan Patrick Kelly, Allison Leo, Adam Sanford, Katherine Tokarz, Shanna VanDerwerker 12. Lisa Brescia 13. Alli Mauzey

*Julia Murney and Kendra Kassebaum (photo by Joan Marcus)*

# OFF-BROADWAY

*Top to bottom:*

*MayuOmana in* BE *at the Union Square Theatre (photo by Ran Biran)*

*Clockwise from top: Hunter Bell, Heidi Blickenstaff, Susan Blackwell, and Jeff Bowen in* [title of show] *at the Vineyard Theatre (photo by Carol Rosegg)*

*Ryan Ward in* Evil Dead: The Musical *at New World Stages (photo by Carol Rosegg)*

Left: Marie-France Arcilla, Erica Schroeder, Erin Crosby, Julie Dingman Evans, Denise Summerford in Shout! The Mod Musical at the Julia Miles Theatre (photo by Joan Marcus)

Below: Andréa Burns, Robin De Jesús, Christopher Jackson, Lin-Manuel Miranda, Karen Olivo, and Janet Dacal in In the Heights at 37 Arts (photo by Joan Marcus)

Burke Moses and Sara Jean Ford in the revival of
The Fantasticks at the Snapple Theater Center
(photo by Joan Marcus)

George Grizzard and Christine Baranski in Manhattan Theatre Club's production of
Paul Rudnick's Regrets Only (photo by Joan Marcus)

David Greenspan, Don
Amendolia, Frederick
Weller, Pedro Pascal,
Romain Frugé, Kelly
AuCoin, Jesse Hooker,
Michael McElroy and
Randy Redd in Second
Stage's production of
Terrence McNally's
Some Men (photo by
Joan Marcus)

Above: The Cast of the Peccadillo Theatre Company's production of Room Service at SoHo Playhouse (photo by Carol Rosegg)

Right: Meryl Streep in the Public Theater production of Mother Courage and Her Children (photo by Michal Daniel)

Below: Donna Murphy and the Company in City Center ENCORES! production of Follies (photo by Joan Marcus)

*Right: Blythe Danner and Gale Harold in the Roundabout Theatre Company's production of Tennessee Williams'* Suddenly Last Summer *(photo by Joan Marcus)*

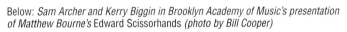

Left: *Curtis McClarin and Lynda Gravatt in August Wilson's* King Hedley II *at the Signature Theatre Company (photo by Carol Rosegg)*

Below: *Sam Archer and Kerry Biggin in Brooklyn Academy of Music's presentation of Matthew Bourne's* Edward Scissorhands *(photo by Bill Cooper)*

*Nilaja Sun in* No Child… *at the Barrow Street Theatre
(photo by Carol Rosegg)*

*Jeremy Shamos and Christopher Fitzgerald in* Gutenberg!
The Musical! *at 59E59 Theaters and the Actors Playhouse
(photo by James Ambler)*

*Brendan Milburn and Valerie Vigoda in* Striking 12 *at the Daryl
Roth Theatre (photo by Joan Marcus)*

Above: *Mare Winningham, Irene Malloy, and Matthew Morrison in Atlantic Theater Company's* 10 Million Miles *(photo by Monique Carboni)*

Left: *Orville Mendoza and Michele Ragusa in Primary Stages production of* Adrift in Macao *(photo by James Leynse)*

Below: *Jill Clayburgh and Blair Brown in Lincoln Center Theater's production of Sarah Ruhl's* The Clean House *(photo by Joan Marcus)*

Above: *Sigourney Weaver and Kristine Nielsen in the Playwrights Horizons production of A.R. Gurney's* Crazy Mary *(photo by Joan Marcus)*

Right: *Fan Yang in* The Gazillion Bubble Show *at New World Stages (photo by Nino Fernando Campagna)*

Below: *Daphne Rubin-Vega and Philip Seymour Hoffman in LAByrinth Theater Company's production of* Jack Goes Boating *(photo by Monique Carboni)*

# THE PORCH

Altered Stages; First Preview: June 1, 2006; Opening Night: June 2, 2006; Closed June 25, 2006; 26 performances

Written by Kari Floren; Presented by Right Down Broadway Productions; Director, Michael Berry; Choreography, Nancy Lemenager; Sets, Tamar Gadish; Costumes, Dana Murdock; Lighting, Russel Phillip Drapkin; Original Music & Sound, Roger Murdock; PSM, Emileena Pedigo; Casting, Stephanie Klapper; Technical Director, Elisha Schaefer; Creative Consultant, Michael McKenzie; Props, Amanda Jane Haley; Carpenter, Joe Powell; Sound Operator, Rod Weber; Press, Publicity Outfitters

**CAST** Ziad **Javier Munoz;** Jean **Lauren Mufson;** Lee **Don Harvey;** Ramona **Shirley Roeca**

**SETTING** A turn of the century house in the mountains of West Virginia; late summer, the present. World premiere of a new play presented in two acts.

**SYNOPSIS** *The Porch* is a comedy about four desperate souls, stuck together at a country bed and breakfast, who are all looking for a place to stop running. The porch becomes a sizzling battleground, and a new day emerges out of the darkness, bringing hope and courage to unlikely allies.

*Lauren Mufson and Javier Munoz in* The Porch
*(photo by Elisha Sachfer)*

# WIT

Acorn Theatre on Theatre Row; June 4, 2006; 1 performance

Written by Margaret Edson; Director, Leigh Silverman

**CAST** Vivian Bearing PhD **Kathleen Chalfant;** Harvey Kelekian **Walter Charles;** Jason Posner MD **Daniel Sarnelli;** Susie Monahan **Paula Pizzi;** Lab Technician **Brian J. Carter;** Lab Technician **Alli Steinberg;** E.M. Ashford **Helen Stenborg;** Lab Technician **Hope Albrecht**

A staged reading of the play presented without intermission.

**SYNOPSIS** Ms. Chalfant, Ms. Stenborg, Ms. Pizzi, Ms. Steinberg, Mr. Charles, Mr. Carter, and Mr. Sarnelli, members of the 1998 original Off-Broadway cast, reunited for this production of Edson's moving drama about a dying cancer patient, a benefit for the Jane Soyer SHARE Fund.

# NOTHING

59E59 Theater A; First preview June 7, 2006; Opening Night: June 11, 2006; Closed July 2, 2006; 31 performances

Adapted by Andrea Hart from the novel by Henry Green; Produced by 59E59 Theaters (Elysabeth Kleinhans, Artistic Director; Peter Tear, Executive Producer); Presented by Sophie Ward & Simon Dutton in association with Nothing Productions Ltd. as part of the Brits Off Broadway 2006; Director, Robert David Macdonald; Restaging/Design, Philip Prowse; Lighting, Gerry Jenkinson; Production Supervisor, Rena Branna; Costume Supervisor, Jane Hamilton; Assistant Director, Geoffrey Cauley; AEA Stage Manager, Jenny Deady; Press, Karen Greco

**CAST** John Pomfret **Simon Dutton;** Mary Pomfret **Candida Benson;** Jane Wetherby **Sophie Ward;** Philip Wetherby **Pete Ashmore;** Liz Jennings **Andrea Hart;** Richard Abbot **Derwent Watson;** Gaspard **Tristram Wymark**

**SETTING** London, post-war. A play presented in two acts. Originally presented at the Citizens Theatre, Glasgow, Scotland.

**SYNOPSIS** Adapted from one of Green's lesser-known novels, *Nothing* is a caustic comedy of manners surrounding the impending marriage of the children of two upper class ex-lovers.

*Candida Benson and Sophie Ward in* Nothing
*(photo by Richard Campbell)*

# ARABIAN NIGHT

East 13th Street Theatre; First Preview: May 31, 2006; Opening Night: June 12, 2006; Closed July 1, 2006; 34 performances

Written by Roland Schimmelpfennig, translated by David Tushingham; Produced by The Play Company (Kate Loewald, Founding Producer; Lauren Weigel, Managing Producer); Director, Trip Cullman; Sets, Louisa Thompson; Costumes, Katherine Ross; Lighting, Lenore Doxsee; Sound, Bart Fasbender; PSM, Marion Friedman; Production Manager, Lester Grant; Casting, Judy Henderson; Associate Producer/Dramaturg, Linda Bartholomai; ASM, Alison De Santis; Props, Desiree Maurer; Associate Production Manager, Jee Han; Technical Director, Joel Sherry; Producing Associates, Rob Marcato, Melissa Hardy; Press, The Karpel Group

**CAST** Hans Lomeier **Stelio Savante;** Fatima Mansur **Roxanna Hope;** Franziska Dehke **Jicky Schnee;** Kalil **Piter Marek;** Peter Karpati **Brandon Miller**

**SETTING** An anonymous housing complex. New York premiere of a play presented without intermission.

**SYNOPSIS** *Arabian Night* is an erotic urban fantasy by one of Germany's most celebrated contemporary playwrights. This nocturnal adventure, part fairy tale, part noir thriller, and part nightmare, tells the story of five people whose destinies become intertwined on a hot summer night. When the building's water supply mysteriously disappears, they are all drawn to the apartment of a sleeping beauty, where they meet their fate.

*Jicky Schnee and Brandon Miller in* Arabian Night
*(photo by Carol Rosegg)*

# BURLEIGH GRIME$

New World Stages—Stage 3; First Preview: May 23, 2006; Opening Night: June 13, 2006; Closed July 16, 2006; 24 previews, 39 performances

Book by Roger Kirby, original music by David Yazbek; Produced by Lewis Productions; Director, David Warren; Musical Staging, Andy Blankenbuehler; Sets, Jim Youmans; Costumes, Gregory Gale; Lighting, Jeff Croiter; Sound, Peter Fitzgerald; General Managers, Angelo Fraboni, Robert Schneider; PSM, Jane Pole; Music Director, Dean Sharenow; Casting, Jamie Fox & Kristine Lewis; Associate Producers, Judith Ann Abrams Productions, Craig L. Burr, Claire & Robert Chamine, Robert L. Chapman Jr., Harold Edgar, Geoffrey R. Hoguet, Robert D. Kissin, Mary Ann & Don LaGuardia; Advertising, Eliran Murphy Group; Press, Shaffer-Coyle Public Relations

**CAST** Coffee Girl/Dancer/Wife **Nancy Anderson;** Hap **Jason Antoon;** George Radbourn **James Badge Dale;** Buck **John Lavelle;** Elizabeth Bigley **Wendy Malick;** Burleigh Grimes **Mark Moses;** Grace Redding **Ashley Williams;** Understudies **Nancy Anderson** (Elizabeth), **Kelly Sullivan** (Grace, Coffee Girl/Dancer/Wife), **Doug Wert** (Burleigh Grimes, George, Hap, Buck)

**MUSICIANS** Jack Petruzzelli (keyboards/bass/guitar), Stephen Ulrich (bass/guitar), David Berger (drums), Dean Sharenow (drums)

**SETTING** New York City, the present. New York premiere of a play with live music presented in two acts.

**SYNOPSIS** George Radbourn is a Wall Street newbie who doesn't recognize that his mentor, Burleigh Grimes, may not be entirely sincere in appearance or agenda. Grimes, a relentless man of infinite calculation, is further assisted in his financial schemes by media powerhouse Elizabeth Bigley. George struggles for survival under the hand of Grimes' flexible business tactics, while also dealing with the arrival of his college sweetheart, Grace Redding, who has to face some difficult choices of her own.

*James Badge Dale, Mark Moses, and Nancy Anderson in*
Burleigh Grime$ *(photo by Carol Rosegg)*

# AFTER THE END

59E59 Theater B; First Preview: June 13, 2006; Opening Night: June 14, 2006; Closed July 2, 2006; 24 performances

Written by Dennis Kelly; Produced by 59E59 Theaters (Elysabeth Kleinhans, Artistic Director; Peter Tear, Executive Producer); Presented by Paines Plough and the Bush Theatre as part of the Brits Off Broadway 2006; Director, Roxana Silbert; Set/Costumes, Miriam Buether; Lighting, Chahine Yavroyan; Sound, Matt McKenzie; Associate Director, George Perrin; Production Manager, Robert Homes; Touring Production/Technical Manager, Rachel Shipp; Stage Manager, Christabel Anderson; AEA Stage Manager, Mandy Berry; Press, Karen Greco

**CAST** Mark **Tom Brooke;** Louise **Loo Brealey**

A psychological thriller performed without intermission.

**SYNOPSIS** Following a nuclear attack, office geek Mark risks his life to rescue the woman he has worshipped from afar, sheltering them both in his nuclear fall-out bunker. Living on rations of tuna and canned chili, Louise begins to suspect that perhaps this nuclear attack never happened.

# TREASON

Perry Street Theatre; First Preview: June 8, 2006; Opening Night: June 15, 2006; Closed July 29, 2006; 7 previews, 46 performances

Written by Sallie Bingham; Produced by Perry Street Theatre Company (Martin Platt and David Elliott, Co-Directors); Director, Martin Platt; Sets, Bill Clarke; Costumes, Martha Hally; Lighting, Jeff Nellis; Sound, Lindsay Jones; Projections, Brian Kim; Props, Judi Guralnick; PSM, Misha Siegel-Rivers; ASM, Kate DeCoste; Casting, Stephanie Klapper; Press, Springer Associates, Joe Trentacosta

**CAST** Ezra Pound **Philip Pleasants;** Dorothy Shakespeare Pound **Jennifer Sternberg;** Marcella Spann **Mary C. Bacon;** Sherri Martinelli **Kathleen Early;** Dr. Winfred Overholser **Peter van Wagner;** Olga Rudge **Nicole Orth Pallavicini;** Whiteside/Micheaux **Damon Gupton;** John Jasper/Allen Ginsberg **David B. Huevelman;** Mary Rudge **Rachel Fowler**

World premiere of a new play presented in two acts.

**SYNOPSIS** Ezra Pound helped make the careers of T.S. Eliot and James Joyce, translated texts from many languages, re-discovered much of the music of Vivaldi, and wrote operas. And he was a womanizer, an anti-Semite, a racist, an absent father, and a traitor to his country. Spanning over twenty years, Bingham's play exposes the man behind the genius through the eyes of five women who loved him.

*David B. Huevelman and Philip Pleasants in* Treason
*(photo by Monique Carboni)*

# STORIES FOR THE WOBBLY HEARTED

59E59 Theater C; First Preview: June 13, 2006; Opening Night: June 15, 2006; Closed June 28, 2006; 14 performances

Written and directed by Daniel Kitson; Produced by 59E59 Theaters (Elysabeth Kleinhans, Artistic Director; Peter Tear, Executive Producer); Presented by Higgledy Piggledy Enterprises as part of the Brits Off Broadway 2006; Press, Karen Greco

Performed by **Daniel Kitson**

American premiere of a solo performance play presented without intermission.

**SYNOPSIS** Kitson makes his New York debut with his Edinburgh Fringe First Award-winning show, a collection of joyous, intimate, funny, sad, poignant and life affirming stories — told by lamplight.

# TAILS

45th Street Theatre; First Preview: June 7, 2006; Opening Night: June 18, 2006; Closed July 2, 2006; 11 previews, 15 performances

Book and lyrics by Mark Masi, music by Jess Platt; Produced by Eric Krebs and Chase Mishkin; Director/Choreographer, Christopher Scott; Sets, Peter Feuchtwanger; Costumes, Cheryl McCarron; Lighting, Mitch Dana & Ben Haga; Sound, Ray Shilke; Music Director/Orchestrations/Arrangements, Mat Eisenstein; Casting, Barry Moss & Bob Kale; PSM, Brian Westmoreland; ASM, Jeff Scott Carey; Production Supervisor, PRF Productions; Press, Keith Sherman and Associates

**CAST** Mildred **Bethe Austin;** Ozzie **Miguel Cervantes;** Speagle **William Thomas Evans;** Howard **Gerry McIntyre;** Sophie **Tracey Stephens;** Understudy **Jeff Scott Carey**

**MUSICIANS** Mat Eisenstein (keyboard), Sam Sadigursky (reeds)

**MUSICAL NUMBERS** Out; Who's Your Daddy?; Ozzie's Lie; Numbers; A Real Go-Getter; I Could Jump; Goodbye, Speagle Goodbye; In Another Place; Show Dog; For the Little Ones; Sorry For You; Breathe It In; Good Mornings; In a Ring; We Are There; Think I'll Take Him Home; Who's Your Daddy? (reprise); Breathe It In (reprise)

A new musical presented in two acts.

**SYNOPSIS** Tails tells the story of five dogs in a dog pound who wait and hope to be chosen for adoption. The dogs include Speagle, the love-smitten mutt; Sophie, the show dog; and a new puppy surrounded by mystery.

*Bethe Austin, Tracey Stephens (front), Gerry McIntyre,*
*Miguel Cervantes, and William Thomas Evans (back) in* Tails
*(photo by Richard Termine)*

## DIE MOMMIE DIE!

Hudson Guild Theatre; June 19, 2006; 1 performance

Written by Charles Busch; Produced by The Actors Fund of America, Tim Pinckney, & Steven Yuhasz; Director, Carl Andress; Sets, Michael Anania; Lighting, Kirk Bookman; Sound, Harris Skiball; Costumes, Michael Bottari & Ronald Case; Stage Manager, Don Myers; Casting, Mark Simon; Press, Chuck Mirachi

**CAST** Angela Arden **Charles Busch;** Edith Sussman **Jenn Harris;** Bootsie Carp **Jayne Houdyshell;** Tony Parker **Christopher Meloni;** Sol Sussman **Tom Mardirosian;** Lance Sussman **Keith Nobbs;** Mourners **Harry Bouvy, Bret Shuford, Sam Turch**

**SETTING** 1967. The entrance and living room of the Sussman home in Beverly Hills. A staged reading of a play presented in two acts.

**SYNOPSIS** *Die Mommie Die!* is a riotous comedy-thriller steeped in the glamour of 1960s Hollywood. Angela Arden, a fallen pop diva is trapped in a hateful marriage to film producer Sol Sussman. Desperate to find happiness with her younger lover, an out-of-work TV actor named Tony Parker, Angela gruesomely murders her husband with the aid of a poisoned suppository. This reading was a benefit for the Actors Fund of America.

## KING LEAR

La MaMa E.T.C. Annex; First Preview: June 16, 2006; Opening Night: June 19, 2006; Closed July 2, 2006; 15 performances

Written by William Shakespeare; Presented by the Actors' Shakespeare Project (Benjamin Evett, Artistic Director; Sara Stackhouse, Executive Producer); Co-Produced by La MaMa E.T.C. (Ellen Stewart, Artistic Director); Director, Patrick Swanson; Design, David R. Gammons; Lighting, Mark O'Maley; Props, Elizabeth Locke; Sound/Music, Bill Barclay; Fight Director, Robert Walsh; Stage Manager, Adele Nadine Traub; ASM, Elizabeth Ross; Technical Director, Mark Tambella; Press, Sam Rudy Media Relations

**CAST** Kent **Allyn Burrows;** Gloucester **Colin Lane;** Edmund **Benjamin Evett;** King Lear **Alvin Epstein;** Cornwall **Michael Forden Walker;** Albany **William Gardiner;** Goneril **Jennie Israel;** Regan **Paula Langton;** Cordelia **Sarah Newhouse;** France **Gabriel Levey;** Burgundy **Bill Barclay;** Edgar **Doug Lockwood;** Oswald **Bill Barclay;** Fool **Ken Cheeseman;** Curan **Dan Domingues;** Old Man **William Gardiner;** Messengers/Knights/Gentlemen/ Servants **Dan Domingues, Gabriel Levey**

Revival of the play presented in two acts. This production of *King Lear* was originally a co-production with the Boston University School of Theatre.

**SYNOPSIS** A new theater company and an old acting pro combine talents to create an imaginative, energetic and unorthodox production of *King Lear,* presented by the Boston based Actors' Shakespeare Project, and starring the legendary eighty-one year old Alvin Epstein as Lear. The original 14 members of the 2005 Boston production reassembled for this limited engagement.

*Alvin Epstein in La MaMa E.T.C.'s production of* King Lear *(photo by Carol Rosegg)*

## LOVE ME TENDER: THE SONGS OF ELVIS PRESLEY

59E59 Theater C; Opening Night: June 29, 2006; Closed July 2, 2006; 4 performances

Arranged by Barb Jungr and Adrian York, inspired by Howard Thompson's idea and James Lee Burke's landscapes; Produced by 59E59 Theaters (Elysabeth Kleinhans, Artistic Director; Peter Tear, Executive Producer); Presented by James Seabright in association with New Greenham Arts (Newbury, U.K.) as part of the Brits Off Broadway 2006; Sets/Lighting, Nick Flintoff; Hair, Fordham White; Press, Karen Greco

Performed by **Barb Jungr;** Piano **Charlie Giordano**

**MUSICAL NUMBERS** Love Letters Straight From Your Heart, Heartbreak Hotel; Wooden Heart, Are You Lonesome Tonight, In The Ghetto, Kentucky Rain, I Shall Be Released, Love Me Tender, Always on My Mind, Tomorrow is a Long Time, Long Black Limousine, Looking For Elvis, Peace in the Valley

A musical performance presented in two acts.

**SYNOPSIS** With her unique vocal style, Barb Jungr performs her art song-styled re-workings of material recorded by Elvis Presley. The performance is based on Jungr's 2005 Linn Records recording of the same name. Critics have compared her to Nina Simone, Peggy Lee, and Edith Piaf, declaring that she is one of the best interpreters of other artists such as Bob Dylan and Jacques Brel.

*Barbara Jungr in* Love Me Tender: The Songs of Elvis Presley *(photo by Piers Allardyce)*

## theAtrainplays: Volume XXI

New World Stages; July 2, 2006; 1 performance

Produced by Lawrence Feeney; Head Writer, Craig Pospisil; Writers: Liz Amberly, Joshua James, Michael Lazan, Stephen O'Rourke, Craig Pospisil, Erica Silberman; Composers/Lyricists: Gaby Alter, Brian J. Nash, Brandon Patton, Jeremy Schonfeld; Directors: David Brind, Edie Cowan, Michael Duling, Susan Einhorn, Barry McNabb, Mark Lonergan; Choreographers: Tricia Brouk, Dwight Edwards; Musical Director, Alec Berlin; Production Supervisor, Andrea "Spook" Testani; PSM, Linda Marvel; ASM, Rock Noel; Lighting, Paul Witte; Original Set Design, Andrew Donovan

**CAST Ashlie Atkinson, Jeb Brown, Stephanie D'Abruzzo, Kevin Del Aguila, Natalie Douglas, Ryan Duncan, Tracy Jai Edwards, Lawrence Feeney, Jenny Fellner, Eric Michael Gillett, Rob Gallagher, Mandy Gonzalez, Cady Huffman, Tim Johnson, Donovan Patton, Christine Pedi, Michael Pemberton, Rene Ruiz, Kate Shindle, Amber Stone, Melanie Vaughan, Doug Wert;** Band **Alec Berlin, Jordan Perlson, Rick Hip-Flores, Chris Tarry**

A collection of short plays and musicals presented without intermission. This presentation was the twenty-first edition of the series.

**SYNOPSIS** Writers script short musicals while riding the entire route of the A train from 207th Street to Rockaway. Composers and lyricists pick up the scripts and ride the train back, composing a score. Casts and directors are chosen by random draw, and the shows are rehearsed and performed all in a twenty-four hour period.

## RIVER DEEP: A Tribute to Tina Turner

Peter Jay Sharp Theatre; Opening Night: July 5, 2006; Closed July 29, 2006; 23 performances

Book by Gabrielle Lansner, music and lyrics by Philip Hamilton; based on *I, Tina* by Tina Turner with Kurt Loder; Additional music by Andy Ezrin, Holly Knight and Michael Chapman; Produced by Gabrielle Lansner and Company; Director/Choreographer, Gabrielle Lansner; Sets, Dean Taucher; Costumes, Liz Prince; Lighting, Jim French; Projections, Stephanie Berger; PSM, Christine Shallenberg; Production Manager, Joe Doran; Marketing/Development, Donna Walker Kuhne; Company Administrator, Aimee McCabe; Graphics, Lisa Powers, Visual Design, Brian Beasley; Press, Shaffer-Coyle Public Relations

**CAST** Tina Turner **Pat Hall;** Narrator **Erica Bowen;** Venatta Fields, an Ikette **McKenzie Frye\*;** Bonnie Bramlett, an Ikette **Heather Lind;** Rhonda Graam, Road Manager **Paula McGonagle;** Back-up Singer **Shekitra Starke**

**MUSICIANS** Daniel Minteris (keyboards), Alex Alexander (percussion), Trevor Exter (electric cello), Ghieli Minucci, and Spiros Exias (guitar)

**MUSICAL NUMBERS** Dancing to the Rhythm and Blues, Summer Song Blues, Southern Nights, Picnic Pick Up/Rapid Relay, Your Star's Gotta Shine, Treat You Like a Lady, See No Evil, Say No Evil, Tina's Chant, In Your Wildest Dreams, Just Let Me Know

Encore presentation of a musical and dance piece presented without intermission. Previously presented January 20–February 4, 2006, at the Peter J. Sharp Theatre.

**SYNOPSIS** *River Deep* is a joyous new musical celebrating the life of music legend Tina Turner featuring a complete original score by composer Philip Hamilton that captures the essential sounds of the 60's and 70's.

*Zainab Jah played the role in the previous engagement of the production

*Erica Bowen, Zainab Jah (front), and Pat Hall (back) in* River Deep: A Tribute to Tina Turner *(photo by Stephanie Berger)*

# CRAZY FOR THE DOG

Bouwerie Lane Theatre; Opening Night: July 11, 2006; Closed August 26, 2006; 42 performances

Written by Christopher S. Boal; Presented by Rachel Reiner Productions LLC in association with the Jean Cocteau Repertory; Director, Eric Parness; Sets, Matthew Allar; Costumes, Sidney Shannon; Lighting, Pamela Kupper; Sound, Nick Moore; Stage Manager, Amy Henault; Production Manager, Evan Schlossberg; Press, Sam Rudy Media Relations

**CAST** Paul **Patrick Melville;** Jenny **Wrenn Schmidt;** Kevin **Ryan C. Tramont;** Sarah **Christine Verleny**

**SETTING** Jenny's apartment, Brooklyn, New York. Now. World premiere of a new play presented in two acts. The show ran June 8–30, 2006 for fourteen additional performances as an Off-Off-Broadway showcase prior to this Off-Broadway extension.

**SYNOPSIS** *Crazy for the Dog* is a twisting, turning new dark comedy that exposes one family's deepest secret, a secret that binds together two siblings even as it threatens to destroy them. Racing through a lifetime of lies and pent-up blame, they cross New York to save not only a defenseless dog, but also their troubled relationship.

*Patrick Melville and Wrenn Schmidt in* Crazy for the Dog
*(photo by Ben Coopersmith)*

# THE CAPITOL STEPS: I'm So Indicted

The Supper Club; Opening Night: July 11, 2006; Closed August 20, 2006; 48 performances

Written and presented by The Capitol Steps, lyrics by Bill Strauss, Elaina Newport, Mark Eaton; Director, Bill Strauss; Producer, Elaina Newport; Media, Mike Thornton

**CAST Mike Thornton, Mike Carruthers, Mike Tilford, Elaina Newport, Ann Schmitt;** Pianists **Marc Irwin, Howard Breitbart**

**MUSICAL NUMBERS** Here's to You, Reverend Robertson, What a Difference Delay Makes, Government Lessons for Little Children: Chicken Little, Juan, What Kind of Fuel Am I?, God Bless My SUV, This is the House That Jack Bribed, Rafael Palmiero's Greatest Hits, Dubai Dubai Doo, How Do You Solve a Problem Like Korea?, Sam Alito; In the Metro, GOP-BS, Rolling Kidney Stones; FU Airlines, Living Will, Old Finger, Can't Get to Church; Three Little Kurds From School, Lirty Dies, If You Only Had a Heart, The Sunni Side of Tikrit, Mexifornia Here I Come, Al (Gore) Shook Up

A musical revue presented in two acts.

**SYNOPSIS** Armed and hilarious with new songs and numbers, the Capitol Steps bring their timely and irreverent spoof of the headlines to the New York stage and promise to bring down the entire house - and Senate. The Capitol Steps perform songs from their new album, *I'm So Indicted*, with special appearances by Dick "Don't Shoot!" Cheney, Donald Rumsfeld, Hillary Clinton, the Supreme Court Justices, and many more!

The Capitol Steps: *Tracey Stephens, Jamie Zemarel, Michael Carruthers, and Ann Johnson in* I'm So Indicted
*(photo by Richard Termine)*

# SECRETS

Theatre at St. Luke's; First Preview: June 28, 2006; Opening Night: July 13, 2006; Closed July 30, 2006; 17 previews, 22 performances

Written by Gerald Zipper; Produced by John Chatterton in association with La Muse Vénale; Director, Ted Mornel; Sets, Josh Iacovelli and Zen Mansley; Lighting/Stage Manager, Josh Iacovelli; Costumes, Elizabeth Flores; ASM, Stuart Marshall; Company Manager/Production Consultant, Louis S. Salamone; General Manager, John Chatterton; Press, David Gersten

**CAST** Hank **Mark Hamlet;** Dora **Lissa Moira;** Matt **Tom Sminkey;** Rhonda **Alyce Mayors;** Len **Darren Lougée;** Lally **Elena Zazanis**

A new play presented in two acts.

**SYNOPSIS** Hidden relationships threaten friendship and love as this evening of wining and dining degenerates into a session of backbiting, snide comments, and a contest to see who can be the cruelest to their respective spouses. When all is said, the participants wonder whether it's worth staying together anymore — but then again, can they adjust to a life alone?

Elena Zazanis, Darren Lougée, Alyce Mayors, and Tom Sminkey in Secrets (photo by Stuart Marshall)

# [title of show]

Vineyard Theatre; Opening Night: July 14, 2006; Closed October 1, 2006, 91 performances

Music and lyrics by Jeff Bowen, book by Hunter Bell; Produced by The Vineyard Theatre, Kevin McCollum, and Laura Camien; Director and Choreography, Michael Berresse; Music Director and Arrangements, Larry Pressgrove; Set, Neil Patel; Costumes, Chase Tyler; Lighting, Ken Billington and Jason Kantrowitz; Sound, ACME Sound Partners; PSM, Martha Donaldson; ASM, Tom Reynolds; Cast recording: Sh-K-Boom/Ghostlight Records 715584414-2

**CAST** Jeff **Jeff Bowen;** Hunter **Hunter Bell;** Susan **Susan Blackwell;** Heidi **Heidi Blickenstaff;** Piano **Larry Pressgrove;** Understudies **Benjamin Howes, Courtney Balan**

**MUSICAL NUMBERS** Untitled Opening Number, Two Nobodies in New York, An Original Musical, Monkeys and Playbills, Part of It All, I Am Playing Me, What Kind of Girl is She?, Die Vampire, Die, Filling Out the Form, September Song (Festival Medley), Secondary Characters, Montage/Photo Shoot, A Way Back to Then, Nine People's Favorite Thing

**SETTING** Place: [place]. Time: [time]. Commercial extension of a new musical presented without intermission. Previously played February 15–April 30, 2006 (see *Theatre World* Volume 62, page 175). Originally presented at the New York Musical Theatre Festival in 2004, and at Ars Nova September 11–27, 2005.

**SYNOPSIS** Two nobodies in New York, Jeff and Hunter, write a musical about two guys writing a musical for a musical theatre festival. With the help of their lady-friends Heidi and Susan and their musical director Larry, they succeed in getting to the festival and continuing the journey to Off-Broadway. In this ultimate meta-musical, the cast fights the creative vampires and the frustrations of the business to make their dreams come true.

(Clockwise from left) Heidi Blickenstaff, Jeff Bowen, Susan Blackwell, and Hunter Bell in [title of show] (photo by Carol Rosegg)

# NO CHILD...

Barrow Street Theatre; First Preview: July 8, 2006; Opening Night: July 16, 2006; Closed June 3, 2007; 311 performances

Written by play by Nilaja Sun; Produced by Epic Theatre Center; Director, Hal Brooks; Set, Narelle Sissons; Costumes, Jessica Gaffney, Lighting, Mark Barton, Sound, Ron Russell; Stage Manager, Tom Taylor; Press, O+M Company Performed by **Nilaja Sun**

**2006-2007 Awards:** Lucille Lortel Award: Outstanding Solo Show; Outer Critics Circle: Outstanding Solo Performance, John Gassner Award for American play; **Theatre World Award:** Nilaja Sun

A new solo performance play presented without intermission. Previously ran at the Beckett Theatre May 10–June 4, 2006.

**SYNOPSIS** *No Child. . .* is an unflinching look into the New York City Public Education system. Sun transforms herself into the teachers, students, parents, administrators, janitors, and security guards who inhabit our public schools every day and are shaping the future of America.

*Nilaja Sun in* No Child… *(photo by Carol Rosegg)*

# A STONE CARVER

SoHo Playhouse; First Preview: July 18, 2006; Opening Night: July 27, 2006; Closed August 27, 2006; 9 previews, 33 performances

Written by William Mastrosimone; Presented by Passage Theatre Company of Trenton, New Jersey (June Ballinger, Producing Artistic Director; David White, Associate Artistic Director); Produced by Darren Lee Cole and Parseghian Planco; Director, Robert Kalfin; Sets, Nathan Heverin; Costumes, Gail Cooper-Hecht; Lighting, Josh Bradford; Sound, Austin Duggan; Fight Director, B.H. Barry; Casting, Irene Stockton; General Management, Darren Lee Cole, Gabriel Voytas; Marketing, Jim Glaub; PSM, Lisa McGinn; ASM, Patrick Healy, Devon Jordon; Assistants to the Director, Heather Arnson, Anna Chazelle; Associate Lighting, Paul Hudson; Press, Karen Greco

**CAST** Agostino **Dan Lauria;** Raffaele **Jim Iorio;** Janice **Elizabeth Rossa**

A new play presented without intermission.

**SYNOPSIS** When a town wants to build a new highway off-ramp and issues eminent domain orders to clear the needed land, one elderly stone carver refuses to leave the home he built with his own hands. His son, a rising politician, tries to convince him to move - and move on. *A Stone Carver* is a powerful drama about a conflict sparked by a son's commitment to progress, a father's respect for the past, and the shifting values between generations.

*Jim Iorio, Elizabeth Rossa, and Dan Lauria in* A Stone Carver *(photo by Cie Stroud)*

# SHOUT! The Mod Musical

Julia Miles Theatre; First Preview: July 11, 2006; Opening Night: July 27, 2006; Closed December 10, 2006; 20 previews, 163 performances

Created by Phillip George and David Lowenstein, mod musings and groovy gab by Peter Charles Morris and Phillip George; Produced by Victoria Lang & P.P. Piccoli, Brent Peek, and Mark Schwartz; Director, Phillip George; Choreography, David Lowenstein; Musical Direction/Orchestrations/Additional Arrangements, Bradley Vieth; Sets, David Gallo; Costumes, Philip Heckman; Lighting, Jason Lyons; Sound, Tony Meola; PSM, Jana Llynn; Stage Manager, Nathan K. Claus; General Manager/Company Manager, Brent Peek Productions, Scott Newsome, Shaun Garrett; Associate Producers, Patricia Melanson, eBroadway Plays/Pat Addiss, Robin Gurwin; Associate Choreography/Dance Captain, Sloan Just; Wigs, Alfonso Annotto; Producing Associate, Jared Fine; Production Management, Dynamic Productions, Brian Rosenblum, Craig Sanogueira; Marketing, The Araca Group; Advertising, Hothouse Ltd.; Press, Boneau/Bryan-Brown, Jackie Green, Juliana Hannett, Heath Schwartz; Cast recording: Rhino 74791

**CAST** Blue Girl **Marie-France Arcilla;** Yellow Girl **Erin Crosby;** Orange Girl **Julie Dingman Evans;** Green Girl **Erica Schroeder;** Red Girl **Denise Summerford;** Gwendolyn Holmes (voiceover) **Carole Shelley;** Understudies **Sloan Just, Casey Clark**

**MUSICIANS** Bradley Vieth (Conductor/keyboard), Christopher Stephens (Keyboard #2), Joe Brady (Percussion)

**MUSICAL NUMBERS** England Swings/Round Every Corner/I Know A Place, I Only Want To Be With You/Tell the Boys, How Can You Tell, Wishin' And Hopin', One Two Three, To Sir With Love, Don't Sleep In The Subway, Son Of A Preacher Man, James Bond Theme/Goldfinger, You Don't Have To Say You Love Me, Diamonds Are Forever, Puppet On A String, Georgie Girl/Windy, Who Am I?, Don't Give Up, I Just Don't Know What To Do With Myself, The Boat I Row, These Boots Are Made For Walkin', I Couldn't Live Without Your Love, You're My World/All I See Is You, Those Were The Days, Shout!, Goin' Back, Downtown

**SETTING** London; The Swingin' 1960s. New York premiere of a new musical presented without intermission. U.S. premiere at the Raymond F. Kravis Center for the Performing Arts, West Palm Beach, Florida. Developed in association with Amas Musical Theatre (Donna Trinkoff, Producing Director) with a staged reading at the 2004 New York Musical Theatre Festival (Kris Stewart, Artistic Director).

**SYNOPSIS**  *Shout!* flips through the years like a musical magazine, tracking five young women as they come of age during the liberating days of the 1960s that made England swing. It is a non-stop journey through the infectious and soulful pop anthems and ballads that made household names of stars like Petula Clark, Dusty Springfield, and Lulu. *Shout!* uses letters to an advice columnist, true confessions, quizzes and advertisements as a frame for the hit songs.

*Denise Summerford, Erin Crosby, Marie-France Arcilla, Erica Schroeder, and Julie Dingman Evans in* Shout! The Mod Musical *(photo by Joan Marcus)*

# ABSINTHE

Spiegeltent at South Street Seaport; Opening Night: August 3, 2006; Closed October 1, 2006; 70 performances

Created and Produced by Ross Mollison and Vallejo Gantner; Director, Brett Haylock. PSM, Derek Brashears

**CAST**  **Camille O'Sullivan, Denis Lock, Hamish McCann, Amy Saunders, Una Mimnagh, Nate Cooper, Ursula Martinez, Tom Noddy, Yulia Pikhtina, David O'Mer, Brett Haylock**

A variety show presented in two acts.

**SYNOPSIS**  Combining the traditions of vaudeville and music hall with Berliner Kabarett, *ABSINTHE - Les Artistes de La Clique* is a variety show on acid, a late-night saunter through the sultriest, strangest circus in town. Fairground attraction collides with sideshow burlesque to transform the elegant, sumptuous confines of the Spiegeltent into something just a little ... below the belt.

*David O'Mer in* Absinthe *(photo by Marc Marnie)*

# BARBARA'S BLUE KITCHEN

Lamb's Theatre; First Preview: July 31, 2006; Opening Night: August 3, 2006; Closed September 2, 2006; 35 performances

Book, music and lyrics by Lori Fischer; Produced by Carolyn Rossi Copeland, Rob Reich, & LAF Music Inc.; Director, Martha Banta; Sets and Lighting, Bobby Bradley; Sound, Damian Chiurco; Assistant Director, Kevin R. Free; Musical Arranger, Daniel Levy; General Manager, The Lamb's Theatre, Mary Kickel; Stage Manager, Allison Laurence; Press, Keith Sherman and Associates

**CAST**  Barbara Jean and characters in Diner  **Lori Fischer;** Dickie Brian Hull/WATR DJ/guitar **Scott Wakefield** or **Kurt Zischke**

**SETTING**  A small diner in Watertown, Tennessee, Summer 1997. A solo performance play with music presented without intermission. This production was the final show to play the Lamb's Theatre

**SYNOPSIS**  *Barbara's Blue Kitchen* follows a day in the life of Barbara Jean, the proprietor of the down-home coffee shop, her regular customers, and the lives that unfold over the blue plate special. The action is peppered with a score of twelve original songs and a healthy dose of southern charm.

*Lori Fisher in* Barbara's Blue Kitchen *(photo by Damien Chiurco)*

## ANAÏS NIN: One of Her Lives

Beckett Theatre; First Preview: August 3, 2006; Opening Night: August 5, 2006; Closed August 26, 2006; 24 performances

Written and directed by Wendy Beckett; Producer, Wendy Beckett; Executive Producer, Matthew Sandblom; Presented by Pascal Productions; Sets/Costumes, Halcyon Pratt; Lighting, Robin A. Paterson; Sound, Travis Walker; Assistant Sound, Sara Bader; PSM, Heather Arnson; ASM, Cambra Overend; Dialogue Coach, Stephen Gabis; Casting, Judy Henderson; Assistant Director, Brett Heath; Press, Katie Rosin

**CAST** Anaïs Nin **Angela Christian;** Henry Miller **David Bishins;** June Miller **Alysia Reiner;** Nin's Father/ Dr. Otto Rank **Rocco Sisto**

**SETTING** 1930s, Paris, France. A new play presented without intermission.

**SYNOPSIS** The play follows the development of a writer who, in the end, must choose her own path if she is to succeed in her literary ambition. Biographically, the play traces the complicated love triangle between Anaïs Nin, author, Henry Miller, and his wife June. A literary ménage a trois is born that is like no other.

*Angela Christian, David Bishins, and Alysia Reiner in*
Anaïs Nin: One of Her Lives *(photo by Richard Termine)*

## CREATION: A Clown Show

Theatre 5; First Preview: August 4, 2006; Opening Night: August 10, 2006; Closed September 10, 2006; 42 performances

Created and conceived by Lucas Caleb Rooney and Orlando Pabotoy; Presented by Gussy Charles Productions; Director, Orlando Pabotoy; Original Music, Peter Friedland, and Javen Tanner; Producer, Ty Jones; Producer/General Manager, Jill Jones; Costumes, Kimberly Glennon; Lighting, Peter West; PSM, Renee Blinkwolt; Production Assistant, Catherine Mancuso; Props, Mary Vorrasi; Technical Director, Mark Vanderhook; Electrician, Marnie Cumings; Set Consultant, Loy Arcenas; Press, David Gibbs, DARR Publicity

**CAST** Clown **Lucas Caleb Rooney;** The Voice **Samuel Stricklen;** Musicians **Peter Friedland, Javen Tanner**

A solo performance clown show presented without intermission.

**SYNOPSIS** *Creation*, a solo clown show in the tradition of Harpo Marx and Bill Irwin, is a physically raucous, delightful romp through the world of the clown, where the silly is celebrated and the simple is beautiful. Embracing make-believe and magic, and returning one to a world of wonder, *Creation* offers a hilarious new view of that old book known as Genesis.

*Lucas Caleb Rooney in* Creation: A Clown Show *(photo by Jill Jones)*

## EVENSONG

The Barrow Group Arts Center; First Preview: August 10, 2006; Opening Night: August 11, 2006; Closed August 27, 2006; 14 performances

Written by Mary Gage; Produced by Broad Horizons Theatre Company in association with Jack W. Batman; Director, Lewis Magruder; Costumes, Emily Pepper; Lighting, Thom Weaver; Original Music, Larry Spivack; Assistant Director, Margo Lemberger; PSM, Gina Verdi; Press, Shaffer-Coyle Public Relations

**CAST** Marie **Mary Ellen Ashley;** Duke **Arthur French;** Clay **Donald Grody;** Helen **Mikel Sarah Lambert;** Sue **Pat Nesbit;** Gwen **Lucille Patton**

A new lyrical play presented without intermission.

**SYNOPSIS** Based on interviews with seniors over eighty living in Michigan, *Evensong* weaves together the lives of six people who speak for a generation of Americans—some born here, others who arrived here with nothing. These men and women toiled, suffered, and survived to help shape this country. *Evensong* celebrates them for the lives they lived and the wisdom they pass along. Though all had led very different lives, each survived the Great Depression and World War II and had completed a long and sometimes harrowing journey from childhood to old age. *Evensong* blends their stories into an American tapestry celebrating life.

*Mikel Sarah Lambert, Arthur French, and Lucille Patton in* Evensong
*(photo by Ben Strothmann)*

*Arian Moayed and Tom Ridgely in* Marco Millions (based on lies)
*(photo by Ryan Jensen)*

## MARCO MILLIONS (based on lies)

Lion Theatre; First Preview: August 4, 2006; Opening Night: August 12, 2006; Closed August 26, 2006; 19 performances

Created and presented by Waterwell, adapted from the play by Eugene O'Neill; Director, Tom Ridgely; Choreographer, Lynn Peterson; Composer, Lauren Cregor; Sets, Dave Lombard; Costumes, Elizabeth Payne; Lighting, Stacey Boggs; Sound, Jessica Paz; Stage Manager, Patricia Drozda; Graphic Design, Brian McMullen; ASM, Krissy Shields; Press, Shaffer-Coyle Public Relations

**CAST** Marco Polo **Arian Moayed;** Kublai Khan (and others) **Rodney Gardiner;** Maffeo Polo (and others) **Tom Ridgely;** Princess Kukachin (and others) **Hanna Cheek;** Narrator (and others) **Kevin Townley**

**MUSICIANS** Lauren Cregor, Gunter Gruner, Jenny Hill, Adam Levine, Joe Morse

A "drop" (dramatic vaudeville with comedy and music) presented without intermission.

**SYNOPSIS** The acclaimed ensemble Waterwell puts its signature irreverent stamp on O'Neill's lesser-known play about the thirteenth century travels of Marco Polo. *Marco Millions (based on lies)*, is the story of a Westerner encountering the East and the collision of cultures and economies that followed. The play is a kaleidoscopic and freewheeling ride that confronts questions of class and race that are as important now as they were in 1928... or 1271.

## THE FANTASTICKS

Snapple Theater Center; First Preview: July 28, 2006; Opening Night: August 23, 2006; still running as of May 31, 2007

Book and lyrics by Tom Jones, music by Harvey Schmidt, suggested by the play *Les Romanesques* by Edmond Rostand; Produced by Steven Baruch, Marc Routh, Richard Frankel, Thomas Viertel; Director, Tom Jones; Original Staging, Word Baker; Sets/Costumes, Ed Wittstein; Lighting, Mary Jo Dondlinger; Sound, Dominic Sack; Casting, Telsey + Company; Musical Director, Dorothy Martin; PSM, Gregory R. Covert; Stage Manager/Dance Captain, Kim Moore; Production Management, Aduro Productions; Production Supervisor, Dan Shaheen; General Management, Richard Frankel Productions, Ed Kaats; Musical Staging, Janet Watson; Company Manager, Leslie Anne Pinney; Press, Barlow · Hartman, Andrew Snyder; Cast recording: Sh-K-Boom/Ghostlight 84415

**CAST** The Narrator **Burke Moses**[+]; The Boy (Matt) **Santino Fontana**[*1]; The Girl (Luisa) **Sara Jean Ford**[*2]; The Boy's Father (Hucklebee) **Leo Burmester**[*3]; The Girl's Father (Bellomy) **Martin Vidnovic;** The Old Actor (Henry) **Thomas Bruce;** The Man Who Dies (Mortimer) **Robert R. Oliver**[+]; The Mute **Douglas Ullman Jr.**[*4]; At the Piano **Dorothy Martin;** At the Harp **Erin Hill**

**STANDBYS** John Deyle[*5] (Hucklebee/Henry/Mortimer), Paul Jackel[*6] (El Gallo/Hucklebee/Bellomy), Betsy Morgan[*7] (The Mute/Luisa), Douglas Ullman Jr. [*4] (Matt)

**MUSICAL NUMBERS** Overture, Try to Remember, Much More, Metaphor, Never Say No, It Depends on What You Pay, Soon It's Gonna Rain, Abduction Ballet, Happy Ending, This Plum is Too Ripe, I Can See It, Plant a Radish, Round and Round, They Were You, Try to Remember (reprise)

133

Revival of the musical presented in two acts. *The Fantasticks* is the world's longest running musical and the longest running Off-Broadway production ever. The original production opened at the Sullivan Street Playhouse on May 3, 1960, and closed January 13, 2002, playing over 17,000 performances (see *Theatre World* Volume 16, page 167 for original credits). In this revival, Tom Jones, author and lyricist, recreates the role of "Henry" The Old Actor under the pseudonym 'Thomas Bruce.'

**SYNOPSIS** *The Fantasticks* tells the story of a young boy and girl who fall madly in love at the hands of their meddling fathers, but soon grow restless and stray from one another. Will their separation provide a deeper appreciation for the love they once shared or create a permanent gulf between them?

+Burke Moses replaced James Moye in previews. Robert R. Oliver replaced MacIntyre Dixon in rehearsals.

*Succeeded by: 1. Douglas Ullman Jr., Anthony Federov 2. Julie Craig, Betsy Morgan 3. John Deyle 4. Nick Spangler 5. Tom Flagg 6. Stuart Marland 7. Betsy Morgan, Julie Craig

*Burke Moses, Sara Jean Ford, and Santino Fontana in* The Fantasticks
*(photos by Joan Marcus)*

*Leo Burmester, Burke Moses, and Martin Vidnovic in* The Fantasticks

# WASPS IN BED

Beckett Theatre; First Preview: September 5, 2006; Opening Night: September 7, 2006; Closed October 15, 2006; 39 performances

Written by Richard Willis Jr., Kieron Quirke, Paul Murray and Nicola Behrmann, story by Raja G. Ogirala and Richard Willis Jr.; Produced by OM Productions; Director, Lisa Marie Meller; Sets, Dustin O'Neill; Costumes, Deanna L. Berg; Lighting, Graham Kindred; Sound, Andrew Eisele; Props, Mary Vorrasi; Casting, Jamibeth Margolis; Advertising, Eliran Murphy Group; Marketing, Katie Rosin; Production Manager, Aron Deyo; PSM, Allison Deutsch; ASM, Andrea Jo Martin; Company Manager, Ginger Dzerk; General Manager, Dean Strober; Executive Producers, Raja G. Ogirala and Raja C. Ogirala; Press, Shaffer-Coyle Public Relations

*Kelly Deadmon and David Alan Basche in* WASPs in Bed
*(photo by Bruce Glikas)*

**CAST** Allan **David Alan Basche**; Betsy **Kelly Deadmon**; Bobby **Rick Gillford**; Raina **Alysia Reiner**; Cal **Richard Short**; Reese **Jessica-Snow Wilson**

**SETTING** July 4th, a cabin in the Berkshires. World premiere of a new play presented in two acts.

**SYNOPSIS** A provocative comedy about the perpetual pursuit of life, love, and happiness, *WASPs in Bed* is about three old friends with new partners who re-unite for Bobby's wedding. When 'the corporates,' married with two kids; 'the artsy types,' about to wed; and 'the politicals,' vehemently opposed to marriage, are all thrust into the political and emotional woods of matrimony, a lovely weekend getaway becomes a pending revolution.

# THE PERSIANS

City Center Mainstage; September 16–20, 2006; 6 performances

National Theatre of Greece's presentation of the play by Aeschylus, translated by Nikoletta Frindzila; Director, Lydia Koniordou; Sets/Costumes, Lili Kendaka; Music, Takis Farazis; Choreography, Apostolia Papadamaki; Lighting, Lefteris Pavlopoulos; Vocal Patterns, Mirka Gamentzaki; U.S. Press, Richard Kornberg and Associates

**CAST** Queen Atossa **Lydia Koniordou;** Darius **Yannis Kranas;** King Xerxes **Christos Loulis;** Messengers **Phaidon Kastris, Takis Sakellariou, Apostolis Pelakanos, Dimitris Kanellos, Sampson Fytros, Yorgos Gallos, Panagiotis Klinis, Yorgos Stamos;** Chorus leaders **Phaidon Kastris, Manolis Dragatsis, Takis Sakellariou, Dimitris Kanellos, Dinos Pontikopoulos, Stephanos Kosmidis, Vassilis Margetis;** Chorus **Apostolis Pelakanos, Ioanna Kotsi, Katerina Liontaki, Sampson Fytros, Yorgos Frindzilas, Yorgos Gallos, Elena Marsidou, Yannis Kotsifas, Vassilis Spiropoulos, Yorgos Stamos, Yorgos Dousis, Alexandros Kalpakidis, Panagiotis Klinis, Yorgis Tsampourakis, Vassilis Zaifidis, Chrysanthi Avloniti, Dimitris Mosxonas;** Musicians **Takis Farazis, Stephanos Logothetis, Stephanos Tortopoglou, Nikos Xinos**

A classic play presented in Greek with English titles performed in two acts. This production received its first performance July 1, 2006 in Delphi, Greece.

**SYNOPSIS** The National Theatre of Greece returns to New York for a limited run of Aeschylus' *The Persians*, the oldest surviving play in history and the only extant Greek tragedy that is non-mythical in theme and based on historic fact.

# FIFTY MILLION FRENCHMEN

Florence Gould Hall; Opening Night: September 17, 2006; Closed October 8, 2006, 4 performances

Music and lyrics by Cole Porter, book by Herbert Fields; Produced by The Lost Musicals Charitable Trust/Lost Musicals U.S. Inc.; Director, Ian Marshall Fisher; Music Director, Mark Mitchell

**CAST** Michael Cummins **Sean McKnight;** Billy Baxter **Keith Merrill;** Monsieur Pernasse **Roger DeWitt;** Marcelle **Catherine Lavalle;** Peter Forbes **Edward Watts;** Tetti/Magician/Waiter/Driver **Jeffrey Stern;** Mrs Gladys Carroll **Mary Ellen Ashley;** Mr Emmitt Carroll **Richard Marshall;** Joyce Wheeler **Katie Adams;** Looloo Carroll **Michelle K Nicklas;** Violet Hildegarde **K.T. Sullivan;** Mrs. De Vere **Sondra Lee;** May De Vere **Christine Pedi;** Mrs Ira Rosen **Donna Coney Island;** Mr. Ira Rosen **Dale Radunz;** Junior Rosen **Eamon Foley;** Grand Duke Ivan Ivanovitch **Maurice Edwards**

**MUSICAL NUMBERS** You Do Something to Me, You've Got That Thing, Find Me a Primitive Man, Where Would You Get Your Coat, Do You Want to See Paris?, Yankee Doodle, Why Shouldn't I Have You?, Somebody's Going to Throw a Big Party, It Isn't Done, I'm in Love, The Queen of Terre Haute, The Tales of the Oyster, My Boyfriend Back Home, Paris, What Did You Do to Me?, You Don't Know Paree, I'm Unlucky in Love, Finale

**SETTING** Paris, 1929. Concert version revival of a musical presented in two acts.

**SYNOPSIS** *Fifty Million Frenchmen* follows a group of well-to-do Americans unleashed in Paris and looking for excitement. A hilarious satire of American's abroad, the musical has not been seen in New York since its 1929 run at the Lyceum Theatre.

# LEMKIN'S HOUSE

McGinn/Cazale Theatre; First Preview: September 13, 2006; Opening Night: September 17, 2006; Closed October 8, 2006; 24 performances

Written by Catherine Filloux; Director, Jean Randich; Produced by Body Politic Theater and Vital Theatre Company; Sets, Sue Rees; Lighting, Matthew Adelson; Sound, Robert Murphy; Costumes, Camille Assaf; Props, Liz Maestri; Fight Choreography, Christopher Edwards; Stage Manager, Joanna Jacobsen; ASM, Megan Schwarz; Director/Dramaturg, Effy Redman; Technical Director, Daniel Jagendorf; Press, Sam Rudy Media Relations

**CAST** Raphael Lemkin **John Daggett;** Promire/Jack/Antonine/Hasan **Christopher McHale;** JP/Militiaman/Victor/Palmer **Christopher Edwards;** Aide/Nausicaa Agathe/Rose/Guard **Constance Winston;** Mother/Caitlin/Tatjana **Laura Flanagan**

Off-Broadway transfer of a play presented without intermission. Previously presented at 78th Street Theatre Lab, February 2006.

**SYNOPSIS** *Lemkin's House* is set in the afterlife of Raphael Lemkin, the Polish-American lawyer whose family died in the Holocaust and who invented the word "genocide." He dedicated his life to the fight to have genocide declared an international crime. Lemkin must recognize that even his law is not enough to change the world. He weighs his ethical accomplishments against his guilt for deserting his own doomed family ultimately seeking not only justice but also forgiveness.

*John Daggett and Laura Flanagan in* Lemkin's House
*(photo by Carol Rosegg)*

# SISTERS

59E59 Theater B; First Preview: September 12, 2006; Opening Night: September 17, 2006; Closed October 8, 2006; 33 performances

Written by Declan Hassett; Presented by The Colorado Festival of World Theatre in association with The City Theatre Dublin; Director/Lighting/Original Music, Michael Scott; Sets, Stuart Marshall; Costumes, Michael McCaffery; Technical Director, Cormac Veale; U.S. Production Manager for City Theatre Dublin, Tommy Joe Lucas, Jr.; Stage Manager, Jenny Deady; Press, Karen Greco

**CAST** Martha/Mary **Anna Manahan**

Setting: 1950s; Ireland. New York premiere of new solo performance play presented in two acts. Originally presented in at City Theatre Dublin, Ireland.

**SYNOPSIS** Tony-winner Anna Manahan creates two extraordinary portraits of Sisters Martha and Mary in *Sisters*, a story of disappointed love, brutal passion, and the horrific consequences of two women's lives. The play's two acts outline the resentments, regrets, and secrets of these two women whose lives have taken very different turns.

*Anna Manahan in* Sisters *(photo by Valerie O'Sullivan)*

# ESOTERICA

DR2 Theatre; First Preview: September 9, 2006; Opening Night: September 19, 2006; Closed December 30, 2006; 99 performances

Written by Eric Walton; Produced by Daryl Roth, Leia Thompson, and David Sonkin; Director, Elysa Marden; Sets, Troy Hourie; Costumes, Jessica Jahn; Lighting, Ben Stanton; Original Music and Sound, Lisa Heffter; PSM, Ana Mari de Quesada; Press, Pete Sanders

Performed by **Eric Walton** and **Reyna de Courcy**

A magic show presented in two acts.

**SYNOPSIS** *Esoterica* is multi-media theatrical tour-de-force in which critically acclaimed actor, magician, and mentalist Eric Walton leads his audience on an unforgettable exploration of the rich and complex tapestry of the human psyche. With his incomparable abilities as a sleight of hand artist, raconteur, poet and showman, Mr. Walton expertly and satirically investigates with his audience matters philosophical, metaphysical, and arcane.

*Eric Walton in* Esoterica

# MACHIAVELLI

ArcLight Theatre; First Preview: September 13, 2007; Opening Night: September 24, 2006; Closed November 5, 2006; 12 previews, 43 performances

Written by Richard Vetere; Produced by San Casciano Productions; Director, Evan Bergman; Sets/Lighting, Maruti Evans; Costumes, Michael Bevins; PSM, Elis C. Arroyo; ASM, April A. Kline; Technical Supervisor, Greg Hirsch; General Management, Ken Denison, Carol Fishman; Executive Producers, Elizabeth Williams, Aruba Productions; Marketing, Martian Entertainment; Company Manager, Sasha DeFazio; Fight Coordinator, Ron Piretti; Sound Coordinator, Brian Petway; Props, Brian Schweppe; Assistant Design, Aaron Paternoster, Gentry Farley; Wig, Marion M. Geist; Press, Pete Sanders, Glenna Freedman

**CAST** Alfonso **Lex Woutas;** Machiavelli **James Wetzel;** Marietta **Liza Vann;** Giuliano **Chip Philips;** Lorenzo **Jason Howard;** Baccina **Stephanie Janssen**

**SETTING** 1513–1527; A prison courtyard in Florence, Italy, and Machiavelli's property outside Florence. A new play presented in two acts. Originally presented Off-Off-Broadway at Manhattan Theatre Source, January 2006.

**SYNOPSIS** Written in commedia style, *Machiavelli* tells the story of how the world's most famous political thinker used his genius to survive and outsmart the ruthless Medici family while bringing democracy to Florence during the Renaissance in the 1500's.

*James Wetzel, Liza Vann, and Stephanie Janssen in* Machiavelli *(photo by Joan Marcus)*

# BUSH IS BAD: Impeachment Edition

Triad Theatre; First Preview: September 21, 2006; Opening Night: September 29, 2006; Closed December 30, 2006, 46 performances

Concept, music, lyrics, and musical direction by Joshua Rosenblum; Produced by Tim Peierls and Shrubbery Productions; Director/Choreographer, Gary Slavin; Graphics, Colin Stokes; Costumes, Anne Auberjonois; Lighting/Sound, Tonya Pierre; Assistant Director/Choreographer, Janet Bushor; Props, Mary Ann Miles; Creative Consultant/Press, Joanne Lessner; Production Coordinator, Ayelet Arbuckle; Marketing, Gary Shaffer; Digital Imaging, Julian Rosenblum; Graphic Design/Design Adaptation, Michael Holmes

**CAST** Janet Dickinson[*1], Neal Mayer, Michael McCoy[*2]; Pianist **David Wolfson**

**MUSICAL NUMBERS** How Can 59 Million People Be So Dumb?, Bush is Bad, New Hope for the Fabulously Wealthy, Das Busch Ist Schlecht, Good Conservative Values, The Gay Agenda, I May Be Gay, I'm Losing You, Karl, Love Song of W. Mark Felt, John Bolton Has Feelings, Too, Crazy Ann Coulter, Lying Liars, Survivor: Beltway Scumbag Edition, The "I" Word , Get Real, The Inauguration Was Marvelous, Good Conservative Values II, Culture of Life, Beaten by a Dead Man, Sure You Betcha, Georgie, In His Own Words, On Our Way to Guantonamo Bay; Wake Me When It's 2009, The Man From Diebold, Heck of a Job, You Can Never Have Enough Bush, Torture Has Been Very Good To Me

Revised edition of the musical revue presented without intermission. The first edition played the Triad October 6, 2005–July 29, 2006 (see *Theatre World* Volume 62, page 103).

**SYNOPSIS** Described as "the hysterical love child of *Forbidden Broadway* and "The Daily Show," *Bush is Bad* is a gleefully partisan, take-no-prisoners look at the current sorry state of affairs in American government.

*Succeeded by 1. Christianne Tisdale, Lori Hammel 2. Tom Treadwell

*Original cast members Neal Mayer, Kate Baldwin, and Michael McCoy in* Bush is Bad: Impeachment Edition *(photo by Carol Rosegg)*

# DRUG BUDDY

Cherry Lane Theatre; First Preview: September 27, 2006; Opening Night: September 30, 2006; Closed October 21, 2006; 16 performances

Written by David Folwell; Produced by the stageFARM Theatre Company (Carrie Shaltz, Founder and Executive Director; Alex Kilgore, Artistic Director); Director, Alex Kilgore; Sets, John McDermott; Lighting, Ed McCarthy; Sound, John Kilgore; PSM, Eliza Johnson; ASM, Kelly Beaulieu; Assistant Director, Christine Renee Miller; Casting, Susan Shopmanker; Production Coordinator, Christine Miller; Marketing, Kate Laughlin; Development, Yufei Hsu; Press, O+M Company, Philip Carrubba

**CAST** Wade **Matthew Stadelmann;** Bodie **Jesse Hooker;** Wendy **Carrie Shaltz;** Travis **Jake M. Smith**

World premiere of a new play presented without intermission.

**SYNOPSIS** *Drug Buddy* is about staying up all-night and waking up transformed into the person you never wanted to become. Wade is recovering from a night of firsts: His first drug experience, his first sexual experience, and his first brush with death. It's been an eventful night—if only he could remember it. Wade's best friend Bodie remembers enough to know that they need to get out of Texas. Fast!

*Matthew Stadelmann and Jesse Hooker in* Drug Buddy
*(photo by Richard Termine)*

## MARIA MARIA

Gerald W. Lynch Theater at John Jay College; First Preview: September 22, 2006; Opening Night: October 1, 2006; Closed October 15, 2006; 11 previews, 17 performances

Book and lyrics by Hye Jung Yu, music by Gyung Chan Cha; Produced by Joa Musical Company, Chris Yongseok Choi, Jack M. Dalgleish, Hyun Chul Kang, in conjunction with the New York Musical Theatre Festival; Director, Cheon Mo Seong; Choreography, In Sook Choi; Musical Director, Moo Youl Choi; Sets, Sook Jin Seo; Costumes, Soo Dong Lee; Lighting, Tae Hwan Koo; Sound, Kook Hyun Kang; Makeup, Sung Hye Kim; Arrangements, Chul Min Kim; Stage Manager, Sung Ye Suk; Assistant Director, Jung Bum Kim; Assistant Choreography, Seung Min Kang; Masque Dance, Seung Chul Lee; Master Section Chief, Hee Chul Shim; Section Chief, Jong Suk Kim; Prcss, O+M Company

**CAST** Maria **Hyo Sung Kang;** Maria (alternates) **Ga In Choi** or **Sonya;** The Blind Woman **Bock Hee Yoon;** Jesus **Sang Woo Park;** Jesus (alternates) **Bo Kang Kim** or **Joon Ho Huh;** The Pharisee **Seung Chul Lee;** The High Priest **Tae Hyung Kim** or **Jong Goo Kim;** Peter **Young Wan Kim;** Lisa and Maria's Mother **Hi Jin Ki;** Judas **Won Suk Ko;** Antipas & Simon **Seong Woog Lee;** Thomas **Ji Seung Ha;** Anais **Soo Jung Kim;** Andre **Sae Joon Hwang;** Band Master **Jung Hee Park;** Drums **Tae Yong Lee**

American premiere of a musical presented in Korean with English titles in two acts.

**SYNOPSIS** In this award-winning Korean musical, Maria is a prostitute who leads a miserable life serving Roman soldiers. Wanting to escape her fate, she makes a deal that will change her life. With the rising popularity of Jesus, his opponents make her an offer to seduce him. If successful, her reward is a chance to go to Rome to redeem her life.

*The Joa Musical Company in* Maria Maria
*(photo courtesy of Joa Musical Company)*

## THE TOOTH OF CRIME

La MaMa E.T.C. Annex; Opening Night: October 3, 2006; Closed October 22, 2006; 28 performances

Written by Sam Shepard; Produced by La MaMa E.T.C. (Ellen Stewart, Artistic Director); Director, George Ferencz; Original Music, Sam Shepard, Musical Director, Bob Jewett, Stage Design, Bill Stabile, Costumes, Sally Lesser; Press, Sam Rudy Media Relations

**CAST** Hoss **Ray Wise;** Becky Lou **Jenne Vath;** Star-man **John Andrew Morrison;** Galactic Jack **Gideon Charles Davis;** Referee **Arthur Adair;** Cheyenne **Cary Gant;** Doc **Raul Aranas;** Crow **Nick Denning**

Revival of the play with music presented in two acts. Originally produced at the Open Space, London, on July 17, 1972.

**SYNOPSIS** *The Tooth of Crime* is about a fading rock star fending off the ambitious newcomer who wants to take his place. La MaMa E.T.C.'s 1983 production is re-presented in celebration of La MaMa's 45th Anniversary, featuring Mr. Ferencz's original direction (who staged the entire production as a rock concert), and original cast members Raul Aranas as "Doc" and Ray Wise in his Obie-award winning performance as "Hoss." This project was done originally in association with Syracuse Stage. Mr. Shepard subsequently rewrote the play in 1987, but allowed La MaMa to use the original script for this production.

*Raul Aranas and Ray Wise in* The Tooth of Crime
*(photo by Mark Roussel)*

# BUSH WARS: A Musical Revenge

Actors Playhouse; First Preview: September 22, 2006; Opening Night: October 4, 2006; Closed November 12, 2006; 8 previews, 25 performances

A musical revue created and directed by Nancy Holson, conceived and produced by Jim Russek; Co-producers, Bob Boyett, Mel & Phyllis Holson; Co-Creator-Director/Choreography, Jay Falzone; Set/Props, Patrice Escandon; Costumes, Elizabeth Payne; Lighting, Scott Borowka; Musical Director, Alexander Rovang; PSM, Jeanne-Marie Fisichella; General Management, Jamie Cesa; Company Manager, Townsend Teague; Properties, Amy Schwartz; Press, Peter Cromarty and Company

**CAST** Satan/Bill Frist/Barbara Bush/Jesus **Jay Falzone;** George W. Bush **Jason Levinson;** Eve/Hallie Burton/Betsy Ross/Professor of Republican Sociology 101 **Mamie Parris;** Blue State Blues Singer/Condoleezza Rice/Supreme Court Justice **Abigail Nessen;** Osama bin Laden/Thomas Jefferson/Border Patrol **Chris Van Hoy;** Pianist **Alex Rovang**

Revised edition of a new political musical revue presented without intermission. Previously played last season at Collective: Unconscious Theatre and Rattlestick Playwrights Theater (see *Theatre World* Volume 62, page 115).

**SYNOPSIS** Told through 16 musical parodies and dozens of costume changes, *Bush Wars* sinks its talons into everything from Dick Cheney literally in bed with the oil companies to the Supreme Court's "right hand turn" and from "Republican training school" to George W. in a soft shoe number with his bosom buddy, Jesus! New material includes a hilarious take on the immigration guest workers program, wire tapping, the re-writing of the Constitution, and voter fraud! The musical takes a funny but insightful look at how America's current government has undermined Democracy itself!

*Jason Levinson and Jay Falzone in* Bush Wars: A Musical Revenge *(photo by Steve Schwartz)*

*Svein Sturla Hungnes and Cast in the Norwegian Company's production of* Peer Gynt *(photo by Lars Erik Skrefsrud)*

# PEER GYNT

Delacorte Theater; October 5–7, 2006; 3 performances

Written by Henrik Ibsen, music by Edvard Grieg; Produced by The Norwegian Company of *Peer Gynt* (Gudbrandsdalen, Norway); Director, Svein Sturla Hungnes; Conductor, Timothy Myers; Choir Leader, Nina Moen; Arrangements, Atle Halstensen; Film Director, Arne Rostad; Orchestra, The American Symphony Orchestra; Production Manager, C. Townsend Olcott II; Stage Manager, Hans Voigt; Lighting, Jeff Nellis; Sound, Dave Meschter; Costumes, Ingrid Nylander/Svein Sturla Hungnes; Makeup, Greta Bremseth; Press, O+M Company

**CAST** Peer Gynt **Svein Sturla Hungnes;** Mother Ase **Kari Simonsen;** Solveig **Linda Øvrebø;** Ingrid/The Greenclad Woman **Mari Maurstad;** The Farmer at Haegstad/The Mountain King/Strange Passenger/Begriffenfeldt **Rune Reksten;** The Button Molder/Bøygen/The Blacksmith/Captain **Stein Grønli;** Other roles **Karoline Krüger, Camilla Granlien**

Concert version of a multimedia play with music presented in two acts. This production has been staged annually at the Peer Gynt Festival on Norway's Lake Gålå since 1989.

**SYNOPSIS** To commemorate the 100th anniversary of Ibsen's death, the Lake Gålå's production of *Peer Gynt* performs for the first time outside of Norway, Ibsen's homeland. Written in verse and concerning the epic quest of a proud anti-hero, Svein Sturla Hungnes' multimedia epic concert staging of the 1867 work features a cast of more than 150 actors, and features the Grieg score performed by the American Symphony Orchestra and the Peer Gynt Chamber Choir.

# THE THUGS

SoHo Rep; First Preview: October 5, 2006; Opening Night: October 7, 2006*; Closed November 12, 2006; 2 previews, 28 performances

Written by Adam Bock; Produced by SoHo Rep; Director, Anne Kauffman; Sets, David Korins; Costumes, Michelle R. Phillips; Lighting, Ben Stanton; Sound, Robert Kaplowitz & Jeremy Lee; Props, Mary Vorrasi; Stage Manager, Sarah Bishop-Stone; Artistic Director, Daniel Aukin/Sarah Benson; Press, Sam Rudy Media Relations

**CAST** Elaine **Saidah Arrika Ekulona;** Bart **Brad Heberlee;** Diane **Carmen Herlihy;** Joey **Chris Heuisler;** Daphne **Keira Keeley;** Mary **Lynne McCollough;** Chantal **Maria Elena Ramirez;** Mercedes **Mary Shultz**

World premiere of a new play presented without intermission.

**SYNOPSIS** *The Thugs* is a new dark comedy about work, thunder, and the mysterious things that are happening on the ninth floor of a big law firm. When a group of temps try to discover the secrets that lurk in the hidden crevices of their workplace, they realize they would rather believe in gossip and rumors than face dangerous realities.

*Performances from October 31–November 12 were under an Off-Broadway contract.

Carmen Herlihy, Lynne McCollough, Mary Shultz, and Saidah Arrika Ekulona in The Thugs *(photo by Monique Carboni)*

# HELL HOUSE

St. Ann's Warehouse; First Preview: October 1, 2006; Opening Night: October 10, 2006; Closed October 29, 2006; 250 performances

Text by Pastor Keenan Roberts; Presented by Arts at St. Ann's (Susan Feldman, artistic director, Sallie D. Sanders, General Manager); Produced and performed by Les Freres Corbusier (Alex Timbers, Artistic Director; Aaron Lemon-Strauss, Executive Director); Director, Alex Timbers; Sets, Garin Marschall; Costumes, Sidney Shannon; Lighting, Tyler Micoleau; Sound and Music, Bart Fasbender; Makeup, David Withrow; Dramaturg, Alexis Soloski; Properties, Stephanie Wiesner; Music Director, Gabriel Kahane; PSM, Alaina Taylor; Stage Managers, Erin Koster & Molly Eustis; Associate Producers, Maggie Rowe, Jaclyn Lafer, Jack Rudy; Press, Richard Kornberg and Associates

**CAST** Jeremy **Teddy Bergman;** Satan **Jeff Biehl;** Chad **David Flaherty;** Pastor Pat **Pat Inglis;** Chrissy **Julie Klausner;** Jan **Julie Lake;** Steve **Rob O'Hare;** Brian **Wil Petre;** God **Jared Reinmuth;** Courtney **Amanda Sayle;** Jessica **Katie Vagnino;** Chris **Mike Walker;** Ensemble **David Abeles, Lindsay Becker, Satya Bhabha, Craig Colfert, Peter Cook, Carla Corvo, Mike Daisey, Max Dana, Sam Forman, Jacob Grigolia-Rosenbaum, Malcolm Groome, Meghan May Hart, Alex Henrickson, Jenny Hildner, Greg Hildreth, Andy Horwitz, Toby Lawless, Brian Levinson, Erica Lipez, Rebecca Miller, Liz Myers, Ani Niemann, Lance Rubin, Rachel Shukert, Amy Staats, Maggie Surovell, Stephen Taylor, Ian Unterman, Liz Vacco, Ben Vershbow, Taylor Wilcox, Katie-Marie Zouhary**

New York premiere of a religious theatrical play/installation and haunted house presented without intermission. The show operated ten performances an evening.

**SYNOPSIS** Les Freres Corbusier's *Hell House* is almost identical recreation of the thousands of hell houses staged by Christian Evangelicals in communities across America during the Halloween season. A multi-room theatrical experience that is part installation art, part play, and part haunted house, *Hell House* features a dozen "rooms" of performance and a company of nearly 100 actors, designers, and technicians, ending in a giant Evangelical rock hoedown, replete with white powdered donuts and a lively game of "Pin the Sin on Jesus." First staged by Jerry Falwell in the 1970s, hell houses take a traditional haunted house's ghosts and ghouls and substitute teenage cheerleaders getting abortions, gay men dying of AIDS, and children reading Harry Potter and then being damned to hell. The Les Freres production marks the first time that a hell house has been seen in the New York area.

Liz Myers, Rebecca Miller, Julie Lake, and Ben Vershbow in Les Freres Corbusier's production of Hell House *(photo by Joan Marcus)*

# ASCENSION

Lion Theatre; First Preview: October 6, 2006; Opening Night: October 11, 2006; Closed November 19, 2006; 5 previews, 39 performances

Written by Edmund De Santis; Produced by Red Light District; Director, Marc Geller; Sets, Aaron Mastin; Costumes, Dennis Ballard; Lighting, Fran Den Danto III; Stage Manager, Christy Thede; Press, Kevin McAnarney

**CAST** Father Calvin Porter **Stephen Hope;** Agnes Sabatino **Lucy McMichael;** Lorenzo Sabatino **Brandon Ruckdashel**

World premiere of a new play presented in two acts. The show ran on an Off-Broadway contract for performances from October 22–November 19.

**SYNOPSIS** *Ascension* is about an ambitious Catholic priest who struggles to hold together the fabric of the world he has created in order to keep his desires at bay. After being drawn into a web of evil and deceit by the schizophrenic wife of a butcher who accuses him of sexually abusing her son eight years earlier, the priest is visited by the angelic young man himself.

# 25 QUESTIONS FOR A JEWISH MOTHER

Theatre at St. Luke's; First Preview: September 27, 2006; Opening Night: October 12, 2006; Closed March 18, 2007; 16 previews, 138 performances

A solo performance play by Kate Moira Ryan, with additional material by Judy Gold; Director, Karen Kohlhaas; Sets/Costumes, Louisa Thompson; Lighting, Jennifer Tipton; Sound, Jorge Muelle; PSM, Ain Rashida Sykes; Press, The Publicity Office

Performed by **Judy Gold**

Revival of a new solo performance play presented without intermission. Previously played last season at Ars Nova Theatre January 18–March 25, 2006 (see *Theatre World* Volume 62, page 116).

**SYNOPSIS** Actress/comedienne Gold and playwright Ryan interviewed over fifty Jewish women of different ages, ethnicities, and occupations across the U.S. to assemble this moving and humorous portrait of what makes a Jewish mother, a Jewish mother

*Judy Gold in* 25 Questions for a Jewish Mother
*(photo by Carol Rosegg)*

*James Martinez, Teddy Canez, and Mateo Gómez in* Elliot, A Soldier's Fugue *(photo by Evan Sung)*

# ELLIOT, A SOLDIER'S FUGUE

El Museo del Barrio's Teatro Heckscher; Opening Night: October 6, 2006; Closed October 29, 2006; 24 performances

Written by Quiara Alegriá Hudes; Produced by Page 73 Productions and El Museo del Barrio; Director, Davis McCallum; Original Music, Michael Friedman; Set, Sandra Goldmark; Costumes, Chloe Chapin; Lighting, Joel Moritz; Sound, Walter Trarbach IV & Gabe Wood; Stage Manager, Nicole Bouclier; Casting, Stephanie Klapper; General Manager, Michele Weathers & R. Erin Craig, La Vie Productions; Press, The Karpel Group

**CAST** Elliot **James Martinez;** Ginny **Sheila Tapia;** Grandpop **Mateo Gómez;** Pop **Teddy Canez**

Revival of the play presented without intermission. World premiere at the Culture Project's 45 Below January 28–February 9, 2006 (see *Theatre World* Volume 62, page 244).

**SYNOPSIS** At eighteen, Lance Corporal Elliot Ortiz crossed over to Iraq. At nineteen, he received the Purple Heart. Now, back from active duty, Elliot is a hometown hero. As Elliot comes to terms with his own memories of war, the military experiences of his father and grandfather unfold, revealing startling similarities that unite the Ortiz men across time.

# MY NAME IS RACHEL CORRIE

Minetta Lane Theatre; First Preview: October 5, 2006; Opening Night: October 15, 2006; Closed December 17, 2006; 80 performances

Adapted by Katharine Viner and Alan Rickman, based on writings by Rachel Corrie; Produced by Dena Hammerstein and Pam Pariseau for James Hammerstein Productions and The Royal Court Theatre, London; Director, Alan Rickman; Sets, Hildegard Bechtler; Lighting, Johanna Town; Sound/Video, Emma Laxton; PSM, Renée Rimland; Production Manager, Aduro Productions; General Manager, Roy Gabay; Associate Producer, John O'Boyle; Associate Director, Tiffany Watt-Smith; ASM, Jerry Dee Lame; Casting, David Caparelliotis; Press, Barlow • Hartman

**CAST** Rachel Corrie **Megan Dodds;** Rachel Corrie (matinee performances and extension) **Bree Elrod;** Understudy **Kerry Bishé**

American premiere of a solo performance play presented without intermission. World premiere in April 2005 at London's Royal Court Theatre and returned for an encore engagement in October 2005. It later played nine weeks at London's Playhouse Theatre in spring 2006. The play was nominated for an Olivier Award for Outstanding Achievement.

**SYNOPSIS** Compiled from writings left behind in the diaries, letters, and e-mails of American activist Rachel Corrie, a twenty-three-year-old protester who was killed by an Israeli bulldozer in Gaza, the play chronicles the human, social, and political evolution in the life and controversial death of a young woman. The play traces the life of Rachel from her early days in Washington State through her experiences as an activist seeking to learn more about the community within Gaza.

*Bree Elrod in* My Name is Rachel Corrie *(photo by Paul Kolnik)*

# THE VOYAGE OF THE CARCASS

SoHo Playhouse; First Preview: October 4, 2006; Opening Night: October 16, 2006; Closed November 5, 2006; 13 previews, 19 performances

Written by Dan O'Brien; Produced by Stage 13 Productions, Thomas & Daria Sullivan; Director, Randy Baruh; Sets, Wilson Chin; Costumes, Olga Ivanov; Lighting, Grant W.S. Yeager; Sound, Drew Levy; Fight Choreographer, Felix Ivanov; PSM, Jennifer Grutza; Assistant Director, Alexa Polmer; General Manager, Darren Lee Cole, Gabriel Voytas; Associate Producers, Shari Fogler, Thomas H. Hanna Jr.; ASM, Raynelle Wright; Dramaturg, Marge Betley; Press, Karen Greco

**CAST** Bane Barrington/Bill **Dan Fogler;** Elijah Kane/Helen **Kelly Hutchinson;** Israel/Bjorn Bjornsen/Dan **Noah Bean**

**SETTING** Time: A hundred years ago or so/Today. Place: Somewhere just south of the North Pole/A small theater in the middle of nowhere. A play presented in two acts. World premiere at the 2004 Deertrees Festival in Harrison, Maine; New York premiere at The Greenwich Street Theatre.

**SYNOPSIS** Weaving Commedia Dell'arte with Theatre Verite, *The Voyage of the Carcass* is a play-within-a-play that looks at people's dreams, both failed and realized. When their Polar expedition goes awry, only three members of the doomed SS Carcass remain. After forty years trapped in the ice, will they make it home alive? But first, they'll take a five-minute break to explore themselves, their roles, and their "issues" as actors dealing with an artic blast of their own. Bill is a struggling mime; his wife Helen is an ad exec and erstwhile actress; Dan is a passive-aggressive playwright.

*Kelly Hutchinson, Noah Bean, and Dan Fogler in* The Voyage of the Carcass *(photo by Mario Ducoudray)*

# CONFESSIONS OF AN IRISH REBEL

Irish Arts Center; First Preview: October 11, 2006; Opening Night: October 18, 2006; Closed November 5, 2006; 6 previews, 14 performances

Created by Shay Duffin; Produced by the Irish Arts Center (Tom Scharff, Executive Director; Brídin Murphy Mitchell, Managing Director); Lighting, Graham Kindred; Stage Manager, Rafi Levavy; Press, Katie Rosin; Business Manager, Agnes Maddox

**CAST** Brendan Behan **Shay Duffin**

Revival of a solo performance play presented without intermission. Previously presented as *Shay Duffin as Brendan Behan* at the Astor Place Theatre, June 9–21, 1981 (see *Theatre World* Volume 38, page 48).

**SYNOPSIS** *Confessions of an Irish Rebel* takes a unique look at Irish history and culture through the life experiences of Irish author and playwright Brendan Behan. Shay Duffin brings Behan to life with both humor and affection. His portrayal provides audiences with an enjoyable experience filled with keen perspectives on all facets of Irish life.

## THE TIMEKEEPERS

TBG Theatre; First Preview: October 11, 2006; Opening Night: October 18, 2006; Closed December 17, 2006; 68 performances

Written by Dan Clancy; Produced by The Barrow Group (Seth Barrish, Artistic Director; Eric Paeper, Executive Director); Director, Lee Brock; Set/Costumes, Markas Henry; Lighting, Tyler Micoleau; Sound, Stefano Zazzera; Stage Manager, Chris Lemme; Props, Alix Steel; ASMs, Rachel McFarland, Eileen Lacy; Assistant Director, Stephen Singer; Press, Shirley Herz, Dan Demello

**CAST** Benjamin **Seth Barrish;** Hans **Eric Paeper;** Capo **Chris Cantwell***

American premiere of a new play presented without intermission.

**SYNOPSIS** *The Timekeepers* is a tale of transcendence in the midst of a world gone mad. At Sachsenhausen Concentration Camp in World War II Germany, a Jewish prisoner and a homosexual prisoner are thrown together in dire circumstances. Their wicked sense of humor, vast differences, and passionate love for opera take them to rich, rarely explored territory.

*Succeeded by John Ahlin

*Seth Barrish and Eric Paeper in The Barrow Group's* The Timekeepers *(photo by Scott Wynn)*

## WHO KILLED BOB MARLEY?

The Gatehouse; Opening Night: October 24, 2006; Closed October 28, 2006; 5 performances

Written by Roger Guenveur Smith; Commissioned, developed, and produced by Harlem Stage/Aaron Davis Hall Inc. for WaterWorks; Original Music, Marc Anthony Thompson; Cinematography, Arthur Jafa; Press, Heidi Riegler Communications

### Performed by **Roger Guenveur Smith**

A solo performance multi-media play with music performed without intermission.

**SYNOPSIS** Smith's solo performance work *Who Killed Bob Marley?* gives insight into Smith's personal life and also provides thoughtful commentary about Rastafarian culture, the bond between father and son, and the blending of fact and fiction in the artistic realm.

## LIVE GIRLS

Urban Stages; First Preview: October 23, 2006; Opening Night: October 25, 2006; Closed November 26, 2006; 22 performances

Written by Victoria Stewart; Produced by Urban Stages (Frances Hill, Artistic Director; Sonia Kozlova, Managing Director); Director, Lou Jacob; Sets, John McDermott; Lighting, Josh Bradford; Costumes, Amela Baksic; Sound, Lindsay Jones; Stage Manager, Ashley B. Delegal; Casting, Susan W. Lovell; Marketing, Michelle Brandon; Press, Brett Singer and Associates

**CAST** Sarah Brown **Pamela Hart;** Sonia Ridge **Suli Holum;** Allison **Jenny Maguire**

New York premiere of a new play presented without intermission.

**SYNOPSIS** Sex and performance art collide in *Live Girls*, a play about an Anna Deavere Smith-like performance artist who interviews a porn star for a piece on social injustice. As expectations are challenged and the interview turns increasingly personal, "reality based" theatre icon Sarah finds that she is asking a new set of questions. What is real and what is performance? What's personal and what's public? Who benefits from art and who are its victims? And when Sarah allows her own assistant to interview her, she begins to ask another question: who's exploiting whom?

*Suli Holum, Pamela Hart, and Jenny Maguire in* Live Girls *(photo by P.A.)*

# PORT AUTHORITY THROW DOWN

Culture Project–45 Below; First Preview: October 20, 2006; Opening Night: October 26, 2006; Closed November 19, 2006; 32 performances

Written by Mike Batistick; Produced by The Working Theatre (Connie Grappo, Artistic Director; Mark Plesent, Producing Director); Director, Connie Grappo; Sets, Sandra Goldmark; Lighting, S. Ryan Schmidt; Costumes, Eleni J. Christou; Sound, John Ivy; Video, Rodger Belknap and Ana Hurka-Robles; Production Manager, Aron Deyo; PSM, Annette Verga-Lagier; ASM, Jessica Pecharsky; Assistant Director, Jake Hirzel; Fight Choreography, Katherine Eckblad; Press, Publicity Outfitters, Timothy Haskell

**CAST** Pervez Bhutto **Debargo Sanyal;** Barb **Annie McNamara;** Nate **Edwin Lee Gibson*;** Nawaz **Aladdin Ullah**

**SETTING** Time: Autumn, 2003. Place: Port Authority Bus Terminal in New York City. World premiere of a new play presented in two acts.

**SYNOPSIS** Pervez Bhutto, a NYC taxi driver, is afraid to return to his Jersey City apartment after the arrest of his brother, a *Daily News* vendor at Port Authority Bus Terminal. In the ten days that follow, he discovers that you can live in a Crown Victoria taxi if you just put your mind to it, that love can come from Akron, Ohio, and that, sometimes, fake hope is all you've got.

*Succeeded by James Murray Jackson Jr.

*Aladdin Ullah and Debargo Sanyal in* Port Authority Throw Down *(photo by Gabe Evans)*

# BHUTAN

Cherry Lane Theatre; First Preview: October 19, 2006; Opening Night: October 29, 2006; Closed December 9, 2006; 11 previews, 42 performances

Written by Daisy Foote; Produced by the Cherry Lane Theatre (Angelina Fiordellisi, Artistic Director; James King, Managing Director) in association with New York Stage and Film; Director, Evan Yionoulis; Sets, Laura Hyman; Costumes, Rebecca Bernstein; Lighting, Pat Dignan; Sound, Bart Fasbender; PSM, Marti McIntosh; Production Manager, Janio Marrero; Casting, Pamela Perrell; Dialect Coach, Maggie Surovell; Press, Publicity Outfitters, Timothy Haskell

**CAST** Mary **Tasha Lawrence;** Frances **Sarah Lord;** Sara **Amy Redford;** Warren **Jedadiah Schultz**

**SETTING** Tremont, New Hampshire, the present. A new play presented without intermission. Previously presented at Cherry Lane's studio space in November 2005.

**SYNOPSIS** Foote's drama follows a New England family's ups and downs after the death of their father. Frances wonders how she wound up here... her mother is driving her crazy, her aunt is stalking a married man, and her brother is in prison. Each day, Frances' future drifts farther and farther away— she dreams of Bhutan but can barely find the front door.

# THE SUNSET LIMITED

59E59 Theater B; First Preview: October 24, 2006; Opening Night: October 29, 2006; Closed November 19, 2006; 28 performances

Written and directed by Sheldon Patinkin; Presented by Steppenwolf Theatre Company (Martha Lavey, Artistic Director; David Hawkanson, Executive Director); Sets, Scott Neale; Costumes, Tatjana Radisic; Lighting, Keith Parham; Sound, Martha Wegener; Stage Manager, Jenny Deady; Press, Karen Greco

**CAST** White **Austin Pendleton;** Black **Freeman Coffey**

**SETTING** A room in a tenement building in a black ghetto of New York City; the present. New York premiere of a new play presented without intermission. World premiere at the Steppenwolf Theatre Company (Chicago, Illinois) May 28, 2006.

**SYNOPSIS** *The Sunset Limited* concerns a startling encounter on a New York subway platform that leads two strangers to a rundown tenement where a life-or-death decision must be made.

*Austin Pendleton and Freeman Coffey in* The Sunset Limited *(photo by Michael Brosilow)*

## DI YAM GAZLONIM (The Pirates of Penzance)

Goldman-Sonnenfeldt Auditorium at JCC; First Preview: October 29, 2006; Opening Night: November 1, 2006; Closed November 17, 2006; Revived March 18–April 1, 2007; 37 performances

Book and lyrics by Al Grand, based on the W.S. Gilbert's libretto; Music by Arthur Sullivan; Produced by the National Yiddish Theater-Folksbiene; Director/English Supertitles, Allen Lewis Rickman; Music Director, Zalmen Mlotek; Sets, Vicki Davis; Lighting, Russel Drapkin; Costumes, K. Laurinda Wilson; Choreography/ASM/Dance Captain, Penny Ayn Maas; Stage Manager, Marci Skolnick; Technical Director, Dennis Eisenberg; Executive Producer, Jennifer Dumas; Press, Beck Lee Media Blitz

**CAST** W.S. Gilbert/Major General **Stephen Mo Hanan;** Fayvl (Frederick) **Jacob Feldman;** Shmuel **I.W. Firestone;** Yankl **D. Zhonzinsky;** Mendl **Eyal Sherf;** Khaskl **Stuart Marshall;** Leybl **Yankl Salant;** Rivke **Genette Lane;** Groyser Gazlen (Pirate King) **Steve Sterner;** Hadasa **Yelena Shmulenson-Rickman;** Yehudis **Ashley Adler;** Khave **Andee Shuster*;** Dvoyre **Susanne Kobb;** Malke (Mabel) **Dani Marcus;** Sergeant of Police **Allan Lewis Rickman**

**FOLKSBIENE BAND** Zalmen Mlotek (Conductor/piano), Stephen Borsuk (keyboard 2), Michael Winograd or Margo Levertett (clarinet)

**SETTING** Cornwall, England in 1897. New adaptation of the operetta performed in Yiddish with English and Russian titles in two acts.

**SYNOPSIS** Cleverly melding two seemingly mismatched languages and cultures, Grand creates a theatrical marvel that is once familiar and at the same time genially foreign. *Di Yam Gazlonim* returned in the spring for an encore limited run after the success of its initial run in the fall.

*Amanda J. Passante performed the role in the spring revival.

*Stephen Mo Hanan, Dani Marcus, and Steve Sterner in the National Yiddish Theatre-Folksbiene's* Di Yam Gazlonim (The Pirates of Penzance) *(photo by Scott Wynn)*

## EVIL DEAD: THE MUSICAL

New World Stages—Stage 1; First Preview: October 2, 2006; Opening Night: November 1 2006; Closed February 17, 2007; 34 previews, 126 performances

Book and lyrics by George Reinblatt, music by Frank Cipolla, Christopher Bond, Melissa Morris, and George Reinblatt; based on Sam Raimi's 80s cult classic films; Presented by Jenkay LLC, Jeffrey Latimer Entertainment, and Just For Laughs Live, by special arrangement with Renaissance Pictures Ltd. and Studio Canal Image, S.A.; Co-Directors, Hinton Battle and Christopher Bond; Choreographer, Hinton Battle; Sets, David Gallo; Costumes, Cynthia Nordstrom; Lighting, Jason Lyons; Sound, Peter Fitzgerald & Kevin Lacy; Special Effects/Makeup, Louis Zakarian; Sound Effects, Michael Laird; Fight Choreography, B.H. Barry; Musical Supervisor, Frank Cipolla; Arrangements/Orchestrations, Eric Svejcar; Musical Director, Daniel Feyer; Press, The Karpel Group; Marketing, Leanne Schanzer Promotions; Advertising, Agency212; PSM, Jane Pole; Technical Supervisor, Matthew Maraffi; Casting, Mungioli Theatricals, Arnold J. Mungioli; Company Manager, Jennifer Kemp; General Management, Snug Harbor Productions, Steven Chaikelson, Brannon Wiles; Producers, Jay H. Harris, Bruce Hills, Jeffrey Latimer, Evi Regev, Gilbert Rozon; Executive Producer, William Franzblau; ASM, Bonnie Brady; Associate General Manager, Jamie Tyrol; Props/Additional Effects, Peter Sarafin; Fight Captain, Brandon Wardell; Dance Captain, Jennifer Byrne; Cast recording: Time Life Records

*The Cast of* Evil Dead: The Musical

**CAST** Linda **Jennifer Byrne;** Cheryl **Jenna Coker;** Shelly/Annie **Renée Klapmeyer;** Ash **Ryan Ward;** Scott/Spirit of Knowby **Brandon Wardell;** Ed/Moose **Tom Walker;** Jake **Darryl Winslow;** Fake Shemp **Ryan Williams**

**UNDERSTUDIES** Tom Walker (Ash), Ryan Williams (Ash, Scott, Ed, Moose, Jake, Spirit of Knowby), Amy Shute (Linda, Cheryl, Shelly, Annie, Fake Shemp)

**BAND** Daniel Feyer (Conductor/keyboards), Jake Schwartz (guitar/banjo), Brad Carbone (drums/percussion)

**MUSICAL NUMBERS** Cabin in the Woods, Housewares Employee, It Won't Let Us Leave, Look Who's Evil Now, What the...?, Join Us, Good Old Reliable Jake, Housewares Employee (reprise), I'm Not a Killer, I'm Not a Killer (reprise), Bit-Part Demon, All the Men in My Life, Ode to an Accidental Stabbing, Do the Necronomicon; It's Time, We Will Never Die, You Blew That B**** Away

New York premiere of a new musical presented in two acts.

**SYNOPSIS** *Evil Dead: The Musical* unearths the old familiar story "boy and friends take a weekend getaway at abandoned cabin, boy expects to get lucky, boy unleashes ancient evil spirit, friends turn into Candarian Demons, boy fights until dawn to survive." As musical mayhem descends upon this sleepover in the woods, "camp" takes on a whole new meaning. Buzzing chainsaws and dancing demons add to the frenzy, slaying audiences with a tale of lust, love, and dismemberment.

# THE MILLINER

East 13th Street Theatre; First Preview: October 24, 2006; Opening Night: November 1, 2006; Closed December 17, 2006; 8 previews, 48 performances

Written by Suzanne Glass; Produced by The Directors Company; Director, Mark Clements; Sets, Todd Ivins; Costumes, Gregory Gale; Lighting, Jeff Nellis; Sound, Nick Borisjuk; Musical Direction/Original Music, Warren Wills; Fight Director, Rick Sordelet; Projections, Melissa M. Spengler; Hats, Lynne Mackey; Press, O+M Company

**CAST** Wolfgang **Michael Gill**; Amalia **Julia Haubner;** Claudia **Caralyn Kozlowski;** Wolfgang's Mother **Maria Cellario**; Frau Hendel **Donna Davis;** Max/Heinz **Steven Hauck**; Gerhardt/Paul **Glenn Kalison**

**SETTING** Before and after World War II, Berlin and London. World premiere of a new play presented in two acts.

**SYNOPSIS** Drawn in part from the author's own family experience, *The Milliner,* a tale of passion, fashion, and music, is about Wolfgang, a talented creator of hats. As a Jew on trial in Germany after the end of the Second World War, Wolfgang tells his tale. Though he is in love with Germany, Wolfgang is forced to leave for England with his wife in 1938 and longs to go home to the culture and cabaret of Berlin. In 1946, despite the Nazi's murder of his mother, he does just that. The consequences of his return to his Motherland are cataclysmic.

# WHEN THE LIGHTS GO ON AGAIN

Triad Theatre; First Preview: October 28, 2006; Opening Night: November 1, 2006; Closed May 27, 2007; 56 performances.

Conceived, written and directed by Bill Daugherty; Produced by Thoroughbred Records & Max Weintraub; Musical Director, Doyle Newmyer; Musical Staging, Lori Leshner; Lighting/Sound, Tonya Pierre; Makeup/Hair, Jimmy Cortes; Press, Peter Cromarty and Company; Cast recording: Thoroughbred Records TBR 104

**CAST** Billy Allen **Bill Daugherty;** Joe Parker **Paul Kropfl;** Nancy Sanders **Christina Morrell;** Connie Sanders **Connie Pachl**

**MUSICIANS** Doyle Newmyer (Musical Director/piano), Jim Conant (guitar), John Loehrke (bass), Chip Fabrizi (drums)

**MUSICAL NUMBERS** Show Your Linen, Miss Richardson, Don't Wake Up My Heart, Humpty Dumpty Heart, Moonlight Serenade, Make Believe Ballroom Time, When The Lights Go On Again (All Over The World), You're A Lucky Fellow, Mr. Smith, No Love, No Nothin', It's A Lovely Day Tomorrow, I Left My Heart At The Stagedoor Canteen, They're Either Too Young Or Too Old, Flat Foot Floogie, He's 1-A In The Army (And He's A-1 In My Heart), The Starlit Hour, We Mustn't Say Goodbye, Any Bonds Today?, Nancy (With The Laughing Face), My Sister And I, G.I. Jive, Don't Sit Under the Apple Tree, (There'll Be A) Hot Time In The Town Of Berlin, The White Cliffs Of Dover

**SETTING** WNEW radio broadcast from the ballroom of the Roosevelt Hotel, the early 1940s. A musical presented in two acts.

**SYNOPSIS** *When the Lights Go On Again* depicts the journey of a vocal group called The Moonlighters and their efforts to help get America through the dark days of World War II. The cast sings over 25 hit songs from that sentimental era. The show pays loving tribute to the men and women who gave their all during World War II and the songs that helped them do it.

*Bill Daugherty, Connie Pachl, Paul Kropfl, and Christina Morrell in* When the Lights Go On Again *(photo by Ben Strothmann)*

# POST MORTEM

Flea Theater; First Preview: October 18, 2006; Opening Night: November 2, 2006; Closed December 16, 2006; 11 previews, 34 performances

Written by A.R. Gurney; Produced by The Flea Theater (Jim Simpson, Artistic Director; Carol Ostrow, Producing Director); Director, Jim Simpson; Sets, Mimi Lien; Costumes, Claudia Brown; Lighting, Brian Aldous; Sound, Jill B.C. DuBoff; Scenic Artist, Gary Levinson; Stage Manager, Jennifer Noterman; Technical Director, Joshua Higgason; Assistant to the Director, Dev Bondarin; Casting, Calleri Casting; Press, Ron Lasko

**CAST** Alice **Tina Benko;** Dexter **Christopher Kromer;** Betsy **Shannon Burkett**

World premiere of a new comedy presented without intermission.

**SYNOPSIS** *Post Mortum* is set in the not-too-distant future when the Christian Right holds sway. Alice, a lowly lecturer in drama at a faith-based state university in the Midwest, and Dexter, an enthusiastic student more interested in his teacher than the theater, become embroiled in the discovery of a play by an obscure late twentieth century playwright named A.R. Gurney. When the authorities destroy the script, these two must piece together the play and with it the future of the world gone mad.

# THE BLUEST EYE

Duke on 42nd Street; Opening Night: November 3, 2006; Closed November 19, 2006; 12 performances

Written by Toni Morrison, adapted by Lydia Diamond; Presented by Steppenwolf Theatre Company (Chicago, Illinois) and the New Victory Theatre; Director, Hallie Gordon; Sets, Stephanie Nelson; Lighting, J.R. Lederle; Costumes, Alison Heryer; Sound, Victoria Delorio; Stage Manager, Deb Styer; Choreographer, Ann Boyd; ASM, Beth Stegman; Dramaturg, Lenora Brown; Press, Darren Molivinsky, John Lanasa

**CAST** Claudia **Libya V. Pugh;** Frieda, Darlene **Monifa M. Days;** Pecola Breedlove **Alana Arenas;** Mama **TaRon Patton;** Pauline Breedlove **Chavez Ravine;** Soaphead Church/Daddy **James Vincent Meredith;** Cholly Breedlove **Victor J. Cole;** Maureen Peel **Noelle Hardy**

New York premiere of a play for young adults presented without intermission.

**SYNOPSIS** Nobel Prize-winner Toni Morrison's heart-wrenching masterpiece is a haunting and tragic portrait of a black girl's coming of age in the racially turbulent 1940s. Ridiculed by her peers and her family, Pecola Breedlove wants nothing more than to be loved. Each evening, she makes the same prayer, for "blue eyes to be pretty, blue eyes to be noticed, blue eyes to be accepted." This story of a young girl with an innocent desire remains poignantly relevant and a disturbing reflection of today s unattainable standards of beauty.

*Alana Arenas and Chavez Ravine in* The Bluest Eye
*(photo by Ben Strothmann)*

# an oak tree

Barrow Street Theatre; First Preview: October 27, 2006; Opening Night: November 4, 2006; Closed January 14, 2007; 86 performances

Written by Tim Crouch; Produced by the Perry Street Theatre and Rosalie Beer, A.J. Epstein, Richard Jordan Productions in association with Barrow Street Theatre; Co-Directors, Tim Crouch, Karl James, & a smith; Score, Peter Gill; Lighting, A.J. Epstein; Sound, Graham Johnson; PSM, Richard Hodge; Press, Springer Associates, Joe Trentacosta

**CAST** The Hypnotist **Tim Crouch;** The Father **Richard Kamins, Angela Reed, Carmela Marner, Gene Marner, David Bridel, Peter Gaitens, Camilla Enders, Johana Arnold, Ed Vassallo, Peter Van Wagner, Rachel Fowler, Lucas Caleb Rooney, Michael Cullen, Mark Blankenship, F. Murray Abraham, Charles Busch, Reed Birney, Randy Harrison, James Urbaniak, Kristin Sieh, Leslie Hendrix, Steve Blanchard, Laurie Anderson, Amy Landecker, John Shuman, Jeremy Beiler, Kelly Calabrese, Michael Countryman, Laila Robins, Pearl Sun, Joan Allen, Maja Wampuszyc, Christopher Cook, Maura Tierney, Alison Fraser, Frances McDormand, Mary Bacon, Tamara Tunie, Ray Dooley, Brooke Smith, John Judd, Richard Kind, Matt Arkin, Craig Wroe, Michael Cerveris, Marin Ireland, Peter Dinklage, Alysia Reiner, Tim Blake Nelson, Chuck Cooper, Ben Walker, Austin Pendleton, Alix Elias, Mark Consuelos, David Pasquesi, Mike Myers, David Rasche, Lili Taylor, Joey Slotnick, Kathleen Chalfant, Hunter Foster, David Hyde Pierce, Stephen Lang, Kathryn Grody, Scott Foley, Jay O. Sanders, Alan Cox, Denis O'Hare, Alan Ruck, Lisa Emery, Frank Wood, David Mogentale, Alexandra Neil, Tom Cavanaugh, Brian Logan, Katie Finnerran, Walter Bobbie, Wendy Vanden Heuval, Tovah Feldshuh, Carolyn McCormick, Maryann Plunkett, Judith Ivey**

American premiere of a new play presented without intermission.

**SYNOPSIS** *an oak tree* is the story of two men brought together by loss: a father whose daughter has been killed in a car accident—and the driver of that car—a provincial stage hypnotist. The two are reunited for the first time since the accident when the hypnotist inadvertently calls him on stage as a volunteer. In a unique theatrical twist, "The Father" is played by a different actor (male or female) at each performance. The second actor walks on stage neither having seen nor read a word of the play they're in...until they're in it. *an oak tree* is a bold, moving, and absurdly comic play about loss, suggestion, and the power of the mind.

*Tim Crouch in* an oak tree *(photo by Lillie Charles)*

## ALL TOO HUMAN: An Evening With Clarence Darrow

45th Street Theatre; First Preview: October 28, 2006; Opening Night: November 5, 2006; Closed December 10, 2006; 7 previews, 30 performances

Written by Henry Miller; Produced by A New Dawn LLC & Town Square Productions Inc.; Director, Laurie Brown Kindred; Sets, Chris Jones; Lighting, Graham Kindred; Sound, Elliott Forrest; Stage Manager, Mary E. Leach; Company Manager, Rebecca Sherman; Assistant to Mr. Miller, Carol Pantel; Marketing/Advertising, Arnie Sawyer Studios; General Manager, Town Square Productions, Don Frantz; Production Consultant, Kevin Conway; Press, The Jacksina Company, Judy Jacksina

### Performed by **Henry Miller**

**SETTING** Time: The 1930s. Place: Various courtrooms, a lecture hall, an apartment in Chicago. World premiere of a new solo performance play presented without intermission.

**SYNOPSIS** *All Too Human* tells the story of Clarence Darrow's fight against religious intolerance, capital punishment, prohibition, the oppression of the workers, and anything else Darrow felt impeded the bringing of enlightenment and culture to the human mind. He argued and won many of the most famous cases ever brought to trial; defending the downtrodden, amoral, maligned, and the misguided. Darrow's career and convictions re-defined the essence of the American legal system. In 1912, he was indicted for bribing a jurist. He hired the infamous Earl Rogers to defend him; but decided to deliver his own summation to the jury. He won. Then came Leopold and Loeb, followed by the Scopes Monkey Trial.

## MIMI le DUCK

New World Stages—Stage 3; First Preview: October 12, 2006; Opening Night: November 6, 2006; Closed December 3, 2006; 28 previews, 30 performances

Book and lyrics by Diana Hansen-Young, music by Brian Feinstein; Produced by Mango Hill Productions LLC, Aruba Productions LLC, in association with Marie Costanza and Paul Beattie; Director, Thomas Caruso; Musical Staging, Matt West; Sets, John Arnone; Costumes, Ann Hould-Ward; Lighting, David Lander; Sound, Tony Smolenski IV, Walter Trarbach; Music Director/Orchestrations, Chris Fenwick; Wigs/Hair, David H. Lawrence; Casting, Dave Clemmons, Geoff Josselson; Marketing, HHC Marketing and Marcia Pendelton; PSM, Charles M. Turner III; Fight Director, Rick Sordelet; Production Supervisor, Greg Hirsch; General Managers, Ken Denison, Carol Fishman; Company Manager, Mark Rowan; ASM, Karen Munkel; Dialects, Shane Ann Younts; Dance Captain, Robert DuSold; Press, Richard Kornberg and Associates, Tom D'Ambrosio

**CAST** Miriam **Annie Golden;** Peter **Marcus Neville;** Ernest Hemingway **Allen Fitzpatrick;** Gypsy **Ken Jennings;** Claude **Robert DuSold;** Madame Vallet **Eartha Kitt;** Ziggy **Tom Aldredge;** Clay **Candy Buckley**

**UNDERSTUDIES** Ron Bagden (Ziggy, Gypsy, Peter), Wayne Schroder (Peter, Claude, Hemingway), Kay Walbye (Miriam, Clay, Vallet)

**ORCHESTRA** Chris Fenwick (Conductor/piano), Suzanne Chaplin (violin), Eli Hludzik (drums), Peter Prosser (cello)

**MUSICAL NUMBERS** Ketchum, Idaho, Red, Paris is a City, 22 Rue Danou, A Thousand Hands, Why Not?, It's All About, Empty or Full, Everything Changes, There Are Times In Life, Don't Ask, Get Outta Here Peter, Is There Room?, The Green Flash, My Mother Always Said, The Only Time We Have is Now, Cozy Dreams Come True, Paris is a City (reprise), Peter's Reprise, All Things New, The Garden Is Green, There is Room

**SETTING** The present, Ketchum, Idaho and Paris, France. A new musical presented in two acts.

**SYNOPSIS** The new musical follows Miriam, a discontented Mormon housewife from Ketchum, Idaho, who, in a moment of desperately crazy inspiration, packs her bags and moves to Paris, leaving behind her husband and her successful career as a painter of duck canvases for the QVC Network. *Mimi le Duck* is as whimsical and unique as the city of Paris, populated by romance and intrigue, gypsy pickpockets, over-the-hill torch singers, and that ever-elusive spark that gives us the guts to change our lives.

*Marcus Neville, Tom Aldredge, Allen Fitzpatrick, Candy Buckley, Ken Jennings, Eartha Kitt, Robert DuSold, and Annie Golden in* Mimi le Duck *(photo by Joan Marcus)*

## CIRQUE de SOLEIL: Delirium

Madison Square Garden; November 8–9, 2006

Created, directed, and designed by Michel Lemieux and Victor Pilon; Presented by Cirque du Soleil and Live Nation; Tour Creative Directors, Gilles Ste-Croix and Carmen Ruest; Costumes, Michel Robidas; Lighting, Alain Lortie; Music Director, Production, and Arrangements, Francis Collard; Original Music, Violaine Corradi, Rene Dupere, Benoit Jutras, Luc Tremplay; Lyrics, Robbie Dillon; Choreographer, Mia Michaels; Sound, Yves Savoie; Props, Anne-Seguin Poirier

**CAST** Nitza, Ric'Key Pageot, Dessy Di Lauro, Jacynthe, Juliana Sheffield, Raffaele Artigliere, Sacha Daoud, El Hadji "Elage" Diouf, Karim Diouf, Andre Faleiros, Elie Haroun, Predrag "Pedja" Manov, Alexis Messier, Jacques "Kuba" Seguin, Kullak Viger Rojas, Andree-Anne Tremblay, Karl Baumann, Adam Read, Irina Akimova, Alexandra Apjarova, Cinthia Beranek, Marek Berlin, Darren Bersuk, Sylvia Camarda, Eve Castelo Branco, Corinne Chachay, Etienne Deneault, Baris Dilaver, Michael Duffy, Sophia Gaspard, Eira Glover, Bimbo Gomero, Ruslan Kiyanitsa, Oleg Kagarlytsky, Andrey Koltsov, Everth Lopez, Anton Makuhin, Christian Patterson, Rob Rubinger, Sebastian Sfedi, Yuriy Shabunin, Serge "Kehino" Takri, Emilie Therrie

National tour of a theatrical event presented in two acts.

**SYNOPSIS** *Delirium i*s a contemporary urban tale, a quest for balance in a world increasingly out of sync with reality. Bill—the main character—is an ordinary man living inside a bubble, more and more recluse in a society where even relationships are "virtual," and where television and computers have become ubiquitous devices that isolate us from one another.

*Cast members of Cirque du Soleil: Delirium*
*(photo by Marie-Josée Lareau © 2006 Cirque du Soleil Inc.)*

Company Manager, Susan L. Brumley; Associate Director/Choreographer, Bethany Pettigrew; Cast recording: Hy-Fy Records

**CAST** Miles Muldoon/He **Michael McEachran;** Julie Lemmon **Anika Larsen;** Violet Zipper **Nicole Ruth Snelson;** Greek/Therapist **Stephen Bienskie;** Greek/Yogi **Natalie Joy Johnson;** Greek/Federal Bureaucrat **Kevin Smith Kirkwood;** Understudies: **Chuck Ragsdale, Courtney Balan**

**MUSICIANS** Seth Weinstein (Conductor/keyboard), Jonah Speidel (keyboard), James Bettincourt (bass), Greg Germann (drums)

**MUSICAL NUMBERS** Only the Paranoid Survive, Love or Fear, I Want What You Want, The Melon Ballet, Julie's Prayer, The Voices in My Head, Violet's Confession, Love Is, Yoga Class, I Want to Know You, Read My Mind, It's Over Miles, When the Music Played, We Can Save the World and Find True Love, Save the People, Oh, God/Read My Mind

**SETTING** New York City, the present. A musical presented in two acts. Previously presented at the 2004 Fringe Festival.

**SYNOPSIS** In this rollicking musical about hot relations at the United Nations, a cowardly bookshop clerk, a sexy diplomat, and an idealistic slacker confront their deepest fears when an office romance leads to international crisis.

*Nicole Ruth Snelson, Kevin Smith Kirkwood, and Michael McEachran in* How to Save the World and Find True Love in 90 Minutes *(photo by Carol Rosegg)*

# HOW TO SAVE THE WORLD AND FIND TRUE LOVE IN 90 MINUTES

New World Stages—Stage 5; First Preview: November 4, 2006; Opening Night: November 12, 2006; Closed December 31, 2006; 10 previews, 57 performances

Book and lyrics by Jonathan Karp, music by Seth Weinstein; Produced by Lawrence Anderson and The Singing Comedians; Director/Choreographer, Christopher Gattelli; Music Director, Seth Weinstein; Sets, Beowulf Boritt; Costumes, David Murin; Lighting, Jeff Croiter; Sound, Peter Hylenski; Casting, Dave Clemmons; Arrangements/Orchestrations, Seth Weinstein and Jonah Speidel; PSM, Thom Schilling; Press, The Karpel Group; Marketing, Leanne Schanzer Promotions; Internet Marketing, Virtucon Marketing; Technical Supervisor, Thomas Schultz; General Management, Anderson LaFrance Entertainment; ASM, Jason A. Quinn;

# STRIKING 12

Daryl Roth Theatre; First Preview: November 6, 2006; Opening Night: November 12, 2006; Closed December 31, 2006; 7 previews, 57 performances

Book, music and lyrics by Brendan Milburn, Valerie Vigoda, and Rachel Sheinkin; Produced by Nancy Nagel Gibbs and Greg Schaffert, in association with Mark Johannes and Amy Danis; Director, Ted Sperling; Sets, David Korins; Costumes, Jennifer Caprio; Lighting, Michael Gilliam; Sound, Robert J. Killenberger; PSM, Kim Vernace; General Management, 321 Theatrical Management; Production Management, Aduro Productions; ASM, Jeffrey Miles Rodriguez; Associate General Manager, Beth Blitzer; Associate Design: Rod Lemmond (set), Carly Dyas (costumes), John Viesta (lighting); Technical Director, Bryan M. Hart; Marketing, Situation Marketing/Damian Bazadona & Steve Tate; Advertising, SpotCo; Press, Shaffer-Coyle Public Relations; Cast recording: PS Classics

**CAST** The Man Who's Had Enough **Brendan Milburn;** SAD Light Seller and Others **Valerie Vigoda;** Party Host and others **Gene Lewin**

**MUSICAL NUMBERS** Snow Song (It's Coming Down), Last Day of the Year, Resolution, The Sales Pitch, Red and Green (And I'm Feeling Blue), Matches for Sale, Say What? Hey La La/Fine Fine Fine, Can't Go Home, Wonderful, Give the Drummer Some, Picture This, Caution to the Wind, It's Not All Right, Wonderful (reprise), Picture This/Snow Song (reprise), Closing

A new musical performed without intermission. Originally presented by the Prince Music Theater, Philadelphia, and subsequently at The Old Globe, San Diego.

**SYNOPSIS** *Striking 12* is the story of a Grumpy Guy who decides to avoid the hectic, loveless world on New Year's Eve, until he's visited by an incandescent salesgirl with the promise to chase away his winter doldrums. Combining pop-rock, musical comedy and old-fashioned uplift with a healthy dose of 21st-century skepticism, this festive tale, performed by the members of the indie pop-rock band Groovelily, ignites the holiday spirit and connects lush musical textures and soaring vocals to make a new music that's all their own.

*Gene Lewin and Valerie Vigoda in* Striking 12 *(photo by Joan Marcus)*

# BUSKER ALLEY

The Kaye Playhouse at Hunter College; November 13, 2006; 1 performance

Book by A.J. Carothers, music and lyrics by Richard and Robert Sherman; Produced by the York Theatre Company (James Morgan, Artistic Director); Director/Design, Tony Walton; Choreography, Lisa Shriver; Music Director, Aaron Gandy; Lighting, Richard Pilbrow; Sound, Peter Fitzgerald; Costumes, Rebecca Lustig; PSM, Peter Lawrence; Stage Managers, Chad Lewis, Andrea Jo Martin, Jim Woolley, Stacey Zaloga; Production Coordinator, Scott Dela Cruz; Press, David Gersten

**CAST** Dame Libby **Glenn Close;** Charlie Laughton **Jim Dale;** Elaine Claire **Elizabeth Inghram;** Max Beardsley **Mike Hall;** Victor Duchesi **John Bolton;** Arthur **George S. Irving;** Gladys **Anne Rogers;** Libby **Jessica Grové;** Prentiss James **Noah Racey;** BBC Announcer **Simon Jones;** Wilson **Bob Fitch;** Keppel **Patrick Wetzel;** Betty **Christy Candler;** Michael **Michael Lane Trautman;** Diane **Diane Wasnak**

**ORCHESTRA** Aaron Gandy (Conductor/piano), Mark York (synthesizer), John Meyers (drums), Brian Drye (trombone), Elizabeth Inghram (flute), Diane Wasnak (accordion/baritone sax/saw)

**MUSICAL NUMBERS** Blow Us a Kiss, Hula Love Song, Never Trust a Lady, When Do I Get Mine?, Strays, Mates, What to Do With 'Er, He Has A Way, Busker Medley, He Has A Way/She Has A Way, Ordinary Couples, Busker Alley, When Do I Get Mine? (reprise), How Long Have I Loved Libby, Baby Me, How Long Have I Loved Libby (reprise), Ordinary Couples/I'm On The Inside, Tin Whistle Tune, Mates, The "New Show" Audition, Wher The 'Ell Is 'Ome, Where Are The Faces?, Paddle Your Own Canoe, Charlie the Busker, Busker Finale, He Had A Way

**SETTING** London, Spring 1938. Concert version of the musical presented in two acts. A benefit for the York Theatre Company.

**SYNOPSIS** *Busker Alley,* a musical adaptation of the 1938 British film *St. Martin's Lane,* concerns a busker (one who entertains in public on London's' famous streets) who falls in love with a much younger woman who longs to be a big star in the theater and leaves him to follow her dreams. *Busker Alley* was set to arrive in Broadway in 1995 as a vehicle for Tommy Tune. After a sixteen-city tour, Tune dropped out of the production with a broken foot, and the planned Broadway premiere at the St. James Theatre was off.

# WOYZECK

St. Ann's Warehouse; Opening Night: November 13, 2006; Closed December 3, 2006; 19 performances

Written by Georg Büchner, adapted, and directed by Daniel Kramer; Presented by London's Gate Theatre; Produced by Tali Pelman, KLN Productions and Arts at St. Ann's; Sets/Costumes, Neil Irish; Lighting, David Howe; Sound, Adrienne Quartly; Choreographer, Ann Yee; Assistant Director, Kendall O'Neill; Production Managers, John Titcombe & Owen Hughes; Stage Manager, Dan Ayling; Costume Supervisor, Isabel Munoz; Aerial Movement, Gavin Marshall; Aerial Training, Melissa Merran; Military Consultant, Charles Mayer; Press, Saks & Company, Blake Zidell, Brian Shimkovitz, Carla Sacks

**CAST** Woyzeck **Edward Hogg;** Andres **Roger Evans;** Sergeant **Clive Brunt;** Drum Major **David Harewood;** Marie **Myriam Acharki;** Margaret **Rachel Lumberg;** Captain **Fred Pearson;** Doctor **Tony Guilfoyle;** Grandmother **Diana Payne-Myers;** Showman **Josh Cole**

American premiere of a London revival of a musical play presented in two acts.

**SYNOPSIS** Daniel Kramer's high-octane, rock and roll *Woyzeck* is a dazzling reinvention of Büchner's classic masterpiece, hailed by critics and audiences as a theatrical tour de force. Obsessed by love, pursued by visions, and overpowered by odds, *Woyzeck* is the harrowing journey of one honest man's downfall and heartbreaking descent into madness.

*Mica Bagnasco in* Duse's Fever *(photo by Epstein)*

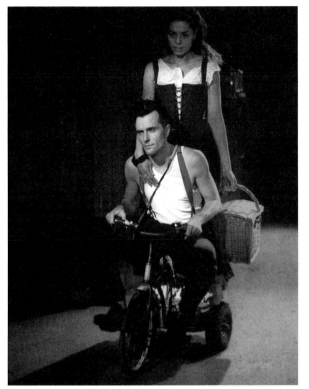

*Edward Hogg and Myriam Acharki in the Gate Theatre of London's production of* Woyzeck

# DUSE'S FEVER

Kirk Theatre; First Preview: November 9, 2006; Opening Night: November 16, 2006; Closed December 2, 2006; 22 perfomances

Written by Mica Bagnasco; Director, Douglas S. Hall; Sets, Kevin Judge; Costumes, David Borella; Lighting, Shawn E. Boyle; Sound, Jeremy J. Lee; Press, Sam Rudy Media Relations, Bob Lasko

**CAST** Nina Gibello **Mica Bagnasco**

**SETTING** Italy, Eleonora Duse's dressing room, December 1923. World premiere of a solo performance play presented without intermission.

**SYNOPSIS** *Duse's Fever* is set in the dressing room of the world-renowned actress Eleonora Duse a few months before her death, where Nina, her devoted dresser of twenty-six years, awaits her cues while Duse is performing on stage in Ibsen's *Hedda Gabler.* Beloved by Chekhov, Shaw, Joyce, Le Gallienne, Barrymore, Chaplin, kings, and commoners, Duse comes to life in through Nina's recollection of the accomplishments and intimate details of the actress's colorful life.

# ZANAHORIAS (Carrots)

Duke on 42nd Street; Opening Night: November 22, 2006; Closed December 10, 2006; 23 performances

Written by Antonio Zancada; translation & adaptation by Miriam Stenning and Francisco Reyes: Produced by Equilicuá Producciones in association with Puy Navarro and The Immediate Theater Company; Director, Alfredo Galván; Choreography, Silvia Sierra; Music, Geoffray Barbier; Sets, Regina García; Lighting, María Cristina Fusté; Costumes, Meghan E. Healey; Makeup, Alex Almeida; Wigs, NIB Hair Center/Omar Santa Cruz; Voice & English-language Speech Coach, Page Clements; Stage Manager, Jessica V. Urtecho; ASM, Christopher G. Paolucci

**CAST** Madame del Sagrado Corazón **Denise Quiñones;** Marqués de ¡Ufff! **Bill Blechingberg;** Condesa de ¡Eh! **Beatriz Córdoba;** Josefine **Iva Gocheva;** Rey ¡Oh! Primero de Puritania **Francisco Reyes;** Marquesa de ¡Ahhh! **Monica Steuer;** Understudy for Ms. Quiñones **Puy Navarro**

**SETTING** The 18th-century in the fictional Kingdom of Puritania. New York premiere of a touring new play presented in two acts; selected performances in English and Spanish. In 2007, the play became the most awarded production by Hispanic theater critics and associations in NYC, and toured Puerto Rico and Latin America.

**SYNOPSIS** In Puritania, where dialectical battles and the coarsest acts occur daily, the most depraved holds the higher social status. But thanks to Madame's talent for manipulation and disguise, this is about to change. Heads will roll, yes. *Zanahorias (Carrots)* is a period piece in essence and style, and a pop culture celebration in the making—*Dangerous Liaisons* reinvented through today's eyes: same kind of backstabbing with slightly more lavish costumes. But, the carrots: what's their significance?

# ROOM SERVICE

SoHo Playhouse; First Preview: November 17, 2006; Opening Night: November 28, 2006; Closed April 8, 2007; 12 previews, 158 performances

Written by John Murray and Allen Boretz; Presented by the Peccadillo Theatre Company; Produced by SoHo Playhouse, Jonathan Reinis Productions, Jeffrey Sine and The StoryLine Project; Director, Dan Wackerman; Sets, Chris Jones; Costumes, Gail Cooper-Hecht; Lighting, Jeffrey E. Salzberg; General Manager, Olson Rhodes; Stage Manager, Michael Joseph Ormond; ASM, Liza Baron; Dramaturg, William M. Peterson, PhD.; Wardrobe, Kat Martin; Associate Producer, Production Consultants Inc.; Press, Peter Cromarty and Company

**CAST** Gordon Miller **David Edwards;** Joseph Gribble **Dale Carman;** Harry Binion **Fred Berman;** Faker Englund **Robert O'Gorman;** Christine Marlowe **Kim Rachelle Harris;** Leo Davis **Scott Evans;** Hilda Manney **Blythe Gruda;** Gregory Wagner **Sterling Coyne;** Simon Jenkins **Raymond Thorne;** Dr. Glass **Jerry Coyle;** Sascha Smirnoff/Senator Blake **Louis Michael Sacco;** Timothy Hogarth, Bank Messenger **Dennis Wit**

**SETTING** A Times Square Hotel, mid-1930s. Transfer of the Off-Off-Broadway revival of a play presented in three acts with one intermission. Previously played at the Bank Street Theatre July 6–August 5, 2006.

**SYNOPSIS** *Room Service* is about the efforts of an unscrupulous producer to find a backer for his new show. Holed up in a hotel with nineteen hungry actors and a ballooning room service bill, he tries to forestall eviction by convincing the show's gullible young playwright to fake his own death. Meanwhile, an emissary from one of the country's wealthiest businessmen turns up with money to invest in the show; that is, until he discovers the hotel doctor bound and gagged in the bathroom. The situation goes from bad to worse as the much-abused hotel manager threatens to have the entire show confiscated by the sheriff on opening night!

*Sterling Coyne, Robert O'Gorman, Fred Berman, and David Edwards in* Room Service *(photo by Carol Rosegg)*

# THE ATHEIST

Center Stage NY; First Preview: November 24, 2006; Opening Night: November 29, 2006; Closed December 23, 2006; 24 performances

Written by Ronan Noone; Produced by Square Peg Productions (Sara Katz and Douglas Mercer, Co-Artistic Directors; Betsey Katz, Managing Director); Director, David Sullivan; Sets, Richard Chambers; Costumes, Jennifer Caprio; Lighting, Stephen Boulmetis; Original Music, Haddon Kime; Sound, Julie Pittman; Technical Director, Tom Fusco; PSM, Misha Siegel-Rivers; Production Assistants, Jen Browne, Harmony Ingraham, Steph Lalley; Graphics, Betsey Katz; Stylist, Krister Atle

**CAST** Augustine Early **Chris Pine**

A solo performance play presented without intermission. This was the inaugural production for Square Peg Productions.

**SYNOPSIS** *The Atheist* is a dark comedy about a journalist's relentless quest for fame. Every good news story needs a good storyteller, but as Augustine Early's headlines become fueled by vengeance and self-interest, secrets hold no sanctuary and a good story always prevails, regardless of the cost.

# THE BIG VOICE: God or Merman?

The Actors Temple Theatre; First Preview: November 25, 2006; Opening Night: November 30, 2006; Closed May 13, 2006; 5 previews, 125 performances

Book, music, and lyrics by Jim Brochu and Steve Schalchlin, additional lyrics by Marie Cain; Produced by Murphy Cross, Paul Kreppel, Edmund Gaynes, BarBar Productions; Director, Anthony Barnao; Sets and Lighting, Clifton Taylor; Costumes, Elizabeth Flores; Sound, David Gotwald; PSM, John M. Atherlay; Associate Producers, Nancy Bianconi, Pamela Hall, Louis S. Salamone; Production Manager, Paul Ziemer, Joe Cangelosi; Production Supervisor, Jana Llynn; Marketing, HHC Marketing; General Management, Jessimeg Productions; Graphics, Stephen Gilewski; Press, Keith Sherman and Associates

**CAST** Steve **Steve Schalchlin**[*1]; Jim **Jim Brochu**[*2]; The Big Voice **Robert Mandan**

**MUSICAL NUMBERS** Why?, I Want to Make Music, The Holy Tour, Jame$ Robert$on, The Closet, Where Is God? Beyond the Light, Near You, Christmastime, Sometimes When I Pray, If God Has Hands, You Are A Stranger, One New Hell, How Do You Fall Back in Love, The Sower and the Scarecrow, Why? (reprise)

**SETTING** Act One: Then and Now. Act Two: Here and There. A musical comedy in two lives presented in two acts. Previously presented at the Belt Theatre as part of the 2004 NYMF Festival.

**SYNOPSIS** Brochu and Schalchlin make a musical of their relationship and hilariously prove that showbiz is as much a calling as the priesthood. This high energy, razzle-dazzle show chronicles the lives of a Baptist from Arkansas and a Catholic from Brooklyn who find eternal salvation in the temple of musical theatre. The biographical musical traces the couple's meeting aboard a ship in the Atlantic Ocean, Steve's struggle with AIDS, the production of their hit Off-Broadway musical *The Last Session*, their separation, and their reconciliation. It's a comedy about a "gay marriage" between two men created by the couple themselves.

*Succeeded by: 1. Carl Danielsen (3/17/06) 2. Dale Radunz (3/17/06)

*Jim Brochu and Steve Schalchlin in* The Big Voice: God or Merman? *(photo by Ed Krieger)*

# AN EVENING HONORING THE LARAMIE PROJECT

Town Hall; December 1, 2006; 1 performance

Written and directed by Moisés Kaufman; Created and presented by the Tectonic Theater Project; Produced by The Matthew Shepard Foundation

**CAST Brian Kerwin, Chad Allen, Stockard Channing, Robert Desiderio, Van Hansis, Peter Hermann, Joshua Jackson, Terry Kinney, Cyndi Lauper, Judith Light, Stephanie March, John McAdams, James Murtaugh, Mary Beth Peil, Kelli Simpkins;** Host **Tipper Gore;** Special performance **Cyndi Lauper;** Presentation to Tectonic Theatre Company **Judy Shepard**

A staged reading of the play presented in two acts. The work premiered in Denver in 2000, followed by a critically acclaimed Off-Broadway run at the Union Square Theatre April 27–September 2, 2000 (see *Theatre World* Volume 56, page 164). An HBO film version featuring many celebrities was first telecast in 2002.

**SYNOPSIS** In this benefit for The Matthew Shepard Foundation, this special reading of *The Laramie Project* — the documentary-like work set in the aftermath of the Laramie murder of a gay twenty-one-year-old college student Matthew Shepard — was performed on the date that would have marked Shepard's thirtieth birthday.

# A YIDDISH VAUDEVILLE

Goldman-Sonnenfeldt Auditorium at JCC; Opening Night: December 3, 2006; Closed December 17, 2006; 15 performances

Curated and compiled by Bruce Adler and Zalmen Mlotek, with Motl Didner; additional material from Miriam Hoffman, Rena Berkowicz-Borow and Allen Lewis Rickman; Produced by the National Yiddish Theatre-Folksbiene; Directors, Bruce Adler and Danny Siretta; Musical Staging, Danny Siretta; Music Director, Zalmen

Mlotek; Sets, Vicki Davis; Costumes, Gail Cooper-Hecht; Lighting, Russel Phillip Drapkin; Sound, Elizabeth Rhodes; Executive Producer, Jennifer Dumas; Stage Manager, Marci Skolnick; ASM, Annette Verga-Lagier; Press, Beck Lee Media Blitz

**CAST Bruce Adler, Dani Marcus, Allen Lewis Rickman, Joanne Borts, Mitch Smolkin;** Folksbiene Band **Steve Sterner** (keyboards), **Matt Temkin** (percussion), **Brian Galssman, Marty Confurius** (bass)

World premiere of a new revue presented without intermission.

**SYNOPSIS** *A Yiddish Vaudeville* includes some of the catchiest, funniest, most heart-breakingly memorable songs, and humor that have sprung from the Yiddish vaudeville tradition. These major highlights were first performed and identified with such legendary performers as Molly Picon, Menashe Skolnik, Shimon Dzign, Max Bozyk, and the husband and wife team of Julius Adler and Henrietta Jacobson. Now, two-time Tony Award nominee Bruce Adler (son of Julius and Henrietta), headlines this new musical revue.

*Allen Lewis Rickman, Dani Marcus, Bruce Adler, Joanne Borts, and Mitch Smolkin in* A Yiddish Vaudeville *(photo by Scott Wynn)*

# GUTENBERG! THE MUSICAL!

59E59 Theater B; First Preview: November 21, 2006; Opening Night: December 3, 2006; Closed December 21, 2007; Transferred to Actors Playhouse; First Preview: January 16, 2007; Second Opening Night: January 21, 2007; Closed May 6, 2007; 14 previews, 159 performances

Written by Scott Brown and Anthony King; Produced by Trevor Brown, Ron Kastner, Terry Allen Kramer, and Joseph Smith; Original Producers, Upright Citizens Brigade Theatre and New York Musical Theatre Festival; Director, Alex Timbers; Musical Director/Arrangements, T.O. Sterrett; Succeeding Musical Director, Kris Kukul; Lighting, Tyler Micoleau; Costumes, Emily Rebholz; Assistant Director, Ian Unterman; PSM, Wesley Apfel; Production Assistant, Brady Amoon; Rehearsal Pianist, Kevin Rockower; Original Arrangements, Barry Wyner; Original Transcriptions, Jeffrey Wraight; Associate Lighting, Anjeanette Stokes; Photography, Keith Trumbo; General Manager, The Splinter Group; Press, Shaffer-Coyle Public Relations

**CAST** Bud Davenport **Christopher Fitzgerald**[*1]; Doug Simon **Jeremy Shamos**[*2]; Understudy **Ryan Karels;** Piano **T.O. Sterrett/Kris Kukul**

**MUSICAL NUMBERS** Prologue, Schlimmer!, I Can't Read, Haunted German Wood, The Press, I Can't Read (reprise), Biscuits, What's the Word, Stop the Press, Tomorrow is Tonight, Second Prologue, Words, Words, Words, Monk With Me, Go to Hell, Festival!, Finale

**SETTING** A backer's audition in New York City, the present. A new musical presented in two acts. Developed at Upright Citizens Brigade Theatre in 2003; World premiere at London's Jermyn Street Theatre, January 2006, both starring the writers in the roles; American premiere at the 2006 New York Musical Theatre Festival featuring the current cast.

**SYNOPSIS** In this two-man musical spoof, a pair of aspiring playwrights performs a backers' audition for their new project — a big, splashy musical about printing press inventor Johann Gutenberg. With an unending supply of enthusiasm, Bud and Doug sing all the songs and play all the parts in their crass historical epic, with the hope that one of the producers in attendance will give them a Broadway contract — fulfilling their ill-advised dreams.

*Succeeded by: 1. David Turner (2/13/07) 2. Ryan Karels (4/3/07), Darren Goldstein (4/10/07)

*Christopher Fitzgerald and Jeremy Shamos in* Gutenberg! The Musical! *(photo by James Ambler)*

# ANNIE

Theatre at Madison Square Garden; Opening Night: December 6, 2006; Closed December 30, 2006; 30 performances

Book by Thomas Meehan, music by Charles Strouse, lyrics by Martin Charnin; based on the "Little Orphan Annie" comics; Presented by NETworks Presentations, Rodger Hess, and TC Theatrical; Director, Martin Charnin; Original Staging, Peter Gennaro; Choreographer, Liza Gennaro; Sets, Ming Cho Lee; Original Costumes, Theoni Aldridge, Lighting, Ken Billlington, Sound, Peter Hylenski; Music Director and Supervision/Additional Orchestrations, Keith Levenson; Music Coordinator, John Mezzio; Additional Costumes, Jim Halliday; Hair, Bernie Ardia; Production Supervisors, Jason Juenker & Jon Harrington; General Managers, Gregory Vander Ploeg, Dawn Marie Bernhard, and Gentry & Associates; Casting, Patricia Pearce Gentry, Bob Cline; PSM, Victoria Navarro; Stage Manager, Molly Meg Legal; Company Manager, Ken Leist; Marketing, TMG-The Marketing Group; Animal Trainer, William Berloni; Executive Producer, Kary M. Walker; Dance Captain, Antoinette DiPietropolo

**CAST** Molly **Anastasia Korbal;** Pepper **Madison Zavitz;** Duffy **Amanda Balon;** July **NicKayla Tucker;** Tessie **Brandy Panfili;** Kate **Gabi Nicole Carruba;** Annie **Marissa O'Donnell;** Miss Hannigan **Kathie Lee Gifford;** Bundles McCloskey/Justice Brandeis **Aaron Kaburick;** Apple Seller/Jimmy Johnson/Morganthau **Richard Costa;** Dog Catcher/Sound Effects Man/Ickes **Harry Turpin;** Sandy **Lola;** Lt. Ward/Fred McCracken/Howe **Allen Kendall;** Sophie the Kettle/Mrs. Pugh/Oxydent Producer/Perkins **Katherine Pecevich;** Grace Farrell **Elizabeth Broadhurst**; Drake **David Chernault;** Cecille/Ronnie Boylan **Julie Cardia;** Annette/Connie Boylan **Kelly Lynn Cosme;** Mrs. Greer/Bonnie Boylan **Liz Power;** Oliver Warbucks **Conrad John Schuck;** Star to Be **Monica L. Patton;** Rooster Hannigan **Scott Willis;** Lily St. Regis **Ashley Puckett Gonzalez;** Bert Healy **Christopher Vettel;** F.D.R. **Allan Baker;** Street People/Warbuck's Staff/New Yorkers/Hooverville-ites **Natalie Backman, Julie Cardia; David Chernault, Kelly Lynn Cosme, Richard Costa, Antoinette DiPietropolo, Brian Michael Hoffman, Aaron Kaburick, Allen Kendall, Billy Kimmel, Monica L. Patton, Katherine Pecevich, Liz Power, Harry Turpin, Christopher Vettel;** Standby for Miss Hannigan **Alene Robertson**

**TOURING MUSICIANS** Keith Levenson (Conductor), Karen Dryer (Assistant Conductor/keyboard), Kelly Ann Lambert (Associate Conductor), John Trombetta (trumpet), Tom Bradford (drums)

**MUSICAL NUMBERS** Maybe, It's The Hard Knock Life, Tomorrow, We'd Like to Thank You Herbert Hoover, Little Girls, I Think I'm Gonna Like It Here, NYC, Easy Street, You Won't Be an Orphan for Long, Maybe (reprise), You're Never Fully Dressed Without a Smile, Easy Street (reprise), Tomorrow (reprise), Something Was Missing, Annie, I Don't Need Anything But You, Maybe (reprise), A New Deal for Christmas

**SETTING** December 11–25, 1933. New York City. National touring production of a musical presented in two acts.

**SYNOPSIS** Kathie Lee Gifford stars as Miss Hannigan (replacing tour regular Alene Robertson) in the Tony award-winning musical *Annie*, a timeless tale of a spunky red head who dreams of a life outside the walls of the orphanage. This classic musical about never giving up hope, based on the 1924 comic strip "Little Orphan Annie" written by Harold Gray (which still holds the record today for the longest-lasting comic strip in history), celebrates its thirtieth anniversary with this touring production.

# MURDER MYSTERY BLUES

59E59 Theater A; First Preview: November 24, 2006; Opening Night: December 7, 2006; Closed December 31, 2006; 44 performances

Adaptation, lyrics, additional dialogue and direction by Janey Clarke, based on short stories by Woody Allen; Produced by London's I'm a Camera (Janey Clarke, Pete Staves, and Karen Meehan, Founding Producers); Composer/Musical Director, Warren Wills; Sets/Lighting, Maruti Evans; Costumes, Michael Bevins; Choreographer, Tamsyn Salter; Fight Director, Tim Davenport; Stage Manager, Sinead Bourke; General Manager, The Splinter Group; Assistant Director, Talya Klein; Assistant Musical Director, Charles Geizhals; Associate Producer, Sarah Frain; ASM, Gregory Konow; Press, Karen Greco

**CAST-MUSICIANS** Lucy Tintree **Stephanie Dodd;** Flo Guiness **Mary Fahl;** Inspector Ford **Jeff Ganz**; Kaiser Lupowitz **Alex Haven;** Lenny Mendel **Michael Murray;** Heather Buttkiss **Andromeda Turre**

American premiere of a new play with music presented in two acts.

**SYNOPSIS** Private Eye Kaiser Lupowitz has seen it all, then a dynamite brunette asks him to find Mr. Big. Will he find the most elusive Guy in the whole of New York? Soon Lupowitz cracks the case and, after dinner and drinks, sees through the mysterious femme fatale's disguise. Based on the short stories of Woody Allen, *Murder Mystery Blues* is a play with original jazz, set in the world of 1940s film noir New York.

*Mary Fahl, Andromeda Turre, Jeff Ganz, Alex Haven, and Stephanie Dodd in* Murder Mystery Blues *(photo by James Ambler)*

# MY MOTHER'S ITALIAN, MY FATHER'S JEWISH & I'M IN THERAPY

Little Shubert Theatre*; First Preview: November 3, 2006; Opening Night: December 8, 2006; still running as of May 31, 2007

Written by Steve Solomon; Produced by Rodger Hess, Abby Koffler, Howard Rapp & Arnold Graham, Leah & Ed Frankel; Director, John Bowab; Sets, Ray Klausen; Lighting, Brian Nason; Sound, Carl Casella; PSM, Jamie Rog; Production Management, Aurora Productions; General Manager, Richards/Climan Inc; Associate Producer, Carol & Andy Caviar; Marketing, Leanne Schanzer Promotions; Press, Keith Sherman and Associates

Performed by **Steve Solomon**

New York premiere of a new solo performance play presented without intermission.

**SYNOPSIS** In his biographical show, *Italian + Jewish = Therapy*, Steve Solomon combines comic voices, sound effects, and astounding characters to bring alive a myriad of people from all walks of life. Billed as "one part lasagna, one part kreplach, and two parts prozac," the show relates to the wacky side of the human condition.

*Transferred to the Westside Theatre (Downstairs) on May 4, 2007

*Steve Solomon in* My Mother's Italian, My Father's Jewish & I'm in Therapy *(photo courtesy of Charles Rapp Enterprises Inc.)*

# A VERY MERRY UNAUTHORIZED CHILDREN'S SCIENTOLOGY PAGEANT

New York Theatre Workshop Mainstage; First Preview: November 29, 2006; Opening Night: December 10, 2006; Closed January 7, 2007; 42 performances

Book, music, and lyrics by Kyle Jarrow, concept by Alex Timbers; Produced by Aaron Lemon Strauss and Les Freres Corbusier in association with New York Theatre Workshop; Director/Choreographer, Alex Timbers; Sets, David Evans Morris; Costumes, Jennifer Rogien; Lighting, Juliet Chia; Properties, Stephanie Wiesner; Music Director, Gabriel Kahane; PSM, Alaina Taylor; Stage Manager, Erin Koster; Stage Managers, Meghan May Hart, Kelly Maizenaski; Casting, Stephanie Klapper; Press, Richard Kornberg & Associates, Don Summa

**CAST** Dahlia Chacon, Hudson Cianni, Lauren Kelly, Jolie Libert, Steven Lobman, Elizabeth Lynn, Sean Moran, Kat Peters, Alex Swift, William Wiggins

Revival of a musical presented without intermission. Originally produced November 2003 at The Tank on 42nd Street and then transferred Off-Broadway to The John Houseman Theatre (see *Theatre World* Volume 60, page 112).

**SYNOPSIS** A self-proclaimed "bizarre new holiday classic"– part avant-garde performance art, part children's theatre—the *Pageant* is based on the actual principles of Scientology and the seriously unbelievable life story of founder L. Ron Hubbard. The cast of kids plays such well-known Scientologists as Tom Cruise, Kirstie Alley, and John Travolta, among others.

*Sean Moran, Jolie Libert, William Wiggins, and Hudson Cianni and Cast in* A Very Merry Unauthorized Children's Scientology Pageant *(photo by Joan Marcus)*

## RAGS

Nokia Theatre; December 11, 2006; 1 performance

Music by Charles Strouse, lyrics by Stephen Schwartz, book by Joseph Stein; Produced by Jamie McGonnigal in association with the Joey DiPaolo AIDS Foundation; Director, Stafford Arima; Choreography, Patricia Wilcox; Music Director, Mark Hartman; Sets, David Korins; Costumes, Michael Bottari and Ronald Case; Lighting, Traci Klainer; Sound, Walter Trarbach and Tony Smolenski IV; Orchestrations, Michael Starobin; Overture Orchestrations, Larry Wilcox, adapted by Larry Blank; Associate Producer/Company Manager, Robert A. Sherrill; Assistant Director, Tye Blue; Associate Music Director, Joshua Clayton; Associate Sets, Rod Lemmond; Associate Lighting, Joel Silver; Production Manager, Spencer Robinson; PSM, Renee Rimland; Stage Manager, Bryce McDonald

**CAST** Americans **Max von Essen, Colin Hanlon;** Rebecca **Carolee Carmello;** David **Struan Erlenborn;** Bella **Eden Espinosa;** Avram **Michael Rupert;** Ben **David A. Austin;** Jack **Adam Heller;** Anna **Anne Nathan;** Mike **Stuart Marland;** Rachel **Lanie Kazan;** Klezmer Leader/Rag Picker **Peter Lockyer;** Rosa **Stacia Fernandez;** Saul **Lewis Cleale;** Bronstein **John Schiappa;** Hamlet **David Josefsberg;** Ophelia **Lisa Jolley;** Nathan **Gregg Edelman;** Big Tim **John Treacy Egan;** Ensemble/Chior **Donna Accorso, Evan Andrews, Mike Babel, Richard Barth, Aaron Berk, James Bullard, Robyn S. Clark, Leslie Clemmons, Kevin Covert, Mike Cruz, Jeff Cyronek, Vibecke Dahle, Shannon Davies, Dan Debenport, Nicole DeCario, Melissa Driscol, Scott Evans, Tim Fitzgerald, Monique French, Tom Gamblin, Johnathan Reid Gealt, Brian M. Golub, Ben Hartley, Lisa Harvie, Shannon Hastings, Mair Heller, Sarah Hund, Eric Imhoff, Valerie Issembert, Chris Janssen, Mara Kaye, Genevieve Koch, Sabra Lewis, Lisa Liaromatis, Dan Maceyak, Jennifer Malenke, Kasey Marino, Emily McNamara, Brian Murphy, Matthew Nowak, Matthew Parker, Marcie Passley, Kate Pazakis, Kevin Reed, Connie Renda, Shoshanna Richman, Spencer Robinson, Ann Rooney, Andrew Ross, Danny Rothman, Katie Schickert, Rebecca Soler, Felicity Stiverson, Justin Stratton, Scott Sussman, Kristina Teschner, Karrah Tines, Jodie Trappe, Marc Tumminelli, Bridget Walders, Erin West, Erin Williams, Joey Williamson;** Dancers **Vibecke Dahle, Ben Hartley, Lisa Harvie, Eric Imhoff, Sabra Lewis, Felicity Stiverson, Gustavo Wons;** Children **Michael Herwitz, Matthew Leonard, Emily Trais**

**MUSICAL NUMBERS** Prologue, Greenhorns, If We Never Meet Again, Brand New World, Penny a Tune, Easy For You, Hart to Be a Prince, Blame It On the Summer Night, For My Mary, Rags, On the Fourth Day of July, Children of the Wind, On The Fourth Day of July (reprise), Yankee Boy, Uptown, Three Sunny Rooms, Wanting, Rags (reprise), What's Wrong With That?, Kaddish, Bread and Freedom, Dancing With the Fools, Finale

A concert version of the musical presented in two acts. Originally presented on Broadway at the Mark Hellinger Theatre August 5–24, 1986 (see *Theatre World* Volume 43, page 10), and revived Off-Broadway at the American Jewish Theatre December 2, 1991 (see *Theatre World* Volume 48, page 113).

**SYNOPSIS** Rebecca, an immigrant, finds herself and her young son, David, very much alone in the brand new world of America. Through Rebecca's encounters and relationships with others experiencing similar struggles, *Rags* tells of the American experience when the "melting pot," was an ideal many hoped to be a part of and reminds us of the intense struggle so many of our immigrant ancestors fought, to make this country what it is today. This 2006 World AIDS Day concert was a benefit for the Joey DiPaolo AIDS Foundation.

## BECOMING ADELE

Clurman Theatre; First Preview: December 15, 2006; Opening Night: December 20, 2006; Closed January 6, 2007; 23 performances

Written by Eric Houston; Produced by Gotham Stage Company (Michael Barra, Producing Artistic Director; Julia Haubner Smith, Co-Artistic Director); Director, Victor Maog; Sets, Antje Ellermann; Costumes, Myrna Colley-Lee; Lighting, Lucas Benjaminh Krech; Sound, Elizabeth Rhodes; Press, Springer Associates, Shane Marshall Brown

**CAST** Adele **Kimberly Stern**

New York premiere of a new play solo performance play presented without intermission.

**SYNOPSIS** *Becoming Adele* is the captivating story of the irrepressible Adele, a spunky Brooklyn waitress, as she tries to carve out a better future for herself and her daughter while learning to live each moment to the fullest as she becomes the Adele she was meant to be.

*Kimberly Stern in* Becoming Adele *(photo by Ben Strothmann)*

# THE SUNSHINE BOYS

Symphony Space; January 7, 2007

Written by Neil Simon, translated by Miriam Hoffman; Director and Narrator, Isaiah Sheffer

**CAST** Willy Clark (Anshel) **Theodore Bikel;** Al Lewis (Velvel) **Fyvush Finkel;** Herschel **Allen Lewis Rickman;** Nurse **Yelena Schmuelenson-Richman**

**SETTING** An apartment in an old hotel on upper Broadway in New York City, a television studio and Willie's apartment. A staged reading of the play presented in Yiddish in two acts. Originally presented on Broadway at the Broadhurst Theatre December 20, 1972 (see *Theatre World* Volume 29, page 42).

**SYNOPSIS** Theodore Bikel and Fyvush Finkel co-star in Neil Simon's landmark comedy *The Sunshine Boys*... in Yiddish! This gala performance was a benefit for the Folksbiene, the National Yiddish Theatre and the North American premiere of Miriam Hoffman's critically acclaimed translation that premiered in Tel Aviv.

# RiddleLikeLove (with a side of ketchup)

Ensemble Studio Theatre; First Preview: January 4, 2007; Opening Night: January 8, 2007; Closed January 29, 2007; 4 previews, 16 performances

Written by Julie Fitzpatrick and Doug Anderson; Produced by Ensemble Studio Theatre (Curt Dempster, Artistic Director), Matt Lawler, with support from the rUDEmECHANICALS Theatre Company; Co-presented with Town Hall Theatre; Director/Piano Accompanist, Douglas Anderson; Set Consultant, Maruti Evans; Lighting, Evan Purcell; Sound, Noah Trepanier; PSM, Jenny Deady; Press, David Gersten

**CAST** Julie/Elizabeth **Julie Fitzpatrick;** ASL Interpretation **Wendy Schneider, Lisa Bixler, Maureen Chalmers, & Ruth Aleskovsky**

A solo performance play presented without intermission. Previously presented by the Godlight Theatre Company at 59E59 March–April 2006. World premiere at Town Hall Theater (Middlebury, Vermont) in 2005.

**SYNOPSIS** They were the best of friends, but soon after Julie went off to become a New York City actor and singer, Elizabeth, an advocate for the deaf, passed away. In this emotional, musical, and wildly funny journey, these two best friends are reunited. Elizabeth reaches across time to comfort her longtime friend and to inspire audiences who are meeting her for the first time.

# BLACKOUT

Kirk Theatre; First Preview: January 6, 2007; Opening Night: January 11, 2007; Closed January 27, 2007; 23 performances

Written by Michael I. Walker, original story by Kevin Quinn and Michael I. Walker; Produced by the Cell Theatre Company (Nancy Manocherian, Artistic Director; Matt Lillo, Managing Director); Director, Kira Simring; Design, Gabriel Hainer Evansohn; Costumes, Kristine Koury; Co-Lighting, Carl Faber; Sound, Travis Walker; PSM, Fran Rubenstein; Marketing, Wren Longo; Casting, Michael Cassara; Production Manager, Mary E. Leach; Technical Director, Tyler I. Hall; Assistant Director, Kerry Flanagan; Associate Set, Emily Fishbaine; Dramaturg, Kevin Quinn; Press, Pete Sanders, Shane Marshall Brown

**CAST** Collin **Ryan Patrick Bachand;** Alex **Teddy Bergman;** Lena **Almeria Campbell;** Maggie **Kate Goehring;** Fitz **Kevin Mambo;** Levi **Darnell Williams**

**SETTING** August 14, 2003, New York City. World premiere of a new play presented in two acts. This production was the inaugural outing for the newly minted Cell Theatre Company.

**SYNOPSIS** When the lights go out on New York City in the blackout of 2003, six strangers collide on a street corner in Hell's Kitchen. Their lives quickly intertwine, but when the power is restored, this newly formed community struggles to hold on to what they found in the dark. Inspired by the works of James Baldwin, *Blackout* is a smart, topical illumination of sex, race, faith, and electrical power.

*Teddy Bergman and Kevin Mambo in* Blackout
*(photo by Jesse-Chan Norris)*

# GET YOUR WAR ON

59E59 Theater B; First Preview: January 9, 2007; Opening Night: January 11, 2007; Closed January 28, 2007; 25 performances

Adapted by Kirk Lynn et al., from the internet comic by David Rees; Produced by Rude Mechanicals of Austin, Texas (Co-Producing Artistic Directors: Madge Darlington, Lana Lesley, Kirk Lynn, Sarah Richardson, Shawn Sides); Presented as part of the Under the Radar Festival 2007, produced by The Public Theater; Director, Shawn Sides; Sets, Leilah Stewart; Costumes, Laura Cannon; Lighting, Brian Scott; Sound, Robert S. Fisher; Technical Design, Madge Darlington; PSM, José Angel Hernández; Press, Sam Rudy Media Relations, Bob Lasko

**CAST** Ron Berry, Lana Lesley, Jason Liebrecht, Kirk Lynn, Sarah E. Richardson

New York premiere of a new play presented without intermission.

**SYNOPSIS** Using David Rees' savage and hysterical internet comic strip "Get Your War On" to combat the mainstream media's cultural amnesia about the sins of the current administration, the Rude Mechs cuss and spit through six years worth of disappointment, horror, and shame. With nothing more than five overhead projectors and public domain clip-art, *Get Your War On* represents stunned and outraged Americans as they react to 9/11, the Bush administration, and its "totally awesome" War On Terror.

*Jason Liebrecht in* Get Your War On *(photo by Jacques-Jean Tiziou)*

*Cynthia Hopkins, Gloria Deluxe, and the Cast of* Must Don't Whip 'Um *(photo by P.A.)*

## MUST DON'T WHIP 'UM

St. Ann's Warehouse; First Preview: January 15, 2007; Opening Night: January 17, 2007; Closed February 4, 2007; 2 previews, 15 performances

Music and text by Cynthia Hopkins; Produced by Arts at St. Ann's and Accinosco; Sets/Video/Production Design, Jim Findlay & Jeff Sugg; Choreography, Cynthia Hopkins, Diane Madden, Annie B Parson, Jordana Che Toback; Costumes, Tara Webb; Lighting, Jason Boyd; Sound, Jim Dawson with Jamie McElhinney; Production Coordinator, Aiyana D'Arcangelo; Directorial Consultation, Brooke O'Hara and D.J. Mendel; Technical Director, Peter Warren

**CAST** Cynthia Hopkins, Jim Findlay, Susan Oetgen, Jeff Sugg; Video Performances **Steve Ciuffo** (The Amazing Russello), **Aleta Claire Findlay** (Young Mary Fern), **Cynthia Hopkins** (Goodwin Stevens), **James Sugg** (Ronnie Falconne)

**THE BAND— Gloria Deluxe** Ben Holmes (trumpet), Kristen Mueller (drums), Reut Regev (trombone), Josh Stark (bass), Philippa Thompson (violin/guitar/percussion/musical saw), Karen Waltuch (viola/percussion)

**MUSICAL NUMBERS** Barrels of Oil, Blow It, Mister, Open Door, Lazarus, Horses to the Mountains, Come On, Love Is the Answer, Birdsong for the Birds, The Teaches of the Leeches, All the Pretty Crosses

World premiere of a musical/concert/multimedia piece performed without intermission. Prior to this engagement, the show played Walker Art Center in Minneapolis, Minnesota.

**SYNOPSIS** *Must Don't Whip 'Um*, is a *Last Waltz*-style staged documentary farewell concert performance of Cameron Seymour—a failed 1970s pop star—on the eve of her disappearance. The show is performed live as a concert by singer-songwriter Cynthia Hopkins, with technical wizards Jim Findlay and Jeff Sugg and the band Gloria Deluxe.

## THE POLISH PLAY

Walker Space at Soho Rep; First Preview: January 13, 2007; Opening Night: January 19, 2007; Closed February 17, 2007; 28 performances

A Conflation of *Macbeth* by William Shakespeare & *Ubu Roi* by Alfred Jarry, devised and directed by Henry Wishcamper; Produced by Katharsis Theater Company; Sets, Takeshi Kata; Costumes, Jenny Mannis; Lighting, Matthew Richards; Sound/Composer, Bart Fasbender; Puppets, Aleksandra Maslik; Fights, Qui Nguyen; Production Manager, Robin Ganek; PSM, Kelly Beaulieu; ASM, Melanie Lyanim; Producing Associate, Lisa Dozier; Props/Scenic Artist, Geoffry Decas; Wigs/Hair/Makeup, Erin Kennedy Lunsford; Casting, Stephanie Klapper; Technical Director, Derek Dickinson; Assistant Director, Erica Lipez; Press, Karen Greco

**CAST** Foley Artist **James Bentley;** Queen Rosamond, Cotice, et al. **Jeff Biehl**; Père Ubu **Jordan Gelber**; MacDuff, et al. **Torsten Hillhouse;** Banquo, et al. **Jacob Knoll;** King Wenceslas, Ross, et al. **Lucas Caleb Rooney;** Mère Ubu **Dana Smith-Croll;** Fleance, Lady MacDuff's Son, et al. **Ryan Ward;** Bougrelas, Lady MacDuff, et al. **Eunice Wong**

World premiere of a new play presented in two acts.

**SYNOPSIS** In *The Polish Play*, the idiot-tyrant Père Ubu, encouraged by his wife and the Three Weird Sisters, ascends the throne of Poland by slaughtering the meek King Wenceslas. Simultaneously a dark tragedy, a broad satire, and an absurdly gruesome Grand Guignol, *The Polish Play* offers one of Western theater's greatest stories as you've never seen it before.

*Jordan Gelber and Dana Smith-Croll in* The Polish Play *(photo by James Ambler)*

# DUTCHMAN

Cherry Lane Theatre; First Preview: January 16, 2007; Opening Night: January 22, 2007; Closed February 24, 2007; 6 previews, 35 performances

Written by Amiri Baraka (a.k.a Leroi Jones); Produced by Cherry Lane Theatre (Angelina Fiordellisi, Founder/Artistic Director; James King, Managing Director); Director, Bill Duke; Sets, Troy Hourie; Costumes, Rebecca Bernstein; Lighting, Jeff Croiter; Sound, Drew Levy & Tony Smolenski IV; Video, Aaron Rhyne; Fight Director, John Edmund Morgan; PSM, Gregory T. Livoti; ASM, Mei Ling Acevedo; Production Manager, Janio Marrero; Casting, Pamela Perrell; Press, Publicity Outfitters, Timothy Haskell

**CAST** Conductor/Drunk **Paul Benjamin**; Young Negro **Justin Carte**r; Clay **Dulé Hill**; Subway Rider **Christina Lind**; Subway Rider **Arthur Lundquist**; Lula **Jennifer Mudge**

Revival of a play presented without intermission. First presented at The Cherry Lane Theatre on March 24, 1964

**SYNOPSIS** This shocking drama tells the story of a white woman who seduces a naïve bourgeois black man on a train, with terrifying results.

*Stefanie Neukirch and Stephanie Silver in* Wake Up Mr. Sleepy! Your Unconscious Mind is Dead! *(photo by Paula Court)*

*Dulé Hill and Jennifer Mudge in* Dutchman *(photo by Gabe Evans)*

# WAKE UP MR. SLEEPY!
# Your Unconscious Mind is Dead!

Ontological Theatre at St. Marks; First Preview: January 18, 2007; Opening Night: January 25, 2007; Closed April 22, 2007; 65 performances

Created and directed by Richard Foreman; Presented by the Ontological-Hysteric Theatre; Managing Director, Shannon Sindelar; Technical Director, Peter Ksander; Stage Manager, Brendan Regimbal; Sound Engineer, Daniel Allen Nelson; Props/ Costumes, Meghan Buchanan, Video Engineer, Kleoni Manoussakis; Lighting Engineers, Joshua Briggs and Peter Ksander; Press, Manny Igrejas; Arts Management, Performing Art Services; Graphic Design, Elka Krajewska

**CAST** Tall Man **Joel Israel;** Short Man **Chris Mirto;** Girl in Pantsuit **Stefanie Neukirch;** Aviator **James Peterson;** Female Voice **Kate Manheim;** Male Voice **Richard Foreman;** Film Cast: **Samuel Alves, Carla Bolito, António Calpi, João Correia, Maria Duarte, Cândido Ferreira, Patrícia Galiano, Carla Galvão, Patrícia Leal, Tiago Manaia, Tita Morgado, Adelina Oliveira, João Pedreiro, André Teodósio**

World premiere of a new experimental multimedia play presented without intermission.

**SYNOPSIS** *Wake Up Mr. Sleepy! Your Unconscious Mind Is Dead!* is Richard Foreman's latest battle cry as he plunges head first into the planet's malaise and digs beneath the surface of our everyday lives and dreams. As it straddles the divide between film and theater, this dramatic extravaganza struggles to unearth the unknowable sources of human inventiveness. This show the second in a series in which Foreman uses a backdrop of digital film shot in countries around the world (in this case Lisbon, Portugal, recent World Cup contenders).

# ABSOLUTE CLARITY

Players Theatre; First Preview: January 31, 2007; Opening Night: February 2, 2007; Closed February 25, 2007; 28 performances

Written by Sophia Romma, loosely based on the play *She, in the Absence of Love and Death* by Edvard Radzinski; Presented by ArtVoice and Cinema Anastasia Productions; Director, Yuri Joffe; Sets, Anastasia Glebova; Costumes, Robert Eggers; Lighting, Russel Drapkin; Sound, Zachary Williamson; Set, Gregg Bellon; Production Manager, Sean Ryan; Stage Manager, Sergio Cruz; ASM, Susan D. Lange

**CAST** LaBelle Watson **Alexandra Bosquet;** Tita Marie Ache **Brianne Berkson;** The Duke **Alexander Elisa;** Clare Kline **Cara Francis;** Daniel Weitz **Mark Light-Orr;** Robert Capria, Sr. **Steve Greenstein;** Patricia Kline **Victoria Guthrie;** Moses **Jason Yachanin;** Joey De Jazz **Patrick Knighton;** Sylvie Weitz **Inbal Samuel;** Musicians **Patrick Knighton, Brianne Berkson, Jason Yachanin, Alexander Elisa**

World premiere of a new play with music presented in two acts.

**SYNOPSIS** In this cinematic, tragicomic coming-of-age story, Claire, a lonely lover, an irreverent dreamer, and rebellious daughter, lives in a world of melodies and double meanings: love is still love, even if it's imagined; death is still death, even if it's an accident. Claire struggles to actualize herself as an artist, fights for independence against her mother, briefly joins a pickpocket-filled jazz band, and revisits the lawyer and judge of her childhood custody trial, triggering disastrous consequences. Her world is populated by women who, like herself, grasp for kernels of happiness, and by men that they love and betray, who also abuse them mercilessly.

# A MIDSUMMER NIGHT'S DREAM

TBG Theatre; First Preview: January 27, 2007; Opening Night: February 3, 2007; Closed February 25, 2007; 28 performances

Written by William Shakespeare; Produced by Theatre by the Blind; Director, Ike Schambelan; Sets, Merope Vachiloti; Costumes, Brad L. Scoggins; Lighting, Bert Scott; Stage Manager, Francis Eric Montesa; ASM, Hollis Hamilton; Dialect Coach, Susan Cameron; Production Manager, Nicholas Lazzaro; Music and Musicians, The Company; Marketing, Michelle Brandon; Development Associate, Ilana Novick; Press, Shirley Herz, Dan Demello

**CAST** Egeus/Oberon/Bottom/Pyramus **George Ashiotis;** Demetrius/Mustardseed/Quince/Prologue **Jon Levenson;** Hermia/Titania/Starveling/Moonshine **Ann Marie Morelli;** Hoppolyta/Helena/Moth/Snout/Wall **Erin O'Leary;** Lysander/Cobweb/Flute/Thisby **Andrew Rein;** Theseus/Puck/Peaseblossom/Snug/Lion **Nicholas Viselli**

A new adaptation of the play presented without intermission.

**SYNOPSIS** Theatre By the Blind's *Midsummer* defies tradition and puts a unique Manhattan spin on the classic about the pangs and intensity of young romance. With only a cast of six, each actor plays an Upper East Side Athenian, an immigrant rude mechanical, and a disco staff fairy. The three worlds collide, but it all ends happily, even though the course of true love never did run smooth.

*George Ashiotis and Ann Marie Morelli in Theatre By The Blind's A Midsummer Night's Dream (photo by Carol Rosegg)*

# THE CRYING WOMAN (La Llorona)

Beckett Theatre; First Preview: February 1, 2007; Opening Night: February 4, 2007; Closed February 24, 2007; 24 performances

Written by Kathleen Anderson Culebro; Produced by Stageplays Theatre Company; Director, Tom Ferriter; Sets, Zhanna Gurvich; Costumes, Vasila Zivanic; Lighting, Jeffrey Koger; Original Music, Cindy O'Connor; Sound, Chris Rummel; Choreography, Ron DeJesus; Wigs/Makeup, Wendy Parson; PSM, Misha Siegel-Rivers; ASM, Rosie Goldman; Casting, Laura Dragomir; Press, Pete Sanders

**CAST** La Llorona **Natasha Tabandera;** Carlos **Mauricio Tafur Salgado;** Irma **Ioana Alfonso;** Liz **Julia Barnett;** Jeffrey **Trevor Jones;** Sergio **Germán Nande**

World premiere of a new play presented in two acts.

**SYNOPSIS** This cross-cultural drama is about an American businessman assigned to open an American fast food restaurant, to sell Mexican food, in Mexico City. When he and his pregnant wife move into the home of a struggling Mexican architec—forced to rent his ancestral home to support his own young family—the hacienda is visited by La Llorona, a spirit who sings her song of sadness in hopes of rescuing the two young couples from danger.

*Natasha Tabandera (standing) and Ioana Alfonso in* The Crying Woman (La Llorona) *(photo by Gerry Goodstein)*

# REAL DANGER

Theatre 5; Opening Night: February 5, 2007; Closed March 3, 2007; 16 performances

Written by by Jeff Hollman; Presented by Emerging Artists Theatre (Paul Adams, Artistic Director and Founder) as part of the "Triple Threat" series; Director, Paul Adams; Music Composition, Louis Fujinami Conti; Stage Manager, Jennifer Russo; Sets, Robert Monaco; Costumes, Amy Elizabeth Bravo; Lighting, Jennifer Granrud; Sound, Ned Thorne; Composer/Original Music, Louis Fujinami Conti; Sound/Wardrobe, Hershey Miller; Sound Supervisor, Aaron David Blank; Production Manager, Deb Guston; Crew: David Bishop, Jenny Lee Mitchell, Erin Hadley; Marketing/Publicity, Katie Rosin, United Stages

**CAST** Ferdy **Eric Chase;** Edward **Ryan Duncan;** Vicki **Carl Monda**

**SETTING** Cleveland, Ohio. World premiere of a new play presented without intermission.

**SYNOPSIS** *Real Danger* begins with a surprise reunion between two friends nine years after they graduated from college. Edward reunites with his soccer teammate, Ferdy and his girlfriend Vickie, to apologize for an old wrong. He learns how Ferdy and Vickie met and how they became fugitives in fear that her former lover would kill them if he found them. For Edward, the reunion moves quickly away from his original purpose and becomes a series of shocking surprises.

# (mis)UNDERSTANDING MAMMY: The Hattie McDaniel Story

Theatre 5; Opening Night: February 7, 2007; Closed March 4, 2007; 16 performances

Written by Joan Ross Sorkin; Presented by Emerging Artists Theatre (Paul Adams, Artistic Director and Founder) as part of the "Triple Threat" series; Director, David Glenn Armstrong; Musical Supervisor, Lance Horne; Associate Director, Daniel Haley; PSM, Jennifer Granrud; Sets, Robert Monaco; Costumes, Amy Elizabeth Bravo; Lighting, Jennifer Granrud; Sound, Ned Thorne; Composer/Original Music, Louis Fujinami Conti; Sound/Wardrobe, Hershey Miller; Sound Supervisor, Aaron David Blank; Production Manager, Deb Guston; Marketing/Publicity, Katie Rosin, United Stages

**CAST** Hattie McDaniel **Capathia Jenkins**

**SETTING** 1952. Motion Picture Country Home and Hospital in Woodland Hills, California. World premiere of a new play with music presented without intermission.

**SYNOPSIS** *(mis)Understanding Mammy* reveals a side of Hattie McDaniel's life that few people knew. Hattie achieved stardom by becoming the first African-American to win an Academy Award, but she paid a high price for fame. By playing a succession of maids and cooks, most notably Mammy in *Gone With the Wind*, she became the target of an unrelenting campaign against "Mammyism" led by Walter White of the NAACP, who thought her roles were shameful and degrading to their race. Despite her own efforts to bring dignity and humanity to her roles, within seven years of winning her Oscar her film career was virtually destroyed.

*Capathia Jenkins in* (mis)Understanding Mammy: The Hattie McDaniel Story *(photo by Jennie Zeiner)*

# IN THE HEIGHTS

37 Arts; First Preview: January 9, 2007; Opening Night: February 8, 2007; Closed July 15, 2007; 33 previews, 181 performances

Music and lyrics by Lin-Manuel Miranda, book by Quiara Alegría Hudes; Conceived by Lin-Manuel Miranda; Produced by Kevin McCollum, Jeffrey Seller, and Jill Furman; Director, Thomas Kail; Choreographer, Andy Blankenbuehler; Music Director, Alex Lacamoire; Sets, Anna Louizos; Costumes, Paul Tazewell; Lighting, Jason Lyons; Sound, Acme Sound Partners; Arrangements/Orchestrations, Alex Lacamoire & Bill Sherman; Music Coordinator, Michael Keller; Casting, Telsey + Company; Marketing, Scott A. Moore; PSM, J. Philip Bassett; General Manager, R. Erin Craig; Technical Supervisor, Randall Etheredge; Company Manager, Lizbeth A. Cone; Stage Manager, Amber Wedin; Assistant Director, Casey Hushion; Assistant Choreographer, Joey Dowling; Assistant to the Choreographer, Luis Salgado; Fight Captain, Michael Balderrama; Associate Design: Donyale Werle, Todd Potter (set), Michael McAleer (costumes), Jennifer Schriever (lighting); Music Copying, Emily Grishman; Rehearsal Pianist, Zachary Dietz; Wigs, Charles LaPointe; Fight Consultant, Ron Piretti; Associate Technical Supervisor, Jason Marsh; Additional Dance Arrangements, Oscar Hernandez; Press, Barlow · Harman, Matt Stapleton, Wayne Wolfe

**CAST** Graffiti Pete **Seth Stewart;** Usnavi **Lin-Manuel Miranda;** Piragua Guy **Eliseo Roman;** Abuela Claudia **Olga Merediz;** Carla **Janet Dacal;** Daniela **Andréa Burns;** Kevin **John Herrera;** Camila **Priscilla Lopez;** Sonny **Robin De Jesus;** Benny **Christopher Jackson;** Vanessa **Karen Olivo;** Nina **Mandy Gonzalez;** Bolero Singer **Doreen Montalvo;** Ensemble **Rosie Lani Fiedelman, Asmeret Ghebremichael, Joshua Henry, Nina LaFarga, Doreen Montalvo, Eliseo Roman, Javier Muñoz\*, Luis Salgado, Rickey Tripp;** Swings **Michael Balderrama** (Dance Captain), **Stephanie Klemons** (Assistant Dance Captain), **Michelle Rios, Shaun Taylor-Corbett**

**UNDERSTUDIES** Michael Balderrama (Graffiti Pete, Piragua Guy), Janet Dacal (Vanessa), Asmeret Ghebremichael (Vanessa, Carla), Joshua Henry (Benny), Nina LaFarga (Nina), Doreen Montalvo (Abuela Claudia, Camila, Daniela), Javier Muñoz (Usnavi, Sonny, Graffiti Pete), Eliseo Roman (Kevin), Rickey Tripp (Benny)

**ORCHESTRA** Alex Lacamoire (Conductor/keyboards), Manny Moreira (guitars), Irio O'Farrill (bass), Andres Patrick Forero (drums/percussion), Doug Hinrichs (percussion), Raul Agraz (trumpet), David Richards (woodwinds)

**MUSICAL NUMBERS** In the Heights, Breathe, Benny's Dispatch, It Won't Be Long Now, Plan B, Inútil (Useless), No Me Diga, 96,000, Paciencia Y Fe (Patience and Faith), When You're Home, Piragua, Siempre (Always), The Club/Fireworks, Sunrise, Hundreds of Stories, Carnaval del Barrio, Atencíon, Alabanza, Everything I Know, Hear Me Out, Goodbye, Finale

**2006-2007 AWARDS:** Drama Desk: Outstanding Ensemble Performance; Lucille Lortel: Outstanding Musical, Outstanding Choreographer; Clarence Derwent Award: Lin-Manuel Miranda; **Theatre World Award:** Lin-Manuel Miranda

**SETTING** Washington Heights, Manhattan. Fourth of July weekend, the present. World premiere of a new musical presented in two acts. Developed at The Eugene O'Neill Theater Center, 2005; initially developed by Back House Productions

**SYNOPSIS** In the Heights follows two days in the life of Washington Heights, the vibrant immigrant neighborhood at the top of Manhattan. From the vantage point of Usnavi's corner bodega, we experience the joys, heartbreaks, and bonds of a Latino community struggling to redefine home. This original musical features a mix of hip-hop, salsa and meringue.

\*Succeeded by John Rua. Temporary cast members: Nancy Ticotin (Camila), Tony Flacon (ensemble)

*Andréa Burns, Karen Olivo, Mandy Gonzalez, and Janet Dacal in* In the Heights *(photos by Joan Marcus)*

*Mandy Gonzales and Christopher Jackson in* In the Heights

# ELEPHANT GIRLS

Theatre 5; First Preview: February 7; Opening Night: February 10, 2007; Closed: March 4, 2007; 2 previews, 14 performances

Written by Carl Gonzalez; Presented by Emerging Artists Theatre (Paul Adams, Artistic Director and Founder) as part of the "Triple Threat" series; Director, Derek Jamison; Stage Manager, Andrew Ronan; Sets, Robert Monaco; Costumes, Amy Elizabeth Bravo; Lighting, Jennifer Granrud; Sound, Ned Thorne; Composer/Original Music, Louis Fujinami Conti; Sound/Wardrobe, Hershey Miller; Sound Supervisor, Aaron David Blank; Production Manager, Deb Guston; Marketing/Publicity, Katie Rosin, United Stages

**CAST** Robina **Sarah Miriam Aziz;** Beth **Amy Bizjak;** Claire **Glory Gallo;** Vickie **Lué McWilliams;** Frances **Vivian Meisner;** Jasmine **Gameela Wright**

**SETTING** Time: A recent Friday, early evening. Place: A living room in New Jersey. World premiere of a new play presented in two acts.

**SYNOPSIS** When a Kozy Kitchen party that the perfect housewife Claire hosts for her family and friends is interrupted by an unexpected guest, six women find themselves exploring the complexities of human behavior and the consequences of their own life choices. What happens to a little girl in the absence of love? What happens when strangers half a world away take up her cause? Inspired by National Geographic's famous cover photo "The Afghan Girl," *Elephant Girls* culminates these women spiraling into a maelstrom of white-hot emotion that leaves their relationships forever changed.

# THE LAST WORD...

Theatre at St. Clements; First Preview: January 30, 2007; Opening Night: February 8, 2007; Closed March 11, 2007; 40 performances

Written by Oren Safdie; Produced by Les Gutman and Elizabeth Cockrell in association with Friendly Fire and Lynn Shaw Productions; Director, Alex Lippard; Sets, Michael V. Moore; Lighting, Lucas Benjamin Krech; Costumes, Kirche Leigh Zeile; Sound, Gabe Wood; PSM, Marci Skolnick; Production Manager, TFI Production Inc./Helena Webb; Associate General Manager, Steven Bloom; Casting, Deborah Brown; General Manager, Cesa Entertainment Inc.; Wardrobe Supervisor/Props, Annie Deardorff; Advertising, Eliran Murphy Group; Press, Sam Rudy Media Relations, Dale Heller, Robert Lasko, Charlie Siedenburg

**CAST** Henry Grunwald **Daniel J. Travanti;** Len Artz **Adam Green**

**SETTING** A Fall in the 1990's. A small, rundown office above a Greenwich Village theatre. New York premiere of a new play presented without intermission. First produced at Malibu Stage Company, California.

**SYNOPSIS** Henry Grunwald, a Viennese Jew who fled the Nazis, retired as the head of an ad agency to fulfill his dream of being a playwright. When he interviews a playwriting student with more modern values to be his assistant, the two engage in a verbal war on one another that ultimately reveals the hidden truths they each have buried deep inside. Can the gap between their two worlds be bridged?

*Daniel J. Travanti and Adam Green in* The Last Word...
*(photo by Carol Rosegg)*

# THE QUANTUM EYE: Magic Deceptions

SoHo Playhouse–The Huron Club; First Preview: September 27, 2007; Opening Night: February 9, 2007; still running as of May 31, 2007 (Friday evenings)

Created by Sam Eaton; Produced and directed by Samuel Rosenthal; Original Music, Scott O'Brien; Art Design, Fearless Design; Assistant Producer, Janet Oldenbrook; Artwork, Glenn Hidlago; House Manger, Janet Oldenbrook; Press, Timothy Haskell; Wardrobe, Larry the Tailor

Performed by **Sam Eaton**

A mentalist/magic show presented without intermission. Programme includes: A Gulity Conscience, One Card, Fourth Dimension, Two Words, Animal Instinct, Digimancy, Mental Sketch, Transmission, Mnemoncis, Strange News

**SYNOPSIS** The spirit of Harry Houdini, and Victorian era New York are alive and none of your secrets are safe from *The Quantum Eye*.... Eaton takes audiences to the outer limits of human perception. His masterful use of prediction, supernormal mentalism, memorization, and calculation will amaze and entertain audiences. It is an extraordinary blend of twenty-first Century mentalism and Victorian-era mystery. *The Quantum Eye* is proof that there is still magic in the air.

*Sam Eaton in* The Quantum Eye: Magical Deceptions
*(photo by Michael Kwiecinski)*

# MY SECRET GARDEN

45th Street Theatre; First Preview: February 2, 2007; Opening Night: February 14, 2007; Closed March 11, 2007, 14 previews, 27 performances

Adapted by Nancy Friday and Christopher Scott, based on Friday's novel; Produced by Maximus Productions in association with Eric Krebs; Director, Christopher Scott; Sets, Bernard Grenier; Lighting, Ben Hagen; Costumes, Michele Reisch; PSM, Brian Westmoreland; Company Manager, Rebecca Sherman; General Management, EKTM/Jonathan Shulman; Production Supervisor, PRF Productions; Press, Judy Jacksina

**CAST** Helen, Lola, etc. **Jane Blas;** Karen, Bella, etc. **McKenzie Frye;** Therapist, Francesca, etc. **Lyn Philistine;** Nancy **Mimi Quillin**

World premiere of a new play presented without intermission.

**SYNOPSIS** *My Secret Garden* tells the story of Nancy Friday and her search for the female sex fantasy. Containing 70s music and sexually explicit material, this new play is adapted from Friday's controversial 1973 novel, which compiled interviews of women discussing (in finite and graphic detail) their sexual fantasies and became an immediate bestseller and target of the world's media.

*Lyn Philistine, Mimi Quillin, Jane Blas, and McKenzie Frye in* My Secret Garden *(photo by Richard Termine)*

# THE GAZILLION BUBBLE SHOW

New World Stages—Stage 3; Previews: January 17–23, 2007; Opening Night: February 15, 2007; still running as of May 31, 2007*

Created and staged by Fan Yang; Produced and Set Design by Fan Yang and Neodus Company Ltd.; Artistic Director, Jamie Jan; Show Director, Steve Lee; Lighting, Jin Ho Kim; Sound, Joon Lee; Gazilllion Bubbles FX, Special Effects, Alex Cheung; Theatrical Special Effects, CITC/Gary and Stephanie Crawford; Original Music, Workspace Co. Ltd.; Laser Design, Abhilash George; Lumalaser, Tim Ziegenbein; Lighting Effects, David Lau; Special Effects Inventor, Dragan Maricic; PSM, Yeung Jin Son; Stage Manager, Min Song; Technical Director, Alan Kho; Production Manager, Vanes D'Andrea; General Management, The Splinter Group; Marketing, HHC Marketing; Marketing Director, Chermaine Cho; Press, Springer Associates, Joe Trentacosta, Gary Springer

Performed by **Fan Yang**

New York premiere of an interactive theatrical event presented without intermission.

**SYNOPSIS** The first interactive stage production of its kind, complete with fantastic light effects and lasers, Fan Yang blends art and science to dazzle audiences with his jaw-dropping masterpieces of bubble artistry that defy gravity and logic as we know it. He holds Guinness World records for the biggest bubble ever blown, the largest bubble wall ever created (a staggering 156 feet!), most bubbles within a bubble, and in May 2006, was able to encapsulate twenty-two people inside a single soap bubble on live television.

*The show went on hiatus March 31–April 19.

*Fan Yang in* The Gazillion Bubble Show
*(photo by Nino Fernando Campagna)*

# WORKING

Zipper Theater; February 19, 2007; 1 performance

Adapted by Stephen Schwartz and Nina Faso, from the book by Studs Terkel, songs by Craig Carnelia, Micki Grant, Mary Rodgers & Susan Birkenhead, Stephen Schwartz, James Taylor; Dance Music by Michele Brourman; Presented by the Zipper Theater, Ryan Hill, & John Johnson in association with The Actors Fund; Director, Gordon Greenburg; Music Director, Steve Marzullo; Musical Staging, Warren Carlyle; Lighting, Jeff Croiter and Jeff Carnevale; Sound, P.J. Boeckel and Peter Fitzgerald; Casting, Telsey + Company; PSM, Sara Jaramillo; ASM, Ryan Mekenian; General Manager, Andrew Jones; Assistant Director, Raymond Zilberberg; Press, Shaffer-Coyle Public Relations

**CAST** Jeb Brown, Merle Dandridge, Ed Dixon, Roderick Hill, Celia Keenan-Bolger, Mary Testa

**BAND** Steve Marzullo (Piano/Conductor), Ben Cohn (2nd keyboard), Kenny Brescia (guitar), Sean McDaniel (drums), Mary Ann McSweeney (bass)

**MUSICAL NUMBERS** All The Livelong Day, I'm Just Movin', Lovin' Al, Nobody Tells Me How, Millwork, If I Could've Been, Mason, Brother Trucker, It's An Art, Joe, Cleaning Women, Fathers and Sons, Something to Point To

Staged concert reading of a musical presented without intermission. Originally presented on Broadway at the 46th Street (Richard Rodgers) Theatre May 14–June 4, 1978 (see *Theatre World* Volume 34, page 48).

**SYNOPSIS** The 1978 musical about real people and their jobs, *Working* receives one of its first New York revivals in this benefit for the Actors Fund of America.

# BFF

DR2 Theatre; First Preview: February 17, 2007; Opening Night: February 25, 2007; Closed March 31, 2007; 37 performances

Written by Anna Ziegler; Produced by Women's Expressive Theater Inc. (Victoria Pettibone, Director of Operations/Executive Producer; Sasha Eden, Creative Director/Executive Producer); Director, Josh Hecht; Sets, Robin Vest; Costumes, Sara Jean Tosetti; Lighting, Clifton Taylor; Original Music/Sound, David Stephen Baker; Projections, Kevin R. Frech; PSM, Ashley B. Delegal; Production Manager, David Nelson; ASM, Taylor Mankowski; Assistant Director, Tasha Gordon-Solmon; Web Design/Art Director, Kayla Silber; Props, Kathryn Kawecki; Casting, Jack Doulin; Associate Producer, Andrea Chalupa; Press, Spin Cycle, Ron Lasko

**CAST** Eliza **Laura Heisler;** Lauren **Sasha Eden;** Seth **Jeremy Webb***

World premiere of a new play presented without intermission.

**SYNOPSIS** *BFF* tells the story of Lauren and her "best friend forever" Eliza. Lauren is a New Yorker who is split in two by time, living in the past and present simultaneously. Haunted by her adolescent past, she is desperate to catch up with her present and explore a new romance. But when Lauren accidentally tells a lie, she is forced to complete a story that, until now, has remained cruelly unfinished.

*Succeeded by Sean Dugan (3/23/07)

*Laura Heisler and Sasha Eden in* BFF *(photo by Max Ruby)*

# SEALED FOR FRESHNESS

New World Stages—Stage 5; First Preview: February 15, 2007; Opening Night: February 24, 2007; Closed April 29, 2007; 10 previews, 86 performances

Written and directed by Doug Stone; Produced by Cannon Entertainment Group in association with Fresh Ice Productions; Sets, Rob Odorisio; Costumes, Rob Bevenger; Lighting, Traci Klainer; Sound, Ken Hypes; General Manager, Maria Producitons Inc, Maria Di Dia; PSM, Elizabeth Grunenwald; Marketing, HHC Marketing; Advertising, Eliran Murphy Group; Production Manager, Aduro Productions Inc.; Casting, Paul Donelan; Executive Producer, Mike Fimiani; Co-Producers, Will Fruma Campbell, F4 Capital Management; Company Manager, Robert E. Schneider; ASM, Shawn Curran; Props, Will Fruma Campbell; Associate Costumes, Jeffrey Johnson-Doherty; Associate Sound, Graham Johnson; Press, O+M Company, Rick Miramontez, Philip Carrubba

**CAST** Bonnie Kapica **Jennifer Dorr White;** Richard Kapica **Brian Dykstra;** Jean Pawlicki **Nancy Hornback;** Tracy Ann McClain **Kate Vandervender;** Sinclair Benevente **J.J. Van Name;** Diane Whettlaufer **Patricia Dalen**

**UNDERSTUDIES** Cynthia Babak (Jean, Diane, Tracey Ann), Shawn Curran (Richard), Elizabeth Meadows Rouse (Sinclaire, Bonnie)

**SETTING** A typical mid-west suburb. 1968. A new play presented in two acts. Previously presented at The Pantheon Theater in 2003.

**SYNOPSIS** Billed as the original "Desperate Housewives," *Sealed for Freshness* is the story of five mid-western women who believe in being good wives, good mothers and good neighbors. They were raised to trade their dreams, hopes and desires for social norms, and now they want them back. These hermetically sealed, airtight lives unravel during a sidesplitting Tupperware party gone awry as they struggle with lost youth, missed opportunities — and deviled egg containers.

*Patricia Dalen, Jennifer Dorr White, Nancy Hornback, J.J. Van Name, Kate Vandevender, and Brian Dykstra (standing) in* Sealed for Freshness *(photo by Carol Rosegg)*

# BOYS JUST WANNA HAVE FUN

Actors Playhouse; First Preview: February 23, 2007; Opening Night: March 2, 2007; Closed June 9, 2007

Written by Anthony Wilkinson and Teresa Anne Cicala; Produced by Andee Productions; Directors/Casting, Sonia Blangiardo and Teresa Anne Cicala; Choreographer, J. Austin Eyer; Sets, Robert Santeramo; Costumes, Bernard Grenier; Lighting, Bob Bessoir; General Management, Cesa Entertainment Inc.; Production Coordinator, Nate Johnson, Nicole Michelle; Technical Director, Ben Folstein; Advertising, Eliran Murphy; Marketing, Hugh Hysell; Makeup, Nathan Johnson; Press, Richard Kornberg & Associates, Billy Zavelson

**CAST** Ralph Rizzo/Rio La Rocca **Anthony Wilkinson;** Danny Delmonico **Tom Baran;** Lauren Vitale/Lola **Rachel Valdati*;** Mateo Dupris **Kevin McIntyre;** Connie Profacci **Randi Kaplan;** Joey Defrancesco **Erik Ransom;** Vinny Marino **Kevin P. Smith;** Brooklyn John **Philip Andrew Brock;** Pontessa Puree/Carmine Lozio **Chad Kessler;** Swings **Concetta Aliotta, Adam Ferguson, Jonathan Lang, Vincent Iannuzzi**

**UNDERSTUDIES** Adam Ferguson (Mateo/Joey), Concetta M. Aliotta (Lauren/Lola/Connie), Jonathan Lang, (Rio/Vinny), Vincent Iannuzzi (Bklyn John/Carmine/Pontessa), Liz Gerecitano (Lauren/Lola/Connie), Philip Andrew Brock (Danny)

World premiere of a new play presented in two acts.

**SYNOPSIS** In the late 1980s, NYPD detectives Ralph and Lauren go undercover at a Staten Island gay bar packed with eccentric regulars to infiltrate an alleged drug ring. Instead, Ralph soon finds himself under the covers with Danny, the local heartthrob. In spite of some disturbing revelations and complications, in time, this unlikely couple may discover their very own happy ending.

*Succeeded by Liz Gerecitano

# HAMLET

St. Ann's Warehouse; First Preview: February 27, 2007; Opening Night: March 4, 2007; Closed March 25, 2007; 24 performances

Adapted by the company from the play by William Shakespeare; Produced by the Wooster Group in association with Arts at St. Ann's; Director, Elizabeth LeCompte; Set, Ruud van Den Akker; Lighting, Jennifer Tipton, Gabe Maxson; Sound, Geoff Abbas, Joby Emmons, Matt Tierney, Dan Dobson; Video, Reid Farrington; Costumes, Claudia Hill; Production, Bozkurt Karasu; Assistant to the Director, Teresa Hartmann; Technical Director, Aron Deyo; Stage and Costume Assistant, Ariella Beth Bowden; Sound Technician, Matt Schloss; Fight Coach, Felix Ivanov; Movement, Natalie Thomas

**CAST** Hamlet/Player **Scott Shepherd;** Claudius/Marcellus/Ghost/Grave-digger/Player **Ari Fliakos;** Gertrude/Ophelia/Player **Kate Valk;** Polonius/Player **Roy Faudree;** Laertes/Rosencrantz/Guildenstern/Player **Casey Spooner;** Horatio/Player **Judson Williams;** Bernardo/Rosencrantz/Guildenstern/Osric/Player **Daniel Pettrow;** Nurse/Player **Dominique Bousquet**

World premiere of an experimental theatrical piece presented in two acts.

**SYNOPSIS** The Wooster Group's *Hamlet* reconstructs a hypothetical theater piece from the fragmentary evidence of Richard Burton's 1964 Broadway production that was recorded in performance and shown as a film for two days only in 2,000 U.S. movie houses. The idea of bringing a live theater experience to thousands of simultaneous viewers in different cities was trumpeted as a new form called "Theatrofilm." This *Hamlet* attempts to reverse the process, like an archeologist inferring an improbable temple from a collection of ruins.

*Scott Shepherd in The Wooster Group's* Hamlet *(photo by Paula Court)*

# THE ATTIC

59E59 Theater B; First Preview: February 21, 2007; Opening Night: March 4, 2007; Closed March 25, 2007; 31 performances

Written by Yoji Sakate, translated by Leon Ingulsrud and Keiko Tsuneda; Produced by The Play Company (Kate Loewald, Founding Producer; Lauren Weigel, Managing Producer); Director, Ari Edelson; Sets, Takeshi Kata; Costumes, Junghyun Georgia Lee; Lighting, Tyler Micoleau; Sound, Bart Fasbender; PSM, Scott Pomerico; Production Manager, Lester Grant; Casting, Vince Liebhart; Literary Associate/Company Manager, Melissa Hardy; Dramaturg, Linda Bartholomai; ASM, Heather Prince; Properties; Desiree Maurer; Associate Production Manager, Jee Han; Technical Director, Nick Warren Gray; Producing Associate, Rob Marcato; Associate Artist, Trip Cullman; Press, The Karpel Group

**CAST** Older Brother **Trey Lyford;** Third Floor Monitor/Corpse/Young Man/Man with Crutches **Caesar Samayoa;** Buyer/Detective 2/Samurai 2/Clerk/Soldier **David Wilson Barnes;** Young Woman/Anchorperson 1/Mother/Lady/Matsu **Fiona Gallagher;** Girl/Middle Aged Man/Woman in White/Take **Emily Donahoe;** Boy/Woman/Middle Aged Woman/Teacher/Anchorperson 2/Ume **Michi Barall;** Detective 1/Samurai 1/Father/Young Man 2/Man with Overalls/Soldier **Ed Vassallo;** Man With a Cap **Brandon Miller**

English language premiere of a new play presented without intermission.

**SYNOPSIS** *The Attic* is a surreal dark comedy by celebrated Japanese writer Yoji Sakate, about hikikomori, a widespread phenomenon in Japan in which young people withdraw into their rooms, refusing any contact with the outside world, sometimes for years. The play imagines a world in which a mysterious corporation manufactures tiny "attics" and sells them to people who "go hikikimori."

*Trey Lyford and Caesar Samayoa in* The Attic *(photo by Carol Rosegg)*

# BILL W AND DR. BOB

New World Stages—Stage 2; First Preview: February 16, 2007; Opening Night: March 5, 2007; Closed June 10, 2007; 21 previews, 111 performances

Written by Stephen Bergman and Janet Surrey; Produced by Bradford S. Lovette, Dr. Michael Weinberg & Judith Weinberg, Evelyn Freed, Milton D. McKenzie, in association with New Repertory Theatre (Rick Lombardo, Producing Artistic Director; Harriet Sheets, Managing Director); Director, Rick Lombardo; Sets, Anita Fuchs; Costumes, Jane Alois Stein; Lighting, Daniel Meeker; Original Music, Ray Kennedy; Sound, Rick Lombardo; Fight Choreography, Ted Hewlett; Casting, Stuart Howard, Amy Schecter, Paul Hardt; PSM, Cheryl Olszowaka; Marketing, Marcia Pendelton, Walk Tall Girl Productions; Promotions, HHC Marketing, Michael Redman; General Management, Albert Poland; Production Management, Aurora Productions; Company Manager, Susan L. Brumley; ASM, Emily Ellen Roberts; Assistant Director, Erick Herrscher; Fight Captain, Deanna Dunmyer; Props Coordinator, Peter Sarafin; Press, Sam Rudy Media Relations

**CAST** Bill Wilson **Robert Krakovski;** Dr. Bob Smith **Patrick Husted;** Man **Marc Carver;** Lois Wilson **Rachel Harker;** Anne Smith **Kathleen Doyle;** Woman **Deanna Dunmyer;** Pianist **Ray Kennedy**

**UNDERSTUDIES** Paul Niebanck (Bill W/Man), Ted Pejovich (Dr. Bob/Man), Katherine Leask (Lois/Woman), Kay Walbye (Anne/Woman)

**SETTING** Many different places from September 1925 to July 1935, except the Prologue and Epilogue, both set in 1939 and 1955. New York premiere of a new play with live music presented in two acts. This cast performed the world premiere production at New Repertory Theatre (Boston, Massachusetts), March 5–26, 2006

**SYNOPSIS** In 1929, famous New York stockbroker Bill Wilson crashes with the stock market and becomes a hopeless drunk. Dr. Bob Smith, a surgeon from Ohio, has also been an alcoholic for thirty years, often going into the operating room with a hangover. Through an astonishing series of events, Bill and Bob meet and form a relationship, each helping to keep the other sober. This is the amazing and often humorous story of the two men who pioneered Alcoholics Anonymous, as well as the story of their wives, who founded Al Anon.

*Robert Krakovski and Patrick Husted in* Bill W and Dr. Bob
*(photo by T. Charles Erickson)*

*Ain Gordon, Kathleen Chalfant, Hazelle Goodman, and Frank Wood in* Spalding Gray: Stories Left to Tell *(photo by Richard Termine)*

# SPAULDING GRAY: STORIES LEFT TO TELL

Minetta Lane Theatre; First Preview: February 20, 2007; Opening Night: March 6, 2007; Closed June 26, 2007; 16 previews, 129 performances

Created by Kathleen Russo and Lucy Sexton, based on the writings and stories of Spalding Gray; Produced by Michael Alden, Eric Falkenstein, and the Naked Angels Theatre Company (Jenny Gersten, Artistic Director); Director, Lucy Sexton; Sets, David Korins; Costumes, Michael Krass; Lighting, Ben Stanton; Original Music and Sound, Fitz Patton; Projections, Leah Gelpe; PSM, Matthew Silver; ASM, Ryan West; Production Manager, Shannon Nicole Case; Associate Set Design, Rod Lemmond; Assistant Set Design, Amanda Phillips; Assisting Lighting Design, Lauren Phillips; Assistant Director, Brittany O'Neill; Press, O+M Company

**CAST** Family **Frank Wood;** Love **Kathleen Chalfant[*1];** Adventure **Hazelle Goodman;** Journals **Ain Gordon[*2];** Career **Richard Kind** (February 20–25), **Fisher Stevens** (February 27–March 7), **Estelle Parsons,** (March 8–11) **Josh Lucas** (March 20–April 8), **Rachel Dratch** (April 10–22), **Bruce Vilanch** (April 24–May 6), **Valerie Smaldone** (May 8–13), **Dylan Walsh** (May 15–20), **Charles Busch** (May 23–June 3), **Whoopi Goldberg** (June 5), **David Boreanaz** (June 6–10), **Christopher Gorham** (June 12–17), **Michelle Trachtenberg** (June 19–24), **Elaine Stritch** (June 26)

**UNDERSTUDIES** Hazelle Goodman (Career), Frank Wood (Journals), Ain Gordon (Love), Ryan West (Family/Adventure)

World premiere of a new play presented without intermission.

**SYNOPSIS** Co-conceived by Gray's widow, Kathleen Russo, *Stories Left to Tell* weaves the late actor-writer's monologues, stories, unpublished letters, and journal entries. The show unfolds chronologically, from recollections of childhood swimming trips with his mother (who also committed suicide) and tales of awkward adolescent sexual encounters, to the joy Gray took in being a father himself. The production includes excerpts from *Sex and Death to Age 14, Terrors of Pleasure, Swimming to Cambodia, Impossible Vacation, Gray's Anatomy, Monster in a Box, It's a Slippery Slope, Morning, Noon and Night,* and *Life Interrupted.*

*Succeeded by : 1. Lisa Kron (for Ms. Chalfant's vacation May 2–June 3) 2. Anthony Rapp (May 15–27), Ain Gordon (May 29–June 10), Darnell Williams (June 11–25), Roger Howarth (June 26)

# MY FAIR LADY

Avery Fisher Hall; Opening Night: March 7, 2007; Closed March 10, 2007; 4 performances

Book and lyrics by Alan Jay Lerner, music by Frederick Loewe, based on George Bernard Shaw's *Pygmalion*; Presented by the New York Philharmonic (Lorin Maazel, Music Director); Executive Producer, Matías Tarnopolsky; Producer, Thomas Z. Shepard; Director, James Brennan; Conductor/Musical Director, Rob Fisher; Choreography, Peggy Hickey; Concert Adaptation, David Ives; Sets, Ray Klausen; Costumes, Gail Baldoni; Lighting, Ken Billington; Sound, Peter Fitzgerald; PSM, Peter Hanson; Props, Ron Groomes; Associate Conductor, Chris Fenwick; Chorus Preparations, Benjamin Whiteley; Rehearsal Pianists, Harriet Wingren, Catherine Venable; Wigs, Mark Rampmeyer; Dialects, Stephen Gabis; ASM, Jeffrey Rodriguez

**CAST** Eliza Doolittle **Kelli O'Hara;** Freddy Eynsford-Hill **Philippe Castagner;** Colonel Hugh Pickering **Charles Kimbrough;** Henry Higgins **Kelsey Grammer;** Cockney Quartet **Matthew Deming, Brian Dougherty, Robb Zimmerman, Ross Benoliel;** Harry **Joe Grifasi;** Jamie **Michael J. Farina;** Alfred P. Doolittle **Brian Dennehy;** Mrs. Pearce **Meg Bussart;** Mrs. Higgins **Marni Nixon;** Zoltan Karpathy **Tim Jerome;** The New York Choral Artists (* indicates Servant Chorus): Sopranos: **Patricia Andress\*, Robin Campbell, Rachel Coloff, Susan Derry\*, Nadja DiGiallonardo, Toni Dolce, Lori Engle\*, Ginger Green, Rebecca Robbins\*, Carla Wesby\*;** Altos: **Christine Arand\*, Becky Baxter\*, Teresa Buchholz\*, Esther David\*, Christine DiGiallonardo, Helen Karloski, Erin Kemp, Katherine Schmidt, Jacqueline Pierce;** Tenors: **Matthew Deming\*, Brian Dougherty, Frank Ream, J.D. Webster\*, Scott Williamson\*, Robb Zimmerman;** Basses: **Adam Alexander\*, Ross Benoliel, Roderick Gomez, Dale Hensley\*, Christopher Job, Steven Moore\*, Christopher Roselli, Joshua South\*, Lewis White;** Dancers **Jessica Hartman, Ellyn Marsh, Jean Michelle Sayeg, Leslie Stevens, Eric Sean Fogel, Ben Franklin, Tim Hausmann, Jody Reynard**

**MUSICAL NUMBERS** Overture and Opening Scene, Why Can't the English, Wouldn't It Be Loverly?, With a Little Bit of Luck, I'm an Ordinary Man, With a Little Bit of Luck (reprise), Just You Wait, The Servants' Chorus, The Rain in Spain, I Could Have Danced All Night, Ascot Gavotte, On the Street Where You Live, Eliza's Entrance, Promenade, Embassy Waltz, Entr'acte, You Did It, Just You Wait (reprise), On the Street Where You Live (reprise), Show Me, The Flower Market, Get Me to the Church on Time, A Hymn to Him, Without You, I've Grown Accustomed to Her Face

Staged concert revival of the musical presented in two acts. The original 1956 Broadway production of the musical starred Rex Harrison, Julie Andrews, and Stanley Holloway. It has had three Broadway revivals, in 1976, 1981, and 1993.

**SYNOPSIS** The New York Philharmonic enters its first foray into a musical theatre staged concert with this production. Adapted from Shaw's 1912 play and Gabrial Pascal's motion picture *Pygmalion*, the story follows a Cockney flower girl who is trained by a bachelor linguistics expert to speak proper English in six months' time as part of a daring challenge.

# THE PIRATES OF PENZANCE

New York State Theater, Lincoln Center; First Preview: March 3, 2007; Opening Night: March 7, 2007; Closed March 31, 2007; 16 performances

Libretto by William S. Gilbert, music by Arthur Sullivan; Produced by New York City Opera in association with Glimerglass Opera; Conductor, Gerald Steichen; Director, Lillian Groag; Choreography, Lynne Hockney; Sets, John Conklin; Costumes, Jess Goldstein; Lighting, Pat Collins; Sound, Abe Jacob

*The company of the New York Philharmonic production of* My Fair Lady *(photo courtesy of the New York Philharmonic)*

**CAST** Samuel **Scott Guinn;** Pirate King **Marc Kudisch;** Frederic **Matt Morgan;** Ruth **Myrna Paris;** Edith **Erin Elizabeth Smith;** Kate **Heather Johnson;** Isabel **Shannon Carson;** Mabel **Sarah Jane McMahon**; Major-General Stanley **Mark Jacoby;** Major Sergeant of Police **Kevin Burdette;** Queen Victoria **Fran Barnes**

Revival of the operetta presented in two acts.

**SYNOPSIS** NYCO presents a traditional production of Gilbert and Sullivan's most known operetta, and the only show in their canon that debuted in America (in 1879). A parody, a satire on class, a poke at Victorian morals, and a spoof of the establishment, *The Pirates of Penzance* is filled with humorous songs, lots of action, some spoken dialogue to further the plot, a happy ending, and a good-natured lampooning of traditional Italian opera.

# TALL GRASS

Beckett Theatre; First Preview: March 3, 2007; Opening Night: March 12, 2007; Closed April 15, 2007; 8 previews, 34 performances

Written by Brian Harris; Produced by Roger Alan Gindi in association with Nutmeg Productions; Director, Nick Corley; Sets, Cameron Anderson; Costumes, Gail Baldoni; Lighting, Josh Epstein; Sound, Sharath Patel; Fight Director, Rick Sordelet; PSM, Sarah Bierenbaum; Stage Manager, Adam Grosswirth; Company Manager, A. Scott Falk; Casting, Judy Henderson; Technical Supervisor, Aduro Productions; Marketing, HHC Marketing; Wigs, Mark Rampmeyer; Props, Rose AC Howard; Assistant Director, Noel Carmichael; Press, Keith Sherman and Associates

**CAST** Paula LeBrek/Margaret/Dottie **Marla Schaffel;** Trevor Palumbo/James/Howard **Mark H. Dold;** Waiter/Dog/Chester **Edward O'Blenis;** Understudy **Jim Price** (Trevor/James/Howard)

Three one-act plays presented without intermission.

**SYNOPSIS** *Tall Grass* is a collection of three dark comedies about three couples with strange problems. A lazy young executive is obsessed with a career-obsessed woman in *The Business Proposal*. A middle-aged couple's sexual fantasy lurches out of control in *The Gerbil*. In *Tall Grass*, octogenarians fight for their lives. *Tall Grass* shows that in romance, those in love still have an axe to grind, especially when they discover what lurks beneath the surface.

# BE

Union Square Theatre; First Preview: February 23, 2007; Opening Night: March 13, 2007; Closed July 1, 2007; 16 previews, 124 performances

Created and directed by Eylon Nuphar and Boaz Berman; Produced by Marc Routh, Tom Viertel, Steven Baruch, Roy Ofer, Mayumana Ltd., Annette Niemtzow and Pamela Cooper; Creative Team, Ido Kagan, Mathew Jessner, David Ottone; Sets, Nizan Refaeli; Costumes, Neta Haker; Lighting, Eyal Tavori; Sound, Amir Schorr; Mayumana Operational Management, Dalya Swissa, Erez Bek, Jack Ben Haim; Production Manager, Aduro Productions; Technical Director, Yanka Swissa; Creative Assistant, Iris Marko; General Manager, Marc Routh Productions/Denise Cooper; Production Coordinator, Dee Wickert; Marketing, Leanne Schanzer Promotions; Advertising, Eliran Murphy Group; Press, Shaffer-Coyle Public Relations

**CAST** Boaz Berman, Sharon Ben Naim, Alba Bonal Garcia, Eva Boucherite Martin, Vicente De Andres, Silvia Garcia De Ves, Michael Feigenbaum, Ido Kagan, Yael Mahler, Taly Minkov, Reut Rotem, Ido Stadler, Aka Jean Claude Thiemele, Hila Yaffe

American premiere of a theatrical performance piece presented without intermission.

**SYNOPSIS** *Be* is a purely theatrical event that combines elements from various art disciplines based on music, movement, acting, dance, and rhythm. An ever-evolving performance piece, it has gone through constant re-creation in its eleven-year history (it was first presented in Tel Aviv in 1996), giving focus to the individual talents of its evolving roster of cast members, who come to the show from all parts of the globe.

*Mayumana in* BE *(photo courtesy of Mayumana Company)*

# WIDOWERS' HOUSES

Kirk Theatre; First Preview: March 4, 2007; Opening Night: March 14, 2007; Closed April 8, 2007; 33 performances

Written by George Bernard Shaw, adapted by Ron Russell with Godfrey L. Simmons Jr.; Produced by Epic Theatre Center; Director, Ron Russell; Sets, Cameron Anderson; Costumes, Margaret E. Weedon; Lighting, Tyler Micoleau, Sound, Ron Russell; Press, O+M Company, Jon Dimond

**CAST** Harry Trench **James Wallert;** William de Burgh Cokane **Godfrey L. Simmons Jr.;** Blanche Sartorius **Rachel Holmes;** Mr. Sartorius **Peter Jay Fernandez;** Parlor Maid **Jessica Richardson;** Lickcheese **Jacob Ming-Trent**

**SETTING** 1992, The Rosa Parks Houses in Harlem, New York. World premiere of a new adaptation of the play presented in two acts.

**SYNOPSIS** In the original play, Shaw twists and mangles the hearts of two idealistic lovers amidst a world of "slumlordery" and exposes the class-obsessed nature of Edwardian England and its callousness towards the poor who struggle to build better lives but are given limited housing options. Epic's adaptation shifts the play to a similar period in New York's recent history, which saw extensive urban renewal in response to a massive housing crisis and the rise of wealth in the African-American business class, but a lack of philanthropic interest in those left behind.

*James Wallert and Rachael Holmes in* Widowers' Houses *(photo by Dixie Sheridan)*

# FUGUE

Cherry Lane Theatre; First Preview: March 13, 2007; Opening Night: March 21, 2007; Closed April 21, 2007; 8 previews, 34 performances

Written by Lee Thuna; Produced by Cherry Lane Theatre (Angelina Fiordellisi, Artistic Director; James King, Managing Director); Director, Judith Ivey; Sets, Neil Patel; Costumes, Gail Cooper-Hecht; Lighting, Pat Dignan; Sound, T. Richard Fitzgerald & Carl Casella; Music, Stanley Silverman; PSM, Scott Pegg; Stage Manager, Kyle Gates; Technical Supervisor, Aduro Productions; Casting, Deborah Brown; General Manager, Roger Alan Gindi; Associate Producer, Martin G. Thuna; Consultant, Jules Ochoa; Company Manager, Cathy Kwon; Fight Consultant, Rick Sordelet; Press, Keith Sherman and Associates, Scott Klein

**CAST** Mary **Deirdre O'Connell;** Zelda **Charlotte Booker;** Dr. Danny Lucchesi **Rick Stear;** Dr. John Oleander **Liam Craig;** Mother **Catherine Wolf;** Noel **Ari Butler;** Tammy **Lily Corvo;** Liz Kruger **Danielle Skraastad**

A play presented in two acts. Originally produced at the Long Wharf Theatre in 1986.

**SYNOPSIS** A woman is found wandering Chicago, her feet blistered and bloody. Doctors at the hospital recognize this as a symptom of the "fugue" state of amnesia, where the patient is literally running away from an intolerable memory. A young psychiatrist assigned to work with her is running from his own demons as well—a mistake he made with a patient that had a devastating effect on his own life. His job is to make her remember, but if she does, will he be repeating the mistake that he made?

*Ari Butler and Deirdre O'Connell in* Fugue *(photo by Carol Rosegg)*

# APOSTASY

Urban Stages; First Preview: March 24, 2007; Opening Night: March 29, 2007; Closed May 6, 2007; 44 performances

Written by Gino Dilorio; Produced by Urban Stages (Frances Hill, Artistic Director; Sonia Kozlova, Managing Director; Lori Ann Laster, Program Director; K.C. Forcier, Development Associate); Director, Frances Hill; Sets, Roman Tatarowicz; Lighting, Josh Bradford; Video and Projections, William Cusick; Sound, David M. Lawson; Costumes, Nadia Fadeeva; Choreographer, Corrine Nagata; PSM, Carol A. Sullivan; Technical Director, Joe Powell; Technical Assistant, Stephen Riscica; Associate Projections, Alex Koch; Assistant Director, Christopher Bonnell; Marketing, Michelle Brandon; Graphics, Sondra Graff; Press, Brett Singer and Associates

**CAST** Sheila **Susan Greenhill;** Rachel **Susan Louise O'Connor;** Dr. Julius Strong **Harold Surratt**

**SETTING** Mid-March, the present. Place: A private cottage in Westchester Hospice. New York premiere of a new play presented in two acts. Originally produced by the New Jersey Repertory Company in 2006.

**SYNOPSIS** Sheila is a successful, middle-aged Jewish businesswoman who has a terminal illness. Until now Judaism has been her security blanket, but its teachings are no longer providing the comfort she seeks. A charismatic black televangelist walks off the TV screen, through Sheila's back door and into her fragile life. The choice is his arms or the arms of her daughter. When you are about to bite the dust, do you take a bite of the apple?

*Harold Surratt, Susan Louise O'Connor, and Susan Greenhill in* Apostasy *(photo by P.A.)*

# LA MAGNANI

ArcLight Theatre; First Preview: March 22, 2007; Opening Night: March 29, 2007; Closed April 29, 2007; 6 previews, 24 performances

Written by Theresa Gambacorta; Produced by Quattro Sorelle Productions; Director, Elizabeth Kemp; Sets, Shawn Lewis, Costumes, Theresa Squire; Lighting, Jorge Arroyo; Original Music and Sound, David Pinkard; Press, Scotti Rhodes

**CAST** Anna Magnani **Theresa Gambacorta**

**SETTING** March 21, 1956. A solo performance play presented without intermission.

**SYNOPSIS** *La Magnani*, celebrates the life of Anna Magnani, one of Italy's most revered actresses and a favorite of Tennessee Williams. With her irreverently messy black hair and eyes whose dark circles framed a vibrant and haunting expression unmatched in its intensity, Anna Magnani carved out an extraordinary cinematic career that defied the glamorous image of her rivals.

# FOR SERVICES RENDERED

Laura Pels Theatre; April 9, 2007; 1 performance

Written by W. Somerset Maugham; Presented by The Acting Company; Director, Maria Aitken; Stage Manager, Michaella K. McCoy

**CAST** Collie Stratton **Jefferson Mays;** Charlotte Ardsley **Roberta Maxwell;** Dr. Prentice **Brian Murray;** Wilfred Cedar **Jay O. Sanders;** Sydney Ardsley **Michael Stuhlbarg;** Leonard Ardsley **Paxton Whitehead;** Gwen Cedar **Lisa Banes;** Eva Ardsley **Francesca Faridany;** Etheyl Bartlett **Susan Lyons;** Howard Bartlett **Daniel Gerroll;** Stage Directions/Gertrude **Kaitlin O'Neal;** Lois Ardsley **Morgan Hallett**

**SETTING** Terrace, dining-room, and drawing-room of the Ardsleys' House, Rambleston, Kent, England. A staged reading of a play presented in two acts. Originally presented on Broadway at the Booth Theatre April 12, 1933.

**SYNOPSIS** Now acclaimed as one of the best plays of Maugham's career, *For Services Rendered* initially shocked audiences by chronicling the devastating impact of World War I on an English family. Maugham, who had previously been praised for his adept and entertaining storytelling skill, had not prepared his audience for this departure.

# SHAKESPEARE BIRTHDAY MARATHON

The Kaye Playhouse at Hunter College; April 9, 2007, 1 performance

Presented by The Shakespeare Society (Michael Sexton, Artistic Director)

**CAST** Peter Ackerman, Cherise Boothe, Philip Bosco, Alyssa Bresnahan, John Cariani, Ruth Carpenter, Michael Cerveris, Kathleen Chalfant, David Costabile, Aisha deHaas, Darius deHaas, Autumn Dornfeld, John Egan, Jennifer Ikeda, Oscar Isaac, John Christopher Jones, Richard Kind, Tom Kozurnplik, Norm Lewis, Kathryn Meisle, Debra Messing, James Naughton, Kristine Nielsen, David Oyelowo, Gerald Pinciss, Jeremy Shamos, Gary Simpson, Daniel Stewart, David Turner, Mark Verdino, Tom Wopat, Lee Wilkof

**SYNOPSIS** This second annual free community event celebrates Shakespeare's birthday with acclaimed actors, singers, and musicians performing scenes, speeches and songs from some of his greatest comedies and romances.

# ARMED AND NAKED IN AMERICA

Duke on 42nd Street; Opening Night: April 11, 2007; Closed April 22, 2007; 12 performances

Written by David Folwell; Produced by Naked Angels and Dan Klores; Sets, David Rockwell; Costumes, Jessica Wegener; Lighting, Jason Lyons; Sound Tony Smolenski IV & Drew Levy; Projections, Batwin + Robin; Properties, Jeremy Lydic & Matthew Hodges

**WEEK A** (April 11–15): *Woman at War* by Alexandra Gersten-Vassilaros, directed by Davis McCallum; Cast: **Zabryna Guevara**; *Myrtle Beach* by Dan Klores, directed by John Gould Rubin; Cast: **Katherine Crockett, David Deblinger, Yul Vazquez, Georgi James**; *Hero* by Deirdre O'Connor, directed by Dave Dalton; Cast: **James McMenamin, Nancy McNulty**; *President and Man* by Louis Cancelmi, directed by Evan Cabnet; Cast: **Lizbeth Mackay, Brandon Miller, Chris Sarandon**; *Szinhaz* by Itamar Moses, directed by Michelle Tattenbaum; Cast: **Brian Avers, Bess Wohl**; *Cards* by Theresa Rebeck, directed by Rebecca Taichman; Cast: **Kate Nowlin, Jeanine Serralles**; *The Machine* by Betty Shamieh, directed by Marisa Tomei; Cast: **Amir Arison, Ron Cephas Jones, Hortencia Colorado, Marshall Factora, Gaby Hoffmann, Reno**; *Sonnets for an Old Century* by Jose Rivera, directed by Davis McCallum; Cast: **Zabryna Guevara**; VIDEOS: *Great American Wars: Episode 6* Video by Movie Geek; Co-creators, Dylan Dawson & Aaron Maurer; *Creation Nation On the Street* by Creation Nation; Creators: Billy Eichner, Benjamin Salka, Robin Taylor

**WEEK B** (April 18-22): *After the Deer Hunter* by Nicole Burdette, directed by Jodie Markell; Cast: **Logan Marshall-Green, Natalia Payne**; *Bully Composition* by Will Eno, directed by Daniel Aukin; Cast: **Elizabeth Marvel, Thomas Jay Ryan**; *Propaganda* by Cindy Lou Johnson, directed by Pam MacKinnon; Cast: **Sarah Sweet**; *The Earliest Uses of Spin* by David Rabe, directed by Evan Yionoulis; Cast: **Deborah Rush, Brennan Brown, Thomas Jay Ryan**; *Amici, Ascoltate* by Warren Leight, directed by Evan Yionoulis; Cast: **Tony Campisi, Ilana Levine, Derek Lucci**; *Ever Less Free* by Pippin Parke, directed by Frank Pugliese; Cast: **Bradley White, Kate Nowlin, Halley Wegryn Gross**; VIDEOS: *A Toast* by The Harvard Sailing Team; Creators: Chris Smith, Rebecca Brey, Jen Curran, Clayton Early, Faryn Einhorn, Katie Larsen, Adam Lustick, Billy Scafuri, Sara Taylor; *60* by Andy Blitz

World premiere of short plays and videos presented without intermission.

**SYNOPSIS** Naked Angels presents its latest "Issue Project" series of short plays inspired by the current state of American culture, politics, and war.

*Seth Rudetsky in* Seth's Broadway 101 *(photo by Jay Brady)*

# SETH'S BROADWAY 101: A Master Class in Divas, Belting, and Hostile Opinions

New World Stages; April 16, 2007; 1 performance

Created, written and hosted by Seth Rudetsky; Produced by Tim Pinckney; Presented by The Actors Fund; Director, Peter Flynn; Music Director, Steve Marzullo; Choreography, Devanand Janki; Set Consultant, Paul Weimer; Lighting Consultant, Jeff Croiter; Costume Supervision, Michael Growler; Sound, Scott Stauffer; PSM, Jeff Davolt; Orchestrations, Jesse Vargas; Line Producer, Patrick Weaver; Marketing, Adam Jay; Program, Tina Royero

**CAST** Laura Benanti, Charles Busch, Kristin Chenoweth, Jen Cody, Natascia A. Diaz, Raúl Esparza, Manoel Felciano, Norm Lewis, Andrea McArdle, Julia Murney, Pam Myers; Ensemble: Mathias Anderson, Holly Ann Butler, Paul Castree, Kate Chapman, Christina Connors, Josh Eckblom, Phil Fabry, Darren Gibson, Jeff Lewis, Emily Lockhart, Loren Latarro, Val Moranto, Jesse Nager, Kat Najat, Naomi Naughton, Kate Pazakis, Nandita Shanoy, Luis Salgado, Rickey Tripp, Jason Veasey

A master class in belting, divas, and hostile opinions presented without intermission. A benefit for The Actors Fund.

**SYNOPSIS** The Actors Fund presents this endlessly entertaining event. Using a full orchestra, audio/visual aids and the talents of some "a-mah-zing" Broadway guest stars, the always hilarious Seth Rudetsky, a leading authority and completely obsessive master of all things Broadway, shows you—up close and personal—what is brilliant about Broadway, how the whole thing works and why it can sometimes be a splitting headache!

## The J.A.P. SHOW—Jewish American Princesses of Comedy

The Actors Temple Theatre; First Preview: April 7, 2007; Opening Night: April 18, 2007; still running as of May 31, 2007

Created by Cory Kahaney; Produced by Foster Entertainment, Maximum Entertainment, Avalon Entertainment, and Judith Marinoff, Director, Dan Fields; Sets, Jo Winiarski; Projections, Aaron Rhyne; Lighting, Jeff Croiter; Assistant Video, Linsey Bostwick; Associate Producer, Victoria Winkelman; Press, Richard Kornberg and Associates, Laura Kaplow-Goldman, Billy Zavelson

**CAST** Cory Kahaney, Jackie Hoffman, Cathy Ladman, Jessica Kirson; Rotating Cast Members **Sherry Davey, Julie Goldman, Betsy Salkind**

World premiere of a stand-up comedy theatrical experience presented without intermission.

**SYNOPSIS** A rotating cast of four comics demonstrates, through their own stories and stand-up, how the Jewish female comics of yore are treasured pioneers without whom they would not exist. With jokes both old and new about sex, husbands, family, and weight issues, these lascivious ladies prove that the stuff cracking-up Bubby and Zayde in the schtetl is still pretty funny. The live performance is peppered with vintage audio and video footage of the original queens of comedy Totie Fields, Jean Carroll, Betty Walker, Pearl Williams, Belle Barth, and Sophie Tucker, enabling these proud princesses to share the stage with their royal forebears.

*Keo Woolford in* I Land *(photo by Matt Zugale)*

*Jessica Kirson and Cory Kahaney in* The J.A.P Show *(photo by Jaisen Crocket)*

## I LAND

Culture Project at 55 Mercer; Opening Night: April 20, 2007; Closed May 17, 2007; 20 performances

Written by Keo Woolford; Produced by the Ma-Yi Theater Company (Jorge Z. Ortoll, Executive Director; Ralph B. Peña, Artistic Director); Director/Co-Creator, Roberta Uno; Choreography, Robert Cazimero & Rokafella; Set/Costumes, Clint Ramos; Lighting, Josh Bradford; Sound, Elton Lin; Projections, Zachary Borovay; PSM, Annette Verga-Lagier; Production Manager, Dave Shelley; Associate Set, Craig Napoliello; Electrician, Lowell Fox; Wardrobe, Erick Medinilla; Sound/Projection Operator, Scott M. Sexton; Light Board, Keleigh Eisen

Performed by **Keo Woolford**

World premiere of a solo performance play presented without intermission. The show had additional performances June 20–24, 2007 at the premiere National Asian American Theatre Festival.

**SYNOPSIS** Keo Woolford, acclaimed actor, former boy band star, and Merrie Monarch Award-winning hula dancer, weaves together hula, hip-hop, traditional Hawaiian talk story, and spoken word. Woolford's semi-autobiographical journey navigates the many worlds where hula lives: from backyard parties to Hollywood kitsch to the realm of the sacred. Along the way, islands—separated by geography and culture—collide: a hotel hula show and conservatory audition; a Catholic high school and an evangelical church service; a moment of pop stardom and the opportunity to learn from a hula master.

## JANE EYRE

Baruch Performing Arts Center—Rose Nagelberg Hall; Opening Night: April 23, 2007; Closed May 5, 2007; 14 performances

Adapted by Polly Teale from the novel by Charlotte Brontë; Produced by The Acting Company (Margot Harley, Producing Artistic Director); Director, Davis McCallum; Sets, Neil Patel; Costumes, Christal Weatherly; Lighting, Michael Chybowski; Original Music/Sound, Michael Freidman & Fitz Patton; Movement Director, Tracy Bersley; Casting, Liz Woodman; Dialect Coach, Gillian Lane-Plescia; Production Manager, Rick Berger; Stage Manager, Josiane M. Lemieux; ASM, Christine Whalen; Director of Development and Communications, Gerry

Cornez; General Manager, Ishanee De Vas; Associate Producing Artistic Director, Douglas Mercer; Staff Repertory Director, Jason King Jones; Company Manager, Beth Reisman; Touring Crew Supervisors, Scott Davis (lighting), Scott Brodsky (props), Jaclyn Hunt (wardrobe), Brendan O'Brien (sound); Wigs, Leah Loukas; Press, Judy Katz Public Relations

**CAST** Cellist **Deborah Friedman;** Jane Eyre **Hannah Cabell;** Bertha **Carie Kawa;** John Reed/Rochester **Christopher Oden;** Bessi/Grace Poole/Blanche Ingram **Amy Landon;** Abigail/Helen Burns/Adele **Kelley Curran;** Mrs. Reed/Mrs. Fairfax **Liv Rooth;** Brocklehurst/Richard Mason **Jeffrey M. Bender;** Pilot the dog/Lord Ingram/Sir John Rivers **Matt Steiner;** Understudies: **Jeffrey M. Bender** (Mr. Rochester), **Kelley Curran** (Jane, Blanche, Bessie, Grace, Woman), **Mina Friedman** (Adele, Helen, Mary, Abigail), **Jason King Jones** (Richard Mason, Sir John Rivers, Lord Ingram, Pilot the Dog), **Amy Landon** (Mrs. Reed, Mrs. Fairfax, Diana Rivers), **Christopher Oden** (Mr. Brocklehurst), **Liv Rooth** (Bertha), **Matt Steiner** (John Reed)

National touring production of a play presented in two acts. This adaptation was originally performed by the Shared Experience Theatre Company at the Wolsey Theatre (Ipswich, England), September 4, 1997.

**SYNOPSIS** *Jane Eyre* is Charlotte Brontë's timeless coming-of-age story of one of literature's most independent and strong-willed women. Jane Eyre is obscure and plain, but locked up in the attic of her imagination lives a woman so passionate, so wild, so full of longing, she must be guarded night and day for fear of the havoc she would wreak. Who is this terrifying woman who threatens to destroy Jane's orderly world: a world where Jane has for the first time fallen in love?

*Christopher Oden and Hannah Cabell in The Acting Company's production of* Jane Eyre *(photo by Richard Termine)*

# LET'S SPEAK TANGO!

Chernuchin Theatre at the American Theatre of Actors; First Preview: April 20, 2007; Opening Night: April 25, 2007; Closed May 6, 2007; 16 performances

Written and directed by Carlo Magaletti; Produced by Valetango Corp.; Tango Choreography, Valeria Solomonoff; Assistant Director, Tatiana Gelfand; Assistant Choreographer, Beverly Durand; Sets, Miha Glockenspiel; Costumes, Jilian Tully; Lighting, William J. Growny; Visual Sound Effects, Mauro De Trizio; Press, O+M Company, Philip Carrubba

**CAST** Giorgio **Carlo Magaletti;** Elisabeth **Katja Lechthaler;** Professor Jeff Pillet Mechanic **Fausto Lombardi;** Tango Dancers: **Diego Blanco, Hernan Brizuela, Miwa Kaneko, Ana Padron, Walter Perez, Heather Gehring;** Swing **Valeria Solomonoff**

U.S. premiere of a new dance play presented in two acts.

**SYNOPSIS** *Let's Speak Tango!* tells the story of a couple who meet while dancing the tango: he's Italian and she German. The play intertwines the use of classical and modern forms of tango with dialogue to force the viewer to listen and focus on the emotion of the dance form. Even though they don't speak the same language the couple understands each other perfectly as they fall in love, learning to communicate by listening to each other through the language of dance. As their relationship grows, Giorgio realizes that the more he learns English, the less the couple understands each other.

*The Cast of The Living Theatre production of* The Brig *(photo by John Ranard)*

# THE BRIG

The Living Theatre; First Preview: April 12, 2007; Opening Night: April 26, 2007; Closed Closed September 16, 2007; 113 performances

Written by Kenneth H. Brown; Produced by The Living Theatre (Judith Malina, Artistic Director/Founder); Director, Judith Malina; Ensemble Training, Steven Ben Israel; Design, Julian Beck and Gary Brackett; Stage Manager, Sarah Matczak; Assistant Director, Claire Lebowitz; ASM, Sarah Michelson; Producer, Hanon Rezinikov; Press, Shirley Herz, Dan Demello

**CAST\*** **Johnson Anthony, Gene Ardor, Kesh Baggan, Steven Scot Bono, Brent Bradley, Brad Burgess, John Kohan, Albert Lamont, Jeff Nash, Bradford Rosenbloom, Jade Rothman, Isaac Scranton, Joshua Striker-Roberts, Morteza Tavakoli, Evan True, Antwan Ward, Louis Williams**

Revival of a play presented in two acts.

**SYNOPSIS** The Living Theatre, a pioneer of the Off-Broadway movement founded in the 1950s by Julian Beck and Judith Malina, inaugurates their new permanent home at 19-21 Clinton Street with Kenneth H. Brown's 1963 drama *The Brig.* The play, which won the Obie Award, is a chilling portrait of military prisons. Brown survived incarceration in a U.S. Marine Corps brig during the Korean War.

\*Succeeding Cast Members: David Copley, Alfretz Costelo, Chris Doi, Andrew Greer, David Markham-Gessner, Tommy McGinn, Rebel-Rocko

# BEAUTY ON THE VINE

Clurman Theatre; First Preview: April 24, 2007; Opening Night: May 2, 2007; Closed June 3, 2007; 41 performances

Written by Zak Berman; Produced by Epic Theatre Center; Sets, Narelle Sissons; Costumes, Gabriel Berry; Lighting, Justin Townsend; Sound, Ryan Rumery; Wig/Makeup, Cookie Jordan; PSM, Jack McDowell; Press, O+M Company

**CAST** Sweet **Howard W. Overshown;** Lauren, Lauren 2, Lauren 3 **Olivia Wilde;** Girl **Jessica Richardson;** Daniel **Victor Slezak\*;** Mother **Barbara Garrick;** Ellie **Helen Coxe**

World premiere of a new play presented in two acts.

**SYNOPSIS** *Beauty On The Vine* is a romantic fable about the power of the human face in an age of extreme plastic surgery. Sweet calls himself a "mutt." But he finds his home when he falls in love with Lauren Chickering, a fast-rising star of right-wing radio, but her success has also inspired a series of events that leads to a brutal murder. Trying to understand the motive and meaning of Lauren's death, Sweet joins Lauren's father on a journey through the looking glass into a highly disturbing Wonderland where appearances are always deceiving.

*Succeeded by David Strathairn (5/29/07)

*Olivia Wilde and Howard W. Overshown in* Beauty on the Vine *(photo by Tao Ruspoli)*

*Jazmin Caratini and Francis Mateo in* Bad Blood/Malasangre *(photo by Gerry Goodstein)*

**SETTING** 1987, Puerto Rico and El Paso, Texas. New York premiere of a play performed in two acts; alternate Spanish and English performances.

**SYNOPSIS** *Bad Blood (Malasangre)* takes a look at the relationship of a young Puerto Rican couple, both professionals, who face the dilemma of her accepting a dream job in El Paso, Texas, or letting their marriage collapse.

# BAD BLOOD (Malasangre)

47th Street Theatre; First Preview: April 25, 2007; Opening Night: May 3, 2007; Closed May 20, 2007; 9 previews, 20 performances

Written by Roberto Ramos-Perea, English translation by Charles Philip Thomas; Produced by The Puerto Rican Traveling Theater Company; Director, Miriam Colón Valle; Sets, Randall Parsons; Costumes, Marion Talan; Lighting, Scott Andrew Cally; Press, Peter Cromarty

**CAST** Mario **Francis Mateo;** Luna **Jazmin Caratini;** Don Augusto **Felipe Javier Gorostiza;** Elsa **Gladys Perez;** Hugo **German Nande**

# THE RECEIPT

59E59 Theater C; First Preview: May 3, 2007; Opening Night: May 6, 2007; Closed May 27, 2007; 5 previews, 25 performances

Devised by Will Adamsdale and Chris Branch; Produced by Fuel (Louise Blackwell, Kate McGrath, Sarah Quelch, Founders) as part of the Brits Off Broadway 2007; Dramaturg, Kate McGrath; Design Help, Mervyn Miller; Closing Song, Corey Dargel; Commissioned and developed at BAC

**Performed by Will Adamsdale and Chris Branch**

American premiere of a new play presented without intermission.

**SYNOPSIS** A man flips out and searches the city for the owner of a receipt. Is he a hero, or an idiot? A little story told by two men, a filing cabinet, and a Moog synthesizer. *The Receipt* premiered at the 2006 Edinburgh Fringe Festival, where it received a Fringe First Award and a Total Theatre Award for Innovation.

*Will Adamsdale and Chris Branch in* The Receipt
*(photo by Sheila Burnett)*

# MEMORY

59E59 Theater A; First Preview: May 5, 2007; Opening Night: May 10, 2007 Closed May 27, 2007; 6 previews, 22 performances

Written by Jonathan Lichtenstein; Produced by Clwyd Theatr Cymru & Emma Lucas as part of the Brits Off Broadway 2007; Director/Lighting, Terry Hands; Design, Martyn Bainbridge; Sound, Matthew Williams; Company Stage Manager, Jane Bullock; Production Management, Caryl Carson, Jim Davis; Electrician, Keith Hemming; Press, Karen Greco

**CAST** Chris/Director **Christian McKay;** Viv/Eva **Vivien Parry;** Lee/Peter **Lee Haven-Jones; ** Olly/Isaac **Oliver Ryan;** Huw/Bashar **Ifan Huw Dafydd;** Dan/Felix **Daniel Hawksford;** Simon/Aron **Simon Nehan**

American premiere of a new play presented without intermission.

**SYNOPSIS** *Memory* explores how we choose to remember events and the consequences of these choices. We are introduced to a group of actors in the rehearsal room with their director. They take us to East Berlin in 1990 just as the wall has come down. A young man arrives at the flat of his grandmother with awkward questions about the past. Meanwhile, a generation later, we witness events in Bethlehem as the Israeli security barrier is going up. The past and the present are explored in a series of compelling scenes and memories are challenged in the search for truth.

# DAUGHTER OF A CUBAN REVOLUTIONARY

DR2; First Preview: May 9, 2007; Opening Night: May 13, 2007; Closed June 2, 2007; 17 performances

Written by Marissa Chibas; Produced by INTAR; co-production with the Center for New Performance at CalArts; Director, Mira Kingsley; Sets, Dan Evans; Costumes, Karen Murk; Lighting, Rebecca M.K. Makus; Sound, Colbert S. Davis IV; Video, Adam Flemming; Press, Richard Kornberg and Associates, Darren Molovinsky

Performed by **Marissa Chibas**

New York premiere of a new solo performance play presented without intermission.

**SYNOPSIS** *Daughter of a Cuban Revolutionary* centers on three towering figures in the life of protean performer Marissa Chibas: her father, Raul Chibas, who co-wrote the manifesto for the Cuban revolution with Fidel Castro; her uncle, Eddy Chibas, the frontrunner for the Cuban presidency in 1951 before committing suicide during a live radio broadcast; and her mother, Dalia Chibas, Miss Cuba runner-up in 1959.

*Lee Haven-Jones, Vivien Parry, and Simon Nehan in* Memory
*(photo by Manuel Harlan)*

# DON'T QUIT YOUR NIGHT JOB

HA! Comedy Club; First Preview: April 26, 2007; Opening Night: May 17, 2007; Closed June 4, 2007

Devised by Steve Rosen, David Rossmer, Sarah Saltzberg, and Dan Lipton; Produced by Jed Bernstein

**CAST** (rotating): **Jill Abramovitz, Eric B. Anthony, Todd Buonopane, Tim Cain, Matt Cavenaugh, Will Chase, Jennifer Cody, Jenn Colella, John Ellison Conlee, Tara Copeland, Deborah S. Craig, Will Erat, Jordan Gelber, Jared Gertner, Jerzy Gwiazdowski, Jeff Hiller, Lisa Jolley, Jason Kravits, Stacie Morgain Lewis, Vasthy Mompoint, Nancy Opel, Greg Reuter, Sandy Rustin, Amy Rutberg, Clarke Thorell, Donna Vivino, Noah Weisberg**; Special Guests: **Hunter Bell, Susan Blackwell, John Bolton, Trevor Braun, Laura Bell Bundy, Natalie Cortez, Stephanie D'Abruzzo, Brian D'Addario, Paige Davis, Melissa Errico, Tovah Feldshuh, Jesse Tyler Ferguson, Hunter Foster, Kat Foster, Jenn Gambatese, Alexander Gemignani, Malcolm Gets, Sean Gilbert, Heather Goldenhersh, Amanda Green, Marvin Hamlisch, Sam Harris, Patrick Henney, Henry Hodges, Brian d'Arcy James, Jay Johnson, Steve Kazee, Derek Keeling, Celia Keenan-Bolger, Richard Kind, Marc Kudisch, Gavin Lee, Andrea Martin, Eric Millegan, Austin Miller, Michael Mulheren, Bebe Neuwirth, Denis O'Hare, Kelli O'Hara, Orfeh, Nicole Parker, Christine Pedi, Michael Riedel, Mo Rocca, Seth Rudetsky, Kate Shindle, Phoebe Strole, Marc Summers, John Tartaglia, Tracie Thoms, Alan Tudyk, Bruce Vilanch, Paul Vogt, Christine Whitehead, Patrick Wilson, Tom Wopat, Tony Yazbeck, John Lloyd Young**

**BAND** Eli Bolin (keyboards), Damien Bassman, Joe Choroszewski, Rich Huntley, Sean McDaniel, or Tim McGregor (drums)

An evening of sketch comedy, music, and improvisation presented without intermission. Previously played once a month at Joe's Pub June 26, 2006–March 12, 2007.

**SYNOPSIS** *Don't Quit Your Night Job* is where Broadway goes to let its hair down. The late night happening of improv, music, sketches, stories, games, and surprises was created by its stars, Steve Rosen, Dan Rossmer, Sarah Saltzberg, and Dan Lipton. It is, truly, where Broadway and improv meet... and make out.

*David Rossmer, Sarah Saltzberg, Dan Lipton, and Steve Rosen of* Don't Quit Your Night Job *(photo by Monique Carboni)*

# PHALLACY

Cherry Lane Theatre; First Preview: May 15, 2007; Opening Night: May 18, 2007; Closed June 10, 2007; 25 performances

Written by Carl Djerassi; Produced by Redshift Productions (Max Evjen, Artistic and Executive Director; Megan Halpern, Artistic and Producing Director); Director, Elena Araoz; Sets, Susan Zeeman Rogers; Costumes, Victoria Tzykun; Lighting, Justin Townsend; Sound, Arielle Edwards; Video/Projections, Katy Tucker; Production Manager, Peter Braasch Dean; PSM, Libby Steiner; Marketing, Sol Lieberman; ASM, C.J. Laroche; Company Manager, Max Evjen; Associate Company Manager, Megan Halpern; Casting, Jack Doulin; Technical Director, Jesse Wilson; Associate Production Manager, Thomas Goerhing; Press, Springer Associates, Joe Trentacosta

**CAST** Dr. Regina Leitner-Opfermann **Lisa Harrow;** Voice of High School Student **C.J. Laroche;** Emma Finger **Carrie Heitman;** Dr. Rex Stolzfuss **Simon Jones;** Dr. Otto Ellenbogen **Vince Nappo**

**SETTING** The recent past in Vienna and in Luxemburg, 1572. American premiere of a new play presented in two acts. World premiere at the New End Theatre, London, April 6, 2005.

**SYNOPSIS** *Phallacy* pits a passionate art historian against a cocksure chemistry professor. As the amazing race between art and science begins, reputations clash, and the authenticity of a priceless statue hangs in the balance.

*Simon Jones and Lisa Harrow in* Phallacy *(photo by Richard Termine)*

# SILVERLAND

59E59 Theater B; First Preview: May 15, 2007; Opening Night: May 20, 2007; Closed June 3, 2007; 7 previews, 17 performances

Written by Benjamin Davis; Produced by Lacuna Theatre Company and Bertold Wiesner as part of the Brits Off-Broadway 2007; Director, Di Trevis; Design, Mark Friend; Movement, Jane Gibson; Lighting, Mark Doubleday; Costumes, Claire Hardaker & Beth Madden; Sound, Albi Gravener; Assistant Director, Lauren Eales; Production Manager Gary Beestone; Stage Manager (U.K.), Di Fraser; ASM (U.K.), Sophie Westendarp; Press, Karen Greco

**CAST** Dario **Cary Crankson;** Ellen **Sophie Hunter;** Gabriel **Tom McClane;** Stockers **Tim Steed;** Mikey **Bradley Taylor;** Cleo **Ony Uhiara**

**SETTING** London, 2011. American premiere of a new play presented without intermission.

**SYNOPSIS** With resources running dangerously low and a volatile and exaggerated climate teetering on the brink of chaos, six characters search for companionship in the face of inevitable change. Three stories unfold over five seasons, portraying a netherworld of wastelands, raves, and dreamscapes where timelines are skewed and reality is split in half.

# FACING EAST

Atlantic Theater Company Stage 2; First Preview: May 25, 2007; Opening Night: May 29, 2007; Closed June 17, 2007; 4 previews, 21 performances

Written by Carol Lynn Pearson; Produced by Plan-B Theatre Company (Salt Lake City, Utah) and Bruce Wayne Bastian; Director/Costumes, Jerry Rapier; Sets, Randy Rasmusen; Lighting/Props, Cory Thorell; Sound, Cheryl Ann Cluff; Stage Manager, Jennifer Freed; Publicity, HHC Marketing

**CAST** Alex **Charles Lynn Frost;** Ruth **Jayne Luke;** Marcus **Jay Perry**

New York premiere of a new play presented without intermission. World premiere played in Salt Lake City prior to this engagement.

**SYNOPSIS** Ruth and Alex McCormick are an upstanding Mormon couple reeling from the suicide of their gay son. Stuck between their faith and their new reality, they encounter their son's partner, Marcus, for the first time.

*Jay Perry (front), Charles Lynn Frost, and Jayne Luke (background) in* Facing East *(photo by Jennifer Zornow)*

# THE ROMANCE OF MAGNO RUBIO

Culture Project 55 Mercer; First Preview: May 19, 2007; Opening Night: May 27, 2007; Closed June 17, 2007; 28 performances

Written by Lonnie Carter, based on a story by Carlos Bulosan; Produced by the Ma-Yi Theater Company as the inaugural production for the first annual National Asian American Theatre Festival (June 11–24, 2007); Director/Sets, Loy Arcenas; Costumes, Clint Ramos; Lighting, James Vermeulen; Original Music/Sound, Fabian Obispo; Movement, Kristin Jackson; Musical Director, Dominick Amendum

**CAST** Nick **Arthur Acuña;** Prudencio **Bernardo Bernardo;** Atoy/Clarabelle **Ramon de Ocampo;** Magno Rubio **Jojo Gonzalez;** Claro **Paolo Montalban**

Revival of a play presented without intermission. Ma-Yi presented the original production at the DR2 Theatre in 2002 with Mr. Gonzalez, Mr. Acuña, and Mr. de Ocampo, and the production won eight Obie Awards in 2003.

**SYNOPSIS** Set in the central valleys of California in the 1930s, the play focuses on Magno Rubio, an illiterate Filipino farm worker and his pen-pal courtship with Clarabelle, a white woman from Arkansas who advertises in the back pages of a "lonely hearts" magazine. Believing he has found the woman of his dreams, the young man fantasizes about their life together, only to soon realize that reality and dreams do not always align.

*Arthur T. Acuña, Paolo Montalban, Ramon De Ocampo, Jojo Gonzalez, and Bernardo Bernardo in* The Romance of Magno Rubio *(photo by Matt Zugale)*

# ESCAPE FROM BELLVUE

Village Theatre; Opening Night: May 31, 2007; Closed August 4, 2007

Written by Christopher John Campion; Produced by R&P Productions; Director, Alex Timbers; Sets, Cameron Anderson; Lighting, David Weiner; Sound, Tom Licameli & Phil Palazzolo; Projections, Jake Pinholster; Video, Chris Cassidy; Music, The Knockout Drops; Executive Producer, WestBeth Entertainment and Kirsten Ames; Press, The Karpel Group

**CAST-BAND** Lead Vocals **Christopher John Campion;** Guitars/Vocals **Tom Licameli;** Bass/Vocals **Phil Mastrangelo;** Drums **Vinny Cimino**

**SONGS** Pilot Light, Tightrope Walker, Circle the Drain, Bermuda Triangle, Wrong Turn, Pieces of Us, City of Love, That Fate Thing, Where Did the Love Go?, Vicious Freaks, Bright Room

An experimental rock-concert/theatrical/multi-media piece presented without intermission. Premiered at The Paradise Factory Theater in New York in December 2005.

**SYNOPSIS** With driving rock 'n' roll and darkly comic monologues, *Escape From Bellevue* takes audiences on a whirlwind ride as Knockout Drops' front man Christopher John Campion chronicles the band's travails in the music biz as well as his own surreal escapades under the influence. The story centers on Campion's three trips to the world's most foreboding and infamous mental institution, Bellevue Hospital, and climaxes with his infamous escape during his second stay —rumored to be the first to escape from the notorious establishment since 1963.

*Christopher John Campion in* Escape From Bellevue
*(photo by Carol Rosegg)*

# FATE'S IMAGINATION

Players Theatre; First Preview: May 25, 2007; Opening Night: May 31, 2007; Closed June 17, 2007; 24 performances

Written by Randall David Cook; Produced by Gotham Stage Company (Producing Artistic Director, Michael Barra; Co-Artistic Director, Julia Haubner Smith); Director, Hayley Finn; Sets, Robin Vest; Costumes, Erin Elizabeth Murphy; Lighting, Lucas Benjaminh Krech; Original Music/Sound, Robert Kaplowitz; Projections, luckydave; General Manager, Michael Barra Productions; Stage Manager, Lyndsey Goode; Production Assistant, Alexis Caldwell; Technical Director, Jason Adams; Casting, Super/Capes Casting; Press, Springer Associates, Shane Marshall Brown

**CAST** Brock **Jed Orlemann;** Lilah **Elizabeth Norment;** Susan Thomas **Donna Mitchell**

World premiere of a new play presented without intermission.

**SYNOPSIS** Lilah, desperate to reconnect with true love, believes she has found it in a chance sexual encounter with Brock, a man half her age. Brock's mother, Susan Thomas, a senator from New York, is determined not to let a family scandal derail her bid for president, but Lilah's seduction knows no bounds as the personal and political collide in this intense sexual drama.

*Jed Orlemann and Elizabeth Norment in* Fate's Imagination
*(photo by Monique Carboni)*

# Played Through / Closed this Season

## AIN'T SUPPOSED TO DIE A NATURAL DEATH

Club T New York; Opening Night: April 7, 2006; Closed June 17, 2006; 24 performances

Music and lyrics by Melvin Van Peebles; Produced by the Classical Theatre of Harlem (Alfred Preisser, Co-Founder and Artistic Director; Christopher McElroen, Co-Founder and Executive Director) in association with AIN'T LLC.; Director, Alfred Preisser; Press, Brett Singer and Associates

**CAST** Sunshine **Jordan Brown;** Tomboy **Chudney Sykes;** Country **Taharaq Patterson;** Fattso **John-Andrew Morrison;** Missy **Robyne Landiss Walker;** Sweet Daddy/Cop **Willie Teacher;** Big Titties **April McCants;** Barmaid **Althea Vyfius;** Blindman/Con **J. Kyle Manzay;** Junebug **Charles Rueben;** Wino/Frog **Glenn Turner;** Funky Girl **Neil Dawson;** The Dyke **Tracy Jack;** Postman **James Tolbert;** Lily **Mo Brown;** Scavenger Lady **Kimberlee Monroe**

Revival of the musical with music presented without intermission. CTH first revived this show October 2004. The original production opened October 20, 1971 at the Barrymore Theatre, transferring to the Ambassador, playing for 325 performances (see *Theatre World* Volume 28, page 15).

**SYNOPSIS** *Ain't Supposed to Die a Natural Death* is a gutsy, lusty narrative of Black street life that explores every aspect of ghetto agony. Peopled by junkies, whores, pimps, lesbians, drag queens, sweating workers, crooked cops, prisoners, lovers, and dreamers, Van Peebles' play is considered a tradition shattering and trend setting work which spawned the choreopoem, spoken word, and rap music.

*Mo Brown in* Ain't Supposed to Die a Natural Death
*(photo by Michael Messer)*

## ALL DOLLED UP

Acorn Theatre; First Preview: April 29, 2006; Opening Night: May 7, 2006; Closed June 11, 2006

Written and composed by Bobby Spillane; Produced by Colin Quinn and Working Stiff Productions; Director, Susan Campanaro; Set, Kenny McDonough and Chris Wiggins; Lighting, Dana Giangrande and Tim Stephenson; Original Music/Sound, Alex Jost; Video, Billy Delace; Press, Shaffer-Coyle Public Relations

**CAST** Sally **Michael Basile;** Frankie/Conductor/Spider **Tomm Bauer;** Newswomen **Jennifer Blood;** Patti **Jamie Bonelli;** Ricky **Matt Gallagher;** Vince/Tom Kelly **John F. O'Donohue;** John **Rocco Parente;** Joey/Bartender **Christo Parenti;** Karen/Jody **Alyssa Truppelli**

**SETTING** 1960s, New York City. A new play presented without intermission. Originally presented at The Producers Club April 2005.

**SYNOPSIS** Based on the story of a real-life cross-dressing mobster, *All Dolled Up* tells the story of Salvatore, a wiseguy from Bensonhurst who is trying to keep his newly discovered dressing fetish a secret from his associates. When his secret is out, the Italian Mafia and Greenwich Village's Gay Community come together in a hilarious scheme to keep "Sally" alive.

## ALTAR BOYZ

New World Stages—Stage 4; First Preview: February 15, 2005; Opening Night: March 1, 2005; 939 performances as of May 31, 2007

Book by Kevin Del Aguila, music, lyrics, and vocal arrangements by Gary Adler and Michael Patrick Walker, conceived by Marc Kessler and Ken Davenport; Produced by Ken Davenport and Robyn Goodman, in association with Walt Grossman, Ruth Hendel, Sharon Karmazin, Matt Murphy, and Mark Shacket; Director, Stafford Arima; Choreography, Christopher Gattelli; Musical Director/Dance Music/Additional Arrangements, Lynne Shankel; Set, Anna Louizos; Costumes, Gail Brassard; Lighting, Natasha Katz; Sound, Simon Matthews; Orchestrations, Doug Katsaros, Lynne Shankel; Casting, David Caparelliotis; PSM, Sara Jaramillo; Hair, Josh Marquette; Production Manager, Andrew Cappelli; Associate Producer, Stephen Kocis; General Manager, Martian Entertainment; Company Manager, Ryan Lympus; ASM, Alyssa Stone; Casting, David Petro; Associate Choreographer, Tammy Colucci; Press, David Gersten and Associates; Cast recording: Sh-K-Boom Records 86050

**CAST** Matthew **Jason Celaya**[*1]; Mark **Tyler Maynard**[*2]; Luke **Andrew C. Call**[*3]; Juan **Ryan Duncan**[*4]; Abraham **Dennis Moench**[*5]; Voice of GOD **Shadoe Stevens;** Understudies **Jim Daly, Joey Khoury**

***ALTAR BOYZ* BAND** Lynne Shankel (Conductor/keyboard), Matt Gallagher (keyboard), David Matos (guitar), Clayton Craddock (drums), Doug Katsaros (music programmer)

**MUSICAL NUMBERS** We Are the Altar Boyz, Rhythm in Me, Church Rulz, The Calling, The Miracle Song, Everybody Fits, Something About You, Body Mind & Soul, La Vida Eternal, Epiphany, Number 918, Finale: I Believe

**SETTING** Here and Now. A musical presented without intermission. For original production credits see *Theatre World* Volume 61, page 142. Originally produced at the New York Musical Theatre Festival, September 2004.

**SYNOPSIS** A struggling Christian boy band (with one nice Jewish boy), trying to save the world one screaming fan at a time, perform their last tour date at the New World Stages. Their pious pop act worked wonders on the home state Ohio bingo-hall-and-pancake breakfast circuit, but will temptation for solo record deals threaten to split the Boyz as take a bite out of the forbidden Big Apple?

*Succeeded by: 1. Kyle Dean Massey, Matthew Buckner 2. Zach Hanna, Ryan J. Ratliff 3. Landon Beard 4. Shaun Taylor-Corbett, Jay Garcia 5. Eric Schneider, Ryan Strand

Tyler Maynard, Ryan Duncan, Jason Celaya, Andrew C. Call, and Dennis Moench in Altar Boyz *(photo by Carol Rosegg)*

# ANNULLA

Theatre at St. Luke's; First Preview: May 4, 2006; Opening Night: May 14, 2006; Closed June 11, 2006

Written by Emily Mann; Produced by Edmund Gaynes and the West End Artists Company; Director, Pamela Hall; Set, Josh Iacovelli, Costumes, Elizabeth Flores, Lighting, Kimberly Jade Tompkins; General Manager, Jessimeg Productions; PSM, Josh Iacovelli; Press, David Gersten & Associates

**CAST** Annulla Allen **Eileen DeFelitta;** Voice of Emily **Neva Small**

**SETTING** Annulla's London kitchen, 1974. New York premiere of a new play presented without intermission.

**SYNOPSIS** In this "interview" play, Annulla Allen, a vibrant woman who had a fascinating history of living as a Polish Jew in Nazi Germany posing as an Aryan, tells a treasure trove of stories how she managed to elude authorities and get her Austrian Jewish husband out of Dauchau.

# THE AWESOME 80s PROM

Webster Hall; First Performance: July 23, 2004 (Friday evenings only); Opening Night: September 10, 2004 (Fridays and Saturdays); 159 performances as of May 31, 2007 (Saturday evening performances only)

Written and produced by Ken Davenport, Co-authored by The Class of '89 (Sheila Berzan, Alex Black, Adam Bloom, Anne Bobby, Courtney Balan, Mary Faber, Emily McNamara, Troy Metcalf, Jenna Pace, Amanda Ryan Paige, Mark Shunock, Josh Walden, Noah Weisberg, Brandon Williams, Simon Wong and Fletcher Young); Director, Ken Davenport; Choreography, Drew Geraci; Costumes, Randall E. Klein; Lighting, Martin Postma; PSM, Carlos Maisonet; Associate Producers, Amanda Dubois, Jennifer Manocherian; Company Manager, Matt Kovich; ASM, Kathryn Galloway; Casting, Dave Clemmons (original), Daryl Eisenberg; Press, David Gersten & Associates

**CAST** Johnny Hughes (The DJ) **Philip Burke**[*1]; Lloyd Parker (The Photographer) **Jaron Vesely**[*2]; Dickie Harrington (The Drama Queen) **Bennett Leak;** Michael Jay (The Class President) **Jake Mosser;** Mr. Snelgrove (The Principal) **Fletcher Young;** Molly Parker (The Freshman) **Lauren Schafler;** Inga Swanson (The Swedish Exchange Student) **Emily McNamara;** Joshua "Beef" Beefarowski (A Football Player) **David Surkin;** Whitley Whitiker (The Head Cheerleader) **Jessica West Regan;** Fender (The Rebel) **Sean Attebury;** Heather #1 (A Cheerleader) **Tiffany Engen;** Heather #2 (The Other Cheerleader) **Megan Gerlach**[*3]; Kerrie Kowalski (The Spaz) **Kathy Searle;** Missy Martin (The Head of the Prom Committee) **Brooke Engen;** Louis Fensterpock (The Nerd) **Noah Weisberg**[*4]; Blake Williams (The Captain of the Football Team) **Major Dodge;** Mrs. Lascalzo (The Drama Teacher) **Jennifer Miller;** Feung Schwey (The Asian Exchange Student) **Anderson Lim;** The Mystery Guest **CP Lacey**

**SETTING** Wanaget High's Senior Prom, 1989. An interactive theatrical experience presented without intermission. For original production credits see *Theatre World* Volume 61, page 121.

**SYNOPSIS** Wanaget High's Senior Prom, 1989. The Captain of the Football Team, the Asian Exchange Student, the Geek, and the Head Cheerleader are all competing for Prom King and Queen. The audience decides who wins, all while moonwalking to retro hits from the decade.

*Succeeded by: 1. Scott Sussman 2. Craig Jorczak 3. Kate Wood Riley 4. Nick Austin

Front: *Jessica West Reagan;* Center: *Jenna Pace, Noah Weisburg;* Back: *Brian Peterson, and Brandon Williams in* The Awesome 80s Prom *(photo by Carol Rosegg)*

# BEAU BRUMMELL

59E59 Theater B; First Preview: May 9, 2006; Opening Night: May 12, 2006; Closed June 11, 2006

Written by Ron Hutchinson; Presented by The Ideas Foundry (Paul Savident, Executive Producer) as part of the Brits Off Broadway 2006; Director, Simon Green; Sets/Costumes, Tom Rand; Lighting, Adam H. Greene; Sound, Mike Walker; Original Music, George Taylor; AEA Stage Manager, Mandy Berry; Press, Karen Greco

**CAST** Beau Brummell **Ian Kelly;** Austin **Ryan Early**

**SETTING** 1821, on the day King George IV passed through Northern France en route to Hanover; New York premiere of a play presented without intermission. Performed in repertory with *Cooking for Kings.*

**SYNOPSIS** *Beau Brummell* is about the legendary British dandy who cut a swathe through late Georgian society by redefining men's fashion and masculinity. The play traces his final precipitous fall into poverty and madness.

# BILLY CONNOLLY LIVE!

37 Arts Theatre A; First Preview: May 9, 2006; Opening Night: May 11, 2006; Closed June 17, 2006; 30 performances

Written by Billy Connolly; Presented by WestBeth Entertainment (Arnold Engelman, President)

Performed by **Billy Connolly**

New York premiere of a solo comedy show performed without intermission.

**SYNOPSIS** The well-known British comedienne brings his uncensored, uncut, and unpredictable stand-up to New York. Billy Connolly has been described as "a genius," his stand up "otherworldly," and his honesty "terrifyingly insightful." Billy is poised to conquer America alone on stage with a microphone, bringing his oxygen-depriving take on all things taboo.

*Billy Connolly*

# BLUE MAN GROUP

Astor Place Theatre; Opening Night: November 7, 1991; 8,241 performances as of May 31, 2007

Created and written by Matt Goldman, Phil Stanton, Chris Wink; Director, Marlene Swartz and Blue Man Group; Artistic Directors, Caryl Glaab, Michael Quinn; Artistic/Musical Collaborators, Larry Heinemann, Ian Pai; Set, Kevin Joseph Roach; Costumes, Lydia Tanji, Patricia Murphy; Lighting, Brian Aldous, Matthew McCarthy; Sound, Raymond Schilke, Jon Weston; Computer Graphics, Kurisu-Chan; Video Design, Caryl Glaab, Dennis Diamond; Stage Manager, Patti McCabe; Executive Director/North American Theatrical Productions, Maureen Moynihan; Resident General Manager, Leslie Witthohn; Senior General Manager, Colin Lewellyn; Associate Artistic Director, Marcus Miller; Senior Performing Director, Chris Bowen; Performing Directors, Chris Bowen, Michael Dahlen, Randall Jaynes, Jeffrey Doornbos, Brian Scott; Presented by Blue Man Productions; Original Executive Producer, Maria Di Dia; Casting, Deb Burton; Press, Manuel Igrejas, Ian Allen

**CAST** (rotating) **Kalen Allmandinger, Gideon Banner, Wes Day, Matt Goldman, John Hartzell, Colin Hurd, Michael Rahhal, Matt Ramsey, Pete Simpson, Phil Stanton, Steve White, Chris Wink**

**MUSICIANS** Tom Shad, Geoff Gersh, Clem Waldmann, Dan Dobson, Jeff Lipstein, Byron Estep, Matt Hankle, Dave Corter

An evening of performance art presented without intermission. For original production credits see *Theatre World* Volume 48, Page 90.

**SYNOPSIS** The three-man new-vaudeville Blue Man Group combines comedy, music, art, and multimedia to produce a unique form of entertainment.

# BUSH IS BAD: The Musical Cure for the Blue-State Blues

Triad Theatre; First Preview: September 15, 2005; Opening Night: September 29, 2005; Closed July 29, 2006

Concept, music, lyrics, and musical direction by Joshua Rosenblum; Produced by Tim Peierls and Shrubbery Productions; Director/Choreographer, Gary Slavin; Graphics, Colin Stokes; Costumes, Anne Auberjonois; Lighting/Sound, Tonya Pierre; Assistant Director/Assistant Choreographer, Janet Bushor; Props, Julian Brightman; Creative Consultant, Joanne Lessner; Production Coordinator, Ayelet Arbuckle; Marketing, Gary Shaffer; Digital Imaging, Julian Rosenblum; Graphic Design/Design Adaptation, Michael Holmes; Press, Kevin McAnarney; Cast recording: Original Cast Records 837101 123426

**CAST** **Janet Dickinson, Neal Mayer, Michael McCoy;** Pianist **Joshua Rosenblum**

A musical revue presented without intermission.

**SYNOPSIS** Described as a cross between *Forbidden Broadway* and *The Daily Show, Bush Is Bad* is a left-eyed look at the current sorry state of affairs in American government.

## cagelove

Rattlestick Playwrights Theater 224 Waverly; First Preview: May 10, 2006; Opening Night: May 15, 2006; Closed June 25, 2006; 6 previews, 30 performances

Written by Christopher Denham; Produced by Rattlestick Playwrights Theater (Artistic Director, David Van Asselt; Managing Director, Sandra Coudert); Director, Adam Rapp; Set, John McDermott; Costumes, Erika Munro; Lighting, Ed McCarthy; Sound, Eric Shim; Fight Direction, Rick Sordelet; PSM, Paige Van Den Burg; Makeup, Pamela May; Press, O+M Company

**CAST** Sam **Daniel Eric Gold;** Katie **Gillian Jacobs;** Ellen **Emily Cass McDonnell**

**SETTING** Sam's apartment, Chicago, Illinois; the present. A new play presented without intermission.

**SYNOPSIS** In *cagelove*, Sam's fiancée Katie has been raped by a former lover. Or has she? With a wedding date looming, Sam fights to save their now fragile relationship, even while undertaking a desperate search to uncover Katie's secret past. Whispers become certainty, certainty becomes obsession and Sam must decide: How far is too far for love?

## CIRQUE de SOLEIL: Corteo

Grand Chapiteu at Randall's Island; First Preview: April 25, 2006; Opening Night: May 4, 2006; Closed July 2, 2006

Created and directed by Daniele Finzi Pascal; Produced by Cirque de Soleil (Guy Laliberté, Founder and CEO); Director of Creation, Line Tremblay; Set, Jean Rabasse; Lighting, Martin Labrecque; Costumes, Dominique Lemieux; Sound, Jonathan Deans; Acrobatic Rigging, Danny Zen; Makeup, Nathalie Gagné; Composer/Music Director, Phillippe Leduc, Maria Bonzanigo, Michel Smith; Acting Coaches, Hugo Gargiulo, Antonio Vergamini; Dramaturgical Analyst, Dolores Heredia

*A scene from* Corteo *(photo by Marie-Josée Lareau © 2006 Cirque de Soleil Inc.)*

**CAST** The Dead Clown **Jeff Raz;** The Loyal Whistler **Robert Stemmons;** The White Clown **Taras Shevchenko;** The Clowness **Valentyna Paylevanyan;** The Little Clown **Grigor Paylevanyan;** The Giant Clown **Victorino Antonio Lujan**

**MUSICIANS** Roger Hewett (Bandleader, keyboards), Gérard Cyr (keyboards), Michel Vaillancourt (guitar), Buddy Mohmed (bass/double bass), Suzie Gagnon (accordion), Kit Chatham (percussion), Gale Hess (violin/clarinet), Paul Bisson & Marie-Michelle Faber (singers)

A theatrical event with music, juggling, acrobats, gymnastics, dance, and more presented in two acts.

**SYNOPSIS** *Corteo* (which means "cortege" in Italian) combines the craft of the actor with the prowess of the acrobat, plunging the audience into a world of playfulness and spontaneity situated in a mysterious region between heaven and Earth. In the show, a clown pictures his own funeral taking place in a carnival atmosphere, watched over by quietly caring angels.

## cloud:burst

59E59 Theater C; First Preview: May 23, 2006; Opening Night: May 30, 2006; Closed June 11, 2006

Written and directed by Chris O'Connell; Presented by Theatre Absolute (Coventry, U.K.; Julie Negus, Producer) as part of the Brits Off Broadway 2006; Sets/Costumes, Janet Vaughan; Lighting, James Farncombe; Soundscape, Andy Garbi; Company Stage Manager, Lizzie Wiggs; AEA Stage Manager, Terri K. Kohler; Marketing/Press, Champberlain AMPR, Karen Greco

**CAST** Dominic **Graeme Hawley**

New York premiere of a solo performance play presented without intermission. Performed in repertory with *Private Peaceful*.

**SYNOPSIS** Dominic is an ordinary man who is consumed by the glare of the media after his daughter is murdered. When the press attention moves elsewhere, he is left to pick up the pieces.

## COOKING FOR KINGS

59E59 Theater B; First Preview: May 10, 2006; Opening Night: May 13, 2006; Closed June 11, 2006

Written by Ian Kelly, based on his biography of Antonin Carême; Presented by The Ideas Foundry (Paul Savident, Executive Producer) as part of the Brits Off Broadway 2006; Director, Simon Green; Sets/Costumes, Tom Rand; Lighting, Adam H. Greene; Sound, Scott George; Original Music, George Taylor; AEA Stage Manager, Mandy Berry; Press, Karen Greco

**CAST** Antonin Carême **Ian Kelly**

**SETTING** The kitchens of the Royal Pavilion in Brighton, the Romanov Pavlovsk Palace, and Antonin Carême. Revival of the solo performance play presented without intermission. This production previously played the Brits Off Broadway 2004. Performed in repertory with *Beau Brummell*.

**SYNOPSIS** *Cooking for Kings* is based on the life of Antonin Carême, the first celebrity chef, and follows his rise to become a chef for Napoleon, the Prince Regent, Tsar Alexander I and others.

# DARK YELLOW

Studio Dante; First preview: May 24, 2006; Opening Night: May 27, 2006; Closed June 17, 2006; 16 performances

Written by Julia Jordan; Produced by Studio Dante (Michael and Victoria Imperioli, Artistic Directors), Tina Thor, and Howard Axel; Director, Nick Sandow; Set/Costumes, Victoria Imperioli; Lighting, Tony Giovannetti; Sound, David Margolin Lawson; Painter, Richard Cerullo; Master Carpenter, Ryczard Chlebowski; Stage Manager, Carrie Tongarm; ASM, Emily Park Smith; Assistant Director, Zetna Fuentes; Casting, Jack Doulin; Press, The Karpel Group

**CAST** Bob **Elias Koteas;** Jenny **Tina Benko;** Tommy **Max Kaplan**

**SETTING** A rural place, somewhere in America. World premiere of a new noir play presented without intermission.

**SYNOPSIS** A murder in a cornfield becomes the focus of an unusual encounter between a local woman and a stranger she meets at the small town bar. As they engage in a game of questions, word play, and sexual intrigue, both strive for a connection while identities and motives remain hidden.

# DRUMSTRUCK

New World Stages—Stage 2; First Preview: May 12, 2005; Opening Night: June 16, 2005; Closed November 16, 2006; 40 previews, 607 performances

An interactive drum-theatre experience conceived by Warren Lieberman, co-created by Kathy-Jo Ross; Presented by Drum Café, Dodger Theatricals, Visual Spirit, in association with Amy J. Moore; Director, David Warren; Sets, Neil Patel; Lighting, Jeff Croiter; Sound, Tom Morse; Dance Consultant, Moving Into Dance; Technical Supervisor, Tech Production Services Inc.; PSM, Bernita Robinson; Promotions, HHC Marketing; Executive Producers, Sally Campbell Morse, James Sinclair; Company Management, Wendeen Lieberman, Bill Schaeffer; Press, Boneau/Bryan-Brown

*The Company of* Drumstruck (*photo by Joan Marcus*)

**CAST** Nicholas Africa Djanie, Vuyelwa Booi, Sebone Dzwanyudzwanyu Rangata, Enock Bafana Mahlangu, Tiny, Kevin Brubaker, Richard Carter, Themba Kubheka, Ronald Thabo Medupe, Molutsi Mogami, Molebedi Sponch Mogapi, LeeAnét Noble

A performance piece presented without intermission. Originally produced in Johannesburg, South Africa, by Drum Café.

**SYNOPSIS** *Drumstruck* is an interactive South African drumming event. Audience members are given a drum and become part of the show.

# FOOLS IN LOVE

MET Theatre at 55 Mercer; First Preview: June 10, 2005; Opening Night: June 23, 2005; Closed December 23, 2006; 525 performances

Conceived by Sarah Rosenberg and Louis Reyes Cardenas, adapted from William Shakespeare's *A Midsummer Night's Dream*; Produced by Millennium Talent Group in association with Manhattan Ensemble Theatre; Director, Sarah Rosenberg; Choreography, Amelia Campbell; Set, Bruce Dean; Costumes, Adriana Desier Durantt; Lighting, Sean Linehan; Sound, Stephanie Palmer; Props, Faye Armon; PSM, Chelsea Morgan Hoffmann; Press, Max Eisen

**CAST** Hermia **Erika Villalba;** Helena **Breeda Wool;** Lysander **Matt Schuneman;** Demetrius **Antony Raymond;** Peter Quince **Tom Falborn;** Bottom **Ryan Knowles;** Flute **Louis Reyes Cardenas;** Snug **Anthony Gallucio;** Tom Snout **Joseph Desantis;** Titania **Margaret Curry;** Oberon **Andy Langton;** Puck **Brandy Wykes;** Peaseblossom **Taylor Stockdale;** Ensemble **Jacqueline Algarin, Amelia Randolph Campbell, Laura Cloutier, Simone Galon, Laura Gosheff, Mike Gomez, Frank Kelly, Nova Mejia, D.J. Paris, Jacqueline Raposo, Eunhye Grace Sakong;** Doo Wop Group **Trevor Allen, Lauren Haughton, Misti Vara, Johanna Bon, D.J. Paris**

**SETTING** 1962, Duke's Diner, California. A play with music presented without intermission. Presented in repertory with *Tempest Tossed Fools*.

**SYNOPSIS** In this new version of the Shakespeare classic geared toward younger audiences, *Fools in Love* uses classic songs from the 50s and 60s as fairies on roller skates explode from the juke box and dance their magic.

# FORBIDDEN BROADWAY: Special Victims Unit

47th Street Theatre; First Preview: October 16, 2004; Opening Night: December 16, 2004; Closed April 15, 2007; 816 performances

Created and written by Gerard Alessandrini; Produced by John Freedson, Jon B. Platt, Harriet Yellin; Directors, Gerard Alessandrini and Phillip George; Music Director, David Caldwell; Set, Megan K. Halpern; Costumes, Alvin Colt; Lighting, Marc Janowitz; Production Consultant, Pete Blue; Associate Producers, Gary Hoffman, Jerry Kravat, Masakazu Shibaoka; General Manager, Ellen Rusconi; PSM, Jim Griffith; Marketing, SRO Marketing; Press, The Pete Sanders Group, Glenna Freedman; Cast recording: DRG 12629

**CAST** **Michael West, Valerie Fagan, Jared Bradshaw, Jeanne Montano;** Piano **David Caldwell;** Understudies **Gina Kreiezmeir, William Selby**

A musical revue of Broadway parodies presented in two acts. For original production credits see *Theatre World* Volume 61, page 134. The production originally opened at the Douglas Fairbanks Theatre and transferred to the 47th Street Theatre on May 29, 2005. The show went on hiatus from March 27–June 9, 2006, and performed in San Diego to allow the resident company Puerto Rican Traveling Theatre to use the space.

**SYNOPSIS** Off-Broadway's longest running revue continues in this latest version, spoofing not only America's obsession with crime drama, but the latest crop of Broadway shows and stars, including *Avenue Q, Wicked, Sweet Charity, Doubt, All Shook Up, The Pajama Game*, Kathleen Turner, Chita Rivera, Rita Moreno, Julie Andrews, Harvey Fierstein, Bernadette Peters, and as always, Ethyl Merman.

*Donna English and Jared Bradshaw in* Forbidden Broadway: Special Victims Unit *(photo by Carol Rosegg)*

# HAMLET

Theatre 5; First Preview: May 16, 2006; Opening Night: May 21, 2006; Closed June 11, 2006; 28 performances

Written by William Shakespeare, Produced by Theatre By the Blind (George Ashiotis and Ike Schambelan, Co-Artistic Directors); Director, Ike Schambelan; Sets, Merope Vachlioti; Costumes, Christine Field; Lighting, Bert Scott; Sound, Nicholas Viselli & Ann Marie Morelli; Production Manager, Nicholas Lazzaro; Fight Director, Matt Opatrny; Stage Manager, Ann Marie Morelli; ASM, Francis Eric Montesa; Marketing, Michelle Brandon; Press; Shirley Herz

**CAST** Guardian: Marcellus/Polonius/Gentleman/Gravedigger/Osric **John Little;** King: Ghost/Claudius/Player King **George Ashiotis;** Queen: Gertrude/Reynaldo/Player Queen/Second Gravedigger **Melanie Boland;** Prince: Francisco/Hamlet/Sailor **Nicholas Viselli;** Lover: Horatio/Ophelia/Rosencrantz **Pamela Sabaugh;** Friend: Bernardo/Laertes/Guildenstern/Player **Nick Cordileone**

Revival of the play presented in two acts.

**SYNOPSIS** In this sleek, visceral, production, a prince receives a charge to avenge his father's murder and wonders if he really saw a ghost or unjustly suspects his uncle. *Hamlet* is about playing, seeming, and acting, fired by showmanship and flauntingly theatrical. Theatre By The Blind strips the artifice and veneer, to reveal the meat, bones, and life- leaping back over 400 years of encrusted tradition to Shakespeare's rules.

# I LOVE YOU, YOU'RE PERFECT, NOW CHANGE

Westside Theatre–Upstairs; First Preview: July 15, 1996; Opening Night: August 1, 1996; 4,517 performances as of May 31, 2007

Lyrics and book by Joe DiPietro, music and arrangements by Jimmy Roberts; Produced by James Hammerstein, Bernie Kukoff, Jonathan Pollard; Director, Joel Bishoff; Musical Director, Kim Douglas Steiner; Sets & Lighting, Neil Peter Jampolis; Costumes, Pamela Scofield; Original Costumes, Candice Donnelly; Sound, Duncan Edwards; Production Supervisor, Matthew G. Marholin; Stage Manager, William H. Lang; General Management, 321 Theatrical Management: Nancy Nagel Gibbs, Marcia Goldberg, Nina Essman; Associate Producer, Matt Garfield; Company Manager, Eric Cornell; Assistant Director/ASM, Wendy Loomis; Casting, Stuart Howard, Amy Schecter & Paul Hardt; Marketing, SRO Marketing; Press, Jim Randolph; Cast recording, Varese Sarabande VSD-5771

**CAST** Jordan Leeds[*1], Colin Stokes[*2], Jodie Langel[*3], Anne Bobby; Standbys **Will Erat, Karyn Quackenbush;** Musicians **Kim Douglas Steiner** (piano), **Patti Ditzel** (violin)

*Adam Arian, Jodie Langel, Ron Bohmer, and Anne Bobby in* I Love You, You're Perfect, Now Change *(photo by Carol Rosegg)*

**MUSICAL NUMBERS** Cantata for a First Date, Stud and a Babe, Single Man Drought, Why Cause I'm a Guy, Tear Jerk, I Will Be Loved Tonight, Hey There Single Guy/Gal, He Called Me, Wedding Vows, Always a Bridesmaid, Baby Song, Marriage Tango, On the Highway of Love, Waiting Trio, Shouldn't I Be Less in Love with You?, I Can Live with That, I Love You You're Perfect Now Change

A musical revue presented in two acts. For original production credits see *Theatre World* Volume 53, Page 116. Originally produced by The American Stage Company (James N. Vagias, Executive Producer). Presented at The Long Wharf Theatre (Arvin Brown, Artistic Director; M. Edgar Rosenblum Executive Director) May 9–June 9, 1996. On August 1, 2006, *I Love You You're Perfect, Now Change* celebrated its tenth anniversary and is the sixth longest running Off-Broadway production. The show has been produced in over 400 cities worldwide. On May 9, 2007, the Chinese production of the show played in repertory with the American company for 23 performances until June 3, 2007, marking the first time in U.S. history that a foreign production of an American musical played in repertory with a show's American company. The show was performed in Mandarin with English supertitles, and the cast included Lin Yilun, one of China's most popular singing stars, along with Yu Yi, Wen Yang, and Ma Qingli.

**SYNOPSIS** A musical comedy with everything you ever secretly thought about dating, romance, marriage, lovers, husbands, wives and in-laws, but were afraid to admit.

*Succeeded by: 1. Ron Bohmer, Will Erat, Jim Stanek 2. Jamie LaVerdiere, Adam Arian, Bryan McElroy, Jim Stanek, Bryan McElroy 3. Courtney Balan

# JACQUES BREL IS ALIVE AND WELL AND LIVING IN PARIS

Zipper Theatre; First Preview: March 5, 2006; Opening Night: March 27, 2006; Closed March 25, 2007; 384 performances

Production conception, English lyrics, and additional material by Eric Blau and Mort Shuman (based on Jacques Brel's lyrics and commentary), music by Jacques Brel; Produced by Dan Whitten, Bob and Rhonda Silver, Ken Grossman, in association with Tiger Theatricals; Director, Gordon Greenberg; Music Director/Arrangements, Eric Svejcar; Choreography, Mark Dendy; Set, Robert Bissinger; Costumes, Mattie Ullrich; Lighting, Jeff Croiter; Sound, Peter Fitzgerald; Production Manager, Aurora Productions; PSM, Sara Jaramillo; Creative Consultant, Howard Bateman; Associate Producer, Kathleen Brochin; General Manager, Richards/Climan Inc.; Assistant Director, Ryan J. Davis; Marketing, HHC Marketing; Casting, Cindi Rush; Press, O+M Company; Cast recording: Sh-K-Boom/Ghostlight Records 7915584416-2

**CAST** Robert Cuccioli, Natascia A. Diaz[1], Rodney Hicks[2], Gay Marshall; Understudies Kevin Del Aguila, Jayne Paterson[3]

**MUSICIANS** Eric Svejcar/Rick Hip-Flores (Conductor/piano/accordion/acoustic guitar/French horn/ trumpet/Hammond B-3), Stephen Gilewski (acoustic and electric bass), Brad Gorilla Carbone (drums and percussion)

**MUSICAL NUMBERS** Le Diable (Ça Va), If We Only Have Love, Alone, I Loved, Jackie, My Childhood, Madeleine, Bachelor's Dance, Fanette, Le Moribond/Goodbye My Friends/My Last Supper, The Desperate Ones, Timid Frieda, Girls and Dogs, The Statue, Sons Of, Amsterdam, The Bulls, Brussels, Ne Me Quitte Pas, The Middle Class, Old Folks, Funeral Tango, My Death, Marieke, Song For Old Lovers, Next, No Love You're Not Alone, Carousel, If We Only Have Love

Revival of a musical revue presented in two acts. For original production credits see *Theatre World* Volume 62, page 124. Originally produced Off-Broadway at the Astor Place Theatre May 17–September 1, 1974, running 125 performances (see *Theatre World* Volume 30, page 92).

**SYNOPSIS** Brel's timeless relevance and enduring passions are celebrated in this diverse revue featuring ballads, tangos, boleros, rock, and classics. With raw human emotion, each piece tells a story, examining themes of love, war, adventure, broken dreams, people from all classes, being young, growing old, and death- but never forgetting that life with all its complexities shows much humor.

*Succeeded by: 1. Jayne Paterson (1/9/07) 2. Constantine Maroulis (1/9/07) 3. Tamra Hayden

*Robert Cuccioli, Gay Marshall, Rodney Hicks, and Natascia Diaz in* Jacques Brel is Alive and Well and Living In Paris *(photo by Carol Rosegg)*

# A JEW GROWS IN BROOKLYN

Lamb's Theatre/37 Arts; First Preview: March 28, 2006; Opening Night: April 10, 2006; Closed June 10, 2007; 304 performances

Written by Jake Ehrenreich; Produced by Growing Up in America LLP, Dana Matthow, Philip Roger Roy and Second Generation Productions; Director, Jon Huberth; Set, Joseph Egan; Costumes, Lisa Ehrenreich; Lighting, Anjeanette Stokes; Sound, David Ferdinand & One Dream Sound; Musical Director, Elysa Sunshine; Press, Keith Sherman and Associates

### Performed by **Jake Ehrenreich;** Musicians **Todd Isler, Zvi Klein, Mark Muller, Elysa Sunshine**

A solo performance musical presented with intermission. The show originally opened at the American Theatre of Actors Chernuchian Theatre and closed May 29–June 6 to transfer to the Lamb's Theatre June 7, 2006. After a run of 100 performances, the show closed September 17, 2006, when the Lamb's Theatre closed, then resumed performances at 37 Arts on October 11, 2006, until the end of its run.

**SYNOPSIS** *A Jew Grows in Brooklyn* is the story of a young man, who as a son of survivors growing up in Brooklyn in the 1960s, wanted nothing more than to be an American. While his Yiddish-speaking parents may have failed to understand the game of baseball, or make sense of rock music, they did more than he may have realized growing up to teach him the lessons of life and to help him appreciate how music, culture, and creativity are truly wellsprings of renewal.

*Jake Ehrenreich and the Band in* A Jew Grows in Brooklyn *(photo by Carol Rosegg)*

## JEWTOPIA

Westside Theatre–Downstairs; First Preview: September 28, 2004; Opening Night: October 21, 2004; Closed April 29, 2007; 27 previews, 1,052 performances

Written by Bryan Fogel and Sam Wolfson; Produced by WEJ Production LLC, William I Franzblau, Jenkay LLC, and Jay H. Harris; Director, John Tillinger; Set, Patrick Fahey; Costumes, Cynthia Nordstom; Lighting, Mike Baldassari; Sound, Kevin Lacy; Stage Manager, Jeff Benish; Associate Producers, John Ballard, Steve Boulay, David Elzer, Epstein/Roberts, Martha R. Gasparian, Kanar/Dickler, Brian Melzer, Elsa Daspin Suisman, Lawrence S. Toppall, Helaine Weissman; General Manager, Richards/Climan Inc.; Production Manager, Terry Jackson; Casting, Arnold Mungioli; Marketing, Leanne Schanzer; Press, Keith Sherman and Associates

**CAST** Marcy Cohen/Arlene Lipschitz **Glynis Bell**[*1]; Chris O'Connell **Bryan Fogel**[*2]; Dennis Lipschitz/Party Guy **Lorry Goldman;** Rachel **Roseanne Ma;** Bad Dates/Jill/Nurse/Allison Cohen **Samantha Daniel**[*3]; Rabbi Schlomo/Irving **Joel Rooks;** Adam Lipschitz **Sam Wolfson**[*4]

**UNDERSTUDIES** David L. Townsend (Chris/Adam), D.L. Schroder (Rabbi Schlomo/Irving/ Dennis/Party Guy), Christine Delaine (Women's roles and Assistant Stage Manager)

A play presented in two acts. For original production credits see *Theatre World* Volume 61, page 126.

**SYNOPSIS** Adam Lipschitz, twenty-nine and single, is obsessed with dating gentile girls because they don't remind him of his mother. One night at a mixer, he meets Chris O'Connell, a single gentile man in search of "jewtopia," where all his decisions will be made for him. In exchange for some coaching on Jewish culture, Chris offers to set Adam up with the perfect girl.

*Succeeded by: 1. Becky London 2. Josh Heine 3. Vanessa Lemonides 4. Jeremy Rische

*The Cast of* Jewtopia *(photo by Carol Rosegg)*

## LOOK MA...NO EARS!

Laurie Beechman Theatre; First Preview: April 29, 2006; Opening Night: May 6, 2006; Closed June 16, 2006

Book by Stephen Winer and Lindsey Alley, music and lyrics by Bob Stein; Produced by Eva Price; Director, Ben Rimalower; Lighting, Allison Greaker and Joey Pieragowski; Costumes, Michael H. Woll; Choreography, James Deportee; Music Director, Bob Stein; Press, Shaffer-Coyle

Performed by **Lindsey Alley;** Musicians **Bob Stein** (Conductor/piano), **Mark Wade** (bass), **Brian Czach** and **Michael Klopp** (drums)

An autobiographical solo performance musical presented without intermission.

**SYNOPSIS** When she was a child, Alley spent seven seasons as a Mouseketeer on *All New Mickey Mouse Club* alongside Keri Russell, Britney Spears, Justin Timberlake, and Christina Aguilera. She then moved to New York to pursue her Broadway dreams. The show is a hilarious musical memoir and an honest, touching tale of a small town girl making it in the big city—with, of course, her mother to thank.

*Lindsay Alley in* Look Ma...No Ears! *(photo by Joy Jacobs)*

## NAKED BOYS SINGING

New World Stages—Stage 4; First Preview: July 2, 1999; Opening Night: July 22, 1999; 2,554 performances as of May 31, 2007 (Weekend performances only)

Written by Stephen Bates, Marie Cain, Perry Hart, Shelly Markham, Jim Morgan, David Pevsner, Rayme Sciaroni, Mark Savage, Ben Schaechter, Robert Schrock, Trance Thompson, Bruce Vilanch, Mark Winkler; Conceived and directed by Robert Schrock; Produced by Jamie Cesa, Carl D. White, Hugh Hayes, Tom Smedes, Jennifer Dumas; Choreography, Jeffry Denman; Music Director, Jeffrey Biering; Original Musical Director and Arrangements, Stephen Bates; Set/Costumes, Carl D. White; Lighting, Aaron Copp; PSM, Heather Weiss/Scott DelaCruz; ASM, Mike Kirsch/Dave August; Dance Captain, Craig Lowry; Press, David Gersten; Original Press, Peter Cromarty; L.A. Cast recording: Café Pacific Records

**CAST** Naked Maid **Michael Chapman;** Radio **Eric Dean Davis;** Robert Mitchum **Frank Galgano;** Entertainer **Brian M. Golub;** Bris **Matthew Kilgore;** Porn Star **George Livengood;** Muscle Addiction **Craig Lowry;** Window **Timothy John Mandal;** Swings **Phil Simmons, Mike Kirsch, Lance Olds;** Piano **Jeffrey Biering**

**MUSICAL NUMBERS** Gratuitous Nudity, Naked Maid, Bliss, Window to Window, Fight the Urge, Robert Mitchum, Jack's Song, Members Only, Perky Little Porn Star, Kris Look What You've Missed, Muscle Addiction, Nothin' But the Radio On, The Entertainer, Window to the Soul, Finale/Naked Boys Singing!

A musical revue presented in two acts. For original production credits see *Theatre World* Volume 56, page 114. Originally opened at The Actors Playhouse; transferred to Theatre Four March 17, 2004; transferred to the John Houseman Theater September 17, 2004; transferred to the 47th Street Theatre November 12, 2004; transferred to the Julia Miles Theatre May 6, 2005; transferred to New World Stages October 14, 2005.

**SYNOPSIS** The title says it all! Caution and costumes are thrown to the wind in this all-new musical revue featuring an original score and a handful of hunks displaying their special charms as they celebrate the splendors of male nudity in comedy, song and dance.

# NOT A GENUINE BLACK MAN

DR2 Theatre; First Preview: May 10, 2006; Opening Night: May 17, 2006; Closed July 16, 2006; 9 previews, 68 performances

Written by Brian Copeland, developed by Brian Copeland and David Ford; Produced by Daryl Roth; Director, Bob Balaban; Lighting/Stage Manager, David Hines; Wardrobe Consultant, Sara Tosetti; General Manager, Adam Hess; Production Manager, Ray Harold; Associate General Manager, Erika Happel; Development, Marcia Pendelton; Company Manager, Steven M. Garcia; Marketing, HHC Marketing and Marcia Pendelton; Press, Pete Sanders

Performed by **Brian Copeland**

**SETTING** New York premiere of a solo performance play presented without intermission. The play holds the record for the longest running solo show in the Bay Area.

**SYNOPSIS** The well-known San Francisco radio talk show host and comic explores how surrounding make us who we are. Brian tells his search of defining himself as black after growing up in the 1970s in San Leandro, California, one of the most notoriously racist white communities in the U.S.

# PERFECT CRIME

Snapple Theater Center; Opening Night: April 18, 1987; 8,192 performances as of May 31, 2007

Written by Warren Manzi; Presented by The Actors Collective in association with the Methuen Company; Director, Jeffrey Hyatt; Set, Jay Stone, Mr. Manzi; Costumes, Nancy Bush; Lighting, Jeff Fontaine; Sound, David Lawson; Stage Manager, Michael Danek; Press, Debenham Smythe/Michelle Vincents, Paul Lewis, Jeffrey Clarke

**CAST** Margaret Thorne Brent **Catherine Russell;** Inspector James Ascher **Richard Shoberg;** W. Harrison Brent **David Butler;** Lionel McAuley **Philip Hoffman;** David Breuer **Patrick Robustelli**

**SETTING** Windsor Locks, Connecticut. A mystery thriller presented in two acts. For original production credits see *Theatre World* Volume 43, page 96. Originally opened at the Courtyard Theatre, subsequently transferred to the Second Stage, 47th St. Playhouse, Intar 53 Theater, Harold Clurman Theatre, Theatre Four, The Duffy Theatre, and currently the Snapple Theater Center. Original cast member Catherine Russell has only missed four performances since the show opened in 1987.

**SYNOPSIS** *Perfect Crime*, Off-Broadway's longest running play, is a murder mystery about a psychiatrist who is accused of killing her husband by a detective who can't quite pin the murder on her. The complication is that the psychiatrist and the detective are in love.

*Brian Copeland in* Not a Genuine Black Man *(photo by Joan Marcus)*

# PRIVATE PEACEFUL

59E59 Theater C; First Preview: May 24, 2006; Opening Night: May 30, 2006; Closed June 11, 2006

Adapted by Simon Reade from the novel by Michael Morpurgo; Presented by the Bristol Old Vic and Scamp Theatre (Louise Callow and Jennifer Sutherland, Founders) as part of the Brits Off Broadway 2006; Director, Simon Reade; Sets/Costumes, Bill Talbot; Lighting, Tim Streader, Sound, Jason Barnes; AEA Stage Manager, Terri K. Kohler; Press, Karen Greco

**CAST** Tommo Peaceful **Alexander Campbell**

American premiere of a solo performance play presented without intermission. Performed in repertory with *cloud:burst*.

**SYNOPSIS** *Private Peaceful* is the story of the final hours of a sixteen-year-old First World War soldier as he awaits a dawn execution by firing squad. Peaceful looks back at his short but joyful past growing up in rural Devon; his exciting first days of school; the accident in the forest that killed his father; his adventures with Molly, the love of his life; and the battles and injustices of war that brought him to the front line.

*Alexander Campbell in* Private Peaceful *(photo by Manuel Harlan)*

# THE RACE

59E59 Theater A; First Preview: May 16, 2006; Opening Night: May 18, 2006; Closed June 4, 2006

Created and devised by Gecko (Amit Lahav and Al Nedjari, Co-Artistic Directors; James Flynn and Katharine Markee, Devisors); Produced by Fuel (Louise Blackwell, Kate McGrath, and Sarah Quelch, Founders) as part of the Brits Off Broadway 2006; Directors, Amit Lahav and Al Nedjari; Technician, Joseph White; Assistant Director, Helen Baggett; Production Manager, Stuart Heyes; Technician, Rachel Bowen; Costumes, Ellen Parry and Gecko; Lighting, Kristina Hjelm and Gecko; Props, Torben Schact and Gecko; Press, Karen Greco

**CAST** Amit Lahav, Al Nedjari, James Flynn, Katharine Markee, Natalie Ayton; Off Stage Performer **Joseph White;** Understudy **Helen Baggett**

New York premiere of a theatrical experience presented without intermission.

**SYNOPSIS** One man is on a collision course with his future, sprinting toward the most important moment of his life. But will he be ready? How can a man prepare to meet his first child? *The Race* chronicles a man trying to reconnect his feelings and truly live. Surfing from image to image on a swell of physical energy, *The Race* is an exhilarating and affirming theatrical experience like no other.

*Amit Lahav (front), Natalie Ayton, Al Nedjari, James Flynn, and Katherine Markee (back) in* The Race *(photo by Simon Alexander)*

# RED LIGHT WINTER

Barrow Street Theatre; First Preview: January 20, 2006; Opening Night: February 9, 2006; Closed June 25, 2006; 23 previews, 158 performances

Written by Adam Rapp; Produced by Scott Rudin/Paramount Pictures, Robyn Goodman, Roger Berlind, and Stuart Thompson; Director, Adam Rapp; Sets, Todd Rosenthal; Costumes, Michelle Tesdall; Lighting, Keith Parham; Sound, Eric Shim; PSM, Richard A. Hodge; Original Casting, Erica Daniels; New York Casting, David Caparelliotis; Production Management, Aurora Productions; General Management, James Triner; Associate Producers, Ruth Hendel, Stephen Kocis; ASM, Monica West; Press, Boneau/Bryan-Brown, Jim Byk, Juliana Hannett, Matt Ross

**CAST** Matt **Christopher Denham;** Davis **Gary Wilmes;** Christina **Lisa Joyce;** Standbys **Jason Fleitz, Monica West**

**SETTING** A hotel room in Amsterdam, Red Light District, and a small apartment in the East Village. New York premiere of a new play presented in two acts. Originally produced at the Steppenwolf Theatre Company, Chicago, Illinois.

**SYNOPSIS** Two college friends spend a wild, unforgettable evening in Amsterdam's Red Light District with a beautiful young prostitute. They find that their lives have changed forever when their bizarre love triangle plays out in unexpected ways a year later in the East Village.

*Christopher Denham, Gary Wilmes, and Lisa Joyce in* Red Light Winter *(photo by Paul Kolnik)*

## SANDRA BERNHARD: Everything Bad & Beautiful

Daryl Roth Theatre; First Preview: March 29, 2006; Opening Night: April 5, 2006; Closed July 9, 2006

Written by Sandra Bernhard; Produced by Daryl Roth; Musical Director, LaFrea Sci; Set, David Swayze; Lighting, Ben Stanton; Sound, Walter Trarbach & Tony Smolenski IV; Production Manager, Shannon Nicole Case; General Manager, Adam Hess; Associate Producer, Joe Watson; Press, Pete Sanders; Show recording: Breaking Records

**CAST** Sandra Bernhard; Band **The Rebellious Jezebels: La Frae Sci, John Pahmer, Eric Jayk, Mark Vanderpoel, Matt Aronoff, Stefani Lippman**

New York premiere of a solo performance theatrical extravaganza presented without intermission.

**SYNOPSIS** Sandra Bernhard, accompanied by the Rebellious Jezebels, performs her brand of wild comedy, reckless rock and roll, and trademark social commentary in her newest work, ripping apart celebrity culture while commenting on events of the time including Britney Spears, Laura Bush, Condoleezza Rice, Bob Dylan, Mariah Carey, and the war on terror.

*Sandra Bernhard and the Rebellious Jezebels (photo by Paul Kolnik)*

## SLAVA'S SNOWSHOW

Union Square Theatre; First Preview: August 24, 2004; Opening Night: September 8, 2004; Closed January 14, 2007; 1,004 performances

Created and staged by Slava Polunin by arrangement with SLAVA and Gwenael Allan; Produced by David J. Foster and Ross Mollison; Co-Producers, Tom Lightburn and Jared Geller; Sets/Costumes, Anna Hannikaninen; Lighting, Oleg Iline; Sound, Rastyam Dubinnikov; General Manager, Simon Bryce; Production Managers, Carolyn Kelson and Jason Janicki; Company Manager, Ginger Dzerk; Advertising, Eliran Murphy Group; Press, Marc Thibodeau, The Publicity Office

**CAST** (rotating) Yellow Clown **Slava Polunin, Derek Scott, Robert Saralp, Fyodar Makarov;** Green Clowns **Ivan Polunin, Nikolai Terentiev, Alexandre Frish, Onofrio Colucci, Boris Hybner, Jason Janicki, Aelita Loukhaeva, Yury Musatov, Elena Ushakova, Stanislav Varkki;** Replacements **Richard Crawford, Oleg Lugovskoy, Georgiy Deliyev, Artem Zhimolokhov, Spencer Chandler**

An Eastern European clown show presented without intermission. For original production credits see *Theatre World* Volume 61, page 121.

**SYNOPSIS** Russia's greatest clowns string together a series of breathtaking images performed to popular music. A giant cobweb stretches over the entire audience; a raging blizzard coats the audience in snow; giant helium-filled beach balls are kept afloat by the viewers. Lyrical, hilarious, poignant, and brilliant.

*Slava Polunin in* Slava's Snowshow

*Cast members from* Stomp, *celebrating its thirteenth year at the Orpheum Theatre (photo by Oleg Micheyev)*

# STOMP

Orpheum Theatre; First Preview: February 18, 1994; Opening Night: February 27, 1994; 5,580 performances as of May 31, 2007

Created and directed by Luke Cresswell and Steve McNicholas; Presented by Columbia Artists Management, Harriet Newman Leve, James D. Stern, Morton Wolkowitz, Schuster/Maxwell, Galin/Sandler, and Markley/Manocherian; Lighting, Mr. McNicholas, Neil Tiplady; Production Manager, Pete Donno; General Management, Richard Frankel/Marc Routh; Press, Chris Boneau/Adrian Bryan-Brown, Jackie Green

**CAST** (rotating) **Marivaldo Dos Santos, Sean Edwards, Fritzlyn Hector-Opare, Brad Holland, Patrick Lovejoy, Stephanie Marshall, Keith Middleton, Jason Mills, Yako Miyamoto, Raymond Poitier, Camille Shuford, Carlos Thomas, Jeremy Tracy, Dan Weiner, Nicholas V. Young**

A percussive performance art piece presented with an intermission. For original production credits see *Theatre World* Volume 50, page 113.

**SYNOPSIS** Stomp is a high-energy, percussive symphony, coupled with dance, played entirely on non-traditional instruments, such as garbage can lids, buckets, brooms, and sticks.

# THE TALK OF THE TOWN

The Oak Room; Opening Night: May 23, 2005; Closed August 7, 2006; 116 performances (Sunday and Monday performances only)

Book, lyrics, and music by Ginny Redington and Tom Dawes; Presented by The Peccadillo Theatre Company (Dan Wackerman, Artistic Director; Kevin Kennedy, Managing Director) and the Algonquin Hotel; Director, Dan Wackerman, Musical Director, Mark Janas; Movement Consultant, Mercedes Ellington; Assistant Director/Stage Manager, Michael Gianakos; Sets/Lighting, Chris Jones; Costumes, Amy C. Bradshaw; Arrangements/Orchestrations, Jeffrey Biering; Dramaturg, William M. Peterson, PhD.; General Manager, Jamie Cesa; Associate General Manager, Rick L. Stevens; Company Manager, Townsend Teague; Press, Brett Singer & Associates, Peter Cromarty

**CAST** Dorothy Parker **Kristin Maloney;** Robert Benchley **Jared Bradshaw;** Alexander Woolcott **Chris Weikel;** Robert Sherwood **Adam J. MacDonald;** Edna Ferber **Donna Coney Island;** Marc Connelly **Stephen Wilde;** George S. Kaufman **Jeffrey Biering;** Pianists **Mark Janas, Justin Depuyt**

**SETTING** New York City, 1920–1930. Transfer of the Off-Off-Broadway musical presented in two acts. Originally presented in association with William Repicci at the Bank Street Theatre on November 4–December 19, 2004. During the run there it officially became an Off-Broadway production from December 5–19, 2004, leading to this production.

**SYNOPSIS** *The Talk of the Town* tells the story of the ten-year friendship of the wittiest literary lights of the 1920s. Loaded with their legendary quips, critiques, and put-downs, this delightful period musical traces the legendary skirmishes (both romantic and otherwise) around the famed Algonquin Round Table.

*The Cast of* The Talk of the Town *(photo by Mark Dawes)*

# TEMPEST TOSSED FOOLS

MET Theatre at 55 Mercer; First Preview: May 18, 2006; Opening Night: May 25, 2006; Closed December 23, 2006; 130 performances

Adapted by Sarah Rosenberg, based on William Shakespeare's *The Tempest*, conceived and directed by Sarah Rosenberg and Louis Reyes Cardenas; Produced by Millennium Talent Group in association with Manhattan Ensemble Theatre; Music, Eric Luke, Louis Reyes Cardenas, and Stephanie Bailey; Set, Bruce Dean; Costumes, Martina Melendez; Lighting, Sean Linehan; Choreography, Robert Gonzalez Jr.; Press, Max Eisen

**CAST** Prospero **Kevin Barry;** Antonio **Nick Denning;** Ariel **Anna Chlumsky;** Caliban **Robert Gonzales Jr.;** Ferdinand **John Buxton;** Trinculo **Brian W. Seibert;** Stephano **Tommy Dickie;** Alonso **Diego Kelman Ajuz;** Miranda **Rebecca Navarro;** Antonio **Brett Berkly;** Sprites **Stephanie Bentley, Stephanie Leigh Coren, Nichole Azalee-Dsuczek**

A play with music for young audiences performed without intermission. Presented in repertory with *Fools in Love*.

**SYNOPSIS** A new musical re-imagining of Shakespeare's *The Tempest*; a tale of magic, revenge, romance, and a comedy involving a magical island filled with sprites, a storm wrecked ship coming to shore, and a creature called Caliban.

# TONY 'n' TINA'S WEDDING

Vinnie Black's Coliseum at Edison Hotel; Opening Night: February 6, 1988; 5,562 performances as of May 31, 2007 (Friday and Saturday evenings only)

Written by Artificial Intelligence; Conceived by Nancy Cassaro; Originally created by Thomas Allen, James Altuner, Mark Campbell, Nancy Cassaro, Patricia Cregan, Elizabeth Dennehy, Chris Fracchiolla, Jack Fris, Kevin Alexander, Mark Nasser, Larry Pellegrini, Susan Varon, Moira Wilson); Produced by Big Apple Entertainment, Raphael Berko, Jeff Gitlin; Director, Larry Pelligrini; Choreography, Hal Simons; Costumes/Hair/Makeup, Juan DeArmas; Stage Manager, Christy Benanti; ASM, Ryan Delorge; Wardrobe and Hair, Rebecca Gaston; Senior Production Coordinator, Drew Seltzer; Production Coordinator, Evan Weinstein; Marketing, Gary Shaffer; Promotions, DeMarcus Reed

**CAST** Valentina Lynne Vitale Nunzio **Joli Tribuzio;** Anthony Angelo Nunzio Jr. **Craig Thomas Rivela;** Connie Mocogni **Dina Rizzoli;** Barry Wheeler **Scott Voloshin;** Donna Marsala **Jessica Aquino;** Dominick Fabrizzi **Anthony Augello;** Marina Gulino **Dawn Luebbe;** Johnny Nunzio **Deno Vourderis;** Josephine Vitale **Anita Salvate;** Joseph Vitale **Rhett Kalman;** Sister Albert Maria **Daniela Genoble;** Anthony Angelo Nunzio Sr. **Mark Nasser;** Madeline Monore **Alison Leigh Mills;** Michael Just **Matthew Knowland;** Father Mark **James J. Hendricks;** Vinnie Black **Alan Tulin;** Loretta Black **Cindi Kostello;** Sal Antonucci **John DiBenedetto;** Donny Dolce **Johnny Tammaro;** Celeste Romano **Lynn Portas;** Carlo Cannoli **Anthony Ventura;** Rocco Caruso **Ray Grappone**

**SETTING** Tony and Tina's wedding and reception. An interactive environmental theatre production. For original production credits see *Theatre World* Volume 44, page 63. Originally played at Washington Square Church and Carmelita's; transferred to St. John's Church (wedding ceremony) and Vinnie Black's Coliseum (reception) until August 1988; transferred to St. Luke's Church and Vinnie Black's Vegas Room Coliseum in the Edison Hotel. The production closed May 18, 2003, then reopened on October 3, 2003. It closed again May 1, 2004, reopened under new co-producers (Raphael Berko and Jeff Gitlin) on May 15th, 2004.

**SYNOPSIS** Tony and Tina are getting hitched. Audience members become part of the exuberant Italian family—attending the ceremony, mingling with relatives and friends, eating, drinking, and dancing to the band.

*Scott Bielecky and Joli Tribuzio in* Tony 'n' Tina's Wedding

# TRYST

Promenade Theatre; First Preview: March 21, 2006; Opening Night: April 6, 2006; Closed June 11, 2006; 17 previews, 77 performances

Written by Karoline Leach; Produced by Morton Wolkowitz, Suitz LLC, and Barbara Freitag; Director, Joe Brancato; Set, David Korins; Costumes, Alejo Vietti; Lighting, Jeff Nellis; Sound, Johnna Doty; Wigs, Paul Huntley; Casting, Laura Stanczyk; PSM, David H. Lurie; General Management, Richard Frankel Productions, Rod Kaats; Production Manager, Theatresmith Inc.; Company Manager, Kim Sellon; General Management Associate, Leslie Anne Pinney; Dialect Coach, Deborah Hecht; Props, Kathy Fabian; Makeup, Angelina Avallone; Press, Peter Cromarty & Company

**CAST** George Love **Maxwell Caulfield;** Adelaide Pinchon **Amelia Campbell;** Standbys **Brent Harris, Emma Bowers**

**SETTING** London and Weston Super Mare, 1910. World premiere of a romance/thriller presented in two acts.

**SYNOPSIS** George Love, a handsome conman who woos loved-starved women, meets Adelaide Pinchon, a desperate woman, who dreams beyond her mundane world at the local millinery store. Mr. Love has a history of illicit affairs, but after meeting the fantasizing shop-girl... there is a twist of fate.

*Amelia Campbell and Maxwell Caulfield in* Tryst
*(photo by Carol Rosegg)*

*Kyle Manzay and Wendell Pierce in* Waiting for Godot
*(photo by Michael Messer)*

# WAITING FOR GODOT

HSA Theatre; First Preview: May 18, 2006; Opening Night: May 21, 2006; Closed June 25, 2006; 29 performances

Written by Samuel Beckett; Produced by Classical Theatre of Harlem (Alfred Preisser, Co-Founder and Artistic Director; Christopher McElroen, Co-Founder and Executive Director); Director, Christopher McElroen; Set, Troy Hourie; Costumes, Kimberly Glennon; Lighting, Aaron Black; Stage Manager, Joan H. Cappello; Dramaturg, Debra Cardona; Press, Brett Singer

**CAST** Vladimir **Wendell Pierce**; Estragon **J. Kyle Manzay**; Pozzo **Chris McKinney**; Lucky **Billy Eugene Jones**; Boy **Tanner Rich**

**SETTING** A country road. A tree. Evening. Revival of the tragicomedy presented in two acts.

**SYNOPSIS** Vladimir and Estragon, two dilapidated bums, fill their days as painlessly as they can as they wait for Godot, a personage who will explain their interminable insignificance, or put an end to it.

# OFF-BROADWAY
## Company Series

Top to bottom:

*Daniel Beaty in* Emergence-SEE! *at the Public Theater*
*(photo by Michal Daniel)*

*Craig Pattison, Will LeBow, Thomas Derrah, Steven Boyer, Michael*
*Wartella, Elizabeth Jasicki, Lucas Steele, Jennifer Ikeda, and Greg*
*Derelian in* Oliver Twist, *produced by Theatre for a New Audience*
*(photo by Michael J. Lutch)*

*Robert Colston and Joanne Camp in* Toys in the Attic *at the Pearl*
*Theatre Company (photo by Joan Marcus)*

# Abingdon Theatre Company

Fourteenth Season

Artistic Directors, Jan Buttram and Pamela Paul; Managing Director, Samuel Bellinger; Associate Artistic Director/Literary Manager, Kim T. Sharp; Marketing, Michael Page/Doug DeVita; Development, Edward J. McKearney, Lori Gardner; Business/Box Office Manager, Rob Weinstein; Rental/Facilities Manager, Stephen Squibb; Casting, William Schill; Dramaturg, Julie Hegner; Press, Shirley Herz, Dan Demello

**Foggy Bottom** by James Armstrong; Director, Rob Urbinati; Sets, Gabriel Evansohn, Lighting, Carl Faber; Costumes, Susan Scherer; Sound, Graham Johnson; PSM, Kate DeCoste; Cast: Dan Cordle (Dick), Jo Mei (Lee), Jeremy Beiler (Bill), Susanna Guzmán (Juanita), Angela Polite (Sadiku), Maja Wampuszyc (Marina), Richard Zekaria (Muhammad), Denise Bessette (Woman)
World premiere of a new play presented in two acts; Dorothy Strelsin Theatre; September 2–24, 2006 (Opened September 10); 23 performances.

**My Deah** by John Epperson; Director, Mark Waldrop; Sets/Lighting, Mark Simpson; Costumes, Ramona Ponce; Sound, Matt Berman; PSM, Kimothy Cruse; Production Manager, Gabriel Hainer Evansohn; Cast: Nancy Opel (Lillie V./My Deah Hedgepeth), Maxwell Caulfield (Gator Hedgepeth), Peter Brouwer (Governor W. J. Bullard/Rufus Lacy), Lori Gardner (Simplicity Bullard), Michael Hunsaker (Coach), Geoffrey Molloy (Brooksie Jones/Skipper), Jay Rogers (Mignon Mullen), Kevin Townley (Myrna Loy Seabrook/Scooter)
Time: Autumn, 2004. Place Northeast Jackson, Mississippi, the home of Gator and My Deah Hedgepeth. World premiere of a new play presented without intermission; June Havoc Theatre; October 12–November 12, 2006 (Opened October 24); 46 performances.

*Maxwell Caulfield, Geoffrey Molloy, Nancy Opel, Kevin Townley, and Michael Hunsaker in* My Deah *(photo by Kim T. Sharp)*

**The Frugal Repast** by Ron Hirsen; Director, Joe Grifasi; Sets, Ray Recht; Costumes, Karin Beatty; Lighting, Matthew McCarthy; Sound, Graham Johnson; Production Manager, Pete Fry; Cast: Harold Todd (Man), Dawn Luebbe (Woman), Kyrian Friedenberg (Boy), David Wohl (Ambroise Vollard), Frank Liotti (Guillaume Apollinaire), Lizbeth MacKay (Gertrude Stein), Julie Boyd (Alice B. Toklas), Roberto DeFelice (Pablo Picasso), Kathleen McElfresh (Picasso's Companion)
Time: 1913. Place: Paris. World premiere of a new play presented without intermission; June Havoc Theatre; January 26–February 25, 2007 (Opened February 7); 32 performances.

*Lori Gardner, Jan Buttram, and Jeremy Beck in* The President and Her Mistress *(photo by Kim T. Sharp)*

**Dreams of Friendly Aliens** by Daniel Damiano; Director, Kim T. Sharp; Sets, Charlie Corcoran; Costumes, Isabel Rubio; Lighting, Matthew McCarthy; Sound, Graham Johnson; Production Manager, Pete Fry; PSM, Genevieve Ortiz; Cast: Lenore Loveman (Fretta Nutella), Jamie C. Ward (Jesse Chavarra), Gene Gallerano (Max Chavarra), Maureen Griffin (Mrs. Ricotta), Brandon Jones (Officer Velazquez), Max Arnaud (Officer Bryant)
World premiere of a play presented in two acts; Dorothy Strelsin Theatre; March 10–April 1, 2007 (Opened March 18); 23 performances.

**The President and Her Mistress** by Jan Buttram; Director, Rob Urbinati; Sets, James F. Wolk; Costumes, Polly J. Byers; Lighting, Matthew McCarthy; Sound, David M. Lawson; PSM, Andrea L. Beukema; Production Manager, Pete Fry; Cast: Jan Buttram (President Rebecca Shine), Susanna Guzman (Vice President Kit Santos), Sherry Skinker (Peggy Shine), Constance Boardman (Candy Powers), Danton Stone (Paul Porter Shine/Moses), Lori Gardner (Poochy/Femme Voices), Jeremy Beck (ZooZoo)
Time: 2156 A.D. Place: Femme House. World premiere of a play presented in two acts; June Havoc Theatre; April 13–May 13, 2007 (Opened April 25); 32 performances.

**The Greenhouse Effect** by Michael Deep; Director, Kate Bushmann; Sets, Andy Krumkalns; Costumes, Ingrid Maurer, Sound, Ken Feldman; Production Manager, Peter Brouwer; PSM, Kate DeCoste; Cast: Michael Deep (Charles Greenhouse)
World premiere of a new solo performance play presented in two acts; Dorothy Strelsin Theatre; June 2–24, 2007 (Opened June 12); 23 performances.

# Atlantic Theater Company

Twenty-first Season

Artistic Director, Neil Pepe; Executive Director, Andrew D. Hamingson; School Executive Director, Mary McCann; General Manager, Melinda Berk; Associate Artistic Director, Christian Parker; Development, Erika Mallin; Production Manager, Lester Grant; Marketing, Jodi Sheeler; Membership, Sara Montgomery; Operations, Anthony Francavilla; Company Manager, Nick Leavens; School Associates, Steven Hawley, Kate Blumberg; Business Manager, Hilary O'Connor; Education, Frances Tarr; School Artistic Director, Geoff Berman; School Production Manager, Eric Southern; Casting, Telsey + Company; Press, Boneau/Bryan-Brown, Joe Perrotta

**Birth and After Birth** by Tina Howe; Director, Christian Parker; Sets, Takeshi Kata; Costumes, Frederick Tilley II; Lighting, Josh Bradford; Sound, Obadiah Eaves; PSM, Matthew Silver; ASM, Jillian M. Oliver; Assistant Director, Joya Scott; Technical Director, Joel Sherry; Fights, Kathryn Ekblad; Cast: Jeff Binder (Bill), Maggie Kiley (Sandy), Jordan Gelber (Nicky), Peter Benson (Jeffrey), Kate Blumberg (Mia)

New York premiere of a play presented in two acts; Mainstage; September 13–October 29, 2006 (Opened September 13); 48 performances. Originally produced by Philadelphia's Wilma Theatre and subsequently Washington, D.C.'s Woolly Mammoth Theatre Company.

*Jeff Binder, Jordan Gelber, Kate Blumberg, Peter Benson, and Maggie Kiley in* Birth and After Birth *(photo by Monique Carboni)*

**The Voysey Inheritance** by Harley Granville-Barker, adapted by David Mamet; Director, David Warren; Sets, Derek McLane; Costumes, Gregory Gale; Lighting, Jeff Croiter; Music Research/Sound, Fitz Patton; Music Director, David Chase; Dialects, Stephen Gabis; PSM, David H. Lurie; ASM, Jillian M. Oliver; Assistant Director, Jon Ferrari; Technical Director, Nicholas Warren-Gray; Associate PM, Jee Han; Props, Desiree Maurer; Cast: Michael Stuhlbarg (Edward Voysey), Samantha Soule (Alice Maitland), Judith Roberts (Mrs. Voysey), Peter Maloney (George Booth), Fritz Weaver (Mr. Voysey), Steven Goldstein (Mr. Peacey), C.J. Wilson (Major Booth Voysey), Geddeth Smith (Reverend Evan Colpus), Katharine Powell (Ethel Voysey), Rachel Black (Honor Voysey), Christopher Duva (Trenchard Voysey), Todd Weeks (Hugh Voysey)

Time/Place: The Voysey House in Chislehurst, England; 1905. Revival of a play with new adaptation presented in two acts; Mainstage; November 15, 2006–March 25, 2007 (Opened December 6); 140 performances.

*Todd Weeks, Judith Roberts, Rachel Black (seated), C.J. Wilson, Samantha Soule, Michael Stuhlbarg, and Katharine Powell in* The Voysey Inheritance *(photo by Monique Carboni)*

**Anon** by Kate Robin; Director, Melissa Kievman; Sets, Chris Muller; Costumes, Anne Kenney; Lighting, Tyler Micoleau; Sound, Eric Shim; PSM, Adam Ganderson; ASM, Jessie Ksanznak; Props, Faye Armon; Company Manager, Eric Louie; Assistant Director, Jaime Castañeda; Cast: Remy Auberjonois (Trip), Michelle Federer (Alison), Kate Nowlin (Gina), Caroline Aaron (Rachelle), Bill Buell (Bert), Shannon Burkett (Becky), Anna Foss Wilson (Gretchen), Jenny Maguire (Pamela), Dana Eskelson (Claudia), Katy Grenfell (Corinne), Danielle Skraastad (Trish), Linda Marie Larson (Mary), Susan Blackwell (Janice), Saidah Arrika Ekulona (Rita)

Place: Manhattan and Queens. Time: Now. World premiere of a new play presented; Atlantic Stage 2; January 24–February 18, 2007 (Opened January 31); 28 performances.

*Michele Federer and Remy Auberjonois in* Anon *(photo by Monique Carboni)*

*Matthew Morrison, Irene Molloy, Skipp Sudduth, and Mare Winningham in* Ten Million Miles *(photo by Monique Carboni)*

**10 Million Miles** Book by Keith Bunin, music and lyrics by Patty Griffin; Director, Michael Mayer; Sets, Derek McLane; Costumes, Michael Krass; Lighting, Jules Fisher & Peggy Eisenhauer; Sound, Brian Ronan; Music Director/Arrangements/Orchestrations, Tim Weil; Music Coordinator, Michael Keller; PSM, James Harker; ASM, Freda Farrell; Assistant Director, Laura Savia; Technical Director, Nicholas Warren-Gray; Movement, Christopher Gattelli; Cast: Matthew Morrison (Duane), Irene Malloy (Molly), Mare Winningham (The Women), Skipp Sudduth (The Men); Band: Tim Weil (keyboards/accordion/vocals), Bobby Baxmeyer (Guitars/Mandolin), Daniel A. Weiss (guitar/dobro/vocals), Ina May Wool (guitar/vocals/percussion), Tony Conniff (electric bass), Warren Odze (drums/percussion)

Musical Numbers: Useless Desires, We Are Water, Be Careful, Mad Mission, What You Are, One Big Love, Kite, A Couple Fools, Love Throw a Line, Mary, Making Pies, Icicles, 10 Million Miles, First Star, Don't Come Easy

Setting: From the southern tip of Florida to the northwest corner of New York, with detours along the way. The present. World premiere of a new musical presented without intermission; Linda Gross Theater (the Atlantic Mainstage was renamed during this production); May 11–July 15, 2007 (Opened June 14); 53 performances.

*Tim Guinee and Meg Gibson in* The Human Error
*(photo by Monique Carboni)*

**Human Error** by Keith Reddin; Director, Tracy Brigden; Sets, Luke Hegel-Cantarella, Costumes, Markas Henry, Lighting, Jeff Croiter, Original Music/Sound, Eric Shim; PSM, Jillian M. Oliver; Company Manager, Juan Carlos Salinas; Cast: Meg Gibson (Miranda), Tim Guinee (Erik), Ray Anthony Thomas (Ron)

World premiere of a new play presented without intermission; Atlantic Stage 2; August 1–26, 2007 (Opened August 8); 28 performances.

# Brooklyn Academy of Music

Founded in 1861

Alan H. Fishman, Chairman of the Board; Karen Brooks Hopkins, President; William I. Campbell, Vice Chairman of the Board; Joseph V. Melillo, Executive Producer

### 2006 Next Wave Festival – 24th Annual – Theatre Events

**The End of Cinematics** Conceived, written and directed by Mikel Rouse; Produced by Mikel Rouse, Krannert Center for the Performing Arts, & Double M Arts and Events, Executive Producers, Mike Ross, Rebecca McBride, Michael Mushalla, Mary Anne Lewis; Production Manager, William Knapp; PSM, Jenny E. Goelz; Sets, Thomas Kamm; Lighting, Hideaki Tsutsui; Costumes, Anne Kenney; Sound, Christopher Thomas Ericson; Video, Jeff Sugg; Photography, Richard Connors; Cast: Cynthia Enfield, Matthew Gandolfo, Christina Pawl, Robert Rivera, Mikel Rouse, Penelope Thomas
A multi-media theatrical piece presented without intermission; Harvey Theater; October 4–7, 2006; 4 performances.

*The Company of* The End of Cinematics *(photo by Dan Merlo)*

**Mycenaean** Composed, written, directed, and produced by Carl Hancock Rux; Lighting/Video/Sound, Pablo N. Molina; Co-Video/Music Programming, Jaco van Schalkwyk; Mask/Co-Sets, Alison Heimstead; Co-Sets, Efren Delgadillo Jr.; Costume Coordinator, Toni-Leslie James; Dramaturgy, Morgan Jeness; Executive Producers, Stephen M. Cohen, Patrick Synmoie; Associate Producer/Company Manager, Pablo N. Molina; Stage Manager, Ginger Castleberry; Associate Design, Jeffrey Teeter (sound), Christopher Kuhl (lighting); Technical Coordinator, Christopher Kuhl; Movement Coach, Christalyn Wright; Vocal Coach/Arranger, Helga Davis; Cast: Carl Hancock Rux (Racine/Hippolytus), Helga Davis (Arachne), Patrice Johnson (Aricia), Tony Torn (Daedalus), David Barlow (Video Documentarian), Ana Perea (Dream Theorist), Darius Mannino (Dreamer/Soldier/Phillippe), Celia Gorman (Dreamer/Naiad/Nathalie), Christalyn Wright (Dreamer/Naiad), Marcelle Lashley (Dreamer/Naiad/Woman), Niles Ford (Dreamer/Soldier/Minotaur), Paz Tanjuaquio (Dreamer/Naiad), Kelly Bartnik (Dreamer/Naiad)
An experimental theatrical piece presented without intermission; Harvey Theater; October 10–14, 2006; 4 performances.

**Nine Hills One Valley** Text, music, design, and direction by Ratan Thiyam; Presented by Ratan Thiyam's Chorus Repertory Theatre of Manipur; Produced by Asia Society and Lisa Booth Management
A play presented in Manpuri with English surtitles without intermission; Howard Gilman Opera House; October 11–14, 2006; 4 performances.

**Violet Fire: A Multimedia Opera** Composed by Jon Gibson, concept and libretto by Miriam Seidel; Produced by Laura Aswad/Real Arts and Culture LLC, Philip Glass and Terry O'Reilly; Director, Terry O'Reilly; Conductor, Ana Zorana Brajovic; Sets/Costumes, Boris Caksiran; Media, Sarah Drury; Jen Simmons; Choreography, Nina Winthrop, Joanna Kotze; Lighting, Mary Louise Geiger; Sound, Jorge Cousineau; Production Manager, Chris Buckley; PSM, Mary-Susan Gregoson; Assistant Director, Ivana Dragutinovic; Interactive Programming/Media Operator, Charles Hoey; ASM, Alex Senchak; Tango Dancer, Anna Drozdowski; Associate Producer, Novak Stanisic; Cast: Scott Murphree (Tesla), Mirjana Jovanovic (White Dove), Nenad Nenic (Reporter), Dragana Stankovic (Katharine Johnson), Ana Lackovic (Margaret Storm), Peter Stewart (Mark Twain), Joanna Kotze (Dove); Chorus: Natasa Radovanovic, Olivera Krljevic, Jelena Pavlovic, Natasa Matic, Zorana Kalpis, Danijela Milosevic, Natasa Drecun, Maja Zivkovic, Ivana Vidmar, Igor Vujaskovic, Boris Postovnik, Boris Babik, Aleksandar Tasic, Vuk Radonnjic, Ivan Kruljac; Standbys: Darko Djordjevic (Tesla), Kristen Hollinsworth (Dove)
American premiere of a multimedia opera presented without intermission; Howard Gilman Opera House; October 18–21, 2006; 3 performances.

**The Wild Duck** by Henrik Ibsen, adapted by Eirik Stubø and Ole Skjebred; Presented by the National Theatre of Norway; Director, Eirik Stubø; Sets/Costumes, Kari Gravklev; Lighting, Ellen Ruge; Masks/Makeup, Birgit Hauga; Dramaturg, Olav Torbjorn Skare; Assistant Director, Oda Radoor; Cast: Bjorn Skagestad (Haaken Werle), Eindride Eidsvold (Gregers Werle), Kai Remlov (Old Ekdal), Gard Eidsvold (Hjalmar Ekdal), Agot Sendstad (Gina Ekdal), Birgitte Larsen (Hedvig), Petronella Barker (Mrs. Sorby), Kim Haugen (Dr. Relling), Fridtjov Saheim (Molvik)
Revival of the play presented in Norwegian with English titles without intermission; Harvey Theater; October 25–29, 2006; 5 performances.

*Tom McDonald, Jason Baughan, Tam Williams, and Alasdair Craig in* Twelfth Night *(photo by Manuel Harlan)*

*The Propeller Company in* The Taming of the Shrew *(photo by Anthony Field)*

**Twelfth Night** by William Shakespeare; Presented by the Chekhov International Theatre Festival; Director, Declan Donnellan; Design, Nick Ormerod; Lighting, Judith Greenwood; Assistant Director, Evgeny Pisarev; Chreography/Movement Consultant, Jane Gibson; Movement Director, Albert Alberts; Movement Coach, Alexandra Konnikova; Music, Vladimir Pankov and Alexander Gusev; Stage Manager, Olga Vasilevskaya; Cast: Vladimir Vdovichenkov (Orsino), Sergey Mukhin (Sebastian), Mikhail Zhigalov (Antonio), Vsevolod Boldin (a sea captain), Yury Makeev (Valentine), Mikhail Dementiev (Curio), Alexander Feklistov (Sir Toby Belch), Dmitry Dyuzhev (Sir Andrew Aguecheek), Dmitry Shcherbina (Malvolio), Igor Yasulovich (Feste), Alexey Dadonov (Olivia), Andrey Kuzichev (Viola), Ilia Ilyin (Maria)
Revival of the play presented in Russian with English titles with intermission; Harvey Theater; November 7–12, 2006; 7 performances.

**the 51st (dream) state** Conceived and written by Sekou Sundiata; Presented in association with Harlem Stage & Aaron Davis Hall Inc.; Director, Christopher McElroen; Score, Graham Haynes; Choreography, David Thomson; Projections, Sage Carter; Sets, Troy Hourie; Lighting, Roderick Murray; Costumes, Liz Prince; Sound, Lucas Indelicato; Vocal Director/Arrangements, Richard Harper; Additional Music, Bill Toles, Sekou Sundiata; Cast: Sekou Sundiata (Poet), Ronnell Bey, La Tanya Hall, Samita Sinha, Bora Yoon (vocalists), Eddie Allen (trumpet), Chris Eddleton (drums), Calvin Jones (bass), Adam Klipple (keyboards), Bill White (guitar), David Thomson (dancer)
A performance piece with poetry, dance, music, and multi-media presented without intermission; Harvey Theater; November 8–11, 2006; 3 performances.

**La Tempete** by William Shakespeare, translated by Normand Chaurette; Presented by 4D Art Production; Directors/Multi-Media Concept, Michel Lemieux, Victor Pilon & Denise Guilbault; Sets, Anick La Bissonniére; Costumes, Michel Robidas; Lighting, Alain Lortie; Music, Michel Smith; Movement, Dave St.-Pierre; Cast: Denis Bernard (Prospero), Manon Brunelle (Ariel/Caliban), Éveline Gélinas (Miranda), Pierre Etienne Rouillard (Ferdinand), Éric Bernier (virtual Antonio), Vincent Bilodeau (virtual Alonso), Pierre Curzi (virtual Gonzalo), Jacques Girard (virtual Stéphano), Patrice Robitaille (virtual Sébastien), Robert Toupin (virtual Trinculo)
Revival of the play presented in French with English titles without intermission; Howard Gilman Opera House; November 15–18, 2006; 3 performances.

**Hedda Gabler** by Henrik Ibsen, translated by Hinrich Schmidt-Henkel; Presented by Schaubühne am Lehniner Platz Berlin; Director, Thomas Ostermeier; Sets, Jan Pappelbaum; Costumes, Nina Wetzel; Lighting, Erich Schneider; Music, Malte Beckenbach; Dramaturgy, Marius von Mayenburg; Video, Sebastien Dupouey; Cast: Lars Eidinger (Jorgen Tesman), Katharina Schüttler (Hedda Tesman), Lore Stefanek (Juliane Tesman), Annedore Bauer (Mrs. Elvsted), Jörg Hartmann (Judge Brack) and Kay Bartholomäus Schulze (Eilert Lovborg)
Revival of the play presented in German with English titles without intermission; Harvey Theater; November 28–December 2, 2006; 6 performances.

**Don Juan in Prague** Adapted and directed by David Chambers from Mozart and DaPonte's *Don Giovanni*; Presented in association with the Strings of Autumn Festival in Prague and the Prague National Theatre; Conductor, Petr Kofron; Arrangement & Digital Composition, Matthew Suttor; Sets, Darcy Scanlin; Projections/Video, Peter Flaherty; Costumes, Irina Kruzhilaina; Lighting, Christopher Akerlind; Sound, Daniel Baker; Executive Producer, David Chambers; Producer, Beth Morrison Projects; Featuring: Iva Bittová and the Agon Orchestra of Prague
A radical multimedia production of the opera sung in Italian with English dialogue presented in two acts; Harvey Theater; December 13–16, 2006; 4 performances.

**Spring Series**

**Three Atmospheric Studies** Created and presented by the Forsythe Company; Director, William Forsythe; Music, David Morrow & Thom Willems; Text, Dana Caspersen, William Forsythe, David Kern; Costumes, Satoru Choko, Dorothee Merg; Sound and Synthesis, Dietrich Krüger & Niels Lanz
A dance-theatre piece presented in three parts with one pause; Howard Gilman Opera House; February 28–March 3, 2007; 4 performances.

**Edward Scissorhands** Devised, directed, and choreographed by Matthew Bourne; new music and arrangements by Terry Davies, based on themes from the original motion picture score composed by Danny Elfman; based on the original motion picture by arrangement with 20th Century Fox (original story and direction by Tim Burton; original screenplay and co-adaptation by Caroline Thompson); Produced by New Adventures, Martin McCallum, and Marc Platt; Sets/Costumes, Lez Brotherston; Lighting, Howard Harrison; Sound, Paul Groothuis; Music Director/Conductor, Andrew Bryan; Associate Director, Scott Ambler; General Manager, Gentry & Associates; Booking, Alan Wasser Associates; Company Managers, Simon Lacey, Adrian R. Young; U.S. Production Supervisor, Seth Wenig; Production Managers, Jon Harrington (U.S.), David Evans (U.K.); Deputy Stage Manager, Marina Kilby; Technical Director, Richard Reiser; Music Consultant, Ted Sperling; Cast: Sam Archer/Richard Winsor (Edward Scissorhands), Madelaine Brennan (Pegg Boggs/Tiffany Covitt/Old Kim/Cheerleader/TV Reporter), Rachel Morrow (Peg Boggs/ Esmerelda Evercreech/Old Kim), Etta Murfitt (Peg Boggs), Scott Ambler (Bill Boggs), Andrew Corbett (Bill Boggs/George Monroe/Manny Grubb/Inventor/Photographer/TV Reporter), Kerry Biggin/Hannah Vassallo (Kim Boggs/Candy Covitt/Cheerleader), Gavin Eden (Kevin Boggs), Drew McOnie (Kevin Boggs/Gerald Monroe/Chase Covitt/Sheldon Grubb/Little Edward), Michela Meazza (Joyce Monroe), Mikah Smillie (Joyce Monroe/Bunny Monroe/Charity Upton/ Marilyn-Ann Evercreech/Tiffany Covitt/ Cheerleader/TV Reporter), Steve Kirkham (George Monroe/TV Reporter), Sophia Hurdley (Bunny Monroe/Sandra Grubb/ Cheerleader), Shaun Walters (Gerald Monroe), Ebony Molina (Charity Upton), Gareth Charlton (Mayor Franklin Upton III), Adam Galbraith (Mayor Franklin Upton III/James "Jim" Upton/Manny Grubb/The Inventor/Photographer), Gemma Payne (Darlene Upton), Mami Tomotani (Darlene Upton/Gloria Grubb), James Leece (James "Jim" Upton/Brad Covitt), Rachel Lancaster (Esmerelda Evercreech/ Marilyn-Ann Evercreech/Candy Covitt/Gloria Grubb/Cheerleader), Matthew Malthouse (Rev. Judas Evercreech), Ross Carpenter (Rev. Judas Evercreech/Gabriel Evercreech), Shelby Williams (Marilyn-Ann Evercreech), Philip Willingham (Gabriel Evercreech/Chase Covitt), Chloe Wilkinson (Tiffany Covitt), Jake Samuels (Brad Covitt), Dena Lague (Sandra Grubb), Luke Murphy (Sheldon Grubb), Gavin Eden (Little Edward), Chloe Wilkinson (Cheerleader/TV Reporter); Standbys: Matthew Malthouse (Edward), Rachel Lancaster (Kim), Gareth Charlton (Bill), Gemma Payne (Joyce), Sam Archer (George), Jake Samuels/Richard Winsor (James)
A new musical play without words presented in two acts; Howard Gilman Opera House; March 14–31, 2007; 23 performances.

**Twelfth Night** and **The Taming of the Shrew** by William Shakespeare, adapted by Edward Hall and Roger Warren; Presented by Propeller; Produced by Watermill Theatre and Old Vic Productions; Director, Edward Hall; Sets/Costumes, Michael Pavelka; Lighting, Ben Ormerod/Mark Howland; Music, Propeller; U.S. Stage Manager, R. Michael Blanco; Cast: *Twelfth Night:* Tony Bell (Feste), Jack Tarlton (Orsino), Jon Trenchard (Curio/a Priest), Tam Williams (Viola/Cesario), Joe Flynn (Sebastian), Dominic Tighe (Captain of a Ship), Dugald Bruce-Lockhart (Olivia), Bob Barrett (Malvolio), Jason Baughan (Sir Toby Belch), Chris Myles (Maria), Simon Scardifield (Sir Andrew Aguecheek), Alasdair Craig (Antonio); *Taming of the Shrew:* Dugald Bruce-Lockhart (Christopher Sly/Petruchio), Tam Williams (Lucentio), Tony Bell (Tranio), Alasdair Craig (Biondello), Bob Barrett (Baptista), Simon Scardifield (Katherine), Jon Trenchard (Bianca), Chris Myles (Gremio/Vincentio), Jack Tarlton (Hortensio), Jason Baughan (Grumio/A Pedant), Joe Flynn (Curtis), Dominic Tighe (Tailor/Widow); Understudy: Tom McDonald

Revivals of the plays in rotating repertory, both presented in two acts; Harvey Theater; March 17–April 1, 2007; 10 performances each.

**Cymbeline** by William Shakespeare; Presented by Cheek by Jowl; Co-produced with barbicanbite07, Les Gémeaux/Sceaux/Scène Nationale, and Grand Théâtre de Luxembourg; Director, Declan Donnellan; Design, Nick Ormerod; Associate and Movement Director, Jane Gibson; Lighting, Judith Greenwood; Music, Catherine Jayes; Sound, Ross Chatfield; Assistant Director, Owen Horsley; Voice Coach, Patsy Rodenburg; Fight Director, Terry King; Casting, Siobhan Bracke; Technical Director, Simon Bourne; Company Manager, Anna Schmitz; Deputy Stage Manager, Dougie Wilson; ASM, Valerie Cohen; Hair/Makeup, Sarah Louise Packman; Props, Kathy Anders & Lisa Buckley; Cast: Gwendoline Christie (Queen), Tom Hiddleston (Posthumus/Cloten), Jodie McNee (Imogen), David Collings (Cymbeline), Richard Cant (Pisanio), Guy Flanagan (Iachimo), Laurence Spellman (Caius Lucius), Jake Harders (Doctor), Lola Peploe/Claire Cordier (Helen), Ryan Ellsworth (Belarius), John MacMillan (Guideruis), Daniel Percival (Arviragus), Mark Holgate (Company), David Caves (Company)
Revival of the play presented in two acts; Harvey Theater; May 2–12, 2007; 11 performances.

**Dense Terrain** Conceived, directed, and choreographed by Doug Varone, music by Nathan Larson; Sets, Allen Moyer; Video, Blue Land Media; Lighting, Jane Cox; Costumes, Liz Prince; Cast: John Beasant III, Daniel Charon, Ryan Corriston, Natalie Desch, Adriane Fang, Stephanie Liapis, Belinda McGuire, Erin Owen, Eddie Taketa, Doug Varone
A theatrical dance piece presented without intermission; Harvey Theater; May 16–20, 2007; 4 performances.

*Kerry Biggin and Sam Archer in* Edward Scissorhands *(photo by Bill Cooper)*

# City Center Encores!

Fourteenth Season

President/CEO, Arlene Shuler; Senior VP/Managing Director, Mark Litvin; Artistic Director, Jack Viertel; Music Director, Paul Gemignani; Scenic Consultant, John Lee Beatty; Sound, Tom Morse; Concert Adaptation, David Ives; Music Coordinator, Seymour Red Press; Company Manager, Michael Zande; Casting; Jay Binder & Jack Bowdan; Press, Helene Davis; Encores Artistic Associates: John Lee Beatty, Jay Binder, Walter Bobbie, David Ives, Kathleen Marshall

**Follies** Book by James Goldman, music and lyrics by Stephen Sondheim; Director/Choreography, Casey Nicholaw; Guest Music Director, Eric Stern; Costume Consultants, William Ivey Long & Gregg Barnes; Lighting, Ken Billington; PSM, Karen Moore; Original Orchestrations, Jonathan Tunick; Associate Music Director, Mark Mitchell; Music Associate, Joshua Clayton; Stage Manager, Andrea O. Saraffian; Associate Director, Jennifer Werner; Cast: Victoria Clark (Sally Durrant Plummer), Katie Klaus (Young Sally), Anne Rogers (Emily Whitman), Robert E. Fitch (Theodore Whitman), Dorothy Stanley (Dee Dee West), Diane J. Findlay (Sandra Crane), Lucine Amara (Heidi Schiller), Leena Chopra (Young Heidi), Mimi Hines (Hattie Walker), Yvonne Constant (Solange LaFitte), Arthur Rubin (Roscoe), Gerry Vichi (Max Deems), Jo Anne Worley (Stella Deems), Christine Baranski (Carlotta Campion), Donna Murphy (Phyllis Rogers Stone), Victor Garber (Ben Stone), Jenny Powers (Young Phyllis), Colin Donnell (Young Ben), Michael McGrath (Buddy Plummer), Curtis Holbrook (Young Buddy), Philip Bosco (Dimitri Weismann), Denise Payne (Young Emily), Barrett Martin (Young Theodore), Shannon Marie O'Bryan (Young Solange), Cameron Adams (Young Hattie), Ashlee Fife (Young Stella), Jenifer Foote (Young Dee Dee), Jennifer Mathie

(Young Carlotta), Natalie King (Young Sandra), Clyde Alves (Kevin), Kristen Beth Williams (Margie), Emily Fletcher (Sally); Ensemble: Cameron Adams, Clyde Alves, Ashlee Fife, Andrew Fitch, Emily Fletcher, Jenifer Foote, Ben Hartley, Natalie King, Brian J. Marcum, Barrett Martin, Jennifer Mathie, Shannon Marie O'Bryan, Denise Payne, Matt Wall, J.D. Webster, Kristen Beth Williams
Musical Numbers: Beautiful Girls, Don't Look at Me, Waiting for the Girls Upstairs, Rain on the Roof, Ah, Paris!, Broadway Baby, The Road You Didn't Take, Bolero d'Amour, In Buddy's Eyes, Who's That Woman?, I'm Still Here, Too Many Mornings, The Right Girl, One More Kiss, Could I Leave You?, Loveland, You're Gonna Love Tomorrow, Love Will See Us Through, The God-Why-Don't-You-Love-Me Blues, Losing My Mind, The Story of Lucy and Jessie, Live, Laugh, Love Setting: A party on the stage of the Weismann Theatre, New York, 1971. Concert version of the musical presented in two acts; City Center; February 8–12, 2007; 6 performances. The original production, directed by Hal Prince, opened at the Winter Garden Theatre on April 4, 1971, running 522 performances (see *Theatre World* Volume 27, page 42).

**Face the Music** Book, music and lyrics by Irving Berlin, book by Moss Hart; Director, John Rando; Choreography, Randy Skinner; Music Director, Rob Fisher; Adaptation, David Ives; Music Coordinator, Seymour Red Press; Scenic Consultant, John Lee Beatty; Costume Consultant, Toni-Leslie James; Sound, Scott Lehrer; PSM, Rolt Smith; Original Orchestrations, Robert Russell Bennett, Maurice De Packh and Frank Tours: Cast: Judy Kaye (Mrs. Myrtle Meshbesher), Lee Wilkof (Martin van Buren Meshbesher), Jeffry Denman (Pat Mason), Meredith Patterson (Kit Baker), Mylinda Hull (Pickles Crouse), Eddie Korbich (Joe Malarkey), Felicia Finley (Streetwalker), Chris Hoch (Rodney St. Clair/Prosecutor), Timothy Shew (O'Rourke), Walter Bobbie (Hal Reisman); Ensemble: Christine Arand, Heather Ayers, Sara Brians, Rachel Coloff, Rick Crom, Susan Derry, Jack Doyle, Jerold

*Victor Garber and Donna Murphy in* Follies *(photo by Joan Marcus)*

*Walter Bobbie and Company in* Face the Music *(photo by Joan Marcus)*

Goldstein, Todd A. Horman, Justin Keyes, Cara Kjellman, Robyn Kramer, Todd Lattimore, Mike Masters, Brent McBeth, Shannon Marie O'Bryan, Wes Pope, Eric Daniel Santagata, Jacqueline Thompson, Kevin Vortmann, J.D. Webster, Anna Aimee White, Kristen Beth Williams; Cast recording: DRG

Musical Numbers: Overture, Lunching at the Automat, Let's Have Another Cup of Coffee, Let's Have Another Cup of Coffee (reprise), The Police of New York, Reisman's Doing a Show, Torch Song, You Must Be Born With It, Castles in Spain (On A Roof in Manhattan), Crinoline Days, My Beautiful Rhinestone Girl, Soft Lights and Sweet Music, The Police of New York, If You Believe, Entr'acte, Well, of All the Rotten Shows, I Say It's Spinach (and the Hell with It), How Can I Change My Luck?, A Toast to Prohibition, The Nudist Colony, I Don't Want To Be Married (I Just Want to Be Friends), Manhattan Madness, The Investigation

Setting: New York City, 1932. Concert version of the musical presented in two acts; City Center; March 29– April 1, 2007; 5 performances.

**Stairway to Paradise** Music, lyrics, and sketches by Nora Bayes, Irving Berlin, Eubie Blake, Henry Blossom, Elissa Boyd, Bob Cole, Betty Comden, B.G. DeSylva, Howard Dietz, Jimmy Durante, Leo Edwards, Dorothy Fields, George Gershwin, Ira Gershwin, Jay Gorney, Murray Grand, Adolph Green, E.Y. Harburg, Lorenz Hart, Victor Herbert, J.W. Johnson, Jerome Kern, Jean Kerr, Walter Kerr, Duke Leonard, Jimmy McHugh, Blanch Merrill, Ed G. Nelson, Jack Norworth, Harry Pease, Andy Razaf, Richard Rodgers, Harold Rome, Arthur Schwartz, Paul Gerard Smith, Jule Styne, P.G. Wodehouse; Conceived by Jack Viertel; Director, Jerry Zaks; Guest Music Director, Rob Berman; Choreographer, Warren

Carlyle; Costume Consultant, William Ivey Long; Lighting, Paul Gallo; PSM, Rolt Smith; Stage Manager, Andrea O. Saraffian; Assistant Musical Director, David Gursky; Music Associate, Joshua Clayton; Cast: Kristin Chenoweth, Kevin Chamberlin, Christopher Fitzgerald, Jenn Gambatese, Ruthie Henshall, Capathia Jenkins, Michael Gruber, Shonn Wiley, J. Mark McVey, Holly Cruikshank, Kendrick Jones; Ensemble: Timothy J. Alex, Robin Campbell, Erin Crouch, Susan Derry, Lianne Marie Dobbs, Emily Fletcher, Bob Gaynor, Laura Griffith, Dale Hensley, Renée Klapmeyer, Barrett Martin, Sean McKnight, James Patterson, Eric Santagata, Kiira Schmidt, Dennis Stowe, Sarrah Strimel, Kevin Vortmann, J.D. Webster, Teal Wicks

Musical Numbers: Overture, The Land Where the Good Songs Go, Everything in America is Ragtime, The Maiden with the Dreamy Eyes, If I Were on the Stage (Kiss Me Again), Oh! How I Hate to Get Up in the Morning, Pack Up Your Sins and Go to the Devil, Manhattan/Mountain Greenery, I Guess I'll Have to Change My Plan, Memories of You, I Know Darn Well I Can Do Without Broadway, I'm an Indian, Get Yourself a Geisha, Doin' the New Low-Down, My Handy Man Ain't Handy No More, I'll Build a Stairway to Paradise, Brother Can You Spare a Dime, Dancing in the Dark, Entr'acte, F.D.R. Jones, Supper Time, The Land Where the Good Songs Go (reprise), Sing Me a Song With Social Significance, Josephine Please No Lean on the Bell, Rhode Island is Famous for You, Triplets, This is the Army Mr. Jones, I Left My Heart at the Stage Door Canteen, Ev'ry Time We Say Goodbye, Going Home Train, Call Me Mister, Guess Who I Saw Today, Catch Our Act at the Met

An original musical review presented in two acts; City Center; May 10–14, 2007; 6 performances.

*Christopher Fitzgerald, Kevin Chamberlin and Kristin Chenoweth in* Stairway to Paradise *(photo by Joan Marcus)*

# Classic Stage Company

Thirty-ninth Season

Artistic Director, Brian Kulick; Executive Director, Jessica R. Jenen; General Manager, Lisa Barnes; Development, Todd Rosen; Associate Artistic Director, Jeff Janisheski; Assistant General Manager, Faye Rosenbaum; Marketing/Development Associate, Anna Hayman; Artistic Associates, Katherine Kovner, Daisy Walker; Audience Services, Stephen Riordan; Casting, James Calleri; Press, The Publicity Office, Michael Borowski, Marc Thibodeau, Candi Adams

**Richard II** by William Shakespeare; Director, Brian Kulick; Sets, Tom Gleeson; Costumes, Oana Botez-Ban; Lighting, Brian H. Scott; Sound, Jorge Muelle; Fight Director, J. David Brimmer; Production Manager, Jee Han; PSM, Robyn Henry; ASM, Gregory T. Livoti; Technical Director, Nicholas Warren-Gray; Original Photography, Howard Schatz; Original Music, Mark Bennett; Cast: Craig Baldwin (Thomas Mowbray/Earl of Northumberland), Michael Cumpsty (Richard II), Bernardo De Paula (Bushy/Lord Ross/Exton), Jon DeVries (John of Gaunt/Earl of Salisbury/Gardener/Groom), David Greenspan (Bagot/Bishop of Carlisle), Doan Ly (Queen Isabel), George Morfogen (Duke of York), Ellen Parker (Duchess of Gloucester/Lady in Waiting/Duchess of York), Jesse Pennington (Aumerle), Graham Winton (Henry Bolingbroke)
Revival of the play presented in two acts; East 13th Street Theatre; September 6–October 15, 2006 (Opened September 17); 40 performances.

**A Spanish Play** by Yasmina Reza, translated by David Ives; Director, John Turturro; Sets, Riccardo Hernandez; Costumes, Donna Zakowska; Lights Christopher Akerlind; Sound, Darron L. West and Emily Wright; Production Manager, Aduro Productions; Projection Design, Robin Silvestri, Batwin & Rubin Productions; Video Camera Operator, Cameron Bossert; Associate Set Design, Chad McArver; PSM, Fred Hemminger; ASM, Cambra Overend; Assistant Director, Daisy Walker; Technical Director, Jared DeBacker; Cast: Zoe Caldwell (Pilar), Katherine Borowitz (Nuria, *Pilar's daughter*), Linda Emond (Aurelia, *Pilar's daughter*), Denis O'Hare (Mariano, *Aurelia's husband*), Larry Pine (Fernan)
Revival of the play presented without intermission; East 13th Street Theatre; January 10–March 4, 2007 (Opened February 1); 54 performances.

*Zoe Caldwell and Larry Pine in* A Spanish Play *(photo by Joan Marcus)*

**Prometheus Bound** by Aeschylus, translated and directed by James Kerr; Produced in association with Aquila Theatre Company (Peter Meineck, Artistic Director; Robert Richmond, Associate Artistic Director; Todd Batstone, Associate Producer); Composer, Dan Lipton; Sets/Costumes, Paul Wills; Lighting, Mark Jonathan; Sound, Christopher Shutt; Production Manager, Nate Terracio; PSM,

Rebecca Goldstein-Glaze; ASM, Basienka Blake; Associate Production Design, James Shouli; Associate Costumes, Sam Fleming; Cast: David Oyelowo (Prometheus), George Bartenieff (Hephaestus/Oceanus), Michael Dixon (Power/Hermes), Julie McNiven (Violence/Io); Chorus: Therese Barbato, Autumn Dornfeld, Erin Krakow, Susannah Millonzi, Sipiwe Moyo
Revival of the play presented without intermission; East 13th Street Theatre; March 13–April 14, 2007 (Opened March 21); 35 performances.

*David Oyelowo in* Prometheus Bound *(photo by Joan Marcus)*

**Additional Events**

**Open Rehearsal Series:** *Edward II* by Christopher Marlowe; Director, Brian Kulick; Featuring the cast of CSC's production of *Richard II*; CSC East 13th Street Theatre; September 24, October 1 & 8, 2006

**First Look Festival – Anton Chekhov** One night only staged reading and workshop productions; January 22, 2007: *The Cherry Orchard* Director, Diane Paulus; Featuring: Kathleen Chalfant; January 29, 2007: *The Seagull* Director, Austin Pendleton; Featuring: Dianne Wiest, Bill Camp, Jessica Hecht, John Mahoney, Michael Stuhlbarg; February 5, 2007: *Uncle Vanya* Director, Erica Schmidt; Featuring: Peter Dinklage; February 12, 2007: *The Three Sisters* Director, Gregory Mosher; Featuring: Elizabeth Marvel

**The Young Company:** *A Midsummer Night's Dream* by William Shakespeare; Presented by the Graduate Acting Program of the Columbia University School for the Arts; Director, Jeff Janisheski; Sets, Jian Jung; Costumes, Oana Botez-Ban; Lighting, Justin Townsend; Sound, Emily Wright; Dramaturg, Eleanor Skimin; Company Manager, Jamie Forshaw; Stage Manager, Shelley Little; ASM, Amy Dalba; Assistant Director, Daniel Glenn; Cast: Blythe Foster, Courtney King, Aryeh Lappin, Charles Linshaw, Kate LoConti, Tania Monia, Soneela Nankani, Juni Ng, Indika Senanayake, Stephanie Shipp, Terence Swiney, Scott Sweatt; February 24–March 4, 2007; 6 performances.

**Monday Night** *Tempest* Five nights of open rehearsals of the play by William Shakespeare presented in association with the Stage Directors and Choreographers Foundation; March 19: Michael Cumpsty as Prospero, directed by Brian Kulick; March 26: Anne Bogart and SITI Company; April 2: David Costabile and Michael Sexton of The Shakespeare Society; April 9: Michael Sexton; April 16: A staged reading in its entirety, directed by Brian Kulick, starring Michael Cumpsty

**The Iliad, Parts I, II, & III** by Homer, translated by Stanley Lombardo; created by Peter Meineck and Robert Richmond; Produced in association with Aquila Theatre Company; Staged readings of the plays presented in three parts; April 17–18, 2007

# Classical Theatre of Harlem

Eighth Season

Co-Founder & Artistic Director, Alfred Preisser; Co-Founder & Executive Producer, Christopher McElroen: Producing/Development Associate, Jaime Carrillo; Artistic Associate, Karan Kendrick; Production Supervisor, Vincent J. DeMarco/Kelvin Productions LLC; Press, Brett Singer and Associates

**King Lear** by William Shakespeare; Co-produced with the Folger Theatre, Washington, D.C.; Director, Alfred Preisser; Sets, Troy Hourie; Costumes, Kimberly Glennon; Lighting, Aaron Black; Stage Manager, Joan H. Cappello; Fight Director, Denise A. Hurd; Assistant Director, Lydia Fort; ASM, Tyshawn Major; Dramaturg, Debra Cardona; Cast: André DeShields (Lear), Ty Jones (Edmund), John Douglas Thompson (Edgar), Jerome Preston Bates (Kent), Robyne Landiss Walker (Goneril), Zainab Jah (Regan), Ken Schatz (Fool), Christina Sajous (Cordelia), Jaime Robert Carrillo (Oswald), Duane Allen (France), Alexander Sovronsky (Servant/Herald/Musician), Noshir Dalal (Burgandy), Shayshahn MacPherson (Knight/Musician), Danny Camiel (Albany), Ted Lange (Gloucester), Francis Mateo (Cornwall)
Revival of a play presented in two acts; HSA Theatre; September 29–November 5, 2006 (Opened February 15); 30 performances. The production toured to Miami and Washington D.C., playing 47 additional performances.

*André De Shields, Zainab Jah, Ty Jones, Alex Sovronsky, Christina Sajous in* King Lear *(photo by Ruth Savronsky)*

**Marat/Sade** *(The Persecution and Assassination of Jean-Paul Marat as Performed by the Inmates of the Asylum of Charenton Under the Direction of the Marquis de Sade)* by Peter Weiss, music by Richard Peaslee; Director, Christopher McElroen, Sets, Troy Hourie; Costumes, Kimberly Glennon; Lighting, Aaron Black; Musical Director, Kelvyn Bell; Fight Director, Denise Hurd, Choreographer, Rajendra Ramoon Maharaj; Dramaturg, Debra Cardona; Technical Director, Jack Brady; Dance Captain, Jake Lemmenes; Fight Captain, Alexander Sovronsky; Cast: Danny Camiel (Kokol), Robert Freeman (Attendant), Andrew Guilarte (Jacques Roux), Nathan Hinton (Marat), Tyshawn Major (Coulmier's Wife), Jonathan Payne (Simone), James Rana (Polpoch), Ron Simons (Coulmier), David Ryan Smith (Rossignol), T. Ryder Smith (Marquis de Sade), Alexander Sovronsky (Attendant), Eric Walton (Herald), Dana Watkins (Charlotte Corday); Patients of the Asylum: Musa Bacon, Lesley Billingslea, Jamal N. Bruce, Jaime Robert Carrillo, Bill Corry, Erwin Falcon, Michael Flood, Jeffrey Glaser, Ricardo Pérez Gonzalez, Glenn Gordon, Donald Kingston, Paul Karasner, Thomas Layman, Jake Lemmenes, Carl Louis, Mitch Maguire, Eric Steven Mills, Kiel Perry, Scott Sortman, Rommel Tolentino, Vladimi Versailles, Richard Vincent Weber, Chandler Wild

Setting: The Asylum of Charenton, France. Revival of a play presented without intermission; HSA Theatre; February 2–March 11, 2007 (Opened March 11); 25 performances. Originally produced on Broadway at the Martin Beck December 27, 1965 (see *Theatre World* Volume 22, page 46).

*Nathan Hinton, Dana Watkins, and Daniel Talbott in* Marat/Sade *(photo by Michael Messer)*

**Electra** by Alfred Preisser, based on the play by Sophocles; Director, Alfred Preisser; Design, Troy Hourie & Aaron Black; Costumes, Kimberly Glennon; Stage Manager, Joan Cappello; Dramaturg, Ashley Kelly Tata; Choreography, Tracy Jack; Cast: Zainab Jah (Electra), Trisha Jeffrey (Chrysothemis), Samuel Ray Gates (Orestes), Petronia Paley (Clytemnestra); Tracy Jack (Choral Leader), Khadeejah Anne Gray (Chorus), Christina Sajous (Chorus), Sandra Shade Miller (Chorus), Valentine Lyashenko (Soldier), Shayshahn MacPherson (Drummer)
New adaptation of the play presented without intermission; HSA Theatre; May 24–June 24, 2007 (Opened May 31); 25 performances.

*Tracey Jack, Sandra Miller, and Zainab Jah in* Electra *(photo by Troy Hourie)*

# The Culture Project

Artistic Director, Allan Buchman; Business Manager, Casey Cordon; General Manager, Dave Friedman; Women Center Stage, Olivia Greer; Box Office Manager, Becky White; Technical Director/Resident Designer, Garin Marschall; Marketing Associate, Wythe Marschall; Resident Director and Producer, Will Pomerantz; Press, Origlio/Miramontez Company

**Amajuba: Like Doves We Rise** Created and directed by Yael Farber; Written by the cast based on their experience; Lighting, Tim Boyd; Lighting Director, Garin Marschall; Production Manager, Catherine Bloch; Production Coordinator, Leigh Colombick; Producers, David Friedman & Lauren Saffa in association with the Farber Foundry (Thomas O. Kriegsmann, Executive Producer); Cast: Tshallo Chokwe, Roelf Matlala, Bongeka Mpongwana, Phillip "Tipo" Tindisa, Jabulile Tshabalala
A theatrical performance piece presented without intermission; 45 Bleecker; July 20–August 20, 2006 (Opened July 25); 28 performances. Originally presented in South Africa, the Edinburgh Fringe Festival, and London's Criterion Theatre.

**The Treatment** by Eve Ensler; Presented as part of the Impact Festival; Director, Leigh Silverman; Sets, Richard Hoover; Costumes, Candice Donnelly; Lighting, Justin Townsend; Sound, Jill B.C. DuBoff; Cast: Dylan McDermott (Man), Portia (Woman)
World premiere of a new play presented without intermission; 45 Bleecker; August 29–October 22, 2006 (Opened September 12); 48 performances.

*Portia and Dylan McDermott in* The Treatment *(photo by Bruce Glikas)*

**Speak Truth to Power** by Ariel Dorfman, based on the book by Kerry Kennedy; Photographs, Eddie Adams; Director, Terry Kinney; Speak Truth to Power Human Rights Initiative, Nan Richardson, Kerry Kennedy; Cast: Carolyn Baeumler, Marsha Stephanie Blake, Megan Byrne, Stephen Kunken, Aasif Mandvi, Lois Markle, Ellen McLaughlin, Charles Parnell, Keith Randolph Smith, Danton Stone; Supplemental Cast (rotating): Gabriel Byrne, Brooke Shields, Rosario Dawson, Griffin Dunne, Kim Fields, Charles Grodin, Julianna Margulies, Lynn Redgrave, Isabella Rossellini, Fisher Stevens
New York premiere of a new play presented without intermission; 45 Bleecker; October 15, 2006–February 27, 2007 (Opened November 14); 14 performances.

**Dai (enough)** Written and performed by Iris Bahr; Director, Will Pomerantz; Sound, Frank Gaeta; Lighting, Garin Marschall; Sound Mastering, Patrick Giraudi
A solo performance play presented without intermission; 45 Bleecker; November 8–December 16, 2006 (Opened November 14); 55 Mercer; January 4–February

25, 2007; 96 performances. The Culture Project relocated to the old Manhattan Ensemble Theatre space at 55 Mercer on January 1, 2007. Previously presented August 28 and October 12–15, 2006, at the Baruch Performing Arts Center Nagelberg Theatre as part of the Impact Festival.

*Iris Bahr in* Dai (enough) *(photo by Bruce Glikas)*

*Lawrence Wright in* My Trip to Al Qaeda *(photo by Bruce Glikas)*

**My Trip to Al-Qaeda** Written and performed by Lawrence Wright, based on his book *The Looming Tower: Al-Qaeda and the Road to 9/11;* Director, Gregory Mosher
World premiere of solo performance play/theatrical seminar presented without intermission; 55 Mercer; March 1–April 14, 2007 (Opened March 6); 40 performances.

## Irish Repertory Theatre

Nineteenth Season

Producing Director, Ciarán O'Reilly; Artistic Director, Charlotte Moore; Managing Director, Patrick A. Kelsey; Membership Manager, Eric Scott; Director of Development, Terry Diamond; Literary Manager, Kara Manning; Dialect Coach, Stephen Gabis; Box Office Manager, Jeffrey Wingfield; Audience Services, Jared Dawson; Wardrobe Supervisor, Andrea Sarubbi; Master Electrician, Paul Jones; Master Carpenter, Donal O'Reilly; Production Coordinator, Mac Smith; Casting, Laura Maxwell Scott, Deborah Brown; Press, Shirley Herz Associates, Dan Demello

**Mr. Dooley's America** by Philip Dunne and Martin Blaine, based on the newspaper articles of Finley Peter Dunne; Director, Charlotte Moore; Sets, Charles Corcoran; Costumes, Linda Fisher; Lighting, Renée Molina; PSMs, Pamela Brusoski, Elis C. Arroyo; Props, Hilary Baldwin; Cast: Des Keogh (Finley Peter Dunne/Mr. Hennessy), Vincent Dowling (Mr. Dooley)
Setting: Mr. Dooley's Saloon, Chicago, at the turn of the century. A play presented in two acts; Mainstage; August 10–September 10, 2006 (Opened August 16); 45 performances. This production was the final production of the eighteenth season.

**The Hairy Ape** by Eugene O'Neill; Director, Ciarán O'Reilly; Sets, Eugene Lee; Costumes, Linda Fisher; Lighting, Brian Nason; Sound, Zachary Williamson & Gabe Wood; Wigs and Hair, Robert-Charles Vallance; Mask/Puppets, Bob Flanagan; Fight Director, Rick Sordelet; PSM, Janice M. Brandine; Stage Manager, Benjamin J. Shuman; Associate Costumes, Catherine Barinas; Associate Lighting, Renée Molina; Props, Deirdre Brennan; Cast: Kerry Bishé (Mildred), Jason Denuszek (Sailor/Second Engineer/Prisoner/Union Man), Gregory Derelian (Yank), Gerald Finnegan (Paddy), Delphi Harrington (Aunt), David Lansbury (Long), Jon Levenson (Sailor/Policeman/Prisoner/Union Man/Ape), Allen McCullough (Secretary/Engineer/Prison Guard), Michael Mellamphy (Sailor/Policeman/Prisoner), Kevin O'Donnell (Sailor/Prisoner/Union Man)
Time: 1920. Place: An ocean liner, and various places around New York City. Revival of the play presented without intermission; Mainstage; September 29–November 26, 2006 (Opened October 5); 63 performances.

*Gregory Derelian in* The Hairy Ape *(photo by Carol Rosegg)*

**An Evening of Irish One-Acts** *Great White American Teeth* by Fiona Walsh, directed by Virginia Scott; Cast: Fiona Walsh; *Swansong* by Conor McDermottroe, directed by David Sullivan; Cast: Tim Ruddy; Lighting, Renée Molina; PSM, Dyanne M. McNamara
Two one-act solo performance plays presented with intermission; W. Scott McLucas Studio Theatre; October 11–November 5, 2006; 24 performances.

**Meet Me in St. Louis** Book by Hugh Wheeler, songs by Hugh Martin and Ralph Blane; based on *The Kensington Stories* by Sally Benson and the MGM motion picture; Director, Charlotte Moore; Music Director, John Bell; Choreography, Barry McNabb; Sets, Tony Straiges; Costumes, Tracy Christensen; Lighting, Brian Nason; Sound, Murmod Inc.; Wigs/Hair, Robert-Charles Vallance; PSM, Elis C. Arroyo; Stage Manager, Janice M. Brandine; Associate Producer, Stuart Wilk; Cast: Becky Barta (Katie), Doug Boes (Warren Sheffield), Merideth Kaye

*Danielle Piacentile, Bonnie Fraser, and Gabrielle Piacentile in* Meet Me in St. Louis *(photo by Carol Rosegg)*

Clark (Rose Smith), Kerry Conte (Lucille Ballard), Colin Donnell (John Truitt), Bonnie Fraser (Esther Smith), John Hickok (Mr. Alonzo Smith), George S. Irving (Grandpa Prophater), Sarah Pfisterer (Mrs. Anna Smith), Danielle Piacentile (Agnes), Gabrielle Piacentile (Tootie), Ashley Robinson (Lon Smith); Orchestra: John Bell (Piano), Melanie Mason (Cello), Diane Montalbine (Violin), Sue Maskaleris (Violin)

Musical Numbers: Meet Me in St. Louis, The Boy Next Door, Meet Me in St. Louis, Whenever I'm With You, You'll Hear a Bell, A Raving Beauty, Skip to My Lou, Drunk Song, Under the Bamboo Tree, Over the Banister, Trolley Song, A Touch of the Irish, The Boy Next Door (reprise), A Day in New York, You'll Hear A Bell (reprise), Wasn't It Fun, The Banjo, You Are For Loving, Have Yourself A Merry Little Christmas, Meet Me in St. Louis (reprise)

Setting: In and around the Smith family home, 5135 Kensington Ave., St. Louis, Missouri, from the fall of 1903 to the Spring of 1904 and the opening of the Louisiana Purchase Exposition. Revival of the musical presented in two acts; Mainstage; December 6, 2006–February 18, 2007 (Opened December 14); 77 performances. Originally produced on Broadway at the Gershwin Theatre, November 2, 1989 (see *Theatre World* Volume 46, page 15).

**Defender of the Faith** by Stuart Carolan; Director, Ciarán O'Reilly; Sets, Charles Corcoran; Costumes, Martha Hally; Lighting, Brian Nason; Sound, Zachary Williamson; PSM, Janice M. Brandine; Stage Manager, April Ann Kline; Fight Director, Rick Sordelet; Assistant to the Director, Helena Gleissner; Props, John Duckworth; Cast: Matt Ball (Danny), Luke Kirby (Thomas), Peter Rogan (Barney), Anto Nolan (Father), David Lansbury (J.J.), Marc Aden Gray (Unknown Man)

Setting: 1986, a farm on the border of Northern and Southern Ireland. American premiere of a play presented without intermission; Mainstage; March 1–April 29, 2007 (Opened March 8); 69 performances.

*David Lansbury & Luke Kirby in* Defender of the Faith
*(photo by Carol Rosegg)*

**Gaslight** by Patrick Hamilton; Director, Charlotte Moore; Sets, James Morgan; Costumes, Martha Hally; Lighting, Brian Nason; Sound, Zachary Williamson; Original Music, Mark Hartman; Wigs and Hair, Robert-Charles Vallance; Fight Director, Rick Sordelet; PSM, Christine S. Lemme; Stage Manager, April Ann Kline; Props and Decor, Deirdre Brennan; Cast: Brian Murray (Inspector Rough), Patricia O'Connell (Elizabeth), Laura Odeh (Bella Manningham), Laoisa Sexton (Nancy), David Staller (Jack Manningham), April Ann Kline and Jon Levenson (Police Officers)

Setting: A house on Angel Street, Pimlico district of London; 1880. Revival of a play (formerly titled *Angel Street*) presented in two acts; Mainstage; May 9–July 8, 2007 (Opened May 17); 70 performances. *Angel Street* premiered on Broadway at the John Golden Theatre, December 5, 1941, and was revived December 26, 1975 at the Lyceum Theatre (see *Theatre World* Volume 32, page 33).

**Tom Crean – Antarctic Explorer** by Aidan Dooley; Presented in association with Northern Stage, Fairbank Productions, and Play On Words Theatre; Lighting, Brian Nason; PSM, Janice M. Brandine; Lighting Assistant, Mac Smith; Artwork/Graphics, Eric A. Scott; Cast: Aidan Dooley (Tom Crean)

A solo performance play presented in two acts; Mainstage; July 17–September 9, 2007 (Opened July 22); 56 performances. Originally produced at the New York International Fringe Festival in 2003.

*Laura Odeh and David Staller in* Gaslight *(photo by Carol Rosegg)*

# The Keen Company

Seventh Season

Artistic Director, Carl Forsman; Producer, Wayne Kelton; Production Manager, Josh Bradford; Artistic Associate, Blake Lawrence; Season Designers: Beowulf Borritt (Sets), Theresa Squire (Costumes), Josh Bradford (Lighting), Daniel Baker (Sound); Casting, Kelly Gillespie, McCorkle Casting; Press, Karen Greco

**Theophilus North** by Matthew Burnet, adapted from the 1973 novel by Thornton Wilder; Director, Carl Forsman; Producer, Wayne Kelton; PSM, Erin Greiner; ASMs, Jessica Johnston, Denise Blacker; Technical Director, Jesse Wilson; Associate Costumes, Renee Mariotti; Cast: Virginia Kull (Eloise Fenwick/Diana Bell/others), Giorgio Litt (Theophilus North), Geddeth Smith (Father/Dr. Bosworth/others), Margaret Daly (Mother/Mrs. Cranston/others), Joe Delafield (Charles Fenwick/George/others), Regan Thompson (Myra Granberry/Sarah), Brian Hutchison (Henry Simmons/Hilary/others)
Setting: 1926, Newport, Rhode Island. New York premiere of a play presented in two acts; Clurman Theatre at Theatre Row; September 5–October 4, 2006 (Opened September 14); 8 previews, 27 performances. Originally produced January 24, 2003 by Geva Theatre Center (Rochester, New York; Mark Cuddy, Artistic Director) and Arena Stage (Washington, D.C.; Molly D. Smith, Artistic Director; Stephen Richard, Executive Director)

**Tea and Sympathy** by Robert Anderson; Director, Jonathan Silverstein; Associate Sets, Jo Winarski; Stage Manager, Erin Maureen Koster; ASMs, Emily Bayer, Krysta Piccoli; Technical Director, Brant Underwood; Music Instructor, Greg Felden; Fight Director, Robert Westley; Cast: Heidi Armbruster (Laura Reynolds), Randy Danson (Lilly Sears), Dan McCabe (Tom Lee), Mark Setlock (Harris), Brandon Espinoza (Al), Jake Levy (Ralph), Ben Hollandsworth (Steve), Craig Mathers (Bill Reynolds), Hal Fickett (Phil), Dan Cordle (Herb Lee); Understudy: Kathy Kaefer (Lilly Sears)
Time: Late May, 1953. Place: A boys' boarding school in New Hampshire. Revival of a play presented in three acts; Clurman Theatre at Theatre Row; March 6–April 14, 2007 (Opened March 15); 8 previews, 28 performances. Originally produced on Broadway at the Ethel Barrymore Theatre September 30, 1953, transferred to the Longacre February 9, 1955, then to the 48th Street Theatre on April 11, 1955, and closed June 18, 1955, running 712 performances (see *Theatre World* Volume 10, page 15).

Right: *The Cast of* Tea and Sympathy *(photo by Josh Bradford)*

Below: *The Cast of* Theophilus North *(photo by Beowulf Boritt)*

# Lincoln Center Theater

Twenty-second Season

Artistic Director, André Bishop; Executive Producer, Bernard Gersten; General Manager, Adam Siegel; Production Manager, Jeff Hamlin; Director of Development, Hattie K. Jutagir; Director of Finance, David S. Brown; Director of Marketing, Linda Mason Ross; Director of Education, Kati Koerner; Musical Theatre Associate Producer, Ira Weitzman; Dramaturg and Director of the LCT Directors Lab, Anne Cattaneo; Associate Directors, Graciela Daniele, Nicholas Hytner, Susan Stroman, Daniel Sullivan; Casting, Daniel Swee; Press, Philip Rinaldi, Barbara Carroll

**The House in Town** by Richard Greenberg: Director, Doug Hughes; Set, John Lee Beatty; Costumes, Catherine Zuber; Lighting, Brian MacDevitt; Original Music and Sound, David Van Tieghem; Stage Manager, James FitzSimmons; ASM, Elizabeth Miller; Company Manager, Josh Lowenthal; Associate Director, Mark Schneider; Associate Set, Yoshinori Tanokura; Associate Lighting, Jen Schriever; Props, Scott Laule; Cast: Becky Ann Baker (Jean Eliot), Dan Bittner (Christopher Valence), Mark Harelik (Sam Hammer), Jessica Hecht (Amy Hammer), Armand Schultz (Con Eliot), Barbara McCulloh (the Hammers' Maid), Matt Dickson (the Hammers' Footman); Understudies: Matt Dickson (Christopher Valence), R. Ward Duffy (Sam Hammer/Con Eliot/Footman), Susan Knight (Amy Hammer/Maid), Barbara McCulloh (Jean Eliot)

Setting: A townhouse on Millionaires' Row, 23rd Street between Ninth and Tenth Avenues, New York City, The first five months of 1929. World premiere of a new play presented without intermission; Mitzi E. Newhouse Theatre; May 24–July 30, 2006 (Opened June 19); 30 previews, 48 performances.

*Mark Harelik, Jessica Hecht, Armand Schultz and Becky Ann Baker in* The House in Town *(photo by Paul Kolnik)*

**The Clean House** by Sarah Ruhl; Director, Bill Rauch; Sets, Christopher Acebo; Costumes, Shigeru Yaji; Lighting, James F. Ingalls; Sound/Composer, André Pluess; Choreographer, Sabrina Peck; Stage Manager, Roy Harris; ASM, Denise Yaney; Company Manager, Matthew Markoff; Assistant Director, Tracy Young; Projections, William Cusick, Ryan Holsopple; Props, Faye Armon; Hair/Wigs/Makeup, Wendy Parson; Dialect Coach, Deborah Hecht; Cast: Vanessa Aspillaga (Matilde), Blair Brown (Lane), Jill Clayburgh (Virginia), John Dossett (Matilde's Father/Charles), Concetta Tomei (Matilde's Mother/Ana); Understudies: Nicole Sheridan (Matilde), Peter Samuel (Charles), Maureen Mueller (Lane/Virginia), Marilyn Dodds Frank (Ana)

Time: The present. Place: A house that is not far from the city and not far from the sea. New York premiere of a new play presented in two acts; Mitzi E. Newhouse Theatre; October 5, 2006–January 28, 2007 (Opened October 30); 27 previews, 88 performances. World premiere produced by Yale Repertory Theatre, 2004.

*Concetta Tomei and John Dossett in* The Clean House *(photo by Paul Kolnik)*

**Dying City** by Christopher Shinn; Director, James Macdonald; Sets/Costumes, Anthony Ward; Lighting, Pat Collins; Sound, Aural Fixation; Stage Manager, Roy Harris; ASM, Denise Yaney; Company Manager, Matthew Markoff; Assistant Director, Evan Cabnet; Props, Faye Armon; Cast: Rebecca Brooksher (Kelly), Pablo Schreiber (Peter/Craig); Understudies: Dana Powers Acheson, Greg Keller

Time: July 2005 and January 2004. Place: New York City. American premiere of a new play presented without intermission; Mitzi E. Newhouse Theatre; February 15–April 29, 2007 (Opened March 4); 20 previews, 65 performances.

*Rebecca Brooksher and Pablo Schreiber in* Dying City *(photo by Paul Kolnik)*

# MCC Theater (Manhattan Class Company)

Twenty-first Season

Artistic Directors, Robert LuPone and Bernard Telsey; Associate Artistic Director, William Cantler; Executive Director, Blake West; General Manager, Barbara L. Auld; Assistant General Manager, Lauren Levitt; Literary Manager/Resident Dramaturg, Stephen Willems; Assistant Literary Manager, Jamie Green; Playwrights' Coalition Coordinator, Mark Schultz; Development, Blake West, Nicole Cardamone; Marketing, Shanta Mali; Education and Outreach, Katie Miller/John DiResta; Audience Services, Jessica Crone; Youth Company Artistic Director, Stephen DiMenna; Production Manager, B.D. White; Resident Director, Doug Hughes; Resident Playwright, Neil LaBute; Technical Director, James Reddington; Casting, Bernard Telsey; Press, Origlio/Miramontez, Jon Dimond

**Nixon's Nixon** by Russell Lees; Director, Jim Simpson; Sets, Kyle Chepulis; Costumes, Claudia Brown; Lighting, Brian Aldous; Sound, Jill B.C. DuBoff; Projections, Brian H. Kim; PSM, Elizabeth Wiesner Paige; Press, Shaffer-Coyle Public Relations; Cast: Gerry Bamman (Richard M. Nixon), Steve Mellor (Henry A. Kissinger)
Setting: The Lincoln Sitting Room in the White House on the eve of Nixon's resignation, August 7, 1974. Revival of the play presented without intermission; Lucille Lortel Theatre; September 20–October 28, 2006 (Opened October 4); 40 performances. Originally produced by MCC September 29–December 23, 1995 with the same cast, transferring to a commercial run at the Westside Theatre Downstairs March 5–May 12, 1996 (see *Theatre World* Volume 52, page 92).

Above: *Frederick Weller and Ron Livingston in* In a Dark Dark House *(photo by Joan Marcus)*

Below: *Lynn Collins and Stephen Kunken in* A Very Common Procedure *(photo by Joan Marcus)*

*Gerry Bamman as Richard M. Nixon and Steve Mellor as Henry A. Kissinger in* Nixon's Nixon *(photo by Joan Marcus)*

**A Very Common Procedure** by Courtney Baron; Director, Michael Greif; Sets, Robin Vest; Costumes, Miranda Hoffman; Lighting, Tyler Micoleau; Original Music & Sound, Fabian Obispo; PSM, Amy McCraney; ASM, Christina Elefante; Cast: Amir Arison (Dr. Anil Patel), Lynn Collins (Carolyn Goldenhersch), Stephen Kunken (Michael Goldenhersch)
New York premiere of a new play presented without intermission; Lucille Lortel Theatre; January 31–March 10, 2007 (Opened February 14); 40 performances.

**In a Dark Dark House** by Neil LaBute; Director, Carolyn Cantor; Sets, Beowulf Boritt; Costumes, Jenny Mannis; Lighting, Ben Stanton; Sound, Robert Kaplowitz; PSM, Joel Rosen; ASM, Elizabeth Wiesner Paige; Assistant Director, Sari Kamin; Cast: Louisa Krause (Jennifer), Ron Livingston (Drew), Frederick Weller (Terry)
World premiere of a new play presented without intermission; Lucille Lortel Theatre; May 16–July 7, 2007 (Opened June 7); 63 performances.

## Manhattan Theatre Club

Thirty-fifth Season

Artistic Director, Lynne Meadow; Executive Producer, Barry Grove; General Manager, Florie Seery; Artistic Development, Paige Evans; Artistic Operations, Mandy Greenfield; Consultant, Daniel Sullivan; Artistic Administration, Amy Gilkes Loe; Casting, Nancy Piccione, David Caparelliotis; Literary Manager, Emily Shooltz; Director of Musical Theatre, Clifford Lee Johnson III; Development, Jill Turner Lloyd; Marketing, Debra A. Waxman; Finance, Jeffrey Bledsoe; Associate General Manager, Lindsey Brooks Sag; Education, David Shookhoff: Subscriber Services, Robert Allenberg; Production Manager, Ryan McMahon; Lighting and Sound Supervisor, Matthew T. Gross; Properties Supervisor, Scott Laule; Costume Supervisor, Erin Hennessy Dean; Company Manager, Erin Moeller; Press, Boneau/Bryan-Brown, Jim Byk, Aaron Meier, Heath Schwartz, Christine Olver

**Regrets Only** by Paul Rudnick; Director, Christopher Ashley; Set, Michael Yeargan; Costumes, William Ivey Long; Lighting, Natasha Katz; Sound, John Gromada; PSMs, Martha Donaldson, Donald Fried; Stage Manager, Kyle Gates; Choreographer, Daniel Pelzig; Hair/Wigs, Paul Huntley; Makeup, Angelina Avallone; Cast: Christine Baranski (Tibby McCullough), Diane Davis (Spencer McCullough), George Grizzard (Hank Hadley), Jackie Hoffman (Myra Kesselman), Siân Phillips (Marietta Claypoole), David Rasche (Jack McCullough), Mary Testa (Myra Kesselman from December 9–January 9); Understudies: Kit Flanagan (Tibby), Sofia Jean Gomez (Spencer), Terry Layman (Hank/Jack), Patricia O'Connell (Marietta/Myra)
Setting: The McCullough's Park Avenue penthouse, the present. World premiere of a play presented in two acts; City Center Stage I; October 19, 2006–January 28, 2007 (Opening Night November 14); 36 previews, 75 performances.

*George Grizzard and Christine Baranski in* Regrets Only
*(photo by Joan Marcus)*

**The American Pilot** by David Greig; Director, Lynne Meadow; Set, Derek McLane; Costumes, Ilona Somogyi; Lighting, Christopher Akerlind; Sound, Obadiah Eaves; Fight Director, J. David Brimmer; PSM, Donald Fried; Stage Manager, Brendan M. Fay; Musician, Benny Koonyevsky; Dialect Coach, Charlotte Fleck; Special Effects, Waldo Warshaw; Assistant Director, Hilary Adams; Cast: Geoffrey Arend (The Translator), Anjali Bhimani (Evie), Brian Bielawski (Soldier #1), Yusef Bulos (The Trader), Josh Casaubon (Soldier #2), Ron Domingo (The Farmer), Aaron Stanton (The American Pilot), Rita Wolf (Sarah), Waleed F. Zuaiter (The Captain); Understudies: Aadya Bedi (Evie/Sarah), Brian Bielawski (The American Pilot), Arian Moayed (Translator/Trader/Soldiers #1 and #2), Thom Rivera (Farmer/Captain/Soldiers #1 and #2)
Place: A small farm, high up in a rural valley, in a country that has been mired in civil war and conflict for many years. American Premiere of a play presented in two acts; City Center Stage II; November 2–December 31, 2006 (Opened November 21); 20 previews, 47 performances.

*Waleed F. Zuaiter and Yusef Bulos (standing), Geoffrey Arend and Aaron Staton (seated) in* The American Pilot *(photo by Carol Rosegg)*

**Our Leading Lady** by Charles Busch; Director, Lynne Meadow; Set, Santo Loquasto; Costumes, Jane Greenwood; Lighting, Brian MacDevitt; Sound, Scott Lehrer; Wig Design, Tom Watson; Makeup, Angelina Avallone; Fight Director, J. David Brimmer; PSM, Donald Fried; Stage Manager, Alison De Santis; Assistant Director, Hilary Adams; Cast: Kate Mulgrew (Laura Keene), Maxwell Caulfield (Harry Hawk), Reed Birney (Gavin De Chamblay), Kristine Nielsen (Verbena De Chamblay), Barbara Bryne (Maude Bentley), Billy Wheelan (W.J. Ferguson), Ann Duquesnay (Madame Wu-Chan), Amy Rutberg (Clementine Smith), J.R. Horne (Major Hopwood); Understudies: Robin Moseley (Maude/Verbena), Rita Rehn (Laura), James Riordan (Gavin/Harry/Major Hopwood)
Time: April 1865. Place: In and around Ford's Theatre in Washington, D.C. World Premiere of a play presented in two acts; City Center Stage II; February 22- April 29, 2007 (Opened March 20): 29 previews, 48 performances.

*Kate Mulgrew and Cast in* Our Leading Lady *(photo by Joan Marcus)*

*Alison Pill and Jeff Daniels in* Blackbird *(photo by Joan Marcus)*

**Blackbird** by David Harrower; Produced by special arrangement with Michael Edwards and Carole Winter; Director, Joe Mantello; Set, Scott Pask; Costumes, Laura Bauer; Lighting, Paul Gallo; Sound, Darron L. West; Fight Director, J. David Brimmer; PSM, Jill Cordle; Stage Manager, Neil Krasnow; Cast: Alison Pill (Una), Jeff Daniels (Ray); Understudies: Stephanie Janssen (Una), John Ottavino (Ray)

American premiere of a play presented without intermission; City Center Stage I; March 15–June 10, 2007 (Opened April 10); 29 previews, 68 performances. Originally presented by the Edinburgh International Festival, August 2005, and at the Albery Theatre in the West End, February 13, 2006.

# Mint Theater Company

Fifteenth Season

Artistic Director, Jonathan Bank; General Manager, Sherri Kotimsky; Box Office Manager, Toni Anita Hull; Casting, Stuart Howard, Amy Schecter & Paul Hardt; Technical Director, Evan Schlossberg; Press, David Gersten and Associates

**Susan and God** by Rachel Crothers; Director, Jonathan Bank; Sets, Nathan Heverin; Costumes, Clint Ramos; Lighting, Josh Bradford; Sound, Jane Shaw; Props, Judi Guralnick; Dramaturg, Heather J. Violanti; Cast: Opal Alladin (Irene Burroughs), Jennifer Blood (Blossom Trexel), Mathieu Cornillon (Leeds), Alex Crammer (Clyde Rochester), Timothy Deenihan (Barrie Trexel), Katie Firth (Charlotte Marleigh), Leslie Hendrix (Susan Trexel), Anthony Newfield (Hutchins Stubbs), Jordan Simmons (Leonora Stubbs), Al Sapienza (Michael O'Hara)
Revival of a play presented in three acts; June 6–July 30, 2006 (Opened June 18); 57 performances.

Tony Newfield, Al Sapienza, and Leslie Hendrix in Susan and God (photo by Richard Termine)

**John Ferguson** by St. John Ervine; Director, Martin Platt; Sets, Bill Clarke; Costumes, Mattie Ullrich; Lighting, Jeff Nellis; Sound, Lindsay Jones; Props, Judi Guralnick; PSM, Heather Prince; ASM, Kimberly Ann McCann; Dialects/Dramaturgy, Amy Stoller; Associate Costumes, Randi Fowler; Assistant Sound, Will Pickens; Cast: Joyce Cohen (Sarah Ferguson), Robertson Carricart (John Ferguson), Marion Woods (Hannah Ferguson), Mark Saturno (James Caesar), Greg Thornton (Henry Witherow), John Keating (John McGrath), Justin Schultz (Andrew Ferguson), Terrence Markovich (Sam Mawhinney/Sergeant Kernighan), Adam Branson (Constable)
Setting: The Kitchen of John Ferguson, in Ulster County, Ireland, late summer in the 1880s. Revival of a play presented in four acts with one intermission; September–October 29, 2006 (Opened September 25); 52 performances.

**The Madras House** by Harley Granville-Barker; Director, Gus Kaikkonen; Sets, Charles Morgan; Costumes, Clint Ramos; Lighting, William Armstrong; Sound, Ellen Mandel; Wigs/Hair, Gerard James Kelly; Props, Jesse Dreikosen; PSM, Allison Deutsch; ASM, Andrea Jo Martin; Dialects and Dramaturgy, Amy Stoller; Associate Costumes, Jessica Pabst; Sound Consultant, Elizabeth Rhodes; Cast: Jonathan Hogan (Henry Huxtable), Laurie Kennedy (Katherine Huxtable/Miss Chancellor), Lisa Bostnar (Minnie Huxtable/Jessica Madras), Mary Bacon (Clara Huxtable/Maid/Marian Yates/Mannequin), Angela Reed (Julia Huxtable/

Robertson Carricart in John Ferguson (photo by Richard Termine)

Freda Brigstock), Allison McLemore (Emma Huxtable/Mannequin), Pamela McVeagh (Jane Huxtable/Mannequin), George Morfogen (Constantine Madras), Roberta Maxwell (Amelia Madras), Thomas M. Hammond (Philip Madras), Mark L. Montgomery (Major Hippisly Thomas), Kraig Swartz (William Brigstock/Mr. Windelsham), Scott Romstadt (Belhaven), Ross Bickell (Eustace Perrin State)
Setting: London, October 1910. Revival of a play presented in four acts with one intermission; January 3–March 25, 2007 (Opened February 15); 55 performances.

**Return of the Prodigal** by St. John Hankin; Director, Jonathan Bank; Sets/Costumes, Clint Ramos; Lighting, Tyler Micoleau; Sound, Jane Shaw; Associate Set/Props, Craig Napoliello; Associate Costumes, Hwi-Won Lee; PSM, Kimothy Cruse; ASM, Rebecca C. Monroe; Cast: Richard Kline (Samuel Jackson), Tandy Cronyn (Mrs. Jackson), Bradford Cover (Henry Jackson), Roderick Hill (Eustace Jackson), Leah Curney (Violet Jackson), Lee Moore (Sir John Faringford), Kate Levy (Lady Farrington), Margot White (Stella Langford), W. Alan Nebelthau (Dr. Glaisher), Cecelia Riddett (Mrs. Pratt), Robin Haynes (Baines the butler)
Setting: Chedleigh Court, the Jacksons' house in Gloucestershire, England; Revival of a play presented in four acts with one intermission; May 23–July 15, 2007 (Opened June 6); 55 performances.

George Morfogen, Roberta Maxwell, and Thomas Hammond in The Madras House (photo by Richard Termine)

# The New Group

Eleventh Season

Artistic Director, Scott Elliott; Executive Director, Geoffrey Rich, Managing Producer, Barrack Evans; Development, Oliver Dow; Associate Artistic Director, Ian Morgan; Marketing, Wren Longo; Company Manager, Ted Hall/Tim McCann; Business Manager, Elisabeth Bayer; Individual Giving, Barbara Toy; Production Supervisor, Peter R. Feuchtwanger/PRF Productions; Casting, Judy Henderson; Press, The Karpel Group, Billy Zavelson, Darren Molovinsky

**Everything's Turning Into Beautiful** by Seth Zvi Rosenfeld; Songs by Jimmie James; Director, Carl Forsman; Sets, Beowulf Boritt; Costumes, Theresa Squire; Lighting, Josh Bradford; Sound, Daniel Baker; General Manager, Amanda Brandes; Associate Producer, Jill Bowman; Assistant Director, Jocelyn Kuritsky; PSM, Erin Grenier; ASM, Dave Polato; Props, R. Jay Duckworth; Cast: Daphne Rubin-Vega (Brenda), Malik Yoba (Sam)
Time and place: New York City, Christmas Eve. World premiere of a new play with music presented in two acts; Acorn Theatre on Theatre Row; July 17–September 2, 2006 (Opened August 3); 45 performances. (This production was the final show of the tenth season).

Above: *Cynthia Nixon in* The Prime of Miss Jean Brodie *(photo by Carol Rosegg)*

Below: *Wallace Shawn in* The Fever *(photo by Carol Rosegg)*

*Daphne Rubin-Vega and Malik Yoba in* Everything's Turning Into Beautiful *(photo by Carol Rosegg)*

**The Prime of Miss Jean Brodie** by Jay Presson Allen, adapted from the novel by Muriel Spark; Director, Scott Elliott; Sets, Derek McLane; Costumes, Eric Becker; Lights, Jason Lyons; Sound, Daniel Baker; Composer, Tom Kochan; PSM, Valerie A. Peterson; Assistant Director, Marie Masters; Dialect Coach, Stephen Gabis; ASM, Fran Rubenstein; Properties, Maribeau Briggs; Hair Design, Jeff Francis; Wig Design, Paul Huntley; Cast: Emily Bicks (Schoolgirl), Lisa Emery (Miss Mackay), Zoe Kazan (Sandy), Cynthia Nixon (Jean Brodie), Caity Quinn (Schoolgirl), Sarah Steele (Monica), Ritchie Coster (Teddy Lloyd), Betsy Hogg (Mary MacGregor), Caroline Lagerfelt (Sister Helena), John Pankow (Gordon Lowther), Matthew Rauch (Mr. Perry), Halley Wegryn Gross (Jenny)
Revival of the play with music presented in two acts; Acorn Theatre on Theatre Row; September 20–December 9, 2006 (Opened October 9); 83 performances.

**The Fever** by Wallace Shawn; Director, Scott Elliott; Sets, Derek McLane; Costumes, Eric Becker; Lighting, Jennifer Tipton; Sound, Bruce Odland; PSM, Valerie A. Peterson; Properties, Jay Duckworth; Cast: Wallace Shawn (The Traveler)
Time: The present. A solo performance play presented without intermission; Acorn Theatre on Theatre Row; January 9–March 1, 2007 (Opened January 31); 61 performances.

**The Accomplices** by Bernard Weinraub; Director, Ian Morgan; Set Design, Beowulf Boritt; Costumes, Theresa Squire; Lighting, Jeff Croiter; Sound Design/Original Music, Matt Sherwin; PSM, Valerie A. Peterson; Assistant Director, Azar Kazemi; Company Manager, Tim McCann; Literary Associate, James Gittins; ASM, Fran Rubenstein; Dialect Coach, Stephen Gabis; Properties, Susan Barras; Cast: Catherine Curtin (Laura Houghteling/Theresa), Jon DeVries (FDR/Ben Hecht), Robert Hogan (Breckenridge Long), Zoe Lister-Jones (Betty), David Margulies (Rabbi Stephen Wise), Andrew Polk (Samuel Merlin/John Pehle/Emanuel Celler), Daniel Sauli (Peter Bergson), Mark Zeisler (Immigration Officer/Samuel Rosenman), Mark Zimmerman (Henry Morgenthau Jr.)
Setting: New York City and Washington, D.C. from 1940–1944. A drama inspired by real events presented in two acts; Acorn Theatre on Theatre Row; March 20–May 5, 2007 (Opened April 9): 50 performances.

# New York Gilbert & Sullivan Players

Thirty-third Season

Artistic Director/General Manager and Director/Conductor/Sets, Albert Bergeret; Sales/Assistant General Manager, David Wannen; Assistant Music Director, Andrea Stryker-Rodda; Technical Director/PSM, David Sigafoose; Press, Peter Cromarty; Librettos by Sir William S. Gilbert; Music by Sir Arthur Sullivan; Lighting, Sally Small; Costumes, Gail Wofford; ASM, Jessica Hertz; Dance Captain, Michael Levesque

**The Yeomen of the Guard** Choreography, Janis Ansley-Ungar; Co-Sets, Richard Manfredi; Co-Costumes, Jan Holland; Cast: Keith Jurosko (Sir Richard Cholmondely), David Root (Colonel Fairfax), Richard Alan Holmes (Sergeant Meryll), David Michael Chase (Leonard Meryll), Stephen Quint (Jack Point), David Wannen (Wilfred Shadbolt), Lucian Russell (The Headsman), Daniel Lockwood (First Yeoman), Alexander Elisa (Second Yeoman), Laurelyn Watson Chase (Elsie Maynard), Erika Person (Phoebe Meryll), Angela Smith (Dame Carruthers), Meredith Borden (Kate), Ensemble of Yeoman: Ted Bouton, Louis Dall'Ava, Michael Galante, Alan Hill Michael Levesque, Paul Sigrist; Citizens of the Tower: Kimberly Deana Bennett, Susan Case, Michael Connolly, Donata Cucinotta, Dianna Dollman, Shana Farr, Alena Gerst Dailey, Katie Hall, Lynelle Johnson, David Macaluso, James Mills, Lance Olds, Lauren Pastorek, Monique Pelletier, Fausto Pineda, Lauren Wenegrat, William Whitefield
Setting: Tower Green, London. Time: Sixteenth Century. Revival of the operetta presented in two acts; New York City Center; January 5–13, 2007; 3 performances

*Louis Dall'Ava, Michael Scott Harris, and Keith Jurosko in* Yeoman of the Guard *(photo by Carol Rosegg)*

**The Mikado** Co-Conductor, Jeffrey Kresky; Sets, Albere; Co-Costumes, Kayko Nakamura; Cast: Keith Jurosko (The Mikado of Japan), Michael Scott Harris/Daniel Lockwood (Nanki-Poo), Stephen Quint/David Macaluso (Ko-Ko), Louis Dall'Ava (Pooh-Bah), Edward Prostak (Pish-Tush), Jennifer Piacenti/Elizabeth Hillebrand (Yum-Yum), Melissa Attebury (Pitti-Sing), Robin Bartunek/Lauren Wenegrat (Peep-Bo), Ensemble: David Auxier, Kimberly Deana Bennett, Susan Case, Derrick Cobey, Michael Connolly, Michael Galante, Robert Garner, Alena Gerst Dailey, Kathleen Gluber Tarello, Alan Hill, Morgan James, Lynelle Johnson, Jenny Millsap, Chris-Ian Sanchez, Rebecca O'Sullivan, Erica Person, Paul Sigrist, Angela Smith, David Wannen, William Whitefield; Swings: Michael Levesque, Lauren Wenegrat
Scene: A Japanese Garden. Revival of the operetta presented in two acts; New York City Center; January 6–14, 2007; 6 performances

*Laurelyn Watson Chase and Stephen Quint in* The Mikado *(photo by Carol Rosegg)*

**The Rose of Persia** Libretto by Basil Hood; Choreography, Janis Ansley-Ungar; Co-Costumes, Louis Dall'Ava; Cast: David Wannen (The Sultan Mahmoud of Persia), Richard Alan Holmes (Hassan), Michael Scott Harris (Yussuf), Edward Prostak (Abdallah), David Auxier (The Grand Vizier), Paul Sigrist (The Physician-in-Chief), Louis Dall'Ava (The Royal Executioner), Ted Bouton (A Soldier of the Royal Guard), Laurelyn Watson Chase (The Sultana Zubeydeh), Carol Ambrogio (Scent-of-Lillies), Kimberly Deana Bennett (Heart's Desire), Megan Loomis (Honey-of-Life), Angela Smith (Dancing Sunbeam), Meredith Borden (Blush-of-Morning), Lauren Pastorek (Oasis-in-the-Desert), Rebecca O'Sullivan (Moon-upon-the-Waters), Alena Gerst Dailey (Song-of-Nightingales), Jenny Millsap (Whisper-of-the-West-Wind); Ensemble: Michael Connolly, Michael Galante, Alena Gerst Dailey, Katie Hall, Alan Hill, Michael Levesque, Daniel Lockwood, David Macaluso, Jenny Millsap, Lance Olds, Rebecca O'Sullivan, Monique Pelletier, Jennifer Piacenti, Lauren Wenegrat
Setting: Court of Hassan's House and the Audience Hall of the Sultan's Palace. An operetta performed in two acts; New York City Center; January 11, 2007; 1 performance.

# New York Theatre Workshop

Twenty-seventh Season

Artistic Director, James C. Nicola; Managing Director, Lynn Moffat; Associate Artistic Director, Linda S. Chapman; Casting, Jack Doulin; Planning/Development, Carl M. Sylvestre; Finance/Administration, Robert Wayne; Marketing/Communications, Robert Marlin; General Manager, Harry J. McFadden; Associate Development, Michaela Goldhaber; Education, Jen Zoble; Marketing/Communications Associate, Cathy Popowytsch; Literary Associate, Geoffrey Scott; Artistic Associates, Michael Greif, Michael Friedman, Ruben Polendo; Production Manager, Michael Casselli, Associate Production Manager, Laura Mroczkowski; Master Electrician, John J. Anselmo Jr.; Technical Director, Efran Delgadillo Jr.; Costume Shop Supervisor, Jeffrey Wallach; Sound Engineer, Asa Wember; Press, Richard Kornberg, Don Summa

**El Conquistador!** Text by Thaddeus Phillips and Tatiana Mallarino, in collaboration with Victor Mallarino; Produced in association with Lucidity Suitcase Intercontinental; Director, Tatiana Mallarino; Sets, Thaddeus Phillips; Lighting/Scenic Engineering, Jeff Sugg; Video Design, Austin Switser; Sound, Jamie McElhinney; PSM, Rachel Zack; Cast: Thaddeus Phillips (Polonio); Video Cast: Christina Campuzano (Johanna), Luis Fernando Hoyos (Mauricio), Helena Mallarino (Beatriz), Tatiana Mallarino (Aminta), Victor Mallarino (Didier), Antonio Sanint (El Loco)
Setting: Bogatá, Columbia, the present. New York premiere of a play/foreign film/telenovela performed in Spanish with English surtitles without intermission; September 20–October 22, 2006 (Opened October 3); 36 performances.

*Thaddeus Phillips in* El Conquistador *(photo by Carol Rosegg)*

Right: *Austin Lysy, Patch Darragh ,and Kandiss Edmundson in*
All That I Will Ever Be *(photo by Carol Rosegg)*

**Kaos** Concept, direction, and choreography by Martha Clarke, text adaptation by Frank Pugliese, based on the stories of Luigi Pirandello and the film *Kaos* by the Taviani Brothers; Sets, Scott Pask; Costumes, Donna Zakowska; Lighting, Christopher Akerlind; Projection Design, Tal Yarden; Music Direction, Jill Jaffe, John T. La Barbera; Dramaturgy, Giovanni Papotto; PSM, Anita Ross; ASM, Cyrille Blackburn; Cast: Felix Blaska, Sophie Bortolussi, George de la Pena, Daria Deflorian, Vito Di Bella, Lorenzo Iacona, Jim Iorio, Gabrielle Malone, Matthew Mohr, Rocco Sisto, Cristina Spina, Rebecca Wender, Robert Wersinger, Julia Wilkins; Musicians: Irving Grossman (trumpet), John T. La Barbera (mandolin/guitar), Richard Sosinsky (contrabass)
A theatrical work with music, dance movement, and text performed in Italian with English titles without intermission; November 10–December 31, 2006 (Opened December 4); 57 performances.

*The Cast of* Kaos *(photo by Carol Rosegg)*

**All That I Will Ever Be** by Alan Ball; Director, Jo Bonney; Sets, Neil Patel; Costumes, Emilio Sosa; Lighting, David Lander; Sound, Darron L. West; Fight Choreography, J. Steven White; PSM, Larry K. Ash; ASM, Tom Dooley; Cast: Patch Darragh (White Guy/Bart/Eddie/Waiter), Kandiss Edmundson (Cynthia/Beth), Austin Lysy (Dwight), Peter Macdissi (Omar), David Margulies (Raymond), Victor Slezak (Chuck Bennett/Phil); Understudies: Marsha Stephanie Blake (Cynthia/Beth), Philip Carlson (Raymond & Chuck Bennett/Phil), Ramiz Monsef (Omar), Nick Westrate (Dwight & White Guy/Bart/Eddie/Waiter)
Setting: Los Angeles, now. World premiere of a new play presented in two acts; January 17–March 11, 2007 (Opened February 6); 60 performances.

**All The Wrong Reasons – A True Story of Neo-Nazis, Drug Smuggling and Undying Love** by John Fugelsang; Director, Pam MacKinnon; Sets/Costumes, Kaye Voyce; Lighting, Mark Barton; Sound, Jeremy J. Lee; PSM, Odessa "Niki" Spruill; ASM, Richard A. Hodge; Cast: John Fugelsang
A solo performance play presented without intermission; March 23–May 6, 2007 (Opened April 15); 50 performances.

# Pan Asian Repertory Theatre

Thirtieth Season

Artistic Producing Director, Tisa Chang; Artistic Associate, Ron Nakahara; General Manager, Fran Smyth; Producing Assistant, Abby Felder; Marketing/Education Associate, Steven Osborn; Resident Workshop Instructor, Ernest Abuba; Resident Fight Coordinator, Michael G. Chin; Bookkeeper, Rosemary Khan; Marketing Consultant, Reva Cooper; Crew Chief, Jared Welch; Master Electrician, Paul Jones; Photo Archivist, Corky Lee; Administrative Assistant, Shigeko Suga; Press, Keith Sherman and Associates

**Yohen** by Philip Kan Gotanda; Director, Seret Scott; Sets, Charlie Corcoran; Costumes, Carol Pelletier; Lighting, Kazuko Oguma; Sound, Cliff Caruthers; Stage Manager, T. Rick Jones; Production Coordinator, Abby Felder; Yohen Pottery, Peter Callas; Pottery, Olivia Sullivan Ridgeway; Cast: Dian Kobayashi (Sumi), David Fonteno (James)
Time: 1986. Place: Gardena, California. New York premiere of a new play presented without intermission; West End Theatre; October 14–November 5, 2006 (Opened October 18); 23 performances.

**Tea** by Velina Hasu Houston; Director, Tina Chen; Sets, Charlie Corcoran; Costumes, Carol Pelletier; Lighting, Victor En Yu Tan; Sound, Genevieve-Marie C. Nicolas; PSM, Elis C Arroyo; ASM, James W. Carringer; Cast: Ako (Atsuko Yamamoto), Akiko Hiroshima (Terruko MacKenzie), Karen Tsen Lee (Himiko Hamilton), Jo Shui (Setsuko Banks), Momo Yashima (Chizuye Juarez)
Time: 1968. Place: Japan, Kansas, and the Netherworld. Revival of a play presented without intermission; West End Theatre; May 20–June 17, 2007 (Opened May 30); 29 performances. Presented as part of the first National Asian American Theatre Festival; originally produced by the Manhattan Theatre Club on October 6, 1987.

Right: *David Fonteno and Dian Kobayashi in* Yohen *(photo by Corky Lee)*

Below: *Jo Shui, Ako, Momo Yashima, Karen Tsen Lee, and Akiko Hiroshima in* Tea *(photo by Corky Lee)*

# Pearl Theatre Company

Twenty-third Season

Artistic Director, Shepard Sobel; Associate Director, Joanne Camp; Producing Director, Mary Ann Ehlshlager; Marketing/Press Director, Heather Morris; General Manager, Shira Beckerman; Assistant to the Artistic Director, Craig Evans; Dramaturg, Kate Farrington; Education, Sean McNall; Audience Services, Colin McKenna; Costume Shop Manager, Katy Conover; Speech and Text Coach, Robert Neff Williams; Casting, Rachel Botchan, Joanne Camp; Season Set Designer, Harry Feiner; Season Lighting Designer, Stephen Petrilli; Technical Director, Gary Levinson

**Arms and the Man** by George Bernard Shaw; Director, Gus Kaikkonen; Stage Manager, Lisa Ledwich; Costumes, Sam Fleming; Sound, Sara Bader; Properties, Melanie Mulder; Stage Management Assistants, Amy Dalba, Autumn Joan Tilson; Cast: Rachel Botchan (Raina Petkoff), Robin Leslie Brown (Catherine Petkoff), Hana Moon (Louka), Bradford Cover (Captain Bluntschli), Richard Bolster (Russian Officer), T.J. Edwards (Nicola), Dominic Cuskern (Major Paul Petkoff), Noel Vélez (Major Sergius Saranoff)
Setting: A small town in Bulgaria during the Serbo-Bulgarian War, November 1885 and March 1886. Revival of the play presented in three acts; Theatre 80 St. Marks Place; September 29–December 23, 2006 (Opened October 8) in repertory with *School for Wives*; 10 previews, 28 performances.

*Rachel Botchan and Bradford Cover in* Arms and the Man
*(photo by Gregory Costanzo)*

**School for Wives** by Moliére, translated by Earle Edgerton; Director, Shepard Sobel; Stage Manager, Yvonne Perez; Costumes, Frank Champa; Sound, Sara Bader; Properties, Melanie Mulder; Commedia Coach; Chris Bayes; Stage Management Assistants, Amy Dalba, Autumn Joan Tilson; Cast: Dominic Cuskern (Chrysalde), Dan Daily (Arnolphe), Bradford Cover (Alain), Rachel Botchan (Georgette), Hana Moon (Agnes), Noel Vélez (Horace), T.J. Edwards (Notary/ Oronte)
Setting: A city square in Rouen. Revival of a play presented in two acts; Theatre 80 St. Marks Place; November 10–December 24, 2006 (Opened November 19) in repertory with *Arms and the Man*; 10 previews, 28 performances.

**Toys in the Attic** by Lillian Hellman; Director, Austin Pendleton; Costumes, Barbara A. Bell; Sound, Sara Bader; Dialect Coach, Amy Stoller; PSM, Pamela Edington; Cast: Rachel Botchan (Carrie Berniers), Robin Leslie Brown (Anna Berniers), Joanne Camp (Albertine Prine), Robert Colston (Henry), R.J. Foster (Mover), Jon Froehlich (Mover 1), Sean McNall (Julian Berniers), Marcus Naylor (Gus), Ivy Vahanian (Lily), William White (Taxi Driver/Mover 2); Understudies: R.J. Foster (Gus), Jon Froehlich (Julian), William White (Henry)
Setting: New Orleans, 1957. Revival of a play in three acts presented with one intermission; Theatre 80 St. Marks Place; January 5–February 18, 2007 (Opening Night January 14); 10 previews, 30 performances.

**The Cave Dwellers** by William Saroyan; Director, Shepard Sobel; Costumes, Devon Painter; Sound, Jane Shaw; Stage Manager, Lisa Ledwich; Cast: Francile Albright (A Woman with a Dog), Barthelemy Atsin (Gorky/The Young Opponent), Collin Batten (The Silent Boy/A Young Man), Dominic Cuskern (The Wrecking Crew Boss), R.J. Foster (Jamie), Robert Hock (The King), Mahira Kakkar (The Girl), Sarah Lemp (The Mother/The Young Queen), Sean McNall (The Father), Marcus Naylor (The Duke), Carol Schultz (The Queen); Understudies: Francile Albright (The Queen), Barthelemy Atsin (The Duke), Collin Batten (The Father), R.J. Foster (The Boss/Gorky), Sarah Lemp (The Girl)
Setting: An abandoned theatre on the Lower East Side, New York, mid 1950s. Revival of a play presented in two acts; Theatre 80 St. Marks Place; February 23–April 8, 2007 (Opened March 4); 10 previews, 30 performances.

*Robert Hock and Mahira Kakkar in* The Cave Dwellers
*(photo by Gregory Costanzo)*

**Biography** by S.N. Behrman; Director, J.R. Sullivan; Costumes, Liz Covey; Sound, Jane Shaw; PSM, Dale Smallwood; Cast: Dominic Cuskern (Melchior Feydak), Tom Galantich (Leander Nolan), Carolyn McCormick (Marion Froude), George McDaniel (Orrin Kinnicott), Sean McNall (Richard Kurt), Fletcher McTaggart (Warwick Wilson), Kyra Miller (Slade Kinnicott), Carol Schultz (Minnie)
Setting: Marion Froude's Fifty-Seventh Street home and studio, over five weeks in 1932. Revival of a play presented in three acts with two intermissions; Theatre 80 St. Marks Place; April 13–May 20, 2007 (Opened April 22); 11 previews, 32 performances.

## Playwrights Horizons

Thirty-sixth Season

Artistic Director, Tim Sanford; Managing Director, Leslie Marcus; General Manager, William Russo; New Play Development, Lisa Timmel; Musical Theatre, Christie Evangelisto; Casting, Alaine Alldaffer; Production Manager, Christopher Boll; Development, Jill Garland; Controller, Daniel C. Smith; Marketing, Eric Winick; Ticket Central, Mike Rafael; School Director, Helen R. Cook; General Management Associate, Sandra Gardner; Assistant to the Artistic Director, Julie Foh; Assistant to the Managing Director/Production Company Manager, Caroline Aquino; Associate Production Manager, Shannon Nicole Case; Technical Director, Brian Coleman; Press, The Publicity Office, Bob Fennell, Marc Thibodeau, Michael S. Borowski, Candi Adams, Matt Fasano

**The Pain and the Itch** by Bruce Norris; Director, Anna D. Shapiro; Sets, Dan Ostling, Costumes, Jennifer von Mayrhauser; Lighting, Donald Holder; Sound, Rob Milburn and Michael Bodeen; PSM, Susie Cordon; ASM, Allison Sommers; Cast: Mia Barron (Kelly), Aya Cash (Kalina), Peter Jay Fernandez (Mr. Hadid), Ada-Marie L. Gutierrez/Vivien Kells (Kayla), Jayne Houdyshell (Carol), Reg Rogers (Cash), Christopher Evan Welch (Clay)
Setting: Thanksgiving. New York premiere of a new play presented in two acts; Mainstage Theatre; September 1–October 15, 2006 (Opened September 21); 48 performances. World premiere at the Steppenwolf Theatre, Chicago, June 30–August 28, 2005

*Ada-Marie L. Gutierrez and Jayne Houdyshell in* The Pain and the Itch *(photo by Joan Marcus)*

**Blue Door** by Tanya Barfield; Director, Leigh Silverman; Sets, Narelle Sissons; Costumes, Toni-Leslie James; Lighting, Mary Louise Geiger; Sound, Ken Travis; Original Music, Daryl Waters; Production Stage Manager, Amy McCraney; Cast: Reg E. Cathey (Lewis), Andre Holland (Simon/Rex/Jesse)
New York premiere of a new play presented without intermission; Peter Jay Sharp Theater; September 28–October 29, 2006 (Opened October 8); 37 performances. Originally produced at the South Coast Repertory Theatre, Costa Mesa, California.

*Reg E. Cathey and Andre Holland in* Blue Door *(photo by Joan Marcus)*

**Floyd and Clea Under the Western Sky** Book and lyrics by David Cale, music by Jonathan Kreisberg and David Cale; Director, Joe Calarco; Sets, David Korins; Costumes, Anne Kenney; Lighting, Chris Lee; Sound, Ken Travis; Music Director and Orchestrations, Jonathan Kreisberg; PSM, Emily N. Wells; ASM, Robyn Henry; Associate Set Design, Rod Lemmond; Cast: David Cale (Floyd Duffner), Mary Faber (Clea Johnson); The Band: Dylan Schiavone (guitars/piano), Jimmy Heffernan (dobro/pedal Steel), Brad Russell (acoustic/electric bass), Bill Campbell (drums/percussion)
Musical Numbers: burntagel@aol.com, One Foot in the Real World, I Dread the Night, Greedy, Safety Net, I'll Be Your Secret, Can I Stay Awhile, Help's on the Way, White Cowboy Hat, A Simple Life, White Cowboy Hat (reprise), Would You Give a Damn?, Left Hook, [We're in it for] The Long Haul
Setting: Great Falls, Montana, and Austin, Texas. New York premiere of a musical presented without intermission; Mainstage Theatre; November 10–December 17, 2006 (Opened December 5); 43 performances. World premiere produced by The Goodman Theatre (Chicago, Illinois), April 2005.

Right: *Mary Faber and David Kale in* Floyd and Clea
*(photo by Joan Marcus)*

**Frank's Home** by Richard Nelson; Presented in association with the Goodman Theatre (Chicago, Illinois); Director, Robert Falls; Sets, Thomas Lynch; Costumes, Susan Hilferty; Lighting, Michael Philippi; Original Music and Sound, Richard Woodbury; PSM, Barclay Stiff; ASM, Brandon Kahn; Cast: Chris Henry Coffey (Kenneth), Holley Fain (Helen Girvin), Mary Beth Fisher (Miriam Noel), Maggie Siff (Catherine), Jeremy Strong (William), Peter Weller (Frank Lloyd Wright), Jay Whittaker (Lloyd), Harris Yulin (Louis Sullivan)

Time: August 31–September 2, 1923. Place: The grounds of Olive Hill, Hollywood, California. New York premiere of a new play presented in two acts; Mainstage Theatre; January 13–February 18, 2007 (Opened January 30); 44 performances.

*Mary Beth Fisher, Peter Weller, Harris Yulin, and Maggie Siff in* Frank's Home *(photo by Michael Brosilow)*

**Essential Self-Defense** by Adam Rapp; Produced in association with Edge Theatre Company (Carolyn Cantor, Artistic Director; David Korins, Producer; Ted Rounsaville, General Manager); Director, Carolyn Cantor; Sets, David Korins; Costumes, Miranda Hoffman; Lighting, Ben Stanton; Sound, Eric Shim; Original Music and Lyrics, Ray Rizzo, Adam Rapp, and Lucas Papaelias; Music Arrangements, Ray Rizzo; Fight Director, Joseph Travers; Wigs/Hair/Makeup, Erin Kennedy Lunsford; PSM, Charles M. Turner III; ASM, Courtney James; Cast: Cheryl Lynn Bowers (Sorrell), Guy Boyd (Chuck the Barber), Michael Chernus (Isaak Glinka), Joel Marsh Garland (Klieg the Butcher), Heather Goldenhersh (Sadie), Lucas Papaelias (Todd/UPS Man/Male Nurse), Ray Rizzo (Bob Beard), Paul Sparks (Yul)

Time: The Present. Place: Bloggs, U.S.A. World premiere of a new play presented in two acts; Peter Jay Sharp Theater; March 15–April 15, 2007 (Opened March 28); 37 performances.

*Heather Goldenhersh and Paul Sparks in* Essential Self Defense *(photo by Joan Marcus)*

**Crazy Mary** by A.R. Gurney; Director, Joe Simpson; Sets, John Lee Beatty; Costumes, Claudia Brown; Lighting Brian Aldous; Original Music, Michael Holland; Wigs, Gerard Kelly; PSM, Janet Takami; ASM, Cambra Overend; Cast: Myra Lucretia Taylor (Pearl), Michael Esper (Skip), Sigourney Weaver (Lydia), Mitchell Greenberg (Jerome), Kristine Nielsen (Mary) Place: The library of a private psychiatric institution on the North Shore of Boston. Time: Today. World premiere of a new play presented in two acts; Mainstage Theatre; May 11–June 26, 2007 (Opened June 3); 50 performances.

*Mitchell Greenberg, Kristine Nielsen, Myra Lucretia Taylor, Michael Esper, and Sigourney Weaver in* Crazy Mary *(photo by Joan Marcus)*

# Primary Stages

Twenty-second Season

Executive Producer, Casey Childs; Artistic Director, Andrew Leynse; Managing Director, Elliot Fox; Associate Artistic Director, Michelle Bossy; Marketing, Louis Bavaro; Development, Erica Raven; Business Manager, Stephanie Coulombe; Production Administrator, Ian Grunes; Production Supervisor, Peter R. Feuchtwanger; Company Manager/Marketing Associate, Jill Simon; Literary Manager, Tessa LaNeve; IT Manager, David L. Goldsmith; Public Relations, Anne Einhorn; Associate to the Artistic Director, Lucy McMichael; Facilities Manager, Keith Daniel; Casting, Stephanie Klapper; Press, Origlio Public Relations, Philip Carrubba

**Indian Blood** by A.R. Gurney; Presented in association with Jamie deRoy; Director, Mark Lamos; Sets, John Arnone; Costumes, Ann Hould-Ward; Lighting, Howell Binkley; Original Music/Sound, John Gromada; Hair, David H. Lawrence; Projections, Leah Gelpe; Fight Director, B.H. Barry; Props Master, Jay Duckworth; PSM, Fredric H. Orner; ASM, Hannah Cohen; Assistant Director, Michael Chamberlin; Associate Lighting, Ryan O'Gara; Cast: Charles Socarides (Eddie), Matthew Arkin (Mr. Kenyon/Uncle Paul), Jeremy Blackman (Lambert), Katherine McGrath (Mrs. Garver/Annie/Mrs. Stawicki), Rebecca Luker (Jane), Jack Gilpin (Harvey), Pamela Payton-Wright (Eddie's Grandmother), John McMartin (Eddie's Grandfather)

Time: Mid-1940s. Place: Buffalo, N.Y. World premiere of a new play presented without intermission; 59E59 Theater A; July 25–September 2, 2006 (Opened August 9); 15 previews, 27 performances. 2007 Outer Critics Circle Award for Best Off-Broadway Play.

**Southern Comforts** by Kathleen Clark; Director, Judith Ivey; Sets, Thomas Lynch; Costumes, Joseph G. Aulisi; Lighting, Brian Nason; Sound, T. Richard Fitzgerald; Music, Paul Schwartz; Fight Director, B.H. Barry; Production Sound, Misha Siegel-Rivers; ASM, Stephanie Gatton; Associate Set Design, Charlie Corcoran; Associate Sound, Carl Casella; Props, Faye Armon, Jay Duckworth, Joel Goss; Cast: Larry Keith (Gus), Penny Fuller (Amanda)

Time: The present. Place: The living room of a Victorian home in a small town in rural Northern New Jersey. New York premiere of a new play presented without intermission; 59E59 Theater A; September 28–November 4, 2006 (Opened October 18); 20 previews, 20 performances.

*Penny Fuller and Larry Keith in* Southern Comforts
*(photo by James Leynse)*

*The Cast of* Indian Blood *(photo by James Leynse)*

**Adrift in Macao** Book and lyrics by Christopher Durang, music by Peter Melnick; Presented in association with by Ina Meibach, Susan Dietz, Jennifer Manocherian, Barbara Manocherian; Associate Producer, Jamie deRoy; Director, Sheryl Kaller; Choreography, Christopher Gattelli; Music Director, Fred Lassen; Sets, Thomas Lynch; Costumes, Willa Kim; Lighting, Jeff Croiter; Sound, Peter Fitzgerald; Orchestrations, Michael Starobin; Music Coordinator, Howard Joines; Casting, Mark Simon; PSM, Emily N. Wells; Music Copyist, Anne Kaye/Kaye-Houston Music; Props Master, R. Jay Duckworth; Associate Set, Charlie Corcoran; Assistant to Ms. Kim, Leanne Mahoney; ASM, Robyn Henry; Assistant Director, Andy Sandberg; Assistant Choreographer, Tara Wilkinson; Associate Sound, Megan Hanniger; Programmer, Bruce Samuels; Dance Captain, Elisa Van Duyne; Cast: Will Swenson (Rick Shaw), Orville Mendoza (Tempura), Michele Ragusa (Corinna), Jonathan Rayson (Trenchcoat Chorus/Joe), Elisa Van Duyne (Trenchcoat Chorus/Daisy), Alan Campbell (Mitch), Rachel deBenedet (Lureena); The Band: Fred Lassen (Conductor/piano/synthesizer), Jan Rosenberg (Associate Conductor/synthesizer), Chuck Wilson (reeds), Marc Schmied (bass), Joe Nero (drums)

Musical Numbers: In a Foreign City, Grumpy Mood, Tempura's Song, Mister McGuffin, Pretty Moon Over Macao, Mambo Malaysian, Sparks, Mitch's Story, Adrift in Macao, So Long, The Chase, Revelation, Ticky Ticky Tock

Time: 1952. Place: Macao, China. New York premiere of a new musical presented without intermission; 59E59 Theater A; January 23–March 4, 2007 (Opened February 13); 23 previews, 22 performances. Originally presented by New York Stage and Film Company and The Powerhouse Theatre at Vassar on July 10, 2002; originally produced by Philadelphia Theatre Company (Sara Garonzik, Producing Artistic Director) October 19–November 20, 2005.

*Rachel deBenedet, Michele Ragusa, Alan Campbell. and Orville Mendoza in* Adrift in Macao *(photo by James Leynse)*

**Exits and Entrances** by Athol Fugard; Presented in association with Dasha Epstein and Jamie deRoy; Director, Director, Stephen Sachs; Sets, Charlie Corcoran; Costumes, Shon LeBlanc; Lighting, Brian Nason; Sound, David B. Marling; PSM, Samone B. Weissman; Props, Maggie Kuypers; Cast: William Dennis Hurley (The Playwright), Morlan Higgins (André)

Time: 1961 and 1956. Place: Port Elizabeth and Capetown, South Africa. New York premiere of a new play presented without intermission; 59E59 Theater A; March 27–April 29, 2007 (Opened April 4); 9 previews, 30 performances. Originally produced at The Fountain Theatre, Los Angeles.

*William Dennis Hurley and Morlan Higgins in* Exits and Entrances *(photo by James Leynse)*

# The Public Theater

Fifty-first Season

Producer, Oskar Eustis; Executive Director, Mara Manus; Managing Director, Michael Hurst/Seth Shepsle; Associate Artistic Director, John Dias; Associate Producers, Peter DuBois, Heidi Griffiths, Mandy Hackett; Institutional Development, Anne M. Scott; Marketing, Tom Michel; Production, Ruth E. Sternberg; Communications, Arlene R. Kriv; Casting, Jordan Thaler & Heidi Griffiths; Press, Sam Neuman

**Macbeth** by William Shakespeare; Director, Moisés Kaufman; Sets, Derek McLane; Costumes, Michael Krass; Lighting, David Lander; Music, Peter Golub; Sound, Acme Sound Partners; Dramaturg, Robert Blacker; Fight Director, Rick Sordelet; Cast: Liev Schreiber (Macbeth), Jennifer Ehle (Lady Macbeth), Tolan Aman (Boy), Teagle F. Bougere (Banquo), Sterling K. Brown (Macduff), Lynn Cohen (Weird Sister 3/Porter), Sanjit De Silva (Donalbain), Seth Duerr (Ensemble), Amefika El-Amin (Ensemble), Stephanie Fieger (Ensemble), Jacob Fishel (Malcolm), Herb Foster (Duncan/Doctor), Philip Goodwin (Ross), Hollie Hunt (Ensemble), Florencia Lozano (Lady Macduff), Joan MacIntosh (Weird Sister 1/Gentlewoman), Graeme Malcolm (Seyton), Michael Markham (Ensemble), Mark L. Montgomery (Lennox), Andrew McGinn (Angus/Murderer 1), Lucas Near-Verbrugghe (Ensemble), Clancy O'Connor (Ensemble), Pedro Pascal (Bloody Sergeant/Murderer 2), Ching Valdes-Aran (Weird Sister 2)
Revival of the play presented in two acts; Delacorte Theater; June 14–July 9, 2006 (Opened June 28); 13 previews, 14 performances.

*Liev Schreiber and Jennifer Ehle in* Macbeth *(photo by Michal Daniel)*

**Mother Courage and Her Children** by Bertolt Brecht, translated by Tony Kushner, original music by Jeanine Tesori; Director, George C. Wolfe; Sets, Riccardo Hernández; Costumes, Marina Draghici; Lighting, Paul Gallo; Sound, Acme Sound Partners; Projections, Batwin + Robin Productions; Flight Effects, Flying by Foy; Orchestrations, Bruce Coughlin; Music Director, Kimberly Grigsby; Music Coordinator, Seymour Red Press; Conductor, Chris Fenwick; PSM, Rick Steiger; Cast: Raul Aranas (The Colonel/Older Soldier/Injured Farmer), Geoffrey Arend (Swiss Cheese), Max Baker (Quartermaster/Soldier with Fur Coat), Ato Essandoh (Young Soldier/Lieutenant), Colleen Fitzpatrick (Old Woman/Mother), Glenn Fleshler (Army Recruiter/Soldier), Michael Izquierdo (General's Servant/Soldier with the Eyepatch/Ensemble), Eugene Jones (Yvette's Manservant/Ensemble), Kevin Kline (Cook), George Kmeck (Sergeant), Jenifer Lewis (Yvette), Paco Lozano (Clerk), Michael Markham (Singing Soldier/Ensemble), Larry Marshall (General/Farmer), Jack Noseworthy (Young Man with Mattress/First Soldier), Austin Pendleton (Chaplain), Sean Phillips (Looting Soldier/Ensemble), Silvestre Rasuk (Young Man with Violin/Farmer's Son), Meryl Streep (Mother Courage), Brittany Underwood (Daughter), Alexandria Wailes (Kattrin), Frederick Weller (Eilif), Jade Wu (Injured Father's Wife/Farmer's Wife), Waleed F. Zuaiter (Sergeant)
Revival of the play with original music presented in two acts; Delacorte Theater; August 8–September 3, 2006 (Opened August 21); 12 previews, 12 performances.

*Kevin Kline, Meryl Streep, and Austin Pendleton in* Mother Courage and Her Children *(photo by Michal Daniel)*

**WRECKS** Written and directed by Neil LaBute; Sets/Costumes, Klara Zieglerova; Lighting, Christopher Akerlind; Sound, Robert Kaplowitz; PSM, Mary Michele Miner; Cole Bonenberger; Cast: Ed Harris
American premiere of a solo performance play presented without intermission; Anspacher Theater; September 29–November 19, 2006 (Opened October 10); 11 previews, 41 performances. World premiere presented at Everyman Palace Theatre, Cork, Ireland.

**Emergence-SEE!** by Daniel Beaty; Director, Kenny Leon; Sets, Beowulf Boritt; Costumes, Reggie Ray; Lighting, Michael Chybowski; Sound, Drew Levy and Tony Smolenski IV; PSM, Barbara Reo; Cast: Daniel Beaty
Time: 2006. Place: New York City. A solo performance play presented without intermission; LuEsther Hall; October 10–November 19, 2006 (Opened October 22); 11 previews, 29 performances. Previously presented at the Midtown International Theatre Festival, July, 2003.

**365 Days/365 Plays** by Suzan-Lori Parks; November 13, 2006–November 12, 2007; 365 Days/365 Plays National Festival presented the works simultaneously across the country, creating the largest collaboration in the history of American theater. The Public Theater spearheaded the New York festival. Over the course of the year, over sixty selected theater companies – curated by The Public and the 365 Days/365 Plays National Festival – performed these brief, brilliant plays. Week 1 (November 13–19): The Public Theater; Week 2 (November 20–26): The Foundry Theatre; Week 3 (November 27–December 3): Guerrilla Girls on Tour; Week 4 (December 4–10): Galapagos Art Space; Week 5 (December 11–17): Queens Theatre in the Park; Week 6 (December 18–24): Hourglass Group; Week 7 (December 25–31): scenedowntown; Week 8 (January 1–7): Polybe + Seats; Week 9 (January 8–14): The New Group; Week 10 (January 15–21): Clubbed Thumb; Week 11 (January 22–28): Ars Nova; Week 12 (January 29–February 4): Barrow Street Theatre; Week 13 (February 5–11): Salt Theater; Week 14 (February 12–18): Drama League Directors Project; Week 15 (February 19–25): The 52nd Street Project; Week 16 (February 26–March 4): New York Theatre Workshop; Week 17 (March 5–11): LightBox; Week 18 (March 12–18): The New York Neo-Futurists at The Makor; Week 19 (March 19–25): New Georges; Week 20 (March 26–April 1): Epic Theatre Center; Week 21 (April 2–8): Pregones Theater; Week 22 (April 9–15): Naked Angels; Week 23 (April 16–22): blessed unrest; Week 24 (April 23–29): The Civilians; Week 25 (April 30–May 6): Banana Bag and Bodice; Week 26 (May 7–14): INTAR Theatre; Week 27 (May 14–20): Atlantic Theater Company; Week 28 (May 21–27): SITI Company; Week 29 (May 28–June 3): New Dance Group Arts Center

*James Saito, Jon Norman Schneider, and James Yaegashi in* Durango *(photo by Michal Daniel)*

**Durango** by Julia Cho; Co-produced with the Long Wharf Theatre (Gordon Edelstein, Artistic Director; Joan Channick, Managing Director); Director, Chay Yew; Sets, Dan Ostling; Costumes, Linda Cho; Lighting, Paul Whitaker; Sound/Additional Music, Fabian Obispo; PSM, Buzz Cohen; Cast: Ross Bickell (Ned/Jerry), James Saito (Boo-Seng Lee), Jon Norman Schneider (Jimmy Lee), Jay Sullivan (The Red Angel/Bob), James Yaegashi (Isaac Lee)
World premiere of a play with songs presented without intermission; Martinson Hall; November 7–December 10, 2006 (Opened November 20); 12 previews, 25 performances. Previously played at the Long Wharf Theatre, Connecticut, September 13–October 15.

**King Lear** by William Shakespeare; Director, James Lapine; Sets, Heidi Ettinger; Costumes, Jess Goldstein; Lighting, David Lander; Music, Stephen Sondheim and Michael Starobin; Sound, Dan Moses Schreier and Phillip Scott Peglow; Fight Director, Rick Sordelet; Music Director, Henry Aronson; PSM, James Latus; Cast: Brian Avers (Edgar), Nicole Bocchi (Young Regan), Larry Bryggman (Earl of Gloucester), Kristen Bush (Cordelia), Michael Cerveris (Earl of Kent), Philip Goodwin (Fool/Old Man), Kevin Kline (Lear), Piter Marek (King of France/Ensemble), Logan Marshall-Green (Edmund), Talicia Martins (Young Cordelia), Ryan McCarthy (Ensemble), Laura Odeh (Regan), Daniel Pearce (Duke of Cornwall), Angela Pierce (Goneril), Michael Rudko (Duke of Albany), Timothy D. Stickney (Oswald), Joaquín Torres (Duke of Burgundy/Curan/Ensemble), Paris Rose Yates (Young Goneril)
Revival of a play with songs presented in two acts; Anspacher Theater; February 9–March 25, 2007 (Opened March 7); 24 previews, 18 performances.

*Kristen Bush, Laura Odeh, Daniel Pearce, Kevin Kline, Michael Rudko and Angela Pierce in* King Lear *(photo by Michal Daniel)*

**Passing Strange** Book, music, and lyrics by Stew, music by Heidi Rodewald; Created in collaboration with and directed by Annie Dorsen; Co-produced and commissioned by Berkeley Repertory Theatre; Sets, David Korins; Costumes, Elizabeth Hope Clancy; Lighting, Kevin Adams; Movement Coordinator, Karole Armitage; Sound, Tony Smolenski IV; Musical Director, Heidi Rodewald; Musical Supervisor, Jon Spurney; PSM, Cynthia Cahill; Cast: de'Adre Aziza (Edwina/Marianna/Sudabey), Daniel Breaker (Youth), Eisa Davis (Mother), Colman Domingo (Franklin/Joop/Mr. Venus), Chad Goodridge (Terry/Christophe/Hugo), Rebecca Naomi Jones (Sherry/Renata/Desi), Stew; Musicians: Heidi Rodewald (bass/vocals), Jon Spurney (keyboards/guitar/vocals), Christian Cassan (percussion), Marc Doten (keyboards)
World premiere of a musical/rock concert presented in two acts; Anspacher Theater; May 1–July 1, 2007 (Opened May 14); 15 previews, 56 performances. Previously presented at Berkeley Repertory Theatre October 19–December 3, 2006, and developed at Sundance Theatre Lab.

*Daniel Breaker, Stew, de'Adre Aziza, Rebecca Naomi Jones and Eisa Davis in* Passing Strange *(photo by Michal Daniel)*

## LAByrinth Theater In residence at The Public Theater

Fifteenth Season

Artistic Directors, Philip Seymour Hoffman and John Ortiz; Executive Director, Steve Asher; Associate Artistic Director, Florencia Lozano; Associate Producer, Marieke Gaboury; Marketing, Siobhan Foley; Development, Veronica R. Bainbridge; Company Manager, Kristina Poe; Marketing Associate, Lyssa Mandel; Literary Manager, Andrea Ciannavei; Press, Boneau/Bryan-Brown, Juliana Hannett, Matt Ross

**A Small, Melodramatic Story** by Stephen Belber; Director, Lucie Tiberghien; Sets, Takeshi Kata; Costumes, Mimi O'Donnell; Lighting, Matthew Richards; Sound, Elizabeth Rhodes; PSM, Paige van den Burg; ASM, Libby Steiner; Cast: Carlo Alban (Cleo), Quincy Tyler Bernstine (O), Lee Sellars (Keith), Isiah Whitlock Jr. (Perry)
Setting: Washington, D.C. World premiere new play without intermission; Shiva Theater; October 10–November 5, 2006 (Opened October 22); 32 performances. The cast reprised the roles they created in the 2005 Barn Series reading of the show.

Beth Cole, Philip Seymour Hoffman, John Ortiz, and Daphne Rubin-Vega in Jack Goes Boating (photo by Monique Carboni)

### Developmental Productions & Special Events

**Intríngulis** by Carlo Alban; Director, David Anzuelo; Lighting, Sarah Sidman; Sound, Rob Kaplowitz; Projections, luckydave; PSM, Libby Steiner; Cast: Carlo Alban; a solo performance play presented without intermission; Martinson Hall on the set of Jack Goes Boating; March 26–April 9, 2007; 6 performances.

**Pretty Chin Up** by Andrea Ciannavei; Director, Michele Chivu; Cast: Andrea Ciannavei, Bronwen Coleman, Cusi Cram, Salvatore Inzerillo, Trevor Long, Sidney Williams; a new play presented without intermission; Shiva Theater; May 15–June 2, 2007; 13 performances.

Lee Sellars and Quincy Tyler Bernstine in A Small, Melodramatic Story (photo by Monique Carboni)

**Jack Goes Boating** by Bob Glaudini; Director, Peter DuBois; Sets, David Korins; Costumes, Mimi O'Donnell; Lighting, Japhy Weideman; Composition and Sound, David Van Tieghem; PSM, Damon W. Arrington; ASM, Paige van den Burg; Cast: John Ortiz (Clyde), Daphne Rubin-Vega (Lucy), Philip Seymour Hoffman (Jack), Beth Cole (Connie)
Setting: New York City. World premiere of a new play performed in two acts; Martinson Hall; February 27–April 29, 2007 (Opened March 18); 72 performances.

Andrea Ciannavei in Pretty Chin Up (photo by Nico Malvaldi)

**The Worst of Bogosian: Solos, Speeches, & Rants circa 1980–2000**
Written and performed by Eric Bogosian; Director, Jo Bonney; a solo performance piece presented without intermission; Martinson Hall; June 12–14, 2007, 3 performances.

# Rattlestick Playwrights Theater

Twelfth Season

Co-Founder and Artistic Director, David Van Asselt; Managing Director, Sandra Coudert; Associate Artistic Director, Lou Moreno; Producing Associate, Doug Nevin; Artistic Associate, Jake Witlen; Box Office Manager, Ira Lopez; Casting, Jodi Collins; Press, Origlio/Miramontez Company, Richard Hillman

**It Goes Without Saying** by Bill Bowers; Developed with and directed by Martha Banta; Sets, John McDermott; Costumes, Michael Growler; Lighting, Ed McCarthy; Sound, Jill B.C. DuBoff; PSM, Steve Henry; Logo, Jonathan Wentz; Graphic Design, Bob Holling; Master Electrician, Doug Filomena; Assistant Sound, Stephen Bettridge; Cast: Bill Bowers
New York premiere of an autobiographical solo performance play presented without intermission; Theatre 224 Waverly; August 30–October 15, 2006 (Opened September 7); 35 performances. World premiere at the Adirondack Theatre Festival, Glens Falls, NY (Martha Banta, Artistic Director; David Turner, Producing Director); subsequently produced at the Berkshire Theater Festival (Kate Maguire, Artistic Director).

*Bill Bowers in* It Goes Without Saying *(photo by Sandra Coudert)*

**Dark Matters** by Roberto Aguirre-Sacasa; Director, Trip Cullman; Sets, Wilson Chin; Costumes, Katherine Roth; Lighting, Matt Richards; Sound, Shane Rettig; Original Music, Michael Friedman; PSM, Emily Ellen Roberts; ASM, Robin Ganek; Marketing, Urbintel Inc.; Assistant Set, Alexandra Stine; Crew: Lara C. Quinones, Nikki Rothenberg, Doug Filomena; Playwrights Associate, Lucy Boyle; Cast: Reed Birney (Michael Cleary), Justin Chatwin (Jeremy Cleary), Michael Cullen (Benjamin Egan), Elizabeth Marvel (Bridget Cleary)
Setting: Rural Virginia home of the Clearys, the present. A new play presented in two acts; Theatre 224 Waverly; November 10–December 22, 2006 (Opened November 20); 32 performances.

**Stay** by Lucy Thurber; Director, Jackson Gay; Sets, Erik Flatmo; Costumes, Jenny Mannis; Lighting, Scott Bolman; Sound, Daniel Baker; Original Music, Aaron Meicht; PSM, Christina Lowe; ASM, Robin Ganek; Marketing, Sol Lieberman; Wigs, Erin Kennedy Lunsford; Fight Choreographer, David Anzuelo; Logo, Ola Maslik; Production Crew, John Sundling, Lee Purdy, Will Pickens; Assistants, Stephanie Rosado, Hylenne Goris; Cast: Jenny Maguire (Floating Girl), Sam Rosen (Tommy), Thomas Sadoski (Billy), Maggie Siff (Rachel), Jess Weixler (Julia); Kim Martin-Cotton (Voice of Martha)
World premiere of a new play presented in two acts; Theatre 224 Waverly; March 11–April 15, 2007 (Opened March 19); 27 performances.

*Reed Birney and Justin Chatwin in* Dark Matters
*(photo by Sandra Coudert)*

*Maggie Siff, Jess Weixler, and Jenny Maguire in* Stay
*(photo by Sandra Coudert)*

# Roundabout Theatre Company

Forty-first Season

Artistic Director, Todd Haimes; Managing Director, Harold Wolpert; Executive Director of External Affairs, Julia C. Levy; Associate Artistic Director, Scott Ellis; Founding Director, Gene Feist; Artistic Development/Casting, Jim Carnahan; Education, Margie Salvante-McCann; General Manager, Sydney Beers; General Manager Steinberg Center, Rebecca Habel; Finance, Susan Neiman; Marketing, David B. Steffen; Development, Jeffory Lawson; Sales, Jim Seggelink; Production Manager, Kai Brothers; Company Manager, Nicholas Caccavo; Casting, Mele Nagler; Press, Boneau/Bryan-Brown, Jessica Johnson

**Suddenly Last Summer** by Tennessee Williams; Director, Mark Brokaw; Sets/Costumes; Santo Loquasto; Lighting, David Weiner; Sound, Peter Golub & Ryan Powers; Original Music, Peter Golub; Hair/Wigs, Tom Watson; PSM, James FitzSimmons; Dialect Coach, Deborah Hecht; Fight Director, Rick Sordelet; ASM, Bryce McDonald; Associate Production Manager, Donald Fried; Assistant Director, Moritz von Stuelpnagel; Associate Set Design, Wilson Chin; Cast: Blythe Danner (Mrs. Venable), Gale Harold (Dr. Cukrowicz), Karen Walsh (Miss Foxhill), Becky Ann Baker (Mrs. Holly), Wayne Wilcox (George Holly), Carla Gugino (Catherine Holly), Sandra Shipley (Sister Felicity); Understudies: Sandra Shipley (Mrs. Venable), Karen Walsh (Catherine Holly), Carolyn Swift (Miss Foxhill/Mrs. Holly/Sister Felicity; Matthew Greer (Dr. Cukrowicz/George Holly)
Time and Place: New Orleans, 1936. The Garden District. Between late summer and early fall. Revival of a play presented without intermission; Laura Pels Theatre; October 20, 2006–January 20, 2007 (Opened November 15); 31 previews, 74 performances. Originally produced at the York Playhouse as the second act of *Garden District* with Williams' one-act play, *Something Unspoken*, January 7, 1958 (see *Theatre World* Volume 14, page 137); *Garden District* was revived at Circle in the Square October 10, 1995 (see Theatre World Volume 52, page 14).

*Blythe Danner and Gale Harold in* Suddenly Last Summer
*(photo by Joan Marcus)*

**Howard Katz** by Patrick Marber; Director, Doug Hughes; Sets, Scott Pask; Costumes, Catherine Zuber; Lighting, Christopher Akerlind; Original Music and Sound by David Van Tieghem; PSM, James FitzSimmons; Dialect Coach, Gillian Lane-Plescia; Fight Director, Rick Sordelet; Stage Manager, Bryce McDonald; Associate Director, Mark Schneider; Associate Production Manager, Michael Wade; Associate Set Design, Jeff Hinchee; Associate Costumes, Michael Zecker; Cast: Max Baker (Bern), Alvin Epstein (Jo), Elizabeth Franz (Ellie), Edward Hajj (Norm), Jessica Hecht (Jess), Patrick Henney (Ollie), Alfred Molina (Howard Katz), Euan Morton (Robin), Charlotte Parry (Nat); Understudies: Nick Wyman (Howard Katz), Nancy Franklin (Ellie), Natalie Gold (Nat/Jess), Stan Lachow (Jo), Kiran Merchant (Norm), Thom Rivera (Norm), Noah Ruff (Ollie), Mark Saturno (Bern/Robin)
Time and Place: London, the present and the past. American premiere of a play presented without intermission; Laura Pels Theatre; February 2–May 6, 2007 (Opened March 1); 32 previews, 77 performances.

*Euan Morton and Alfred Molina in* Howard Katz
*(photo by Joan Marcus)*

*Steven Lang in* Beyond Glory *(photo by Joan Marcus)*

**Beyond Glory** by Stephen Lang, adapted from the book *Beyond Glory: Medal of Honor Heroes in Their Own Words* by Larry Smith; Director, Robert Falls; Sets, Tony Cisek; Lighting, Dan Covey; Costumes, David C. Woolard; Sound, Cecil Averett; Music, Robert Kessler & Ethan Neuberg; PSM, James FitzSimmons; Projections, John Boesche; Casting, Carrie Gardner; Stage Manager, Bryce McDonald; Associate Production Manager, Peter Dean; Cast: Stephen Lang; Voices of the Military: John Bedford Lloyd, Matt Sincell, Anne Twomey; Standby: Tony Campisi
World premiere of a new solo performance play presented without intermission; Laura Pels Theatre; May 25–August 19, 2007 (Opened June 21); 31 previews, 69 performances.

# Second Stage Theatre

Twenty-eighth Season

Artistic Director, Carole Rothman; Executive Director, Ellen Richard; Associate Artistic Director, Christopher Burney; Production Manager, Jeff Wild; Director of Finance, Janice B. Cwill; Director of Management, Don-Scott Cooper; Director of Development, Sarah Bordy; Director of Marketing, Hector Coris; Ticket Services Manager, Greg Turner; Technical Director, Robert G. Mahon III; Literary Manager, Sarah Bagley; Casting, Tara Rubin Casting; Press, Barlow · Hartman, Tom D'Ambrosio

**subUrbia** by Eric Bogosian; Director, Jo Bonney; Sets, Richard Hoover; Costumes, Mimi O'Donnell; Lighting, David Weiner; Sound, Robert Kaplowitz; Fight Director, Rick Sordelet; PSM, Wendy Ouellette; Stage Manager, Sharika Niles; Assistant Director, Sarah H. Haught; Vocal Coach, Samara Bay; Cast: Diksha Basu (Pakeesa), Jessica Capshaw (Erica), Kieran Culkin (Buff), Michael Esper (Pony), Halley Feiffer (Bee-Bee), Daniel Eric Gold (Jeff), Gaby Hoffmann (Sooze), Manu Narayan (Norman), Peter Scanavino (Tim)
Setting: The parking lot of a convenience store, today. Updated revival of a play presented in two acts; September 7–October 29, 2007 (Opened September 28); 61 performances. Originally presented by Lincoln Center Theater, April 20–August 28, 1994 (see *Theatre World* Volume 50, page 133).

*Kieran Culkin and Jessica Capshaw in* subUrbia
*(photo by Joan Marcus)*

**The Scene** by Theresa Rebeck; Director, Rebecca Taichman; Sets, Derek McLane, Costumes, Jeff Mahshie; Lighting, Natasha Katz; Sound, Martin Desjardins; PSM, Kelly Hance; Stage Manager, Shanna Spinello; Movement Consultant, Lisa Leguillou; Cast: Anna Camp (Clea), Patricia Heaton (Stella), Tony Shalhoub (Charlie), Christopher Evan Welch (Lewis)
New York premiere of a new play presented in two acts; December 14, 2006–February 11, 2007 (Opened January 11); 69 performances. World premiere at the 2006 Humana Festival at Actors Theatre of Louisville.

*Patricia Heaton, Christopher Evan Welch, and Tony Shalhoub in*
The Scene *(photo by Joan Marcus)*

**Some Men** by Terrence McNally; Director, Trip Cullman; Sets, Mark Wendland; Costumes, Linda Cho; Lighting, Kevin Adams; Sound, John Gromada; PSM, Lori Ann Zepp; Stage Manager, Stephanie Gatton; Movement Consultant, Lisa Leguillou; Dialect Coach, Stephen Gabis; Cast: Don Amendolia (Aaron/Tommy's Dad/Buffed in Chelsea/Trey/Joseph), Kelly AuCoin (Bernie/Martin), Romain Frugé (Carl/Xerxes/Joel/Kurt/Gary), David Greenspan (Perry/Brad/Padraic/Boytoy/BJ/Pat/Spencer), Michael McElroy (Fritz/Mendy/David Goldman/Randy Hunk/Zach/Lewis/Mel/Nurse Jack), Randy Redd (Piano Man/Jackson/Funeral Director/Downtown11/Mary/Mr. Keys/Busboy), Frederick Weller (Paul/Darren/TopDog/Cliff/Will/Michael/Dick/Richard)
New York premiere of a new play presented in two acts; March 2–April 22, 2007 (Opened March 26); 61 performances. World premiere at the Philadelphia Theatre Company (Sara Garonzik, Producing Artistic Director), May 12–June 11, 2006.

*Pedro Pascal, Michael McElroy, Don Amendolia, Romain Frugé, Randy Redd; in mirror: Jesse Hooker, Kelly AuCoin, and Frederick Weller in*
Some Men *(photo by Joan Marcus)*

**Eurydice** by Sarah Ruhl; Director, Les Waters; Sets, Scott Bradley; Costumes, Meg Neville; Lighting, Russell H. Champa; Sound, Bray Poor; PSM, Michael Suenkel; Stage Manager, Stephanie Gatton; Produced by special arrangement with Bruce Ostler, Bret Adams Ltd.; Cast: Maria Dizzia (Eurydice), Gian-Murray Gianino (Loud Stone), Carla Harting (Little Stone), Ramiz Monsef (Big Stone), Joseph Parks (Orpheus), Charles Shaw Robinson (Father), Mark Zeisler (The Nasty and Interesting Man/Lord of the Underworld)

New York premiere of a new play without intermission; May 30–August 26, 2007 (Opened June 12); 103 performances.

Above: *Mark Zeisler, Maria Dizzia, Ramiz Monsef, Gian-Murray Gianino, and Carla Harting in* Eurydice *(photo by Joan Marcus)*

Right: *Debra Jo Rupp and Ashlie Atkinson in* The Butcher of Baraboo *(photo by Joan Marcus)*

## Second Stage Uptown Series

**The Butcher of Baraboo** by Marisa Wegrzyn; Director, Judith Ivey; Sets, Beowulf Boritt; Costumes, Andrea Lauer; Lighting, Jeff Croiter; Sound, Ryan Rumery; Fight Director, Robert Westley; PSM, Lori Ann Zepp; Stage Manager, Susan Shay; Associate Production Manager, Bradley Thompson; Dialect Coach, Stephen Gabis; Associate Sound, Daniel Baker; Assistant Director, Sari Abraham; Cast: Ashlie Atkinson (Midge), Michael Countryman (Donal), Ali Marsh (Sevenly), Debra Jo Rupp (Valerie), Welker White (Gail)

Setting: Baraboo, Wisconsin. World premiere of a new play presented in two acts; McGinn/Cazale Theatre; May 24–June 30, 2007 (Opened June 11); 18 previews, 24 performances.

**Election Day** by Josh Tobiessen; Director, Jeremy Dobrish; Sets, Steven Capone; Costumes, Mattie Ullrich; Lighting, Michael Gottlieb; Sound, Jill B.C. DuBoff; PSM, Lori Ann Zepp; Stage Manager, Susan Shay; Cast: Michael Ray Escamilla (Edmund), Halley Feiffer (Cleo), Adam Green (Adam), Lorenzo Pisoni (Clark), Katharine Powell (Brenda)

World premiere of a new play presented in two acts; McGinn/Cazale Theatre; July 16–August 25, 2007 (Opened August 1); 16, previews, 28 performances.

*Michael Ray Escamilla, Adam Green, Katharine Powell, and Halley Feiffer in* Election Day *(photo by Joan Marcus)*

# Signature Theatre Company

Fifteenth Season – Part Two

Founding Artistic Director, James Houghton; Executive Director, Kathryn M. Lupina; Associate Artist, Constanza Romero; Transition and Capital Projects Director, Jodi Schoenbrun Carter; Associate Artistic Director, Beth Whitaker; Theatre Advancement, Jennie Greer; Associate General Manager, Adam Bernstein; Production Manager, Chris Moses/Paul Ziemer; Marketing, Nella Vera; Casting, Bernard Telsey; Press, The Publicity Office, Michael Borowski, Candi Adams

Playwright in residence: August Wilson

**Seven Guitars** Director, Ruben Santiago-Hudson; Original Music/Musical Director, Bill Sims Jr.; Sets, Richard Hoover; Costumes, Karen Perry; Lighting, Jane Cox; Sound, Darron L. West; Fight Director, Rick Sordelet; Choreography, Ken Roberson; PSM, John M. Atherlay; Animal Trainer, William Berloni; Associate Artist, Todd Kreidler; ASM, Winnie Y. Lok; Assistant Director, Jade King Carroll; Hair/Wigs, Valerie Gladstone; Associate Set, Casey Smith, Veronica Ferrer; Cast: Kevin Carroll (Canewell), Cassandra Freeman (Ruby), Stephen McKinley Henderson (Red Carter), Brenda Pressley (Louise), Lance Reddick (Floyd Barton), Roslyn Ruff (Vera), Charles Weldon (Hedley)
Setting: The backyard of a house in Pittsburgh in 1948. Revival of the play presented in two acts; Peter Norton Space; July 31–October 15, 2006 (Opened August 24, 2006); 80 performances. Originally produced on Broadway at the Walter Kerr Theatre, March 28, 1996 (see *Theatre World* Volume 42, page 42).

*Lance Reddick, Stephen McKinley Henderson, and Kevin T. Carroll in* Seven Guitars *(photo by Carol Rosegg)*

**Two Trains Running** Director, Lou Bellamy; Sets, Derek McLane; Costumes, Mathew J. LeFebvre; Lighting, Robert Wierzel; Sound, Brett Jarvis; Fight Director, Rick Sordelet; Wigs/Hair/Makeup, Erin Kennedy Lunsford; PSM, Babette Roberts; Associate Artist, Todd Kreidler; ASM, Winnie Y. Lok; Assistant Director, Jade King Carroll; Associate Costumes, Amelia Dombrowski; Cast: Leon Addison Brown (Hambone), Chad L. Coleman (Sterling), Frankie Faison (Memphis), Arthur French (Holloway), Ron Cephas Jones (Wolf), January Lavoy (Risa), Ed Wheeler (West)
Setting: A diner in Pittsburgh, 1969. Revival of the play presented in two acts; Peter Norton Space; November 7, 2006–January 28, 2007 (Opened December 3); 96 performances. Originally produced at Yale Repertory Theatre March 27, 1990; produced on Broadway at the Walter Kerr Theatre April 13, 1992 (see *Theatre World* Volume 48, page 40).

Right: *Cherise Boothe and Russell Hornsby in* King Hedley II
*(photo by Carol Rosegg)*

*Leon Addison Brown and January Lavoy in* Two Trains Running
*(photo by Carol Rosegg)*

**King Hedley II** Director, Derrick Sanders; Sets, David Gallo; Costumes, Reggie Ray; Lighting, Thom Weaver; Sound, Jill B.C. DuBoff; Composer, Stephen Neverson; Fight Director, Rick Sordelet; Production Stage Manager, Winnie Y. Lok; Assistant Director, Brian Tucker; Associate Artist, Todd Kreidler; ASM, Chandra LaViolette; Makeup, Tim Miller; Wigs and Hair, Gregory Bazemore; Properties, Peter Sarafin; Cast: Cherise Boothe (Tonya), Lynda Gravátt (Ruby), Stephen McKinley Henderson (Elmore), Russell Hornsby (King Hedley II), Curtis McClarin (Mister), Lou Myers (Stool Pigeon)
Setting: The backyard in the decaying Hill District of Pittsburgh, 1980s. Revival of the play presented in two acts; Peter Norton Space; February 20–April 22, 2007 (Opened March 11); 70 performances. Originally produced on Broadway at the Virginia Theatre (now the August Wilson Theatre), May 1, 2001 (see *Theatre World* Volume 57, page 47).

# Studio Dante

Third Season

Co-Founders & Artistic Directors, Victoria & Michael Imperioli: Executive Directors, Raisa & Richard Chlebowski; Co-producers, Tina Thor & Howard Axel; Director of Play Development, Francine Volpe; Managing Director, Toni Marie Davies; Casting, Jack Doulin, Meredith Tucker; Press, The Karpel Group, Bridget Klapinski, Darren Molovinsky

**The Given** by Francine Volpe; Directors, Michael Imperioli & Zetna Fuentes; Sets/Costumes, Victoria Imperioli; Lighting, Tony Giovannetti; Fight Coordinator, Peter Bucosi; Choreographer, Deb Demast; Stage Manager, Darren Rosen; ASM, Carrie Tongarm; Master Carpenter, Ryczard Chlebowski; Artwork, Nathaniel Kiloer; Wardrobe, Andrea Cavalluzzo; Painter, Richard Cerullo; Cast: Sharon Angela (Suzie), Remy Auberjonois (Seth), Jason C. Brown (Swanee/Yoga Instructor), Elzbieta Czyzewska (Nettie), Anthony de Sando (Leon), Laura Heisler (Cathea)
World premiere of a new play presented in two acts; October 18–November 11, 2006 (Opened October 21); 16 performances.

*Jason C. Brown, Laura Heisler, and Anthony de Sando in* The Given *(photo by George H. McLaughlin)*

**Chicken** by Mike Batistick; Director, Nick Sandow; Sets/Costumes, Victoria Imperioli; Lighting, Tony Giovannetti; Sound, David Margolin Lawson; PSM, Justin Scribner; ASM, Annette Verga-Lagier; Fight Coordinator, Peter Bucosi; Artwork, Nathanial Kiloer; Casting Assistant, Jenn Haltman; Cast: E.J. Carroll (Wendell), Michael Imperioli (Floyd), Sharon Angela (Lena), Raúl Aranas (Geronimo), Lazaro Perez (Felix), Quincy Tyler Bernstine (Rosalind)
World premiere of a new play presented in two acts; February 28–March 31, 2007 (Opened March 10, 2007); 24 performances.

*Michael Imperioli, E.J. Carroll, and Raúl Aranas in* Chicken *(photo by George H. McLaughlin)*

**From Riverdale to Riverhead** by Anastasia Trania; Director, Nick Sandow; Sets/Costumes, Victoria Imperioli; Lighting, Tony Giovannetti; Sound, David Margolin Lawson; Stage Manager, Darren Rosen; ASM, Annette Verga-Lagier; Assistant Director, Zetna Fuentes; Painter, Elaine Sabel; Artwork, Nathanial Kiloer; Cast: Sharon Angela (Stella), Catherine Curtin (Fannie), Ken Forman (Guard/Detective/Radio Personality), Bess Rous (Rosie), Angelica Torn (Louise)
World premiere of a new play presented in two acts; June 6–30, 2007 (Opened June 9); 14 performances.

(Clockwise from top left) *Bess Rous, Catherine Curtin, Sharon Angela, and Angelica Torn in* From Riverdale to Riverhead *(photo by George H. McLaughlin)*

# Theatre for a New Audience

Eleventh Season

Artistic Director, Jeffrey Horowitz; Managing Director, Dorothy Ryan; General Manager, Theresa von Klug; Development, Ernest A. Hood; Education, Joseph Giardina; Finance, Lisa J. Weir; Capital Campaign, Rachel Lovett; Associate Artistic Director, Arin Arbus; Associate General Manager, Sarah Elkashef; Casting, Deborah Brown; Production Manager, Ken Larson; Technical Director, John Martinez; Press, The Bruce Cohen Group

**The Merchant of Venice** by William Shakespeare; Director, Darko Tresnjak; Sets, John Lee Beatty; Costumes, Linda Cho; Lighting, David Weiner; Sound, Jane Shaw; Voice/Text Consultants, Cicely Berry & J. M. Feindel; Dramaturg, Michael Feingold; Video Artist, Matthew Myhrum; Casting, Deborah Brown; Stage Managers, Renee Lutz & Jamie Rose Thoma; Production Manager, Ken Larson; General Manager, Theresa Von Klug; Wigs, Charles LaPointe; Assistant Director, Susanna Gellert; Associate Dramaturg, Ben Nadler; Technical Director, Pierre Kraitsowitz; Props, Faye Armon; Associate Set, Matthew Myhrum; Associate Lighting, Lauren Phillips; Cast: F. Murray Abraham (Shylock), Kenajuan Bentley (Launcelot Gobbo), Arnie Burton (Balthazar), Cameron Folmar (Solanio), Kate Forbes (Portia), Ezra Knight (Prince of Morocco), John Lavelle (Gratiano), Nichole Lowrance (Jessica), Vince Nappo (Lorenzo), Tom Nelis (Antonio), Saxon Palmer (Bassanio), Matthew Schneck (Salerio), Christen Simon (Nerissa), Marc Vietor (Prince of Arragon/Tubal/Duke of Venice)
Setting: Venice & Belmont Italy. Time: The near future. Revival of the play presented in two acts; Duke on 42nd Street; January 6–March 11, 2007 (Opened February 4); 12 previews, 18 performances. Performed in repertory with *The Jew of Malta*.

**The Jew of Malta** by Christopher Marlowe; Director, David Herskovits; Sets, John Lee Beatty; Costumes, David Zinn; Lighting, David Weiner; Sound, Jane Shaw; Voice/Text Consultants, Cicely Berry & J. M. Feindel; Dramaturg, Michael Feingold; Fight Director, J. Steven White; Casting, Deborah Brown; Stage Managers, Renee Lutz & Jamie Rose Thoma; Production Manager, Ken Larson; General Manager, Theresa Von Klug; Wigs, Charles LaPointe; Assistant Director, Sarah Bishop-Stone; Associate Dramaturg, Ben Nadler; Technical Director, Pierre Kraitsowitz; Props, Faye Armon; Associate Set, Matthew Myhrum; Associate Lighting, Lauren Phillips; Cast: F. Murray Abraham (Barabas), Kenajuan Bentley (First Knight), Arnie Burton (Ithamore), Cameron Folmar (Friar Barnardine/Second Merchant), Kate Forbes (Bellamira/Abbess), Ezra Knight (Selim Calymath/Friar Jacomo), John Lavelle (Lodowick), Nichole Lowrance (Abigail), Vince Nappo (Mathias/First Merchant), Tom Nelis (Martin del Bosco/First Jew), Saxon Palmer (Pilia-Borza/Second Jew), Matthew Schneck (Callapine/First Slave), Christen Simon (Katherine/Third Jew), Marc Vietor (Ferneze)
Place: Malta. Time: 1592. Revival of a play presented in two acts; Duke on 42nd Street; January 17–March 10, 2007 (Opened February 4); 12 previews, 15 performances. Performed in repertory with *The Merchant of Venice*.

*Saxon Palmer, Arnie Burton, and Kate Forbes in* The Jew of Malta *(photo by Gerry Goodstein)*

**Oliver Twist** Adapted & directed by Neil Bartlett from the novel by Charles Dickens; Produced in association with the American Repertory Theatre & Berkeley Repertory Theatre; Sets/Costumes, Rae Smith; Lighting, Scott Zielinski; Sound, David Remedios; Music, Gerard McBurney; Music Adaptor/Director, Simon Deacon; Movement, Struan Leslie; Dialects, Laura Hitt; Casting, Deborah Brown; PSM, Chris De Camillis; General Manager, Theresa Von Klug; ASM, Katherine Shea; Production Manager, Greg Rowland; Dramaturg, Michael Feingold; Associate Dramaturg, Ben Nadler; Cast: Carson Elrod (John Dawkins/The Artful Dodger), Michael Wartella (Oliver Twist), Remo Airaldi (Mr. Bumble), Karen MacDonald (Mrs. Bumble), Thomas Derrah (Mr. Sowerberry/Mr. Grimwig/Mr. Fang), Gregory Derelian (Bill Sykes/Mrs. Sowerberry), Jennifer Ikeda (Nancy), Ned Eisenberg (Fagin), Steven Boyer (Noah Claypool/Tom Chitling), Craig Pattison (Charley Bates), Lucas Steele (Toby Crackit), Will LeBow (Mr. Brownlow), Elizabeth Jasicki (Rose Brownlow/Charlotte Sowerberry)
New York premiere of a play presented in two acts; Gerald W. Lynch Theater at John Jay College; March 29–April 15, 2007 (Opened April 1); 5 previews, 16 performances.

*F. Murray Abraham in* The Merchant of Venice *(photo by Gerry Goodstein)*

# Theatreworks USA – New York

Forty-fifth Season

Artistic Director, Barbara Pasternack; Managing Director, Ken Arthur; Chief Development Officer, Patrick Key; General Manager, David Topchik; Marketing, Barbara Sandek; Education, Beth Prater; Associate Marketing, Steve Cochran; Production Manager, Bob Daley; Company Manager, Teresa Hagar; Casting, Robin D. Carus; Associate Artistic Director, Michael Alltop; Marketing Associate, Paula Marchiel; Marketing Coordinator, Patrick Dwyer; Marketing, Martian Media; Technical Coordinator, B.D. White; Press, Shaffer-Coyle Public Relations

**If You Give a Mouse a Cookie and Other Story Books** Musical Scenes by Jordan Allen-Dutton, Erik Weiner & James-Allen Ford, Kirsten Childs, Jeremy Desmon & Patrick Dwyer, Mindi Dickstein & Daniel Messé, Faye Greenberg & David Evans, Robert Lopez & Jeff Marx, Arthur Perlman & Jeffrey Lunden; based on a production originally directed and choreographed by David Armstrong; Director/Choreographer, Kevin Del Aguila; Sets, Rob Odorisio, Costumes, Martha Bromelmeier; Lighting, Tom Sturge; Sound, Eric Shim; Additional Set Design, Vaughn Patterson; Music Director, Jana Zielonka; Orchestrations, Robert Lopez & Jeff Marx; Additional Orchestrations, Dave Hab, James-Allen Ford; Assistant Director, Ryan J. Davis; Stage Manager, Timothy P. Debo; ASM, Laura Rin; Cast: Farah Alvin, David A. Austin, Nick Blaemire, Stephanie D'Abruzzo, Aurelia Williams, Carla Woods; Understudies: Dominique Elise Porter, Courter Simmons A musical for young audiences presented without intermission; Lucille Lortel Theatre; July 16–August 18, 2006 (Opened July 20); 45 performances.

*Kathleen Chalfant in* Great Expectations *(photo by Joan Marcus)*

*Nick Blaemire, Farah Alvin, David A. Austin, Stephanie D'Abruzzo, Carla Woods, and Aurelia Williams in* If You Give a Mouse a Cookie *(photo by Joan Marcus)*

**Great Expectations** by Bathsheba Doran, based on the novel by Charles Dickens; Director, Will Pomerantz; Music, Michael Picton; Sets/Costumes, Carol Bailey; Lighting, Lenore Doxsee; Sound, Eric Shim; Wigs, Kristian Kraii; Stage Manager, Kate Hefel; ASM, Rebecca Spinac; Tech Director, Joe Reddington; Dialect Coach, Wendy Waterman; Cast: Kathleen Chalfant (Miss Havisham), Christian Campbell (Pip), John Joseph Gallagher (Magwich/Jaggers), Kristen Bush (Mrs. Joe/Estella), Kenneth Boys (Pumblechook/Orlick/Herbert), Paul Niebanck (Joe/Drummle), Emily Donahoe (Biddy), Christian Rolleau (Party Guest); Understudies:

Kara Jackson (Biddy/Estella), Diane Ciesla (Miss Havisham), Christian Rolleau (Pip/Pumblechook), Paul Urcioli (Joe/Magwich/Jaggers) A play with music for young audiences presented without intermission; Lucille Lortel Theatre; November 8–December 3, 2006 (Opened November 16); 29 performances.

**Henry and Mudge** Book and lyrics by Kait Kerrigan, music by Brian Lowdermilk, based on the *Henry and Mudge* books by Cynthia Rylant; Director, Peter Flynn; Choreography, Devanand Janki; Music Director/Conductor: Rick Hip-Flores; Associate Music Director, Gillian Berkowitz; Sets, Paul C. Weimer; Costumes, Rob Bevenger; Lighting, Jeff Croiter; Sound, Eric Shim; Stage Manager, Jeff Davolt; Technical Director, J. Brittain Adams; Orchestrations, Brian Lowdermilk, Greg Pliska; Technical Coordinator, J. Brittain Adams; Tech Director, Joseph Reddington; Stage Manager, Jeff Davolt; Assistant Director, Kate Swan; Cast: Jennifer Cody (Annie), Patrick Boll (Dad), Joseph A. Morales (Henry), Joan Hess (Mom), Todd Buonopane (Mudge); Understudies: David Abeles (Dad/Mudge), Michael Busillo (Henry), Amanda Ryan Paige (Mom/Annie); Orchestra: Rick Hip-Flores (piano), Tara Chambers (cello), Ingrid Gretta Gordon (percussion) Musical Numbers: Living in the Country, Something's Missing, Good Dog, Best Friends, Code Crackers, Annie's on Her Way, My Party Dress, Roll Over, The Woods, Henry and Mudge New York premiere of a musical for young audiences presented without intermission; Lucille Lortel Theatre; December 13, 2006–January 20, 2007 (Opened December 17); 48 performances.

**Anne of Green Gables** Book and lyrics by Gretchen Cryer, music by Nancy Ford, based on the book by Lucy Maud Montgomery; Director, Tyler Marchant; Music Director, W. Brent Sawyer; Orchestrations, Dave Hab; Sets, Beowulf Boritt; Costumes, David Woolard; Lighting, Clifton Taylor; Sound, Eric Shim; Wigs, David H. Lawrence; Props, Jung Griffin; Stage Manager, Ruth E. Kramer; Tech Director, Joseph Reddington; Cast: Erick Devine (Matthew Cuthbert), Bethe B. Austin (Marilla Cuthbert), Heather MacRae (Rachel Lynde), Piper Goodeve (Anne Shirley), Michael Mendiola (Man), Alison Faircloth (Woman), Andrew Gehling/Dustin Sullivan (Gilbert Blythe), Jessica Grové (Dianna Barry); Understudies: Holly Ann Butler (Anne/Diane/Woman), Dustin Sullivan/Adam Laird (Gilbert), Tina Johnson (Marilla/Rachel), Kenneth Boys (Matthew/Man); Orchestra: W. Brent Sawyer (Piano/Conductor), Will Martina (Cello), Jeremy Clayton (Woodwinds) Musical Numbers: Overture, Around the Bend, A Pretty Kettle of Fish, I Can Stay, It's the Strangest Thing, Kindred Spirits, Making Up for Lost Time, Hand in Hand, Two Weeks, It Was Not Because of Gilbert Blythe, Drunk!, The Clock Keeps Ticking, It's the Strangest Thing (reprise), First Day at the Academy, It's Nice to Know, Around the Bend (reprise), Making Up for Lost Time (reprise), Finale World premiere of a musical for young audiences presented without intermission; Lucille Lortel Theatre; March 23–May 5, 2007 (Opened March 29), 41 performances.

*Michael Jansen and Miguel Cervantes in* Henry and Mudge *(photo by Joan Marcus)*

*Heather MacRae, Bethe B. Austin, and Erick Devine in* Anne of Green Gables *(photo by Joan Marcus)*

# Vineyard Theatre

Twenty-fifth Anniversary Season

Artistic Director, Douglas Aibel; Executive Director, Jennifer Garvey-Blackwell; Production & Finance, Reed Ridgley; General Manager, Rebecca Habel; Associate Artistic Director, Sarah Stern; Marketing & Audience Development, Shane Guiter; Production Manager, Ben Morris; Company Manager, Rachel E. Ayers; Marketing Associate, Y. Angel Wuellner; Development Associate, Allison Geffner; Box Office Manager, Dennis Hruska; Casting, Cindy Tolan; Press, Sam Rudy, Bob Lasko, Dale Heller

**The Internationalist** by Anne Washburn; Director, Ken Rus Schmoll; Sets, Andromache Chalfant; Lighting, Jeff Croiter; Costumes, Michelle R. Phillips; Sound, Robert Kaplowitz; PSM, Megan Smith; Cast: Annie Parisse (Sara), Zak Orth (Lowell), Liam Craig (James/Bartender), Gibson Frazier (Nicol/Guard), Nina Hellman (Irene/Anonymous Woman), Ken Marks (Simon/Paul)
A new play presented in two acts; Gertrude and Irving Dimson Theatre; October 19–November 26, 2006 (Opened November 7); 39 performances.

*Paige Howard in* Mary Rose *(photo by Carol Rosegg)*

*Annie Parisse and Gibson Frazier in* The Internationalist *(photo by Carol Rosegg)*

**Mary Rose** by J.M. Barrie; Director, Tina Landau; Sets, James Schuette; Costumes, Michael Krass; Lighting, Kevin Adams; Sound, Obadiah Eaves; Hair/Wigs, Paul Huntley; Makeup, Angelina Avallone; PSM, Megan Smith; Cast: Betsy Aidem (Mrs. Morland), Susan Blommaert (Mrs. Otery), Ian Brennan (Mr. Cameron), Michael Countryman (Mr. Morland), Keir Dullea (Narrator), Tom Riis Farrell (Mr. Amy), Darren Goldstein (Simon), Paige Howard (Mary Rose), Richard Short (Harry)
First American revival of the play presented in two acts; Gertrude and Irving Dimson Theatre; February 1–March 25, 2007 (Opened February 20); 55 performances.

**American Fiesta** Written and performed by Steven Tomlinson; Director, Mark Brokaw; Sets, Neil Patel; Projections, Jan Hartley, S. Katy Tucker; Lighting, David Lander; Original Music, David Van Tieghem; Sound, Jill B.C. DuBoff; PSM, Megan Smith; ASM, Jamie Greathouse
A solo performance comedy-drama presented without intermission; Gertrude and Irving Dimson Theatre; April 14–May 20, 2007 (Opened April 26); 39 performances.

*Steven Tomlinson in* American Fiesta *(photo by Carol Rosegg)*

# Women's Project

Twenty-ninth Season

Producing Artistic Director, Julie Crosby, PhD; Artistic Advisor, Liz Diamond; General Manager, Wei-Jie Chou; Marketing, Jen McClelland; Artistic Associate, Megan E. Carter; Development Consultant, Paul Slee; Development Associate, Devin Nix; Marketing Consultants, Kat Williams, Bruce Cohen; Gala Coordinator, Catherine P. Saxton; Graphic Designer, Heather Honnold; Financial Services, Patricia Taylor; Production Manager, Dynamic Productions (Brian Rosenblum, Craig Sanoguiera, Alison Bond); Press, Carol Fineman/Glenna Freedman

**Victoria Martin: Math Team Queen** by Kathryn Walat; Director, Loretta Greco; Sets, Robert Brill; Costumes, Valerie Marcus Ramshur; Lighting, Sarah Sidman; Sound, Daniel Baker; Original Music, The Broken Chord Collective; PSM, Brian Meister; Casting, Paul Fouquet; Assistant Directors, Sarah Malkin, Kate Marks; ASM, Lyndsey Goode; Technical Director, Alison Bond; Props, Faye Armon; Wardrobe Supervisor, Anne Wingate; Cast: Zachary Booth (Peter), Jessi Campbell (Victoria), Adam Farabee (Jimmy), Tobias Segal (Max), Matthew Stadelmann (Franklin)
World premiere of a new play presented in two acts; Julia Miles Theatre; January 12–February 11, 2007 (Opened January 21); 26 performances.

**transFigures** Conceived and directed by Lear deBessonet, text by Bathsheba Doran, Charles Mee, Erin Sax Seymour, Russell Shorto, Joan of Arc, & Henrik Ibsen; Choreography, Andrea Haenggi; Dramaturgy, Megan E. Carter; Sets, Jenny Sawyers; Costumes, Clint Ramos; Lighting, Ryan Mueller; Sound, Mark Huang; Line Producer, Allison Prouty; Casting, Alaine Alldaffer; PSM, Jack Gianino; Assistant Director, Sari Kamin; Stage Manager, Alex Finch; Technical Director, Alison Bond; Associate Lighting, Benjamin Rollins; Cast: David Adkins (Bill), Dylan Dawson (Joshua), Juliana Francis (Margaret 1/Joan), Nate Schenkkan (Victor/Margaret 2), T. Ryder Smith (Gene/John Salvi), Marguerite Stimpson (Susan)
A performance piece with dance, music, and text presented without intermission; Julia Miles Theatre; April 6 -May 6, 2007 (Opened April 16); 34 performances.

**Girls Just Wanna Have Fund$** Presented with arts>World Financial Center and Debra Simon; PSM, Howard Klein; ASM, Hilary Austin; Included: *Keep the Change* by Joy Tomasko and Christina Gorman; Director, May Adrales; Producers, Maria Goyanes and Karen Grenke; Costumes, Brenda Abbandandolo, Props, Susan Barras; Cast: Davina Cohen, Anthony Manna, Sarah Murphy; *I Want What You Have* by Saviana Stanescu; Director, Gia Forakis; Producer, Leigh Goldenberg; Costumes, Alixandra Englund; Production Assistant, Colleen Jasinski; Cast: LeeAnne Hutchison, Tamilla Woodard, Chriselle Almeida; *Remembrance* by Katori Hall; Director, Jyana Gregory; Producer, Linda Powell; Costumes, Brenda Abbandandolo; Production Assistant, Dan Dinero; Cast: Edwina Findley, Dominique Morisseau; *A Peddler's Tale: Buttons, Guts and Bluetooth* by Andrea Lepcio; Director, Kim Weild; Producers, Patricia McNamara & Amy Kaissar; Costumes, Brenda Abbandandolo; Cast: KK Moggie, Khris Lewin; *The Dime Show* by Molly Rice; Director, May Adrales; Producer, Karen Grenke; Costumes, Brenda Abbandandolo; Props, Susan Barras; Cast: David Berent, Ginger Eckert, Andy Grotelueschen, Sara Moore; *Song* by Addie Brownlee; Producer, Maria Goyanes
A collection of new short plays presented without intermission; various locations throughout the World Financial Center; May 16–May 19, 2007; 13 performances.

*Jessi Campbell, Zachary Booth, Adam Farabee, Matthew Stadelmann, and Tobias Segal in* Victoria Martin: Math Team Queen *(photo by Carol Rosegg)*

*Marguerite Stimpson, T. Ryder Smith, Dylan Dawson, Nate Schenkkan, and David Adkins in* transFigures *(photo by Carol Rosegg)*

*Andy Grotelueschen and Anthony Manna in* Girls Just Wanna Have Fund$ *(photo by Carol Rosegg)*

# York Theatre Company

Thirty-eighth Season

Artistic Director, James Morgan; Chairman of the Board, David McCoy; Founding Director, Janet Hayes Walker; Associate Artistic Director, Brian Blythe; Development, Nancy P. Barry; Company Administrator, Alyssa Seiden; Production Manager, Chris Robinson; Communications Director, Alana Karpoff; Audience Services, Kirk Curtis; Developmental Reading Series Coordinator, Jeff Landsman; Casting, Norman Meranus; Technical Director, Scott F. DelaCruz; Marketing, HHC Marketing; Press, Helene Davis

**Asylum: The Strange Case of Mary Lincoln** Book by June Bingham, music and lyrics by Carmel Owen; Director, Fabrizio Melano; Music Director/Orchestration/Arrangements, Bob Goldstone; Musical Supervisor, Matt Castle; Sets, James Morgan; Costumes, Terese Wadden; Lighting, Chris Robinson; Wigs, Erin Kennedy Lunsford; Musical Staging, Brian Blythe; PSM, Scott DelaCruz; Stage Managers, Jose Docen, Sarah Butke; Cast: Ansel Elgort (Voice of Young Robert), Carolann Page (Mary Lincoln), Edwin Cahill (Robert Lincoln), John Jellison (Doctor Patterson/Abraham Lincoln), Joy Lynn Matthews (Delia), Bertilla Baker (Myra Bradwell), Daniel Spiotta (Franc Wilkie); Orchestra: Bob Goldstone/Danny Percefull (Piano), Joe Brent (violin), Tara Chambers (cello)
Musical Numbers: Mother I Need You, A National Disgrace, Dear Mr. Lincoln, Mother I Need You (reprise), This Is the Solution, Doctor, Crystal Wisdom, I Remember Him, The Run, Lincoln Waltz, Warm Mist, Oregon, The Letter, What A Story, Looking at You, It Won't Be Long Now, What A Story (reprise), Easy For You To Be So Noble, Rockabye Child Jesus, Why Robert, Why, It Won't Be Long Now (reprise)
Setting: The Bellevue Asylum, Batavia, Illinois. Winter 1875. World premiere of a new musical presented in two acts; Theatre at St. Peter's Church; September 5–October 1, 2006 (Opened September 14); 10 previews, 21 performances. This production was the final production of the previous season.

**That Time of the Year** Concept and lyrics by Laurence Holzman and Felicia Needleman, music by Sandford Marc Cohen, Nicholas Levin, Donald Oliver, Kyle Rosen, Brad Ross, Mark Wherry, & Wendy Wilf; Co-produced by Whiskey Down Productions; Director/Choreography, Annette Jolles; Music Director/Orchestrator, Annie Pasqua; Sets, James Morgan; Costumes, Terese Wadden; Lighting, Chris Robinson; Additional Arrangements, James Mironchik; PSM, Scott DelaCruz; Cast: Bridget Beirne, Kerri Jill Garbis, Erin Maguire, Jonathan Rayson, Nick Verina; Orchestra: Annie Pasqua (Conductor/piano), Chris Pagano (percussion), Mort Silver (reeds)
Musical Numbers: That Time of Year, Angelo Rosenbaum, Stay Home Tonight, Rock 'n' Roll Hanukkah, Little Colored Lights, God Only Knows, Country Christmas, That Time of Year: Reprise #1, People With Obligations, You're the Reason Why, Mama's Latkes, Husbands' Blues, Welcome, That Time of Year: Reprise #2, Judith Maccabee, Wong Ho's China Garden, They All Come Home, Underneath the Mistletoe, Time for a Spin, Calypso Christmas, That Time of Year: Reprise #3, Candles in the Window, It's Everywhere, Christmastime, Veronica, Holiday Lament, Miracles Can Happen, That Time of Year: Reprise #4, What Are We Gonna Do…?, That Time of Year: Reprise #5 (Bows)
A new musical revue presented in two acts; Theatre at St. Peter's Church; November 29–December 24, 2006 (Opened December 7); 10 previews, 22 performances.

**Blind Lemon Blues** Created by Alan Govenar and Akin Babatunde; Co-produced by Documentary Arts in association with Central Track Productions; Director/Choreography, Akin Babatunde; Music Arrangements, Akin Babatunde, Calvin Yarbrough, Alisa Peoples Yarbrough; Sets, Russell Parkman; Lighting, Steve Woods; Costumes, Tommy Bourgeois, Choreography Consultant, Norma Miller; Directorial & Dramaturgical Consultant, Obba Babatunde; PSM, Alan Govenar; ASM, Amanda Campbell-Wyatt; Marketing Consultant, Marci Pendleton; Cast: Calvin Yarbrough (Lead Belly), Akin Babatunde (Blind Lemon

*Carolann Page and Joy Lynn Matthews in* Asylum
*(photo by Carol Rosegg)*

*Nick Verina, Bridget Beirne, Jonathan Rayson, Erin Maguire, and Kerri Jill Garbis in* That Time of Year *(photo by Carol Rosegg)*

Jefferson), Ensemble: Benita Arterberry, Timothy Parham, Lillias White, Alisa Peoples Yarbrough; Guitar: Sam Swank
Setting: New York City, 1948. New York premiere of a new biographical musical presented in two acts; Theatre at St. Peter's Church; February 15–25, 2007; 10 performances.

**Musicals In Mufti – Musical Theatre Gems
in Staged Concert Performances – Twentieth Series**

**Take Me Along** Music and lyrics by Bob Merrill, book by Joseph Stein and Robert Russell; based on the play *Ah, Wilderness!* by Eugene O'Neill; Director, Michael Montel; Music Director, Danny Percefull; Musical Staging, Ananda Bena Weber; Lighting, Chris Robinson; PSM, Scott F. DelaCruz; Cast: Lorinda Lisitza (Ensemble), Kenneth Cavett (David Macomber), Robyne Parrish (Belle), Matthew Crowle (Wint), Jay Aubrey Jones (Ensemble), Melissa Bohon (Muriel Macomber), Deborah Jean Templin (Essie Miller), Ryan Driscoll (Art Miller), Jacob Levy (Tommy Miller), Susan Bigelow (Lily Miller), Nick Wyman (Nat Miller), Andrew Rasmussen (Richard Miller), David Schramm (Sid Davis)
Musical Numbers: The Parade, Oh Please, I Would Die, Sid Ol' Kid, Staying Young, I Get Embarrassed, We're Home, Take Me Along, For Sweet Charity, Pleasant Beach House, That's How It Starts, The Pleasant Beach House, Oh Please (reprise), Slight Detail (Promise Me a Rose), Staying Young (reprise), Little Green Snake, Nine O'clock, But Yours, Finale
A musical presented in two acts; Theatre at St. Peter's Church; October 13–15, 2006; 5 performances.

**Carmelina** Music by Burton Lane, lyrics by Alan Jay Lerner, book by Joseph Stein and Alan Jay Lerner, additional lyrics by Barry Harman; Director, Michael Leeds; Music Director, Grant Sturiale; Lighting, Chris Robinson; PSM, Scott F. DelaCruz; ASM, Sarah Butke; Cast: Nat Chandler (Steve Karzinski), Joseph Kolinski (Carleton Smith), Daniel Marcus (Walter Braddock), Camille Saviola (Rosa), Marla Schaffel (Signora Carmelina Campbell), Alison Walla (Gia Campbell), Ray Wills (Vittorio Dela Marta), Eli Zoller (Roberto/Guitarist)
Musical Numbers: Prayer, Carmelina, Someone in April, Signora Campbell, You're a Woman, Love Me Tomorrow, Signora Campbell (reprise), One More Walk Around the Garden, All That I Dreamed He Would Be, It's Time for a Love Song, The Image of Me, I Will Kill Her, Sorry As I Am, I'm a Woman, It's Time for a Love Song (reprise)
Setting: A tiny restaurant in the village of San Forino, somewhere between Sorrento and Naples, present day. A musical presented in two acts; Theatre at St. Peter's Church; October 20–22, 2006; 5 performances.

**Plain and Fancy** Book by Joseph Stein and Will Glickman, music by Albert Hague, lyrics by Arnold Horwitt; Director, David Glenn Armstrong, Music Director, Zachary Dietz; Associate Music Director/Pianist, John Bell; Lighting, Chris Robinson; Associate Director, Daniel Haley; PSM, Scott F. DelaCruz; ASM, Sarah Butke; Cast: Cady Huffman (Ruth Winters), Jordan Leeds (Dan King), Sara DeLaney (Katie Yoder), Erick Devine (Papa Yoder), Rick Hilsabeck (Isaac Miller), Charlotte Rae (Emma Yoder), Dan Sharkey (Ezra Reber), Jim Sorensen (Ike Pilersheim), Adam Laird (Jacob Yoder), Ward Billeisen (Abner Zook), Beth Kirkpatrick (Rachel Beiler), Nancy Anderson (Hilda Miller), Jack Noseworthy (Peter Reber)
Musical Numbers: You Can't Miss It, It Wonders Me, Plenty of Pennsylvania, Young and Foolish, Why Not Katie, Young and Foolish (reprise), Helluva Way to Run a Love Affair, This is All Very New to Me, Plain We Live, Plain We Live (reprise), How Do You Raise a Barn, Follow Your Heart, Follow Your Heart (reprise), City Mouse-Country Mouse, I'll Show Him, Young and Foolish (reprise), Take Your Time and Take Your Pick, Plenty of Pennsylvania (reprise)
Setting: Lancaster County in Pennsylvania, a community for the Amish. A musical presented in two acts; Theatre at St. Peter's Church; October 27–29, 2006; 5 performances.

**Special Events**

**Chris & Adelmo: The Second Coming** Written and performed by Christopher Cain and Adelmo Guidarelli, with Amber L. Spradlin; Director/Stage Manager, Mike Wells, Music Director, Bruce Stasyna; Lighting, Chris Robinson; Vocal Coach, Dr. William D. Riley; Production Supervisor, Scott F. DelaCruz; December 5, 2006–January 6, 2007, 6 performances.

**The People Garden** and **The New Kid** Book, music and lyrics by Paul Armento; Co-produced by The Sandcastle Organization; Director, Paul Armento; Stage Manager, Suzan LaVarco; Sound/Stage Crew, David Lehner, Jon Bernstein; Lighting, Oren Rabinowitz; two musicals for young audiences performed by kids; October 14, 2006–May 19, 2007; 10 and 11 performances respectively.

*Timothy Parham, Benita Arterberry, Alisa Peoples Yarbrough, Lillias White, Akin Babatunde, and Calvin Yarbrough in* Blind Lemon Blues
*(photo by Alan Govenar)*

*Harold Todd and Dawn Luebbe in* The Frugal Repast *at Abingdon Theatre Company (photo by Kim T. Sharp)*

*Carolyn McCormick and Dominic Cuskern in* Biography *at the Pearl Theatre Company (photo by Gregory Costanzo)*

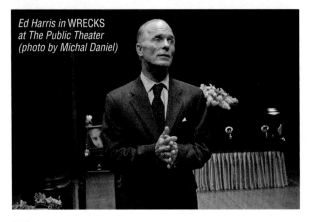

*Ed Harris in* WRECKS *at The Public Theater (photo by Michal Daniel)*

*Richard Kline and Roderick Hill in* Return of the Prodigal *at the Mint Theatre (photo by Richard Termine)*

*Andrew Polk, Daniel Sauli, and Zoe Lister-Jones in* The Accomplices *at The New Group (photo by Carol Rosegg)*

*John Fugelsang in the New York Theatre Workshop's* All the Wrong Reasons *(photo by Carol Rosegg)*

# OFF-OFF-BROADWAY

Top to bottom:

A'lisa D. Miles and Matt DeAngelis in Prospect Theatre Company's production of The Flood at the Chernuchin Theatre (photo by Gerry Goodstein)

Suzanne Rydz and Thomas Ryan in R&R Productions' Love's Divide, which played at Dillons and the Triad Theatre

Seth Rudetsky and Laura Raines in the Gallery Players production of Torch Song Trilogy (photo by Stephen Nachamie)

Ken Matthews in Reverie Productions' Billboard, presented at 59E59 (photo by Zhanna Gurvich)

Arthur French, Bryan Webster, and Timothy D. Stickney in Hamlet, presented by Take Wing and Soar at WorkShop Theater Company's Jewel Box Theater (photo by Joseph Marzullo/Retna Ltd.)

Adrian Wyatt and Andrew Pastides in Makeout Session, presented at TBG Theatre (photo by Jason Woodruff)

Sherry Vine in Theatre Couture's production of Carrie, presented at P.S. 122 (photo by Aaron Corbett)

The cast of the Vortex Theatre Company's HMS Pinafore, presented at the Sanford Meisner Theatre (photo by Jim Baldassare)

Cameron Barnet, Joseph Melendez, Jene Hernandez, and Michael Murnoch in Amas Musical Theatre's Magpie, presented at the Players Theatre (photo courtesy of Donna Trinkoff)

# 13th Street Repertory

Edith O'Hara, Artistic Director/Founder

**Elevator Face Book** lyrics by Chris Widney, music by David Christian Azarow; Director, Amanda Shank; July 13–15

**Terrorism & You** lyrics & direction by Sara Cooper, music & co-direction by Chris Shimojima; July 13–15

**Lucky 13 Short Play Festival** July 20–30; Evening A: *Eleanor* by Julia Sullivan, *Flying Object* by M. John Bohane, *Trouble on the Path* by Joel Stone, *Tushy Glickstein at the Neurotic Olympics* by Michael Stockman, *Lobster Tales* by Michael Stang, *House Across the Street* by Larry Stallings; Evening B: *Me, Myself, and ID* by Matt Faldeman, *Fin and Euba* by Audrey Cefaly, *Where Time Is Money* by Susan Price Monnot, *The Sandman Cometh* by Edward J. Thomas, *Try to Act Normal* by Fredd Sahner, *Love and Death in the Time of the Crayola* by David Schebett

**A Yellow Butterfly Called Sphinxx** by French Christian Palustran; Director, Amanda Shank; July 24–26

**New Sounds in Music** featuring musical groups Myk Freeman Suit and Bing & Ruth; October 1–29

**Pieces of Paradise** by Tennessee Williams; Director, Stephan Morrow; included: *The Municipal Abbatoir, The Palooka, These Are the Stairs You Gotta Watch, Mister Paradise*; October 22–November 15, extended January 22–April 3

**Interview** and **Behind the Invisible Enemy** by Valerie Killigrew; Directors, Matthew Tennie & Karen Raphaeli; November 2–December 2

**A Christmas Carol** by Charles Dickens, adapted by Sandra Nordgren; December 7–January 7

**Outlet** presented by Family Tree Collective; February 21–28

**Five Story Walkup** short plays by John Guare, Neil LaBute, Laura Shaine Cunningham, Clay McLeod Chapman, Daniel Frederick Levin, Quincy Long, Daniel Gallant; Director, Daniel Gallant; March 21–April 14

**Ms. Blusical–Shades of Blu** written, produced & performed by Audra Berger; Music Director, David Lahm; April 18

**Amahlia** by Joel Shatzky; Director, Esther Neff; Music, Ben Tyree; Cast: Andrea Suarez, Joe Lampe, Liche Ariza; April 26–June 2

## Opened-ended Productions

**Ledgends of Laughter** written, directed & performed by Hootch Hoolahan; Opened January 4, 2004

**Line** by Israel Horovitz; Director, Edith O'Hara, 33rd season

**Keep Your Funny Side Up** with Louisa Poster; Opened June 7, 2005

## Non-resident Productions

**Spurn** Multimedia Sketch Comedy Troupe produced by Ross A. McIntyre; Director, Stage Manager, Sheena Crespo; Cast: Lara Jane Dunatov, Matt Klan, Ross A. McIntyre, Bethany Sacks, Jennifer Spragg, Eric Zuckerman; October 4–21

**The Last of the Texas Dollies** by Dan Moyer; presented by Little Red Square; Director, Matthew Patches; April 1–4

# 14th Street Theater

**Nerve** by Adam Szymkowicz; produced by Packawallop Productions and the Hypothetical Theatre Company; Director, Scott Ebersold; Managing Producer, Marc Solomon; Sets, Nicholas Vaughan; Costumes, Jessica Watters; Lighting, Sarah Jakubasz; Choreography, Wendy Seyb; Puppets, Peiyi Wong; PSM, Jenny Snyder; Stage Manager, Catilin Baird; Cast: Susan Louise O'Connor, Travis York; June 8–July 1

**Two Destinies** by Guile Branco; Director, Emanuelle Villorini; Sets, Maya Kaplun; Lighting/Sound, Clarence Gilliard; Cast: Robert Haufrecht, Guile Branco; Piano: Audra Baas; July 7–30

**Fringe Festival 2006 Encores** produced by John Pinckard & Britt Lalfield: *Diving Normal* by Ashlin Halfnight, produced by Electric Pear Productions; Director, Mary Catherine Burke; Cast: Josh Heine, Jayd McCarty, Eliza Baldi; September 5–24; *I Was Tom Cruise* by Alexander Poe, produced by Redux Productions; Directors, Alexander Poe & Joseph Varca; Design, Andrew Boyce, Sarah Cubbage, Joseph Varca; Cast: Jeff Berg, Amy Flanagan, Jeff Addiss, Gideon Banner, Teddy Bergman, Cormac Bluestone, Natasha David, Colby Disarro, Victoria Haynes, Laura Perloe; September 5–22; *The Infliction of Cruelty* by Andrew Unterberg and Sean McManus, produced by Tuesday Club Productions; Director, Joel Froomkin; Design, Jerome Martin, Grant W. Yeager, Alana Israelson; Cast: Elizabeth VanMeter, Holter Graham, Justin Barrett, Aimee DeShayes, Pawel Szajda; September 6–12; *The Deepest Play Ever: The Catharsis of Pathos* by Geoffrey Decas, produced by CollaborationTown; Director, Ryan Purcell; September 9–17; *Danny Boy* by Marc Goldsmith; Director, Christopher Goodrich; September 15–21; *Walmartopia* by Catherine Capellaro & Andrew Rohn, produced by Outside the Big Box; Director, Catherine Capellaro; Choreography, Shannon Barry; Costumes, Kelly Murphy; Lighting, Paul Schaefer; Sound, Ehren Tresner; Props, Kim Zunker; Cast: Tara Ayres, Chris Babiarz, Mikhael Farah, Frank Furillo, John Gustafson, Joe Hammes, Doug Holtz, Jake Jacobson, Kelly Kiorpes, Kelly Kriese, Anna Marquardt, Kelly Murphy, Jennifer Pluff, Stefanie Resnick, Marcy Weiland, Sarah Whelan, Kristy Wilson; September 15–23; *Perfect Harmony* conceived and directed by Andrew Grosso, written and presented by The Essentials; Sets, Eliza Brown; Costumes, Becky Lasky, Lighting, Driscoll Otto; Music Director, Alec Duffy; Cast David Barlow, Autumn Dornfeld, Scott Janes, Vayu O'Donnell, Maria Elena Ramirez, Jeanine Serralles, Marina Squerciati, Margie Stokley, Noah Weisberg, Blake Whyte; September 21–24

**Me, My Guitar, and Don Henley** by Krista Vernoff; produced by Crooked Neck Productions and Rachel Jackson; Director, Peter Paige; Sets, John McDermott; Costumes, Beth Goldenberg; Lighting, John Pinchard; Sound, James Evan Pilato; Stage Manager, Devan Hibbard; Assistant Director, Portia Krieger; Cast: SuEllen Estey, Tara Franklin, Mary Elaine Monti, Stephanie Nasteff, Kaili Vernoff, Jennifer Dorr White; October 7–27

**No Boundaries Play Fest** presented by the Mirror Repertory Company; November 16–19; Series A: *Theatre is The Thing with Tentacles* by Ed Valentine; Director, Mark Defrancis; *Just Another Day in November* by Jonathon Joy; Director, Roseanne Clark; *Circus Chimps* by MacAdam Smith; Director, Mark Defrancis; *Ten Speed Revolution* by John Heimbuch; Director, Alex Burns; Series B: *Song of Bentley* by Daniel Kelley; Director, Anthony Nelson; *Incorporated* by Sarah Hague, Director, Nicholas Uber Leonard; *The Period Fairy* by Jason Kessler; Director, Max Shulman

**the silent concerto** by Alejandro Morales; presented by Packawallop Productions and Hypothetical Theater; Director, Scott Ebersold; Choreography, Wendy Seyb; Sets, Nicholas Vaughan; Costumes, Jessica Watters; Lighting, Douglas Filomena; Sound, Ryan Maeker; Cast: Susan Louise O'Connor, Drew Hirschfeld, Julian Stetkevych; January 3–February 17

**Love and Israel** created and produced by Sissy Block and Ilana Lipski; Director, Ilana Lipski; monologues by Sissy Block, Jonathan Elkins, Benjamin Fleisher, Kelly Hartog, Tania Hershman, Dina Kraft, Ilana Lipski, Rachel Pine, Mindy Raf, Avi Reinharz, Ahron Shapiro, Yossi Tesher; Cast: Sissy Block, Nathan Brisby, Iuliana Gedo, Jordana Oberman, Mindy Raf, Avi Reinharz, Paul Weissman; February 27–28

**volume of smoke** by Clay McLeod Chapman; produced by elsewhere; Director, Isaac Butler; Sets, Tim McMath; Costumes, Sydney Maresca; Lighting, Sabrina Braswell; Original Music, Erik Sanko; Producer, Anne Love; Cast: Katie Dietz, Abe Goldfarb, Daryl Lathon, Ronica V. Reddick, Brian Stillman, Molly Wright Stuart; March 22–April 7

**Opening Doors: A Journey in Musical Theatre** presented by Wingspan Arts; April 14–15

**Alcatraz** by A. Kirchner, based on the poem by Elena Fattakova; presented by The Seven Tigers Company; Director, Andrew Dion; Cast: Drake Andrew, Michael Buoni, Elena Fattakova, Rahti Gorfien, Mark Konrad, Paul Navarra, Daniel J. O'Brien; April 25–May 12

## 29th Street Rep (Altered Stages)

David Mogentale, Artistic Director

**Plays in Motion: Reading Series** *The Conversation* by Francis Ford Coppola, adapted by Kate Harris (September 26); *The 4th Graders Present an Unnamed Love-Suicide* by Sean Graney (October 3); *4 Murders* by Brett Neveu (October 10); *Where You Still Live* by Patricia Henritze (October 17)

### Non-resident Productions

**Three-Ways** by Matthew David Barton; presented by Alamo Theatre; Cast: R.J. Foster, Monica Cortez, Vince Lombardi; August 24–September 2

**Why We Shot John** by Walt Stepp; presented by Cinna Productions, Julie Carpenter; Director, B. Peter Westerhoff; Sets/Costumes, Aaron P. Mastin; Lighting, Stephen Arnold; Sound, Peter Sylvester; PSM, Jesi Thelen; Cast: Bill Dante, Scott Glascock, Charlotte Hampden, Buzz Roddy, Scott Van Tuyl; September 9–October 1

**Wingman** by Robert Cole and John Wooten; Director, John Wooten; Stage Manager, Dale Smallwood; Cast: Gary Cowling, Simon Feil, Matt Fraley, Sebastian LaCause, Jeff Lambert, Kate Stone; October 4–15

**Danny and the Deep Blue Sea** by John Patrick Shanley; presented by Well Urned Productions; Director, JoAnn Oakes; Cast: Leticia Diaz, Gregory Climi; October 16–22

**Love, Death, and Interior Decorating** by Keith Boynton; produced by Fuzzy Dice Productions; Directors, Sandra and Keith Boynton; Sets, KMB/Boynton Expedient Solutions; Lighting, Charles Forster, Costumes, Rachel Ford; Sound, Christine Hong/Boynton & Ford; Stage Manager, James R. Creque IV; Associate Producer, Katharine Croke; Cast: Joan Kubicek, Mike LaVoie, Roya Shanks, Keith Boynton; November 2–18

**Lovehandles** written & directed William Bailey; produced by Small Pond Entertainment, Joane Cajuste, Kelly Vollmer, Michael Roderick; Stage Manager, Drew Honeywell; Assistant Producer, Ron Idra; Lighting/Sound, Kryssy Wright; Cast: Joane Cajuste, Kelly Vollmer, Julian Brennan, Chad Morgan Meador, Kwame Riley, Ken Scudder, Carrie Tavris, John Paul Tilleman, Allison Troesch, Nicole Witkosky; March 15–18

**The View from K Street Steak** by Walt Stepp; presented by Cinna Productions; Director, Tom Herman; Sets, Michael Kearns; Costumes, Cathy Small; Lighting, Charles Foster; Sound, Chris Rummel; PSM, Maureen Rogalski; ASM, Sarah Worrest; Assistant Director, Jeremy Pape; Press, Publicity Outfitters; Cast: Rachel Darden Bennett, Kwaku Driskell, Bill Green, Christopher Hurt, Brian Patrick Mooney, Bill Tatum, Brad Thomason, Samantha Wynn; April 12–May 5

**Mommie's Boys** by Jack Dowd; presented by John Capo Productions; Director, John Capo; Cast: Ryan Coyle, Andrea Marshall-Mooney, Jason Gotay, Diana Prano, Jordan Kaplan, Carol Brooks; May 9–20

**North of Providence** by Edward Allan Baker; presented by Small Pond Entertainment; Director, Glory Sims Bowen; Cast: Chad Meador, Yvonne Roen; May 24–June 3

## 3Graces Theatre Company

Chelsea Silverman, Executive Director; Elizabeth Bunnell and Annie McGovern, Artistic Directors; Kelli Lynn Harrison, Managing Director

**Nickel and Dimed** by Joan Holden, based on "Nickel and Dimed, on [not] Getting by in America" by Barbara Ehrenreich; Director, Dave Dalton; Sets, Victoria Roxo; Costumes, Veneda Truesdale; Lighting, Anjeanette Stokes; Sound/Musical Director, John D. Ivy; Press, Michelle Brandon; PSM, Jennifer B. Havey; Cast: Dorothy Abrahams, Margot Avery, Suzanne Barbetta, Jeremy Beck, Kathleen Bishop, Elizabeth Bunnell, Cherelle Cargill, Richard Ferrone, Annie McGovern, Chelsea Silverman, Nancy Wu; Bank Street Theatre; October 5–28

**Neglect** by Sharyn Rothstein; Director, Catherine Ward; Sets, Victoria Roxo; Costumes, Veneda Truesdale; Lighting, Anjeanette Stokes; Sound/Musical Director, John D. Ivy; Press, Michelle Brandon; PSM, Ange Berneau; Cast: William Jackson Harper, Geany Masai, Ange Berneau; Bank Street Theatre; October 10–25

**Dream of a Common Language** by Heather McDonald; Director, Karen Sommer; Original Music, Chip Barrow, John D. Ivy; Set, Mandy Hart; Lighting, Anjeanette Stokes; Costumes, Veneda Truesdale; Sound, John D. Ivy; Choreography, Dorothy Abrahams; Production Manager, Pamela D. Roberts; ASM, Uys DeBoisson; Cast: David Kahn, Kelli Lynn Harrison, Kerry Watterson, Annie McGovern, Suzanne Barbetta, Ian Christiansen; Hudson Guild Theatre; March 16–April 6

## 3-Legged Dog Theatre Company (3LD Art & Technology Center)

Kevin Cunningham, Art and Business; Victor Weinstock, Managing Director

**The Curse of the Mystic Renaldo The** by Aldo Perez; Director, Victor Weinstock; Technical Director & Sets, Paul DiPietro; Production Manager & Lighting, David Tirosh; Costumes, Allison Keating; Video, Jeff Morey; Sound, Nick Parker, Patrick Klein; Stage Manager, Errin Delperdang; Cast: Aldo Perez, Richard Ginnoccio, Jennifer Mitchell, Musicians: Nick Parker, Patrick Klein; February 22–May 5

**Losing Something** written, directed, and designed by Kevin Cunningham; Costumes/Production Designer, Allison Keating; Sets, Paul DiPietro; Video, Jeff Morey; Sound, Sean Hagerty; Lighting, David Tirosh; Music, Aldo Perez; Dramaturg, Victor Weinstock; Cast: Aldo Perez, Michael Bell, Victoria Chamberlin, Livia DePaolis, Catherine Yeager; April 6–May 5

**Non-resident Productions**

**Dead City** by Sheila Callaghan; presented by New Georges Theatre Company; Director, Daniella Topol; Sets, Cameron Anderson; Costumes, Jenny Mannis; Lighting, Josh Epstein; Sound, Robert Kaplowitz; Video, William Cusick; Assistant Director, Heidi Handelsman; Choreographer, Jessica Hendricks; PSM, Leigh Boone; ASM, Megan Schwarz; Production Manager, Samuel C. Tresler; Technical Director, Seth Allhouse; Press, Jim Baldassare; Cast: April Matthis, Elizabeth Norment, Peter Rini, Shannon Burkett, Rebecca Hart, Dan Illian, Alfredo Narciso; May 26–June 30

# 440 Studios

**Drops** choreographed by Aya Shibahara, music by Peter Rosenblatt and Glen Fittin; Cast: Ralph Colombino, Glen Fittin, Victoria Lundel, Emily Quant, Ryoji Sasamoto, Yuko Sawatani, Peter Rosenblatt, Aya Shibahara; Black Box Theatre; June 14–17

**The Woman's Room** written & directed by Elizabeth Kerins; Cast: Pia Shah; Black Box Theatre; July 14–15

**Remember Me** written & directed by Adam Weir; Black Box Theatre; July 27–28

**I (Heart) Kant** by Ken Urban; presented by the Committee Theatre Company; Director, Dylan McCullough; Sets, Lee Savage; Costumes, Emily Rebholz; Lighting, Thom Weaver; Sound, Elizabeth Rhodes; Stage Manager, Alexandra Cohen-Spiegler; ASM, Jason Weixelman; Cast: Kate Benson, Steven Boyer, Kate Downing, Edelen McWilliams, Frances Mercanti-Anthony; Linhart Theatre; September 8–October 2

**The Asexual Revolution** by Adam Weir; Black Box Theatre; October 27–29

**Testify: Conversations in Congress** presented by Breedingground Productions; Black Box Theatre; November 3–4

**Echoes** by N. Richard Nash; presented by Doubtless Dreamers; Cast: April Lowe, Craig Jessen, Kelly Morris; Black Box Theatre; November 30–December 10

**TASTE: A Reading Series** presented by The Committee Theatre Company; Linhart Theatre; January 11–16; included: *The Vigil or the Guided Cradle* by Crystal Skillman, *Lulu Ascending* by Caridad Svich, and *Sense of an Ending* by Ken Urban

**POPS! Riffs, Rants, and Ramblings on the Current State of Popular Culture Affairs** by Anton Dudley, Jono Hustis, Brian Dykstra, Rob Ackerman, Daphne Greaves, Andrea Lepcio, Robin Rice Lichtig, David Schaller, Justin Scribner, Michael Hartney; presented by At Hand Theatre Company; Black Box Theatre; May 3–5

# 45 Bleecker

**Big Shoot** by Koffi Kwahulé; presented by The Culture Project and RPN Globe; Director/Set, Gabriella Maione; Composer, Michael Galasso; Costumes, Catherine Zuber; Lighting, Justin Townsend; Sound, Kenta Nagai; Fights, J. David Brimmer; PSM, Yvonne Perez; Production Supervisor, Peter R. Feuchtwanger; Cast: Tom Brangle, Patrick Halliday; June 7–July 15

**Godot Has Left the Building** by John Griffin; produced by David Friedman and FourScore Productions in association with The Culture Project; Director, Will Pomerantz; Design, Garin Marschall; Costumes, Naomi Wolff; Sound, Patrick Weaver; Stage Manager, Maeve O'Connor; Cast: Scott Nogi, Edward Griffin, Gabriel Gutierrez, Bert Gurin; 45 Bleecker Below; June 22–July 9

**Cloud Tectonics** by Jose Rivera; produced by Out of Line Productions; Director, James Philip Gates; Sets, Casey Smith; Costumes, Heather Klar; Lighting, Paul Hackenmueller; PSM, Lauren Arneson; Cast: Frederique Nahmani, Luis Vega, Julio Rivera; 45 Bleecker Below; July 13–August 5

**Impact Festival** September 12–October 16; included: *9/12* by David Meth, directed by Chris O'Connor; Cast: Farah Bala, Phil Gardiner, Ariel Estrada, Leslie Jones, Tina Lee, Peter Ratray, Don Striano, Virginia Wing; *Achidi J's Final Hours* by Amy Evans; *Ariel Sharon Stands at the Temple Mount and Dreams of Theodor Herzl* by David Zellnik, directed by Carlos Armesto; Cast: Jeremy Shamos; *Atomic Farmgirl* by C. Denby Swanson; *Cardiac Shadow* by Clay MacLeod Champman; *Dai* written and performed by Iris Bahr; *Enough is Enough* by Joe Sutton; *Free Theater from Belarus*, produced by Aaron Landsman; *Homeland Security* by Stuart Flack, directed by J. Christopher O'Connor; *Heresy* by Sabrina Berman, directed by Marcy Arlin & *The Word Progress on My Mother's Lips Doesn't Ring True* by Matei Visniec, directed by Ian Morgan, presented by Immigrant Theatre Project; *Iraq: Speaking of War* compiled & directed by Karen Malpede, music by Milos Raickovich & Amir El Saffar; Cast: George Bartenieff, Dalia Basiouny, Kathleen Chalfant, Judith Malina, Hanon Reznikov, Najla Said, Amneh Taye, Maysoon Zayid, Waleed Zuaiter, Peter Francis James; *Liz Swados' Political Revue: Mental Missiles* created and directed by Elizabeth Swados, with Utkarsh Ambudkar, Barthelemy Atsin, Matt Citron, Emma Tattenbaum-Fine, Sanaz Ghajarrahimi, Tia N'Deye Jennings, Danielle Levanas, Vella Lovell, Preston Martin, Grace McLean, Anthony Parker, Chloe Ramras; *Philoctetes* by Sophocles, adapted by Bryan Doerries; *Port Authority Throw Down* by Mike Batistick; *Six Actors in Search of a Plot – A Palestinian/Israeli Theater Initiative* by Muhammad Ahmed Zaher, co-authored & directed by Billy Yalowitz; Cast: Shadi Facher Aladeen, Nurit Parente, Hanin Tarabiya, Efrat Ungaro, Ranin Bisharat, Liat Cohen, Shaden Abu el Assal, Oran Dessau; *Speak Truth to Power* edited by Kerry Kennedy, adapted by Ariel Dorfman, directed by Terry Kinney; *Talking to Terrorists* by Robin Soans, directed by E. Christensen; Cast: Anthony Wills Jr, Satya Bhabha, Chinasa Ogbuagu, Elizabeth West, Khris Lewin, John Wright, Darius Suziedelis, Rebecca White; *The People Speak* written & directed by Rob Urbinati, co-written by Anthony Arnove & Howard Zinn, co-directed by Will Pomerantz; *The Peroecution of Brandon Hein* by Charles Grodin, directed by Gordon Edelstein; Cast: Charles Grodin, Kathleen Chalfant, Bob Ari, Julia Gibson, James McMenamin, Kristine Nielsen, Victor Slezak; *The Treatment* by Eve Ensler, *The Veiled Monologues* by Adeheid Roosen; *The Vigil or The Guided Cradle* by Crystal Skillman, directed by Heath Cullens; *The Warrior* by Jack Gihooley, directed by Steven Ditmyer; Cast: Tamara Flannagan & Annie McAdams; *Theatres Against War* by Alexandria Beech, Jason Grote, Akin Salawu, Tommy Smith; directed by Cynthia Croot, Victor Maog, Kristin Marting, Noel Salzman; Cast: Daniel Carlton, Maha Chehlaoui, Kate Cook, Chris Domig, Seraph Erincin, Bridgit Evans, Chris Harcum, Ilyana Kadushin, Donnie Mather, Patrick McNulty, Sophia Skiles, Scott Sowers, Morgan Spector, Sean Tarrant, Deborah Wallace, Mark Watson, Alec Duffy; *Tower of Babel* by Lidy Six & Robert Steijn; *Valient* by Lanna Joffrey, directed by Tamilla Woodard; *Voices UnBroken*

# 45th Street Theatre

**The Happy Idea** by Adé Adémola; presented by Xoregos Performing Company; Director, Sheila Xoregos; Music Director, Eugene Abrams; Cast: Lino Delacore, Lawrence Merritt, Marilyn Bernard, Stephanie Stone; June 8–18

**I Come in Peace** and **Bootleg Islam** two solo performance plays written & performed by Dean Obeidallah and Negin Farsad; September 3–7

**A First Class Man** by David Freeman; produced by Alter Ego Productions; Director, Kareem Fahmy; Sets, Jeffery Eisenmann; Costumes, Chloe Chapin; Lighting, Bryan Keller; Sound, Andrew Papadeas; Cast: Bobby Abid, Chriselle Almeida, Amir Arison, Kelly Eubanks, Steve French, Davis Hall, Timothy Roselle, Doug Simpson, Vikram Somaya, Radhika Vaz; October 5–21

**I'll Be Seeing You...** written and produced by Jennifer Russo; Director, Tracy Podell; Choreography, J. Austin Eyer; Music Director, Nate Patten; Lighting, Connor Mickiewicz; Cast: Jennifer Russo, Elizabeth Kerins, Ben Kaplan, Tripp Pettigrew, Rick Merpi; November 1–4

**Defending the Caveman** by Rob Becker; December 9–10

**The Tempest** by William Shakespeare; presented by Sonnet Repertory Theatre; Director, Neal Freeman; Cast: Frederic Heringes, Melissa Miller, Matthew Conlon, William Connell, Jack Dillon, Carey Van Driest, Patrick Toon; February 15–25

**The Waiting Room** by Samm-Art Williams; produced by The Negro Ensemble Company; Director, Charles Weldon; Sets, George Corrin; Costumes, Marmarra McKinney; Lighting, Ves Weaver; Sound, Anthony J. Dixon; Stage Manager, Elliot Lanes; Cast: Gabrielle Lee, Michael Chenevert, Ed Wheeler, Elain Graham, Gordon MacInnes, David Cochrane, Ebony Jo-Ann, Messeret Stroman; March 16–April 1

**Considering Lear** conceived, produced, and performed by Eric Krebs; April 3–8

**Marie Antoinette: The Color of Flesh** by Joel Gross; produced by Earl Productions and Briana Seferian; Director, Robert Kalfin; Cast: Amanda Jones, Jonathan Kells Phillips, Samantha Ives; April 5–29

**Damn It! I Am a Latino and My Skin Is Black!** written & performed by Luis Lassen; April 12–29

**To Paul** by Joe Silvio; Director, Joe Turci; presented by Take Care! Productions; May 2–6

**Hey You, Light Man!** by Oliver Hailey; presented by Firebrand Theory Theater Company; Director, Jaime Robert Carrillo; Cast: Sari Caine, Gary Ferrar, Vance-Allen Rawles, Christopher Lee, Sonya Tsuchigane, Heidi Azaro; May 18–June 3

# 59E59

**East to Edinburgh** July 11–29; Included – Theatre B: *Fahrenheit 451* by Ray Bradbury; Director, Joe Tantalo; presented by Godlight Theater Company; *Clean Alternatives* by Brian Dykstra; Director, Margarett Perry; presented by Fresh Ice Productions; *Three Mo' Tenors* conceived, directed, and choreographed by Marion. J. Caffey; presented by Wilette M. Klausner; *Twilight: Los Angeles,1992* by Anna Deavere Smith; Director, Linda Ames Key; presented by The Red Chair Players; Theatre C: *Mickey Mouse is Dead* by Justin Sherin; Director, Gordon Garver; presented by Spankin' Yanks; *Pentecostal Wisconsin* written & performed by Ryan Paulson; Director, Virginia Scott; *Businessman's Holiday; Stone and Stone* written, directed & performed by Adam and Todd Stone; *Fargo: A (Mostly) True Story* by Ryan Thoreson and Marie Striden; presented by The Lone Fargoan Company

**Henrik Ibsen + Jon Fosse: Norway Meets New York** produced by Elysabeth Kleinhans and Peter Tear; Sets, Lauren Helpern; Lighting, Mary Louise Geiger; Costumes, Courtney Logan; Sound, David Margolin Lawson; Composer, Cristian Amigo; Dramaturgs, Marie-Louise Miller & Oda Radoor; Movement, Melissa Riker; Two plays presented on a double bill: Ibsen's *Rosmersholm,* adapted by Anna Guttormsgaard and Bridgette Wimberly with Oda Radoor; Director, Timothy Douglas; Cast: Anna Guttormsgaard, Mike Hodge, Neal Lerner, Lizan Mitchell, J. Paul Nicholas, Charles Parnell; Fosse's *deathvariations,* translated and directed by Sarah Cameron Sunde; Cast: Diane Ciesla, Dick Hughes, Natalia Payne, Deborah Knox, David L. Townshend, Charles Borland; Theater B; August 8–September 9

**The Death in Juniper Grove** written & directed by Le Wilhelm; presented by Rage Against Time (R.A.T.) in association with Love Creek Productions; Sets, Lex Liang; Lighting, Megan Bezdek; Costumes, Rachel Sterner; Sound, Cynthia Winstead; Cast: Nancy McDoniel, Kristin Carter, Vito Cottone, Paul A. Nicosia, Jon Oak, Joanie Schumacher, Jaclyn Sokol; Theater C; August 15–September 3

**The Man Himself** by Alan Drury; adapted, directed, and performed by Ami

Dayan; presented by Maya Productions; co-adapted by Mark Williams; Lighting/ Stage Manager, Michael Ou; Film/Graphic Design, Benjamin Flaherty; General Manager, The Splinter Group; Cast: Seth A. Goldstein, Anne Love, and Elisabeth Bayer; Theater C; September 10–October 1

**Trousers** written & directed by Paul Meade and David Parnell; presented by Civic Theatre and Gúna Nua in association with Origin Theatre Company; Sets, Lex Liang; Lighting, James Bedell; Costumes, Elizabeth Flauto; Sound, Zachary Williamson; PSM, Carol A. Sullivan; Press, Mark Cannistraro; Vocal Coach, David Gagnon; ASM, Stephanie Rosenberg; Cast: Gary Gregg, Daniel Freedom Stewart; Theater C; October 5–22

**The Cleric** by Tim Marks; presented by Mind the Gap; Director, Paula D'Alessandris; Sets/Lighting, Maruti Evans; Sound, Brian Petway; Press, Beck Lee; Cast: Richard T. Lester, Armand DesHarnais, James Kloiber, Daniel Haughey, Sean Heeney; Theater C; October 25–November 12

**Romania, Kiss Me!** six short plays presented by The Play Company; *Bus* by Christina Panaite; Director, Liesl Tommy; *Red Bull* by Vera Ion; Director, Marcy Arlin; *Diagnosis* by Iona Moldovan; Director, Tom Caruso; *Romania, Kiss Me!* by Bogdan Georgescu; Director, Kaipo Schwab; *Fuck You, Eu.ro.Pa!* by Nicoleta Esinencu; Director, Jackson Gay; *Our Children* by Christian Panaite; Director, Liesl Tommy; Sets, Clint Ramos; Costumes, Oana Botez-Ban; Lighting, Tyler Micoleau; Sound, Bart Fasbender; Properties, Judi Guralnick; PSM, Nicole Bouclier; Cast: Nadia Bowers, John Boyd, Chris De Oni, Robert Hogan, Julie Jesneck, Rosemary Prinz; Theater C; November 18–December 3

**Billboard** by Michael Vukadinovich; presented by Reverie Productions and Overlap Productions; Director, Tania Inessa Kirkman; Sets, Zhanna Gurvich & Gaetane Bertol; Lighting, Colin D. Young; Costumes, Carla Bellisio; Sound, Elizabeth Coleman; Stage Manager, David A. Vandervliet; Co-Producer, Susanna L. Harris; Associate Producer, Anna Hayman; Press, Karen Greco; Cast: Ken Matthews, Sarah K. Lippmann, Joey Piscopo; Theater C; January 12–February 4

**Gone** by Charles L. Mee; produced by Station 5 in collaboration with The Fifth Floor; Director, Kenn Watt; Cast: Jennifer Wright Cook, Pam Diem, Signe Harriday, Clark Huggins, Peter Richards; Theater B; February 1–11

**6969** by Jordan Seavey; produced by CollaborationTown; Director, Matthew Hopkins; Sets, Geoffrey Decas; Costumes, Leon Dobkowski; Lighting, Mike Riggs; Sound, Brandon Wolcott; Cast: Julia Henderson, Boo Killebrew, Ryan Purcell, Max Rosenak, Dan Stowell, Philip Tara*tula; Theater C; February 8–24

**Blindness** adapted and directed by Joe Tantalo, based on the novel by Jose Saramago; Design, Maruti Evans; Music/Sound, Andrew Recinos; Combat, Josh Renfree; Choreography, Hachi Yu; Cast: Daniel Ball, David Bartlett, Katherine Boynton, Alisa Burket, Enid Cortes, Darren Curley, Timothy Fannon, Kristen Harlow, Lawrence Jansen, Gregory Konow, Deanna McGovern, Nick Paglino, Mike Roche, Cyrus Roxas, Michael Shimkin, Michael Tranzilli, Sam Whitten; Theater C; March 1–April 8

**Rearviewmirror** by Eric Winick; presented by Reverie Productions; Director, Carl Forsman; Sets, Rachel Hauck; Costumes, Rebecca Eastman; Lighting, Colin D. Young; Sound, Ryan Rumery; PSM, Denise Blacker; Cast: Mark Alhadeff, Sarah Nina Hayon, Audrey Lynn Weston; Theater B; March 31–April 22

**Getting Their Act Together Again** written & performed by Gretchen Cryer and Nancy Ford; Theater C; April 10–20

# 78th Street Theatre Lab

**The Florentine** by Michael Hilliard; produced by Project: Theater; Directors, Joseph B. Jung & Garrett Ayers; Cast: Garrett Ayers, Ruark Downey, Brian Frank, Jessi Blue Gormezano, Erin Gorski, Michael Hilliard, Andrew McLeod, Brian Sell; June 8–17

**York** written & performed by David Casteal & Bryan Harnetiaux; Director, Susan Hardie; July 6–9

**Much Ado About Nothing** by William Shakespeare; produced by Folding Chair Classical Theatre; Director, Marcus Geduld; Cast: Jessika Hardy, James Tigger Ferguson, Christian Felix, Angus Hepburn, Will Brunson, Lisa Blankenship, Gowan Campbell, Marcus Geduld; August 3–27

**The Horton Foote Project** A distillation of The Orphans' Home Cycle (*Roots in a Parched Ground, Lily Dale, Valentine's Day,* and *1918)* conceived by Wes Grantom, Amelia McClain, Stephen Plunkett, Lori Wolter; presented by Slant Theatre Project; Director, Wes Grantom; Costumes, Sarah Greene; Lighting, Derek Wright; Stage Manager, Christy Thede; Cast: Amelia McClain, Stephen Plunkett, Chris Grant; Third Floor Theatre; August 6–29

**Something I'll Tell You Tuesday** and **The Loveliest Afternoon of the Year** by John Guare; produced by Project: Theater; Director, Garrett Ayers; Second Floor Theatre; August 10–16

**The Beginning of the And** A play in three parts by Daniel Roberts; produced by Audax Theatre Group; Director, Brian Ziv; Sets, Alex Wilburn, Lights, Lucas Krech; Costumes, Sarah Johnson; Stage Manager, Jessica Pecharsky; ASM, Jodi Witherell; Videography, Scotter McCrea; Cast: *Apps:* Daniel Talbott, Alie Carey, Davis Hall, Scott Sortman, Kevin Perri; *Orange* (co-written by Sam Roberts): Will Brunson, Arleigh Richards, Alie Carey, Kevin Perri; *Ost:* Davis Hall, Arleigh Richards, Romany Reagan, John Kaisner; September 5–16

**Language of Angels** by Naomi Iizuka; produced by Project: Theater; Director, Kevin Dodd; Second Floor Theatre; October 12–21

**The Blood Brothers present An Evening of Grand Guignol Horror** *The Final Kiss* by Maurice Level, and *The Kiss of Blood* by Jean Aragny and Francis Nelson; produced by Nosedive Productions and Blood Brothers; Directors, Pete Boisvert, Patrick Shearer, Stephanie Williams; Lighting, Gabe Evansohn; Sound, Patrick Shearer; Sets, Rebecca Comtois; Costumes, Lauren Cavanaugh; Makeup, Cat Johnson; Cast: Melanie Adelman, Leah Carrell, Rebecca Comtois, Desmond Dutcher, Brendan Farley, Gavin Hoffman, Cat Johnson, Laurel Keane, Anna Kull, Marc Landers, Christopher Yustin; Third Floor Theatre; October 19–28

**A Dolphin Up a Tree** by Kimberly Foster; presented by Magic Bridge Theatre Company; November 5–April 29

**Two Rooms** by Lee Blessing; produced by The Red Fern Theatre Company; Director, Melanie Moyer Williams; Sets, Jesse Dreikosen; Lighting, Gina Scherr; Stage Manager, Laura Luciano; Cast: Jennifer Lucas, David Mason, Emilie Elizabeth Miller, Brian Patacca; November 30–December 10

**The Last Christmas of Ebenezer Scrooge** written & directed by Marvin Kaye; produced by The Open Book; Cast: Marvin Kaye, Stacey Jenson, H. Clark Kee, Nancy Temple, Anne Pasquale, Miller Lide; Second Floor Theatre; December 8–23

**Strings** by Carole Buggé; produced by The Open Book; Director, Marvin Kaye; Cast: Keir Dullea, Mia Dillon, Warren Kelley, Drew Dix, Kurt Elftmann, Andrea Gallo; December 8–January 6

**Kinetic Fortress** by JoAnne C. Maffia; presented by The jojo EXperiment; Technical Director/Video Editor, luckydave; Musicians, Rachel Golub, Christine Perea, JoAnne Maffia; Cast: JoAnne C. Maffia; Video Cast: Jena Necrason, John Nagle, Aidan Koehler, Daniella Rabbani; Second Floor Theatre; February 15–17

**Still Life** by Emily Mann; produced by Retro Productions; Director, Ric Sechrest; Sets/Graphics, Jack & Rebecca Cunningham; Costumes, Rebecca Cunningham; Lighting, Esther M. Palmer; Sound, Jesse Flower-Ambroch; Cast: Heather E. Cunningham, Erik Potempa, Kirsten Vaughan; Third Floor Theatre; February 16–March 3

**The Long Christmas Ride Home** by Paula Vogel; produced by The Red Fern Theatre Company; Director, Melanie Moyer Williams; Sets, Jesse Dreikosen; Costumes, Carmen Bowker; Lighting, Jessica Greenberg; Composer/Music Director, Kristen Lee Rosenfeld; Choreography, Andrea Davey; Puppets, Amy

Mathews; Stage Manager, Laura Luciano; Cast: Laura Anderson, Melissa Bartley, Michael Cherry, Andrea Day, Jenn Dees, Amanda Donelan, Annie Keating, Emilie Elizabeth Miller, Patrick Pizzolorusso, Thomas Poarch, Caroline Reck, Julia Sirna-First; Musician: Leo Adamov; Second Floor Theatre; March 8–19

**The Nibroc Trilogy** Three plays by Arlene Hutton performed in rotating repertory: *Last Train to Nibroc, See Rock City, Gulf View Drive;* produced by the 78th Street Theatre Lab in association with the Journey Company; Director/Sound, Eric Nightengale; Sets, Bradford Olson; Costumes, Shelley Norton; Lighting, Ji-Youn Chang, Gina Scherr; Hair/Wigs, Bobby H. Grayson; PSM, Billie Davis; Cast: Alexandra Geis, Greg Steinbruner, Polly Adams, Ruth Nightengale, Christina Denzinger; Third Floor Theatre; March 17–April 29

**J.B.** by Archibald Macleish; Produced by Project: Theater; Director, Joseph B. Jung; Second Floor Theatre; April 12–28

**Found a Peanut** by Donald Marguiles; produced by The Red Fern Theatre Company; Director, Melanie Moyer Williams; Lighting, Jessica Greenberg; Sets, Adrienne Kapalko; Props, Amanda Donelan; Fight Coordinator, Caroline Reck; Stage Manager, Laura Luciano; Cast: Melissa Dowty, Timothy Fannon, John Dalton Hill, John Mervini, Mike Mihm, Emilie Elizabeth Miller, Jack Perry, Matt Sadewitz; May 3–13

**Oklahoma Smaovar** by Alice Eve Cohen; presented by 78th Street Theatre Lab; Director, Eric Nightengale; Set, Rebecca Lord; Costumes, Sidney Shannon; Stage Manager, Joanna Jacobson; Cast: Gene Gallerano, Cordis Heard, Claire Joseph, Anna O'Donoghue, Scott Daniel Simmons, Leigh Wade; June 21–July 1, 2007

# 92nd Street Y – Lyrics & Lyricists Series

**The Last Girl Singer: Rosemary Clooney and Her Way With Words** Artistic Director, Deborah Grace Winer; Music Director, John Oddo; Director, Mark Waldrop; Musicians: George Rabbai, Marck Vinci, Bucky Pizzarelli, Joe Cocuzzo; Vocalists: James Naughton, Karen Ziemba, Paula West, John Pizzarelli, Debby Boone; January 6–8; **Harnick: Collector's Items (Other People's Lyrics), Part 2** Artistic Director and Piano, Rob Fisher; Host, Sheldon Harnick; Vocalists: Nancy Anderson, John Ellison Conlee; February 10–12; **Say It With Music: Irving Berlin** Artistic Director, Robert Kimball; Host, Charles Osgood; Piano/Vocals, Max Morath; Musicians: Vince Giordano and the Nighthawks; Vocalists: Ivy Austin, Brian d'Arcy James, Jenny Powers; March 17–19; **Thanks for the Memories: The Lyrics of Leo Robin** Artistic Director/Host, Andrea Marcovicci; Music Director, Shelly Markham; Cast: Klea Blackhurst, Brian Byers, Jennifer Sheehan; May 5–7; **Noel Coward and His Ladies** Artistic Director/ Host/Piano, Steve Ross; Script, Barry Day; Vocalists: Steve Ross, Patricia Hodge, Nancy Anderson, Maude Maggart; June 2–4, 2007

# Abingdon Theatre Company & Abingdon Arts Theatre Complex

**Abingdon Theatre Company Staged Readings** June: *Carl aka Karl* by D.T. Arcieri; Director, Page Hearn; July: *The Monkey Jar* by Richard Martin Hirsch; Director, Jocelyn Sawyer; August: Director, Tom Rowan; September: *End of the Road* by Robert Kerr; Director, Andy Volkoff; October: *Treasure* by Tim Slover; Director, Jocelyn Sawyer; November: *Weep No More Today* by Michele Raper Rittenhouse; Director, Marvin Starkman; December: *Big Doolie* by Richard Thompson; Director, Jenn Thompson; January: *Lillian Yuralia* by Barbara Eda-Young; Director, Joe Ragno; February: *Cry Havoc* by Tom Coash; Director, Kim T. Sharp

## Non-resident Productions – June Havoc Theatre

**The Dispute** by Pierre de Marivaux; translated by Neil Bartlett; presented by the National Asian-American Theatre Company (NAATCO); Director, Jean Randich; Design, Mike Rancourt & Jean Randich; Sets, Sue Rees; Lighting, Stephen Petrilli; Costumes, Kirian Langseth-Schmidt; Sound, Robert Murphy; Stage Manager, Henry Akona; Assistant Stage Manager, Simmone Yu; Cast: Jennifer Chang, Alexis Camins, Olivia Oguma, Lanny Joon, Jennifer Chang, Claro de los Reyes, Mel Duane Gionson, Jennifer Ikeda, Mia Katigbak, Annabel LaLonde, Alfredo Narciso; August 4–26

**The Prancing Horse** by Richard Lay; produced by the Sage Theater Company; Director, Martin Ewens; Sets, Tommy Barz; Lighting, Alan Kanevsky; Costumes/ Production Manager, Gretchen Ritchie; Press, Scotti Rhodes; Cast: Romy Nordlinger, Sheila Griffin, Pierre O'Farrell, Tod Engle, Chris Ford; September 14–October 1

**Directorfest 2006** 23rd annual festival of one-acts staged by the Fall Directing Fellows of The Drama League Directors Project; included: *Authorial Intent* by Itamar Moses; Director, Meredith McDonough; *The Blessings of the Animals* by Jonathan Ceniceroz; Director, Alex Torra; *One for the Road* by Harold Pinter; Director, Jaime Castañada; December 7–10

**(Don't Go) Home for the Holidays** composition and musical direction by Greg Bowers; presented by Figgy Productions; AV/Design, Scott Hossner; Costumes, Harmony Arnold; Production Coordinator, Rebecca Zuber; Producer, Jennifer Stark; Associate Producer, Laurence Lombart; Press, Paul Siebold; Performed by The Calamity Carolers of Doom (Salem, Oregon): Greg Bowers, Jennifer Stark, Susan Shoaps, Scott P. Hossner; December 21–30

**Straight to Hell** written & directed by Stephen Stahl, based on the novel by Kathleen Hudon; produced by On the Run Productions; Lighting, Ryan O'Gara; Video, Fin Pictures, Timothy McMcMurty; Sound, Wayne Tresvasani; Music, Bill Jolly; Press, Maya Associates; Cast: Jules Hartley, Carolin Haydee Lopez, John Dalmon, Adam Ratcliffe, Annette Hillary, Paul Hufker; March 14–March 26

**A Midsummer Night's Dream: A Comic Jewish Satire** written and presented by the Dark Lady Players; Adaptation/Dramaturgy, John Hudson; Director, Mahayana Landowne; Choreography, Danielle Quisenberry, Caroline Copeland; Sets, James Simopoulos; Costumes, Jess Lane; Sound, Elliot Lanes; Music, Vortex; Cast: Chanelle Benz, Jen Browne, Amanda Bruton, Monica Cortez, Daniela Dakic, Morganne Davies, Lila Dupree, Megan McGrath, Kirsta Peterson, Stephen Squibb, Peggy Suzuki; March 28–April 1

## Non-resident Productions – Dorothy Strelsin Theatre

**Still Life/Café Coward** two one-acts by Noël Coward; presented by Isle of Shoals Productions; Cast: Brad Thomason, Liv Rooth; August 4–13

**True Story Project: Sex!** conceived and directed by Krista Smith; presented by Visible Theatre; Co-Director, Laura Silence; Cast: Rebecca Bateman, Angela D'Arezzo, Eugenia Francis, Gregg Mozgala, Chris Reed, Esra Gaffin, Michelle Mantione, Katie Labahn, Liz Treston; October 4–November 4

**Krankenhaus Blues** by Sam Forman; presented by Visible Theatre; Director, Donna Mitchell; Music, Helen Yee & Hanna Hens-Piazza; Design, Kimi Maeda; Lighting, Paul A. Jepson; Stage Manager, Emily Alexander-Wilmeth; Cast: Christine Bruno, Angela DeMatteao, Bill Green, Joe Sims; October 5–November 5

**Gauguin/Savage Light** book, music, and lyrics by George Fischoff; Director, Michael Ormond; Choreography, Joe Barros; Cast: Jeff Nardone, Kelly Dynan, Marc Ginsberg; November 8–December 31

**In the Bar of a Tokyo Hotel** by Tennessee Williams; presented by the White Horse Theater Company; Director, Cyndy A. Marion; Sets, Patrick Larsen; Costumes, David B. Thompson; Lighting, Debra Leigh Siegel; Music, Joe Gianono; Dramaturg, Roxane Heinze-Bradshaw; Fight Director, Michael G. Chin; PSM, Elliot Lanes; Cast: Laura Siner, Toshiji Takeshima, Niall O'Hegarty, Greg Homison, Larissa Laurel; February 2–18

**Bed** by Brendan Cowell; presented by One Year Lease Theater Company, Ianthe Demos & Nick Flint; Director, Ianthe Demos; Sets, James Hunting; Costumes, Victoria Tzykun; Lighting, Mike Riggs; Sound, David Chessman; Cast: Nick Flint, Nico Evers-Swindell, Emma Jackson, Sarah-Jane Casey, Nick Stevenson, Ana Lucas; April 11–May 5

# Access Theater

**What Comes Next** by Pamela A. Popeson; presented by Rebellion Dogs Productions; Director, Lorca Peress; Costumes, Peter Janis; Sets, Robert T. Cooke; Lighting, Alex Moore; Tech Design, Michael Gibbons; Stage Manager, Denise R. Zeiler; ASM, Estie Sarvesy; AV, Doug Mestanza; Cast: Stephen Clarke, Joseph Corrao, Marin Gazzaniga, Daniel Hicks, René Keller, Tanya Perez, Angelo Rosso, Dan Teachout, Lane Trippe; July 5–29

**Someone Who'll Watch Over Me** by Frank McGuinness; presented by NYU Graduate Acting Program; July 13–16

**The Crackwalker** by Judith Thompson; presented by New World Theatre; Director/Design, Robert Zick Jr., Set, Gerard J. Savoy; Costumes, Frankie Keane; Stage Manager, Leia Garcia-Benedini; Cast: David Wesley Cooper, Karron Karr, Melanie Kuchinski Rodriguez, Kelly Miller, Marc Adam Smith; October 26–November 12

**The Winter's Tale** by William Shakespeare; presented by Hipgnosis Theatre Company; Director, John Castro; Sets/Lighting, Justin Steeve; Costumes, Drista Thomas; Composer, Luke Mitchell; Stage Manager, Lara Evangelista; Assistant Director, Lindsay Goss; Cast: John Kevin Jones, Sarah Sokolovic, Julian Rozzell, Sara Barker, Demetrios Bonaros, Guthrie Brunk-London, Eric Chase, Kate Dulcich, Hal Fickett, Carlton Franklin, David Laufgraben, David Look, Elizabeth Mirarchi, Margot Newkirk, James Nugent, Justin Steeve, Rachel Tiemann; Gallery Theater; November 2–19

**Project Playwright II** presented by Madair Productions; Works by William Campbell, Robert Charles Gompers, Paul F. Hancock, Erik Christian Hanson, Craig McNulty, Mark Saunders, Michael Small, Andrew W. Turner; Directors, Melani Adair, Tim Farrell, Robert Charles Gompers, Antonio Merenda; Lighting, Brandon Voight; Costumes, Meredith Magoun; Stage Manager, Wren Sheldon; Cast: Marc Baizman, Morgan Baker, Jeff Bloovman, Joe Capozzi, Ed Domingues, Rene Ashli Fulton, Marisa Marquez, Carly Miller, Candice Owens, Werner Pauliks, Amybeth Whissel; November 14–19

**The Apotheosis of Vaclav Drda** by Christopher Cartmill; presented by Gads Hill Theatre Company; March 8–April 1

**Six Degrees of Separation** by John Guare; presented by Well Urned Productions in association with C.A.G.E. Theatre Company and Hudson Shakespeare Company; Director, Jon Ciccarelli; Cast: Michael Hagins, Susan Mirwis, Dan Burkarth, Timothy J. Cox, Elizabeth Yokam, Gerry Kirschbaum, Alice Starr McFarland, Roy Aialon, David King, Manny Liyes, Lauren Kelston, Dan Zimmerman, Michael Rhett; March 15–24

**Marriage is Murder** by Nick Hall; presented by Well Urned Productions; Director, JoAnn Oakes; Cast: Christie Oakes, Gregory Cilmi; March 29–April 8

**Cloud 9** by Caryl Churchill; presented by Whirled Peas Productions; Director, Michael Forte; Cast: Taras Berezowksy, Megan Demarest, Dean Jones, Anais Koivisto, Skid Maher, Kaitlyn Riordan, Jason B. Schmidt; April 12–28

**The Good Thief** by Conor McPherson; produced by Prospect St. Productions, Katie Adams & Kit Wannen; Director, Tom Wojtunik; Artistic Director, Brian Avers; Design, Travis Walker; Costumes, Isabelle Fields; Assistant Director/Stage Manager, Myvonwynn Hopton; Music, Ben Carroll & Corey Musitin; Dramaturg, Marcie Bramucci; Cast: Kit Wannen; May 2–6

**The Landlord** by Jonathan Barsness; produced by Toy Box Theatre Company; Director, Michael Daehn; Composer, Leanne Darling; Costumes, Samm Fromm; Lighting, Chris Robinson; Sets, Chris Kay; Production Manager, David Michael Holmes; Stage Manager, Michelle Van Schyndel; Cast: Jonathan Barsness, Alexander Holt, Katherine Neuman, Mandy Pouilot; May 18–27

**Zeitgeist** written & performed by P.J. Merola; presented by Gentle Machine Productions; May 29–June 3

# Ace of Clubs

**Summer in the Hummer** presented by Billionaires for Bush and Heart of Gold Productions; Artistic Director, Melody Bates; Director, Mahayana Landowne; Choreography, D.J. McDonald; Music, Clifford J. Tasner; Performed by The Billionaire Follies; July 18–August 8

**Dick Cheney's Holiday Spectacular 2006** by Melody Bates, David Bennett and The Billionaire Follies; presented by Billionaires for Bush and Heart of Gold Productions; Artistic Director, Melody Bates; Director, Mahayana Landowne; Choreography, D.J. McDonald; Cast: Tanya Elder, Jamie Jackson, David Bennett, Dave Case, Rob Dapore, Randy Howk, Melody Bates, Yvonne Willrich-Teague, Kellie Aiken, Melissa Collom, Victoria Olson; December 3–20

**New Tricks** A benefit for Theater Askew's production of Jason Schafer's *I Google Myself;* readings from Polly Frost and Ray Sawhill's audio series "Sex Scenes" by Antony Hagopian, Karen Grenke, Sarah Koznin, Jennifer Malloy, Elenna Stauffer, Jake Thomas, Kevin Craig West; Music by Joanna Parson and Pale Male; April 30

# The Actors Company Theatre (TACT)

Scott Alan Evans, Cynthia Harris, and Simon Jones, Co-Artistic Directors; Cathy Bencivenga, General Manager

**Home** by David Storey; Director, Scott Alan Evans; Set, Mimi Lien; Costumes, David Toser; Lighting, Mary Louise Geiger; Sound, Daryl Bornstein; Music, David Macdonald; PSM, Dawn Dumlop/David Aykens; Press, Joe Trentacosta; ASM, Mel McCue; Assistant Director, Jared Ranere; Dialects, Deborah Hecht; Cast: Cynthia Darlow, Cynthia Harris, Simon Jones, Larry Keith, Ron McClary; Beckett Theatre on Theatre Row; December 2–23

**The Sea** by Edward Bond; Director, Scott Alan Evans; Set, Narelle Sissons; Costumes, David Toser; Lighting, Mary Louise Geiger & Lucrezia Briceno; Sound, Daryl Bornstein; Music, Joseph Trapanese; Dialects, Deborah Hecht; PSM, Mel McCue; ASM, Robbie Rescigno; Press, Joe Trentacosta; Cast: Jamie Bennett, Lauren Bloom, Nora Chester, Ruth Eglsaer, Richard Ferrone, Rachel Fowler, Delphi Harrington, Timothy McCracken, Christopher McCutchen, Greg McFadden, Allen Read, Gregory Salata, Caroline Tamas; April 21–May 12

### Salon Series

**The Late Christopher Bean** by Sidney Howard; Director, Kyle Fabel; Cast: James Murtaugh, Zoe Perry, Mary Bacon, Nora Chester, Ashley West, Christopher Toten, Curzon Dobell, Gregory Salata/Simon Jones, James Prendergast; September 23–25

**Kind Lady** by Edward Chodorov; Director, Jenn Thompson; Cast: James Prendergast, Joan Shepard, Francesca Di Mauro, Valerie Wright, Eileen Little, Jamie Bennett, Todd Gearhart, Tuck Milligan, Scott Schafer, Cynthia Darlow, Helen Green; October 14–16

**The Chinese Prime Minister** by Enid Bagnol; Director, Simon Jones; Cast: Larry Conroy, Craig Wichman, Liz Morton, Delphi Harrington, Molly Battles, Rob Breckenridge, Ron McClary, Thom Christopher; January 13–15

**Man & Boy** by Terence Rattigan; Director, Drew Barr; Cast: Rachel Fowler, Joe Delafield, Thom Christopher, James Murtaugh, James Prendergast, Jamie Bennett, Lynn Wright; February 10–12;

**Rain** by John Colton & Clemence Randolph; Director, Jenn Thompson; Cast: Irma-Estel LaGuerre, Matt Fraley, Craig Peugh, Michael Halling, Owen Thompson, James Predergast, Francesca Di Mauro, Valerie Wright, Jerry Jerger, Margaret Nichols, Gregory Salata; March 10–12

**Dandy Dick** by Arthur Wing Pinero; Director, Stephen Hollis; Cast: Scott Schafer, Richard Ferrone, James Murtaugh, Eve Bianco, Sasha Higgins, John Brant, Nicola Victoria Buck, Dana Smith-Croll, Craig Wroe, Steve French; May 19–21

# Actor's Theatre Workshop

**Stone** & **The Maguffin** two one-acts by Edward Bond and Adam Hunault; presented by Stone Soup Theatre Arts; Director, Nadine Friedman; Cast: *Stone:* Seiko Carter, Caroline Reck, Ben Trawick-Smith, Chris Wild; *The Maguffin:* Lauren Birriel, David Bryant, D.R. Hanson, Jacques Laurent, Marsha Martinez, Rachel Rhodes, Maria Schirmer; April 5–28

**Beyond Therapy** by Christopher Durang; presented by New York Deaf Theatre; Director, Garrett Zuercher; Cast: Christopher Tester, Hillary Baack, Aaron Kubey, Anne Tomasetti, Darren Fudenske, Samuel Caraballo; Voiced by Zack Linnert and Caroline Burrow; May 6–20

# Amas Musical Theatre

Donna Trinkoff, Producing Director

**Magpie** Book by Steven M. Jacobson, music by Gary William Friedman, lyrics by Edward Gallardo, additional lyrics by Stevie Holland; World premiere staged reading at TBG Theatre (presented as part of NYMF, September 28): Director, Rajendra Ramoon Maharaj; Musical Director, Martin Bejerano; Cast: Ronny Mercedes, Jessica Fields, Kenyon Adams, John Paul Almon, Kimberly Reid Dunbar, Dennis Holland, Maxx, Joseph Melendez, Doreen Montalvo, Michael Murnoch, Kim Volpe; Developmental production at The Players Theatre, March 9–25: Director, Rejandra Ramoon Maharaj; Music Director, Jana Zielonka; Sets, John Pollard, Lighting, Japhy Weideman; Costumes, Leslie Bernstein; Sound, Danny Erdberg; PSM, Brian Westmoreland; Cast: Ronny Mercedes, Jessica Fields, Kimberly Reid Dunbar, Dennis Holland, Joseph Melendez, Michael Murnoch, J. Cameron Barnett, Jene Hernandez, Gary Lindemann, Julian Rebolledo, Natalie Toro

**Sprang Thang** (Rosetta LeNoire Musical Theatre Academy Production) book, music and lyrics by Goldee Greene; Director, Christopher Scott; Music Director, Marshall Keating; Choreography, Monica Johnson; Set, Matt Morrow; Lighting, Herrick Goldman; Costumes, Cheryl A. McCarron; Players Theatre; May 11–20

**Broadway Soul** conceived, directed, and arranged by Chapman Roberts; Musical Director, Will Barrow; Choreography, Leslie Dockery; Benefit Gala starring B.J. Crosby and Freda Payne; With: Faruma and Floyd Williams, Bertilla Baker, Jean Cheek, McKenzie Frye, Patricia Iacobazzo, Patrick Jude, Sandra-Reaves Phillips, Raun Ruffin, Steve Ruggieri, Glenn Turner; New World Stages; November 13

**Six O'Clock Musical Theatre Lab Series** *Escape from Pterodactyl Island* by Peter Charles Morris; Director, Phillip George; October 26–27; *108 Waverly* book and lyrics by Dan Clancy, music by Lynn Portas; Director, Sam Viverito; Music Director, Edward G. Robinson; Cast: Jared Bradshaw, Billy Bustamante, Michael Deleget, Colin Donnell; Clurman Theatre on Theatre Row; January 16–17; *An Officer and A Gentleman* book by Sharleen Cooper Cohen & Douglas Day Stewart, lyrics and music by Kenneth Hirsch & Robin Lerner; Director, Michael Bush; Players Theatre; April 12–13; *Izzy! A Dizzy Musical Fairy Tale* by Joan Ross Sorkin and Steven Fisher, music and lyrics by Steven Fisher; Cast: Megan Lawrence, Nick Wyman, Jessica Grové, Jim Poulos, Blake Hammond, Kevin Smith Kirkwood, Miche Braden; Lion Theatre on Theatre Row; April 16–17; *The Psalm of Ruby Redd* by Carl Maultsby; Director, Chuck Patterson; Conductor, M. Roger Holland; Cast: Diana Solomon-Glover, David Hughey, Fred Isozaki, N'Kenge, Jess Munoz, Charlotte Small; Players Theatre; May 1–2

# American Globe Theatre

John Basil, Producing Artistic Director

**The Comedy of Errors** by William Shakespeare; Director, Kelley McKinnon; Sets/Lighting, Mark Hankla; Costumes, Jim Parks; Composer, Scott O'Brien; Stage Manager, Kelan Maloney; Cast: Eric Conley, Zenzele Cooper, Todd Courson, Nicholas Daniele, Michael Hagins, Angus Hepburn, Ginna Hoben, Kevin Lind, Julia McLaughlin, Brian Moore, Brandi Rhome, Mat Sanders, Graham Stevens; September 15–October 7

**The Tempest** by William Shakespeare; Director, John Basil; Choreography, Alisa Claire; Set, Kevin Lee Allen; Costumes, Jim Parks; Lighting, Mark Hankla; Original Music/Sound, Scott O'Brien; PSM, Michael R. Mele; Props, Kathleen McDonough; Cast: Inna Beynishes, Ashley Anne Russ, Rebecca MacDougall, Richard Fay, Uma Incrocci, Elizabeth Keefe, Brian Morvant, Christopher Newell, Todd Courson, Mat Sanders, Robert Ierardi, Rainard Rachele, Bob Armstrong, Stanley Harrison; March 15–April 14

# American Theatre of Actors

### Beckmann Theatre

**The Maids** by Jean Genet; produced by Draupadi Ensemble; Director, Laura Parker; Cast: Jessica Hester, Lisette Hazan, Amy Matthews; July 20–August 5

**A Scene with a Red Bird** by Minoru Besuyaku; Producer/Director, Kiyoshi Kiyama; Set, Mitsuru Ishii; Lighting, Seiji Moriwaki; Sound, Akira Oyamada; Music, Yuuki Ando; Costumes, Ai Higushi; Choreography, Yukiyo Nakada; Cast: Aya Hirose, Atsuo Hasegawa, Morihiko Uchiyama, Tsuginobu Honda, Masako Tanka, Yuga Yoshino, Tsugki Hayashi, Tomohisa Miyakawa, Ryuma Uchida, Chikako Hashimoto, Genjiro Mori, Sachiko Takayanagi, Makiko Iwashita, Mariko Kikuchi, Takako Tanaka; October 13–15

**Beware of Greeks-They Know Things!** written & directed by Norman Weinstein; January 3–7

**An Ideal Husband** by Oscar Wilde; produced by Foolish Mortals; Director, Kelly Barrett; Cast: Mark A. Kinch, Erin Liz Hart, Andrew D. Montgomery, Clara Wong, Jaclyn Sokol, Paul Wilcox, Winnie Troha, Alan Salsbury, Lizzie Schwarz, Meghan Powe, Thomas Noel; January 18–28

**Frau Dracula (That Prussian Bitch From Hell)** by J.D. Klein; presented by Love Creek Productions; Director, Le Wilhelm; Cast: Kristin Carter, Philip Galbraith, Nick Giello, Cynthia Granville, A.C. Jermyn, Rachel Lande, Megan Sambataro, Gregg David Shore, Al Smith, Kirsten Walsh; February 14–March 4

**Lady Windermere's Fan** by Oscar Wilde; presented by Foolish Mortals; Director, Lawrence Frank; April 19–29

### Chernuchin Theatre

**Side Show** Book and lyrics by Bill Russell, music by Henry Krieger; Producer/Director, Ryan Mekenian; Music Director, Michael Pettry; Choreography, Billy Griffin; Cast: Dane Agostinis, Kevin Bradley Jr., Nathan Brisby, Jordan Kai Burnett, Dawn Cantwell, Josh Isaacs, Carey McCray; August 31–September 3

**Roundtable Ensemble in Repertory** January 16–February 10; included: **The Mammy Project** written & performed by Michelle Matlock, co-written by Joan Evans; produced by Joshua Weiss; Director, Amy Gordon; **The Taming of the Shrew** by William Shakespeare; Director, Andrew Grosso; presented by Roundtable Ensemble; Cast: B. Brian Argotsinger, Arthur Aulisi, Tom Butler, Autumn Dornfeld, Jonathan Kells Phillips, Alex Smith, Paul Whitthorne, Charissa Chamorro, Natalia de Campos; **Silence** by Moira Buffini; Director, Suzanne Agins; Cast: Helen Piper Coxe, Greg Hildreth, Kelly Hutchinson, Chris Kipiniak, Joe Plummer, Makela Spielman

**The Naked Eye Planets** by Rebecca Tourino; presented by Coyote Rep; Director, Magdalena Zira; Cast: Maria Cellario, Brandon Collinsworth, Glenn Kalison, Jeanne LaSala, Quinn Mander, Emily Rogge, Amanda Sayle, Sean Tarrant, Heidi Tokheim, Diane Tyler; March 9–25

### Sargent Theatre

**Miles to Babylon** by Ann Harson; presented by Evensong Associates; Director, Tom Thornton; Set, Michael Anania; Lighting, Alex Moore; Sound/Stage Manager, Elliot Lanes; Costumes, Alice Bryant Cubicciotti; Cast: Angela Della Ventura, Denise Fiore, Karen Gibson, James Nugent, Rachel Schwartz; October 12–29

**Hamlet: Up Close** presented by Irondale Ensemble Project; Director, Barbara Mackenzie-Wood; November 30–December 3

**Dog Day Afternoon** adapted and directed by Frank Solorzano; presented by Barefoot Theatre Company; Cast: Jeremy Brena, Susan Ferrara, John Gazzale, Victoria Malvagno, Dolores McDougal, Roderick Nash, Amanda Plant, Lorraine Rodriquez, Rafi Silver, Frank Solorzano, Anika Solveig, Joli Tribuzio, Christopher Whalen; March 7–25

**Did You Used to Be R.D. Laing?** written & performed by Mike Maran; Score, David Milligan; March 30–April 7

**Five Years Later** by Jeff Love & Marc Adam Smith; presented by Point of You Productions; Director, Jeff Love; Cast: Melanie Kuchinski Rodriguez, Felicia Eugenia Velasco, Johnny Blaze Leavitt, Marc Adam Smith, Gerard J. Savoy, Paul Weissman, Alyssa Mann, Tina Trimble, Meghan Dickerson, Brandon Beilis, Karron Karr, Ian Fishman; April 11–28

**The Seagull** by Anton Chekhov; presented by Foolish Mortals; Director, Kelly Barrett; Cast: Valerie Austin, Josh Culpepper, Brian Lee Elder, Catherine Hennessey, Mark A. Kinch, Meghan Powe, Omar Prince, Alan Salsbury, Amy Beth Sherman, Tony Travostino, Tony White; May 10–20

### Courtyard Theatre

**Measure for Measure** by William Shakespeare; Director, James Jennings; Cast: Michael Henry Harris, David Demato, Lauren Waisbren, Chad Mills, Gregory O'Conner; Dustin Smallheer, Erin Maya Darke, Kevin C. Woods, Charles Baker, Christopher Thornton, Paul Hansen, Brett Fleischer, Cara Maltz, Katherine Poklemba, Marie Darden; June 7–24

**As You Like It** by William Shakespeare; Director, James Jennings; Cast: Charles Baker, Michael Bordwell, Ned Cray, Marie Darden, Tim Dudek, Bill Growney, William Greville, Paul Hansen, Jessica Lynn Jennings, Raul Julia Jr., Katherine Poklemba, Stephan Scheck, Marvin Schwartz, James Wirt; September 6–23

**A Bard's Day's Night ('s Dream)** written & directed by Jory Levine; produced by Jor-El Productions; Cast: John Bertrand, Russell Jordan, John D'Arcangelo, Wendy Charles, Morgan Jae, Aimee McCabe, Frank Lin, Skyih S. Smith, JessAnn Smith, Alan Pagano, Jory Levine, Daniel Kemna, Joshua Levine, Dan Rice, Dale Davidson, Ledwin Lopez, Torre Reigns, Nick Fondulis, Jonathan Lang, Heather Wildenberger, William Sudan Mason, David Caesar Harrison, Henrik Petersen, Joel Altherr, John Scamardella, Madalyn McKay; September 7–October 1

## Andhow! Theatre Company

Jessica Davis-Irons, Artistic Director; Andrew Irons, Producing Director

**Angel Mountain** by John-Richard Thompson; Director, Jessica Davis-Irons; Sets, Neal Wilkinson; Lighting, Owen Hughes; Sound, Jill B.C. DuBoff; Costumes, Becky Lasky; Cast: Arthur Aulisi, Jessica Dickey, Danny Deferrari, Rachel Peters, Abby Royle, Noah Trepanier; Connelly Theatre; July 6–29

**Dialogue 2006** readings at the Great Room at South Oxford Space; *Dead Dogs* by Greg Steinbruner; Director, Andrew Grosso (November 5); *Men in Trees* by Gilbert Girion; Director, Jessica Davis-Irons (November 12); *Lyric is Waiting* by Michael Puzzo; Director, Jessica Davis-Irons (November 19); *How the Sun Shines* by Margie Stokley; Director, Amanda Charlton (November 26); *7 Santas* by Jeff Goode (December 18)

## ArcLight Theater

**Jitter** by Richard Sheinmel; produced by Lady Like Productions; Director, Clyde Balbo; Costumes, Ramona Ponce; Production Manager, Maysa Andujar; Cast: Dan Almekinder, Camille Burford, Zach McCoy, Collette McGuire, Sara Vanbeckum; June 16–July 1

**The Germans in Paris** by Jonathan Leaf; presented by Verse Theater Manhattan; Director, James Milton; Cast: Jon Krupp, Ross Beschler, David Lamberton, Angelica Torn, Claire Winters, Kathryn Elisabeth Lawson, Brian Wallace, Alexander Bilu, Bruce Barton; January 5–27

**Uncle** by Dean Gray; presented by Blue Heron Theatre; Director, Wayne Maugans; Sets, Daniel Ettinger, Costumes, Martin T. Lopez; Lighting, Paul Bartlett; Sound, David Lawson; Composer, Andrew Rindfleisch; Additional Music, Colin Huggins; Cast: Brian Patacca, Richard Bowden, James Heatherly, Darren Lougee, Nancy McDoniel; February 10–March 4

## ARS Nova

**Creation Nation** created by Billy Eichner with assistance from Robin Taylor (ongoing); **Automatic Vaudeville** hosted by Colette Hawley; Guests: Kevin Cahoon and Ghetto Cowboy, Chelsea Peretti, Varsity Interpretive Dance Squad (Opened June 2, 2005, closed February 8, 2007); **Broadway Spotlights Series** Donna Lynne Champlin (June 4), David Josefsberg (June 5), Mary Faber (February 2 & 7), Todd Buonopane (March 5), Drew Sarich (March 19), Mara Davi (April 2),

Kristin Huffman (May 7), Lauren Pritchard (May 22); **"Unchartered" Series** Ben Birney and Rob Seitelman (June 6), The Songs of Chris Miller and Nathan Tysen (November 12); **Jollyship The Whiz Bang** June 7–14, March 13 & 20; **Kelly Kinsella: Live Under Broadway** June 15; **Holy Cross Sucks!** written & performed by Rob Nash; Director, Jeff Calhoun; June 21–22; **RFK** by Jack Holmes; Director, Larry Moss; Cast: Christopher Cass; June 24–25; **Freestyle Love Supreme** July 13, March 7; **Happy Hour: It Takes 3** July 18–19; **Natalie Joy Johnson with the Pink Champagne Orchestra** July 22–October 13; **Matt Sigl: Unstuck in Time** July 23; **Cipher** July 29; **Fast Food Town** August 16; **Be Frank with Josh and Tamra** August 18; **Cady Huffman: Live at Ars Nova** August 20–21; **The Exquisite Tale of Ronald Pelican** August 23; **The Wau Wau Sisters: Turning Tricks From the Streets** August 24; **Hypochondria** August 24; **Stars in Her Eyes** August 25–26; **Semi-Precious Weapons** September 8–30; **It's All About the Story** October 4–18; **Truth (the heart is a million little pieces above all things)** October 5–November 4; **Let It Sing: The Songs of Alan Zachary and Michael Weiner** October 15; **Letting Go of God** October 19–29; **Funeral** October 31–January 28; **Welcome to My 15 Minutes** November 14; **Perfection** November 15–17; **Kelly Kinsella: Under Pressure** November 16; **Rudolph Unplugged** November 19–20, May 16; **Life in a Marital Institution** November 21–28, May 16, 23; **52 Man Pickup** December 2; **On, Girl** December 5; **Movie Geek** December 8, March 11; **British Invasion: The UK Stars of WHOSE LINE IS IT ANYWAY?** Cast: Steven Frost, Jim Sweeney, Steve Steen, Andy Smart, Richard Vranch January 3–7; **Justin Bohon: Always Someone Cooler** Cast: Justin Bohon with Tory Ross, Nikki Daniels, Jarrod Emick, Michael Scott, Q. Smith Musicians: Stephen Oremus (Music Director), Rick Molina, Sean McDaniel, Michael Blanco; January 8; **At Least it's Pink** by Bridget Everett, Michael Patrick King, Kenny Mellman; Director, Michael Patrick King; Cast: Bridget Everett; January 16–April 1; **Shushie Bush** written & performed by Colette Hawley; January 18; **The Red Beard of Esau** by Rachel Shukert; Director, Alex Timbers; Cast: Elliotte Crowell, Billy Eichner, Sam Forman, Van Hansis, Julie Lake, Maggie Lauren, Austin Lysy, Reg Veneziano, Taylor Wilcox; January 29; **Tom Shillue: Dad 2.0** written & performed by Tom Shillue; January 30; **Out of the Water** by Brooke Berman; Director, Trip Cullman; February 5; **Langhorne Slim** February 6; **The Becky Show** February 11–12; **Shockwave: the Valentine's Mixtape Volume IV** performed by Shockwave February 20; **Without Skin or Hair: The Music of Nick Jones and Benjamin Ickies** February 22; **75 Inches** written & performed by Dick Scanlon; February 26–27; **Electric Fiction** March 6; **All Hail Hurricane Gordo** March 12; **Crabquistador: Scavenger of God** March 13–20; **AV Lounge** March 15, April 26, May 24; **"Out Loud" Gay Play** reading series: *Connecticut* by Kathryn Walat Director, Leigh Silverman (March 26), *Hollywood Nurses* (April 9), *Incendiary* (April 30), *Drip* (May 14); **Dixie's Tupperware Party** by Kris Andersson & Elizabeth Meriwether; Director, Alex Timbers; April 20–July 1; **Daniel Zaitcik: Losses and Reunions** April 23; **Old Springs Pike** April 24, May 29; **Broadway Idol: Jaclyn Huberman** May 8, 13; **Tastiskaink** May 14

## The Ateh Theater Group

Artistic Director, Bridgette Dunlap

**The Girl Detective** adapted and directed by Bridgette Dunlap from the story by Kelly Link; Choreographer, Whitney Stock; Set/Costumes, Emily French; Lighting, Michael Salvas; Sound, Chris Rummel; Cast: Kathryn Ekblad, Tim Eliot, Alexis Grausz, Chris Hale, Charley Layton, John Long, Madeleine Maby, Sara Montgomery, Elizabeth Neptune, Danielle Thorpe, Marie Weller, Ben Wood; Connelly Theater; February 23–March 17

**Alice's Adventures in Wonderland** adapted and directed by Bridgette Dunlap from the book by Lewis Carroll; Set, Emily French; Costumes, Amy VanMullekom; Cast: Kathryn Ekblad, Madeleine Maby, Hannah Miller, Sara Montgomery, Brian Morgan, Elizabeth Neptune, Ben Wood, Hannah Miller, Elizabeth Taylor, Marie Weller; Connelly Theater; February 23–March 17

## Atlantic Theater Company

**Hamlet** by William Shakespeare; presented by Orpheus Productions; Director Anya Saffir; September 7–16

### Atlantic for Kids

**Strega Nona** adapted for the stage from Tomie De Paola's novel by Thomas Olson, lyrics by Thomas Olson and Roberta Carlson, music, music direction, and additional lyrics by Aron Accurso; Director, Jacquelyn Landgraf; Choreography, Alison Beatty; Costumes, Taylor Harrison; Cast: Melanie Levy, Matt Schock, Faryn Einhorn, Clayton Early, Sarah Brill, Michael Caputo, Marie Weller; October 7–29

**A Dolphin Up a Tree** book & lyrics by Kimberly Foster, music & lyrics by John Fleming; Director, Paul Urcioli; Costumes, Catherine Blackhole; Choreography, Casey Moeckel; Cast: Lauren Hines, Brad Mielke, Katie Flahive, Charley Layton; March 3–25

## Axis Company

Jeffrey Resnick, Executive Producer; Randy Sharp, Artistic Director

**Levittown** by Marc Palmeri; Director, George Demas; Design, Kate Aronson-Brown; Lighting, Amy Harper; Sound, Steve Fontaine; Stage Manager, Emily Carr; Cast: Brian Barnhart, Margo Passalaqua, Cecelia Riddett, Joe Viviani, Michael Laurence, Curzon Dobell, Ian Tooley, Joe Fuer; June 22–July 16

**Hospital 2006** a serial play by Axis Company; Director/Music/Lyrics, Randy Sharp; Design, Kate Aronson-Brown; Lighting, David Zeffren; Sound, Steve Fontaine; PSM, Marlene Berner; Film, Ben Wolf; Editor, Mike Huetz; Production Manager, Ian Tooley; Cast: Paul Marc Barnes, Brian Barnhart, David Crabb, George Demas, Joe Fuer, Laurie Kilmartin, Lynn Mancinelli, Sue Ann Molinell, Matt Neely, Edgar Oliver, Marc Palmieri, Margo Passalaqua, Tom Pennacchini, Randy Spence, Jim Sterling, Ian Tooley; September 29–November 11

**Seven in One Blow, or The Brave Little Kid** by the Brothers Grimm; Director/Original Music, Randy Sharp; Stage Manager, Ian Tooley; Design, Kate Aronson-Brown; Lighting, Amy Harper; Sound, Steve Fontaine; Cast: Marc Palmieri, David Crabb, Kate Hettesheimer, Jim Sterling, Brian Barnhart, Randy Sharp, George Demas, Margo Passalaqua, Sue Ann Molinell, Edgar Oliver, Laurie Kilmartin, Marlene Berner; 5th annual presentation; December 1–17

### Non-resident Productions

**Confidence, Women** written & directed by Robert Cucuzza; presented by ACME Acting Lab; Set, Merope Vachlioti; Costumes, Lee Harper/Matthew Simonelli; Lighting, Amy Harper; Stage Manager, Stephanie Usis; Cast: Kelsey Bacon, Regina Betancourt, Ella Bole, Britt Genelin, Gina Guarnieri, Hagar Moor, Kelly Sharp; March 1–17

## Babel Theatre Project

**The Insomnia Project** by Jessica Brickman; Producer, Jeremy Blocker; Director, Geordie Broadwater; Set, Emily Carmichael; Costumes, Lee Harper & Jessica De La Cruz; Lighting, Joshua Randall; Sound, Anthony Gabriele; Stage Managers, Kathryn Ann Pierroz, Stephanie Coulombe; Cast: Ben Vershbow, Julie Lake, Drew Battles, Diana Buirski; Medicine Show Theatre; July 5–29

**The Calamity of Kat Kat and Willie** by Emily Young; Producer, Jeremy Blocker; Director, Heath Cullens; Set, Emily Carmichael; Costumes, Lee Harper & Jessica De La Cruz; Lighting, Joshua Randall; Sound, Anthony Gabriele; Stage Managers, Kathryn Ann Pierroz, Stephanie Coulombe; Cast: Jeremy Bobb, Erik Liberman, Joe Petrilla, Miriam Silverman; Medicine Show Theatre; July 5–29

## Bank Street Theatre

**The Architect of Destiny** by Michael Gianakos; presented by Inch Mile Entertainment; Director, Luke Hancock; Cast: Michael Gianakos, Martha Cary, Luke Hancock, Joe Lattanzi, Jamie Milward, Greg Wands; June 1–10

**Box Americana: A Wal-Mart Retail Fantasia** by Jason Grote; Director, Connie Grappo; June 15–25

**Room Service** by John Murray & Allen Boretz; Director, Dan Wackerman; July 6–August 5; transferred Off-Broadway (see full credits in the Off-Broadway section in this volume)

**Count Down** by Dominique Cieri; presented by Off World Theatre and Double Play Connections; Director, Elyse Knight; Cast: Valerie Blazek, Sandi Carroll, Reina Cedeno, Major Dodge, Megan Ferguson, Kasey Lockwood, Shawand McKenzie, Adepero Oduye, Dania Ramos; November 8–19

**The Mystery of Irma Vep** by Charles Ludlam; presented by D(3) Productions; Director, Stacey Weingarten; Design, Robert DiGiovanni; Producer, Daniel Holzberg; Cast: Daniel Levinson, David Levinson; January 4–6

**Arrivals** by David Gow; produced by Bank Street Theatre Productions, Kevin Kennedy, Weissberger Theater Group, Jay Harris; Director, Dan Wackerman; Set, Chris Jones; Costumes, Gail Cooper-Hecht; Lighting, Joe Hodge; Sound, Margaret Pine; Music, Jesse Harris; Stage Manager, John Handy; ASM/Ensemble, Anais Borck, Brendan Burke; General Manager, Olson Rhodes; Cast: D. Michael Berkowitz, Michael Goodfriend, Susan Jeffries, Laurence Lau, Lanie MacEwan, Sal Mistretta, Brigitte Viellieu-Davis; February 12–March 10

## The Barrow Group Arts Center (TBG Theatre)

**The Legend of Pearl Hart** book and lyrics by Cathy Chamberlain, music by Rich Look; produced by LCO; Director, Lea Orth; Music Director/Arrangements, David Jackson; Choreography, Jim Osorno; Additional Arrangements, Howard Johnson; Sets, Darrell Keister; Lighting, Amith Chandrashaker; Costumes, Amy Kitzhaber; Stage Manager, Jim Losee; ASM, John Rice; Cast: Catherine Hesse, Michael Shane Ellis, Laurie Gamache, Keith Krutchkoff, Arthur Lindquist, Darcy Miller, Trip Plymale, Judith J.K. Polson, George Riddle, Stephanie Schweitzer, Tyler W. Smith, Natasha Soto-Albors, Bradley P. Staubes, Dax Valdes; June 9–24

**'night Mother** by Marsha Norman; Director, Shannon Patterson; Cast: Lucy Avery Brooke, Amy Loughead; July 6–17

**Chekhov & Maria** by Jovanka Bach; Producer/Director, John Stark; Lighting/Sound/Production Manager, Joe Morrissey; Design/ASM, Janet Sacrey; Costumes, Zale Morris; Cast: Ron Bottitta, Gillian Brashear; July 7–30

**Makeout Session** by Kenan Minkoff; Associate Producer, Isaac Klein; Director, Matt Cowart; Design, Travis McHale; Costumes, Elisa Richards; Press, Judy Jacksina; Cast: Andrew Pastides, Adrian Wyatt; October 20–November 12

**Dating Grim** by Dennis Hurley and John Misselwitz; Director, Rodney Hakim; Cast: Kristen Aldrich, Dustin C. Burrell, Eric Clavell, Marshall Elliott, Elizabeth Howard, Stephen Jutras, Marc Landers, Michael Schwendemann, Shelly Smith, Dennis Hurley; December 14–17

**A Steady Rain** by Keith Huff; Director, K. Lorrel Manning; February 28–March 5

**It is said the men are over in the Steel Tower** by Hideo Tsuchida; Director, Ronit Muszkatblit; March 2–18

**Scituate** by Martin Casella; presented by Barry Goralnick & Outcast Productions; Director, David Hilder; Set, Lauren Helpern; Lighting, Traci Klainer; Costumes, Robin McGee; Sound, Bart Fasbender; Press, Joe Trentacosta; Cast: Holly Barron, Constance Boardman, Damian Buzzerio, Curran Connor, Missy Hargraves, Chad Hoeppner, Laurence Lau, Matthew Mabe, Stefanie Zadravec; March 23–April 7

**GayFest NYC** 1st annual; presented by Robert Harris and Jack W. Batman; included: *Revolution* written & directed by Michael D. Jackson; Cast: Cory Boardman (May 9–14); *Competing Narratives* by A.B. Asher; Director, Margarett Perry; Cast: Sebastian LaCause, Michael Vaccaro, Matthew Boston (May 17–21); *A Kiss From Alexander* book and lyrics by Stephan DeGhelder, music by Brad Simmons; Director/Choreographer, D.J. Salisbury; Co-producer, Dennis Grimaldi; Cast: Gavin Esham, Jeremiah James, Charles Logan, Matthew Marks, Eddie Rabon, Craig Ramsey, Brendt Reil, "Knuckles" Simmons, Jamison Stern, Justin Wilcox (May 24–June 2); Readings: *Edward the King* by David Hopes, directed by Sidney J. Burgoyne; *The Casserole Brigade* by Robert John Ford; directed by Martin Casella

# Blue Coyote Theater Group

Robert Buckwalter, Gary Shrader, Kyle Ancowitz, Founders; Stephen Speights, Director

**The Most Wonderful Love** by Matthew Freeman; Director, Kyle Ancowitz; Music, Margaret F. Heskin & Stephen Speights; Sets, Kerry Chipman, Sound, Brandon Wolcott; Costumes, Katherine Harber; PSM, Sarah Locke; Press, Karen Greco; Cast: Frank Anderson, Lenni Benicaso, David DelGrosso, Laura Desmond, Brian Fuqua, Sarah Ireland, Scott Lovelady, Josephine Stewart, Matthew Trumbull; Access Theater; June 12–July 1

**Standards of Decency Project** plays by David Johnston, Matthew Freeman, David Foley, Brian Dykstra, Boo Killebrew, Laura Henry, Kristen Palmer, John Yearley, Stan Richardson; Directors: Gary Shrader, Robert Buckwalter, Stephen Speights, Kyle Ancowitz; Cast: Victor Almanzar, Nathalie Altman, Michael Bell, Lenni Benicaso, R. Jane Casserly, Laura Desmond, Sean Fri, Tasha Guevara, Tracey Gilbert, Vedant Gokhale, Jeff Hiller, Sarah Ireland, Debbie Jaffe, Cat Johnson, Sean Kenin, Violet Krumbein, Daniel Nunez, G. Ivan Smith, Adam Rihacek, Alexis Suarez, Matthew Trumbull, Daniel Wesley, Joseph Yeargain; Access Theater; December 12–January 8

**The Oresteia** by David Johnston; Director, Stephen Speights; Lighting, Evan O'Brient; Costumes, Jonna McElrath; Music, Margaret F. Heskin; Sound, Brandon Wolcott; Masks, Michelle Ross; PSM, Liz Reddick; Cast: Frank Anderson, Kyle Ancowitz, Brendan Bradley, Bryce Gill, Nell Gwynn, Heidi Jackson, Kathy Lichter, Jonna McElrath, Sarah Schoenberg, Gary Shrader, Robyn Weiss; Access Theater; February 17–March 10

# Boomerang Theatre Company

Tim Errickson, Artistic Director

**King Lear** by William Shakespeare; Director, Philip Emeott; Costumes, Carolyn Pallister; Fight Director, Carrie Brewer; Assistant Director, Sue Abbott; Cast: Zack Calhoon, John Dalmon, Bill Fairbairn, Benjamin Ellis Fine, Justin R. G. Holcomb, Richard Kirkwood, Beth Ann Leone, Uriel Menson, Kate Sandberg, David Sedgwick, David Sitler, Sara Thigpen, Aaron Michael Zook; Performed in Central Park, Riverside Park, Prospect Park, & Astoria Park; June 17–July 23

**Anna Christie** by Eugene O'Neill; Director, Cailin Heffernan; Sets, Scott Orlesky; Costumes, Cheryl McCarron; Lighting, Melanie Smock; Sound, Ann Warren; Stage Manager, Mark Wolff; Cast: Steven M. Bari, Dunsten J. Cormack, Michael Kohn, Jennifer Larkin, Linda S. Nelson, Aidan Redmond; Center Stage NY; September 7–24

**Love in the Insecurity Zone** by Mike Folie; Director, Rachel Wood; Sets, Scott Orlesky; Costumes, Cheryl McCarron; Lighting, Melanie Smock; Sound, Ann Warren; Stage Manager, Tzipora Kaplan; Cast: Trevor Davis, Jodi Dick, Catherine Dowling, John C. Fitzmaurice, Justin R.G. Holcomb, Alisha R. Spielmann; Center Stage NY; September 9–30

**The Ugly Man** by Brad Fraser; Director, Christopher Thomasson; Sets, Scott Orlesky; Costumes, Cheryl McCarron; Lighting, Melanie Smock; Sound, Ann Warren; Stage Manager, Sarah Locke; Fight Director, Carrie Brewer; Cast: Paul Caiola, Bret Jaspers, Jennifer Lyn Perez, Aaron Simms, Barbara Drum Sullivan, Jaime West, Joe Whelski; Center Stage NY; September 14–October 1

**First Flight Readings** *What About the Bones?* by Sean Michael Welch (November 30), *The Most Beautiful Lullaby You've Ever Heard* by Greg Romero (December 2); *Parking Lot Lonely Heart* by Colin McKenna (December 3); *Heads* by E. M. Lewis (December 3); *The System* by Isaac Rathbone (December 3)

# The Brick

**The $ellout Festival** June 2–August 30; included: *Bad Girls* by Sibyl Kempson, directed by Shoshona Currier; *Bonbons for Breakfast* by Lisa Ferber, directed by Ivanna Culinan; *Die Hard: The Puppet Musical* created by John Ardolino & James Walton; *Freak Out Under the Apple Tree* by Tom X. Chao; *Girls! Girls! Girls!* directed by Jennifer Schmermund; *Greed: A Musical Love $tory* written & directed by Robert Honeywell; *The Impotent General* by Gary Winter, directed by Meredith McDonough; *I.P.O. – Flipping Unreal Estate* performed by Octavio Campos & Michael Yawney; *King Lear* by William Shakespeare, directed by Michael Gardner; *The Kung Fu Importance of Being Earnest* conceived by Timothy Haskell, adapted and directed by Michael Gardner; *Magic Monkey Dance Company* directed by Yvan Greenberg; *The Nigerian Spam Scam Scam* by Dean Cameron, directed by Paul Provenza; *Red Carpet LIVE!* performed and created by Lisa Levy; *Rosea on the Flesh* by Nerik Elliot & Alie Vidich; *Sexadelic Cemetery (A Bizarre Science Fantasy)* written & directed by Jeff Lewonczyk; *The Soccergirl Second* by Ryan P. Murray; *Stars in Her Eyes* by Clay McLeod Chapman, directed by Moritz von Stuelpnagel; *That's What We're Here For (An American Pageant)* written & directed by Ian W. Hill; *Trav S.D.'s Health and Wealth Elixir Program* written & performed by Trav S.D.; *The True Life Story of [YOUR NAME HERE]* directed by R.J. Tolan

**Havel Fest** the complete plays of Václav Havel presented by Untitled Theatre Company #61; productions at the Brick included: *An Evening with the Family* translated by Carol Rocamora & Tomas Rychetsky, directed by Glory Sims Bowen, presented by FHB Productions; Cast: Jassica Baily, Brenda Crawley, Noemy Hernandez, Eric Christopher Hoelle, Amy Liszka, David Nash, Iracel Rivero, Isaac Scranton, Medina Senghore, David Skigen, Anthony Stevenson, Jonathan Weirich;

on a double bill with *Guardian Angel* translated by Paul Wilson, directed by Jeff Lewonczyk, presented by Piper McKenzie Productions; Cast: Richard Harrington, Trav S.D. (October 27–November 26); *The Garden Party* translated by Jan Novak, directed by Andrea Boccanfuso, produced by Oracle Theatre; Cast: James Bentley, Michael Marion, Kristine Waters, John Kohan, Alley Scott, David Nelson, Steve Russo, Laura Stockton, Sergei Burbank; presented on a double bill with *Mistake* translated by Carol Rocamora & Tomas Rychetsky, directed by Issac Rathbone & Jennifer Rathbone, produced by Oracle Theater; Cast: Laura Stockton, Alley Scott, Kristine Waters, Joe Beaudin, Daryl Brown, David Nelson (October 26–November 19); *Mountain Hotel* translated by Jitka Martinova, directed by Michael Gardner, produced by The Brick Theater; Cast: Gyda Arber, Fred Backus, Bryan Enk, Robert Honeywell, Heath Kelts, Devon Hawkes Ludlow, Alanna Medlock, R. David Robinson, Alyssa Simon, Moira Stone, Art Wallace (November 9–26); *Temptation* translated by Marie Winn, directed by Ian W. Hill, produced by Gemini CollisionWorks; Cast: Fred Backus, Eric C. Bailey, Aaron Baker, Danny Bowes, Walter Brandes, Maggie Cino, Tim Cusack, Jessi Gotta, Christiaan Koop, Roger Nasser, Timothy McCown Reynolds, Alyssa Simon (November 2–26)

**New York Clown Theatre Festival** September 1–November 10

**Absence of Magic** performed by Eric Davis; October 6–14

**Buoffon Glass Menajoree** adapted and directed by Eric Davis from Tennessee Williams' *The Glass Menagerie*; Cast: Lynn Berg, Audrey Crabtree, Aimee German; October 13–November 10, revived March 8–24

**The Death of Griffin Hunter** by Krik Wood Bromley; presented by Inverse Theatre; Director, Howard Howard Thoresen; Cast: Chris Thorn, Christopher Borg, Hettienne Park, Catherine McNelis, Jessica Chandlee Smith, Al Benditt, Bob Laine, Eva van Dok, Timothy McCown Reynolds, Randall Middleton, Josh Hartung; January 10–February 3

**Strom Thurmond Is Not a Racist** and **Cleansed** by Thomas Bradshaw; presented by the Immediate Theater Company; Director, Jose Zayas; Set, Ryan Elliot Kravetz; Sound, Jeremy Wilson; Costumes, Mel Haley; Lighting, Jim French; Cast: *Strom Thurmond:* Hugh Sinclair, Makeda Christodoulos, Peter Schuler; *Cleansed:* Jerry Zellers, Nikole Williams, Barrett Doss, Derrick Sanders, Joseph Carusone, Zach Lombardo, Frank J. Caiati, Siho Ellsmore; Brick Café; February 8–March 3

**Suite** created and directed, Rachel Cohen; Cast: Katie Brack, Rachel Cohen, Elodie Escarmelle, Adrian Jevicki, Kelly Kocinski, Michelle Vargo; April 12–21

**The Present Perfect** by Kourtney Rutherford; Director, Kevin Doyle; Cast: Tim Donovan, Jr., Thomas Guiffre, Christine Holt, Kourtney Rutherford, Jason Schuler; April 26–May 14

# Broadway by the Year

Scott Siegel, Creator and Host; Barbara Siegel, Advisor; Ross Patterson, Musical Director/Arranger; Michael Lavine, Sheet Music Consultant; Ross Patterson Little Big Band, Accompanist

**The Broadway Musicals of 1978** Director, Bryan Batt; Starring: Bryan Batt, Joyce Chittick, Chuck Cooper, Mary Bond Davis, Julie Garnye, Sean Martin Hingston, Nancy Opel, Christine Pedi, Noah Racey, Lennie Watts, Lari White Special Guest Star: Carolee Carmello; June 19

**The Broadway Musicals of 1928** Director, Joel Froomkin; Starring: Nancy Anderson, Joyce Chittick, Jeffry Denman, Max von Essen, Malcolm Gets, Leah Hocking, Eddie Korbich, Bob Martin, Paul Schoeffler, Lumiri Tubo, Lari White; appearances by David Colbert & Luis Vilabon; Town Hall; February 26

**The Broadway Musicals of 1938** Director, Emily Skinner; Starring: Andy Blankenbuehler, Sarah Uriarte Berry, Aaron Lazar, Shannon Lewis, Ray McLeod, Christianne Noll, Connie Pachl, Hugh Panaro, Martin Vidnovic, Barbara Walsh; Town Hall; March 26

**The Broadway Musicals of 1959** Director, Marc Kudisch; Starring: Mary Bond Davis, Manoel Felciano, Mark Jacoby, Marc Kudish, Nancy Lemenager, Sarah Jane McMahon, Josh Prince, Emily Skinner, Bruce Vilanch; Town Hall; April 30

**The Broadway Musicals of 1964** Director, Dan Foster; Cast: Stephanie J. Block, Liz Callaway, Joyce Chittick, Scott Coulter, Gregg Edelman, Xanthe Elbrick, Beth Leavel, Sean Martin Hingston, David Pittu, Devin Richards; Town Hall; June 18

# Broken Watch Theatre Company

Drew DeCorleto, Aristic Director

**Never Tell** by James Christy; Director, Drew DeCorleto; Sets, J. Wiese; Costumes, Rebecca Lustig; Lighting, Dusty Ray; Sound, Jason Rea; Original Music, Drew Sarich; Stage Manager, Jon William Goldman; Video, Jito Lee; Casting, Stephanie Klapper; Press, Springer Associates; Cast: Michael Blum, Lori Garrabrant, Teresa L. Goding, Eva Kaminsky, John Rengstorff, Jason Schuchman, Mark Stelock, Matthew Wilkas; July 22–August 13

**Dibble Does Christmas in New York** by Jerry Robbins; Music by Jeffrey Sage; Director, Drew DeCorleto; Stage Manager, Erin Leigh Lapham; Casting, Stephanie Klapper; Press, Springer Associates; Cast: Mark Setlock, Stephen P. Brumble Jr., Sarah Ecton-Luttrell, William Jackson Harper, E.C. Kelly, Roger Rifkin, Julie Wilder, Barrett Hall; December 9–30

# Collaborative Artists Project 21 (CAP 21)

Frank Ventura, Executive Artistic Director; Eliza Ventura, Artistic Director

**Pages, A New Musical** music and lyrics by Will Van Dyke, book and lyrics by Josh Halloway; Director, Lawrence Arancio; Musical Director, Marshall Keating

**A Womb With a View** conceived, written & performed by Debra Barsha; Director, Frank Ventura; May 22–June 3

### Conservatory Productions

**Evita** music by Andrew Lloyd Webber, lyrics by Tim Rice; Director, Frank Ventura; Musical Director, Jerry Jean; November 2–12; **Cabaret** music by John Kander, lyrics by Fred Ebb, book by Joe Masteroff; Director, Aimee Francis; Musical Director, Michael Hicks; Choreographers, Lori Leshner, Billy Griffin; February 15–25; **Pippin** music and lyrics, Stephen Schwartz, book, Roger O. Hirson; Director/Choreographer, Steven Sofia; Musical Director, Jerry Jean; April 12–22

### Monday Night Readings – Spring 2007

Dorothy Strelsin New Works Series: *Upfronts and Personal* by Ken Levine, directed by Janet Brenner; Cast: Malcolm Gets, Joanna Gleason, David Rasche, David Schramm, Chip Zien; *A Womb with a View* by Debra Barsha and Frank Ventura, directed by Frank Ventura; *The Cosmopolitan* by Lance Horne, Lorin Latarro, and Josh Rhodes, directed by Peter Flynn; Cast: Sal Viviano, Karen Mason, Rick Hilsabeck; *Defending Richard* by Dana Zeller-Alexis, directed by Austin Pendleton; *Little Heart* by Irene O'Garden, directed by Lisa Rothe; *Urban Acts* by Susan Cameron, directed by Eliza Ventura; Barbara Wolff Classics Series: **Carousel** Book and lyrics by Oscar Hammerstein II, music by Richard Rodgers; directed by Eliza Ventura; Musical Director, Paul Johnson; **Oklahoma** book and lyrics by Oscar Hammerstein II, music by Richard Rodgers; directed by Eliza Ventura; Musical Director, Marshall Keating

# Castillo Theatre

Artistic Director, Dan Friedman; Managing Director, Diane Stiles

**Sapphire's Kiss** by Maggie Zarillo-Gouldin; Directors, Fred Newman & Mary Fridley; June 9–25

**Broadway-Sometimes Off** conceived and directed by Fred Newman; created and performed by the Castillo Ensemble; September 15–30

**Outing Wittgenstein** by Fred Newman; Director, Dan Friedman; Cast: James Arden, Natasha Danielian, Drummond Doroski, Athena Freedlander, Emily Gerstell, Luis Gomez, Daniel Gurian, Kenneth Hughes, Paul C. Newport, Michael Padilla, Gary Patent, Morgan Scott, Christine Tracy-Garrison, Serge Velez; October 20–December 10

**Over There/Over Here** by Michael Reyes; presented by Youth Onstage! Experimental Workshop of the All Stars Project; Director, Brian Mullin; Cast: Michael Alcide, Darnelle Cadet, Lisa Edwards, Christlabelsay Elian, Ralph Francois, David Friggle, Johanny Paulino, Gillian L. Rougier, Sita Sarkar; November 10–December 10, January 13, 14, 26

**America (a conversation)** created by the Youth Onstage!; Director, Dan Friedman & Brian Mullin; Cast: Michael Alcide, Darnelle Cadet, Lisa Edwards, Christlabelsay Elian, Ralph Francois, David Friggle, Johanny Paulino, Gillian L. Rougier, Sita Sarkar; February 16–March 4

**It Hasn't Always Been This Way** by Ntozake Shange; co-production with the New Federal Theatre; Director, Dianne McIntyre; Cast: Ntozake Shange, Shireen Dickson, Nina Dominique, Petronia Paley, Charles Wallace; February 21–March 3

**Homeland Security: Bringing Dr. King Up To Date** directed and choreographed by Desmond Richardson; Performed by young performers from the All Stars; March 9–April 4

**Backstage (A Love-Hate Story of the Women's Movement)** written & directed by Fred Newman; Cast: Madelyn Chapman, Melvin Shambry, Gabrielle L. Kurlander; April 27–June 10

**All Stars Hip-Hop Cabaret** director, Dan Friedman & Antoine R.L. Joyce; Performed by Youth Onstage! and the All Stars Talent Show Network; June 1–16

# Center Stage NY

**ONE Solo Arts Festival** 3rd annual solo performance festival presented by terraNova Collective; included: Taylor Mac, Roger Bonair-Agard, Megan Bridge, James Carter, Glenna Miller, Lance Werth, Andrews DuBouchet, Justine Moore, Christen Clifford, Jeff Grow, Livia Scott, Abbie Conant, Lee Barton; June 8–25

**Hamlet (solo)** performed by Raoul Bhaneja; Director, Robert Ross Parker; August 12–13

**Organic Shrapnel** by Charles Cissel; Director, Terese Hayden; October 15

**The Beauty Queen of Leenane** by Martin McDonagh; presented by Perservus Productions; Director, David Storck; Cast: Lisa McLogan Shaheen, Katherine O'Sullivan, Timothy Fannon, Chris Ford; October 27–November 5

**Masquerade: Poems of Calypso and Home** written & performed by Roger Bonair-Agard; Director, Kamilah Forbes; November 7–19

**The Dirty Talk** by Michael Puzzo; Director, Padraic Lillis; Set, Rob Monaco; Lighting, Sarah Sidman; Costumes, Lea Umberger; General Manager, Abby Marcus; Cast: Kevin Cristaldi, Sidney Williams; January 14–February 4

**Men of Steel** by Qui Nguyen; presented by Vampire Cowboys Theatre Company; Director, Robert Ross Parker; Fights, Marius Hanford; Sets/Lighting, Nick Francone; Costumes, Jessica Wegener; Sound, Patrick Shearer; Press, Jim Baldassare; Cast: Noshir Dalal, Sharon Eisman, Jason Liebman, Tom Myers, Melissa Paladino, Jeremy Sarver, Paco Tolson, Temar Underwood; March 15–April 8

**Not Waving** by Ellen Melaver; produced by Square Peg Productions; Director, Douglas Mercer; Cast: Heidi Armbuster, Josh Barrett, Eleanor Handley, Greg Keller, Kristine Nielsen, Tim Spears; March 27

**Thinking Makes It So** written & directed by Damon Krometis; Design, Jennifer Brunk; Stage Manager, Christine Fisichella; Cast: Joe Curnutte; April 11–22

**Stand-Up Girl** by Elizabeth C. Gutterman; Director, Michelle Tattenbaum; Cast: Carole Schweid, Jenn Wehrung; April 25–29

**An Octopus Love Story** by Delaney Britt Brewer; presented by Kids With Guns; Director, Mike Klar; Producers, Ben Cikanek, Jessica Jolly, Mike Klar, James Eun Lim, Robert Patrizi; Set, Brian Sidney Bembridge; Lighitng, John Wolf; Costumes, Heather Klar; Cast: Michael Cyril Creighton, Andrew Dawson, Jenny Greer, Kelli Holsopple, Eric Kuehnemann, Krista Sutton, Josh Tyson; May 2–20

# chashama

Anita Durst, Founder

**The Eaten Heart** by Hannah Bos, Oliver Butler & Paul Thureen, presented by The Debate Society; June 1–4

**2x4** written & performed by James Junio, Ashleigh Lay, Stefanie Maas, Michael Miano, Emily Vick, Scott R. Weigand, Amy Wowak; June 7–11

**He(R)evolution** written & performed by Julia Ahumada Grob; Director, Alli Maxwell; July 27–29

**I Saw the Evil One** written, directed & performed by Craig Flanagan; presented with Normandy Sherwood's window performance installation, *Canary*; August 14–18

**Miss Julie** by August Strindberg; Director, Tara Matkosky; Cast: Elizabeth Lee Malone, Louis Ozawa Changchien, Sandi Carroll; September 7–10

**To Be Loved** by Alex DeFazio; Director, Jody P. Person; presented by Elixer Productions; Producer, Faye Rosenbaum; Original Music, Chris Gardella; Cast: Bobby Abid, Albert Aeed, Kelly Markus, Jesse Soursourian, Elizabeth Sugarman, Brian Sufalko, Brady Niederer; November 30–December 23

**Hustler, WI** written & directed Michael Scott-Price; presented by Asteroid B612; Cast: Ali Stover, Mike Keller, Anthony D. Stevenson; January 23–February 11

**A Series of Grease Fires** by Quasi Theatre; Cast: Jason Klein, Tony Hogrebe, Chloe Liederman, Ben Williams; March 16–17

**The Wedding** written & directed by Teddy Jefferson; March 27–31

**Macbeth** by William Shakespeare; Directors, Darragh Martin, Abigail Broberg; Producer, Jessica Teague; Cast: Jeff Brown, Pardis Dabashi, Lydica Brunner, Lakshimi Sundaram, Gareth Schumacher, Chas Carey, Daniel Mitura, Bert Ma Jordan Fraade, Tyson Brody, Michael Brick, Nate Trunnell, Sarah Lord, Siobhan Gilbert, Jason Resnikoff, Katherine Atwill; March 30–April 2

**Eden** by Marina Shron; Director, Alexandra Aron; April 10

**Peasant** written & performed by Susan Ferrara; Director, Dale Heinen; May 3–25

**You Are Here: A Maze** by Sam Hillmer and Laura Paris; May 6–27

# Cherry Lane Theatre

Angelina Fiordellisi, Founder/Artistic Director; James King, Managing Director

**Tongues: Reading Series 2006–2007** *The Middle East, In Pieces* featuring: *Dog River* by Beau Willimon, directed by Thomas Caruso; Cast: Mozhan Marno, Adam Saunders; *The Black Eyed* (excerpt) by Betty Shamieh, directed by Sam Gold; Cast: Anney Giobbe, Tara Franklin, Lanna Joffrey, Michelle Torres; *9 Parts of Desire* (excerpt) by Heather Raffo, directed by Thomas Caruso; Cast: Mozhan Marno; *Beirut Rocks* by Israel Horovitz, directed by Thomas Caruso; Cast: Peter Stadlen, Augustine Welles, Lucy Boyle, Mozhan Marno; *Petra* by Anne Nelson, directed by Thomas Caruso; Cast: Anne Carney, Anthony Veneziale, Mozhan Marno; *Power Lunch* by Kia Corthron, directed by Leah Gardiner; Cast: Brenda Thomas, Anne Carney, Leila Buck; *HKeele - Talk to Me* written & performed by Leila Buck, directed by Thomas Caruso; *Aces* by Paul Benjamin; Cast: Roger Robinson,0 David Little; *They Call Me Nigger* by Paul Benjamin; Cast: Roger Robinson, David Little, Janio Marrero, Katori Hall, Dulé Hill, Alfredo Narciso; *Smoke In The Mountains* by Beau Willimon, directed by Sam Gold; Cast: Patch Darragh, Paul Sparks, Michael Chernus, Austin Lysy, James Seol; *No Stallions In Manhattan* by Jane Ann Crum, directed by Loretta Greco; *Loons* by Rob Ackerman, directed by Jamie Richards; presented by Joan and Richard Firestone; Cast: Kevin Geer, Cynthia Harris, Robert Hogan, Jared McGuire, Caroline Rhea, Grant Shaud

**Mentor Project 2007 Showcases** Sets, Regina Garcia; Costumes, Rebecca Bernstein; Lighting, Pat Dignan; Sound, Barbara Vlahides; Stage Manager, Mei Ling Acevedo; included: *The Secret Agenda of Trees* by Colin McKenna; Mentor, Lynn Nottage; Director, Sam Gold; Cast: Patch Darragh, Sarah Lord, Gio Perez, Jedadiah Schultz, Sara Surrey; *Topsy Turvy Mouse* by Peter Gil-Sheridan; Mentor, Michael Weller; Director, Daniella Topol; Cast: Rosalyn Coleman, Ted Koch, Kelly Mcandrew, Ian Quinlan, Henny Russell, Gita Reddy; *Training Wisteria* by Molly Smith Metzler; Mentor, Jules Feiffer; Director, Leah C. Gardiner; Cast: Jessica Digiovanni, Angela Ford, Bruce McCarty, Marissa O'Donnell, Matt Stagelmann; Studio Theatre; March 20–May 12

**Cherry Pit Late Nite** *Breaking Walls: A Wall Street Romance* by M. Alexandria Beech; directed by Christian Ely; Cast: Gina Mahoney, Gabriel Portuondo, Matthew Pavoni, Kerry Bishe, Benjamin Ellis Fine, Scott MacArthur, Manny Liyes, Jose Juan Torres; August 17–26; *FUCT Impregnates Your Sister* created and performed by the Comedy troupe FUCT; September 8–15; *The Van Driver Experience* created by Jason Schuler; November 9–11; *Warning Signs* created and performed by Maggie Surovell; November 16–18; *Extreme Girl* written & performed by Barbara Blackburn, directed by Courtney Munch; January 25–27; *Deaf, Dumb and FUCT;* February 2–10

### Non-resident Productions

**Downtown Urban Theatre Festival** 5th annual; included: *The Brighter Burn* by Herb Donaldson; *When Santo Domingo Isn't Enough* by Melissa Fendell; *Black at Michigan* by Dominique Morisseau; *Call Me Crazy...*by Helena D. Lewis; *Georgia* by Gian DiDonna; *Speak Your Mind* by Michael R. Ramirez; *touch* by Francisco Roque; *Trans Plantations* by Janis Astor del Valle; *Freedom* by Emma Terese; *Karen & Tomas (I Touch Myself)* by Mel Nieve; *Hearts and Minds* by Joel R. Johnson; June 14–24

**Kingdom of Not** written and performed by Dan Carbone; Director, Joseph Graham; Design, John Sowle; Producer, Kaliyuga Arts; Studio Theatre; November 4–18

**Twigs** by George Furth; presented by No Frills; November 13 & 20

**Four Play** presented by the Republic Theater Company; included: *The Thirteen Clocks* by James Thurber, adapted by Frank Lowe, directed by Andrew Langton; *The Tempest* by William Shakespeare directed by Jessica Scott;

*The E.C.: Elsinore County,* written & directed by Antony Raymond; *Miss Julie* by August Strindberg, directed by Akiva Daube; December 2006

**Vita and Virginia** by Eileen Atkins; presented by No Frills; Cast: Kathleen Chalfant, Patricia Elliott; November 27–December 11

**Cycle** by Rose Courtney; Director, Craig Carlisle; Choreography, Laura Sheehy; Music Director, Rachel Kaufman; Cast: Charlotte Shrubsole; February 16–March 3

**The Memory of Water** by Shelagh Stephenson; presented by Third Encore Company; Director, Ellen Lichtensteiger; Set, Tim McMath; Costumes, Jessica Cloutier; Lighting, David Roy; Sound, Katherine Miller; Stage Manager, Christy Thede; ASM, Mat Bussler; Cast: Victoria Bundonis, Zoe Frazer, Borden Hallowes, Abby Overton, Todd Reichart, Karen Sternberg; Studio Theatre; May 17–June 2

# Clemente Soto Vélez Cultural Center

**Measure for Measure** by William Shakespeare; presented by Hipgnosis Theatre Company; Director, John Castro; Cast: Erika Bailey, Demetri Bonaros, Nick Brooks, Kate Dulcich, Johan Kevin Jones, Francis Kelly, David Laufgraben, David Look, Elizabeth Mirachi, Margot Newkirk, Julian A. Rozzell Jr., Adelia Saunders, Wayne Alon Scott, Sarah Sokolovic, Justin Steeve, Rachel Tiemann; Flamboyan Theatre; June 15–July 2

**The Kafka Series** presented by Black Moon Theatre Company; Director/Adaptator, Rene Migliaccio; included: *The Metamorphosis* Cast: Eric Pettigrew, Jieun Lee, Juliette Morel; *The Trial* Cast: Yasser Akhtar, Brenda Cooney, Yvette Feuer, Steve Howe, John Maurice, Leah Rudick, Deven Sisler, Lori M. Vincent, Gabriel Williams; Teatro La Tea; September 15–October 28

**Nightmare: Face Your Fear** created and directed by Timothy Haskell; presented by Psycho Clan; September 28–November 3

**King of Dominoes** by Bill Vargas; Director, Michael J. Marvaez; Cast: Michael Philip Del Rio, Jason Flores, Indio Melendez, Teresa Yenque; Teatro La Tea; November 8–December 3

**Why Does It Sting When I Pee?** by Felipe Ossa; Director, Tom Thornton; November 9–19

**Some Historic/Some Hysteric** conceived and directed by Ildiko Lujza Nemeth, co-conceived by Jessica Sofia Mitrani; presented by New Stage Theatre Company; Cast: Catherine Correa, Tino del Casar, Nicole Hafner, Markus Hirnigel, Denice Kondik, Sarah Lemp, Florencia Minniti, Monica Risi, Paula Roman, Gaby Schafer, Jeanne Lauren Smith, Jose Cavazos, Sara Hatfield, Fabiyan Pemble-Belkin, Kaylin Lee Clinton; November 10–December 10

**All Fall Down** written & directed by David Ledoux & Allison Smith; presented by Theatre Recrudescence; Cast: Samantha Anderson, Sal Bardo, Michael Bordwell, Katie Braden, Dave Collins, Candice Goodman, Vincent Ingrisano, Jesse Irwin, James Poling, Erin Leigh Schmoyer, Alley Scott, Julia Susman, Timothy Thurston, Jenna Weinberg; Milagro Theatre; November 29– December 17

**Point Break Live!** adapted by Kathryn Bigelow; presented by New Rock Theater Productions; Director, Jamie Hook; Cast: Topher Mikels, Thomas Blake, George Spielvogel, Ben Robertson, Izzy Abeyta, Scout Durwood, Amber Hubert, Mike Kash, Jonathan Evan Stern, Adam Morris, Conor Tansy; Teatro La Tea; January 25–February 25

**American Family Project** written & directed by Deepa Purohit & Sanjit De Silva; presented by Rising Circle Theater Collective; Cast: Catherine Jhung, Nancy Kim, Kerry Mantle, Arlando Smith, Paula Wilson; Teatro La Tea; March 1–11

**The Secret War** written & directed by Darius Safavi; Cast: Gregory Manley, Nina Shahi, Carlos Ibarra, Ben Forster; Milagro Theatre; April 27–May 20

**A Mouthful of Birds** by Caryl Churchill and David Lan; presented by Breedingground Productions; Director, Tomi Tsunoda; Design, Tomi Tsunoda, Laura Shiffrin, Jo Lampert, Sanaz Ghajarrahimi, Andrew Scoville, Steve O'Shea; Cast: Debbi J. Morgan, Fred Urfer, Doug Paulson, Stephanie Roy, Skyler Sullivan, Morgan Murphey, Mark Lindberg, Theresa Finamore, Jessica Levine, Tomi Tsunoda; May 16–June 2

## Collective: Unconscious

**Pinchbottom's Sub:Conscious** monthy burlesques hosted by Nasty Canasta and Jonny Porkpie; Guest Stars: Anita Cookie, Bambi the Mermaid, Bastard Keith, Belle-Morte Baudelaire, Clams Casino, Creamy Stevens, Delirium Tremens, Dirty Martini, Gigi LaFemme, Harvest Moon, Howling Vic, Jo Boobs, Julie Atlas Muz, Little Brooklyn, Lukki, Miss Firecracker, Miss Saturn, Naughtia Nice, Nelson Lugo, Peekaboo Pointe, Rose Wood, Ruby Valentine, Scarlet Sinclair, Schaffer the Darklord, Scott Rayow, Scotty the Blue Bunny, Seth Herzog, Tigger, Velocity Chyaldd, Veronika Sweet, World Famous *Bob*, Zero Boy; opened May 19, 2006; open run

**Game Boys** by Douglas Harmsen; presented by Partial Comfort Productions; Director, Marc Santa Maria; Cast: Di Johnston, Edwin Sean Patterson, David Sajadi, Paco Tolson; June 8–16

**Underground Zero Festival** July 19–August 5; included: *It Came From New York: The Battle of New York* curated by Michele Carlo, featuring Big Mike, Andy Christie, Peter Lubell, Marie Mundaca, Nancy Richards, Julie Booth; *Broken Dog Legs* written & performed by Emily Conebere, directed by Rachel Rayment; *Jamal Lullabies* written & performed by Emily Conebere, directed by Paul Bargetto; *The Ted Haggard Monologues* by Michael Yates Crowley, directed by Michael Rau; *The Sisters* by Harrison Rivers, directed by Matt Torney; *Why He Drinks Coffee* by Josh Koenigsberg, directed by Matt Torney; *The Moxie Show* curated and hosted by Trav S.D., featuring Ian W. Hill; *Let Us Go Then, You and I* inspired by Samuel Beckett, directed by James Dacre; *The Flying Machine: Journey to the End of the Night* by Jason Lindner, directed by Joshua Carlebach; *Commedia dell'Artemisia* by Kiran Rikhye, directed by Jon Stancato, presented by Stolen Chair Theatre Company; *GO!* directed by Kara Tyler, presented by The Train Station (San Francisco); *SICK: Sick of it All* written & directed by Caleb Hammond; Drama of Works and Exlploding Puppet Productions pieces including "Sid & Nancy Punch & Judy Show," "Puppet Kafka," and "Die Hard: The Puppet Musical"

**Titus X: The Musical** by Shawn Northrip; presented by Fugly Productions and The Tank; Director, Peter Sanfilippo; The Tank; July 27–August 24

**Run the Maze, Burn the Maze** by Edward P. Clapp; presented by Collective Hole Productions in association with The Tank; Director, Rebecca V. Nellis; Cast: Sean Seally, Garrett Feek; September 7–10

**Turning Tables** written & performed by Coffee Cup (a theatre co.); Director, Gita Reddy; Set/Lighting, Shaun Fillion; Costumes, Marion Talan; Cast: Mike Ferrell, Ishah Janssen-Faith, Jack McGowan, Hemmendy Nelson, Phil Vos; September 28–October 15

**SLAM Theater** at The Tank; October 1–22, January 7–28, May 6–June 3

**Obstruction Plays** presented by Slant Theatre Project, obtstructions written by Lee Blessing, Naomi Iizuka, Sarah Ruhl; included: *The Dinner Table* by Dan O'Brien, directed by Suzanne Agins; Cast: Peter Kim, Robert Karma Robertson, Amy Lynn Stewart, Liv Rooth, John Behlmann, Larry Dial, Polly Hubbard; *Priest in a Pool* by Michele Lowe, directed by Adam Knight; Cast: Brian Slaten, Vayu O'Donnell; *Caution: Parents May Be Less Insane Than They Appear* by Lisa Kron, directed by We Grantom; Cast: Kelli Giddish, Garrett Neergaard, Michael Doyle, Marnye Young; *I See London, I See France* written & directed by Evan Cabnet; Cast: Noah Trepanier, Kathleen White, Kelly McCreary; *Blossoming Andromachae* by Marcus Gardley, directed by Lori Wolter; Cast: Arlando Smith, James Seol,

Matthew Dellapina, Robert Karma Robinson, Kelly McCreary; *Unlimited* by Mat Smart, directed by Steve Cosson; Cast: Amy Lynn Stewart, Daoud Heidami, Matthew Dellapina, Nicholas Heck, Therese Barbato, Garrett Neergaard, David Carl, Robert Karma Robinson, Stephen Sanders, Noah Trepanier, John Behlmann, Larry Dial, Peter Kim, Vayu O'Donnell, Brian Slaten; The Tank; November 1–December 2

**La Turista** by Sam Shepard; Director, Rachel Fachner; presented by Solid Hang; Cast: Jonathan Florez, Mary Guiteras, Tom Vaught, Nathan Williams; November 16–19

**Things Are Going to Change, I Can Feel It** by Mike Smart; presented by Immediate Medium Inc.; Director, J.J. Lind; Cast: Gary Bronz, Max Dana, Brady Jenkins, Toby Lawless, Rachel Levy, Ainna Manapat, Maki Takenouchi, Liz Vacco; January 19–21

**The End of the Known World Plays** *Juicy and Delicious* by Lucy Alibar, directed by Zoe Aja Moore; Choreography, Brian Maloney; *The Bird Stories* by James Ryan Caldwell, directed by Bethany Perkins; Cast: Lucy Alibar, Elliotte Crowell, Aidan Kane, James Ryan Caldwell, Ben Maddocks, Brian Maloney, Tom Rothacker, Liz Wisan, Eden Worsley; The Tank; February 24–March 14

**Exposed: Experiments in Love, Sex, Death and Art** written & performed by Annie Sprinkle and Elizabeth Stephens; Director, Neon Weiss; April 26–May 12

## Connelly Theater

**Fools and Lovers** by Gregory Sherman & Gregory Wolfe; Director, Gregory Wolfe; Cast: Djola Branner, David DelGrosso, Kate Greer, Lynn Lobban, Rhonda S. Musak, David Pixley, Yvonne Roen, Jonathan Todd Ross, Emily Shoolin, James Wolfe; September 21–October 15

**All the Way Home** by Tad Mosel, based on *Death in the Family* by James Agee; presented by The Transport Group; Director, Jack Cummings III; Set, Sandra Goldmark; Costumes, Shana Alberg & Katherine Rohe; Lighting, R. Lee Kennedy; Music, Ellen Weiss; Cast: Barbara Andres, Patrick Boll, John Braden, Alice Cannon, Corinne Edgerly, Chandler Frantz, Patrick Gilbert, Joseph Kolinski, Michael Lewis, Tom Ligon, Ben Masur, Joanna Parson, Monica Russell, Irma St. Paule, Letta Serra; October 26–November 18

**The Dark at the Top of the Stairs** by William Inge; presented by The Transport Group; Director, Jack Cummings III; Set, Sandra Goldmark; Costumes, Shana Albery; Lighting, R. Lee Kennedy; Sound, Seth Guterman; PSM, Wendy Patten; Cast: Patrick Boll, Donna Lynne Champlin, Paul Iacono, Liz Mamana, Colby Minifie, Michele Pawk, Jay Potter, Jack Tartaglia, Matt Yeager; March 30–April 21

## CRS Studio Theatre

**Gus and Fred Smash the TV** written & directed by Harold Lehmann; Cast: Jim Ford, Alex Kipp, Robert Weinstein; June 2–18; **Mikros Kosmos** presented by Anemone Dance Theater; Choreography, Sara Baird & Erin Dudley; Music, Kenneth Kirschner; Violin, Christopher Tignor & Miriama Young; October 26–November 4; **The Trial** by Franz Kafka; presented by Egress Theatre Co.; Director, Andrew Bielski; Score, Patrick Penta; Cast: Daryl Brown, Daniel Granke, Jonathan Levy, Jason Smith, Robert Weinstein, Matthew Woods; February 9–March 3; **Unlikely Excursions** created and performed by Cassie Terman and Heather Harpham; presented by CRS and Dharma Road; March 9–10; **My Mirror, My Self** by Maureen Robinson, designed, directed, and performed by Yuki Kawahisa; with Toni Mayo; April 19–28

## Dixon Place

**Ambushed** concept and choreography by Michela Marino-Lerman; Cast: Michela Marino-Lerman, DJ Supreme, Chikako Iwahori, Hannah Leah Dunn, Hank Smith, Claudia Gomez Vorce, Masato Nishitani, Joseph Wiggan, Kendrick Jones II; June 9–24

**Skin Deep** written & performed by Jeffrey Essmann; July 6–7

**Slanty Eyed Mama** written & performed by Kate Rigg; Composer, Lyris Hung; July 19–23

**Concord, Virginia** written & performed by Peter Neofotis; monthly August 7–June 18

**The Idiot King** written & directed by Susana Cook; Score, Julian Mesri; Cast: Consuelo Arias, Lucy Mackinnon, Anni Amberg, Soraya Odishoo, Karen Jaime, Julian Mesri, Jennifer Fomore, Amanda Salane, Jose Garcia Armenter, Susana Cook; August 15–26

**The Nibbler** written & performed by Victoria Roberts; Director, Louise Fagan; September 14–October 7

**The Last Emperor of Flushing** written & performed by Alvin Eng; October 5 & 12

**WARNING! Not for Broadway** festival of experimental musicals curated by Michelle Feldman; included: *Bar Code* by by Debbie Andrews, Mike Blaxill & Ted Lange; *Zuly in the Last Place on Earth* by John Chin, Anthea Fane & Christina Kulick, directed by Mercedes Murphy; *RollerCoaster* by Kenneth Alan Morrill, musical direction by Elaine Kwon; *Kultur Kamp* by Nina Mankin, featuring Taylor Mac; *No More Waiting* by Chris Widney & David Christian Azarow; *Little Mary* by Michele Aldin & Keith Gordon, directed by Lauren Rosen; *The Wings of Yi Sang* by Kyoung-Ae Kang & Paul Nelson; *Caged Sparrows* by Germono Toussaint Bryant; *Runway 69* by Erin Kamler, produced by David Gordon, Eric Kamler, and Shana Waterman; performed at Roulette/20 Greene Street; November 10–12

**what remnants remain** written & performed by Alva Rogers; December 1 & 2

**Revofuckinlution** written & performed by Jack Shamblin; December 4

**Filtered** and **2:55 a.m.** written & performed by Jackie Moynahan and Jen Abrams; January 6

**Scheherazade** created and directed by Yvan Greenberg; Cast: Corey Dargel, Sheila Donovan, Oleg Dubson, and Alexis Macnab; February 10–24

**Crime or Emergency** written & performed by Sibyl Kempson; March 1–16

**Ice Queens: The Faggot War** written & performed by Michael Cross Burke; March 22

**Puppet Blok!** curated by Leslie Strongwater; April 13 & 14

**Play Boy: Or, Ode to America After the Second Civil War** written & directed by Johnny Klein; April 18 & 19

**Sum of Us** written & performed by Michelle Matlock; with Inner Princess; May 10–26

## The D-Lounge

**Assisted Loving** written and performed by Bob Morris; Director, Gordon Greenberg; March–June, 2006; **I Know You Are but What Am I?** written & performed by Taffy McCarthy; October 13–15; **The Country Feedback** by Joel Hanson & **War Mouth** by Ernest Curcio; presented by Boon Theatre; Director, Ernest Curcio; Cast: *The Country Feedback:* Stephen Reyes, Scott Voloshin, Stacey Uria, Jeff Forte, John DeBenedetto; *War Mouth:* Nick Basile, Barbara Ann Rollins,

Danny Bruckert, Joel Hanson; March 11–20; **The Devil and Billy Markham** by Shel Silverstein; presented by Algonquin Theater Productions; Director, Thomas Coté; Music, The Broken Pockets Band: Sean Singer, Seth Foster, Trey Albright; Cast: Brit Herring; March 9–April 14

## The Drilling CompaNY

Hamilton Clancy, Producing Artistic Director; Karen Kitz, Associate Producer

**The Tempest** by William Shakespeare; Director, Kathy Curtiss; Design, Rebecca Lord; Percussion, Thom Garvey; Assistant Director, Stephanie Bashall; Cast: James Davies, Brad Coolidge, Shannon Marshall, Greg Petrov, Greg Couba, Owen Thompson, David Marantz, Roberto Felice, Allesandro Colla, Nicole Longchamp, Alexandra Bosquet, Demetrius Kallas, Tom Gregory, David Douglas Smith, Shira Kobren; parking lot at Ludlow & Broome; July 6–22

**As You Like It** by William Shakespeare; Director, Jesse Ontiveros; Music, Dan Barnhill; Cast: Richard Mover, Erik Bryan Slavin, Dan Barnhill, Tom Lapke, Peter Macklin, Max Hambleton, Michael Gnat, Elizabeth Schmidt, Dana Slamp, Michael Gnat, Erik Bryan Slavin, Dan Barnhill, Tom Lapke, Hamilton Clancy, Anne Popolizio, Dan Barnhill, Neil Shah, Maria McConville, Tom Lapke, Hamilton Clancy, Dan Barnhill, Tom Lapke; parking lot at Ludlow & Broome; July 27–August 12

**Security** eight short plays; PSM, Billie Davis; Lighting, Miriam Crowe; Sets, Rebecca Lord; Sound, Chris Rummel; Percussionist, Thom Garvey; Composer for *Circus Berzerkus*, Rock Wilk; Company Manager, Colleen Cosgrove; Artists, Phillip DeVita, Allen Gaoiran, Marie Roberts; included: *Bells and Whistles* by Brian Dykstra; Director, Laura Strausfeld; Cast: Michael Gnat, Don Carter, David Marantz, Hamilton Clancy, Carol Halstead, Richard Mover; *The Proposal* by Stephen Bittrich; Director, Carol Halstead; Cast: Stephanie Cozart, Josh Foldy; *Zahra* by Neil Olson; Director, Bradford Olson; Cast: Hamilton Clancy, Karen Kitz, David Marantz; *Killing Squirrels in Sleepy Hollow* by P. Seth Bauer; Director, Peter Bretz; Cast: Elowyn Castle, Bill Green, Kwaku Driskell, Jesus A. Del Rosario Jr.; *100 Years War* by Sheri Graubert; Director, Tom Herman; Cast: Rebecca Darke, Randie Shane, Bill Green, *Safety Off* by Kate McCamy Director, Richard Mover; Cast: Michael Gnat, Colleen Cosgrove, Hamilton Clancy; *Don't Quit* by C. Denby Swanson; Director, Matthew Cowart; Cast: Don Carter; *Circus Berzerkus* by Paul Siefken Director, Shana Gold; Cast: Allesandro Colla, Scott Baker, Bill Green, Genia Morgan, Randie Shane; 78th Street Theatre Lab Third Floor Theatre; June 9–July 2

**Security: The Refinery** series of readings and rough stagings of works in development on "dark" nights; authors included: Micheline Auger, Stephen Bittrich, Colleen Cosgrove, Sheri Graubert, Oyamo, Dana Slamp; June 12–26

**Security2** eight short plays; Sets, Rebecca Lord; Lighting, Miriam Crowe; Sound, Chris Rummel; Production Stage Manager, Billie Davis; Art, Phillip De Vita; included: *A Gopher in the Ninth Ward* by Trish Harnetiaux; Director, Eric Nightengale; Cast: Carol Scudder, Michael Gnat; *Crusade* by Justin Boyd; Director, Richard Harden; Cast: Stephen Bittrich, Amber Voiles; *With Benefits* by Colleen Cosgrove; Director, Dave Marantz; Cast: Karla Hendrick, Jane Guyer, Michael Gnat, Geoff Grady, Kristin Wheeler; *Breach of Security* by Brian Christopher Williams; Director, Tom Herman; Cast: Erin Mallon, Josh Foldy, Megan MacKenzie Lawrence, *Hay Outta Hell* by Yvette Sirker; Director, Hamilton Clancy; Cast: Rebecca Darke, Brigitte Barnett, Kwaku Driskell, Allen Jared, Colleen Cosgrove; *Grapeheads* by Sheri Graubert; Director, Hamilton Clancy; Cast: Dan Teachout, Jane Guyer, Rich Orlow, Tanya Perez; *The Knock* by Drew Sachs; Director, Bradford Olson; Cast: Scott Baker, Patrick Edgar; *Continuum* by Reneé Flemings; Director, Liz Dunn Ruiz; Cast: Nikki Andrews, Emilie Byron, Tanya Perez; *Safe* by Don Carter; Director, Rachel Wood; Cast: Ebbe Bassey, Cidele Curo, Mary Fox, Dennis Gagomiros, Darren Lipari, Ron Dreyer, Alessandro Colla; 78th Street Theatre Lab Third Floor Theatre; November 9–19

**Justice** nine short plays; PSM, Amy Cruz; Lighting, Miriam Crowe; Sets, Rebecca Lord; Sound, Chris Rummel; Costumes, Lisa Renee Jordan; Press, Kate McCamy; Art, Phillip De Vita; included: *Just Us* by Brian Dykstra; Director, Desmond Mosley; Cast: Dave Marantz, Patrick Edgar, Kwaku Driskell; *God's Signature* by Stephen Bittrich; Director, Peter Bretz; Cast: Kevin Draine, Amber Voiles, Abhijeet Sheety; *Inheritance* by Eric Henry Sanders; Director, Hamilton Clancy; Cast: Karla Hendrick, David Adams; *Sheet* by Ronan Noone; Director, Bradford Olson; Cast: Jane Guyer; *Dog Justice* by Andrea Moon; Director, Hamilton Clancy; Cast: Veronica Cruz, Colleen Cosgrove, Karla Hendrick; *Habeas Corpus* by Kate McCamy; Director, Richard Mover; Cast: Jane Ray, Hamilton Clancy, Abhijeet Sheety; *By the Book* by Paul Siefken; Director, Richard Harden; Cast: Don Carter, Roberto DeFelice, Patrick Edgar, Kwaku Driskell; *Natural Causes* by C. Denby Swanson; Director, Dan Teachout; Cast: James Davies; *Devin and Josh Are New Anchors: The Death of Jeremy Jeremyson* by Trish Harnetiaux; Director, Jude Domski; Cast: Patrick Edgar, Kwaku Driskell; 78th Street Theatre Lab Third Floor Theatre; May 9–27

**Drilling Company Discovery Series** *The Acquisition* by Stephen Bittrich; Director, Will Pomerantz; Cast: Stephanie Cozart, Ron Dreyer, Douglas Harmsen, Dylan Green, Mikel Sarah Lambert, Dana Slamp, Paul Whitthorne; 78th Street Theatre Lab 3rd floor; May 14; *Over the Line* by Seth Bauer; Director, Gabriele Förster; Cast: Alessandro Colla, Jane Guyer, Megan MacKenzie Lawrence, Darren Lipari, Maria Jane Guyer, Tobias Segal; 78th Street Theatre Lab on the 3rd Floor; May 29

# Duo Theatre

**Hyenas** by Christian Siméon; presented by Stages Theatre Center; Director/Adaptor, Paul Verdier; Cast: Daniel Pettrow; May 25–June 17; **Vassa Zheleznova** by Maxim Gorky; presented by Horizon Theatre Rep; Director, Christopher Carter Sanderson; October 5–29; **The Marilyn Project** written & directed by Michelangelo Alasa; Cast: Stephanie Bentley, Brenda Bush, Greg Pernhajen, Luke Valerio, Reet Roos Varnik; November 30–December 16

# Emerging Artists Theatre Company

Artistic Director, Paul Adams; Associate Artistic Director, Derek Jamison

**EATfest Fall 2006** thirteen short plays; Theatre 5; October 31–November 19; included: *Can't You See We're Acting* by Carl L. Williams, directed by Glenn Schudel; Cast: Peter Byrne, Peter Levine, Hershey Miller, Jennifer Pawlitschek, Jacqueline Sydney; *Customer Disservice* by Gregg Pasternack, directed by Kelly Haydon; Cast: William Reinking, Amol Tripathi; *Five Minutes* by Allan Baker, directed by Kevin Brofsky; Cast: Brian Duguay, Hunter Gilmore, Brian Louis Hoffman, Scott Katzman, Sandra Mills Scott, Gameela Wright; *Fit for Love* by Rich Orloff, directed by Christopher Maring; Cast: Marc Castle, Brian Louis Hoffman, Allyson Morgan; *Forgetting to Remember* by Greg Kalleres, directed by Ian Streicher; Cast: Michael Cuomo, Greg Homison, Rebecca Hoodwin; *Help Thyself* by Greg Kalleres, directed by Derek Jamison; Cast: Matt Boethin, Glory Gallo; *Must the Show Go On?* by Carl L. Williams, directed by Deb Guston; Cast: Paul Adams, Tracee Chimo, Wayne Henry, Lee Kaplan; *Neverland* by Kim Kelly, directed by Rebecca Nyahay; Cast: Michael Batelli, Helen Green, Shannon Marie Kerr; *Our Lady of the Sea* by Aoise Stratford, directed by Troy Miller; Cast: Scott Klavan, Tim Seib, Matt Stapleton; *Recoil* by Karen Schiff, directed by Jonathan Warman; Cast: Ron Bopst, Blanche Cholet; *Room at the Inn* by Barbara Lindsay, directed by Roberto Cambeiro; Cast: Damon Boggess, Daniel Carlton, Karen Stanion; *Sick* by Bekah Brunstetter, directed by Tzipora Kaplan; Cast: Enid Cortes,

Matthew A.J. Gregory, William Jackson Harper, Stacy Mayer, Jeffrey Parrillo, Jess Phillips; *Triple Play* by Marc Castle, directed by Carter Inskeep; Cast: Erik Baker, Jeannie Dalton, Erin Hadley

**EATfest Spring 2007** nine short plays; Theatre 5; March 13–April 1; included: *Postcards from a Dead Dog* by F.J. Hartland, directed by Troy Miller; Cast: Jason Hare, Jacqueline Sydney; *The Questioning* by Frank Higgins, directed by Lorrel Manning; Cast: Alexandra Devin, Suzan Mikiel-Kennedy, Danielle Quisenberry; *ClapTrapp* by Joseph Godfrey, directed by Melissa Attebery; Cast: Amy Bizjak, Laura Dillman, Steve Hauck, Hershey Miller, Courter Simmons, Christopher Voeller; *Vamp* by Ry Herman, directed by Kel Haney; Cast: Tracee Chimo, Blanche Cholet, Philip Guerette, Stacy Mayer; *Tell* by Rodney Lee Rogers, directed by Ian Streicher; Cast: Laura Fois, Ryan Hilliard; *Third Wheel* by Monica Flory, directed by Ned Thorne; Cast: Erik Baker, Aimee Howard, Claire Tyers; *My Name is Art* by Peter Snoad, directed by Kelly Haydon; Cast: Andrea Alton, Tim Intravia, Scott Klavan; *Some are People* by Kathleen Warnock, directed by Mark Finley; Cast: Janice Mann, Karen Stanion; *One of the Great Ones* by Chris Widney, directed by Jonathan Warman; Cast: Jane Altman, Marc Castle

# Ensemble Studio Theatre

Artistic Director, Curt Demptser/William Carden; Executive Director, Paul Alexander Slee; Youngblood Artistic Directors, Graeme Gillis and R.J. Tolan

**Going to the River 2006** A gala festival of staged readings by African-American women playwrights; Elizabeth van Dyke, Producing Artistic Director; included: A Tribute to Kia Corthron; *Walking Women* by Cassandra Medley; *Mail* by Bridgette A. Wimberly, directed by Talvin Wilks; *Raising the Bar: The Sadie Alexander Story* by Jo Tanner; *Formerly Known as Sarah* by Joyce Griffen; *On the Way to Timbucktoo* by Petronia Paley; *Wild Black-Eyed Susans* by Melissa Maxwell; *Salt in a Wound* by Melissa Maxwell; Staged Readings: *The M Odeyssey* by P.J. Gibson, choreography by Dyane Harvey; Workshop Reading: *My Secret Language of Wishes* by Cori Thomas; Special Tribute: *Celebrating Marti,* works by Marti Evans Charles; June 27–July 9

**Octoberfest 2006** included: *David's Play* written & directed by Tom Rowan; Cast: Cory Grant, Josh Heine, Ericka Kreutz, David Lavine, Jake Myers, Brian N. Taylor, Elizabeth Van Meter; October 6–7

**Project 35** Thirty-five evenings of art readings to celebrate EST's 35th anniversary; included: *All Through the Night* by Shirley Lauro; *Bicoastal* by Adam Forgash; *The Big Girls* by Ann Marie Healy; *Bob* by Anton Dudley; *Cat.her.in.e* by Amy Staats; *The Coffee Trees* by Arthur Giron; *Creative Writing* by J. Holtham; *Dying in Boulder* by Linda Faigo-Hall; *Escape Velocity* by James Ryan; *Existing Privilige* by James DeMarse; *Fanny* by Julie Leedes; *Fast Blood* by Judy Tate; *Flora Gardner* by Graeme Gillis; *Footprints in the Snow* by Jeanne Dorsey; *Free Gift Inside* by Edward Allan Baker; *The Garden Variety* by Lloyd Suh; *Hemingway* by Lawrence Luckinbill; *The Lake* by Frank Gilroy; *Massacre (sing to your children)* by Jose Rivera; *May Day* by Conrad Bromberg; *My Before and After* by Michael Louis Wells; *Natural Selection* by Leslie Lyles; *Owners* by Edith Freni; *One Thing I Like to Say Is* by Amy Fox; *Pa's Hat (Liberian Legacy)* by Cori Thomas; *Predators* by Romulus Linney; *Progress in Flying* by Lynn Rosen; *The Sequence* by Paul Mullin; *The Tilted House* by Susan Haar; *Yumee & Jack* by Bill Bozzone; November 10–December 18

**Serendib** by David Zellnik; Director, Carlos Armesto; Set, Ryan Elliot Kravetz; Costumes, Jennifer Caprio; Lighting, Evan Purcell; Sound, Graham Johnson; Music, Katie Down; PSM, Wendy Ouellette; Associate Producer, Robert Askins; Producer, Renee Blinkwolt; Casting, Shane Goldstein; Cast: Joseph Adams, Geeta Citygirl, John Gabriel, Linda Powell, James Rana, P.J. Sosko, Nitya Vidyasager, Richard B. Watson; Main Production of the First Light Festival; March 28–April 22

**First Light Festival 2007** presented by EST/Alfred P. Sloan Foundation Science & Technology Project; 9th annual; March 28–April 27; Program Directors, Carlos Armesto and Graeme Gillis; Workshops: *The Tallest Building in the World* by Matt Schatz; *By Proxy* by Amy Fox; *Galois* by Sung Rno; *Me and Marie Curie* by Alec Duffy; Readings: *Ever More Intelligent* by Alex Timbers; *The Great Dismal* by Gweydian Suilebhan; *Leave a Light On* by Ann Marie Healy; *Chance & Necessity* by Jon Klein; *Doctors Jane and Alexander* by Edward Einhorn; *Perfect and Constant* by Rob Askins

**Shatter** Four world premiere short plays; included: *The Last Day* Adapted by Justin Quinn Pelegano from the novel by Richard Matheson; *Antigone Noir* adapted by Destiny Lilly from Sophocles; *Eyez Watchin'* by André Ford; *Mali and the Arc of the Covenant* written & directed by Andrew Bergh; May 16–22

**EST Marathon 2007** 29th annual festival of new one-act plays; Series A (May 31–June 20): *The News* by Billy Aronson; Director, Jamie Richards; Cast: Diana Ruppe, Geneva Carr, Thomas Lyons, Grant Shaud; *My Dog Heart* by Edith Freni; Director, John Gould Rubin; Cast: Brian Avers, Pepper Binkley, Brian Fenkart; *First Tree in Anarctica* by Julia Cho; Director, Kate Whoriskey; Cast: Michi Barall, Jon Norman Schneider; *The Probabilities* by Wendy MacLeod; Director, Karen Kohlhaas; Cast: Bruce MacVittie; *Things We Said Today* by Neil LaBute; Director, Andrew McCarthy; Cast: Dana Delaney, Victor Slezak; Series B (June 15–30): *Priceless* by Elizabeth Diggs; Director, Mary Robinson; Cast: Morgan Hallett, Michael Izquierdo, Craig Anthony Grant; *Self-Portrait in a Blue Room* by Daniel Reitz; Director, Pamela Berlin; Cast: Larry Pine, Chris Stack; *Casting* by Amy Fox; Director, Nela Wagman; Cast: Sutton Crawford, Polly Adams, Noah Fleiss, Alfredo Narciso; *Milton Bradley* by Peter Sagal; Director, Susan Einhorn; Cast: Jason Schuchman, Stephen Singer; *Beirut Rocks* by Israel Horovitz; Director, Jo Bonney; Cast: Enver Gjokaj, Stephanie Janssen, Marin Ireland, Frank Solorzano

### Youngblood Company

**The True Life Story of [Your Name Here]** by Qui Nguyen, Michael Lew, Courtney Brooke Lauria, Daria Polatin, Emily Conbere, Edith L. Freni, Sharyn Rothstein and Annie Baker; Director, R.J. Tolan; True Life Story eBay bidder: Tom Ritchford; Cast: Lucia Brizzi, Helen Coxe, David Gelles-Hurwitz, Debbie Jaffe, Moira Lael MacDonald, Gregg Mozgala, Steven Sanpietro; The Brick Theater's \$ellout Festival; June 2–July 1

**Thicker Than Water** seven new plays and musicals by EST emerging playwrights; included: *Bike Wreck* by Qui Nguyen, directed by John Gould Rubin; *Group* by Annie Baker, directed by Alex Timbers; *And The Baby Makes Three* by Courtney Brooke Lauria, directed by Melissa Kievman; *Rob* by Sam Forman, directed by Marlo Hunter; *Triage* by Sharyn Rothstein, directed by R.J. Tolan; *The Roosevelt Cousins* by Michael Lew, directed by Moritz von Steulpnagel; *Songs: The Jamal Lullabies* by Emily Conbere, directed by R.J. Tolan; Cast: Catherine Curtin, Jeffrey Nauman, Paco Tolson, Julie Leedes, Pepper Binkley, Lance Rubin, Justin Reinsilber, William Jackson Harper, Arthur Acuna, Gregg Mozgala, Ted Schneider, Bekah Coulter, Allison Jill Posner, Stacey Cervellino, Nicole Stefonek; February 17–March 10

**Neglect** by Sharyn Rothstein; Director, Catherine Ward; Cast: William Jackson Harper, Geany Masai; February 11–March 10

**Bloodworks 2007** readings of new full length plays by Justin Deabler, Emily Conbere, Sharyn Rothstein, Qui Nguyen, Michael Sendrow, Emily Chadick Weiss, Delaney Britt Brewer, Courtney Brooke Lauria, Matt Schatz, Jihan Crowther; Landmark Tavern; May 9–June 20

### Non-resident Productions

**Absence of Magic** created and starring Eric Davis; Director, Sue Morrison; July 5–11

**Boy's Life** by Howard Korder; presented by Panicked Productions, Dan Weisberg & Jessica Delbridge; Director, Glenn De Kler; Stage Manager, Treasa O'Neill; Cast: Andy Hartsman, Rob Egginton, Joe Tomasini, Lindsay Smith, Maura Hannigan, Ross Erin Martineau, Kathryn Lower, Jessica Delbridge; August 4–11

## The Flea Theater

Jim Simpson, Artistic Director; Todd Rosen, Managing Director; Carol Ostrow, Producing Director

**I.E., In Other Words** by Mark Greenfield; Director, Kip Fagan; Set, Michael Casselli; Lighting, Ben Kato; Costumes, Normandy Sherwood; Cast: Josh Adler, Teddy Bergman, Kina Bermudez, Havilah Brewster, Jaime Robert Carrillo, Garrett Hendricks, Bobby Hodgson, Beth Hoyt, Richard Kass, Malcolm Madera, Kelly Miller, Bobby Moreno, Mary Jane Schwartz, Rob Yang; Downstairs @ The Flea; June 1–16

**The Guys** by Anne Nelson; Director, Thomas Kail; Cast: Tom Wopat & Grace Gonglewski or Tim Cummings & Irene Walsh; September 11–23

**'Twas the Night Before** ten-minute works: *Not a Creature Was Stirring* by Christopher Durang, directed by Kip Fagan; *Away in the Manger* by Roger Rosenblatt, directed by Jason Podplesky; *Before the Before and Before That* by Mac Wellman, directed by Amanda Wright; *Christmas Song* written & directed by Len Jenkin; *Holiday Moves* written & directed by Elizabeth Swados; Choreography, Mimi Quillin; Sets, Kyle Chepulis; Costumes, Erin Elizabeth Murphy & Sarah Beers; Sound, Jill B.C. DuBoff; Stage Manager, Lauren Levitt; Cast: Ben Beckely, Elizabeth Hoyt, Leslie Meisel, John Fico, David Skeist, Tanya Fischer, Evan Enderle, Pernell Walker, Katherine Creel, Jonathan Ledoux, Barnett Cohen, Bobby Hodgson, Emily Hyberger, Joseph McLaughlin, Liz Wisan, Ben Horner, Jocelyn Kuritsky, Wil Petre, Mary Schwartz, James Stover, Maiken Wiese, Rob Yang, Cooper Daniels, Brian Morvant, Kendall Rileigh, Julie Ferrell, Megan Raye Manzi, Vadim Newquist, Theresa Ngo, Alexis Macnab, Donal Brophy, Catherine Gowl, David Marcus, James Blanshard, J. Julian Christopher, Dan Cozzens, Emily Firth, Cara Francis, Carson Hinners, Max Jenkins, Rachel Rusch; also performed at The Chelsea Art Museum; December 4–30

**The Director** by Barbara Cassidy; Director, Jessica Davis-Irons; Choreography, Mimi Quillin; Set, Neal Wilkinson; Costumes, Chloe Chapin; Lighting, Peter Ksander; Sound, Jill B.C. DuBoff; Video, Dustin O'Neill; Stage Manager, Lauren Levitt; Cast: Lauren Shannon, Catherine Gowl, Donal Brophy, Barnett Cohen, Jackie Chung, Pernell Walker, Havilah Brewster, Leslie Meisel, Gamze Ceylan, Kristen Ryan, Alexis Macnab, Liz Wisan, Drew Hildebrand, Dalton Wiles; Downstairs @ The Flea; February 21–March 31

**Los Angeles** by Julian Sheppard; Director, Adam Rapp; Set, David Korins; Costumes, Erika Munro; Lighting, Miranda Hardy; Sound/Music, Eric Shim; Co-composers, Ray Rizzo & Amelia Zirin-Brown; Stage Manager, Jess Johnston; Cast: Ben Beckley, Dan Cozzens, Cooper Daniels, Roy Edroso, Evan Enderle, Tanya Fischer, Meredith Holzman, Emily Hyberger, David Skeist, Katherine Waterston, Rob Yang; Downstairs @ The Flea; February 14–April 14

**Smoke and Mirrors** by Jacob Goodrich; Director, Nick Faust; Costumes, Elizabeth R. Payne; Set, Neal Wilinson; Lighting, Joshua Higgason; Sound, Brandon Wolcott; Cast: Ben Horner, Susan Hyon, Jason Dirden, Aurelia Lavizzo, Parrish Hurley, Stas May, Tina Alexis Allen; Downstairs @ The Flea; April 18–June 2

**Non-resident Productions**

**Atta Boy Zimmy** written & performed by Brad Zimmerman; presented by Brockton Productions; July 6–8

**Two September** by Mac Wellman; Director/Set, Loy Arcenas; Costumes, Claudia Brown; Lighting, Brian Aldous; Sound, Jill B.C. DuBoff; Stage Manager, Jennifer Noterman; Cast: Tina Benko, Shannon Burkett, Christopher Kromer; November 29–December 16

# Galapagos Arts Space

**Cruel and Unusual** festival of plays presented by Brooklyn Playwrights Collective; included: *Gertrude Stein's Penis* by Jeffrey Skinner, directed by Jennie Pu; with Diana K. Lee, Brett Vanderbrook, Natalie Neckyfarow; *Sum* by Al Lefcowitz, directed by Joya Scott; with Albert Sanchez Jr., Cody Lindquist, Matt B. Wells; *The Audience/Theatricks* by Maria Micheles, directed by Andy Millon; with Albert Sanchez Jr., Cody Lindquist, Matt B. Wells; *A Dream Play* by Les Hunter, directed by Andy Millon; with Brett Vanderbrook, Stephanie Shaw, Sunrise Marks; *A Long and Happy Marriage* by Will Cordeiro, directed by Kristina Candelarie; with Michael C. Freeland, Alex Crowley, Alisa Frazinni, Liz White, Kristin Hoffmann. *Community Theater Interview with Pere Ubu* by Cornelius Chapman; *STRAY* by Elizabeth Stapp; *The Letters* adapted by Maria Micheles, directed by Joya Scott; with Sunrise Marks, Brett Vanderbrook, Julia Goldstein; May 26–June 23

**Teatro Slovak** by Richard Caliban; June 2–3

**Love Ahoy** monthly dating game; opened June 21, still running

**Zenith 5** by John Moran; Cast: Katherine Brook, Joseph Keckler, Erin Markey, Mina Nishimura, Popo Tso; July 7–28;

**Are You There, Galapagos? It's Me, Carmine** written & performed by Carmine Covelli; August 4–25

**4F** written & performed by The Gossip Factory: Keith Foster, Leigh Diveris, Ryan McWilliams, Ariella Beth Bowden, Andrew Ballard, Mark Johanson, Natasha Gavin, Sarah Elliott, Katie Lawson, Brian McCarthy; September 1–29

**Einstein's Dead and So Are You, A Love Letter to Betsy Ross** created by Red Metal Mailbox; October 6–27

**Little Building** book, lyrics and direction by Nick Jones, music by Benjamin Ickies; Cast: Corey Sullivan, Tamar Schoenberg, Jessica Delfino, Katie McClenahan, Mark Sam Rosenthal, Peter J. Cook, Jarret Berenstein, Jason Quarles; February 9–18

**fuckplays** presented by Working Man's Clothes and The Thursday Problem; included: *The Impotence of Being Ernest* by Joshua Hill, directed by Julie Rossman; *Marriage Play* by Bekah Brunstetter, directed by Diana Basmajian; *Arms and the Octopus* by Casey Wimpee, directed by Isaac Byrne; *Wood* by Justin Cooper, directed by Steven Gillenwater; *Sharpen My Dick* by Greg Romero, directed by Cole Wimpee; *Candy Room* by William Charles Meny; directed by Thomas Caruso; *The Saddest Thing in the History of the World* by Kyle Jarrow, directed by Matthew Hancock; *1.1-1.7* by Eric Sanders, directed by Stephen Brackett; Cast: Adam Belvo, Mick Bleyer, Elliotte Crowell, Jared Culverhouse, John Flynn, Robert Funaro, Kaci Gober, Ebony Hogan, Julian James, Elizabeth Kensek, Michael Mason, Erin McCarson, Nell Mooney, David Mitsch, Will Neuman, Amy Lynn Stewart, Steven Strobel, Mark Thornton, Lucy Walters, Molly Ward, Charlie Wilson, Cole Wimpee, Alessandra Ziviani; April 6–27

# Gallery Players

Heather Siobhan Curran, Board President; Matt Schicker, Board Vice-President;

**The Actor's Nightmare** and **Sister Mary Ignatius Explains It All for You** by Christopher Durang; Director, Doug Howe; Producer, Cathy Bencivenga; Set, Joseph Trainor; Costumes, Jessa-Raye Court; Lighting, Travis I. Walker; Sound, Steve Sabaugh; PSM, Erika Omundson; Cast: B. Brian Argotsinger, Nat Cassidy, Whitney Kirk, Gael Schaefer, Sarah Beth-Lee Williams, Austin Zabito-Valente; September 9–24

**Urinetown, the Musical** book and lyrics by Greg Kotis, music and lyrics by Mark Hollmann; Producer, Katie Adams; Director, Tom Wojtunik; Choreography, Ryan Kasprzak; Music Director, Brenna Sage; Sets, Joseph Trainor; Costumes, David Withrow; Lighting, Travis I. Walker; Sound, Sara Bader; PSM, C.J. LaRoche; Cast: Jon Frazier, Kat Aberle, Joshua James Campbell, Tom Cleary, De'Lon Grant, Allison Guinn, Tauren Hagans, Daniel Haggard, Jean Liuzzi, Jared R. Lopatin, Jennifer McCabe, Catia Ojeda, Jan-Peter Pedross, Adam Riccio, Mitchell Scott Shapiro, Kim Shipley; October 14–November 5

**Torch Song Trilogy** by Harvey Fierstein; Director, Stephen Nachamie; Producer, M.R. Goodley; Composer/Sound, Brenna Sage; Set, Craig M. Napoliello; Costumes, Kathleen Leary; Lighting, Dan Gallagher; PSM, Jodi M. Witherell; Cast: Yolanda Batts, Seth Rudetsky, Brad Thomason, Andrea Wollenberg, Andy Phelan, Marc Tumminelli, Laura Sommer Raines; November 25–December 10

**Dedication or The Stuff of Dreams** by Terrence McNally; Producer, Matt Schicker; Director, Heather Siobhan Curran; Set, David Ogle; Lighting, G. Benjamin Swope; Costumes, Amy Elizabeth Bravo; Sound, Megan Henninger; PSM, Angela Allen; Cast: Burke Adams, John Blaylock, Brian Michael Flanagan, Hanna Hayes, Dennis Keefe, Jessica Krueger, Beth E. Smith; January 13–28

**Violet** book and lyrics by Brian Crawley, music by Jeanine Tesori, based on *The Ugliest Pilgrim* by Doris Betts; Producer, Rene M. Becker; Director, M.R. Goodley; Music Director, Jeffrey Campos; Choreography, Vibecke Dahle; Set, Charlie Corcoran; Lighting, Todd Reemtsma; Costumes, Lillian Rhiger; Fights, Ian Marshall; PSM, Autumn Tilson; Cast: Anne Berkowitz, Brad Thomason, Rhyn McLemore, Collin Howard, Shad Olsen, Jan-Peter Pedross, Sarah Orr, Marcie Henderson, Brian Michael Flanagan, Jeremy Ritz, Yolanda Batts, Julie Galorenzo, Tyler Marcum, Julie Rees; February 17–March 11

**The Learned Ladies** by Molière, translated by Richard Wilbur; Producer, Angela Delaney; Director, Neal Freeman, Set, Hannah Shafran; Lighting, Nik Anderson; Costumes, Andrea Lenci-Cerchiara; PSM, Elena Kopaleichvilli; Cast: Patrick Toon, Heather Curran, Alisha Spielmann, Anna Moore, Fred Heringes, Laura Heidinger, Marc Halsey, Nat Cassidy, Stephen McFarland, Candice Goodman, Joshua Key-Maginnis; March 31–April 15

**Victor/Victoria** book by Blake Edwards, lyrics by Leslie Bricusse, music by Henry Mancini, additional music by Frank Wildhorn; Producers, Robin Mishik-Jett, Heather Siobhan Curran; Director, Matt Schicker; Music Director, Justin Hatchimonji; Choreography, Stacy Mosscotti-Smith; Fight Director, Nickalaus Locke Koziura; Dramaturg, Kate Stopa; Set, Michael M. Kerns; Lighting, David Roy; Costumes, Samantha L. Fromm; PSM, Amanda Jean Nowack; Cast: Meg Benfield, Jamie Birkett, John Blaylock, Melissa D'Amico, Andrea Davey, Chip DuFord, Patrick Field, Tripp Fountain, Andy Frye, David Michael Green, Allison Guinn, Tauren Hagans, D.H. Johnson, Craig Joseph, Dennis Keefe, E.C. Kelly, Lorinne Lampert, Christine Paterson, Thomas Poarch, Michael Reyna, Tom Schubert, Rieko Yamanaka; May 5–27

**10th Annual Black Box New Play Festival** included: *Bury Him* by Joe Lauinger, directed by Alexa Polmer; *A Temporary Lapse* by Judd Lear Silverman, directed by Rich Ferraioli; *Attention Def…Hey Look a Dog!* by Daniel Damiano, directed by Donald Butchko; *The Invited Guest* by Staci Sweden, directed by Marc Stuart Weitz; *Violating Uncle Piggy* by Judd Lear Silverman, directed by Amanda Friou; June 7–24

# Gene Frankel Theatre

**The Adventures of Nervous Boy (A Penny Dreadful)** by James Comtois; presented by Nosedive Productions; Director, Pete Boisvert; Set, Rose A.C. Howard; Lighting, Sarah Watson; Sound, Patrick Shearer; Stage Manager, Stephanie Williams; Cast: Mac Rogers, Rebecca Comtois, Anna Kull, Marc Landers, Patrick Shearer, Ben Trawick-Smith, Tai Verley, Scot Lee Williams; Underground Theatre; June 8–July 8

**Heart's Desire** by Caryl Churchill, directed by Max Seide, & **Jesus Hector Christ** written & directed by Ian Schoen; two one-acts presented by Legitimate Theater Company; Cast: *Heart's Desire:* Allison Abrams, Janice Bishop, Jay Horton, Mimi Jefferson, Cash Tilton; *Jesus Hector Christ:* Eric Brown, Brenda Cooney, Chris Norwood; June 21–July 8

**Dead Certain** by Marcus Lloyd; presented by Expression Theatre of San Francisco; Producer/Director, Andrey Esterlis; Design, Stacy Marshall; Lighting, Chris Paulina; Cast: Diana Brown, Andrey Esterlis; July 12–July 23

**Zastrozzi: The Master of Discipline** by George F. Walker; Director, Felixz Ivanov; September 14–16

**Fallen** by Laura Gale and Joseph Schultz; presented by New York Theatre Experiment; Producer, Rori Bergman; Director, Joseph Schultz; Stage Manager, Emily Ballou; Cast: Dana Berger, Emberli Edwards, Laura Gale, Christel Halliburton, Meghan Love, Leah Reddy, Jaclyn Sokol, Shelly Stover, Nina Wheeler-Cahlfin; September 22–October 1

**Two Hookers & A Dead Pony** by Shel Silverstein; presented by A Chick & Wing Production; Director, Bruce Ornstein; Cast: Kyle Baxter, Julee Cerda, Amy Wendling; October 5–8

**Fiction** by Steven Dietz; October 19–28

**The Libation Bearers** by Aeschylus; presented by The Hammer Theater Collective; Directors, Lauren Benson & Lorelei Ignas; Producer, Megan Zimmer; Cast: Todd Briscoe, Elsa Carette, Katie Quarrier, Liz Alderfer, Julie Mozdy, Jacqui Sherwood, Yael Silverman, Drew Van Der Burg, Paige Howard; November 16–18

**Been So Long** by Che Walker; presented by Break Through Theatre; Director, Rob Barron; October 19–November 4

**Fuddy Meers** by David Lindsay-Abaire; presented by Thirsty Turtle Productions; Director, Beth Lopes; Set/Lighting, Ian Crawford; Costumes, Katja Andreiev; Sound, Fred Nicolaus; Cast: Ali Baynes, Greg Kostal, Mary Quick, Steve Stout, Jake Thomas, Paula Vingelen, Gillian Wiggin; Underground Theatre, November 2–12

**Wonder Woman Week Festival** presented by Groove MaMa Ink and Bricken Sparacino; included performances by Michelle Samuels, Leigh Evans, Victoria McNichol, Samantha Lally, Alisha Martin, Heather Harpham, Gab Cody, Meghan O'Neill, Jessica Hester, Jessica Delfino, Ophira Eisenberg, Jenn Hyjack, Sandria Choi, Kelly Nichols, Guerrilla Girls on Tour, Cassie Terman, Meg Renton, Giulia Rozzi, Tulis McCall, Jennifer Cooke, Lea Bender, Kelly Kinsella, and others; November 27–December 3

**Cornered** four plays presented by EMEE Theater Group; included: *Sure Thing* by David Ives, directed by Marissa Wolf; Cast: Eric Michaels, Meghan Marx; *Jiley Nance and Lednerg – A Dark Humor* by Jacquelyn Reingod, directed by Rod Cassavale; Cast: Elizabeth Allerton, Meghan Mark; *The Wall* by Richard Luachman, directed by Bruce Ornstein; Cast: Ethan Frank, Eric Michaels; *Tickets, Please!* by Anthony Sportiello, directed by Bruce Ornstein; Cast: Elizabeth Allerton, Ethan Frank; December 7–10

**Rebel Without a Niche** written & performed by Kurt Fitzpatrick; January 6

**Soft Click of a Switch** by Carter W. Lewis; Director, Kip Rosser; Cast: Robert Baumgardner, James Leach; January 10–21

**Pvt. Wars** by James McLure; presented by Incumbo Theater Company; Director, Max Montel; Producers, Megan Larche, Mark Montgomery, Ethan Baum; Set, Jane Parrott; Costumes, Meredith Neal; Lighting, Pamela Kupper; Stage Manager/Sound, Melissa Jernigan; Cast: Ethan Baum, Jeffry Denman, Chapin Springer; Underground Theatre; January 25–February 18

**Birdy and the Golden Putter** written & performed by Nick Colt and Jed Zion; Director, Daniel G. O'Brien; March 1–10

**Porn and Happiness (You Can't Have Both)** by David Holstein; Director, Ben Arredondo; March 15–25

**52 Pick-Up** by T.J. Dawe & Rita Bozi; presented by Too Much Free Time Productions; Director, Heather Arnson; Cast: Kurt Fitzpatrick, Natalie Thomas; April 12–21

**Cary from the Cock** created, written & performed by Cary Curran; May 10–26

**Autophobia** plays by Kate Hoffower, Jon Jory, John Stinson, Charles Forbes and Jane Anderson; presented by Lay It Down Productions; Director, Holly-Anne Ruggiero; Cast: Theodora Dunlap, Erin Levendorf, Melaena Cadiz, Rafi Silver, Tim Mele, Mike Duff; May 20–21

# Gingold Theatrical Group: Project Shaw

David Staller, Founder and Artistic Director; The Players Club, Grammercy Park South; monthly public readings of the complete works of George Bernard Shaw; produced and directed by David Staller; Associate Producers, Jerry Wade, Theresa Diamond, Anita Jaffe, Kate Ross; Bill Barbanes

**Getting Married** Host: Michael Riedel; Cast: Penny Fuller, George S. Irving, Simon Jones, Alison Fraser, Paxton Whitehead, Liz Morton, Paul Hecht, Daniel Reichard, Peter Yonka, Laura Odeh, Howard Kissel, Charlotte Rae; June 19; **John Bull's Other Island** Host: Howard Kissel; Cast: Marc Kudisch, Victor Slezak, Adam Feldman, Simon Kendall, Brian Murray, Barrett Foa, John Keating, Merwin Goldsmith, John Martello, Malachy Court, Mary Carver, Kate Baldwin, Charlotte Moore; July 17; **The Apple Cart** Host: Robert Simonson; Cast: Brian Murray, Marian Seldes, Barrett Foa, Donald Corren, George S. Irving, Liz Morton, Peter Bartlett, Lenny Wolpe, Simon Jones, Howard Kissel, David Garrison, Charlotte Moore, Becky Ann Baker, Charlotte Rae, James Murtaugh, David Cote; September 18; **Misalliance** Host: Howard Kissel; Cast: Jeremy McCarter, Ian Kahn, Martin Moran, Sarah Uriarte Berry, Sally Ann Howes, Paxton Whitehead, Brian Murray, Gareth Saxe, Andrea Marcovicci, Christian Borle; October 23; **Captain Brassbound's Conversion** Host: Michael Riedel; Cast: Lenny Wolpe, Tyler Maynard, George S. Irving, Veanne Cox, David Lansbury, Terry Wynne, Anthony Holds, John Keating, Howard Kissel, Tim Artz, Merwin Goldsmith, Adam Feldman, Allen McCullough, Patricia O'Connell; November 20; **The Philanderer** Host: Howard Kissel; Cast: Michael Cerveris, Karen Ziemba, Nancy Anderson, David Garrrison, Timothy Jerome, Peter Bartlett, Liz Morton, Patricia O'Connell; December 18; **Candida** Cast: Blair Brown, Daniel Jenkins, Annie Golden, Mark Saturno, Ed Dixon, Matt Cavenaugh, Charlotte Moore; January 22; **Three One-Acts: The Music Cure/Interlude at the Playhouse/The King, The Constitution and the Lady** Host: Howard Kissel; Cast: Marian Seldes, Paxton Whitehead, Barrett Foa, George S. Irving; February 19; **The Doctor's Dilema** Host: Jeremy McCarter; Cast: Michael Tisdale, Patricia Conolly, Brian Murray, Howard Kissel, Malachy McCourt, Timothy Jerome, Simon Jones, Lenny Wolpe, Kate Baldwin, Mark Saturno, Sarah Moon, Michael Schulman, Brent Harris; March 19; **Androcles and the Lion** Host: Brendan Lemon; Cast: Roma Torre, Bruce Vilanch, Raven Snook, Seth Rudetsky, Jeremy McCarter, Alexis Soloski, Charles Isherwood, Michael Musto, Adam Feldman, Michael Riedel; Howard Kissel, David Finkle, Eric Grode, Frank Scheck, Patrick Pacheco, Michael Schulman, Rex Reed; April 23; **Admirable Bashville** Host: Michael Riedel; Cast: Lacey Kohl, Marc Kudisch, Louis Zorich, James Ludwig, Daniel Jenkins, Kevin Joseph, Graham Rowat, Robert Ian Mackenzie, George S. Irving, Charlotte Moore, Patricia Conolly; May 21

# Harlem Repertory Theater

Keith Lee Grant, Artistic Director

**Dreamgirls** music by Henry Krieger, lyrics and book by Tom Even; Director/Choreographer, Keith Lee Grant; Cast: Alexandra Bernard, Christina Burnette, Natalia Peguero, Danhy Clermont, Isis Kenney, Danyel Fulton, Mabel Gomez, Jean-Pierre Barthelemy, Donovan Thompson, Jose Altidor, Nabil Vinas, Greer Samuels, Monica Delgado, Marcus Dargan, Alex Boucher, Dimitry, Nicholas Betito, Alfredo Millan, Yaritza Pizarro, Edward Corcino, Roderick Warner, Marcel Torres, Lynette Braxton; Aaron Davis Hall at City College; June 23–August 13

**Bye Bye Birdie** music by Charles Strouse, lyrics by Lee Adams, book by Michael Stewart; Director/Choreographer, Keith Lee Grant; Cast: Jose Altidor, Alexandra Bernard, Nicholas Betito, Barbara Blair, Alex Boucher, Lynette Braxton, Krissi Burnette, Danhy Clermont, Marcus Degan, Monica Delgado, Dimitry, Danyel Fulton, Mabel Gomez, Ashley Hatcher, Isis Kenney, Alfredo Millan, Heriberto Oquendo, Yaritza Pizarro, Greer Samuels, Pamela Tabb, Donovan Thompson, Marcel Torres, Nabil Vinas, Roderick Warner; Aaron Davis Hall at City College; August 4–12

**Dutchman** by LeRoi Jones aka Amiri Baraka; Aaron Davis Hall at City College; July 28–August 12

# HERE Arts Center

**How to Stay Bitter Through the Happiest Times of Your Life** written & performed by Anita Liberty; June 7–25

**Her Majesty the King** by Sarah Overman; presented by Dramahaus; Director, Patrick McNulty; Set, Luke Cantarella; Costumes, Katherine Hampton Noland; Music, Josh Farrar; Lighting, Thomas Dunn; Sound, Jason Atkinson; Video, Jeremy Robbins; Press, Ron Lasko; Cast: Justin Adams, Mimi Cozzens, Antonia Fairchild, Michael Keyloun, Jason Kolotouros, Baylen Thomas; June 10–July 1

**Youth Against Violence** presented by vibe Theater Experience and HERE; June 18

**The American Living Room Festival 2006** July 28–August 30; included: *Shadow Play* directed & choreographed by Ariane Anthony; *Cause for Alarm* created & directed by Tina Goldstein; *29 Friends* conceived & choreographed by Megan Metcalf; *Pessimist, Moi?* conceived by & featuring Sophie Amieva; directed by Sarah Sanford; *Looking for Limbo* by Meleana Cadiz, Joseph Keckler & Erin Markey; *Hot Flash* created & performed by Laryssa Husiak; *Removed Exposure* created & performed by Karen Bernard, directed by Maureen Brennan; *Mort* co-created & directed by Kip Fagan, co-created & performed by Nico Vassilakis; *Learning to Listen* written & choreographed by Robin Prichard, performed by Robin Prichard & Alison Malloy; *Your Negro Tour Guide* directed by Jeff Griffin, performed by Torie Wiggins; *Fox(y) Friends* written & directed by Kevin Doyle; *The Dorothy Building* directed & designed by Michael Scott-Price, written by Trav S.D.; *I-95 South* written & directed by Kate Marks; *With Claws and Beak* created by Workhorse, directed by Stephen Buescher; *Thirst* designed & performed by Jil Guyon; *Lee/Gendary* written by Soomi Kim & Derek Nguyen; *WTC* directed by Jonathan Zalben; *The Joy of Lex* created by Alexia Vernon, directed by Jon Stancato; *Tender Trap* created by Catherine Hournihan, performed by Tilt Performance Company; *Belly Dream Real* written & directed by Kate Brehm; *I'm Sorry & I'm Sorry* written, directed & performed by The Candidatos (Kevin Wall & Justin Rose); *The Anguish of Compusure* created by the Unruly Julies, featuring Julie A. O'Baoighill; *Feminists are Funny* written & directed by Aphra Behn; *Remote* directed & performed by Sara Kraft & Ed Purver; *Beautiful Radiant Things* co-created & performed by Jane Ray, co-created & directed by Glynis

Rigsby; *Insomnia/Insexton* adapted & performed by Laila Maria Salins, directed & performed by Leyla Ebtehadj, with Emily Tremaine; *Mrs. Hodges Was Struck By a Train* created & choreographed by Michael Bodel; *Death in Vacant Lot* written by Shuji Terayama, directed by Kameron Steele, featuring The South Wing; *Sketch* choreographed & performed by Amy Larimer; *Vamp* created & performed by Kali Quinn; *3 AM, 89°, No Wind* choreographed & directed by Noel MacDuffie, music by John LaSala; *Woven Room* created & performed by Anya Liftig; *viBe!* written by viBe's ensemble of teenage girls, directed by Dana Edell & chandra thomas; *Between the Shadows* written & directed by Rania Khalil; *Unfamilar Comfort(s)* written by Amanda Weir, directed by Wes Hopper

**Songs of Dragons Flying to Heaven** written & directed Young Jean Lee; Cast: Brian Bickerstaff, Juliana Francis, Haerry Kim, Jun Sky Kim, Jennifer Lim, Becky Yamamoto, Young Jean Lee; September 21–October 20

**The Fortune Teller** created & directed by Erik Sanko, music by Danny Elfman; Cast: Matthew Acheson, Liam Hurley, Erik Sanko, Randall Whittinghill; October 19–31

**Stanley (2006)** created & directed by Lisa D'Amour, co-created and performed by Todd D'Amour; October 26–November 18

**A Love Like Damien's** by Andrea Davis; Director, Andre Lancaster; November 9–December 3

**The Rapture Project** created & performed by Great Small Works (John Bell, Trudi Cohen, Stephen Kaplin, Jenny Romaine); Additional Cast: Shane Baker, Andrea Lomanto, Jessica Lorence, Jessica Lurie; January 4–21

**As You Like It** by William Shakespeare; presented by poortom productions & Joe Plummer; Director, Moritz von Stuelpnagel; Composer, Malcolm Gets; Design, Wilson Chin, Kanae Heike; Costumes, Amy C. Bradshaw; Lighting, Lauren Phillips; Sound, Brandon Lowry; Choreography, Susan Dibble; Fights, Mike Barth; Stage Manager, Jeff Myers; Cast: Joe Plummer, Greg Hildreth, David Foubert, Danny Deferrari, James Saba, Erik Gratton, Dan Amboyer, Matt Gould, Chris Thorn, Eric Michael Anderson; March 15–31

**Orestes 2.0** by Charles Mee; presented by The Immediate Theater Company; Director, Jose Zayas; Set, Ryan Elliot Kravetz; Costumes, Melissa Heley; Lighting, Mark O'Maley; Sound, Jeremy Wilson & Jose Zayas; Cast: Bobby Moreno, Barrett Doss, Peter Schuyler, Joseph Carusone, Hugh Sinclair, Daniel Manley, David Myers, Robert Fuller, Jessica Kaye, Neil Donahue, Julia Arazi, Carleigh Welsh, Paula Ehrenberg, Amanda Sisk, D.J. Thacker, Noah Diamond, Amanda Sisk; March 29–April 21

**Giants** by Laura von Holt; presented by Studio 42; Director, Jen Wineman; Producers, Demos Tsilikoudis, Yasmine Falk; Set, Ryan Elliot Kravetz; Costumes, Christy Rilling; Lighting, Shaun Fillion; Music & Sound, Jane Shaw; PSM, Molly Minor Eustis; Press, Judy Jacksina; Cast: Lisa Barnes, Autumn Hurlburt, Evan Lubeck, Michael Markham; April 9–28

**Food of Life** written & performed by Clea Rivera; Director, Kevin Lawler; May 23–24

**White Hot** by Tommy Smith; Director, May Adrales; Producer, Leigh Goldenberg; Set, Rumiko Ishii; Lighting, Cat Tate; Costumes, Kate Cusack; Sound, Greg Hennigan; Cast: Ben Beckley, Mary Jane Gibson, Joel Israel, Patricia Nelson; Dorothy B. Williams Theatre; June 20–July 2

**The Curse of the Smart Kid** written & directed by David Vining; presented by Cagey Productions; Cast: Ben Beckley, Howling Vic, Albert Cadabra, Nasty Canasta; June 23–25

**Imaginary Lines/Salad Days** written and choreographed by Jillian Sweeney; Director, Jeff Cranor; Cast: Jillian Sweeney, Tara O'Con; June 26–28

**Goodbye April, Hello May** by Ethan Lipton; Director, Patrick McNulty; Choreography, Gabriella Barnstone; Sound, Andy Leviss; Music, Eben Levy; Lighting, G. Benjamin Swope; Costumes, Candace Thompson; Set, Jo Winiarski; Cast: Gibson Frazier, Maria Striar, Kelly Mares, Bill Coelius, Albert Aeed; June 28–July 16

**The American Living Room Festival 2007** presented by HERE at 3LD Art & Technology Center; July 26–September 2, 2007; included: *In the Company of Trees* written & directed by Peter McCabe; *Absolute Brightness* created by Sharptooltheatre; *Sun Sheets and Small Shoes* choreographed by Michael Bodel; *Reading the Water* written by and featuring Monica Hunken, directed by Nadia Foskolou and Benjamin Cerf; *Free and Compulsory: My Year Ineducation* written & performed by Jamie Lyn Smith, directed by Mikki Baloy; *"65"* written & performed by Hal Fickett; *Trigger Happy Jack* by Timothy Braun, performed and directed by Alexis Macnab; *Popart* by Joanne Hudson, directed by Meghan Finn; *Bearshow* choreographed by Johanna S. Meyer and Jennifer Monson, featuring Alejandra Martorell; *Solo: A Two-Person Show* created by Under the Table, performed by Matt Chapman and Josh Matthews; *Steel Net and a High Wire Sing Along* presented by Doorknob Company, directed by Shannon Gillen and Elisabeth Motley; *Flying Brothel* featuring Megan Campisi, Loren Fenton, Kevin Lapin, Liz Vacco, Ben Vershbow; *Quirk* choreographed by Isabella Bruno, featuring Kate Johnson and Pamela James; *Voom* directed and choreographed by Vangeline for the Vangeline Theater; Cast: Pamela Herron, Yukari Coco Koyama, Alethea Vasilas, Vangeline Theater, Kat Mac Millan, Ayako Sana, Myndy K, Katherine Adamenko, Minako Nakashima, Cassandra Rosebeetle; *Medea* adapted and directed by Eddie Kim; *Schiele* developed and presented by Human Company, directed by Royd Climenhaga; *Poli Dégaine (Punchy Draw)* created and performed by La Pendue; *The Passion of Saint Thomas More* by Garrett Fisher, directed and choreographed by Ken Cerniglia and Christy Fisher; *We Declare You a Terrorist* by West Hyler and Tim Lord, directed by West Hyler; *The Angel of History* created by Matthew Torney and Ian Russel; *Strand of Anonymous Pearls* by viBe Theater Experience ensemble, directed by Dana Edell and chandra thomas; *Salt Lake, A New Ballet in 3 Acts* choreographed by Vicky Virgin; *The Error of Their Ways* by Torben Betts, directed by James Dacre; Cast: Annika Boras, Shawtane Bowen, Dina Ann Comolli, Mickey Solis

# Horse Trade Theater Group

Erez Ziv, Managing Director; Morgan Lindsey Tachco, Associate Producer

### Kraine Theater

**Too Much Light Makes the Baby Go Blind** created by Greg Allen; presented by the Neo-Futurists; 30 plays in 60 minutes; Friday and Saturday evenings, open run

**The Australia Project** presented by The Production Company; included: *Bobo an' Spyder an' a Girl from Down Under* by Brett C. Leonard, directed by Robert Glaudini; *Ease* by Betty Shamieh, directed by Daisy Walker; *Ethnic Cleansing Day* by Brett Neveu, directed by Ian Morgan; *I Am Ned Kelly* by Beau Willimon, directed by Mark Armstrong; *Terra Australis Incognito* by Trista Baldwin, directed by Jonathan Silverstein; *Out of Nothing* by Kathryn Walat, directed by Pat Diamond; *Melbourne* by Stephen Belber, directed by Mark Armstrong; *Famished* by Frank Basloe, directed by Stewart J. Zully; *The Fatal Shore* by Kate Moira Ryan, directed by Josh Hecht; *adelaide* by Michael John Garces, directed by Catherine Baker Steindler; *The Sound in the Throat* by Elizabeth Meriwether, directed by Mark Armstrong; *Mushroom* by Ken Urban, directed by Judson Kniffen; *Not Our Last Hurrah* by Courtney Baron, directed by Josh Hecht; Cast: Salvatore Inzerillo, Chris McGarry, Nicolle Bradford, Stewart J. Zully, Mark Thornton, Matt Neely, Timothy Riley, Mary Cross, Todd Gearhart, Paul Swinnerton, Adam Saunders, Kori Schneider, Quentin Maré, Megan McQuillan, Vayu O'Donnell, Michael Szeles, Jeffrey Biehl, Patricia Angelin, Jenny Maguire, Jeffrey Scott Green, Stacey Yen, Natalia Payne, Will Jackson Harper, Jay Smith, Ani Bluhm, David Mawhinney, Mary Cross, Marni Penning, Rick Gradone; June 15–July 2

**Food for Fish** by Adam Szymkowicz; presented by Sanctuary: Playwrights

Theatre; Director, Alexis Poledouris; Cast: Katie Honaker, Anna Hopkins, Luis Moreno, Ana Luis Perera, Caroline Tamas, Orion Taraban; July 6–29

**The World of Ryuji Sawa** created and directed by Ryuji Sawa; July 8 & 9

**The Boys** by Gordon Graham; presented by Outhouse Theatre; Director, Craig Baldwin; Cast: Sarah-Jane Casey, Kimberly Cooper, Angela Ledgerwood, Nick Stevenson, Nico Evers-Swindell, Fiana Toibin, Jeremy Waters; September 8–23

**Le Lycanthrope** by Timothy McCown Reynolds; presented by Horse Trade and loup garou international; Director, Brendan Turk; Cast: Marta Kuersten, Bob Laine, John McConnel, Catherine McNelis, Randall Middleton, Joe Pindelski, Tara Pologar, Tom Reid, Timothy McCown Reynolds, Kelly Spitko; October 9–31

**A Collapse** written & directed by Vincent Marano; presented by Teatro Oscur; Cast: John Blaylock, Ethan Downing, Tod Engle, Jerry Ferris, Don Juhlin, Kathleen O'Neill, Christina Rommanello, Cheri Wicks, Laura Williams; November 8–18

**Love: A Tragic Etude** created and directed by Juan Souki; presented by Century Productions; November 27–December 16

**11** two one-acts presented by Century Productions; included: *Ana 3/11* by Paloma Pedrero, and *A River Apart* by by Michelle Schiefen; November 28–December 22

**Twist: Please, Sir, May I Have Some More?** book, lyrics and direction by Gila Sand, music by Paul Leschen; Music Director/Additional Music, Garrit Guadan; Choreography, Jonathan Alsberry, Luis Vilabon; Cast: Brian Charles Rooney, Reymundo Santiago, Laura Carbonell Smith, Luis Villabon, Denise Estrada, Garrit Guadan, Miron Gusso, Kevin Curtis; December 13–January 18

**Dirty Girl** by Ronnie Koenig; presented by Horse Trade and Firecracker Productions; Director, Robert W. McMaster; Cast: Corrie Beula, Bridget Harvey, Ronnie Koenig, Michael Littner, Jesse Teeters; January 4–27

**Apocalypse Neo: Three Futuristic Views of the Apocalypse** presented by Horse Trade and the NY Neo-Futurists; included: *Monkeyland II (anatk 21.10)* by Rob Neill; Director, Jacquelyn Landgraf; Cast: Jorge Cordova, Ryan Good, Eevin Hartsough, Leslie Korein; *In which the end of thc world...* by Justin Tolley; Director, Mark Armstrong; Cast: Erica Livingston, Lindsay Brandon Hunter, Emma Gordon, Michael Davis, Jarrod Zayas, Justin Tolley; *Revolutions Of a City Of Us* by Crystal Skillman; Director, Chris Dippel; Cast: Tara Perry, Lauren Kincheloe, Sharon Freedman, Jenny Williams, Clay Adams; February 1–10

**Your Face Is a Mess** by Marc Spitz; Director, Carlo Vogel; Cast: Camille Habacker, Ivan Martin; February 14–March 4

**2007 FRIGID New York Festival** 1st annual; March 7–18; included: *BabyLove* written & performed by Christen Clifford, developed & directed by Julie Kramer; *Curriculum Vitae* written & performed by Jimmy Hogg; *Legoland* written & performed by Jacob Richmond with Celine Stubel, presented by Atomic Vaudeville, directed by Britt Small; *G-Men Defectives* created and performed by Ray Besharah & Matthew Domville; *Flamenco Con Fusion* by Ricardo Garcia & Julie Gunn; *Wit's End* written & performed by Sandra Shamas; *We Call Her Benny* written & directed by Suzanne Bachner, presented by The John Montgomery Theatre Company; Cast: Bob Brader, Anna Bridgeforth, Bob Celli, Anna Cody, Thaddeus Daniels, Sean Dill, Francis P. O'Flynn, Candice Owens, Morgan Lindsey Tachco, Danny Wiseman; *The Honeymoon is Officially Over* written & performed by Gemma Wilcox; *Blood Turnip* by Christine Perfetti; Cast: Charmaine Broad, Roxanne Kapitsa, Lynn Mancinelli, Melanie Furjanic, Joshua Seidner, David Davoli

**Requiem Aeternam Deo – A Play for Everyone and Nobody** written & directed by Fulya Peker; presented by The Nietzsche Circle; March 22–April 15

**The Facts of Life: The Lost Episode** by Jamie Morris; Director, Christopher Kenney; Cast: Brooks Braselman, Christopher Kenney, Charlie Logan, Jamie Morris, Jaquay Thomas; March 28–June 27

**Skirts & Flirts** by Gloria Calderon Kellett; Director, Elana K. Smith; Cast: Cobie Smulders, Nadine Velazquez, Joe Manganiello, Scarlett Lam, Drew Powell, Matt Carmody, David Scales, Maya Parish, Lara Wickes, Tressa di Figlia, Kate Micucci, Gloria Calderon Kellett; May 16–19

**While Chasing the Fantastic...** by David Ahonen; presented by The Amoralists; Director, David Levy Horton; Producer, James Kautz; Cast: Kate Adams, Derek Ahonen, Ambrosine Falck, Matt Fraley, Nick Lawson, Matthew Pilieci, Barry Sacker, Rebecca Schall; May 22–June 10

## Red Room

**Last of the Red Hot Dadas** by Keri Reid; presented by Exit Theatre; Director, John Warren; Cast: Christina Augello; June 15–July 1

**Bite** written & directed by Suzanne Bachner; presented by Dysfunctional Theatre, The John Montgomery Theatre Company, and Horse Trade; Cast: Bob Brader, Robert Brown, Jennifer Gill, Theresa Goehring, Amy Overman, Justin Plowman, Naomi Warner, Peter Schuyler; June 16–September 29

**Toasted** written & performed by Elisa DeCarlo; Directoral Consultant, Peter Schlosser; June 17–July 15

**The Orgy of the Dead** adapted from Ed Wood's film and directed by Frank Cwiklik; Cast: Michele Schlossberg, Matthew Gray, Carolyn Demisch, Adam Swiderski, Brandon Beilis, Josh Mertz, Scarlet O'Gasm, Gwen Warkulwiz, Shoshanna Hoffert, Madame Rosebud, Sarah Marck, Jessica Silver, Jessica Savage; June 25–July 11

**The Adventures of Jock Jupiter, Rocket Ranger!** by Todd Michael; presented by Grayce Productions; Director, Neal Sims; Cast: Richard Brundage, Sarah Bunker, Ben Evans, Kevin Kelleher, Todd Michael, Lynne Rosenberg, Neal Sims, Jill Yablon; September 7–30

**The Fake Friends Tour** solo performance pieces: *Paincake* written & performed by Alana Harrison and *Everybody Wants a Piece of Braeson* written & performed by Braeson Herold; September 10–October 23

**Kansas City or Along the Way** by Robert Attenweiler; presented by Disgraced Productions; Director, Seth Duerr; Cast: Becky Benhayon, Adam Groves; October 5–22

**Dumbya's Rapture** written & directed by Eric Diamond; presented by Rough Theater; Cast: Chris Behan, Christopher Cole, Eric Diamond, Maryam Fatima, Charles J. Roby, Fred Ruek, Morgan Lindsey Tachco, Chris Von Hoffman, Joshua Young; October 7–November 4

**The Turn of the Screw** adapted by Jeffrey Hatcher from the novel by Henry James; presented by Twenty Feet Productions; Director, Marc Silberschatz; Cast: Erin Cunningham, Tim Scott; October 27–November 12

**Mono o Mono** Director, Nancy Kelly; included: *On How to Dress Your Children the Day You Are Going to Pretend That They Have Polio* written & performed by Melissa Shaw and *Play/date* written & performed by Emily Helfgot; November 7–27

**Revolver** by Christian Middleton; Director, Sarah Haught; November 16–18

**The Sinister Urge!** by Ed Wood, adapted, directed & designed by Frank Cwiklik; presented by Horse Trade and DO WHAT NOW MEDIA; Cast: Bob Brader, Bryan Enk, Matthew Gray, Shoshanna Hoffert, Jennifer Leigh, Josh Mertz, Mateo Moreno, Melissa Nearman, Kevin Orzechowski, Michele Schlossberg, Jessica Savage, Jessica Silver; November 28–December 19

**The Eight: Reindeer Monologues** by Jeff Goode; presented by The Dysfunctional Theatre Company; Director/Sound, Justin Plowman; Set/Lighting, Jason Unfried; Cast: Steve Orlikowski, Jason Unfried, Allison Sell, Jennifer Gill, Robert Brown, Amy Overman, Peter Schuyler, Theresa Unfried; December 2–20

**Kill Me Like You Mean It** by Kiran Rikhye; presented by Stolen Chair Theatre Company and Horse Trade; Director, Jon Stancato; Cast: Tommy Dickie, Sam Dingman, Cameron J. Oro, Alexia Vernon, Liza Wade White; January 5–27

**Many Worlds** by William Borden; presented by Working Man's Clothes; Director, Isaac Byrne; Cast: Gregory Porter Miller, Greg Horton, Ellen David; February 1–24

**2007 FRIGID New York Festival** 1st annual; March 7–18; included: *The Root of All Squares* created and presented by Black Sheep Theatre (Canada), directed by Dave Dawson, Cast: Ray Besharah, Anne Wyman; *Can't Get Started* by Tom X. Chao, directed by Dave Dawson, Cast: Jayson McDonald, Anne Wyman; RADIOTHEATRE'S *The Island of Dr. Moreau* created, directed & performed by Dan Bianchi, with Elizabeth Burke, William Greville, Aaron Mathias, Robert Nguyen, Wes Shippee, Cash Tilton; *Naught But Pirates* written & performed by Sean Owens; *Pointless Rebellion* written & performed by Elisa DeCarlo, directoral consult by Albert Stern; *The Peculiar Utterance of the Day: Live on Stage!* written & directed by Tom X. Chao; Cast: Gyda Arber, Danny Bowes, Josephine Cashman, Tom X. Chao, Rosalie Purvis; *Jonesie's Cabaret Extravaganza* written and performed by Sara Jones; *Spotless* written & performed by Emily Morwen; *Jesus Christ, I'm Sorry* written & performed by Brent Hirose; *Revival* by Greg Turner, presented by Do Not Disturb Theatre, directed by Sara Sahin; Cast: Erin Fritch, Ellen Lanese, Edward Monterosso, Andre Roman, Alanda Spence

**Suburban Peepshow** by James Comtois; presented by Nosedive Productions; Director, Pete Boisvert; Cast: Zack Calhoon, Lelie E. Hughes, Anna Kull, Marc Landers, Anthony Bertram, Christopher Yustin, Ben VandenBoom, Patrick Shearer, James Comtois; presented with the curtain-raiser **Trailers** by Mac Rogers, directed by Patrick Shearer; Cast: Pete Boisvert, Rebecca Comtois, Mick Hilgers, Cat Johnson, Marc Landers, Stephanie Cox-Williams; April 5–28

**Gift Exchange** by Greg Turner; presented by Do Not Disturb Theatre; Director, Sara Sahin; Cast: Sharon Ann Farrell, Jason Benjamin Gill, Zachary Halley, Kristy Webb; May 9–19

**Spitting in the Face of the Devil** written & directed by Bob Brader, directed and developed by Suzanne Bachner; presented by The John Montgomery Theatre Company and Horse Trade; Lighting, Douglas Shearer May 7–July 16

## UNDER St. Marks

**Other People** by Christopher Shinn; Director, Michael Melamedorff; Music, Patrick Force; Cast: Jimmy King, Cass Bugge, Kevin Creamer, Corey Patrick, Drew DeJesus, Sean North; June 4–17

**Men Eat Mars Bars While Touching Their Penis** by Jennifer Slack-Eaton; presented by Working Man's Clothes Productions; Director, Jared Culverhouse; Cast: Darcie Champagne, Victoria Cengia, Anne Dyas, Amanda Hamilton, Katryn Kinser; June 29–July 15

**Chosen** written & directed by Rick Vorndran; presented by The Dysfunctional Theatre Company; Cast: Robert Brown, Danaher Dempsey, Allison Sell, Amy Oppenheim, Theresa Unfried, Alex Warner; September 17–26

**Revelations** one-acts presented by Rising Sun Perfomance Company; included *Good Enough* written & directed by Kitt Lavoie; *Without* by Laura Rohrman, directed by Kuye Harris; *Cover Magnets* and *Southern Werewolf* by John Patrick Bray, directed by Rachel Klein; *Music to Travel By* written & directed by Andi Stover; July 20–22

**Growing Up Is Hard to Do** conceived and directed by Julie Bain & P. William Pinto; presented by Rising Sun Performance Company; Cast: Julie Bain, Noelle Boostani, David Loewy, Emily MacLeod, P. William Pinto, Robert Richardson, Jovier Sanchez, Kelly Scanlon, Mimi Jefferson; July 27–29

**The Indian Wants the Bronx** by Israel Horovitz; presented by Strain Theatre Company; Director, Greg Parente; September 5–24

**The Strange Box of Dr. Oddbody** by Adam Nowak & Horse Trade Theatre Company; Cast: Adam Nowak, Myles Evans, Rachel Korowitz, Michele O. Medlin, Sarah Nowak, Jane O'Leary, Jeff Scherer, Nate Starkey; October 3–28

**Heartbreak** written & directed by Marc Morales; presented by Edge of Insanity; Cast: Pauly Burke, Solly Duran, Izzy Ruiz, Vedant Gokhale, Vinnie Kay, Deondra Lyonne, Isabella Manso, Patrick McColley, Tom Summers, Anthony Cruz, Heather Thompson, Robert Yang, Melanie A. Maras; October 12–November 4

**Beckett Below** four short plays by Samuel Beckett, presented by ghostcrab; included: *Play* directed by Peter A. Campbell; *Act Without Words II* directed by Ariane Anthony; *That Time* directed by Tim Lee; *Footfalls* directed by Eve Hartmann; November 9–18

**The House of Yes** by Wendy MacLeod; presented by Raben Productions; Director, Katie Raben; Cast: Sarah Moreau, Stephen Squibb, Vivian Neuwirth, Madeleine Maby, Brian Morgan; November 30–December 2

**Laughing Wild** by Christopher Durang; presented by Green Sea Theatre; Director, Jimmy Smith; Cast: Maddalena V. Maresca, Jimmy Smith; December 20–January 10

**Solar Powered Flashlight** impov presented by Rising Sun Performance Company, directed by Crystal Franceschini; Cast: Akia, Crystal Franceschini, Robert Richardson, Kelly Scanlon, Patrick Egan, Sahadev Poudel, Elizabeth Burke, Josh Hyman; January 16, April 1

**The Bad Bruise of Billy MacBean** and **The Gringo of Deli Acapulco** by Eric Brand; presented by Old Kent Road Theater; Director, Noah Burger; Cast: Charlie Hewson & Katie Morris/Scott Eckert & Reema Zaman; January 21–February 13

**Pulcinella's War** written & performed by Antonio Fava; February 24

**2007 FRIGID New York Festival** 1st annual; March 7–18; included: *Harm's Way* written & performed by Mac Wellman; presented by newfangled theatReR; *Andrea* written & performed by Allison Landa; *Orange Murder Suit* by Rob Matsushita, directed by Rick Vorndran; presented by The Dysfunctional Theatre Company; Cast: Theresa Unfried, Allison Sell, Jennifer Gill; *One Lump or Two* directed by Neil Casey; *Crazy Over Love* created and performed by David Tyson; *The Butterfield Tones* written & directed by Robert Attenweiler, co-directed by John Patrick Hayden; presented by Disgraced Productions; Cast: Becky Benhayon, Joe Stipek, Nathan Williams, Wil Petre; *The Light Inside* written, directed & performed by Lindsay Wolf, with Molly O'Neal, Steven Smith; *The Burning Bush* written & performed by Barbara Baumawitz; *Super Glossy* written & performed by Courtney McLean; *Born Ready* by Joseph Jomo Pierre, presented by Obsidian Theatre Company

**The Apologies** short plays presented by No Tea Productions; included: *Mark and Andy in a Cop Drama* by Jeff Sproul, directed by Dan O'hare; Cast: Jeff Sproul, Matt Sears; *Dirigible* written & directed by Lindsey Moore, co-written by Jeff Sproul; Cast: Tom Bartos, Kelly Eads; *Technical Knock-Up* written & directed by Matt Sears; Cast: Jesse Jones, Timothy Mather, Kelly Eads, Matt Sears, Lindsey Moore, D. Robert Wolcheck; *Throwing Porcelain* written & directed by Martin Dockery, co-written by Lucy Baker; Cast: Peter Plano, Annie Meisels; *Semi-Private* written & directed by Lindsey Moore; Cast: Jeff Sproul, Lindsey Moore; *The Dance of the McDictator* written & directed by Darren Kaminsky; Cast: Lindsey Moore, Kelly Eads, Timothy Mather, Tom Bartos, Jeff Sproul, Jesse Jones, Matt Sears, D. Robert Wolcheck; March 29–April 7

**A Paranoid's Guide to History** presented by INRECO; April 12–21

**Mixed Tape 2007** presented by Another Urban Riff; *Track 1* by Lauren Hatcher, directed by Robyn Neilsen; Cast: Kristen Abate, Lawrence Jansen, Jessica Schupack, Julie Wiedeman, Jarrod Zayas; *Track 2* by Lisa Atenasio, directed by Eden Foster; Cast: Kerryn Feehan, Lawrence Jansen, Amber Petty, Tricia McAlpin; *Track 3* by Eden Foster, directed by Marge Lewit; Cast: Lisa Antenasio, Chris Cipriano, Kerryn Feehan, Matthew Watkins, Julie Wiedeman; *Track 4* by Marge Lewit, directed by David Williams; Cast: Megan Armitage, Lisa Atenasio, Karin Freeland, Robyn Neilsen, Nick Paglino, Lucas Wotkowski, Jarrod Zayaz; April 28–May 19

**The Big Funk** by John Patrick Shanley; presented by Anthro-Fab Productions & Tobacco Bar Theatre Company; Director, Dana Panepinto; Cast: Colleen Britt, Ellen Hauck, Toby Knops, Deanna McGovern, Michael Schantz, Jesse Soursourian; May 13–15

**The Most Beautiful Lullaby You've Ever Heard** by Greg Romero; presented by City Attic Theatre; Director, Andrew Merkel; Cast: John Conor Brooke, Dianna Marino, Lucy Walters; May 24–June 2

# Hourglass Group

Elyse Singer, Artistic Director; Carolyn Baeumler and Nina Hellman, Associate Directors

**Trouble in Paradise** by David Simpatico, adapted from Ernst Lubitsch's 1932 film, screenplay by Samson Raphaelson; Score, Steven Bernstein and the Millennial Territory Orchestra; Director/Conceiver, Elyse Singer; Choreography, Carey Bertini; Sets, Lauren Helpern; Costumes, Theresa Squire; Lighting, Traci Klainer; Sound, Katie Down; Props, Faye Armon; Dramaturgy, Erika Rundle & Aniko Szucs; Musical Director, Jill Brunelle; Wigs, Rob Greene & John J. Janas; Assistant Director, Deborah Phillips; Production Management, Dynamic Productions; PSM, Elyzabeth Gorman; ASM, Sunneyva Stapleton; Casting, Deborah Brown; Press, Spin Cycle; Cast: Carolyn Baeumler, Nina Hellman, Jeremy Shamos, Steven Rattazzi, Gordon Stanley, Cynthia Darlow, Liam Craig, Henry Caplan; Hudson Guild Theatre; June 14–July 22

**Real Live Women** solo performance shows; included: *BabyLove* by Christen Clifford, directed by Julie Kramer; *The Chrismahanukwanzakah Monologues* by Yolanda Shoshana; *White Tape* by Linda Mancini; *Cou-Cou Bijoux is alive, and well* by Raquel Cion; *Fifteen Dreams* by Veronique Jeanmarie; *Quiet Frenzy* by Stacey Karen Robinson; D-Lounge at the Daryl Roth Theatre; November 30 & December 6

# Hudson Guild Theatre

**Civil Sex** written and performed by Brian Freeman; presented by Hudson Guild Theatre Company; Director, James Furlong; July 28–August 5

**The Ballad of Eddie and Joe** by David Sard; Director, Lorca Peress; Set, Alan M. Bolle; Lighting, Alex Moore; Costumes, Raul Aktanov; Fights, Stephen Innocenzi; Cast: Michael Citriniti, Angelo Rosso, Ana Mercedes Torres, Stephen Innocenzi, Jerry Rago, Joyce Griffen, Anita Velez-Mitchell; September 8–24

**Season of Change** presented by Dreamscape Theater; included: *Marisol* by Jose Rivera, directed by Shaun Peknic; Cast: Julia Alexandria, Kent Meister, Dawn Timm, Christine Verleny; *True West* by Sam Shepard, directed by Kate Ross; Cast: Zack Calhoon, Jordan Meadows, Brian McFadden, Ruth Ann Phimister; *Truce on Uranus* written and directed by Mark Lindberg; Cast: David A. Ellis, Ricardo Perez-Gonzalez, Jordan Wishner, Sarah Worrest, Suzanne Hall, Emma Canalese; October 6–29

**Ghosts** by Henrik Ibsen; presented by Hudson Guild Theatre Company; Director, Jim Furlong; Cast: David King, Giovanna Henson; February 2–10

**for colored girls who have considered suicide/when the rainbow is enuf** by Ntozake Shange; presented by Hudson Guild Theatre Company; Director, Marvin Kazembe Jefferson; February 3–11

**Mad Forest** by Caryl Churchill; presented by QED Productions; Director, Julia Beardsley O'Brien; Cast: Adam Belvo, Tom Cleary, Micah Freedman, Marguerite French, Matthew Gray, Angus Hepburn, Megan Ketch, Christiaan Koop, Elena McGhee, Mick O'Brien, Andy Waldschmidt; February 15–March 4

**Scenes From an Execution** by Howard Barker; presented by QED Productions; Director, Zander Teller; Cast: Angela Jewell Arnold, Micah Freedman, Charles Hendricks, Elena McGhee, Matt McIver, Julia Beardsley O'Brien, Mick O'Brien, Christian Pedersen, Corey Tazmania; May 25–June 10

## Impact Theater

**Kip, the Enchanted Cat** written & directed by Aaron Michael Zook; presented by Tuckaberry Productions; Cast: Lorinne Lampert, Adam Baritot, Brian Wilson, Sarah Amandes, Dianna Tucker, Robert Steiger; November 4 –December 9

**Female Bonding** by Susan Kaessinger; Director, David Schuman; Cast: Susan Kaessinger, Ed Lacina, Noelle Lynch, Gina Mahoney, Fernando A. Mateo Jr., Sheiva Marie Nader, Michael Nastu, Kara Payne, Christine Rigby, Linda Rucconich; November 9–19

**Winter One-Act Festival** included: Week 1: *Playgroup* by Thelma de Castro, directed by Seth Payeur; Cast: Sarah Haund, Brie Turhoff, Jeanine Gangloff; *Edging the Cliff* by Jae Kramisen, directed by Brian Franko; Cast: Helene Galek, Dan Pfau; *Snow in Galveston* by Schatzie Schaefers, directed by James Monohan; Cast: Pamela Paul, Celia Howard; *CAUTION: The True Imagined Story of My Parents' Romance* by Lauren Yee, directed by Marie Darden; Cast: Amy Chang, Jamie Park, John Wu, Charlie Newell; *Suicide Gal, Won't You Come Out Tonight, Come Out Tonight* by J. Boyer, directed by Corinne Neal; Cast: Andrea Sooch, Anne Popolizio; *The Fears of Harold Shivers* by Dawson Moore, directed by Chris Cotone; Cast: David Licht, Robyn Frank, Anne Popolizio, Everett Patterson, Noah Crowe; Week 2: *Ignorance* by Shannon Murdoch, directed by Shannon Ward; Cast: Arnold Kim, Colleen Allen; *In The Beginning Again* by Lauren D. Yee, directed by Chanda Calentine; Cast: Ann Roser, Alexis Hale, Jon Fornker, Lee Marvin Sebastiany; *Sea Change* by Christine Emmert, directed by Janus Surratt; Cast: Erica Lustig, Jen Namof; *Fin and Euba* by Audrey Ceflay, directed by Michelle Dean; Cast: Sara Foldenauer, Delia Cyrillo; *A Diner A Shiner* by Dan Moyer, directed by Chris Cotone; Cast: Jonathan Raviv, Robyn Frank; *The Story of Izanagi and Izanami* by Kristen Miller, directed by Maura Kelley; Cast: Joan Lunoe, David Walter; February 1–11

**Orphans** by Joel Shatzky; Director, Cara Blouin; Cast: Darlene Heller, Samantha Payne, Liz Racster, Maria Alegre, Isabel Agnes, Nancy Eng; May 5–13

## Impetuous Theater Group

James David Jackson, Artistic Director; Josh Sherman, Managing Director

**Fenway: Last of the Bohemians** by Kelly McAllister and Lisa Margaret Holub; Co-presented with Boomerang Theatre; Director, Tim Errickson; Set, Joe Powell; Costumes, Cheryl McCarron; Lighting, Holly M. Kirk; Sound, Ryan Dowd; Stage Manager, Angela Allen; Cast: Carrie Brewer, Reyna de Courcy, Margaret A. Flanagan, Jack Halpin, James David Jackson, Tom Knutson, Paul Navarra; chashama; November 3–19

**The Chronological Secrets of Tim** by Janet Zarecor; Director, Sarah Ali; Assistant Director, Jessica Pollack; Stage Manager, Rebeka Pinon-Cassidy; Sets, Amanda Haley; Lighting, Holly Kirk; Costumes, Meg Zedler; Sound, Megan Henninger; General Manager, Averia Gaskin; Press, Lanie Zipoy; Technical Director, Brian MacInnis Smallwood; Cast: Liz Bangs, Kira Blaskovich, Corey Ann Haydu, Matt Stevens; May 18–June 3

## The Independent Theater

**The Wild Life** written & directed by Juoyoung Hong; June 9–25

**Triple Threats** by Alec Holland and Melissa Samuels; presented by For Art's Sake Productions; Director, Ryan J. Davis; Cast: Josh Painting, Kat Ross, Richard Taylor; July 27–August12

**After the Flood** Raul Jennings & **Pieces of Home** by Jack Zullo; presented by Common Thread Theater; Directors, Michelle Dean & Y. Angel Wuellner; September 13–23

**The Black Crook** by Charles M. Barras; presented by Room5001 Theatre and Nate Barrall, conceived, adapted and directed by Joshua William Gelb; Cast: Dane Agostinis, Maranda Barskey, Randy Blair, Josh Isaacs, Craig Jorczak, Matt Sadewitz, Sam Tedaldi, Kate Weber; March 7–17

**The Girl Most Likely To...** written & directed by Jodi Smith; presented by NativeAliens Theatre Collective; Cast: Sly Augustus, Kaitlin Bailey, Marielle Carter, Melissa Center, Ethan Downing, Dennis Hurley, John Ierardi, Yasmine Jahanmir, Jack Moran, Brendan Rothman-Hicks, Cynthia Russell; March 20–24

## Irish Arts Center

**The Gold Standard** by Daniel Roberts; Produced by Audax Theatre Group; Director, Alex Lippard; Stage Manager, Jessica Pecharsky; Assistant Director, Brian Ziv; ASM, Jodi Witherall; Set, Michael Moore; Lighting, Graham Kindred; Costumes, Jessica Gaffney; Cast: Sabine Singh, Antony Hagopian, Jordan Charney, Yasu Suzuki, Alie Carey; June 3–July 1

**Bully** by Jerome Walden; presented by Double W Productions; directed by and featuring William Walsh; July 4–23

**The Irish Play** by Tim McGuillicuddy; presented by Hamm & Clov Stage Company; Director, Theodore Mann; Lighting, Jake Fine; Sound, Tom Cassetta; PSM, Leslie Kelly; Fights, Brad Lemons; Cast: Alicia M. Fitzgerald, Jimmy Kerr, Jonathan P. Judge-Russo, Zachary Spicer, Elizabeth Stephensen; May 31–June 30

## LAByrinth Theater Company

**The Barn 2006** 7th annual Reading Series Festival; Shiva Theatre; December 2–20; included: *Becoming Jack* by Justin Reinsilber; Director, Elizabeth Canavan; Cast: Chris Chalk, Salvatore Inzerillo, Dina Janis, Kelley Rae O'Donnell, Melissa Paladino, Richie Petrocelli, Felix Solis, Ed Vassallo, Aaron Roman Weiner; *The Wild Inside* by Cusi Cram; Director, John Gould Rubin; Cast: Julian Acosta, Carlo Alban, Yetta Gottesman, Salvatore Inzerillo, Florencia Lozano, Paula Pizzi; *Penalties & Interest* by Rebecca Cohen; Director, Paula Pizzi; Cast: Julian Acosta, Elizabeth Canavan, Yetta Gottesman, Michael Puzzo; *Sam's Coming* by Kia Corthron; Director, Sarah Sidman; Cast: Marsha Stephanie Blake, Mariana Carreño, Venida Evans, Russell G. Jones, Angela Lewis, Peter McRobbie, Portia, Phyllis Sommerville; *Sweet Storm* by Scott Hudson; Director, Padraic Lillis; Cast: Jamie Dunn, Barrett Martin; Cast: Marsha Stephanie Blake, Mariana Carreño, Venida Evans, Russell G. Jones, Peter McRobbie, Portia, Phyllis Sommerville; *Knives & Other Sharp Objects* by Raúl Castillo; Director, Felix Solis; Cast: Maggie Bofill, Lydia DeSouza, Sarah Hayon, Nathan LeBronn, Richie Petrocelli, Joselin Reyes, Emilz Rodriguez, Martha Wollner; *The Rest of Your Life* by Megan Mostyn-Brown; Director, Meredith McDonough; Cast: Chris Chalk, Beth Cole, Alexis Croucher, Ashley Hanna, Felix Solis, Sidney Williams, Portia;

*History of Invulnerability* by David Bar Katz; Director, John Gould Rubin; Cast: J. Eric Cook, Ritchie Coster, David Deblinger, Carlee McManus, Chris Messina, Richie Petrocelli, Michael Puzzo, Melissa Ross, Alexa Scott-Flaherty; *A View from 151st Street* by Bob Glaudini; Director, Peter DuBois; Cast: Gbenga Akkinagbe, Liza Colon-Zayas, Russell G. Jones, Marisa Malone, Elizabeth Rodriguez, Felix Solis, Craig muMs Grant, David Zayas; *Untitled* written & directed by Stephen Adly Guirgis

# La MaMa Experimental Theatre Club (E.T.C.)

Ellen Stewart, Founder and Director

## First Floor Theatre

**Lunatics' Ball** by Claudia Menza; Director/Set, Harold Dean James; Lighting, Tony Mulanix; Costumes, Ramona Ponce; Cast: Paul Albe, Daniel Clymer, Lynn Eldredge, Joe Kelly, Stella Venner, Cezar Williams; June 8–25

**Abandon** written & directed by Matthew Maguire; presented with Creation Production Company; Cast: Jeff Barry, Victoire Charles, Alexis McGuinness, Genevieve Odabe, Richard Prioleau, Michael Ryan; October 19–November 5

**Home Front** by Daniel Algie; Director, E. Randahl Hoey; Set, Josh Zangen; Lighting, Joel E. Silver; Costumes, Erika Ingrid Lillienthal; Composer, David Lenchus; Casting, Cindi Rush; Cast: Connell Cole, Joseph Jamrog, Anthony Duke Claus, Christy Pusz, Fletcher McTaggert, H. Clark; November 9–26

**The Whore From Ohio** by Hanoch Levin, translated Sandra Silverston; Directors, Geula Jeffet Attar & Victor Attar; Design, Rob Eggers; Lighting, Chaim Gitter & Sebastian Adamo; Music, Yuval Mesner; Cast: Victor Attar, Udi Razzin, Zishan Ugurlu; November 30–December 10

**Earth in Trance** written & directed by Gerald Thomas; Music/Sound, David Lawson; Cast: Fabiana Gugli, Juliano Antunes, Seth Powers; December 14–30

**Party Time** written & directed by Paul Zimet; presented in association with The Talking Band; Set, Lino Fiorito; Lighting, Lenore Doxsee; Music, Peter Gordon; Video, Kit Fitzgerald; Cast: William Badgett, Joe Rosetto; January 10–21

**The Burial At Thebes** by Seamus Heaney, based on *Antigone* by Sophocles; presented in association with The Eleventh Hour Theatre Company; Director, Alexander Harrington; Choreography, Claire Pavlich; Music, Carman Moore; Set, Tony Penna; Lighting, Claire Pavlich; Cast: Frank Anderson, Janice Bishop, Jessica Crandall, Louise Flory, Liz Frost, John McCarthy, Jason Adamo, Rebecca Austin, Judith F. Bradshaw, Maija Lisa Currie, Sarah Ecton-Luttrell, Erik Gratton, Carrie Anne James, Christopher Keogh, Liz Sanders, Randi Sobol, Jason Weiss; January 25–February 11

**La Vie Noir** by Jim Neu; Director, Keith McDermott; Set/Costumes, Meg Zedler; Lighting, Carol Mullins; Sound, Jacob Burckhardt; Music, Harry Moon & Neal Kirkwood; Cast: Deborah Auer, John Costelloe, Agosto Machado, Chris Maresca, Jim Neu, Tony Nunziata, Paco, Mary Schultz, Black-Eyed Susan; February 15–March 4

**Janyl** Created and performed by Yara Arts Group; Director, Virlana Tkacz; Movement, Shigeko Sara Suga; March 9–25

**Kerez (The Treatment)** created by Sakhna Nurlan Asanbekov; performed by Sakhna Theatre; March 29–April 2

**Waxing West** by Saviana Stanescu; presented in association with East Coast Artists; Director, Benjamin Mosse; Set, Kanae Heike; Costumes, Alixandra Gage; Sound, Sharath Patel; Music, Lucian Ban; Stage Manager, Adam Ganderson; Cast: Elizabeth Atkeson, Kathryn Kates, Jason Lawergren, Alexis McGuinness, Tony Namovski, Grant Neale, Dan Shaked, Marnye Young; April 5–22

**Clytemnestra's Tears** written & directed by Avra Sidiropoulou; presented by Persona Theatre Company; performed by Themis Bazaka; May 17–June 3

## The Annex

**Dancing vs. the Rat Experiment** created and presented by Witness Relocation; Director/Choreographer, Dan Safer; Music, Miss Derringer, Skeleton Key, D.J. Dragon, Murder By Death, Douglas Wagner, Mobcat, Arthur Pruvis, The Borromeo String Quartet, Anton Sanko; Set/Lights, Jay Ryan; Costumes/Masks, Pandora Andrea Gastelum; Sound, Tim Schellenbaum; Production Manager, Rebecca Reaves; Cast: Abby Browde, Heather Christian, Sean Donovan, Emmitt George, Mike Mikos, Dan Safer, Laura Berlin Stinger, Orion Taraban, Randy Thompson; October 26–November 12

**Pilgrimage** created & performed by Laughing Stone Dance Theatre; Choreography, Sin Cha Hong; November 6–8

**Several Witty Observations** presented by Dada von Bzdulow Theattre, based on the writings of Witold Gombrowicz; Director, Leszek Bzdyl; Cast: Leszek Bzdyl, Katarzyna Chmielewska, Rafal Dziemidok; November 16–26

**Open Door** created, directed, choreographed and starring Federico Restrepo, in collaboration with Denise Greber, lyrics and music by Elizabeth Swados; Music Director, Kris Kukul; Cast: Neimah Djourabchi, Sara Galassini, Denise Greber, Allison Hiroto, Sharon Mashihi, Romona Mukherjee, Pasha Prakasa, Emily Vick, Chris Wild, Paula Wilson; December 1–17

**A Crazy Sound** written & directed by Dario D'Ambrosi; presented by Teatro Patologico; Set/Costumes, Vittorio Terracina; Lighting, Danilo Facco; Sound, Stefano Zazzera; Music Director, John La Barbera; Cast: Lucy Alibar, Sheila Dabney, Celeste Moratti, Meredith Summers, Emma Lynn Worth, Kat Yew; December 21–30

**Medea** by Euripides; Director/Choreography, Hiroshi Jin; preformed by Company East (Japan); January 4–14

**Concrete** text, music, and direction by Robert Ashley; Cast: Sam Ashley, Tom Buckner, Jacqueline Humbert, Joan la Barbara, Tom Hamilton; January 17–21

**Once There Was a Village** written & directed by Vit Horejs, inspiried by Yuri Kapralov, music by Frank London and the Hungry March Band; presented and perfomed by The Czecholslvak-American Marionette Theatre; January 25–February 11

**Palenque** presented by Oyu Oro; Director/Choreography, Danys Perez; February 15–25

**Republic of Dreams** by Stacy Klein, Carlos Uriona and Matthew Glassman; based on the work of Bruno Schulz; presented in association with Double Edge Theatre and the Polish Cultural Institute; Director, Stacy Klein; Design, Mira Zelechower Aleksiun; Music, Jacek Ostaszewski; Dramaturg, Ilan Stavans; March 8–18

**The Exiles** written, directed, and designed by Theodora Skipitares, based on *Orestes* by Euripides; Lighting, Pat Dignan; Puppets, Cecilia Schiller; Music, Tim Schellenbaum; Video, Kay Hines; Cast: Sheila Dabney, Chris Maresca, Alissa Mello, Nicky Paraiso, Sonja Perryman, Aneesh Sheth, Amanda Villalobos; March 22–April 8

**Trophy Wife** book and direction by Mary Fulham, music by Terry Waldo, lyrics by Paul Foglino; based on *Anna on the Neck* by Anton Chekhov; presented in association with Watson Arts; Choreography, Heidi Latsky; Set, Gregory John Mercurio; Costumes, Ramona Ponce; Lighting, Federico Restrepo; Sound, Tim Schellenbaum; Video, Ray Roy and Eva Mantell; Cast: Hal Blankenship, Sharon Ann Farrell, Brian P. Glover, Joan Jaffe, Jacquelyn Kroschell, Max Lodge, Lisa Passero, Michael Rader, William Ryall, Jack Slattery; April 12–22

**Romeo and Juliet** by William Shakespeare, adaptation, direction, sets, and music by Ellen Stewart; presented in association with Great Jones Repertory Company; Choreography, Renouard Gee and H.T. Chen; Co-Set Design, Mark Tambella, Jun Maeda; Costumes, Radu, Miruna Boruezescu and Kanako Hiyama; Lighting, Federico Restrepo; Co-Music, Genji Ito; Co-Music/Music Director, Michael Sirotta; Cast: Noshir Dalal, George Drance, Brian P. Glover, Malaika Queano, Steven Ryan, Shigeko Suga, Ronny Wasserstrom, Meredith Wright; May 24–June 17

**Something to Crow About** by Alejandro Roces; presented by UST Conservatory of Music and UNESCO Philippines ITI; Design, Len Santos; Stage Manager, Mybel Lynne Quito; Cast: Bernardo Bernardo, Manrico A. Embele, Bobby Superales, Rammel Maglonzo, Armel de Guzman, Angelbert Cruz, Marion Buit, Edna Sanchez, Danilo Nicodemus Pahati, Edralyn Inda, Mylene Ontulan, Thea Perez, Austregelina Alfornon, Ronan Ferrer, Hazel Ceguera, Charisma C. Castro, Lovelle Inoferio, Mary Ann Santiago, Michelle Bautista, Jose Juan D. Reyes, Israel Comandante, Jose Exequiel Vale, Karl Angelo Tangco, Mary Grace Alvarez; June 21–24

### The Club

**Death by Joinery** by Mike Gorman; June 2–11

**Spic & Spam** by Alba Sanchez & Peter J. Brynes; Director, Gary Dini; September 22–October 8

**Marlene Dietrich** performed by Ksenija Prohaska; October 2 & 3

**Modern Living** by Richard Sheinmel; Director, Michael Barron; Sets, John McDermott; Costumes, Jennifer Caprio; Lighting, Jay Scott; Sound, Tim Schellenbaum; Music, Clay Zambo; Cast: Meg Anderson, Christopher Borg, Mick Hilgers, Richard Scheinmel, Nomi Tichman; October 13–29

**Swell(ing) Relatives** written & directed by Valeria Vasilevski; Cast: Lawrence Goldhuber; November 3–12

**The Golf Wars** by Peter Dizozza; Director, Tom Nondorf; Cast: Dennis Hurley, Eric Starker, Shelly Smith, Douglas Williams, Patrick Walsh, Molly Amoroso; November 6

**The Architecture of Seeing – Remix** created by Patricia Hoffbauer & George Emilio Sanchez; December 1–16

**The Pursuit of Happines** performed by Jeffrey Essmann & Susan Burns; December 4

**Christmas in Nickyland** curated by Nicky Paraiso; December 19

**Shenanigans is Back (in the Habit!!)** performed by Geoffrey Decas, Julia Henderson, Boo Killebrew, Ryan Purcell, Jordan Seavey, Noah Starr, Phillip Taratula, T.J. Witham; January 6

**Sylvia So Far** written and directed by Timothy Mathis; Cast: Bianca Leigh; January 12–21

**The Be(a)st of Taylor Mac** written & performed by Taylor Mac; Director, Drew Geraci; January 26–28

**Split Ends** written & performed by Venus Opal Resse; Director, Liesl Tommy; February 1–11

**Food for Thought** by Kim Ima & Onni Johnson; February 16–25

**Presenting Gilda Lilly** by David Leddick & Andrew Sargent; Cast: David Leddick, Nathan Smith; March 2–4

**Tarantella** written & directed by Marisa Buffone; March 16–25

**Dancing With Bishop** poems by Elizabeth Bishop, performed by Saskia Hegt; March 30–April 8

**Lapdog** by Adam Weiner; Cast: Adam Carpenter, Zach Steel, Adam Weiner; April 2

**Go Ahead...Laugh** written and performed by Mary Ann Henderson; Director, Anthony Guerino; April 20

**Antigone** by Jose Watanabe; Director, Gisela Cardenas; May 17–18

**All Her Faces: A Portrait of Dusty Springfield** Conceived, written, directed & performed by Anthony Innéo, in association with SCRIPTS UP! Inc.; Choreography, Gregory Daniels; Costumes, Cheryl Leggi; Sound, Adam Farquharson; Orchestrations/Vocal Arrangements/Musical Director, Jo Lynn Burks; The Band: Sean Jenness, Jo Lynn Burks, Steve Bartosik, Louis Tucci; Back-up Singers: Lauren Echo, Sandra Caldwell, Isabel Santiago, Amy Fox; June 1–10

# Lincoln Center Festival 2006

Nigel Redden, Director

**DruidSynge: The Complete Plays of John Millington Synge** presented by Druid Theatre (Galway, Ireland); included: *Riders to the Sea, The Playboy of the Western World, Deirdre of the Sorrows, The Shadow of the Glen, The Well of the Saints, The Tinker's Wedding;* Director, Garry Hynes; Choreography, David Bolger; Sets, Francis O'Connor; Costumes, Kathy Strachan; Lighting, Davy Cunningham; Sound, John Leonard; Music, Sam Jackson; Stage Manager, Tim Smith; Cast: Sarah-Jane Drummey, Richard Flood, Simone Kirby, Mick Lally, Marcus Lamb, Nick Lee, Louise Lewis, Eoin Lynch, Hannah McCabe, Charlie McCarthy, Aaron Monaghan, Eamon Morrisey, Marie Mullen, Derry Power, Peg Power, Gemma Reeves, Catherine Walsh, John Gaughan; Gerald Lynch Theatre; July 10–23

**Grendel** by Elliot Goldenthal, Julie Taymor, and J.D. McClatchy, based on the novel by John Gardner and the legend of "Beowulf;" presented in association with the Los Angeles Opera; Director, Julie Taymor; Choreography, Angelin Preljocaj; Set, George Tsypin; Costumes, Constance Hoffman; Lighting, Donald Holder; Puppets/Masks, Julie Taymor and Michael Currie; Cast: Eric Owens, Denyce Graves, Desmond Richardson, Laura Claycomb, Jay Hunter Morris, Richard Croft, Raymond Aceto, David Gagnon, Jonathan Hays, Charles Temkey, Hanan Alattar, Maureen Francis, Sarah Coburn; NY State Theatre; July 11–16

**Eraritjaritjaka: Musée Des Phrases** written & directed by Heiner Goebbels, based on texts by Elias Canett; presented in association with Théâtre Vidy-Lausanne; Set/Lighting, Klaus Grünberg; Costumes, Florence von Gerkan; Sound, Willi Bopp; Video, Bruno Deville; Cast: André Wilms, The Mondriaan Quartet; Rose Theater; July 27–29

**Geisha** conceived and directed by Ong Keng Sen, text by Robin Loon; presented in association with TheatreWorks (Singapore); Costumes, Mitsuishi Yanaihara; Lighting, Scott Zielinski; Sound, Toru Yamanaka; Cast: Karen Kandel, Gojo Masanosuke, Kineya Katsumatsu; Gerald Lynch Theatre; July 27–30

# Looking Glass Theatre

Justine Lambert, Artistic Director; Jenn Boehm, Managing Director

**Helix 999** by Kenneth Nowell; Director, Candace O'Neil Cihocki; Set, Jane Parrot; Lighting, Ryan Metzler; Costumes, Skyler Schrempp; Cast: Jennifer Boehm, Mark Comer, Nic Heppe, Julia E.C. Jones, Elizabeth Yocam; October 13–November 18

**Winter 2006 Writer/Director Forum** Writers: Lisa Johnson, Nancy G. McClernan, Mary Flanagan, Dorianne Emmerton, Lauren D. Yee, Moliere; Directors: Rose Ginsberg, Emily Plumb, Maureen Rogalski, Aliza Shane, Ain Rashida Sykes, Erin Winebark; Novermber 30–December 17

**The Vagina Monologues** by Eve Ensler; Director, Rose Ginsberg; Cast: Tania Asnes, Jenn Boehm, Leigh Feldpausch, Hannah Ginsberg, Laura Harrison, Dara Iannuzzi, Heidi Kok, Emily Marro, Christina Norris, Ochuole Ode, Corinne Palermo, Meg Richwine, Mia Ulibarri, Simmone Yu; February 17–18

**Baal** by Bertolt Brecht, translated by Eric Bentley; Composer/Music Director, Alan S. Hewitt; Director, Charmian Creagle; Set, Romanka Zajac; Lighting, Ryan Metzler; Costumes, Rien Schlecht; Choreographer, Amiti Perry; Stage Manager, Chanda Calentine; Cast: Lyndsey Anderson, Sara Jeanne Asselin, Jennifer Boehm, Jane Elliott, John Forkner, Kyle Haggerty, Melissa House, Jadelynn Stahl, Kymberlie Stansell; March 1–25

**Creatures of the Cabaret** short plays by Nancy Gail-Clayton, Karin Diann Williams, Beverly Rana, Letitia Sweitzer, Charmian Creagle, Sean Doran, & Lenore Blumenfeld; Director, Shari Johnson; Cast: Lynsey Becher, Alex Coelho, Meredith Dillard, Abigail Hawk, Kirsten Kollender, Elise Link, Elizabeth Stewart, Daren Taylor, Michael Wantuck, Sharon Zaslaw; March 9–April 7

**Bug Boy Blues** by Lisa Railsback; Director, Candace O'Neil Cichoki; Set, Romanka Zajac; Lighting, Ryan Metzler; Costumes, Tara Hawks; Stage Managers, Danya Nardi, Rachel Klein; Cast: Daniel Gibel, Marci Koltonuk, Brooke Lucas, Pauline Miller, Julie Nelson, Krystal Osbourne, Heather Siler, Jeff Stevens, Erin Sullivan; April 28–June 3

**Odyssey** written & directed by Kate Marks from the classic by Homer; Set, Carolyn Mraz; Lighting, Ryan Metzler; Costumes, Sean Sullivan; Sound, Jason Atkinson; Stage Manager, Toby Bercovici; Cast: Elena Chang, Will Ellis, Fosse E. Emery, Sarah Petersiel, Libya Pugh, Marc Santa Maria, Ben Sumrall, Daren Taylor, Jamie Lea Thompson, Joshua Vink, Anthony Wills Jr., Andrew Zimmerman; May 10–June 3

**Spring 2007 Writer/Director Forum** Writers: Anne Dichele, Dina Ross, Julia Martin, Dina Gregory, Celia McBride, Stephanie Timm, Ruth Tyndall Baker, Aphra Behn, Isabella Russell-Ides, Dianna A. Lewis, Jen Klein, William Shakespeare; Directors: Chanda Calentine, Mariana Carbonell, Rose Ginsberg, Emily Gipson, Jacquelyn Honeybourne, Rachel Klein, Julia Martin, Danya Nardi, Emily Plumb, Maureen Rogalski, Nikki Rothenberg, Aliza Shane, Elizabeth Sturrus, Erin Winebark; June 7–July 1

**Non-resident Productions**

**The Most Fabulous Story Ever Told** by Paul Rudnick; July 27–30

**Weasel Erotica** by King Talent; presented by Baby Hippotamus Productions; Director, Melissa Jo Talent; Cast: Tony King, Amy Kersten, King Talent, Matt "Mo" Talent, Rebecca Sponseller, Jeremy Sykes, Anne McDaniels, Jennifer Sandella; Kimi Winkler; August 4–27

**Circles** by Joseph Byrne; presented by Beyond Skin Theatre Company; Director, Stephen Francis; Cast: Joseph Byrne, Gina dos Santos; September 5–30

**The End of Civilization** by George F. Walker; Director, Alan Langdon; Cast: Michael Healy, Christina Pastor, Jeff Todesco, Corby Proctor, Stacey Kelleher; November 9–19

# Manhattan Repertory Theatre

Ken Wolf, Artistic Director

**Summerfest** included: *Identity* by and featuring Nicholas Linnehan, directed by Ken Wolf, with Sarah Giller, Peter Quinones; *Listerine-a-Strada* written & directed by Tracy Walsch, Amanda Cronk, & Jedidiah Clarke, with Elizabeth Blue, Jedidiah Clarke, Amanda Cronk, Jared Robinson, Jennie Slentz, Paul Snyder, Tracy Walsch; *Sitting on the Edge of the World* directed by Damon Krometis, with Toni Mayo, Melanie Lefebvre, Dan Chen; *RPG* by William Andrew Horn, directed by Jessie Lyn Jarosz, with Punam Bean, John Bodycombe, Meg O'Brien, Kevin Coyle, John Dillon, Billy Horn, Melissa Howes, Cameron J. Oro, Jaimee Segars; *In the Floodplain* by Jacob M. Appel, directed by Rosalie Purvis, with Kathy Devine, Robert Harrington, Russell Kerr, Juliet O'Brien; *Walking on Eggshells* written & performed by Deborah Johnstone, directed by Mary Lee Kellerman; *Conversations with Dog* written & directed by Ken Wolfe, with Anthony J. Ribustello, Jamie Watson, Amber Jean Koerner; *Animum Reflectere, Rachel Must Die* by & featuring Christopher Albate, directed by Jesse Martinez, with Chelsie Castillo, Beverly Lauchner, Ryan Stone, Craig Peugh; *Cherubina* by Paul Cohen, directed by Rebecca Lingafelter, with Laura Heidinger, Teddy Bergman; *Confessions of a Catholic Girl* written & performed by Julia Bugnacki, directed by Ilona Pierce; *Broken Boulevard* by Rudy Cecera; *The Practical Application of Forbidden Fruit* by and feauring David Jeffers, with Kristen Albanese, Renee Brown, Jim deProphetis; *Absent-Minded Gay Angel* by Jessie Lyn Jarosz, directed by Peter Mussared, with Michelle Federico, Jose Laureiro; *Identity Crisis* by Kevin Chew, directed by Arthur An, with Christopher Wang, Melanie Maras, Kevin Smart, Sarah Bernier; *In the Open* by Angela Liao, directed by Don Nguyen, with Vera Miao, Mami Kimura, Shaka Malik; *Finding Elizabeth Taylor* by Becki Heller & Elizabeth Claire Taylor, directed by Tatiana Gomberg, with Elizabeth Claire Taylor; *Carrie and Lil* by Sara Jeanne Asselin, directed by Jessica Franz, with Sari Kamin, Ramona Floyd, Ann Margaret Hollyman, Alton Clemente; *Woody and the Herb* by Bill Barnett, directed by James Jaworski, with Pete Barker, Stewart Schneck; *Telling Yourself It Doesn't Matter* written, directed and featuring Marlene Rhein, with Will Schmincke, Marcella Anise Smith, Stephanie Bush; July 1–August 12

**Fall One-Act Play Festival** included: *Muse* by William Andrew Horn; *Eating Mimi* by Liza Lentini; *The Office* by Kate Hoffower; *Wristbands* by Maureen McSherry; *Piñata* by Zach Messner; *Platonic* by Rudy Cecera; *The Sunshine Foundation for the Arts* by Sara Jeanne Asselin; *Comfort* by Keith Glass; *Always* by Angel Dillemuth; *There's Always a Band* by Isaac Rathbone; *Hallelujah Illinois* by Rachel Wahl; *Clash and Learn* by Ervon Neely; *Realer Than That* by Kitt Loroie; *Damaged Dancers* by Marjorie Suvalle; *Customer Service* by Marlene Rhein & Jennifer Ostrega; *Promiscuity: The One Night Stand Chronicles* by Kassandra Vaughn Harper; *Stuck* by Motry Tomycz; September 27–October 15

**Winterfest** included: *Sensory* by Lucas Hewit; *For You* by Josh Drimmer, directed by Constance Thackaberry, with Holly Ellis, Brian W. Seibert; *The Lead* by Rudy Cecera, directed by Bernard Etienne, with Rudy Cecera, Laura D'Amico, Rosie Mattia, Rachel Holmes, Allison Hirschlag, Jiffy Reed, Kat Garson, Steven Viola; *Perfidia* by Steve Kalvar; *Rachel Must Die* by & featuring Christopher Albate, with Tim Mele, Craig Peugh, Bernadette York; *The King in Yellow* by Duke York; *The Family Abortionist* by Lena Moy-Borgen, directed by Patty Montesi, with Courtney Reed, Eve Gibson, Dan Rabinowitz, Miranda Kahn; *A Rabbi in the Attic* by Jack A. Churilla; *If Condition* by Aaron Carter, directed by Carolina Conte, with Adam Perabo, Ashley Goerhring, Nick Pavlik, Erinn Ruth; *Seconds* by Stephen Lemay; *Bordertown* by Steve Ives, directed by Tom Berger, with Gerard Adimando, Cary Hite, Marta Kuersten, Ron Kuriloff, Michael Littner, Daniel Marmion, Kasey Williams, Clara Wong, Kyle Zingler; *The Jilting of Granny Weatherall* by Barbara Lifton, directed by Gloria Zelaya, with Barbara G. Lifton, Meghan Burke, Tom Cox, Carolina McNeely, Jacob Pinion; *And Young Men Die* by Bill Hammond, directed by Shay Lyn Zanotti, with Jerome McIntosh, Mark Cirnigliare, Sarah Himmelstein, Tosh Marks, Julian Schrenzel; February 7–March 24

**Pop** by Liza Lentini; Cast: Dale Davidson, Mollie Lohinski, Scott MacKenzie, Shashanah Newman, Rick Plaugher, Antony Raymond, Christopher Van Jura; in rep with **Brothers** by Angel Dillemuth and **Shades of Gray** by Felix Otero; April 4–7

**Spring One-Act Festival** included: *Am I Blue?* by Beth Henley, directed by Esther Barlow; Cast: Lara Gold, Gregory Loy; *Special Talents* by Jeannine Coulombe, with Kristen Shea; *Oblivious* written & directed by Dennis Hurley; Cast: Christel Ferguson, James Clifton Huffman, Amy Liszka; *Taz* by Patrick Brian Scherrer; *An Apology for the Play Suicidal Algorithms* by Jason Cutler; Cast: Michael Ashley Harkins, Alice Onco, Sherri Quaid, Nathan Riley, Billy Robinson; *Shy* by Ken Wolf; April 18–21

**All Women Are Crazy, All Men Are Assholes** written & directed by Nick Dujnic; Cast: Cait Doyle, Steve Laferriere, Nick Nerio; in rep with **Everybody Dies in February** by Vanessa Bombardieri; Director, Rosalie Purvis; Music/ Additional Text, James David Jacobs; May 9–12

**American Audition** an Audtion Reality Show; Host: Rudy Cecera; Finalists: Naomi Austin, Amanda Goodman, Sydette Harry, Sarah Paige; April 27, May 5, May 19

### Non-resident Production

**All for One** by Paul Weitz; presented by Due North Theatre Company; Director, Jeremy Colgan; Cast: Beth Briley, Israel Vuffardi, Ryan Christopher, Candice Holdorf, Greg Waits; June 21–25

# Manhattan Theatre Source

**6969** by Jordan Seavey; presented by CollaborationTown; Set, Geoffrey Decas; Costumes, Leon Debkowski; Lighting, Laurel Happel; Sound, Brandon Wolcott; Cast: Jessica Avellone, Terri Gabriel, Julia Henderson, Boo Killebrew, Ryan Purcell, Max Rosenak, Jordan Seavey, Dan Stowell, Phillip Taratula, T.J. Witham; June 1–3

**Brother, Mine** written & directed by Eric C. Dente and k.c. keene; presented by Watermark Ensemble; Cast: Frank Harris, Donald Rizzo, April Ortiz, James Patrick Early, Brian Anthony Wilson; June 18–20

**It Isn't the Moon** by Christina Fragola; presented by Red Wall Productions; Director, Rosalyn Coleman Williams; Cast: Pennie Diamond Quintana, Yvette Ganier, Ian White; June 14–29

**Faces...Voices** by Doreen Perrine; Director, Miriam Eusebio; July 2–4 (performed at WOW Café Theatre from August 17–26)

**Flying Dreams** written & directed by Sharon Fogarty; presented by Making Light; Accompanist; Peter Dizozza; Lighting/Sound, Matt Quint; Cast: Pete Aguero, Sharon Fogarty, Matthew Porter; July 19–29

**Move It!** presented by Parallel Exit; Design, Steve Lucas; Cast: Mike Dobson, Mark Lonergan, Joel Jeske, Brent McBeth, Derek Roland, Ryan Kasprzak; September 11–12

**Estrogenius Festival** 7th annual; September 20–October 14; Week 1 (produced by Fiona Jones): *Bridal Suite* by George Hunka; *Screwballs* by Joan Murray; *A Place for Owls* by Fiona Jones; *Mescalito* by Lucy Boyle; *Loose Girls & Screwdrivers* by Catherine Zambri; Week 2 (produced by Jennifer Gordon Thomas); *Avarice Fantasy* by Miriam Eusebio; *Nu Shu* by Thomas H. Diggs; *Detention* by Maura Kelley; *Decoding Fruit* by Molly Smith Metzler; *Percentages* by Julie Perkins; Week 3 (produced by Shoshona Currier): *Arms* by Bekah Brunstetter; *Cave Krewe* by Kara Corthron; *Night Train* by Gena Acosta; *The Party* by Lynne McMahon; *Triage* by Sharyn Rothstein; Week 4 (produced by Tegan Meyer): *The Doubtful Dead* by

Mercedes Sanchez; *Eleanor* by Julia Dwyer Sullivan; *The Morning After* by Wendy Castor; *The Monotone Poncho Spatula* by Mya Kagan; *The Chicken and the Egg* by Shelly Mazzanoble; Solo Shows September 30: *Free and Compulsory* by Vivian LaRouche; *Under the Overalls: Stories of a Dresser Unraveled* by Kimberly Prentice; *Dad & Me* by Heather Aldridge; *Cracking Composure* by Kat Katsanis; *Good at That* by Leslie Pasternack; *Still Waters* by Valerie Gilbert; *Jews Don't Join the Circus* by Beth Bongar; *Considering in CT* by Adele Bruni; Solo Shows October 14: *Dirty Girl* by Harrison David Rivers performed by Rebecca Simone Stein; *Shirley on the Plane* by Amanda Ronconi; *That First Winter* by Richard Ballon performed by Cheryl King; *Walking on Eggshells* by Deborah Johnstone; *Left* by Jo Hudson; *Malleus, Incus, Stapes* by Claire McCague; *Spleen* by Michelle Maryk; *Remedies* by Julie Kline; *Bawdy and Soul* by Jane Aquilina

**In Public** by George Hunka; Director, Isaac Butler; Cast: Daryl Lathon, Abe Goldfarb, Jennifer Gordon Thomas, Ronnica V. Reddick, Brian Silliman; October 24–28

**Recreating Keiter: I Saw Dad Make the Whole Thing Up** written & performed by Cindy Keiter; presented by Bridge Club Productions; Director, Padraic Lillis; November 1–18

**As Long a Time as a Long Time Is in Longtime Land** by Todd Pate; Director, Barbara Suter; Cast: Todd Pate, Aaron Slavik; November 27–December 2

**Hot Damn Holiday!** presented by GroundUp Productions; Director, Dan Marzollo; Producers, Kate Middleton, Dan Wheeless; Stage Manager, Devan Hibbard; Lighting, Travis McHale; Cast: David DiAngelo, Amy Heidt, Kate Middleton, Guy Olivieri; December 6–16

**MacBeth: A Walking Shadow** adapted and dramaturge by Doug Silver, co-adapted and directed by Andrew Frank; Lighting, Steven Arnold; Sound, Andrew Bellware; Stage Manager, Laura Schlactmeyer; Cast: Ato Essandoh, Lou Carbonneau, Celia Schaefer, Meghan Reilly, Chuck Bunting, Michael Baldwin, Len Childers, Amy Dickenson, James Edward Becton, Ridley Parson, Lex Woutas; January 5–27

**The Sandman** by E.T.A. Hoffmann, adapted by Casey VanWormer; presented by Project: Theater; Director, Kevin Dodd; Stage Manager, Tzipora Kaplan; Design, Ryan Dodd; Choreography, Erin Malley; Cast: Jason Yachanin, Dina Percia, Cate Bottiglione, Matthew A.J. Gregory, Joe Jung, Brian Frank; January 7–9

**Corn Bread and Feta Cheese: Growing Up Fat and Albanian** written & performed by Elza Zagreda; presented by Rocky from the Bronx Productions; February 1–3

**Sacred Hearts** two plays presented by Teatro Oscuro & Present Tense Productions; PSM, Renato Espinoza; included: *The Love Song of Eleanor Purdy* by Germaine Netzband, directed by Michael Raimondi; Cast: Katie Tuminelly, Kim Blair, Robert B. Cordell; February 7–10; *The Truth About Love* by Susannah Nolan, directed by Christine Simpson; Cast: Nancy Nagrant, Joel Brady, Melissa Briggs, Ivanna Cullinan; February 14–17

**Coming or Going** by Lisa Roth; presented by Pretty Little Heads; Director, Leslie Cloninger; Stage Manager, Irene Carroll; Lighting, Kia Rogers; Cast: Amy Dickenson, Tracey B. Wilson, Amanda Hilson, Shannon Yocum, Chris Blessit; February 21–March 10

**Burn This** by Lanford Wilson; presented by GroundUp Productions; Director, Laura Standley; Stage Manager, Devan Hibbard; Cast: Kevin Connell, Anna Fitzwater, Michael Schantz, Victor Verhaeghe; March 14–24

**Clinically Negative (A Viral Comedy)** by Sam Forman, Billy Eichner, Annie Baker, Beau Willimon; presented by mCenterprises; Director, Portia Krieger; Cast: Melissa Firlit, Wil Petre, Shawn Dempewolf, Caroline Slaughter, Megan Messmer; March 26–31

**A Lie of the Mind** by Sam Shepard; Director, Daryl Boling; Music, Minetta Creek; Lighting, Stephen Arnold; Costumes, Michael Bevins; Cast: Todd D'Amour, Hank Davies, Campbell Echols, Cindy Keiter, Emily Mitchell, Ridley Parson, Laura Schwenninger, Jeff Willis; April 4–28

**States of Exception** and **In Private** two plays by George Hunka; Cast: Jason Howard, Abby Royle, Jennifer Gordon Thomas; April 15–17

**A Coupla White Chicks Sitting Around Talking** by John Ford Noonan; Set, David Roman & Ed McNamee; Costumes, Julie Perkins; Sound, Drew Bellware; Stage Manager, Irene Carroll; Director, Steven Bloom; Cast. Monica Russell, Nancy Sirianni; May 9–26

**Genius Andronicus** by Lynda Green; Director, Melissa Firlit; May 5

# The Medicine Show Theatre Ensemble

Barbara Vann, Artistic Director

**The Happiest Girl in the World** book by Fred Saidy & Henry Myers, music by Jacques Offenbach, lyrics by E.Y. Harburg, based on *Lysistrata* by Aristophanes; Director, Barbara Vann; Choreography, Ernesta Corvino, Michael Dion, Stelios Manolakakis; Fights, Linda Lutes; Music Diretor/Pianist, Michael Dion; Set, Paul Gugliotta; Costumes, Uta Bekaia; Lighting, Kia Rogers; Cast: Mark J. Dempsey, Ray Bendana, Sven Salumaa, Kip Potharas, Mark Gering, Cedric Jones, Ilona Farkas, Mary-Ellen Hickey, Jonathan Roufaeal, Samuel H. Perwin, Sarah Engelke, Rachel Black, Amanda Hargrove, Andrea Pinyan, Sky Seals, Nique Haggerty; November 17–December 17

**The Balcony** by Jean Genet; Director, Barbara Vann; Cast: Karen Amatrading, Sara Copeland, Mark Dempsey, Sean Dill, Ron Dreyer, Ilona Farkas, Mark Gering, Felix Gadron, Lauren LoGiudice, Louise Martin, Tassos Pappas, Charles J. Roby, Jose Ramon, Jonathan Roufaeal, Peter Schmitz, Barbara Vann; March 29–April 21

### Non-resident Productions

**One Nation Under** by Andrea Lepcio; presented by At Hand Theatre Company; Director, Tye Blue; Set, Nathan Elsener; Lighting, Josh Starr; Costumes, Michelle Andre; Sound, Nathan Leigh; Stage Manager, Sarah Ripper; Cast: Adrienne Hurd, Toks Olagundoye, Peter Reznikoff, Christopher Abbott, Chrystal Stone, J'nelle Bobb-Semple; August 9–26

**Hurt So Good** written & directed by Johnny Blaze Leavitt; presented by Point of You Productions; Co-director, Suse Sternkopf; Set, Gerard J. Savoy; Costumes, Karron Karr; Fights, Nicole Godino; Production Supervisor, Marc Adam Smith; Cast: Maggie Cino, Jessie J. Fahay, Marlise Garde, Sonia Gardea. Hailey Giles, Nicole Godino, Cedric Jones, Chris Keating, Amy Kersten, Tehila Kronfeld, Johnny Blaze Leavitt, Doralyn Leone, Alyssa Mann, Perryn Pomatto, Minna Richardson, Gerard J. Savoy, Marc Adam Smith, Courtney Tisch, Tina Trimble Savoy, Felicia Eugenia Velasco, Paul Weissman; August 31–September 16

**Twenty Years of Agnes** by Juan Riquelme, directed and adapted by Camilo Fontecilla; presented by Pandora's Box & Shalimar Productions; Cast: Debra Kay Anderson, Jacquelyn Poplar, Atticus Rowe; September 29–October 22

**Horowitz: The Acrobat at Rest** by Stelios Manolakakis; presented by Princess Kisses Theatre Group; Director, Elias Kasman; Costumes, Viviane Galloway; Lighting, Susan Nicholson; Cast: Stellios Manolakakis, Alyssa Simon; January 26–February 17

**The House of Yes** by Wendy Macleod; presented by Theatre Rats; Director, Lauren Reinhard; Set, Alexis Hadsall; Lighting, Michael Guglioti; Costumes, David Withrow; Stage Manager, Marta Tejada; Cast: Christina Brucato, Sarah Burns, Nick Mitchell, Gerry Sheridan, Zac Springer; April 26–May 5

# Metropolitan Playhouse

Alex Roe, Artistic Director; Michael Bloom, Associate Artistic Director

**East Village Chronicles Volume 3: The Notable and The Notorious** seven new plays, included: *Bentl Briv* by Michael Bettencourt; *Nonnie* by Alberto Bonilla; *Flight* by Renee Flemings; *Peter Stuyvesant* by Stephen O'Rourke; *Lucky* by Anthony P. Pennino; *Boss* by Adrian Rodriguez; *Father's Name Was Daddy* by Trav S. D.; Directors: Anne Beaumont, Alberto Bonilla, Sidney Fortner, Anthony P. Pennino; Cast: Wendy Allegaert, John Blaylock, Ian Eaton, Benjamin Scott Grimes, Shellen Kostabi, Robert Kya-Hill, Allison Lane, Marty McDonough, Eric Troy Miller, Stu Richel; June 22–July 2

**The Octoroon** by Dion Boucicault; Director/Set, Alex Roe; Costumes, Melisa Estro; Lighting, Erin Lapham; Cast: Leo Dobson, Alia Chapman, Alex Ubokudom, Tryphena Wade, Justin Stevens, Michael Hardart, Wendy Merritt, Mike Durkin, Margaret Loesser Robinson, Ray McDavitt, Sarah Hankins, David Lamb, Arthur Acuna, John Rengstorff, Andrew Clateman; September 29–October 29

**The Truth** by Clyde Fitch; Director, Yvonne Conybeare; Cast: Shanara Gabrielle, Peter Reznikoff, Christy McIntosh, Jeff Pucillo, Rob Skolits, Amy Smith, Rene Becker, Evan Palazzo; November 10–December 10

**Twainathon** works by or about Mark Twain; included: *Huck Finn* adapted by N. G. McClernan; *The War Prayer* adapted by Michael Durkin; Extracts from *Adam's Diary* adapted by Anthony P. Pennino; *The Report of My Death* by Adam Klasfeld; *The Californian's Tale* adapted by Andrew Firda; *Henry's Lunchroom* by Dan Evans; *An Inconvenient River* by Laura Livingston; *The Man Who Corrupted Hadleyburg* adapted by Michael Bettencourt; *Anhedonia Road* adapted by Chris Harcum; *Fennimore Cooper's Literary Offenses* read by Mikel Sarah Lambert; *A Marvelous Curiosity* compiled by Jeremy X. Halpern; *The Hadleyburg Project* music by Adam Cohen, book & lyrics by Kevin Laub; *beTwixt, beTween & beTWAIN* music, lyrics and adaptation, Danny Ashkenasi; January 15–28

**André** by William Dunlop; Director, Elfin Frederick Vogel; Set, Tilman Schall; Costumes, Lillian Rhiger; Lighting, Christopher Studley; Stage Manager Anthony Long; Cast: Sebastian Conybeare, Kathleen Dobbs, Lee Dobson, Chris Harcum, Ronald Roy Johnson Jr., Shane Colt Jerome, Jacob C. Mirer, Nicholas Richberg, Suzanne Savoy, Joseph Yeargain, March 2–April 1

**Denial** by Peter Sagal; Director, Alex Roe; Lighting, Maryvel Bergen; Costumes, Melissa Estro; Stage Manager, Ernesto Espinoza; Cast: Suzanne Toren, Alia Shakira Chapman, H. Clark Kee, Michael James Anderson, Martin Novemsky, John Tobias; April 13–May 13

**East Village Chronicles Volume 4** eight new plays; included: *60 Guilders Worth* by Anthony P. Pennino; *Stars Over the East Village* by Nathanael Chura; *Unresolved* by Page Hearn; *Apologies to Vietnam* by C. S. Hanson; *The Old New World* by J. P. Chan; *Parkhurst's Descent* by Trav S.D.; *Triangles Everywhere* by Kimberly Wadsworth; *Quiet Howl* by Laura Livingston; *Age of Discovery* by Carlos Jerome; *Sheila Mom* by Richard Sheinmel; Cast: Brian Coats, Andrew Firda, G. R. Johnson, Shelleen Kostabi, Christopher Lukas, Jo Mei, Wendy Merritt, Shaundra Noll, Rob Skolits, Amy Smith, Debargo Sanya; May 31–June 17

Dan Carbone in Kingdom of Not, *presented at Cherry Lane's Studio Theatre (photo by John Sowle)*

Laurence Lau and Michael Gabriel Goodfriend in Bank Street Theatre's Arrivals *(photo by Claudia Mandlik*

Chad Hoeppner and Matthew Mabe in Scituate, *presented by Outcast Productions (photo by Charlie Anderson)*

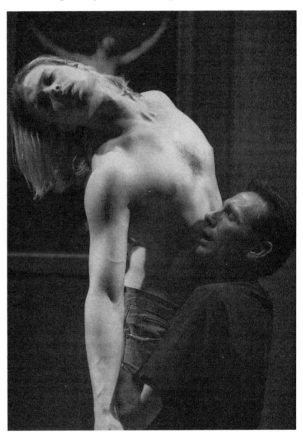

Brandon Ruckdashel and Stephen Hope (back) in Ascension, *presented at the Lion Theatre on Theatre Row (photo by Marc Geller)*

Left: *Jennifer Gill, Justin Plowman, and Amy Overman in* Bite, *presented by Dysfunctional Theatre Company, The John Montgomery Theatre Company and Horse Trade Theater Group at the Red Room (photo by Scott Wynn)*

## Michael Chekhov Theatre Company

Michael Horn, Producing Artistic Director

**Sam Shepard Festival** at the Big, Little Theatre; *When the World Was Green* co-written by Joseph Chaikin, directed by Carol Kastendieck; Music, Woody Regan; Cast: Peter J. Coriaty, Alia Tarraf, Larry Chertoff (June 5–27); *Geography of a Horse Dreamer* directed by Ann Bowen; Cast: Tim Scott, Brian Tracy, Peter Picard, David Elyha, Tom Pavey, Will Schnieder, Mark Stevens; on a double bill with: *Chicago* directed by Tom Amici; Cast: Tim Scott, Liz Sanders, Mark Stevens, Kate Campbell, Kristin Carter, Will Schnieder, Jason Kalus (June 14–July 14); *Angel City* directed by Alisha Silver (June 19–July 11); *Savage Love* co-written by Joseph Chaikin, directed by Jason Kalus; Cast: Jessica Jade Andres, Larry Gutman, Jordan Kamp, Sheila O'Toole, Mary Van Fleet, Becky Lake, Jared Morgenstern; on a triple bill with: *The 4-H Club* directed by Guilherme Parreiras; Cast: Michael Smith Rivera, Vance Clemente, Armand Anthony; and: *The Rock Garden* directed by Alisha Silver; Cast: Thomas Francis Murphy, Duvall O'Steen, J. Robert Zanfardino (August 2–31); *Forensic and the Navigators* directed by Tom Amici; Cast: Ali Costine, Tim Scott, Mark Stevens, Drew Zechman, Matt Bralow; on a double bill with: *States of Shock* directed by Joe Benenati; Cast: Steve Abbruscato, Aaron Firicano, Natalie Barback, Julie Finch, Allen Magnus (September 13–October 6, revived December 14–21); *Shaved Splits* directed by Jason King Jones; Cast: Darcie Champagne, Michael Mason, Doua Moua, Toshi Nakayama, Josh Painting, Samuel H. Perwin (September 24–October 26); *Seduced* directed by Joe Zarro; Cast: Amy Cassel Taft, Vance Clemente, Michael Smith Rivera, Hannah Snyder-Beck (October 22–November 19); *True West* (first production) directed by Ann Bowen; Cast: Peter Picard, Tom Pavey, Mark Stevens, Frieda Lipp (November 22–January 5); *The Unseen Hand* directed by Tom Amici; Cast: Brian Lee Elder, Jason Griffith, Brian Tracy, Stew Miller, Parker Croft; presented on a double bill with: *Back Bog Beast Bait* directed by Alisha Silver; Cast: Brian Lee Elder, Will Schneider, Sylvia Osei, Rel Lavizzo, Donald Lauer (November 26–December 18); *True West* (second production); Director, Jason King Jones; Cast: Tom Amici, Tim Scott, James Pravasilis, Julie Finch (January 9–31); *The God of Hell* directed by Jeffrey Stanley; Cast: Danton Bankay, Bret Haines, Steve Kelly, Susie Abraham (January 14–February 11)

**Happy Hour, the Show: Sex, Relationships & Sometimes Love** by Joelle Arqueros, adapted and directed by Michael Horn; Cast: Missy Buser, Sarah Ashley Cerullo, Gio Crisafulli, Matthew Gologor, Amber Jean Koerner, Joshua Levine, Zach Lombardo, Meghan Reilly, Chala Savino, Tim Scott, Margot Staub; Opened April 1, 2006, still running

**Bad Evidence** by Terry Quinn; Director, Louis Lopardi; Cast: Thomas Francis Murphy, Duvall O'Steen; September 13–October 5

**'night Mother** by Marsha Norman; Director, Max McGuire; Cast: Leslye Anderson, Evangeline Johns; October 26–November 14

## Michael Weller Theatre

**Trojan Women 2.0** by Charles Mee; presented by Milk Can Theatre Company; Director, Lauren Reinhard; Set, Carrie Mossman; Lighting, Michael Guglioti; Costumes, David Withrow; Sound/Music, Nick Moore; Stage Manager, Christine Vartoughian; Cast: Daniel Smith, Deborah Friedman, Elizabeth Days, Jennifer Cintron, Jessica Newton, Joe Sevier, Michael McGuire, Kenneth L. Naanep, Lindsay Drew, Mary Ellen Toomey, Mary Greenawalt, Michelle Miller, Nia Renee Hill, Satomi Blair, Teresa Wentzell, Malachy Orozco; September 9–24

**The Uncertainty Principle** by Bethany Larsen; presented by Milk Can Theatre Company; Director, Julie Fei-Fan Balzer; Cast: Lauren Gleason, Casey McClellan, Tim Downey, Judy Chestnut, Chris Kloko; September 9–24

**The Heart of My Mystery: The Hamlet Project** adapted by Barbara Bosch & Mark Ringer; Director, Barbara Bosch; Composer, Brian Hurley; Cast: Peter Husovsky, Maeve Maguire, Bob Adrian, Bryan Webster, Natasha Pillchik, Rand Mitchell, James Cleveland, Antonio Suarez, Chip Persons, Mark Ringer; October 12–29

**Loose Knit** by Theresa Rebeck; Director, Douglas S. Hall; Cast: Kathryn Gerhardt, Lisa Riegel, Hollie Hunt, Betty McKinley, Laura DiCerto, Michael Edmund, Brian Parker; March 28–April 1

**Growing Pretty** written & directed by Carey Crim; presented by Write Club NYC; Cast: Brandon Bales, Tim Barker, Jenny Burleson, Timothy Flynn, David Sajadi, Carrie Yeager; April 13–28

**The Potluck Plays** presented by Milk Can Theatre Company; included: *Answering* written & directed by Tom Nondorf; *Eggnogstic* by Bethany Larsen, directed by Ryan Ratelle; *PUNCH* written & directed by M.L. Kinney; *Swimming Uptown* by Cheryl Davis, Directed by Jill Landaker; *Salad Days* by Julie Fei-Fan Balzer, directed by Kimberly VerSteeg; *The Cooking King* by Sharon E. Cooper, Directed by Riv Massey; *The Potato Play* written & directed by Melissa Fendell; Cast: Antonia Barba, Satomi Blair, Chris Catalano, Tessa Faye, Candice Fortin, Jean Goto, Jason Griffith, Chris Kloko, Marta Kuerston, Liz Maestri, Steve Maruzzelli, Matthew Murumba, Amira Nader, Shayna Padovano, Brian Pracht, Cynthia Rice, Matt Stapleton, Sonja Sweeney, Adia Tucker, Baris Tuncer, Kirsten Walsh; May 3–13

**Dinner with Friends** by Donald Margulies; Director, Rob O'Neill; May 20–June 2

## Midtown International Theatre Festival

John Chatterton, Founder and Executive Producer; 7th annual; July 17–August 6; Venues included the WorkShop Theatre Mainstage and Jewel Box; Where Eagles Dare Theatre and Studio

*Absence* by Kimberly Patterson; *AfterWords* by Marcus Davidson, Dena Douglass, and Edward Musto; *The Answer Is Horse* by Joya Scott, directed by Julia Holleman; *Countdown* by Vincent Caruso, directed by Jerry Mond; *Das Brat* written & directed by Eric Bland; *Fleeing Katrina* by Rob Florence, directed by Mary Lee Kellerman; *The Girls Of Summer* by Layon Gray; *In A Bucket Of Blood* by John Kearns, directed by Michael Mellamphy; *Invisible Child* by Lisa Barri, directed by Brad Raimondo; *It Is What It Is* by Cinda Lawrence; *Jewish By Injection Only* by Michael Stockman; *Jews Don't Join The Circus* by Beth Bongar; *LOL* by Tony Sportiello, directed by Jerry Less; *Love, Punky* by Robin Hopkins; *The Maternal Instinct* by Monica Bauer, directed by Melissa J. Wentworth; *MentalPause* by Margaret Liston; *Motion And Location* by Lorna Littleway, directed by Sue Lawless; *The Mistake Presents 'Muggy'; Pie Obsessed Drunken Fatties* by Julie Perkins and Marjorie Suvalle; *Props* by Michael Roderick; *The Quiet Model* by L.A. Mitchell, directed by Chelsea Miller; *Remuda* by William Donnelly, directed by Tzipora Kaplan; *Sex & Sealing Wax* by Romy Nordlinger; *Shoot The Dog* by Brittany Rostron, directed by Dennis X. Tseng; *The Siblings* by Edward Elefterion; *The Sit-Down Show* by Desiree Burch; *Stars In My Eyes* by Edward Field, adapted by Michael Boothroyd; *STICKY GIRLS* by Linda Evans, directed by Constance George; *The Sunny Side Of The Street/A Mouth Full Of Water* by Estelle Campagna and Tessa Fontaine; *Surgery* by Karin Diann Williams; *Taxi Stories* by David O'Shea; *Tokyo Vampire* by Dwayne Lawler; *The Turtle Tattoo* by Jonathan Wallace; *Unveiled & Warning Signs* by Michele Cuomo and Maggie Surovell; *Wake Of The Essex* by Lou Rodgers; *The Wastes Of Time* by Duncan Pflaster, directed by David Gautschy; *Where Three Roads Meet* by John Carter, directed by Will Warren; *Who Will Sing For Lena* by Dr. Janice Liddell, PhD.

## Musicals Tonight!

Mel Miller, Producer and Artistic Director

**Me and My Girl** book & lyrics by L. Arthur Rose & Douglas Furber, book revised by Stephen Fry, music by Noel Gay; Director/Choreography, Thomas Mills; Music Director, James Stenborg; Cast: Renee Barnett, Patrick Boyd, Robyn S. Clark, John Alban Coughlan, Michelle Liu Coughlin, Lydia Gladstone, Christopher Guilmet, Annette Hunt, George S. Irving, Liliane Klein, Patrick Maubert, Jeff McLean, Trista Moldovan, Jonathan Osborne, Robyne Parrish, Roger Rifkin, B.J. Scahill, Jacob R. Thompson; McGinn/Cazale Theatre; October 23–November 5

**Shinbone Alley** book & lyrics by Joe Darion, book by Mel Brooks, music by George Leinsinger, based on the stories of George Kleinsinger; Director/Choreography, Thomas Mills; Music Director, Rick Hip-Flores; Cast: Kim Brownell, Erik McEwen, Thursday Farrar, Elena Gutierrez, Gene Jones, Trent Armand Kendall, Lisa Marie Morabito, Val Moranto, Kwame Michael Remy, Leajato Amara Robinson, Justin Sayre, Allyson Tucker, Lee Zarrett; McGinn/Cazale Theatre; November 7–19

**The Happy Time** book by N. Richard Nash, lyrics by Fred Ebb, music by John Kander; Director, Thomas Mills; Music Director, James Stenborg; Cast: Larry Daggett, Annie Edgerton, David Geinosky, George S. Irving, Andy Jobe, Michael Masters, Lauren Mufson, Rachel Alexa Norman, Charly Seamon, Sarah Solie, Timothy Warmen, Michael Wolland; McGinn/Cazale Theatre; March 6–18

**Ernest in Love** book by Anne Croswell, music by Lee Pockriss, lyrics by Anne Cross; based on *The Importance of Being Earnest* by Oscar Wilde; Director/Choreography, Thomas Mills; Music Director, Bill Stanley; Cast: Melissa Bohon, Selby Brown, Sarah Dacey Charles, Jody Cook, Nick Dalton, Kathryn Feeney, Blake Hackler, Michael Jennings, Robert Anthony Jones, Katherine McClain, Lauren Molina, Roger Rifkin, William Ryall, Deborah Jean Templin, Joseph Torello; McGinn/Cazale Theatre; March 20–April 1

**Irene** book by Hugh Wheeler & Joseph Stein, music by Harry Tierney, lyrics by Joseph McCarthy, additional lyrics & music by Charles Gaynor & Otis Clements; Director, Thomas Mills; Music Director, James Stenborg; Cast: Richard Barth, Selby Brown, Marnie Buckner, Jacque Carnahan, Janet Carroll, Jody Cook, Kellie Drinkhahn, Jillian Louis, Michael Jennings Mahoney, Katherine McClain, Laura Pavell, Patrick Porter, Justin Sayre, Micah Sheppard, Jendi Tarde; McGinn/Cazale Theatre; April 17–29

## New Federal Theatre

Woodie King Jr., Artistic Director

**The Taking of Miss Janie** by Ed Bullins; Director, Shuneille Perry; Choreography, Chiquita Ross; Cast: Alia Chapman, Lee Gundersheimer, Garrett lee Hendricks, Royce Johnson, Kate Russell; Abrons Arts Center Experimental Theatre at Henry Street Settlement; November 30–December 23

**Ntozake Shange: A Retrospective** included *Bookie Woogie Landscape, A Photograph: Lovers in Motion, From Okra to Greens/A Different Kind of Love Story, It Hasn't Always Been This Way, Laila's Dream,* and Shange's adaptation of Brecht's *Mother Courage*; Abrons Arts Center at Henry Street Settlement & the Castillo Theatre; February 7–March 4

**Moon on a Rainbow Shawl** by Errol John; presented with the Caribbean American Repertory Theatre; Director, Shirley Parkinson-Wright; Cast: Lola Loui, Erwin E.A. Thomas, Lincoln Brown, David Heron, Najah Johnson, Carla Brothers, Kim Weston-Moran; Abrons Arts Center Recital Hall at Henry Street Settlement; May 10–27

## The New Group (naked)

**Strangers Knocking** by Robert Tenges; Director, Marie Masters; Sets, Peter R. Feuchtwanger; Costumes, Kristine Koury, Lighting, Nicole Pearce; Sound, Bart Fasbender; PSM, Valerie A. Peterson; Stage Manager, Jared Abram DeBacker; Cast: Talia Balsam, Julie Halston, Stella Maeve, Michael Stahl-David, Jonathan Walker; Understudy: Mercer Boffey; Acorn Theatre on Theatre Row; May 14–June 3

**Expats** by Heather Lynn MacDonald; Director Ari Edelson; Sets, Peter R. Feuchtwanger; Costumes, Kristine Koury, Lighting, Nicole Pearce; Sound, Travis Walker; PSM, Jared Abram DeBacker; Stage Manager, Valerie A. Peterson; Assistant Director, James Gittins; Cast: Reiko Aylesworth, James Badge Dale, Jesse Hooker, Jay Klaitz, Matthew Rauch, Taylor Wilcox, Natalia Zvereva; Acorn Theatre on Theatre Row; May 18–June 3

## New Victory Theatre

**Rennie Harris' NY Legends of Hip-Hop** October 6–22; **Little Donkey** presented by Theater Terra (Amsterdam, Netherlands); October 27–November 5; **Speedmouse: The Worst of the Umbilical Brothers** presented by The Umbilical Brothers (Sydney, Australia); November 10–26; **Circus Oz: The Laughing at Gravity Tour** presented by Circus Oz (Melbourne, Asurailia); December 1–31; **Lookingglass Alice** adapted from Lewis Carroll; presented by Lookingglass Theatre Company (Chicago); February 9–25; **Dan Zanes and Friends: Catch That Train!** March 2–11; **Lifeboat** by Nicola McCartney; presented by Catherine Wheels Theatre Company (Scotland); March 16–25; **The Number 14** presented by Axis Theatre Company (Vancouver, Canada); March 30–April 15; **Macbeth** by William Shakespeare; presented by Chicago Shakespeare Theater and Colla Marionette Company (Milan, Italy); April 20–29; **Ragamala** presented by Ragamala Music and Dance Theatre (India); May 4–13; **Cirkus Inferno** presented by The Daredevil Opera Company (Ontario, Canada); May 18–June 10

**New Victory Danish Festival** included: *The Attic Under the Sky* (Carte Blance), *Hans Christian Anderson You Must be an Angel* (Gruppe 38), *Elephant and Crocodile* (Corona La Balance), *DIVA* (Sofie Krog Teater); *Songs From Above* (Teater My/Teater Reflesion); Duke on 42nd Street; May 3–13

## New York Classical Theatre

Stephen Burdman, Artistic Director

**All's Well That Ends Well** by William Shakespeare; Director, Jay Skelton; Stage Manager, Jeremy Wilcox; Design, Victoria Tzykun; Voice/Speech Coach, Barbara Adrian; Publicist, Laurie Sheppard; Cast: Elena Araoz, Bob Armstrong, Michael Carlsen, Stewart Carrico, Janis Dardaris, Torsten Hillhouse, Ingrid Kullberg-Bendz, Michael E. Lopez, Vince Nappo, Taylore Mahogany Scott, Jeffrey Woodard; Central Park; June 1–June 25

**Mary Stuart** by Friedrich Schiller; Director, Stephen Burdman; Design Andrea Huelse; Voice/Speech Coach, Pamela Prather; PSM, Jennifer Russo; Publicist, Laurie Sheppard; Cast: William Connell, Sean Hagerty, Patricia Marie Kelley, James Knight, Michael Marion, Bryant Mason, Don Mayo, Mary Jo McConnell, Alex Pappas, Tyler Pierce, Tim Smallwood, Kim Stauffer; Battery Park; July 2–12

**The Comedy of Errors** by William Shakespeare; Director, Stephen Burdman; Design, Jessica Trejos; Voice/Speech Coach, Barbara Adrian; PSM, Jennifer Russo; Publicist, Laurie Sheppard; Cast: Natalie Knepp, Mary Jo McConnell, Michael Marion, Joe Menino, Grant Neale, Shad Ramsey, Max Vogler, Ashley West, Patrick Zeller, Tessa Zugmeyer; August 3–27

## New York International Fringe Festival

Elena K. Holy, Producing Artistic Director; 10th annual; August 11–27; performances at 13th Street Rep, Access Theater, Actors' Playhouse, Center for Architecture, Cherry Lane Studio, CSC, Connelly Theater, Dance New Amsterdam, DR2 Theatre, The Flea, Gene Frankel Theatre, Henry Street Settlement, Linhart Theater @ 440 Studios, Lucille Lortel Theatre, Manhattan Children's Theatre, Mo Pitkin's, Players Loft, Players Theatre, Village Theatre

...categories (a simple play) by Melissa Osborne; Director, Kel Haney; 24 is 10: The Best of The 24 Hour Plays; The 5 Roses of Jennifer by Annibale Ruccello, translated by Silvia Casertano & Sabina Cangiano; Director, Sabina Cangiano; 58! A Comedy About Bike Messengessengering by Tony Mendoza; Director, Pat McKenna; 6x5, le bonheur, a besoin de témoins written and directed by Shelly DeVito; ABSOLUTE FLIGHT: A Reality Show With Wings by Barbara Blumenthal-Ehrlich; Director, Rosemary Andress; Air Guitar by Mac Rogers, music by Sean Williams, lyrics by Jordana Williams; Director, Paul Urcioli; Americana Absurdum by Brian Park; Director, Paul Urcioli; AmericanBlackout written & directed by Robb Leigh Davis; An American Gospel by Ashley Christopher Leach; Director, Laura Klein; Ana 3/11 by Paloma Pedrero, translated by Phyllis Zatlin; Director, Anjali Vashi; Anima by Christiaan Greer; Director, Emily Meisler; Anna and the Annadroids: The Robots Dream Tour by Anatomical Scenario Movement; Director, Anna Sullivan; The Armageddon Dance Party by David L. Williams; Director, Kara-Lynn Vaeni; Aspiration: Housewife written & directed Carolyn Siegel; Co-director, Jessica Bonenfant; Backstage at Da Fonky B written and directed by Alycya K. Miller; Band Geeks: A Halftime Musical by Becky Eldridge & Amy Petersen, music, lyrics & direction by Andrew Eninger; Behind the Sticks by Adam Mervis; Director, Megan Marod; The Bicycle Man book by Dave Lewman, Joe Liss, Mark Nutter & John Rubano, music & lyrics by Mark Nutter; Big Doolie by Richard Thompson; Director, Jenn Thompson; The Big Picture by Andrew Greer; Director, Lexie Pregosin; Billy The Mime written & directed by Billy The Mime; Billy the Mountain and Other American Card Tricks by Striding Lion Ensemble, inspired by Frank Zappa; Director, Amanda Berg; Black Stuff by LeVan D. Hawkins & Alexander Thomas; Director, Kevin Vavasseur; Bloodties by Ned Massey; Director, Catherine Miller Hardy; BLUE BALLS: In & Out of Uniform with the NYPD by Michael Tester; Director, Rye Mullis; The Blue Martini by Michael Ferrell; Director, Jim Wren; Breakfast for Dinner by Isaac Rathbone; Director, Joni Weisfeld; Breathe…Or You Can Die! written & directed by Anna Zastrow; Breeze off the River by Kyle Baxter; Director, Deloss Brown; Broken Hands by Moby Pomerance; Director, Marc Weitz; The Burning Cities Project by The Dreamscape Theatre; Director, Jennifer McGrath; Chess, The Infinite Monkey Project by Drew Brody; The Chrysalis Stage written & directed by Cobey Mandarino; The City That Cried Wolf by Brooks Reeves; Director, Dan Barnes; Claire's Room by Lisa del Rosso; Director, Phil Nicoletti; A Collapse by Vincent Marano; The Complete Lost Works of Samuel Beckett Found In An Envelope… by The Neo-Futurists; Confessions adapted from Phaedra and directed by Dongshin Chang; contra-tiempo Director/Choreography, Ana Maria Alvarez; Corleone: The Shakespearean Godfother written & directed by David Mann; Corps Values by Brendon Bates; Director, Susan W. Lovell; Crazy written & performed by Gail Marlene Schwartz; Directors, Christopher Tebbetts & Suzanne Boisvert; Danny Boy by Marc Goldsmith; Director, Christopher Goodrich; The Day the Universe Came Closer by Hiram Pines; Director, Jessica Porter; Dear America by Michele Aldin; Director, Lauren Rosen; The Deepest Play Ever: The Catharsis of Pathos by Geoffrey Decas, music and lyrics by Michael Wells; Director, Ryan Purcell; The Delicate Business of Boy and Miss Girl by Carly Mensch; Director, Marina McClure; Democrats Abroad by Chris Earle; Director, Shari Hollett; The Devil and Billy Markham by Shel Silverstein, music by Dave Toomey & Paul Urcioli; Director, Paul Urcioli; Dis/Appearing by Betsy Rosen; Co-writer/Director, Eric Van Wyk; Diving Normal by Ashlin Halfnight; Director, Mary Catherine Burke; Don't Ask by Bill Quigley; Director, Mark Stevens; Don't Spit the Water! by Steve Gadlin & Paul Luikart; Director, Steve Gadlin; Eenie Meanie by Teresa Willis; Director, Elizabeth Swanson; Eleanor alla Barre by Sara Buffamanti; Director, Rebecca Lingafelter; Emergency Exits written & directed by Adena Jacobs & Carla Silbert; Every Nigger Is A Star by Mario Burrell; Director, Jemel McNell; Eye Candy written & directed by Maria Colaco; Faded by Robert Dominguez; Director, Veronica Caicedo; Fallen Angel book, music & lyrics by Justin Murphy, Co-Composer, Roger Butterley; The Fan Tan King by C.Y. Lee, music by Doug Lackney; Director, Tisa Chang; Fando y Lis adapted & directed by Monica Bucciantini, adapted from Fernando Arrabal; Fantasy, Girl by LyaNisha Gonzalez; Director, Selena Ambush; The Fartiste book & story by Charlie Schulman, music & lyrics by Michael Roberts; Director, John Gould Rubin; Fatboy Romeo written & directed by Neal Freeman; Faust by Christopher Marlowe; Director, Josh Allen; Fay Lindsay-Jones Story by Greg Emetaz; Director, Desdemona Chiang; Fear Up: Stories from Baghdad and Guantanamo by Karen Bradley & Marietta Hedges; Director, Joe Brady; Fitz & Walloughs Get it in the End by Paul Hagen, lyrics & music by Micah Bucey & Drew Edwards; Director, Paul Mazza; Flying On The Wing by Michael Perlman; Fornicatically Challenged by Judi Lee Brandwein; Director, Mark Travis; Four One-Legged Men by Gary Corbin; Director, William Martin; Free To Be Friends by Julie Klausner & Sue Galloway; Director, Dyna Moe; The French Defense by Dimitri Raitzin; Director, Aleksey Burago; FULL HOUSE written & directed by Masako Sato; Garbage Boy by Christopher Millis; Director, Ashley Lieberman; Girl Scouts of America by Andrea Berloff & Mona Mansour; Director, James Saba; Godversations by Larry Brenner; Director, Betsy Karic; The Goods Are Odd by Julie Sharbutt & Liz Wisan; Director, Mo Fathelbab; GRACE by Shannon Thomason & Sara Thigpen; Director, Melanie Ashley; Grace Falls book, music & lyrics by Daeil Cha; Director, Ryan Davis, Musical Director, Casey Lee; Griot: He Who Speaks the Sweet Word by Al Letson with Larry Knight Jr. & David Girard, music by DJ Zane 3; Director, Barbara Colaciello; HA! HA! Club by Billie E. Hazelbaker, music by Patrick Barnes, additional lyrics by Bryan Barnes; Director, Frank A. Barnhart, Musical Director, Nancy Nocks; The Happiness of Schizophrenia written & directed by Anthony Wills Jr.; Happy Sauce by Benjamin Lewis; Director, Matt Dickson; Harriet Hopperdoodle's Hair-Brained History Test! written & directed Jeanne Beechwood & Jon Copeland; HENRY KISSINGER: A ROMANTIC COMEDY by John Attanas; Director, Melanie Moyer Williams; Here. This. Now. true stories by Youth Communication, adapted by Tamilla Woodard & Sharahn LaRue McClung; Director, Tamilla Woodard; HERMANAS by Monica Yudovich; Director, Claudia Zelevansky; Higher Power by Sam Ryan; Director, Chris Plante; Hot Black/Asian Action by Quinn D. Eli; Director, Jessica Rotondi; HOUSE by David Bromley; Director, Handan Ozbilgin; How 2 Men Got On in the World written & directed by Emily Mendelsohn; HOW THE WEST WAS SPUN based on texts by Will Rogers, adapted/directed/choreographed by Edward Cardaci, lyrics by Clifford J. Tasner; Hugging the Shoulder written & directed by Jerrod Bogard; I Come in Peace by Dean Obeidallah; Director, Negin Farsad; I Coulda Been a Kennedy by Dennis Trainor Jr.; i want to be MUSASHI: a clown samurai fantasy by Christopher Lueck; Director, Amanda Pekoe; I Was Tom Cruise written & directed by Alexander Poe; Co-Director, Joseph Varca; I, Marlena by Laylage Courie & Kenosha Kid; If You See Something, Say Something by Elna Baker; Director, Joe Schiappa; I'LL SELL THE HOUSE IN WHICH I CAN LIVE NO MORE inspired by the writer Bohumil Hrabal; Director, Jerzy Zon; Imminent, Indeed (or Polly Peachum's Peculiar Penchant for Plosives) written & directed by Bryn Manion; The Impotence of Being Earnest by members of The Princeton Triangle Club; Director, Troy Holland; In Transit by Matt Hoverman; Director, Padraic Lillis; The Inconstant Infection by

Ed Malin; Director, John DeBenedetto; *The Infliction of Cruelty* by Andrew Unterberg & Sean McManus; Director, Joel Froomkin; *The Israeli-Palestinian Conflict: A Romantic Comedy* by Negin Farsad & Alex Zalben, music by Gaby Alter; *It's a Hit A Killer New Musical* by Book by Beth Saulnier, lyrics by Melissa Levis, music by David Weinstein; Director, Julie Kramer; *The Kitchen Sink* written & directed by Meghan Gambling; *LA FEMME EST MORTE or Why I Should Not F%!# My Son* written & directed by Shoshona Currier, additional text by Georges Bataille and Seneca; *The Last Spoken Word* by Francis Kuzler; Director, Philip Emeott; *Letter Purloined* by David Isaacson; Director, the ensemble of Theater Oobleck; *Light & Love* written & directed by S.P. Riordan; *Lizardskin* by Jen Silverman; Director, Katherine Kovner; *LULU* by the Silent Theatre Company, adaptation & music by Isaiah Robinson; Director, Tonika Todorova; *LYING* by Jessica Burr & Matt Opatrny, adapted from the memoir by Lauren Slater; Director, Damen Scranton; *A Man's a Man* by Bertolt Brecht, translated by Eric Bentley; Director, Leah Bonvissuto; *Mary Berry Presents: The Life of Mary Berry* written & directed by William B. Smith; *Melo-llama: A Melodrama* by Sarah Bagley; Director, Moritz von Stuelpnagel; *Mike's Incredible Indian Adventure* by Michael Schlitt; Director, Nancy Keystone; *Minimum Wage* by Charlie LaGreca & Jeff LaGreca, music & lyrics by Sean Altman & the LaGreca Brothers; Director, Jeff LaGreca; *Modern Missionary* by Julia Barnett; Director, Andrew Garman; *Moral Values: A Grand Farce or Me No Likey The Homo Touch-Touch* by Ian McWethy; Director, Jeffrey Glaser; *MOTHERS OF INVENTION* by Laura Poe; Director, Kimmy Gatewood; *Mrs. Darling's Bed 'n' Board* written & directed by Karlton Parris; *MUSCLE-MAN vs. SKELETONMAN: A Love Story... the musical* written, directed & choreographed by Richard J. Hinds and Ginamaria Trello; *My Nasty Bitch Wife* written & directed by Caila Lipovsky; *Naughty Prep School Stories* by Michael Quiñones; Director, Malini Singh McDonald; *Neon Mirage* by Liz Duffy Adams, Dan Dietz, Julie Jenson, Lisa Kron, Tracey Scott Wilson and Chay Yew, music & Lyrics by Rick Hip-Flores; Director, Wendy McClellan; *Never Swim Alone* written & directed by Daniel MacIvor; *Nutmeat: A Burlesque Fairytale* by Megan Campisi, in collaboration with Andres Bezares, Colin Bosio & Caroline Reck; Director, Megan Campisi with Kevin Lapin; *Oblivious to Everyone* written & directed by Jessica Lynn Johnson; Co-Director, Chris Sorensen; *The October Sapphire* written & directed by Nicholas Coyle, music by Andy Clockwise; *Odd Man Out* written & directed by John Holleman and Company; *An Off-White Afternoon* by Eric Meyer; Director, Jason A. Narvy; *Olsen Terror* by Chris Wells, music & lyrics by Chris Wells & Jeremy Bass; Director, Laural Meade; *A One Man Hamlet* based on text by William Shakespeare, adapted by Andrew Cowie; Director, Lauren Pfitzner; *The Onion Lovers* by Robert J. Bonocore; Director, J. Julian Christopher; *Only a Lad* by Andrew Loschert, music and lyrics by Danny Elfman; Director, Rob Seitelman; Music Director, Mary Ann Ivan; *Open House* by Ross Maxwell; Director, Josh Hecht; *Ophelia* by Ashley Minihan; Director, Ilo Orleans; *Pack Light* by Caroline Neisha Taylor; Choreographer, Natalie Joseph-Settle; *PARK-N-RIDE* written & directed by Laura Park; *The Penguin Tango* written & directed by Stephen Svoboda; *PERFECT* written & directed by Tanya Klein; *Perfect Harmony* by Andrew Grosso & The Essentials; Director, Andrew Grosso; *Permanent Whole Life* by Zayd Dohrn; Director, Wesley Savick; *Picking Up The Baby* by Ellen Margolis; Director, Teresa K. Pond; *Piece of Mind* by Mary Crescenzo; Director, Richard Manichello; *PIGGY 1.5* written & directed by David Commander; *Pitched* by S. Melinda Dunlap; Director, Luke Leonard; *The Pool with Five Porches* by Peter Zablotsky; Director, John Ahlers; *The Prostitute of Reverie Valley* by Adam Klasfeld; Director, Sherri Kronfeld; *The Pumpkin Pie Show: la petite mortes* by Clay McLeod Chapman; *Pith!* written & directed by Stewart Lemoine; *Places* written, directed & choreographed by Barbara Thieme; *Planet Samovar* by Harold Todd & Maura Kelley; Director, Maura Kelley; *Pleading Infinity* written & directed by T. J. Walsh; *Plugged: A Rock Opera* by Penelope Corrin, music by Corinne Kessel; Director, John Murphy; *Puppet Government* by Steve Barney; Director, Chris Humphrey; *The RABBI and the CHEERLEADER* by Sandy Wolshin; *Rainy Days & Mondays* by Andrew Barrett; Director, Niegel Smith & Henry Menendez; *Rapunzel* by Karen Rousso with Judy Dulberg & Kerry Wolf, music by Karen Rousso & Holley Bartlett; Director, Karen Rousso; Choreography, Brian Swasey;

*Red Herring* by Michael Albanese; Director, Jonathan Silverstein; *Requiem for New Orleans: a Hip Hop Eulogy* text, music, direction & choreography by James Vesce & Donell Stines; *Reservoir Bitches* by Laura McGhee; Director, Allan Guttman; *The Return of the Wayward Son* written & directed by Brian D. Fraley; *REVENGE OF A KING* by Herb Newsome; Director, Steve Broadnax; *Roadside, Maryland* by Forrest Simmons; Director, David Thigpen; *Romancing The Terrorist: Tajiki Nights* written & directed by Mike Wallach & Negin Farsad; *The Revenants* by Scott T. Barsotti; Directors, Rob Gander &Cara Scarmack; *SHELF LIFE* by Camille M Brown; Director, Matt Hoverman; *A SHOW OF FORCE* created & performed by Donnie Mather; Director, Leon Ingulsrud; *rum & coke* created & performed by Carmen Peláez; Director, Carl Andress; *The Saints of Festus* by Scott Hess; Director, David Drake; *SAKURA no gotoku, Like a cherry tree* written & directed by Keiko Nakano; *Sax & Dixon: This Plane is Definitely Crashing* by Peter McNerney, Matt Sax, John Dixon; Director, Peter McNerney; *The Secret Ruths of Island House* by Claytie Mason & Alissa Mortenson; Director, Cecelia Frye; *Solicitation* by Gib Wallis; Director, Nancy Hendrickson; *Some Kind of Pink Breakfast* by Chris Harcum, music by Debby Schwartz; Director, Bricken Sparacino; *Site-Seeing* by Susan Haedicke & Leslie Felbain; Director, Leslie Felbain; *A Small Hole* by Julia Jarcho, adapted from *Mansfield Park* by Jane Austen; Director, Alice Reagan; *soledad.es* by Raquel Feliu Torres; Director, Sara Serrano; *Something More Pleasant* by Joshua William Gelb; Director, Brittany O'Neill; *suburban STORIES* written & directed by Tom Conklin, based on interviews by Tom Conklin and Sibylla Nash; *Suicide, The Musical* by Helen Stratford; Director/Musical Director, Joe McCanta; Choreographer, Paul Monaghan; *SUNDAY NIGHT LIVE: ON TOUR!* created & performed by the sketchersons; *T.L.C.* by Robert Moulthrop; Director, Marc Silberschatz; *Take On Me (adoption, addiction, and a-ha)* by Christine Simpson; Director, Jesse Jou; *Tea in the Afternoon* by Vanessa Shealy; Director, Frank Pisco; *The Tell-Tale Heart – a musicabre* by Edgar Allan Poe, music & adaptation by Danny Ashkenasi; Director, David L. Carson; *Their Wings Were Blue* by Carmen Betancourt; Director, Jocelyn Sawyer; *This Won't Take Long* by David M. Korn; Director, Shango Amin; *Thought Prints:* written and performed by Bobby Torkova, The *Postal Prestidigitator* by Bobby Torkova, the Postal Prestidigitatior; Director, Virginia Scott; *A Time to be Born: a 1940's New York Musical* by Tajlei Levis, music by John Mercurio, based on the novel by Dawn Powell; Director, Marlo Hunter; *Todd Robbins' Carnival Knowledge* by Todd Robbins; Director Kristen Sanderson; *Tradition!* by Alan Ostroff; Director, Jack Wann; *The Transformation of Dr. Jekyll* created by Rabbit Hole; Director, Edward Elefterion; *Trouble in Shameland* book, music, lyrics & direction by Bryan Putnam; *TRUCE* by Marilee Talkington; Director, Justin Quinn Pelegano; *Tuesdays and Sundays* by Daniel Arnold & Medina Hahn; Director, Wojtek Kozlinski; *Understand To Be Understood* by Mariam Adjose, Dwayne Andrews, Diderot Jean Baptiste, Keninya Odems, Kennyetta Odems, Sasha Silva, & Dean Taylor, Perry Taylor, Desiree Wright; Director/Editor, Juliette Avila; *Uneventful Deaths for Agathon* written & directed by Javierantonio González; *The Unlucky Man in the Yellow Cap* by J.R. Pick, composed by Peter Fish, adapted by Zuzana Justman; Director, Marcy Arlin; *Vice Girl Confidential* by Todd Michael; Director, Neal Sims; *Vile Affections* by Vanda; *Vote McOwskey!* by Jeremiah Murphy with additional material by Laura Dillman, Justin Herfel, & Chris Ryan; Director, Jeremiah Murphy; *Walmartopia* book, music, lyrics, & direction by Catherine Capellaro & Andrew Rohn, Choreography, Shannon Barry; *We Love You, Johnny Hero* text, music, direction & choreography by Sara Cooper & Chris Shimojima; Co-Choreographer, Sara Wolski; *Whiz Kid* by Michael Allen; Director, Helena Prezio; *Women and the Trojan Horse* by Sam Dowling and Nick Warren; Director, Praxis Theatre Laboratory; *THE XXXOTIKA REVIEW* by Carmen Barika; Choreography, Wanjirù Kamuyu; *The Yellow Wallpaper* by Brian Madden; Director, Edward Warren; *Your Place...or Mine?* by Kim Moore, G. Todd Buker, Julia Griswold, & Jillian Weise; Director, Kim Moore

# New York Musical Theatre Festival (NYMF)

Kris Stewart, Founder and Executive Director; Isaac Robert Hurwitz, Producing Director; Geoff Cohen, Executive Producer; 3rd annual; September 10–October 1; performances at 37 Arts, New World Stages, Ars Nova, 92nd Street Makor, Steinhardt Center, 45th Street Theatre, The Sage, Theatre at St. Clements, The Barrow Group Theatre, Red Room, P.S. 122, Lamb's Theatre

**Next Link Productions** *Desperate Measures* book & lyrics by Peter Kellogg, music by David Friedman; *Emerald Man* book & lyrics by Janet Cole Valdez, music by Marc Bosserman & Tom Valdez; *Flight of the Lawnchair Man* music & lyrics by Robert Lindsey-Nassif, book by Peter Ullian, directed by Lynne Taylor-Corbett; *Go-Go Beach* book & lyrics by John Wimbs, music by Michael Shaieb & Brent Lord; *Have a Nice Life* book by Matthew Hurt & Conor Mitchell, music & lyrics by Conor Mitchell; *Hot and Sweet* book, music & lyrics by Barbara Schottenfeld; *Journey to the West* book & lyrics by Robert Taylor & Richard Oberacker, music by Richard Oberacker; *Kingdom* book, music & lyrics by Ian Williams & Aaron Jafferis; *Lunch* book, music & lyrics by Shawn Northrip; *Oedipus for Kids* book & lyrics by Kimberly Patterson & Gil Varod, music by Robert J. Saferstein; *River's End* book & lyrics by Cheryl Coons, music by Chuck Larkin; *Smoking Bloomberg* book, music & lyrics by David Comue, Sam Holtzapple, Warren Loy, Chris Todd; *The Screams of Kitty Genovese* music by Will Todd, libretto by David Simpatico; *Three Sides* music & lyrics by Grant Olding, book by Grant Olding & Toby Davis; *Warrior* book, music & lyrics by Marcus Hummon

**Invited Productions** *Behind the Limelight* music & lyrics by Christopher Curtis; *Captain Gravy's Wavy Navy: Where's the Moon?* book, music & lyrics by David Cooper & Jeffrey Katz; *Gutenberg! The Musical!* book, music & lyrics by Anthony King and Scott Brown; *Having It Almost* book by David Goldsmith & Wendy Perelman, lyrics by David Goldsmith, music by John Kavanaugh, additional songs by Jeff Blumenkrantz, Annie Kessler, Libby Stein, and Stephen Schwartz; *J.O.B. The Hip-Hopera* book & lyrics by Jerome Sable & Eli Batalion, music by Jerome Sable, Eli Batalion & Joe Barrucco; *Party Come Here* book by Daniel Goldfarb, music & lyrics by David Kirshenbaum; *The Children* book & lyrics by Stan Richardson, music by Hal Goldberg; *The Man in My Head* book by Thomas F. DeFrantz, music & lyrics by Michael Wartofsky; *The Night of the Hunter* book & lyrics by Stephen Cole, music by Claibe Richardson; *The Paisley Sisters' Christmas Special* book & lyrics by Jim Ansart, Joel Benjamin, Steve Silverman, music & additional book by Bret Silverman; *The Tragic and Horrible Life of the Singing Nun* book by Blair Fell, music & lyrics by Andy Monroe; *This Could Be Love* book, music & lyrics by Brock Simpson; *Virgins* book & lyrics by Dean Bryant, music by Matthew Frank; *White Noise* book, music & lyrics by Joe Drymala, additional songs, Rick Crom, Glen Kelly, Laurence O'Keefe, Eric Svejcar

**NYMF Dance Series** *All is Love* music by Travis Sullivan & Alex Fortuit; *School Daze* conceived & created by Wendy Seyb; *Common Grounds* book by Sammy Buck, music by Doug Katsaros

**Developmental Series** *Alive in the World* music & lyrics by Paul Scott Goodman; *Chang & Eng* book by Burton Cohen, lyrics by Stephen Hoffman, music by Mark Campbell; *Cumberland Blues* book by Michael Norman Mann, music by Jerry Garcia & Robert Hunter, lyrics by Robert Hunter, additional material by Phil Lesh, Greg Anton; *Drift* book by Craig Pospisil, music & lyrics by Jeremy Schonfeld; *Magpie* book by Steve Jacobson, music by Gary William Friedman, lyrics by Edward Gallardo; *Saint Heaven* by Martin Casella, music & lyrics by Keith Gordon; *The Tales of Custard the Dragon* book by Mary Hall Surface, music by Brad Ross, lyrics by Danny Whitman; *The Chocolate Tree* by Al & Marshall Pailet; *Wallenberg* book & lyrics by Laurence Holzman & Felicia Needleman, music by Benjamin Rosenbluth

**Concerts and Special Events** *Baby Wants Candy* Improv Toupe; *Blue Lou and the Bullyfish…In Concert* by Stephanie Arasim Portnoy; *Little by Little* book by Ellen Greenfield & Annette Jolles, music by Brad Ross, lyrics by Ellen Greenfield & Hal Hackady; *"The MacGuffin?"* by Terry Withers & Jason Rhyne; *The Unauthorized Musicology of Ben Folds*; *Andrew Lippa and a Piano*; *Annie Golden: Velvet Prison*; *The Petersons*; *Old Springs Pike*; *A New Generation of Song*

**NYMF @ Ars Nova** Broadway Idol, NYMF Speakeasy, NYMF-toberfet, Manoel Felciano, Joe Iconis: Things to Ruin, Groovelily, Donna Lynne Champlin: Finishing the Hat, Daniel Reichard in concert, Broadway Spotlight: Merle Dandridge

**Seminars** "Crossing Over: Adapting Musicals from Other Media," "Dream Dialogue: Master Composers Share Their Secrets," "The Business of Show," Masterclass One: Dance, Masterclass Two: Hip Hop, Materclass Three: Pop, Rock and R & B Vocal

**Partner Events** *Angels* book & lyrics by Ken Lai & Marcus Chong, music by Ken Lai; *Illyria* in Concert adapted by Peter Mills & Cara Reichel; *Maria Maria* book & lyrics by Hye Jung Yu, music by Gyungchan Cha; *Moopim* by Saar Harari, music by Brian Prunka; *Soul Searching* music & lyrics by Avi Kunstler, book, additional music & lyrics by Matt Okin; *what@trip!* created, written & directed by Roi Escudero; Museum of Television & Radio Screenings: *The Ballad of Baby Doe*, *Annie Get Your Gun*, *A Salute to Dorothy Loudon*, *One Touch of Venus*, *Wonderful Town*

# Nicu's Spoon

Stephanie Barton-Farcas, Founder and Artistic Director

**Cherish** by Ken Duncum; Director, June Stein; Sets, Michael Kurtz; Lighting, Steven Wolf; Sound/Slides, S. Barton-Farcas; Stage Managers, Sara Bancroft, Laurie Green; Cast: Rebecca Challis, Jeffrey Danneman, Jessica Lions, Alvaro Sena; Abingdon Arts June Havoc Theatre; June 7–25

**Buried Child** by Sam Shepard; Director, Stephanie Barton-Farcus; ASL Project Director, Pamela Mitchell; Technical Director, Steven Wolf; Stage Manager, Howard Goldberg; Cast: Jim Williams, Alvaro Sena, David Marantz, Wynne Anders, Wendy Clifford, Erwin Falcon, Darren Fudenske; Access Theater; October 4–22

**Tales of the Lost Formicans** by Constance Congdon; Director, Brett Maughan; Costumes, Rien Schlecht; Lighting, Steven Wolf; Sound, Tom Cassetta; PSM, Kathleen Conway; Cast: Rebecca Challis, Brian Coffey, Lindsay Goranson, William Huntley III, Jovinna Chan, Russell Waldman, Celia Bressack, Michael Hartney Theatre 54 at Shetler Studios; March 28–April 15

# Ohio Theatre

**Summerworks 2006** presented by Clubbed Thumb; included: *I Have Loved Strangers* by Anne Washburn, directed by Johanna Mckeon; Cast: Jeff Biehl, Elliotte Crowell, Laura Flanagan, Jennifer R. Morris, James Stanely, Jay Smith, T. Ryder Smith; *Alice the Magnet* by Erin Courtney, directed by Pam MacKinnon; Cast: Cohlie Brocato, Maria Dizzia, Sheri Graubert, Quentin Maré; *Quail* by Rachel Hoeffel, directed by Kip Fagan; Cast: Gerry Bamman, Zuleyma Guevara, Elizabeth Meriwether, Benjamin Pelteson, Everett Quinton; June 4–24

**Ice Factory 2006** presented by Soho Think Tank; included: *The WanderLUSTers Present Achtung Grimm!* presented by Concrete Temple Theatre, libretto & direction by Renne Philippi, music & lyrics by Lewis Flinn; *Aruba* by Rob Evans, created & presented by People Can Run; *Particularly in the Heartland* directed by Rachel Chavkin, created & presented by THE TEAM; *The Flight of Icarus* by Aaron Mack Schloff, directed by Samuel Buggeln, presented by Soho Think Tank; *Betrothed* adapted & directed by Rachel Dickstein, score by Vijay Iyer, presented by Ripe Time; *The Jaded Assassin* by Michael Voyer, conceived & directed by Timothy Haskell, presented by Big Time Action Theatre; July 5–August 12

**FIZZ: The Totally Fictionalized Story of America's Most Successful Blunder** by Rogelio Martinez; Director, Sam Gold; Set, Marsha Ginsberg; Costumes, Emily Pepper; Lighting, Ben Stanton; Sound/Videos, Leah Gelpe; Cast: Bryant Mason, Cheryl Lynn Bowers, Mary Ramussen, Matt D'Amico, Keira Naughton; September 9–30

**Ignite 06** presented by Synapse Productions; included: *Dick & Condi: The Lounge Act* by Jamie Jackson, SoHee Youn, John Herin, with Elizabeth June; *Clarisse & Larmon* by Deb Margolin, directed by David Travis, with Kathleen Chalfant & Shawn Elliott; *Sounds of Silence* by Eliza Jane Schneider & Jon Dabach; *The Sniper* by Yussef El Guindi, directed by Alexandra Farkas; *The Drill (or Which Way Out)* by Trish Harnetiaux, directed by Jude Domski; *Party Discipline: A Political Tranformation Seminar* by Subjective Theatre Company, directed by Zachary R. Mannheimer; *Texaco's Last Stand (aka Kill Tex: The Complete Volume)* directed by Leah Bonvissuto; *The Club* by James Christy, directed by Kerry Whigham; *The Wal-Mart Extra-Vocational Theatre Club Presents The Miracle of Corn Syrup* directed by Jeremy Lydic; *Beautiful, Radiant Things* created by Jane Ray, directed by Glynis Rigsby; *Red Bastard is a …?; The Elephant* by Henry Meyerson, directed by Moritz von Stuelpnagel; *Three Simones Walk Into a Bar…* by The TEAM, directed by Rachel Chavkin; *Me and Shirley* by Henry Meyerson, directed by Moritz von Stuelpnagel; *Iraq.doc* by Caryl Churchill, directed by David Travis; *Displaced* by Isabella Bruno; *Grand Marshall* by Clay McLeod Chapman; *The Doorman's Double Duty* written and directed by Robert Lyons; *Darfur, Sudan* by Winter Miller, directed by Daniel Talbott; *God and Country: A Vaudeville* by Clay McLeod Chapman; *Party Lines* by Winter Miller, directed by Daniel Talbot; *Mama, I Want a Nuclear Bomb* by Jonathon Ward; *Child of the Revolution* written & performed by Said Sayrafiezadeh; *A Modest Adjustment* by Daniel Rebellato, directed by Joe Ward; *Stretch: A Fantasia* by Susan Bernfield, directed by Emma Griffin; *Wabenzi (The Big Men)* by Richard Bean, directed by David Travis; *Testimony* by LeeSaar the Company; *Advice to Iraqi Women* by Martin Crimp, directed by Amanda Charlton; *Way to Go!* by Caitlin Miller, directed by Anne Kaufman; October 3–22

**Havel Fest** the complete plays of Václav Havel presented by Untitled Theater Company #61; productions at the Ohio Theatre included: *Audience* translated by Jan Novak, directed by Edward Einhorn, produced by UTC #61; Cast: Dan Leventritt, Scott Simpson; on a double bill with *Protest* translated by Jan Novak, directed by Robert Lyons, produced by Soho Think Tank; Cast: Andy Paris, Richard Toth (October 30–November 25); *The Butterfly on the Antenna* translated by Carol Rocamora & Tomas Rychetsky, directed by Henry Akona, produced by Walking Shadow; Cast: Philip Emeott, Liz Wisan, Dawn Jamieson, Richard Renner; on a double bill with *Motormorphosis* translated by Carol Rocamora & Tomas Rychetsky, directed/designed & performed by Tanya Khordoc and Barry Weil, produced by Evolve Company (November 3–26); *The Conspirators* translated by Carol Rocamora & Tomas Rychetsky, directed by Kay Matschullat (November 13); *Unveiling* translated by Jan Novak, Director, Randy White, produced by Cardinal Stage Company; Cast: Diane Kondrat, Bill Simmons, Mike Price (October 30–November 11); *The Increased Difficulty of Concentration* translated by Stephan Simek, directed by Yolanda Hawkins, produced by True Comedy Theatre; Cast: John Hagan, Brad Holbrook, Shira Kobren, Meret Oppenheim, David Ott, Matthew Park, Amy Quint, Kate Reilly (November 2–26); *Largo Desolato* translated by Tom Stoppard, directed by Eva Burgess, produced by TYNA Collective; Cast: Erik Kever Ryle, Brian Quirk, Jennifer Boutell, Janet Ward, Skyler Sullivan, Nancy Nagrant, Greg Skura, Joshua Briggs, Jon Okabayashi, Jennifer Boutell (November 3–25); *The Memo* translated by Paul Wilson, directed by Edward Einhorn, produced by UTC #61; Cast: Peter Bean, V. Orion Delwaterman, Ryan Dutcher, Talaura Harms, Uma Incrocci, Alice Starr McFarland, Skid Maher, Tom McCarten, Josh Mertz, Shelley Ray, Leah Reddy, Andrew Rothkin, Josh Silverman, Ken Simon, Maxwell Zener (November 1–25); *Redevelopment* translated by James Saunders, directed by Grant Neale, produced by Nomad Theatrical Company; Cast: Sarah Bell, Margaret Catov, Joseph DiSalle, Erik Gratton, Tracy Hostmeyer/Hillary Spector, Elda Luisi, Mark E. Macken, Aole T. Miller, Shad Ramsey, Ric Sechrest, Patrick Zeller, Tessa Zugmeyer (November 4–25)

**The Dreamer Examines His Pillow** by John Patrick Shanley; presented by Ditto Productions; Director, Rusty Owen, Lighting, Ryan Wentworth; Set, Jesse Dreikosen; Costumes, Isabel Rubio; Sound, Frederick Kennedy; Stage Manager, Ewan Walker; Cast: Joe Petcka, David Ditto Tawil, Eleni Tzimas; November 30–December 16

**As Yet Thou Art Young and Rash** based on *Suppliants* by Euripides, adapted and directed by David Herskovits; presented by Target Margin Theater; Sets, Susan Barras; Costumes, Meredith Palin; Lighting, Juliet Chia; Sound, Jane Shaw; Music, David Rosenmeyer; Cast: Satya Bhabha, Mia Katigbak, Mary Neufeld, Tina Shepard, Stephanie Weeks; January 9–February 3

**TMT Greek Labaoratory** presented by Target Margin Theater; included *MEZE; Over There* created by Kathleen Kennedy Tobin; *Dirge* created by Alexis Poledouris; *Beautiful Pooper Scooper* created by Asta Bennie Hostetter; *The Barbie-Steia: Curse of the House of Malibu* created by Michael Levinton & Mallery MacKay-Brook; *AJAX, a furious study on humanity* directed by Gisela Cardenas; *Taking One for the Team* created by Michael Kraskin; January 18–February 3

**The Women of Trachis** by Sophocles, adapted and directed by Kate E. Ryan; presented by Target Margin Theater; Cast: Sara Buffamanti, Todd D'Amour, Birgit Huppuch, Jodi Lin, Rebecca Lingafelter, Debargo Sanyal, Heidi Schreck, Indika Senanyake; Set, Jennifer de Fouchier; Costumes, Amanda Bujak; Lighting, Lucrecia Briceno; January 18–February 3

**The Jaded Assassin** conceived and directed by Tim Haskell and Michael Voyer; produced by David Solomon Rodriguez & Big Time Action Theater; Fight Director, Rod Kinter; Puppets, Faye Armon; Costumes, Wendy Yang; Set, Paul Smithyman; Lighting, Nick Hohn; Cast: Jo-anne Lee, Laine D'Souza, David Solomon Rodriguez, Jason Schumacher, Tonie Tirado, Judi Lewis Ockler, Marius Hanford, Malika Duckworth, Maggie Macdonald, Aaron Haskell, Nick Arens; February 8–March 4

**THE BEST: The OEDI Cycle** presented by Anonymous Ensemble and Soho Think Tank; included *OEDIrx* adapted from *Oedipus Rex* and *OEDI@:us* adapted from *Oedipus at Colonus*; March 21–24

**fuckplays** presented by Working Man's Clothes and The Thursday Problem; see full credits under Galapagos Arts Space; March 28–31

**Miracle in Rwanda** adapted and performed by Leslie Lewis Sword, directed and co-created by Edward Vilga; presented by George Faison & Carl Nelson; April 5–29

**Betrothed** conceived, written & directed by Rachel Dickstein; presented by Ripe Time Theatre Company; Set/Props, Susan Zeeman Rogers; Costumes, Oana Botez-Ban; Lighting, Nicole Pearce; Music, Vijay Iyer; Cast: Laura Butler, Lula Graves, Daniel Irizarry, Ryan Justesen, Mahira Kakkar, Derek Lucci, Paula McGonagle, Gita Reddy, Alok Tewari; May 4–26

# Ontological-Hysteric Theater

Richard Foreman, Founder and Artistic Director; Shannon Sindelar, Managing Director

**The Sewers** by Jason Craig; presented by Banana Bag & Bodice in association with chashama; Director, Mallory Catlett; Composer/Sound, Dave Malloy; Set, Peter Ksander; Lighting, Miranda Hardy; Stage Manager, Morgan Murphy; Cast: Jason Craig, Rod Hipskind, Heather Peroni, Jessica Jelliffe; June 30–July 22

**Untitled Intentional Exercise #1** presented by Stuck Pigs Squealing with Mac Wellman, Oliver Butler, Jason Craig, Jessica Jelliffe; July 26–28

**Under the Sign of the Hourglass...** stories by Bruno Schulz, text by Stephen Cedars; created, directed, and adapted by Anthony Cerrato; Lighting, Owen Hughes; Costumes, Annie Simon; Cast: Joshua Damien Briggs, Rob Skolits, Stephanie Taylor, Vivian Smith, Sarah Politis, Cady Zuckerman, Jon Okabayashi; June 15–24

**PH-S** curated by Morgan von Prelle Pecelli; Artists: Sally Oswald, Risa Shoup, Sara Kraft, Ed Purver, Brendan Regimbal, Jennifer Tsui; July 6–August 17

**Metronoma** created & presented by 31 Down Radio Theater; Director/Sound, Ryan Holsopple; Video, Mirit Tal, Ariel Efron; Lighting, John Luton; Special Effects, Benjamin Brown; Cast: Shauna Kelly, Jonathan Valuckas, Mike Sharpie; August 3–12

**The Hystery of Heat** created and performed by Jackie Milad, Bonnie Jones, Ric Royer, G. Lucas Crane; August 16–19

**First Dark Drama** conceived by Daniel Givens; Director/Movement/Additional Text, Baraka de Soleil; Cast: Sunder Ashni, Christal N. Brown, Baraka de Soleil, Lela Jones, Roger Hall, Mutale Kanyatta, Daniel Givens, Reza Salazar, Francine Sheffield; August 23–26

**Spoleum** written & directed by Daniel Allen Nelson; September 6–10

**Experimental Text 2007** curated by Sally Oswald & Jennifer Tsui; included: *Casting Off* by Bronwen Bitetti, directed by Jeremy Wilhelm; *Do Not Do This Ever Again* written & directed by Karinne Keithley; *Conversations For You and Me* by Rachelle Viader Knowles & Jenny Levison; *Disco Eats Itself* by Tan Lin; *Learning Skills Program* by Johanna Linsley, directed by Katrina Bugaj; *Over the Garden Wall* by Ruth Margraff, directed by Brooke O'Harra; *Copy 8852* by Jason Szalla & John Kearns; May 10–13

**Short Form Festival** curated by Brendan Regimbal & Peter Ksander; included *Keyholes* by Stephen Cedars & Christina Latimer, *Sick* by Caleb Hammond, *Form Equals Nothingness* by Rania Khalil, *The Mysteries of Paris* by Normandy Sherwood, *lpn.then* by Peter Campbell & David Gordon; May 17–19

## Pan Asian Repertory

**Readings & Workshops** *Innocent When You Dream* by Ken Narasaki; Director, Ron Nakahara; Cast: E. Calvin Ahn, Judy Chen, Lydia Gaston, Jackson Loo, Jackson Ning, Kaipo Schwab; December 7; *Stroke* by Chin Woon Ping; Directors, Ernest Abuba and Suli Holum; Choreography, Suli Holum; Cast: Chin Woon Ping; December 15; Actor/Writer Workshop Presentations (led by Ernest Abuba): *Recess* written & performed by Una Aya Osato; *Wong Chin Foo* by Richard Chang; *Born to be Unsed* by Tiffany Rothman, performed by Una Aya Osato; *Mercia* by John Quincy Lee, with Una Aya Osato, Richard Chang, and Tiffany Rothman; Bruce Mitchell Room at 520 Eighth Ave; January 19

## Performance Space 122 (P.S. 122)

Anne Dennin, Artistic Director

**Americana Absurdum** two plays by Brian Parks; Director, John Clancy; included *Vomit & Roses* and *Wolverine Dream;* June 6–25

**The Complete Lost Works of Samuel Beckett As Found In An Envelope (partially burned) In A Dustbin in Paris Labeled "Never to be performed. Never. Ever. EVER! Or I'll Sue! I'LL SUE FROM THE GRAVE!!!"** written and performed by Greg Allen, Benjamin Schneider & Danny Thompson; Director, John Clancy; June 6–25

**America Starts with Me (or The Pursuit of Happiness)** created and performed by The Patriots; presented by Schoolhouse Roxx; Director, Adam Dugas; June 8–10

**In the Spirit–For Real** written & performed by Peggy Pettitt; Director/Set, Remy Tissier; Music, Harry Mann; Lighting, Aimee Schneider; Costumes, Pascaline Tissier; June 15–25

**Orange Lemon Egg Canary** by Rinne Groff; Director, Michael Sexton; Sets, Andromache Chalfant; Lighting, Ben Stanton; Costumes, Oana Botez-Ban; Sound, Eric Shim; Stage Manager, Christine Lemme; Cast: Steve Cuiffo, Aubrey Dollar, Emily Swallow, Laura Kai Chen; July 12–30

**Summer Season at Spiegeltent** 1st annual; included performances by One Ring Zero, Amy Sohn, Ned Vizzini, Mike Daisey, Clay McLeod Chapman; Spiegeltent; August 7

**Tower of Babel** created and performed by Lidy Six & Robert Steijn; Disc Jockey, Cassie6; Video Jockey, Roberta Marques; September 20–23

**Moopim** presented by LeeSaar The Company; Choreography, Saar Harari & Lee Sher; Cast: Ellen Cremer, Rossella Fusco, Saar Harari, Rachel Okimo, Brian Prunka, Lee Sher; September 27–October 8; Encore January 19–21 as part of the COIL Festival 2007

**A Room of One's Own: Women and Power in the New America** written & performed by Coco Fusco; September 28–October 1

**Tale of 2Cities** two plays in repertory: *Part I, Grifters Drifters and Dodgers* and *Part II, Mega Mixicana Waltz* by Heather Woodbury; presented in association with UCLA Live; Director, Dudley Sanders; Cast: Winsome Brown, Michael Ray Escamilla, Tracey A. Leigh, Leo Marks, Diane Rodriguez, Ed Vassallo, Heather Woodbury; October 12–29

**Invisible Messages** created and directed by Peter S. Petralia; presented by Proto-Type; Music, Max Giteck Duykers; Lighting, Rebecca M. K. Makus; Stage Management, Ashley Kosier; Dramaturgy, Glenn Kessler; Cast: Mandy Caughey, Alessandro Magania, Meredith Smart; October 12–29

**Screen Test** created & directed by Rob Roth, text by Romy Ashby & Rob Roth; Costumes, Todd Thomas; Music Director, Sean Pierce, Choreography; Vangeline; Band, Theo & the Skyscrapers; Cast: Rob Roth, Theo Kogan, Maki Shinagawa, Mady Caughey, Pamela Herron, Stacy Lynn Smith, George Graham; performed at Abrons Arts Center at Henry Street Settlement; October 30–November 2

**BAiT (Buenos Aires in Transition)** Shoshana Polanco, Creative Producer; plays included: *A kingdom, a country or a wasteland, in the snow* by Lola Arias, directed by Yana Ross; Lighting, Bryan Keller; Set/Costumes, Zane Pihlstrom; Sound, Sharath Patel &Yana Ross Cast: Heather Lea Anderson, Hayli Henderson, Brian McManamon, Andrea Moro Winslow, James Lloyd Reynolds; *Women Dreamt Horses* by Daniel Veronese, directed by Jay Scheib; Lighting, Justin Townsend; Costumes, Oana Botez-Ban; Set, Peter Ksander; Dramaturg, Peter Campbell; Cast: Caleb Hammond, Aimée Phelan-Deconinck, Jorge Alberto Rubio, Eric Dean Scott, April Sweeney, Zishan Ugurlu; *Ex Antwone* by Federico Leon, directed by Juan Souki; Set, Meinhard Hitti & Tao García; Lighting, Bryan Keller; Sound, Marcelo Añez; Video, Daniel Roversi; Cast: Miguel Govea, Liz Dahmen, James Ryan Caldwell; *Panic* by Rafael Spregelburd, directed by Brooke O'Harra, presented by Theatre of a Two-Headed Calf; Music, Brendan Connelly; Set, Peter Ksander; Lighting, Justin Townsend; Costumes, Anka Lupes; Cast: Rosemary Quinn, Heidi Schreck, Scott Lyons, David Brooks, Nadia Mahdi; November 4–19

**Carrie** by Erik Jackson; Director, Josh Rosenzweig; presented by Theatre Couture; Sets, Tobin Ost; Costumes, David Moyer; Lighting, Paul Hackenmueller; Sound/Music, Robert Kaplowitz; Visual Effects, Basil Twist; Stage Manager, Molly Minor Eustis; Cast: Kate Goehring, David Ilku, Keri Meoni, Kathy Searle, Rafi Silver, Danielle Skraastad, Sherry Vine, Matt Wilkis, Marnye Young; December 2–30

**Three Minutes of Pork and Shoving** choreographed and performed by Scott Heron and HIJACK (Kristin Van Loon & Arwen Wilder); December 14–17

**You Belong to Me: Death of Nations, Part V** written & directed by Josh Fox; presented by Josh Fox and the International WOW; Set/Costumes, Petra Maria Wirth, Judith Kastner, Julien Renard, & Tara Shamskho; Lighting, Charles Foster & Scott Needham; Dramaturg, Frank M. Raddatz; Cast: Beau Allulli, Harold Kennedy German, Carrie Getman, Irene Christ, Beth Griffith, Okwui Okpokwasili, Robert Saietta, Angelika Sautter, Rory Sheridan; January 5–23

**Purity** by Thomas Bradshaw; Director/Sound, Yehuda Duenyas; Set, Clint Ramos; Costumes, Jessica Gaffney; Lighting, Ben Kato; Co-Sound, Jody Elff; Stage Manager, Michelle Leigh Chang; Cast: Kate Benson, Spencer Scott Barros; Albert Christmas; Alexa Scott-Flaherty, Daniel Manley, James Scruggs, Jenny Seaston Stern; January 6–23

**Faker** created by Morgan Thorson; presented as part of COIL Festival 2007; January 17–23

**Feed** & **Glory** two performance pieces written and performed by Jeremy Wade; Musician, Adam Linson; presented as part of COIL Festival 2007; January 17–23

**The Money Conversation** written and performed by Sara Juli; presented as part of COIL Festival 2007; January 20–22

**Edith and Jenny** choreographed and presented by Tamar Rogoff Performance Projects; Performed by Claire Danes and Ariel Rogoff Flavin; January 26–February 4

**Divine Comedy of an Exquisite Corpe** written and performed by Julie Atlas Muz; January 27–February 11

**Every Day Above Ground** by Jodi Essery, inspired by Michael Ondaatje's *The Collected Works of Billy the Kid*; presented by SaBooge Theatre (Canada); Director, Adrienne Kapstein; Set/Lighting, Simon Harding; Music, Jeff Lorenz; Costumes, Jennifer Par; Cast: Trent Pardy, Attila Clemann, Patrick Costello, Graham Cuthbertson, Kayla Fell, Andrew Shaver; February 8–18

**No Where** created and performed by Megan V. Sprenger; February 22–25

**Particularly in the Heartland** by the TEAM; Director, Rachel Chavkin; Sets, Nicholas Vaughan; Costumes, Kristen Sieh; Lighting, Jake Heinrichs; Sound, Matt Hubbs; Dramaturge, Stephanie Douglass and Chantal Pavageaux; Stage Manager, Rebecca Spinac; Cast: Jessica Almasy, Frank Boyd, Jill Frutkin, Libby King, Jake Margolin, Kristen Sieh; February 26–March 18

**Goodness** by Michael Redhill; presented by Volcano (Toronto); Director, Ross Munson; Costumes, Teresa Przybylski; Lighting, Rebecca Picherack; Sound, John Gzowksi; Music Director, Brenna MacCrimmon; Cast: Victor, Ertmanis, Lili Francks, Tara Hughes, Jack Nicholsen, Gord Rand, Amy Rutherford; March 1–11

**1001 Beds** written & performed by Tim Miller; March 8–18

**genesis, no!** choreographed and presented by Adrienne Truscott; Set/Sound/Video, Adrienne Truscott and Carmine Covelli; Cast: Natalie Agee, Carmine Covelli, Neal Medlyn, David Neumann, Adrienne Truscott; March 22–25

***RrrrrrKILLKILLKILL…to infinity (MAKE IT LOOK REAL)*** and ***'It is better to…'*** created and performed by Irish Modern Dance Theatre; Choreography, John Scott, Chris Yon, and Thomas Lehman; March 15–18

**Doublethink** created, presented and performed by Rotozaza (U.K.): Silvia Mercuriali, Ant Hampton, & Neil Bennun; Director, Ant Hampton; March 29–April 1

**5 in the Morning** created, presented and performed by Rotozaza (U.K.): Ant Hampton, Silvia Mercuriali, Greg McLaren, Melanie Wilson, and Catherine Dyson; Director, Ant Hampton; April 5–8

**B.O.B. (Best of Boroughs)** included: *Peripherally Yours…With Love, Staten Island* perfomed by Sara Valentine aka Little Miss Big Mouth, presented by Snug Harbor Cultural Center (Staten Island); *Pent-up: A Revenge Dance* performed by Okwui Okpokwasili, presented by 651 Arts (Brooklyn); *Momma* by Edith L. Freni, presented by Queens Theatre in the Park (Queens); *Hip-Hop to da Head* created, Gabriel "Kwikstep" Dionisio, and Rokafella, presented by Full Circle (Bronx);

*Let the Eagle Scream!* by Nia Love, performed by Blacksmith's Daughter Dance Theatre, presented by Harlem Stage/Aaron David Hall (Manhattan); April 6–22

**Le Petit Mort/Now It's Time to Say Goodbye** created, directed and choreographed by Pavel Zustiak with the Company; Set/Costumes, Nick Vaughn; Video, Tal Yarden; Dramaturg, Rachel Chavkin; Cast: Benjamin Asriel, Gina Bashour, Ellen Cremer, Saar Harari, Marya Wethers, Pavel Zustiak; April 12–15

**Church** written & directed by Young Jean Lee; presented by Young Jean Lee Theater Company; Choreography, Faye Driscoll; Sets, Eric Dyer; Costumes, Normandy Sherwood; Lighting, Mark Barton; Sound, Matthew Tierney; PSM, Sam Seymour; Cast: Greg Hildreth, Karinne Keithley, Weena Pauly, Katie Workum; April 26–May 12

**The Fall and Rise of the Rising Fallen** created, presented, and performed Banana Bag and Bodice; Writer, Jason Craig; Director, Mallory Catlett; Cast: Peter Blomquist, Mallory Catlett, Jennifer Wright Cook, Jason Craig, G Lucas Crane, Miranda Hardy, Rod Hipskind, Peter Ksander, Jessica Jelliffe, Casey Opstad, Morgan von Prelle Pecelli, Heather Peroni, Jamie McElhinney, Morgan Murphy; April 26–May 12

**soloNOVA Arts Festival** 4th annual; presented by terraNOVA Collective; included: *Dear Dad, Confessions of Gogo* written & performed by Monica West, directed by Brad Calcaterra; *Extraordinary Vacancy* written & directed by Anne Goldmann, co-written & directed by Sue Morrison; *Butterfly Suicide* by Samantha Lally, Rebecca Lally & Jeannine Jones, directed by Debbie Jones, performed by Samantha Lally; *By Rail* written & performed by C.J. Critt, directed by Richard Sabellico; *Lucky Pink Wonderland* written & performed by Amanda Duarte, directed & choreographed by Ben Kerrick; *Popsicle's Departure, 1989* written & performed by Madi Distefano, directed by Matt Pfeiffer; *Confessions* written & performed by Milica Paranosic; *The Should Dream* written and performed by Victoria Libertore, directed by Ryan Migge; *Vamping* written & performed by Kali Quinn, directed by Jonathan Maloney; *Miracle Tomato* written & performed by Jessica Cerullo, directed by Ragnar Freidank; Three Solo Dances: *New Solo Dance* choreographed & performed by Larissa Velez, *Lonely* choreographed & performed by Heather Olson, *Ex-Memory: waywewere* choreographed & performed by Jeanine Durning; *Man Up* written & performed by Carlos Andrés Gómez, directed by Tamilla Woodard; May 16–June 3

**The Forest is Young and Full of Love** by Luigi Nono; presented by International Contemporary Ensemble; Director, Habib Azar; Soprano, Tony Arnold; Clarinet, Joshua Rubin, Speakers: Claire Chase, Wendy Richman, Peter Tastsits; Percusion: David Schotzko, David Bowlin, Jennifer Curtis, Kivie Cahn-Lipman; May 22–23

# Personal Space Theatrics

Nicholas Cotz, Artistic Director; Kaia Lay Rafoss, Managing Director

**BecauseHeCan** by Arthur Kopit; Director, Nicholas Cotz; Set, David Esler; Costumes, Kathleen Leary; Lighting, Mike Riotto; Sound, Chris Rummel; Props, Casy Smith; Cast: Daryl Boling, John Henry Cox, Ylfa Edelstein, Karl Gregory, Ronald Guttman; Greenwich Street Theatre; June 9–25

**Myth America** by Stephen Wargo, featuring the writings of Israel Horovitz, Arthur Kopit, Theresa Rebecks, Rachel Axler, Ian Cohen, Brian Dykstra, Jason Grote, Matthew Paul Olmos, Julien Schwab, Saviana Stanescu and Lloyd Suh; Directors, Nicholas Cotz and Adam Fitzgerald; Set/Props, Becca Lord; Costumes, Kathleen Leary; Lighting, Marty Vreeland; Sound, Chris Rummel; Stage Manager, Ryan Parow; Cast: Frank Anderson, Sean-Michael Bowles, Darian Dauchan, Vivia Font, Rich Fromm, Ann Hu, Ken Maharaj, Rob Maitner, Margo Brooke Pellmar, Lori Prince, James Saito; TBG Arts Center; April 15–25

## Peter Jay Sharp Theater at Playwrights Horizons

**Single Black Female** by Lisa Thompson; presented by New Professional Theatre; Director, Colman Domingo; Cast: Soara-Joye Ross, Riddick Marie; June 15–25

**Asking for It** written and performed by Joanna Rush; Director, Lynne Taylor-Corbett; Lighting, Brant Thomas Murray; Sound/Composer, Joachim Horsley; Stage Manager, Tim Kinzel; Peter Jay Sharp Theatre; July 10–24

**FreshPlay Festival** presented by MCC Youth Theater; included: *Ascending to Heaven* by Jennifer Huynh, *Writer's Block* by Kyle-Steven Porter, *Storyteller* by Cara Brumfield, *Directions from a Convict* by Julia Torres, *The Book of the Who* by Holland Hamilton, *The Truth About Coney Island* by MCC Theater Youth Company with Zakiyyah Alexander; August 10–12

## Phare Play Productions

Blake Bradford, Artistic Director; Christine Vinh, Executive Director

**Fall Shorts** included: *Unspoken Arrangements* by Patrick Cleary, directed by Kymm Zuckert; Cast: Tamara Cacchione; *Jesus at the Rehab* by Carl L. Williams, directed by Christine Vinh; Cast: Ria Mae Binaoro, Betsy Head, Brett Maughan, Roland Uruci, Brandon Yeager; *Arms* by Bekah Brunstetter, directed by Brandon Yeager; Cast: Chris Douros, Shelley Virginia, Zarah Kravits; *End Scene* by Brad Jennings, directed by Wayne Yeager; Director, Roy Aialon, Tim Kondrat, Eve Armstrong; *Accused* by Peter Wittenberg, directed by Christine Vinh; Cast: Ryan Patrick, Jasmine Spiess; *Office Work* by Patrick Cleary, directed by Kymm Zuckert; Cast: Kendall Rileigh, Kevin Kaine, Alexander Kruuse Mettin; Grand Theatre at Producers Club; September 22–24

**Inside Carl's Shorts** short plays by Carl Williams; included *His Critical Condition, The Woman Who Shot Santa Clause, Table for Three, What Are Words Worth to a Long Fellow, The Gift of the Magi: The Untold Story, Members of the Club;* Directors, Nicole Serra, Roland Uruci, Casey Duncan, Kymm Zuckert, Eve Armstrong, Christine Vinh; Cast: Edward Monterosso, Jenny Zerke, Benjamin Keaton, Jen Brooks, Niae Knight, Susan Tietze, Mayank Saxena, Jasmine Spiess, Tim Kondrat, Yury Lomakin, Caitlin Davis, Kendall Rileigh, Daralyn Adams, Rusty Harding, Angela Donovan, Amy Lerner, Alexis Adair, Kimberly Bailey; Royal Theatre at the Producers Club; September 22–24

**The Last Cloud** by Blake Bradford; Director, Anne Thibault; Cast: Christopher Eckerdt, Julie Finefrock, Nick May, Kendall Rileigh, Ashley Selett, Joel Veach; Sonnet Theatre at the Producers Club; October 20–22

**Gay Slave Handbook** by Blake Bradford; directed and performed by John Michael Crotty, Benjamin Farber & Nicole Serra; Sonnet Theatre at the Producers Club; October 20–22

**Snake in the Fridge** by Brad Fraser; Director, Blake Bradford; Cast: Vallen Pilgrim, Molly Church, Alicia Green, Will Strong; Grand Theatre at the Producers Club; October 26–31

**Unwrap Your Candy** short plays by Doug Wright; included *Unwrap Your Candy, Lot 13: The Bone Violin, Wildwood Park,* and *Baby Talk;* Directors, Wayne Yeager, Christine Vinh, Carrie Colden; Cast: Wayne Yeager, Lizzie Schwarz, Jeffy Michaels, Matthew Gologor, Casey Duncan, Christine Vinh, Blake Bradford, Brandon Yeager; Grand Theatre at the Producers Club; October 26–31

**The Eight: Reindeer Monolgues** by Jeff Goode; Director, Wayne Yeager; Cast: Dan Parillis, Augustin Correro, Shea Locke, Eve Armstrong, Kevin Sebastian, Casey Duncan, Aaron Kapner, Peggy Queener; Grand Theatre at the Producers Club; December 11–23

**Callback** by Bill Svanoe; presented by Phare Play Productions; Director, Blake Bradford; Cast: Joan Darling & Greg Mullavey or Molly Church & Ax Norman; Lodestar Theatre; December 29–January 14

**Vampingo** and **Moonbite** by Ariana Johns & Jolene Adams, with John Ten Eyck; Directors, Jolene Adams & Greg Mullavey; Cast: Ariana Johns, Kimberly Dillon, Phil Garfinkel, Doua Moua, Shannan Leigh Reeve; Lodestar Theatre; January 24–February 16

**Dark of the Moon** by Howard Richardson and William Berney; presented by Phare Play Productions; Director, Blake Bradford; Cast: Kevin Sebastian, Roland Uruci, Amber Godfrey, Isabelle David, Christine Vinh, Aaron Benham, Linda Hill, Steven Nelson, Vincent Cross, Susanne Gottesman-Traub, Caitlin Davis, Ariel Jacobson, Corrie Desmuke, Kymm Zuckert, Jasmine Spiess, Aaron Kapner, Emily Cohen, Bill Purdy, Tim Kondrat, Emily Mostyn-Brown, Jim deProphetis, Jean Walker, Peter Kilcommons, Gene Connelly, Amanda Cox; Lodestar Theatre; February 23–March 18

**The Complete Works of William Shakespeare (abridged)** by Adam Long, Daniel Singer & Jess Winfield; produced by Phare Play Productions; Director, Christine Vinh; Cast: Michael Climek, Ben Klier, Scott Morales; Lodestar Theatre; April 13–29

**Spring Shorts** included: *Vatican Vince* by Jerrod Bogard, directed by Bennett W. Harrell; Cast: Michael C. Freeland; Cast: Michael C. Freeland, Curtis Burdine, Yury Lomakin, Nanette Drazic, Kristin Skye Hoffmann, Lea McKenna-Garcia; *Marginalia* by Kendall Rileigh, directed by Roland Uruci; Cast: Amber Ford, Michael Weems; *Telling Ma* by R. Lonnie Westeen, directed by Kevin Josephson; Cast: Goldie Zwiebel, Aaron Kapner, Susanne Gottesman-Traub, Elliott Rodriguez; *Mom, Stoned* by Bekah Brunstetter, directed by Karen Dabney; Cast: Katie McConaghy, Peggy Giglio, Carol Neiman; *The Last Posse* by Pat Morgan, directed by Roland Uruci; Cast: Edward Monterosso, Tom Summers, Luis de Amechazurra; *Gay Slave Handbook* by Blake Bradford, directed by Kymm Zuckertt; Cast: Blake Bradford, Christine Vinh, Matt Klan; Lodestar Theatre; April 21–24

**The Cherry Orchard** by Anton Chekhov; Director, Blake Bradford; Cast: Arno Austin, Amber Ford, Marcus D. Harvey, Edward Monterosso, Steven Nelson, Therese Plummer, Peggy Queener, Christopher Reed, Adam Souza, Kate Stratton, Roland Uruci, Goldie Zwiebel, Wilson Nelson; Beckmann Theatre at American Theatre of Actors; May 10–20

**Summer Shorts** included: *Dead Cat* by Ry Heman, directed by Blake Bradford; Cast: Chris Bell, Angela Donovan, Sean Goldman, Jasmine Spiess, Vallen Pilgrim; *The Raft* by Kristyn Leigh Robinson, directed by Brooklyn Scalzo; Cast: Betsy Head, Alex Moshofsky; *1-900-Sex-Date* by Julian Olf, directed by David Pleva; Cast: Peggy Queener, Eric Talon; *The Locker Room* by Judy Klass, directed by Ari Jacobson; Cast: Aidan Diaz, Sean Goldman, Zach Rothman-Hicks, Joel Repman, Molly Church; *I Have It* by Bekah Brunstetter, directed by Karen Dabney; Cast: Jeffrey Parrillo, Katie McConaghy; *The Wake* by Ed Vela, directed by Roland Uruci; Cast: Molly Church, Robyn Gabrielle Lee, Billy Weimer, Eric Talon; Beckmann Theatre at American Theatre of Actors; July 19–22

# Phoenix Theatre Ensemble

Craig Smith, Elise Stone, Michael Surabian, Angela Madden, Jason Crowl, Founders

**The Complete Works of William Shakespeare [abridged]** by Adam Long, Daniel Singer, and Jess Winfield; Director, Michael Surabian; PSM, Kathy Snyder; Costumes, Nicole Frachiseur; Cast: Brian A. Costello, Matt Neely, Scott D. Phillips; New York Improv; October 1–31

**The Sneeze** by Anton Chekov, translated and adapted by Michael Frayn; Director/Sound, John Giampetro; Costumes, Lillian Rhiger; PSM, Shane Van Vliet; Dramaturg, Joanna Donehower; Lighting, Jeffrey E. Salzberg; Cast: Jason O'Connell, Dan Matisa, Laura Piquado; Ace of Clubs; October 14–November 14

**The Lesson** and **The Painting** by Eugene Ionesco; Director, Amy Wagner/Kevin Confoy; Cast: Jennifer Curfman, Sarah Hartman, John Lenartz, Angela Madden, Laura Piquado, Craig Smith; Connelly Theatre; December 7–January 8

**Antigone** by Sophocles, adapted by Jean Anouilh; Director, Gus Kaikkonen; Cast: Kelli Holsopple, Douglas McKeown, Joseph J. Menino, Connelly Theatre; November 28–January 2

**On the Verge, or the Geography of Yearning** by Eric Overmyer; Director, Karen Case Cook; Cast: Angela Madden, Elise Stone, Michael Surabian, Angela Vitale; Connelly Theatre; April 27–May 19

**Maud–The Madness** by Alfred Lord Tennyson; Director, Niegel Smith; Set, Clint Ramos; Lighting, Peter West; Sound, Elizabeth Rhodes; Cast: Jonathan Tindle; Abingdon Arts June Havoc Theatre; May 18–June 9

# Players Theatre

**Art People** by Mark E. Leib; presented by Committed Theatre Company; Director, Tony Giordano; Cast: Charlie Moss, Don Harvey, John Kaisner, Mihaella Mihut, Shelly Ebner, Lauren Stock; November 30–December 17

**Welcome Home Steve** by Craig McNulty; presented by Wizard Oil Productions; Directors, Saida Cooper & Amanda Kate Joshi; Cast: Daniel Marmion, Tyson Murphy, Brittany A. Palazzo, Marie-Rose Pike, Ian Roettger; Loft Theatre; December 6–17

**Triangle** book & lyrics by June Rachelson-Ospa, music by Mark Barkan; Director, Karen Rousso; Music Director, David Fletcher; April 12–15

**Measure for Measure** by William Shakespeare; Director, Meagan Shimizu; Cast: Eric Alba, Danny Adler, Lindsay Bernstein, Alice Dranger, Mikaela Feely-Lehman, Carl Howell, Daniel Kemper, Andrew Levy, Gabriela Marcus, Meredith O'Leary, John Prescod, Patrick Rutnam, Montgomery Sutton; April 26–29

# Producers Club & Producers Club II

**BTW's New Work Series** presented by Beyond the Wall Productions; included: *Fugue for Fred and Four Seasons* by Matte O'Brien, directed by Danya Nardi; *Subverse* by Jeremy Patterson, directed by Greg Cicchino; *The Third Stage* by Matt Johnson, directed by Greg Cicchino; June 1–2

**Alex and the Girls** by Cary Fisher; Cast: Laverne Cox, Candice Owens, Jorge Enrique Rivas, Julia Royter, Meilan Smith, Stephan Varnier; June 12–18

**You're a Good Man, Charlie Brown** by Clark Gessner; presented by Macorannigan Productions; Cast: Michelle Gancedo-Dancer, Jamie Marie Hannigan, Eric Harper, Steven A. Hannigan, Mary Lynch, Steven Maiorano, Ryan P.J. Mulholland, Brianna Diakunczak, Carly Morgan, Jenny Caruso, Gillian Caruso; June 14–18

**Bitter, Bitter, Burnt** by David Sedaris, adapted and directed by Blake Bradford; presented by Etcetera Theatre Company; Cast: David-Wyatt Kuether; Royal Theatre; June 22–24

**Alcibiades the Athenian** by Gerald Kosloff; Director, Samantha Tella; Producer, Samuel Kosloff; Fights, Nick Fondulis; Stage Manager, Anthony Pound; Choreography, Erin Zaruba; Costumes, Jessa-Raye Court; Cast: David A. Rudd, Saluda Camp, Siobhan Parisi, Patrick McDaniel, Keith Blazer, Brian DePetris, Reese Eifler, Shawn Dollinger, Kevin Hoffmann, Nick Fondulis, Tim Romero, Clare Patterson, Shannon Corey, Sameerah Luqmaan-Harris, Julia Roux, Arianna Kosloff; June 28–July 1

**Beer for Breakfast** by Robert Scott Sullivan; presented by Talegate Productions; Director, Jenn Bornstein; Design, Jessica Veres, Bart Schobert, Mike Gnazzo, Mark Marshall; Cast: Meg Bartholomay, Nathan Bock, Julie Campbell-Elliott, Kenneth Hatlee, Ricardo Maldonado, Topher Mikels, Tom Olori; PC II; June 29–July 23

**A Family's Play** written & directed by Shawn Luckey; presented by The Diversity Players of Harlem; Music, Joseph Cornell; Cast: Farah Snipes, Patrick Mitchell, Steve Jean-Baptiste, Gurlaine Jean-Mary, April Lisbeth, Sean Eddy, Nia D. Spaulding, Gwen Majette, C. Truth, Mark Mallek, McGregor Wright, Dwight Ali Williams, Shawn Luckey, Meriam Rodriguez; July 13–16

**Extraordinary Deceptions** magic performed by Michael Gutenplan; PCII; July 28–29

**JungalBook** adapted and directed by Caitlin Heiback; presented by Youth on Target Productions; Cast: Sarah Bellatoni, Leah Carrol, David Futernick, Heather Heels, Chris Maddox, Anthony Mendez, Robyn Schall, Isabel Steuble-Johnson; August 3–5

**Sunlight, Moonlight, Lamplight** created and presented by Prophet in Your Pocket; Director, Rachel Madris; Cast: Sam Sax, Jessica Hendricks, Seth Moore; Crowne Theatre; August 8–13

**The Jackie Simon Show!** by Sean Devaney and Jerrod Bogard; Director, Kristin Skye Hoffman; Royal Theatre; August 22–24

**Love Is Good** by Josh Drimmer; presented by Developing Acts Company; August 23–27

**A Midsummer Night's Dream** by William Shakespeare; presented by Foolish Mortals; Director, Blake Bradford; Cast: Shari Paige Acker, Kelly Barrett, Tamara Cacchione, Molly Church, Casey Duncan, Nancy Elton, Mary Jane Gocher, Sri Gordon, Alicia Green, Suzanne Hall, Erin Elizabeth Hart, Rachel Lande, Catharine Pecile, Nicole Serra, Christine Vinh, Nasreen Z'Navi, Kymm Zuckert; Grand Theatre; August 30–September 10

**My Life As You** by Laura Rohrman; presented by Waverly Writers Collective; Director/Producer, Fritz Brekeller; Cast: Stuart Lopoten, Kelli Porterfield, Ashley Wren Collins, Jeff Branson; PC II; September 14–24

**Starting Here, Starting Now** lyrics by Richard Maltby Jr., music by David Shire; presented by Westminster Conservatory Actors Company; Director, Peter Wright; Cast: Carly Voigt, Kareen Foster, Russell Fischer; September 15–16

**Macdeath** by John Martin and Dudley Stone; presented by HMS Productions; Director, Brian Nelson; Cast: Cyrus E. Newitt, Charles Karel, Christine Rendell, Ellen Mittenthal, David Berent, Cyrus E. Newitt; PCII; October 11–22

**Have You Seen This Man?...The Mel Grovero Project** written & directed by Brandon Kalbaugh; presented by Two Spoons Theatre Company; Cast: Joe MacDougall, Brady Ovson; Cinda Lawrence, Josh Carpenter, Salim Rahman, Brooke Chirone; October 24–29

**Halloween Plays** presented by Developing Acts Company; included: *Who Knows in the Dark?* written & directed by Bettina Bilger; *All Hallowed* by Sharon Surhoff, directed by Rob Aloi; *Something's Brewing* by W. Labier Jones, directed by Marcus Jones; *Charlie House* by Marcus Jones, directed by Paul Nicholas; *Ghoulish Monologues* by Le Wilhelm, directed by Gregg David Shore, Royal Theatre; October 31–November 5

**A Soldier's Play** by Charles Fuller; presented by The Diversity Players of Harlem; Director, Kathy Lindboe; Cast: Shawn Luckey, Erik McKay, Keith Lum, Adrian Washington, Dwight Ali Williams, Jeffrey Smith, Larry Floyd, James Shippy, Daryl Denner, Derrick Sanders, Jacob White, Reginald Barnes, Michael Flood; Grand Theatre; November 7–12

**Bridal Terrorism** by Bill Rosenfield; presented by Diversity Players of Harlem Director, Bill Barry; Cast: Amy Boeding, Bill Barry, Laurence Waltman, Nina Capone, Lorraine Condos, Val Balaj; November 8–12

**Beware: Bernadette! A Musical Fable** written & directed by Leon James Bynum; presented by The Harmony Theatre Company; Music Director, DuPreez Strauss; Choreography, Jennifer Lisette Lopez; Cast: Hamza Z. Ahmed, John Cencio Burgos, Dondrie Burnham, Noah Brendemuehl, Toney Chem, Jennifer Dickson, Miranda Halverson, John Daniel Forslund, Stephen Hershey, Sarah Huo, Jacqueline Langheim, Monroe Moody, Barron Anthony Myers, Marissa Rosen, Mei Sakamoto, Regina Spano, Jamie Leigh White, Rieko Yamanaka; November 15–19

**The Madonna Whore...Confessions of a Dirty Mind** by Tim Douglas; Director, Eric Thal; presented by TwinStar Productions; Cast: Randy Jones, Tim Douglas, Hannah Snyder-Beck; November 29–December 16

**Six Nights to Live Festival** presented by You Are Here Productions; Grand Theatre; December 4–9

**An Ozark Mountain Christmas** by Le Wilhelm; Director, Merry Beamer; PCII; December 7–17

**Mrs. Scrooge! (A New Christmas Carol)** adapted and directed by Peter Mac; Royal Theatre; December 15–16

**Define Happiness** by Deirdre MacNamara; presented by Will Pork Productions; February 14–18

**Love, Greed, and the Pursuit of Happiness** written & directed by Adrienne Moultriez; presented by Yet 2 Evolve Productions; Cast: Shannon Foster, Alfred Rutherford, Brandi Webb, Omar Clyburn, Jamie Park, Michael Alcide; Grand Theatre; February 14–25

**Cigarettes and Chocolate** by Anthony Minghella; presented by Fool's Pear Productions; Director, Jesse Ontiveros; Cast: Brandon Sevier Hillard, Helen Kim, Lisa Margolin, Hannah Mason, Casey McClellan, Madeline Virbasius-Walsh; February 28–March 4

**Family Business** four one-acts presented by Love Creek Productions; included: *The Audition* by Paul DeSena, *Oh, Momma* by Megan Lohne, *Upstairs* by Margaret McCloskey, *How the Nabers Family Found Their Soulfulness* by Janine Nabers; Cast: Jill Abromovich, David Bly, David Gellef-Hurwitz, Rae Schiffino, Eve Packer, Katherine Hamill, Laura Gourdine, Melissa Joyner, Tom Martin, Adrienne Moore, Tai Verley, Robert Wray; Royal Theatre; March 6–10

**Teaspoon Festival of Short Plays** presented by Two Spoons Theatre Company; included: *Oh Nancy* by Dawson Moore, directed by Brandon Kalbaugh; *Medals* by Mark Cornell, directed by Todd Lawson; *No Prune* by Henry Meyterson, directed by Charmaine Broad; *Double Whammy* by Liz Amberly, directed by Marc Jones; *Back In* by Jason R. Montgomery, directed by Tony Capone; *Blind Man's Bluff* by Steven Korbar, directed by Marc Jones; *Wednesdays* by Sue Brody, directed by Paula J. Riley; *Pete's Pot O'Gold* by Brandon Kalbaugh, directed by Joe McDougall; *I Feel Swell* by Henry Meyerson, directed by Paula J. Riley; Cast: Cinda Lawrence, Mario Corry, Renee Petrofes, Allison Poccia, Lindsay Drew, Neil Howard, Gregory Singleton, Davie Pearce, Walt Frasier, Brianne Moncrief, Jessica Mortellaro, Kim Brownell, Ray McDavitt, Anita Wlody, Lynne Rosenberg, Leigh

A. Cambre, Brandon Kalbaugh, Josh Mertz, Shelly Bhalla, Emma Scott, Wendy Merritt, Steve Hill, Kristofer Holz, Evy Lutzky; Royal Theatre; March 22–25

**Random Particles of Matter Floating in Space** by Michael Allen; presented by Jonathan Flha Productions; Director, Denyse Owens; Cast: Jonathan Albert, Elba Sette-Camara, Aaron Haskell; Sonnet Theatre; April 11–21

**The Newlyweds** written & produced by Beverly Orozco; presented by Aditi Pictures; Director, Ben Rivers; Cast: Phillip Hatcher, Jessica Daly, Ben Rivers, Michael Andrews, Liana Velazquez, Sol Crespo, Christopher Williams, Laquayva Anthony, Latreesch Orozco-Simmons, D'Monaye; April 12–22

**As You Like It** by William Shakespeare; presented by Reduxion Theatre Company; Director, Erin Anderson; Lighting, David Nelson; Set, Tyler Woods; Costumes, Jessa-Raye Court; Composer, Mark McDaniels; Stage Manager, Kaoru Kikuchi; Cast: Amanda Moore, Celester Rich, Chad Robison, David Nelson, David Sedgwick, Jennifer Turner, Jessica Angleskhan, Justin R.G. Holcomb, Meagan English, Michael Menger, Samantha Turvill, Sarah Schmitz, Sean Logan, Shawn Renfro; Grand Theatre; April 19–May 5

**Cropped** written & directed by Anita A. Ahiadormey; Cast: Jarett Alexander, Kimberly Courts, Erik McKay, Dalia Rodriguez; Crowne Theatre; April 26–29

**When the World Was Green** by Sam Shepard & Joseph Chaiken; presented by Silver Light Visions; Director, Pam Gittlitz; Cast: Rudy Olivar, Laura Thies; Royal Theatre; May 8–13

**The Revolving Door** written and directed by Tony Vozzo; presented by New Live TV Productions; Cast: Tony Vozzo, Cris Morales, Jacqueline Beaulieu, Anthony Baez, Patrick Egan, Conrad Llerena; May 10–13

**Back 2 Back** *North of Providence* by Edward Allen Baker and *Welded* by Eugene O'Neill; presented by Mare Nostrum Elements; Director, Tim Herman; Cast: Kevin Albert, Cheryl Orsini; May 19–June 3

# Prospect Theater Company

Cara Reichel, Producing Artistic Director; Melissa Huber, Managing Director

**The Flood** Book, music & lyrics by Peter Mills & Cara Reichel; Director, Cara Reichel; Set, Kanae Heike; Costumes, Sidney Shannon; Lighting, Evan Purcell; Orchestrations, Dniel Freyer & Peter Mills; Sound, Shannon Slaton; Stage Manager, Kat West; Music Director, Justin Hatchimonji; Cast: Joe Bergquist, Jennifer Blood, Victoria Bundonis, Nick Cartell, Jamie Davis, Matt DeAngelis, Deborah Grausman, Carol Hickey, Greg Horton, Dan Housek, Suzanne Houston, Amy Hutchins, Jean McCormick, A'lisa D. Miles, Joseph O'Brien, Michael Pesce, Drew Poling, Catherine Porter, Zachary Prince, Jonathan Rayson, Daniel Scott Richards, Zachary Wobensmith, Erica Wright; American Theatre of Actors'Chernuchin Theatre; October 21–November 19

**Tock Tick** book & lyrics by Tom Nevits, music by Gihieh Lee; Director, Jacskon Gay; Music Director, Matt Vinson; Choreography, Stephanie Fittro; Set, Aleksandra Maslik; Costumes, Kate Cusack; Lighting, Cat Tate; Sound, David Erdberg; Stage Manager, C.J. LaRoche; Cast: David Abeles, Maria Couch, David Foley Jr., Christopher Graves, Melissa Hart, Joshua Landay, Mark Mozingo, Robby Sharpe, Laura Beth Wells; West End Theatre; February 3–March 4

**West Moon Street** by Rob Urbinati; Director, Davis McCallum; Set, Lee Savage; Costumes, Naomi Wolff; Lighting, Lily Fossner; Composer, Russell M. Kaplan; Dialects, Ryan Dunn; Production Manager, Mary Leach; PSM, Kat West; Cast: Michael Crane, Avi Glickstein, Jocelyn Greene, Judith Hawking, Melissa Miller, Glenn Peters, Alex Webb, David Ruffin; Hudson Guild Theatre; April 21–May 20

**Prosepect's Dark Nights Series** Spring Series at the Hudson Guild Theatre: *The Stream* by Jackie Baker & Shelly Stover (April 24 & 25), *Statements After An Arrest Under the Immorality Act* by Athol Fugard, directed by Gregory L. Allen (April 28–May 1); *Wendy Saturday* created and performed by Valerie Morel (May 2); *Ophelia: opera in blue* by Sergei Dreznin, text by William Shakespeare; Director, May Adrales; Music Director, Mike Pettry; Design, Kanae Heike, Kate Kusack; Cast: David Mantanga, Ben Beckley, Lucas Howland, Marisa Michelson (May 5–7); *Greg's List: The Musical* compiled & written by Quin Chia, Aaron Coleman & Tom Coppola (May 12–15)

**Benefit Concerts** *The Pursuit of Persephone* book, music & lyrics by Peter Mills, book & direction by Cara Reichel; Cast: Chris Fuller, Jessica Grové, David Abeles, Piper Goodeve, Benjamin Sands; Benefit staged concert reading at the Lucille Lortel Theatre; June 26; *Illyria* book, music & lyrics by Peter Mills, adapted by Cara Reichel & Peter Mills; Director, Cara Reichel; Cast: Jimmy Bennett, Larry Brustofski, Maria Couch, Jeff Edgerton, Jonathan Groff, Jessica Grové, Dan Sharkey, Tina Stafford, Steve Wilson, Michael Winther; Lamb's Theatre; September 11; *The Alchemists* music & lyrics by Peter Mills, book by Peter Mills & Cara Reichel; Host, Malcolm Gets; Cast: David Abeles, Heath Calvert, Jessica Grové, Charles Hagerty, Michael Hunsaker, Richard Todd Adams, Carol Hickey, Greg Horton, Peter Maris, Drew Poling, Navida Stein, Erica Wright, Henry Anderson, Michael Bunting, Brooke Dobossy, Reed Latrowski, Daniel Marconi; Lucille Lortel Theatre; April 9

# Public Theater

**Hip-Hop Theater Festival** 6th annual; created by Danny Hoch; included: *Live From the Front* written & performed by Jerry Quickley, directed by reg e. gaines; *Hollis Mugley's Only Wish* by Keith Josef Adkins; *Skinimin12* written & performed by Jennifer Cendana Armas; *Little Book of Battles* written & performed by Chastity Dotson; *Five 'Til* written & performed by Edwin Lee Gibson, directed by Daphne Richards; *Robocop 525* choreographed & performed by Kenichi Ebina; *Free?* written & performed by Kristina Wong; *Rock, Paper, Scissors* by Ben Snyder, directed by Louis Moreno; June 20–24

**New Work Now!** Festival of New Play Readings; included: *Things We Want* by Jonathan Marc Sherman, directed by Ethan Hawke (October 23), *In the Red and Brown Water* by Tarell McCraney, directed by Tina Landau (October 25), *The Good Negro* by Tracey Scott Wilson, directed by Leisl Tommy (October 29), *Celebrity Row* by Itamar Moses, directed by Oskar Eustis (November 2), *Untitled Darfur Play* by Winter Miller, directed by Joanna Settle (November 3)

**Arab-Israeli Festival** October 24–November 6; included: *iWitness* by Joshua Sobol, adapted & directed by Barry Edelstein; *When The Bulbul Stopped Singing* by David Greig, adapted from the diaries of Raja Shenhadeh, directed by JoAnne Akalaitis; *Untitled* by Najla Said & *La Cosa De Sogni* by Nathalie Handal, directed by Kia Corthron; *The Murder of Isaac* by Motti Lerner, translated by Anthony Berris, directed by Irene Lewis; *Again and Against–The Art of Hoping Indefinitely* by Betty Shamieh, directed by Robert O'Hara; *O Jerusalem* by A.R. Gurney, directed by Jim Simpson

**Under the Radar 2006** (International Edition) January 12–27; included: *A Beautiful View* written & directed by Daniel MacIvor; *Another You* written by and featuring Allen Johnson, directed by Sean Ryan; *Epistle to Young Actors* written & directed by Olivier Py; *Invincible Summer* written & performed by Mike Daisey, directed by Jean-Michele Gregory; *Radio Macbeth* by SITI Company, directed by Anne Bogart and Darron L West; *The Be(a)st of Taylor Mac* written & performed by Taylor Mac, directed by David Drake; *The Brothers Size* by Tarell McCraney, directed by Tea Alagic; *Two Songs* written & performed by John O'Keefe

**In Darfur** by Winter Miller; Director, Joanna Settle; April 13–29

# Push Productions

Tom Escovar, Founder and Managing Director; Michael Kimmel, Creative Director

**Marat/Sade** by Peter Weiss; presented with J. Edward Cecala; Director, Michael Kimmel; Sets/Lighting, Ben Kato; Costumes, Jessica Gaffney; Composer/Musical Director, Scott O'Brien; Choreography, Rachel Klein; Assistant Director/Dramaturg, Tara Good; Associate Producer, Tim Mansfield; PSM, Ana Mari de Quesada; ASM, Claudia Weinstock; Cast: Matt DeVriendt, Tom Escovar, Alan Jestice, Jessica Jolly, Richardson Jones, Carl Louis, Shannon MacMcMillan, Mitchell Malnati, Claire Marie Mannie, Caitlin Mulhern, Brian Reilly, Rob Seitelman, Graham Skipper, Johnny Sparks, Jona Tuck, Kit Williamson; Ensemble: Anneka Fagundes, Iain Hoskins, Amy Wolf; Musicians: Adam Kielman, Jonathan Levy, Mike Lunapiena; June 3–July 1

**Shannon in Ambient Light** by Timothy Mansfield; Director, Michael Kimmel; Sets/Lighting, Ben Kato; Costumes, Jessica Gaffney; Music/Sound, Scott O'Brien; PSM, Sarah Locke; Company Manager, Ana Mari de Quesada; Cast: Stephanie Chambers, Robert Chaney, Matt DeVriendt, Richardson Jones, Amy Wolf; Bottle Factory Theatre; November 1–18

**Kraken** by Len Jenkin; Director, Michael Kimmel; Set/Lighting, Ben Kato; Costumes, Jessica Gaffney; Music/Sound, Scott O'Brien; PSM, Syche Hamilton; Technical Director, Patrick Cecala; Cast: Tom Escovar, Marc Geller, Richardson Jones, Tracy Liz Miller, Heidi Niedermeyer, Eva Patton, Augustus Truhn; May 11–June 2

# RADIOTHEATRE

Creator, Dan Bianchi; Executive Producer, Cynthia Bianchi

**H.G.Wells' The Island of Dr. Moreau** by Dan Bianchi; Produced by Cynthia Bianchi; Director/Music/Design, Dan Bianchi; Sound Engineer, Wes Shippee; Stage Manager, Rob Nguyen; Cast: Liz Burke, William Greville, Aaron Mathias, Rob Nguyen, Patrick O'Connor, Wes Shippee, Cash Tilton; Red Room Theatre; March 9–17

**King Kong** adapted by Dan Bianchi; Produced by Cynthia Bianchi; Director/Music/Design, Dan Bianchi; Sound Engineer, Wes Shippee; Cast: Patrick Flynne, Tom Lacey, Patrick O'Connor, Karyn Plonsky, Cash Tilton, Mark Vance; Red Room; May 24–June 10

# Repertorio Espanol

**Gardel: The Musical** by Eladio Cintrón; Director, Lynette Salas; Musical Director, Carlos Cruz; Choreography, Modesto Lacén; Lighting, Robert Weber Federico; Cast: Miguel Ramos, Mónica Steuer, Ana Padrón, Diego Blanco; Grammercy Arts Theatre; August 4–December 17

**We Women Do It Better** by Roberto Ramos Perea; Director, Angel Gil Orrios; Translator, Charles Philip Thomas; Cast: Soledad Lopez (Spanish) or Merel Julia (English); Grammercy Arts Theatre; May 26–June 18

## Richmond Shepard Theatre

**Disappeared** by Fermin Cabal; Director, Richmond Shepard; Cast: Dawn McGee, Flora Diaz, Lena Armstrong, Leslie Meisel, Anne Connolly, David Gregory; September 7–November 1

**Yashka** by Mike Douglas; presented by TL Productions; Director, Oleg Braude; November 2–November 26

**Modern Medieval** written & performed by David Tyson; November 4–December 23

**The Best Party Ever** written & directed by Annie Ward; Opened December 16; open run

**The Lady Swims Today** written, directed & produced by Howard G. Brown; Set, Kirk Larsen; Lighting, Brett Maughan; Costumes, Lori Santoro; Cast: Maureen Van Zandt, Robert Funaro; February 7–18

**The Dance: The History of American Minstrels** directed and performed by Jason Christophe White and Aaron White; February 22–March 3

**Romance.com** Music, lyrics, book and direction by Joe Simonelli; Cast: Jennifer Nelson, Ben Bleefeld, Pam Delfranco, Michael Sunberg, Rick Makin, Ronnie Marvald; March 30–April 29

## Roy Arias Theatre Center

**Strawberry One-Act Festival** 11th edition; presented by the Riant Theatre; August 4–August 20

**Folie A Deux: Insanity in Paris** by David Stallings; presented by Maieutic Theatre Works; Director, Cristina Alicea; Set, Gabriel Fonseca; Lighting/PSM, Jillian Zeman; Costumes, Tyson Murphy; Cast: Brian Hathaway, Scott Sortman, David Stallings, Hella Bel, Lauren Montgomery; October 6–November 12

**Katrina: A Whole Lotta Water** written & directed by Emmitt Thrower; presented by Wabi Sabi Productions; Music, Shakka; December 14–17

**Vignettes for the Apocalypse** one-acts presented by EndTimes Productions; included: Group 1: *Woo at the Zoo* by Joe Lauinger; Director, Matthew Kreiner; Cast: Jennifer Terpak, Collin MacKenzie Smith, Eddy Munoz; *Let No Man Tear Asunder* by Ed Friedman; Director, Laurie Rae Waugh; Cast: Jay S. Brisk, Lori Feiler, Byron Beane, Alessandro Colla, Sara Gozalo; *Plays for the Sunni Triangle* by Jerrod Bogard; Director, Kristin Skye Hoffmann; Cast: Jerrod Bogard, Tristan Laurence, Ryan Love, Bennett W. Harrell, Micheal C. Freeland, Scott Voloshin, Justin Ness, Sarah Flanagan, Liz White; Group 2: *The National Anthem of Mercury* by Meny Beriro; Director, Greg Cicchino; Cast: Collin MacKenzie Smith, Chris Kateff, Juliet Heller; *The Art of the Pick-Up* by Dave Rosenberg; Director, Matthew Kreiner; Cast: Matthew Watkins, Jamie King, Allyn Rachel; *Occam's Razor* by Wesley St. John; Director, Jared Ranere; Cast: Sara Barker, Reggie Oldham; Group 3: *A Chance Encounter With George W.* by Dave Sweeney; Director, Ilana Landecker; Cast: Byron Beane, J.R. Aducci; *The Long Shot* by Richard Cottrell; Director, Tony Macy-Perez; Cast: Matthew Watkins, Demetrius Kallas; *Over the Asian Airwaves* by Lauren Yee; Director, James E. Duff; Cast: Jessica Ko, Philip Buiser, Richard Hsu, Julee Cerda, John Wu, Katie Dietz; Group 4: *Computer Madness* by Judith Donner Hancock; Director, Michelle Dean; Cast: Sarah Fraunfelder, Alessandro Colla; *Tammy* by Simcha Borenstein; Director, Heather Aronson; Cast: Benna Douglas, Chris Kateff; *Nighthawks* by Evan Guilford-Blake; Director, Tom Herman; Cast: Lodric D. Collins, David Gerald, Oh Rhyne, Kat Garson; February 8–16

**Eva Del Barrio/Isabel Rising** by Houston Brummit & Jimmy Justice; Director, Gloria Zalaya; Music Director, Hobart Spears; Choreography, Adolfo Vazquez; Stage Manager, Hector Palacios; Set, Billy Elder; Cast: Brannon Hall-Garcia, Cyre Rodriguez, Felipe Gorostiza, Roberto Carrasco, Anita Vasan, Gabrielle Garza; February 15–March 11

**Love No Evil** three one-acts: *Blind Love* by Adam Henry, directed by Andy Ottoson; with Malcolm Madera & Gretchen Porro; *Small Talk* by Adam Henry, directed by Andy Ottoson, with Nick Aliberti, Emily Firth, & Alisha Soper; *Violations* by Andy Ottoson, directed by Emily Firth, with Jenn Hopkins; presented by Dalliance Theater; April 17–22

**A Midsummer Night's Dream** by William Shakespeare; presented by New York Neo-Classical Ensemble; Director, Stephen Stout; Cast: Teddy Alvaro, Jessica Jade Andres, James Bartelle, Michael Bartelle, Matthew Berger, Seth Bridges, Kimberly DiPersia, Richard Douglass, Beth Lopes, Grace McLean, Matthew Meixler, Randy Thompson, Gillian Wiggin, Lindsay Wolf; April 19–27

**Hamlet** by William Shakespeare; presented by Gorilla Repertory Theater Company; Director, Christopher Carter Sanderson; May 9–29

## Sage Theater

**Unmasked** by Gail Young; presented by J2 Productions, KMPA Productions, & Paradox Productions; Director, Lizzie Brown; Cast: Marc Balfour, Laurence Cantor, Sara Taylor, Carol Wood, Gail Young; September 6–10

**The Paisley Sisters' Christmas Special** by Jim Ansart, Joel Benjamin, Bret Silverman, Steve Silverman; September 19–26

**The Ticket** book by Eric Ottem, music by Dave Demichelis, music and lyrics by Gary Bragg; presented by Big Break Productions; Director, Michael Raimondi; Choreography, Jacob Brent; Music Directors, Brad Simmons & Rob Lowe; Set, Brian Smallwood; Costumes, Heather Klar; Lighting, Melanie Smock; Sound, Ryan Dowd; PSM, Jon William Goldman; Cast: Julie Barnes, Kim Blair, Timothy Dunn, Hope Harris, Michael Kohn, C. Mingo Long, Annie McGreevey, Corey Skaggs, Joanna Young; Band: Rob Lowe, David DeMichelis, Steve Womer, Steve Holloway; November 7–26

**Just a Matter of Time** book & lyrics by Sandra Dutton, music by Jack Koh; presented by Wayne Sheridan; Director/Choreography, Susan Streater, Music Director, Alan J. Plado, Lighting, Chris Reising; Set, Joe Mathers; Stage Manager, Allison Hope; Cast: Jennifer Kersey, Jean McCormick, Anthony Santelmo Jr., David Demato, Lindsay Goranson, Mary Jane Raleigh, Charlie Newell, Gregory Guy Gorden, Mindy Dougherty, Eric Starker; January 18–31

**Now That You've Seen Me Naked** by Diana Blake; presented by Sage Theater Company; Director, Evan Heird; Music Director/Stage Manager, Michael Leedy; Lighting, Drew Florida; Piano, Aya Kato, Jessie Stacken; Cast: Amy Albert, Diana Blake, Angelina DelCarmen, Ron Hamilton, Chris J. Handley, Ryan Hyde, Rachel McPhee, Perryn Pomatto; February 13–April 7

**Measure for Measure** by William Shakespeare; presented by Charles Drexler/New Lions Theater Company; Director, Lauren Keating; Set, Czerton Lim; Costumes, Summer Jack; Lighting, Paul Toben; Cast: Jordan Barbour, Brian Coats, Nicole D'Amico, Buz Davis, Dinh Q Doan, Charles Drexler, Kelly Hayes, Bobby Hogdson, Erica Lipez, Jared Mercier, Dot Portella, Kiat Sing Teo, Bill Toscano, James Web, Ross Williams; April 13–16

**Mother Load** written & performed by Amy Wilson; presented by Hyde Park & Lafayette, Brian Liebman; Director, Julie Kramer; Lighting, Graham Kindred; Set, Lauren Helpern; Sound, Joe Miuccio; Company Manager, Scott DelaCruz; General Manager, Martian Entertainment; Press, Katie Rosin; April 21–June 22

# Sanford Meisner Theatre

**Hamlet** by William Shakespeare; presented by Reduxion Theatre Company; Director, Tyler Woods; Cast: Erin Anderson, Richard Bolster, Michael Cherry, Kenric Green, Sean Logan, Robert Michael McClure, Samantha Turvill; June 20–July 9

**Alice (squared)** adapted and directed by Cori Silberman; presented by Chris Aniello & Alisa Sommer; Set, Ian Wallace; Costumes, Melissa Daghini; Lighting, Brian Kim; Video, Ana Hurka-Robles; Stage Manager, Jared Goldstein; Cast: Jane Aquilina, Max Arnaud, Kimberly Dilts, Carly Olson, Carrie Ellman, T.J. Fix, Eric Garcia, Candice Palladino, James Walter; September 15–23

**The Marriage Bed** written & directed by Nona Shepphard; presented by Tali Friedman and ASC; Design, Marsha Roddy; Lighting, takis; Sound, Andrew Dodge; Production Coordinator, Mell Wadle; Cast: Nona Shepphard, Tali Friedman; October 6–November 19

**The Ledge** by Jack Hanely; presented by Eavesdrop; Director/Sound/Video, Christopher Eaves; Composer, Alicia Mathewson; Stage Manager, Erin Klee; Cast: Mike Houston; December 1–17

**The Merchant of Venice** by William Shakespeare; presented by Artemis & The Wild Things; Director, Artemis Preeshl; Cast: Ian Byrd, Kate Costello, Joost de Munck, Sarah Donnell, David Ellis, Howard Laniado, Gregg Lauterbach, Brendan Rothman-Hicks, Michael Santora, Sage Suppa, Sarah Tucker, Baris Tuncer, Michael Vaccaro; January 16–20

**H.M.S. Pinafore** adapted from the Gilbert and Sullivan operetta; presented by Vortex Theatre Company (Joshua Randall, Artistic Director; Allison Glenzer, Managing Director); Director, Dave Dalton; Musical Director, Edward Barnes; Choreography, Carrie Cimma; Sets/Lights, Miranda Hardy; Costumes, JessicaWegener; Musicians, Zach Redler, Edward Barnes; Cast: Billy Ernst, Sarah Hartley, Nich Kauffman, David Macaluso, Max Miller, Jendi Tarde, Paul Sigrist; Sanford Meisner Theater; March 3–31

**This Story of Yours** by John Hopkins; presented by Absinthe-Minded Theatre Company; Director, Ralph Scarpato; Cast: Greg Blatto, Peggy Suzuki, Kevin Kelleher, Evan Beskin, Julian Schrenzel, Michael Hagins, Jay McCarey; April 26–May 6

**The Bald Soprano** and **The Lesson** by Eugene Ionesco; presented by Break a Leg Productions; Directors, Joe Benanati & Christopher Bellis; Cast: Phil Garfinkel, Donna Lee Michaels, Jay Aubrey Jones, Teri Black, Martha Lopez Gilpin, Michael Edmund, Michael Gilpin, Judy Jerome, Joan Valentina; May 10–20

**The File on Ryan Carter** written & directed by David Gaard; presented by The Entertainment Agora; Set, Bruce Eyster; Costumes, Michele Reisch; Lighting, Joshua Randall; Sound/PSM, Livia Tabor Hill; Cast: Daniel Koenig, Ryan G. Metzger; May 25–July 8

# Shetler Studios

**In Between the Sheets** by Ian McEwan, adapted & directed by Seth Duerr; presented by York Shakespeare Company; Cast: Mac Brydon, Martin Ewens, David Garry, Nicole Maggi, Paul Rubin, Timothy Smallwood, Kymberly Tuttle, Billy Wheelan, Paulette Williams; Theatre 54; June 4–17

**Changing Violet** written & performed by Deborah Lousie Ortiz, adapted and directed by Terri Muuss; Theatre 54; September 28–November 18

**keepingabreast** written & performed by Jackie Rosenfeld; Director, Rebecca Trent; Theatre 54; November 1–11

**Waves and Beaches** by Jonathan Wallace; presented by Howling Moon Cab Company; Director, Shannon Fillion; January 18–21

**The Spanish Tragedie** by Thomas Kyd; presented by The Queens Players; Director, Rich Ferraioli; Set, Kristen LaSala; Lighting, Matthew Rubin; Cast: Miles Warner, Katie Braden, Cameron Hughes, Kacie Leblong, Malcolm Madera, Rachel Riendeau, Kirk Gostkowski, Melissa Smith, Ryan Metzger, Richard Madden, Dana DiAngelo, Ryan Neal, Tana Leigh Pierce, Ross Pivec; Bridge Theatre; February 13–25

**The Sanitation Chronicles** by Paul Bruno and Mary Humphrey Baldridge; Director, Peter De Maio; Cast: Richard Bey, Danny Cleary, Peter De Maio, Christina George, Joe Albert Lima, Michael Locascio, Vivian Neuwirth, Aidan O'Shea, Bryan Pugh; Theatre 54; April 18–29

**Rose Colored Glass** by Susan Bigelow and Janice Goldberg; Director, Janice Goldberg; Cast: Anita Keal, Emily Zacharias, Brianne Moncrief; Theatre 54; May 5–24

**Pizza Man** by Darlene Craviotto; presented by Wanderlust Productions; Director, Austin Pendleton; Stage Manager, China Hayzer; Cast: Lyndsey Anderson, Micha Lazare, Kyle Wood; Bridge Theatre; May 11–27

# SoHo Rep/Walkerspace

Sarah Benson, Artistic Director; Alexandra Conley, Executive Director

**The Thugs** by Adam Bock; Director, Anne Kauffman; October 5–30; extended October 31–November 19 under and Off-Broadway contract (see full credits in the Off-Broadway section in this volume)

Non-resident Productions

**Mark Smith** by Kate E. Ryan; presented by 13P; Director, Ken Rus Schmoll; Cast: Hannah Cabell, Andrew Dinwiddie, Alissa Ford, Kristen Kosmas, Melissa Miller, Eric Dean Scott; June 5–24

**Cleansed** by Thomas Bradshaw; presented by the Immediate Theatre Company; Director, Elize Day Hittman; Cast: Kaaron Briscoe, Albert Christmas, Nancy Franklin, Aimee McCormack, Bobby Monero, Di Quon; July 7–9

**Blood Wedding** by Federico Garcia Lorca, translated by Lillian Groag; presented by Woodshed Collective; Director, Stephen Squibb & Gabriel Hainer Evansohn; Lighting, Bryan Keller; Sound, Mark Valadez; Music Director, Daniel Rosen; Cast: Kathryn Krasovec, Juliana Huestis, Erikka Danielle Walsh, Steve Kuhel, Tyler Hollinger, Keith Warren, Michele Athena Morgen, Wil Petre, Cassandra Weston, Jennifer Kathryn Marshall, Jocelyn Kuritsky, Charles Sprinkle, Sara Jeanne Asselin, Jake Suffian, Anna Kull; July 21–August 5

**Iphigenia Crash Land Falls on the Neon Shell That Was Once Her Heart (a rave fable)** by Caridad Svich; presented by One Year Lease; Directors, Ianthe Demos & Danny Bernardy; Music, Brian Simerson; Set, James Hunting; Costumes, Kay Lee; Sound, Brian Simerson; Lighting, Mike Riggs; Cast: Danny Bernardy, Nick Flint, Susannah Melone, Brina Stinehelfer, Gregory Walker; September 7–16

**Hotel Oracle** by Bixby Elliot; presented by The Sum Of Us Theatre Company; Director, Stephen Brackett; Set, Nicholas Vaughn; Lighting, Anjeanette Stokes; Costumes, Donald Sanders; Cast: Tessa Gibbons, Raymond James Hill, Katie Honaker, Jim Kane, Paul Keany, Deb Martin; March 8–31

**Mud Blossom** by Ashlin Halfnight; presented by Emergency Theater Project; Director, Kate Pines; Cast: Corinne Edgerly, Jennifer McCabe, Liz Myers; April 14–28

## Stella Adler Studio Theatre

**Hamlet: Evolutions** two plays presented by New World Theatre; included: *Hamlet 1603: The First Quarto* by William Shakespeare, directed by Cynthia Dillon; Cast: Anthony Bagnetto, Robert Cross, Jason Liebman, Kevin Lind, Alyssa Mann, Thomas Poarch, Gabriele Schafer; and *Priscilla* by Jeff Love, directed by Robert Zick Jr.; Cast: Davud Diloreto, Cassie Haynes, Linda Jones, Karron Karr, Jessica Krueger, Paul Weissman; July 7–29

**Glow** by Peter Gil-Sheridan; presented by The Figments; Director, Greg Foro; Cast: Lauren Gleason, Casey McClellan, Lesley Miller, Derek Peith; July 20–29

**The Stronger** by August Strindberg and **The Bald Soprano** by Eugene Ionesco; presented by The End of the Word; Director, Simone Federman; August 11–13

**Serenading Louie** by Lanford Wilson; presented by FHB Productions; Director, Glory Sims Bowen; Cast: Eric Percival, Marci Adlilman, Raissa Dorff, Nathaniel Shaw; March 9–18

## The Storm Theatre

Board of Directors: Peter Dobbins (President), Thomas Gray, Carl Pasbjerg, Jim Scully; Chance Michaels, Producing Director

**Ross** by Terence Rattigan; Director, Stephen Logan Day; Set, Josh Zangen; Costumes, Ruby Randig; Lighting, Bill Sheehan; Sound, Scott O'Brien; Stage Manager, Michaella Kafel; Cast: Emanuele Ancorini, Liam Benzvi, Joe Danbusky, Peter Dobbins, Seán Gormley, Chris Keveney, Gabe Levey, Ted McGuinness, Jamil Mena, Edward Prostak, Anthony Russo, Tim Smallwood, George Taylor, Josh Vasquez, Gabriel Vaughan, Matthew Waterson; October 27–November 18

**Linnea** by John Regis; Director, Peter Dobbins; Set, Todd Edward Ivans; Costumes, Jessica Lustig; Lighting, Bill Sheehan; Sound, Scott O'Brien; Stage Manager, Michelle Kafel; Cast: Stephen Logan Day, David Bodenschatz, Jenn Zarine Habeck, Gabe Levey, Christy Linn, Jamil Mena, Benita Robledo, Ken Trammell, Joshua Vasquez; January 6–February 3

**The Karol Wojtyla Theatre Festival** translations by Boleslaw Taborski; Set, Todd Edward Ivans; Costumes, Jessica Lustig; Lighting, Michael Abrams; Sound, Scott O'Brien; included *The Jeweler's Shop* directed by Robert W. McMaster; Cast: Peter Dobbins, Karen Eke, Chris Keveney, Kristopher Kling, Anthony Russo, Lara Theodos, Elizabeth Wirth; *Our God's Brother* directed by Peter Dobbins & Michelle Kafel; Cast: Nate Begle, Dan Berkey, Charles Casano, Joe Danbusky, Jenn Zarine Habeck, Eric Thorne, William Toth, Matthew Waterson; May 16–June 17

## Summer Play Festival (SPF)

3rd annual; Arielle Tepper, Founder and Executive Producer; July 5–31; performances at the Theatre Row Theatres

*The Butcherhouse Chronicles* by Michael P. Hidalgo, directed by Thomas Caruso; *Father Joy* by Sheri Wilner, directed by Pam MacKinnon; *The Fearless* by Elan Frankel, directed by Scott Schwartz; *Gardening Leave* by Joanna Pinto, directed by Michael Goldfried; *Hardball* by Victoria Stewart, directed by Lou Jacob; *Hitting the Wall* by Barbara Blumenthal-Ehrlich, directed by Drew Barr; *Marge* by Peter Morris, directed by Alex Timbers; *Millicent Scowlworthy* by Rob Handel, directed by Ken Rus Schmoll; *A Wive's Tale* by Christina Ham, directed by Rosemary

Andress, *Spain* by Jim Knable, directed by Jeremy Dobrish; *Training Wisteria* by Molly Smith Metzler, directed by Evan Cabnet; *Swansong* by Patrick Page, directed by David Muse; *Sonia Flew* by Melinda Lopez, directed by Justin Waldman

## Theater for the New City

Crystal Field, Executive Director

**Jesus and Mandy** by Eric Bernat & Robin Carrigan; Director, David Drake; Set, Mark T. Simpson; Costumes, Karl A. Ruckdeschel; Lighting, Garth Reese; Sound, C.P. Roth; Choreography, Robin Carrigan; Production Manager, Karen Mack & Jam Bandit Productions; Stage Manager, Robert P. Mrozek; Cast: Eric Bernat, Eddie Cruz, Afi Ekulona, Stephanie Fittro, John Haegele; June 8–July 2

**Luo Shen** written & directed by Joanna Chan; presented by Yangtze Repertory Theatre of America; Set, Peter Spack; Lighting, Joe Hodge; Costumes, HouJian Xu; Choreography, Master Zhao Naiyi, David Shen; Chorus Masters, Zhao NaiYi, Xiao YunFei, Andrei Drooz; Cast: William YueKun Wu, YiLing Li, Master Fang YuLin, Shawn Deng, Shen Mo, Jenny Hsia, Sophie Li, David Shen, Xiao YunFei, Sam Sung, Deng Yu, Xin Yuan, Solomon Chang; June 8–25

**Tap Dance** written & directed by Crystal Field; Music, Joseph Vernon Banks; Design, Mary Blanchard, Walter Gurbo; Costumes, Myrna Duarte; Sound, Joy Linscheid & David Nolan; Masks, Candice Burridge; Cast: Beryl Armistead, Taylor Borodavka, Celestina Bradsher-Layne, John Buckley, Lily Burd, Mary Cunningham, Alsenio Espinal, Crystal Field, Michael-David Gordon, Lorenzo Iacona, Zainab Johnson, Terry Lee King, Mark Marcante, Craig Meade, Chance Parker, Daniela Pompeu, Primy Rivera, Justin Rodriguez, Dani Roze, Alexander Simmons, Chinatsu Uehara, Michael Vazquez, Angel Lee Vazquez, Christine Woodarek, Tracy Zhang; Musicians: Joseph Vernon Banks, Gary Newton, Kareem A. Walkes, Phil Smith, Michael Grayson; Street Theater performed in NYC Parks; August 5–September 17

**Circus Contraption's Grand American Traveling Dime Museum** August 11–September 23

**Soul Searching** written & directed by Matt Okin & Avi Kunstler; Lighting, Russel Drapkin; Cast: Melissa Schoenberg, Kathryn Comperatore, Ellie Dvorkin, Elana Safar, Shana Solomon, Matt Posner, Scott Harris, Andrew Hubbard; Musicians: Jon Taub, Jason Horowitz, Vitaa; Cabaret Theater; August 31–September 17

**Think of Ben Brantley And Write A Happy Play** written & directed by Bina Sharif; Lighting, Alexander Bartenieff; Sets, Ayesha Jatoi; Cast: Kevin Mitchell Martin, Bina Sharif, Darryl Reilly; Cabaret Theater; September 7–24

**The Funniest Show In The World About The History Of Comedy Performed By Two Brothers In Under Two Hours For Under Twenty Bucks** written, composed, and performed by Josh Bacher & Danny Bacher; Director, Dominick Buccafusco; Choreography, Megeen Corcoran and Moina Sidwell; Costumes, Mama Jean; Lighting, Randy Glickman; Sets, Robert Monaco; Community Space Theater; September 7–October 1

**Allende: The Death of a President** by Rodolfo C. Quebleen; Director, German Jaramillo; Sets/Lighting Luis Cantillo; Music, Pablo Mayor; Costumes, Hersilia Restrepo; Cast: Ramiro Sandoval; Cino Theater; September 21–October 8

**Corrective Lens** written & directed by Ruthy Rosen; Music, Arthur Abrams; Sets, Mark Marcante; Cast: Esther Briskman, Ginger Rich, Sam Antar, Carly Perahia; Cabaret Theater; October 5–22

**Greater Buffalo** by Robyn Burland; Director, Jessica Davis-Irons; Lighting, Drew Florida; Sets, Meganne George; Assistant Director, Ashleigh Hile; Cast: Shira Gregory, Michael Kohn; Community Space Theater; October 7–22

**Voice 4 Vision Puppet Festival** coordinated by Sarah Provost & Jane Catherine Shaw; Lighting, G. Benjamin Swope; Sound, Scott Wiggins; Stage Manager, Neelam Vaswani; included: *The Traveler* by Dramatron Theater (Ken Berman & Frankie Cordero), directed by Tim Lee; Lighting, Michael Spitzer; Sound, Mark Berman; Cast Sarah Frechette; *Warhol* by Drama of Works, directed by Gretchen Van Lente; Design, David Michael Friend; Cast: John Ardolino, Amy Carrigan, Jessica Scott, James Walton; *Slow Ascent* written & directed by Anna Kiraly; Design, Kuba Gontarczyk; *How I Fixed My Engine With Rose Water* by Lake Simons; Music, John Dyer & Rima Fand; Cast: Brendan McMahon, Erin Orr, Chad Lynch, Lake Simons; Cino Theater; October 12–22

**Marx In Soho** by Howard Zinn, directed & performed by Brian Jones; Cabaret Theater; November 3–4

**Job's Passion** by Hanoch Levin, translated by Shay Azoulay; Director, David Willinger; Sets, Joe Barna; Costumes, Lisa Kim; Lighting, Aaron Meadow; Original Music, Ithai Benjamin; Cast: Primy Rivera, Colleen Jason, Michael Climek, E. John Okogun, Oliver Thrun, Arturo Castro, Zoe Mavroudis, Harvey Benjamin, Michael Vazquez, Eric Rasmussen, Freeman Borden, Ana Parsons; Cino Theater; November 9–December 3

**Walk the Mountain** written & performed by Jude Narita; Director, Darling Narita; Sets/Lighting, Jerry Brown; Video, Rod Bradley; November 12–December 3

**New Science** by Jessica Slote, based on the works of Giambattista Vico; Director, Martin Reckhaus; Lighting, Gary Brackett; Cast: Sheila Dabney, Tom Walker, Pamela Mayo, Claire Lebowitz, Johnson Anthony, Debra Wassum, Adela Maria Bolet, Naisha Walton; Cabaret Theater; November 16–26

**Bread and Puppet Theater** included: *The Battle Of The Terrorists and the Horrorists* and *The Everything Is Fine Circus*; Director, Peter Schumann; Johnson Theater; November 30–December 17

**An Optimistic Picture** by Walter Corwin; Director, Jonathan Weber; Lighting, Mark Marcante; Sound, Joy Linscheid & David Nolan; Costumes, Myrna Duarte; Artwork, Will Corwin; Cast: David L. Greenwood, Kathryn Chilson, Giorgio Handman, Jonathan Weber, Jillian Singer; Cabaret Theater; December 7–23

**Woden** written & directed by Gene Ruffini; Sets/Lighting, Jason Sturm; Cast: William Greville, Elizabeth Burke, Robert Armstrong, Jessica Tate, Deborah Johnstone, Carol Ann Palmaro, Bryan Luethy, Dorian Shorts; Cino Theater; December 14–31

**Times Square Angel** by Charles Busch; Director, Carl Andress; Wigs, E. Katherine Carr; Gowns, Michael Bottari & Ronald Case; Cast: Charles Busch, Jim Dale, Jackie Sanders, Marcy McGuigan, Sidney Myer, Carl Andress, Lawernce Bullock, Flotilla DeBarge, Sean Monahan, Andy Halliday, Peter Boroztta, Arnie Kolodner, Theresa Aceves, Julie Halston; Johnson Theater; December 18

**The Love Show in Nutcracker: Rated R** choreographed by Angela Harriell; Sets, Martin Tockman; Costumes, Lezane Trapani; Lighting, Mark Marcante; Sound, Richard Reta; Cast: Jesús Chapa-Malacara, Gregory Dubin, Christopher Dunston, Angela Harriell, Christina Johnson, Kimberly Lantz, Kate Lawrence, Adam Pellegrine, Renee Scalise, Joseph Schles, Amber Shirley, David F. Slone, Esq., Juliana Smith, Emma Stein, Clare Tobin; Community Space Theater; December 14–January 5

**Greener Grasses...** written & directed by Sabura Rashid; Sets, Mark Marcante; Cast: Taqiyyah Haden, Chiquita Camille, Thyais Walsh, Rebecca Thomas, Lisa-Roxanne Walters, Larry Floyd, Andre Dell, Adrian Washington, Bill Weeden, Kenitta Lindsey, Akintola Joboyewa. Johnson Theater; January 11–February 4

**Angry Young Women In Low Rise Jeans With High Class Issues** written & directed by Matt Morillo; Lighting, Amith A. Chandrashaker; Sets, Jana Mattioli; Producers, Matt Morillo & Jessica Durdock; Cast: Devon Pipars, Angelique Letizia, JessAnn Smith, Thomas J. Pilutik, Nicholas J. Coleman, Rachel Nau, Martin Friedrichs; Cino Theater; January 11–February 24

**What Do I Know About War?** by Margo Lee Sherman; Director, Andrea Maddox; Lighting, Cavan Meese; Cast: Margo Lee Sherman; Cabaret Theater; January 19–21

**Kryptonite Hearts** by Charles Battersby, Director, James Duff; Cast: Charles Battersby, Liz Battersby, Jason Griffith, Philip Emeott, Walter Hoffman, Marissa Tiamfook, Lauren Strachen, Stephanie Bush, Jere Williams, Dan Hernandez; Cabaret Theater; January 25–February 11

**Voideville: The Last Show on Earth** written and directed by Gordon Bressack & Ruby Lynn Reyner; Music Director, Steve Greenfield; Choreography, Carolyn Lord; Costumes, Lola Niasse; Sets, Adrian Gallard; Lighting, Sebastian Ademo; Cast: Susie Young, Yvonne Forbes, Jessica Delfino, Jeff Seal, Akynos Shekera, Emma Channing, Gordon Bressack, Ruby Lynn Reyner, Ivan Lenin, D'yan Forest, Kevin Draine, Al Crosby, Fara Greenbaum, Jerry Turner, Julie Atlas Muz, Victoria Libertore (aka Howling Vic), Lavinia Co-op; Community Space Theater; February 1–18

**Thunderbird American Indian Dancers** Annual Dance Concert and Pow-wow; Johnson Theater; February 9–18

**Artfuckers** by Michael Domitrovich; Director, Eduardo Machado; AD, Stefanie Sertich; PSM, Michael Alifanz; Associate Producer, Megan Smith; Sets, Mikiko Suziki; Lighting, Lucas Krech; Costumes, Oana Botez-Ban; Sound, David M. Larson; Cast: Asher Grodman, Tuomas Hiltunen, Jessica Kaye, Nicole LaLiberte, David Marcus; Cabaret Theater; February 15–March 4

**Parental Consent** by Tamara J. Cupic; Director, Franka Fiala; Lighting, Jon D. Andreadakis; Sets, Horacio Molina; Cast: Jessica Tate, Emily Fink, Mary Sarah Agliotta, Warren Lundy, Taquana Stanford; Community Space Theater; March 1–18

**The Further Adventures of Uncle Wiggily: Windblown Visitors** by Laurel Hessing, based on *The Uncle Wiggily Storybook* by Howard R. Garis; Director, Crystal Field; Music, Arthur Abrams; Sets, Donald L. Brooks; Costumes, Myrna Duarte; Lighting, Jason Sturm; Sound, Joy Linscheid & David Nolan; Production Coordinator, Suki Weston; Music Director, A.J. Mantas; Puppets, Spica Wobbe, Morgan Eckert and MoMo Felix; Aerial Dance, Lisa Giobbi; Masks, Candice Burridge & Spica Wobbe; Cast: Freeman Borden, Giovanna DiRauso, Susan Gittens, Lorenzo Iacona, Andrea Maddox, Nalina Mann, Craig Meade, Allison Patrick, Daniela Pompeu, Primy Rivera, Elizabeth Maldonado, Danielle Suder, Oliver Thrun, Chinatsu Uehara, Michael Vazquez, Jonathan Weber, Tracy Zhang, Lei Zhou, Taylor Borodavka, Rockella Caporale; Maya Faerstein-Weiss, Christopher Grant, Daphney Guillaume, Nicholas Guillaume, Natalie Mattson, Paula Merchan, John Preyor, Clara Ruf-Maldonado, Allegra Vacin; Band: Arthur Abrams, A.J. Mantas, Lisa Kline, Kenneth Salters; Johnson Theater; March 2–25

**Betty And The Belrays** written & directed by William Electric Black; Music, William Electric Black & Val Ghent; Choreography, Jeremy Lardieri; Lighting, Federico Restrepo; Cast: Vanessa Burke, Lucille Duncan, Verna Hampton, Cara S. Liander, Nicole Patullo, Chris Reber, Levern Williams; Cabaret Theater; March 8–April 1

**Sleep Over** by Maria Micheles; Director, Kitt Lavoie; Production Manager, T.J. Pallas; Lighting, Justin Partier, Costumes, Jenn Reichert; Cast: Lucy Alibar, Jennifer Curfman, Chris Stack; Cino Theater; March 8–25

**Blood And Rum** written & directed by Ian L. Gordon; Assistant Director Aaron Diehl; Costumes, Aurie Ben-Esri-Ravin; Cast: Cindy Gunraj, Alexa Poller, Artie Ray, Patti-Anne Ali, Sarah Drescher, Patricia McCurdy, Andrew Matthews, Philip Sletteland, Dan Tibbets, Ilana Landecker, Courtney Heller; Community Space Theater; March 22–April 22

**1918: A House Divided** written & directed by Barbara Kahn; Music, Allison Tartalia; Sets, Mark Marcante; Costumes, Amy Kitzhaber; Stage Manager Jan Dekoff; Cast: Victoria Lavington, Erin Leigh Schmoyer, Dan Leeds, Victoria Levin, Kelly Scanlon, Kyle J. Martin, Robert Gonzalez Jr., Matthew Naclerio, Rick Redondo, Faith Wu, Jeanie Tse, Laura Jean Smith, Tina Ward; Cino Theater; April 5–22

**Before God Was Invented** written & directed by Lissa Moira, co-written by Richard West; Design, Zen Mansley; Choreography, Mariana Bekerman; Fights, Jiggers Turner; Music Director, Louisa Bradshaw; Lighting, Adrian Gallard; Cast: Buena Batiste, Louisa Bradshaw, Paulina Brahm, Stefanie Leah Coren, Megan Delay, Andrew Greer, George Isaacs, Ilana Landeckcr, Zen Mansley, Josh Meier, Tom Rothacker, Chase Shellee, Renee Threatte; Cabaret Theater; April 5–22

**My Inner Mark Berman** written by Evan Laurence; Director, Richard Mazda; Cast: Evan Laurence, David F. Slone, Christopher Noffke, Danny Smith, Richard C. Lurie; Cabaret Theater; May 3–20

**In The Schoolyard** written & directed by Paulanne Simmons; Composer, Margaret Hetherman; Sets, Bill Wood; Lighting, Ken Kruk; Sound, Dwight Simmons; Choreography, James Martinelli; Cast: Arthur Brown, Theresa Marinelli, Jimmy Moon, Heather Meagher, Lizzie Czerner, Mickey Corporon, James Martinelli, Richard Bryson, Jody Bell, Jackie Savage, Dave Benger; Community Space Theater; May 3–20

**Love In Tears And Laughter** written & directed by Dr. Joanna Chan; presented by the Yangtze Repertory Theatre of America; Sets, Peter Spack; Lighting, Joe Hodge; Costumes, David Shen; Cast: Qian Ma, ZhiQuang Wang, Joannie Liu, Lei Zhou, YiLing Li, Elizabeth Hammett, Li Chang Lin, David Yang, Wayne Chang, Zhang Kang, Zhang Li, William Wu, Dan Cui, Jin Xin, Kenny Chong, Steve Chu; Johnson Theater; May 31–June 17

**The Poison Man** written & directed by Eugenia Macer-Story; Sets/Lighting, Jason Sturm; Cast: Katie Yamulla, Primy Rivera, Von Jacobs, Ilana Landecker, Nate Steinwachs, Steve Greenstein, Renee Valenti, Francisco Hernandez; Cabaret Theater; June 7–23

**New City, New Blood** play reading series; Curator and Literary Manager, Michael Scott-Price; included: *Greater Buffalo* by Robyn Burland (June 19); *The Pisces Encounter* written by J.B. Heaps (July 24); *Stung* by Robyn Burland (December 11); *Queens Of Heart* by Sabura Rashid (March 12); *Plinko, or The Goddess of Static Cling* by Julia Pearlstein (April 23); *Emergency Contraception: The Musical!* by Sara Cooper & Chris Shimojima (May 14); *Abbatoir* by John Cappelletti (June 11)

# Theater Ten Ten

Judith Jarosz, Producing Artistic Director

**Joe Piscopo's Son** written & performed by Joey Piscopo; Director, Davis Fuller; August 24–26

**Northanger Abbey** adapted from Jane Austen's novel by Lynn Marie Macy; Director, David Scott; Fights, Ricki G. Ravitts; Choreography, Judith Jarosz & Ricki G. Ravitts; Set, Joseph J. Egan; Costumes, Jeanette Aultz Look; Lighting, Bradley James King; Sound, DeLisa White; Dialects, Annalisa Loeffler; PSM, Shauna Horn; Cast: Greg Oliver Bodine, Esther David, Devin Delliquanti, David Fuller, Tatiana Gomberg, Summer Hagen, Sheila Joon, Megan Loomis, Timothy McDonough, Tim Morton, Lisa Riegel, Julian Stetkevych, Sarah Tillson; October 20–November 19

**A Midsummer Night's Dream** by William Shakespeare; Director/Choreography, Judith Jarosz; Lighting, Jay Scott; Set, Matthew Smith; Costumes, Rien Schlecht; PSM/Sound, Shauna Horn; Assistant Director/Fights, Ricki G. Ravitts; Music Director/Composer, Jason Wynn; Cast: Arthur Atkinson, Nat Cassidy, Andrew Clateman, Devin Delliquanti, Lisa Ferraro, David Fuller, Tatiana Gomberg, Annalisa Loeffler, Lynn Marie Macy, Kristopher Monroe, Lisa Riegel, Gael Schaefer, David Tillistrand; February 10–March 11

**Happy End** lyrics by Bertolt Brecht, music by Kurt Weill, original German play by Dorothy Lane, book & lyrics adapted by Michael Feingold; Director, David Fuller; Sets/Lighting, Giles Hogya; Costumes, Viviane Galloway; Musical Director, Michael Harren; Film Director, Joey Piscopo; Assistant Director, Aaron Diehl; PSM, Andy Fitts; ASM, Colleen Darnall; Cast: Tim Morton, Timothy McDonough, Dave Tillistrand, Greg Horton, David Arthur Bachrach, Elizabeth Fye, Joey Piscopo, Aaron Diehl, Judith Jarosz, Megan Loomis, Allen Hale, Sandy York, Lorinda Lisitza, Michael C. O'Day, Cristiane Young; April 27–May 27

# Theatre 315 (Salvation Army Theatre)

**The Burial at Thebes** adapted from Sophocles' *Antigone* by Seamus Heaney; presented by Handcart Ensemble; Director, J. Scott Reynolds; Score, Nathan Bowen; Choreography, Andrea Homer-Macdonald; Masks, Jonathan Becker; Set, David D'Agostini; Lighting, David Kniep; Costumes, Cherie Cunningham; Stage Manager, Erin Williams; Cast: Ron Bopst, Elizabeth A. Davis, Susan Ferrara, Matthew Herrick, Adam Houghton, Tom Houghton, Tom Knutson, Jane Pejtersen; September 7–23

**The Great Divorce** by C.S. Lewis, adapted and directed by George Drance; presented by Magis Theatre Company; Original Music, Elizabeth Swados; Puppets, Ralph Lee; Cast: Thomas Piper, George Drance; January 24–February 11

**Alcestis** by Euripides, adapted by Ted Hughes; presented by Handcart Ensemble; Director, J. Scott Reynolds; Score, Nathan Bowen; Choreography, Andrea Homer-Macdonald; Lighting, David Kniep; Costumes, Jessa-Raye Court; Stage Manager, Valerie Best; Cast: Steve Abbruscato, Ron Bopst, David D'Agostini, Matthew Herrick, Kevin Lapin, Robert Mobley, Nicholas Alexiy Moran, Jane Pejtersen, Laurie Schroeder; April 19–May 5

# Theatre 5

**Wuthering Heights** Adaptation, music, and lyrics by Paul Dick, based on the novel by Emily Bronte; Director, Patrick Diamond; Music Director, Charity Wicks; Set, Lee Savage, Sandra Goldmark, Lighting, Stephen Sakowski; Cast: Dominic Inferrera, Kimberly Burns, Ray Arrucci, Dennis Holland, Sarah Hund, Richard Koon, Eric Monson, Niki Naeve, Danny Rothman, Alexandre De Suze; June 16–July 1

**Five Women Wearing the Same Dress** by Alan Ball; Director, John T. Gorsak; Cast: Brenna McGuire, Danielle Capolon, Lisa Guise, Megan Lappin, Dimitry Michann, Syndi Szabo; September 14–30

**Fraulein Else** by Arthur Schnitzler, adapted and performed by Amy de Lucia; October 8–22

# Theatre Row Theatres

### Beckett Theatre

**Coriolanus** by William Shakespeare; presented by ShakespeareNYC; Director/Design, Beverly Bullock; Lighting, James Bedell; PSM, Christina Martinez; Cast: Adam Raynen, Brian Nocella, Carol Biaggi, Daren Dubner, Donald Warfield, Duncan Hazard, Elizabeth McGuire, Eric Emmanuel, Frank Mihelich, Johnny Lin, Julian Elfer, Katherine Kelly Lidz, Kristopher Kling, Lillian Small, Marcus Dean Fuller, Nicholas Stannard, Peter Herrick, Peter Richards, Sam R. Ross, Seth D. Rabinowitz, Zach Held; June 14–25

**The Imaginary Invalid** by Molière; presented by Resonance Ensemble; Director, Rebecca Patterson; Set, Dustin O'Neill; Costumes, Jenny Fulton; Lighting, Aaron Mason; Sound, Sabrina McGuigan; Cast: Virginia Baeta, Amy Driesler, Valentina McKenzie, Gisele Richardson, Samarra, Carey Urban, Kari Washington; presented in rep with: **The Mail Order Bride** by Charles L. Mee, inspired by *The Imaginary Invalid*; Director, Eric Parness; Set, Dustin O'Neill; Costumes, Sidney Shannon; Lighting, Aaron Mason; Sound, Nick Moore; Cast: John Henry Cox, Booth Daniels, Susan Ferrara, Vivia Font, Sue Jean Kim, Sam Kitchin, Peter McCain, Lori McNally, Melissa Miller, Susan Louise O'Connor; October 27–November 19

**The Vietnamization of New Jersey** by Christopher Durang; presented by the Alchemy Theatre Company; Director, Robert Saxner; Cast: Blanche Baker, Michael Cyril Creighton, Frank Deal, Susan Gross, James Duane Polk, Corey Sullivan, Nick Westrate; January 16–28

**Lipstick on a Pig** by Linda Evans, Director, David Epstein; Cast: Alexis Croucher, John Farrell, Dennis Hearn, Christa Kimlico Jones; May 18–June 3

## Clurman Theatre

**The Equality Play Festival** presented by Diverse City Theater Company; included: *Clean Living* by Robert Askins, directed by Steven Ditmyer; *Cold Flesh* by Jorshinelle Taleon-Sonza, directed by Adam Fitzgerald; *Veils* by Joe Byers, directed by Gregory Simmons; *Onna Field* by Stuart Harris, directed by Carlos Armesto; August 11–26

**The Taming of the Shrew** by William Shakespeare; presented by ShakespeareNYC; Director/Design, Beverly Bullock; Fights, Al Foote III; Lighting, James Bedell; PSM, Steve Barrett; Cast: Adam Raynen, Benjamin Curns, Brian Nocella, David Arthur Bachrach, Denise Cormier, Geoffrey Dawe, Gregg Dubner, Gretchen Howe, Joseph Small, Marc Alan Greece, Miriam Lipner Nicholas Stannard, Peter Herrick, Steven Eng; October 26–November 11

**The Scarlett O'Hara Complex** by Karen Wheeling-Reynolds; presented by Gaff Tape Productions; Director, David Reynolds; Cast: Nicole Vidrine, Dianne Steele, Kathy McGrady Moffett, Beth Livingston, Karen Wheeling-Reynolds, Sarah Smith, Harold Bass, Nat Padgett, Rebecca Clark, David Reynolds; November 30–December 9

**The Monument** by Colleen Wagner; presented by The Clockwork Theatre; Director, Beverly Brumm; Set, Efren Delgadillo Jr.; Lighting, Benjamin C. Tevelow; Costumes, Roxie Zeek; Sound, Reid Hall; PSM, Stephanie Cali; Cast: Ramona Floyd, Jay Rohloff; January 16–28

**Stone Cold Dead Serious** by Adam Rapp; presented by Small Pond Entertainment; Director, Lee Gundersheimer; February 2–18

## Kirk Theatre

**'Nami** by Chad Beckim; presented by Partial Comfort Productions; Director, John Gould Rubin; Set, Heather Wolensky; Costumes, Lex Liang; Lighting, Jason Jeunnette; Sound, Zach Williamson; Stage Manager, Caitlin McAndrews; Cast: Quincy Tyler Bernstine, Michael J.X. Gladis, Eva Kaminsky, Mark Rosenthal, Alfredo Narciso; September 6–30

**The Great Conjurer** by Christine Simpson; presented by Fluid Motion Theater & Film; Director/Set, Kevin Bartlett; Music Director, Benjamin Ickies; Costumes, Deborah J. Caney; Choreography, Wendy Seyb; Lighting, Caroline Abella; Stage Manager, Corinne Neal; Cast: Michael Jerome Johnson, Roseanne Medina, Tzahi Moskovitz, Brian Nishii, Kelly Paredes, Andy Place, Sara Thigpen, Paula Wilson; October 20–November 4

**Lebensraum** by Israel Horovitz; presented by Barefoot Theater; Director, Jonathan Rest; Set, Susan Zeman Rogers; Costumes, Esther Arroyo; Lighting/Sound, Christopher Bailey; PSM, Ashley B. Delegal; Cast: Suli Holum, T. Ryder Smith, Ryan Young; December 17–30

**The Secret of Mme. Bonnard's Bath** written & directed by Israel Horovitz; presented by New York Playwrights Lab; Sets, Jenna McFarland Lord; Costumes, Mimi Maxem; Lighting Christopher J. Bailey; Sound, Julie Pittman; Cast: Michael Bakkensen, Stephanie Janssen, John Shea; February 3–24

**Jump!** by Lisa McGee & **Realism** by Anthony Neilson; presented by The Exchange (formerly Jean Cocteau Repertory); Director, Ari Edelson; Set, Antje Elleman; Lighting, Ben Stanton; Costumes, Oana Botez-Ban; Sound, Bart Fasbender; Cast of *Jump!*: Bree Elrod, Jordan Gelber, Ali Marsh, Stephen Plunkett, Tim Spears, Sarah Grace Wilson, Meredith Zinner; Cast of *Realism:* Bree Elrod, Jordan Gelber, Ali Marsh, Stephen Blunkett, Kathryn Rossetter, Herbert Rubens, Tim Spears; April 15–May 20

**Don Juan in Chicago** by David Ives; presented by Clockwork Theatre; Director, Owen M. Smith; Set, Efren Delgadillo Jr.; Lighting, Benjamin C. Tevelow; Costumes, Jocelyn Melechinskey; Sound, R. Canterberry; PSM, Stephanie Cali; Cast: Stephen Balantzian, Greg Baresi, Mike Cinquino, Doug Nyman, Shayna Padovano, Dayle Pivetta, Virginia Stringel, Vincent Vigilante; May 26–June 9

## Lion Theatre

**Ascension** by Edmund De Santis; Director, Marc Geller; October 6–21; extended on an Off-Broadway contract October 22–November 19 (see full credits in the Off-Broadway section in this volume)

**Days of Wine and Roses** by J.P. Miller; Director, Tony Macy-Perez; Cast: John Haggerty, Arista Burtram; December 14–17

**Extraordinary Deceptions** performed by Michael Gutenplan; December 19–30

**Hello, My Name is...** by Stephanie Rabinowitz; presented by Living Image Arts; Director, Lee Douglas; Set, Ryan Elliot Kravetz; Costumes, Melinda Basaca; Lighting, Scott Hay; Sound, Geoffrey Roecker; Cast: Jonathan Raviv, Randy Falcon, Tracy Shar, Jackie Burns, Mia Aden, Jacob Ming-Trent, Peter Marsh; January 13–28

**Nelson** by Sam Marks; presented by Partial Comfort Productions; Director, Kip Fagan; Cast: Alexander Alioto, Frank Harts, Jordan Mahome; February 7–March 3

**The Merry Wives of Windsor** by William Shakespeare; presented by Oberon Theatre Ensemble; Director, Brad Fryman; Set, Ace Eure; Costumes, Carmen Wrenn; Lighting, Sharon Huizinga; Composer, Mickey Zetts; Associate Director, Cara Reichel; Cast: Stu Richel, Zak Risinger, Mac Brydon, William Laney, Brad Fryman, Mickey Zetts, Matt Miniea, John Gardner, Mary Sheridan, Laura Siner, Kate Ross, Joseph Tomasini, Linda S. Nelson, Henry Anderson, M. Eden Teagle, Vincent LoRusso, Stewart Walker, Ryan Tramont, Walter Brandes; March 8–29

**Sweet Love Adieu** by Ryan J.W. Smith; presented by Oberon Theatre Ensemble in rep with *The Merry Wives of Windsor*; Director, Don Harvey; Set, Ace Eure; Costumes, Carmen Wrenn; Lighting, Sharon Huizinga; Sound, Gennaro Marletta III; Cast: Marcel Simoneau, Tom Lapke, Walter Brandes, Amanda McCroskery, Anne Beaumont, Amanda Nichols, Eve Udesky, Dyanne Court, Kenneth Cavett, Ashley Springer, Charlie Moss; March 15–April 1

**Committed** three short plays: *Off the Cuff* by William K. Powers, directed by Holli Harms; *Men Are Pigs* by Tony Zertuche, directed by Marlo Hunter; *Boxes* by Robert Askins, directed by Lindsay Goss; presented by Living Image Arts; Producer, Lindsay Goss; Set, Scott Needham; Costumes, Melinda C. Basaca; Lighting, Kathleen Dobbins; PSM, Kendra Dolton; ASMs, Jason Kammon, Timothy Nutter, Neal Zupancic; Cast: Mia Aden, Leigh Danya, Dawn Evans, Julie Fitzpatrick, Maria Gabriele, Richard Kent Green, Tyler Hollinger, T.J. Mannix, Peter Marsh, Elzabeth Schmidt, Matthew Sincell, Brandon Walker; April 5–21

**Lunch Hour** by Jean Kerr; presented by Heiress Productions; Director, Maura Farver; Set, Josh Zangen, Lighting, Joel E. Silver, Travis Richardson; Costumes, Kate Blodgett; Stage Manager Angela Allen; Cast: Morgan Baker, Laura Faith, Jeff Pagliano, J.T. Michael Taylor, Mary Willis White; April 26–May 20

## Studio Theatre

**Oblivious to Everyone** written & performed by Jessica Lynn Johnson; Director, Christopher Sorensen; October 27–December 16

**Lady ChardonnEy** by Julio Tumbaco & Jim Gibson; presented by JJ Entertainment; Director, Jason Brantman; Cast: Dee Spencer, Drake Andrew, Elka Rodriguez; January 26–February 11

**Manuscript** by Paul Grellong; Director, Alex Lippard; Set, Michael V. Moore; Costumes, Erin Elizabeth Murphy; Lighting, Graham Kindred; Cast: Greg Cayea, Christine Donlon, Duane Langley; April 4–20

**The Tragedy of John** by Neal Zupancic; presented by Theatre of the Expandable; Director/Set, Corinne Neal; Lighting/Set, Wilburn Bonnell; Sound, Geoffrey Roecker; Stage Manager, Marcus Cooper; Cast: Benjamin G. Bowman, Nathan Brisby, Gregory Engbrecht, John Forkner, Liam Joynt, Desiree Matthews, Christina Shipp; April 26–May 13

# Theatre Three (Mint Theatre Space)

**The Servant of Two Masters** by Carlo Goldoni; presented by the New Globe Theatre; Director, Stuart Vaughan; Cast: Steve Campbell, Nick Fleming, John Hart, Rich Hollman, Grant Kretchik, Ronald Rand, Craig Rising, Gray Stevenson, Alok Tewari, Alessandra Ziviani; December 22–January 21

**The Screwtape Letters** by C.S. Lewis, adapted by Nigel Ford; encore presentation produced by Cornergate Productions; Director, Ralph Irizarry; Cast: Stephen Wargo, Maria Bellantoni, Kevin O'Bryan, Justin Stoney, David Esteve, Holly Hurley, Paul Parker, Sheila Simmons, David Arthur Bachrach; August 4–26

**Brother's Keeper** written & directed by Marc Weiner; presented by Marcus Productions; Set, John Scheffler; Costumes, Melanie Schmidt; Lighting, Nadine Charlsen; Stage Manager, Corrine Slagle; Cast: Adam Murphy, Mariessa Portelance, Stephanie Roy, Gregg Thornsbury, Emily Ward; November 4–19

**The Green Game** written & directed by M. Stefan Strozier and Paul L. Johnson; presented by La Muse Venale Acting Troupe; Choreography, Mindy Upin; Cast: Joe Wissler, April Gentry, McGregor Wright, Ben Bailey, Jessie Fahay, Grace Freeman, Kurt Gorell, Madeline Niro, Mindy Upin, Keri Ann Peterson; March 29–April 22

**Time Being** book, lyrics & direction by Erika Stadtlander, music by Ion Ionescu; presented by Fildwith Ensemble Theatre; Managing Director/Co-director/Stage Manager, Sean Littlejohn; Choreogrpahy, Jessica Northrop; Lighting, Anjeanette Stokes; Costume, Nancy Lindig; Cast: Spencer Adams, Kaydence Frank, Marc Ginsburg, Lizzie Henney, Liz Kimball, Abby Lindig, Eric Nelson, Catia Ojeda, Lauren Orlando, Kristen Rozanski, Lina Silver, Chris Will; April 26–May 13

# T. Schreiber Studio

Terry Schreiber, Founder

**Sweet Bird of Youth** by Tennessee Williams; Director, Terry Schreiber; Set, Hale Tiné; Lighting, Andrea Boccanfuso; Costumes, Karen Ann Ledger; Sound, Christopher Rummel; Stage Manager, Ain Rashida Sykes; Piano, Anthony Aibel; TD, Brian Smallwood; Fights, Robert McCaffrey; Press, Katie Rosin; Cast: Eric Watson Williams, Kelvin Cameron, Ed Avila, Tim Weinert, Shelley Virginia, Robert McCaffrey, Jack Drucker, Gina LeMoine, Jack Nasi, Peter Luna, Joanna Bayless, Morgan Foxworth, David Donahoe, Margo Goodman, Aaron Walker, Andrea

Jackson, Mary Monahan, Pierre LaRochelle, Simeon Lipman, Anthony Aibel; February 15–March 18

**Picasso at the Lapin Agile** by Steve Martin; Director, Cat Parker; Set, George Allison; Lighting, Andrea Boccanfuso; Costumes, Karen Ann Ledger; Sound, Christopher Rummel; PSM, Melanie Bell; Stage Manager, Shane Van Vliet; Cast: Josh Marcantel, Frank Mihelich, Edward Campbell, Todd Cowdery, Jim Aylward, Ivette Dumeng, Richard Zekaria, Maeve Yore, Arela Rivas, Michael Black, Andrea Marie Smith; April 5–May 6

**You Can't Take It with You** by Moss Hart and George S. Kaufman; Director, Peter Jensen; Set, Ryan Scott; Costumes, Summer Lee Jack; Lighting, Eric Larson; Sound, Christopher Rummel; Stage Manager, Shane Van Vliet; Fights, Brian Avers, TD, Brian Smallwood; Vocal Coach, Page Clements; ASM, Miriam Hyfler; Cast: Margot Bercy, Jamie Neumann, Shirine Babb, Jerry Rago, John Mulcahy, Andrew Gregor, Peter Aguero, Peter Judd, Jacqueline van Biene, Blake Hackler, Josh Sienkiewicz, Laurence Cantor, Kathleen H. Isbell, Jim Cyborowski, Helen Louise Azzara, Edward Campbell, Edward Chin-Lyn, Christopher Negrin, Jill Bianchini; May 24–June 24

# Triad Theatre

**A Night in the Old Marketplace** music by Frank London, book & lyrics by Glen Berger; presented by The National Yiddish Theatre–Folksbiene; Director, Alexandra Aron; February 3–14

**Last Jew in Europe** by Tuvia Tenenborn; presented by The Jewish Theater of New York; Director, Andreas Robertz; Set/Scene Paintings, Mark Symczak; Costumes, Elgie C. Johnson; General Manager, Isi Tenenbom; Cantorial Music, Cantor Israel Singer; Cast: Csaba S. Lucas, Lila Donnolo, Michal Gregorewski, Bill Barnett, Aleksandra Popov, Daniel Shafer; March 11–April 3

**Love's Divide** written & performed by Thomas Ryan and Suzanne Rydz; Produced by R&R Productions; Director, J. William Bruce; Sets and Lighting, Francis Vic; Costumes, Fred Goldleaf; Sound, Thomas Ashton; Press, Max Eisen; Triad Theatre; May 3–July 26 (previously played at Dillons October 19–January 7)

# Turtle Shell Productions

Artistic Director, John W. Cooper

**8 Minute Madness Playwright Festival of 2006** 3rd annual; three week competitive short play festival; August 17–September 15

**Stranger Than Fiction** three short plays: *A Love Story, A Queen's Revenge, & The Deserter* written and directed by Norman Beim; Design, John W. Cooper, Maya Animayka, Lisa Weinshrott, Michael L. Kimmel, Sarah Mariece; Cast: Rachel Eve Moses, Christopher Henney, Matthew Schmidt, Ian Campbell Dunn; October 10–27

**On a Darkling Plain** by Norman Beim; Director, John W. Cooper; Cast: Jon Freda, Joan Barber, Bristol Pomeroy, Tom Sminkey; January 10–27

**Five by Tenn** by Tennessee Williams included *Thank You, Kind Spirit, Why Do You Smoke So Much, Lily?, Talk to Me Like the Rain And Let Me Listen…, Hello from Bertha,* and *The Lady of Larkspur Lotion;* Director, John W. Cooper; Set, Ryan Scott, Lighting, Eric Larson; Costumes, A. Christina Giannini; Sound, Roman Battaglia; Cast: Emily Arrington, Kay Bailey, Christie Booker, Susan Capra, Natalie

Carter, Christina Christman, Jovanka Ciares, Elizabeth Clark, Nina Covalesky, Michael Culhane, Barbara Ann Davison, Leon Fallon, Chris Ford, Joyce Feurring, Daniel Kipler, Grace Manzo, Trish Montoya Manzo, Sylvia Mincewicz, Margaret O'Connor, Vincent Oppecker, Candice Palladino, Lennard Sillevis, Rebecca Street; March 8–25

**Fritz and Froyim** book and lyrics by Norman Beim, music by Mark Barkan and Rolf Barnes; based on material from *The Dance of Genghis Cohn* by Roamin Gary; Producer/Director, John W. Cooper; Music Director, Tracy Stark, Choreography, Cheryl Cutlip; General Manager, Jeremy Handelman; Set, Ryan Scott; Costumes, Christina Giannini; Lighting, Eric Larson; Sound, Scott Sexton; Stage Manager, Sarah-Dakotah Farney; Cast: Joan Barber, Erin Cronican, Matthew Hardy, Dennis Holland, T.J. Mannix, Tracy Stark, Richard B. Watson; May 30–June 16

**8 Minute Madness Playwright Festival of 2007** 4th annual; three week competitive short play festival; August 17–September 15

### Non-resident Productions

**The Bronx Balmers** by Jeremy Handelman; presented by Off the Leash Productions; Director, Linda Burson; Set, Maya Kaplun; Lighting, Lisa Weinshrott & Michael L. Kimmel; Sound, Sarah Ibrahim; Costumes, A. Christina Giannini; Stage Manager, TaShawn Jackson; Cast: Michael DeNola, Larry Greenbush, Amanda Nichols, George Santana, Dorcey Winant, Goldie Zwiebel; November 2–19

**The Present's Tiny Point** written & directed by Rob Cardazone; presented by Two Cups and a String Theater; Composer, Bryan Crook; Set, John P. Dessereau; Lighting, Michael P. Jones; Costumes, Jeffrey Fender; Stage Manager, TaShawn Jackson; Music Director, Randy Cohen; Sound/Music Producer, Jerome Kim; Piano, Jodie Moore; Cast: Patrick Knighton, Matthew Cummings, Carter Jackson, Marcy Finestone, Anthony Spaldo, Elizabeth Elson, Kevin Pinassi, Joanna Parson, Matthew Hardy; Thos Shipley; May 11–22

## Urban Stages (Garment District Theatre)

**The Magical Forest of Baba Yaga** by Eugene Schwartz, translated by Stanton Wood; Director, Aleksey Burago; Music, Greg Adair & Colm Clark; Set, Ryan Kravetz; Lighting, Josh Bradford; Costumes, Lioudmila Maisouradze; Stage Manager, Alan Bluestone; Cast: Catherine Kjome, Rainey Lacey, Maria Silverman, Ned Massey, Greg Adair; December 14–January 7

### Non-resident Productions

**Clean** by Bob Epstein; Director, Christopher Maring; Set, Sarah Pearline, Costumes, Katherine Hampton Noland; Lighting, Amith Chandrashaker; Sound, Tim Cramer; Cast: Albert Insinnia, Karl Jacob, John Kudan, Nancy Rodriguez, Cherene Snow, Bjorn Thorstad, Sarah Viccellio; June 16–July 1

**Dammit, Shakespeare!** by Seth Panitch; presented by The University of Alabama & Poor Yorick Productions; Cast: Steve Ray, Stacy Searle, Seth Panitch, Gaye Jeffers, Chris Hardin; August 8–13

**Brutality of Fact** by Keith Reddin; presented by The Cardinal Group; Director, Stephanie Yankwitt; Set, Joe Powell; Lighting, Lily Fossner; Costumes, Melanie Swersey; Cast: Amy La Duz, Donna Robinson, Joy Franz, Melissa Ross, Marshall Correro, D.H. Johnson, Bronwen Coleman, Paris Yates; August 17–September 10

**Almost Made** written & performed by Louie Liberti, developed by Mark Travis; produced by Major Deagan Productions, Racquel Lehrman, Greg Szimonisz; Director, D.W. Brown; Choreographer, Myrna Gawryn; Sets, John McDermott; Lighting, Josh Bradford; October 13–December 3

**Estimated Time of Arrival** five short plays: *Hang Up* by Anthony Minghella, *Hatshop* by Amy Fox, *Double Click* by Amy Fox, *Spilt: Part One* by Michael Weller, *Me Thinks* by Lisa Ebersole; presented by Thirteenth Night Theatre; Director, Drew DeCorleto; Set, David Evans Morris; Costumes, Jessa-Raye Court; Lighting, Juliet Chia; Sound, Michael L. Cooper; Cast: Ethan James Duff, Reese Madigan, Jamie Proctor, Sarah Megan Thomas; January 19–February 10

**Of Mice and Men** by John Steinbeck; presented by Cyclops Productions; Director, Pat Diamond; Cast: James Broderick, Elizabeth A. Davis, Tony F. Devito, General Fermon Judd Jr., Eirik Gislason, Jack Hayflick, Matthew Floyd Miller, Justin Swain, Douglas Taurel; May 10–26

## Vital Theatre Company

Stephen Sunderlin, Producing Artistic Director; Suzu McConnell-Wood, Director of Vital Children's Theatre; Cynthia Thomas, General Manager

**Vital Signs: New Works Festival** 9th annual; included: Series One: *How I Won the War* by Andrea Lepcio, *Tav* by Shawn Hirabayashi, *Souvenirs* by Michael John Garces, *The Remote* by Mark Harvey Levine; Series Two: *Five Wishes* by Thomas H. Diggs, *Antarctica* by Anton Dudley, *Bright.Apple.Crush* by Steven Yockey, *Crimes Against Humanity* by Ross Maxwell; Series Three–Vital R&D: *The Bloomindale Road* by Mark Lowewnstern, *Saffron* by Deen, *Discovering Columbus* by Kim Rosenstock, *It's Giuliani Time* by Aurin Squire, *Double Fantasy* by David Ben-Arie, *Breaking Routine* by Robin Rothstein; November 30–December 17

**The Country Wife** by William Wycherley; produced in association with HoNkBarK Productions; Director, John Ficarra; Costumes, A. Ruckdeschel; Set, Brian Garber; Lighting, Nathan Elsener; Composer, Dana Haynes; Cast: Maurice Edwards, Richard Haratine, Linda Jones, Janna Kefalas, Dolores Kenan, Steve Kuhel, Kristin Prince, Ray Rodriguez, Bridgette Shaw, Joan Slavin, Sam Swartz, Mike Yahn, Robert Lehrer, Brian Linden, Laura LeBleu; January 5–27

### Vital Children's Theatre

**Young King Arthur** music by Scott Zesch, lyrics by Marc Castle, book by Jon Shear & Marc Castle; Director/Choreography, Jason Summers; Music Director, Charles Geizhals; Cast: Eddie Cruz, Liz Gerecitano, Miron Gusso, Garret Lambert, Sarah Levine, Ryan Trepanier; September 23–November 5

**My New York** book by Carla Jablonski, music & lyrics by Rick Hip-Flores; Director, Linda Ames Key; Choreography, Dax Valdes; Cast: Barrett Doss, Sarah Levine, Paul Pino, Dilhya Ross, Dax Valdes, E.J. Zimmerman; November 18–January 7

**Pinkalicious the Musical** book & lyrics by Elizabeth Kann & Victoria Kann, music & lyrics by John Gregor; Director, Suzu McConnell-Wood; Choreography, Dax Valdes; Cast: Korie L. Blossey, Molly Gilman, Alan Houser Meg Phillips, Kristina K. Wilson; January 13–February 25; extended at SoHo Playhouse March 3–May 27

**Game Boy** book by Robin Rothstein, music & lyrics by Matthew Gandolfo; Director, Mary Catherine Burke; Choreography, Vibecke Dahle; Cast: Julia Arazi, Kally Duling, Lance Marshall, Andy McKissick, Kristina K. Wilson, Tim Woods; March 10–April 22

# Where Eagles Dare Theatre

**Shelf: A Tragedy at 45 Degrees** by Molly Goforth; presented by Gansfeld Theatre Company; Director, Katya Campbell; Cast: Elizabeth Kopitke, Molly Goforth, Luke Robertson, Dalane Mason, Paul Rolfes, Clark Gookin, Eric Loscheider; June 21–July 8

**I, Sarah** by Robert W. Cabell; Director, Joe Zingo; presented by ACE Theater of Oregon; Cast: Mindy Nirenstein; June 22–24

**At the Table** by Marcos Barbosa, translated by Mark O'Thomas; presented by LaMicro Theater Company; Director, Pietro Gonzalez; Set/Costumes, Sarah Kishner; Lighting, Kaitlyn Tikkun; Cast: Michael Cunningham, Winston Estevez, Luis Galli, Nandan Sanchoo, Jacob Seelbach, Kevin J. Wagner; October 16–29

**Seascape with Sharks and Dancer** by Don Nigro; presented by Baby Hippopotamus; Director, Kellie Fernald; Stage Manager, Moniera Buck; Cast: Jennifer Sandella, Matt Newton; November 30–December 12

**Green Honey Love** by Gail Wynn Huland El; Director, Hadasah; December 7–16

**Star Power** by Tony Sportiello; presented Algonquin Theatre Productions; Director, Tom Herman; January 15–February 7

**Diet Monologues: The Musical** by Monica Bauer; Director, Heather Guthrie; Music Director, Carl Haan; Cast: Kimberly Stern, Stephen Roath, Eleonore Thomas, Amma Osei, Renee Bergeron; February 12–March 7

**Operation Ajax (A Game of Skill and Chance)** text constructed and directed by Noel Salzman & Tamara Schmidt; additional text construction by Meghan Frank, Mireya Lucio, Armistead Johnson, Rodney Hakim; presented by The Butane Group; Set/Costumes, Arnulfo Maldonado; Lighting, Lucas Krech; Sound, Duncan Cutler; Cast: Jay Smith, Dorothy Abrahams, Albert Aeed, Rodney Hakim, Gavin Starr Kendall, Kelly Markus, Nicholas Warren-Gray; February 14–March 10

**Nosferatu: Land of the Undead** adapted by Stanton Wood; presented by Rabbit Hole Ensemble; Director, Edward Elefterion; Cast: Authur Aulisi, Danny Ashkenasi, Paul Daily, Katie Curri, Laura Bozzone, Emily Hartford, Dan Rice; March 12–21

**What Fools We Lovers Be** by Debbie Williams; produced by Real Arts; April 2–25

**Hanging Woman** by Donna Spector; April 12–21

**Admit Impediments** by Duncan Pflaster; presented by Cross-Eyed Bear Productions; Director, Clara Barton Green; Cast: Tony Chiroldes, Booth Daniels, Alexandra Finger, Paula Galloway, Duncan Pflaster, Nicholas Santasier; April 30–May 23

# Wings Theatre Company

Jeffrey Corrick, Artistic Director; Robert Mooney, Managing Director

**Frankenstein, the Musical** by Robert Mitchell; Director, John Henry Davis; Staging, Haila Strauss; Music Director, Paul Staroba; Cast: Timothy Warmen, Brian Charles Rooney, Martin Giannini, Paul Jackel, Cadden Jones, Kim Volpe; July 13–30

**Autumn Moon: A Werewolf Rock Musical** book, music, and lyrics by David Velarde; Director, Jonathan Cerullo; Cast: Dana Barathy, William Broyles, Jesse Easley, Mishaela Faucher, Sara Fetgatter, Scott Richard Foster, Jeremy Jonet, Marissa Lupp, Rebecca Riker, Amber Shirley, David Weitzer; August 11–September 2

**Beyond Christopher Street** included: *Better Now* by Mark Finley, directed by Steven McElroy; Cast: Chad Austin, Amy Bizjak, Desmond Dutcher; *Work Wife* by David Pumo, directed by Antonio Merenda; Cast: Moe Bertan, Nick Matthews, Karen Stanion; *Ramble* by A.B. Lugo, directed by K. Lorrel Manning; Cast: Michael Cuomo, Carol Nelson; *A Kiss Is Just a Kiss* by Jonathan Kronenberger, directed by Glenn Schudel; Cast: Jason Alan Griffin, Zach McCoy, Andrew Shoffner; November 19–December 16

**Murder Uncensored: The Secret Life of William Desmond Taylor** by George Barthel; Director, Laura J. Kleeman & Raymond O. Wagner; Costumes, Stephen Smith; Lighting, Joe Novak; Cast: Chad Austin, John Buxton, Desmond Dutcher, Mickey Goldhaber, Heather Meagher, Heather Murdock, Kara Nelson, David Rudd, LinDel Sandlin, Holly Vanasse, Raymond O. Wagner; March 9–April 8

**The Jocker** by Clint Jeffries; Director, Jeffrey Corrick; Set, William Ward; Costumes, L.J. Kleeman; Lighting, Eric Larson; Cast: Stephen Cabral, Jason Alan Griffin, Michael Lazar, Nick Matthews, Stephen Tyrone Williams; May 11–June 9

## Non-resident Productions

**An Evening with Shaw** presented by Break a Leg Productions; included: *Fumed Oak* by Noel Coward & *Wanda's Visit* by Christopher Durang; Director, Christopher Bellis; Cast: Michael Kennealy, Martha Lopez Gilpin, Olivea Wooden Virta, Teri Black, Bruce Barton, Michele Fulves; January 29

**Land O'Fire** by Luis Santeiro; presented by New Jersey Theatre Center; Director, Jorge Cacheiro; Set, J. Wiese; Costumes, Debra Otte; Puppets, Stephanie Cathro; Lighting, Joe Doviak; Sound, David Lawson; Music, Marla Meisner; Cast: Dacyl Acevedo, Satomi Blair, Malachy Orozco, David Heron, Jassim Lone, Ian Lassiter, Marisa Marquez; February 16–March 3

**Arts Nouveaux - Une Célébration** presented by Xoregos Performing Company; included *The Confession* by Sarah Bernhardt and *Basking* by Dave DeChristopher; Director/Choreography, Sheila Xoregos; Co-choreography, Rael Lamb; Music by Debussy, Reynaldo Hahn, Ernest Chausson; Costumes, Elgie Chevalier, Carla Gant; Cast: Nicola Barber, Tobias Burns, Aidan Koehler, Kimberly Lantz, Kenneth Linsley, Andrea D'Arcy Mead, Lawrence Merritt, Elizabeth Ruelas; April 12–21

# WorkShop Theater Company

Timothy Scott Harris and Elysa Marden, Artistic Directors; Riley Jones-Cohen, Executive Director

## Mainstage

**Intellectuals** by Scott C. Sickles; Director, David Gautschy; Set, Craig Napoliello; Costumes, Isabelle Fields; Lighting, Deborah Constantine; Sound, Nick DiCeglie, Kevin Reifel, David Gautschy; Stage Manager, Michael Palmer; Cast: Bill Blechingberg, Ellen Dolan, Patricia O'Connell, Kari Swenson Riely, Bill Tatum, Kim Weston-Moran, Jess Cassidy White; September 8–30

**Never Missed a Day** by Ken Jaworowski; Director, Thomas Coté; Set, Amy Vlastelica; Lighting, Evan Purcell; Costumes, Joanie Schumacher; Stage Manager, C.J. LaRoche; Cast: Jed Dickson, Brian Homer, Michael Shelle, Bill Tatum, Shade Vaughn; December 1–16

**The Tragedie of Macbeth** by William Shakespeare; presented in association with the New York Actors Ensemble; Director, Charles E. Gerber; Fights, Galway McCullough; PSM, Michael Palmer; Lighting, Carrie Yacono; Sound, Andy Cohen; Costumes, Amy Kitzhaber; Cast: Gregory Adair, Michael James Anderson,

Susan Angelo, Mick Bleyer, Kenneth Cavett, Alexandra Devin, Letty Ferrer, Mike Finesilver, Brooke Fulton, Justin Gibbs, Noah Keen, Leanne Littlestone, Audrey Maeve Hager, David M. Mead, Edward Myers, Jake Myers, Ben Sumrall, Clare Patterson; January 5–21

**Desire in the Suburbs** adapted from Eugene O'Neill by Frederic Glover; Director, Kathleen Brant; Cast: Timothy Scott Harris, Baz Snider, Dee Dee Friedman; March 14–31

### Plays in Process at the Jewel Box Theater

**Magic and Mayhem** two one-acts: *Deconstructing the Magician* and *The Devil and Billy Markham* written by Nelson Lugo and Shel Silverstein, directed by Thomas Cote; Cast: Nelson Lugo, Brit Herring, Broken Pockets Band; June 1–10, revived August 17–26

**Soundtrack to Cezanne** by Gary Giovannetti, directed by Andrea "Spook" Testani; Cast: Jodie Bentley, Jeremy Brisiel, John Jimerson, Jon Lonoff, Darcie Siciliano; June 15–24

**Niya Tey Soung** by David M. Mead, directed by Arian Blanco; Cast: Lexie Devin, Susan Kim, Kathy Gail MacGowan, Sandy Moore, Paul Singleton; June 28–July 8

**French Kisses** plays from past Samuel French Festivals; included: *Audience* by Mick Stern, directed by Merry Beamer, *Under the Apple Tree* by Bob Manus, directed by Kevin Reifel, *Crossed Wires* by Tony Sportiello, directed by Kathy McGowan; *Threat Level* by Bob Manus & Timothy Scott Harris, directed by David M. Pincus; *The Power and the Glory* by Le Wilhelm, directed by Merry Beamer; Cast: Tracy Newirth, Wende O'Reilly, Paul Singleton, Lexie Devin, Alice Cutler, Liz Forst, Bob Manus, Richard Kent Green, Anne Fizzard; August 14–23

**Liberty–The Musical** by Dana Leslie Goldstein & Jonathan Goldstein, directed by Robert Bruce McIntosh; Cast: Paul Aguirre, Alexandra Devin, Cheryl Dowling, Peter Farrell, Richard Kent Green, Victoria Malvagno, Nedra McClyde, Robert Bruce McIntosh, Kevin McKelvy, Joanie Schumacher, Mark L. Smith; *Uncle Vanya* by Anton Chekhov, translated by Paul Schmidt; Director, Manfred Borman; Cast: Ken Glickfeld, Charlotte Hampden, Susanna Harris, Cordis Heard, Christopher Joseph Jones, Stephan Roylance, Anar Vilas, Dana Watkins; November 9–18

**The Mentee** by Steven Fecter, directed by Elysa Marden; Cast: Reyna de Courcy, Peter McCain, Shelley McPherson; January 11–20

**Three Pairs & a Full House** included *American Thighs* by Gary Giovannetti, directed by Manfred Burman; *Blue Sunset in Timisoara* by Michael Lazan, directed by David Gautschy; *The Farm Bill* by Susan Dworkin, directed by Ahvi Spindell; *One to the Head, One to the Heart* by Ken Jaworowski, directed by Thomas Coté; Cast: Denny Bess, Jeffrey Danneman, Jed Dickson, Lori Faiella, Leslie Gwyn, John Jimerson, Tanya Marten, Shelley McPherson, Peter Stoll, Nicole Taylor; April 11–21

**Couples** by Rich Orloff, directed by David Gautschy; Cast: Anthony Aibel, C.K. Allen, Michael Anderson, Lena Armstrong, Marie-Pierre Beausejour, Peter Farrell, Ken Glickfeld, Justin R. G. Holcomb, Cailin McDonald, Richard Mover, Wende O'Reilly, Vinnie Penna, Jacqueline M. Raposo, Christine Verleny, Jess Cassidy White, L.B. Williams; May 9–19

**Staged Readings** *The Missionary Position* by Lawrence DuKore, directed by Peter Bloch; Cast: Alice Cutler, John Jimerson (September 14–16); *Survival of the Stubbornest* by Theresa Wozunk; Cast: Edward Kasche, Gary Mink, Tracy Newirth, Wende O'Reilly, Ben Sumrall (September 23); One-Acts Plays by David Schmitt (September 30); *I Want to See Carmen Bassillio* by Jim DeMarse (October 12–14); *Radio Ridiculous Presents: A Tale of Two Miserables* by Rich Orloff; Cast: Richard Kent Green, Gary Mink, Tracy Newirth, Laurie Ann Orr, Gerrianne Raphael, Jay Russell (November 2–4); *Pillar of Salt* by William C. Kovacsik, directed by David Gautschy; Cast: Ilana Becker, Jeremy Feldman, Ken Glickfeld, Inga Hyatt, John Jimerson, Edward J. Kasche, Nelson Lugo, Tara MacMullen, Jacob Thompson, Anar Vilas (December 14–16), *Moonlight and Love Songs* by Scott C. Sickles, directed by David Gautschy; Cast: Greg Adair, Libby Hughes, David M.

Mead, Gary Mink, Nicole Taylor, Ryan Tresser, Jess Cassidy White, Jeff Woodman (February 8–10), *Up From Stardom* by Lawrence DuKore, directed by Kevin Reifel; Cast: Ken Glickfeld, Ron Hirt, Debra Ann Khan-Bey, Jeff Paul, Stephanie Weeks (March 24)

**Sundays@Six Readings** *Beavers & Pigs* by Dan Moran (June 3); *Radio Ridiculous* by Rich Orloff (June 4); *Liberty* by Dana Goldstein (June 11); *Kafka's Quest* by Lu Hauser (June 17); *One of Our Own* by Enid Harlow (June 24); *Twilight at the Peace Hotel* by Gary Giovannetti (June 25); *Somewhere Between Heaven and Hell* by Anthony J. Bowman (July 8); *Inch* by Owa (July 9); *Laugh Track* by Robert Strozier (August 13); *Tierra Del Fuego* by Henry Guzman (August 20); *Blue Café & Box Men* by Frank Hertle (September 10); *The Treatment* by Michael Lazan, *The Contour of Shadows* by Liz Amberly (September 24); *Darby O'Gill and the Good People* by Edward Kelly (October 8); *Couples* by Rich Orloff (October 15); One-Acts by Ben Alexander (October 22); *Black Horse* by David Mead (November 12); *Up From Stardom* by Lawrence DuKore (November 19); *The Blue Carbuncle* by Andrew Joffe (December 10); *Umbrellas in the Snow* by Jack Dyville (December 17); *Fire Thief* by Laura Hirschberg (January 7); *Conversations with Max* by Al Tapper (January 14); *Appetites* by Owa (January 21); *The Necessary Disposal* by Bob Ost (January 28); *Freeze* by Richard Broadhurst (February 11); *Rivals* by Robert Grogan (February 18); *Buddies* by Lawrence DuKore (March 4); *Demon Bitch Goddess* by Scott C. Sickles (March 25); *Only Kidding* by Jim Geoghan (April 1); *The Contour of Shadows* by Liz Amberly (April 15); *Taken By Indians* by Alice Van Buren (April 22); *Tropical Heat* by Rich Orloff (May 6); *Women at Window* by Glenn Alterman (May 20)

**Special Events** *Unknown Country 2006: More Plays from Canada* (September 26 & December 3), *Daytime at Nighttime 2006* (November 23), *Greedy* by Alan Freestone, presented by Unrestricted View (London); Cast: Louie Bayliss, Rachel Egan, Felicity Wren, James Wren (January 23–27); The MacIvor Readings: *You Are Here* and *How It Works* by Daniel MacIvor, directed by John Morrison & Elysa Marden (March 18 & 25); *Will-A-Thon: 6 Nights of Shakespeare* directed & conceived by Charles E. Gerber; Cast: Mick Bleyer, Lynda Berge, Ron Crawford, Letty Ferrer, Charles E. Gerber, Cordis Heard, Katrin Hilbe, Katrin Hilbe, Margaret Lewis, David M. Mead, Sandy Moore, Clare Patterson, Stefania Schramm, L.B. Williams (April 23–28)

### Non-resident Productions

**Allies: An Evening of One-Acts** presented by Black Door Theatre Company; included: *Bone China* by K. Alexa Mavromatis, *Fin & Euba* by Audrey Cefaly, *Room at the Inn* by Barbara Lindsay, *Sightlines* by Charles Hall; Directors, Debra Register, Khary Wilson; Set, Colin Key; Lighting, Kate Ashton; Stage Manager, Jeff Cramer; Cast: Donna Blaszczyk, Kristin Cappon, Bronwen Carson, Colin William Key, Sara Laudonia, Gina LeMoine, Josh Marcantel, Barry Jason Schneider, Ryan Sutelan; June 22–29

**Windows** written & directed by Sylvia Bofill; presented by INTAR Theatre; Sets, Jian Junge; Costumes, Oana Botez-Ban; Lighting, Lucas Krech; Sound, David Lawson; Cast: Mercedes Herrero, Carmen de Lavallade, Milena Pérez Joglar; Mainstage; October 18–November 5

**Act Naturally** by Scott Katzman; presented by presented by Intangible Productions; Director, Christopher Manning; Set, David Behring; Costumes, Paulette Keck; Lighting, Melanie Smock; Sound, Nicholas Viselli; PSM, Janice DeKoff; Cast: Scott Katzman, Audrey Amey, Darron Cardosa, Tracee Chimo, Skid Maher, Marlene O'Haire, Gwenyth Reitz; February 8–24

**Hamlet** by William Shakespeare; presented by Take Wing and Soar; Director, Elizabeth Swain; Producer, Debra Ann Byrd, Jacqueline Jeffries; Mainstage; Set, Rob Dutiel; Costumes, Ali Turns; Lighting, Sean Linehan; Sound, David D. Wright; Fights, Ron Piretti; Stage Manager, Glenn Grieves; Cast: Timothy D. Stickney, Petronia Paley, Arthur French, Seth Deurr, Geoffrey Warren Barnes II, Sandford Faison, Larry Floyd, David Heron, Mary Hodges, Michael Leonard James, Tom Martin, Kwame Riley, Miguel Sierra, Carsey Walker Jr., Bryan Webster, Dathan B. Williams; April 13–29

**Half** by Greg Lemoine; presented by White Horse Theater Company; Director, Cyndy A. Marion; Sets, Andis Gjoni; Lighting, Debra Leigh Siegel; Costumes, David B. Thompson; Stage Manager, Elliot Lanes; Cast: Mark Ransom, Jennifer-Scott Mobley, Ken Trammell, Bill Fairbairn; Jewel Box Theater; May 30–June 3

## York Theatre Company

Developmental Reading Series: *Mrs. Lincoln* by June Bingham & Carmel Owen (June 6–8); *Friends Like These* by John McMahon & Jay Jeffries (June 21); *Legend of Sleepy Hollow* by Robert L. Stempin & James Crowley (June 27); *A Good Man* by Philip Goodman & Ray Leslee (August 2–3); *The Brighter Side* by Napua Davoy (September 19); *Oliver's Idea* by Corinna Manetto & Ronald Bazarini (September 21); *Island* by Peter Link, Larry Rosler & Joe Bravaco (September 26); *Unlock'd* by Sam Carner & Derek Gregor (October 23); *Grand and Glorious* by Ed Wilson (October 30); *Bookstore* by Richard Wolf & Jane McAdams (November 1); *Legend of Sleepy Hollow* by Michelle Ackerman (November 2); *Believe* by Brad Howell Houghton (November 5); *Last Smoker in America* by Bill Russell & Peter Melnick (November 6); *Mongrel* by Cornelia Cody (December 8); *Room With a View* by Robert Firpo-Cappiello (December 14); *Bonnie & Clyde* by Hunter Foster (December 15); *Gay Grimms* by Ted Sod, Dan Martin & Michael Biello (January 11); *Sheriff and Caputo* by P.J. Barry (January 22); *Greetings From Yorkville* by Robert Grusecki & Anya Turner (January 29); *The Jello is Always Red* by Clark Gesner (January 30); *A Park Avenue Christmas* by Ed Dixon (January 31); *It's Not What I Say…* by Dan Lanning and R. Bell (February 20); *Stella Rising* by Napua Davoy (February 21); *You Don't Know Jack* by Jay Falzone & Jason Lofredo (February 28)

## Additional Productions and Events

**Accomplice: New York** created by Tom Salamon and Betsy Salamon-Sufott; Cast: James Feuer, Joseph Tomasini, Alan Steele, Joe Luongo, Roland Uruci, Brendan Irving, Lauren Potter, John Cannatella; mystery locations throughout the city; June–November

**Celebrate Good Times (Macbeth)** written & directed by Yuval Sharon; presented by Theater Faction; Set, Rich Murray; Costumes, Jessica Watters; Lighting, Ben Kato; Cast: Jeffrey Meanza, Cara Consilvio, Rajika Puri, Matthew Sullivan, Tyler Hollinger, Jonathan Whittle-Utter, Sarah Fraunfelder, Nicole D'Amico, Matthew Doers, Cherry Duke, Jef Evans, Sarah Fraunfelder, Adriane Lee, Beverly Love, Gregory Marcel, Mark Moorman, Sarah Yahr Tucker, Nadine Zygaj; West End Theatre; June 1–11

**Pocket Full of Change** created & presented by Strike Anywhere Performance Ensemble; Director, Leese Walker; Cast: Andrea Ariel, Donna Bouthillier, Alan Brady, Brian Duguay, Jody Espina, Michel Gentile, Rob Henke, Julie Pasqual, Rolf Sturm, Leese Walker, Jim Whitney; The Brecht Forum; June 2–17

**The Prosecution of Brandon Hein** by Charles Grodin; presented by The Culture Project; Director, Gordon Edelstein; Barrow Street Theatre; Cast: Carey Lowell, Charles Grodin, James McMenamin, Bruce Altman, Bruce McVittie, Julia Gibson; June 5

**Love's Labour's Lost** by William Shakespeare; presented by The Hudson Warehouse; Director, Nicholas Martin-Smith; Cast: Lucas Beck, Chris Behan, Jeff Boles, Todd Butera, Jenny Checchia, Ian Christiansen, Aidan Dee, Meagan English, Joseph Hamel, Mark Isler, Gerald Kline, Frank Magnasco, Jamie Oberlee, Arthur Pellman, Patrick Roeder, Amy Cassel Taft, George Wells; Soldiers and Sailors Monument in Riverside Park; July 6–30

**The Fantasy Party** written & directed by Larry Pellegrini; presented by Jeff Gitlin & Raphael Berko in association with Gary Shaffer; Costumes, Juan De Armas & Concetta Rose Rella; Choreography, Janine Molinari; Edison Hotel, transferred to China Club; opened June 10; still running

**Twelfth Night** by William Shakespeare; presented by Kings County Shakespeare Company; Director, Deborah Wright Houston; Technical Director, Carol Feeley; PSM April A. Kline; Set/Props/Fights, Lucie Chin; Costumes/Wigs Deborah Wright Houston & Lucie Chin; Lighting, Carol Feeley; Press, Jonathan Slaff Associates; Cast: Neimah Djourabchi, Jovis DePognon, Frank Smith, Ashlynne Holder-Mosely, Zohnell Dixon, Ronald Cohen, Ian Gould, Joseph Small, Glenn Urieta, Martina Weber, Rachel Alt, Brie Eley, Nicole Potter, Bruno Peña, Joe Crow Ryan; BRIC Studio at the Strand Theater; June 14–30

**Hamlet** by William Shakespeare; presented by BOFA Productions; St. Malachy's The Actors' Chapel; June 22–24

**God's Country** by Steven Dietz; presented by Thirsty Turtle Productions; Directors, Beth Lopes & Paula Vingelen; Costumes, Katja Andreiev; Lighting, Ian Crawford & Greg Balla; Sound, Fred Nicolaus; Cast: Teddy Alvaro, Joshua Bachove, Justin Fair, Gregory Kostal, Marc LeVasseur, Christian O'Brien, Laurel Reese, Teresa Reilly, Lauren Sowa, Mark Turetsky, Gillian Wiggin; Manhattan Children's Theatre; June 23–July 2

**Manhattan Madcaps of 1924** music by Richard Rodgers, lyrics by Lorenz Hart, book by Isaiah Sheffer; presented by Symphony Space Director, Annette Jones; Set, Ryan Scott; Lighting, Brian Aldous; Costumes, Madeline Cohen; Cast: Katie Allen, Ivy Austin, Christine Bokhour, Sydney J. Borgoyne, Michael Simon Hall, Howard Kay, Staci Runitsky, Nick Verina; Leonard Nimoy Thalia Theatre; July 6–23

**Fresh Fruit Festival 2006** 4th annual; Carol Polcovar, Artistic Director; July 10–23; included: *Love in the World of Fruits* two short plays: *Marla's Devotion* by Linda Eisenstein; *Real Smiles* by Jon M. Spano; Collective: Unconscious; July 14–15; *Come Back to Me* by Jesse Alick; Collective: Unconscious; July 15–16; *Physics of Love* by Jennifer Pawlitschek; Collective: Unconscious; July 15–16; *Why'd Ya Make Me Wear That, Joe?* by Vanda; Dorothy Strelsin Theatre; July 18–21; *To Whom It May Concern* by Aurin Squire; Dorothy Strelsin Theatre; July 19–22; *My Mother Told Me I Was Different: Voices of the Stonewall Rebellion* by Carol Polcovar; Director, David Gaard; Dorothy Strelsin Theatre; July 21–23

**A.F.R.A.I.D.** book, music, & lyrics by Susan Stoderl; presented by Brooklyn Repertory Opera; Director, Brett Wynkoop; Music Director, Hardin Butcher; Cast: Kristina Semos, Pamela Scanlon, Christina Rivera, Janna Tusa, Meghan Dibble, Courtney Schowalter, Ilya Speranza, Cordelia Chenault, Elizabeth Eiel, Tracy Bidleman, Angela Billings, Stefanie Block, Shannon Hunt, Tracey Cooper, Barrett Cobb, Christina Reimer, Francis Devine, Ivy Frenkel, Liora Michelle, Allison Atteberry, Deborah Thomas, Lorene Philips, Amanda White, Nika Leoni, Mary Jane Dingledy, Sarah Arikian, Kathleen Keske, Meryl Sher; Brooklyn Lyceum; July 11–December 12

**The Lisbon Traviata** by Terrence McNally; presented by Ryan Repertory Company; Director/Set/Sound, John Sannuto; Lighting, Barbara Parisi; Co-Sound, Edward Alsina; Co-Set, Michael Perrotta; Cast: Michael Perrotta, Brian Armstrong, Tony Marinelli, Ely Aina Rapoza, Harry Warren Theatre; July 20–30

**What the Thunder Said** created and performed by bluemouth inc.; presented by the Lower Manhattan Cultural Council as part of the "Sitelines" event; Cast: Stephen O'Connell, Richard Windeyer, Lucy Simc, Sabrina Reeves, Ciara Adams, Chad Dembski, Kevin Rees-Cummings, Robert Tremblay; 32 Sixth Avenue; July 25–August 5

**Dear Edwina** by Marcy Heisler and Zina Goldrich; Director, Jen Bender; Music Director, Jose Simbulan; Set. John McDermott; Lighting, Jeff Croiter; Sound, Ezekiel Kendrick; Stage Manager, Alexis P. Prussack; Cast: Scott Coulter, Nathan Klau, Billy Miller, Kelli Rabke, Sandy Rutin, Rob Seitelman, Kate Wetherhead, Becky Lillie Woods; Rattlestick Playwrights Theater; July 27–29

**The Bacchae** by Euripides; presented by The Hudson Warehouse; Director, Ashley Kell-Tata; Soldiers and Sailors Monument in Riverside Park; August 4–27

**The History of Valentyne and Orson** written, created & designed by Ralph Lee; presented by Mettawee River Theater Company; Cast: Ian Lassiter Tom Marion, Jan-Peter Pedross; St. John the Divine's; September 8–17

**The Frogs** adapted from Aristophanes by Jason Tyne; presented by Rising Sun Performance Company; Director, Rachel Klein; Music, Keith Dworkin; Music Director, P. William Pinto, Jovier Sanchez, Amir Levi; Cast: Aaron Oetting, Zachary Zdunich, Elizabeth Burke, Ben Beckley, Jeff Seal, Amir Levi, Tommy Lind, Josh Hyman, Sinem Balkir, Kathleen Schlemmer, Emily Miner, Megan Dahl; Summit Rock in Central Park; September 9–30

**Her Song** written & conceived by Brenda Levitt, co-conceived and music directed by Barry Levitt; Director, Dori Levitt; Cast: Gabrielle Lee, Kate Manning, Kelly McCormick, Trisha Rapier, Gabrielle Stravelli, Heidi Weyhmueller, Emma Zaks; Birdland; opened September 9

**Picasso at the Lapin Agile** by Steve Martin; presented by The Sackett Group; Director, Dov Lebowitz-Nowak; Set, John C. Scheffler; Lighting, Bruce A. Kraemer; Costumes, C.C. Scott; Cast: Peter Bonilla, Sari Caine, Mark Cajigao, Paul Falcetta, Billy Lane, Megan Manzi, Aaron Oetting, Anna Pond, John Scheffler, Carey Seward; Brooklyn Music School Playhouse; September 14–October 1

**Relativity** by Mark Stein; presented by LucGroup; Director, Timmy Quinlan; Stage Manager, Catherine Deciaccio; Cast: Lucas Van Engen, Leigh Feldpausch, Alexis Hyatt, Ellen Lanese, Anthony Spaldo; Phil Bosakowski Theatre; September 14–24

**Moby Dick: The Sermon** by Herman Melville; Director, Joe Rosato; Green-Wood Cemetary Chapel; September 16–December 30

**Dina Martina: Soft Palate, Fallen Arches** created and performed by Grady West; presented by Ron Lasko & Spin Cylce; The Cutting Room; September 22–October 7

**I Wish You a Boat** created & directed by Wendy Ward; Cast: Christine Brumbaugh, Matt W. Cody, Katia Hoerning, Jay T. Johnson, Suzie Mellring, Lara Silva; Ward Studio; September 23–January 27

**Death in Vacant Lot!** translated, adapted and directed by Kameron Steele from Terayama Shuji's *Denen ni Shisu*; presented by The South Wing; Set, Mariano Marquez; Costumes, Carlos Soto; Cast: Ivana Catanese, Gillian Chadsey, Craig Dolezel, Catherine Friesen, James Garver, Jessica Green, LeeAnne Hutchison, Cecile Monteyne, Chris Oden, David Ponce, Jill A. Samuels, Nate Schenkkan, Andrew Schulman; Musicians, Katie Down, Nadia Mahdi, Kevin McWha Steele; LMCC Swing Space; October 4–14

**Ghosts** by Henrik Ibsen; presented by A Rebel Theater; Director/Choreography, Rajendra Ramoon Maharaj; Ngozi Anyanwu, Leticia Bryan, Rory Clarke, Sabrina Collie, Edward Davis, Rodney Gilbert, Sharon King, Mickey Ryan, Arthur Toombs; Abrons Arts Center; October 5–15

**The Trojan Women** by Euripides; presented by the Theatre Group of the Greek Cultural Center; Director, Andreas Tselpos; Cast: Evangelos Alexiou, Eleni Avgousti, Ioanna Gavakou, Electra Maninaki, Eutychia Frangou, Charalambos Gousias, Martha Tompoulidou, Tereza Grimani, Michaella Shiamili, Christina Stefanidis. Greek Cultural Center; October 13–December 17

**The Cartells: A Prime Time Soap…Live!** by Douglas Carter Beane; presented by The Drama Department; Director, Carl Andress; Set, B.T. Whitehill; Costumes, Jeriana Hochberg; Lighting, Kirk Bookman & Julie Seitel; Original Music, Lewis Flinn; Stage Manager, Don Myers; Fights, Rick Sordelet; Casting: Cindy Tolan; Press: Shaffer-Coyle; Cast: Peter Frechette, Joanna Gleason, Brian d'Arcy James, Jason Butler Harner, Joey Slotnick, Kristen Schaal, Peter Hermann, David Rakoff, Vanessa Aspillaga, Keith Davis; presented at and in association with Comix Comedy Club; Episode 1: "The Eye of the Needle" (October 16); Episode 2: "Far Above Rubies" (October 23); Episode 3: "Perish With the Sword" (October 30); Episode 4: "Cast a Stone" (November 6)

**Bad Dog** by Rebecca Stokes; presented by Theatre Forum; Director, Russell Taylor; Set, Aaron Haberer; Costumes, Jennifer Edwards; Lighting, Bobby Bradley; Sound, Kris Chen; PSM, Danielle Campbell; Cast: Sarah Gavitt, Annette Gurrasi, Randy Harmon, Tarek Khan, Evan O'Brien; Church for All Nations; October 27–November 20

**The Charlotte Salomon Project: Life? Or Theater?** conceived & adapted by Jessica Brater & Miriam Fleton Dansky from text by Charlotte Simmons, additional writing by Jacob Burstein-Stern, Elizabeth Emmons, Andrew Gilchrist, Avi Glickstein, & Katya Schapiro; presented by Polybe and Seats; Director, Jessica Brater; Dramaturg, Miriam Felton-Dansky; Producers, Stacey Cooper McMath, Catherine Wallach; Lighting, Marnie Cummings, Natalie Robin; Set, Kanae Heike; Music, Jason Binnick; Costumes, Karen Flood; Cast: Jacob Burstein-Stern, Samantha Debicki, Andrew Gilchrist, Avi Glickstein, Rebekah Mindel, Elaine O'Brien, Molly Parker-Meyers, Katya Schapiro, Lisette Marie Silva, Ari Vigoda; Brooklyn Fire Proof; November 1–19

**Miguel Manara** by Oscar Vladislas de Lubicz-Milosz; presented by Blackfriars Repertory Theatre; Director, Steven Day; Cast: Bill Corey, Liz Douglas, Maureen Dowdell, Kathleen Kaczan, John Nahigian, Thomas Poarch, Esme Von Hoffman, Christopher Zorker, Kevin Kaine; St. Vincent Ferrer Church; November 3–26

**Blade to the Heat** by Oliver Mayer; Director, Thom Garvey; Set, Court Watson; Lighting, Steve O'Shea; Cast: Yash Shah, Ben Cohen, Lina Pava, Stephen Chan; Baruch Performing Arts Center – Rose Nagelberg Theatre; November 14–18

**The Sublet Experiment** by Ethan Youngerman; Director, Michelle Tattenbaum; Costumes, Jessica Pabst; Sound, Tim Boyce; Stage Manager, Karen Dickerson; Cast: Erin Maya Darke, Adam Hyland, Christian Maurice, Marshall Sharer; presented at various apartments throughout the city; November 16–May 20

**The Last Escape** created and performed by Wroclaw Puppet Theatre, based on the writings of Bruno Schulz; presented by JCC Manhattan & Polish Cultural Institute; JCC; November 18–19

**Two from Galilee** created, produced & directed by Tom & Karen Hallet; book by Margorie Holmes, music by Robert Sterling, lyrics by Karla Worley; Cast: Lauren Elizabeth Loss, Ernie Pruneda; Peter Jay Sharp Theatre at Symphony Space; November 21–26

**Blanco** by Pablo Garcia-Gámez; Director, Jorge Merced; Teatro IATI; November 30–December 17

**Fortune and Men's Eyes** by John Herbert; presented by Rusty Spoon Theatre; Director, Douglas Brautigam; Stage Manager, Jen Wiener; Cast: Dan Gallo, Chris Cusano, Thomas Vilorio, Brian Leider, Greg Louis; Interborough Repertory Theater; December 1–17

**Four by Three** plays presented by New Media Repertory; included: *All is Calm* by John Levine, *Poor Hearts* by Edward Musto, *…And Everything Nice* by Edward Musto, *Act Two* by Stanford Pritchard; Director, Miranda McDermott; New Media Repertory Theatre; December 1–8

**Songs for a New World** music & lyrics by Jason Robert Brown; presented by Samsara Theatre Company; Director, Jason Kane; Music Director, Ray Bailey; Cast: Hector Coris, Rick Delancy, Tracy Jai Edwards, Matt Hinkley, Jason Kane, Holli Leggett, Cedric Leiba Jr., Eric Martin, Julie Reyburn, Shelby Rose, Andrea Rutherford, Stephanie Schraer, Alicia St. Louis, Stephanie Streisand; Theatre at St. Luke's December 4–11

**Bring Back Birdie** book by Michael Steward, music by Charles Strouse, lyrics by Lee Adams; presented by Opening Doors Theatre Company (premiere production); Director, Hector Coris; Music Director, Andrew Wheeler; Choreography, Christine Schwalenberg; Producer, Suzanne Adams; Cast: Dana Barathy, Doug Chitel, Desireé Davar, Denise DeMirjian, Scott McLean Harrison, Blayne Levin, Maria Maloney, David Perlman, Jeff Pierce, Marc Tumminelli, Juson Williams; Piano, Jason Sirois; The Duplex Cabaret; December 5–6

**The Agony and the Agony** by Nicky Silver; Director, Terry Kinney; Set, Andromache Chalfant, Costumes, Mattie Ullrich; Lighting, Jeff Croiter, Sound/Music, Obadiah Eaves; Stage Manager, Christine Lemme; Cast: Victoria Clark, Michael Esper, Harry van Gorkum, Cheyenne Jackson, Nicky Silver, Marilyn Torres; Vineyard Theatre Lab Production; December 9

**Among Friends** by Kristine Thatcher; presented by Ryan Repertory Company; Director, Barbara Parisi; Cast: John Sannuto, Tony Marinelli, Brian Armstrong; Harry Warren Theatre; December 16–30

**The Pod Project** an interactive theatrical experience created and directed by Nancy Bannon; produced by Nancy Bannon and Brian MacDevitt; Costumes, Ilona Somogyi; Lighting, Brian MacDevitt; Cast: Bob Moss, Marc Kenison; Stephanie Liapis, Risa Steinberg, Arnie Apostol, Keith Johnson, Megan Brunsvold, Tricia Nelson, Jennifer Gillespie, Rick Meese, Jose Souto, Netta Yerushalmy, Ryan Corriston, Lily Fischer; 20 Greene Street Gallery; January 13–Febrary 11

**No Great Society** presented by Elevator Repair Service; Director, John Collins; Costumes, Colleen Werthmann; Choreogrpahy, Katherine Profeta; Stage Manager, Madeleine Burn; Cast: Susie Sokol, Vin Knight, Scott Shepherd, Ben Williams; New York Theatre Workshop; January 19–22 as part of P.S. 122's COIL festival; January 25–February 11

**A Shelter for Dreams** two one-acts: *Jane's House* by Harriet Rafe, directed by Michael Simon Hall; Cast: Robert Benes, Bridgette Boucher, David Phillip Brooks, Bekka Lindström, Joe Masi, Marilyn Salisbury; *The Usual Space* by Michael Simon Hall, directed by David Bogoslaw; Cast: Anna Ewing Bull, Brad Holbrook; Neighborhood Playhouse; January 26–27

**History Girls** Director, Michael Sexton; presented by The Shakespeare Society; Cast: Kathleen Chalfant, Marian Seldes, Kate Mulgrew, Brian Murray, Joe Plummer, Christopher Evan Welch; Kaye Playhouse; February 12

**Measure for Measure** by William Shakespeare; presented by Blessed Unrest; Director, Jessica Burr; Cast: Paul L. Coffey, Eunjee Lee, Craig Bridger, Laura Wickens, Zenzele Cooper, Celli Pitt; Interart Annex; February 16–March 5

**Floating** by Hugh Hughes and Sioned Rowlands; presented by Hoipolloi; Barrow Street Theatre; February 28–March 3

**Five Boroughs** by John McDermott; Cast: Tony Chiofalo, Jane Guyer, Gayle Robbins, Tony Stacey, Seril James; Iguana Restaurant; March 1–April 21

**Things to Do With Your Mouth** by Melinda Lee; presented by the Lower Manhattan Cultural Council; Design/Composer, Ernesto Klar; 15 Nassua; March 7–10

**Ruff Love, or What You Will** by William Shakespeare, adapted & directed by Deborah Wright; presented by Kings County Shakespeare Company; Cast: Andrew Oswald, Baptista Minola, Brian Rhinehart, Charlie Coniglio, Cotton Wright, Dana Pagliara, Joseph Small, Jovis DePognon, Malena Negrão, Mary Lou Kylis, Neimah Djourabchi, Norah Turnham, Rachel Alt, Roger Dale Stude; March 8–19

**It's a Bird!...It's a Plane!...It's Superman!** book by David Newman & Robert Benton, lyrics by Lee Adams, music by Charles Strouse; presented by Opening Doors Theatre Company; Director, Casey Burden; Producer, Holli Leggett; Music Director, Steven Bednasz; Choreography, Rick Delancy; Cast: Suzanne Adams, Bryce Bermingham, Andrew Cao, Desireé Davar, Blayne Levin, Sarah Lilley, Eric Martin, Ivory McKay, Ravi Roth, Jason B. Schmidt, Michelle Solomon, Rob Ventre; The Duplex Cabaret; March 11–13

**stirring** by Shoshona Currier and Charles Forbes; presented by Shalimar Productions; Director, Shoshona Currier; Cast: Brandon Bales, Matt Bridges, Kim Gainer, Jack P. Dempsey, Rachel Plotkin, Jen Taher, Joey Williamson; Interart Annex; March 16–25

**Romeo and Juliet: Jerusalem** by William Shakespeare; presented by Genesis Repertory; Directors, Mary Elizabeth MiCari, J. Michaels; Lighting, Rob Nguyen & Shaun S. Orbin; Translations/Cultural Advisors, Mimi Asnes & Nesreen Mahmoud; Costumes, Carla Gant; Fights, Douglas Castillo; Cast: Michael Raver, Josh Silverman, Tania Asnes, Sarah Hankins, Justin Maruri, Raphael Kasen, Alex Moshofsky, Adam Gutbezahl, Mary Elizabeth MiCari, J. Michaels, Shawn Watson, Mary Riley, Jennifer Gelber, Kenneth L. Naanep, Brittany Bellizeare, Carissa Cordes, Jason Cutler, Robert Liebowitz, Shaun Orbin, Sarah Leigh Orbin, Dianna Lora; Greek Cultural Center; March 22–April 14

**Platanos & Collard Greens** by David Lamb, based on his novel *Do Platanos Go Wit' Collard Greens?*, produced by Between the Lines Productions, David and Jamillah Lamb; Director, Summer Hill Seven; Cast: Phillip J. Smith, Ben Rivers, Quisha Saunders, Lila Blake Palmer, Sarita Covington, Patricia Aleman, Doni C. Comas; Florence Gould Hall; March 27–July 28

**Seven.11 Convenience Theatre** 5th annual presentation of seven eleven-minute plays presented by Despina & Company; written by Sujit Chawla, Thelma de Castro, Vishakan Jeyakumar, Jon Kern, Janet S. Kim, Michael Lew, Rehana Mirza, Debargo Sanyal; Director, Sanjiv Jhaveri; Music Director, Samrat Chakrabarti; Cast: Ka-ling Cheung, Meetu Chilana, Sam Ghosh, Andrew Guilarte, Jackson Loo, John Rankin, Anita Sabherwal; Abrons Arts Center at Henry Street Settlement; March 29–April 14

**And He Made a Her** by Doric Wilson; presented by TOSOS II with Peculiar Works Project; Director, Mark Finley; Stage Manager, Frederic Graenson; Set, Michael Muccio; Costumes, Chris Weikel; Cast: Matt Rashid, Chris Weikel, Nick Matthews, Roberto Cambeiro, Jamie Heinlein; Laurie Beechman Theatre at the West Bank Café; Fridays, April 6–26

**Expressing Willie** by Rachel Crothers; presented by Women Seeking...A Theatre Company; Director, Christine Mosere; Costumes, Jessa-Raye Court; Set, Brandon Giles; Sound, Katharine Tapp & Lisa Moyer; Choreography, Martha Cataldo-Casey; PSM, Sean Ryan; Cast: Dan Jacoby, Rhonda Ayers, Michael Frederic, Wynne Anders, Simone Lazar, Ann Parker, Maria Silverman, Niko Ruwe, Akiva Penaloza; West End Theatre; April 6–22

**Once Upon a Pandora's Box** by Monica Flory; presented by The New Acting Company; Director, Stephen Michael Rondel; Set/Lighting, Gregg Bellon; Costumes, Julie saltman; Stage Manager, Andrea Ghersetich; Philip Cotloff Center; April 12–May 6

**Jamie...another side of Dean** written & directed by George R. Carr; presented by Veritas Productions; Cast: Mark Thomas, Courtney Allen, Denise Fiore, Jonathan Holtzman, Natalia Klimas, Derrick Brenner; PMT House of Dance; April 19–May 26

**Tune in Tomorrow** by Dave McCracken; presented by DJM Productions; Director, Doug Spagnola; Cast: Colleen Benedict, Dale Church, Rick Lattimer; L'il Peach Theatre; April 19–June 9

**An Evening of Intimate Magic with Eric DeCamps** written & performed by Eric DeCamps; Director, Steve Cuiffo; 3 West Club-The Lincoln Room-Rockefeller Center; May 2–June 20

**God's Ear** by Jenny Schwartz; presented by New Georges; Music/Lyrics, Michael Friedman; Sets, Kris Stone; Costumes, Olivera Gajic; Lighting, Tyler Micoleau; Sound, Leah Gelpe; Dramaturg, Sarah Stern; Props, Lillian Vince; PSM, Megan Schwarz; Cast: Christina Kirk, Gibson Frazier, Monique Vukovic, Judith Greentree, Raymond McAnally, Matthew Montelongo, Annie McNamara; CSC East 13th Street Theatre; May 2–June 2

**Back From the Front** by Lynn Rosen; presented by the Working Theatre; Director, Connie Grappo; Cast: Jen Albano, Peter Bradbury, Karl Kenzler, Haskell King, Christopher Larkin, Aubrey Levy and Annie Torsiglieri; Theatre at Riverside Church; May 3–27

**La Maladie de la Mort** by Marguerite Duras; Director, Bérangère Bonvoisin; presented by French Institute Alliance Française; Cast: Fanny Ardant; Florence Gould Hall; May 4–5

# PROFESSIONAL
# REGIONAL COMPANIES

Top to bottom:

Deanna Dunagan in August: Osage County *at the Steppenwolf Theatre Company (photo by Michael Brosilow)*

The Cast of Urinetown, the Musical *at Geva Theatre Center (photo by Ken A. Huth)*

Tyler Mann, Ricky Ashley and Sara Niemietz in the world premiere of 13 at the Center Theatre Group's Mark Taper Forum *(photo by Craig Schwartz)*

# Actors Theatre of Louisville

Louisville, Kentucky

Forty-third Seasdon

Artistic Director, Marc Masterson; Managing Director, Jennifer Bielstein

## PAMELA BROWN AUDITORIUM

**My Fair Lady** Lyrics and book by Alan Jay Lerner, music by Frederick Loewe; Director/Musical Director, Amanda Dehnert; Sets, David Jenkins; Costumes, Devon Painter; Lighting, Amy Appleyard; Sound, Matt Callahan; Properties, Matt Walston; Choreographer, Kelli Wicke Davis; Choreographer/Assistant Director, Greg Schanuel; Dialect Coach, Don Wadsworth; Stage Manager, Debra Anne Gasper; ASM, Brady Ellen Poole; Dramaturg, Julie Felise Dubiner; Cast: Rachael Warren (Eliza Doolittle), Timothy Crowe (Henry Higgins), George McDaniel (Colonel Pickering), Larry Daggett (Alfred P. Doolittle), Dana Aber (Mrs. Eynsford-Hill/Second Maid), Jessie Austrian (Mrs. Hopkins/First Maid), J. Bernard Calloway (Cockney Quartet/Lord Boxington), Christian Delcroix (Cockney Quartet/Hoxton Man), William Thomas Evans (Cockney Quartet/Selsey Man), Michael Hance (Freddy Eynsford-Hill), Katherine Harber (Mrs. Higgins), Loresa Lanceta (Bystander/Lady Boxington), Nick Locilento (Cockney Quartet/Butler/Second Violin), Abigail Bailey Maupin (Angry Woman), J.P. Moraga (Jamie), Greg Schanuel (Harry/Zoltan Karpathy), Navida Stein (Mrs. Pearce/First Violin), Carly Stotts (Bystander/Maid) Mark Stringham (Charles); Musicians: Bill Corcoran (First Piano/Conductor), Tim Robertson (Second Piano/Vocal Supervisor); August 29–September 23, 2006

*The Cast of* My Fair Lady *(photo by Harlan Taylor)*

**Gem of the Ocean** by August Wilson; Director, Ron O.J. Parson; Sets, Paul Owen; Costumes, Lorraine Venberg; Lighting, Brian J. Lilienthal; Sound, Benjamin Marcum; Properties, Mark Walston; Fight Director, Cliff Williams, III; PSM, Paul Mills Holmes; ASM, Debra Anne Gasper; Dramaturg, Mervin P. Antonio; Cast: Harvy Blanks (Eli), Carl Cofield (Citizen Barlow), Pat Bowie (Aunt Ester Tyler), Tyla Abercrumbie (Black Mary), Larry John Meyers (Rutherford Selig), Thomas Jefferson Byrd (Solly Two Kings), Terrence Riggins (Caesar); October 3–28, 2006

**365 Days/365 Plays** by Suzane-Lori Parks: *Father Comes Home From the Wars* (November 14); *The Great Army in Disgrace* (December 18); *2 Mary's* (January 3); *The Birth of Tragedy* (January 6); *If I Had to Murder Me Somebody* (January 31); *(Again) The Butcher's Daughter* (February 13); also performed January 23–25, 2007 in Actors Theatre lobbies, and January 26, 2007 off-site at Thrown Together Pottery (see credits under Humana Festival listings)

**A Christmas Carol** by Charles Dickens; adapted by Barbara Field; Director, Wendy McClellan; Sets, Paul Owen; Costumes, Lorraine Venberg; Lighting, Deb Sullivan; Sound, Matt Callahan; Properties, Doc Manning & Mark Walston; Music Supervisor, Craig M. Swatt; Dialect Coach, Rinda Frye; PSM, Paul Mills Holmes; ASM, Brady Ellen Poole; Dramaturgs, Diana Grisanti, Cara Pacifico; Cast: William McNulty (Ebenezer Scrooge), Joe Hickey (Bob Cratchit), Tyler Pierce (Fred), Oliver Wadsworth (Marley/Young Marley/Grasper), Ann Hodapp (Mrs. Grigsby/Cook), Aysan Celik (Ghost of Christmas Past/Mrs. Blakely), Sean Sullivan (Boy Scrooge/Simon), Fred Major (Schoolmaster/Undertaker), Angela Sperazza (Fan/Martha Cratchit), Daniel Frith (Young Ebenezer/Snarkers), Flora Diaz (Belle/Mrs. Fred), Sean Andries (Dick Wilkens/Topper), Mark Sawyer-Dailey (Mr. Fezziwig/Old Joe), Pat Bowie (Mrs. Fezziwig/Mrs. Dilber), Maurine Evans (Petunia Fezziwig/Sophia), Nicole Marquez (Marigold Fezziwig/Dorothea), Joseph Benjamin Glaser (Basil Fezziwig/Jeremiah/Tom Cratchit), Lily Stark (Belinda Cratchit/Marjoram, Want), Jeff Snodgrass (Fezziwig Guest/Ghost of Christmas Future), Stacey Robinson (Ghost of Christmas Present/Forrest), Monica Francisco (Mrs. Cratchit), Samuel Blackerby Weible (Tiny Tim/Ignorance), A.J. Glaser (Peter Cratchit/Billy/Fezziwig Kid); Townspeople/Party Guests/Carolers/Children: Taylor Dant, Jada Jefferson, Jane Lee, Jake Millgard, Zachary T. Palamara, Phil Pickens, Mark Stringham; November 21–December 23, 2006

**Sherlock Holmes: The Final Adventure** by Stephen Dietz, based on the original 1899 play by William Gillette and Arthur Conan Doyle; Director, Edward Stern; Sets, Neil Patel; Costumes, Liz Covey; Lighting, Robert Wierzel; Sound, Matt Callahan; Properties, Mark Walston & Doc Manning; Dialect Coach, Don Wadsworth; PSM, Paul Mills Holmes; ASM, Michael D. Domue; Dramaturg, Julie Felise Dubiner; Cast: Joris Stuyck (Sherlock Holmes), Howard Kaye (Doctor Watson), Michael Haworth (Professor Moriarty), Michael Sharon (The King Of Bohemia), Brandy Burre (Irene Adler), David Huber (James Larrabee), Carine Montbertrand (Madge Larrabee), William McNulty (Sid Prince/Clergyman); Police/Passer-bys/Messengers: Loren Bidner, Emily Tate Frank, Zarina Shea, Zdenko Slobodnik, Jeff Snodgrass, Mark Stringham; January 30–February 24, 2007

## BINGHAM THEATRE

**Dracula** Adapted by Hamilton Deane and John L. Balderston from Bram Stoker's novel; Director, William McNulty; Sets, Paul Owen; Costumes, Laura Patterson; Costume Coordinator, John P. White; Lighting, Tony Penna; Sound/Original Music, Benjamin Marcum; Properties, Doc Manning; Fight Director, Cliff Williams, III; Dialect Coach, Rinda Frye; Stage Manager, Brady Ellen Poole; Cast: Elizabeth Wells (Ms. Sullivan), Tyler Pierce (Jonathan Harker), Douglas Rees (Dr. Seward), William McNulty (Van Helsing), Oliver Wadsworth (Renfield), Jake Millgard (Butterworth), Kim Stauffer (Lucy), Misha Kuznetsov (Dracula); Undead Ensemble: Katie Barton, Sophie C. Hill, Eleanor Caudill, Zachary T. Palamara; September 19–October 27, 2006

**The Chosen** Adapted by Aaron Posner and Chaim Potok from the novel by Chaim Potok; Director, Wendy C. Goldberg; Sets, Paul Owen; Costumes, Lorraine Venberg; Lighting, Brian J. Lilienthal; Sound, Matt Callahan; Properties, Doc Manning; Dialect Coach, Don Wadsworth; Stage Manager, Debra Anne Gasper; Dramaturg, Adrien-Alice Hansel; Cast: Matt Seidman (Reuven Malter), Adam Green (Young Reuven Malter), Bernard Burak Sheredy (Reb Saunders), Peter Kybart (David Malter), Peter Stadlen (Danny Saunders); November 7–December 9, 2006

**Mary's Wedding** by Stephen Massicotte; Director, Marc Masterson; Sets, Paul Owen; Costumes, Lorraine Venberg; Lighting, Brian J. Lilienthal; Sound, Matt Callahan; Video, Jason Czaja; Properties, Mark Walston; Dialect Coach, Don Wadsworth; Stage Manager, Debra Anne Gasper; Production Assistant, Melissa Miller; Dramaturg, Mervin P. Antonio; Cast: Will Rogers (Charlie), Nell Geisslinger (Mary/Flowers); January 2–February 3, 2007

## VICTOR JORY THEATRE

**Gone Missing** Written and directed by Steve Cosson from interviews conducted by The Civilians; Music and Lyrics, Michael Friedman; Associate Director, K.J. Sanchez; Sets, Takeshi Kata; Costumes, Sarah Beers; Lighting, Thomas Dunn; Sound, Ken Travis; Musical Director, John D. Zehnder; Choreographer, Jim Augustine; Stage Manager, Frazier Marsh; Properties Coordinator, Deanna Hilleman; Dramaturg, Adrien-Alice Hansel; Cast: Emily Ackerman, Matthew Maher, Jennifer R. Morris, Stephen Plunkett, Robbie Collier Sublett, Alison Weller; September 12–24, 2006

**A Tuna Christmas** by Jaston Williams, Joe Sears, and Ed Howard; Director, Russell Treyz; Sets, Paul Owen; Costumes, John P. White; Lighting, Tony Penna; Sound, Benjamin Marcum; Properties, Joe Cunningham; Stage Manager, Kathy Preher; Production Assistant, Danielle Teague-Daniels; Cast: Bill McKinley (Thurston Wheelis et al), Sheffield Chastain (Arles Struvie et al); November 2, 2006–January 4, 2007

**9 Parts of Desire** by Heather Raffo; Director, K.J. Sanchez; Sets, Mikiko Suzuki; Costumes, Lorraine Venberg; Lighting, Brian J. Lilienthal; Sound, Benjamin Marcum; Properties, Will Griffith; Stage Manager, Brady Ellen Poole; Production Assistant, Danielle Teague-Daniels; Dramaturg, Adrien-Alice Hansel; Cast: Aysan Çelik; Voiceover: Timo Aker; January 18–February 4, 2007

## 31st ANNUAL HUMANA FESTIVAL OF NEW AMERICAN PLAYS

February 25–April 7, 2007

**The Unseen** by Craig Wright; Director, Marc Masterson; Sets, Michael B. Raiford; Costumes, Lorraine Venberg; Lighting, Brian J. Lilienthal; Sound, Matt Callahan; Properties, Doc Manning; Stage Manager, Kathy Preher; Production Assistant, Sara Kmack; Dramaturg, Adrien-Alice Hansel; Cast: Richard Bekins (Wallace), Gregor Paslawsky (Valdez), Richard Furlong (Smeija); Bingham Theatre; February 25–April 1, 2007

**dark play or stories for boys** by Carlos Murillo; Director, Michael John Garces; Sets, Michael B. Raiford; Costumes, Lorraine Venberg; Lighting, Brian J. Lilienthal; Sound, Matt Callahan; Video, Jason Czaja; Properties, Mark Walston; Fight Director, Drew Fracher; Stage Manager, Megan Schwarz; Dramaturg, Mary Resing; Cast: Matthew Stadlemann (Nick), Liz Morton (Molly/Rachel), Will Rogers (Adam), Lou Sumrall (Male Netizen), Jennifer Mendenhall (Female Netizen); Bingham Theatre; March 2–31, 2007

**Strike-Slip** by Naomi Iizuka; Director, Chay Yew; Sets, Paul Owen; Costumes, Christal Weatherly Lighting, Deb Sullivan; Sound, Andre Pluess; Properties, Ron Riall; Fight Director, Lee Look; Stage Manager, Debra Anne Gasper; Production Assistant, Melissa Miller; Dramaturg, Julie Felise Dubiner; Cast: Nelson Mashita (Lee Sung Cho), Keith Randolph Smith (Frank Richmond), Justin Huen (Rafael Guttierez), Ali Ahn (Angie Lee), Romi Dias (Vivana Ramos), Heather Lea Anderson (Rachel Morse), Tim Altmeyer (Dan Morse), Hanson Tse (Vince Lee); Brown Auditorium; March 8–31, 2007

**When Something Wonderful Ends** by Sherry Kramer; Director, Tom Moore; Sets, Paul Owen; Costumes, Lorraine Venberg; Lighting, Brian J. Lilienthal; Video, Jason Czaja; Properties, Mark Walston; Stage Manager, Michele Traub; Dramaturg, Carrie Hughes; Cast: Lori Wilner (Sherry); Victor Jory Theatre; March 10–April 1, 2007

**The As If Body Loop** by Ken Weitzman; Director, Susan V. Booth; Sets, Paul Owen; Costumes, Christal Weatherly; Lighting, Deb Sullivan; Sound, Benjamin Marcum; Properties, Doc Manning; Fight Director, Lee Look; Production Stage Manager, Paul Mills Holmes; Dramaturg, Julie Felise Dubiner; Cast: Marc Grapey (Aaron), Kristin Fiorella (Sarah), Josh Lefkowitz (Glenn), Jana Robbins (Attic Lady), Keith Randolph Smith (Martin); Brown Auditorium; March 15–April 7, 2007

**BACH: An American Bachelor/ette Party Spectacle** Conceived by Whit MacLaughlin and Alice Tuan with text by Alice Tuan; Created by New Paradise Laboratories, Director, Whit MacLaughlin; Sets, Matt Saunders; Costumes, Rosemarie McKelvey; Lighting, Brian J. Lilienthal; Sound, Whit MacLaughlin; Video, Jorge Cousineau; Properties, Ron Riall; Stage Manager, Nancy Pittelman; Production Assistant, Danielle Teague-Daniels, Dramaturg, Adrien-Alice Hansel; Cast: Round 1 and Beyond: McKenna Kerrigan (Betsy Competitive), Jeb Kreager (Matty Jay), Lee Ann Etzold (Betty Lee), Matt Saunders (Becky Steem), Aaron Mumaw (Maya Faye), Mary McCool (Mary Bette); Round 2 and beyond: Aaron Mumaw (Taggis), Matt Saunders (Chet), Jeb Kreager (Smoak), Lee Ann Etzold (Lars), Mary McCool (Mike), McKenna Kerrigan (Wesley); performed off-site at The Connection; March 21–April 1, 2007

*Whit MacLaughline and Alice Tuan in* Batch: An American Bachelor/ette Party Spectacle *(photo by Harlan Taylor)*

**The Open Road Anthology** by Constance Congdon, Kia Corthron, Michael John Garcés, Rolin Jones, A. Rey Pamatmat & Kathryn Walat; music by GrooveLily; Director, Will MacAdams; Sets, Paul Owen; Costumes, Susan Neason; Lighting, Nick Dent; Sound, Benjamin Marcum; Properties, Mark Walston; Musical Supervisor/Arranger, Brigid Kaelin; Stage Manager, Melissa Miller; Dramaturgs, Adrien-Alice Hansel and Julie Felise Dubiner; Cast: 2006–07 Acting Apprentice Company: Timo Aker, Sean Andries, Katie Barton, Loren Bidner, Eleanor Caudill, Maurine Evans, Kristen B. Jackson, Rafael Jordan, Jane Lee, Nicole Marquez, Jake Millgard, Michael Judson Pace, Zachary T. Palamara, Phil Pickens, Zarina Shea, Zdenko Slobodnik, Jeff Snodgrass, Ashley Spearman, Angela Sperazza, Mark Stringham, Emily Tate Frank, Biz Wells; Bingham Theatre; March 23, 25, 30 & April 1, 2007

*Hanson Tse and Nelson Mashita in* Strike-Slip *(photo by Harlan Taylor)*

**365 Days/365 Plays** by Suzan-Lori Parks: *A Play for the First Day of Spring Entitled "How do you Like the War?"* (March 21, 2007); *George Bush Visits The Cheese and Olive* (April 1, 2007); Director, Sean Daniels; Sets, Paul Owen; Costumes, Susan Neason; Lighting, Paul Werner; Sound, Paul L. Doyle; Properties, Mark Walston; Stage Managers, Deb Anne Gasper, Michael D. Domue; Production Assistant; Mellssa Miller; Dramaturg, Kyle J. Schmidt; Cast: Tim Altmeyer, Heather Lea Anderson, Loren Bidner, Emily Tate Frank, Marc Grapey, Justin Huen, Kristen B. Jackson, Rafael Jordan, Jane Lee, Jennifer Mendenhall, Jana Robbins, Zarina Shea, Jeff Snodgrass, Angela Sperazza, Matthew Stadlemann, Lou Sumrall, Samuel Blackerby Weible; Brown Auditorium

**Italian American Reconciliation** by John Patrick Shanley; Director, Jon Jory; Sets, Paul Owen; Costumes, Lorraine Venberg; Lighting, Brian J. Lilienthal; Sound, Matt Callahan; Properties, Mark Walston; Dialect Coach, Don Wadsworth; Movement Supervisor, Mark J. Stringham; PSM, Paul Mills Holmes; ASM, Debra Anne Gasper; Dramaturgs, Diana Grisanti, Cara Pacifico; Cast: Drew Cortese (Aldo Scalicki), Josh Stein-Sapir (Huey Maximilian Bonfigliano), Lee Fitzpatrick (Teresa), Geraldine Librandi (Aunt May), Alexandra Tavares (Janice), Eleanor Caudill (Woman in Audience), Sean Andries, Angela Sperazza (Comedia); Brown Auditorium; April 19–May 14, 2007

**Ten Minute Plays** Sets, Paul Owen; Costumes, Susan Neason; Lighting, Paul Werner; Sound, Benjamin Marcum; Properties, Doc Manning; Fight Director, Lee Look; Stage Managers, Deb Anne Gasper, Michael D. Domue; Dramaturg, Joanna K. Donehower; Included: *I am not Batman* by Marco Ramirez; Director, Ian Frank; Cast: Phil Pickens (A Boy), Zdenko Slobodnik (A Drummer); *Clarisse and Larmon* by Deb Margolin; Director, Jessica Burgess; Cast: Romi Dias (Clarisse), Keith Randolph Smith (Larmon), Timo Aker (Soldier); *Mr. and Mr.* by Julie Marie Myatt; Director, Jessica Burgess; Cast: Maurine Evans (Debra), Mark Stringham (Steven); March 31–April 1, 2007

# Alabama Shakespeare Festival

Montgomery, Alabama

Thirty-fifth Season

Artistic Director, Geoffrey Sherman

**A Midsummer Night's Dream** by William Shakespeare; Created and performed by SITI Company; Director, Anne Bogart; Sets, Neil Patel; Original Lighting, Christopher Akerlind; Touring Lighting, Brian H. Scott; Costumes, Gabriel Berry; Original Music/Sound, T. Griffin; Company Stage Manager, Elizabeth Moreau; ASM, Elizabeth Kegley; Assistant Sound, Matt Hubbs; Managing Director, Megan Wanlass Szalla; Cast: Akiko Aizawa (Hermia/Starveling/Moth), Jeffrey Fracé (Theseus/Oberon/Quince), Karron Graves (Helena/Snug/Mustardseed), Randy Harrison (Lysander/Flute/Cobweb), Ellen Lauren (Hippolyta/Titania), Barney O'Hanlon (Puck), Christopher Spencer Wells (Egeus/Bottom), Stephen Webber (Demetrius/Snout/Peaseblossom); April 23–May 21, 2006

**To Kill a Mockingbird** by Harper Lee, adapted by Christopher Sergel; Director, Paul Barnes; Sets, Bill Clarke; Costumes, Beth Novak; Lighting, Lonnie Alcaraz; Composer, Gregg Coffin; Sound, Brett Rominger; Dramaturg, Susan Willis; Voice/Dialect Coach, Sarah Felder; Movement Coach, Denise Gabriel; Fight Choreographer, Scot Mann; Stage Manager, Mark D. Leslie; ASM, Kimberly J. First; Production Assistant, Melissa Van Swol; Casting, Elissa Myers, Paul Fouquet, Jandiz Estrada; Cast: Greta Lambert (Jean Louise Finch), Trey Morris or Davis Vaughn (Jem), Ashley Joye or Esther Scott Workman (Scout); Stephen Dubberley (Walter Cunningham), Rodney Clark (Atticus Finch), Cheri Lynne (Calpurnia), Nina Frankle (Mrs. Dubose), Dana Benningfield (Mrs. Dubose's neice), Zack Looney or Luke Morris (Dill), Carl Palmer (Nathan Radley), Tom Lawson (Judge Taylor), Greg Thornton (Heck Tate), Carl Palmer (Bob Ewell), Eric D'angelo Moore (Reverend Sykes), Doug Rossi (Mr. Gilmer), Meghan Lisi (Mayella Ewell), Esau Pritchett (Tom Robinson), Stephen Dubberley (Boo Radley); Townspeople: Celeste Burnum, Michael Gatto, Patrick McElwee, Doug Rossi, Tom Lawson; March 5–July 23, 2006

**Twelfth Night** by William Shakespeare; Director, Gavin Cameron-Webb; Sets, Bob Cothran; Costumes, Susan Branch; Lighting, Liz Lee; Composer, Gregg Coffin; Sound, Jake Carter; Dramaturg, Susan Willis; Voice/Dialect Coach, Sarah Felder; Movement Coach, Denise Gabriel; Fight Choreographer, Scot Mann; Stage Manager, Sara Lee Howell; ASM, Kimberly J. First; Production Assistant, Michael Andrew Rodgers; Casting, Elissa Myers, Paul Fouquet, Jandiz Estrada; Cast: Patrick Porter (Orsino), Anthony Reimer (Curio), John-Michael Marrs (Valentine), Mark Robinson, Timothy Daniel Tinney, Layne Weldon (The Duke's Musicians), Lauren Bloom (Viola), Chris Boyd (A Sea Captain), Mark Robinson & Timothy Daniel Tinney (Sailors), Roger Forbes (Sir Toby Belch), Rebecca Koon (Maria), Duane Black (Sir Andrew Aguecheek), Joe Vincent (Feste), Merideth Kaye Clark (Olivia), Paul Hebron (Malvolio) Chris Boyd (Sir Topas), Pantea Ommi & Eboni Witcher (Olivia's attendants), Tim Gittings (Sebastian), Chris Mixon (Antonio), Mark Allan Jeter (Fabian), Mark Robinson, Timothy Daniel Tinney (Officers); March 12–July 23, 2006

**Man of La Mancha** Book by Dale Wasserman, lyrics by Joe Darion, music by Mitch Leigh; Director, Geoffrey Sherman; Musical Director, Thomas Hinds; Assistant Musical Director, Randy Foster; Sets, Paul Wonsek; Costumes, Beth Novak; Lighting, Phil Monat; Sound, Brett Rominger; Dramaturg, Susan Willis; Voice/Dialect Coach, Sarah Felder; Choreography, Denise Gabriel; Stage Manager, Kimberly J. First; ASM, Sara Lee Howell; Production Assistant, Michael Andrew Rodgers; Casting, Elissa Myers, Paul Fouquet, Jandiz Estrada; Cast: Chris Boyd (Captain of the Inquisition), Joe Vincent (Don Miguel de Cervantes/Don Quioxote) Chris Mixon (Manservant/Sancho Panza), Roger Forbes (The Governor/Innkeeper), Ray Chambers (The Duke/Dr.Carrasco/Knight of the Mirrors), Mary Jo Mecca (Aldonza/Dulcinea), Anthony Reimer (Jose), Duane Black (Juan), Mark Robinson (Pedro), Patrick Porter (Anselmo), Timothy Gittings (Paco), Eric D'angelo Moore (Tenorio), John-Michael Marrs (Quito), Rebecca Koon (Maria), Merideth Kaye Clark (Antonia), Timothy Daniel Tinney (Padre), Celeste Burnum (House Keeper), Paul Hebron (Barber), Mark Allan Jeter (Guard), Lauren Bloom (Fermina); April 9–July 23, 2006

**The Trojan Women** by Euripides, translated by Kenneth Cavander; Director, Diana Van Fossen; Sets, Monika Essen; Costumes, Brenda Van der Wiel; Lighting, Phil Monat; Contributing Artist, Nilo Berrocal Vargas; Sound, Jake Carter; Dramaturg, Susan Willis; Voice/Dialect Coach, Sarah Felder; Movement Coach, Denise Gabriel; Movement, Alida José Neslo; Stage Manager, Mark D. Leslie; ASM, Sara Lee Howell; Production Assistant, Melissa Van Swol; Casting, Elissa Myers, Paul Fouquet, Jandiz Estrada; Cast: Esau Pritchett (Poseidon), Greta Lambert (Athene), Geraldine Librandi (Hecuba), Tessa Klein (Cassandra), Cheri Lynne (Andromache), Wesley McDaniels (Astyanax), Dana Benningfield, Meghan Lisi, Pantea Ommi, Alketa Eboni Witcher, Joann Sacco, Angela Dickson, Chalethia Williams (Chorus of Captive Women), Greg Thornton (Talthybius), Rodney Clark (Menelaus), Victoire Charles (Helen), Stephen Dubberley, Michael Gatto, Patrick McElwee, Carl Palmer, Doug Rossi (Soldiers); May 28–July 23, 2006

**Crowns** by Regina Taylor, adapted from the book by Michael Cunningham & Craig Marberry; Director, Janet Cleveland; Sets, Chris Carothers; Costumes, Susan Branch; Musical Director, Bill Sims Jr.; Pianist, Sanchez Dixon; Percussion, Emmitt L. Patton; Lighting, Annmarie Duggan; Sound, Brett Rominger; Dramaturg, Susan Willis; Voice/Dialect Coach, Sarah Felder; Movement Consultant, Denise Gabriel; Stage Manager, Tanya J. Searle; Production Assistant, Michele Fugate; Cast: Margo Moorer (Jeanette), Julia Lema (Velma), Roz Beauty (Yolanda), B.J. Crosby (Mable), James Bowen (Man), Laiona Michelle (Wanda), Avery Sommers (Mother Shaw), Chalethia Williams (Understudy); October 13–November 5, 2006

**Beauty and the Beast** Music by Alan Menken, lyrics by Howard Ashman and Tim Rice, book by Linda Woolverton; Director, Geoffrey Sherman; Choreography, Peggy Hickey; Musical Director, Thomas Hinds; Assistant Musical Director, Randy P. Foster; Sets/Lighting, Paul Wonsek; Costumes, Susan Branch; Sound, Brett Rominger; Dramaturg, Susan Willis; Voice/Dialect Coach, Sarah Felder; Movement Coach, Denise Gabriel; Stage Manager, Kimberly J. First; ASM, Mark

D. Leslie; Dance Captain, Adam Cates; Fight Director, Jason Armit; Cast: Laura Shoop (Belle), Gregg Goodbrod (Beast), Glenn Lawrence (Gaston), Billy Sharpe (Lumiere), Joe Vincent (Maurice), Rodney Clark (Cogsworth), Barbara Broughton (Mrs. Potts), Kraig Swartz (Le Fou), Alex Ellis (Babette), Naden Kreitz, Nathan Looney or Jackson Massey (Chip), Chevy Anz (Madame de la Grand Bouche); Ensemble: Cassie Abate, Chevy Anz, Jessica Blair, Dana Benningfield, Adam Cates, Jessica Chesbro, Ben Franklin, Michael Gatto, Courtney Glass, Megan Grubel, Wes Hart, Tim Hausmann, Mark Alan Jeter, Pete Lay, John-Michael Marrs, Patrick McElwee, Hannah Nieh, Pantea Ommi, Dayla Perkins, Jake Pfarr, Anthony Reimer, Jody Reynard, Mark Robinson, Mavis Scully, Tara Siesener, Joseph Torello, Greg Thornton, Anthony Wayne; November 10–December 23, 2006

**James and the Giant Peach** by Roald Dahl, adapted for the stage by David Wood; Original Music, Gerald V. Castle; Director, Jane Page; Musical Coach, Randy P. Foster; Sets, Michael Fagin; Costumes, Patrick Holt; Lighting, Lonnie Alcaraz; Sound, Kevin Dunayer; Dramaturg, Susan Willis; Voice/Dialect Coach, Sarah Felder; Movement Consultant, Denise Gabriel; Stage Manager, Michele Fugate; ASM, Melissa Van Swol; Cast: Greg Foro (James Trotter), Nathan T. Lange (Old-Green-Grasshopper), Sarah Walker Thorton (Miss Spider/Mrs. Trotter), David Dortch (Centipede), Alison Fredrick (Ladybird/Aunt Sponge), Jerry Ferraccio (Earthworm), Afton C. Williamson (New York Tour Guide/Aunt Spiker/Captain of the Queen Mary), Nick Lawson (Mr. Trotter/Old Man/TV Reporter/First Officer/Second Officer); January 13–February 18, 2007

**Gee's Bend** by Elyzabeth Gregory Wilder; Director, Janet Cleveland; Musical Director/Sound, Brett Rominger; Sets, Michael Schweikardt; Costumes, Rosa M. Lazaro; Lighting, Kathy A. Perkins; Dramaturg, Susan Willis; Voice/Dialect Coach, Sarah Felder; Movement Consultant, Denise Gabriel; Stage Manager, Sara Lee Howell; Production Assistant, Luisa Ann Torres; Cast: Roslyn Ruff (Sadie), Margo Moorer (Nella), Maura Gale (Alice/Asia), Billy Euguene Jones (Macon), Chalethia Williams (Understudy); January 19–February 11, 2007

**Henry VI Part A** by William Shakespeare; Based on *King Henry VI, Part I* and the first three acts of *Henry VI, Part II*; Director, Diana Van Fossen; Composer, James Conely; Orchestrator, Thom Jenkins; Sets/Lighting, Paul Wonsek; Costumes, Beth Novak; Sound, Brett Rominger; Dramaturg, Susan Willis; Voice/Dialect Coach, Sarah Felder; Movement Coach, Denise Gabriel; Fight Directors, Scot Mann, Jason Armit; Stage Manager, Mark D. Leslie; ASM, Kimberly J. First; Casting, Elissa Myers, Paul Fouquet, Jandiz Estrada; Cast: James Beaman (Lord Talbot/Sir John Hume), Dana Benningfield (Simpcox's Wife/First & Second Murdererers), Jeffrey Brick (Richard Plantagenet), Lise Bruneau (Margaret/French Soldier/French Messenger), Ray Chambers (John Duke of Bedford), Nick Cordileone (King Henry VI), David Dortch (Williams/Second Citizen), Roger Forbes (Henry Beaufort/Edmund Mortimer), Michael Gatto (Roger Bolinbroke/Reignier), Paul Hopper (Duke of Gloucester), Mark Allan Jeter (Duke of Somerset), Marcus Kyd (William de la Pole), Nathan Lange (Lawyer/Messenger/Townsman/Papal Legate), Nick Lawson (Basset), John-Michael Marrs (Third Citizen/The Bastard of Orleans), Hollis McCarthy (Eleanor Duchess of Gloucester), Patrick McElwee (Messenger to York/Duke of Alencon), Pantea Ommi (Margery Jourdain), Will Pailen (Thomas Beaufort/Lieutenant of the Tower), Gardner Reed (Joan la Pucelle, a.k.a Joan of Arc), Anthony Reimer (First Citizen/Charles the Dauphin), Adam Richman (The Duke of Burgundy), Mark Robinson (Vernon/John Talbot/English Soldier/Simpcox), Greg Thornton (Earl of Warwick); February 23–June 10, 2007

**Death of a Salesman** by Arthur Miller; Director, Charles Morey; Sets, George Maxwell; Costumes, Brenda Van der Wiel; Lighting, Phil Monat; Sound, Joseph Payne; Dramaturg, Susan Willis; Voice/Dialect Coach, Sarah Felder; Movement Consultant, Denise Gabriel; Stage Manager, Tanya J. Searle; Production Assistant, Michele Fugate; Cast: Rodney Clark (Willy Loman), Greta Lambert (Linda), Drew Parker (Happy), Christian Kohn (Biff), Greg Foro (Bernard), Andrea Cirie (The Woman), Anderson Matthews (Charley), Kenneth Gray (Uncle Ben), Ian Blackman (Howard Wagner), Sarah Walker Thornton (Jenny), Jerry Ferraccio (Stanley), Alison Frederick (Miss Forsythe), Afton C. Williamson; March 2–April 8, 2007

**Henry VI Part B** by William Shakespeare; Based on the last two acts of *King Henry VI, Part II* and *King Henry VI, Part III*; Director, Geoffrey Sherman; Composer, James Conely; Orchestrator, Thom Jenkins; Sets/Lighting, Paul

Wonsek; Costumes, Beth Novak; Sound, Brett Rominger; Dramaturg, Susan Willis; Voice/Dialect Coach, Sarah Felder; Movement Coach, Denise Gabriel; Fight Directors, Scot Mann, Jason Armit; Stage Manager, Mark D. Leslie; ASM, Kimberly J. First; Cast: Dana Benningfield (Edmund/Rebel/Soldier/Attendant), James Beaman (Lord Hastings/Jack Cade/Soldier/Attendant), Jeffrey Brick (Richard Plantagenet/Duke of Buckingham), Lise Bruneau (Margaret), Ray Chambers (Lewis XI King of France/A Father that has killed his Son), Nick Cordileone (King Henry VI), David Dortch (Second Watch/A Son that has killed his Father/Second Lancastrian Soldier/Rebel/Attendant), Roger Forbes (Alexander Iden/First Keeper/Lord Say), Michael Gatto (Sir Humphrey Stafford/Reignier/Duke of Norfolk/Soldier/Attendant), Paul Hopper (Lord Clifford/First Watch), Mark Allan Jeter (Duke of Somerset/Lord Rivers), Marcus Kyd (Clerk of Chatham/George/Soldier/Attendant), Nathan Lange (Third Watch/Smith/Herald/ Soldier/Attendant), Nick Lawson (First Lancastrian Soldier/Michael/Second Keeper/Messenger/Herald/Soldier/Attendant), John-Michael Marrs (Richard/Rebel), Hollis McCarthy (Lady Elizabeth Grey/Rebel/Soldier/Attendant), Patrick McElwee (Edward), Pantea Ommi (Lady Bona/Rebel/Messenger/Herald/Soldier/Attendant), Will Pailen (Duke of Exeter/Lieutenant of the Tower), Gardner Reed (Rebel/Messenger/Herald), Anthony Reimer (Earl of Oxford/Dick/Soldier/Attendant), Anthony Reimer (Dick), Adam Richman (Edward/Duke of Burgandy), Mark Robinson (Young Clifford/Soldier/Attendant), Greg Thornton (The Earl of Warwick), Mikal Webb (Henry Earl of Richmond); March 16–June 10, 2007

**Richard III** by William Shakespeare; Director, Susan Willis; Composer, James Conely; Orchestrator, Thom Jenkins; Sets/Lighting, Paul Wonsek; Costumes, Elizabeth Novak; Sound, Brett Rominger; Dramaturg, Susan Willis; Voice/Dialect Coach, Sarah Felder; Movement Coach, Denise Gabriel; Fight Directors, Scot Mann & Jason Armit; Stage Manager, Mark D. Leslie; ASM, Kimberly J. First; Casting, Elissa Myers, Paul Fouquet, Jandiz Estrada; Cast: David Barber or Seth Meriwether (Richard, Duke of York), James Beaman (Lord Hastings), Dana Benningfield (Prince Edward/Princess Elizabeth/Citizen), Jeffrey Brick (Duke of Buckingham), Lise Bruneau (Queen Margaret), Celeste Burnum (Duchess of York), Ray Chambers (Richard, Duke of Gloucester), Nick Cordileone (Ghost of King Henry VI/Sir James Tyrrel/Lord Mayor of London), David Dortch (Second Messenger/Tressel/Third Citizen/Soldier), Roger Forbes (Bishop of Ely), Michael Gatto (Duke of Norfolk/First Murderer), Paul Hopper (Earl of Derby), Mark Allan Jeter (Anthony Woodville Earl Rivers/Soldier), Marcus Kyd (George, Duke of Clarence/Sir Richard Ratcliff), Nathan Lange (Messenger from Lord Derby/Citizen/Guard/Soldier/Monk), Nick Lawson (Second Murderer/Guard/Soldier), John-Michael Marrs (Cleric/Ratcliff's Soldier/Monk), Hollis McCarthy (Queen Elizabeth), Patrick McElwee (First Messenger/Ghost of Prince Edward/First Citizen/Soldier/Monk), Pantea Ommi (Second Citizen/Monk/Soldier), Will Pailen (Henry Tudor a.k.a King Henry VII/Lieutenant of the Tower), Gardner Reed (Lady Anne), Anthony Reimer (Marquis of Dorset/Earl of Oxford), Adam Richman (King Edward IV/Ratcliff's Soldier/Soldier), Mark Robinson (Lord Grey/Third Messenger/Soldier), Greg Thornton (Sir William Catesby); April 13–June 10, 2007

**Thinking of You** by Peter Hicks; Director, Nancy Rominger; Sets, Peter Hicks; Costumes, Bill Black; Lighting, Reid G. Johnson; Sound, Brett Rominger; Dramaturg, Susan Willis; Movement Coach, Denise Gabriel; Stage Manager, Tanya J. Searle; Production Assistant, Michele Fugate; Cast: Julie Jesneck (Junie Mae Delacroix), Diana Van Fossen (Celeste Delacroix), John Hayden (Sheldon Jennings), Dan Schultz (Leonard Belle), Rodney Clark (Arthur Fragonard), Alison Frederick (Sharon Pendegast); April 20–May 20, 2007

**Menopause, the Muisical** Book and lyrics by Jeanie Linders; Director, Kathryn Conte; Musical Director, Alan Plado; Choreography, Patty Bender; Sets, Bud Clark; National Lighting, Ryan Patridge; Sound, Gary Faller; Stage Manager, Ellen Jones; Production Manager, Michele Fugate; Cast: Nyree Martinez (Soap Star), Paula Estess (Iowa Housewife), Judy Dery (Earth Mother), Fredena Williams & Monique M. Whittington (Professional Woman), Lisa Harris (Understudy), Paula Estess (Dance Captain); Band: Derek Jackson (Conductor/keyboards), Taylor Propp & Abe Becker (bass), Bill Williams (drums); June 1–July 17, 2007

**Doctor Faustus** by Christopher Marlowe; Directors, Michael P. Howley & Geoffrey Sherman; Sets, Paul Wonsek; Props, Brian Baillif; Costumes, Beth Novak; Lighting, Mike Post; Sound, Richelle Thompson; Dramaturg, Susan Willis; Voice/Dialect Coach, Sarah Felder; Movement Consultant, Denise Gabriel; Stage Manager, Luisa Torres; Production Assistants, Mike Jones & Kerrie Riber; Cast: Dana Benningfield (Mephistophilis/Helen of Troy), David Dortch (Martino/Valdes/Pride/Pope), Jerry Ferraccio (Frederick, Cornelius/Gluttony/Raymond), Greg Foro (Dick/Rafe), Alison Fredrick (Good Angel/Cardinal 1/Paramour), Michael Gatto (Bruno/Old Man/Covetousness), Mark Allan Jeter (Doctor Faustus), Nathan Lange (Belzebub/Saxony/Carter), Nick Lawson (Benvolio/Envy), John-Michael Marrs (Scholar 2/Friar/Wrath/ Horse-courser/Alexander), Patrick McElwee (Wagner/Chorus), Pantea Ommi (Lucifer/Hostess/Emperor), Anthony Reimer (Scholar 1/Bishop/Lechery/Servant/Darius), Mark Robinson (Scholar 3/Vintner/Sloth/Duke Vanholt), Sarah Thornton (Evil Angel/Cardinal 2/Duchess), Afton Williamson (Robin/Clown); June 21–June 30, 2007

**Fair and Tender Ladies** Adapted from the novel by Lee Smith, script by Eric Schmiedl, music and lyrics by Tommy Goldsmith, Tom House & Karren Pell; Director, Susan Willis; Musical Director, H. Drew Perkins; Sets, Michael Smith; Costumes, Kristine Kearney; Lighting, Phil Monat: Sound, Richelle Thompson; Dramaturg, Susan Willis; Voice/Dialect Coach, Sarah Felder; Movement Consultant, Denise Gabriel; Stage Manager, Sara Lee Howell; Production Assistant, Michael Aaron Jones; Cast: Greta Lambert (Ivy Rowe), Deb Funkhouser (Silvaney/Miss Thorington/Joli), Kim Ders (Maudy/Beulah/Geneva), Nancy McLemore (Singer/Musician/Mama/Granny Rowe/Mrs. Bostick), H. Drew Perkins (Singer/Musician/Franklin), Tony Roach (Singer/Musician/Mr. Conoway); July 13–August 5, 2007

### SOUTHERN WRITERS' PROJECT FESTIVAL OF NEW PLAYS
### May 18–20, 2007

**Rocket City** by Mark Saltzman; Director, David Ellenstein; Dramaturg, Dick Emmet; Musical Director Brett Rominger; Lighting, Rebecca Dail; Stage Manager, Mark D. Leslie; Production Assistants, Nick Lawson & Sarah Walker Thornton; Cast: Amy Lubin (Lise Bruneau), Jeffrey Brick (Major Hamilton Pike, Jr.), Marcus Kyd (Jed Kessler), Richard McWilliams (Wehrner Von Braun), Lindsay Smiling (Israel Watkins), Paul Hopper (Character Man 1), Rodney Clark (Character Man 2), Greta Lambert (Character Woman 1), Celeste Burnum (Character Woman 2), Michael Gatto (Reader), Eve Loeb (Consultant)

**The Dragonfly Tale** by Lorey Hayes and Bobby Crear; Director, Imani; Dramaturg, Georgette Norman; Lighting, Rebecca Dail; Stage Manager, Trudy Paxton-Mass; Production Assistants, Patrick McElwee & Afton C. Williamson; Cast: Wesley McDaniels (June Bug), Iona Morris (Everlyn Brown), Ron Scott (Clemmy June), Adam Richman (Malcolm Redmond), Hollis McCarthy (Nadine Redmond), Quinton Cockrell (Cut Buddy), Margo Moorer (Vera Mae), Cameron Knight (Teddy Speede), Mark Robinson (Reader)

**The Fall of the House** by Robert Ford; Director, Nancy Rominger; Dramaturg, Marlon M. Bailey; Lighting, Brian Elliott; Stage Manager, Tanya J. Searle; Production Assistants Nathan T. Lange & Jerry Ferraccio; Cast: Kimberly Scott (Munny), Greg Thornton (Edgar Allan Poe, David Poe, Judge), Casaundra Freeman (Janice Berry), Shannon Nicole Lock (Eliza Poe, Cage, Lucy Waitress), Nick Cordileone (Jack), Dan Schultz (Wilson, Social Worker), Tatyana M. Webb (Young Janice, Linney), Anthony Reimer (Reader)

**The Furniture of Home** by Elyzabeth Gregory Wilder; Director, Jamie Lawrence; Dramaturg, OyamO; Lighting, Brian Elliott; Stage Manager, Kimberly J. First; Production Assistants, Greg Foro, Alison Frederick & Daniel King; Cast: Kate Buddeke (Maggie), Council Cargle (Otis), James Beaman (Claiborne), David Dortch (Panama), Luray Cooper (Hayes), Greg Foro (Radio Voice), Pantea Ommi (Reader)

### YOUNG SOUTHERN WRITERS' PROJECT
### ONE-ACT PLAYS COMPETITION READINGS

*Unsaid* by Becca Ansorge; Director, Nick Lawson; Stage Manager, Luisa Ann Torres; Cast: Sarah Walker Thornton (Rose), Nathan T. Lange (Sam), Afton C. Williamson (Victoria), Nick Lawson (Voice of an announcer at Airport/stage directions); *An Accidental Affair* by Brittany Bivins; Director, Ray Chambers; Stage Manager, Luisa Ann Torres; Cast: Alison Frederick (Miss Gracie Mae Lexus), David Dortch (Matthew Lexus), Jerry Ferraccio (Dr. Lucas Henderson), Greg Foro (stage directions); *Children of Ovid* by Daniel King; Director/Stage Directions, Alison Frederick; Stage Manager, Luisa Ann Torres; Cast: Greg Foro (Man), Sarah Walker Thornton (Sarah)

# Alley Theatre

Houston, Texas

Sixtieth Season

Artistic Director, Gregory Boyd; Managing Director, Dean Gladden

**Wait Until Dark** by Frederick Knott; Director, Scott Schwartz; Sets, Linda Buchanan; Costumes, Andrea Lauer; Lighting, Rui Rita; Sound, Ryan Rumery; Fight Direction, Leraldo Anzaldua; Stage Manager, Elizabeth M. Berther; ASM, Terry Cranshaw; Cast: Leraldo Anzaldua (Policeman), Jeffrey Bean (Sgt. Carlino), Maureen Fenninger (Gloria), Elizabeth Heflin (Susy Hendrix), Paul Hope (Sam Hendrix), Kevin Kilner (Mike Talman), John Tyson (Harry Roat, Jr.), Tim Wrobel (Policeman); Hubbard Stage; June 30–July 16, 2006

**Black Comedy** by Peter Shaffer; Director, Gregory Boyd; Sets, Linda Buchanan; Costumes, Andrea Lauer; Lighting, Rui Rita; Sound, Ryan Rumery; Fight Direction, Leraldo Anzaldua; Stage Manager, Elizabeth M. Berther; ASM, Terry Cranshaw; Cast: Cheryl Lynn Bowers (Carol Melkett), Jeffrey Bean (Harold Gorringe), James Belcher (Georg Bamberger), Paul Hope (Schuppanzigh), Annalee Jeffries (Miss Furnival), Melissa Pritchett (Clea), Jamison Stern (Brindsley Miller), John Tyson (Colonel Melkett); Hubbard Stage; July 21–August 6, 2006

**Much Ado About Nothing** by William Shakespeare; Director, Scott Schwartz; Sets, Walt Spangler; Costumes, Fabio Toblini; Lighting, Michael Gilliam; Sound, Jill B.C. DuBoff; Composer, Michael Holland; Choreography, Matt Williams; Dramaturg, Joe Luis Cedillo; Stage Managers, Elizabeth M. Berther, Terry Cranshaw; ASM, Sara Elida Mills; Dialect and Text Work, Jim Johnson; Cast: James Black (Don Pedro), James Belcher (Antonio), Jeffrey Bean (Benedick), Elizabeth Bunch (Hero), Justin Doran (Conrad), Ty Doran or Jacob Teall (Boy), Bettye Fitzpatrick (Friar), Will Fowler (Claudio), Brandon Hearnsberger (Watch/Messenger), Elizabeth Heflin (Beatrice), Paul Hope (Verges), Chris Hutchison (Borachio), Annalee Jeffries (Margaret), Charles Krohn (Leonato), Philip Lehl (Balthasar/Sexton/Watch), Melissa Pritchett (Ursula), David Rainey (Don John), John Tyson (Dogberry); Hubbard Stage; October 6–November 5, 2006

**Tryst** by Karoline Leach; Director, Joe Brancato; Sets, David Korins; Lighting, Jeff Nellis; Costumes, Alejo Vietti; Composer and Sound, Johnna Doty; Stage Manager, Betsy Berther; Dialect/Text Work, Jim Johnson; Cast: Andrea Maulella (Adelaide Pinchin), Mark Shanahan (George Love); Neuhaus Stage; November 9–December 10, 2006

**A Moon for the Misbegotten** by Eugene O'Neill; Director, Gordon Edelstein; Produced in association with Long Wharf Theatre and Hartford Stage Company; Sets, Ming Cho Lee; Costumes, Jennifer Von Maryhauser; Lighting, Jennifer Tipton; Sound, Nick Borisjuk; Fight Director, Brian Byrnes; Stage Manager, Carmelita Becnel; ASM, Terry Cranshaw; Cast: James Black (James Tyrone, Jr.), Wynn Harmon (T. Stedman Harder), Brandon Hearnsberger (Mike Hogan), Annalee Jeffries (Josie Hogan), Bill Raymond (Phil Hogan); Hubbard Stage; January 12–February 4, 2007

*Annalee Jeffries in* Moon for the Misbegotten *(photo by Harlan Taylor)*

**Subject to Fits: A Response to Dostoevskys *The Idiot*** by Robert Montgomery; Director, Gregory Boyd; Sets, Takeshi Kata; Costumes, Fabio Toblini; Lighting, Kevin Rigdon; Music/Sound, John Gromada; Stage Manager, Elizabeth M. Berther; Assistant Director, Alex Harvey; Music Assistant, Deborah Lewis; Cast: Jeffrey Bean (Prince Myshkin), James Belcher (Lebedev), Elizabeth Bunch (Agalaya Yepanchin), Josie de Guzman (Madame Yepanchin), Elizabeth Heflin (Natasha Fillipovna), Chris Hutchison (Ippolit Ivoglin), Charles Krohn (General Ivoglin), Melissa Pritchett and All (Crowdpersons), David Rainey (Paryfron Rogozhin), John Tyson (Ganya Ivolgin); Neuhaus Stage; January 19–February 18, 2007

**Hitchcock Blonde** by Terry Johnson; Director, Gregory Boyd; Set/Projections/Costumes, William Dudley; Lighting, Chris Parry; Sound, Ryan Rumery; Original London Sound, Ian Dickinson; Video Realization, Ian Galloway for Mesmer; Associate Sets, Kevin Rigdon; Fight Director, Leraldo Anzaldua; Stage Manager, Terry Cranshaw; ASM, Sara Elida Mills; Cast: Leraldo Anzaldua (Husband), James Black (Hitch), Elizabeth Bunch (Jennifer), Melissa Pritchett (Blonde), Mark Shanahan (Alex); Hubbard Stage; February 23–March 18, 2007

**To Kill a Mockingbird** by Harper Lee, adapted by Christopher Sergel; Director, Paul Barnes; Associate Director, James Black; Sets, Bill Clarke; Costumes, Elizabeth Novak; Lighting, Rui Rita; Sound, Garth Hemphill; Original Composition, Gregg Coffin; Stage Manager, Carmelita Becnel; ASMs, Sara Elida Milla, Danny Kuenzel; Voice/Dialect Coach, Jim Johnson; Fight Director, Brain Byrnes; Cast: Jeffrey Bean (Mr. Nathan Radley/Bob Ewell), James Belcher (Sheriff Heck Tate), Elizabeth Bunch (Mayella Violet Ewell), Justin Doran (Mr. Gilmer), John Feltch (Atticus Finch), Bettye Fitzpatrick (Mrs. Dubose), Alice M. Gatling (Calpurnia), Brian Hamlin (Townsperson), Chris Hutchison (Walter Cunningham/Arthur 'Boo' Radley), Andrea Hyde (Mrs. Dubose's Attendant/Townsperson), Charles Krohn (Judge Taylor), Jennifer Laporte (Scout), Andrew J. Love (Townsperson), Andrea Maulella (Jean Louise Finch), David Rainey (Tom Robinson), Tommy Waas (Jem), Clarence Whitmore (Reverend Skyes), Wesley Whitson (Charles Baker 'Dill' Harris); Hubbard Stage; March 30–April 29, 2007

*Melissa Pritchett in* Hitchcock Blonde *(photo by T. Charles Erickson)*

**The Clean House** by Sarah Ruhl; Director, David Cromer; Sets, Takeshi Kata; Costumes, Miguel Angel Huidor; Lighting, Kevin Rigdon; Original Composition/Sound, Josh Schmidt; Dialect Coach, Gillian Lane-Plescia; Choreography, Krissy Richmond; Stage Manager, Sara Elida Mills; Dramaturg, Joe Luis Cedillo; Cast: Josie de Guzman (Matilde), Elizabeth Heflin (Lane), Paul Hope (Charles/A Man), Annalee Jeffries (Virginia), Karmín Murcelo (Ana/A Woman); Neuhaus Stage; April 27–May 27, 2007

*Karmin Murcelo and Josie de Guzman in* The Clean House
*(photo by Harlan Taylor)*

**Treasure Island** by Ken Ludwig, adapted from the novel by Robert Louis Stevenson; Director, Gregory Boyd; Sets, Eugene Lee; Costumes, Constance Hoffman; Lighting, Clifton Taylor; Original Music/Sound, John Gromada; Fight Director, Steve Rankin; Assistant Fight Director, Jason Siner; Aerial Sequence Design, Paul Rubin; Technical Director, Jason Duke; Props, Karin Rabe; Stage Manager, Elizabeth M. Berther; Stage Manager, Terry Cranshaw; Cast: Leraldo Anzaldua (Bomba Desperada), Jeffrey Bean (Captain Smollet/Black Dog), James Belcher (Squire Trelawney/Job O'Brien/The Bailiff), James Black (Long John Silver/Town Drunk), Elizabeth Bunch (Jim Hawkins), John Feltch (Dr. Livesey/Captain Flint), Chris Hutchison (Ezekiel Hazard/Tom Morgan/Boy with Barrow/A Cut Purse), Charles Krohn (Billy Bones), Melissa Pritchett (Anne Bonny/Jim's Mother), Mark Shanahan (George Merry), Noble Shropshire (Ben Gunn/Jemmy Rathbone/Reverend Mainwarning/Josiah Bland), John Tyson (Israel Hands/Blind Pew), David Rainey (Justice Death); Hubbard Stage; May 18–June 17, 2007

*John Feltch and Noble Shropshire in* Treasure Island
*(photo by Harlan Taylor)*

# Alliance Theatre

Atlanta, Georgia

Thirty-eighth Season

Artistic Director, Susan V. Booth; Managing Director, Thomas Pechar; Associate Artistic Director, Kent Gash; The Sally G. Tomlinson Artistic Director of Theatre for Youth, Rosemary Newcott

**The 25th Annual Putnam County Spelling Bee** Music & lyrics by William Finn, book by Rachel Sheinkin, conceived by Rebecca Feldman, additional material by Jay Reiss; Director, James Lapine; Choreography, Dan Knechtges; Sets, Beowulf Boritt; Costumes, Jennifer Caprio; Lighting, Natasha Katz; Sound, Dan Moses Schreier; Orchestrations, Michael Starobin; Music Supervisor/Dance Arrangements, Vadim Feichtner; Vocal Arrangements, Carmel Dean; Music Director, Jodie Moore; PSM, Brian J. L'Ecuyer; Associate Director, Darren Katz; Production Supervisor, Andrea "Spook" Testani; Stage Manager, Lori Lundquist; Cast: Katie Boren (Marcy Park), Miguel Cervantes (Chip Tolentino), Alan H. Green (Mitch Mahoney), James Kall (Douglas Panch), Eric Petersen (William Barfee), Jennifer Simard (Rona Lisa Peretti), Sarah Stiles (Logainne Schwartzandgrubenierre), Lauren Worsham (Olive Ostrovsky), Michael Zahler (Leaf Coneybear); August 20–September 16, 2006

*The Cast of* The 25th Annual Putnam County Spelling Bee
*(photo by Greg Mooney)*

**Elliot, A Soldier's Fugue** by Quiara Alegría Hudes; Director, Kent Gash; Sets, Emily Jean Beck; Costumes, English Benning; Lighting, William H. Grant III; Sound, Clay Benning; PSM, lark hackshaw; Dramaturg, Freddie Ashley; Stage Management P.A., Emily Stewart; Cast: Gilbert Cruz (Grandpop), Matthew Montelongo (Pop), Mary Lynn Owen (Ginny), Ivan Quintanilla (Elliot); September 8–October 1, 2006

**Mrs. Warren's Profession** by George Bernard Shaw; Director, Susan V. Booth; Sets, Michael Philippi; Costumes, Linda Roethke; Lighting, Ken Yunker; Original Music/Sound, Rob Milburn & Michael Bodeen; PSM, Pat A. Flora; Dramaturg, Celise Kalke; ASM, Kate McDoniel; Apprentice Stage Manager, Ronnie L. Campbell; Dialect Coach, Marlene Johnson; Cast: James Donadio (Rev. Samuel Gardner), Patricia Hodges (Mrs. Warren), Jason Loughlin (Frank Gardner), Annie Meisels (Vivie Warren), Larry Paulsen (Praed), Peter Van Wagner (Sir George Crofts); September 27–October 22, 2006

**Disney's Aladdin** Music by Alan Menken, lyrics by Howard Ashman and Tim Rice, adaptation and additional lyrics by Jim Luigs; based on the screenplay by Ron Clements & John Musker, Ted Elliot & Terry Rossio; Music Adaptation/Arrangements, Bryan Louiselle; Director, Rosemary Newcott; Sets, Kat Conley; Costumes, Sydney Roberts; Lighting, Ken Yunker; Sound, Clay Benning; Music Director, Christopher Cannon; Choreography, Hylan Scott; PSM, Colleen Janich; Dramaturg, Freddie Ashley; ASM, Jeff McKerley; Stage Management Production Assistant, Liz Campbell; Cast: Nakeisha Daniel (Narrator/Guard #1/Thief/Harem Girls/Matron), Jeanette Illidge (Jasmine), Jeff McKerley (Genie/Princes), Craig A. Meyer (Razoul/Iago), Glenn Rainey (Sultan/Guard #2), Justin Tanner (Aladdin), Scott Warren (Jafar); October 16–November 12, 2006

**A Christmas Carol** by Charles Dickens; adapted by David H. Bell; Director, Rosemary Newcott; Sets, D. Martyn Bookwalter; Costumes, Mariann Verheyen; Lighting, Diane Ferry Williams; Sound, Clay Benning; Musical Direction, Michael Fauss; Assistant Director, Freddie Ashley; PSM, Pat A. Flora; Associate Lighting, Pete Shinn; ASM, Kate McDoniel; Stage Management Apprentice, Ronnie L. Campbell; Cast: Elizabeth Wells Berkes (Belle), Terry Burrell (Bess), Naima J. Carter (Fan/Martha), Ritchie Crownfield (Ensemble), Neal A. Ghant (Bob Cratchit), Bart Hansard (Fezziwig/Christmas Present), Jordan Jackson (Daniel/Turkey Boy), Chris Kayser (Ebenezer Scrooge), Jahi Kearse (Dick Wilkins), Katie Kneeland (Ensemble), Joe Knezevich (Fred), J.C. Long (Peter), Tendal Jaret Mann

*Justin Tanner and Jeff McKerley in* Disney's Alladin
*(photo by Greg Mooney)*

(Tiny Tim), Daniel Thomas May (Marley), Megan McFarland (Christmas Past/Peg), Bernardine Mitchell (Mrs. Dilber/Mrs. Fezziwig), Eric Moore (Topper), Tessa Lene Palisoc (Want), Thomas Piper (Young Scrooge), Keenan Rogers (Wyatt/Ignorance), Morgan Saylor (Belinda), India Scandrick (Melinda), Kinnik Sky (Mrs. Cratchit); November 24–December 24, 2006

**Sister Act, The Musical** Music by Alan Menken, lyrics by Glenn Slater, book by Cheri Steinkellner & Bill Steinkellner; Director, Peter Schneider; Choreography, Marguerite Derricks; Music Supervision, Vocal/Incidental Music Arrangements, Michael Kosarin; Creative Supervisor, Michael Reno; Sets, David Potts; Costumes, Garry Lennon; Lighting, Donald Holder; Sound, Carl Casella & Dominic Sack; Hair/Wigs, Carol F. Doran; Orchestrations, Doug Besterman; Music Director/Conductor, Brent-Alan Huffman; Electronic Music Design, Andrew Barrett for Lionella Productions Ltd.; Dance Arrangements, Mark Hummel; Fight Coordinator, Tim Weske; PSM, Eileen F. Haggerty; ASM, R. Lamar Williams; Assistant Director, Marcus Miller; Associate Choreography, Michelle Elkin; Stage Management Apprentice, Ronnie L. Campbell; Cast: Dawnn Lewis (Deloris Van Cartier), Elizabeth Ward Land (Mother Superior), David Jennings (Sergeant Eddie Souther), Beth Malone (Sister Mary Robert), Amy K. Murray (Sister Mary Patrick), Audrie Neenan (Sister Mary Lazarus), Henry Polic II (Monsignor Howard/Willard/Old Bearded Biker), Harrison White (Curtis Shank), Melvin Abston (TJ/Muscle-T), Dan Domenech (Dinero/Doo-Rag), Badia Farha (Larosa/Sister Mary Frances/Cocktail Waitress), Andi Gibson (Sister Mary Hope/Go-Go Dancer), Wendy James (Sister Mary Augustine/Biker Chick/Swing), Wendy Melkonian (Sister Mary Gabriel/Biker Chick/Swing), Craig A. Meyer (Biker/Swing), Claci Miller (Sister Mary Dominique/Cocktail Waitress), Pátina Renea Miller (Kay-T/Sister Mary Charles/Go-Go Dancer), Lisa Robinson (Sister Mary Ernest/Biker Chick), Danny

Stiles (Bones/Leather), Roberta B. Wall (Sister Mary Bertrand/Maxine); January 17–February 25, 2007

**False Creeds** by Darren Canady; Director, Wendy C. Goldberg; Choreography, Karma Camp; Sets, Todd Rosenthal; Costumes, Anne Kennedy; Lighting, Joshua Epstein; Sound, Clay Benning; Music Composer, Kendall Simpson; PSM, lark hackshaw; Dramaturg, Celise Kalke; Stage Management P.A., Emily Stewart; SDCF Observer, Martin Wilkins; Fight Choreography, Jason Armit; Cast: Joniece Abbott-Pratt (Fannie), Joy C. Hooper (Lydia), Warner Miller (Jason), Alecia Robinson (Janie), chandra thomas (Amelia), Geoffrey D. Williams (Marcus); February 9–March 4, 2007

*Dawnn Lewis The Cast of* Sister Act The Musical
*(photo by Greg Mooney)*

**Go Dog. Go!** Adapted by Allison Gregory and Steven Dietz from the book by P.D. Eastman, music by Michael Koerner; Director, Rosemary Newcott; Sets, Kat Conley; Costumes, Sydney Roberts; Lighting, Ken Yunker; Sound/Co-Composer/Music Director, Clint Thornton; Choreography, Hylan Scott; PSM, Colleen Janich; Dramaturg, Celise Kalke; ASM, Tim Stoltenberg; Production Assistant, Liz Campbell; Cast: Denise Arribas (Green Dog), Scott E. DePoy (Musician Dog), Chris Ensweiler (MC Dog), Enoch King (Yellow Dog), Ayesha Ngaujah (Red Dog), Courtney Patterson (Hattie/Spotted Dog), Tim Stoltenberg (Blue Dog); March 6–30, 2007

**Glengarry Glen Ross** by David Mamet; Director, B.J. Jones; Sets, Leslie Taylor; Costumes, Mariann Verheyen; Lighting, Pete Shinn; Sound, Clay Benning; PSM, Kate McDoniel; Dramaturg, Celise Kalke; Stage Management Production Assistant, Mike Smith; Cast: Brik Berkes (Lingk), David de Vries (Moss), Neal A. Ghant (Roma), Chris Kayser (Levene), Joe Knezevich (Williamson), Larry Larson (Aaronow), Maurice Ralston (Baylen); March 16–April 15, 2007

**Cuttin' Up** by Charles Randolph-Wright, based on the book by Craig Marberry; Director, Kent Gash; Assistant Director/Musical Staging, Byron Easley; Sets, Shaun L. Motley; Costumes, Alvin B. Perry; Lighting, Liz Lee; Original Sound, Timothy M. Thompson; Sound, Clay Benning; Stage Manager, lark hackshaw; Dramaturg, Freddie Ashley; ASM, R. Lamar Williams; Stage Management Apprentice, Ronnie L. Campbell; Barber Shop Coach, Donald Pinckney; Cast: Duane Boutté (Ensemble), Keith Hamilton Cobb (Andre), Carl Cofield (Ensemble), Helmar Augustus Cooper (Howard), Donald Griffin (Ensemble), Marva Hicks (Female Ensemble), E. Roger Mitchell (Ensemble), Eugene H. Russell IV (Rudy); April 11–May 13, 2007

# American Conservatory Theater

San Francisco, California

Fortieth Season

Artistic Director, Carey Perloff; Executive Director, Heather Kitchen

**Travesties** by Tom Stoppard; Director, Carey Perloff; Sets, Douglas W. Schmidt; Costumes, Deborah Dryden; Lighting, Robert Wierzel; Sound, Darron L. West; Choreography, Julia Adam; Dialects, Deborah Sussel; Magic Consultant, Marshall Magoon; Dramaturg, Michael Paller; Casting, Meryl Lind Shaw; Stage Manager, Dick Daley; ASM, Katherine Riemann; Cast: Geordie Johnson (Henry Carr), Anthony Fusco (James Joyce), Gregory Wallace (Tristan Tzara), Geoff Hoyle (Lenin/Bennett), Rene Augesen (Gwendolen), Allison Jean White (Cecily), Joan Mankin (Nadya); September 14–October 15, 2006

Above: *Geoff Hoyle, Joan Mankin, and Allison Jean White in* Travesties *(photo by Kevin Berne)*

Below: *Jacqueline Antaramian, Robert Parsons, Stephen Klum, John Bull, and Jack Willis in* The Little Foxes *(photo by Greg Mooney)*

**The Little Foxes** by Lillian Hellman; Director, Laird Williamson; Sets/Costumes, Robert Blackman; Lighting, Russell H. Champa; Sound, Steve Schoenbeck; Dramaturg, Michael Paller; Casting, Meryl Lind Shaw; Stage Manager, Elisa Guthertz; ASM, Nicole Dickerson; Cast: Margaret Robinson (Addie), Rhonnie Washington (Cal), Julia Gibson (Birdie Hubbard), Robert Parsons (Oscar Hubbard), John Bull (Leo Hubbard), Jacqueline Antaramian (Regina Giddens), Stephen Klum (William Marshall), Jack Willis (Benjamin Hubbard), Grace Heid (Alexandra Giddens), Nicholas Hormann (Horace Giddens); October 27–November 26, 2006

**A Christmas Carol** by Charles Dickens, adapted by Carey Perloff and Paul Walsh, music by Karl Lundeberg; Director, Carey Perloff; Restaging, Domenique Lozano; Choreography, Val Caniparoli; Musical Director, Laura Burton; Sets, John Arnone; Costumes, Beaver Bauer; Lighting, Nancy Schertler; Sound, Jake Rodriguez, Casting, Greg Hubbard and Meryl Lind Shaw; Dramaturg, Michael Paller; Assistant Director, Joel Rainwater; Stage Manager, Dick Daley; ASM, Karen Szpaller; Production Assistant, Megan McClintock; Voice Coach, Jeffrey Crockett; Fight Director, Jud Williford; Speech Coach, Deborah Sussel; Cast: James Carpenter (Ebenezer Scrooge), Jud Williford (Bob Cratchit), Amara Radetsky (Tiny Tim), Lucas Rocco Alifano (Clerk/Dick Wilkins/Ghost of Christmas Future), Ted Welch (Clerk/Topper/Ignorance), Nicholas Hongola (Charitable/Burt/Ghost of Christmas Future), Kurt Uy (Charitable/Jim/Gang Member/Ghost of Christmas Future), Brennen Leath (Fred/Alan/Ghost of Christmas Future), Sharon Lockwood (Mrs. Dilber/Mrs. Fezziwig), Jack Willis (Ghost of Jacob Marley), Christina Owens (Ghost of Christmas Past), Andrew Nayman (Davey), Ariel Farrier-Lindo (Edward/Turkish Fig), Avery Sizelove (Boy Dick/Gang Member), Aidan Mehmet Scott (Boy Scrooge), Elizabeth Levinson (Little Fan/Spanish Onion), Steve Irish (Mr. Fezziwig/Businessman), Brian Stevens (Young Scrooge/Gang Member), Katie Huard (Belle), Jody Flader (Ermengarde/Mrs. Filcher), Margarett Head (Felicity/Mary), Matthew Nicklaw (Giles the Fiddler/Businessman), Christin Sawyer Davis (Ruth/Martha Cratchit), Melisa Ann Hart (Sarah Wilkins/Gang Member), William Halladey Lanier (Rory Wilkins/Turkish Onion), Amara Radetsky (Precious Wilkins), Stephanie Ann Saunders (Dorothy/Annabelle/ Want), Tobiah Richknd (Alfred/Boy in Sunday Clothes), Steven Anthony Jones (Ghost of Christmas Present), Monica Gibbons (Spanish Onion), Megan Apple (French Plum), Lucie Fleming (French Plum), John Bull (Produce Seller/Ghost of Christmas Future), Grace Heid (Produce Seller), Jody Flader (Beth), Graham Outerbridge (Thomas/Businessman), Delia MacDougall (Anne Cratchit), David Beal (Peter Cratchit), Anya Richkind (Belinda Cratchit), Jacqueline Blaska (Sally Cratchit), Caleb Alexander (Ned Cratchit), Seton Brown (Businessman); December 5–December 24, 2006

**The Circle** by W. Somerset Maugham; Director, Mark Lamos; Sets, John Arnone; Costumes, Candice Donnelly; Lighting, York Kennedy; Sound, Jeff Mockus; Dramaturg, Michael Paller; Casting, Meryl Lind Shaw; Dialect Coach, Deborah Sussel; Assistant Director, Adriana Baer; Stage Manager, Joseph Smelser; ASM, Stephanie Schliemann; Cast: James Waterston (Arnold Champion-Cheney, MP), Tom Blair (Butler), Trish Mulholland (Anna Shenstone), Allison Jean White (Elizabeth Champion-Cheney), Craig Marker (Edward Luton), Philip Kerr (Clive Champion-Cheney), Kathleen Widdoes (Lady Catherine Champion-Cheney), Ken Ruta (Lord Hugh Porteus); January 4–February 4, 2007

**Hedda Gabler** by Henrik Ibsen, translated by Paul Walsh; Director, Richard E.T. White; Sets, Kent Dorsey; Costumes, Sandra Woodall; Lighting, Alexander V. Nichols; Original Music/Sound, John Gromada; Dramaturg, Michael Paller; Casting, Meryl Lind Shaw; Assistant Director, Dylan Russell; Stage Manager, Eliza Gethertz; ASM, Heath Belden; Cast: Rene Augesen (Hedda Gabler), Anthony Fusco (Jorgen Tesman), Sharon Lockwood (Miss Juliane Tesman), Finnerty Steeves (Mrs. Thea Elvsted), Jack Willis (Commissioner Brack), Stephen Baker Turner (Ejlert Lovborg), Barbara Oliver (Berte); February 9–March 11, 2007

**After the War** by Philip Kan Gotanda; Director, Carey Perloff; Sets, Donald Eastman; Costumes, Lydia Tanji; Lighting, James F. Ingalls & Nancy Schertler; Sound, Jake Rodriguez; Music, Jennifer Anthony Brown; Choreography, Julia Adam; Dramaturg, Michael Paller; Dialect Coach, Deborah Sussel; Casting, Meryl Lind Shaw; Assistant Director, Laley Lippard; Stage Manager, Kimberly Mark Webb; ASM, Dick Daley; Cast: Hiro Kanagawa (Chester Monkawa), Steven Anthony Jones (Earl T. Wothing), Sala Iwamatsu (Lillian Okamura), Carrie Paff (Mary-Louise Tucker), Francis Jue (Mr. Oiji), Harriett D. Foy (Leona Hitchings), Delia MacDougall (Olga Mikhoels), Ted Welch (Benji Tucker), Sab Shimono (Mr. Goto); March 22–April 22, 2007

*Ted Welch, Sala Iwamatsu, Hiro Kanagawa, and Steven Anthony Jones in* After the War *(photo by Greg Mooney)*

**Blackbird** by David Harrower; Director, Loretta Greco; Sets, Robert Brill; Costumes, David F. Draper; Lighting, Russell H. Champa; Sound, Jake Rodriguez; Original Music, Jorge Boehringer; Dramaturg, Michael Paller; Casting, Meryl Lind Shaw; Dialects, Deborah Sussel; Assistant Director, Erin Gilley; Stage Manager, Elisa Guthertz; ASM, Karen Szpaller; Cast: Steven Culp (Peter/Ray), Jessi Campbell (Una); April 27–May 27, 2007

**The Imaginary Invalid** by Moliere, adapted by Constance Congdon; Director, Ron Lagomarsino; Sets, Erik Flatmo; Costumes, Beaver Bauer; Lighting, Nancy Schertler; Original Music/Sound, Fabian Obispo; Musical Director, Frank Johnson; Dramaturg, Michael Paller; Casting, Meryl Lind Shaw & Greg Hubbard; Assistant to the Director, Nicholas Hongola; Stage Manager, Kimberly Mark Webb; ASM, Katherine Riemann; Cast: John Apicella (Argan), Rene Augesen (Beline), Allison Jean White (Angelique), Jud Williford (Cleante), Gregory Wallace (Claude de Aria), Steven Anthony Jones (Doctor Purgeon), Anthony Fusco (Monsieur de Bonnefoi/Monsieur Fleurant), Nancy Dussault (Toinette), Margarett Head, Maureen McVerry, Brian Stevens (Ensemble); June 7–July 8, 2007

*Jessi Campbell and Steven Culp in* Blackbird *(photo by Erik Tomasson)*

# American Repertory Theatre

Cambridge, Massachusetts

Twenty-seventh Season

Artistic Director, Robert Woodruff; Executive Director, Robert J. Orchard; Associate Artistic Director, Gideon Lester

**Bobrauschenbergamerica** by Charles L. Mee, conceived and produced in association with SITI Company; Director, Anne Bogart; Set/Costumes, James Schuette; Lighting, Brian H. Scott; Sound, Darron L West; Choreography, Barney O'Hanlon; Props, Jason Szalla; Dramaturg, Tanya Palmer; Company Stage Manager, Elizabeth Moreau; Stage Manager, Elizabeth Kegley; Sound Engineer, Mark Huang; ASM, Justin Donham; Cast: Kelly Maurer (Bob's Mom), Ellen Lauren (Susan), Akiko Aizawa (Phil's girl), Leon Ingulsrud (Phil, the Trucker), J. Ed Araiza (Becker), Stephen Webber (Allen), Barney O'Hanlon (Carl), Danyon Davis (Wilson), Tom Nelis (Bob, the Pizza Boy), Jennifer Taher (Roller Girl); Loeb Drama Center; September 9–October 7, 2006

**Wings of Desire** Adapted by Gideon Lester and Dirkje Houtman from the film by Wim Wenders with screenplay by Wim Wenders, Peter Handtke, and Richard Reitinger; Produced in association with Toneelgroep (Amsterdam); Director, Ola Mafaalani; Translation, Gideon Lester & Ko van den Bosch; Sets/Lighting, André Joosten; Costumes, Regine Standfuss; Music/Sound, Andy Moor; Additional Music, Jesse Lenat and Hadewych Minis; Stage Manager, Amy James; Production Associate, Amanda Robbins; Casting, Judy Bowman; Dramaturg, Gideon Lester & Dirkje Houtman; Cast: Bernard White (Damiel), Mark Rosenthal (Cassiel), Mam Smith (Marion), Stephen Payne (Former angel), Frieda Pittoors (Homer), Jesse Lenat & Hadewych Minis (Thoughts/live music), Robin Young (Newsreader), Fred Goessens (Dying Man/Snack Bar Attendant), Andris Freimanis (Child); Loeb Drama Center; November 25–December 17, 2006

**The Onion Cellar** Conceived, written, and designed by Amanda Palmer, Jonathan Marc Sherman, Marcus Stern, and Christine Jones; Director, Marcus Stern; Sets, Christine Jones; Costumes, Clint Ramos; Lighting, Justin Townsend; Sound, David Remedios; Stage Manager, Jennifer Sturch; Dramaturgs, Ryan McKittrick & Neena Arndt; Cast: Remo Airaldi, Claire E. Davies, Thomas Derrah, Brian Farish, Kristen Frazier, Jeremy Geidt, Merritt Janson, Karen MacDonald, Amanda Palmer, Neil Stewart, Brian Viglione; Zero Arrow Theatre; December 9–January 13, 2007

**The Importance of Being Earnest** by Oscar Wilde; Produced, created, de-vised, edited and adapted by Ridiculusmus (David Woods, Jon Haynes, and Jude Kelly); Director, Jude Kelly; Design, Zoe Atkinson; Lighting, Joanne Currey; Music/Sound, David Woods, Jon Haynes, Jude Kelly & Lawrence English; Music Consultant, Lawrence English; Choreography (Galliard), Marcelle Davies; Cast: David Woods, Jon Haynes; Loeb Drama Center; December 21–January 14, 2007

**Britannicus** by Jean Racine, translation by C.H Sisson; Director, Robert Woodruff; Sets, Riccardo Hernandez; Lighting, Christopher Akerlind; Costumes, Kaye Voyce; Sound, David Remedios; Video, Leah Gelpe; Original Music, Alfredo Narciso; Stage Manager, Amy James; Voice/Speech Coach, Nancy Houfek; Casting, Judy Bowman; Cast: Alfredo Narciso (Nero), Kevin O'Donnell (Britannicus), Joan MacIntosh (Agrippina), Merritt Janson (Junia), John Sierros (Burrhus), David Wilson Barnes (Narcissus), Adrianne Krstansky (Albina), Megan Roth (Octavia); Loeb Drama Center; January 20–February 11, 2007

**Oliver Twist** by Charles Dickens, adapted and directed by Neil Bartlett, music by Gerard McBurney; Set and Costumes, Rae Smith; Lighting, Scott Zielinski; Sound, David Remedios: Music Adaptation/Direction, Simon Deacon; Movement, Struan Leslie: Costume Realization, Penny Challen; PSM, Chris De Camillis; Dialects, Laura Hitt; Casting, Deborah Brown; Cast: Carson Elrod (John Dawkins), Michael Wartella (Oliver Twist), Remo Airaldi (Mr. Bumble), Karen MacDonald (Mrs. Bumble), Thomas Derrah (Mr. Sowerberry/Mr. Grimwig/Mr. Fang), Greg Derelian (Bill Sykes/Mrs. Sowerberry), Jennifer Ikeda (Nancy), Ned Eisenberg (Fagin), Steven Boyer (Noah Claypole/Tom Chitling), Craig Pattison (Charley

Bates), Lucas Steele (Toby Crackit), Will LeBow (Mr. Brownlow), Elizabeth Jasicki (Rose Brownlow/Charlotte Sowerberry); Loeb Drama Center; February 17–March 24, 2007

**Invincible Summer** and **Monopoly** Created and performed by Mike Daisey; Director, Jean-Michele Gregory; Zero Arrow Theatre; April 4–May 5, 2007

**No Man's Land** by Harold Pinter; Sets, Michael Griggs; Costumes, David Reynoso; Lighting, Kenneth Helvig; Sound, David Remedios; Stage Manager, Amy James; Voice/Speech Coach, Carey Dawson; Cast: Paul Benedict (Hirst), Max Wright (Spooner), Henry David Clarke (Foster), Lewis D. Wheeler (Briggs); Loeb Drama Center; May 12–June 10, 2007

*Joan MacIntosh in* Brittanicus *(photo by Michael Lutch)*

# Arena Stage

Washington, D.C.

Fifty-sixth Season

Artistic Director, Molly Smith; Executive Director, Stephen Richard

**3 Mo' Divas** Created, directed, and choreographed by Marion J. Caffey; Produced in association with Studio Arena Theatre (Kathleen Gaffney, Artistic Director; Ken Neufield, Executive Director; Jeffrey Schneider, Production Manager), The Citadel Theatre (Bob Baker, Artistic Director; Penny Ritco, Managing Director; Peni Christopher, Company Manager; Dave Horner, Production Manager), and MariMo' Music/Dancap LLC.; Musical Supervision/Orchestrations/Arrangements, Joseph Joubert; Musical Direction, e'Marcus Harper; Additional Arrangements, e'Marcus Harper, Shelton Becton, Danny Holgate, Vivian Reed, Chapman Roberts; Sets, Dale F. Jordan; Costumes, Toni-Leslie James; Lighting, Richard Winkler; Hair/Wigs, Bettie Rogers; Stage Manager, Lloyd Davis Jr.; ASM, Kurt Hall; Production Manager, Carey Lawless; Casting, Eli Dawson, Barry Moss, Bob Kale; Property Master, Chuck Fox; Technical Director, Jim Glendinning; Managing Director, Dancap Productions Inc., Paul Shaw; General Manager/Production Coordinator, Sundance Productions Inc., David Coffman, Jennie Lewis; Cast: Gretha Boston, Andrea Jones-Sojola, Nina Negri, N'Kenge, Jamet Pittman, Vivian Reed; Kreeger Theater; July 15–August 13, 2006

**Cabaret** Book by Joe Masteroff; (based on the play by John Van Druten and stories by Christopher Isherwood); music by John Kander, lyrics by Fred Ebb; Director, Molly Smith; Choreography, David Neumann; Music Director/Conductor, George Fulginiti-Shakar; Sets, Anne Patterson; Costumes, Austin K. Sanderson; Lighting, Joel Moritz; Sound, Phillip Scott Peglow; Hair/Wigs, Bettie O. Rogers; Assistant Choreography, Chris Yon; Assistant Music Director, Jose C. Simbulan; Makeup, Sara Jean Landbeck; Dance Captain/Fight Captain, Jenna Edison; Dramaturg, Mark Bly; Resident Casting, Eli Dawson; Stage Manager, Susan R.

*Nina Negri, Vivian Reed, and Andrea Jones-Sonjola in* 3 Mo' Divas *(photo by Scott Suchman)*

White; ASMs, Amber Dickerson, Kate Olden; Production Manager, Carey Lawless; Technical Director, Jim Glendinning; Property Master, Chuck Fox; Cast: Glenn Seven Allen (Clifford Bradshaw), J. Fred Shiffman (Ernst Ludwig), Brad Oscar (Master of Ceremonies), Dorothy Stanley (Fraulein Schneider), Walter Charles (Herr Schultz), Sherri L. Edelen (Fraulein Kost), Meg Gillentine (Sally Bowles), Julie Burdick (Gretchen/Ensemble), Billy Bustamante (Takeshi/Ensemble), Hillary Heather Elliott (Helga/Ensemble), Deanna Harris (Birgitte/Ensemble), Lynn McNutt (Ruby/Ensemble), Monique L. Midgette (Sparkle/Ensemble), Kyle Pleasant (Rudy/Ensemble), Carlos Ponton (Bobby/Ensemble), Diego Prieto (Victor/Ensemble), Jason Strunk (Arnold/Ensemble), Erica Sweany (Sarah/Ensemble), Jenna Edison, Brett Teresa (Swings); Fichandler Theater; September 8–October 29, 2006

**9 Parts of Desire** by Heather Raffo, Director, Joanna Settle; Sets, Antje Ellermann; Costumes, Kasia Walicka Maimone; Lighting, Peter West; Sound, Obadiah Eaves; Original Choreography, David Neumann; Dramaturg, Michelle T. Hall; Voice/Dialect Coach, Lynne Soffer; Stage Manager, Martha Knight; ASM, Susan R. White; Production Manager, Carey Lawless; Resident Casting, Eli Dawson; Technical Director, Jim Glendinning; Property Master, Chuck Fox; Master Electrician, Christopher V. Lewton; Master Sound Technician, Timothy M. Thompson; Costume Shop Manager, Joseph P. Salasovich; Cast: Heather Raffo; Kreeger Theater; September 29–November 12, 2006

**She Loves Me** Book by Joe Masteroff, music by Jerry Bock, lyrics by Sheldon Harnick; based on a play by Miklos Laszlo; Director, Kyle Donnelly; Choreography, Kenneth Lee Roberson; Music Director/Conductor, William Foster McDaniel; Original Orchestrations, Don Walker; Orchestrations Adaptation, Frank Matosich Jr.; Sets, Kate Edmunds; Costumes, Nan Cibula-Jenkins; Lighting, Nancy Schertler; Sound, Garth Hemphill; Wig Master, Jon Aitchison; Assistant Director, Meredith McDonough; Assistant Music Director, Jose C. Simbulan; Assistant Choreography, Lorna Ventura; Voice/Speech Consultant, Lynn Watson; Dance Captain, Jeremy Leiner; Dramaturg, Michelle T. Hall; Stage Manager, Susan R. White; ASM, Amy K. Bennett; Production Manager, Carey Lawless; Casting, Eli Dawson; TD, Jim Glendinning; Cast: Clifton Guterman (Arpad Laszlo), Jim Corti (Ladislav Sipos), Nancy Lemenager (Ilona Ritter), Sebastian La Cause (Steven Kodaly), Kevin Kraft (Georg Nowack), Hal Robinson (Mr. Maraczek), Brynn O'Malley (Amalia Balash), Michael Scott (Keller/Ensemble), Roger Rosen (Busboy/Ensemble), J. Fred Shiffman (Head Waiter); Ensemble: Jesse Terrill (Violinist), Kurt Boehm, Ashlee Fife, Jennifer Irons, Joe Jackson, Rosalie Tenseth; Swings: Jeremy Leiner, Gia Mora; Fichandler Theater; November 17–December 31, 2006

**Noises Off** by Michael Frayn; Director, Jonathan Munby; Sets, Alexander Dodge; Costumes, Linda Cho; Lighting, Michael Gilliam; Original Music/Sound, Lindsay Jones; Wigs/Hair, Jon Aitchison; Dramaturg, Mark Bly; Fight Director,

Robb Hunter; Dialect Coach, Anita Maynard-Losh; Stage Manager, Amber Dickerson; ASM, Susan Martin; Production Manager, Carey Lawless; Casting, Eli Dawson; Technical Director, Jim Glendinning; Property Master, Chuck Fox; Master Electrician, Christopher V. Lewton; Master Sound Technician, Timothy M. Thompson; Costume Shop Manager, Joseph P. Salasovich; Cast: Helen Carey (Dotty Otley), James Gale (Lloyd Dallas), Stephen Schnetzer (Garry Lejeune), Amelia McClain (Brooke Ashton), Stephen F. Schmidt (Frederick Fellowes), Lynnda Gerguson (Belinda Blair), Susan Lynskey (Poppy Norton-Taylor), Jay Russell (Tim Allgood), Robert J. Prosky (Selsdon Mowbray); Kreeger Theater; December 15, 2006–January 28, 2007

**Gem of The Ocean** by August Wilson; Director, Paulette Randall; Sets, Scott Bradley; Costumes, Ilona Somogyi; Lighting, Allen Lee Hughes; Sound, Timothy M. Thompson; Makeup, Sara Jean Landbeck; Fight Choreography, Cliff Williams III; Production Dramaturg, Mark Bly; Stage Manager, Lloyd David Jr.; ASM, Kurt Hall; Production Manager, Carey Lawless; Casting, Eli Dawson; TD, Jim Glendinning; Property Master, Chuck Fox; Master Electrician, Christopher V. Lewton; Master Sound Technician, Timothy M. Thompson; Costume Shop Manager, Joseph P. Salasovich; Cast: Clayton Lebouf (Eli), Jimonn Cole (Citizen Barlow), Lynnie Godfrey (Aunt Ester Tyler), Pascale Armand (Black Mary), Timmy Ray James (Rutherford Selig), Joseph Marcell (Solly Two Kings), Leland Gantt (Caeser); Fichandler Theater; January 26–March 18, 2007

**Frankie and Johnny in the Claire de Lune** by Terrence McNally; Director, David Muse; Sets, Neil Patel; Costumes, T. Tyler Stumpf; Lighting, Nancy Schertler; Sound, Daniel Baker; Fight Director, Robb Hunter; Dialects, Gary Logan; Dramaturg, Clarence Coo; Stage Manager, Amy K. Bennett; ASM, Kate Olden; Production Manager, Carey Lawless; Casting, Eli Dawson; TD, Jim Glendinning; Property Master, Chuck Fox; Master Electrician, Christopher V. Lewton; Master Sound Technician, Timothy M. Thompson; Costume Shop Manager, Joseph P. Salasovich; Cast: Kate Buddeke (Frankie), Vito D'Ambrosio (Johnny), Stephen Schnetzer (Voice of Radio Announcer); Kreeger Theater; February 23–April 8, 2007

**The Heidi Chronicles** by Wendy Wasserstein; Director, Tazewell Thompson; Sets, Donald Eastman; Lighting, Robert Wierzel; Costumes, Merrily Murray-Walsh; Original Sound, Fabian Obispo; Wigs and Makeup, Jill Kaplan; Line Producer, David Dower; Dramaturgy, Michelle T. Hall, Clarence Coo; Projections, Kirby Malone, Gale Scott White; Vocal Consultant, Lynn Watson; Fight Director, Robb Hunter; Stage Manager, Amber Dickerson; ASM, Kurt Hall; Production Manager, Carey Lawless; Casting, Eli Dawson; TD, Jim Glendinning; Property Master, Chuck Fox; Master Electrician, Christopher V. Lewton; Master Sound Technician, Timothy M. Thompson; Costume Shop Manager, Joseph P. Salasovich; Cast: Ellen Karas (Heidi Holland), Catherine Weidner (Susan Johnston), David Covington (Chris/Mark/Ray/Ensemble), Wynn Harmon (Peter Patrone), Marty Lodge (Scoop Rosenbaum), Hope Lambert (Lisa/Jill/Ensemble), Susan Bennett (Fran/April/Ensemble), Emerie Snyder (Denise/Becky/Ensemble); Fichandler Theater; April 6–May 13, 2007

**Peter and Wendy** Conceived and created by Liza Lorwin (adapter/producer), Julie Archer (designer), Johnny Cunningham (composer) and Lee Breuer (director) from the novel by J.M. Barrie; Lyrics, Johnny Cunningham, J.M. Barrie, Liza Lorwin, Lee Breuer, Jay Ansill, Alan Kelly; Costumes, Sally Thomas; Sound, Edward Cosla; Associate Lighting, Steven L. Shelly; Fight Direction, B.H. Barry; Film, Andrew Moore; Live Sound Effects Score, Jay Peck; Puppetry Director/ Design, Basil Twist & Jane Catherine Shaw; Music Director, Alan Kelly; PSM, Lloyd David Jr.; ASM, Neelam Vaswani; Production Management, Technical Theater Solutions & Rhys Williams; Technical Director, Martin Lechner; Production Consultant, Judith Schoenfeld; Company Manager, Rebecca Josue; Assistant Puppetry Director, Matthew Acheson; Co-Puppet Design/Construction, Julie Archer, Walter Stark, Stephen Kaplin; Cast: Karen Kandel (The Narrator, April 27–May 27), Marsha Stephanie Blake (The Narrator, May 29–June 24); Puppeteers: Eric Wright (Lead, Peter), Lindsay Abromaitis-Smith and Emily DeCola (Peter), Lute Breuer (Lead, Hook), Jessica Scott and Matthew Acheson (Hook), Jessica Scott with Matthew Acheson and Jessica Chandlee Smith (Jane), Emily DeCola

and Lute Breuer (Nana), Lindsay Abromaitis-Smith and Emily DeCola (Smee); Jessica Chandlee Smith (Nana-Croc/The Neverbird), Deana Acheson (Puppeteer Understudy); Musicians: Tola Custy (fiddle), Susan McKeown (singer), Jay Ansill (Celtic harp/vocals), Alan Kelly (accordion), Stephanie Geremia, Ivan Goff (flutes), Aidan Brennan (guitar/vocals), Jerry Busher (percussion/sound effects); Kreeger Theater; April 27–June 24, 2007

**Ennio** Directed and designed by Ennio Marchetto and Sosthen Hennekam; Concept, Ennio Marchetto; Lighting and Sound, Sosthen Hennekam; Production Manager, Carey Lawless; Technical Director, Jim Glendinning; Assistant Technical Director, Steve Greene; Master Electrician, Chris Lewton; Master Sound Technician, Timothy M. Thompson; Costume Shop Manager, Joseph P. Salasovich; Followspot/Crew, Talisa Friedman, Presented as part of the "Arena Presents" series; Cast: Ennio Marchetto, Steve Olson; Fichandler Theater; May 22–June 10, 2007

# Arizona Theatre Company

Tucson, Mesa, and Phoenix, Arizona

Fortieth Season

Artistic Director, David Ira Goldstein; Executive Director, Jessica Andrews; Producing Director, John Kingsbury; Managing Director, Kevin E. Moore

**Twelfth Night** by William Shakespeare; Director, Jon Jory; Sets, Hugh Landwehr; Costumes, David Kay Mickelsen; Lighting, Dennis Parichy; Composer, Peter Ekstrom; Sound, Brian Jerome Peterson; Fight Director, Brent Gibbs; Choreography, Frances Smith Cohen; PSM, Glenn Bruner; Assistant Director, Tamara Fisch; Cast: Stafford Clark-Price (Orsino), Janis Dardaris (Maria), Lisa De Mont (Olivia), Cale Epps (Antonio), Julie Garrison (Ensemble), Roberto Guajardo (Sea Captain/Priest), Sarah Hayes (Valentine), Eddie Levi Lee (Sir Toby Belch), Michael Medeiros (Feste), Everett Quinton (Sir Andrew Aguecheek), Chris Redondo (Ensemble), Kyle Sorrell (Sebastian), Jeff Steitzer (Malvolio), Noah Todd (Curio), Joseph Topmiller (Ensemble), Brenda Withers (Viola); Tucson: September 9–30, 2006; Phoenix: October 5–22, 2006

*Lisa DeMont and Kyle Sorrell in* Twelfth Night *(photo by Tim Fuller)*

**2 Pianos 4 Hands** by Ted Dykstra and Richard Greenblatt; Director, Bruce K. Sevy; Sets, Scott Weldin; Costumes, Kish Finnegan; Lighting, Don Darnutzer; Sound, Brian Jerome Peterson; Assistant Lighting, T. Greg Squires; PSM, Glenn Bruner; Cast: Mark Anders (Ted), Carl Danielsen (Richard); Mesa Arts Center; October 20–29, 2006

**Jitney** by August Wilson; Director, Lou Bellamy; Sets, Vicki M. Smith; Costumes, Matthew J. LeFebvre; Lighting, Michelle Habeck; Sound, John Story; Stage Manager, Mary R. Honour; Assistant Director, Mary K. Winchell; Cast: James T. Alfred (Youngblood), James Craven (Turnbo), Abdul Salaam El Razzac (Shealy), Bus Howard (Doub), Julia Pace Mitchell (Rena), Chuck Patterson (Fielding), Jacinto Taras Riddick (Booster), Adolphus Ward (Philmore), Brian Anthony Wilson (Becker); Tucson: October 22–November 11, 2006; Phoenix: November 16–December 3, 2006

**Ella** Book by Jeffrey Hatcher; Conceived by Rob Ruggiero and Dyke Garrison; Director, Rob Ruggiero; Musical Direction and Arrangements by Danny Holgate; Sets, Michael Schweikardt; Costumes, Alejo Vietti; Lighting, John Lasiter; Sound, Michael C. Miceli; Stage Manager, Bruno Ingram; Cast: George Caldwell (piano/Conductor), Harold Dixon (Norman Granz), Tina Fabrique (Ella Fitzgerald), Rodney Harper (drums), Clifton Kellem (bass), Brian "Lord" Sledge (trumpet); Tucson: November 25–December 20, 2006; Phoenix: December 31, 2006–January 28, 2007; Mesa: February 2–11, 2007

**Souvenir** by Stephen Temperley; Director, Vivian Matalon; Sets, R. Michael Miller; Costumes, Tracy Christensen; Lighting, Ann G. Wrightson; Sounds, David Budries, Phillip Scott Peglow; Wig Designer, David H. Lawrence; Stage Manager, Jack Gianino; Cast: Donald Corren (Cosme McMoon), Judy Kaye (Florence Foster Jenkins); Tucson: September January 13–February 3, 2007, Phoenix: February 8–25, 2007

## REPFEST

**Molly's Delicious** by Craig Wright; Director, Aaron Posner; Sets, Kris Stone; Costumes, Kish Finnegan; Lighting, Don Darnutzer; Sound, Brian Jerome Peterson; Dramaturg, Jennifer Bazzell; PSM, Glenn Bruner; Cast: Stephen D'Ambrose (Alan "Lindy" Linda), Joe Binder (Alec Willoughby), Roberto Guajardo (Ross Willoughby), Barbara Kingsley (Cindy Linda), Andrew Pastides (Jerry Fountain), Adelia Saunders (Alison); Tucson: March 3–April 15, 2007, Phoenix: April 27–May 27, 2007

**I Am My Own Wife** by Doug Wright; Director, Samantha K. Wyer; Sets, Kris Stone; Costumes, Kish Finnegan; Lighting, Don Darnutzer; Sound, Brian Jerome Peterson; Dialect Coach, Dianne Winslow; Dramaturg, Jennifer Bazzell; Stage Manager, Stacey Flores; Cast: Bob Sorenson (Charlotte Von Mahlsdorf); Tucson: March 6–April 15, 2007, Phoenix: April 26–May 20, 2007

**Love, Janis** Conceived, adapted, and directed by Randal Myler; Musical Director, Sam Andrew; Sets, Vicki Smith; Costumes, Lorraine Venberg; Lighting, Don Darnutzer; Sound, Eric Stahlhammer; Projections, Jeffrey Cady; Stage Manager, Dana Victoria Anderson; Cast: Joel Hoekstra (lead guitar), Rod Larkins (trumpet), Eric Massimino (bass), Lisa Otey (keyboards), Rick Peron (trumpet), Sophia Ramos (Janis Joplin singing), Cathy Richardson (Janis Joplin singing), Marisa Ryan (Janis Joplin speaking), Jonathan Sanford (saxophone), Michael Santo (Interviewer), Blake Thompson (rhythm guitar), Jim Wall (percussion); Tucson: March 22–April 9, 2007, Phoenix: April 14–May 27, 2007

# Arkansas Repertory Theatre

Little Rock, Arkansas

Thirty-first Season

Producing Artistic Director, Robert Hupp; General Manager, Mike McCurdy

**Moonlight and Magnolias** by Ron Hutchinson; Director, Robert Hupp; Sets, E. Mike Nichols; Costumes, Olivia Koach; Lighting, Andrew Meyers; Sound, M. Jason Pruzin; Production Manager, Rafael Colon Castanera; Stage Manager, Tara Kelly; Fight Choreographer, D.C. Wright; Cast: Marc Carver (Ben Hecht), Fredric Stone (David O. Selznick), Joseph Graves (Victor Fleming); September 8–24, 2006

**The Second City - Truth Justice or the American Way** Presented by The Second City; Cast: Anthony LeBlanc, Brad Morris, Christina Anthony, Meagan Flanigan, Robyn Norris, T.J. Miller; September 27–October 8, 2006

**The King and I** Book and lyrics by Oscar Hammerstein II, music by Richard Rodgers; Director, Brad Mooy; Music Director, Kristy L. Templet; Choreography, Zhenjun Zhang; Sets, E. Mike Nichols; Lighting, Andrew Meyers; Sound, M. Jason Pruzin; Production Manager, Rafael Colon Castanera; Stage Manager, Shawn Pace; ASM, Danny Kuenzel; Properties, Lynda Kwallek; Cast: Sarah Solie (Anna Leonowens), Charlie Askew (Louis Leonowens), Tom Kagy (Captain Orton/Sir Edward Ramsay), Bobby Martino (The Kralahome), Eng Kian Ooi (The Interpreter), Enrique Acevedo (The King), Luz Lor (Tuptim), Wayne Hu (Lun Tha), Zheng Zhang (Phra Alack), Catherine Mi Eun Choi (Lady Thiang), Allan Mangaser (Prince Chululongkorn), Michiko Takemasa (Eliza), Minami Yusui (Fan Dancer/Topsy), Ayumi Uchida (Little Eva), Zhenjun Zhang (Simon), Brooke Culbertson (Uncle Thomas), Jolli Khoo (Little Buddha), Eun Jung Gonzalez (Principal Palace Dancer/Angel George), Sophia Moschel or Isabella Akel (Princess Ying Yaowlak), Katie Au (Principal Palce Dancer); Royal Children: Will Nicholson, Gracie Stover, Morgan Platt, LaTasha Bryan Snyder, Anna Strack, Annbeth Changyumei Hall, Laura Luz Castillo-Bahena, Irwin Castillo-Bahena, Sky Cardwell, Angel Bahena, Samantha Boyd, Robbin Gordon, Corey Summons Jr., Emma Hurtado, Nia Simone Jackson, Nelson McCain, Caroline McCormick, Jolli Khoo; Ensemble: Rommel O'Choa, Yuhan Ai, Makie Armstrong, Andrew Cheng, Lacy J. Dunn, James Kent, Grace Eunhye Lee, Teresa Wong, Glen Llanes; December 1–31, 2006

**Fences** by August Wilson; Director, Gilbert McCauley; Sets, E. Mike Nichols; Costumes, Olivia Koach; Lighting, William Marshall, Sound, Jason Pruzin; Production Manager, Rafael Colon Castanera; Stage Manager, Nicole Bouclier; Properties, Lynda Kwallek; Cast: Lawrence Evans (Bono), Yaegel Welch (Cory), Lawrence Hamilton (Gabriel), Wendell B. Franklin (Lyons), Kharlissa Lovelace or Nia Simone Jackson (Raynell), Judyann Elder (Rose), Gerard Catus (Troy Maxson); February 2–18, 2007

**Born Yesterday** by Garson Kanin; Director, Cliff Fannin Baker; Sets, E. Mike Nichols; Costumes, Yslan Hicks; Lighting, Ken White; Sound, M. Jason Pruzin; Production Manager, Rafael Colon Castanera; Stage Manager, Tara Kelly; Properties, Lynda Kwallek; Cast: Joan Hess (Billie Dawn), Don Alder (Ed Devery), Mark Enis (Eddie Brock), Ian Moore (Ensemble), Jason Thompson (Ensemble), Scott Coopwood (Harry Brock), Paige Reynolds (Helen/Ensemble), Judy Trice (Mrs. Hedges), Stafford Clark-Price (Paul Verrall), Mark Whitman Johnson (Senator Orvall Hedges); March 16–April 1, 2007

**Bertrand Priest** by Ian Cohen; Director, Brad Mooy; Sets, E. Mike Nichols; Costumes, Olivia Koach; Lighting, Matthew Webb; Sound, M. Jason Pruzin; Production Manager, Rafael Colon Castanera; Stage Manager, Stephen Horton; Properties, Lynda Kwallek; Cast: Matt Walker (Al Steinberg), Molly Collier-Rawn (Anchorperson), Mark Fisher (Bertrand Priest), Eric Martin Brown (Dennis Kennedy), Josie DiVincenzo (Katrina Chernov), Athena (Sherman); April 27–May 13, 2007

**The Full Monty** Music and lyrics by David Yazbek, book by Terrence McNally; Director, Robert Hupp; Music Director, Michael Heavner; Choreography, Lynne Kurdziel Formato; Sets, E. Mike Nichols; Costumes, Olivia Koach & Rafael Castanera; Lighting, Ken White; Sound, M. Jason Pruzin; Production Manager, Rafael Colon Castanera; Stage Manager, Christine Lomaka; ASM, Karyn D. Richardson; Properties, Lynda Kwallek; Cast: Brian Patrick Murphy (Buddy "Keno" Walsh), Christopher Sapienza (Dave Bukatinski), Jason Samuel (Ensemble), Lacy J. Dunn (Estelle Genovese), Matt Bailey (Ethan Girard), Janna Cardia (Georgie Bukatinksy), Larry Daggett (Harold Nichols), SuEllen Estey (Jeanette Burmeister), Peter James Zielinski (Jerry Lukowski), Ethan Paulini (Malcolm MacGregor), Charlie Askew or Joseph Scott (Nathan Lukowski), Jerome Lucas Harmann (Noah "Horse" T. Simmons), Nicole Johndrow (Pam Lukowski), Matthew Tatu (Reg Willoughby), Ragan Renteria (Susan Hershey), Craig Wilson (Teddy Slaughter), Seth Wyatt Kinney (Tony Giordano), Angela C. Howell (Vicki Nichols); June 8–July 1, 2007

# Barter Theatre

Abingdon, Virginia

Seventy-fourth Season

Producing Artistic Director, Richard Rose; Director of Production, Nicholas Piper; Director of Advancement, Jayne Duehring; Managing Director, Joan Ballou

**The Quiltmaker** by Catherine Bush. Director, Katy Brown; Sets, Cheri Prough DeVol; Costumes, Amanda Aldridge; Lighting, Genny Wynn; Sound, Bobby Beck; Stage Manager, Cindi A. Raebel; Dramaturgs, Nicholas Piper & Katy Brown; Cast: Mary Lucy Bivins (Ida May Combs), Janeé Reeves (Juanita Jenkins), Meredith Autry Holcomb (Cindy Taylor Bennett), Nicholas Piper (Jackson Bennett), Michael Poisson (Ronnie Combs), John Hedges (Sheriff Ham Terhune); February 2–April 21, 2007

**Long Shadow** by Conrad Bishop and Elizabeth Fuller; Director, Richard Rose; Sets, Lori Fleenor; Costumes, Kelly Jenkins; Lighting, Richard Rose & Lori Fleenor; Sound, Bobby Beck; Stage Manager, Jessica Borda; ASM, Holley Housewright; Cast: Tom Angland (Woodrow Purvis), Wendy Mitchell Piper (Winona Purvis), Eugene Wolf (Sheriff Carl Timmerman), Tricia Matthews (Sally Timmerman), Frank Green (Lester, deputy sheriff), Matt Greenbaum (Walt, a reporter), Seana Hollingsworth (Ginny Cavendish, a reporter), Rick McVey (Fred Upchurch, farmer), Amy Baldwin (Ruby Upchurch, his daughter), Mike Ostroski (Jamie Upchurch, his son), Matt Greenbaum (Halloween Trick or Treater), Frank Taylor Green (William Ebaugh, a shadow), Mike Ostroski (Brady, a banker), Rick McVey (Oleson, a merchant), Matt Greenbaum (Evans, a realtor), Seana Hollingsworh (Maggie, a bartender), Wendy Mitchell Piper (Lucille, Winona's friend), Tricia Matthews (Ms. Phillips, neighbor), Amy Baldwin (a woman), Rick McVey (Mr. Sturgis, retired merchant), Tricia Matthews (Mrs. Sturgis, his wife), Mike Ostroski (Chris, infantry sergeant on leave), Matt Greenbaum (Thomas O'Donnell, electrician); February 8–April 15, 2007

**Don't Hug Me** Book and lyrics by Phil Olson, music by Paul Olson; Director, Richard Rose; Music Director, James Hollingsworth; Choreography, Richard Rose & Amanda Aldridge; Sets, Cheri Prough DeVol; Costumes, Heather Fleming; Lighting, Heather Eisenhart; Sound, Bobby Beck; Stage Manager, Jessica Borda; Cast: Tricia Matthews (Clara Johnson), Rick McVey (Gunner Johnson), Wendy Mitchell Piper (Bernice Gisselen), Frank Green (Aarvid Gisselsen), Tom Angland (Kanute Gunderson); February 17–May 13, 2007

**Blithe Spirit** by Noel Coward; Director, Nicholas Piper; Sets, Daniel Ettinger; Costumes, Amanda Aldridge; Lighting, Genny Wynn; Sound, Bobby Beck; Stage Manager, Cindi A. Raebel; ASM, Holley Housewright; Cast: Meredith Autry Holcomb (Edith), Amy Baldwin (Ruth Condomine), Mike Ostroski (Charles Condomine), John Hedges (Dr. Bradman), Janeé Reeves (Mrs. Bradman), Mary

*Mike Ostroski, John Hedges, Amy Baldwin, Janeé Reeves, and Mary Lucy Bivins in* Blithe Spirit *(photo courtesy of the Barter Theatre)*

Lucy Bivins (Madame Arcati), Seana Hollingsworth (Elvira); February 22–April 14, 2007

**Lear** Aapted and directed by Richard Rose from *King Lear* by William Shakespeare; Sets, Derek Smith; Costumes, Kimberly Stockton; Lighting, Heather Eisenhart; Sound, Bobby Beck; Voice Coach, Ben Corbett; Dramaturg, Catherine Bush; Fight Choreography, Michael G. Chin; Fight Captain, Mike Ostroski; Stage Manager, Jessica Borda; Cast: Eugene Wolf (Lear), Seana Hollingsworth (Fool, Lear's Executive Assistant), Tricia Matthews (Goneril), Mike Ostroski (Albany), Amy Baldwin (Regan), Ashley Campos (Cordelia), Tom Angland (Kent), Rick McVey (Gloucester), Frank Taylor Green (Edmund), Matt Greenbaum (Edgar), Wendy Mitchell Piper (Oswald); April 20–May 26, 2007

**Married Alive** Book and lyrics by Sean Grennan, music by Leah Okimoto; Director, Katy Brown; Musical Directors, James Hollingsworth & Steve Przybylski; Sets, Cheri Prough DeVol; Costumes, Amanda Aldridge; Lighting, Lynne Chase; Sound, Bobby Beck; Props, Tracy S. Farres; Gospel Choir Designer, Gina Beiswenger; Stage Manager, Cindi A. Raebel; ASM, Holley Housewright; Cast: Amanda Johnson (Erin), Sean Campos (Paul), Cathy Whelan (Diane), Michael Poisson (Ron); April 27–May 26, 2007

**Tradin' Paint** by Catherine Bush; Director, Mary Lucy Bivins; Sets, Cheri Prough DeVol; Costumes, Kimberly Stockton; Lighting, Karen Elb; Sound, Bobby Beck; Dramaturg, Nicholas Piper; Stage Manager, Jessica Borda; Cast: John Hedges (Flagman), Frank Taylor Green (Halley Smoot), Nicholas Piper (Skeeter Jett), Robert Kitchens (Tucker Forbush), Jack Benton (Pierce Garbarino), Seana Hollingsworth (Lucky Tibbs), Matt Greenbaum (Coty Webb), Janeé Reeves (Darla Frye), John Hedges (Football player), John Hedges (Jack), John Hedges (The Boss); May 18–August 26, 2007

**Oliver!** Book, music, and lyrics by Lionel Bart; Director, Paul Russell; Choreography, Amanda Aldridge; Musical Director/Conductor, James Hollingsworth; Assistant Musical Director/Keyboard, Giuseppe Ritorto; Sets, Dale Jordon; Costumes, Amanda Aldridge; Lighting, Dale Jordan; Sound, Bobby Beck; Projections, Bobby Beck & Paul Russell; Dance Captain, Amy Baldwin; Fight Choreography/Captain, Mike Ostroski; Stage Manager, Cindi A. Raebel/Jessica Borda; ASM, Holley Housewright; Dramaturg, Catherine Bush; Cast: Maxey Whitehead (Oliver), Tricia Matthews (Widow Corney), Michael Poisson (Mr. Bumble), Tom Angland (Mr. Sowerberry), Rebecca Reinhardt (Mrs. Sowerberry), Anne Elizabeth Butler (Charlotte), Sean Campos (Noah Claypool), Ben Mackel (Artful Dodger), Eugene Wolf (Fagin), Ezra Colón (Charley), Meredith Autry Holcomb (Nancy), Ashley Campos (Bet), Rick McVey (Bill Sykes), Tom Angland (Mr. Brownlow), Megan Atkinson (Mrs. Bedwin), Rebecca Reinhardt (Milkmaid), Amy Baldwin (Strawberry Seller), Mike Ostroski (Knife Seller), Michael Poisson (Dr. Grimwig); Londoners: Tom Angland, Megan Atkinson, Amy Baldwin, Anne

Elizabeth Butler, Ashley Campos, Sean Campos, Erza Colón, Gwen Edwards, Ben Greenstone, Meredith Autry Holcomb, Tricia Matthews, Mike Ostroski, Michael Poisson, Rebecca Reinhardt; Youth of London: Tori Bartfai, Rachel Boyd, Aria Brinkley, Joseph Brooks, Lexi Clark, Alexandra Eleas, Logan Fritz, Gretchen Gross, Kurtis Gross, Matthew Helton, Hollie Matthews, Sarah Lyn Smith; June 1–August 18, 2007

**Baby** Book by Sybille Pearson, music by David Shire, lyrics by Richard Maltby Jr. Director, Richard Rose; Musical Director, James Hollingsworth; Assistant Musical Director, Giuseppe Ritorto; Piano/Conductor, James Hollingsworth; Keyboard, Giuseppe Ritorto; Percussion, Jay Oberfeitinger: Sets, Daniel Ettinger: Costumes, Kimberly Stockton; Lighting, Daniel Ettinger; Sound, Bobby Beck; Stage Manager, Cindi A. Raebel; ASM, Holley Housewright; Cast: Gwen Edwards (Lizzie Fields), Ben Mackel (Danny Hopper), Tricia Matthews (Arlene MacNally), Rick McVey (Alan MacNally), Seana Hollingsworth (Pam Sakarian), Sean Campos (Nick Sakarian), Janeé Reeves (Ensemble); June 13–August 19, 2007

**More Fun Than Bowling** by Steven Dietz; Director, Mary Lucy Bivins; Sets, Dale Jordan; Costumes, Amanda Aldridge; Lighting, Dale Jordan; Sound, Bobby Beck; Stage Manager, Jessica Borda; Cast: Mike Ostroski (Mister Dyson), Meredith Autry Holcomb (Molly, Jake's daughter), Frank Taylor Green (Jake Tomlinson), Amy Baldwin (Loretta, Jake's third wife), Rebecca Reinhardt (Lois, Jake's second wife); June 22–August 17, 2007

**Harry Chapin: Remember the Music** by Alan Blumenthal, William Roudebush, and Stephen Blumenthal; Director, William Roudebush; Musical Directors, Christopher Ertelt and James Ryan; Sets, Nick Embree; Costumes, Kimberly Stockton; Lighting, E. Tonry Lathrom; Sound, Bobby Beck; Stage Manager, Jessica Borda; Cast: Kimberly Rehfuss, Jennie Eisenhower, Mickey Houlahan, Dan Folino, Paul Bernardo; August 23–September 15, 2007

**America's Blue Yodeler: Jimmie Rodgers** by Doug Pote; Director, Mary Lucy Bivins; Musical Director, Eugene Wolf; Sets, Ben Nicholson; Costumes, Amanda Aldridge; Lighting, Cheri Prough DeVol; Sound, Bobby Beck; Stage Manager, Jessica Borda; Dramaturgs, Catherine Bush and Richard Rose; Cast: Tom Angland (Jimmie Rodgers), Amy Baldwin (All women), Mike Ostroski (All men), Jasper McGruder (Hobo Bob); September 14–November 10, 2007

**Dracula!** Adapted and directed from the Bram Stoker novel by Richard Rose; Sets, Cheri Prough DeVol, Costumes, Amanda Aldridge; Sound, Bobby Beck; Stage Manager, Cindi A. Raebel; Cast: Meredith Autry Holcomb (Mina Seward), Nicholas Piper (Count Dracula), Michael Poisson (Dr. David Seward), Sean Campos (Jonathan Harker), Julia VanderVeen (Sarah Goforth), Tricia Matthews (Professor Eva Van Helsing), Frank Taylor Green (Mister Renfield), Rick McVey (William Spaggs), Ashley Campos (Lucy); September 21–November 17, 2007

**Doubting Thomas** by John Green; Director, Katy Brown; Sets, Cheri Prough DeVol; Costumes, Kimberly Stockton; Lighting, Cheri Prough DeVol; Sound, Bobby Beck; Stage Manager, Cindi A. Raebel; Dramaturg, Catherine Bush; Cast: Sean Campos (Thomas), Meredith Autry Holcomb (Julie), Rick McVey (Pastor Bob), Eugene Wolf (Peter); September 28–November 11, 2007

**Driving Miss Daisy** by Alfred Uhry; Director, Richard Rose; Sets, Daniel Ettinger; Costumes, Amanda Aldridge; Sound, Bobby Beck; Stage Manager, Jessica Borda; Cast: Jasper McGruder (Hoke), Mary Lucy Bivins (Daisy Wertham), Michael Poisson (Boolie Wertham); October 5–November 17, 2007

**Wooden Snowflakes** by Catherine Bush; Director, Richard Rose; Sets, Ben Nicholson; Costumes, Heather Fleming; Lighting, Heather Eisenhart; Sound, Bobby Beck; Stage Manager, Cindi A. Raebel; Dramaturg, Richard Rose; Cast: Tom Angland (Simon Peter Whitaker), Amy Baldwin (Eve Lawson); November 20–December 23, 2007

**A Christmas Carol** Adapted from Dickens by Richard Rose; Director, Nicholas Piper; Sets, Cheri Prough DeVol; Costumes, Amanda Aldridge; Lighting, E. Tony Lathrom; Sound, Bobby Beck; Stage Manager, Jessica Borda; Cast: Michael Poisson (Scrooge), Mary Lucy Bivins, Tricia Matthews, Frank Taylor Green, Rick McVey, Mike Ostroski, Eugene Wolf, Meredith Autry Holcomb; November 23–December 30, 2007

# Bay Street Theatre

Sag Harbor, New York

Fifteenth Season

Co-Artistic Directors, Sybil Christopher and Murphy Davis

**Quartet** by Ronald Harwood; Director, Jack Hofsiss; Sets, Troy Hourie; Costumes, Tracy Christensen; Lighting, Brian Nason; Sound, Tony Melfa; PSM, Nevin Hedley; Musical Supervision, Roger Butterley; Cast: Kaye Ballard (Cecily Robson), Paul Hecht (Wilfred Bond), Simon Jones (Reginald Paget), Siân Phillips (Jean Horton); May 23–June 4, 2006

**The Who's Tommy** by Pete Townshend and Des McAnuff; Director, Marcia Milgrom Dodge; Sets, Gary Hygom; Costumes, Emilio Sosa; Lighting, Paul Miller; Sound, Tony Melfa; Music Director, Roger Butterley; Choreography, Marcia Milgrom Dodge; PSM, Chris Clark; Cast: Ashley Bachner (Specialist's Assistant/ Ensemble), Philip Michael Baskerville (Hawker/Ensemble), Brian Beach (British Officer/Ensemble), Paul Binotto (Uncle Ernie), Shelby Braxton-Brooks (Gypsy/ Ensemble), Gavin Esham (Lover/Ensemble), Noah Galvin (Young Tommy), Nikka Graff Lanzarone (Nurse/Ensemble), Eddie Marco (Harmonica/Ensemble), Mike McGowan (Captain Walker), Euan Morton (Tommy), Liz Pearce (Mrs. Walker), Gregory Treco (Minister/Specialist/Ensemble), Josh Walden (Cousin Kevin/ Associate Choreography), Laura Woyasz (Sally Simpson/Ensemble); June 13–July 9, 2006

**Viva La Vida!** by Diane Shaffer; Director, Susana Tubert; Sets, Narelle Sissons; Costumes, Toni-Leslie James; Lighting, Stephen Strawbridge; Sound, Tony Melfa; PSM, Brian Meister; Cast: Mercedes Ruehl (Frida Kahlo), Rene Pereyra (Diego Rivera), Liza Colón-Zayas (Rosita); July 18–August 6, 2006

**Darwin in Malibu** by Crispin Whittell; Director, Daniel Gerroll; Sets, Gary Hygom; Costumes, Amela Baksic; Lighting, David Weiner; Sound, Tony Melfa; PSM, Chris Clark; Cast: Anna Chlumsky (Sarah), Richard Easton (Wilberforce), Neal Huff (Huxley), Hal Linden (Darwin); August 15–September 3, 2006

*Mercedes Ruehl in* Viva La Vida! *(photo by David Rodgers)*

# Berkeley Repertory Theatre

Berkeley, California

Thirty-ninth Season

Artistic Director, Tony Taccone; Managing Director, Susie Medak; Associate Artistic Director, Les Waters

**Mother Courage** by Bertolt Brecht; Translated by David Hare; Presented in association with La Jolla Playhouse; Director, Lisa Peterson; Music, Gina Leishman; Sets, Rachel Hauck; Costumes, David Zinn; Lighting, Alexander V. Nichols; Sound, Jill B.C. DuBoff; Music Director, Gina Leishman; Fight Director, Steve Rankin; Movement, MaryBeth Cavanaugh; Dramaturg, Shirley Fishman; Stage Manager, Michael Suenkel; ASM, Anjee Nero; Casting, Amy Potozkin (Bay Area), Sharon Bialy and Sherry Thomas (Los Angeles), Tara Rubin (New York); Cast: Ara Anderson (Tuba/Accordion/ Ensemble), Katie Barrett (Yvette Pottier/Ensemble), Ivonne Coll (Mother Courage), David W. Collins (Drummer/Ensemble), Mark Danisovsky (Piano/Accordion/Ensemble), Brent Hinkley (Sergeant/Ensemble), Katie Huard (Kattrin), Drew Hirschfield (Swiss Cheese), Marc Damon Johnson (Recruiting Officer/Ensemble), Patrick Kerr (Chaplain/Ensemble), Justin Leath (Eilif/Ensemble), Jarion Monroe (Cook/Ensemble); September 8–October 22, 2006

**Passing Strange** Book and lyrics by Stew, music by Stew and Heidi Rodewald; Presented in association with The Public Theater; Director/Co-Creator, Annie Dorsen; Choreography, Karole Armitage; Sets, David Korins; Costumes, Annie Smart; Lighting, Kevin Adams; Sound, Jake Rodriguez; Music Directors, Heidi Rodewald and Jon Spurney; Dialect Coach, Dawn-Ellin Fraser; Dramaturg, Madeleine Oldham; PSM, Michael Suenkel; Stage Manager, Cynthia Cahill; Casting, Amy Potozkin; Cast: de'Adre Aziza (Edwina/Mariana/Ensemble), Daniel Breaker (Youth), Eisa Davis (Mother/Ensemble), Colman Domingo (Franklin/Venus/Ensemble), Marc Doten (Multi-instrumentalist), Chad Goodridge (Hugo/Terry/Ensemble), Rebecca Naomi Jones (Sherry/ Desi/Ensemble), Russ Kleiner (percussion), Heidi Rodewald (bass/keyboard/vocalist), Jon Spurney (guitarist/keyboardist), Stew (Narrator); October 19–December 3, 2006

**all wear bowlers** Created by Geoff Sobelle and Trey Lyford; Director, Aleksandra Wolska; Sets, Edward E. Haynes Jr.; Costumes, Tara Webb; Lighting, Randy "Igleu" Glickman; Filmmaker, Michael Glass; Sound, James Sugg; Composer, Michael Friedman; Stage Manager, Michelle Blair; Produced by rainpan 43 productions; Cast: Geoff Sobelle (Earnest), Trey Lyford (Wyatt); November 24–December 23, 2006

**The Pillowman** by Martin McDonagh; Director, Les Waters; Sets, Antje Ellermann; Costumes, Anna R. Oliver; Lighting, Russell H. Champa; Original Music/Sound, Obadiah Eaves; Stage Manager, Michael Suenkel; Fight Director, Dave Maier; Dramaturg, Madeleine Oldham; Casting, Amy Potozkin (Bay Area), Janet Foster (New York); Cast: Tony Amendola (Tupolski), Nancy Carlin (Mother), Erik Lochtefeld (Katurian), Brigette Renee Lundy-Paine (Little Girl), Matthew Maher (Michal), Andy Murray (Ariel), Brendan Reilly (Little Boy), Madeleine Silverman (Little Girl), Howard Swain (Father), Gabriel Vergez (Little Boy); January 12–March 11, 2007

**To the Lighthouse** Adapted by Adele Edling Shank from the novel by Virginia Woolf; Music, Les Waters; Sets, Annie Smart; Costumes, Christal Weatherly; Lighting, Matt Frey; Sound, Darron L. West; Video Designer, Jebediah Ike; Dramaturg, Madeleine Oldham; Dialect Coach, Lynne Soffer; Stage Manager, Elizabeth Moreau; Casting, Amy Potozkin; Cast: Jarion Monroe (William Bankes), Rebecca Watson (Lily Briscoe), Monique Fowler (Mrs. Ramsay), Edmond Genest (Mr. Ramsay), Clifton Guterman (Andrew/Adult James), David Mendelsohn (Charles Tansley), Whitney Bashor (Prue/Adult Cam), Lauren Grace (Minta Doyle/ Mrs. McNabb), Noah James Butler (Paul Rayley), Musicians: Alex Kelly (Cello), Charith Premawardhana (Viola), Justin Mackewich (1st Violin), Sarah Jo Zaharako (2nd Violin); February 23–March 25, 2007

*Erik Lochtefeld and Tony Amendola in* The Pillowman
*(photo by Kevin Berne)*

**Blue Door** A play with original songs by Tanya Barfield; Director, Delroy Lindo; Sets, Kate Edmunds; Costumes, Emilio Sosa; Lighting, Kathy A. Perkins; Sound & Composition, Andre Pluess; Vocal Coach, Lynne Morrow; PSM, Michael Suenkel; Casting, Janet Foster & Amy Potozkin; Cast: Teagle F. Bougere (Simon/Rex/Jesse), David Fonteno (Lewis); April 6–May 20, 2007

**Oliver Twist** by Charles Dickens, adapted, and directed by Neil Bartlett; Composer, Gerard McBurney; Sets/Costumes, Rae Smith; Lighting, Scott Zielinski; Sound, David Remedios; Music Director/Adaptation, Simon Deacon; Movement, Struan Leslie; PSM, Chris De Camillis; Dialects, Laura Hitt; Casting, Deborah Bowen; Flying, Flying by Foy; Cast: Remo Airaldi (Mr. Bumble), Steven Boyer (Noah Claypole/Tom Chitling), Thomas Derrah (Mr. Sowerberry/Mr. Grimwig/Mr. Fang), Gregory Derelian (Bill Sykes/Mrs. Sowerberry), Ned Eisenberg (Fagin), Carson Elrod (John Dawkins/The Artful Dodger), Jennifer Ikeda (Nancy), Elizabeth Jasicki (Rose Brownlow/Charlotte Sowerberry), Will LeBow (Mr. Brownlow), Karen MacDonald (Mrs. Bumble), Craig Pattison (Charley Bates), Lucas Steele (Toby Crackit), Michael Wartella (Oliver Twist); West Coast premiere presented in association with the American Repertory Theatre and Theatre for a New Audience; May 11–June 24, 2007

**Great Men of Genius** Created and performed by Mike Daisey; Director, Jean-Michele Gregory; Lighting, Stephanie Buchner; Lighting Assistant, Frederick Geffken; Electricians, Taryn Roraback &Andrea J. Schwartz; June 6–July 1, 2007

*Monique Fowler and Rebecca Watson in* To the Lighthouse
*(photo by Kevin Berne)*

# Berkshire Theatre Festival

Stockbridge, Massachusetts

Seventy-eighth Season

Artistic Director, Kate Maguire

## MAIN STAGE

**Amadeus** by Peter Shaffer; Director, Eric Hill; Sets, Karl Eigsti; Costumes, Olivera Gajic; Lighting, Matthew E. Adelson; Sound, Nathan Lee; Casting, Alan Filderman; Stage Manager, Jason Hindelang; Cast: Ron Bagden (Baron Gottfried van Swieten), James Barry (Venticelli One), Jonathan Epstein (Antonio Salieri), Tara Franklin (Constanze Weber), Randy Harrison (Wolfgang Amadeus Mozart), Walter Hudson (Joseph II), Bob Jaffe (Count Johann Kilian von Strack), Tom Story (Venticelli Two), Stephen Temperley (Count Franz Orsini-Rosenberg), Ensemble: Robin E. Cannon, Travis G. Daly, Joshua Davis, Aaron Costa Ganis, Sara Oliva, Meg Wieder; June 20–July 8, 2006

**Coastal Disturbances** by Tina Howe; Director, Mark Nelson; Sets; Bill Clark, Costumes, Laurie Churba; Lighting, Dan Kotlowitz; Sound/Composer, Scott Killian; Casting, Alan Filderman; Stage Manager, Linda Harris; Cast: Jeremy Davidson (Leo Hart), Annie Parisse (Holly Dancer), Marcia DeBonis (Faith Bigelow), Victoria Aline Flower (Miranda Bigelow), Jennifer Van Dyck (Arial Took), Rider Stanton (Winston Took), Patricia Conolly (M.J. Adams), Jack Davidson (Dr. Hamilton Adams), Francois Giroday (Andre Sor); July 11–July 29, 2006

**The Night of the Iguana** by Tennessee Williams; Director, Anders Cato; Sets, Carl Sprague; Cosutmes, Murell Horton; Lighting, Jeff Davis; Sound/Composer, Scott Killian; Casting, Alan Filderman; Stage Manager, Jason Hindelang; Cast: Amelia Campbell (Hannah Jelkes), Garret Dillahunt (Reverend T. Lawrence Shannon), Ricky Fromeyer (Pancho), Aaron Costa Ganis (Hank), Joshua Gunn (Pedro), Linda Hamilton (Maxine Faulk), Sam Kitchin (Jack Latta), Charlotte Maier (Miss Judith Fellows), Lauren Orkus (Charlotte Goodall), William Swan (Nonno (Jonathan Coffin); August 1–12, 2006

**The Heidi Chronicles** by Wendy Wasserstein; Director, Vivian Matalon; Sets, Neil Patalon; Costumes, Janus Stefanowicz; Lighting, David Lander; Sound, Dominic Scott Stauffer; Casting, Alan Filderman; Stage Manager, Linda Harris; Cast: Kate Jennings Grant (Heidi Holland), Lynn Hawley (Susan Johnston), Tom Story (Peter Patrone), Scott Lowell (Scoop Rosenbaum), Christopher Corts (Chris Boxer, Mark, Easter Bunny, Waiter, Ray), Jenn Harris (Fran, Lisa, April), Patricia Buckley (Jill, Debbie, Molly, Paula), Laura Heisler (Becky, Clara, Denise); August 15–September 2, 2006

## UNICORN STAGE

**The Illusion** by Pierre Corneille, freely adapted by Tony Kushner; Director, Richard Corley; Sets, Jack Magaw; Costumes, Murell Horton; Lighting, Holly Blomquist; Sound, Andrew Skomorowsky; Fight Director, Anthony J. Simotes; Stage Manager, Barbara Janice Kielhofer; Cast: Ben Beckley (Pridamant of Avignon), Zenzele Cooper (Melibea/ Isabelle/ Hippolyta), Matthew Crider (Matamore), Austin Durant (Alcandre), Kevin Dwyer (Pleribo/ Adraste/ Prince Florilame), Sarah Kauffman (Elicia/ Lyse/ Clarina), Philip Sletteland (Calisto/ Clindor/ Theogenes), Brian Weaver (The Amanuensis); May 25–June 24, 2006

**Where Has Tommy Flowers Gone?** by Terrence McNally; Director, E. Gray Simons III; Sets, Ian Zywica; Costumes, Jessica Risser-Milne; Lighting, Dan Kotlowitz; Sound, E. Gray Simons III; Stage Manager, Steve Horton; Cast: Brian Weaver (Tommy Flowers), Hannah Wilson (Greta/Tommy's Old Flame), Matthew Crider (Matamore), Sarah Kauffman (Tommy's Mother/First Lady), Nicole Marquez (Arnold), Robert Serrell (Ben Delight), Ben Rosenblatt (Hack/Manager/Tommy's Nephew/Tommy's Brother), Morgan Cox (Nedda Lemon), Lizzy Thrasher (Marilyn Monroe/Waitress/Bunny Barnum), Ensemble: Kristi Barron, Rebecca Berowski, Amber Bowman, Katie Edgerton, Laura Ferland, Hesley Harps, Matt Martin, Jessica Perelle, Rachel Ilana Salowitz, Eli Schneider, Alana Renee Waksman; June 28–July 22, 2006

**The Pilgrim Papers** by Stephen Temperley; Director, Vivian Matalon; Sets, R. Michael Miller; Costumes, Tracy Christensen; Lighting, Ann Wrightson; Sound, Craig Kaufman; Stage Manager, Barbara Janice Kielhofer; Cast: Martin Askin (Jones/Billington), Joshua Davis (Standish), Austin Durant (Narrator/ Squanto/Little Mary), Brent Michael Erdy (Robinson/Winslow), Phil Sletteland (Bradford), Arnica Skulstad-Brown (Dorothy), Justin Stoney (Peter/Ned); July 28–August 26, 2006

**Via Dolorosa** by David Hare; Director, Anders Cato; Sets, Chris Boone; Costumes, Olivera Gajic; Lighting, Michael Jarett; Sound, Scott Killian; Assistant Sets, Eliza Rankin; Stage Manager, Mary Costello; Cast: Jonathan Epstein (The Author); August 29–October 21, 2006

*Austin Durant in* Illusion *(photo by Kevin Sprague)*

# Caldwell Theatre Company

Boca Raton, Florida

Thirty-second Season

Artistic Director, Michael Hall

**Lend Me a Tenor** by Ken Ludwig; Director, Joe Warik; Sets, Tim Bennett; Costumes, Erin Amico; Lighting, Aaron Torgerson; PSM, James Danford; Cast: Terrell Hardcastle (Max), Autumn Horne (Maggie), Peter Haig (Saunders), Allan Baker (Tito), Connie SaLoutos (Maria), Bruce Linser (Bellhop), Kim Ostrenko (Diana), Elizabeth Dimon (Julia); July 19–August 13, 2006

*Bruce Linser, Peter Haig, Elizabeth Dimon, Kim Ostrenko, Autumn Horne, Allan Baker, Connie Saloutos, and Terrell Hardcastle in* Lend Me a Tenor *(photo by Sigvision)*

**The Decline and Fall of the Entire World As Seen Through the Eyes of Cole Porter** Music and Lyrics by Cole Porter, based on the New York production assembled and directed by Ben Bagley; Director, Michael Hall; Musical Director/Piano, Eric Alsford; Sets, Tim Bennett; Costumes, Eric Amico; Lighting, Aaron Torgerson; Video Projection Programmer, Sean Lawson; PSM, Jeffry George; Cast: Elizabeth Dimon (Woman #1), Connie SaLoutos (Woman #2), Suzy Jackson (Woman #3), Bruce Linser (Man #1), Terrell Hardcastle (Man #2); August 23–September 17, 2006

**Hunka Hunka Burnin' Love: An Elvis Presley Musical Tribute** Conceived and produced by Jack Lewin, created by Will Friedwald, Jay Leonhart, and Jack Lewin; Director, Kurt Stamm; Sets, Tim Bennett (adapted from the original sets by Todd Engle); Lighting, Jen Kules; Sound, Sean Lawson; Musical Director, Ted Firth; Associate Musical Directors, Dennis Blischak and Phil Hinton; Musical Arrangements, Tedd Firth and John Oddo; Ms. King's Wardrobe, Jump Apparel by Wendye Chaitin; PSM, Molly Elizabeth McCarter; Cast: Kelly King, Ryan Link, Tom LoSchiavo; November 5–December 17, 2006

**Steel Magnolias** by Robert Harling; Director, Michael Hall; Sets, Tim Bennett; Costumes, Eric Amico; Lighting, Thomas Salzman; PSM, George Kapetan; Cast: Elizabeth Dimon (Truvy), Margery Lowe (Annelle), Angie Radosh (Clairee), Lisa Manuli (Shelby), Laura Turnbull (M'Lynn), Pat Nesbit (Ouiser); December 30, 2006–February 11, 2007

**The Lion in Winter** by James Goldman; Director, Michael Hall; Sets, Tim Bennett; Costumes, Eric Amico; Lighting, Thomas Salzman; Sound, Sean Lawson; PSM, Marci A. Glotzer; Cast: Curt Hostetter (Henry II), Erin Joy Schmidt (Alais), Mark Whittington (John), Terrell Hardcastle (Geoffrey), Michael Polak (Richard Lionheart), Pat Nesbit (Eleanor), Bruce Linser (Philip); February 18–April 1, 2007

**The Clean House** by Sarah Ruhl; Director, Michael Hall; Sets, Tim Bennett; Costumes, Eric Amico; Lighting, John Hall; Sound, Sean Lawson; PSM, Molly Elizabeth McCarter; Cast: Karina Barros (Matilde), Pat Nesbit (Lane), Cary Anne Spear (Virginia), Dennis Creaghan (Charles), Harriet Oser (Ana); April 8–May 20, 2007

# Capital Repertory Theatfre

Albany, New York

Twenty-sixth Season

Artistic Director, Maggie Mancinelli-Cahill; Managing Director: Elizabeth Doran

**Five Course Love** Book, music and lyrics by Gregg Coffin; Director and Choreographer, Adam Pelty; Sets, Roman Tatarowicz; Lighting, Stephen Quandt; Costumes, Thom Heyer; Sound, Christopher St. Hilare; Musical Director, Randy Glass; Dance Captain, Tracy J. Wholf; Casting, Stephanie Klapper; PSM, Liz Reddick; Cast: Robert B. Cordell (Matt, Gino, Klaus, Guillermo, Clutch), Tracy J. Wholf (Barbie, Sofia, Gretchen, Rosalinda, Kitty), Michael Lluberes (Dean, Carlo, Heimlich, Ernesto, Pops). Band: Randy Glass (piano), Brendan Coyle (drums), Michael Wicks (bass); July 21–August 19, 2006.

**Intimate Apparel** by Lynn Nottage; Director, Maggie Mancinelli-Cahill; Sets, Roman Tatarowicz; Costumes, Joanne Haas; Lighting, Brian J. Lilienthal; Sound, Christopher St. Hilaire; Stage Manager, Liz Reddick; ASM, Karin Anderson; Cast: Rochelle Hogue (Esther Mills), Venida Evans (Mrs. Dickson), Yvonne Perry (Mrs. VanBuren), George Wynnyczuk (Mr. Marks), Tanesha Gary (Mayme), Maduka Steady (George Armstrong); September 15–October 14, 2006

*Maduka Steady and Tanesha Gary in* Intimate Apparel *(photo by Joe Schuyler)*

**The Underpants** by Steve Martin; Director, Michael Evan Haney; Sets, Robert Klingelhofer; Costumes, Thom Heyer; Lighting, Stephen Quandt; Sound, Jane Shaw; Casting, Stephanie Klapper; PSM, Diane McLean; Cast: Steve Boyer (Benjamin Cohen), Eva Dolan (Gertrute Deuter), Michael Rothaar (Klingelhoff), Marina Squerciati (Louise Maske), Frank Vlastnik (Frank Versati), Kurt Zischke (Theo Maske); November 3–December 2, 2006

**Triple Espresso** by Bill Arnold Michael Pearce Donley and Bob Stromberg; Director, William Partlan; Sets, Nayna Ramey; Lighting, Michael Klaers; Costumes, Kathleen Egan; Sound, John Markiewicz; Stage Manager, Jennifer Hamilton; Cast: Keith Raey (Buzz Maxwell), Danny Jacobs (Hugh Butternut), Duane Dean (Bobby Bean); December 8–31, 2006

**Take Me Out** by Richard Greenberg; Director, Kirk Jackson; Sets, Dan Conway; Costumes, Barbara Wolfe; Lighting, Michael Giannitti; Sound, Neil McFadden; Casting; PSM, Karin Anderson; Cast: William Peden (Kippy Sunderstrom), Jaque Cowart II (Darren Lemming), Jake Suffian (Shane Mungitt), Humberto Domingo Fabre (Martinez), Richard Damasco (Rodriguez), Todd Gebhart (Jason Chenier), Richard Lounello (Toddy Koovitz), Kevin Craig West (Davey Battle), Oliver Wadsworth (Mason Marzac), Nobuo Inubushi (Takeshi Kawabata), Richard Schofield (Skipper/Mr. William Danziger); January 19–February 17, 2007

*Jacques Cowart III and William Peden in* Take Me Out
*(photo by Joe Schuyler)*

**It Ain't Nothin' But the Blues** by Charles Bevel, Lita Gaithers, Randal Myler, Ron Taylor, and Dan Wheetman; Director and Choreographer, Alan Weeks; Music Director, David Malachowski; Sets, Steven Perry; Costumes, Tirza Chappell; Sound, Christopher St. Hilaire; Lighting, Rachel Budin; Stage Manager, Adele Nadine Traub; Cast: Rob Barnes, Cicily Daniels, Jonathan Rosen, Julie Tolivar, Carole Troll, Juson Williams; Band: David Malachowski (guitar), Gary Burke (drums), Bob Green (bass), Pete Levin (piano); March 9–April 7, 2007

**The Crucible** by Arthur Miller; Director, Maggie Mancinelli-Cahill; Sets, Michael Heil; Lighting, Deborah Constantine; Cast: Jeremy Holm (John Procter), Shannon Rafferty (Abigail Williams), Kim Stauffer (Elizabeth Proctor), Terry Rabine (Reverend Parris), Marjorie Johnson (Tituba) Ruth Salter (Sarah Good), Kent Burnham (Reverend John Hale), Carol Charniga (Rebecca Nurse), Dane Knell (Giles Corey), Lauren Holop Kaufman (Betty Parris), Caitlin Davis (Mercy Lewis), Therese Avitabile (Mary Warren), Emily Crockett (Susanna Wallcott), Richard Mawe (Deputy Governor Danforth), Brian Massman (Judge Hathorne), Paula Ginder (Ann Putnam), Richard Harte (Thomas Putnam), Keith Mueller (John Willard), Allan Foster (Francis Nurse), Kris Anderson (Cheever); April 27–May 26, 2007

# CENTERSTAGE

Baltimore, Maryland

Forty-fourth Season

Artistic Director, Irene Lewis; Managing Director, Michael Ross

**The Three Sisters** by Anton Chekhov, translated by Paul Schmidt; Director, Irene Lewis; Sets, Robert Israel; Costumes, Candice Donnelly; Lighting, Mimi Jordan Sherin; Sound, David Budries; Composer/Music Director, Eric Svejcar; Choreography, John Carrafa; Fight Director, J. Allen Suddeth; Production Dramaturg, Gavin Witt; Associate Production Dramaturg, Dina Epshteyn; Casting, Harriet Bass; Stage Manager, Debra Acquavella; ASM, Mike Schleifer; Cast: David Adkins (Vershinin), Christine Marie Brown (Masha), Willy Conley (Fedotik), Gene Farber (Solyony), Kristin Fiorella (Natasha), Mary Fogarty (Anfisa), Joe Hickey (Kulygin), Mahira Kakkar (Irina), Laurence O'Dwyer (Chebutykin), Andy Paterson (Rohde), Stacy Ross/Lise Bruneau (Olga), Matt Bradford Sullivan (Tuzenbach), Evan Thompson (Ferapont), Tony Ward (Andrey); September 15–October 29, 2006

**Death and the Maiden** by Ariel Dorfman; Director, Lillian Groag; Sets, Todd Rosenthal; Costumes, Martha Hally; Lighting, Mark McCullough; Sound, Paul Peterson; Fight Director, J. Allen Suddeth; Production Dramaturg, Otis Ramsey-Zöe; Casting, Janet Foster; Assistant Director, Jillian T. Gaul; Stage Manager, Mike Schleifer; ASM, Debra Acquavella; Cast: Stephen Rowe (Roberto Miranda), Mhari Sandoval (Paulina Salas), Triney Sandoval (Gerardo Escobar); October 26–November 26, 2006

**The Boys From Syracuse** Music by Richard Rodgers, lyrics by Lorenz Hart, book by George Abbott; Director, David Schweizer; Music Director/Orchestrator, Wayne Barker; Choreography, Dan Knechtges; Sets, Allen Moyer; Costumes, David Zinn; Lighting, Christopher Akerlind; Sound, Ryan Rumery; Production Dramaturg, Gavin Witt; Assistant Choreography, Isis Masoud; Assistant Director, Paul Wissman; Casting, Janet Foster; Orchestra Contractor, Chris Hofer; Stage Manager, Debra Acquavella; ASM, Keri Schultz; Cast: Chris Wells (Sorcerer/Duke), Michael Winther (Dromio of Syracuse), Kevin R. Free (Dromio of Ephesus), Stephen Valahovic/Edward Watts (Sergeant), John Ramsey (Aegeon/Goldsmith), Paolo Montalban (Antipholus of Ephesus), Terry Lavell (Tailor/Seeress), Christopher Sergeeff (Tailor's Apprentice/Merchant of Ephesus), Manu Narayan (Antipholus of Syracuse), Kyle DesChamps (Merchant of Syracuse), Laura Lee Anderson (Maid/Courtesan), Rosa Curry/Felicia R. Boswell (Maid/Courtesan), Jessica Wu (Maid/Courtesan), Charlie Parker (Luce), Charlotte Cohn (Adriana), Rona Figueroa (Luciana), Blair Ross (Madame Courtesan); Orchestra: Wayne Barker (keyboards), Matt Belzer (woodwinds), Jared Denhard (trombone), Chris Hofer (bass), Robert LaForce (percussion), Zoltan Racz (accordion); December 8, 2006–January 14, 2007

*The Company of* The Boys From Syracuse *(photo by Richard Anderson)*

**Trouble in Mind** by Alice Childress; Director, Irene Lewis; Sets, David Korins; Costumes, Catherine Zuber; Lighting, Rui Rita; Sound, David Budries; Dialect Coach, Deena Burke; Dramaturg, Catherine Sheehy; Casting, Janet Foster; Stage Manager, Mike Schleifer; ASM, Debra Acquavella; Cast: Starla Benford (Millie Davis), E. Faye Butler (Wiletta Mayer), Thomas Jefferson Byrd (Sheldon Forrester), Maria Dizzia (Judy Sears), Daren Kelly (Bill O'Wray), LeRoy McClain (John Nevins), Garrett Neergaard (Eddie Fenton), Laurence O'Dwyer (Henry), B. Thomas Rinaldi (Stagehand), Craig Wroe (Al Manners); February 2–March 4, 2007

*Garrett Neergaard, E. Faye Butler (foreground), Starla Benford and Maria Dizzia in* Trouble in Mind *(photo by Richard Anderson)*

**Ah, Wilderness!** by Eugene O'Neill; Director, Melia Bensussen; Sets, James Noone; Costumes, Clint Ramos; Lighting, Dan Kotlowitz; Sound, David Remedios; Music Director, Lawrence J. Cione; Fight Director, J. Allen Suddeth; Dialect Coach, Deena Burke; Dramaturg, Dina Epshteyn; Casting, Harriet Bass; Stage Manager, Debra Acquavella; ASM, Mike Schleifer; Cast: Connor Aikin/Bradley Bowers (Tommy Miller), Gloria Biegler (Lily Miller), Tom Bloom (Nat Miller), Bob Braswell (Richard Miller), Eric L. Burton (Bartender), Lawrence J. Cione (Pianist), Leo Erickson (David McComber), Tim Getman (Salesman), Kimesia Hartz (Belle/Muriel McComber), Elizabeth Hess (Essie Miller), Kristen Lewis (Mildred Miller), Timothy Andrés Pabon (Wint Selby), Sandra Struthers (Nora), Peter Van Wagner (Sid Davis), Michael Zlabinger (Arthur Miller); March 16–April 15, 2007

**Thing of Dry Hours** by Naomi Wallace; Director, Kwame Kwei-Armah; Sets, Riccardo Hernández; Costumes, David Burdick; Lighting, Michelle Habeck; Sound, Shane Rettig; Fight Director, J. Allen Suddeth; Speech Consultant, Gillian Lane-Plescia; Dramaturg, Gavin Witt; Casting, Harriet Bass; Stage Manager, Mike Schleifer; ASM, Debra Acquavella; Cast: Steven Cole Hughes (Corbin Teel), Erika LaVonn (Cali Hogan), Roger Robinson (Tice Hogan); April 27–June 3, 2007

# Center Theatre Group

Los Angeles, California

Fortieth Season

Artistic Director, Michael Ritchie, Managing Director, Charles Dillingham

## MARK TAPER FORUM

**Doubt** by John Patrick Shanley; Director, Doug Hughes; Sets, John Lee Beatty; Costumes, Catherine Zuber; Lighting, Pat Collins; Original Music and Sound, David Van Tieghem; Casting, Nancy Piccione/David Caparelliotis; PSM, Charles Means; Stage Manager, Marian Dewitt; Cast: Cherry Jones (Sister Aloysius), Lisa Joyce (Sister James), Adriane Lenox (Mrs. Muller), Chris McGarry (Father Flynn); September 22–October 29, 2006

**Nightingale** by Lynn Redgrave; Director, Joseph Hardy; Sets, Tobin Ost; Costumes, Candice Cain; Lighting, Rui Rita; Sound, Cricket S. Myers; PSM, David S. Franklin; Stage Manager, Michelle Blair; Cast: Lynn Redgrave (Mildred Asher); U.S. Premiere; October 4–November 19, 2006

**13** Music and lyrics by Jason Robert Brown, book by Dan Elish; Director, Todd Graff; Choreography, Michele Lynch; Sets, David Gallo; Costumes, Candice Cain; Lighting, Mike Baldassari; Sound, Duncan Robert Edwards; Projections, Zachary Borovay; Music Director, David O; Casting, Erika Sellin, Jen Rudin Pearson, PSM, William Coiner; Stage Managers, James T. McDermott & Elizabeth Atkinson; Cast: Ricky Ashley (Evan), Caitlin Baunoch (Lucy), Jenáe Burrows (Charlotte), Emma Degerstedt (Kendra), Tinashe Kachingwe (Cassie), Tyler Mann (Archie), Sara Niemietz (Patrice), Ryan Ogburn (Ritchie), J.D. Phillips (Brett), Ellington Ratliff (Simon, Principal), Chloé Smith (Molly), Christian Vandal (Eddie), Seth Zibalese (Malcolm); World Premiere; December 22, 2006–February 18, 2007

**Distracted** by Lisa Loomer; Director, Leonard Foglia; Set/Projections, Elaine J. McCarthy; Costumes, Robert Blackman; Lighting, Russell H. Champa; Sound, Jon Gottlieb; Casting, Erika Sellin; PSM, David S. Franklin; Stage Manager, Michelle Blair; Cast: Stephanie Berry (Mrs. Holly/Dr. Waller/Nurse/Carolyn/Waitress), Johanna Day (Vera), Marita Geraghty (Sherry), Emma Hunton (Natalie), Bronson Pinchot (Dr. Broder/Dr. Jinks/Dr. Karnes/Dr. Zavala), Ray Porter (Dad), Hudson Thames (Jesse), Rita Wilson (Mama); World Premiere; March 15–April 29, 2007

**Yellow Face** by David Henry Hwang; Director, Leigh Silverman; Sets, David Korins; Costumes, Myung Hee Cho; Lighting, Donald Holder; Sound, Darron L. West; Casting, Jordan Thaler, Heidi Griffiths, Erika Sellin; PSM, James T. McDermott; Stage Manager, Elizabeth Atkinson; Cast: Julienne Hanzelka Kim (Leah/Others), Kathryn A. Layng (Jane/Miles/Others), Hoon Lee (DHH), Tzi Ma (HYH/Others), Lucas Caleb Rooney (Stuart, Rocco, Others), Peter Scanavino (Marcus), Tony Torn (The Announcer); World Premiere; May 10–July 1, 2007

## AHMANSON THEATRE (National Touring Shows)

**The Light in the Piazza** Book by Craig Lucas, music and lyrics by Adam Guettel; based on a novel by Elizabeth Spencer; Director, Bartlett Sher; Sets, Michael Yeargan; Costumes, Catherine Zuber; Lighting, Christopher Akerlind; Sound, Acme Sound Partners; Orchestrations, Ted Sperling & Adam Guettel; Music Direction, Kimberly Grigsby; Musical Staging, Jonathan Butterell; Casting, Janet Foster; PSM, David Lober; Stage Manager, Anna Belle Gilbert; Cast: Christine Andreas (Margaret Johnson), Craig Bennett (Priest/Ensemble), Wendi Bergamini (Ensemble), David Burnham (Fabrizio Naccarelli), Laurent Giroux (Ensemble), Laura Griffith (Franca Naccarelli), Jonathan Hammond (Giuseppe Naccarelli), Sean Hayden (Ensemble), Leslie Henstock (Ensemble), Prudence Wright Holmes (Ensemble), Evangelia Kingsley (Ensemble), David Ledingham (Signor Naccarelli), Adam Overett (Ensemble), Elena Shaddow (Clara Johnson), Brian Sutherland (Roy Johnson), Diane Sutherland (Signora Naccarelli); October 31–December 10, 2006

**Edward Scissorhands** Devised, directed, and choreographed by Matthew Bourne; Set/Costumes, Lez Brotherston; Lighting, Howard Harrison; Sound, Paul Groothuis; Music/Arrangements, Terry Davies; Music Director, Andrew Bryan; Cast: Scott Ambler (Bill Boggs), Sam Archer (Edward Scissorhands), Kerry Biggin (Kim Boggs/Candy Covitt/Cheerleader), Madelaine Brennan (Peg Boggs/Tiffany Covitt/Old Kim/TV Reporter), Ross Carpenter (Gabriel Evercreech/Rev. Judas Evercreech), Gareth Charlton (Mayor Franklin Upton, III), Andrew Corbett (Bill Boggs/George Monroe/Manny Grubb/The Inventor/TV Reporter/Photographer), Gavin Eden (Kevin Boggs/Little Edward), Adam Galbraith (Manny Grubb/James (Jim) Upton/Mayor Franklin Upton, III/The Inventor, Photographer), Sophia Dominique Hurdley (Bunny Monroe/Sandra Grubb), Steve Kirkham (George Monroe/TV Reporter), Dena Lague (Sandra Grubb), Rachel Lancaster (Esmeralda

Evercreech/Marilyn-Ann Evercreech/Candy Covitt/Gloria Grubb/Cheerleader), James Leece (James (Jim) Upton/Brad Covitt), Matthew Malthouse (Rev. Judas Evercreech), Drew McOnie (Kevin Boggs/Gerald Monroe/Chase Covitt/Sheldon Grubb/Little Edward), Michela Meazza (Joyce Monroe), Ebony Molina (Mrs. Charity Upton), Rachel Morrow (Esmeralda Evercreech/Peg Boggs/Old Kim), Etta Murfitt (Peg Boggs), Luke Murphy (Sheldon Grubb), Gemma Payne (Darlene Upton), Jake Samuels (Brad Covitt), Mikah Smillie (Joyce Monroe/Bunny Monroe/Charity Upton/Tiffany Covitt/Marilyn-Ann Evercreech/TV Reporter), Mami Tomotani (Gloria Grubb/Darlene Upton), Hannah Vassallo (Kim Boggs/Candy Covitt/Cheerleader), Shaun Walters (Gerald Monroe), Shelby Williams (Marilyn-Ann Evercreech), Philip Willingham (Chase Covitt/Gabriel Evercreech), Chloe Wilkinson (Tiffany Covitt/Cheerleader/TV Reporter), Richard Windsor (Edward Scissorhands); December 12–31, 2006

*Richard Winsor in* Edward Scissorhands *(photo by Bill Cooper)*

**Who's Afraid of Virginia Woolf?** by Edward Albee; Director, Anthony Page; Sets, John Lee Beatty; Costumes, Jane Greenwood, Lighting, Peter Kaczorowski; Sound, Mark Bennett & Michael Creason; Fight Director, Rick Sordelet; Casting, Jay Binder and Jack Bowdan; PSM; Susie Cordon; Stage Manager, Allison Sommers; Cast: Kathleen Early (Honey), David Furr (Nick), Bill Irwin (George), Kathleen Turner (Martha); February 6–March 18, 2007

**Twelve Angry Men** by Reginald Rose; Director, Scott Ellis; Sets, Allen Moyer; Costumes, Michael Krass; Lighting, Paul Palazzo; Sound, Brian Ronan; Original Compositions, John Gromada; Fight Director, Rick Sordelet; Technical Supervisor, Steve Beers; Casting, Jim Carnahan and Mele Nagler; PSM; Michael McEowen; Stage Manager, Megan Schneid; Cast: Charles Borland (Juror Six), Todd Cerveris (Juror Two), T. Scott Cunningham (Juror Twelve), Julian Gamble (Juror Ten), Jeffrey Hayenga (Juror Four), David Lively (Juror Eleven), Alan Mandell (Juror Nine), Randle Mell (Juror Three), Mark Morettini (Juror Seven), Patrick New (Guard), Robert Prosky (Voice of the Judge), Jim Saltouros (Juror Five), Richard Thomas (Juror Eight), George Wendt (Juror One); March 28–May 6, 2007

**Jersey Boys** Book by Marshall Brickman and Rick Elice, music by Bob Gaudio, lyrics by Bob Crewe; Director, Des McAnuff; Sets, Klara Zieglerova; Costumes, Jess Goldstein; Lighting, Howell Binkley; Sound, Steve Canyon Kennedy; Music Direction/Vocal Arrangements/Incidental Music, Ron Melrose; Choreography, Sergio Trujillo; Projections, Michael Clark; Fight Director, Steve Rankin; Orchestrations, Steve Orich; Music Coordinator, John Miller; Technical Supervisor, Peter Fulbright; Casting, Tara Rubin; PSM, Tripp Phillips; Stage Manager, Lori Byars; Cast: John Altieri (Bob Crew/Others), Miles Aubrey (Nick DeVito/Stosh/Norman Waxman/Charlie Calello/Others), Erich Bergen (Bob Gaudio), Sandra DeNise (Church Lady/Angel, Lorraine/Others), Rick Faugno (Frankie Valli), Eric Gutman (Stanley/Hank Majewski/Crewe's PA/Accountant/Joe Long/Others), Leo Huppert (Thug), Michael Ingersoll (Nick Massi), Christopher Kale Jones (Frankie Valli), Nathan Klau (Detective Two/Billy Dixon/Others), Brandon Matthieus (French Rap Star/Detective One/Hal Miller/Barry Belson/Police Officer/Davis/Others), Deven May (Tommy DeVito), Jackie Seiden (Mary Delgado/Angel/Others), Brian Silverman (Thug), Courter Simmons (Joey/Recording Studio Engineer/Others), Joseph Siravo (Gyp DeCarlo/Others), Melissa Strom (Frankie's Mother/Nick's Date/Miss Frankie Nolan/Bob's Party Girl/Angel/Francine/Others); May 25–August 31, 2007

## KIRK DOUGLAS THEATRE

**Nighthawks** by Douglas Steinberg; Director, Stefan Novinski; Sets, Donna Marquet; Costumes, A. Jeffrey Schoenberg; Lighting, Rand Ryan; Original Music Composer, Michael Roth; Casting, Erika Sellin; PSM, Scott Harrison; Cast: Dan Castellaneta (Quig), Dennis Cockrum (Jimmy Nickels), Brian T. Finney (Sam), Joe Fria (Clive), Kelly Karbacz (Lucy), Colette Kilroy (Mae), Morgan Rusler (The Customer); World Premiere; August 27–September 24, 2006

**In the Continuum** by Danai Gurira and Nikkole Salter; Director, Robert O'Hara; Sets, Peter R. Feuchtwanger; Costumes, Sarah Hillard; Lighting, Colin D. Young; Sound, Lindsay Jones; Properties Designer, Jay Duckworth; Casting, Stephanie Klapper; PSM, Samone B. Weissman; Cast: Danai Gurira (Abigail, Others), Nikkole Salter (Nia, Others); November 12–December 10, 2006

**Dogeaters** by Jessica Hagedorn; Director, Jon Lawrence Rivera; Sets, John H. Binkley; Original Costumes, Marya Krakowiak; Costumes, Dianne K. Graebner; Lighting, Steven Young; Sound, Bob Blackburn; Choreography, Kay Cole; PSM, Andrea Lovino; Stage Manager, Scott Harrison; Cast: Robert Almodovar (Freddie Gonzaga/Severo "Chuchi" Alcran/Ka Edgar/Military Man #2), Gino Aquino (Santos Tirador/Lieutenant Pepe Carreon/Tito Alvarez/Young Man), Christine Avila (Leonor Ledesma/Lola Narcisa), Esperanza Catubig (Daisy Avila/Young Woman), Ivan Davila (Andres "Perlita" Alacran), Fran de Leon (Trinidad "Trini" Gamboa), Liza Del Mundo (Barbara Villanueva/Ka Lydia), Ramón de Ocampo (Joey Sands), Antoine Reynaldo Diel (Romeo Rosales/Doorman/Ka Pablo/Kalinga Tribesman), Golda Inquito (Pucha Gonzaga/Jingle Singer), Alberto Isaac (Senator Domingo Avila/"Uncle"), Kennedy Kabasares (Man with Guitar/Waiter #2/Steve Jacobs/Pedro Boomboom Alacran/Kalinga Tribesman), Dom Magwili (General Nicasio Ledesma), Natsuko Ohama (Imelda Marcos), Giovanni Ortega (Chiquiting Moreno), Orlando Pabotoy (Nestor Noralez), Elizabeth Pan (Rio Gonzaga), Ed Ramolete (Mang Berto/Waiter #1/Military Man #1/the Shooter/Kalinga Tribesman), Nick Salamone (Rainer Fassbinder/Father Jean Mallat/Bob Stone), Minerva Vier (Lolita Luna/Jingle Singer); January 14–February 11, 2007

**Sleeping Beauty Wakes** Book by Rachel Sheinkin, music and lyrics by Brendan Milburn and Valerie Vigoda; Director/Choreograper, Jeff Calhoun; Sets, Tobin Ost; Costumes, Maggie Morgan; Lighting, Michael Gilliam; Sound, Eric Snodgrass; ASL Masters, Linda Bove & Betsy Ford; Production Interpreter, Catherine Richardson Kiwitt; Casting, Bonnie Grisan; PSM, William Coiner; Stage Manager, Seth A. Kolarsky; Cast: Erika Amato (Night Terror Patient/Royal Servant/Voice of Clinic Director/Voice of Bad Fairy), Deanne Bray (Clinic Director/Bad Fairy), Clinton Derricks-Carroll (King), Kevin Earley (Insomniac/Royal Messenger/Voice of Prince Charming/Townsperson), Shannon Ford (Drummer/Urashima Taro/Voice of Sleepwalker), Russell Harvard (Orderly/Groundskeeper's Son), Troy Kotsur (Sleepwalker/Prince Charming/Servant), Christia Mantzke (Restless Leg Syndrome Sufferer/Queen/Voice of Snow White), Brendan Milburn (Rip Van Winkle/Voice of Orderly/Voice of Groundskeeper's Son), Valerie Vigoda (Voice of Sleeping Beauty/Snow White), Alexandria Wailes (Beauty); World Premiere; March 31–May 13, 2007

**Come Back, Little Sheba** by William Inge; Director, Michael Pressman; Sets, James Noone; Costumes, Jennifer von Mayrhauser; Lighting, Jane Cox; Sound, Cricket S. Myers; Original Music, Peter Golub; Casting, Bonnie Grisan; PSM, David S. Franklin; Stage Manager, Andrea Iovino; Cast: Roger Aaron Brown (Ed Anderson), Josh Cooke (Turk), Michael Dempsey (Elmo Huston), Jenna Gavigan (Marie), Bill Heck (Bruce), Lyle Kanouse (Postman), Joe Mahon (Messenger), S. Epatha Merkerson (Lola), Alan Rosenberg (Doc), Brenda Wehle (Mrs. Coffman), Matthew J. Williamson (Milkman); June 17–July 15, 2007

# Cincinnati Playhouse in the Park

Cincinnati, Ohio

Forty-seventh Season

Producing Artistic Director, Edward Stern; Executive Director, Buzz Ward

**Of Mice and Men** by John Steinbeck; Director, Edward Stern; Sets, Paul Shortt; Costumes, Kristine Kearney; Lighting, James Sale; Sound, Chuck Hatcher; PSM, Jenifer Morrow; Stage Manager, Suann Pollock; Cast: Marc Aden Gray (George), Brendan Averett (Lennie), Dane Knell (Candy), Kenneth Albers (The Boss), Vince Nappo (Curley), Peter Bretz (Slim), Anne Bowles (Curley's Wife), Christian Kohn (Carlson), Kevin Crowley (Whit), Michael Anthony Williams (Crooks); September 5–October 6, 2006

**In the Continuum** by Danai Gurira and Nikkole Salter; Director, Robert O'Hara; Sets, Peter R. Feuchtwanger; Costumes, Sarah Hillard; Lighting, Colin D. Young; Sound, Lindsay Jones; Properties, Jay Duckworth; PSM, Samone Weissman; Cast: Tinashe Kajese (Abigail and Others), Nikkole Salter (Nia and Others); September 30–October 29, 2006

*Brendan Averett and Marc Aden Gray in* Of Mice and Men *(photo by Sandy Underwood)*

**Ace** Music by Richard Oberacker, book and lyrics by Robert Taylor and Richard Oberacker; Director, Stafford Arima; Choreography, Andrew Palermo; Music Director, David Kreppel; Orchestrator, Greg Anthony; Sets, David Korins; Costumes, Marie Anne Chiment; Lighting, Christopher Akerlind; Sounds, John H. Shivers and David Patridge, First Stage Manager, Andrea L. Shell; Second Stage Manager, Jenifer Morrow; Cast: Noah Galvin (Billy), Traci Lyn Thomas (Mrs. Crandall/Clara Whitlow), Jessica Boevers (Elizabeth), Amy Bodnar (Louise), Duke Lafoon (Edward/Stampley), Matt Bogart (Ace), Chris Peluso (John Robert), Wesley Zurick (School Bully/Ensemble), Evan Martin (Sidekick/Young Charlie/Ensemble), Heather Ayers (Ruth), Gabrielle Boyadjian (Emily), Gabrielle Stravelli

*Chris Peluso in* Ace *(photo by Sandy Underwood)*

(Anique/Ensemble), Susan Kokot Stokes (Teacher/Ensemble), Kelli Barrett (Nurse/Ensemble), James Judy (Toy Store Owner/Colonel Whitlow/Chennault/Ensemble), Richard Barth (Lieutenant Sanders/Sullivan/Ensemble), Danny Rothman (Cooper/Myron/Ensemble), Kevin Reed (Tennaman/Stein/Ensemble); World premiere; October 17–November 17, 2006

**This Wonderful Life** by Steve Murray; conceived by Mark Setlock; Director, Martha Banta; Sets, James F. Wolk; Costumes, Gordon DeVinney; Lighting, Mary Louise Geiger; Sound, Jill B.C. Du Boff; Stage Manager, Suann Pollock; Cast: Harry Bouvy (George Bailey and Others); November 11–December 23, 2006

**A Christmas Carol** by Charles Dickens, adapted by Howard Dallin; Director, Michael Evan Haney; Sets, James Leonard Joy; Costumes, David Murin; Lighting, Kirk Bookman; Sound/Composer, David B. Smith; Lighting Contractor, Susan Terrano; Costume Coordinator, Cindy Witherspoon; Music Director, Rebecca N. Childs; Choreography, Dee Anne Bryll; PSM, Jenifer Morrow; First Stage Manager, Andrea L. Shell; Second Stage Manager, Suann Pollock; Cast: Bruce Cromer (Ebenezer Scrooge), Stephen Skiles (Mr. Cupp/Percy/Rich Father at Fezziwig's), Ron Simons (Mr. Sosser/Tailor at Fezziwig's/Topper/Man with Shoe Shine), Andy Prosky (Bob Cratchit/Schoolmaster Oxlip), Tony Roach (Fred), Gregory Procaccino (Jacob Marley/Old Joe), Dale Hodges (Ghost of Christmas Past/Rose/Mrs. Peake), Evan Martin (Boy Scrooge/Boy at Fezziwig's/Bootblack), Alexandra Roberts (Fan/Guest at Fezziwig's), Keith Jochim (Mr. Fezziwig/Ghost of Christmas Present), Amy Warner (Mrs. Fezziwig/Patience), Ryan Crowder (Dick Wilkins/Streets), Jennifer McConnell (Rich Caroler/Mary at Fezziwig's/Streets), Todd Lawson (Young and Mature Scrooge/Ghost of Christmas Future), Shannon Koob (Belle/Catherine Margaret), Jace Smykil (Rich Caroler/Constable at Fezziwig's), Regina Pugh (Mrs. Cratchit/Laundress), Cullen Cornelius Arbaugh (Peter Cratchit/Gregory/Apprentice at Fezziwig's), Jo Ellen Pellman (Belinda Cratchit/Guest at Fezziwig's), Corri Elizabeth Johnson (Martha Cratchit/Guest at Fezziwig's), Asa Trent Franckewitz (Tiny Tim), Marcy Amell (Poor Caroler/Rich Wife at Fezziwig's), Anthony Trujillo (Poor Caroler/Poulterer/Acountant at Fezziwig's), Nathan Whitmer (Man with Pipe/Baker at Fezziwig's/Streets), Jack Bender (Matthew/Ignorance), Emmye Kearney (Want/Guest at Fezziwig's), Laura Montes (Mrs. Dilber/Guest at Fezziwig's/Streets), Joel Raffee (Lawyer at Fezziwig's/Undertaker/Streets), Gregory Boglin (Charles/Apprentice at Fezziwig's/George); December 2–30, 2006

**Low** Written, produced, and performed by Rha Goddess; Director/Development, Chay Yew; Sound/Composition, Darrin Ross; Additional Composition, Baba Israel and Rha Goddess; Lighting, Sabrina Hamilton; Movement Consultant, Rennie Harris; Stage Manager, Sarah Goshman; Cast: Rha Goddess (Lowquesha and Others); January 10–13, 2007

**The Catholic Girl's Guide to Losing Your Virginity** by Annie Hendy; Director, Richard E. Hess; Stage Manager, Jamie Sullivan; Cast: Annie Hendy (Lizzy); David Zelina (All Other Characters); January 17–21, 2007

**Pure Confidence** by Carlyle Brown; Director, Kent Gash; Sets, Emily Beck; Costumes, Austin K. Sanderson; Lighting, Liz Lee; Sound, Eric Stahlhammer; First Stage Manager, Suann Pollock; Second Stage Managers, Wendy J. Dorn and Andrea L. Shell; Cast: John G. Preston (George DeWitt/Hotel Clerk), William Parry (Colonel Wiley Johnson), Gavin Lawrence (Simon Cato), Maureen Silliman (Mattie Johnson), Ron Riley (Auctioneer/Reporter), Kelly Taffe (Caroline); January 16–February 16, 2007

**1:23** by Carson Kreitzer; Director, Mark Wing-Davey; Set, Douglas Stein & Peter Ksander; Costumes, Kaye Voyce; Lighting, David Weiner; Sound/Composer, Marc Gwinn; Video Designer, Ruppert Bohle; PSM, Jenifer Morrow; Cast: Josh Shirley (McManus), Deborah Knox (Susan), Eva Kaminsky (Andrea), Robert Elliott (Stevens), Rege Lewis (The Carjacker), Shirley Roeca (Juana/La Llorona); World Premiere; February 3–March 4, 2007

**Reckless** by Craig Lucas; Director, Michael Evan Haney; Set/Lighting, Kevin Rigdon; Costumes, Gordon DeVinney; Sound, Jill B.C. DuBoff; First Stage Manager, Andrea L. Shell; Second Stage Manager, Suann Pollock; Cast: Ericka Kreutz (Rachel), Jay Stratton (Tom/Game Show Contestant/Man in Mask/Tom Jr.), Jim Wisniewski (Lloyd), Erin Noel Grennan (Pooty/Talk Show Guest), Michael Brian Dunn (Roy/Tim Timko/Talk Show Host), Bernadette Quigley (Trish/First Derelict/Woman Patient/Game Show Contestant), Amy Warner (Doctors One Through Six), Joel Raffee (Second Derelict/Delivery Boy/Game Show Contestant), Nathan Whitmer (Third Derelict/Game Show Contestant), Laura Montes (Game Show Assistant/Receptionist); March 6–April 6, 2007

**Murderers** by Jeffrey Hatcher; Director, Sarah Gioia; Sets, Joseph P. Tilford; Costumes, Gordon DeVinney; Lighting, Betsy Adams; Stage Manager, Wendy J. Dorn; Cast: Steve Hendrickson (Gerald), Rita Gardner (Lucy), Carolyn Swift (Minka); March 24–April 28, 2007

**Sherlock Holmes: The Final Adventure** by Steven Dietz; based on the original 1899 play by William Gillette and Arthur Conan Doyle; Director, Edward Stern; Sets, Neil Patel; Costumes, Elizabeth Covey; Lighting, Robert Wierzel; Sound, Matt Callahan; PSM, Jenifer Morrow; Stage Manager, Suann Pollock; Cast: Joris Stuyck (Sherlock Holmes), Howard Kaye (Doctor Watson), Michael Haworth (Professor Moriarty), Daniel Freedom Stewart (The King of Bohemia), Brandy Burre (Irene Adler), David Huber (James Larrabee), William McNulty (Sid Prince/Clergyman), Carine Montbertrand (Madge Larrabee); Ensemble: Marcy Amell, Ryan Crowder, Joel Raffee, Jace Smykil, Anthony Trujillo, Nathan Whitmer; April 24–May 25, 2007

**Smoke on the Mountain Homecoming** by Connie Ray, conceived and directed by Alan Bailey; Musical Director/Arrangements, Mike Craver; Sets, Peter Harrison; Costumes, Jeanette deJong; Lighting, Susan Terrano; Stage Manager, Andrea L. Shell; Cast: Tommy Hancock (Stanley Sanders), Scott Wakefield (Burl Sanders), Giorgio Litt (Dennis Sanders), Constance Barron (Vera Sanders),

Angela Brinton Mack (Denise Sanders Culpepper), David Hemsley Caldwell (Reverend Mervin Oglethorpe), Tess Hartman (June Sanders Oglethorpe); May 5–June 24, 2007

*Eva Kaminsky and Josh Shirley in* 1:23 *(photo by Sandy Underwood)*

## City Theatre Company

Pittsburgh, Pennsylvania

Thirty-second Season

Artistic Director, Tracy Brigden; Managing Director, Greg Quinlan

**The Good Body** by Eve Ensler; Director, Tracy Brigden; Sets, Jeff Cowie; Costumes, Michael McAleer; Lighting, Marcus Doshi; Sound, Elizabeth Atkinson; PSM, Patti Kelly; Production Assistant, Lissa Brennan; Cast: Brigitte Viellieu-Davis (Eve), Laurie Klatscher (Woman 1), Erica Bradshaw (Woman 2); October 5–29, 2006

**A Picasso** by Jeffrey Hatcher; Director, Stuart Carden; Sets, Fred Kinney; Costumes, Angela M. Vesco; Lighting, Jim French; Sound, Elizabeth Atkinson; PSM, Patti Kelly; Cast: Mark Zeisler (Pablo Picasso), Rebecca Harris (Miss Fischer); November 9–December 17, 2006

*Rebecca Harris and Mark Zeisler in* A Picasso *(photo by John Schisler)*

**Sister's Christmas Catechism** by Maripat Donovan with Marc Silvia and Jane Morris; Director, Marc Silvia; Sets, Tony Ferrieri; Costumes, Catherine Evans; Production Assistant, Jamie Buczkowski; Cast: Kimberly Richards (Sister); November 24–December 31, 2006

**The Muckle Man** by Roberto Aguirre-Sacasa; Director, Tracy Brigden; Sets, Tony Ferrieri, Costumes, Angela M. Vesco; Lighting, Andrew David Ostrowski; Sound, Jorge Cousineau; PSM, Patti Kelly; Production Assistant, Kelly Marie McKenna; Cast: Robin Walsh (Marina Clarke), James Lloyd Reynolds (Addison Clarke), C.J. Ketchum (Malcolm Clarke),Joe Bender (Harvey Clarke), Tami Dixon (Dora Hand), Brett Mack (Gilbert Messenger), Nathan Blew (Arthur Campbell); January 25–February 18, 2007

*Nathan Blew, Tami Dixon, and Robin Walsh in* The Muckle Man *(photo by John Schisler)*

**Mezzulah, 1946** by Michele Lowe; Director, Erica Schmidt; Sets, Tony Ferrieri; Costumes, Michael Krass; Lighting, Andrew David Ostrowski; Wigs, Elsen Associates, Inc.; Music Director, Thomas Wesley Douglas; PSM, Patti Kelly; Production Assistant, Lissa Brennan; Cast: Theo Allyn (Mezzulah Steiner), Larry John Meyers (Charlie Steiner/Minister), Sheila McKenna (Mary Steiner), Rebecca Harris (Suzannah Hart), Johnny Giacalone (Isaiah Benson), Brett Mack (Horace Steiner), Jenny Wales (Clementine Flynn/Sally Cauley), Jeffrey Carpenter (Errol Hart), Joel Ripka (Fist Adams/Elvira Glass), Gwendolen Morton (Mrs. Bates); March 8–April 1, 2007

*Tony Bingham and Tami Dixon in* The Missionary Position *(photo by John Schisler)*

**The Missionary Position** by Keith Reddin; Director, Tracy Brigden; Sets, Gianni Downs; Costumes, Robert C.T. Steele; Lighting, Andrew Davis Ostrowski; Sound, Elizabeth Atkinson; PSM, Alicia DeMara; Production Assistant, Kelly Marie McKenna; Cast: Tony Bingham (Roger), Rebecca Harris (Maria/Barbara/Pamela/Rebecca/Gretchen), Jeffrey Carpenter (Neil), Tami Dixon (Julie); April 12–May 20, 2007

**Intimate Apparel** by Lynn Nottage; Director, Diane Rodriguez; Sets, Tony Ferrieri; Costumes, Pei-Chi Su; Lighting, Andrew David Ostrowski; Sound, Elizabeth Atkinson; PSM, Patti Kelly; Production Assistant, Lissa Brennan; Cast: Linda Haston (Mrs. Dickson), Tracey A. Leigh (Esther), John Eric Parker (George), Erica Highberg (Mrs. Van Buren), Michael Goodfriend (Mr. Marks), Maria Becoates-Bey (Mayme); May 3–27, 2007

**The Male Intellect: An Oxymoron?** by Robert Dubac; Executive Producer, William I. Franzblau; PSM, Lorraine Mszanski; Cast: Ben Evans (Bobby/The Colonel/Jean-Michel/Fast Eddie/Mr. Linger/Ronnie Cabrezzi); May 31–July 28, 2007

# Cleveland Play House

Cleveland, Ohio

Ninety-first Season

Artistic Director, Michael Bloom; Interim Managing Director, Anne B. DesRosiers

**Rabbit Hole** by David Lindsay-Abaire; Director, Michael Bloom; Sets, Russell Parkman; Costumes, Beth Novak; Lighting, Michael Lincoln; Sound, James C. Swonger; PSM, John Godbout; Cast: Troy Deutsch (Jason), Genevieve Elam (Izzy), Angela Reed (Becca), Kate Skinner (Nat), Danton Stone (Howie); September 15–October 8, 2006

**My Fair Lady** by Alan Jay Lerner and Frederick Loewe; Director, Amanda Dehnert; Sets, David Jenkins; Costumes, Devon Painter; Lighting, Amy Appleyard; Sound, Matt Callahan; Choreography, Kelli Wicke Davis and Greg Schanuel; Dialects, Don Wadsworth; First Piano/Conductor, Bill Corcoran; Second Piano/Vocal Supervisor, Tim Robertson; PSM, Bruno Ingram; Cast: Jessie Austrian (Mrs. Hopkins/First Maid), Dana Aver (Mrs. Eynsford-Hill/Second Maid), Melissa Brobeck (Angry Woman/Person on street), J. Bernard Calloway (Cockney Quartet/Lord Boxington), Timothy Crowe (Henry Higgins), Kathleen Culler (Bystander/

Mrs. Higgins' Maid), Larry Daggett (Alfred P. Doolittle), Christian Delacroix (Cockney Quartet/Angry Man/Hoxton Man), William Thomas Evans (Cockney Quartet/Selsey Man), Michael Hance (Freddy Eynsford-Hill), Katherine Harber (Mrs. Higgins/George the Bartender), Loresa Lanceta (Bystander/Lady Boxington/ Flower Girl), Nick Locilento (Cockney Quartet/Second Violin), George McDaniel (Colonel Pickering), Brian Marshall (Charles), J.P. Moraga (Jamie), Greg Schanuel (Harry/Professor Zoltan Karpathy), Navida Stein (Mrs. Pearce/First Violin), Rachael Warren (Eliza Doolittle); October 6–November 5, 2006

**RFK** Written and performed by Jack Holmes; Director, Seth Gordon; Sets, Neil Patel; Lighting, David Weiner; Sound, James C. Swonger; PSM, John Godbout; October 27–November 19, 2006

**A Christmas Story** by Philip Grecian; Director, Seth Gordon; Sets, Michael Ganio; Costumes, David Kay Mickelsen; Lighting, Richard Winkler; Sound, James C. Swonger; PSM, Matthew E. Sayre; Cast: Alex Biats (Schwartz), Jackson Daugherty (Randy), Naomi Hill (Helen), Angela Holecko (Esther Jane), Charles Kartali (The Old Man), Billy Lawrence (Ralphie), Alex Mayes (Scut Farkas), Christopher McHale (Ralph), Louie Rosenbaum (Flick), Peggy Scott (Miss Shields), Elizabeth Ann Townsend (Mother); November 30–December 23, 2006

*Billy Lawrence in* A Christmas Story *(photo by Roger Mastroianni)*

**Of Mice and Men** by John Steinbeck; Director, Seth Gordon; Sets, Hugh Landwehr; Costumes, David Kay Mickelsen; Lighting, Michael Lincoln; Sound, James C. Swonger; Fight Choreography, Guy Wagner; PSM, John Godbout; Cast: Chet Carlin (Candy), Harry Carnahan (George), Jeremy Holm (Slim), Wiley Moore (Crooks), Vayu O'Donnell (Curley), Amanda Rowan (Curley's Wife), Caleb Sakeres (Whit), Jeffrey Evan Thomas (Lennie), Rohn Thomas (The Boss), John Woodson (Carlson); January 5–28, 2007

**Cuttin' Up** by Charles Randolph-Wright; Director, Israel Hicks; Sets, Michael Carnahan; Costumes, David Kay Mickelsen; Lighting, Phil Monat; Sound, James C. Swonger; PSM, Melissa L.F. Turner; Cast: Harvy Blanks (Kenny/Rev. Carson/ Bernard), Bill Grimmette (Rev. Jenkins/Uncle/Don King), Dorian Logan (Rudy), Iona Morris (Karen/Yvette/Sandra), Maceo Oliver (John/Jermaine/Wheeler), Darryl Alan Reed (Andre), Jacques C. Smith (Howard Jr./Willy, Lou), Adolphus Ward (Howard); February 2–25, 2007

**The Clean House** by Sarah Ruhl; Director, Davis McCallum; Sets, Andromache Chalfant; Composer, Michael Friedman; Costumes, Murell Horton; Lighting, Matthew Richards; Sound, James C. Swonger; PSM, John Godbout; Ursula Cataan (Matilde), Janis Dardaris (Ana), Beth Dixon (Virginia), Patricia Hodges (Lane), Terry Layman (Charles); March 2–25, 2007

*Ursula Cataan in* The Clean House *(photo by Roger Mastroianni)*

**Ella** by Jeffrey Hatcher, conceived by Dyke Garrison and Rob Ruggiero; Musical Director, Danny Holgate; Sets, Michael Schweikardt; Costumes, Alejo Vietti; Lighting, John Lasiter; Sound, Michael C. Miceli; PSM, Bruno Ingram; Cast: George Caldwell (Conductor/piano), Tina Fabrique (Ella), Rodney Harper (drums), Clifton Kellem (bass), George Roth (Norman), Brian Sledge (trumpet); March 23– April 15, 2007

**Lincolnesque** by John Strand; Director, Michael Bloom; Sets, Todd Rosenthal; Costumes, Catherin Norgren; Lighting, Robert Wierzel; Sound, James C. Swonger; PSM, John Godbout; Donald Carrier (Francis), Brian Carter (Leo), Tracey Conyer Lee (Carla, Doctor), Walter Charles (Daly, Secretary of War); April 27–May 20, 2007

# Dallas Theater Center

Dallas, Texas

Forty-eighth Season

Artistic Director, Richard Hamburger

**2 Pianos 4 Hands** by Ted Dykstra and Richard Greenblatt; Director, Richard Greenblatt; Set/Lighting, Steve Lucas; Associate Lighting, Jason Golinsky; Cast: Richard Carsey (Richard), Tom Frey (Ted); August 30–September 24, 2006

**Cat on a Hot Tin Roof** by Tennessee Williams; Director, Richard Hamburger; Sets, Christopher Barreca; Costumes, Anita Yavich; Lighting, Stephen Strawbridge; Sound, Fitz Patton; Cast: Kati Brazda (Mae), Matthew Gray (Gooper), Tippi Hunter (Sookey), Laurie Kennedy (Big Mama), Dakin Matthews (Big Daddy), Jerry Russell (Doctor Baugh), Lorca Simons (Maggie), Rick Stear (Brick), Gary Taggart (Reverend Tooker); October 11–November 5, 2006

*Rick Stear, Dakin Matthews, and Kati Brazda in* Cat on a Hot Tin Roof *(photo by Loli Kantor)*

**A Christmas Carol** by Charles Dickens, adapted by Richard Hellesen, original music by David de Berry; Director & Choreographer, Joel Ferrell; Sets, Bob Lavallee; Costumes, Wade Laboissonniere; Lighting, Matthew Richards; Sound, Brian Branigan; Musical Director, Lindy Heath Cabe; Cast: Robert Langdon Lloyd (Ebenezer Scrooge), Lynn Blackburn (Belle/Ensemble), Laurie Bulaoro (Fred's Wife/Ensemble), Jakie Cabe (Young Scrooge/Ensemble), Chamblee Ferguson (Bob Cratchit/Ensemble), Ian Flanagan (Peter Cratchit/Ensemble), Matthew Gray (Fred/Ensemble), Melissa Renuka Kamath (Laundress/Ensemble), M. Denise Lee (The Ghost of Christmas Present/Ensemble), Shannon J. McGrann (Ms. Cratchit/Ensemble), Dean Nolan (The Ghost of Jacob Marley), Bob Reed (Fezziwig/Ensemble), Taylore Mahogany Scott (Wife's Sister/Ensemble), Lee Trull (Topper/Ensemble), Farrah West (Martha Cratchit/Ensemble), Ashley Wood (The Ghost of Christmas Past/Ensemble); November 24–December 24, 2006

**Moonlight and Magnolias** by Ron Hutchinson; Director, David Kennedy; Sets, John Coyne; Costumes, Barbara Hicks; Lighting, Marcus Doshi; Sound, Ken Travis; Fight Director, Brian Byrnes; Cast: Brad Bellamy (Ben Hecht), Matt Gaydos (David O. Selznick), Jessica D. Turner (Miss Poppenghul), Richard Ziman (Victor Fleming); January 24–February 18, 2007

*Richard Ziman, Matt Gaydos, and Brad Bellamy in* Moonlight and Magnolias *(photo by Linda Blasé)*

**Fences** by August Wilson; Director, Jonathan Wilson; Sets, Scott Bradley; Costumes, Jacqueline Firkins; Lighting, R. Lap-Chi Chu; Sound, Jim Ragland; Fight Director, Mark Olsen; Cast: Che Ayende (Lyons), Don Mayo (Jim Bono), Robert Christopher Riley (Cory), Ray Anthony Thomas (Gabriel), Wandachristine (Rose), Kennedy Williams (Raynell), Wendell Wright (Troy Maxson); March 7–April 1, 2007

**The Taming of the Shrew** by William Shakespeare; Director, Richard Hamburger; Sets, David Zinn; Costumes, Clint Ramos; Lighting, David Weiner; Sound, David Budries; Fight Director, J. David Brimmer; Cast: Mary Bacon (Kate), Jakie Cabe (Grumio), Apollo Dukakis (Baptista Minola), Chamblee Ferguson (Hortensio), Dolores Godinez (Widow/Servant), Matthew Gray (Curtis/Officer), Bryant Mason (Tranio), Marcus Neely (Biondello), Jonno Roberts (Petruchio), Cliff Stephens (Salesman), Jessica D. Turner (Bianca), Noel Vélez (Lucentio), Mark Waltz (Vicentio), John Woodson (Gremio/Tailor); April 18–May 13, 2007

# Delaware Theatre Company

Wilmington, Delaware

Twenty-eighth Season

Producing Director, Anne Marie Cammarato

**The Turn of the Screw** Adapted by Jeffrey Hatcher, from the story by Henry James; Director, Anne Marie Cammarato; Sets, Eric Schaeffer; Costumes, Devon Painter; Lighting, Tyler Micoleau; Sound, Shannon Zura; Composer, Peter Atwater; Dialects, Stanton Davis; Casting, Stephanie Klapper, Meredith Tomason; Stage Manager, Sara J. Tantillo; Cast: Erin Moon (The Woman), Michael Polak (The Man); October 18–November 5, 2006

**Sam Cooke: Forever Mr. Soul** Conceived, written, and direceted by Kevin Ramsey; Music Director, Alva Nelson; Set/Projections, Matthew Myhrum; Costumes, Janus Stefanowicz; Lighting, Troy A. Martin-O'Shia; Sound, Ryan W. Powers; Casting, Stephanie Klapper, Meredith Tomason; Stage Manager, Sara J. Tantillo; Cast: Lawrence Stallings (Sam Cooke), C.S. Treadway (The Voice of the Radio); December 6–24, 2006

**The Retreat From Moscow** by William Nicholson; Director, David Stradley; Sets, Robert Jansen; Costumes, Mattie Ullrich; Lighting, Shannon Zura; Sound, Fabian Obispo; Dialects, Deena Burke; Casting, Stephanie Klapper, Meredith Tomason; Stage Manager, Sara J. Tantillo; Cast: Carole Monferdini (Alice), David McCann (Edward), Christopher Kelly (Jamie); January 24–February 11, 2007

**Driving Miss Daisy** by Alfred Uhry; Director, Meredith McDonough; Sets, Lee Savage; Costumes, Emily Pepper; Lighting, Christopher Studley; Sound, Shannon Zura; Dialect Coach, Stanton Davis; Casting, Stephanie Klapper, Meredith Tomason; Stage Manager, Sara J. Tantillo; Wigs, Leah J. Loukas; Cast: Louisa Flaningam (Daisy), Roscoe Orman (Hoke), Scott Wakefield (Boolie); March 7–25, 2007

**Henry V** by William Shakespeare, adapted by Sanford Robbins; Director, Sanford Robbins; Sets, Fritz Szabo; Costumes, Andrea Barrier; Lighting, Matthew Richards; Stage Manager, Sara J. Tantillo; Speech Coaches, Deena Burke, Steve Tague; Cast: Drew Brehl (Chorus/Archbishop of Canterbury/Pistol/Richard/French King/Captain Jamy), Matthew Burke (Chorus/King Henry); Sarah Fallon (Chorus/Montjoy/Boy/Sir Thomas Grey/English Soldier/Katherine/Alexander Court), Michael Gotch (Chorus/Bishop of Ely/Nym/Henry/The Dauphin/Governor of Harfler/Alice/Earl of Salisbury/John Bates/Monsieur Le Fer), Paul Hurley (Chorus/Duke of Bedford/Mistress Quickly/Duke of Orleans/Captain MacMorris/Michael Williams), Stephen Patrick Smith (Chorus/Earl of Westmoreland/The Constable of France/Captain Fluellen), Steve Tague (Chorus/Duke of Exeter/Bardolph/Captain Gower/Duke of Bourbon); April 18–May 6, 2007

# Denver Center Theatre Company

Denver, Colorado

Twenty-eighth Season

Artistic Director, Kent Thompson; Associate Artistic Director, Bruce K. Sevy; General Manager, Charles Varin; Production Manager, Edward Lapine

**Living Out** by Lisa Loomer; Director, Wendy C. Goldberg; Sets, Lisa M. Orzolek; Costumes, Kevin Copenhaver; Lighting, Charles R. MacLeod; Sound, Matthew C. Swartz; Stage Manager, Christopher C. Ewing; ASM, Kurt Van Raden; Cast: Romi Dias (Ana Hernandez), Makela Spielman (Nancy Robin), Rey Lucas (Bobby Hernandez), Christopher Burns (Richard Robin), Lanie MacEwan (Wallace Breyer), Socorro Santiago (Zoila Tezo), Kathleen McCall (Linda Billings Farzam), Gabriella Cavallero (Sandra Zavala); September 21–October 28, 2006

**Amadeus** by Peter Shaffer; Director, Kent Thompson; Sets, John Iacovelli; Costumes, David Kay Mickelsen; Lighting, Rachel Budin; Sound, Craig Breitenbach; Dialect Coaches, Kathryn G. Maes, Douglas W. Montequin; Stage Manager, Lyle Raper; ASM, Christi B. Spann; Production Assistant, D. Lynn Reiland; Cast: Brent Harris (Antonio Salieri), David Ivers (Venticelli One), Sam Gregory (Venticelli Two), Ivan Lopez (Salieri's Valet), Thaddeus Valdez (Salieri's Cook), Bill Christ (Emperor Joseph II), Randy Moore (Count Johann Kilian von Strack), Michael Mandell (Count Franz Orsini-Rosenberg), Philip Pleasants (Baron Gottfried Van Swieten), Louis Schaefer (Kapellmeister Bonno), Moses Villarama (Priest), Kathleen M. Brady (Teresa Salieri), Anne Marie Nest (Katherina Cavalieri), Stephanie Cozart (Constanze Weber), Douglas Harmsen (Wolfgang Amadeus Mozart), Bradford Shreve (Major Domo), Susanna Florence (Ensemble), Eric Laurits (Ensemble), Maria-Christina Oliveras (Ensemble), Bria Walker (Ensemble); September 28–October 28, 2006

**Season's Greetings** by Alan Ayckbourn; Director, Gavin Cameron-Webb; Sets, Hugh Landwehr; Costumes, Susan E. Mickey; Lighting, Charles R. MacLeod; Sound, Matthew C. Swartz; Fight Director, Geoffrey Kent; Dialect Coaches, Kathryn G. Maes, Douglas W. Montequin; Stage Manager, Mister Erock; ASM, Kurt Van Raden; Production Assistant, D. Lynn Reiland; Cast: Mike Hartman (Harvey Bunker), Paul Hebron (Dr. Bernard Longstaff), Kathleen McCall (Belinda Bunker); Anne Marie Nest (Pattie), Sam Gregory (Neville Bunker), Douglas Harmsen (Eddie), Henny Russell (Rachel), Charlotte Booker (Phyllis Longstaff), Greg Keller (Clive Morris); November 16–December 23, 2006

**A Christmas Carol** by Charles Dickens, adapted by Richard Hellesen, music by David de Berry; Director, Bruce K. Sevy; Musical Director, Gregg Coffin; Sets, Vicki Smith; Costumes, Kevin Copenhaver; Lighting, Don Darnutzer; Sound, Craig Breitenbach; Choreography, Gina Cerimele-Mechley; Original Orchestrations, Thom Jenkins; Dialect Coaches, Kathryn G. Maes, Douglas W. Montequin; Stage Manager, Lyle Raper; ASMs, Christopher C. Ewing, Christi B. Spann; Production Assistant, D. Lynn Reiland; Cast: Philip Pleasants (Ebenezer Scrooge), James Michael Reilly (Bob Cratchit), David Ivers (Fred, A Fiddler, Undertaker's Man), Harvy Blanks (Subscription Gentleman, Old Joe), Ross David Crutchlow (Ghost of Christmas Present, Subscription Gentleman), Raif Henning (A Beggar Child), John Hutton (Ghost of Jacob Marley), Stephanie Cozart (Ghost of Christmas Past. The Charwoman), Bryce Baldwin (Ebenezer the Child), Rachel Obering (Fan, Want), Jeff Cribbs (Ebenezer the Young Man, Party Guest, Merchant), Moses Villarama (Dick Wilkins), Chris Mixon (Fezziwig), Leslie O'Carroll (Mrs. Fezziwig, Party Guest), Maria-Christina Oliveras (Fezziwig Daughter), Christine Rowan (Fezziwig Daughter), Bria Walker (Fezziwig Daughter), Andy Jobe (Suitor, Ghost of Christmas Yet to Come), Jeffrey Roark (Suitor, Merchant), Bradford Shreve (Suitor), Jenn Miller Cribbs (Belle, Martha), Jeffrey Roark (Belle's Husband, Topper), Tina Stafford (Mrs. Cratchit), Sam Van Wetter (Peter), Desirée Samler (Belinda), Max Schwartz (Edward), Ian Farmer (Tiny Tim), Carey Van Driest (Fred's Wife), Christine Rowan (Wife's Sister, The Street Singer), John King (Ignorance), Eric Laurits (Merchant), Kathleen M. Brady (The Laundress), Nick Lormand (Boy in the Street), Eric Laurits (Ensemble), Susanna Florence (Ensemble), Ivan Lopez (Ensemble); November 24–December 24, 2006

**The Pillowman** by Martin McDonagh; Director, Anthony Powell; Sets, Lisa M. Orzolek; Costumes, Christine Dougherty; Lighting, Jane Spencer; Sound/Original Music, Iæden Hovorka; Assistant Director, Jeff Carey; Stage Manager, Mister Erock; Production Assistant, D. Lynn Reiland; Cast: Scott Ferrara (Katurian), Lawrence Hecht (Tupolski), Douglas Harmsen (Ariel), David Ivers (Michal), Maria-Christina Oliveras (Mother), Erik Sandvold (Father), Desirée Samler (Girl), Ry Feder Pruett (Boy), Noah Wilson (Boy); January 11–February 24, 2007

**1001** by Jason Grote; Director, Ethan McSweeny; Sets, Rachel Hauck; Costumes, Murell Horton; Lighting, Charles R. MacLeod; Sound, Matthew C. Swartz; Dramaturg, Allison Horsley; Dialect Coaches, Kathryn G. Maes, Douglas W. Montequin; Movement Coach, Robert Davidson; Fight Director, Geoffrey Kent; Assistant Director, Anthony Luciano; DJ, Sara Thurston; Stage Manager, Christopher C. Ewing; ASM, Kurt Van Raden; Cast: Drew Cortese, Daoud Heidami, Lanna Joffrey, John Livingstone Rolle, Jeanine Serralles, Josh Philip Weinstein; World Premiere; January 18–February 24, 2007

**King Lear** by William Shakespeare; Director, Kent Thompson; Music, Gregg Coffin; Sets, Ralph Funicello; Costumes, Susan Branch; Lighting, York Kennedy; Sound, Craig Breitenbach; Fight Director, Geoffrey Kent; Vocal Coach, Michael Cobb; Assistant Director, Rick Barbour; Stage Manager, Lyle Raper; ASM, Christi B. Spann; Cast: Philip Pleasants (Lear), Sharon Washington (Goneril), Kathleen McCall (Regan), Stephanie Cozart (Cordelia), Robert Jason Jackson (Duke of Albany), Remi Sandri (Duke of Cornwall), Jeffrey Roark (Duke of Burgundy), Moses Villarama (King of France), John Hutton (Earl of Kent), Sam Gregory (Fool), Stephen Weitz (Gentleman), Mike Hartman (Earl of Gloucester), Markus Potter (Edgar), Rodney Hicks (Edmund), William Hahn (Oswald, Captain), Randy Moore (Old Man, Doctor), Susanna Florence (Ensemble), Eric Laurits (Ensemble), Ivan Lopez (Ensemble), Anne Marie Nest (Ensemble), Bradford Shreve (Ensemble), Bria Walker (Ensemble); January 25–February 24, 2007

Jeannine Serralles and John Philip Weinstein in 1001

**Mrs. Warren's Profession** by George Bernard Shaw; Director, Bruce K. Sevy; Sets, Vicki Smith; Costumes, Bill Black; Lighting, Charles R. MacLeod; Sound, Matthew C. Swartz; Stage Manager, Christopher C. Ewing; ASM, Kurt Van Raden; Cast: Richard Sheridan Willis (Praed), John Hutton (Sir George Crofts), Randy Moore (Rev. Samuel Gardner), James Knight (Frank Gardner), Nisi Sturgis (Vivie Warren); March 15–April 21, 2007

**Pure Confidence** by Carlyle Brown; Director, Kent Gash; Sets, Emily Beck; Costumes, Austin K. Sanderson; Lighting, Liz Lee; Sound, Eric Stahlhammer; Stage Manager, Lyle Raper; ASM, Christi B. Spann; Cast: Gavin Lawrence (Simon Cato); Philip Pleasants (Colonel Wiley 'The Fox' Johnson), Maureen Silliman (Mattie Johnson), Heather Alicia Simms (Caroline), Mike Hartman (George DeWitt/Clerk), David Ivers (Auctioneer/Reporter); March 22–April 21, 2007

**The Sweetest Swing in Baseball** by Rebecca Gilman; Director, Wendy C. Goldberg; Sets, Alexander Dodge; Costumes, Anne Kennedy; Lighting, Charles R. MacLeod; Sound, læden Hovorka; Stage Manager, Mister Erock; Production Assistant, D. Lynn Reiland; Cast: Kathleen McCall (Dana), Sam Gregory (Roy/Gary), Megan Byrne (Rhonda/Dr. Gilbert), Brad Heberlee (Brian/Michael), Caitlin O'Connell (Erica/Dr. Stanton); April 5–May 26, 2007

**A Funny Thing Happened on the Way to the Forum** Book by Burt Shevelove and Larry Gelbart, music and lyrics by Stephen Sondheim; Director, Bruce K. Sevy; Musical Director, Gregg Coffin; Choreography, Gina Cerimele-Mechley; Sets, Vicki Smith; Costumes, Kevin Copenhaver; Lighting, Don Darnutzer; Sound, Craig Breitenbach; Conductor, Lee Stametz; Stage Manager, Lyle Raper; ASMs, Christopher C. Ewing, Christi B. Spann; Cast: Ron Orbach (Prologus, Pseudolus), Tim Hausmann (Protean), Terry Lavell (Protean), Ivory McKay (Protean), Mickey Toogood (Protean), Mike Hartman (Senex), Kathleen M. Brady, (Domina), Anderson Davis (Hero), David Ivers (Hysterium), Stephen Berger (Lycus), Stephanie Janette Meade (Tintinabula), Michelle Dyer (Geminae), Kolina Janneck, (Geminae), Elizabeth Clinard (Vibrata), Lauren Pastorek (Gymnasia), Christine Rowan (Philia), Philip Pleasants (Erronius), Glenn Lawrence (Miles Gloriosus); Co-produced with Denver Center Attractions; May 17–July 8, 2007

# Ford's Theatre

Washington, D.C.

Thrity-ninth Season

Producing Director, Paul R. Tetreault; Associate Producers, Mark Ramont and Kristin Fox-Siegmund; Special Project Director, James R. Riley; General Manager, Alfred Butler

**State of the Union** by Howard Lindsay and Russel Crouse; Director, Kyle Donnelly; Cast: Jim Abele, Christopher Bloch, Michael Gabel, Martha Hackett, Naomi Jacobson, Ellen Karas, Floyd King, James Konicek, Hugh Nees, Joe Peck, Kip Pierson, Andrew Polk, Nancy Robinette, Sam Tsoutsouvas, Esther Williamson; September 22–October 22, 2006

**A Christmas Carol** by Charles Dickens, adapted by Michael Wilson; Director, Matt August; Cast: Clinton Brandhagen, Michael Bunce, Michael John Casey, Teresa Castracane, Elliot Dash, Jaclyn DiLauro, Carlos Gonzalez, Michael Goodwin, Bill Hensel, Katie Kleiger, Amy McWilliams, Claudia Miller, Kip Pierson, Richard Poe, Suzanne Richard, Todd Scofield, Erin Sloan; November 15–December 30, 2006

**Jitney** by August Wilson; Presented in association with African Continuum Theatre Company; Director, Jennifer L. Nelson; Cast: Doug Brown, Jessica Francis Dukes, Thembi Duncan, Cleo Reginald Pizana, Ken Yatta Rogers, Fred Strother, Addison Switzer, David Emerson Toney, Craig Wallace, Michael Anthony Williams, Lance Coadie Williams; January 19–February 18, 2007

**Mark Russell…and the Pendulum Swings** February 21–25, 2007

**Meet John Doe** Music and lyrics by Andrew Gerle and Eddie Sugarman; additional story by Matt August; Director, Eric Schaeffer; Cast: Heidi Blickenstaff, Christopher Bloch, Joel Blum, Suzanne Briar, Michael Bunce, Evan Casey, Daniel Cohen, Danielle Eden, Eleasha Gamble, Kimberly McNeese, Channez McQuay, Amy McWilliams, James Moye, Tracy Lynn Olivera, Guy Paul, Joe Peck, Thomas Adrian Simpson, Stephen Gregory Smith, Patrick Ryan Sullivan; March 16–May 27, 2007

# George Street Playhouse

New Brunswick, New Jersey

Thrity-third Season

Artistic Director, David Saint

**The Things You Least Expect** by Joan Vaile Thorne; Director, David Saint; Sets, Michael Anania; Costumes, David Murin; Lighting, Christopher J. Bailey; Sound, Christopher J. Bailey; PSM, C. Renee Alexander; Cast: Mary Beth Piel (Clare), Pamela Payton-Wright (Myra), Jessica Dickey (Caroline), Curtis Mark Williams (Sam); World Premiere; October 3–October 29, 2006

**The Value of Names** by Jeffrey Sweet; Director, James Glossman; Sets, R. Michael Miller; Lighting, Richard Currie; Costumes, Bettina Bierly; Sound, Christopher J. Bailey; PSM, Tom Clewell; Cast: Jack Klugman (Benny), Dan Lauria (Leo), Liz Larsen (Norma); November 14–December 17, 2007

**I Am My Own Wife** by Doug Wright; Director, Anders Cato; Sets, Hugh Landwehr; Lighting, Howell Binkley; Costumes, Jeffrey Van Curtis; Sound, James Swonger; PSM, Tom Clewell; Cast: Mark Nelson (Charlotte von Mahlsdorff); January 16–February 11, 2007

**Souvenir** by Stephen Temperley; Director, Anders Cato; Sets, Karl Eigsti; Costumes, Tracy Christensen; Lighting, Jeff Davis; Sound, Christopher J. Bailey; PSM, C. Renee Alexander; Cast: Liz McCartney (Florence Foster Jenkins), Jim Walton (Cosme McMoon); February 27–March 25, 2007

**Falsettos** Book by William Finn and James Lapine; Music and lyrics by William Finn; Director, David Saint; Sets, Beowulf Borritt; Lighting, Christopher J Bailey; Costumes, Amela Baksic; Sound, Tom Morse; PSM, Tom Clewell; Cast: Michael Winther (Marvin), Malcolm Morano (Jason), Liz Larsen (Trina), Mark Nelson (Mendel), Anne L. Nathan (Dr. Charlotte), Sara Litzsinger (Cordelia), Colin Hanlon (Whizzer); April 10–May 6, 2007

# Georgia Shakespeare Festival

Atlanta, Gerogia

Twenty-second Season

Producing Artistic Director, Richard Garner; Managing Director, Stacy Shaw

**Twelfth Night** by William Shakespeare; Director, Karen Robinson; Sets, Kat Conley; Costumes, Christine Turbitt; Lighting, Liz Lee; Composer, Thom Jenkins; Sound Engineer, Clay Benning; Vocal Coach, Allen O'Reilly; Dramaturg, R. Barton Palmer, Fight Choreography/Fight Captain, Chris Ensweiler; Stage Manager, Karen S. Martin; Production Assistant, Erin B. Zatloka; Cast: Brad Sherrill (Orsino), Zechariah Pierce (Curio/1st Captain), Chad Martin (Valentine/Priest), Courtney Patterson (Viola), Jesse Hinson (Sea Captain/2nd Officer), Allan Edwards (Sir Toby Belch), Tess Malis Kincaid (Maria), Chris Ensweiler (Sir Andrew Aguecheek), Daivd Howard (Feste), Crystal Dickinson (Olivia), Lakisah May (Gentlewoman), Chris Kayser (Malvolio), David Quay (Fabian), Joe Knezevich (Sebastian), Brik Berkes (Antonio); May 2–6, 2007

**Metamorphoses** by Mary Zimmerman, based on the *Myths of Ovid*; Director, Richard Garner; Sets, Tim Conley; Costumes, Christine Turbitt; Lighting, Liz Lee & Mike Post; Composer, Kendall Simpson; Sound, Clay Benning; Vocal Coach, Elisa Carlson; Assistant Sets, Jonathan Williamson; Dramaturg, Christina Wallace; Stage Manager, Margo Khune; Cast: Carolyn Cook (Baucis/others), Crystal Dickinson (Eurydice/others), Brik Berkes (Erysichthon/others), Chris Ensweiler (Phaeton/others), Chris Kayser (Philemon/others), Joe Knezevich (Midas/others), Park Krausen (Alcyone/others), Daniel May (Orpheus/others), Courtney Patterson (Aphrodite/others), Bethany Ann Lind (Myrrha/others); May 23–June 3, 2007

**The Servant of Two Masters** by Carlo Goldoni, translated and adapted by Jeffrey Hatcher & Paolo Emilio Landi; Director, Dan McCleary; Sets, Kat Conley; Costumes, Douglas J. Koertge, Lighting, Liz Lee; Sound, Clay Benning; Juggling Coach, Vincenzo Tortorici; Stage Manager, Roberts Schultz; Cast: Rob Cleveland (Master of Revels), J.C. Long (Deputy Master of Musical Revels), Alex Cole (Deputy Master of Circus Revels), Chris Kayser (Curmudgeon of a Certain Age), Carolyn Cook (Cross-Dressing Leading Lady), Daniel May (Good-Looking Leading Man), Crystal Dickinson (Naughty Supporting Player), Hudson Adams (Reluctant Supporting Player), Zechariah Pierce (Our Young Gallant), Amelia Hammond (Our Young Lady of Perpetual Despair), Park Krausen (a maid), Chris Ensweiler (a servant); June 13–July 28, 2007

*Park Krausen and Chris Ensweiler in* The Servant of Two Masters *(photo by Bill DeLoach)*

**Pericles** by William Shakespeare; Director, Richard Garner; Sets, Kat Conley; Costumes, Sydney Roberts; Lighting, Liz Lee; Sound, Clay Benning; Composer/Musician, Klimchak; Assistant Director, Daniel May; Stage Manager, Margo Khune; Cast: Park Krausen (Gower/Thaisa/Diana), Joe Knezevich (Pericles), Brad Sherrill (Antiochus/Fisherman/Sailor/Bolt), Kristen Burke (Daughter of Antiochus/Lychodrida/Vestal), Daniel May (Thaliard/Fisherman/Sailor/Lysimachus), Rob Cleveland (Helicanus/Philemon/Fisherman), J.C. Long (Escanes/Marshall/Sailor/Pirate), Hudson Adams (Cleon), Carolyn Cook (Dionyza/Lady/Vestal), Chris Kayser (Simonides/Pander), Crystal Dickinson (Cerimon/Bawd), Amelia Hammond (Marina), Alex Cole (Lord of Mytilene/Knight/Servant), David Quay (Knight/Gentleman of Tyre/Pirate), Carl Clemons-Hopkins (Leonin/Guard/Knight), Michael Dalto (Guard/Pirate), Zechariah Pierce (Sailor/Lord/Knight); June 28–July 27, 2007

**Loot** by Joe Orton; Director, Sabin Epstein; Sets, Rochelle Barker, Costumes, Christine Trubitt; Lighting, Liz Lee; Assistant Lighting, Mike Post; Sound; Clay Benning; Dialect Coach, Cynthia Barrett, Combat Consultant, Chris Ensweiler; Stage Manager, Margo Khune; ASM, Cheyenne Grimes; Assistant to the Director, Justin Anderson; Cast: Chris Kayser (McLeavy), Courtney Patterson (Fay), Joe Knezevich (Hal), Daniel May (Dennis), Allen O'Reilly (Truscott), Bruce Evers (Meadows); August 2–19, 2007

**Richard III** by William Shakespeare; Director, Richard Garner; Sets, Kat Conley; Costumes, Sydney Roberts; Lighting, Mike Post; Cast: Joe Knezevich (Richard III), Brik Berkes (Richmond/Hastings), James Donadio (Clarence/Catesby), Daniel May (Buckingham), Neal Ghant (Stanley), Dave Quay (Ratcliff), Tess Malis Kincaid (Margaret), Courtney Patterson (Elizabeth), Yvonne Singh (Duchess); October 11–November 4, 2007

# Geva Theatre Center

Rochester, New York

Thirthy-fourth Season

Artistic Director, Mark Cuddy; Managing Director, Greg Weber; Executive Director, Nan Hildebrandt

**Dial "M" for Murder** by Frederick Knott; Director, Tim Ocel; Mainstage; September 5–October 1, 2006

**Tuesdays With Morrie** by Jeffrey Hatcher and Mitch Albom, based on the book by Mitch Albom; Director, Mark Cuddy; Mainstage; October 10–November 5, 2006

**American Buffalo** by David Mamet; Director, Skip Greer; Nextstage; November 7–26, 2006

**A Christmas Carol** by Charles Dickens, adapted by Richard Hellesen, music by David de Berry; Director, Emma Griffin; Mainstage; November 24–December 24, 2006

**The Underpants** by Carl Sternheim, adapted by Steve Martin; Director, Bruce Jordan; Mainstage; January 3–February 4, 2007

**Our Town** by Thornton Wilder; Director, Mark Cuddy; Mainsatge; February 13–March 11, 2007

**9 Parts of Desire** by Heather Raffo; Nextstage; March 20–April 8, 2007

**Gem of the Ocean** by August Wilson; Director, Timothy Douglas; Mainstage; April 3–29, 2007

**Urinetown, the Musical** Music and lyrics by Mark Hollmann, book and lyrics by Greg Kotis; Director, Mark Cuddy; Mainstage, May 15–June 10, 2007

# Goodman Theatre

Chicago, Illinois

Eighty-second Season

Artistic Director, Robert Falls; Managing Director, Roche Schulfer

**King Lear** by William Shakespeare; Director, Robert Falls; Sets, Walt Spangler; Costumes, Ana Kuzmanic; Lighting, Michael Philippi; Sound, Richard Woodbury; Fight Director, Rick Sordelet; Vocal Coach, Ralph Zito; Casting, Nancy Piccione and Adam Belcuore; Dramaturg, Tom Creamer; PSM, Joseph Drummond; Stage Manager, T. Paul Lynch; Cast: Steve Pickering (Kent), Edward Gero (Gloucester), Jonno Roberts (Edmund), Stacy Keach (Lear), Kim Martin-Cotton (Goneril), Kate Arrington (Regan), Laura Odeh (Cordelia), Kevin Gudahl (Albany), Chris Genebach (Cornwall), Andrew Navarro (Burgundy), Brian Gill (France), Joaquin Torres (Edgar), Dietrich Gray (Oswald), Michael Goldberg (Knight in Lear's retinue), Howard Witt (Fool), Jeffrey Baumgartner (Curan), Steve Schine (Cornwall's Man), Ronald Keaton (Old Man/Gloucester's Tennant), Kareem K. Bandealy (Messenger to Albany and Goneril), Kyle Lemieux (Soldier), Patrick Clear (Medic), David Blixt (Captain), Christopher Johnson (Gloucester's Guard), Cornwall's Guards: David Blixt, Hans Fleischmann, Jose Antonio Garcia; Goneril's Servants: Carolyn Defrin, Ann James, Elise Kauzlaric; Ensemble: Kareem K. Bandealy, Jeffrey Baumgartner, David Blixt, Patrick Clear, Carolyn Defrin, Hans Fleischmann, Jose Antonio Garcia, Brian Gill, Michael F. Goldberg, Ann James, Christopher Johnson, Elise Kauzlaric, Ronald Keaton, Kyle Lemieux, Andrew Navarro, Steve Schine, Matthew Lon Walker; Albert Theatre; September 9–October 15, 2006

**Vigils** by Noah Haidle; Director, Kate Whoriskey; Set/Costumes, Walt Spangler; Lighting, Jason Lyons; Original Music & Sound, Rob Milburn & Michael Bodeen; Projections, John Boesche; Choreography, Randy Duncan; Dramaturg, Tanya Palmer; PSM, Kimberly Osgood; Cast: Johanna Day (Widow), Coburn Goss (Wooer), Marc Grapey (Soul), Steve Key (Body); Owen Theatre; October 14– November 12, 2006

*Johanna Day and Steve Key in* Vigils *(photo by Liz Lauren)*

**Frank's Home** by Richard Nelson; Director, Robert Falls; Sets, Thomas Lynch; Costumes, Susan Hilferty; Lighting, Michael Philippi; Sound, Richard Woodbury; Dramaturg, Tom Creamer; PSM, T. Paul Lynch; Cast: Peter Weller (Frank Lloyd Wright), Maggie Siff (Catherine), Holley Fain (Helen Girvin), Jeremy Strong (William), Harris Yulin (Louis Sullivan), Mary Beth Fisher (Miriam Noel), Jay Whittaker (Lloyd), Chris Henry Coffey; Owen Theatre; November 15–December 23, 2006

**A Christmas Carol** Adapted by Tom Creamer; Director, William Brown; Sets, Todd Rosenthal; Costumes, Heidi Sue McMath; Lighting, Robert Christian; Sound, Lindsay Jones; Composer, Andrew Hansen; PSM, Alden Vasquez; Stage Manager, Sascha Connor; Cast: Justin Amolsch (Musician), Lashawn Banks (Mr. Crumb), Philip James Brannon (Dick Wilkins/Young Man), Ryan Cowhey (Tine Tim), Brian Gill (Bob Cratchit), Lucy Godinez (Johnston/Belinda Cratchit), Dennis Grimes (Scrooge as a Young Man/Ghost of Christmas Future), Steve Haggard (Ghost of Christmas Present/Topper), Matthew D. Heffernan (Pratt/Ignorance/ Turkey Boy), Steven Hinger (Fred), Gregory HIrte (Musician), Katie Jeep (Belle/ Catherine/Young Woman), Bethany Jorgensen (Musician/Philomena), Laney Kraus-Taddeo (Emily Cratchit/Want), John Lister (Schoolmaster/Chestnut Seller), Bradley Mott (Mr.Fezziwig/The Ghost of Christmas Present/Poulterer), William J. Norris (Mr.Ortle), Karen Janes Woditsch (Mrs. Cratchit), Martin Yurek (Ghost of Jacob Marley/Marley as a Young Man/Old Joe); Albert Theatre; November 17– December 30, 2006

*The Company of* A Christmas Carol *(photo by Michael Brosilow)*

**Radio Golf** by August Wilson; Director, Kenny Leon; Sets, David Gallo; Costumes, Susan Hilferty; Lighting, Donald Holder; Sound, Dan Moses Schreier; Original Music, Kathryn Bostic; Dramaturg, Todd Kreidler; Vocal Coach, Erin Annarella; PSM, Narda Alcorn/Marion Friedman; Stage Manager, Joseph Drummond; Cast: Michole Briana White (Mame Wilks), Hassan El-Amin (Harmond Wilks), James A. Williams (Roosevelt Hicks), John Earl Jelks (Sterling Johnson), Anthony Chisholm (Elder Joseph Barlow); Albert Theatre; January 13–February 18, 2007

**Rabbit Hole** by David Lindsay-Abaire; Director, Steve Scott; Sets, Scott Bradley; Costumes, Birgit Rattenborg Wise; Lighting, Robert Christen; Original Music and Sound, Richard Woodbury; PSM, Alden Vasquez; Stage Manager, Sascha Connor; Cast: Amy Warren (Izzy), Lia D. Mortensen (Becca), Daniel Cantor (Howie), Mary Ann Thebus (Nat), Jurgen Hooper (Jason); Albert Theatre; March 20–April 15, 2007

**Oedipus Complex** Adaptor/Director, Frank Galati; Sets, James Schuette; Costumes, Mara Blumenfeld; Lighting, Michael Chybowski; Original Music & Sound, Todd Barton; Vocal/Choral Coach, Linda Gates; Choreographer/ Movement Consultant, Christina Ernst; Dramaturg, Tom Creamer; PSM, Joseph Drummond; Stage Manager, T. Paul Lynch; Cast: Nick Sandys (Freud/Priest of Zeus), Ben Vicellio (Oedipus), Roderick Peeples (Kreon), Jeffrey Baumgartner (Teiresias), Susan Hart (Jocasta), Patrick Clear (Messenger), Bradley Armacost (Shepherd), Safia Hannin or Laney Kraus-Tadeo (Antigone and Ismene); Men of Theibs: Bradley Armacost, Stephen Louis Grush, Kevin Asselin, Derek Hasenstab, Philip James Brannon, Joel Hatch, Cliff Chamberlain, Timothy W. Hull, Patrick Clear, John Phillips, Sean Fortunato, Craig Spidle, Jose Antonio Garcia, Edward Stevens; Albert Theatre; April 28–June 3, 2007

**In the Continuum** Written and performed by Danai Gurira and Nikkole Salter; Director, Robert O'Hara; Sets, Peter R. Feuchtwagner; Costumes, Sarah Hillard; Lighting, Colin D. Young; Sound, Lindsay Jones; Properties, R. Jay Duckworth; Casting, Stephanie Klapper; PSM, Samone B. Weissman; Owen Theatre; May 25–June 24, 2007

**Mirror of the Invisible World** Adapted and directed by Mary Zimmerman; Sets, Dan Ostling; Costumes, Mara Blumenfeld; Lighting, John Culbert; Music/ Sound, Michael Bodeen; Music Arrangements, Michael Bodeen with Gary Kalar, Ronnie Malley, Eve Monzingo; PSM, Alden Vasquez; Stage Manager, Jamie Wolfe; Casting, Adam Belcuore, Stephanie Klapper; Cast: Faran Tahir (King Bahram), Anjali Bhimani (The Indian Princess), Atley S. Loughridge (The Greek Princess), Charlotte Speigner (The Moorish Princess), Sogia Jean Gomez (The Russian Princess), Stacey Yen (The Turkish Princess), Lisa Tejero (The Chinese Princess), Nicole Shalhoub (The Persian Princess), Musicians: Gary Kalar, Ronnie Malley, Eve Monzingo; Albert Theatre; June 23–July 29, 2007

**Honus and Me** Adapted by Steven Dietz from the book by Dan Gutman; Presented in association with Chicago Children's Theatre; Director, Sean Graney; Sets, Todd Rosenthal; Lighting, Heather Gilbert; Cast: Tim Rock, Jane Alderman, Eric Slater, John Steven Crowley, Matthew Hozfeind, Jose Antonio Garcia; July 20–August 26, 2007

# Goodspeed Musicals

East Haddam and Chester, Connecticut

Forty-third Season

Executive Director, Michael P. Price; General Manager, Harriett Guin-Kittner

**Li'l Abner** Book by Norman Panama and Melvin Frank (based on the characters created by Al Capp), original direction & choreography by Michael Kidd; lyrics by Johnny Mercer, music by Gene de Paul; Director, Scott Schwartz; Choreography, Patti Colombo; Sets, David Gallo; Costumes, Michael Krass; Lighting, Kirk Bookman; Music Director, Michael O'Flaherty; Assistant Music Director, William J. Thomas; Orchestrations, Dan DeLange; Cast: Curt Buckler (Earthquake McGoon), Trent Armand Kendall (Marryin' Sam), Glenn Lawrence (Abner), William McCauley (General Bullmoose), Christeena Riggs (Daisy Mae), John Shuman (Pappy Yokum), Andrea Wolff (Mammy Yokum), Michele Ragusa (Appassionata Von Climax); Ensemble: Paul Aguirre, Jennifer Balagna, Adriene Couvillion, Larry Daggett, Dick Decareau, Ryan Donovan, Jeff Hiller, Krista Kurtzberg, Nick Locilento, Kate Marilley, Eddie Rabon, Shane Rhoades, Mark Roland, Sarrah Strimel, Shorey Walker, Christopher Windom; Swings: Ginger Child Smith, Dante Russo, Marcellus Waller; Goodspeed Opera House; April 21–July 2, 2006

**Caraboo, Princess of Javasu** Book by Marsha Norman, lyrics by Beth Blatt, music by Jenny Giering; Director, Gary Griffin; Norma Terris Theatre; May 19–28, 2006

**The 60's Project** Conceived by Janet Brenner, written by Janet Brenner and Ken Levin; Director, Richard Maltby Jr.; Choreography, Lisa Shriver; Music Director, Jason DeBord; Maggie Benjamin (Susan), Rodrick Covington (Samuel), Michael Gillis (Jack), Rodney Hicks (Roy), Megan Lewis (Laura), Andrew Rannells (Billy), Lois Robbins (Lynne), Angela Williams (Rose); Ensemble: Cameron Adams, Mark Bush, Darryl E. Calmese Jr., Claire Karpen, Michael Kadin Craig, Kevin Hale, Miles Johnson, Bobby List, Amy McAlexander, Alexis Sims, Idara Victor; Norma Terris Theatre; August 10–September 3, 2006

*The Cast of* The 60's Project *(photo by Diane Sobolewski)*

**Pirates!** Book and lyrics by Sir William S. Gilbert, music by Sir Arthur S. Sullivan, reconceived by Gordon Greenberg, Nell Benjamin and John McDaniel, with additional book and lyrics by Nell Benjamin; New Music Arrangements/Musical Supervisor, John McDaniel; Director, Gordon Greenberg; Choreography, Warren Carlyle; Sets, Robert Bissinger; Costumes, David C. Woolard; Lighting, Jeff Croiter; Music Director, Michael O'Flaherty; Assistant Musical Director, William J. Thomas; Cast: Farah Alvin (Mabel), Ed Dixon (Major General), Joanna Glushak (Ruth), Gerry McIntyre (Sergeant), John O'Creagh (Samuel), Julia Osborne (Edith), Jason Michael Snow (Frederic), Andrew Varela (Pirate King); Ensemble: Matt Baker, Ryan Bauer-Walsh, Matthew Scott Campbell, Kyle Fichtman, Robyn Kramer, Nick Mannix, Lindsay K. Northen, Michael Rossmy, Roger Preston Smith, Daniel Spiotta, Leah Sprecher, Rebecca Strimaitis, Leonard E. Sullivan, Swings: Jacque Carnahan, Scott Ross; Goodspeed Opera House; October 6–December 10, 2006

**Pippin** Book by Roger O. Hirson, music and lyrics by Stephen Schwartz; Director, Gabriel Barre; Choreography, Mark Dendy; Sets, Beowulf Boritt; Costumes, Liz Prince; Lighting, Kevin Adams; Music Director, Michael O'Flaherty; Music Director/Conductor, Mark Hartman; Orchestrations, Michael Croiter & David Chiappetta; Associate Musical Director, Andrew Graham; Cast: Jason Blaine (Theo), Micky Dolenz (Charlemagne), James Royce Edwards (Lewis), Shannon Lewis (Fastrada), Barbara Marineau (Berthe), Joshua Park (Pippin), Andre Ward (Leading Player), Teal Wicks (Catherine); Ensemble: Sara Antkowiak-Maier, Stephen Brotebeck, Molly Tynes, Jason Dougherty, Dell Howlett, Ryan Kelly, Karl Maier, Lauren Marshall, Candy Olsen, Vincent Rodriquez III, Dana Winkle, Swings: Ashley Arcement, Brandon Tyler Fields; Goodspeed Opera House; July 14–September 24, 2006; National Tour: October 2006–January 2007

**Meet John Doe** Music and book by Andrew Gerle, lyrics and book by Eddie Sugarman; Additional story by Matt August; Director, Michael Baron; Choreography, Karma Camp; Music Director, Albin Konopka; Cast: Joel Blum (Colonel), Keegan Michael Brown (Beany), Donna Lynne Champlin (Ann Mitchell), James Moye (John Doe), Guy Paul (Connell), Patrick Ryan Sullivan (DB Norton), Melanie Vaughan (Mother); Ensemble: David Andrew Anderson, Ronald L. Brown, Rachel Clark, Monique French, Victoria Huston-Elem, Aaron Lee Lambert, Nicole Mangi, Mark Sanders, Jaron Vesely; Norma Terris Theatre; November 9–December 3, 2006

# Guthrie Theater

Minneapolis, Minnesota

Forty-fourth Season

Director, Joe Dowling

**The Great Gatsby** Adapted for the stage by Simon Levy; Director, David Esbjornson; Sets, Thomas Lynch; Costumes, Jane Greenwood; Lighting, Michael Philippi; Composer, Wayne Barker; Sound, Scott W. Edwards; Dramaturg, Amy Wegener; Movement, Marcela Lorca; Voice/Dialect Coach, Lucinda Holshue; Stage Manager, Chris A. Code; ASM, Michele Harms; Assistant Director, Braden Abraham; Cast: Matthew Amendt (Nick Carraway), Lorenzo Pisoni (Jay Gatsby), Heidi Armbruster (Daisy Buchanan), Erik Heger (Tom Buchanan), Cheyenne Casebier (Jordan Baker), Christina Baldwin (Myrtle Wilson), Mark Rhein (George Wilson), Raye Birk (Meyer Wolfshiem), Bob Davis (Chester McKee/Policeman), Kate Eifrig (Lucille McKee/Mrs. Michaelis); July 15–September 10, 2006

*Mark Rhein, Erik Heger, Cheyenne Casebier, and Matthew Amendt in* The Great Gatsby *(photo by Michal Daniel)*

**The Real Thing** by Tom Stoppard; Director, Joe Dowling; Sets, John Arnone; Costumes, Helen Q. Huang; Lighting, Christopher Akerlind; Sound, Scott W. Edwards; Movement, Marcela Lorca; Dramaturg, Carla Steen; Voice/Dialect Consultant, Gillian Lane-Plescia; Stage Manager, Martha Kulig; ASM, Ann K. Terlizzi; Assistant Director, Ben Kernan; Cast: Jay Goede (Henry), Kathryn Meisle (Annie), Lee Mark Nelson (Max), Sally Wingert (Charlotte), Jonas Goslow (Billy), Mike Rasmussen (Brodie), Elizabeth Stahlmann (Debbie); August 5–September 24, 2006

**The Falls** by Jeffrey Hatcher; Co-directors, Michael John Garcés and Bill Rauch; Sets, Christopher Acebo; Costumes, Lynn Jeffries; Lighting, Geoff Korf; Musical Direction/Incidental Music, Andrew Cooke; Sound, C. Andrew Mayer; Movement, Marcela Lorca; Movement Assistant, Randy Reyes; Dramaturg, Michael Bigelow Dixon; Voice/Dialect Consultant, Lucinda Holshue; Stage Manager, Christine Nelson; ASM, Jody Gavin; Assistant Director, Vincent Tycer; Community Dialogue Coordinators, Kathleen Shuler & Harry Waters Jr.; Cast: Sarah Agnew, Leslie Ball, Tamsen Brock, Antonia Brown, Chris Carlson, Michele Celia, Maggie Chestovich, Nicholas J. Christenson, Chango Cummings, DeAnna Cummings, Nesra Cummings, Asma Haidara, Shawn Hamilton, Steve Hendrickson, Peter Howard, Grace Marjean Kibira, John Kunik, Bishara Moallim, Rokia Moallim, Cole Nicholls, Clara Niiska, Arthur Noble, Eleanor Noble, Elizabeth O'Sullivan, Jeany Park, Barbara June Patterson, Mykola Rieland, Isabel Rousmaniere, Ned Rousmaniere, Chris Steller, Frances Stoopes-Yoo, Romanna Vasylevych, Harry Waters Jr., Regina Marie Williams, Robyn Ciera Williams; August 19–September 10, 2006

**Lost in Yonkers** by Neil Simon; Director, Gary Gisselman; Sets, John Arnone; Costumes, David Kay Mickelsen; Lighting, Don Darnutzer; Sound, Scott W. Edwards; Movement, Marcela Lorca; Dramaturg, Michael Lupu; Voice/Dialogue Consultant, Elisa Carlson; Stage Manager, Russell W. Johnson; ASM, Michele Harms; Assistant Director, Robert Goudy; Cast: Michael Booth (Eddie), Rosaleen Linehan (Grandma Kurnitz), Stephen Pelinski (Louie), Finnerty Steeves (Bella), Suzanne Warmanen (Gert), Dylan Frederick or Ryan Howell (Art), Noah Madoff or Ryan McCartan, (Jay); September 23–November 12, 2006

**Edgargo Mine** by Alfred Uhry, based on the book *The Kidnapping of Edgardo Mortara* by David I. Kertzer; Director, Mark Lamos; Sets, Riccardo Hernández; Costumes, Candice Donnelly; Lighting, Mimi Jordan Sherin; Composer, Robert Waldman; Sound, Reid Rejsa; Movement, Marcela Lorca; Dramaturg, Jo Holcomb; Voice/Dialect Coach, Lucinda Holshue; Stage Manager, Chris A. Code; ASM, Ann K. Terlizzi; Assistant Director, Sean Michael Dooley; Cast: Brian Murray (Pope Pius IX), Jennifer Regan (Marianna Mortara), Ron Menzel (Momolo Mortara/Pio Edgardo), Stephen D'Ambrose (Cardinal Antonelli), Nancy Rodriguez (Nina Morisi/Sgra Scazzocchio), J.C. Cutler (Fr. Feletti/Gramont/Il Dottore), Tyson Forbes (Lucidi/Scazzocchio/Riccardo Mortara), Sasha Andreev (Agostini/Fr. Giovanni/Rally Speaker); November 4–December 17, 2006

**A Christmas Carol** by Charles Dickens, adapted by Barbara Field; Director, Gary Gisselman; Sets, Neil Patel; Costumes, Jess Goldstein; Additional Costumes, David Kay Mickelsen; Lighting, Marcus Dilliard; Sound, Scott W. Edwards; Composer, Victor Zupanc; Musical Director, Anita Ruth; Dramaturg, Michael Lupu; Associate Director/Movement Coach, Myron Johnson; Voice/Dialect Coach, Elisa Carlson, Lucinda Holshue; Stage Manager, Martha Kulig; ASM, Jason Clusman; Assistant Director, Rob Goudy; Cast: Priya Anczarski, Lexy Armour, Raye Birk, Michael Booth, Joseph Botten, Maren Bush, Peter Cassada, Aaron Coker, Francesca Dawis, Laura Esping, Larry J. Evans, Susan Fick, Cassie Fox, Nathaniel Fuller, Courtney Glenny, Jonas Goslow, Jon Andrew Hegge, Kate Howell, Kathleen Humphrey, Derek Huntley, Charity Jones, Lily Jones, Michael Kissin, Simone Kolander, Tracey Maloney, Bill McCallum, Kris L. Nelson, Lee Mark Nelson, Ryan Neugent, Isabell Monk O'Connor, Stephen Pelinski, Kelsey Peterjohn, Randy Reyes, Johnathan Ricks, Amanda Schnabel, Doug Scholz-Carlson, Beverly Sotelo, Anna Sundberg, Vern Sutton, Suzanne Warmanen, Sally Wingert, Max Wojtanowicz, Jordan Young; November 26–December 30, 2006

**The Glass Menagerie** by Tennessee Williams; Director, Joe Dowling; Sets, Richard Hoover; Costumes, Ann Hould-Ward; Lighting, Jane Cox; Sound, Scott W. Edwards; Composer, Robert Waldman; Dramaturg, Jo Holcomb; Voice/Dialects, Elisa Carlson; Movement, Marcela Lorca; Stage Manager, Chris A. Code; ASM, Michele Harms; Assistant Director, Ron Menzel; Cast: Jonas Goslow (Jim O'Connor, the Gentleman Caller), Harriet Harris (Amanda), Randy Harrison (Young Tom), Tracey Maloney (Laura) and Bill McCallum (Old Tom); January 20–March 25, 2007

**The Merchant of Venice** by William Shakespeare; Director, Joe Dowling; Sets, Riccardo Hernández; Costumes, Paul Tazewell; Lighting, Matthew Reinert; Composer, Keith Thomas; Sound, Scott W. Edwards; Movement, Marcela Lorca; Dramaturg, Michael Lupu; Voice & Language Consultant, Andrew Wade; Stage Manager, Martha Kulig; ASM, Jason Clusman; Assistant Director, Eric Powell Holm; Cast: Matthew Amendt (Lorenzo), Raye Birk (Balthazar), Michael Booth (Solanio/Salerio), Robert Dorfman (Shylock), Wayne A. Evenson (Salarino), Susan Hofflander (Serving Woman), Richard S. Iglewski (Antonio), Jim Lichtscheidl (Launcelot Gobbo), Ron Menzel (Bassanio), Kris L. Nelson (Leonardo), Lee Mark Nelson (Gratiano), Michelle O'Neill (Portia), Stephen Pelinski (Prince of Arragon/Duke of Venice), Mark Rosenwinkel (Old Gobbo/Tubal), William Sturdivant (Prince of Morocco), Christine Weber (Jessica), Sally Wingert (Nerissa); March 10–May 6, 2007

**Major Barbara** by George Bernard Shaw; Director, Lisa Peterson; Sets, Neil Patel; Costumes, Michael Krass; Lighting, David Weiner; Composer/Sound, Mark Bennett; Dramaturg, Carla Steen; Vocal and Dialect Coach, Elisa Carlson; Movement, Marcela Lorca; Stage Manager, Chris A. Code; ASM, Michele Harms; Assistant Director, Annelise Christ; Cast: Sarah Agnew (Barbara Undershaft),

Paul O'Brien (Andrew Undershaft), Sandra Shipley (Lady Britomart), Joe Paulik (Stephen Undershaft), Jesse Pennington (Adolphus Cusins), Charlie Bethel (Morrison/Bilton), J.C. Cutler (Bill Walker), Laura Esping (Mrs. Baines), Isabell Monk O'Connor (Rummy Mitchens), Stephen Yoakam (Peter Shirley), Hope Cervantes (Jenny Hill), Jonas Goslow (Charles Lomax), Mike Rasmussen (Snobby Price), Vanessa Caye Wasche (Sarah Undershaft); May 5–June 17, 2007

**Boats on a River** by Julie Marie Myatt; Director, Michael Bigelow Dixon; Sets, Victor A. Becker; Costumes, Lynda K. Myers; Lighting, Matthew Reinert; Sound, Reid Rejsa; Video, Heidi Edwards; Dramaturg, Amy Wegener; Vocal and Dialects, Elisa Carlson; Movement, Stuart Pimsler; Video Images, Carol Banker; Stage Manager, Jody Gavin; ASM, Amy Monroe; Assistant Director, Steve Moulds; Cast: Nathaniel Fuller (Sidney Webb), Yoko Fumoto (Tam Webb), Peter Christian Hansen (Ted Thompson), Dale Hodges (Sister Margaret), Kris L. Nelson (Jonathan Black), Mayano Ochi (Lida), Jeany Park (Yen), Randy Reyes (Max), Rebecca J. Wall (Kolab), Aeola Lu (Cambodian Girl), Megan K. Mecklenburg (Cambodian Girl), Anna Northenscold (Cambodian Girl), Isabelle Yang (Cambodian Girl); May 19–June 10, 2007

*Dale Hodges and Rebecca J. Wall in* Boats on a River
*(photo by Michal Daniel)*

**1776** Music and lyrics by Sherman Edwards, book by Peter Stone; Director, John Miller-Stephany; Musical Director/Conductor, Andrew Cooke; Choreography, James Sewell; Sets, James Youmans; Costumes, Mathew J. LeFebvre; Lighting, Donald Holder; Sound, Scott W. Edwards; Dramaturg, Jo Holcomb; Speech and Dialect Coach, Kate Burke; Stage Manager, Martha Kulig; ASM, Jason Clusman; Assistant Director, Sarah Gioia; Cast: Michael Thomas Holmes (John Adams), Peter Michael Goetz (Benjamin Franklin), Tyson Forbes (Thomas Jefferson), Richard White (Richard Henry Lee), Norah Long (Abigail Adams), Robert O. Berdahl (Robert Livingston), Bob Beverage (Caesar Rodney), Raye Birk (Stephen Hopkins), Michael Booth (Rev. John Witherspoon), Mark Bradley (a Painter), Elizabeth Broadhurst (Martha Jefferson), Philip Callen (Dr. Lyman Hall), Sean Michael Dooley (Leather Apron), Wayne A. Evenson (Samuel Chase), Dan Foss (Roger Sherman), Bradley Greenwald (Edward Rutledge), Jon Andrew Hegge (Charles Thomson), Robb McKindles (Joseph Hewes), Lee Mark Nelson (John Dickinson), James Ramlet (Col. Thomas McKean), Mark Rosenwinkel (Andrew McNair), Brian Skellenger (Courier), Brian Sostek (James Wilson), Vern Sutton (Lewis Morris), Peter Thomson (John Hancock), Tony Vierling (Dr. Josiah Bartlett), Jon Whittier (George Read); June 23–August 26, 2007

# Illinois Theatre Center

Park Forest, Illinois

Thirty-first Season

Producing Artistic Director, Etel Billig; Associate Director, Jonathan R. Billig; Technical Director, James Corey

**Waiting for the Parade** by John Murrell; Director,: Etel Billig; Cast: Judy Rossignuolo-Rice, Kira Durbin, Mary Jane Guymon, Jennifer Loftus, Chris Blumer; September 29–October 15, 2006

**The Abandoned El** by Adam Kraar; Director, Etel Billig; Cast: Becca McCoy (Shari), Peter Robel (Robbie); World Premiere; October 27–November 15, 2006

**Kuni-Leml** Book by Nahma Sandrow, music by Raphael Crystal, Lyrics by Richard Engquist; Director, Etel Billig; Choreography, Frank Roberts; Cast: Bernard Rice, Cara Scott, David Lipschutz, Sean Quinlan, Jeny Wasilewski, Frank Roberts, Mike Padden, Reid O'Connell; December 1–16, 2006

**Incognito** Written, directed, and performed by Michael Sidney Fosberg; January 5–21, 2007

**Two Trains Running** by August Wilson; Director, Chuck Gary; Cast: Jason Ball, Inda Craig-Galvan, Lionel Gentle, J.J. McCormick, Michael Kevin Martin, James Pringle, Chuck Gary; February 7–25, 2007

**Candida** by George Bernard Shaw; Director, Etel Billig; Cast: Becca McCoy, David Boettcher, Christopher Merrill, Jack Ryan, Laura Lodewyck, Zachary Clark; March 16–April 1, 2007

**The Last Five Years** Book, music & lyrics by Jason Robert Brown; Director, David Perkovich; Cast: Cory Goodrich (Cathy), Marc Pera (Jamie); April 20–May 6, 2007

*Becca McCoy and Peter Robel in* The Abandoned El
*(photo by Warren Skalski*

# Indiana Repertory Theatre

Indianapolis, Indiana

Thirty-fifth Season

Artistic Director, Janet Allen; Managing Director, Steven Stolen; Associate Artistic Director, Priscilla Lindsay; Playwright-in-Residence, James Still

**The Gentleman from Indiana** by Booth Tarkington, adapted by James Still; Director, Peter Amster; Sets, Russell Metheny; Costumes, Mara Blumenfeld; Lighting, Ann G. Wrightson; Sound, Todd Mack Reischman; Composer, Gregg Coffin; Dramaturg, Richard J. Roberts; Stage Manager, Nathan Garrison; ASM, Krista M. Layfield; Cast: David Alan Anderson (Xenophon Gibbs), Jessica Berns (Hazel Landis), Jason Bradley (John Harkless), Tom Conner (Young William Todd), Adam O. Crowe (Sheriff Jim Bardlock), Joseph Culliton (Judge Briscoe), Catherine Lynn Davis (Mrs. Landis/ Martha Sherwood), Robert Elliott (Fisbee), Charles Goad (Rodney McClune/Kedge Halloway/Bob Skillet/Mr. Macauley), Mark Goetzinger (Old Tom Martin); Sawyer Harvey (Caleb Landis), Robert K Johansen (Homer Tibbs), Jan Lucas (Miss Selena Tibbs), Jason Marr (Tom Meredith), PJ Maske (Minnie Briscoe), Emily Ristine (Helen Sherwood), Daniel Scharbrough (Columbus "Lum" Landis); September 13–October 7, 2006

**Huckleberry Finn** by Mark Twain, adapted by Rita Grossberg Grauer and John Urquhart; Director, Priscilla Lindsay; Sets, Robert M. Koharchik; Costumes, Joel Ebarb; Lighting, Robert A. Shakespeare; Sound; Todd Mack Reischman; Dramaturg, Richard J. Roberts; Stage Manager, James W. Carringer; Fight Choreography, Robert K. Johansen; Cast: Bryant Bentley (Jim), Manon Halliburton (Widow Douglas/Tom Sawyer/Judith Loftus), Jeff Keel (Mark Twain/Duke/Aunt Sally), Robert Neal (Pap/ King), Brian Sheppard (Huckleberry Finn), David W. Wierhake (Musician/Man on the River); October 1–November 4, 2006

**A Christmas Carol** by Charles Dickens, adapted by Tom Haas; Director, Priscilla Lindsay; Sets, Russell Metheny; Costumes, Murell Horton; Lighting, Michael Lincoln; Composer, Andrew Hopson; Choreography, David Hochoy; Associate Lighting, Betsy Cooprider-Bernstein; Musical Director, Christopher Ludwa; Dramaturg, Richard J. Roberts; Stage Manager, Nathan Garrison; ASM, Joel Markus; Young Actor Supervisor, Mary Ferguson; Cast: David Alan Anderson (Portly Gentleman/Christmas Present/Old Joe), Ben Ayres (Willful Smackers/ Christmas Future/Poulterer's Man), Jason Bradley (Young Scrooge/Lamplighter/ Broker), Nick Carpenter (Postboy/Belle's Husband/Broker), Danielle Colucci or Tara Morton (Belinda Cratchit/Fan), Mathew Conwell or Garrett McKenna (Henry Cratchit/Ignorance/Turkey Boy), Gerson Dacanay (Fred/Christmas Past), Charles Goad (Ebenezer Scrooge), Mark Goetzinger (Fezziwig/Topper/Undertaker), Anne Green or Jacqueline White (Betsy Cratchit/Want), Noah Huber or Ciarra Krohne (Tiny Tim/Boy Scrooge), Jennifer Johansen (Belle/Fred's Maid), Robert K. Johansen (Bob Cratchit/Jacob Marley), Constance Macy (Sister of Mercy/Roses Sister/Charwoman), P.J. Maske (Felicity/Martha Cratchit), Kevin Mull or Calvin Smith (Peter Cratchit/Adolescent Scrooge/Dick Wilkins), Brian Nofke (Waiter/ Schoolmaster/Nutley/Broker), Lynne Perkins (Mrs. Cratchit/Mrs. Fezziwig), Angela Plank (Plump Sister/Laundress); November 4–December 24, 2006

**I Have Before Me a Remarkable Document Given to Me By a Young Lady from Rwanda** by Sonja Linden; Director, Risa Brainin; Sets, Russell Metheny; Costumes, Linda Pisano; Lighting, Michael Klaers; Sound, Todd Mack Reischman; Dialect Coach, Candace Taylor; Dramaturg, Richard J. Roberts; Stage Manager, Krista M. Layfield; Casting, Claire Simon Casting; Assistant Director, Georgianna Smith; Cast: Monét Butler (Juliette), Henry Woronicz (Simon); November 15–December 23, 2006

**Gem of the Ocean** by August Wilson; Director, Timothy Douglas; Sets, Tony Cisek; Costumes, Junghyun Georgia Lee; Lighting, Peter Maradudin; Composer, Michael Keck; Sound, Todd Mack Reischman; Dramaturg, Richard J. Roberts; Stage Manager, Nathan Garrison; Casting, Harriet Bass; Co-Produced with Syracuse Stage and Geva Theatre Center; Assistant to the Director, Joanna Winston; Assistant Lighting, Tanya Moake; Fight Choreography, Robert K. Johansen; Vocalist, Kai Mwaafrika; Cast: David Alan Anderson (Caesar Wilks), Chris Chalk (Citizen Barlow), Tracy Griswold (Rutherford Selig), Rachel Leslie (Black Mary), Lizan Mitchell (Aunt Ester), Ernest Perry Jr. (Solly Two Kings), Cedric Turner (Eli); January 17–February 10, 2007

**Twelfth Night** by William Shakespeare, conceived by Janet Allen; Director, Richard J. Roberts; Sets, Robert M. Koharchik; Costumes, Joel Ebarb; Lighting, Ryan Koharchik; Sound, Todd Mack Reischman; Choreography, David Hochoy; Stage Manager, James W. Carringer; Fight Choreography, Robert K. Johansen; Cast: Nick Carpenter (Sebastian), Charles Goad (Malvolio), Jennifer Johansen (Viola), Robert K. Johansen (Feste), Jeff Keel (Sir Toby Belch), Kristin Lennox (Lady Olivia), Robert Neal (Count Orsino), Bill Simmons (Captain/Antonio), Ben Tebbe (Sire Andrew Aguecheek), Milicent Wright (Maria); January 27–February 3, 2007

**Death of a Salesman** by Arthur Miller; Director, Tim Ocel; Sets, Erhard Rom; Costumes, B. Modern; Lighting, Lap-Chi Chu; Composer, Gregg Coffin; Sound, Todd Mack Reischman; Assistant Director, Melissa Rain Anderson; Dramaturg, Richard J. Roberts; Stage Manager, Joel Grynheim; Co-Produced with Syracuse Stage; Fight Choreography, Erik Fredricksen; Lighting Assistant, JoJo Percy, Taylor Fidler-Jarzyniecki, Garrett McKenna; Cast: Andrew Ahrens (Happy Loman), Kenneth Albers (Willy Loman), Ryan Artzberger (Biff Loman), Catherine Lynn Davis (The Woman), Ted Deasy (Howard Wagner/Stanley), Erik Fredricksen

(Ben Loman), Mark Goetzinger (Charley), Kelsey Hanlon (Jenny/Letta), Priscilla Lindsay (Linda Loman), Jennifer Lytle (Miss Forsythe), Sam Misner (Bernard); February 28–March 24, 2007

*Ryan Artzberger, Kenneth Albers, and Andrew Ahrens in* Death of a Salesman *(photo courtesy of Indiana Repertory Theatre)*

**Bad Dates** by Theresa Rebeck; Director, James Still; Sets, Wilson Chin; Costumes, Gail Brassard; Lighting, Michael Lincoln; Original Music, Carrie Newcomer; Sound, Todd Mack Reischman; Dramaturg, Richard J. Roberts; Stage Manager, Krista Layfield; Assistant Lighting, Rachelle Beckerman; Cast: Lauren Lovett (Haley); March 13–April 22, 2007

**The Unexpected Guest** by Agatha Christie; Director, Robert Moss; Sets, Russell Metheny; Costumes, Junghyun Georgia Lee; Lighting, Philip Monat; Sound, Jonathon Herter; Dialect Coach, Candace Taylor; Dramaturg, Richard J. Roberts; Stage Manager, Nathan Garrison; Casting, Alan Filderman; Co-Produced with Syracuse Stage; Assistant to the Director, Heather Harvey; Cast: Ben Ayres (Sergeant Cadwallader), Genevieve Elam (Laura Warwick), Richmond Hoxie (Inspector Thomas), Kathleen Huber (Mrs. Warwick), Robert K. Johansen (Henry Angell), Anthony Marble (Julian Farrar), John G. Preston (Michael Starkwedder), Robb Sapp (Jan Warwick), Michele Tauber (Miss Bennett); April 10–May 6, 2007

## Intiman Theatre

Seattle, Washington

Thirty-fourth Season

Artistic Director, Bartlett Sher; Managing Director, Laura Penn

**Rounding Third** by Richard Dresser; Director, B.J. Jones; Sets, Bill Forrester; Costumes, Dennis Milam Bensie; Lighting, Greg Sullivan; Sound, Joseph Swartz; Stage Manager, Wendiana Walker; ASM, Ryan Nichols; Cast: Michael David Edwards (Michael), Richard Ziman (Don); April 14–May 14 2006

**Richard III** by William Shakespeare; Director, Bartlett Sher; Sets/Lighting, Christopher Akerlind; Costumes, Elizabeth Hope Clancy; Composer/Sound, Peter John Still; Fight Director, J. Steven White; Dialect Coach, Deena Burke; Assistant Director, Sari Ketter; Stage Manager, Lisa Ann Chernoff; ASM, Jamie Soulé; Cast: Hans Altwies (Thomas Rotherham/Henry, Earl of Richmond), Suzanne Bouchard (Queen Margaret), Dale Bowers (Cardinal Bourchier), Megan Cole (Duchess of York), Carter J. Davis (George Stanley), Bradford Farwell (Lord Lovell), Allen Fitzpatrick (King Edward IV), Kristin Flanders (Queen Elizabeth), Daniel E. Flint (Murderer/Sir James Blunt), Allen Gilmore (George, Duke of Clarence/Sir William Catesby), Lenne Klingaman (Lady Anne), Lance McQueen (Sir William Ratcliffe), Michael McQuilken (Musician), Kimo Muraki (Musician), Stephen Pelinski (Richard III), Timothy McCuen Piggee (Lord Hastings), Danielle Elizabeth Powell (Richard, Duke of York), John Pribyl (Lord Stanley), Luc James Rosenthal (Edward, Prince of Wales), Nicholas Stevens (Lord Grey), Tammy Taecker (Mistress Shore), Connor J. Toms (Marquis of Dorset), Michael Winters (Duke of Buckingham), John Wray (Lord Mayor/Sir Robert Brakenbury), R. Hamilton Wright (Earl Rivers/Sir James Tyrell); June 9–July 15, 2006

*Suzanne Bouchard, Stephen Pelinski, and the Company of* Richard III *(photo by Chris Bennion)*

**Heartbreak House** by George Bernard Shaw; Director, Jon Jory; Sets, Christopher Akerlind, Jennifer Zeyl; Costumes, Deb Trout; Lighting, Greg Sullivan; Sound, Stephen LeGrand; Dialect Coach, Judith Shahn; New York Casting, Janet Foster; Stage Manager, Wendiana Walker; ASM, Claire Zawa; Cast: Laurence Ballard (Alfred Mangan), Suzanne Bouchard (Lady Ariadne Utterword), Kate Goehring (Mrs. Hesione Hushabye), Suzy Hunt (Nurse Guinness), Michael Patten (Hector Hushabye, August 22–26), Stephen Pelinski (Hector Hushabye), David Pichette (Mazzini Dunn), Alexandra Tavares (Ellie Dunn), Michael Winters (Captain Shotover), R. Hamilton Wright (Randall Utterword); July 28–August 26, 2006

**Moonlight and Magnolias** by Ron Hutchinson; Director, Timothy Near; Sets, Matthew Smucker; Costumes, Elizabeth Hope Clancy; Lighting, David Lee Cuthbert; Sound, Stephen LeGrand; Fight Director, Geoffrey Alm; New York Casting, Janet Foster; Stage Manager, Melanie R. Mather; ASM, Jamie Soulé; Cast: Tom Beckett (David O. Selznick), Marya Sea Kaminski (Miss Poppenghul), John Procaccino (Victor Fleming), Peter Van Norden (Ben Hecht); September 8–October 7, 2006

**Native Son** by Richard Wright and Paul Green, adapted and directed by Kent Gash; Sets, Edward E. Haynes Jr.; Costumes, Frances Kenny; Lighting, William H. Grant III; Composer, Chic Street Man; Sound, Joseph Swartz; Fight Director, Geoffrey Alm; Dialect Coach, Judith Shahn; New York Casting, Janet Foster.; Stage Manager, Wendiana Walker; Stage Manager, Assistant, Claire Zawa; Cast: Earl Alexander (Gus/The Reverend), Ato Essandoh (Bigger Thomas), Ken Grantham (Mr. Dalton), Kimberly King (Mrs. Dalton), Richard Kline (Max/Newsreel Narrator),

Felicia V. Loud (Bessie/Vera Thomas), Carol Roscoe (Mary Dalton), Lukas Shadair (Buddy Thomas), MJ Sieber (Jan Erlone/Britten), Chic Street Man (Musician), Myra Lucretia Taylor (Mrs. Thomas/Ernie); October 20–November 19, 2006

*Ato Essandoh and Felicia V. Loud in* Native Son
*(photo by Chris Bennion)*

**Black Natvity** by Langston Hughes; Director, Jacqueline Moscou; Choreography, Kabby Mitchell III; Featuring Pastor Patrinell Wright, the Reverend Dr. Samuel B. McKinney, gospel performances by the Total Experience Gospel Choir and the Black Nativity Choir, choreography performed by an ensemble of dancers, and an on-stage band; November 29–December 27, 2006

# Kansas City Repertory Theatre

Kansas City, Missouri

Forty-third Season

Producing Artistic Director, Peter Altman

**Jitney** by August Wilson; Director, Lou Bellamy; Sets, Vicki M. Smith; Costumes, Mathew J. LeFebvre; Lighting, Michelle Habeck; Sound, John Story; PSM, Mary R. Honour; ASM, Beth Ellen Spencer; Cast: James T. Alfred (Youngblood), James Craven (Turnbo), Chuck Patterson (Fielding), Bus Howard (Doub), Abdul Salaam El Razzac (Shealy), Adolphus Ward (Philmore), Brian Anthony Wilson (Becker), Julia Pace Mitchell (Rena), Jacinto Taras Riddick (Booster); September 22–October 15, 2006

**A Christmas Carol** by Charles Dickens; Director, Linda Ade Brand; Sets, John Ezell; Costume Supervisor/Additional Costumes, Antonia Ford-Roberts; Lighting, Shane Rowse; Sound, John Story; Musical Director, Molly Jessup; Choreography, Jennifer Martin; PSM, Terence Orleans Alexander; ASM, Beth Ellen Spencer; Cast: Caroline Adams (Want), Jeanne Averill (Mrs. Cratchit), Tia Battle

(Saphronella), Craig Benton (Bob Cratchit), Robert Gibby Brand (Charles Dickens), Amy Coady (Poulterer's Wife), Jessie Datino (Belle, Laundress), Michael Dragen (Topper/Businessman), Elizabeth Ernst (Ensemble), Chloe Michelle Fey (Belinda Cratchit), Kristen Nicole French (Mrs. Fred), Peggy Friesen (Ghost of Christmas Past/Harpist), Charles Fugate (Fred), Jim Gall (Ghost of Christmas Present), Larry Greer (Marley), Zack Hoar (Tiny Tim), David Tyler Horseman (Ensemble), Jeremy Ims (Toy Vendor), Jessica Ims (Fan), Gary Neal Johnson (Scrooge), Sarah LaBarr (Serious Sister), Brock Christian Lorenzen (Ignorance), Kelcie Nicole Marquardt (Ensemble), Abbi Miller (Martha Cratchit/Giggly Sister), Emilie S. Minnick (Clovia), Alex Montgomery (Peter Cratchit), Merle Moores (Solicitor), Kyle L. Mowry (Undertaker), Nick Padgett (Bobby), Alex Hall Petersen (Scrooge as a boy), Michael Linsley Rapport (Mr. Fezziwig/Businessman), Mark Robbins (Old Joe), Hatchee Brad Shaw (Solicitor/Ghost of Christmas Future), Michael Andrew Smith (Scrooge as a young man), Rusty Sneary (Dick Wilkins), Cameron Benton Stout (Tiny Tim), McKenna Stout (Ensemble), Richard Stubblefield (Albert Hall), Carson Lee Teague (Ensemble), Ian VonFange (Simon), Kathleen Warfel (Mrs. Fezziwig/Charwoman), Rasson Wofford (Urchin); November 18–December 24, 2006

*James T. Alfred, Abdul Salaam El Razzac, and Jacinto Taras Riddick in*
Jitney *(photo by Don Ipock)*

**King Lear** by William Shakespeare; Director, Larry Carpenter; Sets, John Ezell; Costumes, Karin Kopischke; Sound, Tom Mardikes; Lighting, Phil Monat; PSM, Bret Torbeck; ASM, Beth Ellen Spencer; Cast: David DeSantos (Edmund), Gary Holcombe (Kent), Gary Neal Johnson (Gloucester), Denis Arndt (Lear), Kandis Chappell (Goneril), Naomi Peters (Cordelia), Suzanne Bouchard (Regan), John Rensenhouse (Albany), Kurt Rhoads (Cornwall), Ben Newman (Burgundy), David Graham Jones (King of France), David Barlow (Edgar), Logan Ernstthal (Oswald), Larry Paulsen (Fool), Richard Buswell (Edmund's Captain); Assembled Knights and Servants: Jess Atkin, David Bianco, Samuel T. Gaines, David Graham Jones, Todd Carlton Lanker, Anthony Merchant, Matt Rapport; January 19–February 11, 2007

**Love, Janis** Conceived, adapted, and directed by Randal Myler, inspired by the book by Laura Joplin; Music Director, Sam Andrew; Sets, Vicki M. Smith; Costumes, Lorraine Venberg; Lighting, Don Darnutzer; Sound, Eric Stahlhammer; Selected Original Light Show Images, Bill Hamm; Projections Coordinator, Jeffrey Cady; PSM, Mary R. Honour; Assistant to the Stage Manager, Brooke Redler; Cast: Kacee Clanton (Janis Joplin), Mary Bridget Davies (Janis Joplin), Lena Kaminsky (Janis Joplin), Dean Vivian (Interviewer) Musicians: Ken Lovern (keyboards), Terry Swope (lead guitar), Tim Braun (second guitar), Damien "WOO" Salazar (bass), Zack Albetta (drummer), David Sturch (trumpet), Adam Wagner (saxophone); February 2–March 18, 2007

**Sherlock Holmes: The Final Adventure** by Steven Dietz, based on the 1899 play by William Gillette and Arthur Conan Doyle; Director, David Ira Goldstein; Sets Bill Forrester; Costumes, David Kay Mickelsen; Lighting, Dennis Parichy;

Composer, Roberta Carlson; Sound, Brian Jerome Peterson; Associate Director, Kappy Kilburn; Fight Director, Kenneth Merckx, Jr., PSM, Timothy Toothman; ASM, Bryon F. Abens; Cast: Victor Talmadge (Dr. Watson), Mark Robbins (Sherlock Holmes), Preston Maybank (King of Bohemia), Charles Fugate (James Larrabee), Carey Cannon (Irene Adler), Cathy Barnett (Madge Larrabee), Gary Neal Johnson (Sid Prince), Laurence Ballard (Professor Moriarty); Ensemble: Kyle M. Browning, Cassandra Clark, Ryan Meharry; February 23–March 18, 2007

**The Syringa Tree** by Pamela Gien; Director, Sharon Ott; Set/Lighting, Kent Dorsey; Costumes, Lindsay W. Davis; Sounds, Steve LeGrand & John Story; PSM, Mary R. Honour; Assistant to the Stage Manager, Brooke Redler; Cast: Kate Goehring (Elizabeth Grace), Shanesia Davis (Salamina), Peggy Friesen (Eugenie/others), L. Peter Callender (Peter/Zephyr/others/Dubike), Gary Neal Johnson (Dr. Grace/others), Toccarra Cash (Iris/Moliseng); April 27–May 27, 2007

**Under Midwestern Stars** by Esther Blumenfeld; Director, Stephen Rothman; Sets, David Potts; Costumes, Antonia Ford-Roberts; Lighting, Victor En Yu Tan; Sound/Composer, Joe Cerqua; Projections, Jeffrey Cady; PSM, Timothy Toothman; ASM, Beth Ellen Spencer; Cast: Autumn Dornfeld (Rachel), Crista Moore (Lena), Mark Mineart (Joseph); May 11-June 3, 2007

**2 Pianos 4 Hands** by Ted Dykstra and Richard Greenblatt; Director, Bruce K. Sevy; Sets, Scott Weldin; Costumes, Kish Finnegan; Lighting, Don Darnutzer; Sound, Brian Jerome Peterson; PSMs, Deya S. Friedman & Mary R. Honour; Cast: Todd Almond (Ted), Carl J. Danielsen (Richard); May 26–June 24, 2007

# La Jolla Playhouse

La Jolla, California

Thirty-seventh Season

Artistic Director, Des McAnuff; Managing Director, Steven B. Libman

**Zhivago** Book by Michael Weller, music by Lucy Simon, lyrics by Michael Korie and Amy Powers; Director, Des McAnuff; Sets, Heidi Ettinger; Costumes, David C. Woolard; Lighting, Howell Binkley; Sound, Steve Canyon Kennedy; Music Director, Eric Stern; Choreography, Sergio Trujillo; Dramaturg, Allison Horsley; Fight Director, Steve Rankin; Orchestrations, Don Sebesky; Speech/Dialect Coach, Ursula Meyer; Cast: Dominic Bogart, Matt Bogart, Jessica Burrows, Sandy Campbell, Edward Conery, Ryan Drummond, Mark Emerson, David Carey Foster, Jason Heil, Ivan Hernandez, Tom Hewitt, Melissa Hoff, Mackenzie Holmes Christopher Kale Jones, Rebecca Kaasa, Melina Kalomas, David McDonald, Spencer Moses, Eduardo Placer, Graham Rowat, Maureen Silliman, Tina Stafford, Rena Strober, Nick Ullett, Bibi Valderrama, Melissa Van Der Schyff; Understudies: Tom Zohar, Kurt Norby, Emily Kosloski, Graham Rowat, Ryan Drummond, Autumn Bodily, Tina Stafford, Graham Rowat, Melina Kalomas, David Carey Foster; World Premiere; Mandell Weiss Theatre; May 10–July 9, 2006

**Mother Courage** by Bertolt Brecht, translated by David Hare; Presented in association with Berkeley Repertory Theatre; Director, Lisa Peterson; Music, Gina Leishman; Sets, Rachel Hauck; Costumes, David Zinn; Lighting, Alexander V. Nichols; Sound, Jill B.C. DuBoff; Music Director, Gina Leishman; Fight Director, Steve Rankin; Movement Director, MaryBeth Cavanaugh; Dramaturg, Shirley Fishman; Stage Manager, Lisa Porter; ASM, Anjee Nero; Casting, Amy Potozkin (Bay Area), Sharon Bialy and Sherry Thomas (Los Angeles), Tara Rubin (New York); Cast: Ara Anderson (Tuba/Accordion/ Ensemble), Katie Barrett (Yvette Pottier/Ensemble), Ivonne Coll (Mother Courage), David W. Collins (Drummer/Ensemble), Mark Danisovsky (Piano/Accordion/Ensemble), Brent Hinkley (Sergeant/Ensemble), Katie Huard (Kattrin), Drew Hirschfield (Swiss Cheese), Marc Damon Johnson (Recruiting Officer/Ensemble), Patrick Kerr (Chaplain/Ensemble), Justin Leath (Eilif/Ensemble), Jarion Monroe (Cook/Ensemble); Mandell Weiss Forum Theatre; June 20–July 23, 2006

*Jessica Burrows and Ivan Hernandez in* Zhivago *(photo by Kevin Berne)*

**all wear bowlers** Created and performed by Geoff Sobelle and Trey Lyford; Co-produced by rainpan 43 productions; Director, Aleksandra Wolska; Sets, Ed Haynes; Costumes, Tara Webb; Lighting, Randy "Igleu" Glickman; Film Production, Michael Glass; Sound, James Sugg; Film Score, Michael Friedman; PSM, Michelle Blair; Production Manager, Peter J. Davis; Sheila and Hughes Potiker Theatre; August 1–September 3, 2006

**Culture Clash's *Zorro in Hell*** Created, written, and performed by Culture Clash; commissioned by Berkeley Repertory Theatre, La Jolla Playhouse and Zorro Productions Inc.; Director, Tony Taccone; Sets, Christopher Acebo; Costumes, Christal Weatherly; Lighting, Alexander V. Nichols; Sound, Robbin E. Broad; Stage Manager, Kimberly Mark Webb; Fight Director, Dave Maier; Movement Director, Marybeth Cavanaugh; Dramaturg, Shirley Fishman; Cast: Richard Montoya, Ric Salinas, Herbert Sigüenza, Joseph Kamal, Sharon Lockwood; World Premiere; Sheila and Hughes Potiker Theatre; September 30–October 29, 2006

**The Wiz** Book by William F. Brown, music and lyrics by Charlie Smalls, based on *The Wonderful Wizard Of Oz* by L. Frank Baum; Director, Des McAnuff; Orchestrations, Harold Wheeler; Scenic and Environmental Design, Robert Brill; Costumes, Paul Tazewell; Lighting, Howell Binkley; Sound, Peter Fitzgerald; Projections; Michael Clark; Music Director, Ron Melrose; Choreography, Sergio Trujillo; Associate Choreography, Kelly Devine; Dramaturgy, Shirley Fishman; PSM, Frank Hartenstein; Stage Manager, Kelly Martindale; ASM, Michelle

Reupert; Assistant Directors, Holly-Anne Ruggiero & Robert O'Hara; Production Manager, Peter J. Davis; Cast: Charl Brown, Tituss Burgess, E. Faye Butler, Albert Blaise Cattafi, Courtney Corey, Mark Emerson, Dionne D. Figgins, Demond Green, David Alan Grier, Albert Guerzon, Nikki M. James, Dominique Kelley, Ron Kellum, Heather Lee, Orville Mendoza, Alan Mingo, Jr., Anisha Nagarajan, Rashad Naylor, NRaca, Valarie Pettiford, Karine Plantadit, Tera-Lee Pollin, Liz Ramos, Keiana Richard, Marcos Santana and Michael Benjamin Washington; Swings: Jacqueline Maraya Griffin, Jonathan Taylor; Mandell Weiss Theatre; September 26–November 26, 2006

*Tituss Burgess, Nikki M. James, Rashad Naylor, and Michael Benjamin Washington in* The Wiz *(photo by Kevin Berne)*

**The Farnsworth Invention** by Aaron Sorkin; Director, Des McAnuff; Original Music, Andrew Lippa; Sets, Klara Zieglerova; Choreography, Lisa Shriver; Costumes, David C. Woolard; Lighting, Howell Binkley; Sound, Walter Trarbach; Fight Director, Steve Rankin; Vocal Consultation, Ursula Meyer; Dramaturgy, Adam Greenfield; PSM, Rachel J. Perlman; ASM, Stephanie Atlan; Production Manager, Peter J. Davis; Casting, Sharon Bialy & Sherry Thomas (West Coast), Tara Rubin (East Coast); Cast: Jennifer Austin, Nadia Bowers, A.J. Ditty, Ryan Drummond, Amy Ellenberger, Kyle Fabel, Maurice Godin, Morgan Thomas Hollingsworth, Brian Howe, Stephen Lang, Joshua Everett Johnson, Bruce McKenzie, Spencer Moses, Jim Ortlieb, Michael Pemberton, Katharine Powell, Steve Rosen, Jimmi Simpson, James Sutorius, Alexandra Wilson; Page To Stage Workshop Production; Potiker Theatre; February 20–March 25, 2007

*The Cast of* The Farnsworth Invention *(photo by J.T. MacMillan)*

# Long Wharf Theatre

New Haven, Connecticut

Forty-second Season

Artistic Director, Gordon Edelstein; Managing Director, Joan Channick

**Durango** by Julia Cho; Director, Chay Yew; Sets, Dan Ostling; Costumes, Linda Cho; Lighting, Paul Whitaker; Sound and Additional Music Composition, Fabian Obispo; Dialect Coach, Esther Goodheart; PSM, Buzz Cohen; Dramaturg, Beatrice Basso; Cast: James Yaegashi (Isaac Lee), James Saito (Boo-Seng Lee), Ross Bickell (Ned/Jerry), Jon Norman Schneider (Jimmy Lee), Jay Sullivan (The Red Angel/Bob); September 13–October 15, 2006

**Rocket to the Moon** by Clifford Odets; Director, Daniel Fish; Sets, Andrew Lieberman; Costumes, Kaye Voyce; Lighting, Jane Cox; Sound, Corrine K. Livingston; Stage Manager, Alison Cote; ASM, Amy Patricia Stern; Casting, Alaine Alldaffer; Cast: David Chandler (Ben Stark), Christina Kirk (Belle Stark), Andrew Weems (Phil Cooper), Louisa Krause (Cleo Singer), David Margulies (Mr. Prince), Henry Stram (Frenchy), Danny Mastrogiorgio (Willy Wax); October 25–November 19, 2006

*Louisa Krause and David Chandler in* Rocket to the Moon *(photo by T. Charles Erickson)*

**The Santaland Diaries** by David Sedaris, adapted by Joe Mantello; Director, Kim Rubenstein; Sets, Jessica Ford; Costumes, Olivera Gajic; Lighting, Josh Epstein; Sound, Daniel Baker; Stage Manager, Jason Kaiser; Cast: Thomas Sadoski (Man/Crumpet); November 29–December 31, 2006

*Thomas Sadoski in* The Santaland Diaries
*(photo by T. Charles Erickson)*

**The Cocktail Hour** by A.R. Gurney; Director, Kim Rubenstein; Sets, Michael Yeargan, Costumes, Candice Donnelly; Lighting, Pat Collins; Sound, Andre Pluess; Stage Manager, Alison Cote; ASM, Amy Patricia Stern; Cast: John Cunningham (Bradley), Mary Beth Peil (Ann), Rob Campbell (John), Ann Talman (Nina); January 10–February 4, 2007

**Man of La Mancha** Book by Dale Wasserman, music by Mitch Leigh, lyrics by Joe Darion; Director, Charles Newell; Musical Director, Doug Peck; Sets, John Culbert; Costumes, Jacqueline Firkins; Lighting, Mark McCullough; Sound, Ray Nardelli & Josh Horvath; Fight Director, Rick Sordelet; PSM, Cole P. Bonenberger; ASM, Amy Patricia Stern; Cast: Herbert Perry (Miguel De Cervantes), Hollis Resnik (Aldonza/Dulcinea), Jim Corti (Sancho Panza), Matthew Krause (The Duke/Dr. Sanson Carrasco), Stephen Wallen (The Padre), Rena Strober (Antonia), Lucia Spina (Maria/Housekeeper), Benjamin Magnuson (The Barber), Sean Blake (Pedro), Pat McRoberts (The Gypsy); February 21–March 18, 2007

**The Blue Album** Written and performed by David Cale and Dael Orlandersmith; Director, Gordon Edelstein; Sets, Neil Patel; Costumes, Anita Yavich; Lighting, Jennifer Tipton; Sound, John Gromada; Dramaturg, Beatrice Basso; Stage Manager, Jason Kaiser; March 28–April 29, 2007

**Uncle Vanya** by Anton Chekhov, adapted and directed by Gordon Edelstein; Sets, Michael Yeargan; Costumes, Jane Greenwood; Lighting, Christopher Akerlind; Sound, Daniel Baker; Stage Manager, Bret Torbeck, ASM, Amy Patricia Stern; Dramaturg, Beatrice Basso, Cast: Zoaunne Leroy (Marina), Marco Barricelli (Astrov), Mark Blum (Vanya), William Biff McGuire (Serebryakov), Larry Block (Telyegin), Jennifer Dundas (Sonya), Elisabeth Waterston (Yelena), Waltrudis Buck (Maria), Charles Tirrell (Worker); May 9–June 3, 2007

*Elizabeth Waterston and Mark Blum in* Uncle Vanya
*(photo by T. Charles Erickson)*

# McCarter Theatre Center

Princeton, New Jersey

Forty-seventh Season

Artistic Director, Emily Mann; Managing Director, Jeffrey Woodward; Producer Director, Mara Isaacs; Director of Production, David York

**The Birthday Party** by Harold Pinter; Director, Emily Mann; Sets, Eugene Lee; Costumes, Jennifer von Mayrhauser; Lighting Jeff Croiter; Sound, Rob Milburn and Michael Bodeen; Fight Consultant, Rick Sordelet; Casting, Laura Stanczyk; PSM, Cheryl Mintz; Stage Manager, Alison Cote; Cast: Barbara Bryne (Meg), James A. Stephens (Petey), Henry Stram (Stanley), Charlotte Parry (Lulu), Allan Corduner (Goldberg), Randall Newsome (McCann); September 8–October 15, 2006

**Translations** by Brian Friel; Director, Garry Hynes; Set & Costumes, Francis O'Connor; Lighting, Davy Cunningham; Original Music, Sam Jackson; Sound, John Leonard; Casting, Laura Stanczyk, Nancy Piccione, David Caparelliotis; PSM, Richard Costabile; ASM, Kasey Ostopchuck; Co-produced by Manhattan Theatre Club; Cast: David Costabile (Manus), Morgan Hallett (Sarah), Dermot Crowley (Jimmy Jack), Susan Lynch (Maire), Michael FitzGerald (Doalty), Geradline Hughes (Bridget), Niall Buggy (Hugh), Alan Cox (Owen), Graeme Malcolm (Captain Lancey), Chandler Williams (Lieutenant Yolland); October 8–October 29, 2006

**A Christmas Carol** by Charles Dickens, adapted by David Thompson; Director, Michael Unger; Sets, Ming Cho Lee; Costumes, Jess Goldstein; Lighting, Stephen Strawbridge; Original Music & Lyrics, Michael Starobin; Choreography, Rob

*Barbara Bryne in* The Birthday Party *(photo by T. Charles Erickson)*

Ashford; Casting, Laura Stanczyk; Supervising Stage Manager, Cheryl Mintz; Stage Manager, Kasey Ostopchuck; ASM, Hannah Woodward; Cast: Paul Benedict (Ebenezer Scrooge), Lisa Altmore (Mrs. Dilber), Cherise Boothe (Christmas Present), Joseph Collins (Bob Cratchit), Simon Kendall (Young Scrooge), Susan Knight (Mrs. Cratchit), Angela Lin (Belle/Lily), Garrett Long (Fan), Evan Lubeck (Fred), Michael Milligan (Jacob Marley), Anne O'Sullivan (Mrs. Fezziwig), Count Stovall (Mr. Fezziwig/Old Joe); December 3–December 24, 2006

**Lookingglass Alice** Adapted and directed by David Catlin; Sets, Daniel Ostling; Costumes, Mara Blumenfeld; Lighting, Chris Binder; Sound and Composition, Andre Pluess & Ben Sussman; Circus Rigging Design, Scott Osgood; Circus Choreography, Sylvia Hernandez-DiStasi; PSM, Sara Gmitter; Produced in association with Lookingglass Theatre Company; Cast: Larry DiStasi, Anthony Fleming III, Doug Hara, Tony Hernandez, Lauren Hirte; January 9–28, 2007

*Anthony Fleming III and Tony Hernandez in* Lookingglass Alice
*(photo by T. Charles Erickson)*

**Radio Golf** by August Wilson; Director, Kenny Leon; Sets, David Gallo; Costumes, Susan Hilferty; Lighting, Donald Holder; Original Music & Sound, Dan Moses Schreier; Dramaturg, Todd Kreidler; Vocal Coach, Erin Annarella; Casting, Laura Stanczyk; PSM, Narda E. Alcorn; Stage Manager, Marion Friedman; Produced in association with Center Theatre Group/Mark Taper Forum, Huntington Theatre Company, Seattle Repertory Theatre, CENTERSTAGE and Goodman Theatre; Cast: Tonya Pinkins (Mame Wilks), Harry Lennix (Harmond Wilks), James A. Williams (Roosevelt Hicks), John Earl Jelks (Sterling Johnson), Anthony Chisholm (Elder Joseph Barlow); March 18–April 8, 2007

**Mrs. Packard** Written and directed by Emily Mann; Sets, Eugene Lee; Costumes, Jennifer von Mayrhauser; Lighting Jeff Croiter; Original Music & Sound, Rob Milburn and Michael Bodeen; Fight Director, Rick Sordelet; Movement Director, Peter Pucci; Dramaturg, Douglas Langworthy; Casting Laura Stanzyk; PSM, Cheryl Mintz; Stage Manager, Alison Cote; Cast: Kathryn Meisle (Elizabeth Parsons Ware Packard), Dennis Parlato (Dr. Andrew McFarland), John C. Vennema (Theophilus Packard), Fiana Toibin (Mrs. Bonner), Julie Boyd (Mrs. Tenney/Mrs. Sybil Dole), Molly Regan (Mrs. Chapman/Miss Sarah Rumsey/Mrs. Blessing), Georgine Hall (Mrs. Stockton), Jeff Brooks (Dr. J.W. Brown/Mr. Abijah Dole/Dr. Duncanson), Robin Chadwick (Mr. Josephus Smith/Mr. Haslet/Mr. Blackman); World Premiere produced with assistance of The Kennedy Center Fund for American Plays; May 4–June 10, 2007

# Merrimack Repertory Theatre

Lowell, Massachusetts

Twenty-eighth Season

Artistic Director, Charles Towers; Executive Director, Tom Parrish

**Augusta** by Richard Dresser; Director, Charles Towers; Sets, David Evans Morris; Costumes, Deb Newhall; Lighting, Juliet Chia; Sound, Jamie Whoolery; PSM, Emily McMullen; Cast: Kathryn Rossetter (Molly), Jamie Proctor (Claire), Mark Shanahan (Jimmy); September 21–October 15, 2006

**Aunt Dan & Lemon** by Wallace Shawn; Director, Melia Bensussen; Sets, Anita Fuchs; Costumes, Clint Ramos; Lighting, Brian Lilienthal; Sound, Jamie Whoolery; PSM, Emily McMullen; Cast: Jeanine Serralles (Lemon), Dee Nelson (Mother/Flora/June), Allyn Burrows (Father/Freddie/Jasper), Carmen Roman (Aunt Dan), Tamara Hickey (Mindy), Luis Negron (Raimondo), Kyle Fabel (Andy/Marty); October 26–November 19, 2006

**Trying** by Joanna McClelland Glass; Director, Kyle Fabel; Sets, Richard Chambers; Costumes, Deb Newhall; Lighting, Dan Meeker; Sound, Jamie Whoolery; PSM, Emily McMullen; Cast: Nesbitt Blaisdell (Judge Francis Biddle), Nisi Sturgis (Sarah); January 11–February 4, 2007

**Dinah Was** by Oliver Goldstick; Director, Charles Towers; Musical Director, e'Marcus Harper; Sets, Bill Clarke; Costumes, Theresa Squire; Lighting, James Sale; Sound, Jamie Whoolery; PSM, Emily McMullen; Cast: Laiona Michelle (Dinah Washington), J. Bernard Calloway (Boss/Chase), Nadiyah S. Dorsey (Maye/Mama Jones/Violet), W. T. Martin (Spinelli/Greenblatt), John Kooi (Frick/Rollie), Julia Cook (Extra #1), John Kneeland (Extra #2), Michael Morrison (Extra #3), Romero Wyatt (Drummer), Corcoran Holt (Bass), Lawrence Clarke (Saxophone), Greg Diamond (Guitar); February 15–March 11, 2007

**Syncopation** by Allan Knee; Director, Maggie Mancinelli-Cahill; Choreography, Adam Pelty; Sets, Roman Tatarowicz; Cosutmes, Thom Heyer; Lighting, Annmarie Duggan; Sound, Jane Shaw; Associate Lighting, David Upton; PSM, Emily McMullen; Cast: Adam Pelty (Henry), Stacey Harris (Anna); March 22–April 15, 2007

*Laiona Michelle in* Dinah Was *(photo by Meghan Moore)*

*Adam Petty and Stacey Harris in* Syncopation
*(photo by Meghan Moore)*

**Secret Order** by Bob Clyman; Director, Charles Towers; Sets, Bill Clarke; Costumes, Martha Hally; Lighting, Dan Kotlowitz; Sound, Jamie Whoolery; PSM, Emily McMullen; Cast: David Rogers (Roth), Geoff Pierson (Brock), Kelly McCreary (Curiton), Davis Duffield (Shumway); April 26–May 20, 2007

**Reduced Shakespeare Company in Completely Hollywood (abridged)** by Reed Martin and Austin Tichenor; Cast: Reed Martin (Reed), Austin Tichenor (Austin), Dominic Conti (Dominic), Mick Orfe (Mick); December 7–17, 2006

# The Old Globe

San Diego, Califorina

Seventy-second Season

Artistic Director, Jack O'Brien; Executive Director, Louis G. Spisto; Resident Artistic Director, Jerry Patch; Founding Director, Craig Noel

**Christmas on Mars** by Harry Kondoleon; Director, Kirsten Brandt; Sets, Nick Fouch; Costumes, Angela Calin; Lighting, David Lee Cuthbert; Sound, Paul Peterson; Stage Manager, Diana Moser; Cast: Jack Ferver (Nissim), David Furr (Bruno), Colette Kilroy (Ingrid), Sarah Grace Wilson (Audrey); Cassius Carter Centre Stage; June 3–July 9, 2006

**A Midsummer Night's Dream** by William Shakespeare; Director, Darko Tresnjak; Sets, Ralph Funicello; Costumes, Paloma Young; Lighting, York Kennedy; Dramaturg, Dakin Matthews; Original Music & Sound, Christopher Walker; Fight Director, Steve Rankin, Choreographer, Peggy Hickey; Assistant Directors, Lori Petermann & Sarah Rasmussen; Stage Manager, Mary K. Klinger; ASMs, Esther Emery, Tracy Skoczelas, Jenny Slattery; Cast: Matt Biedel (Philostrate/Fairy), J. Paul Boehmer (Theseus/Oberon), Chris Bresky (Servant/Fairy), Chip Brookes (Snout/Wall), Lise Bruneau (Hippolyta/Titania), Melissa Condren (Servant/Fairy), Eve Danzeisen (Hermia), Bayardo De Murguia (Servant/Fairy), Michael Drummond (Puck), Cara Greene (Servant/Fairy), Wynn Harmon (Egeus), Dan Hodge (Starveling/Moonshine), Charles Janasz (Peter Quince), Julie Jesneck (Helena), Aaron Misakian (Servant/Fairy), Michael A. Newcomer (Snug/Lion), Owiso Odera (Lysander), Jonathan Peck (Bottom), Summer Shirey (Servant/Fairy), Kate Turnbull (Servant/Fairy), Michael Urie (Flute/Thisby), David Villalobos (Demetrius), Leah Zang (Servant/Fairy); Lowell Davies Festival Theatre; June 18–September 29, 2006

*Lise Bruneau and J. Paul Boehmer with Leah Zang, Summer Shirey, and Cara Greene in* A Midsummer Night's Dream
*(photo by Craig Schwartz)*

**Othello** by William Shakespeare; Director, Jesse Berger; Sets, Ralph Funicello; Costumes, Linda Cho; Lighting, York Kennedy; Dramaturg, Dakin Matthews; Original Music & Sound, Christopher Walker; Fight Director, Steve Rankin; Assistant Director, James Dublino; Stage Manager, Mary K. Klinger; ASMs, Esther Emery, Tracy Skoczelas, Jenny Slattery; Cast: Matt Biedel (Montano/Servant), Chris Bresky (2nd Gentleman/Sailor), Chip Brookes (1st Gentleman/Servant), Celeste Ciulla (Emilia), Bayardo De Murguia (Officer/Soldier), Wynn Harmon (Lodovico), Rhett Henckel (1st Senator/Soldier), Dan Hodge (Gratiano), Charles Janasz (Duke), Julie Jesneck (Desdemona), Leonard Kelly-Young (Brabantio),

Karl Kenzler (Iago), Aaron Misakian (Sailor/Soldier), Michael A. Newcomer (Cassio), Jonathan Peck (Othello), Summer Shirey (Bianca), Michael Urie (Roderigo), David Villalobos (2nd Senator/Soldier); Lowell Davies Festival Theatre; June 23–October 1, 2006

**Titus Andronicus** by William Shakespeare; Director, Darko Tresnjak; Sets, Ralph Funicello; Costumes, Linda Cho; Lighting, York Kennedy; Dramaturg, Dakin Matthews; Original Music & Sound, Christopher Walker; Fight Director, Steve Rankin; Assistant Directors, Sarah Rasmussen, Lori Petermann; Stage Manager, Mary K. Klinger; ASMs, Esther Emery, Tracy Skoczelas, Jenny Slattery; Cast: Matt Biedel (Martius/Sempronius/Goth-Cook), J. Paul Boehmer (Lucius), Chris Bresky (Quintus/Goth-Cook), Chip Brookes (Publius), Lise Bruneau (Nurse), Celeste Ciulla (Tamora), Melissa Condren (Lavinia), Bayardo De Murguia (Soldier), Michael Drummond (Young Lucius), Cara Greene (Tribune/Goth-Cook), Wynn Harmon (Saturninus), Rhett Henckel (Mutius/Henchman/Messenger), Dan Hodge (Tribune/Clown/Goth-Cook), Charles Janasz (Marcus), Leonard Kelly-Young (Titus), Karl Kenzler (Bassianus), Aaron Misakian (Tribune/Emilius), Michael A. Newcomer (Demetrius), Owiso Odera (Aaron), Kate Turnbull (Tribune/Goth-Cook), Michael Urie (Chiron), David Villalobos (Alarbus/Henchman), Leah Zang (Tribune/Goth-Cook); Lowell Davies Festival Theatre; June 28–September 30, 2006

**The Sisters Rosensweig** by Wendy Wasserstein; Director, David Warren; Sets, Alexander Dodge; Costumes, David Woolard; Lighting, Jeff Croiter; Sound, Paul Peterson; Music Arrangements/Vocal Direction, Cris O'Bryon; Stage Manager, Bret Torbeck; ASM, Moira Gleason; Cast: Mark Blum (Mervyn Kant), Jackie Hoffman (Gorgeous Teitelbaum), Marty Lodge (Nicholas Pym), Deirdre Lovejoy (Pfeni Rosensweig), Stefanie Nava (Tess Goode), Tom Nelis (Geoffrey Duncan), Mark Sullivan (Tom Valiunus), Janet Zarish (Sara Goode); Old Globe Theatre; July 15–August 20, 2006

*T. Ryder Smith in* Lincolnesque
*(photo by Craig Schwartz)*

**Lincolnesque** by John Strand; Director, Joe Calarco; Sets, Michael Fagin, Costumes, Anne Kennedy; Lighting, Chris Rynne; Sound, Lindsay Jones; Stage Manager, Monica Cuoco; Cast: Magaly Colimon (Carla), Leo Marks (Leo), T. Ryder Smith (Francis), James Sutorius (Daly/Secretary of War); World Premiere; Cassius Carter Centre Stage; August 5–September 10, 2006

**Hershey Felder as George Gershwin Alone** Music & lyrics by George and Ira Gershwin, book by Hershey Felder; Director, Joel Zwick; Sets, Yael Pardess; Lighting, Michael T. Gilliam; Sound, Jon Gottlieb; Costumes, Kenneth Cole; PSM, Morgan Cromwell; Production Manager/Technical Director, Matt Marsden; Cast: Hershey Felder (George Gershwin/Playwright); Old Globe Theatre; September 9–October 22, 2006

**Pig Farm** by Greg Kotis; Director, Matt August; Sets, Takeshi Kata; Costumes, Jenny Mannis; Lighting, Chris Rynne; Sound, Paul Peterson; Fight Director; Steve Rankin; Stage Manager, Esther Emery; Cast: Ted Koch (Tom), Ken Land (Teddy), Colleen Quinlan (Tina), Ian White (Tim); World Premiere; Cassius Carter Centre Stage; September 23–October 29, 2006

**Hershey Felder as Monsieur Chopin** by Hershey Felder; Director, Joel Zwick; Sets, Yael Pardess; Lighting, Richard Norwood; Sound, Benjamin Furiga; Wardrobe, Boguslaw; Projections, John Boesche; PSM, Morgan Cromwell; Production Manager/Technical Director, Matt Marsden; Production Consultant, Jeffrey Kallberg, PhD; Cast: Hershey Felder (Frédéric Chopin); Old Globe Theatre; October 26–31, 2006

*Skylar Starrs-Siben and Jay Goede in* Dr. Seuss' How the Grinch Stole Christmas *(photo by Craig Schwartz)*

**Dr. Seuss' How the Grinch Stole Christmas** Book and Lyrics by Timothy Mason, music by Mel Marvin; Director, Jack O'Brien; Sets, John Lee Beatty; Costumes, Robert Morgan; Lighting, Pat Collins; Sound, Paul Peterson; Choreography, John DeLuca; Musical Director, Phil Reno; Associate Director, Brendon Fox; Associate Musical Director/Conductor, Ron Colvard; Stage Managers, Leila Knox and Tracy Skoczelas; Cast: Kevin Bailey (Old Max), Eileen Bowman (Grandma Who), Cassidy Burwell or Caroline Hyatt (Annie Who), Ryan Drummond (Young Max), Scott Dreier (J.P. Who), A.J. Foggiano or Troy Hussman (Boo Who), Jay Goede (Grinch), Mackenzie Holmes or Skylar Starrs

Siben (Cindy-Lou Who), Ari Lerner or Nathan Wetter (Danny Who); Alison Grace Norwood or Bibi Valderrama (Betty Lou Who), Sarah Sumner (Mama Who), James Vasquez (Grandpa Seth Who); Adult Ensemble: Randall Dodge, Ron Christopher Jones, Theresa Layne, Ashley Linton, Spencer Moses, Carly Nykanen, Children's Ensemble: Maddie Shea Baldwin, Halle Hoffman, Ari Krasner, Zev Lerner, Natalya Phillips, Hannah Prater, Keilani Joy Spahn, Celia Tedde, Allie Trimm, Tommy Twomey; Old Globe Theatre; November 11–December 29, 2006

**Much Ado About Nothing** by William Shakespeare; Director, Richard Seer; Sets, Mike Buckley; Costumes, Corey Johnston; Lighting, Chris Rynne; Sound, Paul Peterson; Stage Manager, Crystal Verdon; Cast: Chris Bresky (Claudio), Chip Brookes (Benedick), Joy Farmer-Clary (Hero), Cara Greene (Margaret), Kimberly Greene (Ursula), Rhett Henckel (Don Pedro), Sam Henderson (Borachio), John Keabler (Dogberry), Michael Kirby (Friar Francis/Sexton), Nat McIntyre (Leonato), Aaron Misakian (Don John), Carolyn Ratteray (Verges), Summer Shirey (Antonia), Kate Turnbull (Beatrice); Cassius Carter Centre Stage; November 11–19, 2006

**La Pastorela de la Estrella** by Max Branscomb; Director, William Virchis; Co-presented by Teatro Máscara Mágica; Cassius Carter Centre Stage; December 7–23, 2006

**Ace** Book and lyrics by Robert Taylor and Richard Oberacker, music by Richard Oberacker; Director, Stafford Arima; Musical Director, David Kreppel; Choreography, Andrew Palermo; Orchestrations, Greg Anthony; Sets, David Korins; Costumes, Marie Anne Chiment; Lighting, Christopher Akerlind; Sound, John H Shivers and David Patridge; Stage Manager, Andrea L. Shell; Cast: Michael Arden (John Robert), Heather Ayers (Ruth), Maddie Shea Baldwin (Ensemble), Kelli Barrett (Nurse/Ensemble), Richard Barth (Lieutenant Sanders/Sullivan/Ensemble), Gabrielle Boyadjian (Emily), Ian Brininstool (School Bully/Young Charlie/Ensemble), Lisa Datz (Elizabeth), Noah Galvin (Billy), James Judy (Toy Store Owner/Colonel Whitlow/Chennault/Ensemble), Duke Lafoon (Edward/Stampley), Kevin Reed (Tennaman/Stein/Ensemble), Darren Ritchie (Ace), Danny Rothman (Cooper/Myron/Ensemble), Gabrielle Stravelli (Anique/Ensemble), Susan Kokot Stokes (Teacher/Ensemble), Traci Lyn Thomas (Mrs. Crandall/Clara Whitlow), Betsy Wolfe (Louise); Old Globe Theatre; January 13–February 18, 2007

**The Four of Us** by Itamar Moses; Director, Pam MacKinnon; Sets, Kris Stone; Costumes, Markas Henry; Lighting, Russell Champa; Sound, Paul Peterson; Stage Manager, Tracy Skoczelas; Cast: Sean Dugan (David), Gideon Banner (Benjamin); World Premiere; Cassius Carter Centre Stage; February 3–March 11, 2007

**Restoration Comedy** by Amy Freed; Director, John Rando; Sets, Ralph Funicello; Costumes, Robert Blackman; Lighting, York Kennedy; Stage Manager, Diana Moser; ASM, Jenny Slattery; Cast: Marco Barricelli (Loveless), Chris Bresky (Lory/Ensemble), Chip Brookes (Footman/Ensemble), Peter Frechette (Worthy), Cara Greene (Fistula/Ensemble), Rhett Henckel (Justin/Ensemble), Michael Izquierdo (Young Fashion/Ensemble), John Keating (Snap/Tailor/Parson Bull), Caralyn Kozlowski (Amanda), Amelia McClain (Narcissa/Hoyden), Jonathan McMurtry (Coupler Manlove/Sly/Gardener/Sir Tunbelly), Aaron Misakian (Christopher/Ensemble), Danny Scheie (Lord Foppington aka Sir Novelty Fashion), Christa Scott-Reed (Berinthia), Kimberly Scott (Hillaria/Nurse), Summer Shirey (Ensemble), Kate Turnbull (Amanda's Servant); Old Globe Theatre; March 3–April 8, 2007

**Hold Please** by Annie Weisman; Director, Kirsten Brandt; Sets, Michael Vaughn Sims; Costumes, Mary Larson; Lighting, David Lee Cuthbert; Sound, Paul Peterson; Cast: Kate Arrington (Jessica), Stephanie Beatriz (Erika), Starla Benford (Grace), Kandis Chappell (Agatha); Cassius Carter Centre Stage; March 31–May 6, 2007

**Two Trains Running** by August Wilson; Director, Seret Scott; Sets, Tony Fanning; Costumes, Karen Perry; Lighting, Chris Rynne; Sound, Paul Peterson; Stage Manager, Tracy Skoczelas; ASM, Jami Talbott; Casting, Mele Nagler; Cast: James Avery (Holloway), Willie Carpenter (Hambone), Chuck Cooper (Memphis), Edi Gathegi (Sterling), Roslyn Ruff (Risa), Montae Russell (Wolf), Al White (West); Old Globe Theatre; April 21–May 27, 2007

# Oregon Shakespeare Festival

Ashland, Oregon
Seventy-first Season
Artistic Director, Libby Appel

## ELIZABETHAN STAGE – Allen Pavilion

**The Merry Wives of Windsor** by William Shakespeare; Director, Andrew Tsao; Sets, Richard L. Hay; Costumes, Susan E. Mickey; Lighting, Robert Peterson; Composer, John Tanner; Dramaturg, Dee Anna Phares; Voice/Text Director, Scott Kaiser; Movement/Fight Director, John Sipes; Choreography, Suzee Grilley; Vocal Coach, Kay Hilton; Stage Manager, Gwen Turos; ASM, Melissa L. Wanke; Cast: Shona Tucker (Mistress Margaret Page), Tony DeBruno (Master George Page), Tiffany Adams (Anne Page), Tyler Layton (Mistress Alice Ford), Jonathan Haugen (Master Francis Ford), Hardy Pinnell (John), Todd Bjurstrom (Robert), G. Valmont Thomas (Sir John Falstaff), Marco Barricelli (Bardolph), James Edmondson (Pistol), Kevin Kenerly (Nim), Leah Wessler (Robin), Richard Elmore (Robert Shallow), Shad Willingham (Abraham Slender), Julie Oda (Peter Simple), Brad Whitmore (Sir Hugh Evans), Armando Durán (Doctor Caius), Judith-Marie Bergan (Mistress Quickly), James J. Peck (John Rugby), Erik LaRay Harvey (Host of the Garter Inn), Yorke G. Fryer (Fenton), Kristen Martz (Ensemble), Brandon St. Clair Saunders (Ensemble); June 6–October 6, 2006

**Cyrano De Bergerac** by Edmond Rostand, translated and adapted by Anthony Burgess; Director, Laird Williamson; Sets, William Bloodgood; Costumes, Deborah M. Dryden; Lighting, Robert Peterson; Composer, Todd Barton; Dramaturg, Barry Kraft; Voice/Text Director, Christine Adaire; Movement/Fight Director, John Sipes; Stage Manager, Jill Rendall; ASM, Mandy Younger; Cast: Marco Barricelli (Cyrano de Bergerac), Robin Goodrin Nordli (Roxane), Rex Young (Christian), Derrick Lee Weeden (The Count de Guiche), Robert Vincent Frank (Ragueneau), David Kelly (Henri Le Bret) Dee Maaske (The Duenna), Robynn Rodriguez (Bellerose), Adam Yazbeck (Jodelet), Richard Baird, Mark Peterson, Brandon St. Clair Saunders, Rafael Untalan (Cavalry Men, Musketeers, Guards), Christopher DuVal (M. Dumaine), John Michael Goodson (Young Dumaine), Heather Robison (La Vendeuse), Yorke G. Fryer, John J. O'Hagan (The Marquises), Richard Howard (M. Cuigy), U. Johnathan Troppo (M. Brissaille), René Millán (Lignière), Christine Albright (The Précieuses), Kjerstine Anderson (The Précieuses, Actors of the Théâtre Bourgogne), Michelle Beck (The Précieuses, Actors of the Théâtre Bourgogne), Kelly Curran (The Précieuses, Actors of the Théâtre Bourgogne), Mark Peterson (Pickpocket), G. Valmont Thomas (Montfleury), James Newcomb (Viscount Valvert), Brandon St. Clair Saunders, Adam Yazbeck (Actors of the Théâtre Bourgogne), Hardy Pinnell, S.A. Rogers (Theatre Pages), Edward Condon (Theatre Musician); June 7–October 7, 2006

**The Two Gentlemen of Verona** by William Shakespeare; Director, Bill Rauch; Sets, Christopher Acebo; Costumes, Joyce Kim Lee; Lighting, Robert Peterson; Composer, Paul James Prendergast; Dramaturg, Dee Anna Phares; Voice/Text Director, Christine Adaire; Choreography, Ken Roht; Stage Manager, Amy Miranda Warner; Production Assistant, Mara Filler; Cast: Juan Rivera LeBron (Valentine), Gregory Linington (Proteus), Eileen DeSandre (Speed), Miriam A. Laube (Julia), Catherine E. Coulson (Lucetta), Greta Oglesby (Antonia), Linda Alper (Panthina), David Kelly (Launce), Terwilliger (Crab), Alexander Barnes (Boy), William Langan (Duke of Milan), Sarah Rutan (Silvia), Brad Whitmore (Thurio), James Edmondson (Sir Eglamour), Josiah Phillips (The Duke's Head Butler), Richard Baird (Outlaw/Ensemble), James J. Peck (Outlaw/Ensemble), Vilma Silva (Outlaw), John Michael Goodson (Ensemble), Brandon St. Clair Saunders (Ensemble), Grace Thorsen (Ensemble); June 8–October 8, 2006

## ANGUS BOWMER THEATRE

**The Winter's Tale** by William Shakespeare, Director, Libby Appel, Sets, Rachel Hauck, Costumes, Deborah M. Dryden; Lighting, Robert Peterson; Composer, Todd Barton; Assistant Director, Catherine Baker Steindler; Dramaturg, Patricia M. Troxel; Voice & Text Director, Scott Kaiser; Movement Director, Marcela Lorca; Music Assistant/Vocal Coach, Kay Hilton; Stage Manager, Amy Miranda Warner; ASM, Mandy Younger; Cast: William Langan (Leontes), Miriam A. Laube (Hermione), Alexander Barnes (Mamillius), Jeffrey King (Camillo), Mark Murphey (Antigonus), Tyrone Wilson (Rogero/Shepherd), Rafael Untalan (Cleomenes/Shepherd), Geoffrey Blaisdell (Dion), Greta Oglesby (Paulina), Eileen DeSandre (Emilia/Shepherdess), Kjerstine Anderson (Lady/Mopsa), Michelle Beck (Lady/Dorcas), Richard Baird (Lord/Shepherd), John J. O'Hagan (Lord/Shepherd), Adam Yazbeck (Lord/Shepherd), Rex Young (Polixenes), Juan Rivera LeBron (Florizel), Nell Geisslinger (Perdita), Josiah Phillips (Old Shepherd), Mark Peterson (Clown), Christopher DuVal (Autolycus); February 17–October 29, 2006

**The Diary of Anne Frank** by Frances Goodrich and Albert Hackett, adapted by Wendy Kesselman; Director, James Edmondson; Sets, Richard L. Hay; Costumes, B. Modern; Lighting, Kendall Smith; Sound, David K. Weberg; Dramaturg, Judith Rosen; Voice/Text Director, Scott Kaiser; Stage Manager, Gwen Turos; ASM, Melissa Wanke; Cast: Tony DeBruno (Otto Frank), Linda Alper (Edith Frank), Sarah Rutan (Margot Frank), Laura Morache (Anne Frank), Michael J. Hume (Mr. van Daan), Catherine E. Coulson (Mrs. van Daan), John Tufts (Peter van Daan), Michael Elich (Mr. Dussel), Linda K. Morris (Miep Gies), Brad Whitmore (Mr. Kraler), James J. Peck (Nazi Officer), Todd Bjurstrom, Jeris Schaefer (Dutch Collaborators); February 18–July 9, 2006

**The Importance of Being Earnest** by Oscar Wilde; Director, Peter Amster; Sets, William Bloodgood; Costumes, Mara Blumenfeld; Lighting, Ann G. Wrightson; Sound: Andrew Hopson; Dramaturg, Patricia M. Troxel; Voice and Text Director, Louis Colaianni; Stage Manager, Jill Rendall; ASM, D. Christian Bolender; Assistant Director, Laura Konsin; Cast: Kevin Kenerly (Algernon Moncrieff), Jeff Cummings (John 'Jack' Worthing, J.P.), Richard Elmore (Merriman), Richard Farrell (Merriman), Judith-Marie Bergan (Lady Bracknell), Heather Robison (The Hon. Gwendolen Fairfax), Julie Oda (Cecily Cardew), Dee Maaske (Miss Prism), Geoffrey Blaisdell (Lane), Jonathan Haugen (Rev. Canon Chasuble); February 19–October 29, 2006

**Intimate Apparel** by Lynn Nottage; Director, Timothy Bond; Sets, Richard L. Hay; Costumes, Deborah M. Dryden; Lighting, Darren McCroom; Composer, Michael Keck; Assistant Director, Catherine Baker Steindler; Dramaturg, Deanna Downes; Voice/Text Director, Evamarii Johnson; Stage Manager, Susan L. McMillan; Production Assistant, Angeline Ayriss; Cast: Perri Gaffney (Mrs. Dickson), Gwendolyn Mulamba (Esther Mills), Erik LaRay Harvey (George Armstrong), Terri McMahon (Mrs. Van Buren), Gregory Linington (Mr. Marks), Tiffany Adams (Mayme); April 18–October 28, 2006

**Dr. Jekyll and Mr. Hyde** by David Edgar, based on the novel by Robert Louis Stevenson; Director, Penny Metropulos; Sets, William Bloodgood; Costumes, Deborah M. Dryden; Lighting, Michael Chybowski; Composer, Sterling Tinsley; Dramaturg, Beatrice Basso; Voice/Text Director, Ursula Meyer; Movement/Fight Director, John Sipes; Stage Manager, D. Christian Bolender; Production Assistant, Angeline Ayriss; Cast: James Newcomb (Dr. Henry Jekyll and Mr. Edward Hyde), Richard Farrell (Gabriel John Utterson), Jeff Cummings (Richard Enfield/Parson), Vilma Silva (Katherine Urquart), Jeris Schaefer (Charles), Kelly Curran (Lucy/Maid/Woman on the Platform), Laura Morache (Annie Loder), Robert Sicular (Poole), David Kelly (Dr. Hastie Lanyon/Sir Danvers Carew/M.P./Railwayman); July 26–October 28, 2006

## NEW THEATRE

**Up** by Bridget Carpenter; Director, Michael Barakiva; Sets, Daniel Ostling; Costumes, Robert Morgan; Lighting, James F. Ingalls; Composer & Sound, Irwin Appel; Dramaturg, Lue Morgan Douthit; Voice/Text Director, Louis Colaianni; Choreography, Jim Giancarlo; Stage Manager, Jeremy Eisen; Production Assistant, Angeline Ayriss; Assistant Director, Laura Konsin; Cast: Richard Howard (Walter Griffin), Terri McMahon (Helen Griffin), John Tufts (Mikey Griffin), Christine Albright (Maria), Robin Goodrin Nordli (Aunt Chris), U. Jonathan Toppo (Philippe Petit/Student/UPS Man/Firefighter); February 23–June 23, 2007

**Bus Stop** by William Inge; Director, Libby Appel; Sets, William Bloodgood; Costumes, Deborah Trout; Lighting, Robert Peterson; Composer/Sound: Irwin Appel; Dramaturg, Lue Morgan Douthit; Voice & Text Director, Evamarii Johnson; Fight Choreography, U. Jonathan Toppo; Stage Manager, Jeremy Eisen; Production Assistant, Mara Filler; Cast: Shona Tucker (Grace), Nell Geisslinger (Elma Duckworth), Jeffrey King (Will Masters), Tyrone Wilson (Carl), Tyler Layton (Cherie), Robert Sicular (Dr. Gerald Lyman), Danforth Comins (Bo Decker), Mark Murphey (Virgil Blessing); March 29–October 29, 2006

**King John** by William Shakespeare; Director, John Sipes; Sets, William Bloodgood; Costumes, Shigeru Yaji; Lighting/Projections, Alexander V. Nichols; Sound, Dennis M. Kambury; Dramaturg, Alan Armstrong; Voice/Text Director, Scott Kaiser; Fight Director, John Sipes; Assistant Fight Director, U. Jonathan Toppo; Stage Manager, Susan L. McMillan; ASM, Melissa L. Wanke; Cast: Michael Elich (John), John Tufts (Henry, Melun, Ensemble), Jeanne Paulson (Eleanor of Aquitaine), Emma Harding (Arthur), Robynn Rodriguez (Constance), Linda K. Morris (Blanche), Robert Vincent Frank (Earl of Pembroke/Executioner/Ensemble), Michael J. Hume (Earl of Salisbury), Gwendolyn Mulamba (Lady Faulconbridge), René Millán (Phillip "The Bastard"), Shad Willingham (Robert Faulconbridge/Duke of Austria/Executioner/Ensemble), Richard Elmore (Philip/King of France/Ensemble), Danforth Comins (Lewis/Ensemble), Derrick Lee Weeden (Chatillon/Cardinal Pandulph), Armando Durán (Hubert de Burgh); July 4–October 29, 2006

*Jeanne Paulson and Michael Elich in* King John
*(photo by Jenny Graham)*

# Paper Mill Playhouse

Millburn, New Jersey

Founded in 1934

Associate Artistic Director, Mark S. Hoebee; Managing Director, Diane Claussen

**Godspell** Book by John-Michael Tebelak, music and lyrics by Stephen Schwartz; Director, Daniel Goldstein; Music Director, Loren Toolajian; Choreography, Dan Knechtges; Sets, David Korins; Costume, Mask and Puppet Designer, Miranda Hoffman; Lighting, Ben Stanton; Sound, Randy Hansen; Additional Orchestrations, Loren Toolajian; PSM, Gail P. Luna; Casting, Alison Franck; Press, Shayne A. Miller; Cast: Uzo Aduba, Sarah Bolt, Sara Chase, Robin De Jesus, Joshua Henry, Patrick Heusinger, Dan Kohler, Anika Larsen, Telly Leung, Julie Reiber; September 20–October 22, 2006

**A Wonderful Life** Book and lyrics by Sheldon Harnick, music by Joe Raposo; Director, James Brennan; Music Director, Tom Helm, Choreography, Andy Blankenbuehler; Sets, Charlie Smith, Costumes, Gail Baldoni; Lighting, Richard Winkler; Hair and Wigs, Mark Adam Rampmeyer; Sound, Randy Hansen; PSM, Gail P. Luna; Casting, Alison Franck; Press, Shayne A. Miller; Cast: James Clow (George Bailey), Dale Radunz (Matthew), Jeff Brooks (Clarence), Ed Romanoff (Bob Hepner/Townsperson), Kevin Bernard (Bert), Jessica Mary Murphy (Mrs. Martini), Jerry Galante (Mr. Martini/Townsperson), Robert Creighton (Ernie Bishop), Emilee Dupré (Violet Bick/Townsperson), John Jellison (Tom Bailey/Carter), Jan Pessano (Milly Bailey), Jordan Cable (Harry Bailey), J.B. Adams (Uncle Billy), Kellie Drinkhahn (Karen Zimmer/Dorothy/Townsperson), Seán Martin Hingston (Sam Wainwright), Catherine Brunell (Mary Hatch), Nick Wyman (Henry Potter), Jeremy Davis (Stuart/Bank Teller/Townsperson), Todd Horman (Walt/Townsperson), Jean Marie (Lillian/Mrs. Hatch/Townsperson), Jessica Mary Murphy (Mrs. Bishop/Townsperson), Allison Couture (Ruth Reynolds/Townsperson), Cynthia Leigh Heim (Sarah/Harriet/Townsperson), Ed Romanoff (Accountant), Marisa Malanga (Beth Bailey), Frankie Dolce (Tommy Bailey), Sophie Rudin (Zuzu Bailey), Jacqueline Colmer (Townsperson), Nigel Columbus (Townsperson), Lucy Grebin (Townsperson), Erin Henry (Townsperson), Daniel J. Marconi (Townsperson), Adrian Peña (Townsperson); November 8–December 17, 2006

**Summer and Smoke** by Tennessee Williams; Director, Michael Wilson; Sets, Tony Straiges; Costumes, David C. Woolard; Lighting, Rui Rita; Sound, John Gromada; Hair/Wigs, Denise O'Brien; Choreography, Peter Pucci; Vocal & Dialect Coach, Deborah Dallas Cooney; Fight Director, Mark Olsen; PSM, Barbara Reo; Casting, Alison Franck and Pat McCorkle; Press, Shayne A. Miller; Cast: Jack Davidson (The Rev. Winemiller), Jennifer Harmon (Mrs. Winemiller), Curtis Billings (Dusty/Archie Kramer), Elizabeth Capinera (Pearl/Rosemary), Kevin Anderson (John Buchanan Jr.), Nafe Katter (Dr. Buchanan Sr.), Amanda Plummer (Alma Winemiller), Stephanie Beatriz (Rosa Gonzales), Marta Reiman (Nellie Ewell), Johanna Morrison (Mrs. Bassett), Bill Kux (Roger Doremus), John Ort (Vernon/Townsperson), Mateo Gómez (Papa Gonzales), Olivia D'Ambrosio (Townsperson), Kyle McLaughlin (Townsperson), Rachel Moss (Townsperson); January 10–February 11, 2007

**Romance Romance** Book and lyrics by Barry Harman, music by Keith Herrmann; Director/Choreography, Mark S. Hoebee; Music Director, John O'Neill; Sets and Costumes, David Zinn; Lighting, Jeff Croiter; Sound, Randy Hansen; Hair/Wigs, Charles G. LaPointe; PSM, Brian Meister; Casting, Alison Franck; Press, Shayne A. Miller; Cast: Jessica Bogart (Josefine/Monica), Matt Bogart (Alfred/Sam), Danette Holden (Her/Barb), Mark Ledbetter (Him/Lenny); February 28–April 1, 2007

**Seven Brides for Seven Brothers** Book by Lawrence Kasha and David Landay, lyrics by Johnny Mercer, music by Gene de Paul, new songs by Al Kasha and Joel Hirschhorn; Director, Scott Schwartz; Music Director, Tom Helm; Choreography, Patti Colombo; Sets, Anna Louizos; Costumes, Jess Goldstein; Lighting, Donald Holder; Hair/Wigs, Charles G. LaPointe; Sound, Randy Hansen;

*Jessica and Matt Bogart in* Romance Romance
*(photo by Gerry Goodstein)*

Sound Effects, Christopher "Kit" Bond; Fight Director, J. Allen Suddeth; Dance Music Arrangements, Sam Davis; PSM, Alison Harma; Casting, Alison Franck; Press, Shayne A. Miller; Cast: Michelle Dawson (Milly Bradon), Edward Watts (Adam Pontipee), Randy Bobish (Benjamin), Luke Longacre (Caleb), Karl Warden (Daniel), Travis Kelley (Ephraim), Eric Sciotto (Frank), Christain Delcroix (Gideon), Christina Rae Hedrick (Dorcas), Kate Marilley (Ruth), Denise Payne (Liza), Margot De La Barre (Martha), Stephanie Fittro (Sarah), Sarah Marie Jenkins (Alice), Cameron Henderson (Jeb/Townsperson), Nathan Hershberger (Nathan/Townsperson), Luke Rawlings (Luke/Townsperson), Benjie Randall (Matt/Townsperson), Jason Babinksy (Joel/Townsperson), Ryan Christopher Chotto (Zeke/Townsperson), Nick Sullivan (The Preacher/Townsperson), Andy Paterson (Mr. Hoallum/Townsperson), Tina Stafford (Mrs. Hoallum/Townsperson), Dan Sharkey (Mr. Sander/Townsperson), Becky Barta (Mrs. Sander/Townsperson); April 11–May 31, 2007

*Kate Marilley, Sarah Marie Jenkins, Margot De La Barre, Benjie Randall, Christina Hedrick, and Nathan Hershberger in* Seven Brides for Seven Brothers *(photo by Bruce Bennett)*

**Pirates!** Book and lyrics by Sir William S. Gilbert, music by Sir Arthur S. Sullivan; Director, Gordon Greenberg; Musical Director/Conductor, Shawn Gough; Choreography, Warren Carlyle; Music Supervision/New Arrangements/ Orchestrations, John McDaniel; Sets, Rob Bissinger; Costumes, David C. Woolard; Lighting, Jeff Croiter; Sound, Randy Hansen; Hair/Wigs, Pat Marcus, Stephanie Marletta, & Jim Belcher; Fight Director, Michael Rossmy; Original Sound Effects, Jay Hilton, PSM, Rolt Smith; Casting, Alison Franck; Press, Shayne A. Miller; Cast: Andrew Varela (Pirate King), Ed Dixon (Major-General Stanley), Farah Alvin (Mabel), Liz McCartney (Ruth), Barrett Foa (Fredrick), John O'Creagh (Samuel/Ensemble), Gerry McIntyre (Sergeant), Julia Osborne (Edith/ Ensemble), Ensemble: Timothy J. Alex, Julia Burrows, Kristin Carlson, Michael Daly, Michael Scott Harris, Morgan James, Robyn Kramer, Michael McKinsey, Lucas Richter, Tory Ross, Michael Rossmy, Roger Preston Smith, Daniel Spiotta, Eric LaJuan Summers; June 7–July 8, 2007

*Andrew Varela, John O'Creagh, Daniel Spiotta, and Mike Daly in* Pirates! *(photo by Gerry Goodstein)*

# People's Light & Theatre Company

Malvern, Pennsylvania

Thirty-second Season

Artistic Director, Abigail Adams; Managing Director, Grace Grillet

**The Imaginary Invalid** by Moliére, translated & adapted by James Magruder; Director, Lillian Groag; Sets, Donald Eastman; Costumes, Marla J. Jurglanis; Lighting, Nancy Schertler; Composer, John Glover; Stage Manager/Sound, Charles T. Brastow; Dramaturg, Elizabeth Pool; Cast: Stephen Novelli (Argan), Mary Elizabeth Scallen (Toinette), Joanna Liao (Angelique), Kathryn Petersen (Beline), Peter DeLaurier (Bonnefoi/Beralde), Jud Williford (Cleante), Tom Teti (Diafoirus/Purgon), Benjamin Lloyd (Thomas/Fleurant/President); September 13–October 22, 2006

**Something You Did** by Willy Holtzman; Director, Abigail Adams; Sets, James Krozner; Costumes, Marla J. Jurglanis; Lighting, Dennis Parichy; Original Music/ Soundscape, Michael Keck; Dramaturg, Elizabeth Pool; Stage Manager, Kate McSorley; Cast: Tony Campisi (Gene Biddle), Jordan Charney (Arthur Ross), Melanye Finister (Uneeq/Edmonds/Coradicia Watts), Cathy Simpson (Lenora Renshaw), Amy Van Nostrand (Alison Moulton); October 18–November 19, 2006

**Robin Hood: A Panto** by Kathryn Petersen, original music, arrangements, and musical direction by Vince di Mura; Director, David Bradley; Sets, James F. Pyne Jr.; Costumes, Rosemarie McKelvey; Lighting, Dennis Parichy; Stage Manager/ Sound, Charles T. Brastow; Fight & Movement Choreography, Samantha Bellomo; Cast: Jessica Ball (Barmaid Heloise), Scott Boulware (Will Scarlett), Marla Burkholder (Barmaid Marion), Mark Del Guzzo (Mortimer), Mark Lazar (Mistress Maud), Susan McKey (Madge, Midge's Wife), Christopher Patrick Mullen (Midge, the Miller), John O'Hara (Little John), Tom Teti (Friar Tuck), Carl N. Wallnau (The Sheriff of Nottingham), Erin Weaver (Robin Hood), Kenrick Burkholder (Guard), Cedric Lilly (Guard), Nick Suders (Guard); November 22, 2006–December 31, 2006

**Anne of Green Gables** Adapted by Peter DeLaurier from the novel by L.M. Montgomery; Director, Shannon O'Donnell; Sets, James F. Pyne Jr.; Costumes, Marla J. Jurglanis; Lighting, Dennis Parichy; Composer/Sound, Christopher Colucci; Stage Manager, Kate McSorley; Cast: Erin Clare Hurley (Anne Shirley), Ceal Phelan (Marilla Cuthbert), Peter DeLaurier (Matthew Cuthbert), Foster Cronin (Moody Spurgeon McPherson), Kathryn Petersen (Mrs. Barry/Mrs. Spencer/Voice of Miss Stacy), Marcia Saunders (Mrs. Rachel Lynde), Kim Carson (Diana Barry), Kate Bailey (Jane Andrews), Elena Bossler (Ruby Gillis), Anastasia Currigan (Josie Pye), Daniel Joyce (Gilbert Blythe); January 18–February 11, 2007

*Ceal Phelan and Erin Clare Hurley in* Anne of Green Gables *(photo by Mark Garvin)*

**Tuesdays With Morrie** by Jeffrey Hatcher and Mitch Albom, adapted from Albom's novel; Director, Stephen Novelli; Sets, Lewis Folden; Costumes, Abbie Wysor; Lighting, Gregory Scott Miller; Sound/Stage Manager, Charles T. Brastow; Dramaturg, Elizabeth Pool; David Ingram (Mitch Albom), Robert Spencer (Morrie Schwartz); February 7–March 4, 2007

**Twelfth Night** by William Shakespeare; Director, Abigail Adams; Sets, James F. Pyne Jr.; Costumes, Marla J. Jurglanis; Lighting, Paul Hackenmueller; Sound, Charles T. Brastow; Composer, Vince di Mura; Additional Music, Robert Schumann; Fight & Movement Choreography, Samantha Bellomo; Dramaturgs, Lee Devin & Elizabeth Pool; Cast: Christopher Patrick Mullen (Orsino), Claire Inie-Richards (Curio), Robert Wu (Antonio/Valentine), Miriam Hyman (Viola), Kevin Bergen (Malvolio/Sea Captain), Graham Smith (Sir Toby Belch), Elizabeth Webster Duke (Maria), Lenny Haas (Sir Andrew Aguecheek), Jason Ma (Feste), Mary Elizabeth Scallen (Olivia), Andrew Honeycutt (Sebastian), Mark Lazar (Fabian), Francis J. Coyne (Officer); February 28–April 7, 2007

**The Giver** Adapted by Eric Coble from the novel by Lois Lowry; Director, David Bradley; Sets, James F. Pyne Jr.; Costumes, Rosemarie E. McKelvey; Lighting, Dennis Parichy; Composer/Sound & Projections, Jorge Cousineau; Stage Manager, Kate McSorley; Cast: Peter DeLaurier (Father), Melanye Finister (Mother/Chief Elder), Maggie Fitzgerald (Lily), Cedric Lilly (Jonas), Mark Del Guzzo (Asher), Marla Burkholder (Fiona/Rosemary), Stephen Novelli (The Giver); April 26–May 20, 2007

**Splittin' the Raft** by Scott Kaiser; Director, Jade King Carroll; Sets, Arthur R. Rotch; Costumes, Marla J. Jurglanis; Lighting, Dennis Parichy; Sound, Vincent Olivieri; Musical Director, Vince di Mura; Stage Manager, Charles T. Brastow; Cast: John Douglas Thompson (Jim/Frederick Douglass), Susan McKey (Huck Finn), Cathy Simpson (Widow Douglas/Judge Thatcher/Aunt Sally/Ensemble), Christopher Patrick Mullen (Pap/Mrs. Loftus/Tom Sawyer/Ensemble); May 9–June 10, 2007

**Humble Boy** by Charlotte Jones; Director, Ken Marini; Sets, James F. Pyne Jr.; Costumes, Marla J. Jurglanis; Lighting, Dennis Parichy; Sound, Charles T. Brastow; Fight Consultant, Ahren Potratz; Stage Manager, Kate McSorley; Cast: Pete Pryor (Felix Humble), Alda Cortese (Mercy Lott), Susan Wilder (Flora Humble), Peter DeLaurier (Jim), Stephen Novelli (George Pye), Karen Peakes (Rosie Pye); June 20–July 15, 2007

*Karen Peakes and Pete Pryor in* Humble Boy *(photo by Mark Garvin)*

# Pittsburgh Public Theater

Pittsburgh, Pennsylvania

Thirty-second Season

Artistic Director, Ted Pappas; Managing Director, Mark R. Power

**Oedipus the King** by Sophocles, translated by William Butler Yeats; Director, Ted Pappas; Sets, James Noone; Costumes, David R. Zyla; Lighting, Kirk Bookman; Sound, Zach Moore; Casting, Pat McCorkle; PSM, Ruth E. Kramer; ASM, Amy Monroe; Cast: Jay Stratton (Oedipus, the King of Thebes), Helena Ruoti (Jocasta), Michael McKenzie (Creon), Mark C. Thompson (Priest of Zeus/Chorus), Edward James Hyland (Tiresias), Alex Coleman (First Messenger), Doug Pona (Herdsman), Brian Barefoot (Second Messenger), Darren Eliker (Chorus), Jeffrey Howell (Chorus), Daniel Krell (Chorus), Doug Mertz (Chorus), Joe Warik (Chorus), Aidan Krell (Boy), Nadia Cook-Loshilov (Daughter), Scarlet Buttercup Sparke (Daughter); September 28–October 29, 2006

**The Secret Letters of Jackie and Marilyn** by Mark Hampton & Michael Sharp; Director, Leonard Foglia; Sets, Michael McGarty; Costumes, David C. Woolard; Lighting, Howell Binkley; Hair/Wigs, Paul Huntley; Sound, Zach Moore; Casting, Cindi Rush; Dialects, Don Wadsworth; PSM, Fred Noel; ASM, Alison Paleos; Cast: Gretchen Egolf (Jacqueline Bouvier Kennedy), Carole Shelley (Patty), Heather Tom (Marilyn Monroe); November 9–December 10, 2006

**The Second City Dysfunctional Holiday Revue** Director, Dina Facklis; Musical Director, Joe Grazulis; Stage Manager, Kyle Anderson; Cast: Tim Baltz, Rebecca Hanson, Hans Holsen, Brendan Jennings, Mary Sohn, Dana Quercioli; December 13–16, 2006

**The Chief** by Rob Zellers and Gene Collier; Director, Ted Pappas; Set/Costumes, Anne Mundell; Lighting, Phil Monat; Sound, Zach Moore; PSM, Fred Noel; ASM, Alison Paleos; Cast: Tom Atkins (Arthur J. Rooney, Sr.); January 2–7, 2007

**Cabaret** Book by Joe Masteroff, music by John Kander, lyrics by Fred Ebb; Director/Choreography, Ted Pappas; Sets, James Noone; Costumes, David R. Zyla; Lighting, Kirk Bookman; Sound, Zach Moore; Casting, Mark Simon; Dialects, Don Wadsworth; Assistant Choreography, Carol Schuberg; PSM, Ruth E. Kramer; ASM, Fredric H. Orner; Music Director, F. Wade Russo; Cast: Daniel Krell (Clifford Bradshaw), Harris Doran (The Emcee), Tari Kelly (Sally Bowles), Carrington Vilmont (Ernst Ludwig), Greg Roderick (Customs Officer/Max/Ensemble), Brooks Almy (Fraulein Schneider), Lenora Nemetz (Fraulein Kost), Marcus Stevens (Rudy/Ensemble), Scott Robertson (Herr Schultz), Joseph Domencic (Bobby/Ensemble), Marcus Stevens (Victor), Nicholas Ardell (Taxi Man/Ensemble), Stephanie Lynn Nelson (Kit Kat Girl/Two Ladies), Renee Monique Brown (Kit Kat Girl/Two Ladies), Leasen Almquist (Kit Kat Girl/Gorilla), Daina Michelle Griffith (Kit Kat Girl), Carol Schuberg (Kit Kat Girl); January 25–February 25, 2007

**Life x 3** by Yasmina Reza, translated by Christopher Hampton; Director, Jesse Berger; Sets, Luke Hegel-Cantarella; Costumes, Alejo Vietti; Lighting, John Lasiter; Sound, Zach Moore; Casting, Pat McCorkle; PSM, Alison Paleos; ASM, Rebecca J. Stevens; Cast: Brandon Williams (Henri), Caris Vujcec (Sonia), Susan Angelo (Ines), Rob Breckenridge (Hubert); March 8–April 8, 2007

**The Glorious Ones** Book and lyrics by Lynn Ahrens, music by Stephen Flaherty; Director/Choreography, Graciela Daniele; Sets, Dan Ostling; Costumes, Mara Blumenfeld; Lighting, Stephen Strawbridge; Sound, Zach Moore; Casting, Stanczyk/Cherpakov Casting; Dialect Coach, Don Wadsworth; Assistant to Director, Madeleine Kelly; PSM, Nevin Hedley; ASM, Fredric H. Orner; Orchestrations, Michael Starobin; Musical Direction, Thomas Murray; Cast: Natalie Venetia Belcon (Columbina), John Kassir (Dottore), David Patrick Kelly (Pantalone), Jenny Powers (Isabella Andreini), Paul Schoeffler (Flaminio Scala), Julyana Soelistyo (Armanda Ragusa), Jeremy Webb (Francesco Andreini); April 19–May 20, 2007

**The Gin Game** by D.L. Coburn; Director, Ted Pappas; Sets, James Noone; Costumes, Martha Louise Bromelmeier; Lighting, Kirk Bookman; Sound, Zach Moore; Casting, Pat McCorkle; PSM, Fred Noel; ASM, Rebecca J. Stevens; Cast: Ross Bickell (Weller Martin), Lois Markle (Fonsia Dorsey); May 31–July 1, 2007

# Playmakers Repertory Company

Chapel Hill, North Carolina

Thrity-first Season

Producing Artistic Director, Joseph Haj; Production Manager, Rob McLeod

**I Am My Own Wife** by Doug Wright; Director, Julie Fishell; Sets, Michelle Moody; Costumes, Traci Meek; Lighting, Todd Campbell; Sound, Michèl Marrano; Cast: John Feltch (Charlotte von Mahlsdorf and others); September 13–17, 2006

**The Underpants** by Carl Sternheim, adapted by Steve Martin; Director, Gene Saks; Sets/Costumes, Marion Williams, Lighting, Charlie Morrison, Sound, Michèl Marrano, Cast: Winslow Corbett (Louise Maske), Jeffrey Blair Cornell (Benjamin Cohen), Ray Dooley (Klinglehoff), John Feltch (Frank Versati), Julie Fishell (Gertrude Deuter), Matthew Patterson (Theo Maske), Kenneth P. Strong (King); October 4–29, 2006

**Tuesdays With Morrie** by Jeffrey Hatcher and Mitch Albom, adapted from Albom's novel; Director, Joan Darling; Sets/Costumes, McKay Coble; Lighting, Peter West; Sound, Michèl Marrano; Cast: Greg Mullavey (Morrie Scwartz), Estes Tarver (Mitch Albom); November 15–December 10, 2006

**Stones in His Pockets** by Marie Jones; Director, John Feltch; Sets/Costumes, Marion Jones; Lighting; John Ambrosone; Sound, Michèl Marrano; Cast: David Alley, David Friedlander; January 17–February 11, 2007

**The Bluest Eye** Adapted for the stage by Lydia R. Diamond from the novel by Toni Morrison; Director, Trezana Beverley; Sets, Robin Vest; Costumes, Anne Kennedy; Lighting, Peter West; Sound, Michèl Marrano; Cast: Adrian Bailey (Cholly), Lou Ferguson (Soaphead Church), Allison Reeves (Claudia), Joanna Rhinehart (Mrs. Breedlove), Georgia Southern (Darlene/Frieda), Heaven Stephens (Maureen Peal/White Girl), Danika Williams (Pecola), Kathryn Hunter-Williams (Mama); February 28–March 25, 2007

*Georgia Southern and Allison Reeves in* The Bluest Eye *(photo by Jon Gardiner)*

**The Illusion** by Pierre Corneille, adapted by Tony Kushner; Director, Joseph Haj; Sets, McKay Coble; Costumes, Marion Williams; Lighting, Justin Townsend; Sound, Michèl Marrano; Composer, M. Anthony Reimer; Cast: David Adamson (Pridamont), Janie Brookshire (Melibea/Isabelle/Hippolyta), Jeffrey Blair Cornell (Matamore), Ray Dooley (Alcandre), Nikolas Priest (Amanuensis/Geronte), Allison Reeves (Alicia/Lyse/Clarina), Wesley Schultz (Pleribo/Adraste/Prince Florilame), Chris Taylor (Calisto/Clindor/Theogenes); April 11–May 6, 2007

*Allison Reeves, Janie Brookshire, Ray Dooley, and David Adamson in* The Illusion *(photo by Jon Gardiner)*

**Universes Poetic Theatre Company** Created by Gamal A. Chasten, Lemon, Flaco Navaja, Mildred Ruiz, and Steven Sap; April 26–29, 2007

# Portland Center Stage

Portland, Oregon

Nineteenth Season

Artistic Director, Chris Coleman

**West Side Story** Conceived and originally directed and choreographed by Jerome Robbins, book by Arthur Laurents, music by Leonard Bernstein, lyrics by Stephen Sondheim; Director, Chris Coleman; Music Director, Rick Lewis, Choreography, Joel Ferrell, Sets, G.W. Mercier; Costumes, Jeff Cone; Lighting, Peter Maradudin; Sound, Casi Pacilio; Fight Director, James Armour; Dialect Coach; Teresa Thuman; Stage Manager, Mark Tynan; ASM, Jamie Hill; Production Assistant, Jacob Fenston; Assistant Choreography, Amy Palomino & Kent Zimmerman; Cast: Tony Clarno (Riff), Anderson Davis (Tony), Ryan Jackson (Action), Brian Beach (A-Rab), Tommy Berklund (Baby John), Aaron Hamilton (Big Deal), Scott Sachs (Diesel), Anna Kaiser (Graziella), Kristen J. Smith (Velma), Heather White (Pauline), Amy Palomino (Anybodys), Caesar Samayoa (Bernardo), Carey Brown (Maria), Ivette Sosa (Anita), Matt Caffoni (Chino), Kent Zimmerman (Pepe), Chad Michael (Indio), Oscar Campisi (Anxious), George Nieves (Toro), Danita Salamida (Rosalia), Courtney Laine Mazza (Consuela), Dayna Tietzen (Teresita), Kristen J. Smith (Francisca), Anna Kaiser (Estella, Danny Bruno (Doc/Krupke), Andrew Hickman (Shrank/Glad Hand); October 5–November 12, 2006

**I Am My Own Wife** by Doug Wright; Director, Victor Pappas; Sets, Curt Enderle; Costumes, Jeff Cone; Lighting, Michael Wellborn; Sound, Casi Pacilio; Stage Manager, Jamie Hill; Dialects, Stephanie Gaslin; Dramaturg, Stefan Kay; Production Assistant; Devin Zoller; Cast: Wade McColllum (Charlotte von Mahlsdorf and others); November 7–December 23, 2006

**This Wonderful Life** Conceived by Mark Setlock, written by Steve Murray, based on the screenplay of *It's a Wonderful Life*; Director, Cliff Fannin Baker; Sets, Dex Edwards; Costumes, Jeff Cone; Lighting, Daniel Ordower; Sound, Jen Raynak; Stage Manager, Mark Tynan; Production Assistant, Jacob Fenston; Cast: Matthew Floyd Miller (George Bailey and others); November 20–December 24, 2006

**Misalliance** by George Bernard Shaw; Director, Chris Coleman; Sets, William Bloodgood, Costumes, Jeff Cone; Lighting, Ruth Walkowski; Sound, Casi Pacilio; Dialect Coach, Stephanie Gaslin; Stage Manager, Jamie Hill; ASM, Mark Tynan; Production Assistant, Meghan McNeal; Cast: Steven Cole Hughes (Johnny Tarleton), Ben Steinfeld (Bentley Summerhays), Amanda Soden (Hypatia Tarleton), Linda Ryan (Mrs. Tarleton), Aled Davies (Lord Summerhays), Kenneth Albers (Mr. John Tarleton), Spencer Conway (Joey Percival), Christine Calfas (Lina Szczepanowska), Darius Pierce (Gunner); January 9–February 4, 2007

**Act a Lady** by Jordan Harrison; Director, Cliff Fannin Baker; Sets, Jeff Seats; Costumes, Jeff Cone; Lighting, Don Crossley; Sound, Casi Pacilio; Stage Manager, Mark Tynan; ASM, Creon Thorne; Production Assistant, Jacob Fenston; Accordion Coach, Jacob Fenston; Cast: Act 1: Ebbe Roe Smith (Miles/Lady Romola Von Plofsdorf), James Farmer (True/Countess Mathilde St. Roquefort), Casey McFeron (Casper/Greta the Maid), Sharonlee McLean (Dorothy), Torrey Cornwell (Lorna), Debera Ann Lund (Zina); Act 2: Ebbe Roe Smith (Lady Romola von Plofsdorf), James Farmer (Countess Mathilde St. Roquefort), Casey McFeron (Greta the Maid), Sharonlee McLean (Dorothy/Miles), Torrey Cornwell (Lorna/True), Debera Ann Lund (Zina/Casper); January 30–March 11, 2007

*James Farmer and Casey McFeron in* Act a Lady
*(photo by Joni Shimabukuro)*

**The Thugs** by Adam Bock; Director, Rose Riordan; Sets, Jeff Seats; Costumes, Jeff Cone; Lighting, Don Crossley; Sound, Jen Raynak; Stage Manager, Mark Tynan; ASM, Creon Thorne; Assistant Director, Megan Ward; Production Assistant, Jacob Fenston; Cast: Sharonlee McLean (Mercedes), Debera Ann Lund (Elaine), Laura Faye Smith (Diane), Kelly Tallent (Mary), Kelsey Tyler (Bart), Val Landrum (Daphne), Torrey Cornwell (Chantal), Casey McFeron (Joey); February 9–March 10, 2007

**The Pillowman** by Martin McDonagh; Director, Rose Riordan; Sets, Russell Parkman; Costumes, Jeff Cone; Lighting, Daniel Ordower; Sound, Casi Pacilio; Composer, Twayn Williams; Fight Director, John Armour; Stage Manager, Jamie Hill; ASM, Mark Tynan; Assistant Director, Megan Ward; Production Assistant, Devin Zoller; Cast: Cody Nickell (Katurian), Sean Cullen (Tupolski), James Kennedy (Ariel), Tim True (Michal), Susan Norton (Mother), Damon Kupper (Father), Hayley Rousselle (Girl), Tanner Ward (Boy); February 20 –March 18, 2007

**Fences** by August Wilson; Director, Jonathan Wilson; Sets, Scott Bradley, Costumes, Jacqueline Firkins; Lighting, R. Lap-Chi Chu; Composer/Sound, Jim Ragland; Stage Manager, Michelle Medvin; Fight Director, Mark Olsen; ASM, Mark Tynan; Assistant Director, Hana Sharif; Production Assistant, Jacob Fenston; Cast: Wendell Wright (Troy Maxson), Wandachristine (Rose), Don Mayo (Jim Bono), Robert Christopher Riley (Cory), Ray Anthony Thomas (Gabriel), Che Ayende (Lyons), Makayla Cymon Irvan-Burke or Justyce Chaney (Raynell); Produced in collaboration with Hartford Stage Company and Dallas Theater Center; April 10–May 6, 2007

**Bad Dates** by Theresa Rebeck; Director, Timothy Near; Sets, Matthew Smucker; Costumes, Jeff Cone; Lighting, Daniel Ordower; Sound, Steve Schoenbeck; Associate Sound, Casi Pacilio; Stage Manager, Mark Tynan; Production Assistant, Meghan McNeal; Cast: Carol Halstead (Haley Walker); April 17–June 10, 2007

# Portland Stage Company

Portland, Maine

Thirty-third Season

Artistic Director, Anita Stewart

**The Ugly American** Created and performed by Mike Daisey; Director, Jean-Michele Gregory; June 4–June 26, 2006

**Over the Tavern** by Tom Dudzick; Director, Lisa Difranza; Sets, Anita Stewart; Costumes, Kathleen Brown; Lighting, Bryon Winn; Sound, Christopher Fitze; Stage Manager, Marjorie Gallant; Cast: Peter Bailinson (Rudy Pazinski), Chaney Burlin (Eddie Pazinski), Paul Coufos (Chet Pazinski), Dierdre Friel (Annie Pazinski), August Halm-Perazone (Georgie Pazinksi), Celia Howard (Sister Clarissa), Patricia Randell (Ellen Pazinski); September 26–October 22, 2006

**Two Rooms** by Lee Blessing; Director, Drew Barr; Sets, Russell Metheny; Costumes, Jodi Ozimek; Lighting, Rick Martin; Sound, Peter John Still; Stage Manager, Myles C. Hatch; Cast: Tom Butler (Michael Wells), Moira Driscoll (Ellen Van Oss), Ken Forman (Walker Harris), Caris Vujcec (Lainie Wells); October 31–November 19, 2006

**A Christmas Carol** by Charles Dickens; Director, Anita Stewart; Sets, Anita Stewart; Costumes, Jacqueline Firkins & Susan Thomas; Lighting, Bryon Winn; Composer, Peter John Still; Musical Director, Edward Reichert; Stage Manager, Marjorie Gallant; Cast: Paul Berry (Scrooge), Maureen Buttler (Mrs. Cratchit), Mark Honan (Bob Cratchit), Cristine McMurdo-Wallis (Ghosts), Daniel Noel (Jacob Marley), Edward Reichert (Charles Dickens), Dustin Tucker (Nephew Fred), Sally Wood (Belle); Ensemble: Jane Ackermann, Peter Bailinson, Jackson Beck, Michael Best, Rick Blake, Cecelia Botting, Chaney Burlin, Elsa Curran, Emma Dadmun, Hannah Daly, Nora Daly, Mary Doherty, David Glendinning, August Halm-Perazone, Lynnea Harding, Tim Hartel, Leo Hilton, Charlotte Honan-Warnock, Oona Rosa MacKinnon-Hoban, Bodhi Ouelette, Owen Pence, Philip Rogers, Mitchell Ross, Coral Sandler, Jenny Smick, Charlotte Spritz, Mae Strout, Colin Swords, Elizabeth Tarantino, Valerie Tarantino, Witt Tarantino; November 30–December 24, 2006

**Noises Off** by Michael Frayn; Director, Samuel Buggeln; Sets, Anita Stewart; Costumes, Frank Champa; Lighting, Gregg Carville; Sound, Christopher Fitze; Fight Choreography, Mark Bedell, Stage Manager, Myles C. Hatch; Cast: Scott Barrow (Garry Lejeune/Roger Tramplemain), Kim Ders (Belinda Blair/Flavia Brent), Tavia Gilbert (Poppy Norton-Taylor), J.P. Guimont (Tim Allgood), Mark Honan (Lloyd Dallas), John Little (Frederick Fellows/Philip Brent/ Sheikh), Lisa McCormick (Brooke Ashton/Vicki), Cristine McMurdo-Wallis (Dotty Otley/Mrs. Clackett), Evan Thompson (Selsdon Mowbray/Burglar); January 23–February 18, 2007

**Iron Kisses** by James Still; Director, Risa Brainin; Set/Costumes, Anita Stewart; Lighting, Michael Klaers, Composer, Hans Indigo Spencer; Stage Manager, Marjorie Gallant; Cast: Tom Ford (Billy), Janice O'Rourke (Barbara); February 27–March 18, 2007

**Intimate Apparel** by Lynn Nottage; Director, Lucy Smith Conroy; Sets, Anita Stewart; Costumes, Jacqueline Firkins; Lighting, Bryon Winn; Sound, Matt Cost; Stage Manager, Myles C. Hatch; Cast: Jean Arbeiter (Mrs. Van Buren), Victoire Charles (Mayme), Venida Evans (Mrs. Dickson), Leopold Lowe (George Armstrong), Candice McKoy (Esther Mills), Tzahi Maskovitz (Mr. Marks); March 27–April 22, 2007

**Augusta** by Richard Dresser; Director, Michael Rafkin; Sets, Anita Stewart; Costumes, Susan Picinich; Lighting, Gregg Carville; Sound, Stephen Swift; Stage Manager, Marjorie Gallant; Cast: Charlie Kevin (Jimmy), Sally Wood (Claire), Rae C. Wright (Molly); May 1–May 20, 2007

# Prince Music Theater

Philadelphia, Pennsylvania

Twenty-third Season

Producing Director, Marjorie Samoff; Executive Producer, Alexander Fraser; Associate Artistic Director, Richard M. Parison Jr.

**From Tha Hip** Created and conceived by Clyde Evans Jr. in collaboration with Albert Innaurato, music composed and performed by the Subliminal Orphans; Director, Rajendra Ramoon Maharaj; Music Directors, Charles L. Pateierno & Michael E. Taylor; Choreography, Clyde Evans Jr.; Sets, Bradley Helm; Costumes, Regina M. Rizzo; Lighting, John Hoey; Sound, Nick Kourtides; Stage Manager, Paul Jerue; Cast: Mark Boston, Jon Bulack, Kevin A. Cammarota, David Dorsaima, Virgil Gadson, Haewook Lee, Elaina Parker, Travis Patterson, Justin Valentine, Peggy Walsh, Amanda Washington, Shanika-Nicole Williams; The Band: "Subliminal Orphans"—Joaquin Cotlar, Wiley Griffin, Charlie Patierno, Ken Pendergast, Reg Smith, Michael Tyler (a.k.a. Tu Phace), Amy Yanick (a.k.a. keen); September 19–October 8, 2006

**Always: The Love Story of Irving Berlin** Music and lyrics by Irving Berlin, arrangements by Mark Nadler with assistance by K.T. Sullivan, text by K.T. Sullivan with assistance by Mark Nadler; Director, Richard M. Parison Jr., Lighting, Troy A. Martin-O'Shia; Sound, Nick Kourtides; Stage Manager, Paul Jerue; Cast: Mark Nadler, K.T. Sullivan; October 18–29, 2006

**A Swell Party RSVP: Cole Porter** Music and lyrics by Cole Porter; Arrangements, Mark Nadler; Director, Richard M. Parison Jr; Lighting, Troy A. Martin-O'Shia; Sound, Nick Kourtides; Stage Manager, Paul Jerue; Cast: Mark Nadler and K.T. Sullivan; Musicians: Loren Schoenberg (saxophone), John Loehrke (bass); November 1–5, 2006

**Annie Get Your Gun** Music and lyrics by Irving Berlin, book by Herbert and Dorothy Fields; Director, Richard M. Parison, Jr., Choreography, Mercedes Ellington; Music Director, Eric Barnes; Sets, Todd Edward Ivins; Costumes, Maggie Baker-Atkins; Lighting, Shelley Hicklin; Sound, Otts Munderloh; Hair/Wigs, Jon Carter; Assistant Director, Dawn K. Cowle; Assistant to the Choreography, Jodi Kuhlmann; Native American Consultants, Native Nations Dance Theater; Casting, Janet Foster; PSM, Brian Klinger; ASM, Victoria Hein; Cast: Josie Andrews, Kristina Biddle, Kevin Cammarota, Wesley Cappiello, Anne Connors, Jeffrey Coon, Christopher Coucill, Benjamin Scott Kramer, Jodi Kuhlmann, Erica Mabry, Mary Martello, Andrea McArdle, Michael Newman, Conor O'Brien, Jamieson O'Brien, Michael Philip O'Brien, Cynthia Raff, Caitlin Reilly, Conrad Ricamora, Arthur Ryan, John Scherer, Dan Schiff, Alexis Sims, Elyse McKay Taylor, Andrea Norah Wright; December 2–31, 2006.

*Andrea McArdle in* Annie Get Your Gun *(photo by Mark Garvin)*

**Stormy Weather: Imagining Lena Horne** Conceived and written by Sharleen Cooper Cohen; Director, Michael Bush; Choreography, Randy Skinner; Music Director, Bruce Barnes; Orchestrations, Daryl Waters; Sets, James Noone, Costumes, Linda Cho, Lighting, Traci Klainer, Sound, Nick Kourtides; Casting, Janet Foster; Vocal Arrangements, Bruce Barnes & Daryl Waters; Dance Arrangement, Bruce Barnes & Randy Skinner; Philadelphia Casting, Richard M. Parison Jr.; Assistant Choreography, Jeremy Benton; Assistant Director, Megan Heimbecker; Assistant Music Director, Samuel Heifetz; Assistant Costumes, Emily Pepper, Wig Master, Charles LaPointe, Associate Lighting, Graham Kindred; PSM, Brian Klinger; ASM, Colleen M. Welsh; Cast: Leslie Uggams, Julian Brightman, Carey Brown, Julyza A Commodore, Davis Gaines, Kearran Giovanni, Jared Grimes, Dee Hoty, Julia Lema, Kevyn Morrow, Katie O'Shaughnessey, Destan Owens, Michael Scott, Daniel J. Watts, Dathan B. Williams; February 10–March 4, 2007

**Tiny Dancer** Music, lyrics, and book by Paul Scott Goodman, book co-written by Miriam Gordon; Director, Michael Unger; Music Director, Orchestrations/ Arrangements, Roger Butterly; Sets/Projections, Todd Edward Ivins; Lighting, Derek Hachkowski, Sound, Andrew L. Adams; Casting, Janet Foster; Stage Manager, Bridget A. Cook; Cast: Merideth Kaye Clark, Paul Scott Goodman; Musicians: Roger Butterley (Conductor/piano/guitar/mandolin), Bernard McKenna (guitar), Todd F. Erk (bass), Charles Patierno (drums); March 17–April 1, 2007

**Hair** Book and lyrics by James Rado and Gerome Ragni, music by Galt McDermot; Director, Richard M. Parison Jr.; Choreography, Karen Getz; Music Director, Eric Ebbenga; Sets/Projections, Todd Edward Ivins; Costumes, Mary Folino; Lighting,

Shelley Hicklin; Sound, Otts Munderloh; Hair/Wigs, Jon Carter; Puppets, Spiral Q Puppet Theatre; Assistant Director, Dawn Cowle; Assistant Choreography, Kerri Rose; Associate Music Director, Nick Cheng; Assistant Lighting, J. Dominic Chacon; Casting, Janet Foster; Production Assistant, Jennifer Dillon; PSM, Brian Klinger; Cast: Matthew F. Burrow, Ari Butler, Laura Catlaw, Jaime Cepero III, Nikki Curmaci, Lindsey Gordon, Elizabeth Gross, Gabrielle Hurtt, Rahsaan Kerns, Kathryn M. Lyles, Kalia Lynne, Thom Miller, André Darnell Myers, Michael Ponte, Da'Vine Joy Randolph, Ashley Robinson, Jonathan Shade, Alyse Wojciechowski; May 26–June 24, 2007

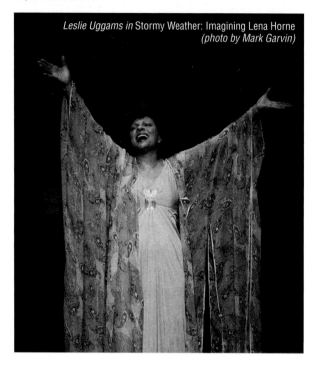

*Leslie Uggams in* Stormy Weather: Imagining Lena Horne
*(photo by Mark Garvin)*

# The Repertory Theatre of St. Louis

St. Louis, Missouri

Fortieth Season

Artistic Director, Steven Woolf; Managing Director, Mark D. Bernstein

## MAINSTAGE

**Ace** Music by Richard Oberacker, book and lyrics by Robert Taylor & Richard Oberacker; Director, Stafford Arima; Choreography, Andrew Palermo; Musical Director, David Kreppel; Orchestrations, Greg Anthony; Sets, David Korins; Costumes, Marie Anne Chiment; Lighting, Chris Akerlind; Sounds, John H. Shivers & David Patridge; Casting, Rich Cole; Stage Manager, Glenn Dunn; ASM, Shannon B. Sturgis; Cast: Noah Galvin (Billy), Traci Lyn Thomas (Mrs. Crandall/Clara Whitlow), Jessica Boevers (Elizabeth), Amy Bodnar (Louise), Duke Lafoon (Edward/Stampley), Matt Bogart (Ace), Chris Peluso (John Robert), Jimmy McEvoy (School Bully/Young Charlie/Ensemble), Ariane Rinehart (Sidekick/Ensemble), Heather Ayers (Ruth), Gabrielle Boyadjian (Emily), Gabrielle Stravelli (Anique/Ensemble), Susan Kokot Stokes (Teacher/Ensemble), Kelli

Barrett (Nurse/Ensemble/Dance Captain), James Judy (Toy Store Owner/Colonel Whitlow/Chennault/Ensemble), Richard Barth (Lieutenant Sanders/Sullivan/Ensemble), Danny Rothman (Cooper/Myron/Ensemble), Kevin Reed (Tennaman/Stein/Ensemble); September 6–October 1, 2006

*Noah Galvin and Gabrielle Stravelli in* Ace
*(photo by Jerry Naunheim Jr.)*

**Of Mice and Men** by John Steinbeck; Director, Edward Stern; Sets, Paul Shortt; Costumes, Kristine Kearney; Lighting, James Sale; Sound, Chuck Hatcher; Casting, Rich Cole; Stage Manager, T.R. Martin; ASM, Tony Dearing; Cast: Marc Aden Gray (George), Brendan Averett (Lennie), Dane Knell (Candy), Kenneth Albers (The Boss), Jon Sampson (Curley), Peter Bretz (Slim), Anne Bowles (Curley's Wife), Christian Kohn (Carlson), Kevin Crowley (Whit), Michael Anthony Williams (Crooks); October 11–November 5, 2006

**The Musical of Musicals – The Musical!** Music and book by Eric Rockwell, lyrics and book by Joanne Bogart; Director/Choreographer, Pamela Hunt; Musical Director, Henry Palkes; Sets, James Morgan; Costumes, Dorothy Marshall Englis; Lighting, Mary Jo Dondlinger; Sound, Tori Meyer; Casting, Rich Cole; Stage Manager, Glenn Dunn; ASM, Shannon B. Sturgis; Cast: Matt Bailey, Joanne Bogart, Edwin Cahill, Kristin Maloney; November 29–December 29, 2006

**Heartbreak House** by George Bernard Shaw; Director, John Going; Sets, John Ezell; Costumes, Elizabeth Covey; Lighting, Dennis Parichy; Sound, Tori Meyer; Casting, Rich Cole; Stage Manager, T.R. Martin; ASM, Tony Dearing; Cast: Ruth Eglsaer (Ellie Dunn), Donna Weinsting (Nurse Guinness), Thomas Carson (Captain Shotover), Andrea Cirie (Lady Utterword), Carole Healey (Hesione Hushabye), Frank Lowe (Mazzini Dunn), Paul DeBoy (Hector Hushabye), Curt Karibalis (Boss Mangan), Matt Bradford Sullivan (Randall Utterword); January 3–January 28, 2007

**The Heidi Chronicles** by Wendy Wasserstein; Director, Michael Evan Haney; Sets, Hugh Landwehr; Costumes, Martha Hally; Lighting, Marcus Doshi; Casting, Rich Cole; Assistant Director, Kelly Lynn Hogan; Stage Manager, Glenn Dunn; ASM, Shannon B. Sturgis; Cast: Effie Johnson (Heidi Holland), Polly Lee (Susan Johnston), James Clow (Peter Patrone), Andy Paris (Scoop Rosenbaum), Avery Clark (Chris/Mark/Ray), Annie Fitzpatrick (Jill/Debbie/Lisa), Maggie Hart (Becky/Clara/Denise); Celeste Ciulla (Fran/Molly/Betsy/April); February 7–March 4, 2007

**Sherlock Holmes: The Final Adventure** by Steven Dietz, based on the original 1899 play by William Gillette and Arthur Conan Doyle; Director, Edward Stern; Sets, Neil Patel; Costumes, Elizabeth Covey; Lighting, Robert Wierzel; Sound, Matt Callahan; Casting, Rich Cole; Stage Manager, Glenn Dunn; ASM, Tony Dearing; Cast: Joris Stuyck (Sherlock Holmes), Howard Kaye (Doctor Watson), Michael Haworth (Professor Moriarty), Michael Sharon (The King of Bohemia), Brandy Burre (Irene Adler), David Huber (James Larrabee), Carine Montbertrand (Madge Larrabee), William McNulty (Sid Prince/Clergyman), Liz Ali, J.J. Perez, Ian Way, Brian White (Police/Passers-By/Messengers); March 21–April 15, 2007

## STUDIO THEATRE

**Ordinary Nation** by Carter W. Lewis; Director, Andrea Urice; Sets, Robert Mark Morgan; Costumes, Dorothy Marshall Englis; Lighting, John Wylie; Sound, Tori Meyer; Casting, Rich Cole; Stage Manager, Shannon B. Sturgis; Cast: George Bartenieff (G.J. Jones), Dana Acheson (Frankie Jones), Gregory Northrop (Nation Jones), Angela Reed (Allison Jones), Curt Hostetter (Gibb Aston); October 25–November 12, 2006

*Dana Acheson and Gregory Northrop in* Ordinary Nation
*(photo by James Visser)*

**A Number** by Caryl Churchill; Director, Susan Gregg; Sets, Narelle Sissons; Costumes, Clyde Ruffin; Lighting, Mark Wilson; Sound, Tori Meyer; Stage Manager, Champe Leary; Cast: Jim Butz (B-2/B-1/Michael Black), Anderson Matthews (Salter); January 17–February 4, 2007

**Woman Before A Glass: A Triptych in Four Parts** by Lanie Robertson; Director, Steve Campo; Sets, Jeff Cowie; Costumes, Alejo Vietti & Elizabeth Flauto; Lighting, Matthew Richards; Sound, J. Hagenbuckle; Associate Director, Tom Wojtunik; Stage Manager, Champe Leary; Cast: Glynis Bell (Peggy Guggenheim); March 14–April 1, 2007

## OFF-RAMP

**The Pillowman** by Martin McDonagh; Director, Steven Woolf; Sets, Adrian W. Jones; Costumes, Alejo Vietti; Lighting, Mary Jo Dondlinger; Sound, Tori Meyer; Fight Director, Brian Peters; Casting, Rich Cole; Stage Manager, Champe Leary; ASM, Mary Jane Probst; Cast: Anderson Matthews (Tupolski), Joseph Collins (Katurian), Paul DeBoy (Ariel), Timothy McCracken (Michal), Ruth Heyman (Mother), Steve Callahan (Father), Dan Ford (Boy), Anna Paniccia (Girl); September 20–October 8, 2006

**Shakespeare's R & J** Adapted by Joe Calarco from the play by William Shakespeare; Director, Paul Mason Barnes; Sets, Scott Neale; Costumes, Garth Dunbar; Lighting, Mark Wilson; Sound, Tori Meyer; Vocal Coach/Combat Director, Bruce Longworth; Casting, Rich Cole; Stage Manager, Kathryn Ballard; Cast: Daniel Zaitchik (Student 1), Bobby Steggert (Student 2), Chris Landis (Student 3), Bob Braswell (Student 4); October 18–November 5, 2006

**Urinetown, the Musical** Music and lyrics by Mark Hollmann, book and lyrics by Greg Kotis; Director, Rob Ruggiero; Choreography, Ralph D. Perkins; Musical Director, F. Wade Russo; Sets, Michael Schweikardt; Costumes, Anne Kenney; Lighting, Peter E. Sargent; Sound, Tori Meyer; Casting, Rich Cole; Stage Manager, Champe Leary; ASM, Mary Jane Probst; Cast: Steve Isom (Officer Lockstock), Zoe Vonder Haar (Penelope Pennywise), Ben Nordstrom (Bobby Strong), Sandie Rosa (Little Sally), Jayne Paterson (Hope Cladwell), Doug Storm (Mr. McQueen), Bill Lynch (Senator Fipp), Jonathan Brody (Old Man Strong/Hot Blades Harry), Rachel Coloff (Soupy Sue/Cladwell's Secretary), Paul Oakley Stovall (Tiny Tom/Dr. Billeaux), Amy Goldberger (Little Becky Two-Shoes/Mrs. Milennium), William Daniels (Robby the Stockfish/UGC Executive #2), Michael J. Farina (Officer Barrel), Tyler Adcock (Billy Boy Bill/UGC Executive #1), Michele Burdette Elmore (Josephine Strong/Old Woman), Erin Anderson (Ensemble Poor), Maggie Hart (Ensemble Poor), Joneal Joplin (Caldwell B. Cladwell); November 15–December 10, 2006

*Ben Nordstrom and The Cast of* Urinetown *(photo by James Visser)*

## THE IMAGINARY THEATRE COMPANY

**The Velveteen Rabbit** by Margery Williams, adapted for the stage by Kim Esop Wylie, music by Joe Dreyer; Director, Kat Singleton; Sets & Costumes, Dorothy Marshall Englis; Stage Manager, Brian Peters; Director of Education, Marsha Coplon; Artistic Supervisor, Jeffery Matthews; Cast: Jason Contini (Boy/Toy Boat), Alan Knoll (Husband/Aunt/Horse/Nana/Wild Rabbit), Meghan Brown (Margery), Christena Doggrell (Velveteen Rabbit/Live Rabbit)

**Hansel and Gretel: The Next Generation** by Kim Esop Wylie, music and lyrics by Neal Richardson; Director, Kat Singleton; Musical Director, Neal Richardson; Set & Costumes, Dorothy Marshall Englis; Stage Manager, Brian Peters; Cast: Christena Doggrell (Gretel), Meghan Brown (Mom), Jason Contini (Hansel), Alan Knoll (Uncle)

**A Thousand Cranes** Adapted by Kathryn Schultz Miller; Director, Jeffery Matthews; Set & Costumes, Dorothy Marshall Englis; Stage Manager, Brian Peters; Cast: Christena Doggrell (Sadako), Meghan Brown (Mother/ Grandmother Oba chan), Alan Knoll (Father), Jason Contini (Kenji)

# San Jose Repertory Theatre

San Jose, California

Twenty-sixth Season

Artistic Director, Timothy Near; Managing Director, Nick Nichols

**2 Pianos 4 Hands** by Richard Greenblatt and Ted Dykstra; Director, Bruce K. Sevy; Sets, Scott Weldin; Costumes, Kish Finnegan; Lighting, Don Darnutzer; Sound, Brian Jerome Peterson; Stage Manager, Laxmi Kumaran; ASM, Jenessa Schwartz; Cast: Mark Anders (Ted); Carl Danielsen (Richard), June 10–July 9, 2006

**Moonlight and Magnolias** by Ron Hutchinson; Director, Timothy Near; Sets, Matthew Smucker; Costumes, Elizabeth Hope Clancy; Lighting, David Lee Cuthbert; Sound, Stephen LeGrand; Stage Manager, Melanie R. Mather; Cast: Tom Beckett (David O. Selznick), Sarah Nealis (Miss Poppenghul), John Procaccino (Victor Fleming), Peter Van Norden (Ben Hecht); October 15–November 12, 2006

**A Christmas Story** by Philip Grecian, based upon the motion picture written by Jean Shepherd, Leigh Brown, and Bob Clark; Director, John McCluggage; Sets, Robert Mark Morgan; Costumes, B Modern; Lighting, Lap-Chi Chu; Sound, Jeff Mockus; PSM, Laxmi Kumaran; ASM, Melissa Berkson; Cast: Dan Haitt (Ralph/Cowboy/Three Lot Owner/ Delivery Man), Nancy Carlin (Mother/Miss Shields), Howard Swain (The Old Man/Santa Claus), Zachary Freier-Harrison (Ralphie Parker), Evan Coleman (Randie Parker), Nick Perry (Flick/Desperado One), Hector Pleins (Schwartz/Desperado Two), Ty Doughty (Scut Farkas/Black Bart), Noel Witcosky (Esther Jane Alberry), Lindsey Meyer (Helen Weathers); November 25–December 30, 200

**Long Day's Journey Into Night** by Eugene O'Neill; Director, Jonathan Moscone; Sets, Annie Smart; Costumes, B. Modern; Lighting, Lap-Chi Chu; Sound, Steve Schoenbeck; PSM, Laxmi Kumaran; ASM, Jaime Abegglen; Cast: Kimberly K. King (Mary Tyrone), Sarah Nealis (Cathleen), Paul Vincent O'Connor (James Tyrone, Sir), Mark A. Phillips (Jamie Tyrone), T. Edward Webster (Edmund Tyrone); January 27–February 25, 2007

**Nixon's Nixon** by Russell Lees; Director, Michael Bulter; Sets, Scott Weldin; Costumes, B. Modern; Lighting, Kurt Landisman; Sound, Jeff Mockus; PSM, Laxmi Kumaran; ASM, Melissa Berkson; Cast: David Pichette (Richard Nixon), Peter Van Norden (Henry Kissinger), Mike Taylor (The Marine); March 24–April 22, 2007

**Rabbit Hole** by David Lindsay-Abaire; Director, Kristin Brandt; Sets, Kate Edmunds; Costumes, B. Modern; Lighting, David Lee Cuthbert; Sound, Jeff Mockus; PSM, Laxmi Kumaran; ASM, Peter Royston; Cast: Andy Murray (Howie); Stacy Ross (Becca); Lynne Soffer (Nat); Jessa Watson (Izzy), James Breedlove (Jason); May 12–June 10, 2007

*Stacy Ross and Andy Murray in* Rabbit Hole *(photo by Pat Kirk)*

# Seattle Repertory Theatre

Seattle, Washington

Forty-fourth Season

Artistic Director, David Esbjornson; Managing Director: Benjamin Moore

**Doubt** by John Patrick Shanley; Director, Warner Shook; Sets, Michael Ganio; Costumes, Frances Kenny; Lighting, Allen Lee Hughes; Composer, Michael Roth; Dialect Coach, Judith Shahn; Cast: Corey Brill (Father Brendan Flynn), Kandi sChappell (Sister Aloysius Beauvier), Melissa D. Brown (Sister James), Cynthia Jones (Mrs. Muller); Septmember 21–October 21, 2006

**Thom Pain (based on nothing)** by Will Eno; Director, Jerry Manning; Sets/Lighting, L.B. Mose; Costumes, Shannin Strom; Cast: Todd Jefferson Moore (Thom Pain); October 5–November 5, 2006

**The Great Gatsby** by F. Scott Fitzgerald, adapted for the stage by Simon Levy; Director, David Esbjornson; Sets, Tom Lynch; Costumes, Jane Greenwood; Lighting, Scott Zielinski; Composer, Wayne Barker; Sound, Scott Edwards; Choreography, Sean Curren; Fight Choreography, Geoffrey Alm; Cast: Matthew Amendt (Nick Carraway), Heidi Armbruster (Daisy Buchanan), Cheyenne Casebier (Jordan Baker), Bradford Farwell (George Wilson), Sean G. Griffin (Meyer Wolfsheim), Erik Heger (Tom Buchanan), Gretchen Krich (Mrs. Mckee/Mrs. Michalis), Lorenzo Pisoni (Jay Gatsby), Kathryn Van Meter (Myrtle Wilson), David J. Wright III (Saxman); Ensemble: Justin Alley, Anna-Lisa Carlson, Trick Danneker, Doug Fahl, Pamela Mijatov, Sabrina Prada; November 2–December 10, 2006

**Memory House** by Kathleen Tolan; Director, Allison Narver; Sets, Matthew Smucker; Costumes, Marcia Dixcy Jory; Lighting, Marcus Doshi; Sound, Dominic Cody Kramers; Cast: Jeanne Paulson (Maggie), Sharia Pierce (Katia); November 16–December 17, 2006

*The Cast of* The Great Gatsby *(photo by Chris Bennion)*

**The Lady from Dubuque** by Edward Albee; Director, David Esbjornson; Sets, John Arnone; Costumes, Elizabeth Hope Clancy; Lighting, James F. Ingalls; Cast: Hans Altwies (Fred), Myra Carter (Elizabeth), Kristin Flanders (Lucinda), Carla Harting (Jo), Charlie Matthes (Sam), Chelsey Rives (Carol), Paul Morgan Stetler (Edgar), Frank X (Oscar); January 11–February 10, 2007

**Blue Door** by Tanya Barfield; Director, Leigh Silverman; Sets, Narelle Sissons; Costumes, Toni-Leslie James; Lighting, ML Geiger; Sound, Ken Travis; Composer, Daryl Waters; Dialect Coach, Deborah Hecht; Cast: Reg E. Cathey (Lewis), Hubert Point-Du Jour (Rex/Simon/Jesse); February 1–March 4, 2007

**Fire on the Mountain** by Randal Myler and Dan Wheetman; Director, Randal Myler; Sets, Vicki Smith; Costumes, Marcia Dixcy Jory; Lighting, Don Darnutzer; Sound, Eric Stahlhammer; Slide Designer, Randal Myler; Cast: Molly Andrews, 'Mississippi' Charles Bevel, Margaret Bowman, Tony Marcus, Lee Morgan, Mike Regan, Ed Snodderly, Dan Wheetman, Trevor Wheetman, Tommy Fleming; February 22–March 24, 2007

**My Name is Rachel Corrie** by Alan Rickman and Katharine Viner, from the writings of Rachel Corrie; Director, Braden Abraham; Sets, Jennifer Zeyl; Costumes, Harmony Arnold; Lighting, L.B. Morse; Sound, Obadiah Eaves; Videographer, Nick Schwarz Hall; Cast: Marya Sea Kaminski (Rachel Corrie); March 15–April 22, 2007

*Marya Sea Kaminski in* My Name is Rachel Corrie
*(photo by Chris Bennion)*

**Gem of the Ocean** by August Wilson; Director, Phylicia Rashad; Sets, John Iacovelli; Costumes, Susan E. Mickey; Lighting, Allen Lee Hughes; Composer, Kathryn Bostic; Sound, Dan Moses Schreier; Production Sound Supervisor, Tim Pritchard; Cast: Crystal Fox (Black Mary), William Hall Jr. (Solly Two Kings), Khalil Kain (Citizen Barlow), Stanley Wayne Mathis (Caesar), Todd Jefferson Moore (Rutherford Selig), Michele Shay (Aunt Ester), Allie Woods (Eli); April 5–May 6, 2007

*Michele Shay and William Hall Jr. in* Gem of the Ocean
*(photo by Chris Bennion)*

## Shakespeare Theatre Company

Washington, D.C.

Twenty-first Season

Artistic Director, Michael Kahn; Managing Director, Nicholas T. Goldsborough

**An Enemy of the People** by Henrik Ibsen, translated by Rick Davis and Brian Johnston; Director, Kjetil Bang-Hansen; Sets/Costumes, Timian Alsaker; Lighting, Charlie Morrison; Sound, Martin Desjardins; Vocal Coach, Gary Logan; Resident A.D., Stephen Fried; Literary Associate, Akiva Fox; PSM, Amber Wedin; ASM, Cary Louise Gillett; Cast: Joseph Urla (Dr. Thomas Stockman), Philip Goodwin (Peter Stockman), Caitlin O'Connell (Mrs. Stockman), Rick Foucheux (Aslaksen), Robin Gammell (Morten Kiil), Tyrone Mitchell Henderson (Billing), Derek Lucci (Hovstad), Peter Rini (Captain Horster), Samantha Soule (Petra), Ben Schiffbauer (Eilif), Connor Aikin (Morten), Nick Vienna (Ensemble); August 29–October 22, 2006

**The Beaux' Stratagem** by George Farquhar, adapted by Thornton Wilder and Ken Ludwig; Director, Michael Kahn; Sets, James Kronzer; Costumes, Robert Perdziola; Lighting, Joel Moritz; Sound, Martin Desjardins; Choreography, Peter Pucci; Fight Director, Paul Dennhardt; Resident Voice/Text Coach, Ellen O'Brien; Resident A.D., Stephen Fried; Directorial Assistant, Merry Alderman; Literary Associate, Akiva Fox; PSM, M. William Shiner; ASM, Cary Louise Gillett; Cast: Veanne Cox (Mrs. Kate Sullen), Christopher Innvar (Jack Archer), Christian Conn (Tom Aimwell), Julia Coffey (Dorinda), Nancy Robinette (Lady Bountiful), Floyd King (Foigard), Ian Bedford (Sullen), Dan Crane (Hounslow), Colleen Delany (Cherry), Drew Eshelman (Boniface), Rick Foucheux (Gloss), Daniel Harray (Sir Charles Freeman), Diane Ligon (A Lady), Hugh Nees (Scrub), Anne Stone (A County Woman), Nick Vienna (Bagshot), Maria Kelly, David Murgittroyd, Matthew Stucky (Servants); November 7–December 31, 2006

*Julia Coffey, Nancy Robinette, Christian Conn, Christopher Innvar, and Veanne Cox in* The Beaux' Stratagem *(photo by Carol Rosegg)*

**Richard III** by William Shakespeare; Director, Michael Kahn; Sets; Lee Savage, Costumes, Jennifer Moeller; Lighting, Charlie Morrison; Composer/Sound, Martin Desjardins; Fight Choreography, David Leong; Assistant Fight Choreography, Paul Dennhardt; Resident Voice/Text Coach, Ellen O'Brien; Resident A.D., Stephen Fried; Literary Associate, Akiva Fox; Directorial Assistant, Alexander Burns; PSM, M. William Shiner; ASM, Benjamin Royer; Cast: Geraint Wyn Davies (Richard), Edward Gero (Duke of Buckingham), Margot Dionne (Queen Elizabeth), Pamela Payton-Wright (Duchess of York), Tana Hicken (Queen Margaret), Claire Lautier (Lady Anne), Andrew Long (Duke of Clarence), Floyd King (King Edward IV) Ralph Cosham (Lord Stanley), Jeff Allin (Sir Richard Ratcliffe), Ian Bedford (Sir James Tyrrel), Donald Carrier (Earl Rivers), Aubrey Deeker (Sir William Catesby), James Denvil (Sir Robert Brakenbury), David Gross (Earl of Richmond), Bill Hamlin (Bishop of Ely), Keith Irby (Sir Walter Herbert), Carl Palmer (Lord Lovell), Lawrence Redmond (Sir James Blunt), Lawrence Redmond (Lord Mayor of London), Carl Palmer (First Murderer), James Ricks (Second Murderer), Raphael Nash Thompson (Hastings), James Denvil (Earl of Oxford), Floyd King (Scrivner), Melora Kordos (Jane Shore), David Murgittroyd (George Stanley), Dan Crane (Lord Grey), Matthew Stucky (Marquess of Dorset), Kent Jenkins (Duke of York), Maria Kelly (Elizabeth), Sean McCoy (Young Clarence), Matthew Williams (Prince of Wales); January 16–March 18, 2007

**Titus Andronicus** by William Shakespeare; Director, Gale Edwards; Sets, Peter England; Costumes, Murell Horton; Lighting, Mark McCullough; Composer/, Martin Desjardins; Fight Director, Rick Sordelet; Resident Voice/Text Coach, Ellen O'Brien; Assistant Director, Alexander Burns; Literary Associate, Akiva Fox; PSM,

M. William Shiner; ASM, Cary Louise Gillett; Cast: Sam Tsoutsouvas (Titus), Valerie Leonard (Tamora), Alex Podulke (Saturninus), William Langan (Marcus Andronicus), Colleen Delany (Lavinia), Michael Brusasco (Bassianus), James Chatham (Young Lucius), Julie-Ann Elliott (A Nurse), David L. Townsend (Chiron), Ryan Farley (Demetrius), Chris Genebach (Lucius), Bill Hamlin (Emilius), Peter Macon (Aaron), Chris Scheeren (Quintus), David Murgittroyd (Martius), Danny Binstock (Mutius), Matthew Stucky (Alarbus); April 3–May 20, 2007

*Chris Genebach and Peter Macon in* Titus Andronicus *(photo by Carol Rosegg)*

**Love's Labour's Lost** by William Shakespeare; Director, Stephen Fried, based on original direction by Michael Kahn; Sets, Ralph Funicello; Costumes, Catherine Zuber; Lighting, Mark Doubleday; Composer, Adam Wernick; Sound, Martin Desjardins; Choreography, Karma Camp; Music Director, George Fulginiti-Shakar; Resident Voice/Text Coach, Ellen O'Brien; Assistant Director, Paul Takacs; Literary Associate, Akiva Fox; Stage Manager, Karen Oberthal; ASM, Che Wernsman; Cast: Amir Arison (King Ferdinand of Navarre), Christian Conn (Dumaine), Mauricio Tafur Salgado (Longavile), Hank Stratton (Berowne), Caroline Bootle (Princess of France), Colleen Delany (Katherine), Sabrina LeBeauf (Rosaline), Tonya Beckman Ross (Maria), Nick Choksi (Moth), Wynn Harmon (Don Adriano de Armado), Michael Milligan (Costard), Anthony Newfield (Boyet), John Robert Tillotson (Holofernes), Drew Eshelman (Sir Nathaniel), Rock Kohli (Anthony Dull), Leo Erickson (Monsieur Marcade), James Rana (Forester), Nitya Vidyasagar (Jaquenetta), Brian Q. Silver (Sitar Player), Rex Daugherty, Michael Feldsher, Stephen McWilliams, Matthew Stucky and Amol Tripathi (Ensemble); May 24–June 3, 2007

**Hamlet** by William Shakespeare; Director, Michael Kahn; Sets, Walt Spangler; Costumes, Murell Horton; Lighting, Charlie Morrison; Composer, Adam Wernick; Sound, Martin Desjardins; Resident Voice/Text Coach, Ellen O'Brien; Fight Director, David Leong; Assistant Fight Director, Paul Dennhardt; Puppets, Aaron Cromie; Kabuki Consultant, David Furumoto; Assistant Director, Alexander Burns; Directorial Assistant, Merry Alderman; Literary Associate, Akiva Fox; PSM, M. William Shiner; ASM, Benjamin Royer; Cast: Jeffrey Carlson (Hamlet), Robert Cuccioli (Claudius), Janet Zarish (Gertrude), Michelle Beck (Ophelia), Robert Jason Jackson (Polonius), Kanajuan Bentley (Laertes), Ted van Griethuysen (Ghost/First Player/Gravedigger), J. Clint Allen (Guildenstern), James Denvil (Player King), Maria Kelly (Player Queen), Bill Largess (Osric), Kenneth Lee (Fortinbras), Pedro Pascal (Horatio), David L. Townsend (Rosencrantz), Craig Wallace (Prologue); Ensemble: Maria Kelly, David Murgittroyd, Erskine Ritchie, Ben Rosenblatt, Nick Vienna, Chris Whitney; June 5–July 29, 2007

# South Coast Repertory

Costa Mesa, California

Forty-third Season

Producing Artistic Director, David Emmes; Artistic Director, Martin Benson; Managing Director, Paula Tomei.

**Nothing Sacred** by George F. Walker; Director, Martin Benson; Sets, James Youmans & Jerome Martin; Costumes, Angela Balogh Calin; Lighting, York Kennedy; Original Music/Music Direction, Michael Roth; Stage Manager, Jamie A. Tucker; ASM, Randall K. Lum; Cast: Daniel Blinkoff (Arkady Kirsanov), Richard Doyle (Nikolai Kirsanov), Angela Goethals (Fenichka), Jeremy Guskin (Gregor), Khrystyne Haje (Anna Odintsov), Jeremy Peter Johnson (Bailiff), Hal Landon Jr. (Piotr), Jeff Marlow (Victor Sitnikov), Isaac Nippert (Sergei), Eric D. Steinberg (Yevgeny Bazarov), John Vickery (Pavel Kirsonov); Segerstrom Stage; September 1–October 8, 2006.

**Bach at Leipzig** by Itamar Moses; Director, Art Manke; Sets, Thomas Buderwitz; Costumes, Maggie Morgan; Lighting, Geoff Korf; Sound, Tom Cavnar; Assistant Director, Darin Anthony; Fight Director, Martin Noyes; Stage Manager, Erin Nelson; Cast: Tony Abatemarco (Georg Balthasar Schott), Stephen Caffrey (Johann Friedrich Fasch), Sean H. Hemeon (The Greatest Organist in Germany), Jeffrey Hutchinson (Georg Lenck), John-David Keller (Georg Friedrich Kaufmann), Timothy Landfield (Johann Christoph Graupner), Erik Sorenson (Johann Martin Steindorff); Argyros Stage; September 24–October 15, 2006.

**Ridiculous Fraud** by Beth Henley; Director, Sharon Ott; Sets, Hugh Landwehr; Costumes, Joyce Kim Lee; Lighting, Peter Maradudin; Sound, Stephen LeGrand; Fight Director, Martin Noyes; Dialects, Cynthia Bassham; Stage Manager, Randall K. Lum; ASM, Nina K. Evans; Cast: Betsy Brandt (Willow Clay), Nike Doukas (Maude Chrystal), Ian Fraser (Lafcad Clay), Matt Letscher (Kap Clay), Matt McGrath (Andrew Clay), Paul Vincent O'Connor (Ed Chrystal), Randy Oglesby (Uncle Baites), Eliza Pryor (Georgia); Segerstrom Stage; October 13–November 19, 2006.

**A Christmas Carol** (27th Annual Production) by Charles Dickens, adapted by Jerry Patch; Director, John-David Keller; Sets, Thomas Buderwitz; Costumes, Dwight Richard Odle; Lighting, Donna & Tom Ruzika; Composer/Arrangements, Dennis McCarthy; Sound, Drew Dalzell; Vocal Director, Dennis Castellano; Choreography, Linda Kostalik; Assistant Director, Hisa Takakuwa; Stage Manager, Erin Nelson; ASM, Chrissy Church; Cast: Mason Acevedo (Ebenezer as a Boy/Want), Christian Barillas (Undertaker/Ebenezer as a Young Man), Daniel Blinkoff (Bob Cratchit), Covi Brannan or Hannah Sullivan (Belinda Cratchet), Jennifer Chu (Lena, Belle/Pursued Maiden/Scavenger), Courtney DeCosky (Elizabeth Shelley/Fan), Richard Doyle (The Spirit of Christmas Past/Solicitor/Gentleman on the Street), Andy Garza (Thomas Shelley), Ryan Gates (Oliver Shelley/Ebenezer as a Boy/Ignorance), Phillip Jarrell or Brendan Kreditor (Boy on the Street), Courtney Kato or Christi Muncey (Teen Girl About Town), John-David Keller (Mr. Fezziwig/Gentleman on the Street), Art Koustik (Joe), Megan Lambert or Sanaz Toossi (Martha Cratchit), Timothy Landfield (Chimney Sweep/The Spirit of Christmas Present), Hal Landon Jr. (Ebenezer Scrooge), Ann Marie Lee (Toy Lady/Sally/Scavenger), Martha McFarland (Solicitor/Mrs. Fezziwig/Scavenger), Omead Moini or Christopher Rybus ("Tiny" Tim Cratchit), Isaac Nippert (Puppeteer/Mr. Topper), Matthew Pancoe or Alex Paul (Peter Cratchit), Jennifer Parsons (Rich Woman/Mrs. Cratchit), Demie Santone or Elizabeth Wilson (Girl About Town/Want), Howard Shangraw (Fred, Gentleman on the Street), Don Took (Jacob Marley's Ghost/The Spirit of Christmas Yet to Come), Dillon Tucker (Constable/Wreath Seller/Jacob Marley as a Young Man/Poulterer); Segerstrom Stage; November 25–December 24, 2006.

**La Posada Mágica (The Magical Journey)** Written and directed by Octavio Solis, music by Marcos Loya; Sets, Christopher Acebo; Costumes, Shigeru Yaji; Lighting, Lonnie Rafael Alcaraz; Musical Director, Marcos Loya; Choreography, Linda Kostalik; Stage Manager, Jamie A. Tucker; Cast: Denise Blasor (Consuelo/

Widow), Danny Bolero (Papi/Jose Cruz), Sol Castillo (Refugio/Buzzard), Marcos Loya, Lorenzo Martinez (Musicians/Ensemble), Miguel Najera (Horacio), Erica Ortega (Mom/Mariluz), Kevin Sifuentes (Eli, Bones/Lauro), Tiffany Ellen Solano (Gracie), Teresa Velarde (Caridad/Widow); Argyros Stage; December 8–23, 2006.

**Pig Farm** by Greg Kotis; Director, Martin Benson; Sets, Thomas Buderwitz; Costumes, Julie Keen; Lighting, Christina L. Munich; Sound, Tom Cavnar; Fight Director, Steve Rankin; Associate Fight Director, Martin Noyes; Stage Manager, Randall K. Lum; Cast: J.D. Cullum (Teddy), Brad Fleischer (Tim), Blake Lindsley (Tina), Steve Rankin (Tom); Argyros Stage; January 7–28, 2007.

**Life Is a Dream** by Pedro Calderon de la Barca, translated and adapted by Nilo Cruz; Original Music, Rob Milburn and Michael Bodeen; Director, Kate Whoriskey; Sets, Walt Spangler; Costumes, Ilona Somogyi; Lighting, Scott Zielinski; Sounds, Rob Milburn and Michael Bodeen; Choreography, Warren Adams; Stage Manager, Erin Nelson; ASM, Nina K. Evans; Cast: Lucia Brawley (Rosaura), Daniel Breaker (Segismundo), Jennifer Chu (Estrella), Matt D'Amico (Clarín), John de Lancie (Basilio), Richard Doyle (Clotaldo), Jason Manuel Olazábal (Astolfo), Luis Vega (Revolutionary Leader/Lead Servant); Ensemble: Michael Irish, Ary Katz, Ceilidh Lamont, Lovelle Liquigan, Tara Louise, Andrew Scott, Luis Vega; Segerstrom Stage; February 2–March 11, 2007.

**The Piano Teacher** by Julia Cho; Director, Kate Whoriskey; Sets/Costumes, Myung Hee Cho; Lighting, Jason Lyons; Sound, Tom Cavnar; Music Consultant, Deborah Wicks La Puma; Stage Manager, Jamie A. Tucker; Cast: Kevin Carroll (Michael), Linda Gehringer (Mrs. K), Toi Perkins (Mary Fields); Argyros Stage; March 11–April 1, 2007.

*Linda Gehringer and Kevin Carroll in* The Piano Teacher
*(photo by Henry DiRocco)*

**My Wandering Boy** by Julie Marie Myatt; Director, Bill Rauch; Sets, Christopher Acebo; Costumes, Shigeru Yaji; Lighting, Lonnie Rafael Alcaraz; Sound, Paul James Prendergast; Video Coordinator, Austin Switser; Assistant Director, Dara Weinberg; Stage Manager, Randall K. Lum; ASM, Chrissy Church; Cast: Purva Bedi (Sally Wright), John Cabrera (Rooster Forbes), Richard Doyle (Wesley Boudin), Brent Hinkley (John), Veralyn Jones (Miranda Stevens), Charlie Robinson (Detective Howard), Elizabeth Ruscio (Liza Boudin); Segerstrom Stage; March 30–May 6, 2007

**System Wonderland** by David Wiener; Director, David Emmes; Sets/Costumes, Myung Hee Cho; Lighting, Lap-Chi Chu; Sound, Tom Cavnar; Fight Director, Martin Noyes; Videographer, Victor Mouledoux; Stage Manager, Erin Nelson; Cast: Shannon Cochran (Evelyn), Robert Desiderio (Jerry), John Sloan (Aaron); Argyros Stage; April 22–May 13, 2007

**Hamlet** by William Shakespeare; Director, Daniel Sullivan; Sets, Ralph Funicello; Costumes, Ilona Somogyi; Lighting, Pat Collins; Composer/Sound; Obadiah Eaves; Fight Director, Robin McFarquhar; Vocal Coaches, Cynthia Bassham & Philip Thompson; Assistant Director, Armando Molina; Stage Manager, Jamie A. Tucker; ASM, Nina K. Evans; Cast: Brooke Bloom (Ophelia), Matt D'Amico (Captain/Marcellus/Lord/Player), Carrie Darrow (Ensemble), David DeSantos (Fortinbras/Cornelius/Player Queen), Richard Doyle (Ghost/Doctor/Fortinbras' Army), Robert Foxworth (Claudius), Linda Gehringer (Gertrude), Graham Hamilton (Laertes), Matthew Henerson (Voltemand/Lucianus/Gravedigger/Fortinbras' Army), Hal Landon Jr. (Player King/Gravedigger/Fortinbras' Army), William Landsman (Ensemble), Hamish Linklater (Hamlet), Louis Lotorto (Osric/Reynaldo/Bernardo/Fortinbras' Army), Henri Lubatti (Rosencrantz/Fortinbras' Army), Jeff Marlow (Guildenstern/Fortinbras' Army), Andrew Matthews (Francisco/Player/Messenger), Dillon Tucker (Ensemble), Michael Urie (Horatio); Segerstrom Stage; May 25–July 1, 2007

*Hamish Linklater and Michael Urie in* Hamlet *(photo by Henry DiRocco)*

### THEATRE FOR YOUNG AUDIENCES

**James and the Giant Peach** by Roald Dahl, adapted by David Wood; Director, Shelley Butler; Sets, Sibyl Wickersheimer; Costumes, Angela Balogh Calin; Lighting, Lonnie Rafael Alcaraz; Sound, Josh Schmidt; Stage Manager, Kristin Ahlgren; ASM, Louis Lotorto; Cast: Diana Burbano (Spider, Others), Gregg Daniel (Grasshopper/Others), Louis Lotorto (Centipede/Others), Alex Miller (James), Jennifer Parsons (Ladybug/Others), Tom Shelton (Earthworm/Others); November 3–19, 2006

**The Prince and the Pauper** by Mark Twain, adapted by Jonathan Bolt; Director, Nicholas C. Avila; Sets, Sara Ryung Clement; Costumes, Alex Jaeger; Lighting, Lonnie Rafael Alcaraz; Sound, Tom Cavnar; Fight Director, Martin Noyes; Stage Manager, Kristin Ahlgren; Cast: Mark Coyan (Miles Hendon, Others), John-David Keller (Lord Chamberlain/Others), Mary Dolson Kildare (Lady Jane/Others), Alex Miller (Prince Edward), Graham Miller (Tom), Tom Shelton (John Canty/Others); February 9–25, 2007

**The Only Child** by Quincy Long, music by Dennis McCarthy; Director, Stefan Novinski; Sets, Donna Marquet; Costumes, Angela Balogh Calin; Lighting, Christina L. Munich; Music Director, Deborah Wicks La Puma; Stage Manager, Erin Nelson; Cast: Larry Bates (Toby), Alison Case (Tina), Jennifer Chu (Lolly), Nicholas Hormann (Mr. Ice Cream), Jennifer Parsons (Mother), Tom Shelton (Father); June 8–24, 2007

## Steppenwolf Theatre Company

Chicago, Illinois

Thirty-first Season

Artistic Director, Martha Lavey; Artistic Director, David Hawkanson

**The Pillowman** by Martin McDonagh; Director, Amy Morton; Sets, Loy Arcenas; Costumes, Ana Kuzmanic; Lighting, Chris Akerlind; Sound, Michael Bodeen, Rob Millburn; Cast: Tracy Letts, Yasen Peyankov, Jim True-Frost, Abigail Leone Droeger, Oliver Kal, Danny McCarthy, Leah Rose Orleans, Elizabeth Rich, Michael Shannon, Quinn Wermeling; Downstairs Theatre; September 14–November 12, 2006

**The Bluest Eye** by Lydia Diamond, based on the novel by Toni Morrison; Director, Hallie Gordon; Sets, Stephanie Nelson; Costumes, Allison Heryer Lighting, J.R. Lederle; Sound, Victoria Delorio; Choreography, Ann Boyd; Cast: Victor J. Cole, Monifa M. Days, Noelle Hardy, TaRon Patton, Libya V. Pugh, Chavez Ravine; Upstairs Theatre (Steppenwolf for Young Adults); October 6–28, 2006

**Elliot, A Soldier's Fugue** by Quiara Alegría Hudes; Presented by Rivendell Theatre Ensemble and Teatro Vista; Director, Lisa Portes; Sets, Kevin Depinet; Costumes, Christine Pascual; Lighting, Jesse Klug; Sound, Joshua Horvath; Stage Manager, Suzette Lynn Taylor; Dramaturg, Ben Calvert; Props, Joanna Iwanickal; Cast: Meighan Gerachis, Gustavo Mellado, Edward F. Torres, Juan F. Villa; Garage Theatre; November 2–December 10, 2006

**Sonia Flew** by Melinda Lopez; Director, Jessica Thebus; Sets, Stephanie Nelson; Costumes, Janice Pytel; Lighting, J.R. Lederle; Sound, Andre Pluess, Ben Sussman; Cast: Alan Wilder, Sandra Delgado, Andrew Perez, Vilma Silva, Jeff Still; Downstairs Theatre; November 30, 2006–February 4, 2007

**Betrayal** by Harold Pinter; Director, Rick Snyder; Sets, Todd Rosenthal; Costumes, Nan Zabriskie; Lighting, Robert Christen; Sound, Andrew Hansen; Stage Manager, Laura Glenn; ASM, Deb Styer; Assistant Director, Katie Schoeneck; Dialect Coach, Linda Gates; Cast: Ian Barford, Tracy Letts, Amy Morton, Guy Barile, Scott Joseph Baker, Shane Kenyon, Nettie Kraft, Abigail Misko; Upstairs Theatre; January 25–May 27, 2007

**Huck Finn** by Mark Twain, adapted by Laura Eason; Director, Edward Sobel; Sets, Keith Pitts; Costumes, Debbie Baer; Lighting, Keith Parham; Sound, Rick Sims; Stage Manager, Lauren Hickman; Dramaturg, Kate Evans; Dialects, Eva Breneman; Cast: Kirk Anderson, Janet Ulrich Brooks, Don Forston, Erik Hellman, Jürgen Hooper, Chike Johnson, Bradley Mott, Stanton Nash, Steve Ratcliff; Downstairs Theatre (Steppenwolf for Young Adults); February 24–March 18, 2007

**The Diary of Anne Frank** by Frances Goodrich and Albert Hackett, adapted by Wendy Kesselman; Director, Tina Landau; Sets, Richard Hoover; Costumes, James Schuette; Lighting, Scott Zielinski; Sound, Michael Bodeen, Rob Milburn; Stage Manager, Malcolm Ewen; ASM, Christine Freeburg; Dramaturg, Rosie Forrest; Assisstant Director, Margot Bordelon; Cast: Robert Breuler, Francis Guinan, Mariann Mayberry, Yasen Peyankov and Alan Wilder, Kirk Anderson,

Jason Bradley, Mark Buenning, Carolyn Faye Kramer, Christopher McLinden, Claire Elizabeth Saxe, Kathy Scambiatterra, Gail Shapiro; Downstairs Theatre; April 5–June 10, 2007

**August: Osage County** by Tracy Letts; Director, Anna D. Shapiro; Sets, Todd Rosenthal; Costumes, Ana Kuzmanic; Lighting, Ann Wrightson; Original Music, David Singer; Sound, Richard Woodbury; Stage Manager, Deb Snyder; ASM, Michelle Medvin; Dramaturg, Edward Sobel; Cast: Francis Guinan, Mariann Mayberry, Amy Morton, Sally Murphy, Jeff Perry, Rondi Reed, Rick Snyder, Deanna Dunagan, Kimberly Guerrero, Fawn Johnstin, Dennis Letts, Troy West; Downstairs Theatre; June 28–August 26, 2007

*Amy Morton and Deanna Dunagan in* August: Osage County *(photo by Michael Brosilow)*

## STEPPENWOLF VISITING COMPANY INITIATIVE

**Ray Bradbury's Dandelion Wine** by Ray Bradbury, adapted from his novel; Director, Eric Rosen; Presented by Chicago Children's Theatre; Upstairs Theatre; November 11–December 31, 2006

**The Sparrow** by The House; Presented by The House Theatre of Chicago; Director, Nathan Allen; Sets, Collette Pollard; Costumes, Ana Kuzmanic; Lighting, Ben Wilhelm; Sound, Michael Griggs; Stage Manager, Brian DesGranges; ASM, Julia Dossett; Dramaturg, Kelly Kerwin; Choreography, Tommy Rapley; Music

Producer, Mike Pryzgoda, Jeremiah Chiu; Film Design/Director, Lucas Merino; Magic Design, Dennis Watkins; Cast: Patrick Andrews, Johnny Arena, Cliff Chamberlain, Carolyn Defrin, Paige Hoffman, Sara Hoyer, Jill Matelan, Lauren McCarthy, Kat McDonnell, Michael E. Smith, Stephen Taylor, Lauren Vitz, Dennis Watkins; Garage Theatre; March 15–April 21, 2007

**Sketchbook 2007** by various; Presented by Collaboraction; Original Music, John Herndon, Yuri Lane, Kevin O'Donnell, Rhymefest, Nick Tremulis; Festival Director, Anthony Moseley; Producers, Sandra Delgado and Kimberly Senior; Program A Cast: Torey Adkins, Lillian Almaguer, Scott Baity Jr., Scott Barsotti, Dana Black, David Blatt, J. C. Brown, Anita Chandwaney, Peter DeFaria, Chris DePaola, Nancy Friedrich, Shannon Hoag, Ted Hoerl, Greta Sidwell Honold, Jürgen Hooper, Mary Hollis Inboden, Mary Mikva, Lily Mojekwu, Denise Parkhurst, Peggy Roeder, Jim Schmid, Rob Skrocki, Riso Straley, Rebekah Ward-Hays, Foster Williams Jr., John Wilson, John Zinn; Program B Cast: Ray Baker, Michael Bencic, Elizabeth Burke, Jacquelin Burke, Josi Burke, Kurt Chiang, Cary Cronholm, Lauren Delfs, Sandra Delgado, Britton Esposito, Jim Faruggio, Kasey Foster, Leonardo Garcia, Steven Gilpin, Danny Goldring, Matthew Gottlieb, Miranda Herbert, Max Lesser, Isabel Liss, Jasmin Maldonado, Guy Massey, Joe McCauley, Bill McGough, Julia Merchant, Amanda Nunez, Nina O'Keefe, Kelly O'Sullivan, Steve Pickering, Lorena Quintana, Sadie Rogers, Michael Salinas, Carlos Serrano, Melissa Serrano, Amy Speckien, Neal Starbird, Nick Tremulis, Haruna Tsuchiya, Bob Turton, Stephanie Vazquez, Jesse Weinberg; Garage Theatre; May 31–July 1, 2007

**500 Clown Frankestein** and **500 Clown Macbeth** Presented by 500 Clown, written and performed by Molly Brennan, Adrian Danzig, and Paul Kalina; Director, Leslie Buxbaum Danzig; Sets, Dan Reilly, Costumes, Tatjana Radisic; Stage Manager, Angie Renaldo; performed in repertory in the Upstairs Theatre; June 14–August 12, 2007

## STEPPENWOLF TRAFFIC

**Citizens of the World** by Laura Eason; Director, Jessica Thebus; Conductor, Josephine Lee; Cast: Robert Breuler, Martha Lavey, James Vincent Meredith, Yasen Peyankov, Kinan Abou-Afach, Cheryl Lynn Bruce, Chicago Children's Choir, Sandra Delgado, John Goodwin, Sherry Hong, Anish Jethmalani, Manose, Brent Roman, Diana Simonzadeh, Chihsuan Yang; Millennium Park; September 11, 2006

**Symphony Space's Selected Shorts** by various; Cast: Martha Lavey, Jim True-Frost, Isaiah Sheffer; Downstairs Theatre; October 16, 2006

**An Evening with Allen Toussaint** Written and performed by Allen Toussaint; Downstairs Theatre; December 18, 2006

**Traffic Jam 2007** Downstairs Theatre (unless noted); February 22, 2007–March 12, 2007: *Kahil El'Zabar and Friends* with Stephen Berry, Ari Brown, Ernest Khabeer Dawkins, Kahil El'Zabar, Robert Griffin, Fareed Haque, Robert Baabe Irving III, Jabari Liu, Norman Palm, Junius Paul, Isaiah Spencer, Corey Wilkes, Enoch Williamson; February 22; *The John Pizzarelli Quartet: Dear Mr. Sinatra;* February 23; *An Evening with Dar Williams;* February 24; *Music & Memories* Director, Sylvia Ewing: Cast: Timuel Black, Tom Burrell, Kevin Coval, Sense, Koko Taylor, Michael Warr, Laura Washington, Avery R Young; February 25; *Stories on Stage: Tilting at Windmills* by Sandra Cisneros, Claude McKay, and Julie Orringer; Director, Cheryl Lynn Bruce; Cast: Alana Arenas, Sandra Delgado, Allen Gilmore, Joseph Minoso; Upstairs Theatre; February 26; *Bill Frisell* Featuring Bill Frisell, Greg Leisz, Jenny Scheinman; March 1; *Howard Fishman: Bob Dylan & The Band's Basement Tapes* with Howard Fishman, Ron Caswell, Michael Daves, Mark McLean, Mazz Swift; March 2; *Sandra Bernhard is Plan B From Outer Space*; March 3; *The Making of a Chef* featuring Grant Achatz and Michael Ruhlman; March 4; An Evening with The Ditty Bops featuring Amanda Barrett and Abby deWald; March 7; *Maude Maggart: Good Girl/Bad Girl* with Yair Evnine, Maude Maggart, Lanny Meyers; March 8; *Jon Brion - Tonight!* March 9; *An Evening with Oleta Adams*; March 10; *Stories on Stage: I Had a Dream* by Sean Ennis and David Haynes; Director, Michael E. Myers; Cast: Thomas J. Cox, Trace Hamilton, Roger Mueller, Vikki J. Myers; Upstairs Theatre; March 12, 2007

**TJ and Dave** Written and performed by TJ Jagodowski and David Pasquesi; Downstairs Theatre; April 30, 2007

**Blues/Hip-Hop Intersection** Director, Sylvia Ewing: Featuring Beatmonstas, Billy Branch, Butter, Kevin Coval, Idris Goodwin, Russ Green, Itch 13, Mae Koen, Amina Norman-Hawkins, Sense, Sons of Blues, Supreme and Avery R. Young; Millenium Park; July 30, 2007

### STORIES ON STAGE SERIES – "THE STUFF OF DREAMS"

Upstairs Theatre

*An Early Morning Snack* by Walter R. Brooks, Angela Johnson, David Lubar, and Megan Whalen Turner; Director, Jessica Thebus; Readers: Amy J. Carle, Thomas J. Cox, Sean Fortuanto, Lindsey Noel Whiting; March 18, 2007; *Fever Dreams* by Aimee Bender, T. Coraghessan Boyle, and Harlan Ellison; Director, Tracy Letts; Readers: Martha Lavey, Christopher Holloway, David Pasquesi; April 23, 2007; *Eyes Wide Open* by Jack Ketchum, Henry Kuttner, Chet Williamson; Director, Ed Sobel; Readers: Christian Stolte, Andrew White, Dexter Zollicoffer; May. 7, 2007; *O Say Can You See?* by David Bezmozgis, Rebecca Curtis, Bathsheba Monk; Director, Steve Scott; Readers: Rengin Altay, Annabel Armour, Matthew Krause; June 11, 2007; *To Sleep, Perchance to Dream* by Lynne Sharon Schwartz, Amy Bloom, David Sedaris; Director, Judy O'Malley; Readers: Rob Riley, Amy Bloom; July 9, 2007

### THE 3rd ANNUAL FIRST LOOK REPERTORY OF NEW WORK

Garage Theatre – August 2–26, 2007

*Tranquillity Woods* by Joel Drake Johnson; Director, Sandy Shinner; Sets, Marcus Stephens, Costumes, Debbie Baer; Lighting, J.R. Lederle; Sound, Gregor Mortis; Stage Manager, Rose Packer; Dramaturg, Gabriel Greene; Cast: Usman Ally, Annabel Armour, Velma Austin, Don Blair, Laurie Larson and Mary Ann Thebus; *When the Messenger Is Hot* by Laura Eason, from the stories of Elizabeth Crane; Director, Jessica Thebus; Sets, Marcus Stephens; Costumes, Debbie Baer; Lighting, J.R. Lederle; Sound, Gregor Mortis; Stage Manager, Lauren V. Hickman; Dramaturg, Heidi Coleman: Assistant Director, Jenny Avery, Kate Walsh; Cast: Kate Arrington, Marilyn Dodds Frank, Coburn Goss, Lauren Katz, Amy Warren; *Gary* by Melinda Lopez; Director, Jonathan Berry; Sets, Marcus Stephens; Costumes, Debbie Baer; Lighting, J.R. Lederle; Original Music, Rick Sims; Sound, Gregor Mortis; Stage Manager, Kim Forbes; Dramaturg, Sarah Gubbins; Assistant Director, Megan Schuchman; Cast: Judy Blue, Brad Bukauskas, Madison Dirks, Rachel Sondag, Rani Waterman

# Trinity Repertory Theatre

Providence, Rhode Island

Forty-third Season

Artistic Director, Curt Columbus; Executive Director, Michael Gennaro

**Cherry Orchard** by Anton Chekhov, translated and directed by Curt Columbus; Sets, Eugene Lee; Costumes, William Lane; Lighting, Deb Sullivan; Sound, Peter Sasha Hurowitz; PSM, Alden Vasquez; Cast: Stephen Berenson (Yepihodov), Angela Brazil (Dunyasha), Nicholas Few (Kolya), Crystal Finn (Varya), Mauro Hantman (Yasha), Jason Hart (Pasha), Steven Jobe (Musician), Phyllis Kay (Lovey Ranevskaya), Brian McEleney (Leonid Gaev), Barbara Meek (Firs), Anne Scurria (Charlotta), Fred Sullivan Jr. (Boris Semyonov-Pischik), Stephen Thorne (Peter Trofimov), Joe Wilson Jr. (Yermolai Lopakin), Emily Young (Anya), Sarah & Joseph Dowling Jr. Theater; September 15–October 29, 2006

**A Christmas Carol** by Charles Dickens, adapted by Adrian Hall and Richard Cumming; Director, Curt Columbus, original music by Richard Cumming; Musical Director, Christine Noel; Sets/Puppets, Blair Thomas; Costumes, William Lane; Lighting, Brian J. Lilienthal; Sound, Peter Sasha Hurowitz; Co-Set Design, Philip Creech; Set Decorator, S. Michael Getz; PSM, Lloyd Davis Jr.; Stage Manager, Michael D. Domue; Timothy Crowe or William Damkoehler (Ebenezer Scrooge), Peter Deffet & Sean Hopkins or Mat Arruda & Marya Errin Jones (Puppeteers), Richard Donnelly or Mark Peckham (Solicitor/The Ghost of Christmas Present/ Old Joe), Morgan Dover-Pearl or Diana Buirski (Belle/Lucy/Mrs. Dilbert/ Poor Wife), Mauro Hantman or Fred Sullivan, Jr. (Bob Cratchit), Jason Hart or Charlie Hudson III (Solicitor/Martin), Phyllis Kay or Janice Duclos (Reader/Mrs. Fezziwig/Mrs. Cratchit), Rama Marshall or Nick Few (Topper/Undertaker's Man), Anne Scurria or Cynthia Strickland (Mrs. Partlet/The Ghost of Christmas Past/ Mother-in-Law), Joe Wilson Jr. or Stephen Thorne (Jacob Marley/Fred/Older Scrooge/Poor Husband); Children's Cast: Dustin Iscm, Patti Laliberte, Teddy McNulty, Darius Ovalles, Rebekah Philip, Demetria Rowan, Austin Adams, Ariel Dorsey, Michael Liebhauser, Destinee Mangum, Bobby Robertson, Max Theroux; Children's Chorus: Kayla Anghinetti, Jillian Bernier, Emily Carter, Mia Ceglie, Jennifer Christensen, Sophie Cram, Nicole DeLuca, Julie Farabaugh, Julianne Fournier, Ashlee Gray, Georgia King, Massi King, Jacqueline Lagueux, Rebecca Mallette, Kelsey McKay, Victoria McMahon, Saydee McQuay, Kaitlyn Moniz, Raquel Perez, Avery Pierce, Noah Pimentel, Tiffany Rabideau, Ashley Robillard, Audrey Robinson, May Rowland, Alexandra Russell, Hannah Schur, Nicolas Schur, Danielle Tocco, Lauren Vermillion Katie West, Kaitlyn Whitman, Alexia Williams, Troy Allen, Jillian Beaulieu, Romie Bois, Emily Boss, Alexis Boyer, Emilia Cadden, Madeline Canfield, Mara Canfield, Emily Costantino, Miranda Dean, Adelae Durand, Christina Drumm, Alicia Evans, Julia Ferragamo, Molly Gregory, Jessica Heutteman, Allison Javery, Ardriana Mahoney, Ellen Martin, Kelsey Martin, Sara Morris, Leah McCarvill, Lauren Medeiros, Gabby Palko, Eryka Perreault, Emily Scott, Madeleine Snow, Delia Sosa, Haley Theroux, Kalen Valliere, Corinne Vanfechtman; Elizabeth and Malcolm Chace Theater; November 17–December 31, 2006

**Dublin Carol** by Conor McPherson; Director, Amy Morton; Set, Eugene Lee; Costumes, Ana Kuzmanic; Lighting,, Deb Sullivan; Sound, Peter Sasha Hurowitz; Stage Manager, Jennifer Grutza; Cast: Danny Mefford (Mark), William Petersen (John), Rachael Warren (Mary); Sarah & Joseph Dowling Jr. Theater; November 30, 2006–January 7, 2007

*The Company of* Our Town *(photo by T. Charles Erickson)*

**Our Town** by Thornton Wilder; Director, Brian McEleney; Sets, Michael McGarty; Costumes, William Lane; Lighting, Brian J. Lilienthal; Sound, Peter Sasha Hurowitz; Speech/Voice Coach, Thom Jones; Stage Manager, Buzz Cohen; Cast: Stephen Berenson (Simon Stimson), Susannah Flood (Emily Webb), Mauro Hantman (Mr. Webb), Rob Jarbadan (Musician), Phyllis Kay (Mrs. Gibbs), Barbara Meek (Stage Manager), Eric Murdoch (George Gibbs), Fred Sullivan, Jr. (Doctor Gibbs), Stephen Thorne (Wally Webb/Professor Willard/Constable Warren/ Sam Craig), Rachael Warren (Mrs. Webb), Joe Wilson Jr. (Joe Crowell/Howie Newsome/Joe Stoddard), Heather Wood (Rebecca Gibbs/Mrs. Soames); Elizabeth & Malcolm Chace Theater; January 26, 2007–March 4, 2007

**A Delicate Balance** by Edward Albee; Director, Kevin Moriarty; Sets, Michael McGarty; Costumes, Ron Cesario; Lighting, Deb Sullivan; Sound, Peter Sasha Hurowitz; Speech/Voice Coach, Thom Jones; PSM, Katie Ailinger; Cast: Angela Brazil (Julia), Timothy Crowe (Tobias), William Damkoehler (Harry), Janice Duclos (Agnes), Anne Scurria (Claire), Cynthia Strickland (Edna); Sarah & Joseph Dowling, Jr. Theater; February 16–March 25, 2007

*Timothy Crowe and Anne Scurria in* A Delicate Balance
*(photo by T. Charles Erickson)*

**The Fantasticks** Music by Harvey Schmidt, book and lyrics by Tom Jones; Director, Amanda Dehnert; Musical Director, Tim Robertson; Choreography, Sharon Jenkins; Sets, Eugene Lee; Costumes, William Lane; Lighting, John Ambrosone; Sound, Peter Sasha Hurowitz; Fight Choreographer, Craig Handel; Speech/Voice Coach, Thom Jones; PSM, Jennifer Grutza; Cast: Stephen Berenson (Bellomy), Nate Dendy (Mute), Mauro Hantman (Mortimer), Brian McEleney (Henry), Fred Sullivan Jr. (Hucklebee), Stephen Thorne (Matt), Rachael Warren (Luisa), Joe Wilson Jr. (El Gallo); Elizabeth & Malcolm Chace Theater; March 30–April 29, 2007

**The Clean House** by Sarah Ruhl; Director, Laura Kepley; Sets, E. David Cosier; Costumes, William Lane; Lighting, Brian J. Lilienthal; Sound, Peter Sasha Hurowitz; Speech/Voice Coach, Thom Jones; PSM, Barbara Reo; Cast: Angela Brazil (Matilde); William Damkoehler (Charles), Janice Duclos (Virginia), Barbara Meek (Ana), Cynthia Strickland (Lane); Sarah & Joseph Dowling Jr. Theater; April 27–June 3, 2007

*Fred Sullivan Jr., Rachael Warren, Stephen Thorne, and Stephen Berenson in* The Fantasticks *(photo by T. Charles Erickson)*

# Williamstown Theatre Fedstival

Williamstown, Massachusetts

Fifty-second Season

Artistic Director, Roger Rees

**Uncle Sam I Am: A 4th of July Celebration** Created and directed by Sam Breslin Wright; Music Director, Kris Kukul; Lighting, Wilburn Bonnell; Sound, David Thomas; Stage Manager, Jaimie van Dyke; Cast: Remy Auberjonois, Greg Hildreth, Sarah Townsend Turner, Liz Wisan; Apprentice Singers: Abby Marsh, Sarah Masse, Ryan Nearhoff, Emily Pinas, Kevin Reed, Dan Reiss, Tro Shaw, Stephen Stocking; Musicians: Chelsea Morgan Hoffman (clarinet), Kris Kukul (piano), Erica Lipez (violin), Joe Tippett (guitar); Nikos Stage, June 27–30

**Anything Goes** Music and lyrics by Cole Porter, original book by Guy Bolton and P.G. Wodehouse, Howard Lindsay, and Russel Crouse; Director, Roger Rees; Music Director, Ed Barnes; Choreography, Tim Foster; Sets, Neil Patel; Costumes, Kaye Voyce; Lighting, France Aronson; Sound, Nick Borisjuk; Stage Manager, Adam Grosswirth; ASM, Gregory T. Livoti; Cast: Tom Bloom (Elisha J. Whitney), Malcolm Gets (Sir Evelyn Oakleigh), Sandra Shipley (Mrs. Harcourt), Nikki Renee Daniels (Hope Harcourt), Greg Hildreth (Bishop Henry T. Dobson); Sharon Lawrence (Reno Sweeney), Lisa Birnbaum, Xanthe Elbrick, Sarah Turner, Liz Wisan (Angels), Matt Cavenaugh (Billy Crocker), Remy Auberjonois (Moonface Martin), Catherine Brunell (Bonnie), Paul O'Brien (Captain), Kirby Ward (Purser), Danny Medford (Reporter/Officer), Joe Plummer (Reporter/Convert), Bill Bateman (Rich Passenger), Crystal Chapman (Rich Passenger), Lance Rubin (Cameraman/ Convert/Officer/Steward/Stoker), Greg Hildreth (Soaked Passenger), Sailors: Kate Blacksmith, Caitlin Cassidy, Ben Diskant, Evan Enderle, Sam Harrell, Benjamin Izzo, Sarah Masse, Ryan Nearhoff, Anastasia Niemann, Emily Pinas, Phillip Pinero, Kevin Reed, Kate Rose, Stephanie Rosenberg, Kyle Schaefer, Elisabeth Schneider, Tro Shaw, Stephen Stocking; Orchestra: Steven Bodner, Ernest Clark, Donna Gouger, Richard Huntley, Joe LaCreta, Ron Lively, Robert Zimmerman; Main Stage; July 5–16, 2006

**Demon Dreams** Book and lyrics by Tommy Smith, music by Michael McQuilken; Director, Amanda Charlton; Choreography, Portia Krieger; Costumes, Emily Rebholz; Lighting, Paul Toben; Sound, David Thomas; Sets, Lara Fabian; Stage Manager, John Ferry; Cast: Charlie Hudson III (Yubon), Brett Dalton (Kubon), Corey Jones (Hibon), Allison Tigard (Sanpon), Erica Newhouse (Nippon), Jenny Gammello (Chipon), Ninjas: Paige Dana, Jaclyn DiLauro, Madeline Duffy-Feins, Bridgette Hayes, Sophie Kargman, Sarah Stevens; Main Stage; July 11–16, 2006

357

*Matt Cavenaugh and Nikki Renee Daniels in* Anything Goes
*(photo by Allison Leger)*

**Lucy and the Conquest** by Cusi Cram; Director, Suzanne Agins; Sets, Mimi Lien; Costumes, Jennifer Caprio; Lighting, Charles Foster, Sound, Rob Kaplowitz; Fight Choreography, Ryan Karels; Stage Manager, Amber Wedin; ASM, Whitney Smith-Nelson; Cast: Jeanine Serralles (Lucy Santiago), David Ross (Tommy/Drew Gold), Bernard White (Juan Ricardo Santiago/Inca Man), Socorro Santiago (Pacha Santiago), Vanessa Aspillaga (Lila), Julian Acosta (The Gring); Nikos Stage; July 12–23, 2006

**Sweet Bird of Youth** by Tennessee Williams; Director, David Jones; Sets, Derek McLane; Costumes, Ilona Somogyi; Lighting, David Weiner; Sound, John Gromada; Dialects, Stephen Gabis; Fight Director, Rick Sordelet; Stage Manager, Matthew Lloyd Silver; ASM, Robyn Henry; Cast: Derek Cecil (Chance Wayne), Margaret Colin (Princess Kosmonopolis), Charlie Hudson III (Fly), Justin Swain (Hatcher), Ted Koch (George Scudder), Gerry Bamman (Boss Finley), Corey Jones (Charles), Christopher Evan Welch (Tom Junior), Beth Fowler (Aunt Nonnie), Bess Wohl (Heavenly Finley), Dan Cozzens (Stuff), Betsy Aidem (Miss Lucy), Brett Dalton (The Heckler), Vayu O'Donnell (Bud), Nick Merritt (Scotty), Erica Newhouse (Violet), Allison Tigard (Edna), Ensemble: Jonathan Bass, Matt Clevy, Charlie Drexler Paul Kite, Jesse Liebman, Matthew Lynch, Megan McGrath, Justin Perez, Nissa Perrott, Alex Polcyn, Briel Pomerantz, Ira Sargent; Main Stage; July 19–30, 2006

**A Nervous Smile** by John Belluso; Director, Maria Mileaf; Sets, Vince Mountain; Costumes, Katherine Roth; Lighting, Nicole Pearce; Sound, Nick Borisjuk; Voice Coach, Stephen Gabis; Stage Manager, David Lurie; ASMs, Kelly Glasgow, Jaimie Van Dyke; Cast: Scott Cohen (Brian), Amy Brenneman (Eileen), Gloria Reuben (Nicole), Deirdre O'Connell (Blanka); Nikos Stage; July 26–August 6, 2006

**Romeo and Juliet** by William Shakespeare; Director, Will Frears; Sets, Takeshi Kata; Lighting, Matthew Richards; Costumes, Jenny Mannis; Sound, David Thomas; Fight Direction, Rick Sordelet; Composer, Michael Friedman; Choreography, Tracy Bersley; Stage Manager, Adam Grosswirth; ASM, Greg T. Livoti; Cast: Nyambi Nyambi (Sampson), Ian Unterman (Gregory), David Ross (Abraham), Zachary Shornick (Balthasar), Greg Hildreth (Benvolio), Remy Auberjonois (Tybalt), Daniel Oreskes (Capulet), Paul O'Brien (Montague), Sandra Shipley (Lady Montague), Ron Cephas Jones (Prince Escalus), Austin Lysy (Romeo), Joe Plummer (Paris), Ezra Miller (Peter/Page), Enid Graham (Lady Capulet), Kristine Nielsen (Nurse), Emmy Rossum (Juliet), Benjamin Walker (Mercutio), Bill Camp (Friar Lawrence), Corey Jones (Apothecary), Daniel Mefford (Friar John), Jenny Gammello, Abby Marsh (Dancing Girls), Ryan Andreas, Nick DeVita, Jon Neidich (Guards), Capulets: Chris Imbrosciano, Kareem Lucas, Kevin Reed, Dan Reiss, Zachary Sniderman, Stephen Stocking; Bande (Los Mercedes) : Joe Tippett (Ramon Manuel Mercedes), Nick Delaney (Manuel Ramon Mercedes), Ryan Nearhoff (El Guapo Mercedes), Lisa Birnbaum (Evita –Estrella Mercedes), Evan Enderle (Bob); Main Stage; August 2–13, 2006

**The Opposite of Sex** Music and lyrics by Douglas J. Cohen, book by Robert Jess Roth and Douglas J. Cohen, Based on the screenplay by Don Roos; Director, Robert Jess Roth; Music Director, Lynne Shankel; Sets, Derek McLane; Costumes, Sarah Laux; Lighting, Norm Schwab; Sound, Nick Borisjuk; Fight Director, Rick Sordelet; Stage Manager, BJ Forman; ASMs, Kelly Beaulieu, John Ferry; Cast: Kerry Butler (Dedee Truitt), Ian Scott McGregor (Randy Cates/Others), Gregg Edelman (Bill Truitt), Lance Rubin (Jason Bock), David Burtka (Matt Matteo), Kaitlin Hopkins (Lucia Dalury), Herndon Lackey (Carl Tippett); Nikos Stage; August 9–20, 2006

**Double Double** by Rick Elice and Roger Rees; Director, Roger Rees; Sets, Neil Patel; Costumes, Jennifer Caprio; Lighting, Charles Foster, Sound, David Thomas; Stage Manager, Jennifer Dewar; ASMs, Alyssa Stone, Elizabeth Unsworth; Cast: Jennifer Van Dyck (Phillipa James), Matt Letscher (Duncan McFee); Main Stage; August 16–27, 2006

*Kerry Butler and Ian Scott McGregor in* The Opposite of Sex
*(photo by Allison Leger)*

# THEATRICAL AWARDS

## 2006 – 2007

Top to bottom:

2007 Theatre World Award Winner Nilaja Sun

2007 Theatre World Award Winners Fantasia and Lin-Manuel Miranda

1994 Theatre World Award Winner Michael Cerveris, Rebecca Brooksher, Mary Beth Lang, and 2007 Theatre World Award Winners Stark Sands and Xanthe Elbrick

# 2007 Theatre World Award Winners

*Eve Best of* The Moon for the Misbegotten

*Mary Birdsong of* Martin Short: Fame Becomes Me

*Erin Davie of* Grey Gardens

*Xanthe Elbrick of* Coram Boy

*Fantasia of* The Color Purple

*Johnny Galecki of* The Little Dog Laughed

*Jonathan Groff of* Spring Awakening

*Gavin Lee of* Mary Poppins

*Lin-Manuel Miranda of* In the Heights

*Bill Nighy of* The Vertical Hour

*Stark Sands of* Journey's End

*Nilaja Sun of* No Child…

# 63rd Annual Theatre World Awards

Tuesday, June 5, 2007, at New World Stages – Theatre 3

Originally dubbed *Promising Personalities* in 1944 by co-founders Daniel Blum, Norman MacDonald, and John Willis to coincide with the first release of *Theatre World*, the now sixty-three-year-old definitive pictorial and statistical record of the American theatre, the Theatre World Awards, as they are now known, are the oldest awards given for debut performances in New York City, as well as one of the oldest honors bestowed on New York actors.

Administered by the Theatre World Awards Board of Directors, a committee of current New York drama critics chooses six actors and six actresses for the Theatre World Award who have distinguished themselves in Broadway and Off-Broadway productions during the past theatre season. Occasionally, Special Theatre World Awards are also bestowed on performers, casts, or others who have made a particularly lasting impression on the New York theatre scene.

The Theatre World Award Janus statuette is an original bronze sculpture in primitive-modern style created by internationally recognized artist Harry Marinsky. It is adapted from the Roman myth of Janus, god of entrances, exits, and all beginnings, with one face appraising the past and the other anticipating the future. Originally cast and mounted on marble in the Del Chiaro Foundry in Pietrasanta, Italy, this year's awards were cast by Sculpture House Casting, New York.

The Theatre World Awards are voted on by the following committee of New York drama critics: Peter Filichia (*Theatermania.com*), Harry Haun (*Playbill*), Matthew Murray (*TalkinBroadway.com*), Frank Scheck (*New York Post*), Michael Sommers (*Newhouse Papers*), Doug Watt (Critic Emeritus, *New York Daily News*), and Linda Winer (*Newsday*). The Theatre World Awards Board of Directors is: Leigh Giroux, (President), Kati Meister (Vice President), Erin Oestreich (Secretary), Scott Denny (Treasurer), Tom Lynch, and Barry Keating.

**THE CEREMONY** Written and Hosted by Peter Filichia; Executive Producers, Scott Denny, Kati Meister, Erin Oestreich; Director, Barry Keating; Music Director/ Accompanist, Lawrence Yurman; Associate Producer, Shane Frampton-Wolters; Associate Director, Jeremy Quinn; Production Manager, Vanes D'Andrea; Stage Manager, Steve Lee; Press, Jim Baldassare; Video Presentation/Graphics, Scott Denny; Program Layout and Design, Mary Botosan; Photographers, Bruce Glikas, John Harrison, Michael Riordan, Aubrey Ruben, Michael Viade; Video Photographers, Richard Ridge and Bradshaw Smith; Lighting, Jin Ho Kim; Sound, Joon Lee; Follow Spot, Hyunwoo Cho; Presented on the set of the production of *The Gazillion Bubble Sho*w designed by Fan Yang and Neodus Co. Ltd.

**PRESENTERS** Alec Baldwin – *Loot* (1986); Michael Cerveris – *The Who's Tommy* (1993); Barbara Cook – *Plain and Fancy* (1955); Jennifer Ehle – *The Real Thing* (2000); Raúl Esparza – *The Rocky Horror Show* (2001); Boyd Gaines – *A Month in the Country* (1980); Rosemary Harris – *The Climate of Eden* (1953); Bambi Linn – *Carousel* (1945); John McMartin – *Little Mary Sunshine* (1960); Estelle Parsons – *Mrs. Dally Has A Lover* (1945); John Tartaglia – *Avenue Q* (2004).

**SPECIAL AWARD** A 2007 Special Award was presented to the Actors Fund in honor the of organization's 125th Anniversary. The award was presented by Theatre World Award winner Patricia Elliott – *A Little Night Music* (1973) and accepted by Actors Fund President and Theatre World Award winner Brian Stokes Mitchell – *Mail* (1988).

**PERFORMANCES AND SPECIAL PRESENTATION** Sharon McNight – *Starmites* (1989): "Diva" (from *Starmites*, music and lyrics by Barry Keating); John Tartaglia – *Avenue Q* (2004) "Second Cousin" (music and lyrics by Gary Adler and Phoebe Kreutz) and "Purpose" (from *Avenue Q,* music by Robert Lopez, lyrics by Jeff Marx); Special Presentation of the Milligan College John Willis Classroom Project: John Cullum – *On a Clear Day You Can See Forever* (1966).

**2007 THEATRE WORLD AWARD JANUS WRANGLER** Mia Faith Hammond

**STAFF FOR NEW WORLD STAGES** Executive Director, Beverly D. Mac Keen; Director of Programming, Michael Coco; Director of Finance, Rainard Rachele; Box Office Treasurer, Gary Powers; Building Operations Manager, Dennis Walls; House Manager, Darren Marshall; Community Resource Manager, Micah Logsdon; Events Manager, Jennifer Jones; Assistant Events Manager, Philip Wilson

**VOLUNTEER STAFF** Greg Bibens, Mark Birch, Kelly Childress, Kim D'Armond, Dan Debenport, Lexie Frare, Allison Graham, Sharon Hunter, John Krieger, Betsy Krouner, Gregg Lauterbach, Nancy Owens, Joanna Parson, John Sala, Scott Sinclair, J. Paul Stephens

**Extraordinary Thanks for Financial Support:** Paul Newman

**Very Special Thanks for Financial Support:** Alec Baldwin, Harry Connick, Jr., James Earl Jones & Cecilia Hart Jones, and Darlene Krenz

**Special Thanks for Financial Support:** Stockard Channing, Blythe Danner, Jamie deRoy, Kati Meister, Chase Mishkin, Christopher Goutman, Nancy Giles, James F. Haag, Jr., and John Lloyd Young

**Special Acknowledgements for Financial Support:** Jane Alexander & Edwin Sherin, John T. Allen, Karen Allen, Maureen Anderman, Howard Atlee-Heinlen, Dylan & Becky Ann Baker, Orson Bean, Richard Benjamin, Tisa Chang-Pan Asian Repertory Theatre, Len Cariou, Thom Christopher, John William Codling, Barbara Cook, David Cryer, Stuart Damon, Jason Danieley, Bambi Linn DeJesus, Bradford Dillman, Rosemary Harris Ehle, Brian D. Farrell, Harvey Fierstein, Angela Fischetti, Bette-Lee Fox, David Fritz, Gail Gerber, Anita Gillette, Joanna Gleason, Marlene J. Gould, Katharine Houghton Grant, Tammy Grimes, Linda Hart, Wayne & Lizbeth Hawley, Joel Higgins, Jayne Houdyshell, Ernestine Jackson, Mark Jacoby, Jonathan Kagan, John Kander, Judy Kaye & David Green, Susan Kellermann, Laurie Kennedy, Raymond & Suzy Lowry, Peter MacNicol, Victor W. Main, Spiro Malas, Daisy Maryles, John McMartin, Hayley Mills, Brian Stokes Mitchell, Virginia A. Moraweck, Mary Murfitt, James Naughton, Charles M. Nolte, Lonny Price, M. Kilburg Reedy, Charles Repole, Cliff Robertson, Jaime L Sanchez, The Shubert Organization Inc. / Gerald Schoenfeld, Elaine Joyce Simon, Sheila A. Smith, Elisa Loti Stein, Russ Thacker, Jane Trese, John & Katherine Turturro, Joan Van Ark, Jennifer Warren, Caroline Winston

Gift Bags Promotions supplied by Applause Theatre and Cinema Books/Hal Leonard Publications; The Araca Group; Farmesthetics, J Records/Arista/Sony BMG; Playbill, Sammy Buck, Sh-K-Boom Records, and Theatermania.

Theatre World Awards after-party generously sponsored by **Trattoria Dopo Teatro,** 125 West 44th Street between 6th Avenue and Broadway; stage decorations donated by **American Foliage and Design Group**; sound equipment generously provided by **Jeremiah Harris/Production Resource Group.**

The Theatre World Awards, Inc. is a 501 (c)(3) nonprofit organization, and our annual presentation is made possible by the generous contributions of previous winners and friends. For more information please visit the website at www.theatreworldawards.org.

Tax-deductible contributions can be sent via Pay Pal® to info@theatreworldawards.org, or checks and money orders sent to:

Theatre World Awards, Inc.
Box 246 Radio City Station
New York, NY 10101-0246

Previous Theatre World Award winner Sharon McNight (Starmites, 1989) entertains the 2007 Theatre World Awards audience

2007 presenter Alec Baldwin (Loot, 1986)

2007 Theatre World Award winner Mary Birdsong (Martin Short: Fame Becomes Me)

2007 Theatre World Award winner Lin-Manuel Miranda (In the Heights)

Estelle Parsons (Mrs. Dally Has a Lover, 1963) presented a 2007 Theatre World Award to her "Roseanne" co-star Johnny Galecki (The Little Dog Laughed)

*Previous Theatre World Award winners Michael Cerveris (Tommy, 1993), Brian Stokes Mitchell (Mail, 1988), and 2007 Awards ceremony entertainer John Tartaglia (Avenue Q, 2004)*

*1955 Theatre World Award winner Jacqueline Brookes (The Cretan Woman)*

*2007 Theatre World Award winner Gavin Lee (Mary Poppins)*

*2007 Theatre World Award winner Eve Best (A Moon for the Misbegotten)*

Left: *2007 Theatre World Award winner Erin Davie* (Grey Gardens)

Right: *2007 presenters and mother-daughter previous winners Jennifer Ehle* (The Real Thing, *2000*) and Rosemary Harris (The Climate of Eden, *1953*)

2007 Theatre World Award winner Jonathan Groff
(Spring Awakening)

*Previous winner Brian Stokes Mitchell (Mail, 1988) accepted the 2007
Special Theatre World for the Actors Fund from previous winner Patricia
Elliott (A Little Night Music, 1973)*

*2007 presenter and previous winner Barbara Cook
(Plain and Fancy, 1955)*

*2007 Theatre World Award winner Fantasia
(The Color Purple)*

*Previous Theatre World Award winner Alice
Playten (Henry, Sweet Henry, 1968) and
2007 ceremony co-producer Kati Meister*

*2007 presenter and
previous winner Boyd
Gaines (A Month in the
Country, 1980) and
2007 presenter and
previous winner John
McMartin (Little Mary
Sunshine, 1960)*

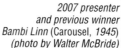

*2007 presenter
and previous winner
Bambi Linn (Carousel, 1945)
(photo by Walter McBride)*

## PREVIOUS THEATRE WORLD AWARD RECIPIENTS

**1944-45:** Betty Comden (*On the Town*), Richard Davis (*Kiss Them For Me*), Richard Hart (*Dark of the Moon*), Judy Holliday (*Kiss Them for Me*), Charles Lang, Bambi Linn (*Carousel*), John Lund (*The Hasty Heart*), Donald Murphy (*Signature* and *Common Ground*), Nancy Noland (*Common Ground*), Margaret Phillips (*The Late George Apley*), John Raitt (*Carousel*)

**1945-46:** Barbara Bel Geddes (*Deep Are the Roots*), Marlon Brando (*Truckline Café* and *Candida*), Bill Callahan (*Call Me Mister*), Wendell Corey (*The Wind is Ninety*), Paul Douglas (*Born Yesterday*), Mary James (*Apple of His Eye*), Burt Lancaster (*A Sound of Hunting*), Patricia Marshall (*The Day Before Spring*), Beatrice Pearson (*The Mermaids Singing*)

**1946-47:** Keith Andes (*The Chocolate Soldier*), Marion Bell (*Brigadoon*), Peter Cookson (*Message for Margaret*), Ann Crowley (*Carousel*), Ellen Hanley (*Barefoot Boy With Cheek*), John Jordan (*The Wanhope Building*), George Keane (*Brigadoon*), Dorothea MacFarland (*Oklahoma!*), James Mitchell (*Brigadoon*), Patricia Neal (*Another Part of the Forest*), David Wayne (*Finian's Rainbow*)

**1947-48:** Valerie Bettis (*Inside U.S.A.*), Edward Bryce (*The Cradle Will Rock*), Whitfield Connor (*Macbeth*), Mark Dawson (*High Button Shoes*), June Lockhart (*For Love or Money*), Estelle Loring (*Inside U.S.A.*), Peggy Maley (*Joy to the World*), Ralph Meeker (*Mister Roberts*), Meg Mundy (*The Happy Journey to Trenton and Camden* and *The Respectful Prostitute*), Douglass Watson (*Antony and Cleopatra*), James Whitmore (*Command Decision*), Patrice Wymore (*Hold It!*)

**1948-49:** Tod Andrews (*Summer and Smoke*), Doe Avedon (*The Young and Fair*), Jean Carson (*Bravo!*), Carol Channing (*Lend an Ear*), Richard Derr (*The Traitor*), Julie Harris (*Sundown Beach*), Mary McCarty (*Sleepy Hollow*), Allyn Ann McLerie (*Where's Charley?*), Cameron Mitchell (*Death of a Salesman*), Gene Nelson (*Lend an Ear*), Byron Palmer (*Where's Charley?*), Bob Scheerer (*Lend an Ear*)

**1949-50:** Nancy Andrews (*Touch and Go*), Phil Arthur (*With a Silk Thread*), Barbara Brady (*The Velvet Glove*), Lydia Clarke (*Detective Story*), Priscilla Gillette (*Regina*), Don Hanmer (*The Man*), Marcia Henderson (*Peter Pan*), Charlton Heston (*Design for a Stained Glass Window*), Rick Jason (*Now I Lay Me Down to Sleep*), Grace Kelly (*The Father*), Charles Nolte (*Design for a Stained Glass Window*), Roger Price (*Tickets, Please!*)

**1950-51:** Barbara Ashley (*Out of This World*), Isabel Bigley (*Guys and Dolls*), Martin Brooks (*Burning Bright*), Richard Burton (*The Lady's Not For Burning*), Pat Crowley (*Southern Exposure*), James Daly (*Major Barbara* and *Mary Rose*), Cloris Leachman (*A Story for a Sunday Evening*), Russell Nype (*Call Me Madam*), Jack Palance (*Darkness at Noon*), William Smithers (*Romeo and Juliet*), Maureen Stapleton (*The Rose Tattoo*), Marcia Van Dyke (*Marcia Van Dyke*), Eli Wallach (*The Rose Tattoo*)

**1951-52:** Tony Bavaar (*Paint Your Wagon*), Patricia Benoit (*Glad Tidings*), Peter Conlow (*Courtin' Time*), Virginia de Luce (*New Faces of 1952*), Ronny Graham (*New Faces of 1952*), Audrey Hepburn (*Gigi*), Diana Herbert (*The Number*), Conrad Janis (*The Brass Ring*), Dick Kallman (*Seventeen*), Charles Proctor (*Twilight Walk*), Eric Sinclair (*Much Ado About Nothing*), Kim Stanley (*The Chase*), Marian Winters (*I Am a Camera*), Helen Wood (*Seventeen*)

**1952-53:** Edie Adams (*Wonderful Town*), Rosemary Harris (*The Climate of Eden*), Eileen Heckart (*Picnic*), Peter Kelley (*Two's Company*), John Kerr (*Bernardine*), Richard Kiley (*Misalliance*), Gloria Marlowe (*In Any Language*), Penelope Munday (*The Climate of Eden*), Paul Newman (*Picnic*), Sheree North (*Hazel Flagg*), Geraldine Page (*Mid-Summer*), John Stewart (*Bernardine*), Ray Stricklyn (*The Climate of Eden*), Gwen Verdon (*Can-Can*)

**1953-54:** Orson Bean (*John Murray Anderson's Almanac*), Harry Belafonte (*John Murray Anderson's Almanac*), James Dean (*The Immoralist*), Joan Diener (*Kismet*), Ben Gazzara (*End as a Man*), Carol Haney (*The Pajama Game*), Jonathan Lucas (*The Golden Apple*), Kay Medford (*Lullaby*), Scott Merrill (*The Threepenny Opera*), Elizabeth Montgomery (*Late Love*), Leo Penn (*The Girl on the Via Flaminia*), Eva Marie Saint (*The Trip to Bountiful*)

**1954-55:** Julie Andrews (*The Boy Friend*), Jacqueline Brookes (*The Cretan Woman*), Shirl Conway (*Plain and Fancy*), Barbara Cook (*Plain and Fancy*), David Daniels (*Plain and Fancy*), Mary Fickett (*Tea and Sympathy*), Page Johnson (*In April Once*), Loretta Leversee (*Home is the Hero*), Jack Lord (*The Traveling Lady*), Dennis Patrick (*The Wayward Saint*), Anthony Perkins (*Tea and Sympathy*), Christopher Plummer (*The Dark is Light Enough*)

**1955-56:** Diane Cilento (*Tiger at the Gates*), Dick Davalos (*A View From the Bridge*), Anthony Franciosa (*A Hatful of Rain*), Andy Griffith (*No Time for Sergeants*), Laurence Harvey (*Island of Goats*), David Hedison (*A Month in the Country*), Earle Hyman (*Mister Johnson*), Susan Johnson (*The Most Happy Fella*), John Michael King (*My Fair Lady*), Jayne Mansfield (*Will Success Spoil Rock Hunter?*), Sarah Marshall (*The Ponder Heart*), Gaby Rodgers (*Mister Johnson*), Susan Strasberg (*The Diary of Anne Frank*), Fritz Weaver (*The Chalk Garden*)

**1956-57:** Peggy Cass (*Auntie Mame*), Sydney Chaplin (*Bells Are Ringing*), Sylvia Daneel (*The Tunnel of Love*), Bradford Dillman (*Long Day's Journey Into Night*), Peter Donat (*The First Gentleman*), George Grizzard (*The Happiest Millionaire*), Carol Lynley (*The Potting Shed*), Peter Palmer (*Li'l Abner*), Jason Robards (*Long Day's Journey Into Night*), Cliff Robertson (*Orpheus Descending*), Pippa Scott (*Child of Fortune*), Inga Swenson (*The First Gentleman*)

**1957-58:** Anne Bancroft (*Two for the Seesaw*), Warren Berlinger (*Blue Denim*), Colleen Dewhurst (*Children of Darkness*), Richard Easton (*The Country Wife*), Tim Everett (*The Dark at the Top of the Stairs*), Eddie Hodges (*The Music Man*), Joan Hovis (*Love Me Little*), Carol Lawrence (*West Side Story*), Jacqueline McKeever (*Oh, Captain!*), Wynne Miller (*Li'l Abner*), Robert Morse (*Say, Darling*), George C. Scott (*Richard III*)

**1958-59:** Lou Antonio (*The Buffalo Skinner*), Ina Balin (*A Majority of One*), Richard Cross (*Maria Golovin*), Tammy Grimes (*Look After Lulu*), Larry Hagman (*God and Kate Murphy*), Dolores Hart (*The Pleasure of His Company*), Roger Mollien (*French Theatre National Populaire*), France Nuyen (*The World of Suzie Wong*), Susan Oliver (*Patate*), Ben Piazza (*Kataki*), Paul Roebling (*A Desert Incident*), William Shatner (*The World of Suzie Wong*), Pat Suzuki (*Flower Drum Song*), Rip Torn (*Sweet Bird of Youth*)

**1959-60:** Warren Beatty (*A Loss of Roses*), Eileen Brennan (*Little Mary Sunshine*), Carol Burnett (*Once Upon a Mattress*), Patty Duke (*The Miracle Worker*), Jane Fonda (*There Was a Little Girl*), Anita Gillette (*Russell Patterson's Sketchbook*), Elisa Loti (*Come Share My House*), Donald Madden (*Julius Caesar*), George Maharis (*The Zoo Story*), John McMartin (*Little Mary Sunshine*), Lauri Peters (*The Sound of Music*), Dick Van Dyke (*The Boys Against the Girls*)

**1960-61:** Joyce Bulifant (*Whisper to Me*), Dennis Cooney (*Every Other Evil*), Sandy Dennis (*Face of a Hero*), Nancy Dussault (*Do Re Mi*), Robert Goulet (*Camelot*), Joan Hackett (*Call Me By My Rightful Name*), June Harding (*Cry of the Raindrop*), Ron Husmann (*Tenderloin*), James MacArthur (*Invitation to a March*), Bruce Yarnell (*The Happiest Girl in the World*)

**1961-62:** Elizabeth Ashley (*Take Her, She's Mine*), Keith Baxter (*A Man for All Seasons*), Peter Fonda (*Blood, Sweat and Stanley Poole*), Don Galloway (*Bring Me a Warm Body*), Sean Garrison (*Half-Past Wednesday*), Barbara Harris (*Oh, Dad, Poor Dad, Mamma's Hung You in the Closet and I'm Feeling So Sad*), James Earl Jones (*Moon on a Rainbow Shawl*), Janet Margolin (*Daughter of Silence*), Karen Morrow (*Sing, Muse!*), Robert Redford (*Sunday in New York*), John Stride (*Romeo and Juliet*), Brenda Vaccaro (*Everybody Loves Opal*)

**1962-63:** Alan Arkin (*Enter Laughing*), Stuart Damon (*The Boys from Syracuse*), Melinda Dillon (*Who's Afraid of Virginia Woolf?*), Robert Drivas (*Mrs. Dally Has a Lover*), Bob Gentry (*Angels of Anadarko*), Dorothy Loudon (*Nowhere to Go But Up*), Brandon Maggart (*Put It in Writing*), Julienne Marie (*The Boys from Syracuse*), Liza Minnelli (*Best Foot Forward*), Estelle Parsons (*Mrs. Dally Has a Lover*), Diana Sands (*Tiger Tiger Burning Bright*), Swen Swenson (*Little Me*)

**1963-64:** Alan Alda (*Fair Game for Lover*), Gloria Bleezarde (*Never Live Over a Pretzel Factory*), Imelda De Martin (*The Amorous Flea*), Claude Giraud (*Phédre*), Ketty Lester (*Cabin in the Sky*), Barbara Loden (*After the Fall*), Lawrence Pressman

(*Never Live Over a Pretzel Factory*), Gilbert Price (*Jerico-Jim Crow*), Philip Proctor (*The Amorous Flea*), John Tracy (*Telemachus Clay*), Jennifer West (*Dutchman*)

**1964-65:** Carolyn Coates (*The Trojan Women*), Joyce Jillson (*The Roar of the Greasepaint – The Smell of the Crowd*), Linda Lavin (*Wet Paint*), Luba Lisa (*I Had a Ball*), Michael O'Sullivan (*Tartuffe*), Joanna Pettet (*Poor Richard*), Beah Richards (*The Amen Corner*), Jaime Sanchez (*Conerico Was Here to Stay* and *The Toilet*), Victor Spinetti (*Oh, What a Lovely War*), Nicolas Surovy (*Helen*), Robert Walker (*I Knock at the Door* and *Pictures in the Hallway*), Clarence Williams III (*Slow Dancing on the Killing Ground*)

**1965-66:** Zoe Caldwell (*Slapstick Tragedy*), David Carradine (*The Royal Hunt of the Sun*), John Cullum (*On a Clear Day You Can See Forever*), John Davidson (*Oklahoma!*), Faye Dunaway (*Hogan's Ghost*), Gloria Foster (*Medea*), Robert Hooks (*Where's Daddy?* and *Day of Absence*), Jerry Lanning (*Mame*), Richard Mulligan (*Mating Dance* and *Hogan's Ghost*), April Shawhan (*3 Bags Full*), Sandra Smith (*Any Wednesday*), Leslie Ann Warren (*Drat! The Cat!*)

**1966-67:** Bonnie Bedelia (*My Sweet Charlie*), Richard Benjamin (*The Star-Spangled Girl*), Dustin Hoffman (*Eh?*), Terry Kiser (*Fortune and Men's Eyes*), Reva Rose (*You're A Good Man, Charlie Brown*), Robert Salvio (*Hamp*), Sheila Smith (*Mame*), Connie Stevens (*The Star-Spangled Girl*), Pamela Tiffin (*Dinner at Eight*), Leslie Uggams (*Hallelujah, Baby*), Jon Voight (*That Summer – That Fall*), Christopher Walken (*The Rose Tattoo*)

**1967-68:** David Birney (*Summertree*), Pamela Burrell (*Arms and the Man*), Jordan Christopher (*Black Comedy*), Jack Crowder – a.k.a. Thalmus Rasulala (*Hello, Dolly!*), Sandy Duncan (*Ceremony of Innocence*), Julie Gregg (*The Happy Time*), Stephen Joyce (*Stephen D.*), Bernadette Peters (*George M*), Alice Playten (*Henry, Sweet Henry*), Michael Rupert (*The Happy Time*), Brenda Smiley (*Scuba Duba*), Russ Thacker (*Your Own Thing*)

**1968-69:** Jane Alexander (*The Great White Hope*), David Cryer (*Come Summer*), Blythe Danner (*The Miser*), Ed Evanko (*Canterbury Tales*), Ken Howard (*1776*), Lauren Jones (*Does a Tiger Wear a Necktie?*), Ron Leibman (*We Bombed in New Haven*), Marian Mercer (*Promises, Promises*), Jill O'Hara (*Promises, Promises*), Ron O'Neal (*No Place to Be Somebody*), Al Pacino (*Does a Tiger Wear a Necktie?*), Marlene Warfield (*The Great White Hope*)

**1969-70:** Susan Browning (*Company*), Donny Burks (*Billy Noname*), Catherine Burns (*Dear Janet Rosenberg, Dear Mr. Kooning*), Len Cariou (*Henry V* and *Applause*), Bonnie Franklin (*Applause*), David Holliday (*Coco*), Katharine Houghton (*A Scent of Flowers*), Melba Moore (*Purlie*), David Rounds (*Child's Play*), Lewis J. Stadlen (*Minnie's Boys*), Kristoffer Tabori (*How Much, How Much*), Fredricka Weber (*The Last Sweet Days of Isaac*)

**1970-71:** Clifton Davis (*Do It Again*), Michael Douglas (*Pinkville*), Julie Garfield (*Uncle Vanya*), Martha Henry (*The Playboy of the Western World, Scenes From American Life,* and *Antigone*), James Naughton (*Long Days Journey Into Night*), Tricia O'Neil (*Two by Two*), Kipp Osborne (*Butterflies Are Free*), Roger Rathburn (*No, No, Nanette*), Ayn Ruymen (*The Gingerbread Lady*), Jennifer Salt (*Father's Day*), Joan Van Ark (*School for Wives*), Walter Willison (*Two by Two*)

**1971-72:** Jonelle Allen (*Two Gentlemen of Verona*), Maureen Anderman (*Moonchildren*), William Atherton (*Suggs*), Richard Backus (*Promenade, All!*), Adrienne Barbeau (*Grease*), Cara Duff-MacCormick (*Moonchildren*), Robert Foxworth (*The Crucible*), Elaine Joyce (*Sugar*), Jess Richards (*On The Town*), Ben Vereen (*Jesus Christ Superstar*), Beatrice Winde (*Ain't Supposed to Die a Natural Death*), James Woods (*Moonchildren*)

**1972-73:** D'Jamin Bartlett (*A Little Night Music*), Patricia Elliott (*A Little Night Music*), James Farentino (*A Streetcar Named Desire*), Brian Farrell (*The Last of Mrs. Lincoln*), Victor Garber (*Ghosts*), Kelly Garrett (*Mother Earth*), Mari Gorman (*The Hot l Baltimore*), Laurence Guittard (*A Little Night Music*), Trish Hawkins (*The Hot l Baltimore*), Monte Markham (*Irene*), John Rubinstein (*Pippin*), Jennifer Warren (*6 Rms Riv Vu*), Alexander H. Cohen (Special Award)

**1973-74:** Mark Baker (*Candide*), Maureen Brennan (*Candide*), Ralph Carter (*Raisin*), Thom Christopher (*Noel Coward in Two Keys*), John Driver (*Over Here*),

Conchata Ferrell (*The Sea Horse*), Ernestine Jackson (*Raisin*), Michael Moriarty (*Find Your Way Home*), Joe Morton (*Raisin*), Ann Reinking (*Over Here*), Janie Sell (*Over Here*), Mary Woronov (*Boom Boom Room*), Sammy Cahn (Special Award)

**1974-75:** Peter Burnell (*In Praise of Love*), Zan Charisse (*Gypsy*), Lola Falana (*Dr. Jazz*), Peter Firth (*Equus*), Dorian Harewood (*Don't Call Back*), Joel Higgins (*Shenandoah*), Marcia McClain (*Where's Charley?*), Linda Miller (*Black Picture Show*), Marti Rolph (*Good News*), John Sheridan (*Gypsy*), Scott Stevensen (*Good News*), Donna Theodore (*Shenandoah*), Equity Library Theatre (Special Award)

**1975-76:** Danny Aiello (*Lamppost Reunion*), Christine Andreas (*My Fair Lady*), Dixie Carter (*Jesse and the Bandit Queen*), Tovah Feldshuh (*Yentl*), Chip Garnett (*Bubblin'gBrown Sugar*), Richard Kelton (*Who's Afraid of Virginia Woolf?*), Vivian Reed (*Bubblin' Brown Sugar*), Charles Repole (*Very Good Eddie*), Virginia Seidel (*Very Good Eddie*), Daniel Seltzer (*Knock Knock*), John V. Shea (*Yentl*), Meryl Streep (*27 Wagons Full of Cotton*), A Chorus Line (Special Award)

**1976-77:** Trezana Beverley (*for colored girls…*), Michael Cristofer (*The Cherry Orchard*), Joe Fields (*The Basic Training of Pavlo Hummel*), Joanna Gleason (*I Love My Wife*), Cecilia Hart (*Dirty Linen*), John Heard (*G.R. Point*), Juliette Koka (*Piaf…A Remembrance*), Andrea McArdle (*Annie*), Ken Page (*Guys and Dolls*), Jonathan Pryce (*Comedians*), Chick Vennera (*Jockeys*), Eva LeGallienne (Special Award)

**1977-78:** Vasili Bogazianos (*P.S. Your Cat Is Dead*), Nell Carter (*Ain't Misbehavin*), Carlin Glynn (*The Best Little Whorehouse in Texas*), Christopher Goutman (*The Promise*), William Hurt (*Ulysses in Traction, Lulu,* and *The Fifth of July*), Judy Kaye (*On the 20th Century*), Florence Lacy (*Hello, Dolly!*), Armelia McQueen (*Ain't Misbehavin*), Gordana Rashovich (*Fefu and Her Friends*), Bo Rucker (*Native Son*), Richard Seer (*Da*), Colin Stinton (*The Water Engine*), Joseph Papp (Special Award)

**1978-79:** Philip Anglim (*The Elephant Man*), Lucie Arnaz (*They're Playing Our Song*), Gregory Hines (*Eubie!*), Ken Jennings (*Sweeney Todd*), Michael Jeter (*G.R. Point*), Laurie Kennedy (*Man and Superman*), Susan Kingsley (*Getting Out*), Christine Lahti (*The Woods*), Edward James Olmos (*Zoot Suit*), Kathleen Quinlan (*Taken in Marriage*), Sarah Rice (*Sweeney Todd*), Max Wright (*Once in a Lifetime*), Marshall W. Mason (Special Award)

**1979-80:** Maxwell Caulfield (*Class Enemy*), Leslie Denniston (*Happy New Year*), Boyd Gaines (*A Month in the Country*), Richard Gere (*Bent*), Harry Groener (*Oklahoma!*), Stephen James (*The 1940's Radio Hour*), Susan Kellermann (*Last Licks*), Dinah Manoff (*I Ought to Be in Pictures*), Lonny Price (*Class Enemy*), Marianne Tatum (*Barnum*), Anne Twomey (*Nuts*), Dianne Wiest (*The Art of Dining*), Mickey Rooney (Special Award)

**1980-81:** Brian Backer (*The Floating Light Bulb*), Lisa Banes (*Look Back in Anger*), Meg Bussert (*The Music Man*), Michael Allen Davis (*Broadway Follies*), Giancarlo Esposito (*Zooman and the Sign*), Daniel Gerroll (*Slab Boys*), Phyllis Hyman (*Sophisticated Ladies*), Cynthia Nixon (*The Philadelphia Story*), Amanda Plummer (*A Taste of Honey*), Adam Redfield (*A Life*), Wanda Richert (*42nd Street*), Rex Smith (*The Pirates of Penzance*), Elizabeth Taylor (Special Award)

**1981-82:** Karen Akers (*Nine*), Laurie Beechman (*Joseph and the Amazing Technicolor Dreamcoat*), Danny Glover (*Master Harold…and the Boys*), David Alan Grier (*The First*), Jennifer Holliday (*Dreamgirls*), Anthony Heald (*Misalliance*), Lizbeth Mackay (*Crimes of the Heart*), Peter MacNicol (*Crimes of the Heart*), Elizabeth McGovern (*My Sister in This House*), Ann Morrison (*Merrily We Roll Along*), Michael O'Keefe (*Mass Appeal*), James Widdoes (*Is There Life After High School?*), Manhattan Theatre Club (Special Award)

**1982-83:** Karen Allen (*Monday After the Miracle*), Suzanne Bertish (*Skirmishes*), Matthew Broderick (*Brighton Beach Memoirs*), Kate Burton (*Winners*), Joanne Camp (*Geniuses*), Harvey Fierstein (*Torch Song Trilogy*), Peter Gallagher (*A Doll's Life*), John Malkovich (*True West*), Anne Pitoniak (*'night Mother*), James Russo (*Extremities*), Brian Tarantina (*Angels Fall*), Linda Thorson (*Streaming*), Natalia Makarova (*On Your Toes* Special Award)

**1983-84:** Martine Allard (*The Tap Dance Kid*), Joan Allen (*And a Nightingale*

Sang), Kathy Whitton Baker (*Fool For Love*), Mark Capri (*On Approval*), Laura Dean (*Doonesbury*), Stephen Geoffreys (*The Human Comedy*), Todd Graff (*Baby*), Glenne Headly (*The Philanthropist*), J.J. Johnston (*American Buffalo*), Bonnie Koloc (*The Human Comedy*), Calvin Levels (*Open Admissions*), Robert Westenberg (*Zorba*), Ron Moody (Special Award)

**1984-85:** Kevin Anderson (*Orphans*), Richard Chaves (*Tracers*), Patti Cohenour (*La Boheme* and *Big River*), Charles S. Dutton (*Ma Rainey's Black Bottom*), Nancy Giles (*Mayor*), Whoopi Goldberg (*Whoopi Goldberg*), Leilani Jones (*Grind*), John Mahoney (*Orphans*), Laurie Metcalf (*Balm in Gilead*), Barry Miller (*Biloxi Blues*), John Turturro (*Danny and the Deep Blue Sea*), Amelia White (*The Accrington Pals*), Lucille Lortel (Special Award)

**1985-86:** Suzy Amis (*Fresh Horses*), Alec Baldwin (*Loot*), Aled Davies (*Orchards*), Faye Grant (*Singin' in the Rain*), Julie Hagerty (*The House of Blue Leaves*), Ed Harris (*Precious Sons*), Mark Jacoby (*Sweet Charity*), Donna Kane (*Dames at Sea*), Cleo Laine (*The Mystery of Edwin Drood*), Howard McGillin (*The Mystery of Edwin Drood*), Marisa Tomei (*Daughters*), Joe Urla (*Principia Scriptoriae*), Ensemble Studio Theatre (Special Award)

**1986-87:** Annette Bening (*Coastal Disturbances*), Timothy Daly (*Coastal Disturbances*), Lindsay Duncan (*Les Liaisons Dangereuses*), Frank Ferrante (*Groucho: A Life in Revue*), Robert Lindsay (*Me and My Girl*), Amy Madigan (*The Lucky Spot*), Michael Maguire (*Les Misérables*), Demi Moore (*The Early Girl*), Molly Ringwald (*Lily Dale*), Frances Ruffelle (*Les Misérables*), Courtney B. Vance (*Fences*), Colm Wilkinson (*Les Misérables*), Robert DeNiro (Special Award)

**1987-88:** Yvonne Bryceland (*The Road to Mecca*), Philip Casnoff (*Chess*), Danielle Ferland (*Into the Woods*), Melissa Gilbert (*A Shayna Maidel*), Linda Hart (*Anything Goes*), Linzi Hateley (*Carrie*), Brian Kerwin (*Emily*), Brian Stokes Mitchell (*Mail*), Mary Murfitt (*Oil City Symphony*), Aidan Quinn (*A Streetcar Named Desire*), Eric Roberts (*Burn This*), B.D. Wong (*M. Butterfly*), Tisa Chang and Martin E. Segal (Special Awards)

**1988-89:** Dylan Baker (*Eastern Standard*), Joan Cusack (*Road* and *Brilliant Traces*), Loren Dean (*Amulets Against the Dragon Forces*), Peter Frechette (*Eastern Standard*), Sally Mayes (*Welcome to the Club*), Sharon McNight (*Starmites*), Jennie Moreau (*Eleemosynary*), Paul Provenza (*Only Kidding*), Kyra Sedgwick (*Ah, Wilderness!*), Howard Spiegel (*Only Kidding*), Eric Stoltz (*Our Town*), Joanne Whalley-Kilmer (*What the Butler Saw*); Pauline Collins of *Shirley Valentine* (Special Award), Mikhail Baryshnikov (Special Award)

**1989-90:** Denise Burse (*Ground People*), Erma Campbell (*Ground People*), Rocky Carroll (*The Piano Lesson*), Megan Gallagher (*A Few Good Men*), Tommy Hollis (*The Piano Lesson*), Robert Lambert (*Gypsy*), Kathleen Rowe McAllen (*Aspects of Love*), Michael McKean (*Accomplice*), Crista Moore (*Gypsy*), Mary-Louise Parker (*Prelude to a Kiss*), Daniel von Bargen (*Mastergate*), Jason Workman (*Jason Workman*), Stewart Granger and Kathleen Turner (Special Awards)

**1990-91:** Jane Adams (*I Hate Hamlet*), Gillian Anderson (*Absent Friends*), Adam Arkin (*I Hate Hamlet*), Brenda Blethyn (*Absent Friends*), Marcus Chong (*Stand-up Tragedy*), Paul Hipp (*Buddy*), LaChanze (*Once on This Island*), Kenny Neal (*Mule Bone*), Kevin Ramsey (*Oh, Kay!*), Francis Ruivivar (*Shogun*), Lea Salonga (*Miss Saigon*), Chandra Wilson (*The Good Times Are Killing Me*), Tracey Ullman (*The Big Love* and *Taming of the Shrew*), Ellen Stewart (Special Award)

**1991-92:** Talia Balsam (*Jake's Women*), Lindsay Crouse (*The Homecoming*), Griffin Dunne (*Search and Destroy*), Laurence Fishburne (*Two Trains Running*), Mel Harris (*Empty Hearts*), Jonathan Kaplan (*Falsettos* and *Rags*), Jessica Lange (*A Streetcar Named Desire*), Laura Linney (*Sight Unseen*), Spiro Malas (*The Most Happy Fella*), Mark Rosenthal (*Marvin's Room*), Helen Shaver (*Jake's Women*), Al White (*Two Trains Running*), *Dancing at Lughnasa* cast (Special Award), Plays for Living (Special Award)

**1992-93:** Brent Carver (*Kiss of the Spider Woman*), Michael Cerveris (*The Who's Tommy*), Marcia Gay Harden (*Angels in America: Millennium Approaches*), Stephanie Lawrence (*Blood Brothers*), Andrea Martin (*My Favorite Year*), Liam Neeson (*Anna Christie*), Stephen Rea (*Someone Who'll Watch Over Me*), Natasha

Richardson (*Anna Christie*), Martin Short (*The Goodbye Girl*), Dina Spybey (*Five Women Wearing the Same Dress*), Stephen Spinella (*Angels in America: Millennium Approaches*), Jennifer Tilly (*One Shoe Off*), John Leguizamo (Special Award), Rosetta LeNoire (Special Award)

**1993-94:** Marcus D'Amico (*An Inspector Calls*), Jarrod Emick (*Damn Yankees*), Arabella Field (*Snowing at Delphi* and *4 Dogs and a Bone*), Aden Gillett (*An Inspector Calls*), Sherry Glaser (*Family Secrets*), Michael Hayden (*Carousel*), Margaret Illman (*The Red Shoes*), Audra McDonald (*Carousel*), Burke Moses (*Beauty and the Beast*), Anna Deavere Smith (*Twilight: Los Angeles, 1992*), Jere Shea (*Passion*), Harriet Walter (*Three Birds Alighting on a Field*)

**1994-95:** Gretha Boston (*Show Boat*), Billy Crudup (*Arcadia*), Ralph Fiennes (*Hamlet*), Beverly D'Angelo (*Simpatico*), Calista Flockhart (*The Glass Menagerie*), Kevin Kilner (*The Glass Menagerie*), Anthony LaPaglia (*The Rose Tattoo*), Julie Johnson (*Das Barbecü*), Helen Mirren (*A Month in the Country*), Jude Law (*Indiscretions*), Rufus Sewell (*Translations*), Vanessa Williams (*Kiss of the Spider Woman*), Brooke Shields (Special Award)

**1995-96:** Jordan Baker (*Suddenly Last Summer*), Joohee Choi (*The King and I*), Karen Kay Cody (*Master Class*), Viola Davis (*Seven Guitars*), Kate Forbes (*The School for Scandal*), Michael McGrath (*Swinging on a Star*), Alfred Molina (*Molly Sweeney*), Timothy Olyphant (*The Monogamist*), Adam Pascal (*Rent*), Lou Diamond Phillips (*The King and I*), Daphne Rubin-Vega (*Rent*), Brett Tabisel (*Big*), *An Ideal Husband* cast (Special Award)

**1996-97:** Terry Beaver (*The Last Night of Ballyhoo*), Helen Carey (*London Assurance*), Kristin Chenoweth (*Steel Pier*), Jason Danieley (*Candide*), Linda Eder (*Jekyll & Hyde*), Allison Janney (*Present Laughter*), Daniel McDonald (*Steel Pier*), Janet McTeer (*A Doll's House*), Mark Ruffalo (*This Is Our Youth*), Fiona Shaw (*The Waste Land*), Antony Sher (*Stanley*), Alan Tudyk (*Bunny Bunny*), *Skylight* cast (Special Award)

**1997-98:** Max Casella (*The Lion King*), Margaret Colin (*Jackie*), Ruaidhri Conroy (*The Cripple of Inishmaan*), Alan Cumming (*Cabaret*), Lea Delaria (*On the Town*), Edie Falco (*Side Man*), Enid Graham (*Honour*), Anna Kendrick (*High Society*), Ednita Nazario (*The Capeman*), Douglas Sills (*The Scarlet Pimpernel*), Steven Sutcliffe (*Ragtime*), Sam Trammel (*Ah, Wilderness!*), Eddie Izzard (Special Award), *The Beauty Queen of Leenane* cast (Special Award)

**1998-99:** Jillian Armenante (*The Cider House Rules*), James Black (*Not About Nightingales*), Brendan Coyle (*The Weir*), Anna Friel (*Closer*), Rupert Graves (*Closer*), Lynda Gravátt (*The Old Settler*), Nicole Kidman (*The Blue Room*), Ciáran Hinds (*Closer*), Ute Lemper (*Chicago*), Clarke Peters (*The Iceman Cometh*), Toby Stephens (*Ring Round the Moon*), Sandra Oh (*Stop Kiss*), Jerry Herman (Special Award)

**1999-2000:** Craig Bierko (*The Music Man*), Everett Bradley (*Swing!*), Gabriel Byrne (*A Moon for the Misbegotten*), Ann Hampton Callaway (*Swing!*), Toni Collette (*The Wild Party*), Henry Czerny (*Arms and the Man*), Stephen Dillane (*The Real Thing*), Jennifer Ehle (*The Real Thing*), Philip Seymour Hoffman (*True West*), Hayley Mills (*Suite in Two Keys*), Cigdem Onat (*The Time of the Cuckoo*), Claudia Shear (*Dirty Blonde*), Barry Humphries (Special Award)

**2000-2001:** Juliette Binoche (*Betrayal*), Macaulay Culkin (*Madame Melville*), Janie Dee (*Comic Potential*), Raúl Esparza (*The Rocky Horror Show*), Kathleen Freeman (*The Full Monty*), Deven May (*Bat Boy*), Reba McEntire (*Annie Get Your Gun*), Chris Noth (*The Best Man*), Joshua Park (*The Adventures of Tom Sawyer*), Rosie Perez (*References to Salvador Dali Make Me Hot*), Joely Richardson (*Madame Melville*), John Ritter (*The Dinner Party*), *Stones in His Pocket* cast: Seán Campion & Conleth Hill (Special Awards)

**2001-2002:** Justin Bohon (*Oklahoma!*), Simon Callow (*The Mystery of Charles Dickens*), Mos Def (*Topdog/Underdog*), Emma Fielding (*Private Lives*), Adam Godley (*Private Lives*), Martin Jarvis (*By Jeeves*), Spencer Kayden (*Urinetown*), Gretchen Mol (*The Shape of Things*), Anna Paquin (*The Glory of Living*), Louise Pitre (*Mamma Mia!*), David Warner (*Major Barbara*), Rachel Weisz (*The Shape of Things*)

**2002-2003:** Antonio Banderas (*Nine*), Tammy Blanchard (*Gypsy*), Thomas Jefferson Byrd (*Ma Rainey's Black Bottom*), Jonathan Cake (*Medea*), Victoria Hamilton (*A Day in the Death of Joe Egg*), Clare Higgins (*Vincent in Brixton*), Jackie Hoffman (*Hairspray*), Mary Stuart Masterson (*Nine*), John Selya (*Movin' Out*), Daniel Sunjata (*Take Me Out*), Jochum ten Haaf (*Vincent in Brixton*), Marissa Jaret Winokur (*Hairspray*), Peter Filichia (Special Award), Ben Hodges (Special Award)

**2003-2004:** Shannon Cochran (*Bug*), Stephanie D'Abruzzo (*Avenue Q*), Mitchel David Federan (*The Boy From Oz*), Alexander Gemignani (*Assassins*), Hugh Jackman (*The Boy From Oz*), Isabel Keating (*The Boy From Oz*), Sanaa Lathan (*A Raisin in the Sun*), Jefferson Mays (*I Am My Own Wife*), Euan Morton (*Taboo*), Anika Noni Rose (*Caroline, or Change*), John Tartaglia (*Avenue Q*), Jennifer Westfeldt (*Wonderful Town*), Sarah Jones (*Bridge and Tunnel* Special Award)

**2004-2005:** Christina Applegate (*Sweet Charity*), Ashlie Atkinson (*Fat Pig*), Hank Azaria (*Spamalot*), Gordon Clapp (*Glengarry Glen Ross*), Conor Donovan (*Privilege*), Dan Fogler (*The 25th Annual Putnam County Spelling Bee*), Heather Goldenhersh (*Doubt*), Carla Gugino (*After the Fall*), Jenn Harris (*Modern Orthodox*), Cheyenne Jackson (*All Shook Up*), Celia Keenan-Bolger (*The 25th Annual Putnam County Spelling Bee*), Tyler Maynard (*Altar Boyz*)

**2005-2006:** Harry Connick, Jr. (*The Pajama Game*), Felicia P. Fields (*The Color Purple*), Maria Friedman (*The Woman in White*), Richard Griffiths (*The History Boys*), Mamie Gummer (*Mr. Marmalade*), Jayne Houdyshell (*Well*), Bob Martin (*The Drowsy Chaperone*), Ian McDiarmid (*Faith Healer*), Nellie McKay (*The Threepenny Opera*), David Wilmot (*The Lieutenant of Inishmore*), Elisabeth Withers-Mendes (*The Color Purple*), John Lloyd Young (*Jersey Boys*)

*The class of 1948:* Theatre World *founder Daniel Blum, Estelle Loring, Ralph Meeker, Meg Mundy, Patrice Wymore, Edward Bryce, Peggy Maley, and Mark Dawson*

*The class of 1950: Charlton Heston, Lydia Clarke, Charles Nolte, Daniel Blum, Roger Price, Phil Arthur, Don Hanmer, Priscilla Gillette, Nancy Andrews, Grace Kelly, and Marcia Henderson*

*The class of 1962: James Earl Jones, Sean Garrison, Don Galloway, Peter Fonda, Brenda Vaccaro,* Theatre World *founder Daniel Blum, Janet Margolin, and Keith Baxter*

*The class of 1963: (Front) Alan Arkin Julienne Marie, presenter Carol Channing, Melinda Dillon, Liza Minnelli; (Middle row) Stuart Damon, Dorothy Loudon,* Theatre World *founder Daniel Blum, Diana Sands, Brandon Maggart; (Back) Robert Drivas, Swen Swenson, and Bob Gentry*

# Major New York Theatrical Awards

## AMERICAN THEATRE WING'S ANTOINETTE PERRY "TONY" AWARDS

Sunday, June 10, 2007, at Radio City Music Hall; the 61st annual Tony Awards are presented in recognition of distinguished achievement in the Broadway theatre. The 2006–2007 Tony Awards Nominating Committee (appointed by the Tony Awards Administration Committee) included: Victoria Bailey, executive; Joe Benincasa, executive; Susan Birkenhead, lyricist; Edward Burbridge, scenic designer; Robert Callely, executive; Ben Cameron, executive; Bettie Corwin, executive; John Dias, producer/dramaturg; Mercedes Ellington, choreographer; Sue Frost, producer/company manager; Joanna Gleason, actor; David Henry Hwang, playwright; Andrew Jackness, scenic designer; Betty Jacobs, historian/script consultant; Robert Kamlot, manager; Todd London, artistic director; Brian Stokes Mitchell, actor; John Nakagawa, producer; Peter Neufeld, manager; Lynn Nottage, playwright; Gilbert Parker, executive; Jonathan Reynolds, playwright/screenwriter; Steve Suskin, author; Jac Venza, executive; Tom Viola, executive; Franklin Weissberg, judge.

**Best Play:** *The Coast of Utopia* by Tom Stoppard; produced by Lincoln Center Theater, Andre Bishop, Bernard Gersten, Bob Boyett

**Nominees:** *Frost/Nixon* by Peter Morgan; produced by Arielle Tepper Madover, Matthew Byam Shaw, Robert Fox, Act Productions, David Binder, Debra Black, Annette Niemtzow/Harlene Freezer, The Weinstein Company, The Donmar Warehouse; *The Little Dog Laughed* by Douglas Carter Beane; produced by Roy Gabay, Susan Dietz, Morris Berchard, Steve Bozeman, Ted Snowdon, Jerry Frankel/Doug Nevin, Jennifer Manocherian/Ina Meibach, Second Stage Theatre, Carole Rothman, Ellen Richard; *Radio Golf* by August Wilson; produced by Jujamcyn Theaters, Margo Lion, Jeffrey Richards/Jerry Frankel, Tamara Tunie/Wendell Pierce, Fran Kirmser, Bunting Management Group, Georgia Frontiere and Open Pictures, Lauren Doll/Steven Greil & The AW Group, Wonder City, Inc./Townsend Teague, Jack Viertel, Gordon Davidson

**Best Musical:** *Spring Awakening* produced by Ira Pittelman, Tom Hulce, Jeffrey Richards, Jerry Frankel, Atlantic Theater Company, Jeffrey Sine, Freddy DeMann, Max Cooper, Mort Swinsky/Cindy and Jay Gutterman/Joe McGinnis/Judith Ann Abrams, ZenDog Productions/CarJac Productions, Aron Bergson Productions/Jennifer Manocherian/Ted Snowdon, Harold Thau/Terry Schnuck/Cold Spring Productions, Amanda Dubois/Elizabeth Eynon Wetherell, Jennifer Maloney/Tamara Tunie/Joe Cilibrasi/StyleFour Productions

**Nominees:** *Curtains* produced by Roger Berlind, Roger Horchow, Daryl Roth, Jane Bergére, Ted Hartley, Center Theatre Group; *Grey Gardens* produced by East of Doheny, Staunch Entertainment, Randall Wreghitt/Mort Swinsky, Michael Alden, Edwin W. Schloss, Playwrights Horizons; *Legally Blonde The Musical* produced by Hal Luftig, Fox Theatricals, Dori Berinstein, James L. Nederlander, Independent Presenters Network, Roy Furman, Amanda Lipitz, Broadway Asia, Barbara Whitman, FWPM Group, Hendel/Wiesenfeld, Goldberg/Binder, Stern/Meyer, Lane/Comley, Bartner-Jenkins/Nocciolino, Warren Trepp, MGM On Stage, Darcie Denkert, Dean Stolber

**Best Book of a Musical:** Steven Sater, *Spring Awakening*

**Nominees:** Rupert Holmes & Peter Stone, *Curtains*; Doug Wright, *Grey Gardens*; Heather Hatch, *Legally Blonde The Musical*

**Best Original Score** (music and/or lyrics): Duncan Sheik and Steven Sater, *Spring Awakening*

**Nominees:** John Kander, Fred Ebb, and Rupert Holmes, *Curtains*; Scott Frankel and Michael Korie, *Grey Gardens*; Laurence O'Keefe and Nell Benjamin, *Legally Blonde The Musical*

**Best Revival of a Play:** *Journey's End* produced by Boyett Ostar Productions, Stephanie P. McClelland, Bill Rollnick, James D'Orta, Philip Geier

**Nominees:** *Inherit The Wind* produced by Boyett Ostar Productions, The Shubert Organization, Lawrence Horowitz, Jon Avnet/Ralph Guild, Roy Furman, Debra Black/Daryl Roth, Bill Rollnick/Nancy Ellison Rollnick, Stephanie McClelland; *Talk Radio* produced by Jeffrey Richards, Jerry Frankel, Jam Theatricals, Francis Finlay, Ronald Frankel, James Fuld, Jr., Steve Green, Judith Hansen, Patty Ann Lacerte, James Riley, Mary Lu Roffe/Mort Swinsky, Sheldon Stein, Terri & Timothy Childs/StyleFour Productions, Irving Welzer/Herb Blodgett; *Translations* produced by Manhattan Theatre Club, McCarter Theatre Center, Lynne Meadow, Barry Grove, Emily Mann, Jeffrey Woodward

**Best Revival of a Musical:** *Company* produced by Marc Routh, Richard Frankel, Tom Viertel, Steven Baruch, Ambassador Theatre Group, Tulchin/Bartner Productions, Darren Bagert, Cincinnati Playhouse in the Park

**Nominees:** *The Apple Tree* produced by Tom Viertel, Roundabout Theatre Company, Todd Haimes, Harold Wolpert, Julia C. Levy; *A Chorus Line* produced by Vienna Waits Productions; *110 in the Shade* produced by Roundabout Theatre Company, Todd Haimes, Harold Wolpert, Julia C. Levy

**Best Performance by a Leading Actor in a Play:** Frank Langella, *Frost/Nixon*

**Nominees:** Boyd Gaines, *Journey's End*; Brian F. O'Byrne, *The Coast of Utopia*; Christopher Plummer, *Inherit the Wind*; Liev Schreiber, *Talk Radio*

**Best Performance by a Leading Actress in a Play:** Julie White, *The Little Dog Laughed*

**Nominees:** Eve Best, *A Moon for the Misbegotten*; Swoosie Kurtz, *Heartbreak House*; Angela Lansbury, *Deuce*; Vanessa Redgrave, *The Year of Magical Thinking*

**Best Performance by a Leading Actor in a Musical:** David Hyde Pierce, *Curtains*

**Nominees:** Michael Cerveris, *LoveMusik*; Raúl Esparza, *Company*; Jonathan Groff, *Spring Awakening*; Gavin Lee, *Mary Poppins*

**Best Performance by a Leading Actress in a Musical:** Christine Ebersole, *Grey Gardens*

**Nominees:** Laura Bell Bundy, *Legally Blonde The Musical*; Audra McDonald, *110 in the Shade*; Debra Monk, *Curtains*; Donna Murphy, *LoveMusik*

**Best Performance by a Featured Actor in a Play:** Billy Crudup, *The Coast of Utopia*

**Nominees:** Anthony Chisholm, *Radio Golf*; Ethan Hawke, *The Coast of Utopia*; John Earl Jelks, *Radio Golf*; Stark Sands, *Journey's End*

**Best Performance by a Featured Actress in a Play:** Jennifer Ehle, *The Coast of Utopia*

**Nominees:** Xanthe Elbrick, *Coram Boy*; Dana Ivey, *Butley*; Jan Maxwell, *Coram Boy*; Martha Plimpton, *The Coast of Utopia*

**Best Performance by a Featured Actor in a Musical:** John Gallagher, Jr., *Spring Awakening*

**Nominees:** Brooks Ashmanskas, *Martin Short: Fame Becomes Me*; Christian Borle, *Legally Blonde The Musical*; John Cullum, *110 in the Shade*; David Pittu, *LoveMusik*

**Best Performance by a Featured Actress in a Musical:** Mary Louise Wilson, *Grey Gardens*

**Nominees:** Charlotte d'Amboise, *A Chorus Line*; Rebecca Luker, *Mary Poppins*; Orfeh, *Legally Blonde The Musical*; Karen Ziemba, *Curtains*

**Best Scenic Design of a Play:** Bob Crowley & Scott Pask, *The Coast of Utopia*

**Nominees:** Jonathan Fensom, *Journey's End*; David Gallo, *Radio Golf*; Ti Green and Melly Still, *Coram Boy*

**Best Scenic Design of a Musical:** Bob Crowley, *Mary Poppins*

**Nominees:** Christine Jones, *Spring Awakening*; Anna Louizos, *High Fidelity*; Allen Moyer, *Grey Gardens*

**Best Costume Design of a Play:** Catherine Zuber, *The Coast of Utopia*

**Nominees:** Ti Green and Melly Still, *Coram Boy*; Jane Greenwood, *Heartbreak House*; Santo Loquasto, *Inherit the Wind*

**Best Costume Design of a Musical:** William Ivey Long, *Grey Gardens*

**Nominees:** Gregg Barnes, *Legally Blonde The Musical*; Bob Crowley, *Mary Poppins*; Susan Hilferty, *Spring Awakening*

**Best Lighting Design of a Play:** Brian MacDevitt, Kenneth Posner, and Natasha Katz, *The Coast of Utopia*

**Nominees:** Paule Constable, *Coram Boy*; Brian MacDevitt, *Inherit the Wind*; Jason Taylor, *Journey's End*

**Best Lighting Design of a Musical:** Kevin Adams, *Spring Awakening*

**Nominees:** Christopher Akerlind, *110 in the Shade*; Howard Harrison, *Mary Poppins*; Peter Kaczorowski, *Grey Gardens*

**Best Choreography:** Bill T. Jones, *Spring Awakening*

**Nominees:** Rob Ashford, *Curtains*; Matthew Bourne and Stephen Mear, *Mary Poppins*; Jerry Mitchell, *Legally Blonde The Musical*

**Best Direction of a Play:** Jack O'Brien, *The Coast of Utopia*

**Nominees:** Michael Grandage, *Frost/Nixon*; David Grindley, *Journey's End*; Melly Still, *Coram Boy*

**Best Direction of a Musical:** Michael Mayer, *Spring Awakening*

**Nominees:** John Doyle, *Company*; Scott Ellis, *Curtains*; Michael Greif, *Grey Gardens*

**Best Orchestrations:** Duncan Sheik, *Spring Awakening*

**Nominees:** Bruce Coughlin, *Grey Gardens*; Jonathan Tunick, *110 in the Shade*; Jonathan Tunick, *LoveMusik*

**Special Theatrical Event:** *Jay Johnson: The Two and Only*

**Regional Theatre Tony Award:** Alliance Theatre (Atlanta, Georgia)

**PAST TONY AWARD WINNERS** (Awards listed are Best Play followed by Best Musical, and as awards for Best Revival and the subcategories of Best Revival of a Play and Best Revival of a Musical were instituted, they are listed respectively): **1947:** No award given for musical or play **1948:** *Mister Roberts* (play) **1949:** *Death of a Salesman, Kiss Me, Kate* (musical) **1950:** *The Cocktail Party, South Pacific* **1951:** *The Rose Tattoo, Guys and Dolls* **1952:** *The Fourposter, The King and I* **1953:** *The Crucible, Wonderful Town* **1954:** *The Teahouse of the August Moon, Kismet* **1955:** *The Desperate Hours, The Pajama Game* **1956:** *The Diary of Anne Frank, Damn Yankees* **1957:** *Long Day's Journey into Night, My Fair Lady* **1958:** *Sunrise at Campobello, The Music Man* **1959:** *J.B., Redhead* **1960:** *The Miracle Worker, Fiorello!* & *The Sound of Music* (tie) **1961:** *Becket, Bye Bye Birdie* **1962:** *A Man for All Seasons, How to Succeed in Business Without Really Trying* **1963:** *Who's Afraid of Virginia Woolf?, A Funny Thing Happened on the Way to the Forum* **1964:** *Luther, Hello, Dolly!* **1965:** *The Subject Was Roses, Fiddler on the Roof* **1966:** *The Persecution and Assassination of Marat as Performed by the Inmates of the Asylum of Charenton Under the Direction of the Marquis de Sade, Man of La Mancha* **1967:** *The Homecoming, Cabaret* **1968:** *Rosencrantz and Guildenstern Are Dead, Hallelujah Baby!* **1969:** *The Great White Hope, 1776* **1970:** *Borstal Boy, Applause* **1971:** *Sleuth, Company* **1972:** *Sticks and Bones, Two Gentlemen of Verona* **1973:** *That Championship Season, A Little Night Music* **1974:** *The River Niger, Raisin* **1975:** *Equus, The Wiz* **1976:** *Travesties, A Chorus Line* **1977:** *The Shadow Box, Annie* **1978:** *Da, Ain't Misbehavin, Dracula* (innovative musical revival) **1979:** *The Elephant Man, Sweeney Todd* **1980:** *Children of a Lesser God, Evita, Morning's at Seven* (best revival) **1981:** *Amadeus, 42nd Street, The Pirates of Penzance* **1982:** *The Life and Adventures of Nicholas Nickelby, Nine, Othello* **1983:** *Torch Song Trilogy, Cats, On Your Toes* **1984:** *The Real Thing, La Cage aux Folles, Death of a Salesman* **1985:** *Biloxi Blues, Big River, Joe Egg* **1986:** *I'm Not Rappaport, The Mystery of Edwin Drood, Sweet Charity* **1987:** *Fences, Les Misérables, All My Sons* **1988:** *M. Butterfly, The Phantom of the Opera, Anything Goes* **1989:** *The Heidi Chronicles, Jerome Robbins' Broadway, Our Town* **1990:** *The Grapes of Wrath, City of Angels, Gypsy* **1991:** *Lost in Yonkers, The Will Rogers' Follies, Fiddler on the Roof* **1992:** *Dancing at Lughnasa, Crazy for You, Guys and Dolls* **1993:** *Angels in America: Millenium Approaches, Kiss of the Spider Woman, Anna Christie* **1994:** *Angels in America: Perestroika, Passion, An Inspector Calls* (play revival), *Carousel* (musical revival) **1995:** *Love! Valour! Compassion!, Sunset Boulevard, The Heiress, Show Boat,* **1996:** *Master Class, Rent, A Delicate Balance, King and I* **1997:** *The Last Night of Ballyhoo, Titanic, A Doll's House, Chicago* **1998:** *Art, The Lion King, A View from the Bridge, Cabaret* **1999:** *Side Man, Fosse, Death of a Salesman, Annie Get Your Gun* **2000:** *Copenhagen, Contact, The Real Thing, Kiss Me, Kate* **2001:** *Proof, The Producers, One Flew Over the Cuckoo's Nest, 42nd Street* **2002:** Edward Albee's *The Goat, or Who Is Sylvia?, Thoroughly Modern Millie, Private Lives, Into the Woods* **2003:** *Take Me Out, Hairspray, Long Day's Journey Into Night, Nine* **2004:** *I Am My Own Wife, Avenue Q, Henry IV, Assassins* **2005:** *Doubt, Monty Python's Spamalot, Glengarry Glen Ross, La Cage aux Folles* **2006:** *The History Boys, Jersey Boys, Awake and Sing!, The Pajama Game*

## DRAMA DESK AWARDS

Sunday, May 20, 2007, at LaGuardia Concert Hall-Lincoln Center; 52nd annual; Host: Kristen Chenoweth. Presented for outstanding achievement in the 2006–2007 season for Broadway, Off-Broadway, and Off-Off-Broadway productions, voted on by an association of New York drama reporters, editors and critics: Barbara Siegel – Chairperson (Theatermania.com and TalkinBroadway.com), William Wolf (WolfEntertainmentGuide.com, Drama Desk President); Glenda Frank (*Plays International,* nytheatre-wire.com), Tony Phillips (*New York Press*); Andrew Probst (American Theater Web, XM Satellite Radio), and Richard Ridge (Broadway Beat TV); Executive Producer, Robert R. Blume; President, William Wolf.

**New Play:** *The Coast of Utopia* by Tom Stoppard

**New Musical:** *Spring Awakening* by Steven Sater and Duncan Sheik

**Revival of a Play:** *Journey's End* by R.C. Sherriff

**Revival of a Musical:** *Company* by Stephen Sondheim and George Furth

**Book:** Rupert Holmes and Peter Stone, *Curtains*

**Composer:** Duncan Sheik, *Spring Awakening*

**Lyricist:** Steven Sater, *Spring Awakening*

**Actor in a Play:** Frank Langella, *Frost/Nixon*

**Actress in a Play:** Eve Best, *A Moon for the Misbegotten*

**Featured Actor in a Play:** Boyd Gaines, *Journey's End*

**Featured Actress in a Play:** Martha Plimpton, *The Coast of Utopia*

**Actor in a Musical:** Raul Esparza, *Company*

**Actress in a Musical:** (tie) Audra McDonald, *110 in the Shade*; Donna Murphy, *LoveMusik*

**Featured Actor in a Musical:** Gavin Lee, *Mary Poppins*

**Featured Actress in a Musical:** Debra Monk, *Curtains*

**Solo Performance:** Vanessa Redgrave, *The Year of Magical Thinking*

**Director of a Play:** Jack O'Brien, *The Coast of Utopia*

**Director of a Musical:** Michael Mayer, *Spring Awakening*

**Choreography:** Andy Blankenbuehler, *In the Heights*

**Orchestrations:** (tie) Mary Mitchell Campbell, *Company*; Jonathan Tunick, *LoveMusik*

**Set Design of a Play:** Bob Crowley and Scott Pask, *The Coast of Utopia*

**Set Design of a Musical:** Bob Crowley, *Mary Poppins*

**Costume Design:** Catherine Zuber, *The Coast of Utopia*

**Lighting Design:** Kenneth Posner, Brian MacDevitt, Natasha Katz, *The Coast of Utopia*

**Sound Design:** Gregory Clarke, *Journey's End*

**Unique Theatrical Experience:** *Edward Scissorhands*

**Outstanding Ensemble Performances:** *In the Heights*; *Lebensraum*

**Special Awards:** John Kander and Fred Ebb for forty-two years of excellence in advancing the art of musical theater; Austin Pendleton for being a renaissance man of the American theater; Transport Group for its breadth of vision and its presentation of challenging production; National Yiddish Theatre Folksbiene for preserving for ninety-two consecutive seasons the cultural legacy of Yiddish speaking theater of America

## VILLAGE VOICE OBIE AWARDS

Monday, May 21, 2007, at the Skirball Center; 52nd annual; Hosts: Cynthia Nixon and T.R. Knight. Presented for outstanding achievement in Off- and Off-Off-Broadway theater in the 2006–2007 season; Judges: Michael Feingold (Committee Chair and *Village Voice* chief theatre critic), Kristen Childs (playwright and former winner), Ain Gordon (playwright/director/actor and former winner), Adam Rapp (playwright and former winner), Anne Dennin (theater administrator), Jeremy McCarter (*New York Magazine* theatre critic), Alexis Soloski (*Village Voice* theatre critic).

**Performance:** Donna Lynne Champlin, *The Dark at the Top of the Stairs*; Ain Gordon, *Stories Left to Tell*; David Greenspan, *Faust & Some Men;* Nina Hellman, *Trouble in Paradise*; Nancy Opel, *My Deah*; Roslyn Ruff, *Seven Guitars*; James Saito, *Durango*; Michael Stuhlbarg, *The Voysey Inheritance*; Nilaja Sun, *No Child*; Harris Yulin, *Frank's Home*; Winsome Brown, Michael Ray Escamilla, Tracey A. Leigh, Leo Marks, Diane Rodriguez, Ed Vassallo, Heather Woodbury, *Tale of Two Cities*; Sustained excellence of performance: Betsy Aidem, Andre De Shields, Ron Cephas Jones

**Direction:** Lou Bellamy, *Two Trains Running*; Anne Kauffman, *The Thugs*; Matthew Maguire, *Abandon*; Eirik Stubo, *The Wild Duck*; Chay Yew, *Durango*

**Playwriting:** Adam Bock, *The Thugs*

**Design:** Rae Smith, set and costume design of *Oliver Twist*; Beowulf Boritt, sustained excellence in set design; Robert Kaplowitz, sustained excellence in sound design

**Special Citations:** Daniel Beaty, *Emergence-SEE!*; Edward Hall and Propeller, *Taming of the Shrew*; Tim Crouch, *an oak tree*; The Living Theatre Ensemble and director Judith Malina, *The Brig*

**Emerging Playwright Award:** Young Jean Lee

**Ross Wetzsteon Memorial Award** ($2,000): Rattlestick Playwrights Theatre

**Lifetime Achievement:** Alvin Epstein

**Obie Theater Grants** ($5,000): Transport Group, Peculiar Works Project, Synapse Productions, The Play Company

**PAST OBIE BEST NEW PLAY WINNERS** (If year is missing, no award was given that season; some seasons multiple plays were awarded): **1956:** *Absalom, Absalom* **1957:** *A House Remembered* **1959:** *The Quare Fellow* **1961:** *The Blacks* **1962:** *Who'll Save the Plowboy?* **1964:** *Play* **1965:** *The Old Glory* **1966:** *The Journey of the Fifth Horse* **1970:** *The Effect of Gamma Rays on Man-in-the-Moon Marigolds* **1971:** *The House of Blue Leaves* **1973:** *The Hot L Baltimore* **1974:** *Short Eyes* **1975:** *The First Breeze of Summer* **1976:** *American Buffalo, Sexual Perversity in Chicago* **1977:** *Curse of the Starving Class* **1978:** *Shaggy Dog Animation* **1979:** *Josephine* **1981:** *FOB* **1982:** *Metamorphosis in Miniature, Mr. Dead and Mrs. Free* **1983:** *Painting Churches, Andrea Rescued, Edmond* **1984:** *Fool for Love* **1985:** *The Conduct of Life* **1987:** *The Cure, Film Is Evil, Radio Is Good* **1988:** *Abingdon Square* **1990:** *Prelude to a Kiss, Imperceptible Mutabilities in the Third Kingdom, Bad Benny, Crowbar, Terminal Hip* **1991:** *The Fever* **1992:** *Sight Unseen, Sally's Rape, The Baltimore Waltz* **1994:** *Twilight: Los Angeles, 1992* **1995:** *Cryptogram* **1996:** *Adrienne Kennedy* **1997:** *One Flea Spare* **1998:** *Pearls for Pigs and Benita Canova* **2001:** *The Syringa Tree* **2004:** *Small Tragedy*

## OUTER CRITICS CIRCLE AWARDS

Thursday, May 24, 2007 at Sardi's Restaurant; 57th Annual. Presented for outstanding achievement in the 2006–2007 season. Winners are voted on by theatre critics of out-of-town periodicals and media.

**Broadway Play:** *The Coast of Utopia*

**Broadway Musical:** *Spring Awakening*

**Off-Broadway Play:** *Indian Blood*

**Off-Broadway Musical:** *In the Heights*

**New Score:** *Spring Awakening*

**Revival of a Play:** *Journey's End*

**Revival of a Musical:** *Company*

**Director of a Play:** Jack O'Brien, *The Coast of Utopia*

**Director of a Musical:** Michael Mayer, *Spring Awakening*

**Choreography:** Andy Blankenbuehler, *In the Heights*

**Actor in a Play:** Frank Langella, *Frost/Nixon*

**Featured Actor in a Play:** Boyd Gaines, *Journey's End*

**Actor in a Musical:** Raul Esparza, *Company*

**Featured Actor in a Musical:** David Pittu, *LoveMusik*

**Actress in a Play:** Eve Best, *A Moon for the Misbegotten*

**Actress in a Musical:** Donna Murphy, *LoveMusik*

**Featured Actress in a Play:** Martha Plimpton, *The Coast of Utopia*

**Featured Actress in a Musical:** Karen Ziemba, *Curtains*

**Scenic Design:** Bob Crowley and Scott Pask, *The Coast of Utopia*

**Costume Design:** Catherine Zuber, *The Coast of Utopia*

**Lighting Design:** Brian MacDevitt, Kenneth Posner and Natasha Katz, *The Coast of Utopia*

**Solo Performance:** Nilaja Sun, *No Child…*

**John Gassner Playwriting Award:** Nilaja Sun, *No Child…*

## LUCILLE LORTEL AWARDS

Monday, May 7, 2007 at New World Stages; 22nd Annual; Host: Bobby Cannavale and Bebe Neuwirth. Presented by the League of Off-Broadway Theatres and Producers for outstanding achievement Off-Broadway. The 2006-2007 awards committee consisted of Jamie Blankenship, Mark Dickerman, John Clinton Eisner, Barrack Evans, Kurt Everhart, David Finkle, Russell Lehrer, Nicolas Nagler, Victor

Pappas, Barbara Pasternack, Zachary Pincus-Roth, Mark Rossier, David Savran, Tom Smedes, and Barbara Wolkoff.

**Play:** *Stuff Happens*, by David Hare, produced by The Public Theater

**Musical:** (tie) *In the Heights*, by Quiara Alegría Hudes and Lin-Manuel Miranda, *Spring Awakening* by Duncan Sheik and Steven Sater, produced by Atlantic Theater Company

**Outstanding Revival:** *Two Trains Running*, by August Wilson, produced by Signature Theatre Company

**Outstanding Solo Show:** *No Child*, by Nilaja Sun

**Actor:** Peter Francis James, *Stuff Happens*, produced by The Public Theater

**Actress:** Gloria Reuben, *Stuff Happens*, produced by The Public Theater

**Featured Actor:** Arthur French, *Two Trains Running*, produced by Signature Theatre Company

**Featured Actress:** Sherie Rene Scott, *Landscape of the Body,* produced by Signature Theatre Company

**Direction:** Daniel Sullivan, *Stuff Happens*, produced by The Public Theater

**Choreography:** Andy Blankenbuehler, *In the Heights*

**Scenery:** Derek McLane, *The Voysey Inheritance*, produced by Atlantic Theater Company

**Costumes:** Gregory Gale, *The Voysey Inheritance*, produced by Atlantic Theater Company

**Lighting:** Kevin Adams, *Spring Awakening*, produced by Atlantic Theater Company

**Sound:** Martin Desjardins, *columbinus*, produced by New York Theatre Workshop

**Body of Work:** Classical Theatre of Harlem

**Edith Olivier Award:** Rick Sordelet

**Playwrights Sidewalk Award:** Christopher Durang

**Lifetime Achievement Award:** Kevin Kline

**Special Award:** The Actors Fund

**PAST LUCILLE LORTEL AWARD WINNERS** (Awards listed are Outstanding Play and Outstanding Musical, respectively, since inception): **1986:** *Woza Africa!*, no musical award **1987:** *The Common Pursuit*; no musical award **1988:** no play or musical award **1989:** *The Cocktail Hour*; no musical award **1990:** no play or musical award **1991:** *Aristocrats*; *Falsettoland* **1992:** *Lips Together, Teeth Apart*; *And the World Goes 'Round* **1993:** *The Destiny of Me*; *Forbidden Broadway* **1994:** *Three Tall Women*; *Wings* **1995:** *Camping with Henry & Tom*; *Jelly Roll!* **1996:** *Molly Sweeney*, *Floyd Collins* **1997:** *How I Learned to Drive*; *Violet* **1998:** (tie) *Gross Indecency* and *The Beauty Queen of Leenane*; no musical award **1999:** *Wit*; no musical award **2000:** *Dinner With Friends*; *James Joyce's The Dead* **2001:** *Proof*; *Bat Boy: The Musical* **2002:** *Metamorphoses*; *Urinetown* **2003:** *Take Me Out*, *Avenue Q* **2004:** *Bug*; *Caroline or Change* **2005:** *Doubt*; *The 25th Annual Putnam County Spelling Bee* **2006:** *The Lieutenant of Inishmore*; *The Seven*

## NEW YORK DRAMA CRITICS' CIRCLE AWARD

Monday, May 14, 2007, at the Algonquin Hotel; 72nd Annual. Presented by members of the press in the New York area. New York Drama Critics' Circle Committee: President, Adam Feldman (*Time Out New York*), Clive Barnes (*The New York Post*), Melissa Rose Bernardo (*Entertainment Weekly*), David Cote (*Time Out New York*), Joe Dziemianowicz (*The Daily News*), Michael Feingold (*The Village Voice*), Robert Feldberg (*The Bergen Record*), Elysa Gardner (*USA Today*), Eric Grode (*The New York Sun*), John Heilpern (*The New York Observer*), Jacques le Sourd (*Gannett Newspapers*), Jeremy McCarter (*New York*), David

Rooney (*Variety*), David Sheward (*Back Stage*), John Simon (*Bloomberg News*), Michael Sommers (*The Star-Ledger/Newhouse* Newspapers), Terry Teachout (*The Wall Street Journal*), Linda Winer (*Newsday*), Richard Zoglin (*Time*).

**Best Play:** *The Coast of Utopia* by Tom Stoppard

**Best American Play:** *Radio Golf* by August Wilson

**Best Musical:** *Spring Awakening* by Steven Sater and Duncan Sheik

**Special Citation**: *Journey's End* by R.C. Sherriff (Broadway revival)

**PAST DRAMA CRITICS' CIRLCE AWARD WINNERS** (From 1936 to 1962, the New York Drama Critics' Circle presented awards for Best American Play, Best Foreign Play, and Best Musical, although some years no awards were given in specific categories. For entries below during those years, the first entry (unless otherwise indicated) is for Best American Play, (F) for Best Foreign Play, and (M) for Best Musical. For listings from 1962 to the present, the first listing (unless otherwise indicated) is for Best Play, and proceeding listings are as follow: (A) – Best American Play, (F) – Best Foreign Play, (M) – Best Musical, depending on which awards were cited. Special Citations, periodically presented through the years, are indicated as such.): **1936:** *Winterset* **1937:** *High Tor* **1938:** *Of Mice and Men, Shadow and Substance* (F) **1939:** *The White Steed* (F) **1940:** *The Time of Your Life* **1941:** *Watch on the Rhine, The Corn Is Green* (F) **1942:** *Blithe Spirit* (F) **1943:** *The Patriots* **1944:** *Jacobowsky and the Colonel* (F) **1945:** *The Glass Menagerie* **1946:** *Carousel* (M) **1947:** *All My Sons, No Exit* (F), *Brigadoon* (M) **1948:** *A Streetcar Named Desire, The Winslow Boy* (F) **1949:** *Death of a Salesman, The Madwoman of Chaillot* (F), *South Pacific* (M) **1950:** *The Member of the Wedding, The Cocktail Party* (F), *The Consul* (M) **1951:** *Darkness at Noon, The Lady's Not for Burning* (F), *Guys and Dolls* (M) **1952:** *I Am a Camera, Venus Observed* (F), *Pal Joey* (M), *Don Juan in Hell* (special) **1953:** *Picnic, The Love of Four Colonels* (F), *Wonderful Town* (M) **1954:** *Teahouse of the August Moon, Ondine* (F), *The Golden Apple* (M) **1955:** *Cat on a Hot Tin Roof, Witness for the Prosecution* (F), *The Saint of Bleecker Street* (M) **1956:** *The Diary of Anne Frank, Tiger at the Gates* (F), *My Fair Lady* (M) **1957:** *Long Day's Journey into Night, The Waltz of the Toreadors* (F), *The Most Happy Fella* (M) **1958:** *Look Homeward Angel, Look Back in Anger* (F), *The Music Man* (M) **1959:** *A Raisin in the Sun, The Visit* (F), *La Plume de Ma Tante* (M) **1960:** *Toys in the Attic, Five Finger Exercise* (F), *Fiorello!* (M) **1961:** *All the Way Home, A Taste of Honey* (F), *Carnival* (M) **1962:** *The Night of the Iguana, A Man for All Seasons* (F), *How to Succeed in Business Without Really Trying* (M) **1963:** *Who's Afraid of Virginia Woolf?, Beyond the Fringe* (special) **1964:** *Luther, Hello Dolly!* (M), *The Trojan Women* (special) **1965:** *The Subject Was Roses, Fiddler on the Roof* (M) **1966:** *Marat/Sade, Man of La Mancha* (M), *Mark Twain Tonight - Hal Holbrook* (special) **1967:** *The Homecoming, Cabaret* (M) **1968:** *Rosencrantz and Guildenstern Are Dead, Your Own Thing* (M) **1969:** *The Great White Hope, 1776* (M) **1970:** *Borstal Boy, The Effect of Gamma Rays on Man-in-the-Moon Marigolds* (A), *Company* (M) **1971:** *Home, The House of Blue Leaves* (A), *Follies* (M), **1972:** *That Championship Season, The Screens* (F), *Two Gentlemen of Verona* (M), *Sticks and Bones* (special), *Old Times* (special) **1973:** *The Changing Room, The Hot L Baltimore* (A), *A Little Night Music* (M) **1974:** *The Contractor, Short Eyes* (A), *Candide* (M) **1975:** *Equus, The Taking of Miss Janie* (A), *A Chorus Line* (M) **1976:** *Travesties, Streamers* (A), *Pacific Overtures* (M) **1977:** *Otherwise Engaged, American Buffalo* (A), *Annie* (M) **1978:** *Da, Ain't Misbehavin'* (M) **1979:** *The Elephant Man, Sweeney Todd* (M) **1980:** *Talley's Folly, Betrayal* (F), *Evita* (M), Peter Brook's *Le Centre International de Créations Théâtricales* at La MaMa ETC (special) **1981:** *A Lesson from Aloes, Crimes of the Heart* (A), *Lena Horne: The Lady and Her Music* (special), *The Pirates of Penzance* at New York Shakespeare Festival (special) **1982:** *The Life and Adventures of Nicholas Nickleby, A Soldier's Play* (A) **1983:** *Brighton Beach Memoirs, Plenty* (A), *Little Shop of Horrors* (M), Young Playwrights Festival (special) **1984:** *The Real Thing, Glengarry Glen Ross* (F), *Sunday in the Park with George* (M), Samuel Beckett (special) **1985:** *Ma Rainey's Black Bottom* **1986:** *A Lie of the Mind, Benefactors* (A), *The Search for Signs of Intelligent Life in the Universe* (special) **1987:** *Fences, Les Liaisons Dangereuses* (F), *Les Misérables* (M) **1988:** *Joe Turner's Come and Gone, The Road to Mecca* (F), *Into the Woods* (M) **1989:**

*The Heidi Chronicles, Aristocrats* (F), *Bill Irwin: Largely New York* (special) **1990:** *The Piano Lesson, Privates on Parade* (F), *City of Angels* (M), **1991:** *Six Degrees of Separation, Our Country's Good* (F), *The Will Rogers Follies* (M) Eileen Atkins - *A Room of One's Own* (special) **1992:** *Dancing at Lughnasa, Two Trains Running* (A) **1993:** *Angels in America: Millenium Approaches, Someone Who'll Watch Over Me* (F), *Kiss of the Spider Woman* (M) **1994:** *Three Tall Women, Twilight: Los Angeles, 1992* - Anna Deavere Smith (special) **1995:** *Arcadia, Love! Valour! Compassion!* (A), Signature Theatre Company's Horton Foote Season (special) **1996:** *Seven Guitars, Molly Sweeney* (F), *Rent* (M), New York City Center's *Encores!* (special) **1997:** *How I Learned to Drive, Skylight* (F), *Violet* (F), *Chicago* - Broadway revival (special) **1998:** *Art, Pride's Crossing* (A), *The Lion King* (M), *Cabaret* – Broadway revival (special) **1999:** *Wit, Closer* (F), *Parade* (M), David Hare (special) **2000:** *Jitney, James Joyce's The Dead* (M), *Copenhagen* (F) **2001:** *The Invention of Love, The Producers* (M) *Proof* (A) **2002:** *Edward Albee's The Goat, or Who is Sylvia?, Elaine Stritch: At Liberty* (special) **2003:** *Take Me Out, Talking Heads* (F), *Hairspray* (M) **2004:** *Intimate Apparel,* Barbara Cook (special) **2005:** *Doubt, The Pillowman* (F) **2006:** *The History Boys, The Drowsy Chaperone* (M), John Doyle, Sarah Travis and the cast of *Sweeney Todd* (special), Christine Ebersole (special)

## DRAMA LEAGUE AWARDS

Friday, May 11, 2007; Broadway Ballroom at The Marriott Marquis; 73rd Annual. Presented for distinguished achievement in the New York theater; winners are selected by members of the League.

**Play:** *The Coast of Utopia*

**Musical:** *Spring Awakening*

**Revival of a Play:** *Journey's End*

**Revival of a Musical:** *Company*

**Performance:** Liev Schreiber, *Talk Radio*

**Julia Hansen Award for Excellence in Directing:** Michael Mayer

**Achievement in Musical Theatre:** John Kander and Fred Ebb

**Unique Contribution to Theater:** Broadway Cares/Equity Fights AIDS

## PULITZER PRIZE AWARD WINNERS FOR DRAMA

Established in 1917; Administered by the Pulitzer Prize Board, Columbia University; Lee C. Bollinger, President. Winner is chosen by a jury, composed of three to four critics, one academic and one playwright, however the board has final authority over choice. Presented for an outstanding drama or musical presented in New York or regional theater. The award goes to the playwright but production of the play as well as the script, is taken into account.

**2007 Winner:** *Rabbit Hole* by David Lindsay-Abaire

**PAST PULITZER PRIZE WINNERS** (If year is missing, no award was presented that year): **1918:** *Why Marry?* by Jesse Lynch Williams **1920:** *Beyond the Horizon* by Eugene O'Neill **1921:** *Miss Lulu Bett* by Zona Gale **1922:** *Anna Christie* by Eugene O'Neill **1923:** *Icebound* by Owen Davis **1924:** *Hell-Bent for Heaven* by Hatcher Hughes **1925:** *They Knew What They Wanted* by Sidney Howard **1926:** *Craig's Wife* by George Kelly **1927:** *In Abraham's Bosom* by Paul Green **1928:** *Strange Interlude* by Eugene O'Neill **1929:** *Street Scene* by Elmer Rice **1930:** *The Green Pastures* by Marc Connelly **1931:** *Alison's House* by Susan Glaspell **1932:** *Of Thee I Sing* by George S. Kaufman, Morrie Ryskind, Ira and George Gershwin **1933:** *Both Your Houses* by Maxwell Anderson **1934:** *Men in White* by Sidney Kingsley **1935:** *The Old Maid* by Zoe Atkins **1936:** *Idiot's Delight* by Robert E. Sherwood **1937:** *You Can't Take It with You* by Moss Hart and George S. Kaufman **1938:** *Our Town* by Thornton Wilder **1939:** *Abe Lincoln in Illinois* by Robert E.

Sherwood **1940:** *The Time of Your Life* by William Saroyan **1941:** *There Shall Be No Night* by Robert E. Sherwood **1943:** *The Skin of Our Teeth* by Thornton Wilder **1945:** *Harvey* by Mary Chase **1946:** *State of the Union* by Howard Lindsay and Russel Crouse **1948:** *A Streetcar Named Desire* by Tennessee Williams **1949:** *Death of a Salesman* by Arthur Miller **1950:** *South Pacific* by Richard Rodgers, Oscar Hammerstein II, and Joshua Logan **1952:** *The Shrike* by Joseph Kramm **1953:** *Picnic* by William Inge **1954:** *The Teahouse of the August Moon* by John Patrick **1955:** *Cat on a Hot Tin Roof* by Tennessee Williams **1956:** *The Diary of Anne Frank* by Frances Goodrich and Albert Hackett **1957:** *Long Day's Journey Into Night* by Eugene O'Neill **1958:** *Look Homeward, Angel* by Ketti Frings **1959:** *J.B.* by Archibald MacLeish **1960:** *Fiorello!* by Jerome Weidman, George Abbott, Sheldon Harnick, and Jerry Bock **1961:** *All the Way Home* by Tad Mosel **1962:** *How to Succeed in Business Without Really Trying* by Abe Burrows, Willie Gilbert, Jack Weinstock, and Frank Loesser **1965:** *The Subject Was Roses* by Frank D. Gilroy **1967:** *A Delicate Balance* by Edward Albee **1969:** *The Great White Hope* by Howard Sackler **1970:** *No Place to Be Somebody* by Charles Gordone **1971:** *The Effect of Gamma Rays on Man-in-the-Moon Marigolds* by Paul Zindel **1973:** *That Championship Season* by Jason Miller **1975:** *Seascape* by Edward Albee **1976:** *A Chorus Line* by Michael Bennett, James Kirkwood, Nicholas Dante, Marvin Hamlisch, and Edward Kleban **1977:** *The Shadow Box* by Michael Cristofer **1978:** *The Gin Game* by D.L. Coburn **1979:** *Buried Child* by Sam Shepard **1980:** *Talley's Folly* by Lanford Wilson **1981:** *Crimes of the Heart* by Beth Henley **1982:** *A Soldier's Play* by Charles Fuller **1983:** *'night, Mother* by Marsha Norman **1984:** *Glengarry Glen Ross* by David Mamet **1985:** *Sunday in the Park with George* by James Lapine and Stephen Sondheim **1987:** *Fences* by August Wilson **1988:** *Driving Miss Daisy* by Alfred Uhry **1989:** *The Heidi Chronicles* by Wendy Wasserstein **1990:** *The Piano Lesson* by August Wilson **1991:** *Lost in Yonkers* by Neil Simon **1992:** *The Kentucky Cycle* by Robert Schenkkan **1993:** *Angels in America: Millenium Approaches* by Tony Kushner **1994:** *Three Tall Women* by Edward Albee **1995:** *Young Man from Atlanta* by Horton Foote **1996:** *Rent* by Jonathan Larson **1998:** *How I Learned to Drive* by Paula Vogel **1999:** *Wit* by Margaret Edson **2000:** *Dinner with Friends* by Donald Margulies **2001:** *Proof* by David Auburn **2002:** *Topdog/Underdog* by Suzan-Lori Parks **2003:** *Anna in the Tropics* by Nilo Cruz **2004:** *I Am My Own Wife* by Doug Wright **2005:** *Doubt* by John Patrick Shanley

# Regional and Other Theatrical Awards

## AMERICAN THEATRE CRITICS ASSOCIATION AWARDS

### Steinberg New Play Award and Citations

March 31, 2007; Ceremony at the Humana Festival at Actors Theatre Louisville; founded in 1977. The Harold and Mimi Steinberg/ATCA Awards honor new plays that had their world premieres in the previous year in professional productions outside New York City. From 1977–1984 ACTA gave only one play a citation. After 1985, three citations were awarded. Currently the principal citation comes with a $25,000 prize and others are awarded a $7,500 prize.

**2007 Citations:** *Hunter Gatherers* by Peter Sinn Nachtrieb (principal); Citations: *Opus,* by Michael Hollinger; *Guest Artist,* by Jeff Daniels

**Past Recipients** (after 1986, first entry is the principal citation): **1977:** *And the Soul Shall Dance* by Wakako Yamauchi **1978:** *Getting Out* by Marsha Norman **1979:** *Loose Ends* by Michael Weller **1980:** *Custer* by Robert E. Ingham **1981:** *Chekhov in Yalta* by John Driver and Jeffrey Haddow **1982:** *Talking With* by Jane Martin **1983:** *Closely Related* by Bruce MacDonald **1984:** *Wasted* by Fred Gamel **1985:** (no principal citation) *Scheherazade* by Marisha Chamberlain, *The Shaper* by John Steppling, *A Shayna Maidel* by Barbara Lebow **1986:** *Fences* by August Wilson; *Fugue* by Lenora Thuna; *Hunting Cockroaches* by Janusc Glowacki **1987:** *A Walk in the Woods* by Lee Blessing; *The Film Society* by John Robin Baitz; *Back to the World* by Stephen Mack Jones **1988:** *Heathen Valley* by

Romulus Linney; *The Voice of the Prairie* by John Olive; *The Deal* by Matthew Witten **1989:** *The Piano Lesson* by August Wilson; *Generations* by Dennis Clontz; *The Downside* by Richard Dresser **1990:** *2* by Romulus Linney; *Pick Up Ax* by Anthony Clarvoe; *Marvin's Room* by Scott McPherson **1991:** *Two Trains Running* by August Wilson; *Sincerity Forever* by Mac Wellman; *The Ohio State Murders* by Adrienne Kennedy **1992:** *Could I Have This Dance* by Doug Haverty; *American Enterprise* by Jeffrey Sweet; *Miss Evers' Boys* by David Feldshuh **1993:** *Children of Paradise: Shooting a Dream* by Steven Epp, Felicity Jones, Dominique Serrand, and Paul Walsh; *Black Elk Speaks* by Christopher Sergel; *Hurricane* by Anne Galjour **1994:** *Keely and Du* by Jane Martin **1995:** *The Nanjing Race* by Reggie Cheong-Leen; *Rush Limbaugh in Night School* by Charlie Varon; *The Waiting Room* by Lisa Loomer **1996:** *Amazing Grace* by Michael Cristofer; *Jungle Rot* by Seth Greenland; *Seven Guitars* by August Wilson **1997:** *Jack and Jill* by Jane Martin; *The Last Night of Ballyhoo* by Alfred Uhry; *The Ride Down Mount Morgan* by Arthur Miller **1998:** *The Cider House Rules, Part II* by Peter Parnell; *Jitney* by August Wilson; *The Old Settler* by John Henry Redwood **1999:** *Book of Days* by Lanford Wilson; *Dinner With Friends* by Donald Margulies; *Expecting Isabel* by Lisa Loomer **2000:** *Oo-Bla-Dee* by Regina Taylor; *Compleat Female Stage Beauty* by Jeffrey Hatcher; *Syncopation* by Allan Knee **2001:** *Anton in Show Business* by Jane Martin; *Big Love* by Charles L. Mee; *King Hedley II* by August Wilson **2002:** *The Carpetbagger's Children* by Horton Foote; *The Action Against Sol Schumann* by Jeffrey Sweet; *Joe and Betty* by Murray Mednick **2003:** *Anna in the Tropics* by Nilo Cruz; *Recent Tragic Events* by Craig Wright; *Resurrection Blues* by Arthur Miller **2004:** *Intimate Apparel* by Lynn Nottage; *Gem of the Ocean* by August Wilson; *The Love Song of J. Robert Oppenheimer* by Carson Kreitzer **2005:** *The Singing Forest* by Craig Lucas; *After Ashley* by Gina Gionfriddo; *The Clean House* by Sarah Ruhl; *Madagascar* by J.T. Rogers **2006:** *A Body of Water* by Lee Blessing; *Red Light Winter* by Adam Rapp; *Radio Golf* by August Wilson

### M. Elizabeth Osborn Award

Established in 1993. Presented by the American Theatre Critics Association in memory of TCG and American Theatre play editor M. Elizabeth Osborn to an emerging playwright; $1,000 prize and recognition in The Best Plays Theater Yearbook edited by Jeffrey Eric Jenkins. No award was presented this season.

**Past Recipients: 1994:** Anne Galjour **1995:** Charlie Varon **1996:** Richard Kalinoski **1997:** Keith Glover **1998:** Rebecca Gilman **1999:** Dan O'Brien **2000:** Coby Goss **2001:** S.M. Shephard-Massat **2002:** Mia McCullough **2003:** John Walch **2004:** Rolin Jones **2005:** J.T. Rogers **2006:** Ken LaZebnik

### The ASCAP Foundation Awards

The ASCAP Foundation provides Awards to emerging composers and songwriters and recognition to honor the achievements of established composers and songwriters. **2006 Awards: The Sammy Kahn Award:** John Francis; **The ASCAP Foundation Life In Music Award:** Laurence Rosenthal; **The Richard Rodgers Award:** Marvin Hamlisch; **The Richard Rodgers New Horizon Award:** Scott Frankel and Michael Korie; **The Robert Allen Award:** Rosi Golan; **The Harold Arlen Film and TV Award:** Aaron Sapp

### AUDELCO AWARDS - THE "VIVS"

Monday, November 20, 2006; Harlem Stages/Aaron Davis Hall – Marion Anderson Theatre; 34th annual. Presented for excellence in Black Theatre for the 2005–2006 Season by the Audience Development Committee, created by Vivian Robinson. Co-Chairs: Phylicia Rashad, Vinnie Burrows, Kene Holliday, Kim Sullivan.

**Dramatic Production of the Year:** *Intimate Apparel* by Lynn Nottage (Roundabout Theatre Company)

**Lead Actor:** André DeShields, *Dream on Monkey Mountain* (Classical Theatre of Harlem)

**Lead Actress:** Viola Davis, *Intimate Apparel* (Roundabout Theatre Company)

**Supporting Actor:** Kim Sullivan, *Dream on Monkey Mountain* (Classical Theatre of Harlem)

**Supporting Actress:** Lynda Gravátt, *Intimate Apparel* (Roundabout Theatre Company)

**Musical Production of the Year:** *Caroline, or Change*

**Performance in a Musical/Female:** Tonya Pinkins, *Caroline, or Change*

**Performance in a Musical/Male:** Chuck Cooper, *Caroline, or Change*

**Director/Musical Production:** George C. Wolfe, *Caroline, or Change*

**Director/Dramatic Production:** Joyce Sylvester, *Freeda Peoples* (Billie Holiday Theatre)

**Outstanding Ensemble Performance:** New Federal Theatre's *Great Men of Gospel:* Jeff Bolding, Ralph Carter, Cliff Terry, Gary E. Vincent, and Montroville C. Williams

**Solo Performance:** Sarah Jones, *Bridge and Tunnel* (Culture Project)

**Choreography:** Dyane Harvey, *Great Men of Gospel* (New Federal Theatre)

**Outstanding Musical Director:** Linda Twine, *Caroline, or Change*

**Lighting Design:** Aaron Black, *Dream on Monkey Mountain* (New Federal Theatre)

**Set Design:** Derek McLane, *Intimate Apparel* (Roundabout Theatre Company)

**Costume Design:** Catherine Zuber, *Intimate Apparel* (Roundabout Theatre Company)

**Sound Design:** Jon Weston, *Caroline, or Change*

**Best Playwright:** Lynn Nottage (*Intimate Apparel* and *Fabulation*)

**Pioneer Awards:** P.J. Gibson, Arthur French, Allie Woods, Emily C. Martinez

**Rising Star Honoree:** Zora Howard

**Board of Directors Awards:** Philip Rose, A. Peter Bailey, J.E. Franklin

### BARRYMORE AWARDS

October 23, 2006; Merriam Theater; 12th Annual; Host: Mary Martello. Presented by the Theatre Alliance of Greater Philadelphia for excellence in theatre in the greater Philadelphia area for the 2005-2006 season.

**Production of a Play:** *Richard III* (Lantern Theater Company)

**Production of a Musical:** *Winesburg, Ohio* (Arden Theatre Company)

**Direction of a Play:** Terrence J. Nolen, *Opus* (Arden Theatre Company)

**Direction of a Musical:** Terrence J. Nolen, *Winesburg, Ohio* (Arden Theatre Company)

**Musical Direction:** Thomas Murray, *Winesburg, Ohio* (Arden Theatre Company)

**Leading Actor in a Play:** Pete Pryor, *Richard III* (Lantern Theater Company)

**Leading Actress in a Play:** Jacqueline Antaramian, *Nine Parts of Desire* (Wilma Theater)

**Leading Actor in a Musical:** Brian Hissong, *Winesburg, Ohio* (Arden Theatre Company)

**Leading Actress in a Musical:** Rachel deBenedet, *Adrift in Macao* (Philadelphia Theatre Company)

**Supporting Actor in a Play:** John Zak, *The Tempest* (Philadelphia Shakespeare Festival)

**Supporting Actress in a Play:** Amanda Schoonover, *Killer Joe* (Theatre Exile)

**Supporting Actor in a Musical:** Orville Mendoza, *Adrift in Macao* (Philadelphia Theatre Company)

**Supporting Actress in a Musical:** Michele Ragusa, *Adrift in Macao* (Philadelphia Theatre Company)

**Set Design:** Bradley Helm, *Daughters of Genius* (1812 Productions)

**Lighting Design:** John Stephen Hoey, *9 Parts of Desire* (Wilma Theater)

**Costume Design:** Janus Stefanowicz, *Intimate Apparel* (Philadelphia Theatre Company)

**Sound Design:** Nick Kourtides, *Mission to Mercury* (Pig Iron Theatre Company)

**Original Music:** Andre Pluess & Ben Sussman, *Winesburg, Ohio* (Arden Theatre Company)

**Choreography/Movement:** Mercedes Ellington, *Dreamgirls* (Prince Music Theater)

**New Play:** *Opus* by Michael Hollinger (Arden Theatre Company)

**Ensemble in a Play:** *Killer Joe* (Theatre Exile)

**Ensemble in a Musical:** *Mission to Mercury* (Pig Iron Theatre Company)

**F. Otto Haas Award for Emerging Philadelphia Theatre Artist:** Ben Dibble

**Excellence in Theatre Education/Community Service:** InterAction (InterAct Theatre Company)

**Lifetime Achievement Honoree:** Robert Hadley

**Ted & Stevie Wolf Award for New Approaches to Collaborations:** Arden Theatre Company & Vertigo String Quartet, *Opus*

**Suzanne Roberts Theatre Alliance College Scholarship Award:** Joseph Pizzi

**Joseph Cairns Jr. and Ernestine Bacon Cairns Memorial Scholarship:** Erika Wasko

**Special Recognition Award:** ComedySportz Philadelphia

## BAY AREA THEATRE CRITICS CIRCLE AWARDS

Founded in 1977. Presented by members of the print and electronic media for outstanding achievement in theatre in the San Francisco Bay Area for the 2006 calendar year.

**Entire Production/Drama:** *The Miser* (Berkeley Repertory Theatre); *Salome* (Aurora Theatre)

**Principal Performance Female/Drama:** Rita Moreno, *The Glass Menagerie* (Berkeley Repertory Theatre); Susi Damilano, *Reckless* (San Francisco Playhouse)

**Principal Performance, Male/Drama:** James Carpenter, *The Master Builder* (Aurora Theatre); L. Peter Callender, *World Music* (TheatreFirst)

**Supporting Performance, Female/Drama:** Delia MacDougall, *Merry Wives of Windsor* (California Shakespeare Theater); Nancy Carlin, *The Immigrant* (San Jose Rep); Sue Trigg, *Noises Off* (Willows Theatre)

**Supporting Performance, Male/Drama:** Dan Hiatt, *The Immigrant* (San Jose Rep)

**Director/Drama:** Barbara Damashek, *Laughter on the 23rd Floor* (Center REPertory)

**Set Design/Drama:** Bill English, *Roulette* (San Francisco Playhouse); Donald Eastman, *The Rivals* (American Conservatory Theater)

**Sound Design/Drama:** Dave Malloy, *Merry Wives of Windsor* (California Shakespeare Theater); Jeff Mockus, *Old Wicked Songs* (Marin Theatre Company)

**Lighting Design/Drama:** Jon Retsky, *Mystery Plays* (San Francisco Playhouse); Nancy Schertler, *The Rivals* (American Conservatory Theater)

**Costume Design/Drama:** Anna R. Oliver, *Restoration Comedy* (California Shakespeare Theater); Beaver Bauer, *The Rivals* (American Conservatory Theater); Fumiko Bielefeldt, *M. Butterfly* (TheatreWorks); Lydia Tanji, *Merry Wives of Windsor* (California Shakespeare Theater)

**Original Score/Drama:** Gina Leishman, *Mother Courage* (Berkeley Repertory Theatre)

**Choreography or Fight Direction/Drama:** Chris Black, *Salome* (Aurora Theatre); David Maier, *Zorro in Hell* (Berkeley Repertory Theatre)

**Solo Performance/Drama:** Ron Severdia, *A Christmas Carol* (Humbug Theater); Tim Miller, *1001 Beds* (New Conservatory Theatre Center); W. Allen Taylor, *Walkin' Talkin' Bill Hawkins* (The Marsh Berkeley)

**Ensemble/Drama:** *The Immigrant* (San Jose Rep); *The Marriage of Figaro* (Center REPertory)

**Entire Production/Musical:** *Seven Brides for Seven Brothers* (Broadway by the Bay); *Urinetown* (Foothill Music Theatre); *Vanities* (TheatreWorks)

**Principal Performance, Female/Musical:** Jessica Raaum, *Annie Get Your Gun* (Foothill Music Theatre)

**Principal Performance, Male/Musical:** Rick Williams, *1776* (Willows Theatre)

**Supporting Performance, Female/Musical:** Mary-Pat Green, *Putting It Together* (San Francisco Playhouse); Maureen McVerry, *Pardon My English* (42nd Street Moon); Tiffany Marie Austin, *Miss Saigon* (Broadway by the Bay)

**Supporting Performance, Male/Musical:** David Sattler & Paul Araquistain, *Miss Saigon* (Broadway by the Bay)

**Director/Musical:** Alex Perez, *Miss Saigon* (Broadway by the Bay)

**Music Director:** Catherine Snider, *Urinetown* (Foothill Music Theatre), Mark Hanson, *Miss Saigon* (Broadway by the Bay)

**Set Design/Musical:** Joe Ragey, *Annie Get Your Gun* (Foothill Music Theatre); Walt Spanger, *Happy End* (American Conservatory Theater)

**Sound Design/Musical:** Jeff Curtis, *Happy End* (American Conservatory Theater)

**Lighting Design/Musical:** Michael Ramsaur, *Miss Saigon* (Broadway by the Bay)

**Costume Design/Musical:** Candice Donnelly, *Happy End* (American Conservatory Theater); Janis Bergmann, *Annie Get Your Gun* (Foothill Music Theatre)

**Choreography:** Berle Davis, *Seven Brides for Seven Brothers* (Broadway by the Bay); Robyn Tribuzi, *Miss Saigon* (Broadway by the Bay)

**Original Script/Musical:** Morris Bobrow, *Shopping! The Musical* (AWAT Productions); Jay Kuo, *The Insignificant Others* (New Conservatory Theatre Center)

**Original Score:** David Kirshenbaum, *Vanities* (TheatreWorks)

**Ensemble/Musical:** *Passing Strange* (Berkeley Repertory Theatre)

**Touring Productions:** *Doubt* (Carol Shorenstein Hays, Manhattan Theatre Club); *Hairspray* (American Musical Theatre of San Jose); Matthew Bourne's *Swan Lake* (Best of Broadway)

**Paine Knickerbocker Award:** New Conservatory Theatre Center & A Traveling Jewish Theatre

**Barbara Bladen Porter Award:** Kim Taylor

**Special Awards:** Cal Performances & Ross Valley Players

## BISTRO AWARDS

April 9, 2007; Gotham Comedy Club; 22nd Annual. Presented by *Back Stage* Magazine for outstanding achievement in the cabaret field; winners selected by a committee consisting of Elizabeth Ahlfors (*Cabaret Scenes*), David Finkle (*Back Stage*'s Bistro Bits columnist), John Hoglund (former Bistro Bits columnist), Erv Raible (Executive/Artistic Director of the Cabaret Conference at Yale University), Roy Sander (former Bistro Bits columnist) and Chuck Taylor (*Billboard*); produced by Sherry Eaker,created by the late *Back Stage* cabaret critic Bob Harrington.

**Vocalist:** Keith David at the Metropolitan Room; Douglas Ladnier at Danny's Skylight Room

**Debut:** Valarie Pettiford at the Metropolitan Room

**Major Engagement:** Jeff Harnar at Feinstein's at the Regency; Rebecca Luker at Feinstein's at the Regency

**Major Jazz Engagement:** Kurt Elling at Birdland

**Jazz Vocalist:** Andrew Suvalsky at the Metropolitan Room

**Musical Duo:** Klea Blackhurst and Billy Stritch in *Dreaming of a Song: The Music of Hoagy Carmichael* at the Metropolitan Room; Faith Prince and Tom Wopat in *Let's Fall in Love* at Feinstein's at the Regency

**Musical Group Performance:** Tom Andersen, Scott Coulter, and Tim DiPasqua in *Southern Comfort: A Down-Home Country Music Jamboree* at Laurie Beechman Theater at the West Bank Café

**Musical Comedy Performance:** Jay Rogers in *Eat, Drink, and Be Mary* at the Metropolitan Room; Kristine Zbornik at the Metropolitan Room

**Unique Artist:** Jose Luis Rodriguez at Danny's Skylight Room

**Return to Cabaret:** Charles Cochran at Danny's Skylight Room

**Tribute Show:** Terese Genecco in *Drunk With Love: A Tribute to Frances Faye* at the Metropolitan Room

**Piano Bar Entertainer:** Ray Fellman for *The After Party* at the Laurie Beechman Theater at the West Bank Café; David Shenton at Helen's Piano Lounge; Rick Unterberg at the Townhouse

**Comedian:** Bob Smith at Gotham Comedy Club

**Song of the Year:** "One Thing" by Tim DiPasqua

**Special Material:** "Almost (99 I Love Yous)" by Joe Iconis and Robert Maddock

**Recording:** Mary Foster Conklin for *Blues for Breakfast: Remembering Matt Dennis;* Barbara Fasano for *Written in the Stars*

**Musical Director:** Shelly Markham for his performances with Andrea Marcovicci in *By Request* at the Oak Room at the Algonquin

**Instrumentalist:** Sean Smith

**Instrumentalist Group:** The Ross Patterson Little Big Band at Danny's Skylight Room

**Technical Director:** Tim Flannery at the Oak Room at the Algonquin

**Special Awards:** Chris Mazzilli, Steve Mazzilli, and Lennie Watts for outstanding achievement at the Metropolitan Room; Donald Schaffer for outstanding cabaret achievement at Danny's Skylight Room; Erv Raible with Wendy Lane Bailey for the Cabaret Conference at Yale University; Mike Greensill for consistent excellence as musical conductor and arranger

**Ira Eaker Special Achievement Award:** Sheera Ben-David

**Bob Harrington Lifetime Achievement Award:** Betty Buckley

## BROADWAY.COM AUDIENCE AWARDS

May 31st, 2007; 8th Annual. The Broadway.com Audience Awards give real theatergoers a chance to honor their favorite Broadway and Off-Broadway shows and performers.

**New Broadway Musical:** *Spring Awakening*

**New Broadway Play:** *The Coast of Utopia*

**Broadway Musical Revival:** *Les Misérables*

**Broadway Play Revival:** *Talk Radio*

**New Off-Broadway Musical:** *In the Heights*

**New Off-Broadway Play:** *My Mother's Italian, My Father's Jewish and I'm in Therapy*

**Leading Actor in a Broadway Musical:** Jonathan Groff, *Spring Awakening*

**Leading Actress in a Broadway Musical:** Christine Ebersole, *Grey Gardens*

**Leading Actor in a Broadway Play:** Liev Schreiber, *Talk Radio*

**Leading Actress in a Broadway Play:** Angela Lansbury, *Deuce*

**Featured Actor in a Broadway Musical:** John Gallagher Jr., *Spring Awakening*

**Featured Actress in a Broadway Musical:** Orfeh, *Legally Blonde*

**Featured Actor in a Broadway Play:** Ethan Hawke, *The Coast of Utopia*

**Featured Actress in a Broadway Play:** Tonya Pinkins, *Radio Golf*

**Diva Performance:** Kristin Chenoweth, *The Apple Tree*

**Solo Performance:** Vanessa Redgrave, *The Year of Magical Thinking*

**Onstage Pair:** Jonathan Groff & Lea Michele, *Spring Awakening*

**Ensemble Cast:** *Spring Awakening*

**Breakthrough Performance (Male):** Jonathan Groff, *Spring Awakening*

**Breakthrough Performance (Female):** Lea Michele, *Spring Awakening*

**Replacement (Male):** John Tartaglia, *Beauty and the Beast*

**Replacement (Female):** Fantasia, *The Color Purple*

**New Broadway Song:** "Omigod, You Guys," *Legally Blonde*

**Long-Running Broadway Show:** *Wicked*

**Long-Running Off-Broadway Show:** *Altar Boyz*

## CARBONELL AWARDS

April 9, 2007; Broward Center for the Performing Arts – Amaturo Theatre; 31st annual; Host: Bruce Adler. Presented for outstanding achievement in South Florida theater during the 2006 calendar year.

### Regional Awards

**George Abbott Award for Outstanding Achievement in the Arts:** Michael Spring

**Bill Von Maurer Award for Theatrical Excellence:** Florida Stage

**Howard Kleinberg Award:** New World School of the Arts, Miami

**Fred Diekmann Emerging Artist Award:** Kameshia Duncan (actress)

**New Work:** *Cradle of Man* by Melanie Marnich (Florida Stage)

**Ensemble:** *Lend Me a Tenor,* produced by the Caldwell Theatre Company

**Production of a Play:** GableStage, *The Pillowman* (GableStage)

**Director of a Play:** Joseph Adler, *The Pillowman* (GableStage)

**Actor in a Play:** Antonio Amodeo, *The Pillowman* (GableStage)

**Actress in a Play:** Lisa Morgan, *Who's Afraid of Virginia Woolf?* (Palm Beach Dreamworks)

**Supporting Actor in a Play:** Peter Haig, *The Price* (Palm Beach Dreamworks)

**Supporting Actress in a Play:** Connie SaLoutos, *Lend Me a Tenor* (Caldwell Theatre Company)

**Production of a Musical:** *The Tin Pan Alley Rag* produced by Maltz Jupiter Theatre

**Director of a Musical:** Jiri Zizka, *The Tin Pan Alley Rag* (Maltz Jupiter Theatre)

**Actor in a Musical:** Tally Sessions, *The Tin Pan Alley Rag* (Maltz Jupiter Theatre)

**Actress in a Musical:** Tina Fabrique, *Ella* (Florida Stage)

**Supporting Actor in a Musical:** Reggie Whitehead, *The Full Monty* (Actors' Playhouse)

**Supporting Actress in a Musical:** Lourelene Snedeker, *Irving Berlin's White Christmas* (Actors' Playhouse)

**Musical Direction:** Brad Ellis, *The Tin Pan Alley Rag* (Maltz Jupiter Theatre)

**Choreography:** Ron Hutchins, *Five Guys Named Moe* (Stage Door Theatre)

**Scenic Design:** Richard Crowell, *Splitting Infinity* (Florida Stage)

**Lighting Design:** Richard Crowell, *Splitting Infinity* (Florida Stage)

**Costume Design:** Erin Amico, *Intimate Apparel* (GableStage)

**Sound Design:** Matt Corey, *The Pillowman* (GableStage)

### Stock/Roadshow Awards

**Production:** *Wicked,* Broward Center for the Performing Arts

**Director:** Joe Mantello, *Wicked*

**Choreography:** Twyla Tharp, *Movin' Out*

**Actor:** Mark Nelson, *I Am My Own Wife*

**Actress:** Stephanie J. Block, *Wicked*

**Supporting Actor:** David Garrison, *Wicked*

**Supporting Actress:** Gwen Hollander, *Little Women*

**Scenic Design:** Eugene Lee, *Wicked*

**Lighting Design:** Kenneth Posner, *Wicked*

**Costume Design:** Susan Hilferty, *Wicked*

## CONNECTICUT CRITICS' CIRCLE AWARDS

June 4, 2007; Goodspeed Opera House; 17th Annual. Presented for outstanding achievement in Connecticut theater, selected by statewide reviews, feature writers, columnists, and broadcasters, for 2006–2007 season.

**Production of a Play:** *Uncle Vanya* (Long Wharf Theatre)

**Production of a Musical:** *Singin' in the Rain* (Goodspeed Musicals)

**Actress in a Play:** Donna Wandrey, *Murderers* (TheatreWorks)

**Actor in a Play:** (tie) Marco Barricelli, *Uncle Vanya* (Long Wharf Theatre); James Lecesne, *I Am My Own Wife* (Hartford Stage)

**Actress in a Musical:** Hollis Resnik, *Man of La Mancha* (Long Wharf Theatre)

**Actor in a Musical:** Jon Peterson, *George M.* (Seven Angels Theatre)

**Direction of a Play:** Gordon Edelstein, *Uncle Vanya* (Long Wharf Theatre)

**Direction of a Musical:** Rob Ruggiero, *Make Me a Song: The Music of William Finn* (TheatreWorks)

**Choreography:** Warren Carlyle, *Singin' in the Rain* (Goodspeed Musicals)

**Set Design:** Scott Bradley, *Eurydice* (Yale Repertory Theatre)

**Lighting Design:** Russel H. Champa, *Eurydice* (Yale Repertory Theatre)

**Costume Design:** Angela Wendt, *Singin' in the Rain* (Goodspeed Musicals)

**Sound Design:** David Remedios, *No Exit* (Hartford Stage/ART)

**Ensemble Performance:** *A Grand Night for Singing* (Ivoryton Playhouse)

**Touring Production:** *Monty Python's Spamalot*

**Debut Award:** Vanessa Kai, *Far East* (Stamford Theater Works)

**Tom Killen Memorial Award:** James Bundy, Artistic Director of Yale Rep

## CRAIG NOEL AWARDS

January 29, 2007; 5th annual. Presented by the San Diego Theatre Critics Circle for outstanding achievement in the greater San Diego theatre in the 2006 calendar year.

**Choreography:** Kirby Ward, *Thoroughly Modern Millie* (Moonlight Stage Productions)

**Original Music for a Play:** Gina Leishman, *Mother Courage and Her Children* (La Jolla Playhouse)

**Set Design:** Robert Brill, *The Wiz* (La Jolla Playhouse)

**Lighting Design:** Chris Rynne, *Lincolnesque* (The Old Globe)

**Costume Design:** Lewis Brown, *The Constant Wife* (The Old Globe)

**Lead Performance in a Musical, Female:** (tie) Nikki M. James, *The Wiz* (La Jolla Playhouse); Sarah Sumner, *Urinetown* (Starlight Musical Theatre)

**Lead Performance in a Musical, Male:** (tie) Doug Bilitch, *Urinetown* (Starlight Musical Theatre); Thom Sesma, *The Times They Are A-Changin'* (The Old Globe)

**Featured Performance in a Musical, Female:** Rena Stober, *Zhivago* (La Jolla Playhouse)

**Featured Performance in a Musical, Male:** (tie) Matt Bogart, *Zhivago* (La Jolla Playhouse); Ron Chaoularton, *My Fair Lady* (Cygnet Theatre)

**Music Direction:** Pamela Fuller, *Urinetown* (Starlight Musical Theatre)

**Lead Performance in a Play, Female:** (tie) Kandis Chappell, *Collected Stories* (North Coast Repertory Theatre); Lisa Renee Pitts, *Intimate Apparel* (San Diego Repertory Theatre); Sharon Lockwood, *Culture Clash's Zorro in Hell* (La Jolla Playhouse)

**Lead Performance in a Play, Male:** (tie) Joshua Everett Johnson, *Copenhagen* (Cygnet Theatre); Jonathan McMurty, *Trying* (The Old Globe); T. Ryder Smith, *Lincolnesque* (The Old Globe)

**Featured Performance in a Play, Female:** Katie Barrett, *Mother Courage and Her Children* (La Jolla Playhouse)

**Featured Performance in a Play, Male:** (tie) Charles Janasz, *Titus Andronicus* (The Old Globe); James Sutorius, *Lincolnesque* (The Old Globe)

**Ensemble:** Sandy Duncan, Ned Schmidtke, Samantha Soule in *A Body of Water* (The Old Globe)

**Touring Production:** *Doubt* (Broadway San Diego)

**Direction of a Musical:** (tie) Brian Wells and David Brannen, *Urinetown* (Starlight Musical Theatre); Des McAnuff, *The Wiz* (La Jolla Playhouse)

**Direction of a Play:** Ethan McSweeny, *A Body of Water* (The Old Globe)

**Musical Production:** (tie) *Urinetown* (Starlight Musical Theatre); *The Wiz* (La Jolla Playhouse)

**Dramatic Production:** *A Body of Water* (The Old Globe)

**Des McAnuff New Visions Award:** Delicia Turner Sonnenberg

**Artistic Visionary Award:** Des McAnuff, La Jolla Playhouse


## DRAMATIST GUILD AWARDS

Established in 2000, these awards are presented by the Dramatists Guild of America to outstanding writers at the Dramatists Guild Annual Benefit and Awards Gala. **2007 Winners: Elizabeth Hull-Kate Warriner Award** (to the playwright whose work deals with social, political or religious mores of the time): Steven Sater and Duncan Sheik, *Spring Awakening;* **Frederick Loewe Award for Dramatic Composition:** Scott Frankel; **Flora Roberts Award:** Ed Bullins; **Lifetime Achievement:** Horton Foote; **Wendy Wasserstein Prize** (to an accomplished and promising female writer): Linda Ramsey


## ED KLEBAN AWARD

16th and 17th Annual. Presented by New Dramatists in honor of Edward Kleban; award is given annually to both a librettist and a lyricist ($100,000 to each recipient payable over two years); Board of Directors: Andre Bishop, Sheldon Harnick, Richard Maltby, Jr., Francis Neuwirth (Treasurer), Alan J. Stein (Secretary), John Weidman, Maury Yeston (President). Judges: Rick Elice, Carol Hall, Charles Kopelman. **2006 Winners:** Laurence Holzman and Felicia Needleman (co-librettists); Robert L. Freedman and Steven Lutvak (co-lyricists); **2007 Winners:** Jeremy Desmon (librettist); Joe Iconis (lyricist)


## ELLIOT NORTON AWARDS

Monday, May 21, 2007; Cutler Majestic Theatre; 25th annual. Presented for outstanding contribution to the theater in Boston; voted by a Boston Theater Critics Association selection committee comprising Terry Byrne, Carolyn Clay, Iris Fanger, Louise Kennedy, Joyce Kullhawik, Robert Nesti, Ed Siegel and Caldwell Titcomb.

**Visiting Production:** *Doubt* (Presented by Jon B. Platt)

**Outstanding Production, Large Company:** *Mauritius* (Huntington Theatre Company)

**Outstanding Production, Midsized Company:** *Miss Witherspoon* (Lyric Stage Company)

**Outstanding Production, Small Company:** *A Midsummer Night's Dream* (Boston Theatre Works)

**Outstanding Production, Fringe Company:** *Stuff Happens* (Zeitgeist Stage Company)

**Outstanding Musical Production:** *Caroline, or Change* (SpeakEasy Stage Company)

**Director, Large Company:** Nicholas Martin, *Love's Labour's Lost* (Huntington Theatre Company)

**Director, Midsized Company:** David R. Gammons, *Titus Andronicus* (Actors' Shakespeare Project)

**Director, Small/Fringe Company:** Jon Lipsky, *Coming Up for Air: An AutoJAZZography* (Alliger Arts) and *King of the Jews* (Boston Playwrights Theatre)

**Design, Large Company:** Christine Jones (set) and Justin Townsend (lighting), *The Onion Cellar* (American Repertory Theatre)

**Design, Small/Midsize Company:** Dewey Dalley (sound), *Miss Witherspoon, 9 Parts of Desire* (Lyric Stage Company), and *The Women* (SpeakEasy Stage Company)

**Musical Performance:** Leigh Barrett, *Ragtime* (New Repertory Theatre) and *Souvenir* (Lyric Stage Company)

**Solo Performance:** Stan Strickland, *Coming Up for Air: An AutoJAZZography* (Alliger Arts)

**Actor, Large Company:** Michael Aronov, *Mauritius* (Huntington Theatre Company)

**Actor, Small/Midsized Company:** Larry Coen, *The Plexiglass Menagerie* (The Gold Dust Orphans), *Silent Night of the Lambs* (The Gold Dust Orphans), *Miss Witherspoon* (Lyric Stage Company), *The Taming of the Shrew* (Commonwealth Shakespeare Company), and *Samurai 7.0: Under Construction* (Beau Jest Moving Theatre)

**Actress: Large Company:** Joan MacIntosh, *Britannicus* (American Repertory Theatre)

**Actress, Small/Midsized Company:** Paula Plum, *Miss Witherspoon* (Lyric Stage Company)

**Norton Prize for Sustained Excellence:** Eugene Lee

**25th Anniversary Awards:** Mayor Thomas Menino, Robert Woodruff, American Repertory Theatre, Jon Platt, Jon Kimbell, North Shore Music Theatre; Special Citation: The Harvard Theater Collection


## THE EQUITY AWARDS

**St. Clair Bayfield Award** Established in 1973 in memory of Equity member St. Clair Bayfield, the Award honors the best performance by an actor in a Shakespearean play in the New York metropolitan area. **2006 Winner:** George Morfogen, *Richard II* (Classic Stage Company)

**Joe A. Callaway Award** Established by Equity member Joe A. Callaway in 1989 to encourage participation in the classics and non-profit theatre. **2006 Winners:** Lily Rabe, *Heartbreak House* (Roundabout Theatre Company); Michael Stuhlbarg, *The Voysey Inheritance* (Atlantic Theater Company)

**Clarence Derwent Awards** 63rd annual; Given to a female and male performer in a supporting role by Actors Equity Association, based on work in New York that demonstrates promise. **2007 Winners:** Leslie Kritzer, *Legally Blonde*; Lin-Manuel Miranda, *In the Heights*

**Lucy Jordan Award** Established in 1992 to honor the legacy of Lucy Finney Jordan, a former ballerina and chorus "gypsy" who, for many years, was the "face" of Actors' Equity in the Western Region as the Union's Outside Field Rep. The award is given to those who demonstrate a lifetime commitment to the theatre and especially, helping other theatre artists. **2006 Winner:** Don Toner, Austin Playhouse Managing Artistic Director and Producer

**Rosetta LeNoire Award** Established in 1988, the award was named in honor of the actress Rosetta LeNoire, who was also the first recipient, not only because of her body of work in the theatre - and her work with the then titled Actors' Equity Association's Ethnic Minorities Committee - but also for founding the AMAS Repertory Theatre Company. **2006 Winners:** Mia Katigbak and National Asian-American Theatre Company

**Paul Robeson Award** Established in 1974 to recognize a person who best exemplified the principles by which Mr. Robeson lived. It was created by donations from members of the acting profession. **2006 Winner:** Bill Cosby

**Richard Seff Award**  Established in 2003, this annual award is given to a male and female character actor who is 50 years old or older and who has been a member of the Actors' Equity for 25 years or longer, for the best performance in a featured or unfeatured supporting role in a Broadway or Off-Broadway production. **2006 Winners:** Jayne Houdyshell, *Well;* Jim Dale, *The Threepenny Opera*

**Roger Sturtevant Musical Theatre Award**  3rd Annual; established in 2005 in memory of Roger Sturtevant, a beloved box office treasurer and part-time casting director. This award is presented to Equity Membership Candidates who have demonstrated outstanding abilities in the musical theatre field. **2007 Winners:** Janine Romano, Scott Reardon

**Patrick Quinn Award**  1st Annual; Established in memory of beloved actor, humanitarian and former AEA President, Patrick Quinn who passed away in September, 2006; presented to a person who has worked tirelessly for the betterment of actors. **2007 Winner:** Jeanna Belkin, AEA Councilor

**ACCA Award**  1st Annual; Presented to an outstanding Broadway chorus. **2007 Winner:** *Legally Blonde*

## FRED EBB AWARD

November 28th, 2006; American Airlines Theatre Penthouse Lounge; 2nd annual. The Fred Ebb Award recognizes excellence in musical theatre songwriting, by a lyricist, composer, or songwriting team that has not yet achieved significant commercial success. The award is meant to encourage and support aspiring songwriters to create new works for the musical theatre. The prize includes a $50,000 award. **2006 Winner:** Robert L. Freedman and Steven Lutvak; Past Recipient: **2005:** John Bucchino

## GEORGE FREEDLEY MEMORIAL AWARD

Established in 1968 to honor the late George Freedley, theatre historian, critic, author, and first curator of the New York Public Library Theatre Collection, this award honors a work about live theatre published in or distributed in the United States during the previous year. **2006 Winner:** *The Masks of Anthony and Cleopatra* by Marvin Rosenberg; **Special Jury Prize:** *Lady in the Dark: Biography of a Musical* by Bruce D. McClung, and *Wagner and the Art of the Theatre* by Patrick Carnegy

## GEORGE JEAN NATHAN AWARD

With his preamble "it is my object and desire to encourage and assist in developing the art of drama criticism and the stimulation of intelligent playgoing," the late George Jean Nathan provided in his will for a prize known as the George Jean Nathan Award for Dramatic Criticism. The prize consists of the annual net income of half of Mr. Nathan's estate, which "shall be paid to the American who has written the best piece of drama criticism during the theatrical year (July 1 to June 30), whether it is an article, an essay, treatise or book." The award now amounts to $10,000 and in addition, the winner receives a trophy symbolic of, and attesting to, the award. **2005–2006 Winner:** Charles Isherwood of the New York Times

## GLAAD MEDIA AWARDS

March 26, 2007; Marriott Marquis; 18th annual. Presented by the Gay and Lesbian Alliance Against Defamation for fair, accurate and inclusive representations of gay individuals in the media as a means of eliminating homophobia and discrimination based on gender identity and sexual orientation.

**2007 Winners in the Theater: New York Theater – Broadway & Off-Broadway:** (tie) *25 Questions for a Jewish Mother* by Kate Moira Ryan, with Judy Gold; *The Little Dog Laughed* by Douglas Carter Beane; **New York Theater – Off-Off-Broadway:** *Candy and Dorothy* by David Johnston; **Los Angeles Theater:** *Bluebonnet Court* by Zsa Zsa Gershick

## HELEN HAYES AWARDS

Monday, April 16, 2007; The Warner Theatre; 23rd annual; Host: Jason Kravits. Presented by the Washington Theatre Awards Society in recognition of excellence in Washington, D.C. for the 2006–2007 Season.

**Play:** *Measure for Measure* (Folger Theatre)

**Musical:** *Caroline, or Change* (Studio Theatre)

**Lead Actress, Musical:** Julia Nixon, *Caroline, or Change* (Studio Theatre)

**Lead Actor, Musical:** Will Gartshore, *Assassins* (Signature Theatre)

**Lead Actress, Play:** Andrew Long, *Frozen* (Studio Theatre Second Stage)

**Lead Actor, Play:** Johanna Day, *The Rainmaker* (Arena Stage)

**Supporting Actress, Musical:** Donna Migliaccio, *Assassins* (Signature Theatre)

**Supporting Actor, Musical:** Andy Brownstein, *Assassins* (Signature Theatre)

**Supporting Actress, Play:** Kate Eastwood Norris, *A Midsummer Night's Dream* (Folger Theatre)

**Supporting Actor, Play:** Philip Goodwin, *An Enemy of the People* (The Shakespeare Theatre Company)

**Director, Play:** (tie) Michael Kahn, *Love's Labour's Lost* (The Shakespeare Theatre Company); Aaron Posner, *Measure for Measure* (Folger Theatre)

**Director, Musical:** Joe Calarco, *Assassins* (Signature Theatre)

**Set Design, Play or Musical:** James Kronzer, *The Beaux' Stratagem* (The Shakespeare Theatre Company)

**Costume Design, Play or Musical:** Catherine Zuber, *Love's Labour's Lost* (The Shakespeare Theatre Company)

**Lighting Design, Play or Musical:** Charlie Morrison, *The Elephant Man* (Theatre Center)

**Sound Design, Play or Musical:** Martin M. Neilson, *A Prayer for Owen Meany* (Round House Theatre)

**Musical Direction, Play or Musical:** George Fulginiti-Shakar, *Cabaret* (Arena Stage)

**Choreography:** Irina Tsikurishvili, *Frankenstein* (Synetic Theater)

**Ensemble:** *The Resistible Rise of Arturo Ui* (Catalyst Theater Company)

**Production, Non-resident:** *In the Continuum*, produced by Woolly Mammoth Theatre Company

**Lead Actress, Non-resident:** Danai Gurira, *In the Continuum* (Woolly Mammoth Theatre Company)

**Lead Actor, Non-resident:** David Burnham, *The Light in the Piazza* (National Tour)

**Supporting Performer, Non-resident:** Jeff Dumas, *Monty Python's Spamalot* (National Tour)

**Charles MacArthur Award for Outstanding New Play or Musical, Non-resident:** Renee Calarco, *Short Order Stories* (Charter Theatre Company)

## HENRY HEWES DESIGN AWARDS

November 9, 2006; Sardi's Restaurant; 42nd annual. Sponsored by the American Theatre Wing, these awards are presented for outstanding design originating in the U.S. for the 2005–2006 theatre season. The award (formerly known as the Maharam Theatre Design Award up until 1999) is named after the former theatre critic for the *Saturday Review* who passed away July 20, 2006. The awards are selected by a committee comprising of Jeffrey Eric Jenkins (chair), Tish Dace, Michael Feingold, Glenda Frank, Mario Fratti, Randy Gener, and Joan Ungaro.

**Scenic Design:** Allen Moyer, *Grey Gardens*

**Lighting Design:** Howell Binkley, *Jersey Boys*

**Costume Design:** Anita Yavich, *Measure for Pleasure*

**Notable Effects:** Ruppert Bohle (projections), Wang Bo & Stephen Kaplin (puppetry), *Cathay: Three Tales of China*

## IRNE AWARDS

Monday, March 19, 2007; Boston Center for the Arts. Founded in 1997 by Beverly Creasey and Larry Stark. Presented by The Independent Reviewers of New England for extraordinary theatre in the Boston area during the 2006 calendar year.

### Large Theatre

**Best New Play:** *Mauritius* by Theresa Rebeck (Huntington Theatre Company)

**Best Musical:** *Hairspray* (North Shore Music Theatre)

**Best Drama or Comedy:** *Mauritius* (Huntington Theatre Company)

**Set Design:** Eugene Lee, *Mauritius* (Huntington Theatre Company)

**Lighting:** Andre Joosten, *Wings of Desire* (A.R.T.)

**Costumes:** Erin Chainani, *Les Liaisons Dangereuses* (Huntington Theatre Company)

**Sound:** John A. Stone, *Ain't Misbehavin* & *Jesus Christ Superstar* (North Shore Music Theatre)

**Choreography:** Eileen Grace, *The Will Rogers Follies* (Reagle Players)

**Solo Performance:** Patti LuPone, *Lady with the Torch* (Reagle Players)

**Ensemble:** *Twelve Angry Men* (Roundabout Theatre Company National Tour/ Broadway Across America at the Colonial Theatre)

**Actress, Drama or Comedy:** Marin Ireland, *Mauritius* (Huntington Theatre Company)

**Actor, Drama or Comedy:** Remo Airaldi, *Island of Slaves* (A.R.T.)

**Supporting Actress, Drama or Comedy:** Geneva Carr, *Rabbit Hole* (Huntington Theatre Company)

**Supporting Actor, Drama or Comedy:** Anthony Chisholm, *Radio Golf* (Huntington Theatre Company)

**Actress, Musical:** Birdie Carroll, *Hairspray* (North Shore Music Theatre)

**Actor, Musical:** Jared Gertner, *The 25th Annual Putnam County Spelling Bee* (National Tour, J. Platt, Producer)

**Supporting Actress, Musical:** Maryann Zschau, *Thoroughly Modern Millie* (Reagle Players)

**Supporting Actor, Musical:** Joe Wilson, Jr., *Ain't Misbehavin'* (North Shore Music Theatre)

**Music Director:** Janet Roma, *The 25th Annual Putnam County Spelling Bee* (National Tour, J. Platt, Producer)

**Director, Musical:** Frank Roberts and Troy Magino, *Thoroughly Modern Millie* (Reagle Players)

**Director, Drama or Comedy:** Jerry Mouawad, *No Exit* (A.R.T.)

**Visiting Production:** *Twelve Angry Men* (Roundabout Theatre Company National Tour/Broadway Across America at the Colonial Theatre)

### Small Theatre

**Best New Play:** *Dark As a Thousand Midnights* by Jacqui Parker (Our Place Theatre Project at the African-American Theater Festival)

**Best Musical:** *Ragtime* (New Rep)

**Best Drama or Comedy:** *The Women* (SpeakEasy Stage Company)

**Set Design:** Janie E. Howland, *Five By Tenn* (SpeakEasy Stage Company)

**Lighting:** Karen Perlow, *Five By Tenn* (SpeakEasy Stage Company)

**Costumes:** Dewey Dellay, *Five By Tenn* (SpeakEasy Stage Company)

**Sound:** Gail A. Buckley, *The Women* & *Caroline, or Change* (SpeakEasy Stage Company)

**Choreography:** Josie Bray, *Little Shop of Horrors* (Animus Ensemble)

**Solo Performance:** Lanna Joffrey, *9 Parts of Desire* (Lyric Stage)

**Ensemble:** *The Women* (SpeakEasy Stage Company)

**Actress, Drama or Comedy:** Paula Plum, *The Goat, or Who Is Sylvia?* (Lyric Stage)

**Actor, Drama or Comedy:** Bates Wilder, *Frozen* (New Rep)

**Supporting Actress, Drama or Comedy:** Maureen Keller, *The Women* (SpeakEasy Stage Company)

**Supporting Actor, Drama or Comedy:** William Young, *Five By Tenn* (SpeakEasy Stage Company)

**Actress, Musical:** Jacqui Parker, *Caroline, or Change* (Speak Easy Stage Company)

**Actor, Musical:** Peter Carey, *1776* (Lyric Stage)

**Supporting Actress, Musical:** Merle Perkins, *Caroline, or Change* (Speak Easy Stage Company)

**Supporting Actor, Musical:** Timothy John Smith, *1776* (Lyric Stage)

**Music Director:** Todd Gordon, *Ragtime* (New Rep)

**Director, Musical:** Rick Lombardo, *Ragtime* (New Rep)

**Director, Drama or Comedy:** Scott Edmiston, *The Women* & *Five By Tenn* (SpeakEasy Stage Company)

**Visiting Production:** *The Two and Only* (Zero Arrow–A.R.T.)

## JONATHAN LARSON PERFORMING ARTS FOUNDATION AWARDS

Jonathan Larson's dream was to infuse musical theatre with a contemporary, joyful urban vitality. After twelve years of struggle as a classic "starving artist," his dream came true with the phenomenal success of *Rent*. To celebrate his creative spirit and honor his memory, Jonathan's family and friends created the Jonathan Larson Performing Arts Foundation. The mission of the Foundation is to provide financial support and encouragement to a new generation of musical theatre composers, lyricists, and bookwriters, as well as nonprofit theatre companies that develop and produce their work. **2007 Recipients:** Matt Gould, Melissa Li and Abe Rybeck, Robert Maddock, J. Oconer Navarro, Benj Pasek and Justin Paul, Mike Pettry, St. Ann's Warehouse

# JOSEPH JEFFERSON AWARDS

## Equity Wing Awards

October 29, 2007, at the North Shore Center for Performing Arts, Skokie, Illinois; 39th Annual. Presented for achievement in Chicago Equity theater from August 1, 2006–July 31, 2007; given by the Jefferson Awards Committee.

**New Work, Play:** *August: Osage County* by Tracy Letts (Steppenwolf Theatre Company)

**New Work, Musical:** *The Snow Queen* by Michael Smith and Frank Galati (Victory Gardens Theater)

**New Adaptation:** Mary Zimmerman, *Argonautika: The Voyage of Jason and the Argonauts* (Lookingglass Theatre Company)

**Production of a Play:** *August: Osage County,* produced by Steppenwolf Theatre Company

**Production of a Musical:** *Ragtime,* produced by Porchlight Music Theatre Chicago

**Production of a Revue:** *The All Night Strut,* produced by Marriott Theatre

**Director of a Play:** Anna D. Shapiro, *August: Osage County* (Steppenwolf)

**Director of Musical:** L. Walter Stearns, *Ragtime* (Porchlight Music Theatre)

**Director of a Revue:** Marc Robin, *The All Night Strut* (Marriott Theatre)

**Actor in a Principal Role, Play:** Ben Carlson, *Hamlet* (Chicago Shakespeare Theater)

**Actress in a Principal Role, Play:** Deanna Dunagan, *August: Osage County* (Steppenwolf)

**Actor in a Supporting Role, Play:** Maury Cooper, *The Price* (Shattered Globe Theatre)

**Actress in a Supporting Role, Play:** Penny Slusher, *Another Part of the Forest* (Writers Theatre)

**Actor in a Principal Role, Musical:** David Hess, *Shenandoah* (Marriott Theatre)

**Actress in a Principal Role, Musical:** Ernestine Jackson, *Raisin* (Court Theatre)

**Actor in a Supporting Role, Musical:** Aaron Graham, *Ragtime* (Porchlight Music Theatre)

**Actress in a Supporting Role, Musical:** Sara R. Sevigny, *Assassins* (Porchlight Music Theatre)

**Actress in a Revue:** Molly Andrews, *Fire on the Mountain* (Northlight Theatre)

**Actor in a Revue:** "Mississippi" Charles Bevel, *Fire on the Mountain* (Northlight Theatre)

**Ensemble:** *August: Osage County* (Steppenwolf Theatre Company)

**Scenic Design:** Todd Rosenthal, *August: Osage County* (Steppenwolf)

**Costume Design:** Mara Blumenfeld, *Mirror of the Invisible World* (Goodman Theatre)

**Lighting Design:** John Culbert, *Mirror of the Invisible World* (Goodman Theatre)

**Sound Design:** Richard Woodbury, *King Lear* (Goodman Theatre)

**Choreography:** Marc Robin, Beverly Durand, Mark Stuart Eckstein, Sylvia Hernandez-DiStasi, and Sasha Vargas, *The All Night Strut* (Marriott Theatre)

**Original Incidental Music:** Michael Bodeen, *Mirror of the Invisible World* (Goodman Theatre)

**Musical Direction:** Eugene Dizon, *Ragtime* (Porchlight Music Theatre)

**Cameo Performance:** Douglas Vickers, *The Best Man* (Remy Bumppo Theatre Company)

**Solo Performance:** Lance Stuart Baker, *Thom Pain* (Theatre Wit) and Matt Sax, *Clay* (Lookingglass Theatre Company and About Face Theatre)

**Other:** Michael Montenegro, Puppet Design, *The Puppetmaster of Lodz* (Writers Theatre)

## Non-Equity Awards

June 11, 2007, at the Park West; 33rd Annual. Formerly called the Citations, the Non-Equity Awards are for outstanding achievement in professional productions played from April 1, 2006–March 31, 2007 which played at Chicago theaters not operating under union contracts; given by the Jefferson Awards Committee.

**Production, Play:** (tie) *Blues for an Alabama Sky,* produced by Eclipse Theatre Company; *The Sparrow,* produced by The House Theatre of Chicago

**Production, Musical:** (tie) *Fiorello,* produced by TimeLine Theatre Company; *Side Show,* produced by Bohemian Theatre Ensemble

**Ensemble:** (tie) *Marathon '33* (Strawdog Theatre Company); *The Sparrow* (The House Theatre of Chicago)

**Director of a Play:** (tie) Nathan Allen, *The Sparrow* (The House Theatre of Chicago); Steven Fedoruk, *Blues for an Alabama Sky* (Eclipse Theatre Company)

**Director of a Musical or Revue:** (tie) Nick Bowling, *Fiorello* (TimeLine Theatre Company); Stephen M. Genovese, *Side Show* (Bohemian Theatre Ensemble)

**New Work, Play:** (tie) Chris Matthews, Jake Minton, Nathan Allen, *The Sparrow* (The House Theatre of Chicago); David Alan Moore, *In Times of War* (Stage Left Theatre)

**New Adaptation:** Frances Limoncelli, *Gaudy Night* (Lifeline Theatre)

**Actress in a Principal Role, Play:** (tie) Deborah Hearst, *Fat Pig,* Profiles Theatre; Michelle Courvais, *Boy Gets Girl* (Eclipse Theatre Company)

**Actor in a Principal Role, Play:** Peter Oyloe, *Equus* (Actors Workshop Theatre)

**Actress in a Supporting Role, Play:** (tie) Charlette Speigner, *Blues for an Alabama Sky* (Eclipse Theatre Company); Danica Ivancevic, *Faith Healer* (Uma Productions); Lindsay Weisberg, *One Fine Day* (Stage Left Theatre)

**Actor in a Supporting Role, Play:** Alfred Kemp, *Blues for an Alabama Sky* (Eclipse Theatre Company)

**Actress in a Principal Role, Musical or Revue:** (tie) Andrea Prestinario and Vanessa Panerosa, *Side Show* (Bohemian Theatre Ensemble); Cat Davis, *Mack and Mabel* (Circle Theatre)

**Actor in a Principal Role, Musical:** Michael Mahler, *My Favorite Year* (Bailiwick Repertory)

**Actress in a Supporting Role, Musical or Revue:** Danielle Brothers, *Flora the Red Menace* (Theo Ubique Theatre Company/Michael James)

**Actor in a Supporting Role Musical or Revue:** (tie) Eric Lindahl, *Side Show* (Bohemian Theatre Ensemble); Terry Hamilton, *Fiorello!* (TimeLine Theatre Company)

**Scenic Design:** Courtney O'Neill, *Mud* (The Hypocrites)

**Costume Design:** Jesus Perez, *Mack and Mabel* (Circle Theatre)

**Lighting Design:** Jared Moore, *Angels in America, Part Two: Perestroika* (The Hypocrites and Bailiwick Repertory)

**Sound Design:** Michael Griggs and Mikhail Fiksel, *Angels in America, Part Two: Perestroika* (The Hypocrites and Bailiwick Repertory)

**Choreography:** Tommy Rapley, *The Sparrow* (The House Theatre of Chicago)

**Original Incidental Music:** Kevin O'Donnell, *The Sparrow* (The House Theatre of Chicago)

**Musical Direction:** Doug Peck, *Fiorello!* (TimeLine Theatre Company)

**Fight Choreography:** Matt Hawkins, *Hatfield and McCoy* (The House Theatre of Chicago)

**Object Design:** *The Golden Truffle* (Redmoon Theater)

**Projections Design:** Lucas Merino, *The Sparrow* (The House Theatre of Chicago)

**Puppet Design:** Kass Copeland, *Once Upon a Time (or the Secret Language of Birds)* (Redmoon Theatre)


## KENNEDY CENTER

**Honors** 29th annual; December 3, 2006 (broadcast on CBS December 26, 2006); for distinguished achievement by individuals who have made significant contributions to American culture through the arts: Zubin Mehta, Dolly Parton, William "Smokey" Robinson, Steven Spielberg, and Andrew Lloyd Webber

**Mark Twain Prize** 9th annual; October 15, 2006 (Broadcast on PBS November 20, 2006); for American humor: Neil Simon


## KEVIN KLINE AWARDS

March 26, 2007; Roberts Orpheum Theatre; 2nd Annual; Host: Ken Page. Presented for outstanding achievement in professional theatre in the Greater St. Louis area for the 2006 calendar year; produced by The Professional Theatre Awards Council (Steve Isom, Executive Director); winners were selected by a floating pool of forty-five judges.

**Production of a Play:** *I Am My Own Wife* (Repertory Theatre of St. Louis)

**Director of a Play:** John Going, *I Am My Own Wife* (Repertory Theatre of St. Louis)

**Production of a Musical:** *Urinetown, the Musical* (Repertory Theatre of St. Louis)

**Director of a Musical:** Rob Ruggiero, *Urinetown, the Musical* (Repertory Theatre of St. Louis)

**Musical Direction:** Henry Palkes, *The Musical of Musicals – The Musical!* (Repertory Theatre of St. Louis)

**Choreography:** Pamela Hunt, *The Musical of Musicals – The Musical!* (Repertory Theatre of St. Louis)

**Costumes:** (tie) Marie Anne Chiment *Ace* (Repertory Theatre of St. Louis); Anne Kenney, *Urinetown, the Musical* (Repertory Theatre of St. Louis)

**Lighting:** Chris Akerlind, *Ace* (Repertory Theatre of St. Louis)

**Set:** David Korins, *Ace* (Repertory Theatre of St. Louis)

**Sound:** John H. Shivers, David Patridge, *Ace* (Repertory Theatre of St. Louis)

**New Play or Musical:** *Ace* by Richard Oberacker and Robert Taylor (Repertory Theatre of St. Louis)

**Ensemble in a Play:** *The Probe: An Inquiry in to the Meteoric Rise and Spectacular Fall of Orson Welles in Hollywood* (HotCity Theatre Company and Theatre de la Belle Bete)

**Ensemble in a Musical:** *Urinetown, the Musical* (Repertory Theatre of St. Louis)

**Lead Actor in a Musical:** Noah Galvin, *Ace* (Repertory Theatre of St. Louis)

**Lead Actor in a Play:** Arnie Burton, *I Am My Own Wife* (Repertory Theatre of St. Louis)

**Lead Actress in a Musical:** Jayne Paterson, *Urinetown, the Musical* (Repertory Theatre of St. Louis)

**Lead Actress in a Play:** Donna Weinsting, *From Door to Door* (New Jewish Theatre)

**Supporting Actor in a Musical:** Joneal Joplin, *Urinetown, the Musical* (Repertory Theatre of St. Louis)

**Supporting Actor in a Play:** Jim Butz, *Julius Caesar* (Shakespeare Festival of St. Louis)

**Supporting Actress in a Musical:** Sandie Rosa, *Urinetown, the Musical* (Repertory Theatre of St. Louis)

**Supporting Actress in a Play:** Lavonne Byers, *Polish Joke* (HotCity Theatre)

**Production for Young Audiences:** *You're A Good Man Charlie Brown* (Stages St. Louis)


## LOS ANGELES DRAMA CRITICS CIRCLE

March 19, 2007, at El Portal Theatre; 38th Annual; Host: Wenzel Jones. Presented for excellence in theatre in the Los Angeles and Orange County during the 2006 calendar year.

**Productions:** *Grace* by Craig Wright (Furious Theatre Company at Pasadena Playhouse Carrie Hamilton Theatre); *The Brothers Karamazov* Adapted by Anthony Clarvoe (Circle X Theatre Co. at [Inside] the Ford); *A Marvelous Party* (Laguna Playhouse)

**T.H. McCulloh Award for Best Revival:** *A Touch of the Poet* by Eugene O'Neill (A Noise Within)

**Direction:** John Langs, *The Brothers Karamazov* (Circle X Theatre Co. at [Inside] the Ford); Art Manke, *Bach at Leipzig* (South Coast Repertory); Michael Michetti, *A Picture of Dorian Gray* (The Theatre @ Boston Court); Dámaso Rodriguez, *Grace* (Furious Theatre Company at Pasadena Playhouse Carrie Hamilton Theatre)

**Writing:** Craig Wright, *Grace* (Furious Theatre Company at Pasadena Playhouse Carrie Hamilton Theatre)

**Adaptation:** Anthony Clarvoe, *The Brothers Karamazov* (Circle X Theatre Co. at [Inside] the Ford)

**Musical Direction:** Steven Smith, *A Man of No Importance* (Musical Theatre Guild at the Alex Theatre)

**Musical Score:** Lori Scarlett, *The Break Up Notebook: The Lesbian Musical* (Hudson Backstage Theatre)

**Choreography:** Janet Miller, *The Marvelous Wonderettes* (El Portal Forum Theatre)

**Lead Performance:** Dorie Barton, *Lobster Alice* (Blank Theatre Company's 2nd Stage Theatre); Jodi Carlisle, *A Hole in the Dark* (Blank Theatre Company's 2nd Stage Theatre); Laurence Fishburne, *Fences* (Pasadena Playhouse); Salome Jens, *Leipzig*, West Coast Jewish Theatre and The Group at Strasberg at The Lee Strasberg Institute's Marilyn Monroe Theatre); Cherry Jones, *Doubt* (Center Theatre Group – Ahmanson Theatre); Dan Mailley, *La Bête* (Sacred Fools Theater)

**Ensemble Performance:** *The Brothers Karamazov* (Circle X Theatre Co. at [Inside] the Ford); *The Marvelous Wonderettes* ((El Portal Forum Theatre)

**Solo Performance:** Lynn Redgrave, *Nightingale* (Center Theatre Group – Mark Taper Forum)

**Scenic Design:** Brian Sidney Bembridge, *The Brothers Karamazov* (Circle X Theatre Co. at [Inside] the Ford); Tom Buderwitz, *Equinox* (Odyssey Theatre)

**Lighting Design:** Brian Sidney Bembridge, *The Brothers Karamazov* (Circle X Theatre Co. at [Inside] the Ford); Robert Wilson, *The Black Rider: The Casting of the Magic Bullets* (Center Theatre Group – Ahmanson Theatre)

**Costumes/Hair/Wigs/Makeup Design:** Thomas G. Marquez, *Beehive* (Valley Musical Theatre at the El Portal Theatre)

**Sound Design:** Robbin E. Broad, *The Brothers Karamazov* (Circle X Theatre Co. at [Inside] the Ford); Jon Gottlieb, *iWitness* (Center Theatre Group – Mark Taper Forum); Robert Oriol, *A Picture of Dorian Gray* (The Theatre @ Boston Court)

**Margaret Harford Award** (for Sustained Excellence in Theatre): Troubadour Theater Company

**Polly Warfield Award** (for outstanding single season by a small to mid-sized theatre): Chance Theater

**Ted Schmitt Award** (for outstanding world premiere play in Los Angeles): Richard Montoya, *Water and Power* (Culture Clash)

**Angstrom Award** (for career achievement in lighting design): Christian Epps

**Joel Hirschhorn Award** (for outstanding achievement in musical theatre): Gerald Sternbach

**Bob Z Award** (for outstanding achievement in set design): Joel David

**Comedy/Improv Duo or Group:** The Next Big Broadway Musical

**Revue/Special Production:** *Johnny Mercer Sings – The Songs He Didn't Write*

**Variety Production/Recurring Series:** Trudi Mann's Fabulous Open Mic for Singers

**Piano Bar/Restaurant Singing Entertainer:** Leslie Anderson

**Piano Bar/Restaurant Instrumentalist:** Jerry Scott

**Singer/Songwriter:** John Wallowitch

**Musical Director:** Ted Firth

**Director:** Lina Koutrakos

**Technical Director:** Jean-Pierre Perreaux

**Song:** "Beautiful Mistake" music by John Bucchino, lyrics by Amanda McBroom

**Special Musical Material:** "Not Another Cabaret," words and music by Jason Wynn

**Recording:** Barbara Fasano, *Written in the Stars*

**Jazz Recording:** Mary Foster Conklin, *Blues for Breakfast: Remembering Matt Dennis*

**Hanson Award:** Leslie Orofino

## MAC AWARDS

Tuesday, May 01, 2007; B.B. King's; 21st Annual. Presented annually by the Manhattan Association of Cabarets and Clubs to honor achievements in cabaret, comedy, jazz, and live entertainment in the previous year.

**2007 Board of Directors Awards:** Lincoln Center American Songbook Series, Karen Mason, Seth Rudetsky's Broadway Chatterbox

**Time Out New York Special Achievement Award:** Leslie Kritzer, *Leslie Kritzer Is Patti LuPone at Les Mouches*

**Lifetime Achievement Awards:** Dody Goodman, Jan Wallman

**Female Vocalist:** Barbara Fasano

**Male Vocalist:** Patrick DeGennaro

**Female Jazz Vocalist:** Laurie Krauz

**Male Jazz Vocalist:** John De Marco

**Major Jazz Vocalist:** Judy Barnett

**Major Artist, Female:** Lina Koutrakos

**Major Artist, Male:** Billy Stritch

**New York Debut-Female:** Esther Beckman

**New York Debut-Male:** Rob Langeder

**Cabaret Comedy/Musical Comedy, Female:** Kristine Zbornik

**Cabaret Comedy/Musical Comedy, Male:** Jay Rogers

**Impersonation:** Jimmi James

**Stand-up Comic, Female:** Poppi Kramer

**Stand-up Comic, Male:** Michael Brill

**Major Stand-up Comic-Female:** Julie Goldman

**Major Stand-up Comic-Male:** Greg Giraldo

**Musical Comedy Duo or Group/Special Production:** Thomas Honeck, *Dreaming Wide Awake*

**Jazz Duo or Group:** Barry Levitt Quartet

**Vocal Duo or Group:** Eric Comstock & Barbara Fasano

## MARGO JONES CITIZEN OF THE THEATER MEDAL

Presented by the Ohio State University Libraries and College of the Arts to a citizen of the theater who has made a lifetime commitment to the theater in the United States and has demonstrated an understanding and affirmation of the craft of playwriting. There was no award presented this season.

**Past Recipients: 1961:** Lucille Lortel **1962:** Michael Ellis **1963:** Judith Rutherford Marechal; George Savage (university award) **1964:** Richard Barr; Edward Albee and Clinton Wilder; Richard A. Duprey (university award) **1965:** Wynn Handman; Marston Balch (university award) **1966:** Jon Jory; Arthur Ballet (university award) **1967:** Paul Baker; George C. White (workshop award) **1968:** Davey Marlin-Jones; Ellen Stewart (workshop award) **1969:** Adrian Hall; Edward Parone and Gordon Davidson (workshop award) **1970:** Joseph Papp **1971:** Zelda Fichandler **1972:** Jules Irving **1973:** Douglas Turner Ward **1974:** Paul Weidner **1975:** Robert Kalfin **1976:** Gordon Davidson **1977:** Marshall W. Mason **1978:** Jon Jory **1979:** Ellen Stewart **1980:** John Clark Donahue **1981:** Lynne Meadow **1982:** Andre Bishop **1983:** Bill Bushnell **1984:** Gregory Mosher **1985:** John Lion **1986:** Lloyd Richards **1987:** Gerald Chapman **1988:** no award **1989:** Margaret Goheen **1990:** Richard Coe **1991:** Otis L. Guernsey Jr. **1992:** Abbot Van Nostrand **1993:** Henry Hewes **1994:** Jane Alexander **1995:** Robert Whitehead **1996:** Al Hirschfeld **1997:** George C. White **1998:** James Houghton **1999:** George Keathley **2000:** Eileen Heckart **2001:** Mel Gussow **2002:** Emilie S. Kilgore **2003-2004:** Christopher Durang and Marsha Norman **2005-2006:** Jerome Lawrence and Robert E. Lee

## MUSICAL THEATER HALL OF FAME

This organization was established at New York University on November 10, 1993. Inductees: Harold Arlen, Irving Berlin, Leonard Bernstein, Eubie Blake, Abe Burrows, George M. Cohan, Betty Comden, Dorothy Fields, George Gershwin, Ira Gershwin, Adolph Green, Oscar Hammerstein II, E.Y. Harburg, Larry Hart, Jerome Kern, Burton Lane, Alan Jay Lerner, Frank Loesser, Frederick Loewe, Mary Martin, Ethel Merman, Cole Porter, Jerome Robbins, Richard Rodgers, Harold Rome.

## NATIONAL ARTS CLUB AWARDS

### Joseph Kesselring Fellowship and Honors

National Arts Club member Joseph Otto Kesselring was born in New York in 1902. He was an actor, author, producer, and playwright. Mr. Kesselring died in 1967, leaving his estate in a trust, which terminated in 1978 when the life beneficiary died. A bequest was made to the National Arts Club "on condition that said bequest be used to establish a fund to be known as the Joseph Kesselring Fund, the income and principal of which shall be used to give financial aid to playwrights, on such a basis of selection and to such as the National Arts Club may, in its sole discretion, determine." A committee appointed by the president and the governors of the National Arts Club administers the Kesselring Prizes. It approves monetary prizes annually to playwrights nominated by qualified production companies whose dramatic work has demonstrated the highest possible merit and promise and is deserving of greater recognition, but who as yet has not received prominent national notice or acclaim in the theater. The winners are chosen by a panel of judges who are independent of the Club. In addition to a cash prize, the first prize winner also receives a staged reading of a work of his or her choice. In the fall of 2007, the Club redefined the award to consist of the Kesselring Fellowship, and created a new category called the Kesselring Honors. 2007 Committee Members: O. Aldon James, Stanley Morton Ackert III, Arnold J. Davis, Michael Parva, Jason deMontmorency, Dary Derchin, Alexandra Roosevelt Dworkin, John T. James, Raymond Knowles.

**2007 Fellowship Winner:** Jordan Harrison; **2007 Honors:** Will Eno, Rinne Groff, Marcus Gardley

**Previous Fellowship Recipients: 1980:** Susan Charlotte **1981:** Cheryl Hawkins **1982:** No Award **1983:** Lynn Alvarez **1984:** Philip Kan Gotanda **1985:** Bill Elverman **1986:** Marlane Meyer **1907:** Paul Schmidt **1988:** Diane Ney **1989:** Jo Carson **1990:** Elizabeth Egloff, Mel Shapiro **1991:** Tony Kushner **1992:** Marion Isaac McClinton **1993:** Anna Deavere Smith **1994:** Nicky Silver **1995:** Amy Freed, Doug Wright **1996:** Naomi Wallace **1997:** No Award **1998:** Kira Obolensky **1999:** Heather McDonald **2000:** David Auburn **2001:** David Lindsay-Abaire **2002:** Melissa James Gibson **2003:** Bridget Carpenter **2004:** Tracey Scott Wilson **2005:** Deb Margolin **2006:** Mark Schultz

**Previous Honors Recipients** (if year is missing none was presented): **1980:** Carol Lashof **1981:** William Hathaway **1983:** Constance Congdon **1985:** Laura Harrington **1986:** John Leicht **1987:** Januzsz Glowacki **1988:** Jose Rivera, Frank Hogan **1989:** Keith Reddin **1990:** Howard Korder **1991:** Quincy Long, Scott McPherson **1992:** José Rivera **1993:** Han Ong **1996:** Nilo Cruz **1997:** Kira Obolensky, Edwin Sanchez **1998:** Erik Ehn **1999:** Stephen Dietz **2000:** Jessica Hagedorn **2001:** Dael Orlandersmith **2002:** Lydia Diamond **2003:** Lynn Nottage **2004:** John Borello **2005:** Tanya Barfield **2006:** Bruce Norris

### Medal of Honor

Presented by the National Arts Club for outstanding service in the arts. **2006– 2007 Winners:** Barbara Cook, Actress and Singer; Albert Maysles and the creative team behind the musical *Grey Gardens;* Tony Walton, Stage Director and Designer

### National Medals of the Arts

For individuals who and organizations that have made outstanding contributions to the excellence, growth, support, and availability of the arts in the United States, selected by the President of the United States from nominees presented by the National Endowment. **2006 Winners**: William Bolcom, Cyd Charisse, Roy DeCarava, Wilhelmina Holladay, Interlochen Center for the Arts, Erich Kunzel, Preservation Hall Jazz Band, Gregory Rabassa, Viktor Schreckengost, Ralph Stanley

## NEW DRAMATISTS LIFETIME ACHIEVEMENT AWARD

To an individual who has made an outstanding artistic contribution to the American theater. **2007 Winner:** Edward Albee

## NEW YORK INNOVATIVE THEATRE AWARDS

3rd Annual; September 24, 2007, at FIT's Haft Auditorium. Presented annually to honor individuals and organizations who have achieved artistic excellence in the Off-Off-Broadway theatre. The New York IT Awards committee recognizes the unique and essential role Off-Off-Broadway plays in contributing to American and global culture, and believes that publicly recognizing excellence in independent theatre will expand audience awareness and appreciation of the full New York theatre experience. Staff: Jason Bowcutt, Executive Director; Shay Gines, Executive Director; Nick Micozzi, Executive Director; Awards Committee: Paul Adams (Artistic Director, Emerging Artists Theatre), Dan Bacalzo (Managing Editor, Theatermania), Christopher Borg (Actor, Director), Jason Bowcutt (Executive Director, New York IT Awards), Tim Errickson (Artistic Director, Boomerang Theatre Co.), Thecla Farrell (Outreach Coordinator, Castillo Theatre Co.), Constance Congdon (Playwright), Shay Gines, (Executive Director, New York IT Awards), Ben Hodges (Editor in Chief, *Theatre World),* Leonard Jacobs (National Theatre Editor, *Back Stage),* Ron Lasko (Public Relations, Spin Cycle), Blake Lawrence, Bob Lee, Nick Micozzi (Executive Director, New York IT Awards), Risa Shoup, (Programming Director, Chashama), Nicky Paraiso (Curator for Performance, La MaMa E.T.C.), Jeff Riebe (The January Initiative), Akia Squiterri (Artistic Director, Rising Sun Performance Company).

**Outstanding Actor in a Featured Role:** Joe Plummer, *As You Like It* (poortom productions)

**Outstanding Actress in a Featured Role:** Boo Killebrew, *6969* (CollaborationTown)

**Outstanding Solo Performance:** Mike Houston, *The Ledge,* (eavesdrop)

**Outstanding Original Short Script:** Daniel Reitz, *Rules of the Universe,* (Rising Phoenix Repertory)

**Outstanding Original Full-Length Script:** Saviana Stanescu, *Waxing West* (East Coast Artists)

**Outstanding Original Music:** Leanne Darling, *The Landlord* (Toy Box Theatre Company)

**Outstanding Choreography/Movement:** Dan Safer, *Dancing vs. the Rat Experiment* (La MaMa E.T.C. in association with Witness Relocation)

**Outstanding Sound Design:** Ryan Maeker and Tim Schellenbaum, *Dancing vs. the Rat Experiment* (La MaMa E.T.C. in association with Witness Relocation)

**Outstanding Costume Design:** David Withrow, *Bug Boy Blues* (The Looking Glass Theatre)

**Outstanding Lighting Design:** Peter Hoerburger, *The Present Perfect* (The Operating Theater)

**Outstanding Set Design:** George Allison, *Picasso at the Lapin Agile* (T. Schreiber Studio)

**Outstanding Actress in a Lead Role:** Susan Louise O'Connor, *the silent concerto* (Packawallop Productions)

**Outstanding Actor in a Lead Role:** Max Rosenak, *6969* (CollaborationTown)

**Outstanding Director:** Daniel Talbott, *Rules of the Universe* (Rising Phoenix Repertory

**Outstanding Ensemble:** *6969* (CollaborationTown); Boo Killebrew, Julia Lowrie Henderson, Ryan Purcell, Max Rosenak, Phillip Taratula, Daniel Walker Stowell

**Outstanding Performance Art Production:** *Dancing vs. The Rat Experiment* (La MaMa E.T.C. in association with Witness Relocation)

**Outstanding Production of a Musical:** *Urinetown, the Musical* (The Gallery Players)

**Outstanding Production of a Play:** *Buoffon Glass Menajoree* (Ten Directions)

**Artistic Achievement Award:** Doric Wilson

**Stewardship Award:** Alliance of Resident Theatres/New York

**Caffe Cino Fellowship Award** ($1,000 grant): Rising Phoenix Repertory

## OTTO RENÉ CASTILLO AWARDS

Monday, May 21, 2007; Castillo Theatre All Stars Project; 9th annual. Presented to artists for and theatres from around the world in recognition for contributions to Political Theatre. The Otto Award is named for the Guatemalan poet and revolutionary Otto Rene Castillo, who was murdered by that country's military junta in 1968. **2007 Winners:** Cornerstone Theater Company, Dah Teatar, International WOW Company, Ellen Stewart of La MaMa E.T.C.

## OVATION AWARDS

Orpheum Theatre; November 12, 2007; Host: Neil Patrick Harris. Established in 1989, the L.A. Stage Alliance Ovation Awards are Southern California's premiere awards for excellence in theatre for the 2006–2007 season.

**World Premiere Play:** *Film Chinois* by Damon Chau (Grove Theatre Center)

**World Premiere Musical:** *Sleeping Beauty Wakes* by Rachel Sheinkin, Brendan Milburn, and Valerie Vigoda (Center Theatre Group and Deaf West Theatre)

**Touring Production:** *Jersey Boys* (Center Theatre Group)

**Lead Actor in a Play:** Alan Mandell, *Trying* (The Colony Theatre Company)

**Lead Actress in a Play:** Judy Kaye, *Souvenir* (Richmark Entertainment and Janice Montana)

**Lead Actor in a Musical:** Hershey Felder, *Hershey Felder as George Gershwin Alone* (Geffen Playhouse)

**Lead Actress in a Musical:** Michelle Duffy, *Can-Can* (Pasadena Playhouse)

**Featured Actor in a Play:** (tie) Hugo Armstrong, *Bleed Rail* (The Theatre @ Boston Court); Dan Alemshah, *The Fat of the Land* (The New Theatre)

**Featured Actress in a Play:** Judith Moreland, *Miss Julie* (Fountain Theatre)

**Featured Actor in a Musical:** David Engel, *Can-Can* (Geffen Playhouse)

**Featured Actress in a Musical:** Vicki Lewis, *Hotel C'est L'Amour* (The Blank Theatre Company)

**Solo Performance:** Dael Orlandersmith, *The Gimmick,* (Fountain Theatre)

**Ensemble Performance:** The cast of *Jitney* (Stagewalker Productions)

**Director of a Play:** Stuart Rogers, *The Long Christmas Ride Home* (Theatre Tribe)

**Director of a Musical:** David Lee, *Can-Can* (Pasadena Playhouse)

**Choreographer:** Lee Martino, *On Your Toes* (Reprise! Broadway's Best)

**Musical Direction:** (tie) Dan Wheetman, *Back Home Again: A John Denver Holiday Concert* (Rubicon Theatre Company and Harold Thau Productions); Brendan Milburn, *Sleeping Beauty Wakes* (Center Theatre Group)

**Play:** Intimate theatre: *Jitney* by August Wilson (Stagewalker Productions); Large theatre: *Souvenir* by Stephen Temperley (Richmark Entertainment and Janice Montana)

**Musical:** Intimate theatre: *The Marvelous Wonderettes* by Roger Bean (El Portal Theatre); Large theatre: *Hershey Felder as George Gershwin Alone* (Geffen Playhouse)

**Set Design:** Intimate theatre: Tom Buderwitz, *Paradise Lost: Shadows and Wings* (The Theatre @ Boston Court); Large theatre: (tie) Roy Christopher, *Can-Can* (Pasadena Playhouse); Keith Mitchell, *The Value of Names* (Falcon Theatre)

**Lighting Design:** Intimate theatre: Steven Young, *Paradise Lost: Shadows and Wings* (The Theatre @ Boston Court); Large theatre: Michael Gilliam, *Hershey Felder as George Gershwin Alone* (Geffen Playhouse)

**Sound Design:** Intimate theatre: Martin Carrillo, *Paradise Lost: Shadows and Wings* (The Theatre @ Boston Court); Large theatre: Jon Gottlieb, *Hershey Felder as George Gershwin Alone* (Geffen Playhouse)

**Costume Design:** Intimate theatre: Audrey Fisher, *Tryst* (Black Dahlia Theatre); Large theatre: Tracy Christiansen, *Souvenir* (Richmark Entertainment and Janice Montana)

**The Career Achievement Award:** Annette Bening

**The James A. Doolittle Leadership in Theatre Award:** Community Redevelopment Agency of the City of Los Angeles

**Community Outreach Award:** The Actors Fund

## PITTSBURGH CIVIC LIGHT OPERA'S RICHARD RODGERS AWARD

June 2, 2007; Hilton Hotel, Pittsburgh; founded in 1988; recognizes the lifetime contributions of outstanding talents in musical theatre; Presented by The Pittsburgh Civic Light Opera in conjunction with the families of Richard Rodgers and Oscar Hammerstein II. **2007 Recipient:** Shirley Jones

**Past Recipients: 1988:** Mary Martin **1989:** Dame Julie Andrews **1991:** Harold Prince **1992:** Sir Cameron Mackintosh **1993:** Stephen Sondheim **1996:** Lord Andrew Lloyd Webber **2000:** Gwen Verdon **2002:** Bernadette Peters

## PRINCESS GRACE AWARDS

November 2, 2006; Cipriani on 42nd Street, New York; 24th Annual. Presented by the Princess Grace Foundation – USA, for excellence in theatre, dance, and film across the United States. **2006 Winners in Theatre:** Adam Rapp (Playwright), Suzanne Agins (Williamstown Theatre Festival), Alice Reagan (Target Margin Theatre), Christopher Brown (lighting designer of Mud/Bone), Maureen Towey (Director, Sojourn Theatre), Chi-wang Yang (Director, California Institute of the Arts), James McManus (Playwright, New Dramatists), Michael Braun (Actor, Yale School of Drama).

## RICHARD RODGERS AWARDS

For staged readings of musicals in nonprofit theaters, administered by the American Academy of Arts and Letters and selected by a jury including Stephen Sondheim (chairman), Lynn Ahrens, John Guare, Sheldon Harnick, Jeanine Tesori, and John Weidman. **2007 Winners:** *Calvin Berger* by Barry Wyner; *Main-Traveled Roads* by Paul Libman and Dave Hudson

## ROBERT WHITEHEAD AWARD

For outstanding achievement in commercial theatre producing, bestowed on a graduate of the fourteen-week Commercial Theatre Institute Program who has demonstrated a quality of production exemplified by the late producer, Robert Whitehead. The Commercial Theatre Institute (Jed Bernstein, Director) is the nation's only formal program that professionally trains commercial theatre producers. It is a joint project of the League of American Theatres and Producers, Inc., and Theatre Development Fund. There was no award presented in 2007.

**Previous Recipients**: **1993:** Susan Quint Gallin; Benjamin Mordecai **1994:** Dennis Grimaldi **1995:** Kevin McCollum **1996:** Randall L. Wreghitt **1997:** Marc Routh **1998:** Liz Oliver **1999:** Eric Krebs **2000:** Anne Strickland Squadron **2001–2003:** No Award **2004:** David Binder **2005–2006:** No Award

## SOCIETY OF STAGE DIRECTORS AND CHOREOGRAPHERS (SSDC) AWARDS

**Mr. Abbot Award** Lifetime achievement honor presented exclusively for directors and choreographers annually. **2007 Recipient:** Daniel Sullivan

**Callaway Award** Also known as the "Joey," this award, created in 1989, is issued for excellence in the craft of direction and/or choreography for Off and Off-Off-Broadway. **2006–2007 Winners:** Thomas Kail and Andy Blankenbuehler, *In the Heights*

## SUSAN SMITH BLACKBURN PRIZE

February 26, 2007; New York City; 29th annual; Presenter: Marsha Norman. Presented to women who have written works of outstanding quality for the English-speaking theater. The Prize is administered in Houston, London, and New York by a board of directors who chooses six judges each year. 2006–2007 Judges: Jill Clayburgh, Oskar Eustis, Deborah Findlay, John Guare, Alastair Macaulay, Anna Mackmin. This year, four finalists were chosen to split the top award, each receiving $4,000. Other finalists received $1,000. **2007 Top Finalists:** Lucy Caldwell, *Leaves;* Sheila Callaghan, *Dead City;* Stella Feehily, *O Go My Man,* and Abbie Spallen, *Pumpgirl;* **Other Finalists:** Julia Cho, *The Piano Teacher;* Katie Douglas, *Rust;* Amy Fox, *One Thing I Like to Say Is;* Julia Jordan, *Dark Yellow;* C. Michèle Kaplan; *'Bot;* Nell Leyshon, *Comfort Me With Apples;* Tamsin Oglesby, *The War Next Door;* Francine Volpe, *The Given*

## THEATRE DEVELOPMENT FUND AWARDS

**Astaire Awards** Established in 1982 by the Anglo-American Contemporary Dance Foundation and administered by Theatre Development Fund since 1991, these awards recognize outstanding achievement in dance on Broadway each season. No award was presented this season.

**Irene Sharaff Awards** Founded in 1993 to pay tribute to the art of costume design, this annual award presentation has become an occasion for the costume design community to come together to honor its own. The winners of the five awards are decided upon by the TDF Costume Collection Advisory Committee. **2007 Winners: Lifetime Achievement Award:** Bob Mackie; **Young Master Award:** Murell Horton; **Artisan Award:** Kermit Love; **Memorial Tribute:** Rouben Ter-Arutunian; **The Robert L.B. Tobin Award:** Santo Loquasto

## THE THEATER HALL OF FAME

January 29, 2007; Gershwin Theatre; 36th Annual; Host: Phylicia Rashad. The Theater of Hall of Fame was created in 1971 to honor those who have made outstanding contributions to the American theater in a career spanning at least twenty-five years, with at least five major credits.

**2007 Inductees:** Brian Friel, George Hearn, Willa Kim, Eugene Lee, Patti LuPone, Wendy Wasserstein, August Wilson, Elizabeth Wilson.

**Previous Inductees:** George Abbott, Maude Adams, Viola Adams, Stella Adler, Edward Albee, Theoni V. Aldredge, Ira Aldridge, Jane Alexander, Mary Alice, Winthrop Ames, Judith Anderson, Maxwell Anderson, Robert Anderson, Julie Andrews, Margaret Anglin, Jean Anouilh, Harold Arlen, George Arliss, Boris Aronson, Adele Astaire, Fred Astaire, Eileen Atkins, Brooks Atkinson, Lauren Bacall, Pearl Bailey, George Balanchine, William Ball, Anne Bancroft, Tallulah Bankhead, Richard Barr, Philip Barry, Ethel Barrymore, John Barrymore, Lionel Barrymore, Howard Bay, Nora Bayes, John Lee Beatty, Julian Beck, Samuel Beckett, Brian Bedford, S.N. Behrman, Norman Bel Geddes, David Belasco, Michael Bennett, Richard Bennett, Robert Russell Bennett, Eric Bentley, Irving Berlin, Sarah Bernhardt, Leonard Bernstein, Earl Blackwell, Kermit Bloomgarden, Jerry Bock, Ray Bolger, Edwin Booth, Junius Brutus Booth, Shirley Booth, Philip Bosco, Alice Brady, Bertolt Brecht, Fannie Brice, Peter Brook, John Mason Brown, Robert Brustein, Billie Burke, Abe Burrows, Richard Burton, Mrs. Patrick Campbell, Zoe Caldwell, Eddie Cantor, Len Cariou, Morris Carnovsky, Mrs. Leslie Carter, Gower Champion, Frank Chanfrau, Carol Channing, Stockard Channing, Ruth Chatterton, Paddy Chayefsky, Anton Chekhov, Ina Claire, Bobby Clark, Harold Clurman, Lee J. Cobb, Richard L. Coe, George M. Cohan, Alexander H. Cohen, Jack Cole, Cy Coleman, Constance Collier, Alvin Colt, Betty Comden, Marc Connelly, Barbara Cook, Katharine Cornell, Noel Coward, Jane Cowl, Lotta Crabtree, Cheryl Crawford, Hume Cronyn, Russel Crouse, Charlotte Cushman, Jean Dalrymple, Augustin Daly, Graciela Daniele, E.L. Davenport, Gordon Davidson, Ossie Davis, Ruby Dee, Alfred De Liagre Jr., Agnes DeMille, Colleen Dewhurst, Howard Dietz, Dudley Digges, Melvyn Douglas, Eddie Dowling, Alfred Drake, Marie Dressler, John Drew, Mrs. John Drew, William Dunlap, Mildred Dunnock, Charles Durning, Eleanora Duse, Jeanne Eagles, Fred Ebb, Ben Edwards, Florence Eldridge, Lehman Engel, Maurice Evans, Abe Feder, Jose Ferber, Cy Feuer, Zelda Fichandler, Dorothy Fields, Herbert Fields, Lewis Fields, W.C. Fields, Jules Fisher, Minnie Maddern Fiske, Clyde Fitch, Geraldine Fitzgerald, Henry Fonda, Lynn Fontanne, Horton Foote, Edwin Forrest, Bob Fosse, Rudolf Friml, Charles Frohman, Robert Fryer, Athol Fugard, Eva Le Gallienne, John Gassner, Larry Gelbart, Peter Gennaro, Bernard Gersten, Grace George, George Gershwin, Ira Gershwin, William Gibson, John Gielgud, W.S. Gilbert, Jack Gilford, William Gillette, Charles Gilpin, Lillian Gish, John Golden, Max Gordon, Ruth Gordon, Adolph Green, Paul Green, Charlotte Greenwood, Jane Greenwood, Joel Grey, Tammy Grimes, George Grizzard, John Guare, Otis L. Guernsey Jr., A.R. Gurney, Tyrone Guthrie, Uta Hagen, Sir Peter Hall, Lewis Hallam, T. Edward Hambleton, Oscar Hammerstein II, Walter Hampden, Otto Harbach, E.Y. Harburg, Sheldon Harnick, Edward Harrigan, Jed Harris, Julie Harris, Rosemary Harris, Sam H. Harris, Rex Harrison, Kitty Carlisle Hart, Lorenz Hart, Moss Hart, Tony Hart, June Havoc, Helen Hayes, Leland Hayward, Ben Hecht, Eileen Heckart, Theresa Helburn, Lillian Hellman, Katharine Hepburn, Victor Herbert, Jerry Herman, James A. Herne, Henry Hewes, Gregory Hines, Al Hirschfeld, Raymond Hitchcock, Hal Holbrook, Celeste Holm, Hanya Holm, Arthur Hopkins, De Wolf Hopper, John Houseman, Eugene Howard, Leslie Howard, Sidney Howard, Willie Howard, Barnard Hughes, Henry Hull, Josephine Hull, Walter Huston, Earle Hyman, Henrik Ibsen, William Inge, Bernard B. Jacobs, Elise Janis, Joseph Jefferson, Al Jolson, James Earl Jones, Margo Jones, Robert Edmond Jones, Tom Jones, Jon Jory, Raul Julia, Madeline Kahn, John Kander, Garson Kanin, George S. Kaufman, Danny Kaye, Elia Kazan, Gene Kelly, George Kelly, Fanny Kemble, Jerome Kern, Walter Kerr, Michael Kidd, Richard Kiley, Sidney Kingsley, Kevin Kline, Florence Klotz, Joseph Wood Krutch, Bert Lahr, Burton Lane, Frank Langella, Lawrence Langner, Lillie Langtry, Angela Lansbury, Charles Laughton, Arthur Laurents, Gertrude Lawrence, Jerome Lawrence, Ming Cho Lee, Robert E. Lee, Lotte Lenya, Alan Jay Lerner, Sam Levene, Robert Lewis, Beatrice Lillie, Howard Lindsay, John Lithgow, Frank Loesser, Frederick Loewe,

Joshua Logan, William Ivey Long, Santo Loquasto, Pauline Lord, Lucille Lortel, Dorothy Loudon, Alfred Lunt, Charles MacArthur, Steele MacKaye, Judith Malina, David Mamet, Rouben Mamoulian, Richard Mansfield, Robert B. Mantell, Frederic March, Nancy Marchand, Julia Marlowe, Ernest H. Martin, Mary Martin, Raymond Massey, Elizabeth Ireland McCann, Ian McKellen, Siobhan McKenna, Terrence McNally, Helen Menken, Burgess Meredith, Ethel Merman, David Merrick, Jo Mielziner, Arthur Miller, Marilyn Miller, Liza Minnelli, Helena Modjeska, Ferenc Molnar, Lola Montez, Victor Moore, Robert Morse, Zero Mostel, Anna Cora Mowatt, Paul Muni, Brian Murray, Tharon Musser, George Jean Nathan, Mildred Natwick, Nazimova, Patricia Neal, James M. Nederlander, Mike Nichols, Elliot Norton, Sean O'Casey, Clifford Odets, Donald Oenslager, Laurence Olivier, Eugene O'Neill, Jerry Orbach, Geraldine Page, Joseph Papp, Estelle Parsons, Osgood Perkins, Bernadette Peters, Molly Picon, Harold Pinter, Luigi Pirandello, Christopher Plummer, Cole Porter, Robert Preston, Harold Prince, Jose Quintero, Ellis Rabb, John Raitt, Tony Randall, Michael Redgrave, Ada Rehan, Elmer Rice, Lloyd Richards, Ralph Richardson, Chita Rivera, Jason Robards, Jerome Robbins, Paul Robeson, Richard Rodgers, Will Rogers, Sigmund Romberg, Harold Rome, Lillian Russell, Donald Saddler, Gene Saks, William Saroyan, Joseph Schildkraut, Harvey Schmidt, Alan Schnider, Gerald Schoenfeld, Arthur Schwartz, Maurice Schwartz, George C. Scott, Marian Seldes, Irene Sharaff, George Bernard Shaw, Sam Shepard, Robert F. Sherwood, J.J. Shubert, Lee Shubert, Herman Shumlin, Neil Simon, Lee Simonson, Edmund Simpson, Otis Skinner, Maggie Smith, Oliver Smith, Stephen Sondheim, E.H. Sothern, Kim Stanley, Jean Stapleton, Maureen Stapleton, Frances Sternhagen, Roger L. Stevens, Isabelle Stevenson, Ellen Stewart, Dorothy Stickney, Fred Stone, Peter Stone, Tom Stoppard, Lee Strasburg, August Strindberg, Elaine Stritch, Charles Strouse, Jule Styne, Margaret Sullivan, Arthur Sullivan, Jessica Tandy, Laurette Taylor, Ellen Terry, Sada Thompson, Tommy Tune, Gwen Verdon, Robin Wagner, Nancy Walker, Eli Wallach, James Wallack, Lester Wallack, Tony Walton, Douglas Turner Ward, David Warfield, Ethel Waters, Clifton Webb, Joseph Weber, Margaret Webster, Kurt Weill, Orson Welles, Mae West, Robert Whitehead, Richard Wilbur, Oscar Wilde, Thornton Wilder, Bert Williams, Tennessee Williams, Lanford Wilson, P.G. Wodehouse, Peggy Wood, Alexander Woollcott, Irene Worth, Teresa Wright, Ed Wynn, Vincent Youmans, Stark Young, Florenz Ziegfeld, Patricia Zipprodt

## Founders Award

Established in 1993 in honor of Earl Blackwell, James M. Nederlander, Gerald Oestreicher, and Arnold Weissberger; the Theater Hall of Fame Founders Award is voted by the Hall's board of directors to an individual for his of her outstanding contribution to the theater. There was no award presented this season.

**Past Recipients: 1993:** James M. Nederlander **1994:** Kitty Carlisle Hart **1995:** Harvey Sabinson **1996:** Henry Hewes **1997:** Otis L. Guernsey Jr. **1998:** Edward Colton **1999:** no award **2000:** Gerard Oestreicher; Arnold Weissberger **2001:** Tom Dillon **2002:** No Award **2003:** Price Berkley **2004:** No Award **2005:** Donald Seawell **2006:** No Award

## TOURING BROADWAY AWARDS

Monday, April 16, 2007; Crown Plaza Times Square; 7th annual. Presented by the Broadway League for excellence in touring Broadway in the 2006 season. Winners selected by League presenters representing over 240 markets.

**Best New Touring Musical:** *Monty Python's Spamalot* by Eric Idle, (Produced by Boyett Ostar Productions, The Shubert Organization, Arielle Tepper, Stephanie McClelland/Lawrence Horowitz, Elan V. McAllister/Allan S. Gordon, Independent Presenters Network, Roy Furman, GRS Associates, Jam Theatricals, Concert Productions International, Live Nation

**Best Touring Play:** *Doubt* by John Patrick Shanley (Produced by Carole Shorenstein Hays, MTC Productions Inc. [Lynne Meadow, Artistic Director; Barry Grove, Managing Director], Roger Berlind, and Scott Rudin)

**Best Design of a Touring Production:** *Monty Python's Spamalot,* Scenic and Costumes, Tim Hatley; Lighting, Hugh Vanstone

**Best Score of a Touring Production:** *The Light in the Piazza,* Music and lyrics by Adam Guettel

**Best Direction of a Touring Production:** Mike Nichols, *Monty Python's Spamalot*

**Best Choreography of a Touring Production:** Twyla Tharp, *Movin' Out*

**Best Long-Running Tour Musical:** *Chicago* (Produced by Barry & Fran Weissler)

**Touring Broadway Achievement Award:** Tom Hewitt

**Touring Broadway Audience Choice Award:** *Wicked*

## UNITED STATES INSTITUTE FOR THEATRE TECHNOLOGY (USITT) AWARDS

Awards presented at the USITT Conference and Stage Expo, March 14–17, 2007, in Phoenix, Arizona.

**USITT Award** First presented in 1967, this award recognizes a lifetime contribution in the performing arts community in any capacity. Recipients of this award do not need to be members of the Institute nor must they have any connection to USITT. **2007 Winner:** Irene Corey, Theatrical Designer, Innovator, and Author

**Thomas DeGaetani Award** First presented in 1983, this award honors an outstanding lifetime contribution to the performing arts community by an individual living and/or working in the area where the Annual Conference & Stage Expo is Held. **2007 Recipient:** David Saar, Childsplay Theatre (Tempe, Arizona)

**Joel E. Rubin Founder's Award** First Presented in 1970, this award is presented to a USITT member in recognition of outstanding and continued service to the Institute. **2007 Recipient:** Zelma H. Weisfeld

**Distinguished Achievement Awards** First presented in 1998, this award recognizes achievement by designers and technicians with established careers in the areas of scenic design, lighting design, technical direction, costume design, theatre architecture, theatrical consulting, production management, sound design, arts management, and costume direction. The recipient does not have to be a member of USITT. **2007 Recipients:** Architecture: Hugh Hardy, Malcolm Holzman, Norman Pfeiffer; Costume Design & Technology: Katherine Marshall; Management: Jessica L. Andrews; Scenic Design: Robert Moody; Harold Burris-Meyer Distinguished Career in Sound Design: David Collison

**International Health & Safety Award** First presented in 1985, this award is recognizes outstanding contribution towards health and safety in the performing arts. It is only given in those years where there is important activity in the area of the Conference and Expo, and can be presented to an individual for career-long dedication as well as for specific initiatives. **2007 Recipient:** Jerry Gorrell, Theatre Safety and Standards Development

**Golden Pen Award** First presented in 1986, this award is presented to an author of an outstanding major, recent publication in the field of design and production for the performing arts. **2007 Recipient:** Andrew B. Harris, *The Performing Set: The Broadway Designs of William and Jean Eckart*

**Herbert D. Greggs Awards** First presented in 1979 and 1998, respectively, the Herbert D. Greggs Award (highest honor) and the Herbert D. Greggs Merit Award promote innovative, in-depth writing about theatre design and technology in *TD&T*. **2007 Greggs Award Recipient:** Arnold Wengrow, "Marjorie Kellogg: What I Care About Is Real Things;" **2007 Greggs Merit Award:** Kimberly Poppiti, "Galloping Horses: Treadmills and Other Theatre Applicances in Hippodramas"

**Architecture Awards** Created in 1994 and sponsored by the USITT Architecture Commission, these awards honors excellence in the design of theatre projects. Honor Awards (the highest designation) and Merit Awards are evaluated by a panel of distinguished jurors for creative image, contextual resonance, community contribution, explorations in new technologies, and functional operations. **2007 Honor Awards:** Haworth Tompkins, The Egg, Theatre Royal Bath (Bath, UK); Kuwabara Payne McKenna Blumberg, Young Centre for the Performing Arts (Toronto, Cananda); **2007 Merit Awards:** Keith Williams, The Unicorn Theatre (London, UK); Polshek Partnership & HDR Architecture, Holland Performing Arts Center (Omaha, Nebraska); Haworth Tompkins, Young Vic Theatre (London, UK)

**Special Citations** Special Citations recognize outstanding achievement in any area of the performing arts by an individual or an organization. The initial Special Citation was presented in 1963. **2007 Recipients:** Tharon Musser (lighting designer); Utah Shakespeare Festival

**Rising Star Award** Established by LDI and *Live Design* magazine, this award is given annually to a young professional at the beginning of his or her career; recipients must be in the first four years of professional (non-academic) work following the completion of his or her highest degree. **2007 Recipient:** John Horan (lighting designer)

**YD & T Awards** These awards are presented to young designers and technicians for recognition at the beginning of their careers, and made possible by gifts to USITT. **2007 Recipients:** *KM Fabrics Technical Production Award:* Jonathan Reed; *Robert E. Cohen Sound Achievement Award:* Dave Mickey; *USITT Barbizon Lighting Award:* Holly Blomquist; *USITT Rose Brand Scene Design Award:* Kathryn Kawecki; *USITT Zelma H. Weisfeld Costume Design & Technology Award:* Brandon McWilliams; *USITT Kryolan Corporation Makeup Design Award:* Jillian Carter Rivers; *USITT Frederick A. Buerki Golden Hammer Scenic Technology Award:* Joseph Hamlin; *USITT Clear-Com Stage Management Award:* Tarin Hurstell; *USITT W. Oren Parker Scene Design Award:* Adam Koch; *USITT Stage Technology Lighting Design Award:* John Jacobson

## WILLIAM INGE THEATRE FESTIVAL AWARDS

April 25–28, 2007; 26th annual. Presented for distinguished achievement in American theater.

**2007 Honorees:** Jerry Bock & Sheldon Harnick

**15th Annual Otis Guernsey New Voices in Playwrighting Award:** J.T. Rogers

**Jerome Lawrence Award** (for outstanding contributions to the national theater): Mike Wood

**Previous Festival Honorees: 1982:** William Inge Celebration; **1983:** Jerome Lawrence **1984:** William Gibson **1985:** Robert Anderson **1986:** John Patrick **1987:** Garson Kanin **1988:** Sidney Kingsley (in Independence), Robert E. Lee (on the road) **1989:** Horton Foote **1990:** Betty Comden & Adolph Green **1991:** Edward Albee **1992**: Peter Shaffer **1993:** Wendy Wasserstein **1994:** Terrence McNally **1995:** Arthur Miller **1996:** August Wilson **1997:** Neil Simon **1998**: Stephen Sondheim **1999:** John Guare **2000:** A.R. Gurney **2001:** Lanford Wilson **2002:** John Kander & Fred Ebb **2003:** Romulus Linney **2004:** Arthur Laurents **2005:** Tina Howe **2006:** 25th Anniversary retrospective

**Previous New Voices Recipients: 1993:** Jason Milligan **1994:** Catherine Butterfield **1995:** Mary Hanes **1996:** Brian Burgess Cross **1997:** Joe DiPietro **1998:** David Ives **1999:** David Hirson **2000:** James Still **2001:** Mark St. Germain **2002:** Dana Yeaton **2003:** Theresa Rebeck **2004:** Mary Portser **2005:** Lynne Kaufman **2006:** Melanie Marnich

# LONGEST-RUNNING SHOWS

*Top to bottom:*

*Michael Crawford and Sarah Brightman in* The Phantom of the Opera *(1988) (photo by Clive Barda)*

*Janis Paige and John Raitt in* The Pajama Game *(1954) (photo by Talbot)*

*Alison Fraser, Jasmine Guy, Pattie Darcy (seated), Laura Theodore, Gina Taylor, and Carol Maillard in* Beehive *(1986) (photo by Gerry Goodstein)*

Leo Burmester and Jennifer Butt in the original company of Les Misérables (1987)
(photo by Michael Le Poer/Bob Marshak)

Wayne Cilento and cast of A Chorus Line (1975)
(photo by Martha Swope)

Walter Matthau and Art Carney in The Odd Couple (1965)
(photo by Henry Grossman)

Charles Nelson Reilly, Robert Morse, and the original cast of How to Succeed in Business Without Really Trying (1961) (photo by Friedman-Ables)

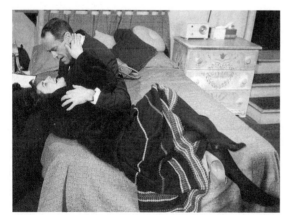

Henry Fonda and Anne Bancroft in Two for the Seesaw (1958)
(photo by Arthur Cantor)

Barbara Barrie, Dean Jones, and Charles Kimbrough in Company (1970)
(photo by Martha Swope)

# Longest-Running Shows on Broadway

*Production is still running as of May 31, 2007; performance count includes performances up to and including that date.

**The Phantom of the Opera***
**8,066 performances**
Opened January 26, 1988

**Cats**
**7,485 performances**
Opened October 7, 1982
Closed September 10, 2000

**Les Misérables**
**6,680 performances**
Opened March 12, 1987
Closed May 18, 2003

**A Chorus Line**
**6,137 performances**
Opened July 25, 1975
Closed April 28, 1990

**Oh! Calcutta** (revival)
**5,959 performances**
Opened September 24, 1976
Closed August 6, 1989

**Beauty and the Beast***
**5,396 performances**
Opened April 18, 1994

**Rent***
**4,614 performances**
Opened April 29, 1996

**Chicago** (musical, revival)*
**4,382 performances**
Opened November 19, 1996

**Miss Saigon**
**4,097 performances**
Opened April 11, 1991
Closed January 28, 2001

**The Lion King***
**4,005 performances**
Opened November 13, 1997

**42nd Street**
**3,486 performances**
Opened August 25, 1980
Closed January 8, 1989

**Grease**
**3,388 performances**
Opened February 14, 1972
Closed April 13, 1980

**Fiddler on the Roof**
**3,242 performances**
Opened September 22, 1964
Closed July 2, 1972

**Life With Father**
**3,224 performances**
Opened November 8, 1939
Closed July 12, 1947

**Tobacco Road**
**3,182 performances**
Opened December 4, 1933
Closed May 31, 1941

**Hello, Dolly!**
**2,844 performances**
Opened January 16, 1964
Closed December 27, 1970

**My Fair Lady**
**2,717 performances**
Opened March 15, 1956
Closed September 29, 1962

**The Producers**
**2,502 performances**
Opened April 19, 2001
Closed April 22, 2007

**Cabaret** (1998 revival)
**2,378 performances**
Opened March 19, 1998
Closed January 4, 2004

**Annie**
**2,377 performances**
Opened April 21, 1977
Closed January 22, 1983

**Mamma Mia!***
**2,366 performances**
Opened October 12, 2001

**Man of La Mancha**
**2,328 performances**
Opened November 22, 1965
Closed June 26, 1971

**Abie's Irish Rose**
**2,327 performances**
Opened May 23, 1922
Closed October 21, 1927

**Oklahoma!**
**2,212 performances**
Opened March 31, 1943
Closed May 29, 1948

**Smokey Joe's Café**
**2,036 performances**
Opened March 2, 1995
Closed January 16, 2000

**Hairspray***
**1,997 performances**
Opened August 15, 2002

**Pippin**
**1,944 performances**
Opened October 23, 1972
Closed June 12, 1977

**South Pacific**
**1,925 performances**
Opened April 7, 1949
Closed January 16, 1954

**The Magic Show**
**1,920 performances**
Opened May 28, 1974
Closed December 31, 1978

**Aida**
**1,852 performances**
Opened March 23, 2000
Closed September 5, 2004

**Gemini**
**1,819 performances**
Opened May 21, 1977
Closed September 6, 1981

**Deathtrap**
**1,793 performances**
Opened February 26, 1978
Closed June 13, 1982

**Harvey**
**1,775 performances**
Opened November 1, 1944
Closed January 15, 1949

**Dancin'**
**1,774 performances**
Opened March 27, 1978
Closed June 27, 1982

**La Cage aux Folles**
**1,761 performances**
Opened August 21, 1983
Closed November 15, 1987

**Hair**
**1,750 performances**
Opened April 29, 1968
Closed July 1, 1972

**The Wiz**
**1,672 performances**
Opened January 5, 1975
Closed January 29, 1979

**Born Yesterday**
**1,642 performances**
Opened February 4, 1946
Closed December 31, 1949

**The Best Little Whorehouse in Texas**
**1,639 performances**
Opened June 19, 1978
Closed March 27, 1982

**Crazy for You**
**1,622 performances**
Opened February 19, 1992
Closed January 7, 1996

**Ain't Misbehavin'**
**1,604 performances**
Opened May 9, 1978
Closed February 21, 1982

**Avenue Q***
**1,599 performances**
Opened July 31, 2003

**Mary, Mary**
**1,572 performances**
Opened March 8, 1961
Closed December 12, 1964

**Evita**
**1,567 performances**
Opened September 25, 1979
Closed June 26, 1983

**The Voice of the Turtle**
**1,557 performances**
Opened December 8, 1943
Closed January 3, 1948

**Jekyll & Hyde**
**1,543 performances**
Opened April 28, 1997
Closed January 7, 2001

**Barefoot in the Park**
**1,530 performances**
Opened October 23, 1963
Closed June 25, 1967

**Brighton Beach Memoirs**
**1,530 performances**
Opened March 27, 1983
Closed May 11, 1986

**42nd Street** (revival)
**1,524 performances**
Opened May 2, 2001
Closed January 2, 2005

**Dreamgirls**
**1,522 performances**
Opened December 20, 1981
Closed August 11, 1985

**Mame**
**1,508 performances**
Opened May 24, 1966
Closed January 3, 1970

**Grease** (revival)
**1,505 performances**
Opened May 11, 1994
Closed January 25, 1998

**Wicked***
**1,496 performances**
Opened October 30, 2003

**Same Time, Next Year**
**1,453 performances**
Opened March 14, 1975
Closed September 3, 1978

**Arsenic and Old Lace**
**1,444 performances**
Opened January 10, 1941
Closed June 17, 1944

**The Sound of Music**
**1,443 performances**
Opened November 16, 1959
Closed June 15, 1963

**Me and My Girl**
**1,420 performances**
Opened August 10, 1986
Closed December 31, 1989

**How to Succeed in Business Without Really Trying**
**1,417 performances**
Opened October 14, 1961
Closed March 6, 1965

**Hellzapoppin'**
**1,404 performances**
Opened September 22, 1938
Closed December 17, 1941

**The Music Man**
**1,375 performances**
Opened December 19, 1957
Closed April 15, 1961

**Funny Girl**
**1,348 performances**
Opened March 26, 1964
Closed July 15, 1967

**Mummenschanz**
**1,326 performances**
Opened March 30, 1977
Closed April 20, 1980

**Movin' Out**
**1,303 performances**
Opened October 24, 2002
Closed December 11, 2005

**Angel Street**
**1,295 performances**
Opened December 5, 1941
Closed December 30, 1944

**Lightnin'**
**1,291 performances**
Opened August 26, 1918
Closed August 27, 1921

**Promises, Promises**
**1,281 performances**
Opened December 1, 1968
Closed January 1, 1972

**The King and I**
**1,246 performances**
Opened March 29, 1951
Closed March 20, 1954

**Cactus Flower**
**1,234 performances**
Opened December 8, 1965
Closed November 23, 1968

**Sleuth**
**1,222 performances**
Opened December 8, 1965
Closed October 13, 1973

**Torch Song Trilogy**
**1,222 performances**
Opened June 10, 1982
Closed May 19, 1985

**1776**
**1,217 performances**
Opened March 16, 1969
Closed February 13, 1972

**Equus**
**1,209 performances**
Opened October 24, 1974
Closed October 7, 1977

**Sugar Babies**
**1,208 performances**
Opened October 8, 1979
Closed August 28, 1982

**Guys and Dolls**
**1,200 performances**
Opened November 24, 1950
Closed November 28, 1953

**Amadeus**
**1,181 performances**
Opened December 17, 1980
Closed October 16, 1983

**Cabaret**
**1,165 performances**
Opened November 20, 1966
Closed September 6, 1969

**Mister Roberts**
**1,157 performances**
Opened February 18, 1948
Closed January 6, 1951

**Annie Get Your Gun**
**1,147 performances**
Opened May 16, 1946
Closed February 12, 1949

**Guys and Dolls** (1992 revival)
**1,144 performances**
Opened April 14, 1992
Closed January 8, 1995

**The Seven Year Itch**
**1,141 performances**
Opened November 20, 1952
Closed August 13, 1955

**Bring in 'da Noise, Bring in 'da Funk**
**1,130 performances**
Opened April 25, 1996
Closed January 19, 1999

**Butterflies Are Free**
**1,128 performances**
Opened October 21, 1969
Closed July 2, 1972

**Pins and Needles**
**1,108 performances**
Opened November 27, 1937
Closed June 22, 1940

**Plaza Suite**
**1,097 performances**
Opened February 14, 1968
Closed October 3, 1970

**Fosse**
**1,093 performances**
Opened January 14, 1999
Closed August 25, 2001

**They're Playing Our Song**
**1,082 performances**
Opened February 11, 1979
Closed September 6, 1981

**Grand Hotel** (musical)
**1,077 performances**
Opened November 12, 1989
Closed April 25, 1992

**Kiss Me, Kate**
**1,070 performances**
Opened December 30, 1948
Closed July 25, 1951

**Don't Bother Me, I Can't Cope**
**1,065 performances**
Opened April 19, 1972
Closed October 27, 1974

**The Pajama Game**
**1,063 performances**
Opened May 13, 1954
Closed November 24, 1956

**Shenandoah**
**1,050 performances**
Opened January 7, 1975
Closed August 7, 1977

**Annie Get Your Gun** (1999 revival)
**1,046 performances**
Opened March 4, 1999
Closed September 1, 2001

**The Teahouse of the August Moon**
**1,027 performances**
Opened October 15, 1953
Closed March 24, 1956

**Damn Yankees**
**1,019 performances**
Opened May 5, 1955
Closed October 12, 1957

**Contact**
**1,010 performances**
Opened March 30, 2000
Closed September 1, 2002

**Never Too Late**
**1,007 performances**
Opened November 26, 1962
Closed April 24, 1965

**Big River**
**1,005 performances**
Opened April 25, 1985
Closed September 20, 1987

**The Will Rogers Follies**
**983 performances**
Opened May 1, 1991
Closed September 5, 1993

**Any Wednesday**
**982 performances**
Opened February 18, 1964
Closed June 26, 1966

**Sunset Boulevard**
**977 performances**
Opened November 17, 1994
Closed March 22, 1997

**Urinetown**
**965 performances**
Opened September 20, 2001
Closed January 18, 2004

**A Funny Thing Happened
on the Way to the Forum**
**964 performances**
Opened May 8, 1962
Closed August 29, 1964

**The Odd Couple**
**964 performances**
Opened March 10, 1965
Closed July 2, 1967

**Anna Lucasta**
**957 performances**
Opened August 30, 1944
Closed November 30, 1946

**Kiss and Tell**
**956 performances**
Opened March 17, 1943
Closed June 23, 1945

**Show Boat** (1994 revival)
**949 performances**
Opened October 2, 1994
Closed January 5, 1997

**Dracula** (1977 revival)
**925 performances**
Opened October 20, 1977
Closed January 6, 1980

**Bells Are Ringing**
**924 performances**
Opened November 29, 1956
Closed March 7, 1959

**The Moon Is Blue**
**924 performances**
Opened March 8, 1951
Closed May 30, 1953

**Monty Python's Spamalot***
**921 performances**
Opened March 17, 2005

**Beatlemania**
**920 performances**
Opened May 31, 1977
Closed October 17, 1979

**Proof**
**917 performances**
Opened October 24, 2000
Closed January 5, 2003

**The Elephant Man**
**916 performances**
Opened April 19, 1979
Closed June 28, 1981

**Kiss of the Spider Woman**
**906 performances**
Opened May 3, 1993
Closed July 1, 1995

**Thoroughly Modern Millie**
**904 performances**
Opened April 18, 2002
Closed June 20, 2004

**Luv**
**901 performances**
Opened November 11, 1964
Closed January 7, 1967

**The Who's Tommy**
**900 performances**
Opened April 22, 1993
Closed June 17, 1995

**Chicago** (musical)
**898 performances**
Opened June 3, 1975
Closed August 27, 1977

**Applause**
**896 performances**
Opened March 30, 1970
Closed July 27, 1972

**Can-Can**
**892 performances**
Opened May 7, 1953
Closed June 25, 1955

**Carousel**
**890 performances**
Opened April 19, 1945
Closed May 24, 1947

**I'm Not Rappaport**
**890 performances**
Opened November 19, 1985
Closed January 17, 1988

**Hats Off to Ice**
**889 performances**
Opened June 22, 1944
Closed April 2, 1946

**Fanny**
**888 performances**
Opened November 4, 1954
Closed December 16, 1956

**Children of a Lesser God**
**887 performances**
Opened March 30, 1980
Closed May 16, 1982

**Follow the Girls**
**882 performances**
Opened April 8, 1944
Closed May 18, 1946

**Kiss Me, Kate** (revival)
**881 performances**
Opened November 18, 1999
Closed December 30, 2001

**City of Angels**
**878 performances**
Opened December 11, 1989
Closed January 19, 1992

**Camelot**
**873 performances**
Opened December 3, 1960
Closed January 5, 1963

**I Love My Wife**
**872 performances**
Opened April 17, 1977
Closed May 20, 1979

**The 25th Annual Putnam County Spelling Bee***
**867 performances**
Opened May 2, 2005

**The Bat**
**867 performances**
Opened August 23, 1920
Unknown closing date

**My Sister Eileen**
**864 performances**
Opened December 26, 1940
Closed January 16, 1943

**No, No, Nanette** (revival)
**861 performances**
Opened January 19, 1971
Closed February 3, 1973

**Ragtime**
**861 performances**
Opened January 18, 1998
Closed January 16, 2000

**Song of Norway**
**860 performances**
Opened August 21, 1944
Closed September 7, 1946

**Chapter Two**
**857 performances**
Opened December 4, 1977
Closed December 9, 1979

**A Streetcar Named Desire**
**855 performances**
Opened December 3, 1947
Closed December 17, 1949

**Barnum**
**854 performances**
Opened April 30, 1980
Closed May 16, 1982

**Comedy in Music**
**849 performances**
Opened October 2, 1953
Closed January 21, 1956

**Raisin**
**847 performances**
Opened October 18, 1973
Closed December 7, 1975

**Blood Brothers**
**839 performances**
Opened April 25, 1993
Closed April 30, 1995

**You Can't Take It With You**
**837 performances**
Opened December 14, 1936
Unknown closing date

**La Plume de Ma Tante**
**835 performances**
Opened November 11, 1958
Closed December 17, 1960

**Three Men on a Horse**
**835 performances**
Opened January 30, 1935
Closed January 9, 1937

**The Subject Was Roses**
**832 performances**
Opened May 25, 1964
Closed May 21, 1966

**Black and Blue**
**824 performances**
Opened January 26, 1989
Closed January 20, 1991

**The King and I** (1996 revival)
**807 performances**
Opened April 11, 1996
Closed February 22, 1998

**Inherit the Wind**
**806 performances**
Opened April 21, 1955
Closed June 22, 1957

**Anything Goes** (1987 revival)
**804 performances**
Opened October 19, 1987
Closed September 3, 1989

**Titanic**
**804 performances**
Opened April 23, 1997
Closed March 21, 1999

**No Time for Sergeants**
**796 performances**
Opened October 20, 1955
Closed September 14, 1957

**Fiorello!**
**795 performances**
Opened November 23, 1959
Closed October 28, 1961

**Where's Charley?**
**792 performances**
Opened October 11, 1948
Closed September 9, 1950

**The Ladder**
**789 performances**
Opened October 22, 1926
Unknown closing date

**Fiddler on the Roof** (2004 revival)
**781 performances**
Opened February 26, 2004
Closed January 8, 2006

**Forty Carats**
**780 performances**
Opened December 26, 1968
Closed November 7, 1970

**Lost in Yonkers**
**780 performances**
Opened February 21, 1991
Closed January 3, 1993

**The Prisoner of Second Avenue**
**780 performances**
Opened November 11, 1971
Closed September 29, 1973

**M. Butterfly**
**777 performances**
Opened March 20, 1988
Closed January 27, 1990

**The Tale of the Allergist's Wife**
**777 performances**
Opened November 2, 2000
Closed September 15, 2002

**Oliver!**
**774 performances**
Opened January 6, 1963
Closed November 14, 1964

**The Pirates of Penzance** (1981 revival)
**772 performances**
Opened January 8, 1981
Closed November 28, 1982

**The Full Monty**
**770 performances**
Opened October 26, 2000
Closed September 1, 2002

**Woman of the Year**
**770 performances**
Opened March 29, 1981
Closed March 13, 1983

**My One and Only**
**767 performances**
Opened May 1, 1983
Closed March 3, 1985

**Sophisticated Ladies**
**767 performances**
Opened March 1, 1981
Closed January 2, 1983

**Bubbling Brown Sugar**
**766 performances**
Opened March 2, 1976
Closed December 31, 1977

**Into the Woods**
**765 performances**
Opened November 5, 1987
Closed September 3, 1989

**State of the Union**
**765 performances**
Opened November 14, 1945
Closed September 13, 1947

**Starlight Express**
**761 performances**
Opened March 15, 1987
Closed January 8, 1989

**The First Year**
**760 performances**
Opened October 20, 1920
Unknown closing date

**Broadway Bound**
**756 performances**
Opened December 4, 1986
Closed September 25, 1988

**You Know I Can't Hear You When the Water's Running**
**755 performances**
Opened March 13, 1967
Closed January 4, 1969

**Two for the Seesaw**
**750 performances**
Opened January 16, 1958
Closed October 31, 1959

**Joseph and the Amazing Technicolor Dreamcoat**
**747 performances**
Opened January 27, 1982
Closed September 4, 1983

**Death of a Salesman**
**742 performances**
Opened February 10, 1949
Closed November 18, 1950

**for colored girls who have considered suicide/when the rainbow is enuf**
**742 performances**
Opened September 15, 1976
Closed July 16, 1978

**Sons o' Fun**
**742 performances**
Opened December 1, 1941
Closed August 29, 1943

**Candide** (1974 revival)
**740 performances**
Opened March 10, 1974
Closed January 4, 1976

**Gentlemen Prefer Blondes**
**740 performances**
Opened December 8, 1949
Closed September 15, 1951

**The Man Who Came to Dinner**
**739 performances**
Opened October 16, 1939
Closed July 12, 1941

**Nine**
**739 performances**
Opened May 9, 1982
Closed February 4, 1984

**Call Me Mister**
**734 performances**
Opened April 18, 1946
Closed January 10, 1948

**Victor/Victoria**
**734 performances**
Opened October 25, 1995
Closed July 27, 1997

**West Side Story**
**732 performances**
Opened September 26, 1957
Closed June 27, 1959

**High Button Shoes**
**727 performances**
Opened October 9, 1947
Closed July 2, 1949

**Finian's Rainbow**
**725 performances**
Opened January 10, 1947
Closed October 2, 1948

**Claudia**
**722 performances**
Opened February 12, 1941
Closed January 9, 1943

**The Gold Diggers**
**720 performances**
Opened September 30, 1919
Unknown closing date

**Jesus Christ Superstar**
**720 performances**
Opened October 12, 1971
Closed June 30, 1973

**Carnival!**
**719 performances**
Opened April 13, 1961
Closed January 5, 1963

**The Diary of Anne Frank**
**717 performances**
Opened October 5, 1955
Closed June 22, 1955

**A Funny Thing Happened**
**on the Way to the Forum** (revival)
**715 performances**
Opened April 18, 1996
Closed January 4, 1998

**I Remember Mama**
**714 performances**
Opened October 19, 1944
Closed June 29, 1946

**Tea and Sympathy**
**712 performances**
Opened September 30, 1953
Closed June 18, 1955

**Junior Miss**
**710 performances**
Opened November 18, 1941
Closed July 24, 1943

**Footloose**
**708 performances**
Opened October 22, 1998
Closed July 2, 2000

**Last of the Red Hot Lovers**
**706 performances**
Opened December 28, 1969
Closed September 4, 1971

**The Secret Garden**
**706 performances**
Opened April 25, 1991
Closed January 3, 1993

**Company**
**705 performances**
Opened April 26, 1970
Closed January 1, 1972

**Seventh Heaven**
**704 performances**
Opened October 30, 1922
Unknown closing date

**Gypsy**
**702 performances**
Opened May 21, 1959
Closed March 25, 1961

**The Miracle Worker**
**700 performances**
Opened October 19, 1959
Closed July 1, 1961

**That Championship Season**
**700 performances**
Opened September 14, 1972
Closed April 21, 1974

**The Music Man** (2000 revival)
**698 performances**
Opened April 27, 2000
Closed December 30, 2001

**Da**
**697 performances**
Opened May 1, 1978
Closed January 1, 1980

**Cat on a Hot Tin Roof**
**694 performances**
Opened March 24, 1955
Closed November 17, 1956

**Li'l Abner**
**693 performances**
Opened November 15, 1956
Closed July 12, 1958

**The Children's Hour**
**691 performances**
Opened November 20, 1934
Unknown closing date

**Purlie**
**688 performances**
Opened March 15, 1970
Closed November 6, 1971

**Dead End**
**687 performances**
Opened October 28, 1935
Closed June 12, 1937

**The Lion and the Mouse**
**686 performances**
Opened November 20, 1905
Unknown closing date

**White Cargo**
**686 performances**
Opened November 5, 1923
Unknown closing date

**Dear Ruth**
**683 performances**
Opened December 13, 1944
Closed July 27, 1946

**East Is West**
**680 performances**
Opened December 25, 1918
Unknown closing date

**Come Blow Your Horn**
**677 performances**
Opened February 22, 1961
Closed October 6, 1962

**The Most Happy Fella**
**676 performances**
Opened May 3, 1956
Closed December 14, 1957

**Defending the Caveman**
**671 performances**
Opened March 26, 1995
Closed June 22, 1997

**The Doughgirls**
**671 performances**
Opened Dec. 30, 1942
Closed July 29, 1944

**The Impossible Years**
**670 performances**
Opened October 13, 1965
Closed May 27, 1967

**Irene**
**670 performances**
Opened November 18, 1919
Unknown closing date

**Boy Meets Girl**
**669 performances**
Opened November 27, 1935
Unknown closing date

**The Tap Dance Kid**
**669 performances**
Opened December 21, 1983
Closed August 11, 1985

**Beyond the Fringe**
**667 performances**
Opened October 27, 1962
Closed May 30, 1964

**Who's Afraid of Virginia Woolf?**
**664 performances**
Opened October 13, 1962
Closed May 16, 1964

**Blithe Spirit**
**657 performances**
Opened November 5, 1941
Closed June 5, 1943

**A Trip to Chinatown**
**657 performances**
Opened November 9, 1891
Unknown closing date

**The Women**
**657 performances**
Opened December 26, 1936
Unknown closing date

**Bloomer Girl**
**654 performances**
Opened October 5, 1944
Closed April 27, 1946

**The Fifth Season**
**654 performances**
Opened January 23, 1953
Closed October 23, 1954

**Jersey Boys***
**655 performances**
Opened November 6, 2006

**Rain**
**648 performances**
Opened September 1, 1924
Unknown closing date

**Witness for the Prosecution**
**645 performances**
Opened December 16, 1954
Closed June 30, 1956

**Call Me Madam**
**644 performances**
Opened October 12, 1950
Closed May 3, 1952

**Janie**
**642 performances**
Opened September 10, 1942
Closed January 16, 1944

**The Green Pastures**
**640 performances**
Opened February 26, 1930
Closed August 29, 1931

**Auntie Mame**
**639 performances**
Opened October 31, 1956
Closed June 28, 1958

**A Man for All Seasons**
**637 performances**
Opened November 22, 1961
Closed June 1, 1963

**Jerome Robbins' Broadway**
**634 performances**
Opened February 26, 1989
Closed September 1, 1990

**The Fourposter**
**632 performances**
Opened October 24, 1951
Closed May 2, 1953

**The Music Master**
**627 performances**
Opened September 26, 1904
Unknown closing date

**Two Gentlemen of Verona** (musical)
**627 performances**
Opened December 1, 1971
Closed May 20, 1973

**The Color Purple***
**624 performances**
Opened December 1, 2005

**The Tenth Man**
**623 performances**
Opened November 5, 1959
Closed May 13, 1961

**The Heidi Chronicles**
**621 performances**
Opened March 9, 1989
Closed September 1, 1990

**Is Zat So?**
**618 performances**
Opened January 5, 1925
Closed July 1926

**Anniversary Waltz**
**615 performances**
Opened April 7, 1954
Closed September 24, 1955

**The Happy Time** (play)
**614 performances**
Opened January 24, 1950
Closed July 14, 1951

**Separate Rooms**
**613 performances**
Opened March 23, 1940
Closed September 6, 1941

**Affairs of State**
**610 performances**
Opened September 25, 1950
Closed March 8, 1952

**Oh! Calcutta!**
**610 performances**
Opened June 17, 1969
Closed August 12, 1972

**Star and Garter**
**609 performances**
Opened June 24, 1942
Closed December 4, 1943

**The Mystery of Edwin Drood**
**608 performances**
Opened December 2, 1985
Closed May 16, 1987

**The Student Prince**
**608 performances**
Opened December 2, 1924
Unknown closing date

**Sweet Charity**
**608 performances**
Opened January 29, 1966
Closed July 15, 1967

**Bye Bye Birdie**
**607 performances**
Opened April 14, 1960
Closed October 7, 1961

**Riverdance on Broadway**
**605 performances**
Opened March 16, 2000
Closed August 26, 2001

**Irene** (revival)
**604 performances**
Opened March 13, 1973
Closed September 8, 1974

**Sunday in the Park With George**
**604 performances**
Opened May 2, 1984
Closed October 13, 1985

**Adonis**
**603 performances**
Opened circa. 1884
Unknown closing date

**Broadway**
**603 performances**
Opened September 16, 1926
Unknown closing date

**Peg o' My Heart**
**603 performances**
Opened December 20, 1912
Unknown closing date

**Master Class**
**601 performances**
Opened November 5, 1995
Closed June 29, 1997

**Street Scene** (play)
**601 performances**
Opened January 10, 1929
Unknown closing date

**Flower Drum Song**
**600 performances**
Opened December 1, 1958
Closed May 7, 1960

**Kiki**
**600 performances**
Opened November 29, 1921
Unknown closing date

**A Little Night Music**
**600 performances**
Opened February 25, 1973
Closed August 3, 1974

**Art**
**600 performances**
Opened March 1, 1998
Closed August 8, 1999

**Agnes of God**
**599 performances**
Opened March 30, 1982
Closed September 4, 1983

**Don't Drink the Water**
**598 performances**
Opened November 17, 1966
Closed April 20, 1968

**Wish You Were Here**
**598 performances**
Opened June 25, 1952
Closed November 28, 1958

**Sarafina!**
**597 performances**
Opened January 28, 1988
Closed July 2, 1989

**A Society Circus**
**596 performances**
Opened December 13, 1905
Closed November 24, 1906

**Absurd Person Singular**
**592 performances**
Opened October 8, 1974
Closed March 6, 1976

**A Day in Hollywood/A Night in the Ukraine**
**588 performances**
Opened May 1, 1980
Closed September 27, 1981

**The Me Nobody Knows**
**586 performances**
Opened December 18, 1970
Closed November 21, 1971

**The Two Mrs. Carrolls**
**585 performances**
Opened August 3, 1943
Closed February 3, 1945

**Kismet** (musical)
**583 performances**
Opened December 3, 1953
Closed April 23, 1955

**Gypsy** (1989 revival)
**502 performances**
Opened November 16, 1989
Closed July 28, 1991

**Brigadoon**
**581 performances**
Opened March 13, 1947
Closed July 31, 1948

**Detective Story**
**581 performances**
Opened March 23, 1949
Closed August 12, 1950

**No Strings**
**580 performances**
Opened March 14, 1962
Closed August 3, 1963

**Brother Rat**
**577 performances**
Opened December 16, 1936
Unknown closing date

**Blossom Time**
**576 performances**
Opened September 29, 1921
Unknown closing date

**Pump Boys and Dinettes**
**573 performances**
Opened February 4, 1982
Closed June 18, 1983

**Show Boat**
**572 performances**
Opened December 27, 1927
Closed May 4, 1929

**The Show-Off**
**571 performances**
Opened February 5, 1924
Unknown closing date

**Sally**
**570 performances**
Opened December 21, 1920
Closed April 22, 1922

**Jelly's Last Jam**
**569 performances**
Opened April 26, 1992
Closed September 5, 1993

**Golden Boy** (musical)
**568 performances**
Opened October 20, 1964
Closed March 5, 1966

**One Touch of Venus**
**567 performances**
Opened October 7, 1943
Closed February 10, 1945

**The Real Thing**
**566 performances**
Opened January 5, 1984
Closed May 12, 1985

**Happy Birthday**
**564 performances**
Opened October 31, 1946
Closed March 13, 1948

**Look Homeward, Angel**
**564 performances**
Opened November 28, 1957
Closed April 4, 1959

**Morning's at Seven** (revival)
**564 performances**
Opened April 10, 1980
Closed August 16, 1981

**The Glass Menagerie**
**561 performances**
Opened March 31, 1945
Closed August 3, 1946

**I Do! I Do!**
**560 performances**
Opened December 5, 1966
Closed June 15, 1968

**Wonderful Town**
**559 performances**
Opened February 25, 1953
Closed July 3, 1954

**The Last Night of Ballyhoo**
**557 performances**
Opened February 27, 1997
Closed June 28, 1998

**Rose Marie**
**557 performances**
Opened September 2, 1924
Unknown closing date

**Strictly Dishonorable**
**557 performances**
Opened Sept. 18, 1929
Unknown closing date

**Sweeney Todd, the Demon Barber of Fleet Street**
**557 performances**
Opened March 1, 1979
Closed June 29, 1980

**The Great White Hope**
**556 performances**
Opened October 3, 1968
Closed January 31, 1970

**A Majority of One**
**556 performances**
Opened February 16, 1959
Closed June 25, 1960

**The Sisters Rosensweig**
**556 performances**
Opened March 18, 1993
Closed July 16, 1994

**Sunrise at Campobello**
**556 performances**
Opened January 30, 1958
Closed May 30, 1959

**Toys in the Attic**
**556 performances**
Opened February 25, 1960
Closed April 8, 1961

**Jamaica**
**555 performances**
Opened October 31, 1957
Closed April 11, 1959

**Stop the World—I Want to Get Off**
**555 performances**
Opened October 3, 1962
Closed February 1, 1964

**Florodora**
**553 performances**
Opened November 10, 1900
Closed January 25, 1902

**Noises Off**
**553 performances**
Opened December 11, 1983
Closed April 6, 1985

**Ziegfeld Follies (1943)**
**553 performances**
Opened April 1, 1943
Closed July 22, 1944

**Dial "M" for Murder**
**552 performances**
Opened October 29, 1952
Closed February 27, 1954

**Good News**
**551 performances**
Opened September 6, 1927
Unknown closing date

**Peter Pan** (revival)
**551 performances**
Opened September 6, 1979
Closed January 4, 1981

**How to Succeed in Business Without Really Trying** (revival)
**548 performances**
Opened March 23, 1995
Closed July 14, 1996

**Let's Face It**
**547 performances**
Opened October 29, 1941
Closed March 20, 1943

**Milk and Honey**
**543 performances**
Opened October 10, 1961
Closed January 26, 1963

**Within the Law**
**541 performances**
Opened September 11, 1912
Unknown closing date

**Pal Joey** (revival)
**540 performances**
Opened January 3, 1952
Closed April 18, 1953

**The Sound of Music** (revival)
**540 performances**
Opened March 12, 1998
Closed June 20, 1999

**What Makes Sammy Run?**
**540 performances**
Opened February 27, 1964
Closed June 12, 1965

**The Sunshine Boys**
**538 performances**
Opened December 20, 1972
Closed April 21, 1974

**What a Life**
**538 performances**
Opened April 13, 1938
Closed July 8, 1939

**Crimes of the Heart**
**535 performances**
Opened November 4, 1981
Closed February 13, 1983

**Damn Yankees** (revival)
**533 performances**
Opened March 3, 1994
Closed August 6, 1995

**The Unsinkable Molly Brown**
**532 performances**
Opened November 3, 1960
Closed February 10, 1962

**The Red Mill** (revival)
**531 performances**
Opened October 16, 1945
Closed January 18, 1947

**Rumors**
**531 performances**
Opened November 17, 1988
Closed February 24, 1990

**A Raisin in the Sun**
**530 performances**
Opened March 11, 1959
Closed June 25, 1960

**Godspell**
**527 performances**
Opened June 22, 1976
Closed September 4, 1977

**Fences**
**526 performances**
Opened March 26, 1987
Closed June 26, 1988

**The Solid Gold Cadillac**
**526 performances**
Opened November 5, 1953
Closed February 12, 1955

**Biloxi Blues**
**524 performances**
Opened March 28, 1985
Closed June 28, 1986

**Irma La Douce**
**524 performances**
Opened September 29, 1960
Closed December 31, 1961

**The Boomerang**
**522 performances**
Opened August 10, 1915
Unknown closing date

**Follies**
**521 performances**
Opened April 4, 1971
Closed July 1, 1972

**Rosalinda**
**521 performances**
Opened October 28, 1942
Closed January 22, 1944

**The Best Man**
**520 performances**
Opened March 31, 1960
Closed July 8, 1961

**Chauve-Souris**
**520 performances**
Opened February 4, 1922
Unknown closing date

**Blackbirds of 1928**
**518 performances**
Opened May 9, 1928
Unknown closing date

**Dirty Rotten Scoundrels**
**627 performances**
Opened March 3, 2005
Closed September 3, 2006

**Doubt**
**525 performances**
Opened March 9, 2005
Closed July 2, 2006

**The Gin Game**
**517 performances**
Opened October 6, 1977
Closed December 31, 1978

**Side Man**
**517 performances**
Opened June 25, 1988
Closed October 31, 1999

**Sunny**
**517 performances**
Opened September 22, 1925
Closed December 11, 1926

**Victoria Regina**
**517 performances**
Opened December 26, 1935
Unknown closing date

**Fifth of July**
**511 performances**
Opened November 5, 1980
Closed January 24, 1982

**Half a Sixpence**
**511 performances**
Opened April 25, 1965
Closed July 16, 1966

**The Vagabond King**
**511 performances**
Opened September 21, 1925
Closed December 4, 1926

**The New Moon**
**509 performances**
Opened September 19, 1928
Closed December 14, 1929

**The World of Suzie Wong**
**508 performances**
Opened October 14, 1958
Closed January 2, 1960

**The Rothschilds**
**507 performances**
Opened October 19, 1970
Closed January 1, 1972

**On Your Toes** (revival)
**505 performances**
Opened March 6, 1983
Closed May 20, 1984

**Sugar**
**505 performances**
Opened April 9, 1972
Closed June 23, 1973

**The Light in the Piazza**
**504 performances**
Opened March 17, 2005
Closed July 2, 2006

**Shuffle Along**
**504 performances**
Opened May 23, 1921
Closed July 15, 1922

**Up in Central Park**
**504 performances**
Opened January 27, 1945
Closed January 13, 1946

**Carmen Jones**
**503 performances**
Opened December 2, 1943
Closed February 10, 1945

**Saturday Night Fever**
**502 performances**
Opened October 21, 1999
Closed December 30, 2000

**The Member of the Wedding**
**501 performances**
Opened January 5, 1950
Closed March 17, 1951

**Panama Hattie**
**501 performances**
Opened October 30, 1940
Closed January 13, 1942

**Personal Appearance**
**501 performances**
Opened October 17, 1934
Unknown closing date

**Bird in Hand**
**500 performances**
Opened April 4, 1929
Unknown closing date

**Room Service**
**500 performances**
Opened May 19, 1937
Unknown closing date

**Sailor, Beware!**
**500 performances**
Opened September 28, 1933
Unknown closing date

**Tomorrow the World**
**500 performances**
Opened April 14, 1943
Closed June 17, 1944

# Longest-Running Shows Off-Broadway

* Production is still running as of May 31, 2007, and performance count includes performances up to that date.

**The Fantasticks**
**17,162 performances**
Opened May 3, 1960
Closed January 13, 2002

**Blue Man Group***
**8,241 performances**
Opened November 17, 1991

**Perfect Crime***
**8,192 performances**
Opened April 5, 1987

**Stomp***
**5,580 performances**
Opened February 27, 1994

**Tony 'n' Tina's Wedding***
**5,562 performances**
Opened May 1, 1987

**I Love You, You're Perfect, Now Change***
**4,517 performances**
Opened August 1, 1996

**Nunsense**
**3,672 performances**
Opened December 12, 1985
Closed October 16, 1994

**The Threepenny Opera**
**2,611 performances**
Opened September 20, 1955
Closed December 17, 1961

**Naked Boys Singing***
**2,554 performances**
Opened July 22, 1999

**De La Guarda**
**2,475 performances**
Opened June 16, 1998
Closed September 12, 2004

**Forbidden Broadway 1982–87**
**2,332 performances**
Opened January 15, 1982
Closed August 30, 1987

**Little Shop of Horrors**
**2,209 performances**
Opened July 27, 1982
Closed November 1, 1987

**Godspell**
**2,124 performances**
Opened May 17, 1971
Closed June 13, 1976

**Vampire Lesbians of Sodom**
**2,024 performances**
Opened June 19, 1985
Closed May 27, 1990

**Jacques Brel is Alive and Well and Living in Paris**
**1,847 performances**
Opened January 22, 1968
Closed July 2, 1972

**Forever Plaid**
**1,811 performances**
Opened May 20, 1990
Closed June 12, 1994

**Vanities**
**1,785 performances**
Opened March 22, 1976
Closed August 3, 1980

**The Donkey Show**
**1,717 performances**
Opened August 18, 1999
Closed July 16, 2005

**Menopause the Musical**
**1,712 performances**
Opened April 4, 2002
Closed May 14, 2006

**You're A Good Man, Charlie Brown**
**1,597 performances**
Opened March 7, 1967
Closed February 14, 1971

**The Blacks**
**1,408 performances**
Opened May 4, 1961
Closed September 27, 1964

**The Vagina Monologues**
**1,381 performances**
Opened October 3, 1999
Closed January 26, 2003

**One Mo' Time**
**1,372 performances**
Opened October 22, 1979
Closed 1982–83 season

**Grandma Sylvia's Funeral**
**1,360 performances**
Opened October 9, 1994
Closed June 20, 1998

**Let My People Come**
**1,327 performances**
Opened January 8, 1974
Closed July 5, 1976

**Late Nite Catechism**
**1,268 performances**
Opened October 4, 1995
Closed May 18, 2003

**Driving Miss Daisy**
**1,195 performances**
Opened April 15, 1987
Closed June 3, 1990

**The Hot L Baltimore**
**1,166 performances**
Opened September 8, 1973
Closed January 4, 1976

**I'm Getting My Act Together and Taking It on the Road**
**1,165 performances**
Opened May 16, 1987
Closed March 15, 1981

**Little Mary Sunshine**
**1,143 performances**
Opened November 18, 1959
Closed September 2, 1962

**Steel Magnolias**
**1,126 performances**
Opened November 17, 1987
Closed February 25, 1990

**El Grande de Coca-Cola**
**1,114 performances**
Opened February 13, 1973
Closed April 13, 1975

**The Proposition**
**1,109 performances**
Opened March 24, 1971
Closed April 14, 1974

**Our Sinatra**
**1,096 performances**
Opened December 8, 1999
Closed July 28, 2002

**Beau Jest**
**1,069 performances**
Opened October 10, 1991
Closed May 1, 1994

**Jewtopia**
**1,052 performances**
Opened October 21, 2004
Closed April 29, 2007

**Tamara**
**1,036 performances**
Opened November 9, 1989
Closed July 15, 1990

**One Flew Over the Cuckoo's Nest** (revival)
**1,025 performances**
Opened March 23, 1971
Closed September 16, 1973

**Slava's Snowshow**
**1,004 Performances**
Opened September 8, 2004
Closed January 14, 2007

**The Boys in the Band**
**1,000 performances**
Opened April 14, 1968
Closed September 6, 1970

**Fool For Love**
**1,000 performances**
Opened November 27, 1983
Closed September 29, 1985

**Forbidden Broadway: 20th Anniversary Celebration**
**994 performances**
Opened March 20, 2002
Closed July 4, 2004

**Other People's Money**
**990 performances**
Opened February 7, 1989
Closed July 4, 1991

**Cloud 9**
**971 performances**
Opened May 18, 1981
Closed September 4, 1983

**Secrets Every Smart Traveler Should Know**
**953 performances**
Opened October 30, 1997
Closed February 21, 2000

**Sister Mary Ignatius Explains it All for You & The Actor's Nightmare**
**947 performances**
Opened October 21, 1981
Closed January 29, 1984

**Altar Boyz***
**939 performances**
Opened March 1, 2005

**Your Own Thing**
**933 performances**
Opened January 13, 1968
Closed April 5, 1970

**Curley McDimple**
**931 performances**
Opened November 22, 1967
Closed January 25, 1970

**Leave It to Jane** (revival)
**928 performances**
Opened May 29, 1959
Closed 1961–62 season

**The Mad Show**
**871 performances**
Opened January 9, 1966
Closed September 10, 1967

**Hedwig and the Angry Inch**
**857 performances**
Opened February 14, 1998
Closed April 9, 2000

**Forbidden Broadway Strikes Back**
**850 performances**
Opened October 17, 1996
Closed September 20, 1998

**When Pigs Fly**
**840 performances**
Opened August 14, 1996
Closed August 15, 1998

**Scrambled Feet**
**831 performances**
Opened June 11, 1979
Closed June 7, 1981

**The Effect of Gamma Rays on Man-in-the-Moon Marigolds**
**819 performances**
Opened April 7, 1970
Closed June 1, 1973

**Forbidden Broadway SVU**
**816 performances**
Opened December 16, 2004
Closed April 15, 2007

**Over the River and Through the Woods**
**800 performances**
Opened October 5, 1998
Closed September 3, 2000

**A View From the Bridge** (revival)
**780 performances**
Opened November 9, 1965
Closed December 11, 1966

**The Boy Friend** (revival)
**763 performances**
Opened January 25, 1958
Closed 1961–62 season

**True West**
**762 performances**
Opened December 23, 1980
Closed January 11, 1981

**Forbidden Broadway Cleans Up Its Act!**
**754 performances**
Opened November 17, 1998
Closed August 30, 2000

**Isn't It Romantic**
**733 performances**
Opened December 15, 1983
Closed September 1, 1985

**Dime a Dozen**
**728 performances**
Opened June 13, 1962
Closed 1963–64 season

**The Pocket Watch**
**725 performances**
Opened November 14, 1966
Closed June 18, 1967

**The Connection**
**722 performances**
Opened June 9, 1959
Closed June 4, 1961

**The Passion of Dracula**
**714 performances**
Opened September 28, 1977
Closed July 14, 1979

**Love, Janis**
**713 performances**
Opened April 22, 2001
Closed January 5, 2003

**Adaptation & Next**
**707 performances**
Opened February 10, 1969
Closed October 18, 1970

**Oh! Calcutta!**
**704 performances**
Opened June 17, 1969
Closed August 12, 1972

**Scuba Duba**
**692 performances**
Opened November 11, 1967
Closed June 8, 1969

**The Foreigner**
**686 performances**
Opened November 2, 1984
Closed June 8, 1986

**The Knack**
**685 performances**
Opened January 14, 1964
Closed January 9, 1966

**Fully Committed**
**675 performances**
Opened December 14, 1999
Closed May 27, 2001

**The Club**
**674 performances**
Opened October 14, 1976
Closed May 21, 1978

**The Balcony**
**672 performances**
Opened March 3, 1960
Closed December 21, 1961

**Penn & Teller**
**666 performances**
Opened July 30, 1985
Closed January 19, 1992

**Dinner With Friends**
**654 performances**
Opened November 4, 1999
Closed May 27, 2000

**America Hurrah**
**634 performances**
Opened November 7, 1966
Closed May 5, 1968

**Cookin'**
**632 Performances**
Opened July 7, 2004
Closed August 7, 2005

**Oil City Symphony**
**626 performances**
Opened November 5, 1987
Closed May 7, 1989

**The Countess**
**618 performances**
Opened September 28, 1999
Closed December 30, 2000

**The Exonerated**
**608 performances**
Opened October 10, 2002
Closed March 7, 2004

**Hogan's Goat**
**607 performances**
Opened March 6, 1965
Closed April 23, 1967

**Drumstruck**
**607 performances**
Opened June 16, 2005
Closed November 16, 2006

**Beehive**
**600 performances**
Opened March 30, 1986
Closed August 23, 1987

**Criss Angel Mindfreak**
**600 performances**
Opened November 20, 2001
Closed January 5, 2003

**The Trojan Women**
**600 performances**
Opened December 23, 1963
Closed May 30, 1965

**The Syringa Tree**
**586 performances**
Opened September 14, 2000
Closed June 2, 2002

**The Dining Room**
**583 performances**
Opened February 24, 1982
Closed July 17, 1982

**The Musical of Musicals –The Musical!**
**583 Performances**
Opened December 16, 2003; Closed January 25, 2004
Reopened June 10, 2004; Closed October 3, 2004
Reopened February 10 2005; Closed November 13, 2005

**Krapp's Last Tape & The Zoo Story**
**582 performances**
Opened August 29, 1960
Closed May 21, 1961

**Three Tall Women**
**582 performances**
Opened April 13, 1994
Closed August 26, 1995

**The Dumbwaiter & The Collection**
**578 performances**
Opened January 21, 1962
Closed April 12, 1964

**Forbidden Broadway 1990**
**576 performances**
Opened January 23, 1990
Closed June 9, 1991

**Dames at Sea**
**575 performances**
Opened April 22, 1969
Closed May 10, 1970

**The Crucible** (revival)
**571 performances**
Opened 1957
Closed 1958

**The Iceman Cometh** (revival)
**565 performances**
Opened May 8, 1956
Closed February 23, 1958

**Forbidden Broadway 2001: A Spoof Odyssey**
**552 performances**
Opened December 6, 2000
Closed February 6, 2002

**The Hostage** (revival)
**545 performances**
Opened October 16, 1972
Closed October 8, 1973

**Wit**
**545 performances**
Opened October 6, 1998
Closed April 9, 2000

**What's a Nice Country Like You Doing in a State Like This?**
**543 performances**
Opened July 31, 1985
Closed February 9, 1987

**Forbidden Broadway 1988**
**534 performances**
Opened September 15, 1988
Closed December 24, 1989

**Gross Indecency: The Three Trials of Oscar Wilde**
**534 performances**
Opened September 5, 1997
Closed September 13, 1998

**Frankie and Johnny in the Claire de Lune**
**533 performances**
Opened December 4, 1987
Closed March 12, 1989

**Six Characters in Search of an Author** (revival)
**529 performances**
Opened March 8, 1963
Closed June 28, 1964

**All in the Timing**
**526 performances**
Opened November 24, 1993
Closed February 13, 1994

**Fools in Love**
**525 performances**
Opened June 23, 2005
Closed December 23, 2006

**Oleanna**
**513 performances**
Opened October 3, 1992
Closed January 16, 1994

**Making Porn**
**511 performances**
Opened June 12, 1996
Closed September 14, 1997

**The Dirtiest Show in Town**
**509 performances**
Opened June 26, 1970
Closed September 17, 1971

**Happy Ending & Day of Absence**
**504 performances**
Opened June 13, 1965
Closed January 29, 1967

**Greater Tuna**
**501 performances**
Opened October 21, 1982
Closed December 31, 1983

**A Shayna Maidel**
**501 performances**
Opened October 29, 1987
Closed January 8, 1989

**The Boys From Syracuse** (revival)
**500 performances**
Opened April 15, 1963
Closed June 28, 1964

*Jerry Orbach, Rita Gardner, Kenneth Nelson, William Larsen, Hugh Thomas, Richard Stauffer, the original cast of* The Fantasticks (1960) *(photo by Friedman-Abeles)*

*Ed Harris and Dennis Ludlow in* Fool For Love (1983) *(photo by Gerry Goodstein)*

*John Neville-Andrews and Diz White in* El Grande de Coca-Cola (1973) *(photo by Terrence Le Goubin)*

*Conrad Fowkes, Bill Macy, Henry Calvert, James Barbosa, Cynthia Harris, Ronnie Gilbert, Brenda Smiley, Joyce Aaron in* American Hurrah (1966) *(photo by Slade-Grossman)*

# OBITUARIES

Elizabeth Allen

June Allyson

Red Buttons

Roscoe Lee Browne

Peter Boyle

Betty Comden

John Conte

Yvonne DeCarlo

Ellen Hanley

Kitty Carlisle Hart

Arthur Hill

Barnard Hughes

Mary Orr

Bruno Kirby

Calvin Lockhart

Carrie Nye

Tom Poston

Charles Nelson Reilly

Jack Warden

Jane Wyatt

**Eve Adamson**, 68, Beverly Hills, CA-born actress/director/producer, died Oct. 8, 2006, in Manhattan, NY, of unknown causes, found in her bed. In 1971 as founder of the Jean Cocteau Repertory theatre company in New York, she organized a group of actors in a converted storefront in the East Village and eventually grew the organization into a highly respected producing organization. A fan of the absurdist tradition, Ms. Adamson named the company after the French avant-garde Jean Cocteau and began its first season of rotating repertory in 1973. Receiving a grant from the state of New York, the company moved into the Bouwerie Lane Theater in 1974 and established a lasting presence in the Off-Off-Broadway theatre world. She was artistic director for eighteen years during which time the company presented scores of classical works in repertory. The company presented the last Tennessee Williams play to have it premiere during his lifetime, *Something Cloudy, Something Clear*, in 1981. Stepping down as artistic director of the Cocteau in 1989, she directed nationally and in Europe and occasionally staged plays as well at the Cocteau. Ms. Adamson directed the debut production of the Phoenix Theater Ensemble, a group of longtime Cocteau actors who broke off from the Cocteau to form their own theatre company.

**Tim Albrecht**, 41, Great Falls, MT-born performer/choreographer, died Dec. 9, 2006, in Los Angeles, CA, in his sleep, of unknown causes. Broadway credits include *Ain't Broadway Grand* and *Showboat* (1995). Other credits include *Broadway Bares* benefits for Broadway Cares/Equity Fights AIDS. National credits as a choreographer also include the tenth season of *The View* on television and the principal choreographer for *The Rosie O'Donnell Show*. Known also for his work at the Diamond Head Theatre in Hawaii, credits there include *The Full Monty, Suessical*, and *Cinderella*. Film credits include *The Intern, Camp*, and *Pretty Dead Girl*. He was also a member of the Kennedy Theatre performing company. Survivors include his parents, Ken and Bunky Albrecht, and a sister, Denise.

**Elizabeth Allen** (Elizabeth Ellen Gillease), 72, Jersey City, NJ-born actress, died Sept. 19, 1996, in Fishkill, NY, of kidney failure. Broadway credits include *Romanoff and Juliet, The Gay Life* (1962 Tony nomination), *Do I Hear a Waltz?* (1965 Tony nomination), *Sherry!* and *42nd Street*. National tour credits include *Cactus Flower* and *California Suite*. Best known as the *Away we go!* Girl on *The Jackie Gleason Show* during the 1950s, her other television credits include *The Paul Lynde Show, Bracken's World, C.P.O Sharkey, Another World, Kojak, Mannix*, and *Texas*. She was also a member of the Helen Hayes Repertory Company in New York for several years. Film credits include *From the Terrace, Diamond Head, Donovan's Reef, Cheyenne Autumn, Star-Spangled Girl*, and *The Carey Treatment*. Survivors include her sister-in-law, Marion Gillease.

**June Allyson** (Eleanor [Ella] Geisman, aka Jan Allyson, aka Jane Allyson), 88, Bronx, NY-born actress/singer, died July 8, 2006, in Ojai, CA, of pulmonary respiratory failure and acute bronchitis. Her Broadway credits include *Sing Out the News, Higher and Higher, Very Warm for May, Panama Hattie, Best Foot Forward*, and *40 Carats*. National tours include *No, No Nanette*. Film credits include *Girl Crazy, Thousands Cheer, Music for Millions, Two Sisters from Boston, Till the Clouds Roll By, The Secret Heart, High Barbaree, Good News, Two Girls and a Sailor, The Bride Goes Wild, Too Young to Kiss, Remains to Be Seen, Her Highness and the Bellboy, The Sailor Takes a Wife, Little Women, The Three Musketeers, Words and Music, Too Young to Kiss, The Girl in White, Battle Circus, Meet the People, Woman's World, The Stratton Story, The Glenn Miller Story, Strategic Air Command, The McConnell Story, Executive Suite, Best Foot Forward, My Man Godfrey, A Stranger in My Arms, The Shrike, The Reformer and the Redhead, Right Cross, They Only Kill Their Masters, The Opposite Sex, You Can't Run From It, Interlude*, and *Blackout*. Television credits include *The DuPont Show With June Allyson* from 1959-1961, which she hosted and occasionally starred in, *The Judy Garland Show, The Love Boat*, and *Murder, She Wrote*. She became a national spokesperson for Depend undergarments in 1985, and the June Allyson Foundation, founded in 1997, raises money for incontinence research and education. Her 1983 autobiography was entitled *June Allyson*. She was married four times, to Dick Powell, Glenn Maxwell twice, and David Ashrow, who survives her, as does a daughter, Pamela Allyson Powell, of Santa Monica, CA, son, Richard, of Reseda, CA, grandson in Van Nuys, CA, and brother, Arthur Peters, of Ventura, CA. A celebration of Ms. Allyson's life was held Oct. 7, 2006, in Ojai, CA.

**Tige Andrews**, 86, Brooklyn, NY-born actor, died Jan. 27, 2007, at his home in the San Fernando Valley of California, of a heart attack. An Emmy-nominated actor for his work on television in *The Mod Squad*, his Broadway credits include *Mister Roberts, Stockade*, and *Threepenny Opera*. He was a graduate of the American Academy of Dramatic Arts in New York. Survivors include daughters Barbara, Gina, and Julianna, and sons John, Steve, and Tony. His wife of forty-six years, Norma Thornton, died in 1996.

**Isabel Bigley Barnett**, 80, Bronx, NY-born actress, died September 30, 2006, in Rancho Mirage, CA, of pulmonary disease. A Tony winner for her role as the original Sarah Brown in *Guys and Dolls*, she stayed with the original production for three years. She was the last surviving member of the Broadway classic. Her other Broadway credits include *Oklahoma!* and *Me and Juliet*. She attended the Royal Academy of Dramatic Art in London, England, and her West End credits include *Oklahoma!* and where she performed in the first BBC broadcast musical production, *Gay Rosalinda*. She starred in *Café Continental*, a weekly television show filmed in London and broadcast in the United States, and performed in *Bagatelle*, a well-received nightclub act. On television, she appeared frequently on *The Ed Sullivan Show, Colgate Comedy Hour*, and *Goodyear Theater*. A well-known philanthropist, she and her husband established a graduate program in arts policy and administration at Ohio State University, the first of its kind in the United States. Together, they funded the Lawrence and Isabel Barnett Fellowships and endowed the Barnett Arts and Public Policy Symposiums. Isabel Barnett donated her theater memorabilia for the Isabel Bigley Barnett Collection at the Jerome Lawrence and Robert E. Lee Theatre Research Institute at Ohio State. She and her husband were also very active with the ALS Association, dedicated to finding the cause of Lou Gherig's Disease. There they established the Lawrence and Isabel Barnett Post-Doctoral Fellowships for research. She was also active in California in the Coachella Valley in philanthropic causes. Elected to the Board of Trustees of the McCallum Theatre in Palm Desert, CA, in 2000, she became the first chair of the McCallum Theatre Board in 2005. She was also on the Board of the Palm Springs Air Museum. She and her husband co-chaired the 2003 and 2004 galas there. Her husband of fifty-three years, Lawrence Barnett, six children, Lawrence Jr., Robert Barnett, William Barnett, Claudia Scott, James Barnett, and Laurey Treiger, sixteen grandchildren, and four great-grandchildren survive her.

**John Bishop** (John Dickson Bishop), 77, Mansfield, OH-born writer/director, died Dec. 20, 2006, in Bad Heilbrunn, Germany, of cancer. He was a resident of Encino, CA, at the time of his death. Broadway credits as a writer include *The Trip Back Down* and *The Musical Comedy Murders of 1940*. He was a resident playwright for the Circle Repertory Theatre, where his credits included *Borderlines, The Great Grandson of Jedediah Kohler*, and *Confluence*. He also performed as an actor at the Cleveland Playhouse. Plays he directed at Circle Repertory include Rafael Lima's *El Salvador*, and Joe Pintauro's *Beside Herself*. His film credits as a screenwriter include *The Package*, starring Gene Hackman and Tommy Lee Jones, as well as *Drop Zone*. A lifelong softball player, Mr. Bishop also wrote the script for the multimedia presentation *The Baseball Experience*, now playing at the National Baseball Hall of Fame and Museum in Cooperstown, N.Y. He is survived by his wife, Lisa Maurer Bishop, sons Michael, Matthew, and Christopher, and two grandchildren.

**Peter Boyle**, 71, Norristown, PA-born actor, died Dec. 12, 2006, in New York, NY, of multiple myeloma and heart disease. Studying with Uta Hagen in New York, his Broadway credits include *Paul Sills' Story Theatre* and *The Roast*. National tours include *The Odd Couple*. Early in his career he was a member of the Second City improvisation troupe in Chicago. Film credits include *Young Frankenstein, The Candidate, Wizard, Taxi Driver*, and *Monster's Ball*. An Emmy winner for a role on *The X Files*, he starred for nine years, from 1996-2005, opposite Doris Roberts on television in *Everybody Loves Raymond*. He received seven Emmy nominations for that role, as well as one nomination for his role as Senator Joseph McCarthy in the 1977 television miniseries *From Here to Eternity*. His wife, Loraine, daughters Lucy and Amy, and two sisters, Alice Duffy and Sidney Boyle, survive him.

**Ruth Brown**, 78, Portsmouth, VA-born actress, died Nov. 24, 2006, in Las Vegas, NV, of a heart attack and stroke. A 1989 Tony winner for her role in *Black and Blue*, a role she recreated in the television version of the same play, her other Broadway credits include *Amen Corner*. Film roles include *Hairspray* and *Honeydripper*.

**Roscoe Lee Browne**, 81, Woodbury, NJ-born actor, died April 11, 2007, in Los Angeles, CA, of cancer. His Broadway credits include *The Cool World*, *General Seeger, Tiger, Tiger Burning Bright, The Ballad of the Sad Café, Danton's Death, A Hand Is on the Gate* (also directed), *My One And Only*, and *Two Trains Running* (Tony Award nominee, Best Supporting Actor). He also taught comparative literature and French at Lincoln University in New Jersey and was a nationally known track and field star before turning his interest to theatre. He performed at the New York Shakespeare Festival before joining James Earl Jones in 1961 in the original cast of *The Blacks* Off-Broadway. Other Off-Broadway credits include *Benito Cereno*. Television credits include *All in the Family, The Cosby Show*, for which he won an Emmy Award, *Soap, A Different World*, and *Law And Order*. Film credits include *The French Connection, Topaz, The Liberation of L.B. Jones, and The Mambo Kings*. Known widely for his strength as a vocal performer, he narrated the movie *Babe*, as well as participated in spoken-word works with the Boston Pops, the Los Angeles Philharmonic, and other orchestras.

**Red Buttons** (Aaron Chwatt), 87, Manhattan, NY-born actor/comic, died July 13, 2006, at his home in Los Angeles, CA, of vascular disease. Broadway credits *Vickie, Winged Victory, Barefoot Boy With Cheek, Hold It!* and *Buttons On Broadway*. A Best Supporting Actor Academy Award winner as well as Golden Globe winner for his role as Airman Joe Kelly in the film *Sayonara*, other film credits include *Hatari! The Longest Day, Winged Victory, 13 Rue Madeleine, Footlight Varieties, Imitation General, The Big Circus, Ticklish Affair, One, Two, Three, Five Weeks in a Balloon, The Longest Day, Your Cheatin' Heart, Up From the Beach, Harlow, Stagecoach* (1966), *They Shoot Horses, Don't They?, Who Killed Mary What's 'ername? The Poseidon Adventure, 18 Again!, Gable and Lombard, Viva Knieval, Pete's Dragon, Movie, Movie, C.H.O.M.P.S., When Time Ran Out, It Could Happen To You,* and *The Story of Us*. Joining the army in 1943, he spent the remainder of World War II in its entertainment unit, performing in the hit *Winged Victory*, written by Moss Hart. Beginning his career as a Borcht Belt comic in the Catskills and in Burlesque clubs in the 1940s and early 1950s, he became a staple on television in the early 1950s in guest appearances in shows such as *Suspense* and eventually when given his own variety show, *The Red Buttons Show*, which began in 1952 and ran for several seasons on CBS. Picked up the third year by NBC, his series was finally cancelled in May 1955. He then became a fixture of nightclubs and in television guest appearances, ultimately known for briefly starring in *The Double Life of Henry Phyfe* in 1966 and for stints on *The Dean Martin Celebrity Roast* in the 1970s, as the White Rabbit in the 1985 musical miniseries *Alice in Wonderland*, and in the recurring role of Al Baker on *Knots Landing* in the 1980s, and in *Street Time* on Showtime in 2002. He also made notable guest appearances on *E.R.* and *Roseanne*. The Academy of Radio and Television Arts and Sciences named Comedian of the Year by in 1954. His first two marriages ended in divorce, and his third wife, Alicia, died in 2001. Their daughter, Amy Nogress, son, Adam, as well as a brother and a sister survive him.

**Betty Comden** (Elizabeth Cohen), 89, Brooklyn, NY-born lyricist/librettist, writer/source material provider, died Nov. 23, 2006, in Manhattan, NY, of heart failure. During a professional partnership that lasted over sixty years and until the death of partner Adolph Green in 2002, Betty was among the first Theatre World Award winners in 1945 (for *On the Town*). Her Broadway credits in any number of artistic capacities include *On the Town* (and 1971 and 1998 revivals), *Billion Dollar Baby, Two on the Aisle, Wonderful Town* (Best Musical Tony Award, and 2003 revival), *Peter Pan* (and 1979, 1990, 1991,1998, and 1999 revivals), *Bells Are Ringing* (Best Musical Tony nomination and 2001 revival), *Say, Darling, A Party with Betty Comden and Adolph Green* (and 1977 revival), *Do Re Mi* (Best Musical Tony Award), *An Evening with Yves Montand, Subways Are for Sleeping, Dylan, Fade Out-Fade In, Hallelujah, Baby!* (Best Musical Tony Award), *Applause* (Best Musical Tony Award), *Lorelei, On the Twentieth Century* (Best Book of a Musical Tony Award, Best Original Score Tony Award, and 2005 benefit revival), *The Madwoman of Central Park West, A Doll's Life* (Best Book of a Musical Tony Award nomination), *Singin' in the Rain* (Best Book of a Musical Tony Award nomination), *Barbara Cook: A Concert for the Theatre, Jerome Robbins' Broadway, The*

*Will Rogers Follies* (Best Original Score Tony Awards), *Elaine Stritch At Liberty, Barbara Cook's Broadway* and *Isn't It Romantic*. Meeting almost always daily with collaborator Green until his death, they were one of the most successful and long-lived partnerships in the history of the theatre. Joining with Judy Holliday, Alvin Hammer, and John Frank, they formed a cabaret act named *The Revuers* and performing at the venue the Village Vanguard in the 1930s. The gig resulted in Comden and Green's performance in the 1944 film *Greenwich Village*, but they returned quickly to revues and worked consistently in nightclubs. Comden's numerous film credits include *The Band Wagon* (Academy Award nomination), *Take Me Out to the Ball Game, It's Always Fair Weather* (Academy Award nomination), *Good News, The Barkleys of Broadway, Singin' in the Rain, On the Town, Bells Are Ringing, Garbo Talks, Slaves of New York*. Comden and Green were the recipients of the 1991 Kennedy Center honors for their contributions to American musical theatre. 1999 saw a tribute in a two-night program at Carnegie Hall, and a star-studded memorial for Adolph Green was held in October 2002. Her memoir *Off Stage* was published in 1995. Her only husband, Steven Kyle, a designer and businessman, died in 1979. Son Alan died in 1990, and daughter, Susanna Kyle, of Manhattan, New York, survives her.

**John Conte**, 90, Palmer, MA-born actor, died Aug. 26, 2006, in Rancho Mirage, CA, of natural causes. With Broadway credits including *Allegro* and *Arms and the Girl*, he also founded and owned the NBC affiliate in Palm Desert, CA, which became the third largest station in the Coachella Valley of California, was a founding sponsor of the Eisenhower Medical Center, and helped to create the McCallum Theatre in Palm Desert, CA. His numerous television credits as an actor include *Your Show of Shows, Matinee Theatre, The Silver Theatre, Studio One, The Untouchables, Perry Mason,* and *Bonanza*. Film credits include *The Man With the Golden Arm* with Frank Sinatra in 1955. Married three times, the first two marriages ended in divorce, and he is survived by third wife, Sirpuhe, son Christopher Conte of Los Angeles, CA, stepdaughters Louise Danellan of Los Angeles, CA, and Joyce Stein of Indian Wells, CA, and six grandchildren.

**Pat Corley**, 76, Dallas, TX-born actor, died Sept. 11, 2006, in Los Angeles, CA, of congestive heart failure. Broadway credits include *Blues for Mister Charlie, The Secret Affairs of Mildred Wild, Of Mice and Men, and Sweet Bird of Youth*. His numerous film credits include *Coming Home, True Confessions,* and *Against All Odds*. And from 1988-1996, he appeared on television with Candice Bergen on *Murphy Brown* as Phil the Bartender. Other television credits include *The Bay City Blues, Hill Street Blues,* and *The Executioner's Song*. His numerous film credits include *The Super Cops, The Bad News Bears in Breaking Training, Coming Home, Nightwing, The Onion Field, The Rose, The Black Marble, The Hand, True Confessions, Hanky Panky, Night Shift,* and *Against All Odds*. Survivors include his sons Jerry and Kevin, daughters Troy Corley and Christina Pratt, and twelve grandchildren. A daughter, Michelle, died in 1996.

**Yvonne DeCarlo** (Peggy Yvonne Middleton), 84, Vancouver, British Columbia-born actress, died January 8, 2007, at the Motion Picture & Television facility in suburban Los Angeles, CA, of heart failure. Her Broadway credits include *Follies* She is best known for her stint as Lily Munster from 1964-66 on television's *The Munsters*. Signed to a contract in 1942 with Paramount Pictures, her numerous film roles numbered near 100 and include *Harvard Here I Come! Slave Girl, Casbah, Desert Hawk, Frontier Gal, Black Bart, River Lady, Calamity Jane and Sam Bass, The Gal Who Took the West, This Gun For Hire, Road to Morocco, Lucky Jordan, Youth on Parade, Rhythm Parade, The Crystal Ball, Salute for Three, For Whom the Bell Tolls, So Proudly We Hail!, Let's Face It, True to Life, Standing Room Only, The Story of Dr. Wassell, Rainbow Island, Kismet, Practically Yours, Here Come the Waves, Bring on the Girls, The Deerslayer, Criss Cross, Flame of the Islands, Tomahawk, The San Francisco Story, The Captain's Paradise, Tonight's the Night, Passion, Raw Edge, The Ten Commandments, Salome-Where She Danced, Song of Scheherazade, Brute Force, Buccaneer's Girl, The Desert Hawk, Tomahawk, Hotel Sahara, Silver City, Scarlet Angel, Hurricane Smith, Sombrero, Sea Devils, Fort Algiers, Border River, Passion, Tonight's the Night/Happy Ever After, The Contessa's Secret, Shotgun, Flame of the Islands, Magic Fire, Raw Edge, Death of a Scoundrel, Band of Angels, Timbuktu, Mary Magdalene, Law of the Lawless, Arizona Bushwhackers, The Delta Factor, The Seven Minutes, Arizona*

*Slim, It Seemed Like a Good Idea at the Time, Won Ton Ton, The Dog Who Saved Hollywood, House of Shadows, Guyana, Cult of the Damned, Silent Scream, The Man With Bogart's Face/Sam Marlow, Private Eye, Play Dead, Liar's Moon, Vultures in Paradise, Cellar Dweller, Mirror, Mirror, Oscar, The Naked Truth, Desert Kickboxer, The Sorority House Murders, Season of the Heart, Blazing Stewardess/ Texas Layover, Satan's Cheerleaders, Nocturna: Granddaughter of Dracula, McClintock* (with John Wayne), *A Global Affair* (with Bob Hope), *Hostile Guns* (with George Montgomery), *The Power* (with George Hamilton), *American Gothic* (with Rod Steiger), as well as *Munster Go Home!*, and *Here Come the Munsters!* Also an opera singer in her early years at the Hollywood Bowl, her 1987 autobiography was entitled *Yvonne: An Autobiography.* Her marriage to Hollywood stunt man Bob Morgan ended in divorce, but produced two sons, Bruce and Michael. Son Michael survives her, as does a stepdaughter, Bari Morgan.

**Curt Dempster**, 71, Detroit, MI-born stage manager/theatre founder/producer, died Jan. 19, 2007, in New York, NY. As founder of the Ensemble Studio Theater in New York, NY, his theatre produced over 6000 plays since being founded in 1971. His Broadway credits as a stage manager include *The Investigation, Krapp's Last Tape/The Zoo Story,* and *Happy Days.* As artistic director of Ensemble Studio Theatre, Broadway credit includes *Open Admissions.* His several film credits include *Desperately Seeking Susan, The Manhattan Project,* and *Last Ball.*

**Alfred Desio** (Alfred De Sio, Al DeSio, Al De Sio), 74, Geneva, NY-born dancer, died Feb. 14, 2007, in Los Angeles, CA, of complications from bladder cancer. An inventor of a kind of enhanced tap dancing called Tap-Tronics, the system allows tap dancers to make their own music using microphones in their shoes, the tap sounds that result are then picked up by the microphones and relayed to transmitters, receivers, synthesizers, and other electronic equipment. His Broadway credits include *West Side Story, Donnybrook!, Kean, She Loves Me, I'm Solomon, Zorba,* and *Coco.* He is survived by his wife and collaborator, Louise Reichlin. He also taught at the University of Southern California, the Colburn School of Performing Arts, and Loyola Marymount University, as well as directed a tap-dancing program for children. He also helped his wife run the Los Angeles Choreographers and Dancers dance company.

**Vilma Ebsen**, 96, Belleville, IL-born actress/singer/dancer, died March 12, 2007, in Pacific Palisades, CA, in her sleep. Becoming the dance director of the dance department at Rollins College in Orlando, FL, she joined her brother Buddy in New York in 1928, a year after graduating from high school. Following a rave review by critic Walter Winchell who caught her and brother Buddy's act at an Atlantic City revue, as a vaudeville team the Ebsens' credits included a stint at the Palace Theatre in *Broadway Stars of the Future,* followed by Broadway credits including *Whoopee!, Flying Colors, Ziegfeld Follies of 1934,* and a role on her own in *Between the Devil.* The duo's sole film credit was *Broadway Melody of 1936,* after which time she relocated to California and founded the Ebsen School of Dancing in Pacific Palisades, CA, with sister Helga in 1943, which focused on ballet and tap dancing for children. It operated until the mid-1990s. Her first marriage to seven-time Academy Award-nominated film composer Robert Emmett Dolan ended in divorce and her marriage to second husband Stanley Biggs, an inventor and professional tennis player, also ended in divorce. Buddy Ebsen died in 2003. Two sons, Robert Dolan and Michael Biggs, two granddaughters, and four great-grandchildren survive her.

**Robert Arthur Fennell** (Bob Fennell), 48, Yonkers, NY-born press agent, died November 12, 2006, at his family's home in Yonkers, NY, of liver cancer. Since 1996, Fennell was the co-owner of The Publicity Office, handling the press for such clients as this season's *Grey Gardens,* long running hit shows *Wicked, The Phantom of the Opera, The 25th Annual Putnam County Spelling Bee,* last season's revival of *Three Days of Rain* starring Julia Roberts, as well the 2004 revival of *A Raisin in the Sun* starring Sean Combs, the 2002 revival of *Man of La Mancha,* and *The Diary of Anne Frank* starring Natalie Portman. He represented over one hundred Broadway, Off-Broadway and touring productions in his short career, including *Putting It Together, James Joyce's The Dead, The Green Bird, Follies, Jane Eyre, Festen, Angels in America, Skylight, Hamlet, Fortune's Fool, Stomp, The Vagina Monologues,* The Royal National Theatre, and The Royal

Shakespeare Company. His company also handled the press for Off-Broadway non-profits Playwrights Horizons and The Signature Theatre Company. Fennell was a graduate of Fordham University and New York University Tisch School of the Arts. In addition to his work as a press agent, he was an adjunct lecturer at Brooklyn College. Prior to his work as a press agent, the lifelong New York resident worked as an actor and a carpenter. Fennell was an initial associate of Boneau/Bryan-Brown in 1991. Mr. Fennell is survived by his longtime companion, Stacy Shane; his mother, Katherine Fennell; sisters Mary Ann Brendler of Monroe, NY; Susan D'Agostino of Ardsley, NY; Katherine Hoffnagle of Hastings, NY; Elizabeth Frare of Valley Cottage, NY; and Nancy Case of Greenwich, CN, as well as three nephews and six nieces.

**Richard Martin Gilman**, 83, Brooklyn, NY-born literary and drama critic, died Oct. 28, 2006, in Kusatsu, Japan, following a ten year battle with lung cancer. A professor at the Yale School of Drama from 1967-1998 with students there including Christopher Durang, Wendy Wasserstein, and Albert Innaurato, he also was a lecturer or visiting professor at Columbia University, Stanford University, and Barnard College. He served in the Marine Corps in the South Pacific from 1943-1946, before becoming a drama critic at *Commonweal,* and then the same at *Newsweek* from 1964-67. He was the author of six books: *The Confusion of Realms, The Making of Modern Drama, Common and Uncommon Masks, Decadence: The Strange Life of an Epithet, Faith, Sex, Mystery: A Memoir, The Drama Is Coming Now: The Theatre Criticism of Richard Gilman, 1961-1991,* and *Chekhov's Plays.* He was a drama critic at *Commonweal* following his stint in the Marine Corps, and was the president of the PEN American Center from 1981-1983 (the largest of the eight-two centers of the international association of writers) as well as the 1971 recipient of the George Jean Nathan Award for drama criticism. Two previous marriages, one to Esther Morgenstern, a painter and dancer, in 1949, and the other to Lynn Nesbit, the literary agent, in 1966, ended in divorce. In 1992, he married Yasuko Shiojiri, who had translated his books into Japanese. She survives him, as do daughters Priscilla and Claire Gilman, of Manhattan, NY, son, Nicholas, of Mexico City, Mexico, a sister, Edith Axelrod, of New Jersey, and four grandchildren.

**Murray Grand**, 87, Philadelphia, PA-born composer and lyricist, died March 7, 2007, in Santa Monica, CA, of emphysema. His Broadway credits include *Once Over Lightly, Leonard Sillman's New Faces of 1952,* and *New Faces of 1956.* His Off-Broadway credits include *Chic.* During World War II, he accompanied stars such as Betty Grable, Gypsy Rose Lee, and Beatrice Lillie, when they toured with the USO. He began his career playing gigs at such New York nightclubs as the Fireside Inn, Upstairs at the Downstairs, Bon Soir, Jack Delaney's, and the Village Green. His standard "Guess Who I Saw Today," considered one of the twenty-five most important nightclub songs of all time, appeared in *Leonard Sillman's New Faces of 1952,* and was eventually recorded by such performers as Nancy Wilson and Sarah Vaughan. International musical production credits include *Triple Galop* in Paris, France, *The Dancing Heiress* in London, England, and the *Caesar's Palace Revue* in Las Vegas, NV. His film credits as a pianist include *Tempest* and *Moscow on the Hudson.* He also composed music for the revival tour of the Joan Collins and Linda Evans show *Legends!* He is survived by a sister.

**Ellen Hanley**, 80, Lorain, OH-born actress, died Feb. 12, 2007, in Norwalk, CT, of a stroke, following a lengthy battle with cancer. Making her Broadway debut in *Annie Get Your Gun* (with Ethel Merman) in 1946, she appeared in *Barefoot Boy With Cheek* (with Nancy Walker and Red Buttons) in 1947, winning a Theatre World Award for her performance. Other Broadway credits include *Two's Company* (with Bette Davis), *First Impressions,* the Pulitzer Prize-winning *Fiorello!, The Fig Leaves Are Falling,* and *1776.* Off-Broadway credits include *The Boys from Syracuse* in 1963. Touring extensively in summer stock shows in the 1940s and 1950s, she was also a regular performer in Julius Monk's revues in the 1950s. Her 1951 marriage to performer Ronnie Graham ended in divorce. Daughter, Nora Graham, son, Julian, of Bridgewater, CT, sister, Patricia Hanley, of New York, brother, playwright William Hanley of Ridgefield, CT, and several grandchildren, survive her.

**Jay Harnick**, 78, Chicago, IL-born performer/director/producer/manager, died Feb. 27, 2007, at the Isabella House in New York, NY, following a long illness. As founder and artistic director of Theatreworks USA from 1961 until his retirement in 2000, he oversaw the nation's largest touring children's theater company, bringing performances to forty-nine states and Canada and assembling a repertoire of 117 musicals and plays. Theatreworks USA also provided starts to the careers of actors such as F. Murray Abraham and Henry Winkler. His Broadway credits include *Gentleman Prefer Blondes, Alive and Kicking, John Murray Anderson's Almanac, Phoenix '55*; as a production stage manager, *Tartuffe*; as an assistant director, *The Office*; and as a producer, *The Sudden and Accidental Re-education of Horse Johnson.* Other credits include *Abduction From the Seraglio* with the New York City Opera and a tour of *Fiddler on the Roof.* Survivors include his wife, actress Barbara Barrie, brother, lyricist Sheldon Harnick, daughter, sister, Gloria, daughter, Jane Harnick, son, Aaron, and a granddaughter.

**Kitty Carlisle Hart** (Catherine Conn), 96, New Orleans, LA-born actress/arts advocate, died April 17, 2007, in New York, NY, of heart failure. One of the most visible, enduring, and effervescent personalities of twentieth century theatre as well as New York society, her fame ranged from her marriage to Moss Hart, to her staple of appearances as a pioneer on television game shows of the 1950s, 1960s, and 1970s, to her service as chairperson of the New York State Council of the Arts for twenty years, from 1976-1996. Her Broadway credits include *Champagne, Sec, White Horse Inn, Three Waltzes, Walk With Music, The Rape of Lucretia, Anniversary Waltz*, and *On Your Toes.* Educated in Europe in the classics, her career in the theatre started by performing in stage shows in between movies several times a day. She played many a summer stock company, and sang "The Star Spangled Banner" at many World War II bond rallies. She also played the *subway circuit*, in the Brooklyn and the Bronx. A perennial in the early days of game shows, she appeared on *To Tell the Truth* from 1956-1977. Her film roles include *Hollywood Canteen, A Night at the Opera, Murder at the Vanities, She Loves Me Not, Here Is My Heart, Larceny with Music, Radio Days*, and *Six Degrees of Separation.* She made many Decca recordings early in her career but didn't make her Metropolitan Opera debut until the age of fifty-six, in *Die Fledermaus.* She filled her later years following retirement from her career as a performer and arts advocate by performing on cruise ships and up to November 2006, at a fundraiser at Lincoln Center. Performing well up until the end of her life, her one-woman show in which she toured was entitled *My Life on the Wicked Stage.* Her autobiography, *Kitty: An Autobiography*, was published in 1988, she was named a "living landmark" by the New York Landmarks Conservancy in 1998, and was named as well to the Theater Hall of Fame in 1999. Her marriage to dramatist Moss Hart in 1946 ended with his death in 1961, and she is survived by her two children from that marriage, daughter, Catherine Hart, a physician in New York City, Christopher Hart, a producer in Los Angeles, CA, and three grandchildren.

**Melissa Hayden** (Mildred Herman), 83, Toronto, Canada-born ballerina dancer, died Aug. 9, 2006, in Winston-Salem, NC, of pancreatic cancer. Her Broadway credits include with the Ballet Theatre in 1946, and *Allegro* in 1947. She was a member of the American Ballet Theatre from 1945-1947, and again from 1953-1954, and also essentially a founding member of George Balanchine's City Ballet, attending from 1948-1973. Mayor John Lindsay presented her with New York City's Handel Medallion in 1973. Some of her most famous performances include Titania in *Midsummer Night's Dream*, Eurydice in *Orpheus*, Sugarplum Fairy in *The Nutcracker*, and Odette in *Swan Lake*, all Balanchine productions. Following her retirement from performing, she established herself as an influential teacher, heading the ballet department at Skidmore College and the School of Pacific Northwest Ballet in Seattle, WA, where she was also briefly artistic director. From 1983 until her death, she taught at the North Carolina School of the Arts in Winston-Salem, NC, where she taught more than 6,000 students. Her television appearances include *The Kate Smith Show* and film appearances include *Limelight.* Her husband, Donald Coleman, son, Stuart Coleman, of Scarsdale, NY, daughter, Jennifer C. Damsky, of Manhattan, NY, and five grandchildren, survive her.

**Joseph Hayes**, 88, Indianapolis, IN-born author/playwright, died Sept. 11, 2006, in St. Augustine, FL, of complications from Alzheimer's disease. His

Broadway credits include *Leaf and Bough, The Desperate Hours* 1955 Best Play Tony Award), *The Happiest Millionaire*, and *Calculated Risk.* His film credits include *The Desperate Hours*, based on his novel and play of the same name, and *Bon Voyage!* His wife and collaborator, Marrijane, died in 1991. He is survived by sons, Daniel Hayes, of Georgetown, FL, Gregory, of Atlanta, and Jason, of Juneau, AK, and five grandchildren. *In 1955, for a photographic display accompanying an article about the Broadway play, *Life* magazine posed some of the actors in a house outside Philadelphia, where a similar home invasion had taken place three years earlier. James J. Hill, the father of the family that had been taken hostage, sued Time Inc., *Life's* parent company, arguing that the article and photographs had conflated his story with the fictional, and very different, events in Mr. Hayes's book, entitling the Hill family to damages. In 1967, the case went before the United States Supreme Court, where Richard M. Nixon, then a Wall Street lawyer, represented Mr. Hill. The court ruled in favor of *Time*, citing the absence of proof of "actual malice." (Actual malice is a legal term meaning knowledge of falsity or reckless disregard for the truth.) The ruling expanded the proof of malice requirement to cases involving people who are not public figures but are in the news, a significant decision in First Amendment law.

**Benjamin Hendrickson**, 55, died July 2, 2006, in Huntington, NY, of a self-inflicted gunshot wound to the head. His Broadway credits include *The Three Sisters* (and 1975 revival), *The Beggar's Opera, Measure for Measure, Next Time I'll Sing to You, The Robber Bridegroom, Edward II, The Time of Your Life, The Elephant Man, Strider*, and *Awake and Sing!* Best known for his work on *As The World Turns*, he won an Emmy Award for his work on that show.

**Henry Hewes**, 89, Boston-born theatre critic, died July 18, 2006, in Manhattan, NY. The founder of the American Theater Critics Association in 1974, his first job in the industry was as a copy boy to Brooks Atkinson at *The New York Times*, eventually working his way up to writing profiles up to the Sunday arts pages. He then joined *The Saturday Review*, where eventually he became the chief critic, serving in that capacity from 1955-1973. His tenure there was marked by his attention to international and regional theatre productions. He also helped create the American Theatre Wing's design awards, now called the Hewes Awards. He was also a past president of the New York Drama Critics Circle and the Drama Desk, and the editor from 1960-1964 of the *Best Plays* anthology. He was elected to the Theater Hall of Fame in 2002. His wife, Jane, sons, Henry, Tucker, and Havelock, and six grandchildren, survives him.

**Arthur Hill** (Arthur Edward Spence Hill), 84, Melfort, Saskatchewan, Canada-born actor, died Oct. 22, 2006, in Pacific Palisades, CA, of complications from Alzheimer's disease. His early career consisting of touring Canada in theatrical productions and performances on the BBC, he performed in London's West End before eventually landing on Broadway in *The Matchmaker*, followed by *Look Homeward, Angel, The Gang's All Here, All the Way Home, Who's Afraid of Virginia Woolf?* (1963 Best Actor in a Play Tony Award and New York Drama Critics Award), and *More Stately Mansions.* His numerous film credits include *In the Cool of the Day, Harper, A Bridge Too Far, The Ugly American*, and *The Andromeda Strain.* On television, he could be seen in *Alfred Hitchcock Presents, The Defenders, Ben Casey, The Untouchables, The F.B.I., Mission: Impossible, The Fugitive, Marcus Welby, M.D., The US Steel Hour, Hallmark Hall of Fame*, and *Studio One.* And for three years he was the face of *Owen Marshall, Counselor at Law*, which ran from 1971-1974. He served the Royal Candian Air Force in World War II. His first wife, Peggy Hassard, died in 1990 of complications of Alzheimer's disease, after which time he retired from acting. Survivors include his wife, Anne-Sophie Taraba, son, Douglas, of Los Angeles, CA, a daughter, a stepdaughter, and sisters, Pat and Eunice, both of Winnipeg, Canada.

**Grant Hossack**, 69, composer/conductor/orchestrator/musical supervisor, died Jan. 6, 2007, of cancer. Broadway credits include *Travesties* and *The Moony Shapiro Songbook.* A prolific composer in London's West End, he was also musical director for the BBC2 radio orchestra, along with composing award-winning music for the British television series *Nanny.*

**Barnard Hughes** (Barnard Aloysius Kiernan Hughes), 90, Bedford Hills, NY-born actor, died July 11, 2006, in New York, NY, following a brief illness. A 1978

Best Actor in Play Tony Award winner as well as a Drama Desk Award winner for his role in *Da*, his other Broadway credits include *Please, Mrs. Baribaldi, The Ivy Green, Dinosaur Wharf, A Majority of One, Advise and Consent, The Advocate, Nobody Loves an Albatross, Hamlet, I Was Dancing, How Now, Dow Jones, The Wrong Way Light Bulb, Sheep on the Runway, Abelard and Heloise, Much Ado About Nothing* (Best Featured Actor in a Play Tony nomination), *Uncle Vanya, The Good Doctor, All Over Town, V.I.P Night on Broadway, Angels Fall, End of the World, The Iceman Cometh, Prelude to a Kiss,* and *Waiting in the Wings*. Off-Broadway credits include *Translations*. Credits in Ireland include *You Can't Take It With You* at the Abbey Theater, and reprising his role in *Da* at the Olympia Theater. Film credits include *Midnight Cowboy, The Hospital, Cold Turkey, Where's Poppa, Oh, God! Maxie, The Lost Boys, Doc Hollywood, Tron, Sister Act 2, Da* (reprising his stage role), *Where's Poppa*, and *Cradle Will Rock*. An Emmy Award winner for his guest role in *Lou Grant*, his other television credits include *Playhouse 90, Kraft Theatre, Doc, The Guiding Light, As The World Turns, All in the Family, The Bob Newhart Show, Blossom,* and *The Cavanaughs*. He was a veteran of World War II. In 2000 he was awarded with a Special Drama Desk Award for lifetime achievement. He is survived by his wife of fifty-six years, actress Helen Stenborg, alongside whom he acted for many years, even up until 1999, son, director Doug Hughes, daughter, Laura Hughes, of New York, NY, and grandson, Samuel Hughes Rubin.

**Betty Hutton** (Elizabeth June Thornburg), 86, Battlefield Creek, MI-born actress, died March 12, 2007, in Palm Springs, CA, of complications from colon cancer. Her Broadway credits include *Two For The Show, Panama Hattie, Betty Hutton and Her All-Star International Show* (1952 and 1953), *Fade Out-Fade In,* and *Annie*. Her film roles include *Annie Get Your Gun, The Greatest Show on Earth, The Fleet's In, Star Spangled Rhythm, Happy Go Lucky, The Miracle of Morgan's Creek, And the Angels Sing, Duffy's Tavern, Cross My Heart, Red, Hot, and Blue, Let's Dance, Sailor Beware, Let's Face It, Here Come the Waves, The Stork Club, Incendiary Blonde, The Perils of Pauline, Somebody Loves Me, Dream Girl,* and *Spring Reunion*. Her own television series, *The Betty Hutton Show*, lasted a single season, from 1959-60. Receiving a master's degree in psychology in the early 1980s from Salve Regina in Newport, RI, she eventually taught at Emerson College and made occasional broadcast appearances late in her career. Her four marriages, the first to Charles O'Curran, a dance director, the second to Ted Briskin, a manufacturer, the third to Alan Livingston, a recording company executive, and the fourth, to Pete Candoli, a jazz trumpeter, all ended in divorce. She is survived by her daughters, Candy and Lindsay, from her marriage to Ted Briskin, and Caroline, from her marriage to Pete Candoli.

**George Charles Izenour**, 94, New Brighton, PA-born designer, died March 28, 2007, in Philadelphia, PA. Based on his college thesis, Izenour pioneered theatre design with the development of his Izenour System. He developed an electronic dimming system for stage lighting, the first of its kind. It allowed one operator watching a performance from the back of the theatre to do what previously took two to three operators to manage. Used in television studios and theatres across the country, the Izenour System eventually made its way to Broadway. He similarly invented a system to move scenery via a winch, by remote control. In the 1950s, he built a theatre for the Loeb Drama Center at Harvard University that could convert from a proscenium stage to a thrust in 15 minutes. Other commissions followed, including those in Canada, Israel, Venezuela, and across the United States. In 1939, a grant from the Rockefeller Foundation allowed him to move to the Yale School of Drama to establish the electromechanical laboratory, where he worked for thirty-eight years. As an engineering consultant, he advised the Metropolitan Opera Company and the Julliard School of Music and helped to design more than 100 theatres across the country. At the time of his death, he was a partner in the theater design company he founded, George C. Izenour Associates. A wife and son predeceased him. There are no immediate survivors.

**George Jenkins**, 98, Baltimore, MD-born designer, died April 6, 2007, in Santa Monica, CA, in his sleep and of natural causes. A double Tony nominee in 1957 for his work on *The Happiest Millionaire* as well as *Too Late the Phalarope*, he also received a Tony nomination in 1960 for *The Miracle Worker* and another in 1961 for *13 Daughters*. He received a 1977 Drama Desk Award nomination for

Outstanding Set Design for *Sly Fox*. Other Broadway credits as an assistant to Jo Mielziner include *The Boys from Syracuse, Stars in Your Eyes, Watch on the Rhine, The Wookey,* and *The Land is Bright*. His stand-alone credits include *Early to Bed, Mexican Hayride, Allah Be Praised! I Remember Mama, Dark of the Moon, Common Ground, Memphis Bound!, Are You With It, Strange Fruit, The French Touch, Tonight at 8:30, Time for Elizabeth, Lost in the Stars, The Curious Savage, Bell, Book, and Candle, Three Wishes for Jamie, Touchstone, Gently Does It, The Immoralist, The Bad Seed, Ankles Aweigh, The Desk Set, Rumple, Two for the Seesaw, Once More, With Feeling, Cue for Passion, Tall Story, Jolly's Progress, One More River, Critic's Choice, A Thousand Clowns, Step on a Crack, Jennie, Catch Me if You Can, Generation, The Royal Hunt of the Sun, Wait Until Dark, The Only Game in Town, Night Watch, Sly Fox* (and 2004 revival). Perhaps best known for his design (with George Gaines) of the 1976 film *All the President's Men*, his other film credits include *Klute, The Parallax View, The Secret Life of Walter Mitty, The Bishop's Wife, Wait Until Dark, The Subject Was Roses, 1776, The Paper Chase, Funny Lady, Mickey One, Night Moves, Comes a Horseman, The China Syndrome, Starting Over, Sophie's Choice,* and *Presumed Innocent*. He worked in the early days of television on such shows as *Philco TV Playhouse* and designed shows for the Philadelphia, PA group Plays and Players for several years before making the move to New York City. Later in life he taught at University of California at Los Angeles. He was divorced from his first wife, Barbara, and his second wife of fifty years, Phyllis Adams Jenkins, died in 2004. His daughter survives him from his first marriage, Jane Jenkins Dumais, three granddaughters, including Wylie Griffin, and two great-granddaughters.

**Robert Earl Jones**, 96, Senatobia, MS-born actor, died Sept. 7, 2006, in Englewood, NJ, at the Actor's Fund of America home, of natural causes. He was a longtime resident of New York City. His Broadway credits include his 1945 debut in *The Hasty Heart*, followed by *Set My People Free, Caesar and Cleopatra, Fancy Meeting You Again, Mister Johnson, Infidel Caesar, The Moon Besieged, More Stately Mansions, All God's Chillun Got Wings, Death of a Salesman, Unexpected Guests, Mule Bone,* and *The Gospel at Colonus*. Off-Broadway credits include *Moon on a Rainbow Shawl*. A prizefighter under the name of Battling Bill Stovall, he became a sparring partner of Joe Louis in Chicago, IL, in his early life. Taking a job in New York City with the Works Progress Administration, he later moved into acting, but was blacklisted in the 1950s due to political affiliations. His film roles include Luther Coleman in *The Sting, The Cockfighter, The Cotton Club, Witness, One Potato, Two Potato, Terror in the City, Mississippi Summer, Lying Lips,* and *The Notorious Elinor Lee*. His television credits include *Kojak* and *Lou Grant*. He was presented with a Lifetime Achievement Award from the National Black Theatre Festival, received an Oscar Micheaux Award, and was inducted into the Black Filmmakers Hall of Fame. His two marriages ended in divorce, the first to Ruth Connoly, the second to Jumelle P. Jones. Sons, the actor James Earl Jones, and Michael Earl Jones, of Chandler, AZ, and one grandchild, survive him.

**Scott Kelman**, 70, performance art guru/activist, died Feb. 22, 2007, in Portland, OR, of complications of pneumonia. Beginning his career in experimental theatre in the 1960s and 1970s, he eventually opened the Factory Place theatre in downtown Los Angeles in 1981, and finally Pipeline Inc., which garnered much national attention and local awards for incorporating homeless persons, among others. Productions of note were *Peter, Paul and Henry, Angel's Flight,* and *Tao Soup*. Relocating to Portland, OR in the 1990s, he founded the Brooklyn Bay Performance Space and taught his "kelmanwords" performance process, a mindfulness and body-based approach to creativity. Among those Kelman brought initially to the stage were Whoopi Goldberg, Harry Shearer, and the performance artists John Fleck, Kedric Robin Wolfe, Jan Munroe, and Hirokazu. Survivors include a sister, Pepi Kelman, and godson and archivist, Jay Green.

**Bruno Kirby** (Bruno Giovanni Quidaciolu Jr.), 57, New York, NY-born actor, died Aug. 14, 2006, in Los Angeles, CA, of complications from recently diagnosed leukemia. His Broadway credit includes *Lost In Yonkers*. Off-Broadway he appeared in *Bunny Bunny*, about his friendship with the late actress Gilda Radner. His film credits include *The Young Graduates, The Harrad Experiment, Sleepers, Tin Men, When Harry Met Sally, This Is Spinal Tap, Good Morning, Vietnam, The Godfather: Part II, The Basketball Diaries, Donnie Brasco, City Slickers,* and *The Freshman*.

His television credits include *The Super*, HBO's *Entourage*, and *Homicide: Life on the Street*. His father, wife, Lynn Sellers, stepmother, Roz, brother, John, and stepbrother, Brad Sullivan, survive him.

**Florence Klotz** (Kathrina E. Klotz, aka Flossie Klotz), 86, Brooklyn, NY-born costume designer, died of heart failure, Nov. 1, 2006, in New York, NY. A six-time Best Costume Design Tony Award winner for *Follies* (1971, and Drama Desk Award), *A Little Night Music* (1973), *Pacific Overtures* (1976, and Drama Desk Award), *Grind* (1985), *Kiss of the Spiderwoman* (1993, and Drama Desk Award), and *Showboat* (1995, and Drama Desk Award), her other Broadway credits as an assistant include *The King and I, A Tree Grows in Brooklyn, Two on the Aisle, Pal Joey, Of Thee I Sing, Wish You Were Here, My 3 Angels, Carnival in Flanders, Silk Stockings, Cat on a Hot Tin Roof, Pipe Dream, The Ponder Heart, Mr. Wonderful, Orpheus Descending, Jamaica, Time Remembered, Flower Drum Song, J.B., The Sound of Music, A Loss of Roses, Toys in the Attic, Invitation to a March, Do Re Mi, The Gay Life, Lord Pengo*, and in her own right include *Carousel* (1957), *Jerome Robbins' Ballet: U.S.A.* (and 1961 revival), *A Call on Kuprin, Take Her, She's Mine, Romulus, Never Too Late, On an Open Roof, Nobody Loves an Albatross, The Owl and the Pussycat, One by One, Mating Dance, The Best Laid Plans, It's A Bird…It's a Plane…It's Superman!, Paris is Out!, Norman, Is That You?, Sondheim, A Musical Tribute, Dreyfus in Rehearsal, Legend, Side by Side by Sondheim, On the Twentieth Century* (1978 Drama Desk Award), *Harold and Maude, Goodbye Fidel, The Little Foxes, A Doll's Life, Peg, Jerry's Girls, Rags, Roza*, and *City of Angels* (Tony nomination). Her film credits include *A Little Night Music* and *Something for Everyone*. In addition to her Tonys, Klotz won five Drama Desk Awards, three L.A. Critic Circle Awards, and two Outer Critics' Circle Awards. In 2002, she received the Patricia Zipprodt Award from the Fashion Institute of Technology, and in 2005, she won the Irene Sharaff Lifetime Achievement Award. Among her survivors are her niece, Suzanne DeMarco, and her cousin, Paula Silbert.

**Henry LeTang**, 91, Harlem, New York-born performer/dancer, died April 26, 2007, in his sleep at Desert Springs Hospital in Las Vegas, NV. A Best Choreography Tony Award winner in 1989 for his work on *Black and Blue*, his other Broadway credits include *My Dear Public*, followed by *Dream With Music, Shuffle Along* (1952), *Eubie* (Tony nomination), *Sophisticated Ladies* (1981 Tony Award nomination, Drama Desk Award nomination). A teacher to Chita Rivera, Gregory Hines, Savion Glover, Betty Hutton, Billie Holliday, and Lena Horne, among many, many others, he opened his own dance studio in Harlem at the age of seventeen and only stopped coaching at his home a few months prior to his death. His film credits include *The Cotton Club* and *Tap*. His first two marriages ended in divorce, and his third wife, the former Ellie Epps, died in 2002. He is survived by his son, Henry LeTang Jr., son Jon, sister, Edith LeTang, and ten grandchildren.

**Calvin Lockhart**, 72, Bahamas-born actor, died March 29, 2007, in the Bahamas, of complications following a stroke. His Broadway credits include *The Cool World* and *Reggae*. Best known for his roles in "Blackploitation" films, his credits in that medium include *Joanna, Cotton Comes to Harlem, Halls of Anger, Melinda, Let's Do It Again*, and *Coming to America*. He is survived by his wife, Jennifer Miles-Lockhart, and two sons.

**Salem Ludwig**, 91, Brooklyn, NY-born actor, died April 1, 2007, in New York, NY. His Broadway credits include *Miracle in the Mountains, All You Need is One Good Break, An Enemy of the People, Camino Real, The Trip to Bountiful, Inherit the Wind, The Disenchanted, Rhinoceros, The Three Sisters, Moonchildren, The American Clock, I'm Not Rappaport, A Month of Sundays*, and *Park Your Car in Harvard Yard*. Also appearing in more than forty films and television programs, his career was cut short in that medium by being blacklisted in the 1950s. His credits in television in film include *I Love You Alice B. Toklas!, Never Love a Stranger, What's So Bad About Feeling Good? For the Love of Money, The Object of My Affection, All in the Family, The Sopranos, Unfaithful, The Savages*.

**Hal Lynch**, 79, Birmingham, AL-born actor, died Oct. 5, 2006, in Opp, AL, of suicide. His Broadway credits include *Spoon River Anthology*. Best known for his roles on television and film, his numerous film roles include *Stagecoach*, and

television credits include *Star Trek, The Wild, Wild West, Gunsmoke, The Big Valley, The Mod Squad, Mayberry F.F.D., Mannix*, and *Emergency*.

**Mako** (Makoto Iwamatsu), 72, Kobe, Japan-born actor, died July 21, 2006, in Somis, CA, of esophageal cancer. Best known for his role as the Reciter in *Pacific Overtures* in 1976, he received a Tony nomination for his role in the production, followed by another Broadway appearance in *Shimada*. He received an Academy Award nomination for his work in the film *The Sand Pebbles* (with Steve McQueen), becoming one of only a few Japanese actors to have achieved the honor. His other film credits include *Conan the Barbarian, Conan the Destroyer, Seven Years in Tibet, Pearl Harbor*, and *Memoirs of a Geisha*. Television credits include *McHale's Navy, 77 Sunset Strip*, and *I Spy*. He served the United States in World War II, and enrolled at the Pasadena Playhouse following the war to study acting. He helped found the East West Players, America's first Asian-American repertory company, based in Los Angeles, CA, serving as artistic director there until 1989. Other credits include *The Music Lessons* and David Henry Hwang's *FOB* at The Public Theater. His survivors include his wife, actress/director/dancer/choreographer Shizuko Hoshi, daughters, Sala Icsman of Hamburg, NJ, and Mimosa Skelton of Camarillo, CA, sister, Momo Yashima, of Los Angeles, CA, and two grandchildren.

**Daniel McDonald**, 46, Scranton, PA-born actor, died Feb. 15, 2007, at his home in New York, NY, of brain cancer. Having studied at the Royal Academy of Dramatic Art in London, England, he was a Theatre World Award winner as well as a Best Actor in a Musical Tony Award nominee and Drama Desk Award nominee for his role in 1997's *Steel Pier*. His other Broadway credits include *High Society* and *Mamma Mia!* His national tour credits include *Contact*. His television credits include *Sex and the City, Law & Order, CSI: Miami*, and *Murder She Wrote*. His wife, Mujah Maraini-Melehi, and two children, Fosco and Ondina, survive him.

**Robert Mitchell** (Robert Deatrick Mitchell), 77, Passaic, NJ-born designer, died Aug. 18, 2006, in Manhattan, NY, of epithelioid hemangioendothelioma, a rare disease of the blood vessels. His Broadway credits include *Medea* (1973), *Beatlemania, The Basic Training of Pavlo Hummel* (with Al Pacino), and *Oedipus Rex* (1984). Off-Broadway credits include *Screens* at the Brooklyn Academy of Music, and he designed a production of *Oedipus Tyrannos* in the ancient theater at Epidaurus, the first American to do so. He also worked during his career with the Pennsylvania Ballet and Les Grands Ballets Canadiens of Montreal, and with the band Emerson, Lake, & Palmer. His partner of forty-five years, Patrick Horrigan, and a brother, Fred, of Lovell, ME, survive him.

**Sheridan "Sherry" Morley**, 65, British-born theatre critic and biographer, died in his sleep Feb. 16, 2007, in London, England. The son of famous British actor Robert Morley, he was born the day his father opened as Sheridan Whiteside in Moss Hart's *The Man Who Came to Dinner*. Raised with the glitterati of show business on both sides of the Atlantic Ocean, his maternal grandmother was the actress Gladys Cooper, the actor Robert Hardy was uncle by marriage, and his godfather was Noël Coward. His biography of Coward, entitled *A Talent to Amuse*, was published in 1969. His other works include biographies of Gertrude Lawrence, Marlene Dietrich, Katherine Hepburn, Audrey Hepburn, David Niven, James Mason, his father Robert Morley, and John Gielgud, the publication for the latter being held until after Gielgud's death in order to shield the subject him from the scrutiny of revelations about his homosexuality. He taught at The University of Hawaii, followed by a stint as a late-night newscaster and commentator on British independent television and the BBC, where he was featured on *Late Night Line-Up*. He also served as an arts writer for the *Times of London*, as well as other publications. He later became deputy features editor and then television critic for the *Times of London*, and in 1975 he became arts editor and theater critic of the humor magazine *Punch*, position for which he held until the magazine folded in 1992. In addition, he wrote articles for the *International Herald Tribune* and *Playbill* stateside. Other assignments included drama critic for *The Spectator, The New Statesman*, and *The Daily Express*. As a dramatist himself, he devised and staged *Noël and Gertie*, a show about Noël Coward and Gertrude Lawrence, which had a moderate run in London's West End. He also directed Corin Redgrave in Noël Coward's *Song at Twilight* also in the West End. His first marriage, to

Margaret Gudejko, to whom he was married from 1965-1990, ended in divorce. His second wife, the critic and writer Ruth Leon, survives him, as does a son and two daughters from his first marriage.

**Barry Nelson** (Barry Robert Haakon Nielsen), 86, San Francisco, CA-born actor/director, died April 7, 2007, while traveling in Bucks County, PA, of undisclosed causes. Gaining lasting notoriety as the first actor to portray the character of James Bond in a one-hour television production in 1954 of Ian Fleming's *Agent 007*, he performed in an adaptation of *Casino Royale* for the CBS anthology series *Climax!* His Broadway credits include his debut in *Winged Victory*, followed by *Light Up the Sky, The Rat Race, The Moon Is Blue* (with Barbara Bel Geddes), *Wake Up, Darling, Mary, Mary* (again with Barbara Bel Geddes), *Nobody Loves an Albatross, Cactus Flower* (with Lauren Bacall), *Everything in the Garden, The Only Game in Town, The Fig Leaves Are Falling, The Engagement Baby, Seascape* (with Deborah Kerr), *The Norman Conquests, The Act* (with Liza Minnelli, Best Actor in a Musical Tony nomination). His film credits include *Shadow of the Thin Man, Johnny Eager, Dr. Kildare's Victory, A Yank on the Burma Road, The Human Comedy, Bataan, A Guy Named Joe, Mary, Mary* (with Debbie Reynolds), *Pete and Tillie, Airport,* and *The Shining.* His television credits in addition to the role of James Bond include *The Hunter, My Favorite Husband* (with Joan Caulfield, from 1953-1957), *Hudson's Bay, The Twilight Zone, Cannon, Taxi, Dallas,* and *The Love Boat.* A veteran of World War II, he also appeared on the stage and film versions of *Winged Victory.* His first marriage, to actress Teresa Celli, ended in divorce in 1951. His wife, Nansi, survives him.

**Walter Nicks**, 81, dancer/choreographer/teacher, died April 3, 2007, in Brooklyn, NY. His Broadway credits include *My Darlin' Aida, House of Flowers,* and *Jamaica.* Having trained with Katherine Dunham in the 1940s, he became a master of her technique and became associate director of dance at the Dunham School from 1947-1953. He also studied with José Limón, Robert Joffrey, Karel Shook, Louis Horst, and Doris Humphrey, and danced with the Benny Goodman Jazz Revue in the 1940s. He formed a small company in 1953 named El Ballet Negro de Walter Nicks, in Mexico. He performed additionally in Cuba, the Dominican Republic, Puerto Rico, and Haiti. In the 1950s he taught in New York at the Phillips-Fort Studio and choreographed several Harry Belafonte specials. The American Dance Festival honored him for his teaching in 2000, and in 2002 the International Association of Blacks in Dance saluted him for his contributions to dance.

**Carrie Nye** (Carolyn Nye McGeoy), 69, Greenwood, MS-born performer, died July 14, 2006, in New York, NY, of lung cancer. Making her Broadway debut in 1960 in *A Second String,* her other Broadway credits include *Mary, Mary, Half a Sixpence* (Tony nomination), *A Very Rich Woman, Cop-Out,* and *The Man Who Came to Dinner.* Off-Broadway credits include *The Trojan Women* and *Real Inspector Hound.* But it was at the Williamstown Theater Festival and other regional theatres that she made her most lasting mark. Her numerous credits over decades at the Williamstown Theater Festival include *A Streetcar Named Desire, The Skin of Our Teeth,* and *Nude With Violin.* She also performed *Troilus and Cressida* at the White House for President John F. Kennedy. Other regional credits include those at the New Jersey Shakespeare Festival, the Adelphi Festival in Garden City, NY, and the Phoenix Theater Company in Purchase, NY. Her television credits include *Divorce His* and *Divorce Hers* (with Elizabeth Taylor and Richard Burton), most notably as Tallulah Bankhead in *The Scarlett O'Hara War,* for which she was nominated for an Emmy Award, and in roles on *The Guiding Light.* Her film roles include those in *Creepshow* and *Hello Again.* The meticulous rebuilding of Tick Hall, a Stanford White house in Montauk and the house she and husband Dick Cavett owned on Long Island that burned in 1997, was chronicled in the 2003 documentary, *From the Ashes: The Life and Times of Tick Hall.* Her husband, whom she met at Yale Drama School and married in 1964, survives her.

**Mary Orr** (Mary Caswell Orr, aka Mary Orr Denham), 95, Brooklyn, NY-born author/performer, died Sept. 22, 2006, in Manhattan, NY, of pneumonia. She was responsible for penning a short story that became a radio dramatization and what eventually became the basis for the screenplay of *All About Eve.* Receiving $800.00 for her work, what was then entitled *The Wisdom of Eve* appeared in *Cosmopolitan* in May 1946. Based on an actual woman who would wait outside the door of

actress Elisabeth Bergner while she performed in 1943's *The Two Mrs. Carrolls* on Broadway, the story goes that the attendant woman then became Ms. Bergner's secretary, and then proceeded to take her acting career as well as husband (director Paul Czinner). Ms. Orr would marry the director of *The Two Mrs. Carrolls,* Reginald Denham, in 1947. With Denham, her Broadway author credits include *Wallflower, Dark Hammock, Round Trip, Be Your Age,* and *Applause.* Her credits as an actress include *Berlin, Child of Manhattan, Chrysalis, Jupiter Laughs, Dark Hammock, Sherlock Holmes,* and *The Desperate Hours.* Her husband Reginald Denham having died in 1983, her survivors include her nieces Jessica Ivan, of Hartville, OH, and Lenschen Witte, of Alliance, OH, and three step-grandchildren.

**Chris Parry**, 54, British-born designer, died Jan. 19, 2007, in San Diego, CA, of undisclosed causes. A Best Lighting Design Tony Award winner and Drama Desk Award winner for his work on *The Who's Tommy,* his other Broadway credits include *Les Liasons Dangereuses* (1987 Tony nomination), *Search and Destroy, Translations, A Midsummer's Night Dream* (1996 Drama Desk nomination), and *Not About Nightingales* (1999 Outstanding Lighting Design Drama Desk Award, Tony nomination). His film credits include *The Who's Tommy, the Amazing Journey,* and he was on the teaching staff of the University of San Diego.

**Margaret Perry**, 94, Denver, CO-born actress/director/production crewmember, died April 7, 2007, in Colorado. The daughter of actress Antoinette Perry (for whom the Tony Awards are named), her Broadway credits include her debut in 1931 in *After All,* followed by *Ceiling Zero, Now You've Done It, The Greatest Show on Earth, The First Mrs. Fraser, The Shop at Sly Corner, Love Me Long,* and *Mr. Barry's Etchings.* Her film credits include *Go West, Young Man, New Morals for Old,* and *Ceiling Zero.* Her three marriages include those to actor Burgess Meredith and art director Paul Fanning.

**Steven Pimlott**, 53, Stockport, England-born producer/director, died Feb. 14, 2007, at his home near Colchester in Essex, England, of lung cancer. Broadway credits as a director include *Joseph and the Amazing Technicolor Dreamcoat* (1993) and *Bombay Dreams.* The artistic director of the Chichester Festival Theater in southern England, his credits there include *Rose Tattoo.* He was a producer of the English National Opera from 1974-1976, and an associate director of the Royal Shakespeare Company from 1996-2002, and credits there include *Julius Caesar, As You Like It, Richard III, Hamlet, Measure for Measure,* and *Antony and Cleopatra.* In 2007 Queen Elizabeth II named him an officer of the Order of the British Empire for his "services to drama." His mother, Marian Pimlott, wife, Daniela Bechly, an opera singer, sister, Ruth, two sons, Oskar and Raphael, and daughter, Phoebe, survive him.

**Anne Pitoniak**, 85, Westfield, MA-born actress, died April 22, 2007, in New York, NY, of complications from cancer. Making her Broadway debut in 1983 at the age of sixty-one in *'night Mother,* she won a Theatre World Award and a Tony nomination. Her other Broadway credits include *The Octette Bridge Club* (1985 Drama Desk Award, Outstanding Featured Actress in a Play), *Picnic* (1994 Tony nomination), *Amy's View, Uncle Vanya, Dance of Death,* and *Imaginary Friends.* Spending most of her life before Broadway acting in television and radio commercials, she began studying at the Lee Strasberg Theater Institute in 1975. She became a resident actor at the Actors Theater of Louisville in Kentucky in 1977. There she appeared in the Humana Festival of New American Plays, where her roles included those in *Agnes of God* and Jane Martin's *Talking With,* which transferred Off-Broadway. Her television roles included those in *Third Watch* and *Law & Order: SVU.* A veteran of the U.S.O, she performed in Japan during W.W. II. Survivors include her son, Christian Milford, daughter, Susan, a grandson, and two sisters and a brother.

**Rupert Pole**, 87, Los Angeles, CA-born actor/forest ranger, was found at his home July 15, 2006, in the Silver Lake section of Los Angeles, CA, following a recent stroke. Anais Nin's literary executor as well as widower, his Broadway credits include *Mr. Sycamore* and *Common Ground.* Overseeing the estate of his late wife, who died in 1977, he presided over the publication of four unexpurgated volumes of her erotic journals, chronicling liaisons with Henry Miller, Otto Rank, and her own father, were hailed as major works of twentieth century nonfiction. Pole, who was then a forest ranger and also taught literary history at Thomas Starr

King Middle School in Silver Lake, released all of these. His mother was married to Lloyd Wright, architect and son of Frank Lloyd Wright. Having been married in 1923 to Hugo Guiler, after moving to the West Coast with Pole, Nin shuttled back and forth between the East and West coasts, a bigamist and keeping the truth from both husbands, having married Pole also in 1955. No reported survivors.

**Tom Poston** (Thomas Gordon Poston), 85, Columbus, OH-born actor, died May 30, 2007, in Los Angeles, CA, following a brief illness. With Broadway credits including *Cyrano de Bergerac, Stockade, The Grand Prize, Will Success Spoil Rock Hunter? Goodbye Again, Shinbone Alley, Drink to Me Only, Golden Fleecing, The Conquering Hero, Mary, Mary, Forty Carats, But, Seriously...,* and *A Funny Thing Happened on the Way to the Forum,* he still found his greatest success on television, winning his first of three Emmy Awards for his role on *The Steve Allen Show,* as The Man Who Can't Remember His Name. When the show moved to Los Angeles in 1959, Poston stayed in New York. Eventually finding himself on the West Coast, however, his television credits there included most notably Franklin Delano Bickley on *Mork and Mindy,* and George Utley on *Newhart,* playing a handyman who wasn't very handy. He also appeared on another Newhart sitcom, *Bob.* He was a panelist for ten years on *To Tell the Truth,* and among his numerous television credits are those on *Studio One, The Phil Silvers Show, The Defenders, Get Smart, The Bob Newhart Show, The Love Boat, St. Elsewhere, The Simpsons, Coach, Murphy Brown, Home Improvement, Touched by an Angel, Will and Grace, Dream On, Just Shoot Me,* and *That '70s Show.* His film roles include *Cold Turkey, The Happy Hooker, Rabbit Test, Christmas with the Kranks, Beethoven's 5th,* and *The Princess Diaries 2: Royal Engagement.* In his early days, he performed as an acrobat with the Flying Zepleys, and was a veteran of the Army Air Corps in Europe during World War II. Poston was married four times. The first, to Jean Sullivan, ended in divorce. The second, to Kay Hudson, ended in divorce. He later remarried Hudson and their marriage lasted until her death in 1998. Having had a fling with her before they both married other people, he and actress Suzanne Pleshette reunited in 2000 and married in 2001. She survives him, as does a daughter from his first marriage, Francesca Poston, of Nashville, TN, son, Jason Poston, of Los Angeles, CA, and Hudson Poston, of Portand, OR, (from his marriage to second wife Kay Hudson), and sister, Rosalie Cassou, of Fredericksburg, VA.

**Richard Warren Pugh**, 55, died June 9, 2006, in New York, NY, of complications from diabetes. His Broadway credits include *Sweeney Todd, The Music Man, Copperfield, Zorba,* and *The Phantom of the Opera,* of which he was an original member, and of which he was a member when he died. He was also a second vice president of Actors' Equity Association from 1991-2000, and his film credits include *Pocahontas.*

**Patrick Quinn** (Patrick Dominic Quinn), 56, Philadelphia, PA-born actor/Actors' Equity administrator, died Sept. 24, 2006, of a heart attack, at his country home in Bushkill, PA. He lived in Manhattan. Having recently been appointed to the highest staff position at Equity, he was to take over his new position in months. A member of Actors' Equity since 1970, he was elected to the council in 1977. In 2000, he was elected president, holding the position for six years, and helping negotiate a new four-year contract for the union. He raised dues for the first time in twenty years, and guided the union through 9/11 and afterwards. In 1987 he helped create Equity Fights AIDS, a nonprofit begun by the union, that later merged with Broadway Cares. Debuting on Broadway in 1976 in *Fiddler on the Roof,* his other Broadway credits include *Lend Me a Tenor, Beauty and the Beast, A Class Act,* and *The Sound of Music* (1998). He performed often at the Paper Mill Playhouse and at the Walnut Street Theater in Philadelphia, PA. He was a director of *Secrets Every Smart Traveler Should Know,* an Off-Broadway revue that ran for three years. His television credits include *Bosom Buddies* and *Law and Order.* He was the founder of the Charade Dinner Theater in Philadelphia, and performed in numerous regional theatre productions including *Man of La Mancha.* He is survived by his partner of twelve years, Martin Casella, three brothers, James, of Naples, FL, Gerard, of Coatesville, PA, and John, of Doylestown, PA, and sister, Liz Anne Antonucci, of Bloomington, MN.

**Charles Nelson Reilly**, 76, Bronx, NY-born actor/director, died May 25, 2007, in Los Angeles, CA, of complications from pneumonia. A 1962 Best Featured Actor in a Musical Tony Award winner for the role of Bud Frump in *How to Succeed in Business Without Really Trying,* his other Broadway credits as an actor include *Bye Bye Birdie, Hello, Dolly!* (Tony nomination), *Skyscraper,* and *God's Favorite.* As a director his Broadway credits include *The Belle of Amherst* (with Julie Harris), *Paul Robeson, Break a Leg, Charlotte, The Nerd,* and *The Gin Game* (with Charles Durning and Julie Harris; Tony nomination). A 2002 Outstanding Solo Performance Drama Desk Award nominee for his role in *Save it for the Stage: The Life of Reilly,* his other Off-Broadway credit includes the direction of *Private Lives* at the Lucille Lortel Theatre. He was best known for his many campy television appearances, most notably for his years on the game show *Match Game* and in ninety-five appearances on *The Tonight Show* with Johnny Carson. His partner, Patrick Hughes, survives him.

**Lloyd Richards** (Lloyd George Richards), 87, Toronto, Canada-born actor/director/producer, died June 29, 2006, his eighty-seventh birthday, of heart failure. One of the most influential participants in twentieth century American theatre, and even more especially so as an African-American, he began his professional life by moving to New York, fresh from volunteering for the Army Air Corps in World War II. Meeting Paul Mann, he began to study with and later taught with Mann at his actors' workshop. A 1960 Best Director Tony nominee for his work on his Broadway debut, *A Raisin in the Sun,* his other Broadway credits include *The Egghead* and *A Phoenix Too Frequent/Freight* as a performer. Moving into directing, his Broadway credits include *The Long Dream, The Moon Beseiged, I Had a Ball, The Yearling,* and *Paul Robeson.* As dean of the Yale School of Drama and artistic director of the Yale Repertory Theater (1979-1991), as well as the National Playwrights Conference at the Eugene O'Neill Theater Center in Connecticut (from 1968-1999), he oversaw the Broadway productions of *A Lesson From Aloes* (Best play Tony Award nominee), *MASTER HAROLD...and the boys, Ma Rainey's Black Bottom, Blood Knot, Fences* (1987 Best Play Tony Award, Best Direction of a Play Tony Award, Drama Desk Outstanding New Play Drama Desk Award, Outstanding Director of a Play Drama Desk Award nominee, *A Walk in the Woods* (1988 Best Play Tony Award nominee), *Joe Turner's Come and Gone* (1988 Best Play Tony Award nominee, Best Direction of a Play Tony Award nominee) Outstanding New Play Drama Desk Award, Outstanding Director of a Play Drama Desk Award nominee), *Long Day's Journey Into Night (*1989 Outstanding Revival Drama Desk Award nominee), *Ah, Wilderness!* (1989 Best Revival Tony Award nominee), *The Piano Lesson* (1990 Best Play Tony Award nominee, Best, Outstanding New Play Drama Desk Award, Outstanding Director of a Play Drama Desk Award nominee), *The Cemetery Club, Two Trains Running,* and *Seven Guitars* (1996 Best Direction of a play Tony Award nominee, Outstanding Director of a play Drama Desk Award nominee). Facilitating August Wilson's place by presenting so many of his works as a major playwright of the twentieth century, he also fostered the careers of Wendy Wasserstein, Christopher Durang, Lee Blessing, and David Henry Hwang, among many, many others. He was perhaps the greatest single influence upon playwrights in the latter half of the twentieth century. As the artistic director of the Yale Repertory Theatre, he accepted the 1991 Regional Theatre Tony Award. He also taught at New York University in the 1960s, before beginning his tenure at Yale. He is survived by his wife of fifty-nine years, Barbara Davenport, son, Scott Davenport Richards, of Montclair, NJ, and son, Thomas, of Pontedera, Italy.

**Ian Richardson**, 72, Edinburgh, Scotland-born actor, died unexpectedly Feb. 9, 2007, at his home in London, England. His Broadway credits include *Marat/Sade* (1965) with the Royal Shakespeare Company, *My Fair Lady* (1976 Outstanding Actor in a Musical Drama Desk Award, Best Actor in a Musical Tony Award nomination), and *Lolita.* He appeared with the Royal Shakespeare Company as well in *Love's Labour's Lost* and *The Merchant of Venice,* among many, many other roles, including Prospero, Angelo, and Cassius ,in England. He also toured internationally with Diana Rigg and Derek Jacoby in *The Hollow Crown,* and appeared in the West End in *The Creeper.* Early in his career he worked as a radio announcer and attended the Glasgow College of Dramatic Art. But he was best known for his television performances, most notably for the role of Francis Urquhart in the BBC series *House of Cards,* of which there were two sequels. He also played in a television adaptation of John le Carré's *Tinker, Tailor, Soldier, Spy,* and Sherlock Holmes in two television movies. His wife, actress Maroussia Frank, two sons, Jeremy and Miles, several grandchildren, and two sisters, survive him.

**Howard Rosenstone**, 68, died June 7, 2006, in Manhattan, NY, of pulmonary failure. With clients such as David Mamet and Wallace Shawn, he also performed in the David Mamet/Shel Silverstein crime comedy *Things Change*. His partner, John O'Connor, and sister, Elaine Auerback, of Roxbury, NY, survive him.

**Laurence Sacharow**, 68, Brooklyn, NY-born director, died Aug. 16, 2006, in Manhattan, NY, of leukemia. With Off-Broadway credits including *Five of Us* (Obie Award), *The Concept, Young Playwrights Festival* (1988), *Three Tall Women* (1993 Lucille Lortel Award), *The Golem,* and *Beckett/Albee,* he was also the artistic director of River Arts Rep, which he founded in 1979. He also directed the American premieres of *Viva Detroit* and *Hunting Cockroaches*. A pioneer of biographical theatre, he assembled eight residents of a drug rehabilitation center on Staten Island where he worked and created *The Concept,* with the residents as actors and himself as director—a show which premiered at *Café La Mama,* and later transferred to the Off-Broadway Sheridan Square Playhouse. The play was later presented at the White House as well as the United Nations, and a 1994 version toured Russia. Another of his biographical pieces, *The Road Home: Stories of Children of War,* was based on survivors of violence from around the world. Since 1989 he was the director of the theater program at Fordham University's Lincoln Center campus theater program. He was a veteran of the U.S. Army, and is survived by his wife, Michelle, daughters Anya Sacharow and Nina, and a grandson.

**Vincent Sardi Jr.**, 91, New York, NY-born proprietor of the famous Broadway restaurant landmark *Sardi's,* died Jan. 4, 2007, in Berlin, VT, of complications of a urinary tract infection. With actors' caricatures hanging on the wall who were appearing on Broadway and its central location to the theatre district, *Sardi's* restaurant became a place where dreams were made and broken for decades. Founded in 1921, Vincent took the restaurant over from his father around 1945, keeping it until it was sold in 1985. He took control again five years later, and then retired in 1987. His grandson, Sean Ricketts, currently manages the restaurant. He was a veteran of the Marines in World War II.

**Lanna Saunders**, 65, New York, NV-born actress, died March 10, 2007, in Sherman Oaks, CA, of multiple sclerosis. Her Broadway credits include *Sunrise at Campobello, Milk and Honey, Never Live Over a Pretzel Factory, The Changeling,* and *Philadelphia, Here I Come!* Best known for her long-running role as Sister Marie on *Days of Our Lives* on television from 1979-1985, her other television and film credits include *Body Heat, Ruby and Oswald, The Waltons, Fantasy Island,* and *Hart to Hart*. Her husband, actor Lawrence Pressman, and son, actor David Pressman, survives her. Born into a show business family, her father was actor Nicholas Saunders and her grandfather was Russian actor Nicholas Soussanin.

**Nicholas Saunders** (Nikita Soussanin), 92, Kiev, Ukraine-born actor/translator, died August 16, 2006, in Los Angeles, CA, of lung cancer. His Broadway credits include *The Bridal Crown, Lady in the Dark, Happily Ever After, The Magnificent Yankee, The Fifth Season, A Call on Kuprin, Take Her, She's Mine, The Passion of Josef D., Scenes and Revelations,* and *Zoya's Apartment.* Perhaps best known for his role as Captain Barker on *The Phil Silvers Show,* he also worked as a Russian language announcer and later for Radio Liberty as a producer. Since the 1980s, he and partner Frank Dwyer had translated dozens of plays by Anton Chekov from from Russian into English, including *The Wood Demon, Chekhov x 4* (2005 L.A. Drama Critics Award). Born into a show business family, his father was Russian actor Nicholas Soussanin and his stepmother actress Olga Baclonova. His daughter was actress Lanna Saunders.

**Harold Scott**, 70, Morristown, NJ-born actor/producer and first black artistic director of a major American regional theatre, died July 16, 2006, in Newark, NJ. As a performer, his Broadway credits include *The Cool World, After the Fall, Marco Millions, The Changeling, Incident at Vichy, The Cuban Thing, The Gingham Dog, Les Blancs, The Mighty Gents,* and as a director include *Paul Robeson* (and revival), and *Garden District.* Off-Broadway credits include his performance in Genet's *The Blacks* as well as *Deathwatch* (1959 Obie Award), *Death of Bessie Smith, Boys in the Band, A Raisin in the Sun* (1986), *The Member of the Wedding,* and *The Old Settler.* Making history as the artistic director of the Cincinnati Playhouse in the Park from 1972-1974, as well as being the first black person to do so, his numerous other regional theatre credits include those at Arena Stage, Seattle Repertory

Theatre, Indiana Repertory Theatre, and Syracuse Stage. And for almost twenty years, he was the head of the directing program at the Mason Gross School of the Arts at Rutgers University. No immediate survivors.

**Sidney Sheldon**, 89, Chicago, IL-born writer/producer, died Jan. 30, 2007, in Los Angeles, CA, of pneumonia. A Tony winner for Best Musical for 1959's *Redhead,* his other Broadway writing credits include *The Merry Widow, Jackpot, Dream with Music, Alice in Arms,* and *Roman Candle.* A Best Original Screenplay Academy Award winner for *The Bachelor and the Bobby Soxer,* his numerous film credits include *Annie Get Your Gun, Easter Parade, Three Guys Named Mike,* and *You're Never Too Young.* His television credits include *The Patty Duke Show, Hart to Hart,* and he won an Emmy Award for his executive production of *I Dream of Jeannie.* Some of the many television adaptations of his novels include *The Other Side of Midnight, Rage of Angels, Master of the Game, Windmills of the Gods, The Sands of Time,* and *A Stranger in the Mirror.* He was a veteran of the US Army/Air Corps during W.W. II.

**Michael Smuin**, 68, Missoula, MT-born dancer/choreographer, died April 23, 2007, in San Francisco, CA, of a heart attack. A Drama Desk and Tony Award winner for his choreography of *Anything Goes,* his other Broadway credits as a performer include *Little Me* (1962), followed by choreography credits including *Sophisticated Ladies, Canciones de mi Padre, Shogun, The Musical,* and *Private Lives.* Choreographing for the American Ballet Theater in New York before returning to the San Francisco Ballet as artistic director, he eventually founded the Smuin Ballet in 1994, with credits including *Stabat Mater* and *Bluegrass/Slyde.* He won Emmy Awards for his choreography of *Romeo and Juliet, The Tempest,* and *Song for Dead Warriors.* He is survived by son, Shane, and brothers Stephen and Douglas.

**Michael Shurtleff** (Charles Gordon Shurtleff), 86, Oak Park, IL-born casting director/author, died Jan. 28, 2007, in Los Angeles, CA, of lung cancer and other health problems. Penning one of the most influential books on the actor's audition process, *Audition* is still considered the definitive book on the subject. A casting director early in his career for David Merrick, he counted among the talent he helped introduce Elliott Gould, Barbra Streisand, and Jerry Orbach. Shows for which he help cast include *Irma la Douce, Oliver!, I Can Get It for You Wholesale, Pippin, Chicago,* and *Jesus Christ Superstar.* He started his independent casting service Casting Consultants in 1962, and other shows he worked on include *The Apple Tree* and *1776.* In Hollywood, shows he cast included *The Graduate* and *The Sound of Music.* Also a successful Off-Broadway playwright, his *Call Me by My Rightful Name,* starring Robert Duvall, Alvin Ailey, and Joan Hackett, opened in 1961. His survivors include two brothers, John and Roger.

**Susan Raab Simonson**, 37, Greenbrae, CA-born theatre producer, died Nov. 27, 2006, in Los Angeles, CA, of breast cancer. Known nationally as associate producer of L.A. Theatre Works, a company that recorded live productions for later broadcast over satellite and public radio, she helped mount classical as well as contemporary works for LATW's *The Play's the Thing* live radio theatre series created in association with the Smithsonian Institution in Washington, D.C. Plays she chose and cast include *On the Waterfront, The Ride Down Mt. Morgan, Agnes of God,* and *Proof.* Also a veteran producer of stage productions in San Francisco and having attended American Conservatory Theatre, she also worked at Tim Robbins' Actors' Gang theater company. Survivors include husband Academy Award winning filmmaker Eric Simonson, infant son, Henry, parents Joan and Robert Raab, brothers Steve and Michael, sister-in-law Julie, nieces Ella and Soskia, and nephew Nicholas.

**Arnold Sundgaard** (Arnold Olaf Sundgaard), 96, St. Paul, MN-born lyricist/playwright, died Oct. 22, 2006, in Dallas, TX, of congestive heart failure. Broadway writing credits include *Everywhere I Roam, The First Crocus, Rhapsody, The Great Campaign,* and *Of Love Remembered.* Lyricist credits include *The Young Abe Lincoln.* His other theatre credits include *Spirochete: A History,* about the war against syphilis, produced by the Federal Project in 1938. With Kurt Weill he wrote the libretto for the 1948's *Down in the Valley,* and with Alec Wilder he wrote *How Lovely Is Christmas,* recorded by Bing Crosby. He also wrote the librettos for nearly a dozen operas, including *The Lowland Sea* with Wilder in 1952. With

Douglas S. Moore, he wrote *Giants in the Earth*, an opera based on the novel by O.E. Rolvaag. Moore's score for *Giants of the Earth* won the Pulitzer Prize for music in 1951. With illustrator Eric Carle he turned to children's books with publications including *The Lamb and the Butterfly*, and with illustrator Dominic Catalano, *The Bear Who Loved Puccini*. He also taught at Columbia University, Bennington College, and University of Texas. Survivors include two daughters, Joy Kaiser, of Palo Alto, CA, and Jill Jones, of Belmont, MA, son Stephen, of Dallas, TX, nine grandchildren, and twelve great-grandchildren.

**Roy Tobias**, 78, Philadelphia, PA-born dancer/teacher, died Aug. 16, 2006, in Seoul, Korea, of a condition he had had for thirteen years that made it difficult for him to eat. Having joined American Ballet Theater at age sixteen, his Broadway credits include performances with that theatre company, as well as *High Button Shoes* and *Carousel*. His other performance credits include the Grand Ballet du Marquis de Cuevas in Paris, France, and the Ballet Society, with which he danced, from 1950-1960. Noted roles included Balanchine's *Agon*, as well as *Nutcracker, Divertimento No. 15*, Jerome Robbins' *Fanfare*, and Bolender's *The Still Point*. From 1961-1963 he taught ballet in Japan, eventually relocating to Korea full time in the 1980s, where his credits included those at the Korean National Ballet Company, Universal Ballet, and Seoul Ballet Theater, where he worked until 2003. His companion, Jae-Soo Lee, of Seoul, Korea, survives him.

**Jack Warden**, 85, Newark, NJ-born actor, died July 19, 2006, in New York, NY. His Broadway credits include *A View from the Bridge, Golden Boy, Lullaby, The Body Beautiful, The Man in the Glass Booth*, and *Stages*. A ranked professional middleweight boxer early in his career, he became best known for his work on television and film, and was a two-time Academy Award nominee (for his roles in two Warren Beatty movies, *Shampoo* and *Heaven Can Wait*). His other numerous film roles include *12 Angry Men, All the President's Men, Death on the Nile, The Champ, ...And Justice for All, Being There, The Great Muppet Caper, The Verdict, September, The Presidio, Bullets Over Broadway*, and *Things to Do in Denver When You're Dead*, among scores of others spanning five decades. An Emmy Award winner for his portrayal of football coach George Halas in the 1971 television movie *Brian's Song*, his other small screen credits include *Mr. Peepers, N.Y.P.D., Jigsaw John*, and *Crazy Like a Fox*. For five years he was a company member at the Dallas Alley Theater. He was a veteran of the U.S. Navy in W.W. II as well as the U.S. Merchant Marine and the U.S. Army. No reported survivors.

**Ruth Webb** (Ruth Thea Ford), 88, New York, NY-born performer/talent agent, died Dec. 4, 2006, in Los Angeles, CA, of a long pulmonary illness. With Broadway credits including *Marinka, Early to Bed, On the Town*, and *The Walking Gentleman*, from 1962 and until her death she was president and chief executive of the Ruth Webb Talent Agency. Her client list came to include Kathryn Grayson, Rhonda Fleming, Dorothy Lamour, Donald O'Connor, Gloria Swanson, Gig Young, Ann Sothern, Mickey Rooney, Tiny Tim, Phyllis Diller, Bert Parks, Rose Marie, as well as the notorious such as Tonya Harding, Joey Buttafuoco, Sydney Biddle Barrows, Kato Kaelin, Gennifer Flowers, Tammy Faye Bakker Messner, and John Wayne Bobbitt. Two sons, Michael Benajam of Los Angeles, CA, and Jack Webb of Miami, FL, three grandchildren, and one great-grandchild survive her. Also surviving are her companion of thirty-five years, Jamie Stellos, and Mr. Stello's wife, Nancy.

**Edward Weston**, 81, Chicago, IL-born actor/Actors' Equity union leader, died Sept. 6, 2006, in Venice, CA, of a thyroid condition. His Broadway credits include *Allegro*. European tours include *Oklahoma!* Other theatre credits include *Gentleman Prefer Blondes* and a touring production of *Best Foot Forward*, and

he appeared in many live television shows and films, most notably as a backup singer to Jerry Lewis. As the Western regional director of Actors' Equity from 1968-1990, he was instrumental in crafting the 99-seat theater plan that allowed Actors' Equity members in Los Angeles to work in small venues without insisting they be paid union scale. In 1978 he was presented with the Los Angeles Drama Critics Circle Margaret Hartford Award for his union work. He was also active with the Actors' Fund later in his life. And being made award of a program to help retired dancers segue into new professions, he helped launch a similar plan in the U.S. in 1985. He was a veteran of W.W. II, and is survived by a brother, Seymour Goldfarb of Boynton Beach, FL.

**Jane Wyatt**, 96, Campgaw, NJ-born actress, died Oct. 20, 2006, in Bel Air, CA, in her sleep. Best known as Margaret Anderson, wife of Jim Anderson (actor Robert Young) on *Father Knows Best*, she won three Emmy Awards for her work on that television program that ran between 1954 and 1960. She also received a citation from the California Assembly for "consistency in outstanding performance as Margaret Anderson in *Father Knows Best*." Her Broadway credits include *Give Me Yesterday, Dinner at Eight, The Fatal Alibi, The Mad Hopes, Evensong, Conquest, For Services Rendered, The Joyous Season, Lost Horizons, The Bishop Misbehaves, Save Me the Waltz, Night Music, Quiet, Please! Hope for the Best*, and *The Autumn Garden*. Other notable television roles include that of Spock's mother on *Star Trek*, as the moderator-host of an ABC daytime series *Confidential for Women*, in 1967, and as Dr. Auschlander's wife on *St. Elsewhere*. An apprentice at the Berkshire Playhouse in Stockbridge, MA, early in her career, her credits include film roles in *One More River, Great Expectations, Hope for the Best, None But the Lonely Heart, Gentleman's Agreement, Canadian Pacific, Task Force, Boomerang, Pitfall, Lost Horizon*, and *Star Trek IV: The Voyage Home*. A brush with the blacklist in the 1950s was responsible for some of her film work lessening. Her charity work included that with the March of Dimes, which she had worked with since its founding in 1938, and with Los Angeles Beautiful. Sons Christopher Ward, of Piedmont, CA, and Michael Ward of Los Angeles, CA, two grandsons, including Nicholas Ward, granddaughter, and seven great-grandchildren, survive her.

**Gretchen Wyler** (Gretchen Patricia Wienecke), 75, Bartlesville, OK-born actress/activist, died May 27, 2007, in Camarillo, CA, of breast cancer. With Broadway credits include *Guys and Dolls, Silk Stockings, Damn Yankees, Rumple, Bye Bye Birdie*, and *Sly Fox* (1976 Outstanding Actress in a Play Drama Desk nomination), she became perhaps best known for her animal rights activism also during her life. Made the first female board member by the American Society for the Prevention of Cruelty to Animals, she also sat on the board of directors for the Fund for Animals and was vice chairwoman until 1991, when she founded the animal rights group Ark Trust. Ark Trust merged with the Humane Society of the United States, and she served as vice president of the Hollywood office of that organization until her retirement in 2006. She created the Genesis Awards in 1986, which recognize the media and entertainment industries for incorporating animal protection themes into their work. She also crusaded to end horse-slaughtering factories, the use of steel-jaw leg hole traps, to prohibit the use of animal testing in research and development by cosmetics and drug companies, as well as worked tirelessly to improve animal conditions in zoos and circuses. Her position of the Los Angeles Zoo directors advisory committee allowed her to keep close watch over that organization, and she became a somewhat controversial figure for doing so. Her sister, Peggy Hanson of Pacific Palisades, CA, and brother, Lou Wienecke of Granbury, Texas, survive her.

# Index

419

**John Willis (Editor Emeritus)** was editor in chief of both *Theatre World* and has been editor of its companion series *Screen World* for forty-three years. *Theatre World* and *Screen World* are the oldest definitive pictorial and statistical records of each American theatrical and foreign and domestic film season, and are referenced daily by industry professionals, students, and historians worldwide.

Mr. Willis has also served as editor of *Dance World*, *Opera World*, and *A Pictorial History of the American Theatre 1860–1985*. Previously, he served as assistant to *Theatre World* founder Daniel Blum on *Great Stars of the American Stage*, *Great Stars of Film*, *A Pictorial History of the Talkies*, *A Pictorial History of Television*, and *A Pictorial Treasury of Opera in America*.

For over forty years he presided over the presentation of the annual Theatre World Awards, incorporated in 1997 as a 501 (c)(3) nonprofit organization. Begun in 1945 and presented by past winners, they are the oldest awards given to actors for a Broadway or Off-Broadway debut role.

On behalf of *Theatre World*, Mr. Willis received a 2001 Tony Honor for Excellence in the Theatre, the 2003 Broadway Theater Institute Lifetime Achievement Award, a 1994 special Drama Desk Award, and in 1993, the first Outstanding Special Lucille Lortel Award. On behalf of *Screen World*, he received the prestigious 1998 National Board of Review Wiliam K. Everson Award for Film Preservation. He has also received a Professional Excellence Award from his alma mater, Milligan College.

He has served on the nominating committees of the Tony Awards and the New York University Musical Hall of Fame, and has served on the national board of directors for the Clarence Brown Theatre at the University of Tennessee in Knoxville, TN, as well as the past board of directors of the National Board of Review. In addition, Mr. Willis is retired from the New York public school system.

In 1993, the auditorium in which he had performed as a high school student was renovated and christened the John Willis Performing Arts Center at Morristown-Hamblen High School East, in Morristown, TN. And in 2007, a classroom in the new Milligan College theatre complex was named in his honor.

**Ben Hodges (Editor in Chief)** served as an editorial assistant for seven years on the 2001 Special Tony Honor Award-winning *Theatre World*, becoming the associate editor to John Willis in 1998 and editor in chief in 2007. *Theatre World*–at sixty-four–is the most complete annual pictorial and statistical record of the American theatre, including Broadway, Off-Broadway, Off-Off-Broadway, and regional theatre productions, and is referenced daily by students, historians, and industry professionals worldwide.

Also an assistant for seven years to John Willis for the prestigious Theatre World Awards given for Broadway and Off-Broadway debut performances, Ben was elected to the Theatre World Awards board of directors in 2002 and served as executive producer for the annual ceremony from 2002-2007. In 2003 he was presented with a Special Theatre World Award in recognition of his ongoing stewardship of the event. He also served as executive producer for the LAMBDA Literary Foundation "Lammy" Awards, given for excellence in LGBT publishing.

*The Commercial Theater Institute Guide to Producing Plays and Musicals*, which Hodges co-edited with late Commercial Theater Institute director Frederic B. Vogel, was released by Applause Theatre and Cinema Books in 2007, and with contributions by twenty-eight Broadway producers, general managers, attorneys, and publicists, has become the definitive resource in its field, as well as adopted as a course book by North Carolina School for the Arts, among other colleges and universities.

*Forbidden Acts*, the first collected anthology of gay and lesbian plays from the span of the twentieth century, edited and with an introduction by Hodges, was published by Applause Theatre and Cinema Books in 2003 and became a finalist for the 2004 LAMBDA Literary Award for Drama. It has been adopted as a course book by New York University, Cornell University, Salisbury University, University of Las Vegas, and University of Louisville, among other colleges and universities.

His *Out Plays: Landmark Gay and Lesbian Plays from the Twentieth Century*, edited and with an introduction by Hodges, featuring a foreword by Harvey Fierstein and a new introduction to *The Boys in the Band* by Mart Crowley, was released by Alyson Books in spring 2008. With *Out Plays*, Hodges becomes the most prolific anthologist of published gay and lesbian American plays.

His *The Play That Changed My Life*, with essays by scores of America's foremost American playwrights including Edward Albee, Christopher Durang, Suzan-Lori Parks, and Marsha Norman, is due from Applause Theatre and Cinema Books in 2009.

As an actor, director, and/or producer, Ben has appeared in New York with The Barrow Group Theater Company, Origin Theater Company, Daedalus Theater Company, Monday Morning Productions, the Strawberry One-Act Festival, Coyote Girls Productions, Jet Productions, New York Actors' Alliance, and Outcast Productions. Additionally, he has appeared in numerous productions presented by theatre companies that he founded, including the Tuesday Group and Visionary Works. On film, he can be seen in *Macbeth: The Comedy*.

In 2001, Ben became director of development and then served as executive director for Fat Chance Productions Inc. and the Ground Floor Theatre, a New York-based nonprofit theatre and film production company. *Prey for Rock and Roll* was developed by Fat Chance from their stage production (the first legit production to play CBGBs) into a critically acclaimed feature film starring Gina Gershon and *The Sopranos*' Emmy winner Drea de Matteo. *Prey for Rock and Roll* debuted at the Sundance Film Festival in 2003 and won Best Feature at the 2003 Santa Cruz Film Festival. Additionally, Fat Chance produced the American premiere of award-winning Irish playwright Enda Walsh's *Misterman* Off-Broadway, and a host of readings, workshops, and productions in their Ground Floor Theatre, their mission statement being to present new works by new artists.

In 2003, frustrated with the increasingly daunting economic prospects involved in producing theatre on a small scale in New York, Ben organized NOOBA, the New Off-Off Broadway Association, an advocacy group dedicated to representing the concerns of expressly Off-Off-Broadway producers in the public forum and in negotiations with other local professional arts organizations; their chief objective the reformation of the Actors' Equity Basic Showcase Code. He also serves on the New York Innovative Theatre Awards Committee, selecting outstanding individuals for recognition Off-Off-Broadway, and as vice-president of Summer Stage New York, a professional summer theatre program in Fayetteville, New York.

In 2005 Ben founded and served for two years as executive director of The Learning Theatre Inc., a 501(c)(3) nonprofit organization incorporating theatre into the development and lives of learning disabled and autistic children. He currently serves on the board of directors.

In support of his projects and publications, Ben has appeared on nationwide radio on *The Joey Reynolds Show*, *The Michael Dresser Show*, and on television on New York 1 and *Philly Live* in Philadelphia, PA–the only live televised LGBT call-in show in the United States. Reviews and articles on Ben, his projects, or publications have appeared in *The New York Times*, *The New Yorker*, *GQ*, *Elle*, *Genre*, *Back Stage*, *Time Out New York*, *Playbill*, *Next*, *New York Blade*, *Library Journal*, *The Advocate*, *Chicago Free Press*, *Philadelphia Gay News*, *Houston Voice*, *Stage Directions*, *Between the Lines*, *The Flint Journal*, and *Citizen Tribune*, as well as the web sites CurtainUp.com and in Peter Filichia's Diary on Theatermania.com. He has made guest appearances in support of his publications at the Good Beans Café in Flint, Michigan, at the Common Language Bookstore in Ann Arbor, Michigan, at A Different Light in both Los Angeles and San Francisco, The Open Book in Sacramento, and at Giovanni's Room in Philadelphia, as well as at the DR2 Theatre D-2 Lounge in New York City.

He holds a BFA in Theatre Acting and Directing from Otterbein College in Westerville, Ohio, is an alumnus of the Commercial Theater Institute, and is a candidate for a 2012 Juris Doctor degree from Seton Hall University School of Law in Newark, New Jersey. He lives in New York City. For more information or to schedule speaking engagements, please visit benhodges.com, or e-mail benjaminhodges@gmail.com.

**Scott Denny (Associate Editor)** Scott Denny is and actor and singer and has worked professionally for over twenty years. Originally from Terre Haute, Indiana, he attended Western Kentucky University in Bowling Green, Kentucky and holds a degree in performing arts. His professional theatrical credits include Richard Henry Lee in the national tour of *1776*, Uncle Wes in the Las Vegas and national touring production of *Footloose,* and the assistant company manager and swing performer on the first national tour of Susan Stroman's production of *The Music Man.* Regionally he has appeared in *Evita, The Wizard of Oz,* and *The King and I* at Houston's Theatre Under the Stars, regional premieres of *Silver Dollar* and *Paper Moon* at Stage One in Wichita, Kansas. His summer stock and dinner theatre credits include *Me and My Girl, Gypsy, She Loves Me, The Best Little Whorehouse in Texas,* among several others. In New York he has appeared Off-Off-Broadway in *Election Day, Like You Like It, Vanity Fair,* and in several readings and workshops. He screen credits include the independent films *Red Hook* and *Redefining Normal.* Scott served as assistant editor on *Theatre World* Volume 60, and as associate editor on Volume 61 and 62. In the fall of 2006 Scott was nominated to the Board of Directors of the Theatre World Awards where he now serves as the Treasurer. He served as an associate producer for the 2006 Theatre World Awards, and as co-producer of the 2007 Awards. Scott also works as a production assistant for the Macy's Thanksgiving Day Parade and Macy's Annual Events. For the past five years he has worked on and off for Cruise Everything, a cruise travel agency in Ft. Myers, Florida, specializing in incentive groups. In 2003 and 2006 he served as the group manager and entertainment coordinator for two cruises for QVC's Quacker Factory host Jeanne Bice.

**Allison Graham (Associate Editor)** is from Columbus, Ohio. She graduated magna cum laude from Otterbein College in 2004, where she studied music and dance. In New York, Allison sings as a member of St. Bartholomew's Choir and St. John the Divine's "Nightwatch" program, and is a part of the National Chorale's Avery Fisher Series at Lincoln Center.

**Lisa Kuhnen (Assistant Editor)** is an actor, singer, and dancer, currently living in New York City. She has performed at numerous regional theaters including the Cleveland Playhouse, Great Lakes Theatre Festival, and Syracuse Stage. Lisa has a Bachelor of Fine Arts from Syracuse University where she studied musical theatre with a concentration in dance.